THE GERMAN
RESEARCH COMPANION

THE GERMAN

RESEARCH COMPANION

Shirley J. Riemer

LORELEI
P•R•E•S•S

Publisher's Cataloging in Publication

Riemer, Shirley J.

  The German research companion / by Shirley J. Riemer,

      p. cm.

    Includes bibliographical references and index.

  1. German Americans – Genealogy – Handbooks, manuals, etc. 2. Germany – Genealogy – Handbooks, manuals, etc. 3. Austria – Genealogy – Handbooks, manuals, etc. 4. Switzerland – Genealogy – Handbooks, manuals, etc. I. Title.

E184.G3R54 1997   929.1'08931

                        QBI97-40166

ISBN: 0-9656761-4-5

Library of Congress Catalog Card Number: 97-70445

Lorelei Press, P.O. Box 221356, Sacramento, CA 95822-8356

Printed by: Bertelsmann Industry Services

Every generation revolts against its fathers and makes friends with its grandfathers.

Lewis Mumford

Acknowledgments

Writing a book must surely be the loneliest of tasks. Therefore, good friends like these, who pitched in to help with the effort, are all the more appreciated:

Rainer Thumshirn, of Heimstetten, Germany, contributed to the work as writer, fact-checker, and responder to inquiries. He kept the fax machine warm through many months. Rainer deserves the greatest admiration for his uncanny ability to dig information out of obscure corners of Germany.

John and Mary Heisey, of York, Pennsylvania, both devoted history buffs, kept the mails busy by sending off packets full of suggestions, clippings, statistics, and plenty of genealogy-related reading material for mulling over. Their generous support of the project never waned.

Hannelore Köhler of the German Information Center in New York was especially helpful in ferreting out requested information and in offering the Center's resources over a period of many months. Other staff members at the Center went out of their way as well to assist.

Nell Witalis of Aliquippa, Pennsylvania, a friend since we were five, gave up many hours from her busy life to pound away at her computer on behalf of the enterprise. Fortunately for me, Nell can be counted on always to project the let's-get-this-job-done approach to a task.

Steve Aunan, of Sacramento, California stands way up there when it comes to coaxing computer programs to perform all the tricks they promise. On more than one occasion, Steve solved an "impossible" problem.

Artist Jim Stutzman of Millersburg, Pennsylvania came up with the book's cover design which expresses *precisely* the mood and style I requested – not a common occurrence in author-artist collaborations.

Members of the Sacramento German Genealogy Society displayed two years' worth of patience as the writing went on and on. Their encouragement and understanding fed the project's momentum.

Amanda Breslin, adored granddaughter of San Luis Obispo, California, took on the role of head cheerleader, keeping the e-mail messages flowing in with frequent "stay-with-it" pleas. She should go into the business – any writer would profit from her brand of enthusiasm and encouragement.

To these friends and the many others – who waited and waited – go my warmest thanks.

Shirley J. Riemer

Introduction

This book is intended not as a guide for performing German family history research, but rather as an auxiliary tool – to help family historians discover previously unknown resources, to check on facts related to the research, and most of all to offer clues toward solving ancestral mysteries.

Readers are encouraged to use this book as one means of becoming acquainted with the environment in which their German ancestors lived. Merely to fill in the blanks on one's pedigree chart does little toward that end. What was the discussion of the day in our ancestors' kitchens? How did they scrape together a living? What was their relationship to their church or synagogue? How were their children schooled?

These were flesh and blood hard-working folks, visited by frustrations and sorrows as well as by hopes and joys. Certainly our family members' lives are worth the recording of much more than their names with dates and places of birth, marriage and death.

The more we learn about what was going on in our German ancestors' times, the more clues we are likely to gain. And these clues can send us down a research path that might otherwise never have occurred to us.

It is not a popular idea to suggest that a researcher "waste time" in browsing. Yet this book was created with the notion that it might interest fellow enthusiasts who practice this secret pleasure.

Much of the material found on these pages was discovered as a result of quite idle browsing in libraries in Germany and the United States. The discovered data, gathered so randomly, seemed too intriguing not to share with others who also feel the excitement of German family research.

Open up this book to a random page. Browse away. No one will ever know.

Table of Contents

Chapter 1
Germany: some basics

Chapter 2
Emigration

Chapter 3
Immigration

Chapter 4
Arrival in America

Chapter 5
Church and civil records

Chapter 6
Archives and repositories

Chapter 7
German genealogy aids

Chapter 8
Genealogical tools

Chapter 9
Geography

Chapter 10
American military resources

Chapter 11
Land in America

Chapter 12
United States census

Chapter 13
Newspapers, American records

Chapter 14
Using libraries

Chapter 15
Fraternal organizations

Chapter 16
German education, universities

Chapter 17
Language

Chapter 18
German life

Chapter 19
Naming practices

Chapter 20
German military resources

Chapter 21
Religions

Chapter 22
Germans from Russia

Chapter 23
Pennsylvania

Chapter 24
Beyond Germany

Chapter 25
Eastern and Alsace neighbors

Chapter 26
Business and trade

Chapter 27
Keeping track of time

Chapter 28
This and that

Chapter 29
Cultural institutions

Chapter 30
Libraries, museums, publishers

Chapter 31
Societies, organizations

Chapter 32
Tourism, chambers of commerce, and more

Chapter 1

Germany:

some basics

CHRONOLOGY OF EVENTS IN GERMAN HISTORY

1000-100 B.C.: The Germani tribes occupy the lands from the Baltic Sea to the Danube River, and from the Rhine to the Oder River.

9 B.C. - 9 A.D.: The Romans move eastward to the Elbe River. In 9 A.D. they withdraw to the Rhine.

481-511: The king of the Franks, Clovis, establishes the Frankish Empire.

768-814: Charlemagne (Karl der Große) rules what is to become the Holy Roman Empire. In 800 he is crowned emperor of the Holy Roman Empire of German Nations: First Reich

843: Treaty of Verdun: empire divided among Charlemagne's three grandchildren: Charles the Bold — West Franks; Louis the German — East Franks (nucleus of the future German state); Lothar — Middle Kingdom (Alsace-Lorraine)

919-1024: German tribes unified

969-1806: First German Empire ("Holy Roman Empire of the German Nation")

1000-1500: Jewish expulsions: from German areas (1000-1350), from Hungary (1300s), and from Austria (1400s)

1123-24: Plague sweeps France and Germany

1141-1181: "Saxons" (mostly Franks) invited to settle in Transylvania to defend Hungary's eastern border.

1152-1190: Reign of Frederick I (Barbarossa), of the Hohenstaufen dynasty, who converts the Slavs to Christianity. Age of chivalry.

1200: Early Gothic period begins (Rheims, Cologne, constructed)

1241: Hanseatic League formed

1273-1806: Hapsburg dynasty begins; ends with abolition of Holy Roman Empire by Napoleon in 1806

1348-1365: More than 25 million Europeans die in the Bubonic plague

1417: Frederick of Nürnberg of Hohenzollern family appointed Elector of Brandenburg

c. 1440: In Mainz, Johann Gutenburg invents the art of printing with movable type.

1517: Protestant Reformation begins; Luther fastens 95 theses on Wittenberg church door. First significant non-Catholic religions among Germanic people.

1518-1523: Ulrich Zwingli begins the Reformation in Switzerland, leading to formation of Reformed (Calvinist) Church

c. 1520: Anabaptist movement develops in Switzerland and Germany

1521: Luther's arrest by Charles V, for Diet of Worms. Luther translates New Testament into German, devising new written form of German.

1524: Peasants influenced by Luther's teachings rise up against their feudal overlords and are crushed in the bloody rebellion.

1524: Protestant church records begin in Nürnberg.

1530: Augsburg Confession (creed) adopted by Lutherans

1534: A standardized German language is established with the publication of the Old Testament in Luther's translation of the Bible from Hebrew and Greek into vernacular German.

1545: Catholic Counter-Reformation begins.

1555: Peace of Augsburg: subjects must adopt the religion of their respective local rulers or emigrate.

1556: Palatinate becomes Lutheran.

1562: Wars of Religion in France between Catholics and French Calvinists (Huguenots)

1563: Council of Trent. Catholic priests ordered to start keeping baptism and marriage records.

1568: Protestants in the Spanish Netherlands, including Belgium, are persecuted by the Duke of Alva. Walloon Calvinists flee, especially to the Palatinate, Hesse, and Brandenburg; Dutch-Flemish-Frisian Mennonites flee to Danzig area

1583: Gregorian calendar is adopted by most Catholic countries of Europe — by Prussia in 1612, by most Protestant countries in 1700, by Great Britain in 1752, and by Russia in 1917.

1600: Surnames in common use throughout German areas (in some areas as early as 1100)

1618-1648: Thirty Years War devastates Holy Roman Empire. France emerges as Europe's leading power. Many records are burned. Population drops from 20 million to 13 million.

1622: Pfalz suffers great destruction in the war. January 1 declared as beginning of the year (which previously began on March 25)

1633: Outbreak of plague in Bavaria

1639-60: Grain crisis in Europe

1648: Peace of Westphalia ends Thirty Years War. Holy Roman Empire dissolved. France gets Alsace-Lorraine. By this time there are 350 different German states. Switzerland officially recognized as independent from the Holy Roman Empire. Reformed Church members granted same rights as that Lutherans had been granted almost 100 years earlier.

1650: Introduction of church records in most German areas (but in Switzerland about 1525)

1652: Famine in Lorraine and surrounding lands

1653: Germans from Heidelberg introduce vineyards and winemaking to America.

1654: Spain occupies Palatinate

1671-77: William Penn first visits Germany to propagate Quaker faith.

1678-79: Alsace acquired by France

1681: William Penn founds Pennsylvania

1683: First permanent German settlement in the United States is founded at Germantown, Pennsylvania. Encouraged by American Quaker William Penn, Franz Daniel Pastorius organizes the immigration of 13 Mennonite families from Krefeld, beginning German group immigration to North America.

1685: King Louis XIV of France revokes the Edict of Nantes, which had granted freedom of religion. Persecution and forcible conversion of Huguenots (French Protestants) causes hundreds of thousands to flee to Switzerland, Germany, the

Netherlands, Great Britain and North America. Friedrich Wilhelm, the Great Elector, helps many immigrate to Brandenburg.

1689-97: War of the League of Augsburg results in French burning down many towns in the Palatinate and mass flight of the population

1694: Johann Kelpius leads a group of German mystics to America and forms a brotherhood on Wissahickon Creek near Philadelphia.

1700: The last German Protestant areas finally switch to the Gregorian calendar

1701: Frederick III, elector of Brandenburg, renames his duchy the Kingdom of Prussia and becomes King Frederick I.

1708: Joshua Kocherthal brings 61 Protestant emigrants from the Rhenish Palatinate to America; thousands more from the region follow in 1709.

1709: Thousands more of the Palatine Germans, fleeing destruction caused by the invading French, emigrate to the Hudson River Valley and Pennsylvania. Large numbers of emigrants, called Palatines (*Pfälzer*), leave the Pfalz region of Germany for England and America.

1710: A group of German and Swiss immigrants settle New Bern, North Carolina.

1710-11: First relatively large-scale immigration of Swiss and Palatines to the American colonies.

1711: An estimated 500,000 die of plague in Austria and German areas.

1714: Christopher von Graffenried brings ore miners from Siegen, Westphalia, to Virginia to work Governor Spotswood's iron mines.

1719: Peter Becker brings the first German Baptist "Dunkers" to Germantown. The sect's founder, Alexander Mack, comes to America with another group ten years later.

1727: The German population of Pennsylvania numbers around 20,000.

1722: Austro-Hungarian monarchs begin

Title page of the first Bible printed in America, by Christopher Saur, 1743

inviting Germans to settle parts of their empire.

1730: Beginning of community at Ephrata (Pennsylvania)

1731-38: Expulsion of Salzburger Protestants from the Austrian Empire, some of whom come to America, most going to East Prussia and other European areas.

1732: Benjamin Franklin publishes the first German language newspaper in America, the *Philadelphische Zeitung.*

1732: Conrad Beissel, a Seventh Day Dunker from the Palatinate, founds the Ephrata Cloisters near Lancaster, Pennsylvania.

1733: Members of the Schwenkfelder sect from Silesia settle in Montgomery County, Pennsylvania.

1734: Refugees from Salzburg arrive in Savannah, Georgia

1736: The Herrnhuters, or Moravians, found their first settlement, in Georgia, under the leadership of August Gottlieb Spangenberg.
1740-86: Under Frederick II of Prussia (Frederick the Great), Prussia becomes a great power.
1740-48: War of Austrian Succession between Prussia and Austria; Prussia wins new territories
1742: Nikolaus Ludwig, Count of Zinzendorf and Pottendorf, founds the Moravian settlement of Bethlehem, Pennsylvania.
1743: Christopher Saur of Philadelphia prints a German-language Bible, the first complete Bible ever to be published in America.
1748: George Washington first encounters German immigrants in the Shenandoah Valley.
1749: Settlement of New Germantown (Braintree), Massachusetts
1749-53: Peak of Germanic immigration to colonial America, mostly from near the Rhine valley about 1750.
1750: Beginning of Pennsylvania-German emigration to North Carolina. Also, the first Germans arrive in Nova Scotia.
1753: Hanoverians found the town of Lunenburg, to become the most important ship-building center of Nova Scotia. Moravians begin settlement on the Wachovia tract, North Carolina
1754: The Schwenkfelder sect of Pennsylvania establishes the first Sunday School in America.
1755: Beginning of French and Indian War
1756-1763: Germans play a significant role in fighting the French in the French and Indian War.
1756-63: Seven Years War. An Anglo-Prussian alliance faces off against a coalition of Austria, Saxony, France, and Russia. Prussia wins more territory and goes on to become a great power.
1759: Michael Hillegas opens America's first music store in Philadelphia.

1763: Catherine the Great begins inviting Germans to settle in Russia, granting them free land, freedom from military service, many other special privileges
1764-67: Heavy immigration of Germans to Volga River region in Russia
1766: France acquires Lorraine.
1772-95: Partition of Poland by Russia, Prussia and Austria in three stages: 1772, 1793, and 1795. Poland disappears as an independent country until 1918
1775-83: American Revolution, with independence declared in 1776; 30,000 Hessian and other German mercenaries fight for Great Britain. Thousands remain in United States and Canada after the war.
1776: Henry Miller's newspaper *Staatsbote* is the first paper in America to print the news of the Declaration of Independence.
1778: General Friedrich Wilhelm von Steuben takes over the training of the Continental Army.
1781: Palatine immigration (since 1709) to the United States continues.
1781: Freedom of religion guaranteed in Austria, opening the way for immigration of Protestants.
1781-1864: Serfdom abolished in northern Europe. Key dates: Austria (1781, again in 1848 after being reinstituted); France (1789); Prussia (1807); all German territory (by 1848); Hungary (1853-54); Russia (1861); Russian Poland and Romania (1864).
1782-1787: Heavy German immigration to Danube region of southern Hungary, Galicia and Bukovina, all recently acquired by Austria under Emperor Joseph II
1783: German Loyalists settle in Upper Canada, where the town of Berlin (whose name was changed to Kitchener during World War I) will become the center of a predominantly German area.
1785-1844: Jews required to adopt family names in all Austrian-ruled lands except Hungary (1785-87), in France and Germany (1802-12), and in Russia and Poland

(1844)

1786: German Mennonites from Pennsylvania begin to emigrate to Ontario, more heavily after 1807.

1789: Paris mob storms Bastille; *Declaration of Rights of Man and of Citizen* is published.

1789: Frederick Augustus Mühlenberg becomes first Speaker of United States House of Representatives.

1789-1824: Heaviest German immigration to Black Sea region of Russia (now Ukraine)

1789-1917: Jews emancipated, being granted equality by law in France (1789), Prussia (1850); Austro-Hungarian Empire (1867); Germany (1871); Switzerland (1874) and Russia (1917)

1792: France starts civil registration west of the Rhein. Some church records are interrupted.

1792-1815: Napoleonic wars against revolutionary France by Prussia, Austria and other countries. Napoleon forces end of Holy Roman Empire in 1806, with Hapsburg family continuing to rule Austria, but no longer influential in German lands. Rhenish Confederation founded in 1806. France starts civil registration west of the Rhine. Some church records are interrupted.

1794: Changing of surnames is forbidden in Prussia.

1795: Franco Prussian War. Prussia defeated.

1798: Switzerland declares neutrality.

c. 1800: Industrial Revolution well underway

1803: The disruption of trade following the resumption of war between England and France makes emigration from continental Europe practically impossible.

1803-15: Napoleonic Wars. Napoleon annexes Rhine, abolishes 112 states and free cities, which are absorbed by larger kingdoms, and secularizes monasteries, giving their lands as rewards to friends for loyalty.

1804: Napoleon creates French Empire and proclaims himself emperor. Code Napoleon is issued as a comprehensive compilation of French civil laws.

1804: George Rapp, founder of a communal religious sect, establishes the settlement of Harmony in Pennsylvania.

1805-07: Napoleon compels the emperor Francis I of Austria to renounce his title and position, bringing the Holy Roman Empire of the German Nation to an end.

1806-1813: The German states neighboring France unite under Napoleon's protection in the Confederation of the Rhine. Bavaria and Württemberg are raised to status of kingdoms; new states and grand duchies are created. Areas ruled by 16 German princes become allied to France.

1806-1867: Austrian Empire

1807: Prussians again defeated by Napoleon

1808: First locomotive built

1811: Decree ending use of patronymic surnames in Ostfriesland

1812: War of 1812 brings immigration to a complete halt

1813-15: Prussian rallies German states to rise and drive the French from German soil. War of Liberation. Napoleon defeated at Battle of Leipzig. Spirit of national unity sweeps through German states.

1814: Treaty of Ghent ends War of 1812. First great wave of U.S. immigration begins, with 5 million immigrants between 1815 and 1860.

1814: Napoleon weakens. German states begin to reorganize under the leadership of Prussia.

1815: Napoleon defeated at Waterloo. Congress of Vienna restores Prussian territories, reduces number of independent states to 39 by increasing new territories of Prussia and Austria. The German Confederation is formed with Austria presiding.

1816: Crop failures and famine spark first significant emigration from Germany and Luxumbourg to the United States.

1817: Lutherans and Reformed Churches

are ordered to merge into Evangelical Church in Prussia, and merge elsewhere about the same time.

1818: Black Ball Line of sailing packets begins regular Liverpool-New York service; Liverpool becomes main port of departure for Irish and British along with considerable numbers of Germans and Norwegians.

1819: U.S. Congress passes the :Passenger Act, ending redemptioner trade.

1819: The first steamship crosses the ocean, from Savannah to Liverpool, in 29 days, ushering in a new era of transatlantic travel.

1826-37: Cholera ravages Europe, with 900,000 victims in 1831 alone.

1828: Patronymic naming is abolished in Schleswig-Holstein (then part of Denmark).

1830: Gradually increasing German emigration to United States and Canada, coinciding with beginning of Industrial Revolution at home

1830s: German-Americans introduce gaily-decorated Christmas trees to America.

1830-48: Local and regional patriotism begins to give way to a new spirit of national patriotism previously unknown by Germans. It is Napoleon who more than any other influence spreads pan-German thought.

1835: The male chorus "Männerchor von Philadelphia" is the first German-American "Gesangsverein" (choral society).

1837: Laws in Pennsylvania and Ohio permit public school to be conducted in German.

1838-54: Main wave of emigration of "Old Lutherans," who rejected the Evangelical merger — to New York, Wisconsin, Missouri, Michigan and Texas. About one third go to Australia and Canada

1840: Cunard Line founded, beginning era of steamship lines especially designed for passenger transportation between Europe and the United States.

1840-75: Worldwide cholera, millions of deaths

1841: Heinrich Hoffman von Fallersleben writes text to *Deutschland über Alles* hymn as the rallying cry of liberals urging national over Bavarian, Saxon, or Rhenish patriotism.

1843-59: First large wave of Germans to the United States (1846-1857), especially from the Palatinate and the Rhineland. This emigration peaks in 1854 and is largely stopped by the Panic of 1857. Most German immigration to Texas occurs during this period.

1844: Prince Carl von Solms-Braunfels brings first German settlers to Texas; the next year he founds town of New Braunfels.

1845: First propeller-driven steamship crosses Atlantic

1846: Crop failures in Germany and Holland, followed by foreclosures, encourage more Germans to emigrate to America.

1847: The Missouri Synod of the Lutheran Church is organized in protest against Americanization and liberalization of the Lutheran Church in America.

1848: German Revolution. A self-appointed group of liberals meets in the Pauls Kirche in Frankfurt/Main to draft a constitution for a new German nation to include all Germans states except Austria. Emigration to the United States increases.

1848: German Revolution. Forty-Eighter Friedrich Hecker is greeted by a crowd of 20,000 German-Americans upon his arrival in New York.

1848: Revolution in Germany fails, resulting in emigration of political refugees to America

1849: Mass emigration of the Forty-Eighter political refugees to the United States.

1849: Gold discovered in California

1850: First *Turnverein* in the United States opens in Cincinnati; bloody clashes between anti-foreign nativists, or "Know-

Nothings," and German Americans begin and continue throughout decade.

1850: Hamburg passenger lists begin to document the origins or places of residence of Europeans leaving for the Americas, Africa, and Australia.

1853: Immigrant Heinrich Steinweg founds the piano-manufacturing firm Steinway & Sons in New York.

1854-1855: Anti-foreign movement active in New York City; immigrants beaten by mobs; depression of 1854; two-year cholera outbreak reaches peak in late 1854 aboard ships and at port

1855-90: Castle Garden serves as a processing center for immigrants

1855: Know-Nothings — anti-Catholic, anti-alien — at height of their power

1856: First kindergarten in the United States is organized by Margaretha Meyer Schurz, wife Carl Schurz, in Watertown, Wisconsin.

1857: Economic Panic of 1857 in United States

1857: Depression in United States (Panic of 1857)

1861-65: American Civil War, in which 23 percent of the 2,213,363 soldiers in the Union army are German-Americans; 500 officers in the Union army born in Germany.

1862: Morrill Act makes free land available in the United States.

1862: Otto von Bismarck begins long career as a powerful leader in Prussia (later Germany)

1863-75: Cholera causes deaths of millions, in 1866 killing 300,000 in Eastern Europe.

1864: War with Denmark. Prussia conquers Schleswig-Holstein.

1865-74: Second large wave of emigrants to the United States, peaking in 1873, largely to avoid military service and to escape the ruin of cottage industries

1866-1867: South German states join Prussia and North German states to form the North-German Confederation.

1866: Seven Weeks War. Bismarck leads Prussia in the defeat of Austria, forcing Austria to share power with Hungary as Austro-Hungarian Empire is established in 1867.

1867: Karl Marx publishes Volume I of *Das Kapital.*

1867-1918: Austro-Hungarian Empire

1869: Carl Shurz becomes first German-born citizen to be elected to the United States Senate.

1870-71: German-Americans hail the defeat of France in the Franco-Prussian War and the unification of Germany on January 18, 1871. Prussia's victory over France leads to creation of the (Second) German Empire, taking Alsace and part of Lorraine from France. Second German Reich begins; Otto von Bismarck becomes first chancellor.

1871: Special privileges of Germans are revoked in Russia, sparking emigration to North and South America.

1871-1907: Anti-Jewish pogroms in Russia. Many Jews emigrate to the United States.

1871-1918: Second German Empire

1873-79: Depression in the United States (Panic of 1873)

1874: Prussia introduces civil registration. In 1876 it is required in the rest of the German Empire.

1874: The migration of German-speaking Mennonites from Russia to the prairies of Manitoba begins.

1876: Civil registration is required throughout Germany and begins wherever it is not already in effect.

1877: Carl Schurz becomes Secretary of Interior, holding this office until 1881.

1880s: Industrialization of Germany. Colonizing increases, especially in Africa.

1880-1890: Largest number of Luxembourg emigrants come to the United States.

1880-93: Third wave of German emigrants to the United States, peaking in 1882

1881-88: Large numbers of Swiss emigrants come to the United States.

1888-1918: Reign of Kaiser Wilhelm II, also known as the "Wilhelmine Age."

1889-90: Influenza epidemic, affecting 40 percent of the world, causes deaths in the millions

1892-1954: Ellis Island serves as the United States Immigration Center, through which about 20 million immigrants pass.

1893-94: Renewed worldwide outbreak of cholera

1910-20: Largest number of Swiss emigrants come to the United States

1914: Assassination of Archduke Franz Ferdinand triggers World War I.

1914-18: World War I. German economy in ruins. Alsace-Lorraine returned to France. Parts of eastern Germany ceded to Lithuania and Poland. Bolshevik Revolution of 1917 and civil war cause emigration from Russia.

1917, April 6: United States declares war against Central Powers; German-Americans suffer wave of severe discrimination as America enters World War I.

1917-19: Influenza epidemic, with deaths estimated as high as 50 million

1918: Kaiser abdicates. End of the second German Reich. Treaty of Versailles. Poland recreated, Germany forced to give up territories which Prussia had annexed in the 18th century. Alsace-Lorraine returned to France. Czechoslovakia becomes independent nation. The Weimar Republic is declared.

1919, June 8: Versailles Peace Treaty signed. Germany loses Alsace and Lorraine to France, Eupen and Malmédy to Belgium, part of Jutland to Denmark; Danzig becomes a free state; West Prussia with Posen and Upper Silesia come under Polish rule.

1919-33: Weimar Republic, ill-fated German effort at parliamentary democracy

1920s: Following calming of anti-German sentiment, many German skilled workers and technicians migrate to Canada to work in industrial centers of Ontario.

1921: Treaty of Riga establishes boundaries of new Poland.

1921: Hitler establishes the Nazi Party.

1921-23: Extreme inflation in Germany ($1 = 4 billion marks)

1921-24: Immigration severely curtailed by new American laws

1923: Adolf Hitler's beer-hall Putsch in Munich

1929-34: The Great Depression: Mass unemployment in Germany during worldwide financial crisis. One third of the potential work force is unemployed.

1933: Start of the emigration of German artists and intellectuals to the United States.

1933: Third Reich begins with Hitler's assumption of power as chancellor. Nazi rule begins. Hitler's anti-Semitic campaign drives many German Jews to seek refuge in the United States, but United States quotas imposed in 1929 limit number allowed into the country.

1938, November 9-10: *Reichskristallnacht* pogrom carried out throughout Germany, opening way for the Nazis' attempt to exterminate European Jewry entirely.

1938: Hitler annexes Austria. Munich Pact provides legal framework for Nazi occupation of largely German-speaking Sudeten areas of Czechoslovakia.

1939-45: Germany occupies the rest of Czechoslovakia and invades Poland, thus starting World War II. Many German records destroyed in war.

1939-45: World War II. East Prussia divided between Poland and Russia. Most of Pomerania, West Prussia, Brandenburg, and Silesia come under Polish administration.

1941, December 11: Hitler declares war on the United States.

1941-1945: One-third of the 11 million soldiers in the United States armed forces in World War II are of German descent.

1944-48: Mass flight from Eastern Europe before the advancing Soviet armies. Population of West Germany increases 25% as 14 million ethnic Germans arrive.

1945, May 8: Unconditional surrender of

Germany to the Allies. Germany is then divided into four zones of occupation: American, British, French, and Soviet sectors; Berlin is divided on the same basis.
1945: Hitler commits suicide. End of Third Reich
1948, June: Beginning of the Berlin Blockade and the western allies' Berlin Airlift, which lasts 10 months
1948: The Displaced Persons Act allows additional ethnic Germans, expelled from Eastern Europe, to immigrate to America.
1949: The Federal Republic of West Germany and the German Democratic Republic of East Germany are created.
1950s: About 250,000 Germans, many of them skilled workers, migrate to Canadian cities.
1955: The Federal Republic of West Germany becomes a member of NATO. The German Democratic Republic of East Germahy becomes a member of the Warsaw Pact.
1957: The European Economic Community is established, of which West Germany is a part.
1961, August 13: Construction of Berlin wall begins.
1969-70: West Germany signs a nonaggression treat with the U.S.S.R. and recognizes the Oder-Neisse line as Poland's western frontier.
1973: Both East and West Germany are admitted to the United Nations.
1987: *Glasnost* leads to emigration of many ethnic Germans and Jews from the Soviet Union and East Central Europe.
1989, November 9: Fall of the Berlin Wall
1990, October 3: German reunification completed with joining of German Democratic Republic and Federal Republic of Germany
1993, January 1: Former Czechoslovakia splits into Czech Republic and Slovakia.

FACTS ABOUT THE FEDERAL REPUBLIC OF GERMANY *(Bundesrepublik Deutschland))*

Geographic location
Central Europe, common borders with Denmark (68 km), the Netherlands (577 km), Belgium (167 km), France (451 km), Switzerland (334 km), Austria (784 km), Luxembourg (138 km), the Czech Republic (646 km), and Poland (456 km).
Total area
356,910 sq km; land area 349,520 sq km
Comparative area
Slightly smaller than Montana
Capital
Berlin (The shift from Bonn to Berlin will take place over a period of years with Bonn retaining many administrative functions and several ministries.)
Ports, seaboard and interior
Berlin, Bonn, Brake, Bremen, Bremerhaven, Cologne, Dresden, Duisburg, Emden, Hamburg, Karlsruhe, Kiel, Lübeck, Magdeburg, Mannheim, Rostock, Stuttgart
Jurisdictional history
◆**January 18, 1871:** German Empire unification
◆ **1945:** Divided into four zones of occupation (United Kingdom, United States, Union of Soviet Socialist Republics, and later France) following World War II
◆**May 23, 1949:** Federal Republic of Germany (or West Germany) proclaimed, which consisted of the former zones of the United Kingdom, United States, and France
◆**October 7, 1949:** German Democratic Republic (or East Germany) proclaimed and included the former USSR zone
◆**October 3, 1990:** unification of West Germany and East Germany; on this date the states of Mecklenburg-Vorpommern, Brandenburg, Sachsen-Anhalt, Thüringen, and Sachsen were established and became part of the Federal Republic of Germany;

the eleven districts of East Berlin merged with the state of Berlin.

♦ **March 15, 1991:** rights of all four occupation powers relinquished; return to full sovereignty

Constitution

The Basic Law of May 23, 1949 for West Germany became (with some modifications) the constitution for reunited Germany on October 3, 1990.

Suffrage

18 years of age; universal

Executive branch

Head of state: Federal President; elected for five years by the Federal Assembly *(Bundestag* plus the same number of delegates from the States*)*; President Dr. Roman Herzog since July 1, 1994

Head of government

Elected by the Federal Parliament *(Bundestag)* for its duration (maximum of four years); Chancellor Dr. Helmut Kohl since October 4, 1982

Cabinet

Appointed by the president upon the proposal of the chancellor

Major political parties

♦Christian Democratic Union (CDU), in all Germany except Bavaria
♦Christian Social Union (CSU), only in Bavaria
♦Free Democratic Party (FDP)
♦Social Democratic Party (SPD)
♦Green Party *(Die Grünen)*
♦Party of Democratic Socialism (PDS)
♦Republikaner
♦National Democratic Party (NPD)
♦Communist Party (DKP)

Legislative branch

Bicameral chamber (no official name for the two chambers as a whole)

Federal Parliament *(Bundestag)*

Elected by direct popular vote under a system combining direct and proportional representation; a party must win 5 percent of the national vote or three direct mandates to gain representation; for reunited Germany, first elected on December 2, 1990; term of office is four years

Relative sizes of United States and Germany
Source: German Information Center, *Federal Republic of Germany: Questions and Answers,* Susan Steiner,ed., New York, 1996

Federal Council *(Bundesrat)*

State governments are directly represented; each has three to six votes (depending on size), which must be voted as a block.

Judicial branch

Federal Constitutional Court *(Bundesverfassungsgericht)*; criminal courts *(Strafgerichte)*; civil courts *(Zivilgerichte)*; administrative courts *(Verwaltungsgerichte)*; tax courts *(Finanzgerichte)*; labor dispute courts *(Arbeitsgerichte)*; social affairs courts *(Sozialgerichte)*

Population

81.3 million; including foreigners)

Ethnic divisions

German 95.1%, Turkish 2.3%, Italians 0.7%, Greeks 0.4%, Poles 0.4%, other 1.1%

Religions

Protestant 45%, Roman Caholic 37%, unaffiliated or other 18%

States *(Länder)*

Baden-Württemberg, Bayern, Berlin, Brandenburg, Bremen, Hamburg, Hessen, Mecklenburg-Vorpommern, Nieder-

sachsen, Nordrhein-Westfalen, Rheinland-Pfalz, Saarland, Sachsen, Sachsen-
Anhalt, Schleswig-Holstein, Thüringen

Diplomatic representation in the United States

Chancery at 4645 Reservoir Road NW,
Washington, DC 20007; tel. (202) 298-
4000

Consulate(s) general

Atlanta, Boston, Chicago, Detroit,
Houston, Los Angeles, Miami, New York,
San Francisco, Seattle

Embassy

Deichmanns Aue 29, 53170 Bonn;
mailing address: Unit 21701, Bonn; APO
AE 09080; tel. [49] (228) 3392663; branch
office, Berlin

Consulate(s) general

Frankfurt, Hamburg, Leipzig, Munich,
and Stuttgart

Flag

Three equal horizontal bands of black
(top), red, and gold

THE THREE GERMAN EMPIRES

Historically there have been two periods when Germany was a realm (*Reich*)
ruled by an emperor (*Kaiser*).

First empire

The first German Reich was called the
"Holy Roman Empire of the German Nation."

It began in the tenth century and lasted
850 years until its dissolution in 1806 by
Napoleon's conquest of Europe. This
Reich was ruled by the dual power of the
Kaiser and of the feudal nobles who
elected him.

From the fifteenth century on, the Austrian House of Hapsburg supplied the heirs
to the throne.

Second empire

The second German Reich was
founded by the German federated states,
leaving out Austria, after the Franco-Prussian War of 1870-71. Otto von Bismarck,

who was then Prime Minister of Prussia,
played the decisive role in forging the second Reich, which lasted until Kaiser
Wilhelm II abdicated in 1918 as a result
of the first World War.

Third empire

Adolf Hitler, who became chancellor
in 1933, designated National Socialist
(Nazi) Germany the "Third Reich."

The Third Reich ended when Germany
capitulated on May 8, 1945, thus ending
the second World War.

Source: Federal Republic of Germany:
Questions and Answers, ed. Susan Steiner.
German Information Center, New York, 1996

SIGNIFICANCE OF 'REICH' AND 'EMPIRE'

The term "empire" is from *imperium,*
Latin for "command and the power to issue it," as well as "the area subjected to
this power."

The German term is *Reich*, related to
Latin *regnum*: "rule, government over
country and people," which in the Middle
Ages meant "kingly rule." From early
medieval times, *imperium* and *Reich* were
taken as practically synonymous. They
were also universalized to signify "worldwide rule," though the extent and limits
of the "world" to which this claim related
varied considerably from moment to moment. The constant theme was the reference to imperial Rome, where from the
days of Augustus *imperium* had signified
"empire."

The *Reich* was the *Kaiserreich* (*Kaiser* from Caesar, the paradigmatic Roman
ruler); the *imperium* was the *imperium
romanum* which, according to the historical theory prevailing throughout the Christian Middle Ages, was expected to last to
the end of time.

The medieval (German) empire was
therefore the successor to, and continua-

tion of, the ancient Roman Empire, the authority and sway of which were guaranteed by Scriptural prophecy to endure until the return of Christ (Dan. 2:31-45).

Source: *Dictionary of the Middle Ages*, Vol. 5, ed. Joseph R. Strayer. Charles Scribner's Sons, New York, 1985

HOLY ROMAN EMPIRE OF THE GERMAN NATION

The Holy Roman Empire of the German Nation
(Heiliges Römisches Reich Deutscher Nation)

Since Konrad II, the East Frankonian Empire was known as the *Romanum Imperium* (*Römisches Reich*, or the Roman Empire).

It was called the *Sacrum Imperium* (*Heiliges Reich*, or Holy Empire) since 1157, and since the mid-thirteenth century the name *Sacrum Romanum Imperium* (Holy Roman Empire) gradually came into use.

The addition, *Nationis Germaniae* (*Deutscher Nation,* or German Nation) was only added in the fifteenth century.

The German (or Roman) king was selected by a College of Electors since 1356 (the Golden Bull). However, starting with Otto I, the German Kaiser was crowned by the pope, a tradition that ended with Karl V in 1530.

Since the fifteenth and sixteenth centuries, the Holy Roman Empire was dominated by power struggles between the Kaiser and the *Reichsständen* (the Imperial Diet) until after the Peace of Westfalia when German history took place almost solely on the level of the many territorial states.

In 1806 the Holy Roman Empire of the German Nation was dissolved.

PRUSSIAN AND GERMAN EMPIRE RULERS

The Hohenzollerns
(In 1417 the Hohenzollerns were granted the Electorate of Brandenburg.)
Electors of Brandenburg *(Kurfürsten von Brandenburg):*
◆Friedrich I (1417-1440)
◆Friedrich II (1440-1470)
◆Albrecht Achilles (1480-1486)
◆Johann Cicero (1486-1499)
◆Joachim I (1499-1535)
◆Joachim II (1535-1571)
◆Johann Georg (1571-1598)
◆Joachim Friedrich (1598-1608)
◆Johann Sigismund (1608-1619)
◆Georg Wilhelm (1619-1640)
◆Friedrich Wilhelm, der Große Kurfürst (1640-1688)
◆Friedrich III. (1688-1701)
Kings of Prussia
(Könige von Preußen)
◆Friedrich III, König in Preußen under the name of Friedrich I (1701-1713)
◆Friedrich Wilhelm I (1713-1740)
◆Friedrich II, der Große (1740-1786)
◆Friedrich Wilhelm II (1786-1797)
◆Friedrich Wilhelm III (1797-1840)
◆Friedrich Wilhelm IV (1840-1861)
◆Wilhelm I (1861-1871)
The German Empire
(Das Deutsche Reich)
In 1871 King Wilhelm I of Prussia was proclaimed as the German Kaiser and thus the basis for the empire was reestablished.
Kaisers *(Kaiser):*
◆Wilhelm I (1871-1888)
◆Wilhelm II (1888-1918)
Chancellors *(Kanzler):*
◆Otto von Bismarck (1871-1890)
◆Georg Leo von Caprivi (1890-1894)
◆ Chlodwig Fürst zu Hohenlohe-Schillingsfürst (1894-1900)
◆Bernhard von Bülow (1900-1909)
◆ Theobald von Bethmann-Hollweg (1909-1917)
◆Georg Michaelis (1917)

◆Georg von Gertling (1917-1918)
◆Max von Baden (1918)
The Weimar Republic
(Die Weimarer Republik)
Presidents of the Republic:
◆Friedrich Ebert (1919-1925)
◆Paul von Hindenburg (1925-1934)
Chancellors:
◆Philipp Scheidemann (1919)
◆Gustav Bauer (1919-1920)
◆Hermann Müller (1920)
◆Konstantin Fehrenbach (1920-1921)
◆Joseph Wirth (1921-1922)
◆Wilhelm Cuno (1922-1923)
◆Gustav Stresemann (1923)
◆Wilhelm Marx (1923-1925)
◆Hans Luther (1925-1926)
◆Wilhelm Marx (1926-1928)
◆Hermann Müller (1928-1930)
◆Heinrich Brüning (1930-1932)
◆Franz von Papen (1932)
◆Kurt von Schleicher (1932-1933)
The Third Empire
(Das Dritte Reich)
◆Adolf Hitler, Führer und Reichskanzler (1934-1945)
◆Karl Dönitz (1945)
The two Germanys
(Die Beiden deutschen Staaten)
After the fall of the German Empire on May 8, 1945, the four powers, the USA, USSR, Great Britain, and France, took over the government.

Germany was divided into four occupied zones, by the Potsdam Agreement of August 2, 1945.

In the western zones was established the Federal Republic of Germany; in the Soviet occupied zone, the German Democratic Republic.

Federal Republic of Germany
(Bundesrepublik Deutschland)
Presidents (Bundespräsidenten):
◆Theodor Heuss (1949-1959)
◆Heinrich Lübke (1959-1969)
◆Gustav Heinemann (1969-1974)
◆Walter Scheel (1974-1979)
◆Karl Carstens (1979-1984)
◆Richard von Weizsäcker (1984-1994)

Chancellors (Bundeskanzler):
◆Konrad Adenauer, CDU (1949-1963)
◆Ludwig Erhard, CDU (1963-1966)
◆Kurt Georg Kiesinger, CDU (1966-1969)
◆Willy Brandt, SPD (1969-1974)
◆Helmut Schmidt, SPD (1974-1982)
◆Helmut Kohl , CDU (since 1982); since October 3, 1990 ,chancellor of united Germany
German Democratic Republic
(Deutsche Demokratische Republik)
Heads of state (Staatschefs):
◆Wilhelm Pieck (1949-1960)
◆Walter Ulbricht (1960-1973)
◆Willi Stoph (1973-1976)
◆Erich Honecker (1976-1989)
◆Manfred Gerlach (1989-1990)
First Secretary of the ZK of the SED
(Erste Sekretäre des ZK der SED):
◆Walter Ulbricht (1950-1971)
◆Erich Honecker (1971-1989)
◆Egon Krenz (Oct. - Dec. 1989)
◆After the downfall of communist East Germany: L. de Maizière, Ministerpräsident, 12 April - 2 October 1990

Source: *Meyers Memo: Das Wissen der Welt nach Sachgebieten.* Meyers Lexikonverlag. Mannheim, 1991.

THE SECOND GERMAN EMPIRE (1871-1918)

The Second German Empire (1871-1918) was composed of 26 entities.

(Anglicized forms of the names are shown in brackets and parentheses.)
Four kingdoms [Königreiche]:
◆Preußen (Prussia)
◆Bayern (Bavaria)
◆Sachsen (Saxony)
◆Württemberg (Wuerttemberg)
Six grand duchies [Großherzogtümer]:
◆Baden
◆Hessen (Hesse)
◆Mecklenburg-Schwerin

◆Mecklenburg-Strelitz
◆Oldenburg
◆ Sachsen-Weimar-Eisenach (Saxe-Weimar-Eisenach)
◆**Five duchies [*Herzogtümer*]:**
◆ Sachsen-Anhalt (Anhalt, Saxony-Anhalt)
◆Braunschweig (Brunswick)
◆Sachsen-Altenburg (Saxe-Altenburg)
◆Sachsen-Koburg-Gotha (Saxe-Coburg-Gotha)
◆ Sachsen-Meiningen-Hilburghausen (Saxe-Meiningen-Hilburghausen)
Seven principalities [*Fürstentümer*]:
◆Lippe, Lippe-Detmold
◆Reuß-ältere Linie] (Reuss-elder line), also called *Reuß-Greitz* (Reuss-Greitz)
◆ Reuß-jüngere Linie (Reuss-younger line), also called Reuß-Schleitz-Gera (Reuss-Schleitz-Gera)
◆Schaumburg Lippe
◆Schwarzburg-Rudolstadt
◆Schwarzburg-Sondershausen
◆Waldeck
Three independent cities, sometimes translated as free towns or Hanseatic cities [*Hansestädte*]:
◆Bremen
◆Hamburg
◆Lübeck
One imperial state [*Reichsland*]
◆Elsaß-Lothringen [Alsace-Lorraine]

PROVINCES OF THE KINGDOM OF PRUSSIA (Königreich Preußen)

Königreich Preußen consisted of about 65 percent of the land area and population of the Second German Empire. It had an extra level of administration above the district — the province [Provinz].

The 13 Prussian provinces
◆Brandenburg
◆Ostpreußen (East Prussia)
◆Hannover
◆Hessen-Nassau [Hesse-Nassau]

◆Hohenzollern
◆Pommern [Pomerania]
◆Posen [Poznan]
◆Provinz Sachsen [Province of Saxony]
◆Rheinprovinz [Rhine Province]
◆Schleswig-Holstein
◆Schlesien [Silesia]
◆Westfalen [West Phalia]
◆Westpreußen [West Prussia]

THURINGIA (Thüringen)

Smaller Saxon states in the area between the Thuringian Forest on the south, the Harz Mountains on the north, the Werra River on the west, and the Saale River on the east were sometimes grouped together and called Thüringen.

Thüringen also included parts of the Kingdom of Saxony, the Kingdom of Bavaria, and the Saxony Province of the Kingdom of Prussia.

The eight independent states of Thüringen were
Grand duchy
◆ Sachsen-Weimar-Eisenach (Saxe-Weimar-Eisenach)
Duchies
◆Sachsen-Altenburg (Saxe-Altenburg)
◆Sachsen-Koburg-Gotha (Saxe-Coburg-Gotha)
◆ Sachsen-Meiningen-Hilburghausen (Saxe-Meiningen-Hilburghausen)
Principalities
◆Reuß-ältere Linie (Reuss-elder line), also known as Reuß-Greitz (Reuss-Greitz)
◆ Reuß-jüngere Linie (Reuss-younger line), also known as Reuß-Schleitz-Gera (Reuss-Schleitz-Gera)
◆Schwarzburg-Rudolstadt
◆Schwarzburg, Sondershausen
Following World War I, Thüringen became a political state.

Source: William J. Toeppe, "Dewey and His System (Part 3A), *German Genealogical Society Newsletter* , Vol. IV, No. 6, July 1995

PRUSSIAN PROVINCES: SOME HISTORICAL PERSPECTIVES

Schleswig-Holstein

Prior to the war between Prussia and Austria on one side, with Denmark on the other in 1864, Schleswig and Holstein were parts of the Kingdom of Denmark. As a result of the 1864 war, Denmark lost Schleswig and Holstein. One source says that Prussia and Austria controlled Schleswig and Holstein as a condominium with Austria having more control in Schleswig and Prussia having more control in Holstein.

In the Prussian-Austrian War of 1866, Austria lost all control in this area. Following this war, Schleswig-Holstein became a single province in the Kingdom of Prussia.

Following World War I, the northern part of Schleswig was restored to Denmark.

Prussian Province of Hesse-Nassau

Prior to the Prussian-Austrian War of 1866, the Grand Duchy of Hesse-Cassel, the Duchy of Nassau and the Independent City of Frankfurt am Main existed as independent states. Following this war, these states were combined into the Prussian Province of Hesse-Nassau.

Grand Duchy of Hesse-Darmstadt, or Hesse

Prior to 1866, the Grand Duchy of Hesse-Darmstadt co-existed with the Grand Duchy of Hesse-Cassel. When the Grand Duchy of Hesse-Cassel was reduced to a Prussian province, the Grand Duchy of Hesse-Darmstadt became the Grand Duchy of Hesse [Großherzogtum Hessen].

Principalities of Hohenzollern

The ruling family of Prussia was the House of Hohenzollern. A member of the family acquired the Margraviate (Markgrafschaft) of Brandenburg.

Brandenburg was the seat of power for this branch of the family, although through a political trick, the Brandenburg ruler became the King in Prussia in 1700. The Hohenzollern principalities of Hohenzollern-Sigmaringen and Hohenzollern-Heckingen were held by other branches of the family.

As a result of the revolutions of 1848, the Hohenzollern princes [Fürsten] resigned their Hohenzollern principalities. In accordance with an agreement of 1695, the principalities reverted to the Brandenburg branch of the family (The King in Prussia). Although the King in Prussia named a new Prince of Hohenzollern, this prince was not granted the right to rule Hohenzollern as an independent state.

Hohenzollern was reduced to one Prussian province in 1850.

Kingdom of Hannover

Prior to the Prussian-Austrian War of 1866, the Kingdom of Hannover existed as an independent state. As a result of that war, Hannover was reduced to a Prussian province following the war.

Rhineland

Prior to the first French Revolution of 1789, the Rhineland comprised a number of counties [Grafschaften], each ruled by a count [Graf], and church states, each ruled by a prince-bishop [Fürstbischof]. These counts and prince-bishops held their states directly under the emperor of the Holy Roman Empire of the German Nation as tenants-in-chief [Unmittelbare].

When the French occupied the Rhineland in 1792, these lands were taken and converted into French departments. The lords were paid for their states.

When the French were removed in about 1815, the lands were not restored to the previous lords but were organized into the Rhine Province [Rheinprovinz] of the Kingdom of Prussia.

Source: William J. Toeppe, "Dewey and His System (Part 3A), *German Genealogical Society Newsletter*, Vol. IV, No. 6, July 1995

THE GERMAN STATES (LÄNDER)

Map courtesy of the Germany Information Center, New York

CURRENT JURISDICTIONS OF SECOND GERMAN EMPIRE (1871-1918) MEMBER STATES AND THEIR MAJOR PROVINCES

Former state or province   **Present country/countries**

Anhalt, Duchy *(Herzogtum)* .... former East Germany =Germany (E)
Baden, Grandduchy *(Großherzogtum)* .... former West Germany=Germany (W)
Bayern (Bavaria), Kingdom *(Königreich)*. Provinces: .... Germany (W)
     Franken (Franconia)
     Pfalz (Palatinate)
     Oberpfalz (Upper Palatinate)
     Schwaben (Swabia)
Braunschweig, Duchy *(Herzogtum)* .... Germany (W)
Bremen, Free City *(Freie Stadt, Freie und Hansestadt)* .... Germany (W)
Elsaß-Lothringen (Alsace-Lorraine), Imperial Province *(Reichslande)* .... France
Hamburg, Free City *(Freie Stady, Freie und Hansestadt)* .... Germany (W)
Hessen (Hesse), Grandduchy *(Großherzogtum)* .... Germany (W)
Lippe-Detmold, Principality *(Fürstentum)* .... Germany (W)
Lübeck, Free City *(Freie Stadt, Freie und Hansestadt)* .... Germany (W)
Mecklenburg-Schwerin, Grandduchy *(Großherzogtum)* .... Germany (E)
Mecklenburg-Strelitz, Grandduchy *(Großherzogtum)* .... Germany (E)
Oldenburg, Grandduchy *(Großherzogtum)* .... Germany (W)
Preußen (Prussia), Kingdom *(Königreich)*. Provinces:
     Brandenburg .... Germany (E)
     Hannover (Hanover) .... Germany (W)
     Hessen-Nassau .... Germany (W)
     Hohenzollern .... Germany (W)
     Holstein .... Germany (W)
     Ostpreußen (East Prussia) .... Poland, Lithuania, Russia
     Pommern (Pomerania) .... Germany (E), Poland
     Posen .... Poland
     Rheinland .... Germany (W)
     Schlesien (Silesia) .... Poland
     Schleswig .... Germany (W), Denmark
     Westfalen .... Germany (W)
     Westpreußen (West Prussia) .... Poland
Reuss-Greiz,[+] Principality *(Fürstentum)* .... Germany (E)
Reuss-Schleiz-Gera,[+] Principality *(Fürstentum)* .... Germany (E)
Sachsen (Saxony), Kingdom *(Königreich)* .... Germany (E)
Sachsen-Weimar-Eisenach,[+] Principality *(Fürstentum)* .... Germany (E)
Sachsen-Koburg und Gotha,[+] Principality *(Fürstentum)* .... Germany (E)
Sachsen-Altenburg,[+] Principality *(Fürstentum)* .... Germany (E)
Sachsen-Meiningen,[+] Principality *(Fürstentum)* .... Germany (E)
Schaumburg-Lippe, Principality *(Fürstentum)* .... Germany (W)
Schwarzburg-Rudolstadt,[+] Principality *(Fürstentum)* .... Germany (E)
Schwarzburg-Sondershausen,[+] Principality *(Fürstentum)* .... Germany (E)
Thüringische Staaten[1] .... Germany (E)
Waldeck, Principality *(Fürstentum)* .... Germany (W)
Württemberg, Kingdom *(Königreich)* .... Germany (W)

[1]Thüringen during this period was the name of a geographical region, not that of a state or a province thereof. The states marked above with (+) were known together as *Thüringische Staaten.*

GERMAN CITIES WITH POPULATIONS OVER 100,000 IN 1905

Locality	State	Population
Berlin	Preußen	2,040,148
Hamburg	Hamburg	802,793
München	Bayern	538,393
Dresden	Sachsen	516,996
Leipzig	Sachsen	502,570
Breslau	Preußen	470,751
Köln	Preußen	428,503
Frankfurt/Main	Preußen	334,951
Nürnberg	Bayern	294,344
Düsseldorf	Preußen	253,099
Hannover	Preußen	250,032
Stuttgart	Württemberg	249,443
Chemnitz	Sachsen	244,405
Magdeburg	Preußen	240,661
Charlottenburg	Preußen	239,512
Essen	Preußen	231,396
Stettin	Preußen	224,078
Königsberg	Preußen	219,862
Bremen	Bremen	214,953
Duisberg	Preußen	192,227
Dortmund	Preußen	175,575
Halle	Preußen	169,899
Altona	Preußen	168,301
Strassburg	Elsaß-Lotheringen	167,342
Kiel	Preußen	163,710
Elberfeld	Preußen	162,682
Mannheim	Baden	162,607
Danzig	Preußen	159,685
Barmen	Preußen	156,148
Rixdorf	Preußen	153,650
Gelsenkirchen	Preußen	147,037
Aix-la-Chapelle	Preußen	143,906
Schöneberg	Preußen	140,992
Braunschweig	Braunschweig	136,423
Posen	Preußen	137,067
Kassel	Preußen	120,446
Bochum	Preußen	118,455
Karlsruhe	Baden	111,200
Krefeld	Preußen	110,347
Plauen	Sachsen	105,182
Wiesbaden	Preußen	100,953

Source: *Encyclopedia Britannica*, University Press, New York, 1910, 11th ed.

STATES OF THE GERMAN EMPIRE, 1871-1918, IN ENGLISH AND GERMAN

English	German
Alsace-Lorraine (State)	Elsaß-Lothringen (Reichsland)
Anhalt (Duchy)	Anhalt (Herzogtum)
Baden (Grandduchy)	Baden (Großherzogtum)
Bavaria (Kingdom)	Bayern (Königreich)
Berlin (City)	Berlin (Stadt)
Brandenburg (Province)	Brandenburg (Provinz)
Bremen (Free City-State)	Bremen (Freistadt)
Brunswick (Duchy)	Braunschweig (Herzogtum)
East Prussia (Province)	Ostpreußen (Provinz)
Hamburg (Free City-State)	Hamburg (Freistadt)
Hanover (Province)	Hannover (Provinz)
Hesse (Grandduchy)	Hessen (Großherzogtum)
Hesse-Nassau (Province)	Hessen-Nassau (Provinz)
Hohenzollern (State)	Hohenzollern (Reichland)
Lippe (Principality)	Lippe (Fürstentum)
Lübeck (Free City-State)	Lübeck (Freistadt)
Mecklenburg-Schwerin (Grandduchy)	Mecklenburg-Schwerin (Großherzogtum)
Mecklenburg-Strelitz (Grandduchy)	Mecklenburg-Strelitz (Großherzogtum)
Oldenburg (Grandduchy)	Oldenburg (Großherzogtum)
Pomerania (Province)	Pommern (Provinz)
Posen (Province)	Posen (Provinz)
Prussia (Kingdom)	Preußen (Königreich)
Reuß-Greiz (Principality)	Reuß ältere Linie (Fürstentum)
Reuss-Schleiz-Gera (Principality)	Reuß jüngere Linie (Fürstentum)
Rhineland (Province)	Rheinland (Provinz)
Saxe-Altenburg (Duchy)	Sachsen-Altenburg (Herzogtum)
Saxe-Coburg-Gotha (Duchy)	Sachsen-Coburg-Gotha (Herzogtum)
Saxe-Meiningen (Duchy)	Sachsen-Meiningen (Herzogtum)
Saxe-Weimar-Eisenach (Grandduchy)	Sachsen-Weimar-Eisenach (Großherzogtum)
Saxony (Kingdom)	Sachsen (Königreich)
Saxony (Province)	Sachsen (Provinz)
Schaumburg-Lippe (Principality)	Schaumburg-Lippe (Fürstentum)
Schleswig-Holstein (Proviince)	Schleswig-Holstein (Provinz)
Schwarzburg-Rudolstadt (Principality)	Schwarzburg-Rudolstadt (Fürstentum)
Schwarzburg-Sondershausen (Principality)	Schwarzburg-Sondershausen (Fürstentum)
Silesia (Province)	Schlesien (Provinz)
Waldeck (Principality)	Waldeck (Fürstentum)
West Prussia (Province)	Westpreußen (Provinz)
Westphalia (Province)	Westfalen (Provinz)
Württemberg (Kingdom)	Württemberg (Königreich)
Germany (Empire)	Deutschland (Reich)

Source: Steven W. Blodgett, *Germany Genealogical Research Guide*. The Genealogical Department of the Church of Jesus Christ of Latter-day Saints, 1989. Reprinted by permission of the author.

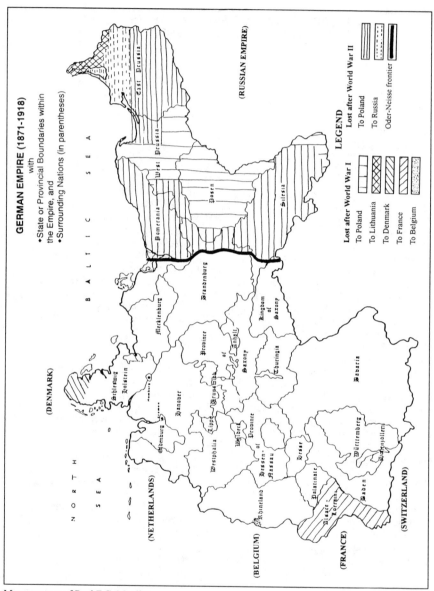

GERMAN EMPIRE (1871-1918)
with
•State or Provincial Boundaries within the Empire, and
•Surrounding Nations (in parentheses)

LEGEND

Lost after World War I

To Poland
To Lithuania
To Denmark
To France
To Belgium

Lost after World War II

To Poland
To Russia
Oder-Neisse frontier

Map courtesy of Paul F.C. Mueller

ENCLAVES AND EXCLAVES

Many states of the Second German Empire were composed of parts in different areas of the Empire. A state might completely surround a part of another state whose main part was distant. This completely surrounded state was an enclave as far as the surrounding state was concerned. These situations arose when a ruling noble family would obtain land outside the main areas ruled by them.

To the state which owned the surrounded part, the surrounded part was an exclave. In other situations, one part of a state might be separated from another part but not completely surrounded by a single state. If the separated part was a small part of the total area of the state, the separated part might also have been called an exclave.With the elimination of the ruling of these areas by the noble families following World War I, the need to recognize these enclaves and exclaves was eliminated.

Source: William J. Toeppe, ed. *Newsletter,* German Genealogical Society of America, Vol. IV, No. 6, 1995. Reprinted by permission.

THE BASIC LAW, OR CONSTITUTION (*Grundgesetz*)

The German constitution is called the *Grundgesetz* (Basic Law) and was put into effect in May 1949 for West Germany.

The name *Grundgesetz* was chosen to emphasize the provisional character of this constitution. As its preamble declared, a definite constitution was to be formulated by the Parliament of a reunited Germany. However, the *Grundgesetz* proved to be so successful that it was retained under the same name by reunited Germany with only minor changes.

In contrast to other constitutions, in which civil liberties are placed in the preamble or in amendments, the Basic Law places civil liberty protection in the constitution itself.

The first paragraph of Article I states that the dignity of the individual must not be threatened.

The third paragraph lists basic rights that all executive and judicial authorities are bound to defend. These include freedom in writing and painting; outlawing of sterilization or medical experiments (even with volunteers); equal rights for men and women; include nondiscrimination regarding sex, descent, race, language, and religious or political views.

Article IV guarantees freedom of religion and conscience, the free profession of religious or philosophic views, and the right to refuse to serve in the military for reasons of conscience. Article V protects freedom of opinion, research, and teaching. Article VI protects marriage and the family. The right of assembly and the right to join and found organizations are also guaranteed. The Basic Law draws heavily from the Bill of Rights and American civil liberties, with additional anti-Nazi-inspired guarantees.

The Basic Law adopts the principle of the American Constitution in that powers of the federal government are expressed and enumerated, while those of the *Länder* (states) are residual. But it also borrows from the Swiss in building its definition of federalism with the heavy intermingling of federal and state governments in their direct effect on the people. The state administrations serve as executors of federal law in many cases.

Sources:
♦Judith M. Gansberg, Stalag: USA. *The Remarkable Story of German POWs in America.* Thomas Y. Crowell Company, New York, 1977.
♦Rainer Thumshirn of Heimstetten, Germany

THE GERMAN FLAG

1813-1818: During War of Liberation against Napoleon, university students wear the black-red-gold colors as a symbol of the struggle for German unity

1817: The tri-colors are flown by students from the University of Jena and other universities at the rally at the Wartburg Castle in Erfurt.

1832: The flag is again displayed at the castle of Hambach when some 30,000 Germans demonstrate for the cause of unity, justice, and freedom. Many German princes take this action as a sign of subversion and ban the flag.

1848: The colors become the symbol of the German Confederation.

1852: After the failure of the revolution in this year, the tri-colors are outlawed, in the interest of "law and order."

1871: Following Bismarck's leadership in the unification of Germany, he chooses the a flag of black-white-red, the colors of Prussia and other northern German states combined.

1918: With the creation of the Weimar Republic, the tricolor of black-red-gold becomes the national flag of Germany, although reactionary forces are vehemently opposed to the flag they identify with liberalism and democracy. (One of their cries: "Down with the black-red-mustard Republic.")

1933: With the Nazis' rise to power, the black-red-gold tricolor is replaced with the pre-World War I black-red-white, which is in turn replaced with the swastika *(Hakenkreuz)* on September 15, 1935.

1933-1935: Display of the black-red-gold becomes a criminal offense.

1949: Since this date, the constitutionally adopted "schwarz-rot-gold" has served as the national colors of the Federal Republic of Germany.

Source: "Banner of Unity, Flag of Hope," by Gerhard Weiss. *German Life*, August/ September 1995.

REUNIFICATION OF GERMANY

On October 3, 1990, less than one year after the opening of the Berlin Wall, the German Democratic Republic acceded to the Federal Republic and adopted its laws. The accession took place in three steps:

1. On May 18, 1990, the Federal Republic of Germany and the German Democratic Republic signed a treaty establishing monetary, economic and social union between the two states.

This took effect on July 1, when the West German D-Mark was introduced into East Germany together with West Germany's laws, rules, and regulations governing such matters as commerce, taxation, and social security .

2. On August 31, 1990, a second treaty was signed under which the five East German states – Mecklenburg-Vorpommern, Brandenburg, Saxony-Anhalt, Thuringia, and Saxony – acceded to the Federal Republic of Germany under Article 23 of the Basic Law.

This, the formal unification treaty, took effect on October 3, 1990.

3. On September 12, 1990, the Federal Republic of Germany, the German Democratic Republic, France, the Soviet Union, Britain and the United States concluded a "Treaty of the Final Settlement with Respect to Germany."

With this treaty, the four Powers agreed to the establishment of a "united Germany" consisting of the territories of the Federal Republic of Germany, the German Democratic Republic and all of Berlin. In doing so, they also agreed to relinquish their rights and responsibilities relating to Berlin and Germany as a whole. They also permitted united Germany to be a member of alliances. The Soviet Union thus agreed to united Germany's continuing membership in NATO. The Soviet Union agreed to withdraw its forces from the territory of the GDR by the end of 1994.

Source: German Information Center, *Federal Republic of Germany: Questions and Answers,* ed. Susan Steiner. New York, 1996.

NATIONAL ANTHEM

The national anthem of the Federal Republic of Germany is the third stanza of the *Lied der Deutschen.*

The lyrics of the anthem were written by August Heinrich Hoffman von Fallersleben (1798-1874), and the melody was composed by Joseph Haydn (1732-1809).

THE SWASTIKA (Hakenkreuz)

The swastika was understood to represent a sun wheel. In 1933 a decree was issued in Germany that the national flags were to be the black, white and red tricolor (from top: black, white, red) and the *Hakenkreuz.* the two flags were to be hoisted together.

The *Hakenkreuz* had a red background, a white disk in the middle, on which was superimposed the swastika, the emblem of the Nazi Party.

On September 15, 1935 it became the national flag.

After World War II, the occupying powers ordered that no flags or emblems of the Nazi regime were to be flown.

Sources:
♦*Flags of the World,* ed. E.M.C. Barraclough. Frederick Warne & Co., New York, 1971
♦Wilfried Fest, *Dictionary of German History 1806-1945.* St. Martin's Press, New York, 1978

CAPITALS OF GERMANY

Berlin was the capital of Germany between 1871 and 1945.

Prior to that there was no German capital because Germany did not exist as a single state.

During the years when two German states existed (1949-1990), Bonn was the capital of West Germany and Berlin (East) was the capital of East Germany.

When East Germany merged with West Germany, it was agreed that Berlin would become the capital of united Germany.

The Bonn government is in the process of moving to Berlin and wants to complete the move by the end of the century.

Source: German Information Center, *Federal Republic of Germany: Questions and Answers,* ed. Susan Steiner. New York, 1996

'CRYSTAL NIGHT,' 1938

On November 9-10, 1938, Nazi officials led attacks on Jews, synagogues and businesses owned by Jews throughout Germany in a pogrom that came to be known as "Crystal Night" (*Reichskristallnacht*).

Nearly 100 people were killed, 267 synagogues were set ablaze, and some 30,000 Jews were arrested for deportation to concentration camps.

Planning may begin in 1998 for a "Topography of Terror" documentation center on the Nazi era, to be built on the site where the Gestapo had its headquarters.

Source: *The Week in Germany,* German Information Center, New York, November 15, 1996.

POPULATION OF GERMAN EMPIRE STATES, 1871

Kingdoms

Prussia	24,691,433
Bavaria	4,863,450
Saxony	2,556,244
Württemberg	1,818,539

Grand Duchies

Baden	1,461,562

Hesse 852,894
Mecklenburg-Strelitz 96,982
Oldenburg 314,459
Duchies
Brunswick 311,764
Saxe-Meiningen 187,957
Saxe-Altenburg 142,122
Saxe-Coburg-Gotha 174,339
Anhalt 203,437
Principalities
Schwarzburg-Sondershausen 76,523
Schwarzburg-Rudolstadt 67,191
Waldeck 56,224
Reuss-Greiz 45,094
Schaumburg-Lippe 32,059
Lippe 111,135
Free Towns
Lübeck 52,158
Bremen 122,402
Hamburg 338,974
Imperial Territory
Alsace-Lorraine 1,549,738

German Empire 41,058,792

Source: *Encyclopedia Britannica: Dictionary of Arts, Sciences, Literature, and General Information,* University Press, New York, Eleventh Edition., 1910

FOUNDING DATES OF GERMAN STATES (*Bundesländer*)

Baden-Württemberg 1952
Bayern 1946
Berlin 1946
Brandenburg 1990
Freie Hansestadt Bremen 1947
Freie Hansestadt Hamburg 1949
Hessen 1945
Mecklenburg-Vorpommern 1990
Niedersachsen 1946
Nordrhein-Westfalen 1946
Rheinland-Pfalz 1946
Saarland 1957
Sachsen 1990
Sachsen-Anhalt 1990
Schleswig-Holsteiin 1946

Thüringen 1990

POLITICAL STRUCTURE, MODERN GERMANY

Modern Germany has a six-level political hierarchy:
1. Federal Republic of Germany [*Bundesrepublik Deutschland*]
2. State [*Land*]
3. District [*Bezirk* or *Regierungsbezirk*]*
4. Circle [*Kreis*]**
5. Official Community [*Gemeinde*]
6. Habitation
*Not applicable to the city states or Saarland; **Not applicable to city states

Source: William J. Toeppe, "Dewey and His System (Part 3A), *German Genealogical Society Newsletter* , Vol. IV, No. 6, July 1995

PLACE-NAME PREFIXES

The following place-name prefixes are shown with their meanings (in parentheses) and examples of their use:
Alt (old): .... Alt Meiershof
Am (at the): .... Am Sonnenberg
Bad (bath, spa): .... Bad Kissingen
Groß (large): .... Groß Buckow, Großgartach
Hinter (back): .... Hinter Bollhagen, Hinterweiler
Hohe (high): .... Hohe Mühle, Hohenkirchen
Im (in the): .... Im Holze
Klein (small): .... Klein Eschefeld
Neu (new): .... Neu Grambow, Neuhardenberg
Nieder (lower):   Nieder Neuendorf, Niederzimmern
Ober (upper): .... Oberbachheim
St. (*Sankt*) .... St. Martin
(meaning saint)
Schloß (castle, palace): Schloß Neuhaus
Unter (lower): .... Untergrombach
Vorder (front): .... Vor Wangern

ABBREVIATIONS USED ON GERMAN MAPS

A. .... Alps (Alpen)
Arch. .... archipelago (Archipel)
B. .... creek (Bach)
B. ... mountain, mountains (Berg, Berge)
B. .... bay (Bucht)
b., bch. .... creek (-bach)
bg., bgn. .... mountain (-berg, -bergen)
bg. .... castle (-burg)
Bhf. .... train station (Bahnhof)
Br. .... well (Brunnen)
D. .... German (Deutsch)
df. .... village (-dorf)
Fj. .... fjord (Fjord)
Fl. .... river(Fluß)
Ft. .... fort (Fort)
G. .... Gulf (Golf)
Geb. .... mountain range (Gebirge)
Gl. .... glacier (Gletscher)
Gr. .... Great- (Groß)
H. .... behind, in back of (hinter)
H. .... hill, high (Höhe, Hügel,
                                        Hoch, Hohen)
hfn. .... harbor (-hafen)
H.I. .... peninsula (Halbinsel)
hm. .... -home (-heim)
hsn. .... place, town (-hausen)
I., Iⁿ .... island (Insel, Inseln)
K. .... cape (Kap)
K., Kan. .... channel (Kanal)
Kl. .... small (Klein-)
Kr. .... county (Kreis)
lbn. .... -live (-leben)
Ld. .... land (Land)
lgn. .... (-lingen)
M., Mitt. .... middle (Mittel)
Nd., Ndr. .... Low-, Lower- (Nieder-)
Ob. .... Upper- (Ober-)
P. .... pass (Paß)
Q. .... spring, source (Quelle)
R. .... reef (Riff)
rde. .... -rode (-rode)
S. .... lake (See)
Schl. .... palace (Schloß)
Schn. .... rapids (Schnellen)
Sd. .... sound (Sund)

Sp. .... peak (Spitze)
St. .... stone (Stein)
St. .... Saint (Sankt)
Str. .... stream (Strom)
Str. .... street, strait (Straße)
T., Th., t., th. .... valley (Tal, Thal,
                                         -tal, -thal)
U. .... Lower- (Unter-)
V. .... volcano (Vulkan)
W. .... west (West)
wd. .... -wood (-wald)
wlr. .... -hamlet (-weiler)

Source: *Minerva Atlas*, Leipzig, 1927

PLACE-NAME ENDINGS TYPICAL IN VARIOUS GERMAN AREAS

-a: Posen, Sachsen, Schlesien
-ach: Baden, Bayern, Elsaß-Lothringen
-ath: Rheinland
-au: Hessen-Nassau, Ostpreußen, Westpreußen, Posen, Sachsen (prov.), Sachsen, Schlesien
-bach: Baden, Bayern, Elsaß-Lothringen, Hessen-Nassau, Hessen, Rheinland, Württemberg
-beck: Hannover, Westfalen
-bek: Schleswig-Holstein
-berg: Baden, Bayern, Pfalz, Brandenburg, Braunschweig, Elsaß-Lothringen, Hannover, Hessen-Nassau, Hessen, Mecklenburg, Oldenburg, Ostpreußen, Westpreußen, Pommern, Rheinland, Sachsen (prov.), Sachsen, Schlesien, Westfalen, Württemberg
-brok: Oldenburg
-bruck: Hannover
-brucken: Pfalz
-bull: Schleswig-Holstein
-burg: Baden, Bayern, Pfalz, Brandenburg, Braunschweig, Elsaß-Lothringen, Hannover, Hessen-Nassau, Hessen, Mecklenburg, Oldenburg, Ostpreußen, Westpreußen, Pommern, Rheinland, Sachsen (prov.), Sachsen, Schlesien, Westfalen, Württemberg

-**by:** Schleswig-Holstein
-**chen:** Elsaß-Lothringen
-**dorf:** Brandenburg, Braunschweig,
Elsaß-Lothringen, Hannover, Hessen-
Nassau, Mecklenburg, Oldenburg,
Ostpreußen, Rheinland, Sachsen (prov.),
Schlesien, Schleswig-Holstein
-**e:** Sachsen (prov.)
-**en:** Ostpreußen, Rheinland, Sachsen
(prov.), Sachsen, Schlesien, Westfalen,
Württemberg
-**erk:** Rheinland
-**feld:** Sachsen, Württemberg
-**felde:** Braunschweig, Westpreußen
-**gard:** Pommern
-**gen:** Baden, Elsaß-Lothringen, Westfalen, Württemberg
-**hagen:** Baden, Mecklenburg, Pommern
-**hain:** Hessen-Nassau
-**hausen:** Bayern, Brandenburg, Braunschweig, Hannover, Hessen-Nassau,
Sachsen (prov.), Westfalen
-**haven:** Hannover
-**helm:** Bayern, Pfalz, Elsaß-Lothringen,
Hessen, Württemberg
-**hofen:** Elsaß-Lothringen
-**horn:** Oldenburg
-**ich:** Rheinland
-**ig:** Sachsen
-**in:** Brandenburg, Mecklenburg, Pommern, Posen
-**ing:** Bayern, Schleswig-Holstein
-**ingen:** Braunschweig
-**itz:** Mecklenburg, Westpreußen, Pommern, Posen, Sachsen (prov.), Sachsen,
Schlesien
-**kehmen:** Ostpreußen
-**ken:** Ostpreußen
-**kirchen:** Hessen-Nassau, Oldenburg,
Rheinland
-**lau:** Brandenburg
-**lin:** Brandenburg
-**litz:** Brandenburg
-**low:** Brandenburg
-**lund:** Schleswig-Holstein
-**mar:** Hessen-Nassau
-**mark:** Brandenburg
-**nau:** Baden
-**nitz:** Brandenburg

-**now:** Brandenburg
-**o:** Posen
-**ow:** Mecklenburg, Pommern
-**pitz:** Brandenburg
-**reuth:** Bayern
-**rode:** Branschweig, Hannover
-**rum:** Braunschweig
-**rup:** Schleswig-Holstein
-**scheid:** Rheinland
-**schin:** Posen
-**see:** Westpreußen, Pommern
-**stadt:** Bayern, Pfalz, Hessen, Sachsen
(prov.), Württemberg
-**stede:** Oldenburg
-**stedt:** Braunschweig, Hannover, Sachsen (prov.), Schleswig-Holstein
-**stein:** Bayern, Hessen-Nassau, Hessen,
Westfalen
-**stett:** Baden
-**sum:** Hannover
-**thal:** Brandenburg
-**walde:** Brandenburg, Westpreußen
-**weiler:** Elsaß-Lothringen
-**witz:** Brandenburg, Schlesien
-**wo:** Posen
-**zig:** Brandenburg, Westpreußen, Posen
Reprinted by permission of Larry O. Jensen.
From, *A Genealogical Handbook of German
Research*. Rev. ed. Pleasant Grove, Utah, 1995.

SOME IMPORTANT GAZETTEERS FOR GERMAN RESEARCH

The following gazetteers (geographi-
cal dictionaries) are especially useful for
German research:
♦*Meyers Orts- und Verkehrs-Lexikon des
Deutschen Reichs* [Meyer's Directory of
Places and Commerce in the German
Empire] (Dr. E. Ütrecht, ed.. Leipzig,
Germany: Bibliographisches Instutut. 5th
ed. 1912, 1913).
The gazetteer, covering the pre-World
War I German Empire, is generally used
to find the locations of civil registration
offices and to determine whether the town
has a parish of a particular religion. The

Germany section of the Family History Library Catalog is organized around the locality entries in this gazetteer. FHL Film 496,640 for A-K; 496,641 for L-Z. Fiche 6000001-29; FHL book 943/E5mo.

♦*Müllers Großes deutsches Ortsbuch*, [Mullers Large German Gazetteer] (Fritz Müller; Wuppertal-Barmen: Post- und Ortsbuchverlag Postmeister A.D. Friedrich Müller, 1958. 18th edition 1974.) Covers modern German place names before 1990 reunification. Cross-referenced to the Shell Atlas] FHL book: Ref 943 E5m 1958. Film 1,045,448. Fiche 6000343-54.

♦*Müllers Verzeichnis der jenseits der Oder-Neisse gelegenen, unter fremder Verwaltungsstehenden Ortschaften*. Revised by M. Dremmerer. Wuppertal-Barmen, Germany: Post und Ortsverlag. 1958. [Mueller's Gazetteer of Localities Lying East of the Oder-Neisse (Line, which Are) under Foreign Administration].

Lists Polish names and former German names of villages which are now in Poland and Russia. FHL book 943 E5m 1958 Supp. Film 1,045,448; fiche 6000343-54.

♦*Amtliches Gemeinde- und Ortsnamenverzeichnis der deutschen Ostgebiete unter Fremder Verwaltung* [Official Gazetteer for the Localities in the (Former) German East under Foreign Administration] (Remagen: Selbstverlag der Bundesanstalt für Landeskunde, 1955.) Covers pre-World War II areas. Provides name changes for former German localities that became part of Poland and Russia after World War II. Volume 1 contains Elsaß-Lothringen and the rest of France, and Eupen-Malmedy and the rest of Belgium.

Volume 2 contains northern Schleswig and the rest of Denmark, Memelland and the rest of Lithuania, and the ceded areas of Ostpreußen, West-preußen, Posen, Oberschlesien and the rest of Poland.

FHL book: Ref 943.8 E5b. Film 824,243, item 2. Fiche 6053256 (11 fiche).

Polish-to-German name changes are on Film 1045449.

♦ *Deutsch-Fremdsprachiges Orts-namenverzeichnis*, 3 vols. [Gazetteer of Places, with German and Foreign Language Names] (Kredel, Otto and Thierfelder, Franz. Berlin: Deutsche Verlagsgesselschaft, 1931)

Post-World War I place names of localities outside the Germanic countries that formerly had German names. FHL book: Ref Q 940 E5kt. Film 583,457.

♦ *Spis Miejscowo ci Polskiej Rzeczypospolitej Ludowej*, 2 Vols.[List of Place Names in the People's Republic of Poland] (Warsaw, 1967) Gives present Polish names for former German counties.

FHL book: Ref 943.8 E5s. Film 844922; Fiche 6000369-6000383.

READING GERMAN PLACE NAMES

For help in reading misspelled or hard-to-read German place names, see this 14-page publication:

Ernest Thode, *Interpreting ~~Mispelled Misspelt~~ Misspelled German Place-Names*. Ernest Thode, RR7, Box 306, Kern Road, Marietta, OH 45750-9437. $6.00 + $1 postage and handling.

MAJOR GAZETTEERS FOR EASTERN EUROPE

Austria: *Gemeindelexikon der in Reichsrate vertretenen Königreiche und Länder* [Gazetteer of the crownlands and territories represented in the imperial council]. Vienna. K.K. Statistisches Zentralkommission, 1903-1908.
Austro-Hungarian Empire: *Allgemeines geographisches statistisches Lexikon aller österreichischen Staaten* [General Gazetteer of all Austro-Hungary]. Vienna.

28   The German Research Companion

Franz Raffelsperger, 1845-1853.
Hungary: *Magyarország Helységnévtára*
[Gazetteer of Hungary], János Dvorzák,
comp. Budapest: "Havi Füzetek," 1877.
German Empire: Ütrecht, E., comp.
*Meyers Orts- und Verkehrs- Lexikon des
Deutschen Reichs* [Meyer's gazetteer and
directory of the German Empire]. Leipzig:
Bibliographisches Institut, 1912.
Prussia: *Gemeindelexikon für das
Königreich Preußen* [Gazetteer for the
Kingdom of Prussia]. Berlin: Verlag des
Königlichen statistischen Landesamts,
1907-1909.
Russian Empire: Sulimierski, Filip, ed.
*Slownik Geograficzny Królestwa
Polskiego i Innych Krajów Slowiañskich*
[Geographical dictionary of the Kingdom
of Poland and other Slavic countries]. 15
Vol. Warsaw: Sulimierski i Walewski,
1880-1902.
Czechoslovakia: *Administratives Ge-
meindelexikon der Cechoslovakischen
Republik* [Administrative Gazetteer of the
Czechoslovak Republic]. Prague. Statis-
tischen Staatsamte, 1927-1928.
**Areas of Hungary later in Czechoslo-
vakia:** *Majtán, Milan. Názvy Obci na
Slovensku za Ostatných Dvesto Rokov*
[Place names in Slovakia during the last
200 years]. Bratislava. Slovenská Akadé
mie Vied, 1972.
Poland: *Spis Miejscowosci Polskiej
Rzeczypospolitej Ludowej* [Gazetteer of
Polish People's Republic Localities].
Warsaw: Wydawnictwakomunikacj i
lacznosci, 1968; also Bystrzycki, Tadeusz.
*Skorowidz Miejscowosci Rzecypos-politej
Polskiej* [Listing of Localities of the Polish
Republic]. Przemysl: Wydawnictwa
ksiaznicy naukowej, 1934. Gazetteer of
the early republic of Poland from 1918 to
1939.
Romania: *Indicatorul Localitatilor din
Romania* [Index of Localities of
Romania]. Bucuresti: Editura Academiiei
Republicii Socialiste Romania, 1974.
Yugoslavia: *Imenik mesta u Jugoslaviji*
[Place names in Yugoslavia]. Beograd:

Novinski Ustanova Sluzbeni List SFRJ,
1972

REGIONAL GAZETTEERS

The multi-volume set of gazetteers, *The
Atlantic Bridge to Germany*, by Charles
M. Hall (Everton Publishers, Inc., Logan,
Utah) provides maps, lists of community
names, and archive information about the
various entities of the Second Empire (including Alsace-Lorraine) and Switzerland,
with each volume concentrating on a given
area.
These volumes are helpful in locating
ancestral towns.
For example, a typical volume offers
an index to the Gemeinde (communities)
of an area, the list of *Kreise* (counties),
many regional maps, bibliographic listings
of resources pertinent to the area, and types
of records available at specific archives.
The series includes the following:
Volume 1: Baden-Württemberg
Volume 2: Hessen-Rheinland-Pfalz
Volume 3: Bavaria
Volume 4: Saarland, Alsace-Lorraine,
Switzerland
Volume 5: Bremen, Hamburg, and
Schleswig-Holstein
Volume 6: Mecklenburg
Volume 7: Northrhine-Westphalia
Volume 8: Prussia
Volume 9: Saxony, Thuringia, nine
duchies

THE 16 STATES (*LÄNDER*): POPULATION, CAPITALS AND OTHER CITIES

"Other cities" named below are those
with populations of more than 100,000.
◆ **Baden-Württemberg** (9.8 million).
Capital: Stuttgart. Other cities, Freiburg,
Heidelberg, Heilbronn, Karlsruhe, Mann-
heim, Pforzheim, Ulm
◆ **Bayern** (11-4 million). Capital Mün-

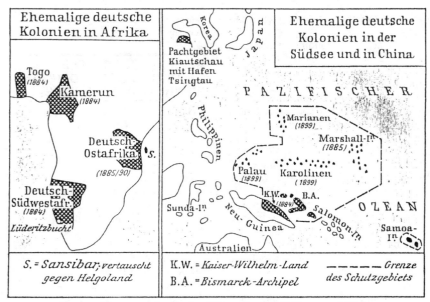

Former German colonies in Africa, the South Seas, and China
(Hans Muggenthaler, Geschichte für Mittelschulen, vol. 3. Kösel-Verlag München, 1962)

chen. Other cities, Augsburg, Erlangen, Fürth, Ingolstadt, Nürnberg, Regensburg, Würzburg
◆**Berlin** (3.4 million). Capital: Berlin.
◆ **Brandenburg** (2.6 million). Capital Potsdam. Other city, Cottbus
◆**Bremen** (0.68 million). Capital: Bremen
◆**Hamburg** (1.7 million). Capital: Hamburg
◆**Hessen** (5.8 million). Capital: Wiesbaden. Other cities, Darmstadt, Frankfurt a. M., Kassel, Offenbach
◆**Mecklenburg-Pommern** (1.9 million). Capital: Schwerin. Other city, Rostock
◆**Niedersachsen** (7.4 million). Capital: Hannover. Other cities, Braunschweig, Göttingen, Hildesheim, Salzgitter, Wolfsburg
◆**Nordrhein-Westfalen** (17.3 million). Capital Düsseldorf. Other cities, Aachen, Bielefeld, Bonn, Dortmund, Duisberg, Essen, Hamm, Köln, Leverkusen, Münster, Paderborn, Recklinghausen,

Siegen
◆**Rheinland-Pfalz** (3.8 million). Capital: Mainz. Other cities, Koblenz, Ludwigshaven
◆**Saarland** (1.1 million). Capital: Saarbrücken.
◆**Sachsen** (4.8 million). Capital: Dresden. Other cities, Chemnitz, Leipzig, Zwickau
◆**Sachsen-Anhalt** (2.9 million). Capital: Magdeburg. Other cities, Dessau, Halle
◆ **Schleswig-Holstein** (2.6 million). Capital: Kiel. Other city, Lübeck
◆**Thüringen** (2.6 million). Capital: Erfurt. Other cities, Gera, Jena

GERMAN COLONIES

By Rainer Thumshirn
    The age of European colonialism began around 1500, when Spanish, Portuguese, French, Dutch and English sailors discovered new overseas territories and

took them into possession for their countries.

Settlement and economic exploitation of these lands were a major factor in the rise of the respective home countries to major powers.

Germany, inward-looking, divided into a multitude of small states, and lacking a sizable fleet, could not try to join this dividing-up of the world except for two short-lived ventures: one into Venezuela 1528-1555 by the merchants Ehingen and Welser, and another by Prussia into Africa's Gold Coast 1683-1718.

While on one hand tens of thousands of German emigrants helped to settle and develop many of the new colonies, on the other hand they usually severed ties to their former homelands which did not gain any advantages from their former subjects' colonization efforts.

This changed only in the 1880s, when German explorers and merchants urged the newly established *Deutsches Reich* to acquire colonies of its own, before none were left. Chancellor Bismarck realized that the remaining available areas for colonization were of little economic value and acquired some of them for the *Deutsches Reich* without enthusiasm.

They were officially called *Schutzgebiete* (protectorates), and Bismarck is said to have avoided the term colony.

These areas were,
♦Togo, Kamerun [Cameroon], Deutsch-Ostafrika [Tanzania] and Deutsch-Südwestafrika [Namibia] in Africa
♦Kiautschau and Tsingtau in China
♦The South Sea Islands of Palau, the Marianas, Caroline Islands, Solomon Islands, and parts of New Guinea. (The Melanesian Islands off the northeast coast of New Guinea are still called Bismarck Archipelago today.)

The acquisitions were short-lived however, as they were lost after World War I when they were taken over by other countries or put under the jurisdiction of the League of Nations.

Source: Rainer Thumshirn, of Heimstetten, Germany

AREA IN SQUARE MILES OF STATES OF THE GERMAN EMPIRE (1900 STATISTICS)

Kingdoms

Preußen	134,463
Bayern	29,282
Württemberg	7,528
Sachsen	55,787

Imperial Territory

Elsaß-Lothringen	5,668

Grand Duchies

Baden	5,821
Hessen	2,965
Mecklenburg-Schwerin	5,135
Mecklenburg-Strelitz	1,131
Oldenburg	2;,479
Sachsen-Weimar	1,388

Duchies

Braunschweig	1,424
Sachsen-Meiningen	953
Sachsen-Koburg und Gotha	755
Sachsen-Altenburg	511
Anhalt	998

Principalities

Waldeck	433
Lippe	469
Schwarzburg-Rudolstadt	363
Schwarzburg-Sondershausen	333
Schaumburg-Lippe	131
Reuß-Greitz	122
Reuß-Schleitz-Gera	31

Free Cities

Bremen	99
Hamburg	158
Lübeck	115

Total: 208,830

Source: Max Kade Institute, Madison, Wisconsin

MAPS AND ATLASES
FOR PRACTICAL USE

by Betty Heinz Matyas

Maps for United States research
◆ State maps: AAA maps have good indexes and details
◆ County maps: *The Handy Book for Genealogists* (Everton Publishers) shows changes in county borders
◆ Township maps: *Township Atlas of the United States*, by J. L. Andriot, is available through the National Archives and genealogy or university libraries
Map scale
A map scale (*Maßstab*, in German) is expressed as a ratio between map distance and ground distance. For example, the scale 1:100,000 in the metric system indicates that 1 represents 1 kilometer of ground distance, and 100,000 represents 100,000 centimeters of map distance.
Maps for driving in Germany
◆ Falk's *Der Große Auto Atlas Bundesrepublik Deutschland*, 1996 (revised annually) is highly recommended. In book form (7½" x 11" closed), when opened fits comfortably on the lap. Each of the five maps has fold-out sections as needed. With a map scale of 1:500,000, this atlas has an easy-to-read index with the current zip codes given. Names of towns are easily visible in strong type, and *Tankstelle* (gas) and *Rastplatz* (rest stop) locations are indicated.
◆ The **Shell Eurokarte Deutschland** folds to 5" x 10", with a scale of 1:750,000. It is difficult to read in the car; the print is small. Maps produced by many other map publishers have these same problems
Maps for German research
◆ The *Atlas of the German Empire, 1892* (published by Thomsen's Genealogical Center, Bountiful, Utah) covers the period of greatest emigration. It contains 24 indexed maps of the German regions and those now in Poland, with scales varying

between 1:850,000 and 1:1,700,000.
◆ The set of Jensen and Storrer maps (**"Maps of the German Empire of 1871"**) is similar. The map of the 1871 German Empire which has the most detail in a scale of 1:100,000 is on film and fiche through the Family History Library. *Karte des Deutschen Reiches* (FHL film #068,814 and FHL fiche #6000063-6000197) consisting of 674 maps, was originally produced for military purposes. It includes all cities, towns, villages, hamlets, manorial estates, and groups of houses. It is suitable for conducting an area search to gather more information on ancestors in neighboring settlements. This map is of special significance because it is coordinated wih listings in the gazetteer, *Meyers Orts- und Verkehrs Lexikon*.
Older maps
Older maps, which may be useful because of boundary or governmental changes,may be found in university and city public libraries. These may not, however, have the advantage of modern topographical methods developed by the end of the eighteenth century. Copies of old maps can be purchased in large libraries such as the state libraries in Berlin and Munich, and in the Library of Congress.
Small-scale maps
These, showing large areas with less detail, varying from about 1:500,000 to 1:2,000,000, are used to ascertain the location of one state or country as it relates to another, or to locate a large region within a state – for example, the Black Forest in Württemberg, the Vogtland in Sachsen, and the borders of a former duchy or principality.
Large-scale maps
These, showing small villages, their main streets, and building locations, vary from about 1:25,000 to 1:200,000. These two scales are the most commonly used.
The 1:200,000
'workhorse' scale
With infrequent exception, the 1:200,000 scale map is of greatest use and

contains all the small villages, including the church location, the *Güter* (noble working estates), moors, and areas of recreational value, any of which may provide clues toward determining an ancestsor's place of origin.

* **Shell maps.** Of superb quality in this scale are the 36 individual Shell maps, called *Die Generalkarte* (not to be confused with the Shell Eurokarte mentioned above), produced by Mairs Geographischer Verlag in Stuttgart. These maps may be obtained at German Shell gas stations and in bookstores, as well as from Genealogy Unlimited in Orem, Utah.

Auto Atlas Deutschland. This atlas, also of superior quality, is published by RV Verlag and is updated every two years. In a size of about 8½" x 11", this atlas provides detailed maps for the entire country. There are 229 maps, a listing of zip codes, and 75 inner-city maps with street indexes, in a scale of 1:20,000. RV publishes an equally excellent atlas for Poland.

ADAC Maxi Atlas Deutschland. This German Auto Club atlas provides much the same content as the *RV Atlas.* Its scale is 1:150,000, allowing for larger print size, but the atlas is rather awkward to handle (15½" tall). It contains no separate city maps.

Topographical maps

Each state of Germany has a *Landesvmessungsamt* (topographical survey office) which produces a series of maps of its state in scales of 1:25,000, 1:50,000, 1:100,000, and 1:500,000. (See "German Historical Maps" in the next section.) Planned for the future are maps in still larger scales of 1:10,000, 1:5,000, and 1:2,500 for certain areas of Germany. For genealogists, the 1:25,000 scale map is probably of most interest.

City maps

Falk's Stadtplan has street maps for about 100 cities on a scale of 1:15,000. Städte-Verlag, which publishes *Freizeit* (leisure-time, recreational) maps, offers 600 city maps at 1:10,000 to 1:100,000 scale. In the RV Atlas are 75 inner-city maps at 1:20,000, indexed. *Atlasco Stadtplan* presents its descriptions in German and English, side by side.

Boundary markings

Many maps show towns, but not the state borders, or conversely, they show state outlines with only a smattering of towns. The *RV Atlas* indicates state boundaries by pink diagonally striped lines. The National Geographic Society sells a political/traveler's map of Germany, issued in 1991, showing plenty of towns, with plainly marked boundaries of the states.

German zip code book

The *Postleitzahlenbuch* (German zip code book) can also help. Listed are all the towns of a certain name, with the zip code number for each; the town, or one close by, will be on the zip code map. If a town is very small, it may carry the number of an adjacent larger place, which is noted on the small town's entry in the zip code listing, and it can then be found on a regular map. If the town has been incorporated into a larger town or city, however, it will not appear in the zip code book.

Meyers gazetteer

There are clues in *Meyers Orts- und Verkehrs Lexikon* to help find a town on a map. Immediately following a town's name is its location – country, state; then nearby services, like courts and administrative offices, post office and telegraph; and also the train station, if it is not within the town itself. The town can then be searched on one's own map, or on *Karte des Deutschen Reiches*, FHL film #068,814, as previously noted.

Map sources

Landesvermessungs. These are the land survey maps for each German state from its *Landesvermessungsamt* (survey office) in Germany. These maps are also available under the title, German Empire Maps, from Genealogy Unlimited. (See next page, "German Historical Maps.")

◆**Genealogy Unlimited,** P.O. Box 537, Orem, UT 84059, for –
a) German Empire Maps (also known as *Landesvermessungs* maps); these are special ordered, in scales of 1:25,000 and 1:200,000. Send a stamped self-addressed envelope for a map grid.
b) *Die General Karte,* by Shall/Mairs, individual regional maps. Send a stamped self-addressed envelope for a map grid.
c)RV Atlas of the German Empire 1892.
◆**The National Geographic Society**, P.O. Box 98171, Washington, DC 20077-9794 for Germany Political/Traveler's Map #20058, published 1991. Ask for a map list.
◆*Städte-Verlag,* Steinbeisstsr. 9, 70736 Fellbach bei Stuttgart, Germany for –
a) *Freizeit Wanderpläne* [leisure-time

maps]
b) *Stadtplan* (city maps)
Ask for a map list and shipping cost.
◆*Karte des deutschen Reiches.* FHL film #068,814

Source: *Der Blumenbaum,* Vol. 14, No. 1, 1996

GERMAN HISTORICAL MAPS

Historical maps are available through the topographical survey office *(Landesvermessungsamt)* of a given German state.
Baden-Württemberg
Landesvermessungsamt Baden-Württemberg

Germany after 1945
(Map courtesy of the German Information Center)

Büchsenstr. 54
70174 Stuttgart
Tel: +49-711-1232831
Fax: +49-711-1232979
Bayern
Bayerisches Landesvermessungsamt
Alexandrastr. 4
80538 München
Tel: +49-89-21621735
Fax: +49-89-21621770
Berlin
Senatsverwaltung für Bau- und
Wohnungswesen
Abt. V - Vermessungswesen
Mansfelder Str. 16
10713 Berlin
Tel. +49-30-8675628
Fax: +49-30-8673117

Brandenburg
Landesvermessungsamt Brandenburg
Aussenstelle Potsdam
Heiinrich-Mann-Allee 103
14467 Potsdam
Tel. +49-331-87491
Fax: +49-331-872387
Bremen
Kataster- und Vermessungsverwaltung
Bremen
Wilhelm-Kaisen-Brücke 4
28195 Bremen
Tel. +49-421-3611
Fax: +49-421-3614947
Hamburg
Vermessungsamt der Freien und
Hansestadt Hamburg
Wexstr. 7

20355 Hamburg
Tel. +49-40-349132169
Fax: +49-40-349133196
Hessen
Hessisches Landesvermessungsamt
Schaperstr. 16
65195 Wiesbaden
Tel: 49-611-535236
Fax: 49-611-535309
Mecklenburg-Vorpommern
Landesvermessungsamt Mecklenburg-
Vorpommern
Lübecker Str. 289
19059 Schwerin
Tel. +49-385-48216
Fax: +49-385-48398
Niedersachsen
Niedersächsisches Landesverwaltungsamt
Landesvermessung
Warmbüchenkamp 2
30159 Hannover
Tel. +49-511-3673288
Fax: +49-511-3673540
Nordrhein-Westfalen
Landesvermessungsamt Nordrhein-West-
falen
Muffendorfer Str. 19-21
53177 Bonn
Tel. +49-228-846535 of +49-228-846536
Fax: +49-228-846502
Rheinland-Pfalz
Landesvermessungsamt Rheinland-Pfalz
Ferdinand-Sauerbruch-Str. 15
56073 Koblenz
Tel. +49-261-492232
Fax: +49-261-492492
Saarland
Landesvermessungsamt des Saarlandes
Von der Heydt 22
66115 Saarbrücken
Tel. +49-681-9712241
Fax: +49-681-9712200
Sachsen
Landesvermessungsamt Sachsen
Olbrichtplatz 3
01099 Dresden
Tel. +49-351-5983608
Fax: +49-351-5983202

Sachsen-Anhalt
Landesamt für Landesvermessung und
Datenverarbeitung Sachsen-Anhalt
Barbarastr. 2
06110 Halle/Saale
Tel. +49-345-4772440
Fax: +49-345-4772002
Schleswig-Holstein
Landesvermessungsamt Schleswig-
Holstein
Mercatorstr. 1
24106 Kiel
Tel. +49-431-3832015
Fax: +49-431-3832099
Thüringen
Thüringer Landesverwaltungsamt
Landesvermessungsamt
Schmidtsted ter Ufer 7
99084 Erfurt
Tel. +49-361-51301
Fax: +49-361-26910

**For maps of the German Empire,
borders of 1935**
Institut für Angewandte Geodäsie
Stauffenbergstr. 13
10785 Berlin
Tel. +49-30-2611156 or +49-30-2611157
Fax: +40-30-2629499

ATLAS FOR GERMANIC GENEALOGY

**Ernest Thode, *Atlas for Germanic
Genealogy*. Heritage House, Marietta,
Ohio, 1982. 3rd edition 1988.**

This atlas, instead of showing
geographi details, provides such information as the geographic areas for particular religions, the geographic reasons that
an ancestor may have emigrated from a
particular port, the given names and surnames that are peculiar to specific areas,
and the geographic regions that may have

jurisdiction over records for a given region.

SANBORN MAPS

In 1867, Daniel A. Sanborn started up his business, the National Insurance Diagram Bureau. Still in operation today, the company is responsible for the mapping of more than 13,000 towns and cities in the United States.

The maps were produced for fire insurance companies which were easily wiped out following major fires. They served the purpose of documenting property owned and destroyed The maps show building outlines, street names, street address numbers, number of stories of the structures, general building use, and construction details.

As the mapping business developed, there were added to the maps fire protection devices and the location of potential fire hazards. Insurers used this information to evaluate risks and to set premiums.

The oldest extant fire insurance map of a United States city is a map of Charleston, South Carolina, published in 1790.

These fire insurance maps can locate an ancestor's home and place of business, showing all details such as sheds, garages, wells, and the number of rooms.

Availability

The Library of Congress has a huge collection of fire insurance maps. Reproductions of the Sanborn maps are available from the Library of Congress, Photoduplication Service, Washington, DC 20540. Tel. (202) 707-5640. Maps published more than 75 years ago are in the public domain and can be reproduced without restriction. The Library of Congress is permitted to reproduce 50 or fewer paper copies or color slides from Sanborn maps for noncommercial customers.

Many public libraries have duplicate sets of Sanborn maps.

The Sanborn Map Company is located at 629 Fifth Avenue, Pelham, NY 10803. To order, specify the exact community, house number or building, or boundary of area by streets. Prices range from $10 for 11 x 14 copies to $25 for photostats of map sheets approximately 22" x 26".

Sources:
♦ "Sanborn City Maps," by Jo White Linn, C.G., C.G.L., *Heritage Quest*, #32.
♦"Fire insurance maps are 'hot' with collectors," by Diane L. Oswald, *AntiqueWeek*, August 5, 1996.
♦ "Fire insurance documents may offer valuable information about ancestors," by John W. Heisey, *AntiqueWeek*, September 9, 1996.

Chapter 2
Emigration

TIMELINE OF EMIGRATION LAWS AND POLICIES IN GERMANY

1724: A Palatinate ordinance threatened confiscation of property in response to the heavy emigration to Pennsylvania. Further Palatine ordinances followed in 1752, 1753, 1764, 1766, 1767, 1769, 1770, and 1779 "to counteract with the necessary vigour the evil whose injuriousness grows the longer it persists." (Between 1709 and 1815, Württemberg issued 18 similar ordinances.)

1768: Emperor Joseph II's edict prohibited "all migration by German imperial subjects to foreign countries having no connection with the empire." The edict contained severe punishments to be imposed on those who disobeyed, called for the immediate arrest of those involved in secret emigration, and even imposed a ban on assemblies. A contemporary document from Upper Hesse reads, "The alleged reasons, namely a great burden of debt and insufficient food supplies, are not enough to justify the supplicants fleeing in such arbitrary manner from their hereditary sovereign and from the country in which they were born, brought up and hitherto nourished; on the contrary, it is their bounden duty to remain in the country and . . . to hope for the return of better and more blessed times."

1815 and following: With the establishment of the German Confederation in 1815 came a liberalization of emigration policy. Also, several individual states wrote the principle of freedom of emigration into their constitutions or granted that freedom through ordinances or laws. As early as 1803 Baden took such measures, followed by Württemberg in 1815, Prussia in 1818, and Hesse in 1821. In almost all states of the Confederation, conditions were laid down before permission to emigrate was granted: Men had to have completed their military service, men with families required the consent of their wives, and all debts had to be paid.

1832: In an early example of beginnings

of government protection of emigrants, the city state of Bremen passed an ordinance protecting emigrants from bad treatment, at the same time cultivating the city's traffic in emigration as it sought to compete with the ports of Rotterdam, Antwerp and LeHavre.

The ordinance of 1832 set out guidelines by which shipowners were required to keep passenger lists, to have food supplies for 90 days on board, and to provide proof of the seaworthiness of their ships.

1837 onwards: Similar ordinances were adopted in Hamburg.

1846-47: Following the great wave of emigration in these years, the Frankfurt National Assembly tried but failed to adopt a uniform emigration policy. In 1878 a similar bill was presented to the Reichstag, but it too failed.

1897: Finally, a uniform, imperial ruling, the Imperial Act on Emigration, was achieved, which contained detailed regulations for agents and entrepreneurs involved in the transport of emigrants. Its goal was to steer emigrants into territories where colonies would serve the interests of the empire.

1975: The Federal Republic of Germany enacted a law superseding that of 1897 by which freedom of migration was established, with the government serving in an advisory capacity only.

Source: Ingrid Schöberl, "Emigration Policy in Germany and Immigration Policy in the United States," *Germans to America: 300 Years of Immigration, 1683-1983*, ed. Günter Moltman, Institute for Foreign Relations, Stuttgart, in cooperation with Inter Nationes, Bonn, Bad Godesberg, 1982.

THE REDEMPTIONERS

Redemption was a system of payment for ship passage through labor given by emigrant passengers.

La Vern Rippley, in his book *The Ger-*

man Americans[1] (which should be required reading for German family history searchers) offers the following explanation of "redemptioning":

"Shipping companies often transported European emigrants to America without directly charging the passengers.

"Occasionally, a local ruler in a German principality also resorted to selling his 'sons' to a shipper or a foreign government for what little they would bring on the auction block. 'Redemptioning' was, therefore, the process by which agents loaded ships with able-bodied men and proceeded to anchor in an American port where the newcomers were sold to the highest bidder.

"Since the shipping company had born the costs of transportation without charging the passenger, potential employers in America reimbursed the shipper when paying the going price for an emigrant who in turn worked for as many years as were necessary to redeem the cost of passage. In a land where the sale of black slaves was taken for granted, we should not be surprised to learn that the redemption of Germans was scarcely frowned upon by anyone.

"American laws binding the contracts of redemption continued in effect until 1819 when the United States Congress passed a law, not abolishing redemption, but limiting the weight of passengers permitted on ships docking at United States ports . . . .

"This action effectively outlawed shipment in steerage, which brought with it an end to the system of redemption because the law ruled out the possibility of huge profits."

Further information

German Immigratrion Servant Contracts: Registered at the Port of Philadelphia, 1817-1831. Farley Grubb. Baltimore, MD, Genealogical Publishing Co., 1994.

[1]La Vern J. Rippley, *The German Americans.* University Press of America, New York, 1984.

HOW 'REDEMPTIONING' WORKED

Gottlieb Mittelberger, an emigrant to Pennsylvania from Württemberg in 1750, wrote this account of his first-hand experiences with the redemptioner system:

"When the ships have landed at Philadelphia after their long voyage, no one is permitted to leave them except those who pay for their passage or can give good security; the others who cannot pay must remain on board the ships till they are purchased, and are released from the ships by their purchasers.

"The sick always fare the worst, for the healthy are naturally preferred and purchased first; and so the sick and wretched must often remain on board in front of the city for two or three weeks, and frequently die, whereas many a one if he could pay his debt and was permitted to leave the ship immediately might recover. . . .

"The sale of human beings in the market on board the ship is carried on thus: Every day Englishmen, Dutchmen, and High German people come from the city of Philadelphia and other places, some from a great distance, say 60, 90, and 120 miles away,and go on board the newly arrived ship that has brought and offers for sale passengers from Europe, and select among the healthy persons such as they deem suitable for their business, and bargain with them how long they will serve for their passage money, for which most of them are still in debt. When they have come to an agreement, it happens that adult persons bind themselves in writing to serve three, four, five, or six years for the amount due by them, according to their strength and age. But very young people, from 10 to 15 years, must serve until they are 21 years old.

"Many persons must sell and trade away their children like so many head of cattle; for if their children take the debt upon themselves, the parents can leave the ship free and unrestrained; but as the par-

ents often do not know where and to what people their children are going, it often happens that such parents and children, after leaving the ship, do not see each other again for years, perhaps no more in all their lives.

"When people arrive who cannot make themselves free, but have children under five years of age, they cannot free themselves by them; for such children must be given to somebody without compensation to be brought up, and they must serve for their bringing up till they are 21 years old. Children from five to ten years, who pay half price for their passage, must likewise serve for it until they are 21 years old; they cannot, therefore, redeem their parents by taking the debt of the latter upon themselves. but children above 10 years can take part of their parents' debts upon themselves.

"A woman must stand for her husband if he arrives sick, and in like manner a man for his sick wife, and take the debt upon herself or himself, and thus serve five or six years not alone for his or her own debt, but also for that of the sick husband or wife.

"But if both are sick, such persons are sent from the ship to the hospital, but not until it appears probable that they will find no purchasers. As soon as they are well again they must serve for their passage, or pay if they have means.

"It often happens that whole families, husband, wife and children, are separated by being sold to different purchasers, especially when they have not paid any part of their passage money.

"When a husband or wife has died at sea, after the ship has completed more than half her trip, the survivor must pay or serve not only for himself or herself, but also for the deceased.

"When both parents died after the voyage was more than half completed, their children, especially when they are young and have nothing to pawn or pay, must stand for their own and their parents' passage, and serve till they are 21 years old.

"When one has served his or her term, he or she is entitled to a new suit of clothes at parting and if it has been so stipulated, a man gets in addition a horse, and a woman a cow.

"When a servant has an opportunity to marry in this country, he or she must pay for each year he or she would still have to serve £5 or £6.

"But many a one who has thus purchased and paid for his bride, has subsequently repented of his bargain, so that he would gladly have returned his dear ware and lost his money in addition.

"If a servant in this country runs away from his master who has treated him harshly, he cannot get far. Good provision has been made for such cases so that a runaway is soon recovered. He who detains or returns a deserter receives a good reward.

"If such a runaway has been away from his master a single day, he must serve an entire week for it; if absent a week, then a month, and for a month, half a year. But if the master does not care to keep the runaway when he gets him back, he may sell him for as many years as he has still to serve."[1]

[1]*The Pennsylvania-German Society Proceedings and Addresses at Ephrata, Oct. 20, 1899.* Vol. X, 1900; Chapter III.

FOOD ON BOARD IMMIGRANT SHIPS

The food served on German-immigrant ships in the 1850s seems to have been fairly standardized. This is an example of a week's menu:
Sunday: salt meat, meal pudding, and prunes
Monday: salt bacon, pea soup, and potatoes
Tuesday: salt meat, rice, and prunes
Wednesday: smoked bacon, sauerkraut,

and potatoes
Thursday: salt meat, potatoes, and bean soup
Friday: herring, meal, and prunes
Saturday: salt bacon, pea soup, and potatoes

Source: Richard O'Connor, *The German-Americans: An Informal History.* Little, Brown and Co., Boston, 1968.

PACKING FOOD FOR THE OCEAN JOURNEY

In 1822, not long after his arrival in America, the nineteen-year-old German immigrant Louis Jüngerich wrote a long letter to his mother, brother, and sister in Hessen, from the farm where he was living in Lancaster County, Pennsylvania.

In his letter he gave specific instructions for any family members who were anticipating a trip to America, including advice on what food to pack for the trip.

He advises his relatives back home to sign onto a ship for the the ocean voyage only (to "cut the cost of provisioning by thirty Gulden"), and then to obtain food supplies on their own, to last 90 days. (The voyage could be expected to last that long.)

His list of recommended provisions to pack *for each person* for the voyage are as follows:

- 55 pounds of ship's zwieback or hardtack
- "6, 8, 9, or 10, or even 12 pounds of butter, depending on circumstances"
- 2 bushels of potatoes or more
- salt
- 15 pounds of flour
- 8 pounds of rice
- 4 pounds of barley
- "any amount of peas, beans, and some meat stock for a fresh soup"
- vinegar to drink ("absolutely necessary"; described by Jüngerich as "ship's water"; vinegar was considered helpful for digestion and was as an antidote to scurvy)
- tea, sugar, chocolate, and brandy ("as you wish")
- 20 pounds of well salted beef
- 6 pounds of bacon for fat
- lemons
- dried plums ("and other small items")
- pepper

Cooking utensils recommended for the ship passage included,

- "2 tin kettles to cook meals, and one for liquids"
- spoons, knives, forks and cups

The young immigrant reported to his family his favorite meal aboard ship:

"Our best meals were as follows: I took the ship's zwieback or hardtack that was handed out to us and butter, soaked the zwieback so that it became spongy, and cooked it in water, adding the butter. This was our best dish and could not compare with what was given out on the ship only at the noon hour."

(A translation note on this item of the letter explains that the zwieback referred to was not "the familiar twice-toasted rusks, but rather a biscuit-like bread product baked especially to travel well and remain palatable in the process.")

Source: Levine, Neil Ann Stuckey, Ursula Roy, and David J. Rempel Smucker, "Trans-Atlantic Advice: An 1822 Letter by Louis C. Jüngerich (1803-1882)," *Pennsylvania Mennonite Heritage,* Vol. XIX, No. 3, July 1996

OVERVIEW OF GERMAN EMIGRATION TO AMERICA

- **Colonial period:** 65,000 to 100,000 Germans (about 8% or 9% of total population of the colonies)
- **1816-1914:** 5.5 million Germans
- World War I to present: About 1.5 million more Germans
- **Altogether:** More than 7 million Germans (this number does not take into account return migration)
- **Peak years of German immigration:** 1854 (215,000); and 1882 (250,000)
- **Second half of nineteenth century:** Americans born in Germany as a rule made up more than 30 percent of all Americans born abroad and more than 4 percent of the total population
- **Total immigration to the United States since 1920:** More than 46 million, of which Germans made up the largest share, about 15 percent. The table on the next page indicates patterns of German immigration in a 150-year period, as well as the relative concentration of Germans among all immigrants.

Source: Günter Moltmann, "Three Hundred Years of German Emigration to North America," translated by William D. Graf. Günter Moltmann, ed., *Germans to America: 300 Years of Immigration 1683-1983,* Institute for Foreign Cultural Relations, Stuttgart, in cooperation with Inter Nationen, Bonn-Godesberg, 1982.

GERMAN IMMIGRATION BY DECADE

Decade	Total Immigration	German Immigration	German as Percentage of Total Immigration
1820-29	128,502.	5,753	4.5
1830-39	538,381	124,726	23.2
1840-49	1,427,337	385,434	27.0
1850-59	2,814,554	976,072	34.7
1860-69	2,081,261	723,734	34.8
1870-79	2,742,137	751,769	27.4
1880-89	5,248,568	1,445,181	27.5
1890-99	3,694,294	579,072	15.7
1900-09	8,202,388	328,722	4.0
1910-19	6,347,380	174,227	2.7
1920-29	4,295,510	386,634	9.0
1930-39	699,375	119,107	17.0
1940-49	856,608	117,506	14.0
1950-59	2,499,268	576,905	23.1
1960-69	3,213,749	209,616	6.5
1970	373,326	10,632	2.8
Total	45,162,638	6,917,090	15.3

U.S. Bureau of Census

THE FIRST GERMANS IN AMERICA

An historic marker is to be placed at Jamestown by the German Heritage Society of Greater Washington, DC in the spring of 1997 to commemorate the arrival of the first Germans in America in James-town in 1608.

The text of the marker, headed, "First Germans at Jamestown," reads,

"The first Germans to land in Jamestown, the first permanent English settlement in Virginia, arrived aboard the Mary and Margaret about October 1, 1608.

"These Germans were glass makers and carpenters. In 1620, German mineral specialists and saw millwrights followed to work and settle in the Virginia colony.

"These pioneers and skilled craftsmen were the forerunners of the many millions of Germans who settled in America and became the single largest national group to populate the United States."

This Jamestown marker, confirming the history of the arrival of the first Germans in America, is an important step toward celebration of the German-American quadricentennial in the year 2008.

The project is sponsored by the German Heritage Society of Greater Washington DC, 3413 Canberra Street, Silver Spring, MD 20904. Tel (301) 572-6803. The society is seeking public support for this project.

Source: *Society for German American Studies Newsletter*, Vol. 17, No. 4, Dec. 1996.

HAMBURG HISTORIC EMIGRATION OFFICE

For years the staff of the Hamburg Historic Emigration Office (*Das Historische Auswandererbüro Hamburg*) searched its passenger records for clients whose ancestors departed from Hamburg. Then in 1995 the office closed, but within two months it was reopened by Elizabeth Stroka who had worked at the office as a family history researcher for almost ten years. The sponsor of the Hamburg Historic Emigration Office is still the Hamburg Tourist Board (*Tourismus-Zentrale Hamburg GmbH*).

Ms. Stroka's main source of information in her research is the passenger lists.

The charge for a search is $75 for each departure year and each different initial of a family name. The fee is the same whether or not the search is successful. A search may take up to one month to complete.

The passenger lists are available as well in the United States, on microfilm, but there may nevertheless be a desire on the part of some searchers to use the services of the Historic Emigration Office because the handwriting of the records is often difficult to read, and the various symbols and abbreviations may be unfamiliar. Also, it takes some time to learn how to use the lists and how to translate them.

Ms. Stroka is an American who has been living in Germany for 30 years. She speaks and writes fluent German.

A search from the Historic Emigration Office requires the exact year of emigration; the first and last names of the emigrant; the age at the time of emigration, if known; the hometown or region where the ancestor lived, if known; the ancestor's profession, if known; the name of the ship, if known; the name and age of other family members who emigrated at the same time; and any other details that may be helpful.

Visitors to the Historic Emigration Office are welcomed. Call first to make an appointment.

The address: Historic Emigration Office, c/o Elizabeth Stroka, Burchardstraße 14, 20095 Hamburg, Germany.

HAMBURG PASSENGER LISTS

The Hamburg Passenger lists may be accessed either through the microfilms of the Family History Library or through the Historic Emigration Office in Hamburg, Germany.

Using the microfilms

To find the microfilm numbers for the Hamburg Passenger Lists, search the "Locality" section of the Family History Library Catalog: Go to "Germany, Hamburg, Hamburg" - "Emigration and Immigration."

On the compact disc version of the Family History Library Catalog, select the computer number search and enter 11064.

Direct and Indirect lists

♦Direct Lists (with index): for passengers traveling directly, non-stop, from Hamburg to an American destination

♦Indirect (with index): for passengers who traveled from Hamburg to an American destination, but who made a stop between the two points

Indexes

Most of the Hamburg passenger lists have been indexed. The lists for 1850-1854 do not require indexing because they are arranged alphabetically.

The two sets of indexes are,

1. The 15-year index to the Direct Hamburg Passenger Lists, 1856-1871

2. The regular indexes

Steps in using the indexes

♦If the departure was between 1850 and 1854, search the alphabetical passenger *lists* for those years.

♦If the departure was between 1856 and 1871, search the 15-year index first (but this is not a complete list).

◆If the person is not found in the 15-year index, search the regular index. (Both the direct and the indirect passenger lists have regular indexes, divided into segments for a year or part of a year. The direct indexes begin in 1854 and end in 1934. The indirect indexes begin in 1854 and end in 1910.)

Index contents

The index entry shows:
◆Name of ship
◆Departure date
◆Name of passenger
◆Name of ship's captain
◆Name of destination port
◆Page number on which information is found on the actual passenger lists

Availability

The microfilmed lists and indexes may be borrowed from the Family History Library in Salt Lake City, through its local Family History Centers. For more information see:
◆*The Hamburg Passenger Lists* (Salt Lake City, Utah; Genealogical Society of UT, 1984; FHL fiche 6000034)
◆*Register and Guide to the Hamburg Passenger Lists, 1850-1934.* Research Paper Series C, No. 30. Salt lake City: The Genealogical Department of The Church of Jesus Christ of Latter-day Saints.

HAMBURG POLICE RECORDS

Because Hamburg was a major port city, thousands of Germans (and those of other ethnic groups) took up temporary residence there before departing the country. In accordance with the regulations in force in the German lands, it was necessary for travelers to register at the resident registration office, whose records have been preserved. Usually it was the police department that was in charge of such registrations.

The information in these records is often better than that of the passenger lists, and they begin several years earlier than

the Hamburg passenger lists that are available.

The resident registers give the former residence of the traveler as well as the actual place of birth. The passenger lists, however, give only the last place of residence.

The types of records available through the Family History Library are,
◆ Passport Applications (*Reisepaß Protokolle*), 1852-1929
◆Register of Non-citizen Resident Servants (*Allgemeine Fremden Meldeprotokolle*) 1843-1890
◆Register of Male and Female Non-citizen Laborers and Domestics (*Fremde Männliche und Weibliche Dienstboden*) 1834-1899
◆ Register of Guilded Journeymen *(Fremde zünftige Gesellen)* 1850-1867

Check the Family History Library Catalog for microfilm and microfiche numbers, listed under Germany - Hamburg- "Emigration and Immigration," "Occupations," and "Population."

STEAMSHIP ARRIVALS
Morton Allan Directory

The Morton Allan Directory of European Passenger Steamship Arrivals[1] lists ships arriving in United States ports – at New York for the years 1890 to 1930, and at New York, Philadelphia, Boston, and Baltimore in the years 1904-1926.

This source lists by years the names of the shipping lines, their ports of departure and stops, the names of the ships, and their specific dates of arrival in the United States ports named above..

The directory lists ports from a wide range of countries in the western hemisphere, including several in Great Britain (mostly Liverpool). The shipping lines whose European points of departure may have relevance for researchers of German emigrants, are listed below. The European ports listed below are not necessarily ports of origin. All American cities shown here are ports of debarkation.

American Merchant Line: Hamburg (1930 only); New York
American Line: Hamburg; Antwerp (1924 only); New York
Anchor Line: Havre (1926 only); New York
Baltic S.S. Corp. of America: Havre; Danzig; New York
Baltic-America Line: Hamburg; Danzig; New York
Cunard Line: Havre; Hamburg; New York
French Line: Havre; Bordeaux; Danzig (1920 only); New York
Hamburg American Line: Hamburg; New York; Philadelphia; Baltimore; Boston
Holland American Line: Rotterdam, Amsterdam, Boulogne; New York; Boston
North German Lloyd: Bremen; New York; Baltimore; Philadelphia
North-West Transportation Line: Rotterdam; Hamburg; New York
Polish-American Navigation Corporation: Danzig (1921 only); New York
Red Star Line: Antwerp; Danzig (1920 and after); Hamburg (1924 only); New York; Philadelphia; Boston
Royal Mail Steam Packet Company: Hamburg (1921 and after); New York
Royal Holland Lloyd: Amsterdam; New York
Russian-American Line: Rotterdam; New York
U.S. Mail Steamship Company: Hamburg; Danzig; New York
United States Line (1921 and after): Bremen; Danzig; New York
United American Lines, Inc. (1922 and after): Hamburg; New York
Uranium Steamship Company: Rotterdam; New York
White Star Line: Antwerp (1927 and after); Bremen (1922 only); Hamburg (1923 and after); New York

[1]*Morton Allan Directory of European Passenger Steamship Arrivals: For the Years 11890 to 1930 at the Port of New York and for the Years 1904 to 1926 at the Ports of New York, Philadelphia, Boston and Baltimore,* Genealogical Publishing Company, Inc., Baltimore, 1993.

Peasants paying dues: farm produce, a sheep and a goose; 1479

TRAVEL IN STEERAGE, 19TH CENTURY

Up to the second half of the nineteenth century, the transport of emigrants was only a subsidiary branch of cargo transport, and emigrants consequently traveled in cargo ships temporarily adapted for the conveyance of passengers. A deck was built between the upper deck and the hold, thus providing he necessary space for passengers. (In German, this was known as the *Zwischendeck.*)The accommodation in the steerage was primitive, as can be imagined. The berths, which were removed again at the end of the passage, since the space was needed on the return journey for cargo, were knocked together out of mere planks, narrow and mostly too short. Mattresses and bedding had to be provided by the passengers themselves. There were few latrines, and ventilation was provided for the most part only through ten hatches. The steerage was at once a bedroom, dining-room and living-room. There were no separate quarters for women or the sick.

All the passengers were crowded into the poorly-lighted deck by day and night. Only if the weather was good was it possible for them to emerge onto the upper deck. Medical care was not available; in an emergency, the sufferer was dependent on the captain's medical knowledge. Feeding was the passengers' own concern; they had to provide their own food and crockery, and the only amenity provided for them was a ration of water. For the preparation of food there were usually only one or two fireplaces, often leading to quarrels between passengers about their use. Many went for days without a hot meal.

By about the end of the 1870s, the steamship had replaced the sailingship for emigrants. This development improved conditions almost at once. The passage was reduced to seventeen days — nine in the fast steamers introduced in the 1890s. Since the ships were fitted expressly for passenger transport, they were better ventilated. The employment of physicians and the segregation of the sexes had been introduced before the end of emigration by sail. Food became more plentiful, especially since it had become possible to keep provisions fresh until the end of the passage.

Gradually the passengers were also offered a degree of service. After the steerage had been equipped, toward the end of the 1880s, with chairs and benches, eating in the bunks or even standing up, which had hitherto been the practice, became a thing of the past. The provision of mattresses, bedding and crockery was taken over by the forwarding agents. Shortly before the First World War, some ships were fitted out with special dining rooms for steerage passengers, in which they were served by stewards. At the beginning of the 1920s, a third class, consisting of four-berth cabins, was introduced on all emigrant ships, and the steerage disappeared completely.

Source: *Germans to America: 300 Years of Immigration 1683-1983.* ed. Günther Moltmann. Institute for Foreign Cultural Relations, Stuttgart.

EARLY RAIL TRAVEL

On September 27,1825 the Englishman George Stephenson's steam powered railway carried 450 people at 15 miles per hour over the 25-mile route from Stockton to Darlington, thus opening the way for practical use of the new technology. His success won him a contract to build a line from Liverpool to Manchester.

Several people had previously built self-propelled steam engines, but efforts to build a steam-powered railway had failed due to the cost of construction and the relative inefficiencies of the engine. Thousands of miles of railroad were built during the middle of the19th century.

Within a few years of Stephenson's 1825 triumph, railroads had been built in Belgium, Italy, Austria and the Netherlands. France built its first in 1832, the Russians in 1837. The first German railroad opened on December 7, 1835, powered by der Adler (the eagle), a Stephenson-built locomotive, and provided transportation between Nürnberg and Fürth. By 1850, 3,000 miles of railroads were in operation in Germany. It was possible to travel from Munich to Hamburg, Stettin, the Rhineland, or Silesia by rail. Anyone going to America after 1850 most certainly could have traveled at least part of the way across the continent by rail.

Source: Excerpted from "How Our Ancestors Got to the Sea," by Bruce Walthers and Rolf Wasser. *The German Connection*, Vol. 18, No. 2 , 1994.

RIVER TRAVEL

After 1807 when Fulton built the first commercially successful steamboat,

The dyer, 1521

steam-powered boats became increasingly popular on Germany's waterways.

Germany has a large number of rivers, but they converge into relatively few seaports.

The important ones for transatlantic travelers were the Rhine, Weser, Elbe, and the Oder. The Rhine and its tributaries, (the Lippe, Ruhr, Mosel, Lahn, Nahe, Main, Neckar, Regnitz, Saar, Sieg, Tauber, etc.) end in Rotterdam.

The Weser that passes Bremen on its way to Bremerhaven on the North Sea includes the Aller, Fulda, Hunte, and Werra.

The Elbe brings the waters of the Elbe, Havel, Mulde, Saxon Saale, Schwarze Elster and Weisse Elster to the North Sea at Hamburg.

The Neisse and Warta join the Oder before it gets to Stettin.

The Danube and its tributaries, (the Enns, Inn, Naab, Regen, Traub, and others), however, empty into the Black Sea. Germany also has many canals.

Many immigrants also left from Le Havre, the French seaport at the mouth of the Seine, which flows through Paris on its way to the English Channel. Undoubt-edly, in France and western Germany, "all roads led to Paris." For those who chose this route, it was probably easier, safer, and/or more economical than a North Sea or Baltic port.

See the geographic positions of these rivers on the next page.

Source: Excerpted from "How Our Ancestors Got to the Sea," by Bruce Walthers and Rolf Wasser. *The German Connection*, Vol. 18, No. 2 (1994).

GERMAN HARBORS AND INLAND WATERWAYS

The total volume at Germany's North Sea and Baltic ports was 161.4 million metric tons in 1991. The most important seaports with numbers of respective metric tons are,

Hamburg	60.33
Wilhelmshaven	17.76
Bremen	14.12
Bremerhaven	13.98
Lübeck	11.32
Rostock	7.44

The most important waterway is the Rhine River, accounting for two-thirds of the inland waterway goods transportation.

A network of canals links the major rivers to the European waterways system. The *Rhein-Main-Donau-Kanal* (Rhine-Main-Danube Canal) was finished in 1993 and connects the North Sea with the Black Sea via the Rhine, Main and Danube rivers. The Nord-Ostsee Kanal connects the North and Baltic seas.

The major inland ports are Duisburg, Mannheim, Hamburg, Cologne, Ludwigshafen, Wesseling, Gelsenkirchen, and Karlsruhe. Inland ships make use of a network of rivers, canals and lakes totaling some 4,400 kilometers (2,700 miles).

Source: German Information Center, *Federal Republic of Germany: Questions and Answers*, ed. Susan Steiner , New York, 1996

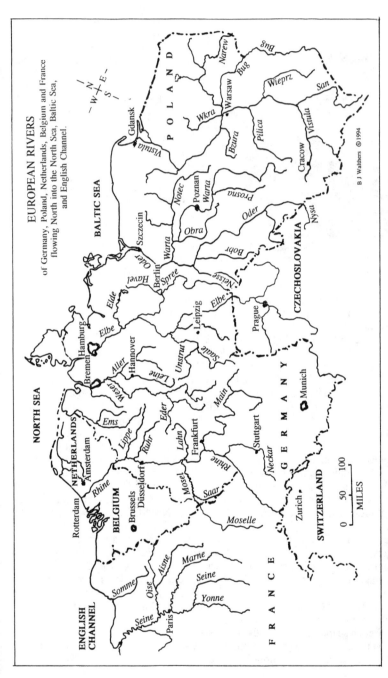

EUROPEAN RIVERS
of Germany, Poland, Netherlands, Belgium and France
flowing North into the North Sea, Baltic Sea,
and English Channel.

B J Walthers ©1994

SOME EARLY RAILROAD LINES
IN ENGLAND AND CONTINENTAL EUROPE

1825 ...... Stockton to Darlington, England (20 miles)
1827 ...... Kerschmarm to Budweiss, Austria(started in 1827)
1827 ...... St. Etienne to Andrezieux, France (used horsepower until 1832)
1830 ...... Mancester to Liverpool, England
1831 ...... Rotterdam to Amsterdam, Netherlands (North Sea port)
1832 ...... Linz to Budweiss, Austria-Hungary (used horsepower until 1837)
1832 ...... St. Etienne To Lyon, France (38 miles, begun in 1828)
1835 ...... Brussels to Malines, Belgium
1835 ...... Nürnberg to Fürth, Bavaria (using a Stephenson-built locomotive)
1836 ...... Linz to Gmunden, Austria (opened in 1836)
1837 ...... Linz to Budweiss, Austria (originally horse-drawn)
1837 ...... Paris to St. Germain, France (13 miles, originally horsedrawn)
1837 ...... Vienna to Brno, Austria
1838 ...... Berlin to Posdam, Prussia
1838 ...... Brunswick to Wolfenbüttel, Brunswick
1839 ...... Haarlem to Amsterdam, Netherlands(Rhine, North Sea port; opened in 1839)
1839 ...... Cologne to Müngersdorf, Prussia
1839 ...... Frankfurt to Hattersheim, Hesse
1839 ...... Leipzig to Dresden, Saxony (carried 412,000 passengers the first year)
1839 ...... Magdeburg, Prussia to Calbe (Saale), Saxony/Anhalt
1839 ...... Munich to Maisach, Bavaria
1839 ...... Naples to Portici, Italy
1839/40 . Paris to Versailles, France (two competing lines)
1840 ...... Berlin to Wittenberg, Prussia (first section finished)
1840 ...... Frankfurt to Wiesbaden, Hessen
1840 ...... Magdeburg, Prussia, to Leipzig, Saxony
1840 ...... Mannheim to Heidelberg, Baden
1841 ...... Berlin, Prussia, to Köthen, Saxony/Anhalt
1841 ...... Berlin to Stettin, Prussia (Oder, Baltic port)
1841 ...... Düsseldorf to Elberfeld, Prussia
1841 ...... Strasbourg to Basel, Switzerland (the first international line)
1842 ...... Bergedorf to Hamburg, Hamburg (Elbe, North Sea port)
1842 ...... Minden to Cologne, Prussia
1843 ...... Angermünde to Stettin, Prussia (Oder, Baltic port)
1843 ...... Cologne, Prussia to Brussels-Antwerp, Belgium
1844 ...... Hamburg, Hamburg to Altona, Schleswig-Holstein
1846 ...... Stargard to Stettin, Prussia (Oder, Baltic port)
1847 ...... Celle, Hannover to Harburg-Wilhelmsburg-Hamburg, Hamburg
.... (Elbe, North Sea port)
1847 ...... Copenhagen to Roskilde, Denmark (first in Scandanavia)
1847 ...... Wunstorf, Hannover, to Bremen, Bremen (Weser, North Sea port)
1847 ...... Zürich, Switzerland, to Baden
1848 ...... Barcelona to Mataro, Spain
1848 ...... Mürzzuschlag to Gloggnitz, Austria (started in 1848, finished about 1854)
1848 ...... Schwerin to Wismar, Mecklenburg (Baltic port)   *[See next page]*

1850 ...... Bad Kleinen to Rostock, Mecklenburg (Baltic port)
1851 ...... Moscow to St. Petersburg, Russia (Baltic port)
1856 ...... Cologne, Prussia, to Amsterdam/Rotterdam, Netherlands (Rhine, North Sea port)
1856 ...... Münster/Westphalia, Prussia to Emden, Hannover (Ems, North Sea port)
1862 ...... Bremen to Bremerhaven, Bremen (Weser, North Sea port)
1867 ...... Oldenburg, Oldenburg, to Bremen, Bremen (Weser, North Sea port)

©Copyright 1997 Bruce Walthers von Alten and Rolf Wasser, originally published in *The German Connection*, Vol. 18, No. 2. Reprinted with permission.

RIVERS OF EUROPE

Name of river	Length (km)	Mouth
Volga *(Wolga)*	3,531	Caspian Sea *(Kaspisches Meer)*
Danube *(Donau)*	2,850	Black Sea *(Schwarzes Meer)*
Dnieper *(Dnjepr)*	2,200	Black Sea *(Schwarzes Meer)*
Don	1,870	Sea of Azov (Asowsches Meer)
Rhine *(Rhein)*	1,320	North Sea *(Nordsee)*
Elbe	1,165	North Sea *(Nordsee)*
Vistula *(Weichsel)*	1,047	Baltic Sea *(Ostsee)*
Loire	1,020	Atlantic Ocean *(Atlantischer Ozean)*
Tagus *(Tajo, Tejo)*	1,007	Atlantic Ocean *(Atlantischer Ozean)*
Meuse *(Maas)*	925	North Sea *(Nordsee)*
Ebro	910	Mediterranean *(Mittelmeer)*
Oder	854	Baltic Sea *(Ostsee)*
Rhone *(Rhône)*	812	Mediterranean *(Mittelmeer)*
Seine	776	English Channel *(Ärmelkanal)*
Weser (with *Werra*)	732	North Sea *(Nordsee)*
Po	652	Adriatic Sea *(Adriatisches Meer)*
Garonne	650	Bay of Biscay *(Golf von Biskaya)*
Tiber	405	Tyrrhenian Sea *(Tyrrhenisches Meer)*
Thames *(Themse)*	346	North Sea *(Nordsee)*

Source: *Brockhaus Enzyklopädie*, Sechster Band. F.A. Brockhaus, Mannheim, 1988.

EARLY 19TH CENTURY SHIPS

Fulton was not the first to build a steam-powered ship, but his (1807) paddle-wheel design was the first commercially successful model. Germany undoubtedly had steam-powered boats within a few years. The design was also used in ocean service, even though paddle-wheels on a rolling ship were often lifted completely out of the water and the exposed mechanism was easily damaged. **1819:** *The American Savannah*, using steam as auxiliary power, was the first steam-powered ship to cross the Atlantic. It used its engines for 105 hours of the 29-day voyage and was out of fuel when it arrived. The first all-steam-powered crossing was made by a British-built ship

Oil mill, Jena

(the *Curaçao*) in 1827.

1838: The British sidewheeler *Sirius* became the first ship to offer regularly scheduled service under steam power. The transatlantic crossing took 18½ days.

1843: The *Great Britain*, launched in 1843 became the first passenger ship with a screw propeller to cross the Atlantic. (The screw propeller had been invented in Bohemia in 1827.)

Sail and steam existed together well into the twentieth century, however. The largest sailing ship ever built, the *Preußen*, was launched in 1902.

Source: Excerpts from "How Our Ancestors Got to the Sea," by Bruce Walthers von Alten and Rolf Wasser. *The German Connection*, Vol. 18, No. 2 , 1994.

PACKING FOR THE VOYAGE TO AMERICA

An immigrant who arrived in America from Oldenburg in about 1835, Liwwät Knapke Böke has left among her prolific writings and drawings[1] these three lists, the first two of which appear to be those prepared for herself and for Bernard Böke, who she had hoped would travel with her to America. (They traveled separately; not long after Liwwät's arrival, they were married in Cincinnati.) From their home village of Neuenkirch in Oldenburg, the length of the voyage to the Bremen departure point was 60 miles.) Following is a summary of the items on the packing lists.

His list

Items to be worn or carried: underpants, shirt, towel, gloves, hardtack, pants, suspenders, candles, snow boots, handkerchief, tallow, stockings, hat, nightshirt, wool coat, chewing tobacco and an iron needle

Items to be transported in a satchel: crucifix, prayer book, baptismal certificate, rosary, bottle of holy water, soap, drinking cup, salve, cream and a hand towel

Items to be packed in a trunk: books,

mirror, bed linen, lamp black, ink in a bottle with a stopper, pliers, cow hide, strap or belt, mallet, scissors, twine, hood, tacks, file, sealing wax and a seal
To be packed in another trunk : pot cover, spoon, knife, blankets, pillows, towels, silver and dishes, bucket, medicine, bed linens, plate, cloths, shirts, a kettle, a feather tick, an apron, and stockings
Planned for carrying in a pouch: sugar, flour, groats, salt, chocolate wafers, potatoes, a coat, bacon, meat, bread, dried apples, cracklings, lard, a pin for closing clothes, shoes, rice, beans, sauerkraut, honey, a bed spread and scarves

Her list
To be worn or carried: long underwear, stockings, belt, jacket, gloves, woolen petticoat, apron, dress, handkerchief, snowboots, button skirt, nightgown, candles, towel, hardtack
Items to be packed in a satchel: crucifix, prayerbook, rosary, bottle of holy water, drinking cup, salve, baptismal certificate, soap
Items to be packed in a trunk: books, mirror, bed linen, muslin, ink in a bottle with stopper, sanitary napkins, paper, quill pens, pillows, chemise, dresses, snow cap, blankets, feather tick, woolen blanket, stockings, nightgowns
In another trunk was to go: knife, spoons, forks, hatpin, ball of thread, towels, aprons, needles, yarn, plate, thread, purse, thimble, buttons, cotton thread, silk thread, dish rag, shoes
To carry in a pouch: Sugar, flour, salt, groats, bacon, meat, bread, dried apples, rice, beans, potatoes, sauerkraut

The seeds list
Bags of vegetable and berry seeds: peas (three varieties); beans (four varieties); turnips (several varieties); beets (three varieties); carrots (two varieties); onions (three varieties); cabbage (three varieties); pickle cucumbers (three varieties); miscellaneous (spinach, rhubarb, kohlrabi, leeks); berries (three varieties)

Small bags of grain seeds: seed corn, oats, wheat, clover, barley, rye
Small bags of fruit seeds: apples, cherries, peaches, pears, quince, plums, apricots
Small bags of flower seeds: margarita, snapdragon, peonies, lady slipper, morning glory, tulips or crocuses

[1]*Liwwät Böke 1807-1882; Pioneer*, comp., ed., Luke B. Knapke. The Minster Historical Society, Minster, Ohio, 1985. ($22.00 plus $3.00 shipping and handling, to Minster Historical Society, P.O. Box 51, Minster, OH 45865)

A SELECT BIBLIOGRAPHY FOR RESEARCHING PASSENGER LISTS

•Burgert, Annette K., *Eighteenth Century Emigrants from German-Speaking Lands to North America*. Vols. 16 and 29. Pennsylvania German Society, Breinigsville, Pa., 1983 and 1985.
•Colletta, John P., *They Came in Ships*. Ancestry Publishing, Salt Lake City, 1989.
•Ferguson, Laraine K., "Hamburg, Germany, Gateway to the Ancestral Home." *German Genealogical Digest*, Vol. 2, no. 1, 1985.
•Filby, P. William, *Passenger and Immigration Lists Bibliography, 1538-1900: Being a Guide to Published Lists of Arrivals in the United States and Canada*. Gale Research Co., Detroit, 1988.
•Filby, P. William, with Mary K. Meyer, eds. *Passenger and Immigration Lists Index: A Guide to Published Arrival Records of about 500,000 Passengers Who Came to the United States and Canada in the 17th, 18th, and 19th Centuries*. 3 vols. Gale Research Company, 1981. Supplemental volumes.
•Glazier, Ira A., and P. William Filby, eds. *Germans to America: Lists of Passengers Arriving at U.S. Ports*, 1850-1855. Scholarly Resources, Wilmington, Del., 1988

Emigration agents in Hamburg, 1864

•National Archives Trust Fund Board, *Immigrant and Passenger Arrivals: A Select Catalog of National Archives Microfilm Publications.* National Archives Trust Fund Board, Washington, D.C., 1983

•Schenk, Trudy, and Ruth Froelke, comps. *The Württemberg Emigration Index.* Ancestry, Salt Lake City, 1986-88.

•Strassburger, Ralph Beaver, comp., and William John Hinke, ed. *Pennsylvania German Pioneers: A Publication of the Original Lists of Arrivals in the Port of Philadelphia from 1727 to 1808.* Vols. 42,

43, 44. Pennsylvania German Society, Norristown, Pa., 1934.

•Tepper, Michael H., *American Passenger Arrival Records: A Guide to the Records of Immigrants Arriving at American Ports by Sail and Steam.* Genealogical Publishing Co., 1988.

•Yoder, Don, ed. *Pennsylvania German Immigrants, 1709-1786: Lists Consolidated from Yearbooks of The Pennsylvania German Folklore Society.* Genealogical Publishing Co., Baltimore, 1980.

•Zimmerman, Gary J., and Marion Wol-

fert, comps. *German Immigrants: Lists of Passengers Bound from Bremen to New York, 1847-1854.* Genealogical Publishing Co., Baltimore, 1985.

MARITIME MUSEUMS

◆**Steamship Historical Society of America**
300 Ray Drive, Suite #4
Providence, RI 02906
or, Librarian, SSHSA Collection
Langsdale Library, University of Baltimore
1420 Maryland Avenue
Baltimore, MD 21201-5779
Tel. (410) 837-4334
The Steamship Historical Society of America maintains one of the largest libraries in North America devoted exclusively to steamboat and steamship history. Its holdings include materials about steamships from the 1830s to the present, as well as engravings, drawings, and photographs of freight and passenger vessels. The library is open for research Monday-Friday,

8:30 am to 3:30 pm; patrons are advised to make appointments in advance). Copies of pictures not restricted may be purchased by mail or in person.)
◆**Maine Maritime Museum**
243 Washington Street
Bath, ME 04530
Tel. (207) 443-1316
◆Mariner's Museum
100 Museum Drive
  Newport News, VA 23606-3759; Fax (757) 591-7320; Web site:www.mariner. org. The museum's Research Library and Archives is open Monday-Saturday, 9 am to 5 pm; call in advance to confirm hours.
◆**Mystic Seaport**
75 Greenmanville Avenue
P.O. Box 6000
Mystic, CN 06355-5327
Tel. (860) 572-5315; Fax (860) 572-5327; e-mail: Tricia@mystic.org
The G.W. Blunt White Library specializes in American maritime history and has ships register finding aids. Open Monday-Friday 10::30 am - 5 pm, also first Thursday and Saturday of the month with reduced staff. Library address: P.O. Box

6000, Mystic, CT 06355. Tel. (860) 572-5367; Fax: (860) 572-5394.

◆Phillips Library,
Peabody Essex Museum
East India Square
Salem, MA 01970
(508) 745-1876; Fax (508) 744-0036

Phillips Library has 400,000 rare books and more than 1 million photographs. It is open Tuesdays, Wednesdays, and Fridays from 10 am to 5 pm, and Thursdays from 1 pm to 8 pm. In June, July and August, the library is open on Mondays, 10 am to 5 pm as well.

◆San Diego Maritime Museum
1492 North Harbor Drive
San Diego, CA 92101
Tel. (619) 234-9153

This museum has a Master Ship Index database. Open daily 9 am - 8 pm (9 pm in summer) including holidays.

◆San Francisco Maritime Museum
J. Porter Shaw Library
860 Beach Street
San Francisco, CA 94109-1110
Tel.: (415) 556-9870

The 14,000-volume library focuses on commercial maritime history, with holdings on sail and steam on the West Coast and in the Pacific Basin from 1520 to the present. It provides reference service. Open Tuesday 5 am - 8 pm, Wednesday, Thursday, and Friday 1-5 pm, Saturday 10 am - 5 pm.

◆Texas Seaport Museum (at Pier 21)
2016 Strand
Galveston, TX 77550-1631
Tel.: (409) 763-1877

GERMANS TO AMERICA
(Passenger lists)

Germans to America: Lists of Passengers Arriving at U.S. Ports, edited by **Ira A Glazier and P. William Filby.**

This is a set of 50 volumes (as of early 1996) of indexed sources of German surname immigrants. Current plans call for the release of from four to six volumes per year until all of the series, covering the years 1850 to 1893, is complete. The earliest date (Vol. 1) is 2 January 1850; the ending date of Volume 54 is June 1884.

The series reproduces information from original passenger lists filed by vessels entering United States ports from abroad. Ships that departed from German ports or carried passengers who declared themselves to be of German origin are included, with first and last names, age, sex, occupation, date of arrival, and province and village of origin (when available) provided for each emigrant.

The entries for 1850 through 1855 cover only ships on which at least 80 percent of passengers had German names; the entries since 1856 include all passengers with German names.

A complete index of names is included at the end of every volume.

Publisher: Scholarly Resources, 104 Greenhill Avenue, Wilmington, DE 19805-2897. Tel. 800-772-8937. Fax: 302-654-3871

Dates covered by volume

vol. 1	Jan 1850 - May 1851
vol. 2	May 1851 - Jun 1852
vol. 3	Jun 1852 - Sep 1852
vol. 4	Sep 1852 - May 1853
vol. 5	May 1853 - Oct 1853
vol. 6	Oct 1853 - May 1854
vol. 7	May 1854 - Aug 1854
vol. 8	Aug 1854 - Dec 1854
vol. 9	Dec 1854 - Dec 1855
vol. 10	Jan 1856 - Apr 1857
vol. 11	Apr 1857 - Nov 1857
vol. 12	Nov 1857 - Jul 1859
vol. 13	Aug 1859 - Dec 1860
vol. 14	Jan 1861 - May 1863
vol. 15	Jun 1863 - Oct 1864
vol. 16	Nov 1864 - Nov 1865
vol. 17	Nov 1865 - Jun 1866
vol. 18	Jun 1866 - Dec 1866
vol. 19	Jan 1867 - Aug 1867
vol. 20	Aug 1867 - May 1868
vol. 21	May 1868 - Sep 1868
vol. 22	Oct 1868 - May 1869

vol. 23	Jun 1869 - Dec 1869	vol. 39	Jun 1881 - Aug 1881
vol. 24	Jan 1870 - Dec 1870	vol. 40	Aug 1881 - Oct 1881
vol. 25	Jan 1871 - Sep 1871	vol. 41	Nov 1881 - Mar 1882
vol. 26	Oct 1871 - Apr 1872	vol. 42	Mar 1882 - May 1882
vol. 27	May 1872 - Jul 1872	vol. 43	May 1882 - Aug 1882
vol. 28	Aug 1872 - Dec 1872	vol. 44	Aug 1882 - Nov 1882
vol. 29	Jan 1873 - May 1873	vol. 45	Nov 1882 - Apr 1883
vol. 30	Jun 1873 - Nov 1873	vol. 46	Apr 1883 - Jun 1883
vol. 31	Dec 1873 - Dec 1874	vol. 47	Jul 1883 - Oct 1883
vol. 32	Jan 1875 - Sep 1876	vol. 48	Nov 1883 - Apr 1884
vol. 33	Oct 1876 - Sep 1878	vol. 49	Apr 1884 - Jun 1884
vol. 34	Oct 1878 - Dec 1879	vol. 50	Jul 1884 - Nov 1884
vol. 35	Jan 1880 - Jun 1880	vol. 51	Dec 1884 - Jun 1885
vol. 36	Jul 1880 - Nov 1880	vol. 52	Jul 1885 - Apr 1886
vol. 37	Dec 1880 - Apr 1881	vol. 53	May 1886 - Jan 1887
vol. 38	Apr 1881 - May 1881	vol. 54	Jan 1887 - Jun 1887

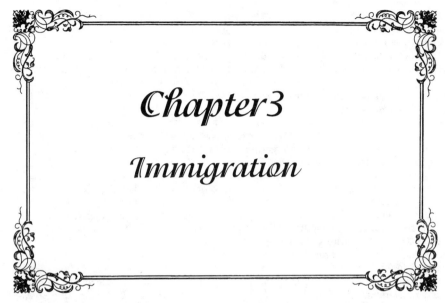

Chapter 3

Immigration

PORTS OF DEBARKATION

by Friedrich R. Wollmershäuser[1]

During the 18th century, emigrants usually used transportation on boats or rafts downstream to ports of overseas embarkation (mainly Rotterdam). As a result of the Navigation Act of the 17th century, European goods (and immigrants bound for the English colonies) had to be transported via England as of 1664. Therefore, all such ships had to touch an English port (usually London or Cowes) before leaving for America.

The completion of the German railroad system in the 1840s enabled the emigrants to choose among several competing ports of embarkation. All such choices may have depended upon the passage rates and the conditions offered by the travel agent, knowledge of experiences of other emigrants who had traveled from specific ports, and whether the emigrant was leaving his country illegally (and thus, trying to go abroad as quickly as possible, chose a foreign port).

The following are some ports of embarkation from which emigrants traveled, with related comments on the passenger lists and supporting records discovered so far:

Libau (Russia)

Served as a port of embarkation for emigrants from Russia, including Russia-Germans. No information available.

Stettin
(today Szczecin, Poland)

This port had very limited importance from 1869 onward. Passenger lists for the years 1869 to 1898 have been preserved at the Greifswald state archives (*Vorpommersches Landesarchiv* Greifswald).[2]

Hamburg

No emigration lists preserved for the period before 1850. The Staatsarchiv Hamburg (SAHbg) has the following lists for the period after 1850:

1850-1855: Passenger lists contain name, often also the first name and occupation, place of birth or former residence, name of ship, port of destination, date of departure

1855 - : Passenger lists contain first and last name, age, former place of residence, country or province, occupation, numbers or names of family members, destination, name of ship and captain, date of departure

Direct emigration
(from Hamburg to an overseas
destination port)
1850-1914: 280 volumes, 140 index volumes (*SAHbg Auswanderungsamt VIII.A.Nr 1f.*).The lists for 1850-1855 are arranged according to the first letter of the surname; later lists are arranged by ships with a separate index. There is a gap between January and 25 September 1853 (in the lists of direct emigration only).
1871-1887: 2 volumes. Persons who traveled overseas, but not in emigrants' ships (*ibid.* Nr 3)
1850-1914: Lists of emigrants' ships leaving Hamburg (*ibid.* Nr 4)
Indirect emigration
(from Hamburg to an English
port and then overseas)
1854-1910: 122 volumes, 25 index volumes. (*SAHbg Auswanderungsamt VIII.C.Nr 1*)
Marriages of emigrants
1850-1853, 1857-1865: Certificates of marriages performed before the U.S. consul at Hamburg, usually among emigrants who could not get a marriage license at home. (For details, see Clifford Neal Smith, *Encyclopedia of German-American Genealogical Research,* New York: R.R. Bowker 1976, p. 197)
Indexes to these lists
♦The regular indexes beginning in 1855 are organized only by the first letter of the surname, and they are difficult to use.
♦An incomplete card index to the years 1856-1871 was compiled by a group of Church of Jesus Christ of Latter-day Saints volunteers in 1969. It is unknown how complete this index is.
♦The card index to the direct lists 1850-1870 and the indirect lists 1850-1867 was compiled during the last few decades by

the Hamburg genealogist Karl Werner Klüber. This index is kept at the Staatsarchiv Hamburg.
♦The indexes to the Germans to America book series includes passenger arrivals of ships from Hamburg.
　The original passenger lists and the original indexes are no longer available for public use, although they have been microfilmed. There are several ways to obtain access to these films:
♦The films may be searched in the Family History Centers of the Family History Library of the Church of Jesus Christ of Latter-day Saints.
♦A professional genealogist in or near Hamburg may be retained [see page 43].

References
♦ Erika Suchan-Galow, *"Hamburger Quellen zur Auswandererforschung." Deutsches Archiv für Landes- und Volksforschung* 7 (1943) 90-98 (Hamburg as a port of embarkation, survey of available sources).
♦Karl-Werner Klüber, "Die Hamburger Schiffslisten." *Archiv für Sippenforschung* 0(1964) 386-390 (and other articles by the same author with a description of the Hamburg passenger lists and name lists of passengers).
♦Karl-Egbert Schultze, *"Zur Bearbeitung der Hamburger Auswandererlisten, insbesondere: kann man sie drucken?" Zeitschrift für niedersächsische Familienkunde* 41(1966) 7-9
♦Karl-Werner Klüber, *"Die Hamburger Auswanderlisten (Schiffslisten)". Mitteilungen der westdeutschen Gesellschaft für Familienkunde* 56 (1968) 278-282 (response by K.W. Klüber to Schultze's considerations)
♦The Genealogical Department of The Church of Jesus Christ of Latter-day Saints (ed.), *The Hamburg Passenger Lists.* Salt Lake City 1976 (Hamburg as a port of emigration, description of the lists and their indexes, case studies).
♦Birgit Gelberg, *Auswanderung nach*

Übersee. Soziale Probeme der Auswand-ererbeförderung in Hamburg und Bremen von der Mitte des 19. Jahrhunderts bis zum ersten Weltkrieg. (Beiträge zur Geschichte Hamburgs 10). Hamburg: Christiansen 1973 (social problems connected with the transportation of emigrants).

♦ The Hamburg Passenger Lists," *The Genealogical Helper* 44 (1990) 28.

♦ Martin A. Diestler, "Some suggestions on tracing emigrants through Hamburg police records," *The Palatine Immigrant,* vol. 14, no. 1 (March 1989) pp. 16-18

**Partial publications
of the Hamburg passenger lists**

Note: PILB = William F. Filby (ed.), *Passenger and Immigration Lists Bibliography, 1538-1900. Being a Guide to Published Lists of Arrivals in the United States and Canada.* Detroit (MI): Gale 1981.

This list contains also some passenger lists taken from American arrival lists.

1845 to New Orleans: see PILB 6127.

1849 ship *Deutschland*: see PILB 3967.

1849-1851 Karl Werner Klüber, "Deutsche Auswanderung nach Australien 1849-1851." Genealogie 15 (1966) 186-194 (emigrants to Australia, partially from the Hamburg passenger lists).

1849-1855: see PILB 3879 (entries in the Hamburg passenger lists compared with emigration announcements in the gazettes of the Bavarian districts of Oberpfalz and Oberfranken).

1850: see PILB 3948 (emigrants from Thuringia).

1850: Karl Welrner Klüber, "Badische Auswanderer nach Übersee." Badische Familienkunde 8 (1965) 131-138 (emigrants from Baden).

1850-1851: see PILB 3941 (emigrants from Bavaria).

1850-1851: see PILB 3935 (emigrants from the Prussian Rhine Province).

1850-1852: see PILB 3886 (emigrants from Anhalt and the Prussian districts of Magdeburg and Merseburg).

1850-1855: see PILB 3960 (emigrants from the city of Leipzig)

HARBURG

Harburg was in the Kingdom of Hannover, across the Elbe River from Hamburg. Transportation of emigrants started 10 April 1851 (see the *Karlsruher Zeitung* 16 April 1851) but never gained much importance.

Reference

♦ Hans-Georg Mercker, *Alphabetisches Register der von und über Harburg ausgewanderten Personen von 1841 bis 1884.* Typescript 1964, one copy located at the Genealogische Gesellschaft, Sitz Hamburg e.V. in Hamburg (list of emigrants from and through the port of Harburg, 1841-54, and returning emigrants).

EMDEN

This port was in the Kingdom of Hannover, Ostfriesland. Transportation of emigrants never gained importance. Some passenger lists were published for 1855-1857. See PILB 9670.

BREMEN

Due to limited storage space and to the authorities' assumption that the emigrants were lost to their native country, the Bremen passenger lists were destroyed in 1875, except for the two preceding years. This procedure continued until about 1907. The emigration lists from 1905 to May 1914 were preserved.

They contained surname and first name of the emigrants, age, number of persons, last residence including country or province, name of ship and country or port of destination. Non-German emigrants were also listed. Passenger lists of ships to England were missing. Those of ships to East Asia, Australia, North and South America were incomplete. These lists were taken to the *Statistisches Landesamt* (Bureau of Statistics) in Bremen in 1931.

In addition, there were police registers from 1898 to 30 July 1914 with the names of German emigrants who traveled in steerage and by third class. These lists were preserved in the *Nachweisungsbüro für Auswanderer* in Bremen.

In 1941 three students extracted records on 8,500 emigrants from Westphalia for the years 1898 to 1914. A small part of this material is preserved in Nordrhein-Westfälisches Staatsarchiv Münster, section Verein für das Deutschtum im Ausland (VDA), cartons 55, 56, and 128.

As this work progressed, duplicates of the lists for 1905 to 1914 were discovered in a shed on the Lloyd platform of the Bremen main railroad station. An evaluation was begun by the Deutsches Auslands-Institut (DAI), Stuttgart, in 1941.

Twenty students were ordered to the Marburg State Archives where they could feel safe from air raids, and the lists (600 kilograms) were trucked there from Bremen. The students limited the task to extractions of Germans or people of German descent. About 80 percent of the lists' emigrants were Slavs, Hungarians, and Jews.

At the end of four weeks, only a fifth of the entries had been extracted, mainly for the years 1907-1908 and 1913-1914. The lists and the extracts were taken to the DAI and stored there. The extracts for German emigrants were sorted into the Central Emigration File (now in the Bundesarchiv Koblenz, R 57 Kartei 1).

The others, mainly Eastern European extracts, were sorted according to the country of origin and year (now in the Bundesarchiv Koblenz, R 57 Kartei 12). The address of these archives: Am Wöllershof 12, 56068 Koblenz, Germany. These card files were microfilmed by the LDS church.

The lists in Bremen were totally destroyed in an air raid on October 6, 1944. The duplicates in Stuttgart were probably destroyed when the DAI building was hit by bombs on September 12 and 19/20, 1944. Possibly they were stored for safe keeping somewhere in the Württemberg

countryside at the end of the war. They have not been recovered.

In 1989, the archives of the Bremen chamber of commerce (Handelskammer) had only a very few passenger lists from 1834, 1854, and 1866. The lists for 1920-1923 and 1925-1939 were returned to East Germany in 1988.

Bibliography

◆Bodo Heyne, *"Über bremische Quellen zur Auswanderungsforschung."* Bremisches Jahrbuch 41 (1944) 358-369 (survey of available passenger lists from 1834 on). Quoted as "Heyne"

◆Gustav Wehner, *"Das Schicksal der Bremer Auswanderer-Listen"* Norddeutsche Familienkunde 1 (1952) 74-78, 96-98, 113-118. Quoted as "Wehner"

◆ Rolf Engelsing, *Bremen als Auswandererhafen 1683/1880. Ein Beitrag zur bremischen Wirtschaftsgeschichte des 19. Jahrhunderts.* (Veröffentlichungen aus dem Staatsarchiv der Freien Hansestadt Bremen 29). Bremen: Schünemann 1961. (Detailed account of the city of Bremen as a port of emigration).

◆Peter Marschalck (comp.), *Inventar der Quellen zur Geschichte der Wanderungen, besonders der Auswanderung, in Bremer Archiven.* (Veröffentlichungen aus dem staatsarchiv der Freien Hansestadt Bremen 53). Bremen: Staatsarchiv Bremen 1986.

◆Gunnar Nebelung, *"Auswanderung über Bremerhaven,"* Genealogie 41 (1992) 250.

Bremen lists

Following are publications of Bremen passenger lists and of passenger arrival lists for ships arriving from Bremen:

1826-1828: Lists of emigrants to Brazil: Staatsarchiv Bremen 2-C.12.e. Published by Peter Marschalck, *"Brasilienauswanderer aus dem Saar-Hunsrück-Raum in Bremen 1826-1828."* *Zeitschrift für die Geschichte der Saargegend* 34 (1986).

1832-1849: Friedrich Spengemann, *Die Reisen der Segelfregatten "Isabella"*

"Pauline" "Meta" und "Uhland" nach Nordamerika. Bremen: Vahland & Co. 1937. (Passenger lists taken from a logbook, indexed in Wehner 75ff.). **1834:** 67 passenger lists of the shipping companies F. D. Lüdering and Westhoff & Meier still existed in 1944 (Heyne p. 363) Two of these lists have been published. **1834:** Ship Ferdinand, see Heyne p. 368 (76 persons to Baltimore) **1834:** Ship Wallace, see Heyne p. 369 (76 persons to New York) All of these lists were stored at a safe place at the end of the war but have not been recovered. **1842:** Ship Friedrich Lucas, see PILB 5270. **1845:** To New Orleans, see PILB 6127. **1845:** To Texas, see PILB 2474-2476. **1847-1854:** Gary J. Zimmerman, Marion Wolfert (eds.), *German Immigrants. Lists of Passengers Bound from Bremen to New York, 1847-1854.* Baltimore: Genealogical Publishing Company, 1985 (includes only those passengers whose German place of origin is given in the New York passenger arrival lists) **1848-1869 (mainly 1850-1855):** Numerous passenger lists have been published in print in the contemporary paper *Allgemeine Auswanerrungs-Zeitung* and are currently being published by the author (30,060) **1848:** Ship Burgundy (shipwrecked), see PILB 5153. **1850:** Ships Itzstein and Welcker, see PILB 3967. **1851:** Ship Reform (and Magnet) to Galveston, see PILB 2514 **1854:** Ship Johann Georg, see Alfred Rubarth, *"Auswanderer" Zeitschrift für niederdeutsche Familienkunde 51* (1976) 92-93 (26 names). **1855-1862:** Gary J. Zimmerman, Marion Wolfert (eds), *German Immigrants. Lists of Passengers Bound from Bremen to New York, 1855-1862.* Baltimore: Genealogical Publishing company, 1986 (con-

tinuation of the book listed above for 1847-1854) **1863-1867:** Gary J. Zimmerman, Marion Wolfert (eds.), *German Immigrants. Lists of Passengers Bound from Bremen to New York, 1863-1867.* Baltimore: Genealogical Publishing company, 1988 (continuation of the book listed above for 1855-1862). **1864:** Karen P. Neuforth (ed.), "Passenger List: The Bark Atalanta Bremen to New York, 1864," *Omnibus 11* (1990) 692ff. **1875-1876:** see PILB 2966 **1875:** Ship Ohio, see PILB 2969 **1876:** Ship Mosel, see PILB 2971. **1882:** Ship Salier, see PILB 6206. **1886:** Hans Arnold Plöhn, *"Im Februar 1886 nach New York ausgereiste Personen,"* Zeitschrift für niederdeutsche Familienkunde 54 (1979) 73-74 (emigrants on the steamer Ems to New York, 20 February 1886, from American sources).

Although the actual passenger lists are lost, the Bremen state archives has records about the births, marriages and death on board Bremen ships from 1834 until 1939. Questions about a particular ship and the passage can usually be answered, often when only a picture of the ship is available.

(Staatsarchiv Bremen, Am Staatsarchiv 1, 28203 Bremen, Germany).

LIVERPOOL

Apparently many German emigrants took the train from Hull to Liverpool and embarked there to continue their journey at the cheap British fares.

No passenger lists have been preserved for Liverpool before 1890, probably none for England before that year at all.

To have a search done in the Passenger Lists Outwards, it is necessary to know the name of the ship, the year and month of departure, and the port from which the ship sailed.

Presumably a search in the Passenger Lists Inwards requires similar data.

These records are open to public search at the Public Record Office (Ruskin Av-

enue, Kew, Richmond, Surrey TW9
4DU).

References
♦"From the Old World to the New. The
Half-Way House to the West." *The
Liverpool Review*, 5 and 12 May 1888 (ob-
servations on emigrants' housing and
transportation in Liverpool).
♦Public Record Office, Lists and In-
dexes Supplementary Series No. IX,
Board of Trade Records to 1913, London:
1964

GLASGOW
Known to have been a port of embarkation for Russia-Germans in 1879, 1905,
and 1911. No additional information available.

AMSTERDAM
According to a letter from Gemeente-
archief Amsterdam, 18 January 1987,
there are passenger lists in the Archives
of the Waterschout (Port Administration).
No passenger lists at all have been found,
but it is doubtful whether any were kept.

ROTTERDAM
Rotterdam is at the mouth of the Rhine
River and was thus the main port of embarkation during the 18th century. Only the
passenger arrival lists for the port of Philadelphia have been preserved for the years
1727 to 1808. These were edited by
Strassburger and Hinke.
The available passenger lists of the
mass emigration of 1709 have been published:
♦Walter Allen Knittle, *Early Eighteenth
Century Palatine Emigration*. Philadelphia 1927, Reprints Baltimore: Genealogical Publishing Company 1965, 1970
(pp. 243-282 include the Rotterdam sailing
lists of 1709, the London Census of the
Palatines of 1709, not in the original order
and with some errors).
♦Lou D. MacWeathy, *The Book of Names*
(etc.), St. Johnsville (NY) 1933, Reprint
Baltimore: Genealogical Publishing
Company 1969 (pp. 75-111 the London
Census of the Palatines of 1709, with some
errors).

♦Henry Z. Jones, John P. Dern, "Palatine
Emigrants Returning in 1710."
♦Karl Scherer (ed.), *Pfälzer-Palatines.*
Kaiserslautern: Heimatstelle Pfalz 1981,
52-77 (lists of passengers who returned
from London to Rotterdam in 1710).
♦ Henry Z. Jones, Jr., *The Palatine
Families of New York. A Study of hte
German Immigrants Who Arrived in
Colonial New York in 1710.* 2 vols.
Universal City (CA): privately published
by the author, 1985 (this is not a
publication of the passenger lists, but an
extensive investigation on those emigrants
who later settled in colonial New York and
New Jersey).
♦John P. Dern, *London Churchbooks and
the German Emigration of 1709. Die
deutsche Auswanderung von 1709 in den
Londoner Kirchenbüchern. (Schriften zur
Wanderungsgeschichte der Pfälzer* 26).
Kaiserslautern: Heimatstelle Pfalz 1968
(listed here as it pertains to the 1709
emigration).
Note: According to a letter from
Gemeente Rotterdam, Archiefdienst (Robert Fruinstraat 52, 3021 XE Rotterdam,
Netherlands), 18 January 1987, the Archives of the Waterschout were destroyed
in the Second World War, including the
passenger lists.
The archives of the Holland-Amerika
Line shipping company contain "passage-
staten" and "passagiers-registers" from
1900 on. These passenger lists contain
many Germans.

ANTWERP
General information: G. Kurgan, E.
Spelkens, *Two Studies on Emigration
through Antwerp to the New World.*
Brussels: Center for American Studies
1976 (contains an essay by G. Kurgan-van
Hententryk on Belgian emigration to the
United States and other overseas countries
at the beginning of the 20th century, and a
statistical investigation by E. Spelkels on
Antwerp as a port of emigration 1843-
1913).
Only the embarkation lists of 1855

have survived and been published: Charles M. Hall (ed.), *The Antwerp Emigration Index*. Salt Lake City: Heritage International (NY) – name, age, place of origin, name of ship and place where passport was issued, for about 5,100 emigrants, many of them from Germany.

Registers for other years were destroyed by German troops in 1914.

The Ludwigsburg State Archives preserves a list of Württemberg emigrants on the ship *Vaterlands-Liebe*, leaving Antwerp for Philadelphia in May 1817 (Staatsarchiv Ludwigsburg D 41, Büschel 4408, reproduced in Günter Moltmann (ed.) *Aufbruch nach Amerika*. Tübingen: Wunderlich 1979, 263-268).

Additional records in the City Archives of Antwerp have been checked for names of German emigrants: hotel registers 1801-1821 and 1858-1887 (MA2641, MA2645, MA2669, MA2672), lists of emigres 1793-1815 (MA447/1, MA450/1) sojourn registers 1840-1871 (MA2670/1-12, MA2671/1), general records on German emigrants 1850-1856 (MA674/1), passport and visa registers 1798-1857 (MA2643, MA2644) passenger arrivals from FROM Rotterdam and London 1843-1844 (MA2636). Most of these lists are incomplete. None contains German emigrants in transit.

LE HAVRE

The port of LeHavre was mainly used by emigrants from southern Germany during the period from about 1830 to 1870.

General information: Jean Braunstein, *"L'emigration allemande par le port du Havre au XIXe siecle."* Annales de Normandie 34 (1984) 95-104 (statistical evaluation of the available data).

The passenger lists are kept at the Archives Departementales de la Seine Maritime, Cours Clemenceau, 76036 Rouen Cedex, France (6 P 6 no. 1-600 for 1750-1898, also for later years).

They give name, description and destination of the ship (mostly to French colonies), name, sometimes age and occupation of the passengers, their place of birth or residence (or the place where their passport was issued), and the names or numbers of family members.

These lists were delivered by the captains when they returned to LeHavre, which may have been one or two years after their departure.

They are filed by the date of delivery and therefore they are hard to locate. Only passenger lists for French ships were delivered, and therefore these lists cover only a small part of the emigrants through this part.

A card index to about 40,000 passenger entries was discovered in the 1980s and thus saved from destruction. This information was supplied by M. Jean-Paul Portellette of LeHavre, who is in charge of the preparation of a letter-by-letter series of publications containing the data from this index.

For details one may write to Cercle Genealogique et Heraldique de Normandie, 17 rue Louis Malliot, 76000 Rouen, France (without any guarantee of receiving an answer).

Supporting information

The civil registration (*Etat civil*) registers do not contain entries on German emigrants who were married or had a child born in LeHavre. Entries of this kind might be found in the registers of the churches (mainly of the Saint Francois Church). The marriages from 1867 to 1870 have been published:

Jean-Paul and Elisabeth Portelette (eds.), *"La Chapelle des Allemands du Havre."* Revue genealogique normande no. 17 (1986) 11-14 (list of 148 marriages, not giving the places of origin, which are also not given in the original records, Archives Departementales de la Seine Maritime, I J 368).

The names of 3987 satisfied and a few disappointed passengers from 1848 to 1855, mainly 1850 to 1854 are being published by the author under the title *Vielen Dank, Herr Bielefeld.*

Sources replacing the passenger lists of various ports

◆Lists of emigrants signing a letter of thanks to the travel agent for his goods and services. These lists were then published by the agent for advertising purposes. Lists of this type are found in many German newspapers of the 1850s and sometimes 1860s.

◆ Ship passenger lists published in the *Allgemeine Auswanderungs-Zeitung* (printed in Rudolstadt 1846-1871). Two lists of this type (for the ships *Itzstein & Welcker* leaving Bremen for New Orleans, and Helena Sloman, Hamburg to New York, both in 1850) were published by Karl Werner Klüber (see PILB 3967 and 3921).

Final notes

◆*Clues* (a magazine of the American Historical Society of Germans from Russia) regularly publishes lists of Russia-German passengers to American and Canadian ports.

◆The remaining passenger arrival lists of the US-American ports from 1850 onward are being published in the following book series:
Ira A. Glazier, P. William Filby (eds), *Germans to America. Lists of Passengers Arriving at U.S. Ports* [1850-1855], vol. 1ff Wilmington DE: Scholarly Resources 1988ff. and continued.

◆Michael Palmer, "Published Passenger Lists: A Review of German Immigrants and Germans to America." *German Genealogical Society of America Bulletin* vol. 4 (1990) pp. 69, 71-90, and not continued (a very detailed account on the available United States arrival lists and the completeness and quality of their publication).

Footnotes

[1]Friedrich R. Wollmershäuser, M.A., an Accredited Genealogist, lives at Herrengasse 8-10, 89610 Oberdischingen, Germany
[2]The author is preparing these passenger lists for publication.
©Friedrich R. Wollmershäuser, 1997

TIMELINE OF IMMIGRATION LAWS IN THE UNITED STATES

1819: Under An Act Regulating Passenger Ships and Vessels, ship captains had to submit to customs officials a list of passengers, describing name, age, sex, vocation, country of origin, and country of destination of each passenger. Passengers ill with contagious diseases had to be quarantined. States carried out provisions of this law.

1847 and 1848: Congress passed laws on accommodation of passengers on ships.

1855: An act of Congress superseded the laws of 1819, 1847, and 1848, whereby it stated the amount of space to which immigrants were entitled aboard ship and required issue of at least one hot meal per day for steerage passengers.
The law was not very effective in correcting the problems of abuse to immigrants.

1864: An Act to Encourage Immigration provided for the naming of a Commissioner of Immigration, in order to encourage contract labor, to increase the numbers of farm workers, and to build American industry.
Immigrants were granted exemption from military service for as long as they remained citizens of a foreign country and did not voluntarily apply for American citizenship. The act was repealed four years later, but competition among the states to attract new citizens grew.

1875: The Immigration Act of 1875 provided for inspection of vessels by state officials. The law barred the admission of ex-convicts as well as Chinese and Japanese who were brought to the United States against their will.

1882: An act was passed by which every immigrant was charged a poll tax of 50 cents.
Subsequent increases had the effect of reducing immigration. In the 1880s authority over immigration, including

"The Only Way to Handle It"
(Literary Digest, May 7, 1921)

enforcement of the Federal statutes, remained at the state level.

1885: A law was passed prohibiting contract labor. It was designed to end the practice of signing up foreign laborers to work in America for low wages. No immigrant could have a job or a promise of a job before landing.

1891: The Immigration Act of 1891 provided for the federal government to take over entirely the job of processing immigrants. Federal inspectors examined immigrants on arrival. All immigrants had to pass a medical exam and answer questions about their background and intentions in America. Shipping lines were forbidden to solicit immigrants in foreign countries. The law also barred from admission persons suffering from "loathesome or dangerous diseases," those convicted of crimes involving "moral turpitude," polygamists, and those whose passage was paid for by others. Those rejected for immigration were deported at the expense of the shipping companies which had transported them to the United States. As a result of this law, all duties previously deferred to the States were

transferred by the June 30, 1891 to United States inspection officers. The Bureau of Immigration began operations in the Treasury Department as the first Federal immigration agency. Besides its headquarters in Washington, DC, the Bureau opened 24 inspection stations (including Ellis Islalnd in January 1892) at ports of entry along both borders and in major seaports.

1903: The Bureau of Immigration was moved to the newly established Department of Commerce and Labor and given broader responsibilities.

1903, 1907: Further laws were passed to impose stricter standards of admission, the object being to exclude untrained workers and anarchists.

1917: A law was enacted prescribing a literacy test for immigrants, affecting primarily eastern and southeastern Europeans.

1921: From this date, all immigration was controlled by a quota system. Starting in this year, quotas allowed only three percent of the share of a nationality in the total American population, as determined by the 1910 census.

1924: The quota was reduced to two percent, with the calculation based on the 1890 census. (In that census year, immigration from eastern and southeastern countries had not been so high.)

1929: American consuls in the countries of emigration were given the decision as to the granting of visas, thus influencing immigration. (In 1921 the maximum immigration for Germany was set at 68,051, which dropped to 51,227 following the act of 1924, and was reduced to 25,967 in 1929. In 1923, Germany exhausted its quota within six months. After 1930, German immigration to the United States almost came to a stop.)

1965: New regulations gave every country a limit of 20,000 immigrants, but not more than 290,000 persons could be admitted annually (170,000 from the eastern and 120,000 from the western hemisphere).

Sources: "Emigration Policy in Germany and Immigration Policy in the United States," by Ingrid Schöberl. *Germans to America: 300 Years of Immigration 1683-1983,* ed. Günter Moltmann, Institute for Foreign Relations, Stuttgart, in cooperation with Inter Nationes, Bonn. Bad Godesberg, 1982. Also, U.S. Immigration and Naturalization Service

NATURALIZATION TIMELINE

1607-1740: Naturalization was granted through the British Crown or Parliament, but colonial governors also granted naturalization for the colony (but not for British citizenship).

1740: Naturalization by colonies required seven years' residency in the colony, an oath of allegiance to the Crown, profession of Christian belief in a colonial court, and evidence of taking of the sacrament in a Protestant and Reformed Congregation (exemptions allowed for Jews and Quakers).

Revolutionary War period: Most of the newly formed states required an oath of allegiance, demonstration of good character, and a specified period of residency, and a disavowal of allegiance to a foreign power.

1790: Under the Constitution, the control of the several states was replaced with federal naturalization, requiring one year's state residence, two years' residence in the United States, and a loyalty oath taken in a court.

1795: Requirements for naturalization were residency in the United States for five years, one year's residency in the state where naturalized, a declaration of intent three years before the oath, an oath of allegiance, good moral character, renunciation of any title of nobility, and the foreswearing of allegiance to the reigning foreign sovereign.

1798: The requirement changed to 14 years' residency, with the declaration of intent to be filed 5 years before the loyalty oath.

1802: Provisions as required in 1795 (above) were restored. Any court which kept records (U.S., state, county, city) could carry out the declaration and oath. The alien was to register with the court, which was "to ascertain the name, birthplace, age, nation and allegiance of each alien, together with the country whence he or she migrated. ..." Automatic citizenship was provided for wives and children of naturalized males and for men who received an honorable discharge for U.S. military service.

1828: The registry requirements of the 1802 law were repealed, but by the late 1820s, the registry and declaration were frequently united as one document. Procedures of the naturalization process: 1) Report and Registry of Aliens, 1798-1828, either separate from of combined with 2) the Declaration of Intention, 3) the Petition for Naturalization, 4) the order of the court granting citizenship, based upon the petition and oath of allegiance, and 5) Certificate of Naturalization. (Note: the first two steps did not always occur at the same time or in the same court.)

1868: With enactment of the Fourteenth Amendment, national citizenship was guaranteed and extended to all persons born or naturalized in the United States and subject to its jurisdiction.

1906: The Bureau of Immigration and Naturalization was created and given authority to make rules, one of which was that the courts had to use only officially produced blank forms and records. (Before 1906, the courts were totally responsible for the naturalization process.)

1913: The Division of Naturalization became the Bureau of Naturalization, which it remained until 1933 when the name was changed to the Immigration and Naturalization Service, in the Department of Labor. This agency was transferred to the Department of Justice in 1940.

1929: An act provided a major refinement

of the 1906 law, among other matters clarifying the requirements for registry of aliens and providing for certificates of derivative naturalization. American consuls in countries of emigration were given the responsibility for deciding who could and could not emigrate.

1930: Due to strict implementation of American immigration restrictions, German migration to the United States almost completely stopped after this year.

NATURALIZATION RECORDS: AN OVERVIEW

Naturalization papers are records of a court procedure granting U.S. citizenship to noncitizens. They usually include three documents — a Declaration of Intention to become a citizen, Petition, and Naturalization Certificate. Prior to 1906, the court record was the only record of a naturalization. After implementation of the Basic Naturalization Act of 1906, a second copy of the records was sent to the then new Bureau of Naturalization in Washington, DC, now part of the U.S. Immigration and Naturalization Service.

Note

Naturalization records exist only for those immigrants who sought citizenship. No such records were drawn for persons who gained citizenship by being born in the United States, by being the wife or child of a naturalized male, or by other derivative citizenship processes.

The main attraction for naturalization was that it provided the right to vote; it was never required for residency. For many German immigrants, naturalization may not have been particularly appealing. In 1901, for example, 65.4 percent of eligible German aliens were naturalized.

Evidence of time and place of naturalization may be found in federal and state censuses, passenger manifests, homestead applications, passport applications, and voter registrations. Filby's "Passenger and Immigration Lists Index" may also provide clues.

DOCUMENTS INCLUDED IN THE NATURALIZATION PROCESS

♦ **Declarations of Intent (commonly known as "First Papers")**

Through the Declaration of Intent, the applicant renounced allegiance to a foreign government and stated an intention to become a United States citizen. It usually appeared two years before other documents. (Between 1798 and 1828, an immigrant, upon arrival, may have filed at a local court of record for a "certificate of report and registry.") The Declaration of Intent was sometimes not required if the applicant served in the military with an honorable discharge, or entered the country as a minor. If an alien filed a Declaration of Intent but never followed through with the final papers, the document should nevertheless have remained on file.

♦ **Naturalization petitions (or "Second," or "Final Papers")**

Naturalization petitions were used to make formal applications for citizenship by those who had met residency requirements and who had declared their intention to become citizens.

Usually the residency requirement was five years in the United States, and one year in the state in which application was being filed.

♦ **Naturalization depositions**

These depositions are formal statements by other persons supporting the applicant's petition for naturalization.

♦ **Records of Naturalization/Oaths of Allegiance**

These records document the granting of U.S. citizenship to petitioners. Such records, later filed in the form of certificates, may typically appear in the court of naturalization in chronological arrangement, often in bound volumes which include surname indexes.

Sometimes the records of a petitioner are bound in the form of a "petition and record."
◆**Final Certificate**
The certificate of citizenship was given to the immigrant.

INFORMATION FOUND IN NATURALIZATION RECORDS

Before September 27, 1906, there was no uniform method of creating naturalization records. As a result, pre-1906 records may contain little information, or many contain a wealth of data. Records before 1906 do not give birth date or town of birth.

After September 26, 1906, naturalization records take a standard format and contain prescribed information. They include the place and date of birth of the immigrant and other family members, port of arrival, vessel name, and date of arrival.

Usual content of records:
◆**Declarations of Intent prior to 1906:** name, country of birth or allegiance, date of application, and signature. Some provide the date and port of arrival in the United States.
◆ **Declarations of Intent after 1906:** applicant's name, age, occupation, and personal description; date and place of birth; citizenship; present address and last foreign address; vessel and port of embarkation for the United States; date of application and signature
◆ **Naturalization petitions**: name, residence, occupation, date and place of birth, citizenship, personal description; date of emigration; ports of embarkation and arrival; marital status; names, dates, places of birth, and residence of applicant's children; date at which U.S. residence commenced; time of residence in state; name changes; and signature.

Frequently interfiled with these petitions are copies of declarations of intention, certificates of arrival, and certificates

of completion of citizenship classes. Petitions after 1930 often include photographs of the applicants.
◆**Naturalization depositions:** period of applicant's residence in a certain locale and other information, including witnesses' appraisals of the applicant's character.
◆**Certificate of Naturalization/Oaths of Allegiance:** the petition for naturalization, affidavits of the petitioner and witnesses, the oath of allegiance, and the order of the court admitting the petitioner to citizenship
◆ **Petition and Record:** documents gathered together into a "Petition and Record," providing the petition for naturalization, affidavits of the petitioner and witnesses, the oath of allegiance, and the order of the court admitting the petitioner to citizenship

THE SEARCH FOR NATURALIZATION RECORDS

◆ For naturalizations occurring before September 27, 1906, there are court records only, which may be found in court houses, state and federal archives, historical societies, and libraries. If the court near where the immigrant lived does not have naturalization records, it can provide information as to where such records are kept.
◆Beginning September 27, 1906, there were two copies of naturalization records filed — one with the court and one with the Bureau of Immigration and Naturalization, now part of the Immigration and Naturalization Service. Also, copies of the records are usually kept with the records of court which handled them or at a state archives.
Court copies
◆Most (but not all) Federal court records are now in the custody of the National Archives.
◆Many state and local court records are
(continued on page 71)

Naturalization Records Timeline

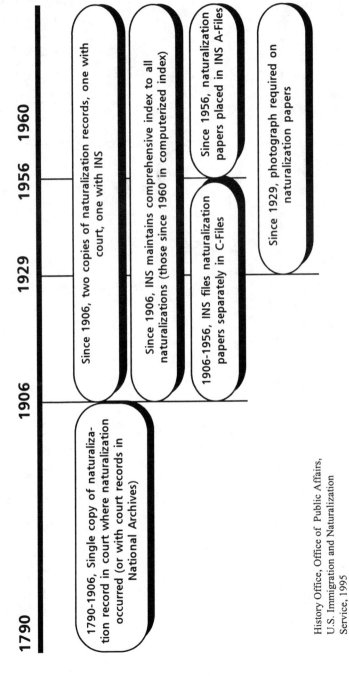

1790   1906   1929   1956 1960

1790-1906, Single copy of naturalization record in court where naturalization occurred (or with court records in National Archives)

Since 1906, two copies of naturalization records, one with court, one with INS

Since 1906, INS maintains comprehensive index to all naturalizations (those since 1960 in computerized index)

1906-1956, INS files naturalization papers separately in C-Files

Since 1956, naturalization papers placed in INS A-Files

Since 1929, photograph required on naturalization papers

History Office, Office of Public Affairs,
U.S. Immigration and Naturalization
Service, 1995

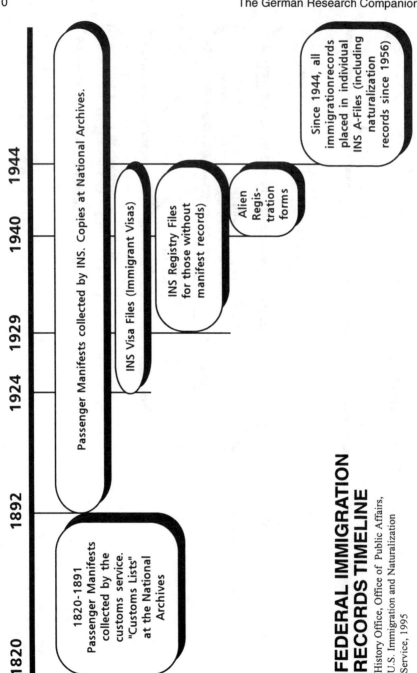

FEDERAL IMMIGRATION RECORDS TIMELINE

1820   1892   1924   1929   1940   1944

1820-1891 Passenger Manifests collected by the customs service. "Customs Lists" at the National Archives

Passenger Manifests collected by INS. Copies at National Archives.

INS Visa Files (Immigrant Visas)

INS Registry Files for those without manifest records)

Alien Regis-tration forms

Since 1944, all immigrationrecords placed in individual INS A-Files (including naturalization records since 1956)

History Office, Office of Public Affairs, U.S. Immigration and Naturalization Service, 1995

stored by other institutions, such as a State Archives.

♦County records are listed in the Family History Library Catalog under the the state, then the county, then "Naturalization and Citizenship."

♦For any court naturalization record, write the Clerk of Court in the county (or counties) where it is likely the immigrant may have applied.

National Archives

The regional archives hold original records of naturalizations filed in most of the federal courts (and, in some cases, non-federal courts) located in their regions. The available records span the period from 1790 to 1950, but coverage varies from region to region Due to the variability in records and finding aids available in each region, researchers should contact the appropriate regional archives for specific information.

Immigration and Naturalization Service (INS)

The INS holds records of naturalizations from September 26, 1906 to the present, but INS records are available only through Freedom of Information Act (FOIA)/Privacy Act (PA) request.

However, copies of most records held by the INS may also be available at public institutions without FOIA/PA restrictions.

Locating the records

♦Homestead and passport applications, normally stored in the National Archives, include the name of the court where a naturalization was certified.The naturalization records are often found with these respective applications.

wIn the FHLC, search under one of the following: [State] - Naturalization and Citizenship; [State], [County], - Naturalization and Citizenship; and [State], [County], [City] - Naturalization and Citizenship.

♦The National Archives' 11 regional archives hold original records of naturalizations filed in most of the federal courts (and, in some cases, nonfederal courts) located in their regions.

The available records span the periods from 1790 to 1950, but covrage varies from region to region.

Due to the variability in records and finding aids which are available in each region, researchers should contact the appropriate regional archives for specific information.

♦ When the 1870 census shows an immigrant to have become a citizen, it is apparent that naturalization papers exist.

♦Check censuses, homestead records, passports, voting registers, and military papers for indications that an immigrant met citizenship requirements.

♦An excellent guide detailing this topic is found in the *Research Outline: United States*, published by the Family History Library and available at Family History Centers.

DERIVATIVE CITIZENSHIP

Derivative citizenship is that which is based on the citizenship of another person or on service performed by an applicant. Included below are provisions of derivative citizenship, not including group citizenship (which includes blocks of people such as Native Americans or Chinese).

1790: Children of naturalized citizens automatically became citizens

1790-1922: During this timespan, the wife became naturalized when her husband gained citizenship.)

1804: Widows and minor children of a deceased applicant who had filed his declaration of intention but who died before the naturalization proceeding, could be declared citizens upon taking the oath required by law.

1824: Minor aliens who had lived in the United States three years before age 21 and for two years thereafter could apply for naturalization. (Repealed in 1906)

1922: An 1855 law granting citizenship to a woman by marriage to a citizen was repealed. Under this law, a married woman now had to be naturalized on her own.

CITIZENSHIP: MILITARY SERVICE AND LAND PURCHASE

1862: An alien of age 21 or more with an honorary discharge from the regular or volunteer armies could petition to become a citizen without any previous declaration of intention and with proof of one year's residence. This legislation applied to any war, including the Mexican, Indian, and the Spanish-American wars.

1894: The same privilege of naturalization was given without filing a declaration of intent to a man who had been honorably discharged after five consecutive years in the Navy or one enlistment in the Marine Corps.

1918: The various laws regarding naturalization of soldiers, sailors and veterans were consolidated, and rules for aliens serving in World War I were liberalized.

Land Purchase

1862: The Homestead Act required that before a settler could purchase land under the Act, he either had to be a U.S. citizen or had to have filed a declaration of intention. The National Archives has Homestead records before May 1, 1908; the Bureau of Land Management has them for the period after that date. The most valuable of the homestead records are the applications.

Chapter 4
Arrival in America

CHRONOLOGY OF IMMIGRANT PROCESSING IN AMERICA

Castle Garden

Castle Garden, at the Battery on the tip of Manhattan, was originally built as a fort, called Castle Clinton (named for DeWitt Clinton, governor of New York), one of five forts built to defend New York harbor.

1807-1811: Circular gun battery emplacement is built

1824: The fort, now named Castle Garden, serves as a fashionable amphitheater. Later, in 1845, renovated as a concert hall where public figures including Lafayette, Kossuth, and President Jackson were received, and where artists such as Jenny Lind were presented.

1850: Increasing immigration through New York harbor demands a centralized receiving station. Disembarking from 1,912 ships, 212,796 newcomers arrive.

1855 (1 August): Castle Garden, on the Battery at the tip of Manhattan, officially opens as the first United States receiving station for immigrants arriving through the nation's principal port of entry at New York City. More than 7 million newcomers come to the United States between 1855 and 1890.

1864: Castle Garden becomes a recruiting quarters for the Union Army; many German and Irish immigrants sign up for service as soon as they arrive in New York

1876: Fire destroys most of the structure, but service to immigrants continues.

1881: Some 455,600 immigrants pass through Castle Garden, more than doubling the past average annual rate, and increasing to 476,000 the following year.

1882: First federal immigration law enacted; bars lunatics, convicts and those likely to become public charges.

1882: Outbreak of anti-semitism in Russia spurs sharp rise in Jewish immigration.

1885: Foran Act prohibits importing contract labor, does not prohibit individuals from assisting immigration of relatives and friends.

1886 (28 October): Statue of Liberty

dedicated, as resistance to immigration becomes stronger.

1887: Castle Garden's facilities are found hopelessly inadequate for flow of immigration.

1890: Last group passes through Castle Garden. Federal government assumes full control of immigration for previous state-contracted management of New York Port.

1891: New legislation places all national immigration under full federal control, creating the Bureau of Immigration under the Department of the Treasury; legislation adds health requirements to immigration restrictions. Russian pogroms spur large volume of Jewish immigration. Immigration through the Barge Office represents 80 percent of the national total.

1896-1941: Castle Garden serves as the New York City Aquarium

1950: Castle Garden is declared a national monument

ELLIS ISLAND

In its 52 years as an immigration station, detention center, and deportation center (1892-1954), Ellis Island served as the gateway to America for an estimated 16 million or more immigrants.

1892 (1 January): Ellis Island Immigration Center formally opens as an immigration station; first and second cabin passengers processed on board and directly disembark in Manhattan.

1892: Immigration through the New York port totals 445,987, showing a shift from northern and western Europeans to southern and eastern Europeans.

1893: Shipowners are required to prepare manifests containing detailed information on individual immigrant passengers.

1893: Cholera epidemic and national economic depression result in immigration decrease, to continue for several years.

1894: Immigration Restriction League organized, favoring the "old" (northern

and western European) over the "new" (southern and eastern European) immigrants.

1897: Literacy test for immigrants, aimed at restricting Italian influx, vetoed by President Cleveland

1897 (13 June): Fire destroys Ellis Island's wooden buildings, along with immigration records dating from 1855-1890 housed in old Navy magazine. Processing temporarily transferred back to Barge Office (14 June) — until 17 December 1900.

1898: U.S. immigration reaches low point of 229,299, with New York port's share only 178,748, following years of national economic depression.

1900 (17 December): New Ellis Island Immigration Station reopens as an immigration station, on a larger scale, with a total of 2,251 immigrants received for inspection on this day. The new complex, unlike the former station, is situated to retain some green space and show to best advantage to approaching ships.

1902: Procedures to ensure efficient, honest and sanitary treatment of immigrants are instituted.

1903: Immigration control transferred to the newly established Department of Commerce and Labor.

1903: New legislation denies entry to anarchists and prostitutes, imposes fines on steamship companies bringing in immigrants with loathsome or contagious diseases.

1903: On one day, 12,600 immigrants arrive at New York Port, with nearly half required to remain in steerage for several days due to inadequate facilities to process all in a day or provide overnight quarters at Ellis Island. This is to become a common occurrence over the next several years.

1904: New 160-foot "Ellis Island" ferry completed, with capacity for 600. Steerage immigrants transported to Ellis from docks at the Battery by barges and tugs provided by steamship companies; when cleared for admission, new ferry runs them hourly to their "new land" at New York.

1905: There are 821,169 immigrants processed at Ellis Island, with many logistical problems regarding numerous detainees frequently required to remain for several days.

1907: Climax of immigration, with 1,004,756 received at Ellis Island.

1909: Following a sharp falloff in 1908, immigration again rising.

1911: Greatest number of exclusions to date; 13,000 immigrants of the 650,000 arrivals at Ellis Island are deported.

1914-18: World War I ends period of mass migration to the United States. 1914: 1,218,480 total U.S. immigration; 878,052 through New York Port. 1915: 326,700 admitted, 178,416 through New York Port (a 75% increase). 1918: Only 28,867 immigrants enter New York Port.

1917: Literacy test for immigrants adopted, having been defeated in seven previous proposals from 1896-1915.

1917: United States enters war. German merchant ship crews held in New York Harbor at Ellis Island; suspected enemy aliens are taken to Ellis under custody.

1918-19: U.S. Army Medical Department and U.S. Navy take over main facilities of Ellis Island; inspection of arriving aliens conducted on board ship or at docks.

1919: Thousands of suspected alien radicals interned at Ellis Island; hundreds deported under new legislation based on principal of guilt by association with any organization advocating revolt.

1920: Ellis Island Station reopened for immigration inspection, while continuing to function as a deportation center.

1920: Immigration takes a noticeable upturn, with 225,206 aliens admitted through New York.

1921: Immigration rises to nearly pre-war proportions; 560,971 immigrants pass through the New York Port — of a national total of 805,228.

1921: Emergency immigration restriction law introduces the quota system, weighted in favor of natives of northern and western Europe; the number of any given European nation's immigrants to the United States annually can not exceed 3 percent of foreign-born persons from that nation living in the United States in 1910. An annual total of admissible immigrants is set at 358,000, with not more than 20 percent of the quota to be received in any given month. Steamship companies rush to land each month's quota of immigrants in keen competition, overloading the processing capacities of Ellis Island.

1921-23: Steamship companies find steerage no longer profitable; new liners are designed instead with comfortable third-class cabins, marking the passage of the steerage era.

1924: National Origins Act (or, the Second Quota Law) further restricts immigration, changing the quota basis from the census of 1910 to that of 1890, and reducing annual quota immigration to 164,000. The Act further requires selection and qualification of immigrants at countries of origin, with inspections conducted by staff of U.S. consuls in Europe.

1924: Mass immigration ends; Ellis Island no longer used for primary inspection of immigrants, who are now inspected in countries of origin.

1929: National Origins Act amended, with new quotas based on 1920 census, and the maximum number of admissions annually lowered to 150,000. Act increases bias against southern and eastern Europeans.

1930: Principal function of Ellis Island changed to detention station. Immigration sharply reduced during economic depression following stock market crash.

1931: Many aliens voluntarily seek deportation to escape economic depression.

1933: In contrast to only 4,488 incoming aliens through Ellis Island, there are 7,037 outgoing aliens.

1933: Hitler initiates anti-Semitic campaign; Jewish refugees come to United

Castle Garden

States, but quota system barriers not lifted to admit large numbers in jeopardy in Germany.

1933: Immigration and Naturalization Bureaus are merged.

1940: Alien Registration Act requires registration of all aliens, adds to the list of deportable classes, and calls for finger-printing arriving aliens.

1941: United States enters World War II. Ellis Island again used for detention of suspected alien immigrants.

1946: War Brides Act provides for admission of foreign-born wives of American servicemen.

1950: Internal Security Act excludes arriving aliens who were ever members of Communist and Fascist organizations.

1952: Immigration and Naturalization Act makes the quota system even more repressive.

1953-56: Refugee Relief Act granted visas to some 5,000 Hungarians after 1956 revolution; President Eisenhower invites 30,000 more on parole.

1954: Ellis Island Station is vacated, declared excess federal property, and closed

1965: Ellis Island added by Presidential Proclamation to the Statue of Liberty National Monument

1976: The site is opened to the public for limited seasonal visitation

1984: Ellis Island closed for $160 million restoration

1990 (10 September): Ellis Island re-opened with extensive museum exhibits and facilities.

Partially based on: *The Ellis Island Source Book,* by August C. Bolino, Kensington Historical Press, Washington, DC, 1985 (chapter IX, Appendix A1; author took information from Tedd McCann, et al. *Ellis Island Study*, Washington: National Park Service, May 1978, pp. C-1 to C-18; D 1-2; E1 to E3)

STATUE OF LIBERTY

Original name of statue: "Liberty Enlightening the World"
Designer: Alsatian sculptor and architect Frédéric Auguste Bartholdi, with engineering assistance from Alexandre Gustave Eiffel, later to become famous for the Eiffel Tower in Paris
Location: Liberty Island, a small island southwest of Manhattan in Upper New York Bay, Liberty Island (called Bedloe's Island before 1956)
Size, weight: 151 feet, 1 inch high, weighing 225 tons, on a 142-foot high pedestal. Right arm, 42 feet long and 12 feet in diameter at its thickest point, extends 300 feet above sea level. Head is 10 feet wide. Each eye is 2.5 feet wide.
Construction: Hand-hammered copper plates over an iron skeleton; 142 steps in side the statue
Presentation from France to the United States: July 4, 1884
Dedication of statue, "Liberty Enlightening the World,": October 28, 1886, as a memorial to the alliance between France and the American colonists who fought for independence in the Revolutionary War in America.
The statue's later influence: During World War I, the statue took on greater symbolism Its image was used to boost sales of what came to be known as "Liberty Bonds" to help support the war effort. Thus the statues title, "Liberty Enlightening the World became more commonly known as the "Statue of Liberty."
National Monument: In 1924, the Statue of Liberty was declared a national monument. In 1933, the National Park Service first took on the responsibility for maintaining the statue.

'THE NEW COLOSSUS'

"The New Colossus," was written in 1883 by American poet Emma Lazarus.
The sonnet is engraved on the pedestal of the Statue of Liberty.

Not like the brazen giant of Greek fame,
With conquering limbs astride from
land to land;
Here at our sea-washed, sunset gates
shall stand
A mighty woman with a torch, whose
flame
Is the imprisoned lightning, and her name
Mother of Exiles. From her beacon-hand
Glows world-wide welcome; her wild
eyes command
The air-bridged harbor that twin
cities frame.
"Keep, ancient lands, your storied
pomp!" cries she
With silent lips. "Give me your tired,
your poor,
Your huddled masses yearning to
breathe free,
The wretched refuse of your teeming
shore.
Send these, the homeless, tempest-tost
to me.
I lift my lamp beside the golden door!"

THE AMERICAN IMMIGRANT WALL OF HONOR

At the end of 1997, registration closes for immigrant ancestor names to be included on The American Immigrant Wall of Honor at the Ellis Island Immigration Museum on Ellis Island in New York. For a $100 donation, the name of either an individual or a family may be permanently engraved on the Wall, which overlooks New York Harbor.

This memorial, the largest wall of names in the world, lists more than 500,000 individuals and families.

The Wall is arranged in two alphabetical listings: Those names registered before 1993 are listed on panels 7 through 484; those registered between 1993 and 1995 are listed on panels 485 through 578.

To determine on which panel a name is inscribed, check the Wall of Honor computer, which displays all registered immigrant names with the corresponding panel number on which each name may be found. In addition to the immigrant's name and the position on the wall, the computerized information includes the country of origin and the donor's name.

Whether an ancestor first set foot on American soil at Ellis Island or entered through another gateway, the name may be included on the Wall.

Donations to The American Immigrant Wall of Honor fund the creation of The American Family Immigration History Center.

Each Wall of Honor donor receives a certificate personalized with the name and country of the individual being honored. Contributions of $1,000, $5,000 and $10,000 receive special places of honor. Contributions are tax-deductible.

All new submissions will be engraved on the Wall by the end of 1998.

For information on how to participate, write to: The Statue of Liberty-Ellis Island Foundation, Inc., P.O. Box Ellis,New York, NY 10163. Tel. (212) 883-1986.

THE ELLIS ISLAND
ORAL HISTORY PROJECT

At the Oral History Studio on the second floor of the Ellis Island Immigration Museum the visitor may listen to interviews made by about 1,200 immigrants and former immigration employees, who have shared their Ellis Island memories. About 300 additional interviews are in the process of transcription. The Oral History Library is a project of the Statue of Liberty-Ellis Island Foundation.

Individual interviews are listed in the library's computers by name, country of origin, immigration date, ship, and a few by topic. In order to review interviews given by German-Americans, it is possible to display on the library computers a list of all Germans in the database, alphabetically arranged by surnames. Women are listed by both maiden and married names. Each interview runs from about 10 minutes to two hours.

The Oral History Library is equipped with 20 listening stations and 50 sets of headphones. Up to four people at one time can listen to the same interview.

Taped interviews may be purchased on standard cassettes at a cost of $10.00 per hour of interview.

Project leaders continue to seek potential interviewees who entered the United States through Ellis Island or who worked at the station during its years of operation.

To hear to one or more of these oral-history interviews, make an appointment with a librarian by calling (212) 363-5807. The fax number is (212) 363-6302.

ELLIS ISLAND GRAFITTI

"Why should I fear the fires of hell? I have been through Ellis Island."
Inscription written on Ellis Island wall by an immigrant

THE STATUE OF LIBERTY
NATIONAL MONUMENT
AND ELLIS ISLAND
IMMIGRATION MUSEUM

Ellis Island and the Statue of Liberty are located in New York Harbor.

The Ellis Island Immigration Museum, on Ellis Island in New York Harbor, is located in the Main Building of the former immigration station complex and tells the story of 400 years of American immigration.

Highlights of the museum
♦ The historic Great Hall, or Registry Room, where new arrivals were processed, now restored to its 1918-1924 appearance
♦ "Through America's Gate," a step-by-step view of the Ellis Island immigrant process
♦ "Ellis Island Galleries," illustrates the history of the Island and its restoration and containing displays of actual immigrant artifacts brought from the Old World and donated to the museum by descendants of the immigrants.
♦ "Peak Immigration Years, 1880-1924," which covers the immigrants' journey to America and the many aspects of their settlement throughout the United States
♦ The Oral History Archives, where visitors may hear taped reminiscences of Ellis Island immigrants and former Ellis Island employees
♦ "The Peopling of America," a graphic, colorful look at the history of immigration to America
♦ Two theaters, featuring the film, "Island of Hope, Island of Tears"
♦ More than 30 galleries of artifacts, historical photos, posters, maps etc.
♦ A Learning Center and student orientation center (reservations required)
♦ The American Immigrant Wall of Honor

Hours
Both the Statue of Liberty and the Ellis Island Immigration Museum are open daily except Christmas Day. Winter hours: 9:30 am - 5 pm. Summer hours: 9:30 am - 5:30 pm

Tickets
Prices (tickets are good for both monuments): $7.00 adults; $5.00 seniors; $3.00 children (3-17); under 3, free. For group tickets call (212) 269-5755.

Transportation
Boats leave daily from the Battery in Lower Manhattan and Liberty State Park in New Jersey about every half hour from 9:30 am to 3:30 pm. The schedule is subject to change. For specific departure times, call Circle Line - Statue of Liberty Ferry Company at (212)269-5755. The ferry runs between the Statue of Liberty and Ellis Island.

UNITED STATES IMMIGRATION AND NATURALIZATION SERVICE

The first immigration office in the federal government was created in 1864 by a law intended to encourage immigration. Under this law, the President appointed a commissioner of immigration within the State Department to regulate the transportation and settlement of "emigrants," but the law had no effect on the commissions, boards, or other officers who were responsible for immigration in each of the states. The commissioner's office was abolished when the law was repealed four years later.

Other federal laws were passed in the 1880s to prevent the admission of undesirable aliens and to control contract labor, but authority over immigration, including enforcement of the federal statutes, remained at the state level. At the same time, the number of immigrants coming to America was rising rapidly.

In 1888, Congress established a select committee to investigate problems caused by the divided authority over immigration. It recommended consolidating this authority within a single federal agency and drafted legislation that Congress enacted as the Immigration Act of 1891.

Signed by President Benjamin Harrison on March 3, 1891, the law established complete and definite federal control over immigration by providing for an office of the Superintendent of Immigration under the Secretary of the Treasury.

As a result of this new law, all the duties previously deferred to the states were transferred by the end of fiscal year (June 30) 1891 to United States inspection officers, and the Bureau of Immigration began operations in the Treasury Department on July 12, 1891, as the first federal immigration agency.

Besides its headquarters in Washington, D.C., the Bureau opened 24 inspection stations (including Ellis Island in January 1892) at ports of entry along both borders and in major seaports. The Marine Hospital Service began conducting medical inspections of arriving immigrants. From this early structure, the immigration side of the present Immigration and Naturalization Service (INS) evolved. In 1903, the Bureau of Immigration was moved to the newly established Department of Commerce and Labor and given broader responsibilities.

Naturalization

The naturalization side of INS did not come into being until Congress passed the Naturalization Act of 1906. Before then, naturalization was a function of the courts. The new law created the Bureau of Immigration and Naturalization and made it responsible for administering and enforcing U.S. immigration laws, supervising the naturalization of aliens, and keeping naturalization records.

This combined function lasted only seven years, however, and naturalization became a separate bureau again in 1913 when the Department of Commerce and Labor was split into two departments.

Both functions moved to the new Department of Labor which left the Commissioner-General in charge of the Bureau of Immigration and a new Commissioner for the Bureau of Naturalization was named. They remained separate until 1933 when they were consolidated by Executive Order to form the Immigration and Naturalization Service, still within the Department of Labor. INS moved to the Department of Justice in June 1940 in a reorganization meant to provide more effective control over aliens at a time of increasing international tensions.

Today the INS is responsible for enforcing laws regulating admission of for-eign-born persons (aliens) to the United States and for administering various immigration benefits including naturalization of resident aliens.

Source: U.S. Immigration and Naturalization Service, 1996

INS DISTRICT OFFICES

Note: Numbers preceding each address indicate U.S. Immigration and Naturalization Service district office numbers.

2: INS, Government Center, JFK Federal Building, Room 1700, Boston, MA 02203

3: INS, 26 Federal Plaza, Room 14-102, New York, NY 10278

4: INS, 1600 Callowhill Street, Philadelphia, PA 19130

5: INS, Equitable Tower One, 100 South Charles Street, 12th Floor, Baltimore, MD 21201

6: INS, 7880 Biscayne Boulevard, Miami, FL 33138

7: INS, 130 Delaware Avenue, Buffalo, NY 14202

8: INS, 333 Mt. Elliott Street, Federal Building, Detroit, MI 48207-4381

9: INS, 10 W. Jackson Boulevard, Suite 600, Chicago, IL 60604

10: INS, 2901 Metro Drive, Suite 100, Bloomington, MN 55425

11: INS, 9747 N. Conant Avenue, Kansas City, MO 64153

12: INS, 815 Airport Way, South, Seattle, WA 98134

13: INS, Appraisers Building, 630 Sansome Street, Room 232, San Francisco, CA 94111-2280

14: INS, 8940 Four Winds Drive, San ANtonio, TX 78239

15: INS, 700 E. San Antonio, El Paso, TX 79901

16: INS, 300 N. Los Angeles Street, Los

Angeles, CA 90012
17: INS, 595 Ala Moana Boulevard, Honolulu, HI 96813
18: INS, 2035 N. Central, Phoenix, AZ 85004
19: INS, 4730 Paris Street, Denver, CO 80239
20: INS, 8101 N. Stemmons Freeway, Dallas, TX 75247
21: INS, 970 Broad Street, Federal Building, Newark, NJ 07102
22: INS, 739 Warren Avenue, Portland, ME 04103
24: INS, A.J.C. Federal Building, 1240 East Ninth Street, Room 1917, Cleveland, OH 44199
25: INS, 4420 North Fairfax Drive, Arlington, VA 22203
26: INS, MLK Federal Building, 77 Forsyth Street, SW, Room 117, ATlanta, GA 30303
27: INS, Carlos Chardon Street, Hato Rey, PR 00917
28: INS, 701 Loyola Avenue, Room T-8011, New Orleans, LA 70113
29: INS, 3736 S. 132nd Street, Omaha, NE 68144
30: INS, 2800 Skyway Drive, Helena, MT 59601
31: INS, Federal Building, 511 Northwest Broadway, Portland, OR 97209
32: INS, 620 East 10th Avenue, Suite 102, Anchorage, AK 99501
38: INS, 509 North Belt, Houston, TX 77060
39: INS, 880 Front Street, Suite 1234, San Diego, CA 92188
40: INS, 2102 Teege Road, Harlingen, TX 78550-4667

Source: History Office, Office of Public Affairs, United States Immigration and Naturalization Service, 1995

REQUESTING INS RECORDS

To request a search of, and copies of INS records either by submitting Form G-639 or by writing a letter. All requests for searches should include the immigrant's full name (with any alternate spellings), date of birth, and place of birth. Information about the immigrant's entry into the United States (date, port, vessel) or his or her naturalization (date, court, certificate number) is helpful.

When requesting records dating from about 1892 to 1952, mention that the request may require a "manual search." Mail the request to the attention of "FOIA/PA" at the INS District Office serving the area where you live.

UNITED STATES PASSPORT APPLICATIONS

United States passport applications are rich in primary information concerning immigrants.

Passport requirements

The National Archives reports that except for a short time during the Civil War, passports were not required of U.S. citizens traveling abroad before World War I. They were frequently obtained when not required, however, because of the added protection they might afford. The National Archives has passport applications received by the Department of State, with related records, 1791-1925. The records are in Record Group 59 or Record Group 84.

Contents of passport applications

A passport application varies in content, the information being ordinarily less detailed before the Civil War than afterward. It usually contains the name, signature, place of residence, age, and personal description of the applicant; names or number of persons in the family intending to travel; the date; and, where appropriate, the date and court of naturalization. It sometimes contains the exact date and place of birth of the applicant and of spouse and minor children, if any, accompanying the applicant, and, if the applicant was a naturalized citizen, the date and port of arrival in the United States, name of vessel on which the applicant arrived, and date and court of naturalization.

For the period 1906-1925, each application includes name of applicant, date and place of birth, name and date and place of birth of spouse or children (when applicable), residence and occupation at time of application, immediate travel plans, physical description, and photograph. Often accompanying applications are transmittal letters and letters from employers, relatives, and other attesting to the applicant's purpose for travel abroad.

Record locations
(passports issued before 1923)

Records of all United States passports issued prior to 1923 are maintained by the National Archives.

Before 1906

For records issued before 1906, write to National Archives, General Reference Branch, Washington, DC 20408.

1906-1922

For records issued between 1906 and 1922, write to National Archives, Suitland Reference Branch, Textual Reference Division, Suitland, MD 20409. (As of 1996, the National Archives is continuing to consolidate all its genealogical records, including passport records, at the National Archives Building in downtown Washington, DC.)

Record location
(passports issued since 1923)

Records of passports issued since 1923 are maintained by the Department of State, Passport Services Directorate. Genealogical researchers wishing to gain access to its records should submit a typed or clearly printed request bearing signature and including full name, date and place of birth of the file subject, and the dates the file subject may have applied for a United States passport. Also included should be a fee of $15 for *each* subject. Checks or money orders should be made payable to the U.S. Department of State. (Address: Department of State, Washington, DC 20520.)

In addition, if the file subject was born after 1900, the Department of State requires either *notarized* consent for the file subject authorizing release of the information for his/her passport record to the requestor, or convincing evidence of death in the form of a newspaper obituary or a death certificate.

Important note

Unless a person who travelled abroad or intended to travel abroad had obtained United States citizenship, it is useless to initiate a search of the passport files.

GERMAN IMMIGRANT AID SOCIETIES

In the eighteenth and nineteenth centuries many ethnic groups in America formed organizations to look out for the welfare of their immigrant countryfolk who were often destitute and suffering from lack of employment and disadvantages related to the clash of cultures.

The first organization to dedicate itself to the welfare of German immigrants was the German Society of Philadelphia, founded in 1764, which responded to the miserable conditions faced by the German redemptioners.

The functions filled by these societies included locating housing and employment, finding relatives, and the changing and transferring of money. The societies saw themselves as guardians of national honor, a goal which unfortunately often provoked hostile reactions among other Americans.

The German Society of New York was the most active of the societies aiding German immigrants because it was New York where most of them entered the country. This society worked closely with the Commissioners of Emigration and, after 1892, with officials at Ellis Island.[1]

[1]Dirk Hoerder and Diethelm Knauf, ed., *Fame, Fortune and Sweet Liberty: The Great European Emigration*. (Bremen: Edition Temmen, 1992)

BENJAMIN FRANKLIN, ON 'THE GERMAN PROBLEM'

"Why should Pennsylvania, which was founded by Englishmen, become a colony of foreigners, who will soon be so numerous that they will be Germanizing us instead of our Anglicizing them?"

FOUNDING DATES OF GERMAN IMMIGRANT AID SOCIETIES

These aid societies are listed in chronological order according to founding dates:
◆**Deutsche Gesellschaft von Pennsylvanien** [German Society of Pennsylvania], Philadelphia, Pa. Founded December 26, 1764
◆**German Friendly Society**, Charleston, South Carolina. Founded 1766 [No longer in existence by 1892]
◆**Deutsche Gesellschaft von New York** [German Society of New York], New York, N.Y. Founded August 20, 1784
◆**Deutsche Gesellschaft von Maryland** [German Society of Maryland], Baltimore, Maryland. Founded February 6, 1817
◆**Deutsche Gesellschaft von New Orleans, Louisiana** [German Society of New Orleans, Louisiana], New Orleans, Louisiana. Founded May 24, 1847.
◆ **Deutscher Hilfsverein von Boston** [German Relief Society of Boston], Boston, Massachusetts. Founded February 6, 1847.
◆**Deutsche Gesellschaft von St. Louis** [German Society of St. Louis], St. Louis, Missouri. Founded 1847

◆**Allgemeine Deutsche Unterstützungs-Gesellschaft** [German Public Assistance Society], San Francisco, California. Founded January 7, 1854.
◆**Deutsche Gesellschaft von Chicago** [German Society of Chicago], Chicago, Illinois. Founded August 1, 1854
◆ **Deutscher Einwanderungs- und Unterstützungs Verein** [German Immigration and Assistance Society], Cincinnati, Ohio. Founded 1854
◆**Allgemeine Deutsche Unterstützungs-Gesellschaft** [German Public Assistance Society], Portland, Oregon. Founded February 7, 1871
◆**Deutsche Gesellschaft von Lehigh County** [German Society of Lehigh County], Allentown, Pennsylvania. Founded November 9, 1871
◆**Einwanderer Hilfsverein** [Immigrants Relief Society], Pittsburg, Pennsylvania. Founded April 15, 1880
◆**Deutsche Gesellschaft von Milwaukee** [German Society of Milwaukee], Milwaukee, Wisconsin. Founded May 28, 1880
◆**Deutsche Gesellschaft von Kansas City** [German Society of Kansas City], Kansas City, Missouri. Founded July 14, 1882
◆**Deutsch-Amerikanische Gesellschaft** [German-American Society], Rochester, New York. Founded October 8, 1883
◆**Allgemeine Deutsche Unterstützungs-Gesellschaft** [German Public Assistance Society], Seattle, Washington. Founded February 22, 1884
◆**Deutsche Gesellschaft von Dorchester** [German Society of Dorchester], Dorchester, Wisconsin. Founded May 5, 1885
◆ **Deutsche Gesellschaft** [German Society], St. Paul, Minnesota. Founded October 10, 1889
◆**Deutsche Gesellschaft von New Haven** [German Society of New Haven], New Haven, Connecticut. Founded March 2, 1890
◆ **Deutsche Gesellschaft** [German Society], Petersburg, Virginia. Founded

The Erie Railroad's ferry at Castle Garden, 1874

April 29, 1890
◆**Deutsch-Amerikanische Gesellschaft von Virginien** [German-American Society of Virginia], Richmond, Virginia. Founded September 8, 1890
Source: *German Day Celebration of the German Society of Pennsylvania* (program), 1892

[1]This house was opposite Castle Garden (the immigration station) in New York.

Source: James Sigurd Lapham, "The German-American, New York City 1860-1890," Ph.D. dissertation, St. John's University, New York, 1977

IMMIGRANT AID BY THE LUTHERAN CHURCH IN NEW YORK CITY

The Care Given German Immigrants at the German Lutheran and Emigrant House, 1871 and 1889

	Type and Amount of Care Given	
	In 1871	In 1889
Letters exchanged	3,125	xxx
Meals Given	915	1,850
Persons Lodged	410	12,439
Persons Employed	404	xxx
Calls at Office	5,604	xxx
Lodging	xxx	12,058

THE 'ENGLISH LANGUAGE VOTE' NEVER TAKEN

"The Mühlenberg myth" says that in the United States in the 1770s, a vote was taken to decide whether German or English should be the national language and that English won by one vote. The tie-breaker was a German, one Frederick Augustus Mühlenberg, the first Speaker of the House — or so the story goes.

In the late 1700s the German language was prevalent, especially in Virginia, Maryland, and Pennsylvania. The German language was especially concentrated in

Pennsylvania, where Germans made up 33 percent of the state population in the 1790s.

When Pennsylvania's State Librarian Thomas L. Montgomery searched in 1927 through Pennsylvania state archives for documentation of the vote, he found no mention of it. In May 1990, The U.S. State historian wrote that he was "unable to document that a vote in the U.S. Congress ever took place with regard to making German the national language. . . ."

Despite the strong use of German in Pennsylvania, the United States census figures for 1790 show that a mere 6 percent of the population spoke German.

Mühlenberg, as Speaker of the House, did cast a tie-breaking vote during his congressional career, on April 26, 1796.

This vote concerned the Jay Treaty, which played a role in keeping Americans neutral in the French and Indian War. The treaty dealt with Americans, English, Indians, and French, but not Germans or the German language.

Source: "A Ballot for Americans: A Famous Vote That Was Never Taken," by Michelle Buswinka, *Munich Found*, April 1992

GERMAN-AMERICAN DAY

On October 6, 1683, a group of Mennonites from Krefeld disembarked from the *Concord* in Philadelphia, representing the first group immigration of Germans to America. Upon their arrival they established a community later known as Germantown.

Three hundred years later, in 1983, President Ronald Reagan declared October 6 that year as German-American Day.

In 1986 a drive was undertaken to make the day an every-year observance. On August 6, 1987, Congress approved S.J. Resolution 108, designating October 6, 1987 as German-American Day. President Reagan signed Public Law 100-104 on August 18 and on October 2, 1987 issued a proclamation to this effect. Every year since 1987, the President has proclaimed October 6 as German-American Day, in honor of the contributions made by German immigrants to the life and culture of the United States.

The German-American Joint Action Committee (GAJAC) was founded in 1990 to coordinate celebrations for this day. GAJAC is made up of the German-American National Congress (DANK), the Steuben Society of America, and the United German-American Committee (VDAK).

Through celebration of German-American Day, the term "German" is used in a cultural rather than a political sense, thus including the German-speaking Swiss, Alsatians, Austrians, Germans from Eastern Europe, and German Jews.

GERMAN IMMIGRANT CASUALTIES ABOARD SHIP

Number of German immigrants arriving in New York City 1865-1867 and number of deaths due to transatlantic travel (number of deaths shown in parentheses):

Baron von Steuben

1865: 11,264 (128)
1866: 14,335 (387)
1867: 8,788 (199)

Source: James Sigurd Lapham, "The German-Americans of New York City 1860-1890," Ph. D. dissertation, St. John's Univeersity, New York, 1977

GERMAN-AMERICANS IN THE 1990 CENSUS

The first group of German settlers arrived in the American colonies in 1683, where they established what later became known as Germantown.

By 1800, about 9 percent of the total population of the United States had ties to Germany. Mass immigration started after 1815 and reached a high during the 1880s when more than 1.5 million Germans arrived.

The peak year was 1882, when a record 250,000 Germans immigrated. At the turn of the century, German immigration began to slow.

Since the 1970s, only about 150,000 Germans have come to the United States. Over three centuries, about 8 million Germans have come to what is now the United States.[1]

German descendants in the 1990 census

Dr. Don Heinrich Tolzman, president of the Society for German-American Studies, provides the following analysis of the 1990 U.S. Census as it relates to the German-American element:[2]

Final results of the 1990 United States Census indicate that the total United States population in that year was 248,709,873. The five major groups and their percentages of the total population are as follows:

1. German   57,985,595   (23.3%)
2. Irish   38,739,548   (15.6%)
3. English   32,655,779   (13.1%)
4. Italian   14,714,939   (5.9%
5. Polish   9,366,106   (3.8%)

The German category does not include Germans from other German-speaking states and regions of Europe and the Americas. Hence, to the German statistic, the following can be added:

1. Alsatian   16,465
2. Austrian   870,531
3. Luxemburger   49,061
4. Swiss-German (estimated) 700,000
5. German-Russian   10,153
6. Pennsylvania German   305,841

These six additional German ethnic groups total 1,952,051. The total of all seven German ethnic categories is 59,937,646.

The results clearly indicate that German-Americans constitute a full one-fourth of the population. German-Americans can take pride in the fact that they are without question the major ethnic group in America, just as they can rightfully be proud of their long history, dating back to the arrival of the first Germans in America in Jamestown, Virginia in 1608.

[1]"German Americans," German Embassy, March 1996; eds. Ekkehard Brose, Betsy Wittleder, Ina-Marie Blomeyer, Andrea Metz. [2]*UGAC-USA Newsletter*, 3 September 1992

GERMAN IMMIGRANT CASUALTIES ABOARD SHIP

Number of German immigrants arriving in New York City 1865-1867 and number of deaths due to transatlantic travel (number of deaths shown in parentheses):

1865: 11,264 (128)
1866: 14,335 (387)
1867: 8,788 (199)

Source: James Sigurd Lapham, "The German-Americans of New York City 1860-1890," Ph. D. dissertation, St. John's Univeersity, New York, 1977

Emigrants in steerage of a passenger ship. (1886)

BEHIND THE GERMAN MIGRATIONS

A book in circulation during the mid-nineteenth century, *Hand- und Reisebuch für Auswanderer* {Handbook and Travel Guide for Emigrants], by Traugott Bromme, offers these reasons for German emigration:

"The innate human urge to forge ahead, to improve one's position, as well as distress, dependent situations, pressures from all sides, often among the best of the most highly placed persons, are reasons why thousands are leaving their fatherland, seeking a new homeland, thousands more are preparing to follow them, and hundreds of thousands are dejectedly and longingly watching the emigrants whom they, for lack of funds, are unable to follow, even though they desire a change, an improvement in their situation just as ardently as the fortunate ones."[1]

A twentieth century writer, Peter Marschalck, has written,

"There is a natural outflow from areas containing too many people in a space toward those with too few people in a space.

"Space is the (not only material) possibility of existence (e.g. political oppression is too small a space for the possibility of political existence; overpopulation is too small a space for the possibility of economic existence) . . . .

"The relationship between people and space, whenever it is not in equilibrium, strives for equilibrium in the long term by adaptation and in the short term by migrations."[2]

· An 1851 emigrant song went like this:

Mein Vetter schrieb noch kürzlich mir
aus diesem schönen Land
Und Ich bleib' wahrlich nicht mehr
hier, will hin zum schönen Land
Rosinen, Mandeln ißt man da, wie
hierzuland das Brot
Denn in dem Land Amerika hat man
gar keine Not[3]

Translation

My cousin wrote me just a while ago
from this beautiful land
And I really won't stay here much
longer, I want to go to the beautiful land
Raisins, almonds are eaten there as in
this country one eats breat
For in the land of America there is no
want.

[1] Traugott Bromme, Hand- und Reisebuch für
Auswanderer nach den Vereinigten Staaten von
Nord-Amerika

[2] Peter Martschalck, *Deutsche
Überseewanderung im 19. Jahrhundert*
[German Migration Overseas in the 19th
Century], Stuttgart 1973.

[3] Test of the poem in Karl Andree,
"Umwandlungen im Weltverkehr der Neuzeit"
[Changes in World Traffic in Modern Times],
Deutsche Vierteljahrsschrift, 18 (1855).

Source for all of the above: Günter Moltmann,
*Germans to America: 300 Years of Immigra-
tion, 1683 to 1983*. Institute for Foreign
Cultural Relations in cooperation with Inter
Nationes, Bonn-Bad Godesburg, 1982.

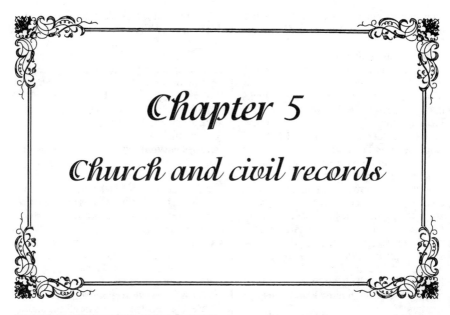

Chapter 5
Church and civil records

GERMAN CHURCH RECORDS

Church records are about the only primary sources of records before 1875 for emigrants from German areas (except west of the Rhine, Baden, Würrtemberg, Hessen, and Frankfurt).

Church registers began between 1530 and 1750. The primary motive for creating them was the church's interest in recording the religious events associated with baptisms, marriages, and burials of persons living in its respective parishes.

The aristocrats ruling most Protestant communities were responsible for early church registers, beginning in countries with advanced administrative systems (as, for example, Saxony and parts of Thuringia or the old dukedom of Württemberg) in the mid 16th century, and about a century later in other parts of Protestant Germany. Keeping of church records varied depending on religious practices in various lands. Sometimes part of a population was Lutheran, another Presbyterian (Calvinist),

each keeping separate church records. In Prussia within its borders of 1817, in Nassau and in the Rhenish part of the grand-dukedom of Hessen, the Lutherans and Calvinists were united in 1818. Since then, only combined "Protestant" (*evangelisch*) church registers exist rather than separate registers for each denomination.

Catholic church registers were written in Latin until the early 19th century (by mandate of the Council of Trent (*Trient*) of 1563).

Almost all Protestant registers were written in German, since the Reformation. Reformed Church records date from 1650. Only the French, Dutch and Czech Protestants had church registers in their own language — until the nineteenth century. In East Frisia and northern Schleswig, older church registers were occasionally written in the Frisian or Danish languages respectively.

Small denominations like the Mennonites and the Moravian Brethren (called "Herrnhuter" in Germany) often had their own church registers. The registers of the oldest Moravian settlement in Germany, Herrnhut in Saxony, began in 1739.

Most church registers in Germany are kept in the parish archives. Some, in the formerly French communities west of the Rhine, can still be found in the local mayor's office, in compliance with a French decree of May 1798. Some are kept in certain special archives, as in Brühl near Cologne, or in Detmold.

To determine what records should be available for a specified parish and where to write for information on these records, consult church record inventories. These are listed in the "Locality" section of the Family History Library Catalog under "Church Records." For more information, see *Research Outline: Germany*, published by the Family History Library, Salt Lake City, Utah. This inexpensive outline is available through most Family History Centers.

GERMAN CHURCH BOOKS *(Kirchenbücher)*

Church books, or parish registers, contain records made by priests and pastors concerning births, baptisms, marriages, deaths, and burials. Church books sometimes include account books (recording fees for tolling bells, fees for masses for the dead, and so forth, lists of confirmations, lists of members, and family registers.

Types of church records
Kirchenbücher Zweitschriften: Parish register transcripts, or duplicates
These date from 1807 in Bavaria; from 1740 in Mecklenburg; from 1899 in Prussia; and from 1808-1875 in Württemberg.
Taufregister: **christening/baptism registers**
These records usually provide the child's name and sex; baptism date, and sometimes birthdate; place of baptism; name

of mother; name and occupation of father; legitimacy of birth; name and occupation of mother's father; names and residence of witnesses or godparents' (unless child is illegitimate, when the father's name is seldom mentioned)
Geburtsregister: **birth registers**
These usually provide the child's name, date of birth, legitimacy, parents and godparents' names
Konfirmationsregister: **Confirmation registers**
Confirmation usually occurred at age 14 for Protestants, and at about age 12 for Catholics. Usually the records provided (at the discretion of the recording minister) name of participant; age; date/place of event; and sometimes name and occupation of father, and name of mother. Some registers give only the names and dates of confirmation.
Trauregister: **marriage registers**
These registers usually provided the name and age of the bride; marriage date and place; residence/occupation of bridegroom; name of clergyman; names of bridegroom's parents, their residence and fathers' occupations; name of bride, her age, and names of her parents; occupation of her father; names of witnesses, their residences and occupations; and name of previous spouse if the bride or bridegroom was widowed.
Sterberegister: **death registers**
Usually provided are the name of the deceased, profession, age at death (sometimes cause of death), occupation, date/place of death, date/place of burial, and surviving spouse and children's names.
Begräbnisse: **burials**
These records usually provided the name of the deceased, date and place of death or burial, message, place of residence, cause of death, and survivors' names.
Familienbücher, Familienregister: **family registers**
This record type is almost always found in southern Germany, especially in Baden

Light cavalry of Bavarian troops in the war of 1870-71

and Württemberg, dating from the early nineteenth century.

Provided are names, birth dates/places, marriage dates, sometimes death dates of man/wife, their parents' names, birth dates/places, children's names in order of birth, birthdates, and birthplaces. Each family was given a family number.

SYMBOLS FOUND IN GERMAN CHURCH RECORDS

The following symbols were commonly written into many church record books:

* = geboren (born)

∞ = verheiratet (married)

† = gestorben (died)

(*) = außereheliche Geburt (illegitimately born)

〰 = getauft (christened)

ₒ = verlobt (engaged)

□ = begraben (buried)

† * = Totgeburt (stillborn)

O|O = geschieden (divorced)

✕ = gefallen (killed in action)

o-o = uneheliche Verbindung (common-law marriage, illegitimate union)

In older records can be found these symbols:

⋎̇ = getauft (christened)

Ψ = geboren (born)

⋋̇ = verheiratet (married)

⋀ = gestorben (died)

⋔ = begraben (buried)

CIVIL REGISTRATION
(Reichspersonenstandsgesetz)

Originally the marital status of a person was recorded by the local clergyman. Parish registers documented births, baptisms, marriages, children, and deaths of the populations.

Civil registration was introduced west of the Rhine by the French in 1798, in the grand-duchy of Baden in 1810, in the Free City of Frankfurt in 1850, in the kingdom of Prussia on October 1, 1874, and in all of the German Empire on January 1, 1876, with the *Reichspersonenstandsgesetz* (Imperial marital status law).

Civil registers in the area west of the Rhine, which was part of the Napoleonic French Empire until 1814, were written in French, but in that year the German language began to replace French.

These registers *(Zivilstandsregister)* held at the *Standesamt* (registry office) contain records of births, deaths, marriages, and children – thus continuing the work of parish registers.

The official responsible for keeping these records, and also for performing weddings, is the *Standesbeamter* (registrar). In small towns and villages, the mayor also was (and often still is today) the registrar.

Once the registry records are no longer considered current (there is no strict nationwide time limit for this), they are transferred to the *Stadtarchiv* (city archive) or *Kreisarchiv* (county archive) – if a small town or village does not have an archive of its own.

A Standesamt usually does not reveal any of its data or provide copies of documents to researchers, except for the immediate family. For accessibility of records once they are transferred to the archives, see "Datenschutz."

Source: Rainer Thumshirn, of Heimstetten, Germany

SOME OTHER CIVIL RECORDS

◆*Passagierlisten*: **passenger lists**
Hamburg passenger list information includes date of embarkation, husband's name, place of origin, occupation, and age; given names and ages of wife and children; sometimes port of destination

◆*Steuerlisten, -bücher*: **tax lists, books**
Providing names and addresses, these date from the beginning of the 15th century.

◆*Leichenpredigten*: **funeral sermons**
Following the Reformation, funeral sermons replaced the elaborate funeral mass of the Catholic church, taking the form instead of a graveside eulogy, which often recounted the life of the deceased person in considerable detail. These sermons were afterwards printed and circulated to friends and family of the deceased. Funeral sermons are found from the period beginning about 1500 until around 1800.

◆ *Auswandererlisten, Auswandererakten*: **emigration lists/records**
Usually these provide name of emigrant, date and place of emigration (sometimes destination), date and place of birth, place of residence, occupation, given names and ages of wife and children. Not all emigrants were listed. These lists date from the early 19th century.

◆*Testamente, Testamentsakten*: **wills**
Usually these documents contained names of heirs and their relationship to the deceased, probate records, name and sometimes age of testator, residence, relationships, description of property, date of will and probate, and witnesses. These records, dating from the 13th century, are found in the *Amtsgerichte* (local courthouses).

◆*Volkszählungslisten, Bauernverzeichnisse, Einwohnerlisten*: **census records**
Originally called Tax and Tithing Records (*Steuer- und Zehntregister*), these exist only in specific areas and times.

Usually provided are name, age, place

of origin, occupation, and residence. Census records occur in Mecklenburg: 1677-1689, with intervals, and in 1819; in Schleswig-Holstein, 1803-1860; and in some other areas. They date from the 16th to 18th century.

◆*Bürgerbücher/-listen*: **burgher rolls, citizenship registrations.**
New immigrants applying for citizenship in a town had to produce a birth or baptism certificate with names and profession of the parents, and if possible the grandparents. Some citizenship records contain the burgher's genealogy. Found in *Stadtarchive,* (state archives), they date from the 13th to the mid-19th century.

◆*Polizeiregister/Einwohnermeldelisten*: **police registers, citizenship registration lists.** Usually provided are the name and address of every permanent resident. Kept at the *Einwohnermeldeamt* (town registration office) and dating from about 1830, these records replaced the *Bürgerbücher.*

◆*Grundbücher*: **land books**
These land books contain descriptions of specific parcels of land, the owners' names, and records of mortgages on property. Kept by the *Amtsgericht* (lower court), they date from the 11th century and sometimes earlier.

◆*Adressbücher*: **city directories**
Provided are names and addresses of residents of a given locality. Dating from the early 1800s, these directories are found in local archives. See Ribbe and Henning's *Taschenbuch für Familiengeschichtsforschung* for lists of years in which *Adressbücher* exist for many localities in Germany.

◆*Gildenbücher, Zunftbücher, Innungsbücher*: **apprentice and guild books**
Usually provided are names, parents' names, occupation, and residence of employer. Dating from the 16th to 19th centuries, the availability of these books is scattered.

◆*Kriegslisten, Militärakten*: **military records**
These records are found in local and state archives near areas where soldiers were stationed.

◆*Dorfsippenbücher, Ortssippenbücher*: **local histories**
These are lineage books showing the genealogy of most residents of a particular village.

◆*Hausbücher*: **house books**
Dating from the 16th to the 19th century, these histories of houses generally include house owners' names, occupations, and social and economic status.

See below for a more extensive list of civil records.

GERMAN RECORD TYPES

Abendmahlgästelisten: communion attendance lists
Abmeldescheine: permits to move away from a place
Achtbücher: proscription books (names of persons tried in absentia)
Adreßbücher: address books (similar to city directories)
Allgemeine Akten: general documents
Almosenliste: welfare lists
Amtsbücher: civil records
Anniversarien: records of donations given for saying prayers on anniversaries of deaths
Arbeitsbücher: employment books
Archivinventare: archive inventories
Armen- und Wohltätigkeitssachen: welfare matters
Armenregister: registers of the poor, welfare lists
Atlanten: atlases
Aufgebote: marriage banns/marriage registers
Aufgelöste Ehen: divorces
Aushebungsrollen: conscription lists (muster rolls)
Aushebungsverzeichnisse: conscription lists (muster rolls)
Auswandererverzeichnisse: emigrant lists
Auswanderungsakten: emigration

records
Auswanderungsgesuche: emigration
applications
Auswanderungslisten: emigration
records
Beerdigungsregister: burial registers
Begräbnisregister: burial register
Begräbnisse, Ordnungen bei: orders of
precedence for funerals
Beiakten: supplementary records
Berufsakten: occupational records
Berufsangehörigenverzeichnisse: lists
of members of a profession
Bestattungsbücher: burial books
Bevölkerungslisten: population lists
Bevölkerungsverzeichnisse: population
lists
Bibliothekskataloge: library catalogs
Bibliotheksverzeichnisse:library
catalogs
Bruderschaftsurkunde: brotherhood
(fraternity) records
Bürgerbücher: citizen rolls
Bürgerlisten: citizen rolls
Dezennaltabellen: decennial index of
vital records (west-Rhine)
Dorfsippenbücher: village lineage
books
Ehebücher: marriage records
Ehelichkeitserklärung: declaration of
legitimacy
Eheregister: marriage registers
Ehescheidung: divorce, dissolved
marriage
Ehestiftunen: matchmakings, donations
on the occasion of a marriage by the
couple (not *to* the couple)
Eheverkündigungen: marriage
proclamations (banns)
Eheverträge: marriage contracts
Einbürgerungen: naturalizations
Einnahmeregister: receipt registers
Einwanderungen: immigrations
Einwohnerlisten: lists of inhabitants
Einwohnermelderegister: inhabitant
registration registers
Einwohnerverzeichnisse: census
records
Erbebücher: inheritance books

Familienbücher: family books
Familiengeschichten: family histories
Familienregister: family registers
Firmungen: confirmations
Flurbücher: field or parcel records
Geburtsbrief: birth letters/certificates
Geburtsregister: birth registers
Geburtsscheine: birth certificates
Geburtsurkunden: birth certificates
Geburtszeugnisse: birth certificates
Gefangener: See *Kriegsgefangener*
Gerichts und Polizeisachen: court and
police matters
Gerichtsakten: court documents
Gerichtsbücher: court books
Gerichtsprotokolle: court minutes
Geschlechterbücher: family lineage
books
Gesellenbücher: journeymen books
Gildenbücher: guild books
Glockenbücher: bell-tolling books
Grabregister: grave registers
Grundbücher: land records
Güterbücher: chattel records
Handbücher: handbooks, manuals
Hausbücher: books recording owners of
houses
Häuserbücher: See *Hausbücher*
Hauslisten: house directories
Heimatsscheine: place of origin
certificates
Heiratsbeilage: marriage documents
(supplements)
Heiratsprotokolle: marriage records
Heiratsurkunden: marriage records
Heiratsverzeichnis: marriage indexes
Herkunftszeugnisse: certificates of
origin
Hochschulmatrikeln: student registers
Hypothekenbücher: mortgage books
Impflisten: vaccination records
Innungsbücher: guild books
Inventare: inventories
Jahrbücher: yearbooks
Jüdische Akten: Jewish documents
Kaufbücher: property records
Kaufverträge: contracts of sales
Kirchenbücher: church books
Kirchenbücherverzeichnisse: parish

register inventories
Kirchenchroniken: church chronicles
Kirchengeschichte: church histories
Kirchenvisitationen: church visitations
Kirchenzweitschriften: church duplicates
kirchliche Adressbücher: church directories
Klosterverzeichnisse: monastery records
Kommunikanten: communicants
Konfirmationsregister: confirmation registers
Kopfzahlregister: census registers
Kriegsgefangener: prisoner of war
Lagerbücher: property/warehouse records, military levy books
Landkarten: maps
Lebensabrisse: biographical sketches
Lebensbilder: biogaphical sketches
Lebensläufe: biographical sketches
Legitimationen: legitimations
Lehnbriefe: fief certificates
Lehnbücher: fief records
Lehrlingsbücher: apprentice books
Leichenpredigten: funeral sermons
Mannzahlregister: census registers
Matrikeln: see *Universitätsmatrikeln*
Meisterbuch: book of masters
Melderegister: registers of residents
Militärakten: military records
Militärkirchenbücher: military church-book records
Militärurkunden: military records
Mitgliederlisten: membership lists
Musterrollen: military lists
Musterungslisten: military lists
Nachlässe: estates
Nachlaßprotokolle: estate records
Namenregister: indexes
Necrologien: records of recent deaths
Offizier-Stammlisten: lists of officers and their assignments
Ortslexika: gazetteers
Ortssippenbücher: locality lineage books
Passagierlisten: passenger lists
Personenstandsregister: registry of vital statistics
Pfarrerverzeichnisse: lists of clergymen
Politische Akten: public records

Polizeiregister: police registers
Proklamationsbücher: banns register
Prozessakten: court records
Quelle: sources
Ranglisten: military lists
Rassenkunde: ethnology
Ratsrechnungen: municipal accounting records
Reiseführer: travel guide books
Reversen: lists of properties reverted to the owners
Scheidungsprozesse: divorce records
Schiffslisten: passenger lists
Schöffenbücher: records of the jurors of the court of first instance
Schulakten: school records
Schulberichte: school records
Schuldbücher: records of indebtedness
Schülerverzeichnisse: alumni lists
Seelenregister: person registers (census records)
Staatsdienstakten: civil service records
Stadtbücher: city records
Stadtchroniken: city chronicles
Stadtrechnungen: municipal account books
Stammrollen: military rosters
Standesamtregister: vital record office registers
Sterberegister: death registers
Sterbeurkunde: death record
Steuerbücher: tax books
Steuerlisten: tax lists
Steuerregister: tax lists
Synodalbücher: synod records
Tagebücher: diaries, journals
Taufregister: christening registers
Telefonbücher: telephone books
Testamente: wills
Testamentsakten: probate records
Todesanzeigen: obituaries
Todesregister: death register
Toten-Annalen: annals of the dead
Totengeläutbücher: death bell tolling books
Trauregister: marriage registers
Überschreibungen: property transfer records
Universitätsmatrikeln: university enroll-

ments, registrations
Untertanenurkunden: serf records
Urkunden: certificates/documents
Vaterschaftsanerkennung: acknowledgements of fatherhood
Verehelichungen: marriages
Verkaufsbriefe: contracts of sales
Verlobungen: engagements (to marry); promises of donations to a church
Verlustlisten: casualties lists
Verschiedene Akten: various documents
Verwaltungsakten: administration documents
Visitationen: (church) inspections
Völkerkunde: ethnology
Volkszählungslisten: census lists
Volljährigkeitserklärung: declaration of majority (age)
Vormünderbücher: guardian books
Vormundschaften: guardian records
Wahlfähigkeitslisten: election lists
Wanderbücher: documents carried by journeymen (*Geselle*) on their journeys
Wanderzettel: guild attestation to member's competence
Wörterbücher: dictionaries
Zehntregister: tithe registers
Zeitungen: newspapers
Zivilstandsamturkunde: civil registry record
Zivilstandsregister: vital records registers
Zunftbücher: guild records
Zuzugsgenehmigungen: permits to move into other areas
Zweitschriften: transcripts, duplicates

PARISH REGISTERS

by Friedrich R. Wollmershäuser[1]

What are parish registers?
Parish registers are books maintained by parish offices to record ecclesiastical events. These records include,
♦Baptisms (recorded with or without the date of birth
♦Confirmations (around the age of 14)
♦Marriages, or banns before marriages, or

permissions to marry in another parish
♦Burials (with or without the date of death)
♦Lists of parish members (often at the beginning of the first volume to replace entries of a lost previous volume)
♦Lists of persons taking the communion or sacrament
♦Family registers (*Seelenregister, Familienregister*) as compilations of family groups on one page
♦Later remarks about the whereabouts of parish members
♦Copies of baptismal or marriage records shown by people when they moved into the parish
♦Lists and biographies of clergymen
♦Historical and miscellaneous notes
The following records are not parish registers:
♦Books maintained by parish offices to record financial, construction, and other matters
♦ Vital registers maintained by state authorities
♦Private records of sacristans, cemetery administrations, etc.
♦Accounts of baptismal, marriage and burial fees
♦Proceedings of moral courts (*Kirchenconventsprotokolle, Kirchenzensurprotokolle).*
These types of records may replace parish missing parish registers:
♦Duplicates of parish registers (from about 1780 to 1876 only)
♦Printed parish registers (in the newspapers of many towns)
♦Abstracts which were made at a time when the parish registers were still there
♦State vital registers, the earliest starting in 1798
Birth registers
♦Birth certificates (*Geburtsschein, Mannrecht*)
♦Entries on penalties for illegitimate births
♦Entries in registers of bonded serfmen
Marriage registers
♦marriage contracts

◆Marriage licenses
◆Entries concerning the payment of a marriage fee (*Brautlauf, Salzscheibe*)
Death registers
◆Death notices in newspapers
◆Death dates in probate records, which often include detailed notifications about the death of the deceased (*Sterbefallanzeigen*)
◆Tombstones
◆Funeral Sermons
◆Entries on the death tax of bonded serfmen (*Hauptrecht*)
◆Petitions of widows, entries on a second marriage
◆Orphans records
Time period
The time in which these parish registers existed varies considerably. In the Protestant territories, the oldest ones usually start when the Reformation was introduced in the pertinent domain (from the 1520s onward); in Catholic lands after the Council of Trent (*Trient*) of 1563. Many of these old books were destroyed during the Thirty Years War (1618-1648), by the French invasions around 1690, and during the Second World War (1939-1945).

At first, most parishes used just one book for all record categories; therefore the entries should be expected to be arranged separately in chronological order for each category. Such order was often not maintained, however, and it can thus be difficult to reconstruct the sequence of the entries. In the older books, entries may be arranged according to places within the parish, by the fathers of the baptized, or by the initials of their first names.

The scope of the entries may vary from bishopric to bishopric and from one location to another. Only when the ecclesiastical and country authorities published guidelines on the recording of events from the mid-1700s onward do the entries take on a uniform appearance.

The reliability of parish register entries is somewhat questionable. There can be found among the older books contemporary corrections and additions of previously missing entries. Also, later remarks are added by recent genealogists to correct errors (sometimes these corrections are wrong, however).
Where can parish registers by found?
Originally, parish registers were kept at the local parish offices, but they may have been forwarded to other places, such as,
◆To another parish office if the original parish no longer exists
◆To a central parish register office in a city
◆To a central ecclesiastical archive
◆To the local civil registration office
◆To a state archive
◆To a municipal archive

In addition, most German countries required the preparation of duplicates (verbatim copies) of the original registers, which had to be stored separate from the original registers or delivered annually to the district court, from about 1800 until the establishment of civil registration offices *(Standesämter)*, at the latest in 1876. Before 1800, some Catholic bishoprics required the yearly submission of duplicates to the bishop's archives.

The Church of Jesus Christ of Latter-day Saints has copied many original parish registers and duplicates on microfilm. Therefore, parish registers may be searched in the Family History Centers as well as at the books' repositories.
Hints and cautions in the use of parish registers
◆Make sure the initial entry is correct. When starting with a known birth date, verify it before searching the marriage and death entries of the parents.
◆Become aware of the organization of the books and the methods of recording the entries. In many Catholic localities, wives were recorded in the death registers only by their maiden names. One would need to know whether this was the case in a given locality before one begins a search.
◆Look for biological inconsistencies. A woman giving birth at age 50 is just as

The wedding mass

suspicious as a first child being born five years after the marriage of the parents.

•Don't trust indexes. If an index does not prove helpful, search through the original register page by page. The entry may be recorded and indexed by a slightly different name (Clais, instead of Klais, for example), or by a quite different name (if an illegitimate child was recorded with the mother's surname and later accepted the surname of the presumed father, for example).

•When the date of a death entry of a man shows his widow to be still fairly young, look for her second marriage before searching for the record of her death. She may have remarried and be registered in the death register under the surname of her second husband

•Places of origin are sometimes listed in unexpected places in the registers, such as,

–In an entry on a relative

–In an entry of the sponsors of the children

– In an entry on the confirmation of a child

–At the death of the person

–In the death entry of a person's father, father-in-law or other relative

•In the records of a group of people who moved to the same place at the same time from the same area of origin

•In the record of a person's mother who moved to a new location when she married.

•Abstract all information given in an entry. Every detail could be important for further research – like the word *weiland* in a marriage entry (indicating that a person was deceased), or the mention of someone's ruler, or the person's nickname, or the occupation.

•Be careful not to mix up two bearers of the same name.

•If it is not certain that the birth entry belongs to the person being searched, check the death, confirmation, and marriage registers to find out if the child survived childhood.

♦Interpret obsolete dates, such as the Tuesday after the Sunday Rogate of 1769. Observe the historical calendar reforms.

♦ Become aware of local customs, especially as they concern name-giving and the selection of sponsors.

The author: Friedrich R. Wollmershäuser, M.A., Accredited Genealogist, Herrengasse 8-10, 89610 Oberdischingen, Germany. © Friedrich R. Wollmershäuser, 1997.

BEGINNINGS
OF CIVIL REGISTRATION

Civil registration records (*Zivilstands-register* or *Personenstandsregister)* are birth, marriage and death records kept by the government.

Civil Registration of births, marriages and deaths by civil officials began in Germany 1 January 1876. In the Prussian provinces it began 1 October 1874. Some earlier registration for particular areas was also kept.

♦**National civil registration:** 1 January 1876
♦**Prussia:** 1 October 1874
♦**Baden:** 1 January 1870 - (marriages only)
♦**Bavaria (Pfalz – west of the Rhine):** 1 May 1798-
♦**Bremen:** 1811 -
♦**Alsace-Lorraine:** 1792 -
♦**Hamburg:** 1811-1815; 1866- (births, deaths; 1596- (marriages)
♦**Hessen (parts west of the Rhine):** 1 May 1798-
♦**Duchy of Nassau:** 1 November 1817 -
♦**Frankfurt (Grand Duchy):** 1 January 1810 - 1 February 1814
♦**Frankfurt (free city):** 1 May 1851-
♦**Lübeck:** 1811 -
♦**Oldenburg (parts west of the Rhine):** 1 May 1798 -
♦**Rheinland (parts west of the Rhine):**

1 May 1798 -
♦**Rheinland (Berg - Grand Duchy):** 1 January 1810-1815
♦**Westfalen:** 1 January 1808-1814
♦ **Württemberg:** 15 November 1807 (family books)

Civil records became the prime source for research after the date of their introduction because of their completeness, informational content and accessibility, and the availability of indexes. The reliability of civil registers is excellent. The percentage of the population covered is probably over 90 percent after 1876. Prior to that, political factors influenced the registry office so heavily that the percentage was much lower.

Source: *Germany: Genealogical Research Guide,* by Steven W. Blodgett. The Genealogical Department of the Church of Jesus Christ of Latter-day Saints, Salt Lake City, Utah, rev. 1989. Reprinted by permission of the author.

CHURCH INVENTORIES,
DIRECTORIES

Church inventories
Church inventories are useful for determining, for the purpose of searching church records, to what parish a particular village or town belonged. To access church inventories for a given German state, check the Family History Library Catalog as follows: Germany - Church Records - Inventories, Registers, Catalogs Germany, [State] - Church Records - Inventories, Registers, Catalogs.

A useful source for locating church inventories is this book, which lists titles by locality:
Steven W. Blodgett, *Germany: Genealogical Research Guide.* FHL book 943 D27bs; film 1,573,115 item 2; fiche 6001630

Church directories
Church directories generally provide lists of parishes in a diocese and the vil-

Christmas market in Munich, 1895

lages belonging to specific parishes. Addresses of parish churches and of diocese headquarters are also included.

To search Roman Catholic dioceses for a particular parish, see the *General-Schematismus der katholischen Geistlichkeit Deutschlands* (Directory of the Catholic clergy of Germany. FHL film 1,340,500.

To search Protestant jurisdictions, see *Deutsches kirchliches Adreßbuch* (German church directory). FHL book 943 K24d 1934; film (1929 edition) 476,672.

GERMAN CENSUSES

Census records are found under terminologies such as *Volkszählungen* (censuses), *Bevölkerungsliste* (population lists), *Bürgerlisten* (citizen lists), *Einwohnerlisten* (resident lists), *Hausbesitzerverzeichnis* (list of house owners), *Mannzählregister* (population count), *Seelenlisten* (church memberships), and *Untertannenlisten* (list of serfs).

Those records identified as *Volkszählungen* are found in the Family History Library Catalog under "Census." Records identified by other names (see the list above) are usually listed under the subject heading "Population."

In Germany, no national census was taken until the late 1800s, but local censuses began as early as the 1500s, most of them appearing in the late 1700s and early 1800s. Most were taken on a city or district level, but some were taken on a kingdom, province, or duchy level.

Censuses provided information on required military service, income taxes, the local populace for the indirect taxes, and custom assessment of the populace.

Census records may be found mixed in with other record groups.

It is wise to write to an archive to obtain a copy of its printed inventory in order to determine whether censuses are included.

For an excellent overview of German census records, see *German Genealogical Digest,* Vol. VI, No. 1, 1990.

In addition to searching the Family History Library Catalog, it may be necessary to write to the appropriate *Stadtarchiv* (municipal archive) or the *Standesamt* (district registry office) to learn whether census records are available.

Source: "Insights to Research: German Census and Other Population Records," *German Genealogical Digest,* Vol. VI, No.1.

CHURCH VOCABULARY

Abt	abbot
Äbtissin	abbess
Bischof	bishop
Bistum	diocese
Dechant, Dekan	dean
Erzbischof	archbishop
Erzbistum	archdiocese
Erzherzogtum	archduchy
Fürstbischof	prince bishop
geistlicher Beamter	ecclesiastical official
Geistlicher	clergyman, minister
Gemeinde	congregation
Gemeindeschreiber	parish clerk
Glöckner	sexton, bell ringer
Hilfsgeistlicher	curate, assistant
Hochstift	independent bishopric, subject only to the Reich (similar to *Freie Reichstadt*)
Kantor	cantor, choir director, organist
Kaplan	chaplain
Kirchenbuch/-bücher	parish register/s
Kirchendiener	(church) sexton
Kirchner	(church) sexton
Kirchenpfleger	church caurator
Kirchenrat	Protestant church official
Kirchenschöffe	church assessor

Küster	church caretaker, sexton
Meßner	sexton
Oberpfarrer	rector, head minister
Pfarrer	minister, pastor
Prediger	preacher
Priester	priest
Propst	dean, provost
Rektor	dean
Vikar	vicar
Vorsänger	choir leader

DATENSCHUTZ (Privacy laws)

By Rainer Thumshirn

After a landmark ruling in 1983 by the *Bundesverfassungsgericht* (Supreme Court), privacy of personal data is taken very seriously in Germany. Strict laws now regulate what kind of personal data may be collected by authorities and private organizations, how they may be processed and used, and to whom they may be released.

The framework is contained in the *Bundesdatenschutzgesetz* (Federal Privacy Law) with corresponding State Privacy Laws. *Datenschutzbeauftragte* (Data Protection Commissioners) supervise observance of these laws and follow up on complaints by individuals.

They also issue annual reports on their findings to the respective legislatures who appoint them.

Obviously, this affects genealogists (who, by definition, do research in personal data which are thus protected) in restricting access to two important sources: the *Einwohnermeldedatei* (residents' registration files) and the *Stadt- und Kreisarchive* (City and County Archives).

All residents in Germany are required by the *Meldegesetz* (Registration Law) of their respective States to register with the local *Einwohnermeldeamt* (residents' registration office). Personal data like name, maiden name, former and present address, citizenship, birthday, marital status, religion, legal guardian, criminal record, and date of death are filed there for official use. If a person moves, all these data are transferred to the *Einwohnermeldeamt* of the new residence.

This system has basically been in effect in most of Germany for approximately 200 years.

When these files are no longer current (there is no strict nationwide time limit for this), they are transferred to the *Stadtarchiv* (City Archive) or *Kreisarchiv* (County Archive) – if a small town or village does not have an archive of its own).

Access to these data is restricted by Privacy Laws referred to above.

For purposes like genealogical research, according to provisions in the *Meldegesetz* (registration law), the *Einwohnermeldeamt* (resident's registration office) will usually provide a *Melderegisterauskunft* (information on registry files) consisting of the name and current address of a person – of the last address if deceased. In most cases a written request is required and a fee is charged.

The *Stadt- und Kreisarchive* can be more generous, as they do not deal with current data. Also, they are not regulated by specific laws but use the *Bundesarchivgesetz* (Federal Archives Law) more or less literally as a guideline.

Accordingly, all available data usually (local variations may apply) are released when a valid reason (such as genealogical research) is given for the request *and* if the person in question has been dead for at least 30 years.

If no date of death is known, the deadline for release of personal data is 110 years after the person's birth date.

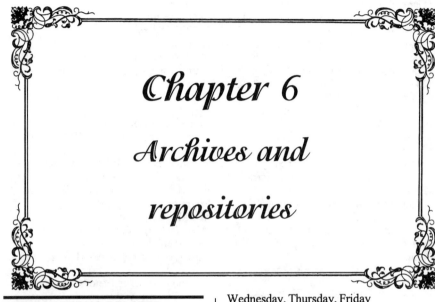

Chapter 6
Archives and repositories

GERMAN TERMS RELATED TO ARCHIVAL RECORDS

◆ *Bundesland:* land of the Federal Republic of Germany
◆ *Regierungsbezirk:* primary administrative division of the country; a district
◆ *Landkreis:* administrative division of a *Regierungsbezirk*; similar to a county
◆ *kreisfreie Stadt:* town with the administrative rank of a *Landkreis*
◆ *Hauptstaatsarchiv, Landeshauptarchiv:* archives corresponding to the area of a Bundesland
◆ *Staatsarchiv, Landesarchiv:* archives corresponding to the area of a *Regierungsbezirk*
◆ *Kreisarchiv:* archives corresponding to the area of a *Landkreis*
◆ *Stadtarchiv:* town archives
◆ *Universitätsarchiv:* university archives
◆ *Bistum:* diocese, bishopric
◆ *Diözese:* diocese
◆ *Diözesanarchiv:* archives of a diocese
◆ *Öffnungszeiten:* opening hours
Mo, Di, Mi, Do, Fr: Monday, Tuesday, Wednesday, Thursday, Friday
◆ *Veröffentlichungen:* publications
◆ *siehe auch:* see also
◆ *zurück zu:* back to

STATE ARCHIVES IN GERMANY *(Staatsarchive)*

Names of states in the list of state archives *(Staatsarchive)* below are shown first with their German names, followed by their anglicised names in parentheses.

The word *Außenstelle* indicates a branch archive. The *Hauptstaatsarchiv* is the main archive for the state.

Baden-Württemberg
(Baden- Wuerttemberg)
Baden-Württembergisches Hauptstaatsarchiv Stuttgart, Konrad-Adenauer-Str. 4, 70173 Stuttgart
◆ Staatsarchiv Ludwigsburg, Schloß Ludwigsburg, Schloßstr. 30, 71634 Ludwigsburg
— *Außenstelle Hohenlohe-Zentralarchiv Neuenstein*: Schloß, 74632 Neuenstein (Württemberg)

◆Generallandesarchiv Karlsruhe, Nörd-
liche Hildapromenade 2, 76133 Karlsruhe
◆Staatsarchiv Freiburg, Colombistr. 4,
79098 Freiburg i Br., Postfach 323, 79003
Freiburg i. Br.
◆Staatsarchiv Sigmaringen, Karlstr. 1+3,
72488 Sigmaringen, Postfach 526, 72482
Sigmaringen
◆Staatsarchiv Wertheim, Bronnbach Nr.
19, 97877 Wertheim
Bayern (Bavaria)
◆ Bayerisches   Hauptstaatsarchiv,
Schönfeldstr. 5, 80539 München
◆ Staatsarchiv Amberg, Archivstr. 3,
92224 Amberg
◆Staatsarchiv Augsburg, Salomon-Idler-
Str. 2, 86159 Augsburg
◆ Staatsarchiv Bamberg, Hainstr. 39,
96047 Bamberg, Postfach 2668, 96017
Bamberg
◆Staatsarchiv Coburg, Herrngasse 11,
96450 Coburg
◆Staatsarchiv Landshut, Burg Trausnitz,
84036 Landshut
◆Staatsarchiv München, Schönfeldstr. 3,
80539 München, Postfach 22 11 52, 80501
München
◆Staatsarchiv Nürnberg, Archivstr. 17,
90110 Nürnberg
◆ Staatsarchiv Würzburg, Residenz-
Nordflügel, 97070 Würzburg
Berlin
◆Landesarchiv Berlin, Kalckreuthstr. 1-2,
10777 Berlin (Schöneberg)
— *Außenstelle Breite Straße:* Breite Str.
30-31, 10178 Berlin
Brandenburg
◆Brandenburgisches Landeshauptarchiv,
An der Orangerie 3, 14469 Potsdam,
Postfach 60 04 49, 14404 Potsdam
— *Außenstelle Bornim:* Am Windmühl-
enberg, 14469 Potsdam
— *Außenstelle Cottbus:* Gulbener Str. 24,
03046 Cottbus
— *Außenstelle Frankfurt/Oder:* Große
Scharrnstr. 59, 15230 Frankfurt/Oder
— Außenstelle Lübben: Gerichtsstr. 4,
15907 Lübben

Bremen
◆Staatsarchiv Bremen, Am Staatsarchiv
1, 28203 Bremen
Hamburg
◆Staatsarchiv der Freien und Hansestadt
Hamburg, ABC-Str. 19 A, 20354
Hamburg
Hessen
(Hesse)
◆Hessisches Hauptstaatsarchiv,
Mosbacher Str. 55, 65187 Wiesbaden
◆ Hessiches Staatsarchiv Darmstadt,
Karolinenplatz 3, 64289 Darmstadt
◆ Hessisches Staatsarchiv Marburg,
Friedrichsplatz 15, Postfach 540, 35037
Marburg
Mecklenburg-Vorpommern
(Mecklenburg-Western Pomerania)
◆Mecklenburgisches Landeshauptarchiv
Schwerin, Graf-Schack-Allee 2, 19053
Schwerin
◆Vorpommersches Landesarchiv Greifs-
wald, Martin-Andersen-Nexö-Platz 1,
17489 Greifswald, Postfach 323, 17463
Greifswald
Niedersachsen
(Lower Saxony)
◆ Niedersächsisches Hauptstaatsarchiv
Hannover, Am Archiv 1, 30169 Hannover
◆ Niedersächsisches Staatsarchiv in
Aurich, Oldersumer Str. 50, 26603 Aurich
◆ Niedersächsisches Staatsarchiv in
Bückeburg, Schloß, 31675 Bückeburg,
Postfach 1350, 31665 Bückeburg
◆ Niedersächsisches Staatsarchiv in
Oldenburg, Damm 43, 26135 Oldenburg
◆ Niedersächsisches Staatsarchiv in
Osnabrück, Schloßstr. 29, 49074 Osna-
brück
◆Niedersächsisches Staatsarchiv in Stade,
Am Sande 4 C, 21682 Stade
◆ Niedersächsisches Staatsarchiv in
Wolfenbüttel, Forstweg 2, 38302 Wolfen-
büttel
Nordrhein-Westfalen
(North Rhine Westphalia)
◆ Nordrhein-Westfälisches Haupt-
staatsarchiv, Mauerstr. 55, 40476
Düsseldorf

◆Nordrhein-Westsfälisches Staatsarchiv Münster, Bohlweg 2, 48147 Münster
◆Nordrhein-Westfälisches Staatsarchiv Detmold und Nordrhein-Westfälisches Personenstandsarchiv Westfalen-Lippe, Willi-Hofmann-Str. 2, 32756 Detmold
◆ Nordrhein-Westfälisches Personenstandsarchiv Rheinland, Schloß Augustusburg (Eingang Schloßstr. 12), 50321 Brühl

Rheinland-Pfalz
(Rhineland-Palatinate)
◆ Landeshauptarchiv Koblenz, Karmeliterstr. 1/3, 56068 Koblenz, Postfach 1340, 56013 Koblenz
◆Landesarchiv Speyer, Otto-Mayer-Str. 9, 67346 Speyer, Postfach 1608, 67326 Speyer

Saarland
◆Landesarchiv Saarbrücken, Scheidter Str. 114, 66123 Saarbrücken, Postfach 102431, 66024 Saarbrücken

Sachsen
(Saxony)
◆ Sächsisches Hauptstaatsarchiv, Archivstr. 14, 10097 Dresden, Postfach 100450, 01074 Dresden
— *Außenstelle Bautzen:* Seidauer Str. 2, 02625 Bautzen
— *Außenstelle Chemnitz,* Schulststr. 38, 09125 Chemnitz, Postfach 525, 09005 Chemnitz
— *Außenstelle Freiberg:* Kirchgasse 11, 09599 Freiberg
— *Depot Kamenz:* Macherstr. 41, 01917 Kamenz
◆ Sächsisches Staatsarchiv Leipzig, Reichsgerichtsgebäude, Beethovenstr. 4, 04107 Leipzig, Postfach 100947, 04009 Leipzig
◆Deutsche Zentralstelle für Genealogie, Schongauerstr. 1, 04329 Leipzig

Sachsen-Anhalt
(Saxony-Anhalt)
◆Landesarchiv Magdeburg-Landeshauptarchiv, Hegelstr. 25, 39104 Magdeburg, Postfach 4023, 39015 Magdeburg
— *Außenstelle Wernigerode:* Lindenallee 21 (Orangerie), 38855 Wernigerode,

Postfach 61, 38842 Wernigerode
— *Außenstelle Möckern:* Schloß, 04159 Möckern
◆ Landesarchiv Merseburg, König-Heinrich-Str. 83, 06217 Merseburg
◆Landesarchiv Oranienbaum, Schloß, 06782 Oranienbaum

Schleswig-Holstein
◆ Landesarchiv Schleswig-Holstein, Prinzenpalais, 24837 Schleswig

Thüringen (Thuringia)
◆ Thüringisches Hauptstaatsarchiv Weimar, Marstallstr. 2, 99423 Weimar, Postfach 726 99408 Weimar
◆Thüringisches Staatsarchiv Altenburg, Schloß 7. 04600 Altenburg, Postfach 149, 04581 Altenburg
◆ Thüringisches Staatsarchiv Gotha, Schloß Friedenstein, 99867 Gotha, Postfach 296, 99854 Gotha
◆ Thüringisches Staatsarchiv Greiz, Oberes Schloß 7, 07973 Greiz
◆Thüringisches Staatsarchiv Meiningen, Schloß Bibrabau, 98617 Meiningen, Postfach 272, 98606 Meiningen
◆Thüringisches Staatsarchiv Rudolstadt, Schloß Heidecksburg, 07407 Rudolstadt

Source: *Archive in der Bundesrepublik Deutschland, Österreich und der Schweiz.* 15. Ausgabe, Ardey-Verlag Münster, 1995

COUNTY ARCHIVES
(Kreisarchive) IN GERMANY

Kreis Aachen: Kreisarchiv, Kreisverwaltung, Bachstr. 39, 52066 Aachen, Postfach 910, 52010 Aachen
Landkreis Ahrweiler: Kreisarchiv, Kreisverwaltung, Wilhelmstr. 24/30, 53474 Bad Neuenahr-Ahrweiler; Postfach 1369, 53458 Bad Neuenahr-Ahrweiler
Alb-Donau-Kreis: Landratsamt Alb-Donau-Kreis, Haupt- und Personalamt, Registratur- und Archivwesen, Schillerstr. 30, 89077 Ulm/Donau
Landkreis Altenburg: Landratsamt [Altenburg], Kreisarchiv, Lindenaustr. 9,

04600 Altenburg (Außenstelle Schmölln, Kreisarchiv, Postfach 141, 04621 Schmölln, Amtsplatz 8, 04626 Schmölln, Dienstsitz: Karl-Marx-Str. 1 b-c, 04621 Schmölln)
Landkreis Altenkirchen: Kreisarchiv, Kreisverwaltung, Parkstr. 1, 57610 Altenkirchen
Landkreis Anklam: See Landkreis Ostvorpommern
Landkreis Annaberg: Kreisarchiv, Paulus-Jenisius-Str. 24, 09456 Annaberg-Buchholz
Landkreis Angermünde: Kreisarchiv. Schwedter Str. 20, 16278 Angermünde
Landkreis Anhalt-Zerbst: Kreisarchiv [Zerbst], Fritz-Brandt-Str. 16, 39261 Zerbst
Landkreis Apolda: See Landkreis Weimar-Land
Landkreis Arnstadt: See Ilm-Kreis
Landkreis Artern: See Kyffhäuser-Kreis
Aschersleben-Straßfurter-Landkreis: Kreisarchiv [Aschersleven], Briete Str. 22, 06449 Aschersleben (Außenstelle Staßfurt, Kreisarchiv, Bernburger Str. 12, 39418 Staßfurt)
Landkreis Aue: Landratsamt Aue, Dezernat I, Kreisarchiv/Heimatpflege, Wettiner Str. 64, 08280 Aue; Postfach 10319, 08273 Aue
Landkreis Auerbach: Kreisarchiv [Auerbach], Friedrich-Engels-Str. 22, 08223 Falkenstein
Landkreis Bad Doberan: Kreisarchiv, August-Bebel-Str. 3, 18209 Bad Doberan
Landkreis Bad Freienwalde: Kreisarchiv, Schulstr. 1, 16259 Bad Freienwalde
Landkreis Bad Langensalza: See Unstrut-Hainich-Kreis
Landkreis Bad Salzungen: See Wartburgkreis
Landkreis Barnim: Kries- und Stadtarchiv [Eberswalde], Heegermühler Str. 75, 16225 Eberswalde, Postfach 100448, 16204 Eberswalde (Außenstelle Bernau, Kreisarchiv, Breitscheidstr. 59, 16321 Bernau)
Landkreis Bautzen: Kreisarchiv, Bahnhofstr. 9, 02625 Bautzen
Landkreis Beeskow: See Landkreis Oder-Spree
Landkreis Belzig: Kreisarchiv, Niemöller-Str. 1-2, 14806 Belzig
Landkreis Bernau: See Landkreis Barnim
Landkreis Bernburg: Stadt- und Kreisarchiv, Karlsplatz 37, 06406 Bernburg
Landkreis Berkastel-Wittlich: Kriesarchiv, Schloßstr. 10, 54516 Wittlich
Landkreis Biberach an der Riß: Kreiskultur- und Archivamt, Rollinstr. 9, 88400 Biberach an der Riß; Postfach 1662, 88396 Biberach an der Riß
Landkreis Birkenfeld: Kreisarchiv, Kreisverwaltung, Schloßallee 11, 55765 Birkenfeld; Postfach 301240, 55760 Birkenfeld
Landkreis Bischofswerda: Kriesarchiv, Kirchstr. 25, 01877 Bischofswerda
Landkreis Bitterfeld, Kriesarchiv, Glück-Auf-Str. 2, 06749 Bitterfeld
Bodenseekreis: Kreisarchiv, Pestalozzistr. 5, 88677 Markdorf
Landkreis Böblingen, Kriesarchiv, Landratsamt, Parkstr. 16, 71034 Böblingen; Postfach 1640, 71006 Böblingen
Landkreis Bördekreis: Kriesarchiv [Oschersleben], Bahnhofstr. 5, 39387 Oschersleben (Außenstelle Wanzleben, Kreisarchiv, Ritterstr. 17-19, 39164 Wanzleben)
Kreis Borken: Kriesarchiv, Kreisverwaltung, Burloer Str. 93, 46325 Borken, Postfach, 46322 Borken
Landkreis Borna: Kreisarchiv, Leipziger Str. 75, 04552 Borna
Landkreis Brand-Erbisdorf, Kreisarchiv, Dr.-W.-Külz-Str. 15, 09618 Brand-Erbisdorf
Landkreis Brandenburg-Land: Kriesarchiv, Bäckerstr. 29, 14770 Brandenburg
Landkreis Breisgau-Hochschwarzwald: Kreisarchiv, Landratsamt, Stadtstr. 2, 79104 Freiburg im Breisgau
Landkreis Bützow: Kreisarchiv, Kreisverwaltung, Schloßplatz 6, 18246 Bützow

Landkreis Burg: See Landkreis Jerichower Land
Burgenlandkreis: Kreisarchiv [Naumburg], Georgenberg 6, 06618 Naumburg (Außenstelle Nebra, Kreisarchiv, 06642 Nebra) (Außenstelle Zeitz, Zentrales Stadt- und Kreisarchiv, Schloßstr. 6, 39249 Zeitz)
Landkreis Calau: Kreisarchiv, J.-Gottschalkstr. 36, 03205 Calau
Landkreis Calw: Kreisarchiv, Vogteistr. 44, 75365 Calw
Landkreis Celle: Kreisarchiv, Kreisverwaltung, Trift 26,Gebäude 6, 29221 Celle
Landkreis Chemnitz: Kreisarchiv, Rußdorfer Str. 1, 09212 Limbach-Oberfrohna
Kreis Coesfeld: Kreisarchiv, Postfach 1543, 48651 Coesfeld
Landkreis Cottbus-Land: Kreisarchiv, Karl-Liebknecht-Str. 30, 03046 Cottbus
Landkreis Cuxhaven: Archiv des Landkreises Cuxhaven, Markstr. 2, 21762 Otterndorf (Niederelbe)
Landkreis Delitzsch: Stadt- und Kreisarchiv, Landratsamt, Markt 10/11, 04509 Delitzsch
Landkreis Demmin: Kreisarchiv, A.-Pompe-Str. 12-15, 17109 Demmin
Landkreis Diepholz: Kreisarchiv, Kreisverwaltung, Postfach, 49356 Diepholz
Landkreis Dippoldiswalde: Kreisarchiv, Dr.-Külz-Str. 1, 01744 Dippoldiswalde
Döbeln: Kreisarchiv, Landratsamt, Dez. III, Straße des Friedens 20, 04720 Döbeln
Landkreis Dresden: Kreisarchiv, Landratsamt, Riesaer Str. 7, 01129 Dresden; Postfach 230100, 01111 Dresden
Kreis Düren: Stadt- und Kreisarchiv, Rathaus, Kaiserplatz, 52349 Düren; Postfach, 52348 Düren
Landkreis Eberswalde: See Landkreis Barnim
Landkreis Eichsfeld: Kreisarchiv [Heiligenstadt], Petristr. 34, 37308 Heilbad Heiligenstadt (Außenstelle Worbis, Kreisarchiv, Friedensplatz 1, 37339 Worbis)
Landkreis Eilenburg: Kreisarchiv, Kranoldstr. 15, 04838 Eilenburg
Landkreis Eisenach: See Wartburgkreis
Landkreis Eisenberg: See Holzlandkreis
Landkreis Eisenhüttenstadt: Kreisarchiv, Glashüttenstr. 6, 15890 Eisenhüttenstadt
Landrkreis Eisleben: See Landkreis Mansfelder Land
Landkreis Emmendingen: Kreisarchiv, Bahnhofstr. 2/4, 79312 Emmendingen
Landkreis Emsland: Kreisarchiv, Postfach 1562, 49705 Meppen
Kreis Ennepetal: (placed in Staatsarchiv Münster)
Enzkreis: Kreisarchiv, Landratsamt, Zähringeralle 3, 75177 Pforzheim; Postfach 1080, 75110 Pforzheim
Erftkreis: Kreisarchiv, Willy-Brandt-Platz 1, 50126 Bergheim
Landkreis Erfurt: See Landkreis Sömmerda
Landkreis Esslingen: Kreisarchiv, Landratsamt, Pulverwiesen 11, Postfach 145, 73726 Esslingen am Neckar
Kreis Euskirchen: Kreisarchiv, Kreisverwaltung, Jülicher Ring 32, 53879 Euskirchen; Postfach 1146, 53861 Euskirchen
Landkreis Finsterwalde: Kriesarchiv, Sonnewalder Str. 2-4, 03238 Finsterwalde
Landkreis Flöha (Sachsen): Kreis- und Verwaltungsarchiv, Landratsamt, Augustusburger Str. 88, 09557 Flöha
Landkreis Forst: Kreisarchiv, Promenade 26, 03149 Forst
Landkreis Freiberg: Kreisarchiv, Hauptstr. 87, 09633 Krummenhennendorf
Landkreis Freital: Kreisarchiv, Uhlandstr. 13, 01705 Freital
Landkreis Freudenstadt: Kreisarchiv, Landratsamt, Landhausstr. 4, 72250 Freudenstadt; Postfach 620, 72236 Freudenstadt
Landkreis Fürstenwalde: See Landkreis Oder-Spree
Landkreis Fürth: Landratsamt, Stresemannplatz 11, 90763 Fürth

Landkreis Gadebusch: See Landkreis Nordwestmecklenburg
Landkreis Gardelegen: See Landkreis Westliche Altmark
Landkreis Geithain: Kreisarchiv, Bahnhofstr. 6, 04643 Geithain
Landkreis Genthin: See Landkreis Jerichower Land
Landkreis Gera: See Landkreis Greiz
Landkreis Gießen: Kreisarchiv, Postfach 110760, 35352 Gießen
Landkreis Gifhorn: Kreisarchiv, Schloßstr. 1, 38518 Gifhorn
Landkreis Glauchau: Kreisarchiv, Heinrich-Heine-Str. 7, 08371 Glauchau
Landkreis Göppinigen: Kreisarchiv, Schloß Filseck, 73066 Uhingen; Postanschrift: Landratsamt, Postfach 809, 73008 Göppingen
Landkreis Görlitz: Kreisarchiv, Postplatz 18, 02826 Görlitz
Landkreis Göttingen: Kreisarchiv, Reinhäuser Landstr. 4, 37083 Göttingen
Landkreis Gotha: Landratsamt Gotha, Kreisarchiv, Postfach 47, 99867 Gotha, 18.-März-Str. 50, 99867 Gotha (Dienstsitz: Bürgeraue 2, 99867 Gotha)
Landkreis Gräfenhainichen: See Landkreis Wittenberg
Landkreis Greifswald: See Landkreis Ostvorpommern
Landkreis Greiz: Landratsamt [Greiz], Kreisarchiv, Postfach 166, 07962 Greiz; Dienstsitz: Dr.-Rathenau-Platz 11, 07962 Greiz (Außenstelle Gera; Kreisarchiv, Postfach 68, 07501 Gera; Dienstsitz: Puschkinplatz 3, 07545 Gera. Außenstelle Zeulenroda, Verwaltungsarchiv, Postfach 7 und 11, 07931 Zeulenroda; Dienstsitz: Goethestr. 17, 07937 Zeulenroda)
Landkreis Grimma: Kreisarchiv, Leipziger Platz 6, 04668 Grimma
Landkreis Grimmen: See Landkreis Nordvorpommern
Landkreis Grevesmühlen: See Landkreis Nordwestmecklenburg
Lankreis Großenhain: Kreisarchiv, Meißner Str. 41a, 01558 Großenhain
Landkreis Guben: Kreisarchiv, Uferstr.

22, 03161 Guben
Landkreis Güstrow: Kreisarchiv [Güstrow], 18273 Güstrow
Kreis Gütersloh: Kreisarchiv, Wasserstr. 14, 33378 Rheda-Wiedenbrück
Kreis Gummersbach: See Oberbergischer Kreis
Landkreis Hagenow: Kreisarchiv, Landratsamt, Hagenstr. 23, 19230 Hagenow
Landkreis Hainichen: Kulturamt, Kreisarchiv Hainichen, Am Landratsamt 3, 09648 Mittweida (The Hainichen district is expected to join with the Rochlitz district)
Landkreis Halberstadt: Kreisarchiv, Friedrich-Ebert-Str. 42, 38820 Halberstadt
Landkreis Haldensleben: See Ohre-Kreis
Landkreis Hameln-Pyrmont: Kreisarchiv, Am Stockhof 2, 31785 Hameln
Landkreis Hannover: Kreisarchiv, Schloßstr. 1, 31535 Neustadt am Rübenberge
Landkreis Harburg: Kreisarchiv, Rote-Kreuz-Str. 6, 21423 Winsen/Luhe
Landkreis Havelberg: See Landkreis Östliche Altmark
Landkreis Heidenheim: Kreisarchiv, Landratsamt, Felsenstr. 36, 89518 Heidenheim an der Brenz, Postfach 1580, 89505 Heidenheim an der Brenz
Landkreis Heilbronn: Kreisarchiv, Landratsamt, Lerchenstr. 40, 74072 Heilbronn
Landkreis Heiligenstadt: See Landkreis Eichsfeld
Kreis Heinsberg: Kreisarchiv, Valkenburger Str. 45, 52525 Heinsberg
Kreis Herford: Kommunalarchiv, Archiv des Kreises und der Stadt: See Stadtarchiv Herford
Landkreis Herzberg: Kreisarchiv, Ludwig-Jahn-Str. 2, 16835 Herzberg
Landkreis Hettstedt: See Landkreis Mansfelder Land
Landkreis Hildburghausen: Kreisarchiv [Hildburghausen], Friedrich-Rückert-Str. 22, 98646 Hildburghausen (Außenstelle

Suhl, Kreisarchiv, Köhlersgehäu 12, 98544 Zella-Mehlis
Landkreis Hildesheim: Kreisarchiv, Bischof-Janssen-Str. 31, 31134 Hildesheim
Hochsauerlandkreis: Kreisarchiv, Kreisverwaltung, Steinstr. 27, 59870 Meschede
Hochtaunuskreis: Kreisarchiv, Schulstr. 27, 61440 Oberursel
Kreis Höxter: Kreisarchiv, Kreisverwaltung, 37671 Höxter
Hohenlohekreis: Kreisarchiv, Hohenlohe-Zentralarchiv, Schloß, 74632 Neuenstein
Landkreis Hohenmölsen: See Landkreis Weißenfels
Landkreis Hohenstein-Ernstthal: Kreisarchiv, Am Bach 1, 09353 Oberlungwitz
Holzlandkreis: Landratsamt [Eisenberg], Kreisarchiv, Schloß 1-6, 07607 Eisenberg (Außenstelle Jena, Kreisarchiv, Postfach 100337 Jena; Dienstsitz: Ammerbach 108, 07745 Jena; Außenstelle Stadtroda, Kreisarchiv, Schloßstr. 2, 07646 Stadtroda)
Landkreis Hoyerswerda: Kreisarchiv, Landratsamt, S.-G-Frentzel-Str. 1, 02977 Hoyerswerda
Ilm-Kreis: Stadt- und Kreisarchiv [Arnstdt], Ritterstr. 14, 99310 Arnstadt (Außenstelle Ilmenau, Kreisarchiv, Krankenhausstr. 12, 98693 Ilmenau)
Landkreis Ilmenau: See Ilm-Kreis
Landkreis Jena: See Holzlandkreis
Landkreis Jerichower Land: Kreisarchiv [Burg], Magdeburger Str. 44, 39288 Burg (Außenstelle Genthin)
Landkreis Jessen: See Landkreis Wittenberg
Landkreis Jüterbog: Kommunalarchiv Jüterbog, Am Dammtor 16, 14913 Jüterbog
Landkreis Kamenz: Kreisarchiv, Rosa-Luxemburg-Str. 1, 01911 Kamenz
Landkreis Karlsruhe: Kreisarchiv im Generallandesarchiv Karlsruhe, Nördliche Hildapromenade 2, 76133 Karlsruhe

Kreis Kleve: Kreisarchiv, Kapuzinerstr. 34, 47608 Geldern
Landkreis Klingenthal: See Landkreis Auerbach
Landkreis Klötze: See Landkreis Westliche Auerbach
Landkreis Königs Wusterhausen: Kreisarchiv, Thälmannplatz 4, 15771 Königs Wusterhausen
Landkreis Köthen: Kreisarchiv, Springstr. 28, 06366 Köthen
Landkreis Konstanz: Landratsamt Konstanz, Benediktinerplatz 1, 78467 Konstanz, Postfach 101238, 78412 Konstanz; Kreisarchiv. Rathaus, Löwengasse 12, 78315 Radolfzell am Bodensee, Postfach 1480, 78304 Radolfzell am Bodensee
Kyffhäuser-Kreis: Landratsamt [Sondershausen], Kriesarchiv, Postfach 15, 99701 Sondershausen, Markt 8, 99706 Sondershausen, Dienstsitz: Dickkopf (Außenstelle Artern, Kreisarchiv, Bergstr. 4, 06556 Artern)
Landkreis Kyritz: Kreisarchiv, Perleberger Str. 2, 16866 Kyritz
Kreis Herzogtum Lauenburg: Archiv des Kreises, Am Markt 10, 23909 Ratzeburg; Postfach 1140, 23901 Ratzeburg
Landkreis Leipzig: Kreisarchiv, Landratsamt Leipzig, Tröndlinring 3, 04105 Leipzig (The districts of Borna, Geithain and Leipzig-Land are expected to join together.)
Landkreis Lobenstein: See Saale-Orla-Kreis
Landkreis Löbau: Kreisarchiv, Georgewitzerstr. 25, 02708 Löbau
Landkreis Luckau: Kreisarchiv, Karl-Marx-Str. 21, 15926 Luckau
Landkreis Luckenwalde: Kreis-und Verwaltungsarchiv, Grabenstr. 23, 14943 Luckenwalde
Landkreis Ludwigsburg: Kreisarchiv, Landratsamt, Hindenburgstr. 40, 71638 Ludwigsburg; Postfach 760, 71607 Ludwigsburg
Landkreis Ludwigslust: Kreisarchiv,

Alexandrienstr. 5/6, 19288 Ludwigslust
Landkreis Lübben: Kreisarchiv, Lohmühlengasse 12, 15907 Lübben
Lankreis Lübz: See Landkreis Parchim
Landkreis Lüchow-Dannenberg: Kreisarchiv, Königsberger Str. 10, 29439 Lüchow
Landkreis Lüneburg: Kreisarchiv, Auf dem Michaeliskloster 4, 21335 Lüneburg
Märkischer Kreis: Kreisarchiv und Landeskundliche Bibliothek des Märkischen Kreises, Bismarckstr. 15, 58762 Altena
Landkreis Märkisch-Oderland: Kreisarchiv, Klosterstr. 14, 15331 Strausberg
Main-Kinzig-Kreis: Kreisarchiv, Barbarossastr. 16-18, 63571 Gelnhausen; Postfach 1465, 63569 Gelnhausen
Main-Tauber-Kreis: See Staatsarchiv Wertheim (Archivverbund Main-Tauber)
Main-Taunus-Kreis: Kreisarchiv, Am Kreishaus 1-5, 65719 Hofheim am Taunus; Postfach 1480, 65704 Hofheim am Taunus
Landkreis Mansfelder Land: Kreisarchiv [Eisleben], Bahnhofstr. 29, 06295 Eisleben (The holdings of Kreis Hettstedt may also be found here.)
Landkreis Marienberg: See Mittlerer Erzgebirgkreis
Landkreis Mecklenburg-Strelitz: Kreisarchiv [Neubrandenburg], Bienenweg 1, 17033 Neubrandenburg (Außenstelle Neustrelitz, Kreisarchiv, Woldegker Chaussee 35, Haus 4, 17235 Neustrelitz; Postfach 1145, 17221 Neustrelitz)
Landkreis Meiningen: See Schmalkalden-Meiningen
Landkreis Meißen: Kreisarchiv, Loosestr. 17/19, 01662 Meißen
Landkreis Merseburg-Querfurt: Zentralregistratur (Archiv) [Merseburg], Domplatz 9, 06217 Merseburg (Außenstelle Querfurt, Kreisarchiv, Burgring 31, 06268 Querfurt
Kreis Mettmann: Kreisarchiv, Schloß Linnep, Linneper Weg 17, 40885 Ratingen-Breitscheid; Postfach 105147,

40858 Ratingen
Kreis Minden-Lübbecke, Kommunalarchiv Minden [archive of the city of Minden and Kreis Minden-Lübbecke], Tonhallenstr. 7, 32423 Minden; Postfach 3080, 32387 Minden
Mittlerer Erzgebirgskreis: Kreisarchiv [Marienberg], Bergstr. 07, 09496 Marienberg
Landkreis Mühlhausen: See Unstrut-Hainich-Kreis
Landkreis Müritz: Kreisarchiv, Kietzstr. 10/11, 17192 Waren
Landkreis Nauen: Kreis- und Verwaltungsarchiv, Goethestr. 59/60, 14632 Nauen
Landkreis Naumburg: See Burgenlandkreis
Landkreis Nebra: See Burgenlandkreis
Landkreis Neubrandenburg: See Landkreis Mecklenburg-Strelitz
Landkreis Neuhaus am Rennweg: See Landkreis Sonneberg
Landkreis Neuruppin: Kreisarchiv, Virchowstr. 14/15, 16816 Neuruppin
Kreis Neuss: Kreisarchiv, Burg Friedestrom, Schloßstr. 1, 41541 Dormagen-Zons
Landkreis Neustrelitz: See Landkreis Mecklenburg-Strelitz
Landkreis Nienburg/Weser: Kreisarchiv, Kreishaus am Schloßplatz, 31582 Nienburg/Weser; Postfach 1000, 31580 Nienburg/Weser
Landkreis Niesky: Kreisarchiv, Robert-Koch-Str. 1, 02906 Niesky
Kreis Nordfriesland: Kreisarchiv, Schloß vor Husum, 25813 Husum
Landkreis Nordhausen: Kreisarchiv, Grimmelallee 20, 99734 Nordhausen
Landkreis Nordvorpommern: Kreisarchiv Stralsund, Tribseer Damm 1a, Postfach 1165, 18401 Stralsund (Außenstelle Grimmen, Kreisarchiv, Bahnhofstr. 12/13, 18507 Grimmen; Außenstelle Ribnitz-Damgarten, Kreisarchiv, Damgartner Chaussee 40, 18311 Ribnitz-Damgarten)
Landkreis Nordwestmecklenburg:

Kreisarchiv Grevesmühlen, Börzower Weg 1, 23936 Grevesmühlen (Außenstelle Gadebusch, Kreisarchiv, Postfach 1263, 19202 Gadebusch; Außenstelle Wismar, Kreisarchiv, Rostocker Str. 76, 23970 Wismar)

Oberbergisher Kreis: Kreisarchiv Moltkestr. 42, 51643 Gummersbach; Postfach 1549, 51605 Gummersbach

Odenwaldkreis: Kreisarchiv, Landratsamt, Michelstädter Str. 12, 64711 Erbach

Landkreis Oder-Spree: Kreisarchiv [Fürstenwalde], Hegelstr. 22, 15517 Fürstenwalde (Außenstelle Beeskow, Kreisarchiv, Rudolf-Breitscheid-Str. 7, 15841 Beeskow

Landkreis Oelsnitz/Vogtland: Kreisarchiv, Schloßstr 32, 08606 Oelsnitz/Vogtland; Postanschrift: Landratsamt Oelsnitz, SG 11 - Archiv, Stephanstr. 9, 08606 Oelsnitz

Landkreis Östliche Altmark: Kreisarchiv [Stendal], Schönbeckstr. 23, 39576 Stendal (Außenstelle Havelberg, Kreisarchiv, Genthiner Str. 17, 39539 Havelberg; Außenstelle Osterburg, Kreisarchiv, Ernst-Thälmann-Str. 1, 39606 Osterburg (Altmark))

Ohre-Kreis: Kreis- und Stadtarchiv [Haldensleben], Bülstringer Str. 30, 39340 Haldensleben (Außenstelle Wolmirstedt)

Kreis Olpe: Kreisarchiv, Kurfürst-Heinrich-Str. 34, 57462 Olpe (Biggesee); Postfach 1560, 57445 Olpe (Biggesee)

Landkreis Oranienburg: Kreisarchiv, Poststr. 1, 16515 Oranienburg

Ortenaukreis: Kreisarchiv, Landratsamt, Badstr. 20, 77652 Offenburg; Postfach 1960, 77609 Offenburg

Landkreis Oschatz: Kreisarchiv Oschatz, Friedrich-Naumann-Promenade 9, 04758 Oschatz

Landkreis Oschersleben: See Bördekreis

Ostalbkreis: Kreisarchiv, Landratsamt, Stuttgarter Str. 41, 73430 Aalen; Postfach 1440, 73404 Aalen

Landkreis Osterburg: See Landkreis Östliche Altmark

Landkreis Osterholz: Kreisarchiv, Amt 41, Postfach 1262, 27702 Osterholz-Scharmbeck

Landkreis Osterode am Harz: Kreisarchiv, Herzberger Str. 5, 37520 Osterode am Harz

Landkreis Ostvorpommern (Usedom-Peene-Kreis): Kreisarchiv [Anklam], Demminer Str. 71-74, 17389 Anklam (Außenstelle Wolgast, Kreisarchiv, Burgstr. 7, 17438 Wolgast; Außenstelle Greifswald-Land, Kreisarchiv, Martin-Andersen-Nexö-Platz 1, 17489 Greifswald)

Kreis Paderborn: Kreisarchiv, Lindenstr. 12, 33142 Büren

Landkreis Parchim: Kreisarchiv, Moltkeplatz 2, 19370 Parchim; Postfach 53 und 54, 19361 Parchim

Landreis Pasewalk: See Landkreis Uecker-Randow

Landkreis Peine: Kreismuseum und -archiv, Stederdorfer Str. 17, 31224 Peine; Postfach 1360, 31221 Peine

Landkreis Perleberg: Kreisarchiv, Berliner Str. 49, 19348 Perleberg

Kreis Pinneberg: Kreisarchiv, Moltkestr. 10, 25421 Pinneberg; Postfach 1751, 25407 Pinneberg

Landkreis Pirna: Kreisarchiv, Zehistaer Str. 9, 01796 Pirna

Landkreis Plauen: Kreisarchiv, Kreisverwaltung, Neundorfer Str. 96, 08523 Plauen

Kreis Plön: Kreisarchiv, Hamburger Str. 17/18, 24306 Plön

Landkreis Pößneck: See Saale-Orla-Kreis

Landkreis Potsdam: Kreis- und Verwaltungsarchiv Potsdam, Friedrich-Ebert-Str. 79/81, 14469 Potsdam

Landkreis Prenzlau: Kreisarchiv, Leninstr. 21, 17291 Prenzlau

Landkreis Pritzwalk: Kreisarchiv, Meyenburger Tor, 16928 Pritzwalk

Landkreis Quedlinburg: Kreisarchiv, Heilige Geist Str. 7, 06484 Quedlinburg

Landkreis Querfurt: See Landkreis Merseburg-Querfurt

Landkreis Rastatt: Landratsamt Rastatt,

Kreisarchiv, Herrenstr. 13, 76437 Rastatt; Postfach 1863, 76408 Rastatt
Landkreis Rathenow: Kreisarchiv, Platz der Freihiet 1, 14712 Rathenow
Landkreis Ravensburg: Landratsamt Ravensburg, Kreisarchiv, Postfach 1940, 88189 Ravensburg; Dienstgebäude: Friedensstr. 6 (= Hauptgebäude)
Kreis Recklinghausen: Kreisarchiv, Kreisverwaltung, Kurt-Schumacher-Allee 1, 45657 Recklinghausen; Postfach 100864 und 100865, 45608 Recklinghausen
Landkreis Reichenbach (Vogtland): Kreisarchiv, Dr.-Külz-Str. 6, 08468 Reichenbach (Vogtland
Rems-Murr-Kreis: Kreisarchiv, Alter Postplatz 10, 71332 Waiblingen
Landkreis Reutlingen: Kreisarchiv, Bismarckstr. 16, 72764 Reutlingen; Postfach 2143, 72711 Reutlingen
Rheinisch-Bergischer-Kreis: Kreisarchiv, Am Rübezahlwald 7, 51469 Bergisch Gladbach
Rhein-Neckar-Kreis: Kreisarchiv, Trajanstr. 66, 68526 Ladenburg; Postfach 1206, 68521 Ladenburg
Rhein-Sieg-Kreis: Kreisarchiv, Kaiser-Wilhelm-Platz 1, 53721 Siegburg, Postfach 1551, 53705 Siegburg
Landkreis Ribnitz-Damgarten: See Landkreis Nordvorpommern
Landkreis Riesa: Kreisarchiv, Kirchstr. 46, 01591 Riesa-Gröba
Landkreis Rochlitz: Kreisarchiv, Waldstr. 2, 09306 Wechselburg; Post: Landratsamt Rochlitz/Hainichen, DI-Kulturamt, Archivwesen, Am Landratsamt 3, 09648 Mittweida
Landkreis Röbel: Kreisarchiv, Bahnhofstr. 13, 17207 Röbel
Landkreis Roßlau: See Landkreis Anhalt-Zerbst
Landkreis Rostock: Kreisarchiv, Friedrich-Engels-Str. 6-8, 18055 Rostock
Landkreis Rotenburg/Wümme: Kreisarchiv, Bremer Str. 38, 27432 Bremervörde; Postf. 1363, 27423 Bremervörde
Landkreis Rottweil: Kreisarchiv,

Landratsamt, Archiv- und Kulturamt, Königstr. 36, 78628 Rottweil
Landkreis Rudolstadt: See Schwarza-Kreis
Landkreis Rügen: Kreisarchiv, Billrothstr. 5, 18528 Bergen
Saale-Orla-Kreis: Kreisarchiv [Schleiz], Oschitzer Str. 4, Postfach, 07907 Schleiz (Außenstelle Lobenstein, Kreisarchiv, Heinrich-Behr-Str., 07356 Lobenstein; Außenstelle Pößneck, Kreisarchiv, Wohlfarthstr. 3-5 07381 Pößneck)
Landkreis Saalfeld: See Schwarza-Kreis
Landkreis Saalkreis: Kreisarchiv, Wilhelm-Külz-Str. 10, 06108 Halle/Saale
Stadtverband Saarbrücken: Archiv, Amt 10 (Hauptamt), Schloßplatz 6/7, 66119 Saarbrücken
Landkreis Saarlouis: Kreisarchiv, Landratsamt, Kaiser-Wilhelm-Str. 6, 66740 Saarlouis; Postfach 1840, 66718 Saarlouis
Landkreis Salzwedel: See Landkreis Westliche Altmark
Landkreis Sangerhausen: Kreisarchiv, Rudolf-Breitscheid-Str. 20-22, 06526 Sangerhausen
Landkreis Schleiz: See Saale-Orla-Kreis
Kreis Schleswig-Flensburg: Kreisarchiv, Suadicanistr. 1, 24837 Schleswig
Landkreis Schmalkalden-Meiningen: Kreisarchiv [Meiningen], Schloß Bibrabau, Schloßplatz 1, 98617 Mein-ingen (Außenstelle Schmalkalden, Kreis- und Stadtarchiv, Schloßküchenweg 15, 98574 Schmalkalden
Landkreis Schmölln: See Landkreis Altenburg
Landkreis Schönebeck/Elbe: Kreisarchiv Schönebeck, Cokturhof, 39218 Schönebeck/Elbe
Landkreis Schwäbisch Hall: Kreisarchiv, Landratsamt, Münzstr. 1, 74523 Schwäbisch Hall; Postfach 100440, 74504 Schwäbisch Hall
Schwarza-Kreis: Kreisarchiv [Saalfeld], Schloßstr. 24, 07318 Saalfeld; Postfach 2244, 07308 Saalfeld (Außenstelle Rudolstadt, Kreisarchiv, Schwarzburger

Chaussee 12, 07407 Rudolstdt, Postfach 85, 07392 Rudolstadt
Landkreis Schwarzenberg: Kreisarchiv, August-Bebel-Str. 11, 08340 Beierfeld, Kreisverwaltung, Hofgarten 1, 08340 Schwarzenberg
Schwarzwald-Baar-Kreis: Kreisarchiv, Am Hoptbühl 2, 78048 Villingen-Schwenningen
Landkreis Schwerin: Kreisarchiv, Wismarsche Str. 132, 19053 Schwerin
Landkreis Sebnitz: Kreisarchiv, Promenade 32, 01855 Sebnitz
Landkreis Seelow: Kreisarchiv, Puschkinplatz 12, 15306 Seelow
Landkreis Senftenberg: Kreisarchiv, Dubinaweg 1, 01968 Senftenberg
Landkreis Sigmaringen: Kreisarchiv, Landratsamt, Leopoldstr. 4, 72488 Sigmaringen; Postfach 440, 72482 Sigmaringen
Landkreis Sömmerda: Kreisarchiv [Sömmerda], Kreisverwaltung, Bahnhofstr. 9, 99610 Sömmerda (Außenstelle Erfurt-Land, Kreisarchiv, Postfach 206, 99005 Erfurt; Dienstsitz: Juri-Gagarin-Ring 110, 99084 Erfurt)
Kreis Soest: Kreisarchiv, Villa Plange, Sigefridwall 8, 59494 Soest; Postfach 1752, 59491 Soest
Landkreis Soltau-Fallingbostel: Kreisarchiv, Vogteistr. 19, 29683 Fallingbostel
Landkreis Sondershausen: See Kyffhäuser-Kreis
Landkreis Sonneberg: Kreisarchiv [Sonneberg], Postfach 158, Bahnhofstr. 66, 96515 Sonneberg (Außenstelle Neuhaus am Rennweg, Kreisarchiv, Sonneberger Str. 1, 98724 Neuhaus am Rennweg
Landkreis Spremberg: Kriesarchiv, Schloßbezirk 3, 03130 Spremberg
Landkreis Stadtroda: See Holzlandkreis
Landkreis Staßfurt: See Aschersleben-Staßfurter-Landkreis
Kreis Steinburg: Gemeinsames Archiv des Kreises Steinburg und der Stadt Itzehoe, Markt 1, 25524 Itzehoe
Kreis Steinfurt: Kreisarchiv, Tecklenburger Str. 8, 48565 Steinfurt; Postfach 1420, 48544 Steinfurt
Landkreis Stendal: See Landkreis Östliche Altmark
Landkreis Sternberg: See Landkreis Parchim
Landkreis Stollberg: Kreisarchiv, Hohndorfer Str., 09366 Oelsnitz/Erzgebirge
Kreis Stormarn: Kreisarchiv, Stormarnhaus, Mommenstr. 11, 23843 Bad Oldesloe
Landkreis Stralsund: See Landkreis Nordvorpommern
Landkreis Strasburg: See Landkreis Uecker-Randow
Landkreis Strausberg: See Landkreis Märkisch-Oderland
Landkreis Suhl: See Landkreis Hildburghausen
Landkreis Templin: Kreisarchiv, Prenzlauer Allee 7, 17268 Templin
Landkreis Teterow: See Landkreis Güstrow
Landkreis Torgau: Kreisarchiv, Schloßstr. 27, 04860 Torgau
Landkreis Traunstein: Kreisarchiv, Landratsamt, Ludwig-Thoma-Str. 2, 83278 Traunstein; Postfach 1509, 83265 Traunstein
Landkreis Tübingen: Kreisarchiv, Doblerstr. 13-21, 72074 Tübingen; Postfach 1929, 72009 Tübingen
Landkreis Tuttlingen: Kreisarchiv, Landratsamt, Bahnhofstr. 100, 78532 Tuttlingen; Postfach 4453, 78509 Tuttlingen
Landkreis Ueckermünde: See Landkreis Uecker-Randow
Landkreis Uecker-Randow: Kreisarchiv [Pasewalk], Am Markt 1, 17309 Pasewalk, Postfach 1242, 17302 Pasewalk (Außenstelle Strasburg, Kreisarchiv, Markt 22, 17335 Strasburg; Außenstelle Ueckermünde, Kreisarchiv, Ueckerstr. 47, 17373 Ueckermünde)
Landkreis Uelzen: Kreisarchiv, Veerßer Str. 53, 29525 Uelzen; Postfach 1761, 29507 Uelzen

Kreis Unna: Kreisarchiv, Kreisverwaltung, Friedrich-Ebert-Str. 17, 59425 Unna, Postfach 2112, 59411 Unna
Unstrut-Hainich-Kreis: Kreisarchiv [Mühlhausen], Bonatstr. 50, 99974 Mühlhausen (Thüringen). (Außenstelle Bad Langensalza, Kreisarchiv, An der Alten Post 3, 99947 Bad Langensalza; Dienstsitz: Thamsbrücker Str. 20, 99947 Bad Langensalza)
Usedom-Peene-Kreis: See Landkreis Ostvorpommern
Landkreis Verden: Kreisarchiv, Bremer Str. 4, 27283 Verden (Aller), Postfach 1509, 27281 Verden
Kreis Viersen: Kreisarchiv, Thomasstr. 20, 47906 Kempen
Landkreis Waldshut: Archiv des Landkreises, Dr.-Rudolf-Eberle-Str. 34, 79774 Albbruck
Landkreis Wanzleben: See Bördekreis
Landkreis Waren: See Landkreis Müritz
Kreis Warendorf: Kreiszentralarchiv, Kreisverwaltung, Waldenburger Str. 2, 48231 Warendorf
Wartburgkreis: Dienstelle Bad Salzungen, Kreisarchiv, Andreasstr. 11, 36433 Bad Salzungen; Dienstsitz: August-Bebel-Str. 2, 36433 Bad Salzungen; Dienstelle Eisenach, Kreisarchiv, Markt 22, 99817 Eisenach
Landkreis Weimar-Land: Kreisarchiv [Apolda], Bahnhofstr. 44, 99510 Apolda; Postfach 134, 99503 Apolda, Dienstsitz: Dorngasse 4, 99510 Apolda. (Außenstelle Weimar, Kreisarchiv, Schwanseestr. 17, 99423 Weimar)
Landkreis Weißenfels: Kreisarchiv [Weißenfels], Am Stadtpark 6, 06667 Weißenfels (Außenstelle Hohenmölsen, Kreisarchiv, Ernst-Thälmann-Str. 58, 06679 Hohenmölsen)
Landkreis Weißwasser (Oberlausitz): Kreisarchiv, Jahnstr. 53, 02943 Weißwasser (Oberlausitz); Postfach 6, 02931 Weißwasser (Oberlausitz))
Landkreis Werdau: See Landkreis Zwickau
Landkreis Wernigerode: Kreisarchiv,

Rudolf-Breitscheid-Str. 10, 38855 Wernigerode
Kreis Wesel: Kreisarchiv, Kreisverwaltung, Reeser Landstr. 31, 46483 Wesel
Landkreis Westliche Altmark: Kreisarchiv [Salzwedel], Karl-Marx-Str. 32, 29410 Salzwedel (Außenstelle Gardelegen, Kreisarchiv, Philipp-Müller-Str. 13, 39638 Gardelegen; Außenstelle Klötze, Kreisarchiv, Poppauer Str. 42, 38486 Klötze)
Landkreis Wismar: See Landkreis Nordwestmecklenburg
Landkreis Wittenberg: Kreisarchiv [Wittenberg], Landratsamt, Möllensdorfer Str. 13a, 06886 Wittenberg (Außenstelle Gräfenhainichen, Kreisarchiv, Karl-Liebknecht-Str. 12, 06773 Gräfenhainichen; Außenstelle Jessen, Robert-Koch-Str. 18, 16917 Jessen)
Landkreis Wittstock: Kreisarchiv, Walter-Schulz-Platz, 16909 Wittstock/Dosse
Landkreis Wolgast: See Landkreis Ostvorpommern
Landkreis Wolmirstedt: See Ohre-Kreis
Landkreis Worbis: See Landkreis Eichsfeld
Landkreis Wurzen: Kreisarchiv, Friedrich-Ebert-Str. 2, 04808 Wurzen
Landkreis Zeitz: See Burgenlandkreis
Landkreis Zerbst: See Landkreis Anhalt-Zerbst
Landkreis Zeulenroda: See Landkreis Greiz
Landkreis Zittau: Landratsamt, Kreisarchiv, Hochwaldstr., 02763 Zitta
Zollernalbkreis: Kreisarchiv, Hirschbergstr. 29, 72336 Balingen
Landkreis Zossen: Kreis- und Verwaltungsarchiv Zossen, Jasminweg 18/19, 15834 Rangsdorf
Landkreis Zschopau: Kreisarchiv, August-Bebel-Str. 17, 09405 Zschopau
Landkreis Zwickau: Landratsamt Zwickauer Land, Kreisarchiv, Schulstr. 7, 08412 Werdau, Postfach 4, 08401 Werdau (Außenstelle, Reichenbacher Str. 158, 08056 Zwickau

Source: *Archive in der Bundesrepublik Deutschland, Österreich und der Schweiz.* Ardey-Verlag, Münster, 1995

TOWN/CITY ARCHIVES (Stadtarchive) IN GERMANY

Aachen: Stadtarchiv, Fischmarkt 3, 52062 Aachen

Aalen: Stadtarchiv, Marktplatz 30, 73430 Aalen, Postfach 1740, 73407 Aalen

Abenberg: Stadtarchiv, Stillaplatz 1, 91183 Abenberg, Postfach 8, 91181 Abenberg

Abensberg: Stadtarchiv, Rathaus, 93326 Abensberg

Achern: Stadtarchiv, Rathausplatz 1, 77855 Achern

Achim: Stadtarchiv, Rathaus Achim, Am Westerfeld 15, 28832 Achim-Uesen

Ahaus: Stadtarchiv, Rathausplatz 1, 48683 Ahaus, Postfach 1462 48681 Ahaus

Ahlen: Stadtarchiv. See Kreis Warendorf

Aichach: Stadtarchiv, Am Plattenberg 20, 86551 Aichach, Postfach 1110, 86542 Aichach

Aichtal: Stadtarchiv, Waldenbucher Str. 30, 72631 Aichtal

Aindling: Marktarchiv, Waldweg 1½, 86447 Aindling

Aken: Stadtarchiv, Stadtverwaltung, 06385 Aken

Albstadt: Stadtarchiv, Bildungszentrum, Johannesstr. 5, 72458 Albstadt-Ebingen

Aldenhoven: Gemeindearchiv, 52457 Aldenhoven, Postfach 1363, 52447 Aldenhoven

Alfeld: Stadtarchiv, Museum der Stadt Alfeld, Am Kirchhof 4/5, 31061 Alfeld (Leine)

Alfter: Gemeindearchiv, Rathaus, 53347 Alfter

Alsfeld: Stadtarchiv, Beinhaus, Post: Stadtverwaltung, 36304 Alsfeld, Postfach 560, 36295 Alsfeld

Altdorf: Stadtarchiv, Oberer Markt 2, Postfach 24, 90518 Altdorf b. Nürnberg

Altena: Stadtarchiv, Rathaus, Lüdenscheider Str. 22, 58762 Altena

Altenau: See Clausthal-Zellerfeld

Altenbeken: Gemeindearchiv, Gemeindeverwaltung, 33184 Altenbeken

Altenberge: Gemeindearchiv, Kirchstr. 25, 48341 Altenberge

Altenburg: Stadtarchiv, Markt 1, 04600 Altenburg

Altenstadt: Gemeindearchiv, Rathaus, Frankfurter Str. 11, 63674 Altenstadt

Alzenau: Stadtarchiv, Postfach 1280, Hanauer Str. 1, 63755 Alzenau

Alzey: Archiv der Stadt, Ernst-Ludwig-Str. 42, 55232 Alzey

Amberg: Stadtarchiv, Zeughausstr. 1, Postfach 2155, 92224 Amberg (Oberpfalz)

Amerang: Gemeindearchiv, Rathaus, Wasserburger Str. 11, 83123 Amerang

Amorbach: Stadtarchiv, Stadtverwaltung, Kellereigasse 1, Postfach 1280, 63916 Amorbach

Andernach: Stadtmuseum und -archiv, Hochstr. 99, 56626 Andernach

Angermünde: Stadtarchiv, Berliner Str. 42, 16278 Angermünde

Annaberg-Buchholz: Archiv, Postfach 53, 09441 Annaberg-Buchholz

Annweiler am Trifels: Verbandsgemeindearchiv, Rathaus, Meßplatz 1, 76855 Annweiler am Trifels

Anröchte: Gemeindearchiv, Rathaus, Hauptstr. 72-74, 59609 Anröchte

Ansbach: Stadtarchiv, Karlsplatz 7/9, 91522 Ansbach

Arnsberg: Stadt- und Landständearchiv, Rathausplatz 1, 59759 Arnsberg, Postfach 2340, 59713 Arnsberg

Arnstadt: Stadtarchiv. See Ilm-Kreis

Arolsen: Stadtarchiv, Große Allee 26, 34454 Arolsen

Arzberg: Stadtarchiv, Stadtverwaltung, Friedrich-Ebert-Str. 6, 95659 Arzberg (Oberfranken), Postfach 1145, 95653 Arzberg (Oberfranken)

Aschaffenburg: Stadt- und Stiftsarchiv, Schönborner Hof, Wermbachstr. 15, 63739 Aschaffenburg

Ascheberg: Gemeindearchiv, Talstr. 8,

59387 Ascheberg, Postfach 2154, 59380 Ascheberg
Aschersleben: Stadtarchiv, Stadtverwaltung, Bahnhofstr. 1, 06449 Aschersleben
Asperg: Stadtarchiv, Schulstr. 12, 71674 Asperg, Postfach 1254, 71674 Asperg
Attendorn: Stadtarchiv, Rathaus, 57439 Attendorn, Postfach 420, 57428 Attendorn
Aub: Stadtarchiv, Rathaus, Marktplatz 1, 97239 Aub
Augsburg: Stadtarchiv, Fuggerstr. 12, 86150 Augsburg
Auma (Thüringen): Stadtverwaltung, Stadtarchiv, Marktberg 9, 07955 Auma (Thüringen)
Babenhausen: Stadtarchiv, Burgmannenhaus, Post: Stadtverwaltung, 64832 Babenhausen (Hessen), Postfach 1109, 64824 Babenhausen (Hessen)
Backnang: Stadtarchiv, Maubacher Str. 60-22, 71522 Backnang, Postfach 1569, 71505 Backnang
Bad Abbach: Stadtarchiv, Markt Bad Abbach, Kaiser-Karl-V.-Allee 12, 93077 Bad Abbach
Bad Bellingen: Stadtarchiv, 79415 Bad Bellingen
Bad Bentheim: Stadtarchiv, Stadtverwaltung, Schloßstr. 2 A, 48455 Bad Bentheim
Bad Bergzabern: Verbandsgemeindearchiv, Schloß, 76887 Bad Bergzabern
Bad Berka: Stadtarchiv, Zeughausplatz 11, 99438 Bad Berka, Post: Stadtverwaltung Bad Berka, Marktplatz 10, Postfach 20, 99438 Bad Berka
Bad Berleburg: Stadtarchiv, Stadtverwaltung, Poststr. 42, 57319 Bad Berleburg
Bad Bevensen: Archiv der Samtgemeinde Bevensen sowie der Stadt Bad Bevensen, Hauptamt, Rathaus, Lindenstr. 1, 29549 Bad Bevensen
Bad Blankenburg: Stadtverwaltung Bad Blankenburg, Stadtarchiv, Markt 1, 07422 Bad Blankenburg, Dienstsitz: Bürgerhaus, Untere Markststr. 16, 07422 Bad Blankenburg
Bad Buchau: Stadtarchiv, Stadtverwaltung, 88422 Bad Buchau
Bad Camberg: Stadtarchiv, Stadtverwaltung, Am Amthof 15, 65520 Bad Camberg
Bad Driburg: Stadtarchiv, Stadtverwaltung, Rathausstr. 2, 33014 Bad Driburg
Bad Dürkheim: Stadtarchiv, Stadthaus, Mannheimer Str. 24, 67098 Bad Dürkheim
Bad Dürrheim: Stadtarchiv, Postfach 1465, 78068 Bad Dürrheim
Bad Ems: Stadtarchiv, Postfach 1153, Römerstr. 97, 56130 Bad Ems
Baden-Baden: Stadtarchiv, Küferstr. 3, 76530 Baden-Baden, Postfach 621, 76520 Baden-Baden
Bad Friedrichshall: Stadtarchiv, Stadtverwaltung, 74177 Bad Friedrichshall
Bad Hersfeld: Stadtarchiv, Am Treppchen 1, 36251 Bad Hersfeld
Bad Homburg: Stadtarchiv, Gotisches Haus, Tannenwaldweg 102, 61350 Bad Homburg
Bad Honnef: Stadtarchiv, Stadtverwaltung, 53604 Bad Honnef, Postfach 1740, 53587 Bad Honnef
Bad Kissingen: Stadtarchiv, Villa Bringfriede, Promenadestr. 6, 97688 Bad Kissingen
Bad König: Stadtarchiv, Magistrat der Stadt, Schloßplatz 3, 64732 Bad König
Bad Königshofen im Grabfeld: Stadtarchiv, Marktplatz 2, 97631 Bad Königshofen im Grabfeld
Bad Kreuznach: Stadtarchiv, Schloßparkmuseum, Dessauer Str. 49, 55545 Bad Kreuznach, Postfach 563, 55529 Bad Kreuznach
Bad Laasphe: Stadtarchiv, Stadtverwaltung, Mühlenstr. 20, 57334 Bad Laasphe
Bad Langensalza: Stadtverwaltung Bad Langensalza, Stadtarchiv, Markt 1, 99947 Bad Langensalza, Dienstsitz: Kleinspehnstr. 20/21, 99947 Bad Langensalza
Bad Lauterberg im Harz: Stadtarchiv, Rathaus, Ritscherstr. 13, 37431 Bad Lauterberg im Harz, Postfach 340, 37423

Bad Lauterberg im Harz
Bad Liebenwerda: Stadtarchiv Bad Liebenwerda, Markt 1, 04924 Bad Liebenwerda
Bad Lippspringe: Stadtarchiv, Stadtverwaltung, Friedrich-Wilhelm-Weber-Platz 1, 33175 Bad Lippspringe, Postfach 1480, 33169 Bad Lippspringe
Bad Mergentheim: Stadtarchiv, Hans-Heinrich-Ehrler-Platz 35, 97980 Bad Mergentheim
Bad Münder am Deister: Stadtarchiv, Rathaus, 31848 Bad Münder, Postfach 1140, 31841 Bad Münder
Bad Münstereifel: Stadtarchiv, Marktstr. 11, 53902 Bad Münstereifel, Postfach 1240, 53896 Bad Münstereifel
Bad Nauheim: Stadtarchiv, Rathaus, Friedrichstr. 3, 61231 Bad Nauheim, Postfach 1669, 61216 Bad Nauheim
Bad Neuenahr-Ahrweiler: Stadtarchiv, Hauptstr. 116, 53474 Bad Neuenahr-Ahrweiler, Postfach 101051, 53448 Bad Neuenahr-Ahrweiler
Bad Neustadt an der Saale: Stadtarchiv, Alte Pfarrgasse 3, 97616 Bad Neustadt an der Saale, Postfach 1640, 97615 Bad Neustadt an der Saale
Bad Oeynhausen: Stadtarchiv, Bahnhofstr. 43, 32545 Bad Oeynhausen, Postfach, 32543 Bad Oeynhausen
Bad Oldesloe: Stadtarchiv, Rathaus, Markt 5, 23843 Bad Oldesloe
Bad Pyrmont: Stadtarchiv, Bismarckstr. 14, 31812 Bad Pyrmont, Postfach 1630, 31798 Bad Pyrmont
Bad Reichenhall: Stadtarchiv, Stadtverwaltung, Rathausplatz 1 und 8, 83435 Bad Reichenhall, Postfach 1140, 83421 Bad Reichenhall
Bad Sachsa: Stadtarchiv, Bismarckstr. 1, 37441 Bad Sachsa, Postfach 1260, 37438 Bad Sachsa
Bad Säckingen: Stadtarchiv, Bürgermeisteramt, Rathausplatz 1, 79713 Bad Säckingen, Postfach 1143, 79702 Bad Säckingen
Bad Salzdetfurth: Stadtarchiv, Rathaus, Oberstr. 6, 31162 Bad Salzdetfurth

Bad Salzuflen: Stadtarchiv, Martin-Luther-Str. 2, 32105 Bad Salzuflen
Bad Salzungen: Stadtverwaltung Bad Salzungen, Stadtarchiv, Postfach 5, 36421 Bad Salzungen, Dienstsitz: Ratsstr. 2, 36433 Bad Salzungen
Bad Schandau: Stadtarchiv, Ernst-Thälmann-Str. 3, 01814 Bad Schandau
Bad Schussenried: Stadtarchiv, Stadtverwaltung, 88427 Bad Schussenried
Bad Schwalbach: Stadtarchiv, Stadtverwaltung, 65307 Bad Schwalbach
Bad Schwartau: Stadtarchiv, Schillerstr. 8, 23611 Bad Schwartau
Bad Segeberg: Stadtarchiv, Oldesloer Str. 20, 23795 Bad Segeberg
Bad Soden: Stadtarchiv, Magistrat der Stadt, 65812 Bad Soden am Taunus
Bad Sooden-Allendorf: Stadtarchiv, Stadtverwaltung, Rathaus, 37242 Bad Sooden-Allendorf
Bad Tennstedt: Verwaltungsmeinschaft Bad Tennstedt, Stadtarchiv, Markt 1, 99955 Bad Tennstedt
Bad Urach: Stadtarchiv, Elsachstr. 7, Städt, Kurverwaltung, 72574 Bad Urach (Württemberg)
Bad Vilbel: Stadtarchiv, Altes Rathaus, Am Marktplatz 5, 61118 Bad Vilbel
Bad Waldsee: Stadtarchiv, nächst St. Peter, Klosterhof 3, 88339 Bad Waldsee, Postfach 1420, 88331 Bad Waldsee
Bad Wildungen: Stadtarchiv, Stadtverwaltung, 34537 Bad Wildungen, Postfach 1563, 34525 Bad Wildungen
Bad Wilsnack: Amts- und Stadtarchiv, Am Markt 1, 19334 Bad Wilsnack
Bad Wimpfen: Stadtarchiv, 74206 Bad Wimpfen, Postfach 120, 74200 Bad Wimpfen
Bad Windsheim: Stadtarchiv, Stadtverwaltung, Marktplatz 1, 91438 Bad Windsheim, Postfach 260, 91425 Bad Windsheim
Bad Wörishofen: Stadtarchiv, Rathaus, Bgm.-Ledermann-Str. 1, 86825 Bad Wörishofen, Postfach 1663, 86819 Bad Wörishofen
Baesweiler: Stadtarchiv, Mariastr. 2,

52499 Baesweiler, Postfach 1180, 52490 Baesweiler

Balingen: Stadtarchiv, Postfach 1840, 72336 Balingen

Ballenstedt: Stadtarchiv, Stadtverwaltung, Rathausplatz 12, 06493 Ballenstedt

Bamberg: Stadtarchiv, Untere Sandstr. 30a, 96049 Bamberg

Barnstorf: Samtgemeindearchiv, Am Markt 4, 49406 Barnstorf, Postfach 140, 49406 Barnstorf

Barntrup: Stadtarchiv, Stadtverwaltung, Mittelstr. 38, 32683 Barntrup, Postfach 1320, 32679 Barntrup

Barsinghausen: Stadtarchiv, Rathaus II am Bahnhof, 30890 Barsinghausen

Barth: Stadtarchiv, Teergang 2, 18356 Barth

Bassum: Stadtarchiv, Mittelstr. 4, 27211 Bassum

Baunatal: Stadtarchiv, Marktplatz 14, 34225 Baunatal

Bautzen: Stadtarchiv, Stadtverwaltung, Lessingstr. 7c, 02625 Bautzen, Postfach 1109, 02607 Bautzen

Bayreuth: Stadtarchiv, Maxstr. 64, Postfach 101052, 95410 Bayreuth

Bebra: Stadtarchiv, Hauptamt, Rathausmarkt 1, 36179 Bebra

Beckum: Stadtarchiv. See Kreis Warendorf

Bedburg: Stadtarchiv, Stadtverwaltung, 50181 Bedburg, Postfach 1253, 50173 Bedburg

Beelen: Gemeindearchiv. See Kreis Warendorf

Beerfelden: Stadtarchiv, Metzkeil 1, 64743 Beerfelden

Beeskow: Stadtarchiv, Liebknechstr. 13/14, 15848 Beeskow

Belgern: Stadtarchiv, Markt 3, 04874 Belgern

Bensheim: Archiv der Stadt Bensheim, An der Stadtmühle 3, 64625 Bensheim

Berchtesgaden: Archiv des Marktes, Rathausplatz 1, 83471 Berchtesgaden

Bergen: Stadtarchiv, Am Museum 2, 29303 Bergen, Postfach 1199, 29296 Bergen

Bergisch Gladbach: Stadtarchiv, Hauptstr. 310, 51465 Bergisch Gladbach, Postfach 200920, 51439 Bergisch Gladbach

Bergkamen: Stadtarchiv, Rathaus, 59192 Bergkamen

Bergneustadt: Stadtarchiv, Othestr. 2-4, 51702 Bergneustadt

Bernau: Stadtarchiv, Bürgermeisterstr. 1, 16321 Bernau

Bernburg: Stadtarchiv. See Landkreis Bernburg

Bersenbrück: Archiv der Samtgemeinde, Rathaus, Lindenstr. 2, 49593 Bersenbrück

Besigheim: Stadtarchiv, Marktplatz 12, 74354 Besigheim

Biberach: Stadtarchiv Biberach. See Landkreis Biberach

Biblis: Gemeindearchiv, Rathaus, Darmstädter Str. 25, 68647

Biebesheim: Gemeindearchiv, Bahnhofstr. 2, 64584 Biebesheim/Rhein, Postfach 1145, 64580 Biebesheim/Rhein

Bielefeld: Stadtarchiv und Landesgeschichtliche Bibliothek, Rohrteichstr. 19, 33602 Bielefeld, Postfach 100111, 33501 Bielefeld

Bietigheim-Bissingen: Stadtarchiv, Hauptstr. 61/63, 74321 Bietigheim-Bissingen, Postfach 1762, 74307 Bietigheim-Bissingen

Bingen am Rhein: Stadtarchiv, Stadtverwaltung, 55411 Bingen am Rhein, Postfach 1751, 55387 Bingen am Rhein

Bischofswerda: Stadtarchiv, Rudolf-Breitscheid-Str. 7, 01877 Bischofswerda, Postfach 1173, 01871 Bischofswerda

Bischofswiesen: Gemeindearchiv, Rathaus, 83483 Bischofswiesen

Bitterfeld: Stadtarchiv, Markt 7, 06749 Bitterfeld

Blankenfelde: Amtsarchiv Blankenfelde-Mahlow, Karl-Marx-Str. 4, 15827 Blankenfelde

Blankenheim: Gemeindearchiv, Rathausplatz 16, 53945 Blankenheim

Blaubeuren: Stadtarchiv, Karlstr. 2, 89143 Blaubeuren

Blomberg: Stadtarchiv, 32825 Blomberg,

Postfach 1452, 32820 Blomberg
Bocholt: Stadtarchiv, Münsterstr. 76, 46397 Bocholt
Bochum: Stadtarchiv, Kronenstr. 47, 44789 Bochum, Postfach 102269, 44777 Bochum
Bockenem: Stadtarchiv, Rathaus, 31167 Bockenem
Bodenwerder: Stadtarchiv, Stadtverwaltung, Münchhausenplatz 1, 37619 Bodenwerder
Böblingen: Stadtarchiv, Rathaus, 71032 Böblingen
Bönen: Gemeindearchiv, Bahnhofstr. 235, 59199 Bönen
Bomlitz: Gemeindearchiv, Schulstr. 4, 29699 Bomlitz
Bonn: Stadtarchiv und Stadthistorische Bibliothek, Stadthaus, Berliner Platz 2, 53103 Bonn
Borgentreich: Stadtarchiv, Am Rathaus 13, 34434 Borgentreich, Postfach 4, 34432 Borgentreich
Borgholzhausen: Stadtarchiv, Rathaus, Schulstr. 5, 33829 Borgholzhausen, Postfach 1261, 33826 Borgholzhausen
Borken: Stadtarchiv, Stadtverwaltung, Im Piepershagen 17, Postfach 1764, 46322 Borken
Borna: Stadtarchiv, Markt 1, 04552 Borna
Bornheim: Stadtarchiv, Rathausstr. 2, 53332 Bornheim
Bottrop: Stadtarchiv, Blumenstr. 12-14, Postfach 101554, 46215 Bottrop
Bovenden: Plesse-Archiv, Rathausplatz 1, 37120 Bovenden
Brackenheim: Stadtarchiv, Verwaltungsstelle Hausen, Nordhausener Str. 4, 74336 Brackenheim-Hausen (Württemberg)
Brake (Unterweser): Stadtarchiv, Rathaus, Schrabberdeich 1, 26919 Brake (Unterweser), Postfach 1453, 26914 Brake (Unterweser)
Brakel: Stadtarchiv, Rathaus, Am Markt, 33034 Brakel
Brandenburg: Stadtarchiv, Altstädtischer Markt 8, 14770 Brandenburg
Brand-Erbisdorf: Stadtarchiv, Haasen-

weg, 09618 Brand-Erbisdorf, Postfach 17, 09614 Brand-Erbisdorf
Braunlage: Stadtarchiv, Stadtverwaltung, Herzog-Johann-Aolbrecht-Str. 2, 38700 Braunlage
Braunschweig: Stadtarchiv, 38100 Braunschweig, Löwenwall 18 B, Postfach 3309, 38023 Braunschweig
Breckerfeld: Stadtarchiv, Rathaus, Frankfurter Str. 38, 58339 Breckerfeld, Postfach 180, 58333 Breckerfeld
Breisach am Rhein: Stadtarchiv, Rathaus, Münsterplatz 1, 79206 Breisach am Rhein
Bremerhaven: Stadtarchiv, Stadthaus 5, Postfach 210360, 27524 Bremerhaven
Bremervörde: Stadtarchiv, Rathaus, Rathausmarkt 1, 27432 Bremervörde, Postfach 1465, 27424 Bremervörde
Bretten: Stadtarchiv, Untere Kirchgasse 9, 75015 Bretten
Brieselang: Amtsarchiv Brieselang, Vorholzstr. 57, 14656 Brieselang
Brilon: Stadtarchiv, Amtshaus, 59929 Brilon
Bruchhausen-Vilsen: Samtgemeindearchiv, Vilser Schulstr. 17, 27305 Bruchhausen-Vilsen
Bruchsal: Stadtarchiv, Am Alten Schloß 4, 76646 Bruchsal, Postfach 2320, 76613 Bruchsal
Brüggen: Gemeindearchiv, Klosterstr. 38, 41379 Brüggen, Postfach 1252, 41374 Brüggen
Brühl: Stadtarchiv, Rathaus, Franziskanerhof, Alte Feuerwache, 50321 Brühl
Buchen: Stadtarchiv, Wimpinaplatz 3, 74722 Buchen (Odenwald)
Buchholz in der Nordheide: Archiv der Stadt, Königsberger Str. 9, 21244 Buchholz in der Nordheide
Büchen: Amtsarchiv Büchen, Amtsplatz, 21514 Büchen
Bückeburg: Stadtarchiv, Schloß, 31675 Bückeburg, Postfach 1350, 31665 Bückeburg
Büdingen: Stadtarchiv, Zum Stadtgraben 7, Post: Stadtverwaltung, 63654 Büding-

en, Postfach 1360, 63643 Büdingen
Bühl: Stadtgeschichtliches Institut, Hauptstr. 92, 77815 Bühl, Postfach 1420, 77804 Bühl
Bünde: Stadtarchiv, Saarlandstr. 5, 32257 Bünde
Büren: Stadtarchiv, Rathaus, Königstr. 16, 33142 Büren
Büttelborn: Gemeindearchiv, 64572 Büttelborn, Postfach 102, 64570 Büttelborn
Burg auf Fehmarn: Stadtarchiv, Rathaus, Am Markt 1, 23769 Burg auf Fehmarn, Postfach 1140, 23763 Burg auf Fehmarn
Burg bei Magdeburg: Stadtarchiv. See Landkreis Jerichower Land
Burgbernheim: Stadtarchiv, Rathaus, Rathausplatz 1, Postfach 47, 91593 Burgbernheim
Burgdorf: Stadtarchiv, Rathaus II, Vor dem Hann. Tor 1, 31303 Burgdorf
Burghausen: Stadtarchiv, Rathaus, 84489 Burghausen, Postfach 1240, 84480 Burghausen
Burgkunstadt: Stadtarchiv, Vogtei 5, 96224 Burgkunstadt, Postfach 1255, 96220 Burgkunstadt
Buttstädt: Stadtverwaltung Buttstädt, Stadtarchiv, Lohstr. 6a, 99628 Buttstädt (Thuringen)
Butzbach: Stadtarchiv Butzbach, Solms-Braunfelser-Hof (Museum), Färbgasse 16, Post: Marktplatz 1, 35510 Butzbach
Buxtehude: Stadtarchiv, Stavenort 5, 21614 Buxtehude, Postfach 1555, 21605 Buxtehude
Calw: Stadtarchiv, Im Zwinger 20, 75365 Calw
Camburg: Stadtverwaltung Camburg, Stadtarchiv, Rathausstr. 1, 07774 Camburg
Castrop-Rauxel: Stadtarchiv, Europaplatz 1, 44575 Castrop-Rauxel
Celle: Stadtarchiv, Westerceller Str. 4, 29227 Celle
Cham: Stadtarchiv, Spitalplatz 22, 93413 Cham
Chemnitz: Stadtarchiv, Aue 16, 09112 Chemnitz
Clausthal-Zellerfeld: Archiv der Samtgemeinde Oberharz mit den Mitgliedsgemeinden Altenau, Clausthal-Zellerfeld, Schulenberg im Oberharz und Wildemann, Hindenburgplatz 8, 38678 Clausthal-Zellerfeld
Coburg: Stadtarchiv, Rosengasse 1, 96450 Coburg, Postfach 3042, 96419 Coburg
Cochem: Stadtarchiv, Stadtverwaltung, Markt 1, 56812 Cochem, Postfach 1444, 56804 Cochem
Coesfeld: Stadtarchiv, Walkenbrückenstr. 25, 48653 Coesfeld, Postfach 1729, 48637 Coesfeld
Cossebaude: Gemeindearchiv, Gemeindeverwaltung, Dresdner Str., 01462 Cossebaude
Coswig: Stadtarchiv, Hauptstr. 18/20, 01640 Coswig
Cottbus: Stadtarchiv Cottbus, August-Bebel-Str. 85, 03046
Creglingen: Stadtarchiv, Rathaus, 97993 Creglingen, Postfach 20, 97991 Creglingen
Crimmitschau: Stadtarchiv, Leipziger Str. 76, 08451 Crimmitschau
Cuxhaven: Stadtarchiv, Altenwalder Chaussee 2, 27474 Cuxhaven
Dahlem: Gemeindearchiv, Rathaus, Hauptstr. 23, 53949 Dahlem
Dahme (Mark): Amtsarchiv Dahme, Hauptstr. 48/49, 15936 Dahme (Mark)
Dannenberg/Elbe: Gemeindearchiv (Samtgemeinde), 29451 Dannenberg, Postfach 1260, 29446 Dannenberg/Elbe
Darmstadt: Stadtarchiv, Karolinenplatz 3, 64289 Darmstadt
Dassel: Stadtarchiv, Postfach, 37582 Dassel
Datteln: Stadtarchiv, Verwaltungsgebäude, Kolpingstr. 1, 45711 Datteln
Deggendorf: Stadtarchiv, Östlicher Stadtgraben 28, 94469 Deggendorf
Delitzsch: Stadtarchiv. See Landkreis Delitzsch
Delmenhorst: Stadtarchiv, Rathaus, 27747 Delmenhorst

Dessau (Anhalt): Stadtarchiv, Lange Gasse 22, 06844 Dessau (Anhalt)
Dieburg: Stadtarchiv, Stadtverwaltung, 64807 Dieburg, Postfach 1207, 64802 Dieburg
Diemelstadt-Rhoden: Stadtarchiv, Stadtverwaltung, 34474 Diemelstadt-Rhoden
Diepholz: Stadtarchiv, Rathausmarkt 1, 49356 Diepholz, Postfach 1620, 49346 Diepholz
Dießen am Ammersee: Gemeindearchiv, Marktplatz 1, 86911 Dießen am Ammersee
Dietenheim: Stadtarchiv, Königstr. 63, 89165 Dietenheim
Dietzenbach: Stadtarchiv, Stadtverwaltung, Offenbacher Str. 11, 63128 Dietzenbach, Postfach 1120, 63111 Dietzenbach
Diez: Stadtarchiv, Stadtverwaltung, Pfaffengasse 27, 65582 Diez (Lahn)
Dillenburg: Stadtarchiv, Stadtverwaltung, Postfach 429, 35664 Dillenburg
Dillingen: Stadtarchiv, Königstr. 38, 89407 Dillingen an der Donau, Postfach 1210, 89402 Dillingen an der Donau
Dingelstädt: Stadtverwaltung Dingelstädt, Stadtarchiv, Geschwister-Scholl-Str. 28, 37351 Dingelstädt
Dingolfing: Stadtarchiv, Rathaus, 84130 Dingolfing
Dinkelsbühl: Stadtarchiv, Rathaus, Segringer Str. 30, 91550 Dinkelsbühl
Dinslaken: Stadtarchiv, Rathaus, Platz d'Agen 1, 46535 Dinslaken, Postfach 100540, 46525 Dinslaken
Ditzingen: Stadtarchiv, Am Laien 4, 71254 Ditzingen, Postfach 1455, 71252 Ditzingen
Doberlug-Kirchhain: Stadtarchiv, Rathaus, Am Markt 8, 03251 Doberlug-Kirchhain
Döbeln: Stadtarchiv, Rathaus, Obermarkt 1, 04720 Döbeln
Dörentrup: Gemeindearchiv, Hauptstr. 2, 32694 Dörentrup, Postfach 1154, 32690 Dörentrup
Donaueschingen: Stadtarchiv, Rathaus, Rathausplatz 1, 78166 Donaueschingen
Donauwörth: Stadtarchiv, Rathaus, 86609 Donauwörth, Postfach 1453, 86604 Donauwörth
Donzdorf: Stadtarchiv - Heimatgeschichtliche Sammlungen, Stadtverwaltung, Hauptstr. 44, 73072 Donzdorf, Postfach 1363, 73069 Donzdorf, Dienstsitz: Hauptstr. 60, 73072 Donzdorf
Dorfen: Stadtarchiv, Justus-von-Liebig-Str. 5, 84405 Dorfen
Dormagen: Stadtarchiv, Gabrielstr. 6, 41542 Dormagen, Postfach 100120, 41538 Dormagen
Dornburg: Stadtverwaltung Dornburg, Stadtarchiv, Markt 21, 07778 Dornburg
Dornstetten: Stadtarchiv, 72280 Dornstetten
Dorsten: Stadtarchiv, Im Werth 6 (Bildungzentrum Maria-Lindenhof), 46282 Dorsten
Dortmund: Stadtarchiv, Friedensplatz 5, 44122 Dortmund, Postfach 105053
Dossenheim: Gemeindearchiv, Am Rathausplatz 1, 69221 Dossenheim, Postfach 1165, 69215 Dossenheim
Dransfeld: Archiv der Samtgemeinde und Stadt, Kirchplatz 1, 37125 Dransfeld
Dreieich: Stadtarchiv, Buchschlager Allee 8, 63303 Dreieich, Postfach 102020, 63266 Dreieich
Dresden: Stadtarchiv, Marienallee 3, 01099 Dresden, Postfach 120020, 01001 Dresden
Drolshagen: Stadtarchiv, Hagener Str. 9, 57489 Drolshagen
Duderstadt: Stadtarchiv, Christian-Blank-Str.1, 37115 Duderstadt, Postfach 1160, 37104 Duderstadt
Dülmen: Stadtarchiv, Stadtverwaltung, Markt 1-3, 48249 Dülmen, Postfach 1551, 48236 Dülmen
Düren: Stadtarchiv. See Kreis Düren
Düsseldorf: Stadtarchiv, Heinrich-Ehrhardt-Str. 61, 40468 Düsseldorf
Duisburg: Stadtarchiv, Karmelplatz 5, 47049 Duisburg
Eberbach (Baden): Stadtarchiv, Stadtverwaltung, 69412 Eberbach (Baden),

Postfach 1134, 69401 Eberbach (Baden)
Ebermannstadt: Stadtarchiv, Rathaus, 91320 Ebermannstadt, Postfach 43, 91316 Ebermannstadt
Ebersbach an der Fils: Stadtarchiv, Postfach 1129, 73055 Ebersbach an der Fils
Ebersberg: Stadtarchiv, Rathaus, Marienplatz 1, 85560 Ebersberg
Eberswalde: Stadtarchiv. See Landkreis Barnim
Eckernförde: Stadtarchiv, Gartenstr. 10, 24340 Eckernförde, Postfach 1420, 24334 Eckernförde
Edenkoben: Stadtarchiv, Verbandsgemeinde, 67480 Edenkoben (Landesarchiv Speyer serves as the depository)
Egestorf: Gemeindearchiv, Hinter den Höfen 9, 21272 Egestorf
Eggenfelden: Stadtarchiv, Rathausplatz 1, Postfach 1220, 84307 Eggenfelden
Ehingen: Stadtarchiv, Stadtverwaltung, Marktplatz 1, 89584 Ehingen (Donau)
Ehrenfriedersdorf: Stadtarchiv, Stadtverwaltung, Markt 1, 09427 Ehrenfriedersdorf
Eichstätt: Stadtarchiv, Marktplatz 11, 85072 Eichstätt, Postfach 1344, 85067 Eichstätt
Eilenburg: Stadtarchiv, Marktplatz 1, 04838 Eilenburg
Einbeck: Stadtarchiv, Steinweg 11, 37574 Einbeck, Postfach 1824, 37559 Einbeck
Eisenach: Stadtverwaltung Eisenach, Stadtarchiv, Am Markt 24, 99817 Eisenach
Eisenberg: Stadtverwaltung Eisenberg, Stadtarchiv, Postfach 22, 07601 Eisenberg, Dienstsitz: Markt 27, 07607 Eisenberg
Eisenhüttenstadt: Stadtarchiv, Am Trockendock 1a, 15890 Eisenhüttenstadt
Eisfeld: Museum Otto Ludwig, Museum für regionale Volkskunde, Stadtarchiv, Markt 2, Schloß, 98673 Eisfeld
Lutherstadt Eisleben: Stadtarchiv, Markt 1, 06295 Lutherstadt Eisleben
Eislingen: Stadtarchiv, Rathaus, 73054 Eislingen

Eitorf: Gemeindearchiv, Markt 1, 53783 Eitorf
Elbmarsch: Samtgemeindearchiv, Elbuferstr. 98, 21436 Marschacht
Ellingen: Stadtarchiv, Franziskanerkloster, Hausner Gasse 7, 91792 Ellingen
Ellwangen: Stadtarchiv, Stadtverwaltung, Spitalstr. 4, 73479 Ellwangen (Jagst)
Elsdorf: Gemeindearchiv, Gladbacher Str. 111, 50189 Elsdorf, Postfach 1155, 50182 Elsdorf
Elsterberg: Stadtarchiv, Markt 1, 07985 Elsterberg
Elsterwerda: Stadtarchiv, Hauptstr. 13, 04910 Elsterwerda
Elterlein: Stadtarchiv, Rathaus/Markt, 09481 Elterlein
Eltville am Rhein: Stadtarchiv, Stadtverwaltung, Matheus-Müller-Str. 3, 65343 Eltville am Rhein, Postfach 65334 Eltville am Rhein
Elze: Stadtarchiv, Rathaus, Hauptstr. 61, 31008 Elze, Postfach 1353, 31003 Elze
Emden: Stadtarchiv, Rathaus am Delft, Postfach 2254, 26721 Emden
Emmendingen: Stadtarchiv, Kirchstr. 7, 79312 Emmendingen (Baden)
Emmerich: Stadtarchiv, Stadtverwaltung, Martinikirchgang 2, 46446 Emmerich
Emsbüren: Gemeindearchiv, Markt 18, 48488 Emsbüren
Emsdetten: Stadtarchiv, Am Markt 1, 48282 Emsdetten, Postfach 1254, 48270 Emsdetten
Endingen: Stadtarchiv, Rathaus, 79346 Endingen
Engen: Stadtarchiv, Rathaus, 78234 Engen (Hegau)
Enger: Stadtarchiv, Kirchplatz 10 (Widukind-Museum), 32130 Enger
Ennepetal: Stadtarchiv, Lindenstr. 8, 58256 Ennepetal
Ennigerloh: Stadtarchiv. See Kreis Warendorf
Eppingen: Stadtarchiv, Bürgermeisteramt, Rathausstr. 14, 75031 Eppingen, Postfach 265, 75021 Eppingen
Eppstein: Stadtarchiv, Rathaus II,

Rossertstr. 21, 65817 Eppstein (Taunus)
Erbach: Stadtarchiv, Stadtverwaltung, Neckarstr. 3, 64711 Erbach
Erding: Archiv der Stadt, Landshuter Str. 1, 85435 Erding
Erftstadt: Stadtarhiv, Rathaus, Holzdamm 10, 50374 Erftstadt
Erfurt: Stadt- und Verwaltungsarchiv, Gotthardstr. 21, 99084 Erfurt, Postfach 243, 99005 Erfurt
Erkelenz: Stadtarchiv, Johannismarkt 17, 41812 Erkelenz
Erkrath: Stadtarchiv, Bahnstr. 16, 40699 Erkrath
Erlangen: Stadtarchiv, Cedernstr. 1, 91054 Erlangen
Erwitte: Stadtarchiv, Stadtverwaltung, 59597 Erwitte, Postfach 1065, 59591 Erwitte
Eschborn: Stadtarchiv, Eschenplatz 1, 65760 Eschborn (Taunus), Postfach 5980, 65734 Eschborn (Taunus)
Eschede: Samtgemeindearchiv, Am Glockenkolk 1, 29346 Eschede
Eschershausen: Stadtarchiv, Postfach 1269, 37629 Eschershausen
Eschwege: Stadtarchiv, Stadtverwaltung, Postfach 1560, 37269 Eschwege
Espelkamp: Stadtarchiv, Rathaus, Wilhelm-Kern-Platz 1, 32339 Espelkamp
Essen: Stadtarchiv, Steeler Str. 29, 45121 Essen
Esslingen: Stadtarchiv, Marktplatz 20, 73728 Esslingen am Neckar, Postfach 269, 73726 Esslingen am Neckar
Esterland: Amtsarchiv Esterland, Hauptstr. 58, 03253 Schönborn
Ettlingen: Stadtarchiv, Schloß, 76261 Ettlingen, Postfach 0762, 76261 Ettlingen
Euskirchen: Stadtarchiv, Kölner Str. 75, 53879 Euskirchen, Postfach 1169, 53861 Euskirchen
Eutin: Stadtarchiv, Sparkasse Ostholstein, Am Rosengarten, 23701 Eutin, Postfach 328, 23693 Eutin
Everswinkel: See Kreis Warendorf
Extertal: Gemeindearchiv und Fotothek, Bösingfeld, 32699 Extertal
Falkenberg (Uebigau): Amtsarchiv

Falkenberg (Uebigau), Markt 3, 04895 Falkenberg/Elster
Falkenberg-Höhe: Amtsarchiv Falkenberg-Höhe, Lindenstr. 2, 15848 Falkenberg (Mark)
Falkensee: Stadtarchiv, Falkenhagener Str. 45, 14612 Falkensee
Falkenstein (Vogtland): Stadtarchiv, Clara-Zetkin-Str. 1, 08223 Falkenstein (Vogtland)
Fallingbostel: Stadtarchiv, Stadtverwaltung, Vogteistr. 1, 29683 Fallingbostel
Fehrbellin: Amtsarchiv Fehrbellin, Johann-Sebastian-Bach-Str. 6, 16833 Fehrbellin
Fellbach: Stadtmuseum und Archiv, Hintere Str. 26, 70734
Feuchtwangen: Stadtarchiv, Rathaus, Hindenburgstr. 5/7, 91555 Feuchtwangen, Postfach 1257, 91552 Feuchtwangen
Filderstadt: Stadtarchiv, Lange Str. 83, 70794 Filderstadt-Sielmingen, Postfach 1180, 70772 Filderstadt
Finnentrop: Gemeindearchiv, 57413 Finnentrop, Postfach 220, 57402 Finnentrop
Finsterwalde: Stadtarchiv, Schloßstr. 7-8, 03238 Finsterwalde
Flensburg: Stadtarchiv, Rathaus, 24937 Flensburg, Postfach 2742, 24917 Flensburg
Flöha: Stadtarchiv, Augustusburger Str. 90, 09557 Flöha
Forchheim: Stadtarchiv, St.-Martin-Str. 8, 91301 Forchheim, Postfach 85, 91299 Forchheim
Forst (Lausitz): Stadtarchiv, Promenade 9, 03149 Forst (Lausitz)
Frankenberg (Sachsen): Stadtarchiv, Markt 15, 09669 Frankenberg (Sachsen)
Frankenthal: Stadtarchiv, Rathaus, 67227 Frankenthal (Pfalz)
Frankfurt am Main: Institut für Stadtgeschichte, Karmelitergasse 5, 60311 Frankfurt am Main
Frankfurt/Oder: Stadtarchiv, Collegienstr. 8/9, 15230 Frankfurt/Oder
Frauenau: Gemeindearchiv, Rathaus, Rathausplatz 4, 94258 Frauenau

Frechen: Stadtarchiv, Rathaus, 50226 Frechen, Postfach 1960, 50209 Frechen
Freiberg (Sachsen): Stadtarchiv, Obermarkt 24, 09596 Freiberg (Sachsen)
Freiburg im Breisgau: Stadtarchiv, Grünwälder Str. 15, 79098 Freiburg im Breisgau
Freilassing: Stadtarchiv, Stadtverwaltung, Münchener Str. 15, 83395 Freilassing, Postfach 1620, 83383 Freilassing
Freising: Stadtarchiv, Rathaus, Obere Hauptstr. 2, 85354 Freising
Freren: Stadtarchiv, Stadtverwaltung, Markt 1, 49832 Freren
Freudenberg: Stadtarchiv, Stadtverwaltung, Bahnhofstr. 18, 57258 Freudenberg
Freudenstadt: Stadtarchiv, Stadtverwaltung, Marktplatz 1, 72250 Freudenstadt
Friedberg (Bayern): Stadtarchiv, Pfarrstr. 6, 86313 Friedberg (Bayern), Postfach 1453, 86313 Friedberg (Bayern)
Friedberg (Hessen): Stadtarchiv im Bibliothekszentrum Klosterbau, Augustinergasse 8, 61169 Friedberg (Hessen), Postfach 100964, 61149 Friedberg (Hessen)
Friedrichroda: Stadtverwaltung, Stadt- und Kurbibliothek, Stadtarchiv, Hauptstr. 45, 99894 Friedrichroda
Friedrichsdorf: Stadtverwaltung, Hugenottenstr. 55, 61381 Friedrichsdorf, Postfach 1340, 61364 Friedrichsdorf
Friedrichshafen: Stadtarchiv, Katharinenstr. 55, 88045 Friedrichshafen
Friedrichstadt: Stadtarchiv, Westerlilienstr. 7, 25840 Friedrichstadt
Fritzlar: Stadtarchiv, Rathaus, 34560 Fritzlar
Fröndenberg: Stadtarchiv, Rathaus, Kirchplatz 2, 58730 Fröndenberg
Fürstenau: Stadtarchiv, Postfach 1160, 49578 Fürstenau
Fürstenfeldbruck: Stadtarchiv, Fürstenfeld 3d, Post: Hauptstr. 31, 82256 Fürstenfeldbruck, Postfach 1645, 82245 Fürstenfeldbruck
Fürstenwalde: Stadtarchiv Fürstenwalde, Eisenbahnstr. 18, 15517

Fürstenwalde (im Aufbau)
Fürth: Stadtarchiv, Schloßhof 12, 90768 Fürth
Füssen: Kloster- und Stadtarchiv, Lechhalde 3, 87629 Füssen
Fulda: Stadtarchiv, Palais Buttlar, Bonifatiusplatz 1-3, 36037 Fulda
Furth im Wald: Stadtarchiv, 93437 Furth im Wald
Furtwangen: Stadtarchiv, Marktplatz 4, 78120 Furtwangen, Postfach 30, 78113 Furtwangen
Gaggenau: Stadtarchiv, Hauptstr. 71, 76571 Gaggenau, Postfach 1520, 76555 Gaggenau
Gaildorf: Stadtarchiv, Schloßstr. 20, 74405 Gaildorf, Postfach 150, 74402 Gaildorf
Gangelt: Gemeindearchiv, Burgstr. 10, 52538 Gangelt
Gangkofen: Archiv des Marktes, Marktplatz 21, 84140 Gangkofen
Garbsen: Stadtarchiv, Lehmstr. 1, 30826 Garbsen
Gardelegen: Stadtarchiv, Rathausplatz 10, 39638 Gardelegen
Garmisch-Partenkirchen: Marktarchiv, Rathausplatz 1, 82467 Garmisch-Partenkirchen
Gartz/Oder: Amtsarchiv Gartz, Stettiner Str. 15, 16307 Gartz/Oder
Gedern: Stadtarchiv, Stadtverwaltung, 63688 Gedern
Geesthacht: Stadtarchiv, Krügersches Haus, Bergedorferstr. 28, 21502 Geesthacht
Gehrden: Stadtarchiv, Kirchstr. 1-3, 30989 Gehrden
Gehren: Stadtverwaltung Gehren, Stadtarchiv, Obere Marktstr. 1, 98708 Gehren
Geilenkirchen: Stadtarchiv, Markt 9, 52511 Geilenkirchen
Geisa: Stadtverwaltung Geisa, Stadtarchiv, Marktplatz 27, 36419 Geisa
Geislingen an der Steige: Stadtarchiv, Altes Rathaus, Hauptstr. 19, 73312 Geislingen an der Steige, Postfach 1162, 73301 Geislingen an der Steige

Geithain: Stadtarchiv, Leipziger Str. 17 (Stadtbibliothek), 04643 Geithain
Geldern: Stadtarchiv, Kulturamt, Issumer Tor 36, 47608 Geldern
Gellersen: Archiv der Samtgemeinde, Dachtmisser Str. 1, 21391 Reppenstedt
Gelnhausen: Stadtarchiv, ehem. Augustaschule, Am Obermarkt, Post: Stadtverwaltung, 63571 Gelnhausen, Postfach 1763, 63557 Gelnhausen
Gelsenkirchen: Institut für Stadtgeschichte, Stadtarchiv, Bildungszentrum, Ebertstr. 19, 45875 Gelsenkirchen, Postfach 100101
Gemünden am Main: Stadtarchiv, Stadtverwaltung, Scherenbergstr. 5, 97737 Gemünden am Main
Gengenbach: Stadtarchiv, Bürgermeisteramt, 77723 Gengenbach, Postfach 1165, 77717 Gengenbach
Genthin: Stadtarchiv, Lindenstr. 2, 39307 Genthin
Georgsmarienhütte: Stadtarchiv, Museum Villa Stahmer, Carl-Stahmer-Weg 13, 49124 Georgsmarienhütte
Gera: Stadtarchiv, Prof.-Simmel-Str. 1, 07548 Gera, Postfach 100, 07501 Gera
Gerlingen: Stadtarchiv, Urbanstr. 5/1, 70839 Gerlingen
Germersheim: Stadtarchiv, Stadtverwaltung, Kolpingplatz 3, 76726 Germersheim
Gernrode: Stadtarchiv, Stadtverwaltung, Marktstr. 20, 06507 Gernrode
Gernsbach: Stadtarchiv, Stadtverwaltung, 76593 Gernsbach, Postfach 1154, 76584 Gernsbach
Gernsheim: Stadtarchiv, Stadthaus, Stadthausplatz 1, 64579 Gernsheim/Rhein, Postfach 1262, 64574 Gernsheim
Gerolzhofen: Stadtarchiv, Rathaus, Brunnengasse 5, 97447 Gerolzhofen
Gescher: Stadtarchiv, Marktplatz 1, 48712 Gescher, Postfach 1361, 48706 Gescher
Geseke: Stadtarchiv Wichburgastr. 9, 59590 Geseke, Postfach 1442, 59585 Geseke
Gevelsberg: Stadtarchiv, Am Schultenhof 1, 58265 Gevelsberg, Postfach 2360 und 2380, 58265 Gevelsberg
Geyer: Stadtarchiv, Altmarkt 1, 09468 Geyer
Giengen an der Brenz: Stadtarchiv, Kirchplatz 2, 89537 Giengen an der Brenz
Giesen: Gemeindearchiv, Rathausstr. 27, 31180 Giesen
Gießen: Stadtarchiv, Behördenzentrum, Ostanlage 45, 35390 Gießen, Postfach 110820, 35353 Gießen
Gifhorn: Stadtarchiv, Schloßstr., 38518 Gifhorn
Gladbeck: Stadtarchiv, Willy-Brandt-Platz 2, 45956 Gladbeck
Glinde: Stadtarchiv, Rathaus, Markt 1, 21509 Glinde
Glückstadt: Stadtarchiv, Brockdorff-Palais, Am Fleth 43, 25348 Glückstadt
Goch: Stadtarchiv, Stadtverwaltung, Markt 2, 47574 Goch
Göppingen: Stadtarchiv, Alter Kasten, Schloßstr. 14, 73033 Göppingen, Postfach 1149, 73011 Göppingen
Görlitz: Stadtarchiv, Untermarkt 8, 02826 Görlitz
Göttingen: Stadtarchiv, Neues Rathaus, Hiroshimaplatz 4, 37083 Göttingen, Postfach 3831, 37028 Göttingen
Golßener Land: Amtsarchiv Golßener Land, Hauptstr. 41, 15938 Golßen
Goslar: Stadtarchiv, Zehntstr. 24, 38640 Goslar, Postfach 2569, 38615 Goslar
Grabow: Stadtarchiv, Am Markt 1, 19300 Grabow
Grafenau: Stadtarchiv, Rathausgasse 1, 94481 Grafenau
Grebenau: Stadtarchiv, Stadtverwaltung, Amthof 2, 36323 Grebenau
Greifswald: Stadtarchiv, Stadtverwaltung der Hansestadt Greifswald, Postfach 253, 17461 Greifswald
Greven: Stadtarchiv, Rathausstr. 6, 48268 Greven
Grevenbroich: Stadtarchiv, 41513 Grevenbroich
Grimma: Stadtarchiv, Markt 17, 04668 Grimma
Groitzsch: Stadtarchiv, Markt 1, 04539

Groitzsch
Gronau/Leine: Stadtarchiv, Blankestr. 16, 31028 Gronau/Leine
Groß-Bieberau: Stadtarchiv, Stadtverwaltung, Marktstr. 28, 64401 Groß-Bieberau
Großbottwar: Stadtarchiv, Im Schulzentrum Lindenstr., 71723 Großbottwar
Großbreitenbach: Stadtverwaltung Großbreitenbach, Stadtarchiv, Markt 11, 98701 Großbreitenbach
Großeutersdorf: Gemeindeverwaltung Großeutersdorf, Gemeindearchiv, Am Kirchberg, 07768 Großeutersdorf
Groß-Gerau: Stadtarchiv, Stadtverwaltung, Marktplatz, 64521 Groß-Gerau, Postfach 1561, 64505 Groß-Gerau
Groß Pankow: Amtsarchiv Groß Pankow, Steindamm 51, 16929 Groß Pankow
Groß Räschen: Amtsarchiv Groß Räschen, Ernst-Thälmann-Str. 47, 01983 Groß Räschen
Groß-Umstadt: Stadtarchiv, Unterdorf 41, 64823 Groß-Umstadt/Raibach, Der Magistrat der Stadt, Markt 1, 64823 Groß-Umstadt
Grünberg: Stadtarchiv, Stadtverwaltung, Postfach 1265, 35301 Grünberg/Hessen
Guben: Stadtarchiv, Stadtverwaltung, Uferstr. 22-26, 03172 Guben
Güglingen: Stadtarchiv, Stadtverwaltung, 74361 Güglingen
Günzburg: Stadtarchiv, Schloßplatz 1, 89312 Günzburg
Güstrow: Stadtarchiv, Markt 1, 18273 Güstrow
Gütersloh: Stadtarchiv, Hohenzollernstr. 30a, 33330 Gütersloh
Gummersbach: Stadtarchiv, Rathausplatz 1, 51643 Gummersbach, Postfach 100852, 51608 Gummersbach
Gundelfingen an der Donau: Stadtarchiv, Postfach 28, 89421 Gundelfingen an der Donau
Gunzenhausen: Stadtarchiv, Rathaus, Marktplatz 23, 91710 Gunzenhausen
Haar: Gemeindearchiv, Bahnhofstr. 7, 85540 Haar b. München
Hachenburg: Stadtarchiv, Mittelstr. 2,

57627 Hachenburg, Postfach 1308, 57622 Hachenburg
Hagen (Westfalen): Stadtarchiv, Rathausstr. 12, Postfach 4249, 58042 Hagen (Westfalen)
Hainichen: Gemeindeverwaltung Hainichen, Gemeindearchiv, Dorfstr. 27, 07778 Hainichen
Halberstadt: Stadtarchiv, Domplatz 49, 38820 Halberstadt
Haldensleben: Stadtarchiv. See Ohre-Kreis
Halle/Saale: Stadtarchiv, Rathausstr. 1, 06108 Halle/Saale
Halle (Westfalen): Stadtarchiv, Kiskerstr. 2, 33790 Halle (Westfalen), Postfach 1563 und 1564, 33780 Halle (Westfalen)
Hallenberg: Stadtarchiv, Stadtverwaltung, Rathausplatz 1, 59969 Hallenberg, Postfach 1155, 59965 Hallenberg
Haltern: Stadtarchiv, Stadtbücherei, Lavesumer Str. 19, 45721 Haltern
Hameln: Stadtarchiv, Osterstr. 2 (Hochzeitshaus), 31785 Hameln
Hamm: Stadtarchiv, Altes Amtshaus Pelkum, Kamener Str. 177, 59077 Hamm, Postanschrift: Stadtverwaltung Hamm, Postfach 2449, 59061 Hamm
Hamminkeln: Gemeindearchiv, Rathaus, Brüner Str., 46499 Hamminkeln
Hanau: Stadtarchiv, Schloßplatz 2, 63450 Hanau
Hann. Münden: Stadtarchiv, Schloßplatz 5, 34346 Hann. Münden, Postfach 1528, 34335 Hann. Münden
Hannover: Stadtarchiv, Am Bokemahle 14-16, 30173 Hannover
Hanstedt: Gemeindearchiv, Gemeindeverwaltung, 21271 Hanstedt
Harburg: Stadtarchiv, Schloßstr. 1, 86655 Harburg
Haren/Ems: Stadtarchiv, Neuer Markt 1, 49733 Haren/Ems
Harpstedt: Gemeindearchiv (Samtgemeinde), Amtshof, 27243 Harpstedt
Harsefeld: Samtgemeindearchiv, Herrenstr. 25, 21698 Harsefeld
Harsewinkel: Stadtarchiv, Münsterstr. 14, 33428 Harsewinkel

Hartenstein: Stadtarchiv, Marktplatz 9, 08118 Hartenstein
Harzgerode: Stadtarchiv, Stadtverwaltung, Markt 1, 06493 Harzgerode
Haselünne: Stadtarchiv, Krummer Dreh 18/19, 49740 Haselünne
Haslach im Kinzigtal: Stadtarchiv, Rathaus, 77716 Haslach im Kinzigtal
Hattingen: Stadtarchiv, Stadtverwaltung, Im Welperfeld 23, 45527 Hattingen
Hatzfeld/Eder: Stadtarchiv, Stadtverwaltung, 35116 Hatzfeld/Eder
Hechingen: Bürgermeisteramt, Stadtarchiv, Postfach 222, 72375 Hechingen
Heide: Archiv der Stadt, Neue Anlage 5 (Bürger-Haus), 25746 Heide
Heideblick: Amtsarchiv Heideblick, Luckauer Str. 21, 15926 Langengrassau
Heidelberg: Stadtarchiv, Heiliggeiststr. 12, 69117 Heidelberg
Heidenheim an der Brenz: Stadtarchiv, Rathaus, Grabenstr. 15, 89522 Heidenheim an der Brenz
Heilbronn: Stadtarchiv, Eichgasse 1 (Deutschhof), 74072 Heilbronn/Neckar
Heiligenhaus: Stadtarchiv, Hauptstr. 157 (Rathaus), 42579 Heiligenhaus, Postfach 100553, 42570 Heiligenhaus
Heiligenstadt: Stadtverwaltung Heilbad Heiligenstadt, Stadtarchiv, Postfach 337, 37303 Heilbad Heiligenstadt, Ägidienstr. 20, 37308 Heilbad Heiligenstadt, Dienstsitz: Kollegiengasse 10, 37308 Heilbad Heiligenstadt
Heimbach: Stadtarchiv, Hengebachstr. 14, 52396 Heimbach
Heldrungen: Stadtverwaltung Heldrungen, Stadtarchiv, Hauptstr. 49/50, 06577 Heldrungen
Helmstedt: Stadtarchiv, Rathaus, Markt 1, 38350 Helmstedt, Postfach 1640, 38336 Helmstedt
Hemer: Stadtarchiv, Hauptstr. 201, 58651 Hemer
Hennef: Stadtarchiv, Beethovenstr. 21, 53773 Hennef
Heppenheim: Stadtarchiv, Großer Markt 1, 64646 Heppenheim, Postfach 1808, 64636 Heppenheim

Herbolzheim: Stadtarchiv, Friedrichstr. 2 A, 79336 Herbolzheim
Herborn: Stadtarchiv, Rathaus, 35745 Herborn
Herdecke: Stadtarchiv, Kulturhaus, Goethestr. 14, 58313 Herdecke, Postfach, 58311 Herdecke
Herford: Kommunalarchiv, Archiv des Kreises und der Stadt, Elverdisser Str. 12, 32052 Herford
Hermsdorf: Stadtverwaltung Hermsdorf, Stadtarchiv, Eisenbergerstr. 56, 07629 Hermsdorf
Herne: Stadtarchiv, Eickeler Str. 7, Postfach 101820, 44651 Herne
Herrenberg: Stadtarchiv, Marienstr. 21, 71083 Herrenberg, Postfach 1209, 71071 Herrenberg
Hersbruck: Stadtarchiv, Rathaus, Postfach 540, 91214 Hersbruck
Herten: Stadtarchiv, Kurt-Schumacher-Str. 16-22, 45699 Herten
Herzberg am Harz: Stadtarchiv, Rathaus, 37412 Herzberg am Harz, Postfach 1340, 37403 Herzberg am Harz
Herzebrock-Clarholz: Gemeindearchiv, Clarholzer Str. 76, 33442 Herzebrock-Clarholz
Herzogenaurach: Stadtarchiv, Marktplatz 11, 91074 Herzogenaurach
Herzogenrath: Stadtarchiv, 52134 Herzogenrath, Postfach 1280, 52112 Herzogenrath
Hessisch Oldendorf: Stadtarchiv, Stadtverwaltung, Marktplatz 13, 31840 Hessisch Oldendorf, Postfach 128, 31833 Hessisch Oldendorf
Hettstedt: Stadtarchiv, Stadtverwaltung, Markt, 06333 Hettstedt
Heusenstamm: Stadtarchiv, Im Herrengarten 1, 63150 Heusenstamm
Hiddenhausen: Gemeindearchiv, Rathausstr. 1, 32120 Hiddenhausen
Hilchenbach: Stadtarchiv, Rathaus, Markt 13, 57271 Hilchenbach, Postfach 1360, 57261 Hilchenbach
Hildburghausen: Stadtarchiv. See Landkreis Hildburghausen
Hilden: Stadtarchiv, Am Holterhöfchen

34, 40724 Hilden
Hildesheim: Stadtarchiv und Stadtbibliothek, Am Steine 7, 31134 Hildesheim
Hille: Marktarchiv, Am Rathaus 4, 32479 Hille (Hartum)
Hindelang: Gemeindearchiv, Eisenhammerweg 35, 87541 Hindelang
Hinterzarten: Stadtarchiv, Hauptamt, 79856 Hinterzarten
Hirschberg/Saale: Verwaltungsgemeinschaft Hirschberg/Saale, Stadt-archiv, Marktstr. 2, 07927 Hirschberg/Saale
Hirschhorn/Neckar: Städtisches Archiv, Rathaus, Neckarsteinacher Str. 8-10, 69434 Hirschhorn/Neckar, Postfach 1151, 69430 Hirschhorn/Neckar
Hitzacker: Archiv, Stadtverwaltung (Samtgemeinde), Am Markt 1, 29456 Hitzacker
Hochheim am Main: Stadtarchiv, Stadtverwaltung, Kulturamt, Burgeffstr. 30, 65239 Hochheim am Main, Postfach 1140, 65233 Hochheim am Main
Hockenheim: Stadtarchiv, Stadtverwaltung, Rathausstr. 1, 68766 Hockenheim
Höchberg: Gemeindearchiv, Gemeindeverwaltung, 97204 Höchberg
Höchst im Odenwald: Gemeindearchiv, Montmelianer Platz 4, 64739 Höchst im Odenwald
Höchstadt an der Aisch: Stadtarchiv, Altes Kommunbrauhaus, 91315 Höchstadt an der Aisch
Höchstädt an der Donau: Stadtarchiv, Bahnhofstr. 10, 89420 Höchstädt an der Donau
Höxter: Stadtarchiv, Stadthaus am Petritor, 37671 Höxter
Hof an der Saale: Stadtarchiv, Unteres Tor 9, 95028 Hof an der Saale, Postfach 1665, 95015 Hof an der Saale
Hofgeismar: Stadtarchiv, Rathaus, Markt 1, 34369 Hofgeismar
Hofheim am Taunus: Stadtarchiv, Kulturamt, Chinonplatz 2, 65719 Hofheim am Taunus, Postfach 1340, 65703 Hofheim am Taunus
Hohe Elbegeest: Amtsarchiv. See Archivgemeinschaft Schwarzenbek

Hohenstein-Ernstthal: Stadtarchiv, Altmarkt 30, 09337 Hohenstein-Ernstthal
Hohenwart: Marktarchiv, 86557 Hohenwart
Holzminden: Stadtarchiv, Bahnhofstr. 31, 37603 Holzminden, Postfach 1404, 37594 Holzminden
Holzwickede: Gemeindearchiv, Rathaus, Postfach, 59439 Holzwickede
Homberg/Ohm: Stadtarchiv, Rathaus, 35315 Homberg/Ohm
Homburg/Saar: Stadtarchiv, Am Marktplatz, 66424 Homburg/Saar, Postfach 1653, 66407 Homburg/Saar
Hoppegarten: Amtsarchiv Hoppegarten, Lindenstr. 14, 15366 Dahlwitz-Hoppegarten
Horb am Neckar: Stadtarchiv, Oberamteigasse 2, 72160 Horb am Neckar
Horn-Bad Meinberg: Stadtarchiv, Stadtverwaltung, Rathausplatz 4, 32805 Horn-Bad Meinberg
Hornburg: Stadtarchiv, Heimatmuseum, 38315 Hornburg
Hoya: Stadtarchiv, Postfach 150, 27318 Hoya
Hoyerswerda: Stadtarchiv, Schloßplatz 1, 02977 Hoyerswerda
Hude: Gemeindearchiv, Parkstr. 53, 27794 Hude
Hückelhoven: Stadtarchiv, Parkhofstr. 76, 41836 Hückelhoven, Postfach 1360, 41825 Hückelhoven
Hückeswagen: Stadtarchiv, Stadtverwaltung, Postfach 166, 42499 Hückeswagen
Hüfingen: Stadtarchiv, Stadtverwaltung, 78183 Hüfingen
Hüllhorst: Gemeindearchiv, Löhner Str. 1, 32609 Hüllhorst
Hünxe: Gemeindearchiv, Dorstener Str. 24, 46569 Hünxe
Hürtgenwald-Kleinhau: Gemeindearchiv, August-Scholl-Str. 5, 52393 Hürtenwald-Kleinhau
Hürth: Stadtarchiv, Rathaus, Friedrich-Ebert-Str. 40, 50354 Hürth, Postanschrift: Stadt Hürth, 50351 Hürth
Hütten: Amtsarchiv Hütten, Schulberg

6, 24358 Ascheffel
Hungen: Stadtarchiv, Kaiserstr. 7, 35410 Hungen
Husum: Stadtarchiv. See Kreis Nordfriesland
Ibbenbüren: Stadtarchiv, Alte Münsterstr. 16, 49477 Iibbenbüren, Postfach 1565, 49465 Ibbenbüren
Ichenheim: Stadtarchiv, Ortsverwaltung, 77741 Neuried-Ichenheim
Idar-Oberstein: Stadtarchiv, Am Markt 2, 55743 Idar-Oberstein
Idstein: Stadtarchiv, Stadtverwaltung, 65510 Idstein, Postfach 1140, 65501 Idstein
Iffezheim: Gemeindearchiv, Bürgermeisteramt, Hauptstr. 54, 76473 Iffezheim
Ilmenau: Stadtverwaltung Ilmenau, Stadtarchiv, Am Markt 7, 98693 Ilmenau, Dienstsitz: Naumannstr. 22, 98693 Ilmenau
Ilsede: Gemeindearchiv, Eichstr. 3, 31241 Ilsede
Immenstadt im Allgäu: Stadtarchiv, 87509 Immenstadt im Allgäu, Postfach 1461, 87504 Immenstadt im Allgäu
Ingelheim am Rhein: Stadtarchiv, Stadtverwaltung, Postfach 60, 55218 Ingelheim am Rhein
Ingolstadt: Stadtarchiv, Auf der Schanz 45, 85049 Ingolstadt, Postfach 210964, 85024 Ingolstadt
Iphofen: Stadtarchiv, Rathaus, 97346 Iphofen
Iserlohn: Stadtarchiv, An der Schlacht 14, 58644 Iserlohn
Isny (Allgäu): Stadtarchiv, Rathaus, 88316 Isny (Allgäu), Postfach 1162, 88305 Isny (Allgäu)
Isselburg: Stadtarchiv, Stadtverwaltung, Markt 14/16, 46419 Isselburg
Issum: Gemeindearchiv, Herrlichkeit 7-9, 47661 Issum
Itzehoe: Gemeinsames Archiv des Kreises Steinburg und der Stadt Itzehoe. See Kreis Steinburg
Jena: Stadtarchiv, Löbdergraben 18, 07743 Jena
Joachimsthal-Schorfheide: Amtsarchiv Joachimsthal-Schorfheide, 16247 Joachimsthal
Jöhstadt: Stadtarchiv, Markt 185, 09477 Jöhstadt
Jork: Gemeindearchiv, Am Gräfengericht 2, 21635 Jork
Jüchen: Gemeindearchiv, Postfach 1101, 41353 Jüchen
Jülich: Stadtarchiv, Kulturhaus, Kleine Rurstr. 20, 52428 Jülich, Postfach 1220, 52411 Jülich
Jüterbog: Stadtarchiv Jüterbog, Markt 1, 14913 Jüterbog
Kaarst: Stadtarchiv, Am Neumarkt 2, 41564 Kaarst
Kahl am Main: Gemeindearchiv, Aschaffenburger Str. 1, 63792 Kahl am Main
Kahla: Stadtverwaltung Kahla, Stadtarchiv, Markt 10, 07768 Kahla
Kaiserslautern: Stadtarchiv, Rathaus, Postfach 1320, 67653 Kaiserslautern
Kalkar: Stadtarchiv, Hanselaerstr. 5, 47546 Kalkar, Postfach 1165, 47538 Kalkar
Kalletal: Gemeindearchiv, Rintelner Str. 5, 32689 Kalletal
Kamen: Stadtarchiv, Rathausplatz 1, 59174 Kamen, Postfach 1580, 59172 Kamen
Kamenz: Stadtarchiv, Markt 1, 01917 Kamenz
Karben: Stadtarchiv, Bürgerzentrum, Rathausplatz 1, Post: Stadtverwaltung, 61184 Karben, Postfach 1107, 61174 Karben
Karlsruhe: Stadtarchiv, Markgrafenstr. 29, 76133 Karlsruhe, Post: Stadt Karlsruhe, Stadtbibliothek, Archiv, Sammlungen, Ständehausstr. 2, 76133 Karlsruhe bzw. 76124 Karlsruhe
Karlstadt: Stadtarchiv, Stadtverwaltung, Helfensteinstr. 2, 97753 Karlstadt
Kassel: Stadtarchiv, Marstallgebäude, Wildemannsgasse 1, 34117 Kassel
Kaufbeuren: Stadtarchiv, Hauberrisserstr. 8, 87600 Kaufbeuren, Postfach 1752, 87577 Kaufbeuren
Kehl: Stadtarchiv, Haupt- und Verkehrsamt, Großherzoz-Friedrich-Str. 19, 77694

Kehl
Kelheim: Stadtarchiv, Alleestr. 21, 93309 Kelheim
Kelkheim (Taunus): Stadtarchiv, Stadtverwaltung, Gagernring 6, 65779 Kelkheim (Taunus), Postfach 1560, 65765 Kelkheim
Kempen: Stadtarchiv. See Kreis Viersen
Kempten (Allgäu): Stadtarchiv, Rathausplatz 3-5, 87435 Kempten (Allgäu)
Kenzingen: Stadtarchiv, Rathaus, Hauptstr. 15, 79341 Kenzingen, Postfach 1119, 79337 Kenzingen
Kerken: Gemeindearchiv, Dionysiusplatz 4, 47647 Kerken, Postfach 1164, 47639 Kerken
Kerpen: Stadtarchiv, Rathaus, Jahnplatz 1, 50171 Kerpen, Postfach 2109, 50151 Kerpen
Kevelaer: Stadtarchiv, Stadtverwaltung, Postfach 75, 47612 Kevelaer
Kiefersfelden: Gemeindearchiv, Rathausplatz 1, 83088 Kiefersfelden
Kiel: Stadtarchiv, Rathaus, Fleethörn, 24103 Kiel
Kierspe: Stadtarchiv, ehem. Amtshaus, Friedrich-Ebert-Str. 380, 58566 Kierspe
Kindelbrück: Verwaltungsgemeinschaft Kindelbrück, Stadtarchiv, Puschkinplatz 1, 99638 Kindelbrück
Kirchberg: Stadtarchiv, Neumarkt 2, 08107 Kirchberg
Kirchheim unter Teck: Stadtarchiv, Wollmarktstr. 48, 73230 Kirchheim unter Teck
Kirchhundem: Gemeindearchiv, Hundemstr. 35, 57399 Kirchhundem
Kirchlengern: Gemeindearchiv, Am Rathaus 2, 32278 Kirchlengern
Kirchseeon: Gemeindearchiv, Rathausstr. 1, 85614 Kirchseeon
Kirn: Stadtarchiv, Kirchstr. 3, 55606 Kirn, Postfach 93, 55602 Kirn
Kitzingen: Stadtarchiv, Landwehrstr. 23, 97318 Kitzingen
Kitzscher: Stadtarchiv, Ernst-Schneller-Str. 1, 04567 Kitzscher
Kleve: Stadtarchiv, Tiergartenstr. 41, 47533 Kleve, Postfach 1960, 47517 Kleve

Klingenthal: Stadtarchiv, Kirchstr. 14, 08248 Klingenthal
Koblenz: Stadtarchiv, Burgstr. 1, 56068 Koblenz, Postfach 2064, 56020 Koblenz
Köln: Historisches Archiv der Stadt, Severinstr. 222-228, 50676 Köln
Königslutter am Elm: Stadtarchiv, Rathaus, Postfach 26, 38154 Königslutter am Elm
Königstein im Taunus: Stadtarchiv, Stadtverwaltung, Postfach, 61462 Königstein im Taunus
Königswinter: Stadtarchiv, 53637 Königswinter
Königs Wusterhausen: Stadtarchiv, Karl-Marx-Str. 23, 15711 Königs Wusterhausen
Köthen: Stadtarchiv, Stadtverwaltung, Markt 1-3, 06366 Köthen
Konstanz: Stadtarchiv, Benediktinerplatz 5, 78467 Konstanz
Korbach: Stadtarchiv, Stadtverwaltung, Postfach 340, 34497 Korbach
Korntal-Münchingen: Stadtarchiv, Bürgermeisteramt, Rathausgasse 2, 70825 Korntal-Münchingen, Postfach 1405, 70810 Korntal-Münchingen
Kornwestheim: Stadtarchiv, Stadtverwaltung, Jakob-Sigle-Platz 1, Postfach 1840, 70806 Kornwestheim
Korschenbroich: Stadtarchiv, Arndtstr. 27, 41352 Korschenbroich
Kranenburg: Gemeindearchiv, Klever Str. 4, 47559 Kranenburg
Kranichfeld: Stadtverwaltung Kranichfeld, Stadtarchiv, Alexanderstr. 7, 99448 Kranichfeld
Krefeld: Stadtarchiv, Girmesgath 120, 47803 Krefeld, Postfach 2740, 47727 Krefeld
Kreuzau: Gemeindearchiv, Bahnhofstr. 7, 52372 Kreuzau
Kreuztal: Stadtarchiv, Stadtverwaltung, Siegener Str. 5, 57223 Kreuztal
Krölpa: Verwaltungsgemeinschaft Krölpa, Archiv, Pößneckerstr. 24, 07387 Krölpa
Kronach: Stadtarchiv, Rathaus, Marktplatz 5, 96317 Kronach, Postfach 1761,

96307 Kronach
Kronberg im Taunus: Stadtarchiv, Stadtverwaltung, Katharinenstr. 7, 61476 Kronberg im Taunus, Postfach 1280, 61467 Kronberg im Taunus
Krumbach (Schwaben): Stadtarchiv, Nattenhauserstr. 5, 86381 Krumbach (Schwaben)
Kühbach: Marktarchiv, Markt Kühbach, Schönbacher Str. 1, 86556 Kühbach
Künzelsau: Stadtarchiv, Stadtverwaltung, Stuttgarter Str. 7, 74653 Künzelsau
Kürten: Gemeindearchiv, Marktfeld 1, 51515 Kürten
Kulmbach: Stadtarchiv, Pestalozzistr. 8, 95326 Kulmbach
Laatzen: Stadtarchiv, Amt für Kultur, Schulen und Sport, Marktplatz 13, 30880 Laatzen, Postfach 110545, 30860 Laatzen
Laer: Gemeindearchiv, Kulturamt der Gemeinde Laer, Mühlenhoek 1, 48366 Laer
Lage: Stadtarchiv, Clara-Ernst-Platz 5, 32791 Lage (Lippe)
Lahnstein: Stadtarchiv, Altes Rathaus, Hochstr. 34, 56112 Lahnstein, Postfach 2180, 56108 Lahnstein
Lahr: Stadtarchiv, Rathaus, Rathausplatz 4, 77933 Lahr (Schwarzwald)
Laichingen: Stadtarchiv, Bürgermeisteramt, 89150 Laichingen
Lampertheim: Stadtarchiv, Stadtverwaltung, Römerstr. 102, 68623 Lampertheim, Postfach 1120, 68601 Lampertheim
Landau in der Pfalz: Stadtarchiv und Museum, Marienring 8, 76829 Landau in der Pfalz
Landsberg am Lech: Stadtarchiv, Lechstr. 132 ½, 86899 Landsberg am Lech
Landshut: Stadtarchiv, Stadtresidenz, Altstadt 79, 84026 Landshut
Landstuhl: Stadtarchiv, Verbandsgemeindeverwaltung, 66849 Landstuhl
Langen: Stadtarchiv, Kulturhaus, Altes Amtsgericht, Darmstädter Str. 27, 63225 Langen
Langenau: Stadtarchiv, Stadtverwaltung, Pfleghof, 89129 Langenau

Langenberg: Gemeindearchiv, Klutenbrinkstr. 5, 33449 Langenberg
Langenfeld (Rheinland): Stadtarchiv, Rathaus, Konrad-Adenauer-Platz, 40764 Langenfeld (Rheinland)
Langenhagen: Stadtarchiv, Niedersachsenstr. 3, 30853 Langenhagen
Langenzenn: Archiv der Stadt, Denkmalplatz 4, 90579 Langenzenn
Langerwehe: Gemeindearchiv, Postfach 1240, 52379 Langerwehe
Langewiesen (Thüringen): Stadtverwaltung Langewiesen, Stadtarchiv, Ratsstr. 2, 98704 Langewiesen
Laubach (Hessen): Stadtarchiv, Stadtverwaltung, Rathaus, Friedrichstr. 11, 35321 Laubach (Hessen), Postfach 1242, 35317 Laubach (Hessen)
Lauda-Königshofen: Stadtarchiv, Bürgermeisteramt, 97922 Lauda-Königshofen
Lauenburg: Stadtarchiv, Elbstr. 2, 21481 Lauenburg
Lauf an der Pegnitz: Stadtarchiv mit Städt, Sammlungen, Spitalstr. 5, 91205 Lauf an der Pegnitz
Laufen: Stadtarchiv, Rathausplatz 3, 83410 Laufen
Lauffen am Neckar: Stadtarchiv, Stadtverwaltung, Rathaus, 74348 Lauffen am Neckar
Lauingen: Archiv der Stadt, Rathaus, 89415 Lauingen
Laupheim: Stadtarchiv, Marktplatz 1, 88471 Laupheim
Lauscha: Stadtverwaltung Lauscha, Stadtarchiv, Postfach, 98734 Lauscha, Dienstsitz: Bahnhofstr. 12, 98724 Lauscha
Lauterbach (Hessen): Stadtarchiv, Obergasse 44, Schulanbau zum "Güldenen Esel", Post: Stadtverwaltung, Rathaus, 36341 Lauterbach (Hessen)
Leer (Ostfriesland): Stadtarchiv, Rathausstr. 1, 26789 Leer, Postfach 2060, 26770 Leer
Lehrte: Stadtarchiv, 31275 Lehrte
Leichlingen: Stadtarchiv, Stadtverwaltung, Am Büscherhof 1, 42799 Leichlingen, Postfach 1665, 42787 Leichlingen

Leinfelden-Echterdingen: Stadtarchiv, Schloßbergweg 17, 70771 Leinfelden-Echterdingen, Postfach 100351, 70747 Leinfelden-Echterdingen
Leipzig: Stadtarchiv, Torgauer Str. 74, 04318 Leipzig, Postfach 780, 04007 Leipzig
Leisnig: Stadtarchiv, Markt 1, 04703 Leisnig
Lemförde: Samtgemeindearchiv, Bahnhofstr. 10 A, 49488 Lemförde
Lemgo: Stadtarchiv, Rampendal 20a, 32655 Lemgo, Postfach 740, 32655 Lemgo
Lengenfeld: Stadtarchiv, Hauptstr. 1, 08485 Lengenfeld
Lengerich: Stadtarchiv, Rathausplatz 1, 49525 Lengerich, Postfach 1540, 49525 Lengerich
Lenggries: Gemeindearchiv, Rathausplatz 1, 83661 Lenggries
Lennestadt: Stadtarchiv, Kölner Str. 57, 57368 Lennestadt-Grevenbrück
Leonberg: Stadtarchiv, Altes Rathaus Eltingen, Carl-Schmincke-Str. 37, 71229 Leonberg, Postfach 1753, 71226 Leonberg
Letschin: Amtsarchiv Letschin, Bahnhofstr. 30a, 15324 Letschin
Leutkirch: Stadtarchiv, Stadtverwaltung, 88299 Leutkirch, Postfach 1260, 88292 Leutkirch
Leverkusen: Stadtarchiv, Landrat-Trimborn-Platz 1 und Stadtgeschichtliches Dokumentationszentrum, Haus-Vorster-Str. 6, 51379 Leverkusen (Opladen), Post: Postfach 101140, 51311 Leverkusen
Lich: Städtisches Archiv, Unterstadt 1, 35423 Lich
Lichtenau: Archiv des Marktfleckens Lichtenau, Gemeindeverwaltung, 91586 Lichtenau
Lichtenfels: Stadtarchiv, Rathaus, Marktplatz 5, 96215 Lichtenfels
Lichtenstein: Stadtarchiv, Poststr. 4, 09350 Lichtenstein
Liebenwalde: Amtsarchiv Liebenwalde, Am Markt 20, 16559 Liebenwalde
Lienen: Gemeindearchiv, Hauptstr. 14, 49536 Lienen

Limburg an der Lahn: Stadtarchiv, Schloß, 65549 Limburg an der Lahn
Lindau/Bodensee: Stadtarchiv, Altes Rathaus, Reichsplatz, 88131 Lindau/Bodensee
Linden: Stadtarchiv, Stadtverwaltung, Konrad-Adenauer-Str. 25, 35440 Linden, Postfach 1155, 35436 Linden
Lindlar: Gemeindearchiv, Borromäusstr. 1, 51789 Lindlar
Lingen/Ems: Stadtarchiv, Postfach 2060, 49803 Lingen/Ems
Linz am Rhein: Stadtarchiv, Klosterstr. (Servitessenkirche), 53545 Linz am Rhein, Postfach 101, 53542 Linz am Rhein
Lippstadt: Archiv- und Museumsamt, Soeststr. 8, 59555 Lippstadt, Postfach 2540, 59535 Lippstadt
Lobenstein: Stadtverwaltung Moorbad Lobenstein, Stadtarchiv, Postfach 130, 07353 Lobenstein, Dienstsitz: Markt 1, 07356 Lobenstein
Löbau: Stadtarchiv, Altmarkt 1, 02708 Löbau, Postfach 180, 02701 Löbau
Löhne: Stadtarchiv, Stadtverwaltung, Oeynhausener Str. 41, 32584 Löhne
Lörrach: Stadtarchiv, Bürgermeisteramt, Rathaus, Luisenstr. 16, 79539 Lörrach, Postfach 1260, 79537 Lörrach
Lohmar: Stadtarchiv, Hauptstr. 83, 53797 Lohmar
Lohne: Stadtverwaltung, Vogtstr. 26, 49393 Lohne
Lommatzsch: Stadtarchiv, Rathaus, 01623 Lommatzsch
Lorch: Stadtarchiv, Stadtverwaltung, Hauptstr. 19, 73547 Lorch
Lorsch: Stadtarchiv, Kaiser-Wilhelm-Platz 1, 64653 Lorsch
Lucka: Stadtverwaltung Lucka, Stadtarchiv, Postfach 55, 04611 Lucka, Dienstsitz: Pegauer Str. 17, 04613 Lucka
Luckau: Stadtarchiv, Am Markt 34, 15926 Luckau
Luckenwalde: Stadtarchiv, Stadtverwaltung, Markt 10, 14943 Luckenwalde
Ludwigsburg: Stadtarchiv, Kaiserstr. 14, 71636 Ludwigsburg, Postfach 249, 71602 Ludwigsburg

Ludwigsfelde: Stadtarchiv, Potsdamer Str. 48, 14974 Ludwigsfelde
Ludwigshafen am Rhein: Stadtarchiv, Rottstr. 17, 67061 Ludwigshafen, Postfach 211225, 67012 Ludwigshafen
Lübbecke: Stadtarchiv, Am Markt (Altes Rathaus), 32312 Lübbecke, Postfach 1453, 32294 Lübbecke
Lübeck: Archiv der Hansestadt, Mühlendamm 1-3, 23552 Lübeck
Lüchow: Stadtarchiv, Burgstr., 29439 Lüchow
Lüdenscheid: Stadtarchiv, Stadtverwaltung, Rathausplatz 2, 58507 Lüdenscheid
Lüdinghausen: Stadtarchiv, Borg 2, 59348 Lüdinghausen, Postfach 1531, 59335 Lüdinghausen
Lügde: Stadtarchiv, Stadtverwaltung, 32676 Lügde, Postfach 1352 und 1353, 32670 Lügde
Lüneburg: Stadtarchiv, Rathaus, Postfach 2540, 21315 Lüneburg
Lünen: Stadtarchiv, Stadtverwaltung, Rathaus, 44530 Lünen
Magdeburg: Stadtarchiv, Bei der Hauptwache 4-6, 39104 Magdeburg, Post: Landeshauptstadt Magdeburg, Der Oberbürgermeister, Stadtarchiv, 39090 Magdeburg
Mainz: Stadtarchiv, Rheinallee 3 B, 55116 Mainz
Mannheim: Stadtarchiv, Collinicenter, 68161 Mannheim
Marbach am Neckar: Stadtarchiv, Marktstr. 25, 71672 Marbach am Neckar, Postfach 1115, 71666 Marbach am Neckar
Marburg: Stadtarchiv, Friedrichsplatz 15, 35037 Marburg, Post: Magistrat der Stadt Marburg, 35035 Marburg
Marienberg: Stadtarchiv, Markt 1, 09496 Marienberg
Marienmünster: Stadtarchiv, Schulstr. 1, 37696 Marienmünster (Vörden)
Markdorf: Stadtarchiv, Stadtverwaltung, Rathaus, 88677 Markdorf (Baden), Postfach 1240, 88670 Markdorf (Baden)
Markgröningen: Stadtarchiv, Finstere Gasse 3, 71706 Markgröningen, Postfach 1262, 71703 Markgröningen

Markneukirchen: Stadtarchiv, Am Rathaus 2, 08258 Markneukirchen
Marktoberdorf: Stadtarchiv, Rathaus, Jahnstr. 1, 87616 Marktoberdorf
Marktredwitz: Stadtarchiv, Neues Rathaus, Egerstr. 2, 95615 Marktredwitz, Postfach 609, 95606 Marktredwitz
Marl: Stadtarchiv, Rathaus, Creiler Platz 1, 45768 Marl
Marsberg: Stadtarchiv, Lillerstr. 8, 34431 Marsberg, Postfach 1341, 34419 Marsberg
Massenheim: Stadtarchiv. See Hochheim am Main
Maulbronn: Stadtarchiv, Rathaus, Klosterhof 31, 75433 Maulbronn, Postfach 47, 75429 Maulbronn
Mayen: Stadtarchiv, Genovevaburg, Eifeler Landschaftsmuseum, 56727 Mayen
Mechernich: Stadtarchiv, Postfach 1260, 53894 Mechernich-Kommern
Meckenheim (Rheinland): Stadtarchiv, Stadtverwaltung, 53340 Meckenheim (Rheinland), Postfach 1180, 53333 Meckenheim (Rheinland)
Meerbusch (Büderich): Stadtarchiv, Karl-Borromäus-Str. 2a, 40667 Meerbusch (Büderich), Postfach 1664, 40641 Meerbusch (Büderich)
Meersburg (Bodensee): Stadtarchiv, Kulturamt der Stadt Meersburg, Postfach 1140, 88701 Meersburg (Bodensee)
Meinerzhagen: Stadtarchiv, Altes Rathaus, Oststr. 5, 58540 Meinerzhagen
Meiningen: Stadtarchiv, Schloß Bibrabau, Schloßplatz 1, 98617 Meining-en
Meißen: Stadtarchiv, Kleinmarkt 5, 01662 Meißen
Meldorf: Stadtarchiv, Dithmarscher Landesmuseum, Bütjestr. 2-4, Landwirtschaftsmuseum, Jungfernstieg 4, 25704 Meldorf
Melle: Stadtarchiv (Stored in Niedersächsischen Staatsarchiv in Osnabrück)
Mellrichstadt: Stadtarchiv, Hauptstr. 4, 97638 Mellrichstadt
Memmingen: Stadtarchiv, Ulmer Str. 19, 87700 Memmingen, Postfach 1853, 87688 Memmingen

Menden (Sauerland): Archiv der Stadt, Altes Rathaus, Postfach 660, 58688 Menden (Sauerland)
Mengen: Stadtarchiv, Stadtverwaltung, 88512 Mengen
Meppen: Stadtarchiv, Markt 43, 49716 Meppen
Merseburg: Historisches Stadtarchiv, Stadtverwaltung, Wilhelm-Liebknecht-Str. 1, 06217 Merseburg
Merzenich: Gemeindearchiv, Valdersweg 1, 52399 Merzenich
Meschede: Stadtarchiv, Vervaltungsstelle Freienohl, Hauptstr. 38-40, 59872 Meschede
Meßkirch: Stadtarchiv, Rathaus, Conradin-Kreutzer-Str. 1, 88605 Meßkirch
Metelen: Stadtarchiv, Sendplatz 18, 48629 Metelen
Mettingen: Gemeindearchiv, Rathausplatz 1, 49497 Mettingen
Mettmann: Stadtarchiv, Neanderstr. 85, 40822 Mettmann
Metzingen: Stadtarchiv, Postfach 1363, 72544 Metzingen
Meuselwitz: Stadtverwaltung Meuselwitz, Stadtarchiv, Postfach 331, 04607 Meuselwitz, Dienstsitz: Rathausstr. 1, 04610 Meuselwitz
Meyenburg: Stadtarchiv, Freyensteiner Str. 42, 16945 Meyenburg
Michelstadt: Stadtarchiv, Löwenhof, Marktplatz, Post: Stadtverwaltung, Frankfurter Str. 3, 64720 Michelstadt
Michendorf: Amtsarchiv Michendorf, Potsdamer Str. 33-37, 14552 Michendorf
Miesbach: Stadtarchiv, Stadtverwaltung, Rathausplatz 1, 83714 Miesbach, Postfach 29, 83711 Miesbach
Milda: Gemeindeverwaltung Milda, Gemeindearchiv, Dorfstr. 60, 07751 Milda
Miltenberg: Stadtarchiv, Rathaus, 63897 Miltenberg, Postfach 1740, 63887 Miltenberg
Mindelheim: Stadtarchiv, Verwaltung Städtische Museen, Hermelestr. 4, 87719 Mindelheim
Minden: Kommunalarchiv Minden

(Archiv der Stadt Minden und des Kreises Minden-Lübbecke), Tonhallenstr. 7, 32423 Minden, Postfach 3080, 32387 Minden
Mittenwald: Marktarchiv, Dammkarstr. 3, 82481 Mittenwald
Mittweida: Stadtarchiv, Rochlitzer Str. 1, 09642 Mittweida
Mölln: Stadtarchiv, Stadthaus, Wasserkrüger Weg 16, 23879 Mölln
Mönchengladbach: Stadtarchiv, Aachener Str. 2, 41050 Mönchengladbach
Mörfelden-Walldorf: Stadtarchiv, Westendstr. 8 und Flughafenstr. 37, 64546 Mörfelden-Walldorf
Moers: Stadtarchiv, Unterwallstr. 17, 47441 Moers
Monheim: Stadtarchiv, Tempelhofer Str. 13, 40789 Monheim
Monschau: Stadtarchiv, Laufenstr. 84, 52156 Monschau
Montabaur: Stadtarchiv, Josef-Kehrein-Schule, Gelbachstr., 56410 Montabaur
Moosburg an der Isar: Stadtarchiv, Stadtplatz 13, 85368 Moosburg an der Isar
Moringen: Stadtarchiv, Amtsfreiheit 8, 37186 Moringen
Morsbach/Sieg: Gemeindearchiv, Bahnhofstr. 2, 51597 Morsbach/Sieg
Mosbach (Baden): Stadtarchiv, Hauptstr. 29, 74821 Mosbach (Baden), Postfach 1162, 74819 Mosbach (Baden)
Much: Gemeindearchiv, Hauptstr. 57, 53804 Much
Mühlacker: Stadtarchiv, Stadtverwaltung, Postfach 1163, 75415 Mühlacker
Mühlberg: Stadtarchiv, Schloßplatz 1, 04931 Mühlberg
Mühldorf am Inn: Stadtarchiv, Rathaus, 84453 Mühldorf am Inn
Mühlhausen: Stadtverwaltung Mühlhausen, Stadtarchiv, Postfach 29 und 40, 99961 Mühlhausen, Dienstsitz: Ratsstr. 19, 99974 Mühlhausen
Mühlheim an der Donau: Stadtarchiv, Stadtverwaltung, 78570 Mühlheim an der Donau
Mühltroff: Stadtarchiv, Postfach, 07917 Mühltroff

Mülheim an der Ruhr: Stadtarchiv, Aktienstr. 85, 45473 Mülheim an der Ruhr, Postfach 101953, 45466 Mülheim an der Ruhr
Müllheim (Baden): Stadtarchiv, Rathaus, Bismarckstr. 3, 79379 Müllheim (Baden)
Münchberg (Oberfranken): Stadtarchiv, Kirchplatz 7, 95213 Münchberg (Oberfranken), Postfach 467, 95213 Münchberg (Oberfranken)
Müncheberg: Amts- und Stadtarchiv Müncheberg, Rathausstr. 1, 15372 Müncheberg
München: Stadtarchiv, Winzererstr. 68, 80797 München
Münnerstadt: Stadtarchiv, Postfach 129, 97702 Münnerstadt
Münsingen: Stadtarchiv, Bachwiesenstr. 7, 72525 Münsingen, Postfach 1140, 72521 Münsingen
Münster: Stadtarchiv, Hörsterstr. 28, 48143 Münster
Münzenberg: Stadtarchiv, Hauptstr. 22, 35516 Münzenberg, Stadtteil Gambach
Munderkingen: Stadtarchiv, Stadtverwaltung, 89597 Munderkingen
Murnau: Archiv des Marktes, Untermarkt 13, 82418 Murnau am Staffelsee
Mylau: Stadtarchiv, 08499 Mylau
Nagold: Stadtarchiv, Badgasse 3, 72202 Nagold, Postfach 1444, 72194 Nagold
Nassau: Stadtarchiv, Rathaus, Postfach 1107, 56371 Nassau
Nauen: Stadtarchiv, Rathausplatz 1, 14641 Nauen
Naumburg: Stadtarchiv, Stadtverwaltung, Georgenberg 6, 06618 Naumburg
Neckargemünd: Stadtarchiv, Rathaus Villa Menzer, Dilsberger Str. 2, 69151 Neckargemünd
Neckarsteinach: Städt. Archiv, Hauptstr. 7, 69239 Neckarsteinach
Neckarsulm: Stadtarchiv, Binswanger Str. 3, 74172 Neckarsulm
Nennhausen: Amtsarchiv Nennhausen, Platz der Jugend, 14715 Nennhausen
Nettersheim: Gemeindearchiv, Krausstr. 2, 53947 Nettersheim
Netzschkau (Vogtland): Stadtarchiv, Markt 12/13, 08491 Netzschkaau (Vogtland)
Neubrandenburg: Stadtarchiv, Stadtverwaltung Neubrandenburg, Postfach 1814, 17008 Neubrandenburg; Dienstsitz: Friedrich-Engels-Ring 53, 17033 Neubrandenburg
Neuburg an der Donau: Stadtarchiv, Bahnhofstr. B 142, 86633 Neuburg an der Donau
Neuenrade: Stadtarchiv, Stadtverwaltung, Alte Burg 1, 58809 Neuenrade
Neu-Isenburg: Stadtarchiv, Rathaus, Hugenotten-Allee 53, 63263 Neu-Isenburg
Neukirchen-Vluyn: Stadtarchiv, Hans-Böckler-Str. 26, 47504 Neukirchen-Vluyn
Neumünster: Stadtarchiv, Grossflechen 68 und Parkstr. 17, 24534 Neumünster, Post: Stadtverwaltung, Postfach 2640, 24516 Neumünster
Neunburg vorm Wald: Stadtarchiv, 92431 Neunburg vorm Wald
Neunkirchen: Stadtarchiv, Rathaus, Postfach 1163, 66511 Neunkirchen
Neuötting: Stadtarchiv, Rathaus, 84524 Neuötting
Neuseddin: Verwaltungsgemeinschaftsarchiv Neuseddin, Kiefernweg 5, 14554 Neuseddin
Neuss: Stadtarchiv, Oberstr. 15, 41460 Neuss
Neustadt (Sachsen): Stadtarchiv, Markt 1, 01841 Neustadt (Sachsen)
Neustadt an der Aisch: Stadtarchiv, An der Bleiche 1, 91413 Neustadt an der Aisch, Postfach 1669, 91406 Neustadt an der Aisch
Neustadt an der Donau: Stadtarchiv, Stadtplatz 1, 93333 Neustadt an der Donau, Postfach 1452, 93330 Neustadt an der Donau
Neustadt an der Dosse: Amtsarchiv Neustadt, Bahnhofstr. 6, 16845 Neustadt an der Dosse
Neustadt in Holstein: Stadtarchiv, Stadtverwaltung, Am Markt 1, 23730 Neustadt in Holstein
Neustadt an der Orla: Stadtverwaltung,

Stadtarchiv, Markt 1, 07801 Neustadt an der Orla

Neustadt an der Weinstraße: Stadtarchiv, Klemmhof, 67433 Neustadt an der Weinstraße, Postfach 100962, 67409 Neustadt an der Weinstraße

Neustrelitz: Stadtarchiv, Markt 1, 17235 Neustrelitz

Neu-Ulm: Stadtarchiv, Rathaus, Augsburger Str. 15, 89231 Neu-Ulm

Neuwied: Stadtarchiv, Landeshauptarchiv Koblenz - Außenstelle Rommersdorf -mit Stadtarchiv Neuwied, Abtei Rommersdorf, 56566 Neuwied

Neu Wulmstorf: Gemeindearchiv, Bahnhofstr. 39, 21629 Neu Wulmstorf, Postfach 1120, 21624 Wulmstorf

Nidda: Stadtarchiv, Stadtverwaltung, Rathaus, 63667 Nidda, Postfach 1250, 63659 Nidda

Nideggen: Stadtarchiv, Stadtverwaltung, Rathaus, Zülpicher Str. 1, 52385 Nideggen, Postfach 1161, 52383 Nideggen

Niederer Fläming: Amtsarchiv Niederer Fläming, Chausseestr. 12a, 14913 Hohenseefeld

Niedergörsdorf: Amtsarchiv Niedergörsdorf, Dorfstr. 14, 14913 Niedergörsdorf

Niederkassel: Stadtarchiv, Rathausstr. 19, 53859 Niederkassel

Niederzier: Gemeindearchiv, Postfach 1120, 52380 Niederzier

Nieheim: Stadtarchiv, Rathaus, 33039 Nieheim

Nienburg (Weser): Stadtarchiv, "Villa Holscher", Verdener Str. 24, 31582 Nienburg (Weser), Postfach 1780, 31567 Nienburg (Weser)

Nördlingen: Stadtarchiv, Hallgebäude, Weinmarkt 1, 86720 Nördlingen

Nörvenich: Gemeindearchiv, Bahnhofstr. 25, 52388 Nörvenich

Nordenham: Stadtarchiv, Enjebuhrer Str. 10, 26954 Nordenham-Abbehausen

Norderney: Stadtarchiv, 26548 Norderney

Nordhausen: Stadtarchiv, Markt 1, Postfach 132, 99732 Nordhausen

Nordhorn: Stadtarchiv, Bahnhofstr. 24, 48529 Nordhorn, Postfach 2429, 48522 Nordhorn

Northeim: Stadtarchiv, St. Blasien, Am Münster 30, 37154 Northeim

Nortorf: Stadtarchiv, Rathaus, Niedernstr. 6, 24589 Nortorf, Postfach 1162, 24585 Nortorf

Nossen: Stadtarchiv, Rathaus, Markt 31, 01683 Nossen

Nottuln: Gemeindearchiv, Stiftsplatz 7, 48301 Nottuln

Nürnberg: Stadtarchiv, Egidienplatz 23, 90403 Nürnberg, Post: 90317 Nürnberg

Nürtingen: Stadtarchiv, Hauptamt, 72622 Nürtingen, Postfach 1920, 72609 Nürtingen

Oberammergau: Gemeindearchiv, Schnitzlergasse 5, 82487 Oberammergau

Oberharz: See Clausthal-Zellerfeld

Oberhausen (Rheinland): Stadtarchiv (Schloß Oberhausen), Konrad-Adenauer-Allee 46, Postfach 101505, 46042 Oberhausen (Rheinland)

Oberkirch: Stadtarchiv, Kultur- und Verkehrsamt, Eisenbahnstr. 1, 77704 Oberkirch

Oberlungwitz: Stadtarchiv, Hofer Str. 203, 09353 Oberlungwitz

Obermoschel: Stadtarchiv, Rathaus, 67823 Obermoschel

Oberndorf am Neckar: Stadt- und Zeitungsarchiv, Stadtverwaltung, Klosterstr. 14, 78727 Oberndorf am Neckar, Postfach 1105, 78720 Oberndorf am Neckar

Obernkirchen: Stadtarchiv (Stored in Niedersächsischen Staatsarchiv Bückeburg)

Oberstdorf: Gemeindearchiv, Marktplatz 2, 87561 Oberstdorf, Postfach 1540, 87561 Oberstdorf

Oberursel (Taunus): Stadtarchiv, Schulstr. 32, 61440 Oberursel (Taunus)

Oberviechtach: Stadtarchiv, Haus der Bäuerin 1, 92526 Oberviechtach

Oberwiesenthal: Stadtarchiv, Stadtverwaltung, Markt 8, Postfach 44, 09482 Kurort Oberwiesenthal

Ochsenfurt: Stadtarchiv, Rathaus, 97199

Ochsenfurt, Postfach 1153, 97195 Ochsenfurt
Ochsenhausen: Stadtarchiv, Stadtverwaltung, 88416 Ochsenhausen
Ochtrup: Stadtarchiv, Prof. -Gärtner -Str. 4, 48607 Ochtrup
Odenthal: Gemeindearchiv, Altenberger-Dom-Str. 31, 51519 Odenthal
Oederan: Stadtarchiv, Markt 5, 09569 Oederan
Öhringen: Stadtarchiv, Stadtverwaltung, Marktplatz 15, 74613 Öhringen, Postfach 1209, 74602 Öhringen
Oelde: Stadtarchiv. See Kreis Warendorf
Oelsnitz (Vogtland): Stadtarchiv, Markt 1, 08606 Oelsnitz (Vogtland)
Oer-Erkenschwick: Stadtarchiv, Christoph-Stöver-Str. 2 (Realschule), Oer-Erkenschwick
Oerlinghausen: Stadtarchiv, Hauptstr. 14 A, 33813 Oerlinghausen, Postfach 1344, 33806 Oerlinghausen
Oestrich-Winkel: Stadtarchiv, Stadtverwaltung, Hauptstr. 31, 65375 Oestrich-Winkel, Postfach 1108, 65370 Oestrich-Winkel
Offenbach: Stadtarchiv, Herrnstr. 61, 63065 Offenbach am Main
Offenburg: Stadtarchiv, Ritterstr. 10, 77652 Offenburg
Olbernhau: Stadtarchiv, Stadtverwaltung, Grünthaler Str. 28, 09526 Olbernhau
Oldenburg (Oldenburg): Stadtarchiv, Damm 41, Postfach 2427, 26105 Oldenburg
Olfen: Stadtarchiv, Kirchstr. 5, 59309 Olfen, Postfach 134, 59396 Olfen
Olpe/Biggesee: Stadtarchiv, "Altes Lyzeum", Franziskanerstr. 6/8, 57462 Olpe/Biggesee
Olsberg: Stadtarchiv, Stadtverwaltung, 59939 Olsberg, Postfach 1462, 59933 Olsberg
Ortenberg: Stadtarchiv, Kasinostr., Post: Stadtverwaltung/Hauptamt, Lauterbacher Str. 2, 63683 Ortenberg
Ortrand: Amts- und Stadtarchiv Ortrand, 01990 Ortrand
Oschatz: Stadtarchiv, 04758 Oschatz

Ostbevern: Gemeindearchiv. See Kreis Warendorf
Osterholz-Scharmbeck: Stadtarchiv, Rathausstr. 1, 27711 Osterholz-Scharmbeck
Osterode am Harz: Stadtarchiv, Altes Rathaus, Martin-Luther-Platz 2, 37520 Osterode am Harz, Postfach 1720, 37507 Osterode am Harz
Ostfildern: Stadtarchiv, Klosterhof Nellingen, 73760 Ostfildern, Postfach 1120, 73740 Ostfildern
Ottobeuren: Stadtarchiv, Rathaus, Marktplatz 6, 87724 Ottobeuren
Owen/Teck: Stadtarchiv, Bürgermeisteramt, Postfach 1151, 73277 Owen/Teck
Paderborn: Stadtarchiv, Marienplatz 2a, 33095 Paderborn
Parchim: Stadtarchiv, Putlitzer Str. 56, 19370 Parchim
Passau: Stadtarchiv, Rathausplatz 2, 94032 Passau, Postfach 2447, 94014 Passau
Pausa: Stadtarchiv, Newmarkt 1, 07952 Pausa
Peine: Stadtarchiv, Windmühlenwall 26, 31224 Peine, Postfach 1760, 31207 Peine
Peitz: Amtsarchiv Peitz, Markt 1, 03185 Peitz
Penig: Stadtarchiv, Markt 6, 09322 Penig
Perleberg: Stadtarchiv, Rathaus, Großer Markt, 19348 Perleberg
Petershagen: Stadtarchiv, Rathaus, Bahnhofstr. 63, 32469 Petershagen, Postfach 1120, 32458 Petershagen
Pfaffenhofen an der Ilm: Stadtarchiv, Hauptplatz 1, 85276 Pfaffenhofen an der Ilm
Pforzheim: Stadtarchiv, Brettener Str. 19, 75177 Pforzheim
Pfullendorf: Stadt- und Spitalarchiv, Bürgermeisteramt, 88630 Pfullendorf (Baden)
Pfullingen: Stadtarchiv, Bürgermeisteramt, 72793 Pfullingen
Pfungstadt: Stadtarchiv, Stadtverwaltung, Kirchstr. 12-14, Postfach 64319 Pfungstadt
Philippsburg: Stadtarchiv, Rote-Tor-Str.

10, 76661 Philippsburg
Pirmasens: Stadtarchiv, Stadtverwalt-ung, 66953 Pirmasens
Pirna: Stadtarchiv, Klosterhof 3, 01796 Pirna
Plauen (Vogtland): Stadtarchiv, Unterer Graben 1, 08523 Plauen (Vogtland)
Plettenberg: Stadtarchiv, Bahnhofstr. 103, 58840 Plettenberg
Plochingen: Stadtarchiv, Stadtverwalt-ung, Schulstr. 5, 73207 Plochingen
Plön: Archiv der Stadt, Schloßberg 4, 24306 Plön
Pößneck: Stadtarchiv, Rathaus, Markt 11, 07381 Pößneck, Postfach 126, 07373 Pößneck
Pöttmes: Marktarchiv, v.-Gumppenberg-Str. 19, 86554 Pöttmes
Pohlheim: Stadtarchiv, 35415 Pohlheim, Postfach 1154, 35411 Pohlheim
Porta Westfalica: Stadtarchiv, Kempstr. 1, 32457 Porta Westfalica, Postfach 1463, 32440 Porta Westfalica
Potsdam: Stadtarchiv, Freidrich-Ebert-Str. 79-81, 14469 Potsdam
Premnitz: Amtsarchiv Premnitz, Liebigstr. 43, 14727 Premnitz
Prenzlau: Stadtarchiv, Am Steintor 4, 17291 Prenzlau
Preußisch Oldendorf: Stadtarchiv, Rathausstr. 3, 32361 Preußisch Oldendorf, Postfach 1260, 32353 Preußisch Oldendorf
Prien am Chiemsee: Marktarchiv, Rathaus, Hauptverwaltung, Rathausplatz 1, 83209 Prien am Chiemsee
Prüm: Stadtarchiv, Rathaus, 54595 Prüm, Postfach 1060, 54591 Prüm
Püttlingen/Saar: Stadtarchiv, Postfach 101240, 66338 Püttlingen/Saar
Pulheim: Stadtarchiv, Rathaus, Alte Kölner Str. 26, 50259 Pulheim, Postfach 1345, 50241 Pulheim
Quakenbrück: Stadtarchiv, 49610 Quak-enbrück (Stored in Niedersächsischen Staatsarchiv in Osnabrück)
Quedlinburg: Stadtarchiv, Stadtverwalt-ung, Markt 1, Postfach 97, 06472 Quedlinburg

Querfurt: Stadtarchiv, Stadtverwaltung, Markt 1, 06268 Querfurt
Radeberg: Stadtarchiv, Markt 19, 01454 Radeberg
Radebeul: Stadtarchiv, Gohliser Str. 1, 01445 Radebeul, Postfach 010121, 01435 Radebeul
Radevormwald: Stadtarchiv, 42477 Radevormwald
Radolfzell: Stadtarchiv, Löwengasse 12, 78315 Radolfzell am Bodensee
Rahden: Stadtarchiv, Lange Str. 9, 32369 Rahden
Rain: Stadtarchiv, Hauptstr. 60, 86641 Rain
Rastatt: Stadtarchiv, Herrenstr. 11, 76437 Rastatt
Rastenberg: Stadtarchiv, Markt 1, 99636 Rastenberg
Rathenow: Stadtarchiv, Jahnstr. 34, 14712 Rathenow
Ratingen: Stadtarchiv, Mülheimer Str. 47, 40878 Ratingen
Raunheim: Stadtarchiv, Rathaus, Schulstr. 2, 65479 Raunheim
Ravensburg: Stadtarchiv, Kuppelnaustr. 7, 88212 Ravensburg, Postfach 2180, 88191 Ravensburg
Recke: Gemeindearchiv, 49509 Recke, Postfach 1252, 49506 Recke
Recklinghausen: Stadt- und Vestisches Archiv, Hohenzollernstr. 12, 45659 Recklinghausen
Rees: Stadtarchiv, Sahlerstr. 8, 46459 Rees
Regen: Stadtarchiv, Stadtverwaltung, Rathaus, 94209 Regen
Regensburg: Stadtarchiv, Keplerstraße 1, 93047 Regensburg, Postfach 110643, 93019 Regensburg
Rehau (Oberfranken): Stadtarchiv, Stadtverwaltung, Martin-Luther-Str. 1, 95111 Rehau (Oberfranken), Postfach 1560, 95105 Rehau (Oberfranken)
Rehden: Samtgemeindearchiv, Schulstr. 18, 49452 Rehden
Rehna: Stadtarchiv, Mühlenstr. 1, 19217 Rehna
Reichenbach (Vogtland): Stadtarchiv,

Markt 6, 08468 Reichenbach (Vogtland)
Reinbek: Stadtarchiv, Rathaus, Hamburger Str. 7, 21465 Reinbek
Reinheim: Stadtarchiv, Kirchstr. 24 (IM Hofgut), Stadtverwaltung, Cestasplatz 1, 64354 Reinheim
Remagen: Stadtarchiv, Rathaus, 53424 Remagen
Remda: Verwaltungsgemeinschaft Remda, Stadtarchiv, Rudolstädter Str. 8-10, Haus II, 07407 Remda
Remscheid: Stadtarchiv, Honsberger Str. 4, 42849 Remscheid
Remseck am Neckar: Stadtarchiv, Bürgermeisteramt, 71686 Remseck am Neckar, Postfach 1163, 71480 Remseck am Neckar
Renchen: Stadtarchiv, Stadtverwaltung, Hauptstr. 57, 77871 Renchen
Rendsburg: Archiv der Stadt, Am Gymnasium 4, 24768 Rendsburg
Rethem (Aller): Stadtverwaltung, Lange Str. 4, 27336 Rethem (Aller), Postfach 1240, 27335 Rethem (Aller)
Reutlingen: Stadtarchiv, Rathaus, Marktplatz 22, 72764 Reutlingen, Postfach 2543, 72715 Reutlingen
Rheda-Wiedenbrück: Stadtarchiv, Rathausplatz 13, 33378 Rheda-Wiedenbrück, Postfach 2309, 33375 Rheda-Wiedenbrück
Rhede: Hauptamt, Archiv, Rathausplatz 9, 46414 Rhede, Postfach 64, 46406 Rhede
Rheinbach: Stadtarchiv, Himmeroder Wall 6, 53359 Rheinbach, Postfach 1128, 53348 Rheinbach
Rheinberg: Stadtarchiv, Alte Kellnerei, Innenwall 104, 47495 Rheinberg, Postfach, 47493 Rheinberg
Rheine: Stadtarchiv, Marktstr. 12, 48431 Rheine, Postfach 2063, 48410 Rheine
Rheinfelden (Baden): Stadtarchiv, Kirchplatz 2, 79618 Rheinfelden (Baden), Postfach 1560, 79605 Rheinfelden (Baden)
Rheurdt: Gemeindearchiv, Rathausstr. 35, 47509 Rheurdt
Rhinow: Amtsarchiv Rhinow, Lilienthalstr. 3, 14728 Rhinow
Ribnitz-Damgarten: Stadtarchiv, Im Kloster 3, 18303 Ribnitz-Damgarten
Riedenburg: Stadtarchiv, Postfach 28, 93337 Riedenburg
Riedlingen: Stadtarchiv, Stadtverwaltung, 88499 Riedlingen
Rieneck: Stadtarchiv, Bürgerzentrum, Schulgasse 4, 97794 Rieneck
Rietberg: Stadtarchiv, Rügenstr. 1, 33397 Rietberg
Rinteln: Stadtarchiv, Marktplatz 7 (Bürgerhaus), 31737 Rinteln, Postfach 1460, 31724 Rinteln
Rodewisch: Stadtarchiv, Wernesgrüner Str. 32, 08228 Rodewisch
Rodgau: Stadtarchiv, Stadtteil Dudenhofen, Altes Rathauss, Georg-August-Zinn-Str.1 und Stadtteil Jügesheim, Neues Rathaus, Hintergasse 15, 63110 Rodgau
Roding: Stadtarchiv, Stadtverwaltung, Schulstr. 12, 93426 Roding
Rödermark: Stadtarchiv, Stadtverwaltung, 63322 Rödermark
Rödinghausen: Gemeindearchiv, Heerstr. 2, 32289 Rödinghausen
Römhild: Stadtverwaltung Römhild, Stadtarchiv, Griebelstr. 28, 98631 Römhild, Dienstsitz: Schloß "Glücksburg", 98631 Römhild
Rommerskirchen: Gemeindearchiv, Nettesheimer Weg (Schulgebäude), 41569 Rommerskirchen, Postfach 101160, 41565 Rommerskirchen
Romrod: Stadtarchiv, Stadtverwaltung, 36329 Romrod
Rosendahl: Gemeindearchiv, Hauptstr. 30, 48720 Rosendahl, Postfach 1109, 48713 Rosendahl
Rosengarten: Ortsteilarchive Westheim, Rieden und Uttenhofen, Post: Gemeindeverwaltung, 74538 Rosengarten
Rosengarten: Gemeindearchiv, Bremer Str. 42, 21224 Rosengarten-Nenndorf, Postfach 240, 21222 Rosengarten-Nenndorf
Rosenheim (Oberbayern): Stadtarchiv, Max-Bram-Platz 2a, 83022 Rosenheim (Oberbayern)

Rostock: Archiv der Hansestadt Rostock, Hinter dem Rathaus 5, 18050 Rostock

Rot am See: Gemeindearchiv, Rathaus, Raiffeisenstr. 1, 74585 Rot am See

Rotenburg/Wümme: Stadtarchiv, Rathaus, Große Str. 1, 27356 Rotenburg/Wümme

Roth (Mittelfranken): Stadtarchiv, Hauptstr. 1, 91154 Roth (Mittelfranken), Postfach 40, 91142 Roth (Mittelfranken)

Rothenburg ob der Tauber: Stadtarchiv, Büttelhaus, Milchmarkt 2, 91541 Rothenburg ob der Tauber

Rottenburg am Neckar: Stadt- und Spitalarchiv, Obere Gasse 12, 72108 Rottenburg am Neckar, Postfach 29, 72101 Rottenburg am Neckar

Rottweil: Stadtarchiv, Engelgasse 13, 78628 Rottweil, Postfach 1753, 78617 Rottweil

Rudolstadt: Stadtarchiv, Rathaus, Markt 7, 07407 Rudolstadt

Rüdesheim: Stadtarchiv, Stadtverwaltung, Rathaus, Markt 16, 65385 Rüdesheim am Rhein

Rümmingen: Gemeindearchiv, Rathaus, Lörracher Str. 9, 79595 Rümmingen

Rüsselsheim: Stadtarchiv, In der Festung, Hauptmann-Scheuermann-Weg 4, 65428 Rüsselsheim

Rüthen: Stadtarchiv, Stadtverwaltung, Hochstr. 14, 59602 Rüthen, Postfach 1026, 59598 Rüthen

Ruhpolding: Gemeinde Ruhpolding, Gemeindearchiv, Postfach 1180, 83318 Ruhpolding

Saalburg: Stadtverwaltung Saalburg, Stadtarchiv, Markt 1, 07929 Saalburg

Saalfeld: Stadtarchiv, Rathaus, Markt 1, 07318 Saalfeld

Saarbrücken: Stadtarchiv, Nauwieserstr. 3, 66111 Saarbrücken

Saarlouis: Stadtarchiv, Alte Brauereistr., Kaserne VI, 66740 Saarlouis

Sachsenheim (Württemberg): Stadtarchiv, Äußerer Schloßhof, 74343 Sachsenheim (Württemberg), Postfach 1260, 74338 Sachsenheim (Württemberg)

Salem: Gemeindearchiv, Bürgermeister- amt, 88682 Salem-Neufrach

Salzgitter: Stadtarchiv, Nord-Süd-Str. 155, 38206 Salzgitter

Salzhausen: Archiv der Samtgemeinde, 21376 Salzhausen

Salzwedel: Stadtarchiv, Stadtverwaltung, Mönchskirche 7, 29410 Salzwedel

Sangerhausen: Stadtarchiv, Stadtverwaltung, Markt 1, 06526 Sangerhausen

Sankt Augustin/Sieg: Stadtarchiv, Rathaus, Markt 1, 53757 Sankt Augustin/Sieg

Sankt Goar: Stadtarchiv, Grundschule, Heerstr., Post: Stadtverwaltung, Heerst. 130, 56329 Sankt Goar

Sankt Ingbert/Saar: Stadtarchiv, Stadtverwaltung, Am Markt 12, 66386 Sankt Ingbert/Saar

Sankt Wendel (Saarland): Stadtarchiv, Mia-Münster-Haus (Mott), 66606 Sankt Wendel (Saarland)

Sarstedt: Stadtarchiv, Kirchplatz 2, 31157 Sarstedt, Post: Steinstr. 22, 31157 Sarstedt

Sassenberg: Stadtarchiv. See Kreis Warendorf

Saterland: Gemeindearchiv, Ramsloh, Hauptstr. 507, 26683 Saterland, Postfach 1164, 26677 Saterland

Saulgau: Stadtarchiv, Bürgermeisteramt, Postfach 1151, 88340 Saulgau

Sayda: Stadtarchiv, Schulgasse 7, 09619 Sayda

Schaafheim: Gemeindearchiv, Gemeindeverwaltung, Wilhelm-Leuschner-Str. 3, 64850 Schaafheim

Schauenburg: Gemeindearchiv, Raiffeisenstr. 5, 34270 Schauenburg

Scheibenberg: Stadtarchiv, Rudolf-Breitscheid-Str. 35, 09481 Scheibenberg

Schelklingen: Stadtarchiv, Stadtverwaltung, 89601 Schelklingen

Schieder-Schwalenberg: Stadtarchiv, Domäne 3, 32816 Schieder-Schwalenberg, Postfach 1265, 32807 Schieder-Schwalenberg

Schiltach: Stadtarchiv, Stadtverwaltung, Postfach 1144, 77757 Schiltach

Schleiden (Eifel): Historisches Archiv

der Stadt, Blankenheimer Str. 2-4 (Behördenhaus), 53937 Schleiden (Eifel)
Schleiz: Stadtarchiv, Bahnhofstr. 1, 07907 Schleiz
Schleswig: Stadtarchiv, Plessenstr. 7, 24837 Schleswig
Schlettau: Stadtarchiv, Markt 1, 09487 Schlettau
Schliersee: Gemeindearchiv, Rathaus, 83727 Schliersee
Schlitz: Stadtarchiv, An der Kirche 4, 36110 Schlitz
Schloß-Holte/Stukenbrock: Gemeindearchiv, Rathausstr. 2, 33758 Schloß-Holte/Stukenbrock
Schlüchtern: Stadtarchiv, 36381 Schlüchtern
Schmalkalden: Stadtarchiv (See Landkreis Schmalkalden-Meiningen)
Schmallenberg: Stadtarchiv, Stadtverwaltung, 57392 Schmallenberg, Postfach 1140, 57376 Schmallenberg
Schneeberg: Stadtarchiv, Kirchgasse 3, 08289 Schneeberg
Schönau am Königsee: Gemeindearchiv, Rathaus, 83471 Schönau am Königsee
Schönebeck/Elbe: Stadtarchiv, Burghof 1, 39218 Schönebeck/Elbe
Schöneck (Vogtland): Stadtarchiv, Sonnenwirbel 3, 08261 Schöneck (Vogtland)
Schöningen: Stadtarchiv, Rathaus, 38364 Schöningen
Schöppingen: Gemeindearchiv, 48624 Schöppingen, Postfach 1107, 48620 Schöppingen
Schongau: Stadtarchiv und Stadtmuseum, Christophstr. 55-57, 86956 Schongau
Schopfheim: Stadtarchiv, Hauptstr. 29, 79650 Schopfheim, Postfach 1160, 79641 Schopfheim
Schorndorf (Württemberg): Stadtarchiv, Archivstr. 4, 73614 Schorndorf (Württemberg), Postfach 1560, 73605 Schorndorf (Württemberg)
Schotten (Hessen): Stadtarchiv, Stadtverwaltung, 63679 Schotten (Hessen)
Schramberg: Stadtarchiv, Im Schloß,

78713 Schramberg
Schriesheim: Stadtarchiv, Rathaus, 69198 Schriesheim
Schrobenhausen: Stadtarchiv, Lenbachplatz 18, 86529 Schrobenhausen, Postfach 1380, 86523 Schrobenhausen
Schüttorf: Stadtverwaltung, Rathaus, 48459 Schüttorf, Postfach 1420, 48459 Schüttorf
Schulenberg: (See Clausthal-Zellerfeld)
Schwabach (Mittelfranken): Stadtarchiv, Stadtverwaltung, 91126 Schwabach (Mittelfranken), Postfach 2120, 91114 Schwabach (Mittelfranken)
Schwabmünchen: Stadtarchiv, Fuggerstr. 50, 86830 Schwabmünchen, Postfach 1252, 86827 Schwabmünchen
Schwäbisch Gmünd: Stadtarchiv, Augustinerstr. 3, 73525 Schwäbisch Gmünd
Schwäbisch Hall: Stadtarchiv, Am Markt 5 und Nonnenhof 4, 74523 Schwäbisch Hall
Schwalbach am Taunus: Stadtarchiv, Stadtverwaltung, Marktplatz 1-2, 65824 Schwalbach am Taunus, Postfach 2710, 65820 Schwalbach am Taunus
Schwandorf (Bayern): Stadtarchiv, Stadtverwaltung, Kirchengasse 1, 92421 Schwandorf (Bayern), Postfach 1880, 92409 Schwandorf (Bayern)
Schwarzenbach an der Saale: Stadtarchiv, 95126 Schwarzenbach an der Saale
Schwarzenbek: Stadtarchiv, Rathaus, Ritter-Wulf-Platz 1, 21493 Shwarzenbek
Schwedt/Oder: Stadtverwaltung, Schwedt/Oder, Dezernat Kultur und Bildung, Kulturamt, Stadtarchiv, Bahnhofstr. 21, 16303 Schwedt/Oder, Postfach 66, 16284 Schwedt/Oder
Schweinfurt: Stadtarchiv , Friedrich-Rückert-Bau, Martin-Luther-Platz 20, 97421 Schweinfurt
Schwelm: Stadtarchiv, Haus Martfeld 1, 58332 Schwelm
Schwenningen: (See Villingen-Schwenningen)
Schwerin: Stadtarchiv, Platz der Jugend 12-14 und Johannes-Stelling-Str. 2, 19053

Schwerin
Schweringen: Gemeindearchiv, Dorfstr.
5, 27333 Schweringen
Schwerte: Stadtarchiv, Brückstr. 14,
58239 Schwerte
Schwetzingen: Stadtarchiv, Bürgermeist-
eramt, Hebelstr. 1, 68723 Schwetzingen,
Postfach 1920, 68721 Schwetzingen
Sebnitz: Stadtarchiv, Kirchstr. 5, 01855
Sebnitz, Postfach 182, 01851 Sebnitz
Seevetal: Gemeindearchiv, Am Schul-
teich 1, 21217 Seevetal
Selbitz (Oberfranken): Stadtarchiv,
Rathaus, 95152 Selbitz (Oberfranken)
Selfkant: Gemeindearchiv, Gemeinde-
direktor, Hauptamt, 52538 Selfkant,
Postfach 1315, 52539 Selfkant
Seligenstadt (Hessen): Stadtarchiv,
Rathaus, Post: Stadtverwaltung, Postfach
63500 Seligenstadt (Hessen)
Selm: Stadtarchiv, Rathaus, 59379 Selm
Senden: Gemeindearchiv, Münsterstr. 30,
Postfach 1251, 48303 Senden
Sendenhorst: Stadt- und Heimatarchiv,
Stadtverwaltung, Rathaus, Kirchstr. 1,
48324 Sendenhorst
Siegburg: Stadtarchiv, Stadtverwaltung,
Nogenter Platz 10, 53721 Siegburg,
Postfach 53719 Siegburg
Siegen: Stadtarchiv, Oranienstr. 15,
57072 Siegen, Postfach 100352, 57003
Siegen
Simmern: Rhein-Hunsrück-Archiv,
Schloß, 55469 Simmern
Simmerath: Gemeindearchiv, Rathaus,
52152 Simmerath
Sindelfingen: Stadtarchiv, Rathausplatz
1, 71063 Sindelfingen, Postfach 180,
71043 Sindelfingen
Singen (Hohentwiel): Stadtarchiv,
August-Ruf-Str. 7, 78224 Singen
(Hohentwiel), Postfach 760, 78207 Singen
(Hohentwiel)
Sinsheim: Stadtarchiv, Wilhelmstr. 14-
16, 74889 Sinsheim, Postfach 74877
Sinsheim
Sömmerda: Stadtarchiv, Marktplatz 2-
4, 99610 Sömmerda
Soest: Stadtarchiv, Jakobistr. 13, 59494

Soest, Postfach 2252, 59491 Soest
Solingen: Stadtarchiv, Gasstr. 22b, 42657
Solingen
Soltau: Stadtarchiv, Altes Rathaus, 29614
Soltau, Postfach 1444, 29604 Soltau
Sondershausen: Stadtverwaltung
Sondershausen, Stadtarchiv, Postfach 30,
99701 Sondershausen, Dienstsitz: Markt
7, 99706 Sondershausen
Sonneberg: Stadtarchiv, Stadtverwalt-
ung, Bahnhofsplatz 1, 96515 Sonneberg,
Postfach 169, 96504 Sonneberg
Sonnewalde: Stadtarchiv, Schloßstr. 21,
03249 Sonnewalde
Sonsbeck: Gemeindearchiv, Herrenstr. 2,
47665 Sonsbeck
Sonthofen: Stadtarchiv, Rathausplatz 1,
87527 Sonthofen
Spaichingen: Stadtarchiv, Stadtverwalt-
ung, 78549 Spaichingen
Spenge: Stadtarchiv, Stadtverwaltung,
Rathaus, Lange Str. 52-56, 32139 Spenge
Speyer: Stadtarchiv, Maximilianstr. 12,
67346 Speyer
Spiegelau: Gemeindearchiv, 94518 Spie-
gelau
Sprendlingen: Stadtarchiv, Stadtverwalt-
ung, 6079 Sprendlingen
Springe: Stadtarchiv, Hauptamt, Auf dem
Burghof 1, 31832 Springe
Sprockhövel: Stadtarchiv, 45549 Sprock-
hövel, Postfach 922040, 45541 Sprock-
hövel
Stade: Stadtarchiv, Johannisstr. 5, 21677
Stade
Stadthagen: Stadtarchiv, 31655 Stadt-
hagen, Postfach 327, 31653 Stadthagen
Stadtlengsfeld: Stadtverwaltung Stadt-
lengsfeld, Stadtarchiv, Amtsstraße 8,
36467 Stadtlengsfeld
Stadtlohn: Stadtarchiv, Stadtverwaltung,
Postfach 1465, 48695 Stadtlohn
Starnberg: Stadtarchiv, Stadtverwaltung,
Vogelanger 2, 82319 Starnberg, Postfach
1680, 82306 Starnberg
Staßfurt: Stadtarchiv, Bernburger Str. 13,
39418 Staßfurt
Staufen (Breisgau): Stadtarchiv, Bürg-
ermiesteramt, 79219 Staufen (Breisgau)

Steinach: Stadtverwaltung Steinach, Stadtarchiv, Postfach 81, 96520 Steinach, Dienstsitz: Marktplatz 4, 96523 Steinach
Steinbach: Stadtarchiv, 76487 Baden-Baden Steinbach
Steinfurt: Stadtarchiv An der Hohen Schule 13, 48565 Steinfurt, Postfach 2480, 48553 Steinfurt
Steinhagen: Gemeindearchiv, Am Pulverbach 25, 33803 Steinhagen
Steinheim (Westfalen): Stadtarchiv, Marktstr. 2, 32839 Steinheim (Westfalen)
Stelle: Gemeindearchiv, Unter den Linden 18, 21435 Stelle
Stendal: Stadtarchiv, Markt 1, 39576 Stendal
Sternberg: Stadtarchiv, Mühlenstr. 14, 19406 Sternberg
Stockach: Stadtarchiv, Rathaus, Adenauerstr. 4, 78333 Stockach
Stolberg (Rheinland): Stadtarchiv, Rathausstr. 11-13, 52222 Stolberg (Rheinland), Postfach 1820, 52205 Stolberg (Rheinland)
Straelen (Niederrhein): Stadtarchiv, Kuhstr. 21, 47638 Straelen (Niederrhein), Postfach 1353, 47630 Straelen (Niederrhein)
Stralsund: Stadtarchiv, Badenstr. 13, 18439 Stralsund
Straubing: Stadtarchiv, Rathaus, Theresienplatz 20, 94315 Straubing, Postfach 0352, 94303 Straubing
Strausberg: Stadtarchiv, Markt 10, 15344 Strausberg
Stuhr: Gemeindearchiv, 28816 Stuhr, Postfach 2130, 28808 Stuhr
Stuttgart: Stadtarchiv, Silberburgstr. 191, 70178 Stuttgart
Südlohn: Gemeindearchiv, Gemeindeverwaltung, Postfach 1030, 46349 Südlohn
Suhl: Stadtarchiv, Stadtverwaltung, Straße der Opfer des Faschismus 5, 98527 Suhl, Postfach 640, 98504 Suhl
Sulingen: Stadtarchiv, Lange Str. 67, 27232 Sulingen, Postfach 1240, 27223 Sulingen
Sulz am Neckar: Stadtarchiv, Stadt-

verwaltung, 72172 Sulz am Neckar, Postfach 1180, 72168 Sulz am Neckar
Sulzbach-Rosenberg: Stadtarchiv, Spitalgasse 21, 92237 Sulzbach-Rosenberg, Postfach 1254, 92230 Sulzbach-Rosenberg
Sundern: Stadtarchiv, Stadtverwaltung, 59846 Sundern, Postfach 1109, 59831 Sundern
Syke: Stadtarchiv, Nienburger Str. 5, 28857 Syke, Postfach 1365, 28847 Syke
Sylt: Sylter Archiv, Stadtarchiv, Alte Post, 25980 Westerland
Tangermünde: Stadtarchiv, Arneburger Str. 94, 39590 Tangermünde
Tann (Rhön): Stadtarchiv, Stadtverwaltung, 36142 Tann (Rhön)
Tanna: Stadtverwaltung Tanna, Stadtarchiv, Markt 1, 07922 Tanna
Tannroda/Ilm: Stadtverwaltung Tannroda, Stadtarchiv, Bahnhofstr. 18, 99448 Tannroda/Ilm
Taucha: Stadtarchiv, Schloßplatz 13, 04425 Taucha
Taunusstein: Stadtarchiv, Magistrat, Stadtteil Hahn, Erich-Kästner-Str. 5, 65232 Taunusstein, Postfach 1552, 65223 Taunusstein
Telgte: Stadtarchiv, Rathaus, Hauptamt, Baßfeld 4-6, 48291 Telgte, Postfach 220, 48284 Telgte
Teltow: Stadtarchiv, Potsdamer Str. 47, 14513 Teltow
Tettnang: Stadtarchiv, Bürgermeisteramt, 88069 Tettnang
Thale: Stadtarchiv, Stadtverwaltung, Rathausstr. 1, 06502 Thale
Themar: Stadtverwaltung Themar, Stadtarchiv Themar, Postfach 58, 98657 Themar, Dienstsitz: Markt 1, 98660 Themar
Tirschenreuth: Stadtarchiv, Maximilianplatz 35, 95643 Tirschenreuth
Titisee-Neustadt: Stadtarchiv, Stadtverwaltung, Rathaus, 79822 Titisee-Neustadt
Tittmoning: Stadtarchiv, Postfach 1106, 84525 Tittmoning
Titz: Gemeindearchiv, Hauptamt, Landstr. 4, 52445 Titz

Tönning: Archiv der Stadt, Rathaus, 25832 Tönning
Toppenstedt: Gemeindearchiv, Lehmelweg 4, 21442 Toppenstedt
Torgau: Stadtarchiv, Markt 1, 04860 Torgau
Tostedt: Samtgemeindearchiv, Schützenstr. 24, 21255 Tostedt
Traunstein (Oberbayern): Stadtarchiv, Stadtplatz 39, 83278 Traunstein (Oberbayern), Post: Stadtarchiv, Stadt Traunstein, Große Kreisstadt, 83276 Traunstein (Oberbayern)
Trebbin: Amtsarchiv Trebbin, Markt 1-3, 14959 Trebbin
Treuchtlingen: Stadtarchiv, Rathaus, 91757 Treuchtlingen
Treuen: Stadtarchiv, Markt 7, 08233 Treuen, Postfach 10032, 08229 Treuen
Triebes: Verwaltungsgemeinschaft Triebes, Stadtarchiv, Schäferstr. 2, 07950 Triebes
Trier: Stadtarchiv, Weberbach 25, 54290 Trier
Triptis: Stadtverwaltung Triptis, Stadtarchiv, Postfach 8, 07817 Triptis, Dienstsitz: Markt 1, 07819 Triptis
Troisdorf: Archiv der Stadt Troisdorf, Am Schirmhof, 53827 Troisdorf-Sieglar
Trostberg: Stadtarchiv, Hauptstr. 24, 83308 Trostberg
Tübingen: Stadtarchiv, Am Markt 1, 72070 Tübingen, Postfach 2540, 72015 Tübingen
Tuttlingen: Stadtarchiv, Rathaus, Rathausstr. 1, 78532 Tuttlingen
Twistringen: Stadtarchiv, Rathaus, Lindenstr. 14, 27239 Twistringen, Postfach 1265, 27234 Twistringen
Überlingen: Stadtarchiv, Stadtverwaltung, Rathaus, 88662 Überlingen (Bodensee), Postfach 101863, 88648 Überlingen (Bodensee)
Uelzen: Stadtarchiv, An der Sankt Marienkirche 1, Postfach 2061, 29525 Uelzen
Ulm: Stadtarchiv, Schwörhaus, Weinhof 12, 89073 Ulm, Postfach 3940, 89070 Ulm

Ulrichstein: Stadtarchiv, Hauptstr. 9, 35327 Ulrichstein
Ummerstadt: Stadtarchiv. See Landkreis Hildburghausen
Unkel: Stadtarchiv, Graf-Blumenthal-Str. 13, 53572 Unkel
Unna: Stadtarchiv, Klosterstr. 12, 59423 Unna, Postfach 2113, 59411 Unna
Unterhaching: Gemeindearchiv, 82008 Unterhaching
Usingen: Stadtarchiv, Stadtverwaltung, Postfach, 61250 Usingen
Uslar: Stadtarchiv, Graftplatz 3, 37170 Uslar
Vaihingen an der Enz: Stadtarchiv, Spitalstr. 8, 71665 Vaihingen an der Enz
Varel: Stadtverwaltung, Rathaus, Windallee 4, 26316 Varel, Postfach 1669, 26306 Varel
Vechta: Stadtarchiv (Stored in Niedersächsischen Staatsarchiv in Oldenburg)
Velbert: Stadtarchiv, Zum Hardenberger Schloß 4, 42553 Velbert
Velen: Gemeindearchiv, Ramsdorfer Str. 19, 46342 Velen, Postfach 1260, 46335 Velen
Vellmar: Stadtarchiv, Stadtverwaltung, Rathausplatz 1, 34246 Vellmar
Ventorf: Gemeindearchiv (See Archivgemeinschaft Schwarzenbek)
Verden (Aller): Stadtarchiv, Ritterstr. 22, 27283 Verden (Aller)
Verl: Gemeindearchiv, Paderborner Str. 3/5, 33415 Verl
Versmold: Stadtarchiv, Schulstr. 14, 33775 Versmold, Postfach 1464, 33762 Versmold
Vettweiß: Gemeindearchiv, Gereonstr. 14, 52391 Vettweiß, Postfach 1124, 52389 Vettweiß
Vienenburg: Stadtverwaltung, 38690 Vienenburg
Viernheim: Stadtarchiv, Stadtverwaltung, 68519 Viernheim, Postfach 1640, 68506 Viernheim
Viersen: Stadtarchiv, Wilhelmstr. 12, 41747 Viersen
Villingen-Schwenningen: Stadtarchiv, Lantwattenstr. 4, 78050 Villingen-

Schwenningen, Postfach 1260, 78002 Villingen-Schwenningen
Vilshofen: Stadtarchiv, Bürg 3, 94474 Vilshofen
Vlotho: Stadtarchiv, Lange Str. 60, 32602 Vlotho, Postfach 1705, 32591 Vlotho
Völklingen/Saar: Stadtarchiv, Neues Rathaus, Hindenburgplatz, 66333 Völklingen/Saar
Voerde (Niederrhein): Stadtarchiv, Rathausplatz 20, 46562 Voerde (Niederrhein)
Vohburg an der Donau: Stadtarchiv, Rathaus, Ulrich-Steinberger-Platz 12, 85088 Vohburg an der Donau
Volkach: Stadtarchiv in der Kartause Astheim, Verwaltungsgemeinschaft, 97332 Volkach
Vreden: Stadtarchiv, Burgstr. 14, 48686 Vreden, Postfach 1351, 48691 Vreden
Wachenheim an der Weinstraße: Stadtarchiv, Weinstr. 16, 67157 Wachenheim an der Weinstraße
Wachtberg: Gemeindearchiv, Rathausstr. 34, 53343 Wachtberg
Wachtendonk: Gemeindearchiv, Rathaus, Weinstr. 1, 47669 Wachtendonk
Wadersloh: Gemeindearchiv (See Kreis Warendorf)
Wächtersbach: Stadtarchiv, Stadtverwaltung, Postfach 1164, 63601 Wächtersbach
Waiblingen: Stadtarchiv, Kurze Str. 25, 71332 Waiblingen, Postfach 1751, 71328 Waiblingen
Waldbröl: Stadtarchiv, 51545 Waldbröl, Postfach 1620, 51536 Waldbröl
Waldfeucht: Gemeindearchiv, Lambertusstr. 13, 52525 Waldfeucht
Waldkirch: Stadtarchiv, Marktplatz 5, 79183 Waldkirch
Waldkraiburg: Stadtarchiv, Stadtplatz 26, 84478 Waldkraiburg, Postfach 1180, 84464 Waldkraiburg
Waldsassen: Stadtarchiv, Stadtverwaltung, Basilikaplatz 3, 95652 Waldsassen
Waldshut-Tiengen: Stadtarchiv, Stadtverwaltung, Kaiserstr. 28-32, 79761 Waldshut-Tiengen, Postfach 1941, 79746 Waldshut-Tiengen

Walsrode: Stadtarchiv, Rathaus, Lange Str. 22, 29664 Walsrode, Postfach 1440, 29654 Walsrode
Waltrop: Stadtverwaltung, Rathaus, Münsterstr. 1, Postfach 120, 45722 Waltrop
Wangen: Stadtarchiv, Rathaus, 88239 Wangen im Allgäu, Postfach 1154, 88227 Wangen im Allgäu
Warburg: Stadtarchiv, Sternstr. 35, 34414 Warburg
Waren: Stadtarchiv, Lange Str. 22, 17192 Waren
Warendorf: Stadtarchiv. See Kreis Warendorf
Warstein: Stadtarchiv, Rathaus, Dieplohstr. 1, 59581 Warstein
Wassenberg: Stadtarchiv, Roermonder Str. 25-27, 41849 Wassenberg, Postfach 1220, 41846 Wassenberg
Wasserburg am Inn: Stadtarchiv, Stadtverwaltung, 83512 Wasserburg am Inn, Postfach 1680, 83506 Wasserburg am Inn
Wasungen: Stadtverwaltung Wasungen, Stadtarchiv, Markt 7, 98634 Wasungen
Weeze: Gemeindearchiv, Cyriakusplatz 13/14, 47652 Weeze, Postfach 1265, 47649 Weeze
Wegberg: Stadtarchiv, Rathausplatz 25, 41844 Wegberg
Wehr: Stadtarchiv, Bürgermeisteramt, Hauptstr. 16, 79664 Wehr
Weida: Stadtverwaltung Weida, Stadtarchiv, Petersberg 2, 07570 Weida
Weiden in der Oberpfalz: Stadtarchiv, Kulturzentrum Hans Bauer, Pfarrplatz 4, 92637 Weiden in der Oberpfalz
Weikersheim: Stadtarchiv, Stadtverwaltung, Postfach 9, 97990 Weikersheim
Weil am Rhein: Stadtarchiv, Stadtverwaltung, Schillerstr. 1, 79576 Weil am Rhein
Weil der Stadt: Stadtarchiv, Stadtverwaltung, Postfach 1120, 71261 Weil der Stadt
Weilburg: Historisches Archiv der Stadt, Schloßplatz 1 , 35781 Weilburg, Postfach

1420, 35781 Weilburg
Weilerswist: Gemeindearchiv, Bonner Str. 29, 53919 Weilerswist
Weilheim an der Teck: Stadtarchiv, Marktplatz 6, 73235 Weilheim an der Teck, Postfach 1154, 73231 Weilheim an der Teck
Weilheim (Oberbayern): Stadtarchiv, Admiral-Hipper-Str. 20, 82362 Weilheim (Oberbayern), Postfach 1664, 82360 Weilheim (Oberbayern)
Weimar: Stadtarchiv, Postfach 14, 99421 Weimar, Dienstsitz: Markt 1, 99423 Weimar
Weingarten (Württemberg): Stadtarchiv, Schützenstr. 3/1, 88250 Weingarten (Württemberg)
Weinheim (Bergstraße): Stadtarchiv, Schulstr. 5/1, 69469 Weinheim (Bergstraße), Postfach 100961, 69449 Weinheim (Bergstraße)
Weinstadt: Stadtarchiv, Postfach 1327, 71373 Weinstadt
Weißenburg in Bayern: Stadtarchiv, Postfach 569, 91780 Weißenburg in Bayern
Weißenfels: Stadtarchiv, Nikolaistr. 13, 06667 Weißenfels
Weißensee: Stadtverwaltung Weißensee, Stadtarchiv, Marktplatz 26, 99631 Weißensee
Weismain: Stadtarchiv, Stadtverwaltung, Am Markt 19, 96260 Weismain, Postfach 27, 96258 Weismain
Welzow: Stadtarchiv Welzow, Rathaus, 16278 Welzow
Wemding: Stadtarchiv, Postfach 29, 86650 Wemding
Wentorf: Gemeindearchiv, Hauptstr. 2, 21465 Wentorf bei Hamburg
Werdau: Stadtarchiv, Markt 12, 08412 Werdau
Werder/Havel: Stadtarchiv, Eisenbahnstr. 13/14, 14542 Werder/Havel
Werdohl: Stadtarchiv, Stadtverwaltung, Goethestr. 51, 58791 Werdohl
Werl: Stadtarchiv, Rathaus, Hedwig-Dransfeld-Str. 23, 59457 Werl, Postfach 6040, 59455 Werl

Wermelskirchen: Stadtarchiv, Stadtverwaltung, 42929 Wermelskirchen, Postfach 1110, 42904 Wermelskirchen
Werne: Stadtarchiv, Kirchhof 9, 59368 Werne, Postfach 1552, 59358 Werne
Werneuchen: Amtsarchiv Werneuchen, Am Markt 5, 16356 Werneuchen
Wernigerode: Stadtarchiv, Burgstr. 49, 38855 Wernigerode
Wertheim: Stadtarchiv. See Staatsarchiv Wertheim (Archivverbund Main-Tauber)
Werther (Westfalen): Stadtarchiv, Kulturamt, Mühlenstr. 2, 33824 Werther (Westfalen)
Wesel: Stadtarchiv, Rathaus, Klever-Tor-Platz 1, 46483 Wesel
Wesseling: Stadtarchiv, 50379 Wesseling, Postfach 1564, 50389 Wesseling
Westerkappeln: Gemeindearchiv, Große Str. 13, 49492 Westerkappeln
Westerstede: Stadtarchiv, Albert-Post-Platz 19, 26653 Westerstede
Wetter (Ruhr): Stadtarchiv, Burgstr. 17, 58300 Wetter (Ruhr), Postfach 146, 58287 Wetter (Ruhr)
Wettringen: Gemeindearchiv, Kirchstr. 19, 48493 Wettringen
Wetzlar: Stadtarchiv, Rathaus, Hauser Gasse 17, 35578 Wetzlar, Postf. 2120, 35573 Wetzlar
Weyhe: Gemeindearchiv, Ortsteil Sudweyhe, Im Mühlengrunde 15 (Wassermühle), Post: Rathausplatz 1, 28844 Weyhe, Postfach 1160, 28838 Weyhe
Wiehe: Stadtverwaltung, Stadtarchiv, Postfach 6, 06571 Wiehe; Dienstsitz: Leopold-von-Ranke-Str. 33, 06571 Wiehe
Wiesbaden: Stadtarchiv, Im Rad 20, 65197 Wiesbaden, Postfach 3920, 65029 Wiesbaden
Wiesensteig: Stadtarchiv, Hauptstr. 25, 73349 Wiesensteig
Wiesloch: Stadtarchiv, 69168 Wiesloch, Postfach 1520, 69156 Wiesloch
Wietze: Gemeindearchiv, Steinförder Str. 4, 29321 Wietze
Wildemann: (See Clausthal-Zellerfeld)
Wildenfels: Stadtarchiv, Poststr. 26, 08134 Wildenfels

Wilhelmshaven: Stadtarchiv, Rathausplatz 10, 26382 Wilhelmshaven, Postfach 1180, 26359 Wilhelmshaven
Wilkau-Haßlau: Stadtarchiv, Dezernat Hauptverwaltung, Postfach 9, 08110 Wilkau-Haßlau
Willich: Stadtarchiv, Albert-Oetker-Str. 98-102, 47877 Willich
Wilster: Stadtarchiv, Klosterhof 28, 25554 Wilster
Windischeschenbach: Stadtarchiv, Rathaus, Hauptstr. 34, 92670 Windischeschenbach
Winnenden: Stadtarchiv, Marktstr. 47, 71364 Winnenden, Postfach 280, 71350 Winnenden
Winsen/Aller: Gemeindearchiv, Am Amtshof 8, 29308 Winsen/Aller
Winsen/Luhe: Stadtarchiv, Rathausstr. 1, 21423 Winsen/Luhe, Postfach 1240, 21412 Winsen/Luhe
Winterberg (Westfalen): Stadtarchiv, Stadtverwaltung, 59955 Winterberg (Westfalen), Postfach 1005, 59941 Winterberg (Westfalen)
Winterstein: Gemeindeverwaltung Winterstein, Gemeindearchiv, Liebensteiner Str. 14, 99891 Winterstein
Wipperfürth: Stadtarchiv, Marktplatz 1, 51688 Wipperfürth, Postfach 1460, 51678 Wipperfürth
Wismar: Stadtarchiv, Vor dem Fürstenhof 1, 23966 Wismar
Witten: Stadtarchiv, Stadt Witten, 58449 Witten
Wittenberg: Stadtarchiv der Lutherstadt, Schloß, 06886 Lutherstadt Wittenberg
Wittenberge: Stadtarchiv, August-Bebel-Str. 10, 19322 Wittenberge
Witzenhausen: Stadtarchiv, Stadtverwaltung, Rathaus, 37213 Witzenhausen
Wörth am Main: Stadtarchiv, Postfach 20, 63939 Wörth am Main
Wolfach: Stadtarchiv, Rathaus, Hauptstr. 41, 77709 Wolfach
Wolfratshausen: Stadtarchiv, Marienplatz 1, 82515 Wolfratshausen, Postfach 1460, 82504 Wolfratshausen
Wolfsburg: Stadtarchiv, Porschestr. 43c,

38440 Wolfsburg, Postfach 100944, 38409 Wolfsburg
Wolfstein: Stadtarchiv, Rathaus, Hauptstr. 2, 67752 Wolfstein
Wolgast: Stadtarchiv, Pestalozzistr. 42, 17438 Wolgast
Wolmirstedt: Stadtarchiv, August-Bebel-Str. 24, 39326 Wolmirstedt
Worms: Stadtarchiv, Raschi-Haus, Hintere Judengasse 6, 67547 Worms, Postfach 2052, 67510 Worms
Wriezen: Amtsarchiv Wriezen, Freienwalder Str. 50, 16269 Wriezen
Wülfrath: Stadtarchiv, Wilhelmstr. 189, 42489 Wülfrath
Würselen: Stadtarchiv, Stadtverwaltung, Morlaixplatz 1, 52146 Würselen, Postfach 1160, 52135 Würselen
Würzburg: Stadtarchiv, Neubaustr. 12, 97070 Würzburg
Wunsiedel: Stadtarchiv, Rathaus, 95632 Wunsiedel, Postfach 140, 95620 Wunsiedel
Wunstorf: Stadtarchiv, Stadtverwaltung, Südstr. 1, 31515 Wunstorf, Postfach 1280, 31502 Wunstorf
Wuppertal: Stadtarchiv, Friedrich-Engels-Allee 89-91, 42285 Wuppertal (Barmen)
Wyk auf Föhr: Föhrer Inselarchiv, c/o Stiftung Nordfriesland, Im Schloß, 25813 Husum
Xanten: Stadtarchiv, Rathaus, Karthaus 2, 46509 Xanten, Postfach 1164, 46500 Xanten
Zaberfeld: Gemeindearchiv, Schloßberg 5, 74373 Zaberfeld
Zeitz: Stadtarchiv. See Burgenlandkreis
Zella-Mehlis: Stadtverwaltung Zella-Mehlis, Stadtarchiv, Rathausstr. 1, 98544 Zella-Mehlis, Dienstsitz: Friedebergstr. 60, 98544 Zella-Mehlis
Zimmern: Gemeindeverwaltung Zimmern, Gemeindearchiv, Dorfstr. 33, 07778 Zimmern
Zirndorf (Mittelfranken): Stadtarchiv, Rathaus, Fürther Str. 8, 90513 Zirndorf (Mittelfranken), Postfach 1160, 90505 Zirndorf (Mittelfranken)

Zittau: Stadtarchiv, Neustadt 47, 02763 Zittau, Postfach 228, 02754 Zittau
Zossen: Amtsarchiv Zossen, Marktplatz 20/21, 15806 Zossen
Zschopau: Stadtarchiv, Altmarkt 2, 09405 Zschopau
Zülpich: Stadtarchiv, Stadtverwaltung, Markt 21, 53909 Zülpich, Postfach 1354, 53905 Zülpich
Zweibrücken: Stadtarchiv, Stadtverwaltung, Herzogstr. 1, Postfach 171, 66468 Zweibrücken
Zwickau: Stadtarchiv, Lessingstr. 1, 08058 Zwickau

Source: *Archive in der Bundesrepublik Deutschland, Österreich und der Schweiz,* Ardey-Verlag, Münster, 1995.

LUTHERAN CHURCH ARCHIVES

Lutheran Church:
central and state archives
(Evangelische Kirche:
Zentral- und Landsarchive)
Evangelisches Zentralarchiv in Berlin, Jebensstr. 3, 10623 Berlin
Vereinigte Evangelisch-Lutherische Kirche Deutschlands, Archiv des Lutherischen Kirchenamts, Richard-Wagner-Str. 26, 30177 Hannover, Postfach 510409, 30634 Hannover
Evangelische Landeskirche Anhalts, Landeskirchenamt, Landeskirchliches Archiv, Friedrichstr. 22, 06844 Dessau
Evangelische Landeskirche in Baden, Evangelischer Oberkirchenrat, Landeskirchliches Archiv, Blumenstr. 1, 76133 Karlsruhe
Evangelisch-Lutherische Kirche in Bayern, Landeskirchliches Archiv, Veilhofstr. 28, 90489 Nürnberg
Evangelische Kirche in Berlin-Brandenburg: See Evangelisches Zentralarchiv in Berlin
Evangelisch-lutherische Landeskirche in Braunschweig, Landeskirchliches Archiv, Alter Zeughof 1, 38100 Braun-

schweig
Bremische Evangelische Kirche, Landeskirchliches Archiv, Franziuseck 2-4, 28199 Bremen, Postfach 106929, 28069 Bremen
Evangelisch-Lutherische Landeskirche Hannovers, Landeskirchliches Archiv, Am Steinbruch 14, 30449 Hannover
Evangelische Kirche in Hessen und Nassau, Zentralarchiv, Ahastr. 5a, Post: Paulusplatz 1, 64285 Darmstadt
Evangelische Kirche von Kurhessen-Waldeck, Landeskirchliches Archiv, Heinrich-Wimmer-Str. 4, 34131 Kassel-Wilhelmshöhe
Lippische Landeskirche, Archiv der Lippischen Landeskirche, Leopoldstr. 27, 32756 Detmold
Evangelisch-Lutherische Landeskirche Mecklenburgs, Landeskirchliches Archiv, Münzstr. 8, Postfach 011003, 19010 Schwerin
Nordelbische Evangelisch-Lutherische Kirche, Nordelbisches Kirchenamt, Dänische Str. 21-35, 24103 Kiel, Postfach 3449, 24033 Kiel
-Archiv der Nordelbischen Evangelisch-Lutherischen Kirche: Nordelbisches Kirchenarchiv Kiel, Dänische Str. 21-35, 24103 Kiel
-Archiv des Kirchenkreises Alt-Hamburg, Neue Burg 1, 20457 Hamburg
Evangelisch-reformierte Kirche in Nordwestdeutschland und Bayern, (Synode der evangelisch-reformierten Kirchen in Nordwestdeutschland und Bayern), Archiv des Synodalrates der Evangelisch-reformierten Kirche, Saarstr. 6, 26789 Leer, Postfach 1380, 26763 Leer
Evangelisch-Lutherische Kirche in Oldenburg, Archiv des Evangelisch-Lutherischen Oberkirchenrats, Philosophenweg 1, 26121 Oldenburg, Postfach 1709, 26007 Oldenburg
Evangelische Kirche der Pfalz, Zentralarchiv, Domplatz 6, 67346 Speyer, Postanschrift: 67343 Speyer
Pommersche Evangelische Kirche, Landeskirchliches Archiv, Postfach 187,

17461 Greifswald, Bahnhofstr. 35/36,
17489 Greifswald, Besucheradresse
[visitors' address]: Karl-Marx-Platz 15
Evangelische Kirche im Rheinland,
Archiv, Hans-Böckler-Str. 7, 40476
Düsseldorf, Postfach 320340, 40418
Düsseldorf
Evangelische Archivstelle Koblenz, Kar-
meliterstr. 1-3, 56068 Koblenz
**Evangelische Kirche der Kirchen-
provinz Sachsen,** Evangelisches Konsis-
torium, Am Dom 2, 39104 Magdeburg
**Evangelisch-Lutherische Landes-
kirche Sachsens,** Landeskirchenarchiv,
Lukasstr. 6, 01069 Dresden
**Evangelische Kirche der Schlesischen
Oberlausitz,** Konsistorium, Schlaurother
Str. 11, 02827 Görlitz
**Evangelisch-Lutherische Kirche in
Thüringen,** Landeskirchliches Archiv,
Schloßberg 4 a, 99817 Eisenach
Evangelische Kirche von Westfalen,
Landeskirchliches Archiv, Altstädter
Kirchplatz 5, 33602 Bielefeld, Postfach
101051, 33510 Bielefeld
**Evangelische Landeskirche in Würt-
temberg,** Landeskirchliches Archiv,
Gänsheidestr. 4, 70184 Stsuttgart,
Postfach 101342, 70012 Stuttgart

CATHOLIC CHURCH ARCHIVES AT BISHOPRICS, DIOCESES AND CATHEDRALS *(Katholische Kirche: Bistums-, Diözesan- und Domarchive)*

Bistum Aachen, Diözesanarchiv, Kloster-
platz 7, 52062 Aachen, Postfach 210,
52003 Aachen
-Domarchiv Aachen, Ritter-Chorus-Str. 7,
52062 Aachen
Bistum Augsburg, Archiv des Bistums
Augsburg, Hafnerberg 2, 86152 Augsburg
Erzbistum Bamberg, Archiv des Erz-
bistums Bamberg, Domplatz 3, 96049
Bamberg, Postfach 120153, 96033
Bamberg
Erzbistum Berlin, Diözesanarchiv

Berlin, Götzstr. 65, 12099 Berlin
Diözese Dresden-Meißen, Bischöfliches
Ordinariat, Käthe-Kollwitz-Ufer 84,
01309 Dresden
Bistum Eichstätt, Diözesanarchiv,
Luitpoldstr. 1, 85072 Eichstätt
Bistum Erfurt, Bistumsarchiv, Her-
mannsplatz 9, 99084 Erfurt, Postfach 296,
99006 Erfurt, Besucheradresse [visitors'
address]: Domstr. 9, Eingang [entrance on]
Stiftsgasse
Bistum Essen, Bistumsarchiv, Zwölfling
16, 45127 Essen, Postfach 100464, 45004
Essen
-Münsterarchiv, Zwölfling 16, 45127
Essen
Erzbistum Freiburg, Erzbischöfliches
Archiv, Herrenstr. 35, 79098 Freiburg im
Breisgau
Bistum Fulda, Bistumsarchiv, Bischöf-
liches Generalvikariat, Paulustor 5, 36037
Fulda, Postfach 147, 36001 Fulda
Bistum Görlitz, Ordinariatsarchiv, Carl-
von-Ossietzky-Str. 41, 02826 Görlitz,
Postfach 127, 02802 Görlitz
Erzbistum Hamburg: See Osnabrück
Bistum Hildesheim, Bistumsarchiv,
Pfaffenstieg 2, 31134 Hildesheim,
Postfach 100263, 31102 Hildesheim
Erzbisbum Köln, Historisches Archiv,
Gereonstr. 2-4, 50670 Köln
Bistum Limburg, Diözesanarchiv
Limburg, Roßmarkt 4, 65549 Limburg
(Lahn), Postfach 1355, 65533 Limburg
(Lahn)
Bistum Magdeburg, Bischöfliches
Zentralarchiv, Generalvikariat, Max-Josef-
Metzger-Str. 1, 39104 Magdeburg
Bistum Mainz, Dom- u. Diözesanarchiv,
Heringsbrunnengasse 4, 55116 Mainz,
Postfach 1560, 55005 Mainz
Erzbistum München und Freising,
Archiv, Karmeliterstr. 1 (Eingang [ent-
rance on] Pacellistr.), 80333 München,
Postfach 330360, 80063 München
Bistum Münster, Bistumsarchiv, Georgs-
kommende 19, 48143 Münster
-Außenstelle Xanten des Bistumsarchivs
Münster, Kapitel 21, 46509 Xanten

-Bischöflich Münstersches Offizialat Vechta, Offizialatsarchiv, Kolpingstr. 25, 49377 Vechta
Bistum Osnabrück, Bischöfliches Generalvikariat, Diözesanarchiv, Große Domsfreiheit 10, 49074 Osnabrück
Erzbistum Paderborn, Erzbistumsarchiv Paderborn, Domplatz 3, 33098 Paderborn
wBistum Passau, Archiv des Bistums Passau, Luragogasse 4, 94032 Passau
Bistum Regensburg, Bischöfliches Zentralarchiv Regensburg, St.-Peters-Weg 11-13, 93047 Regensburg, Postfach 110228, 93015 Regensburg
Bistum Rottenburg-Stuttgart, Diözesanarchiv Rottenburg, Eugen-Bolz-Platz 1, 72108 Rottenburg am Neckar, Postfach 9, 72101 Rottenburg am Neckar
Bischöfliches Amt Schwerin, Bistumsarchiv, Landower Str. 14-16, 19057 Schwerin
Bistum Speyer, Archiv des Bistums Speyer, Kleine Pfaffengasse 16, 67346 Speyer, Postanschrift [postal address]: 67343 Speyer
Bistum Trier, Bistumsarchiv, Jesuitenstr. 13b, 54290 Trier, Postfach 1340, 54203 Trier
Bistum Würzburg, Diözesanarchiv, Bruderhof 1a, Post: Domerschulstr. 2, 97070 Würzburg

OTHER ECCLESIASTICAL ORGANIZATIONS (*Sonstigekirchliche Einrichtungen*)

Deutscher Hugenotten-Verein e.V. [German Huguenot Society], Archiv, Hafenplatz 9 A, 34385 Bad Karlshafen
Das Rauhe Haus, Archiv, Beim Rauhen Hause 21, 22111 Hamburg
Zentralarchiv zur Erforschung der Geschichte der Juden in Deutschland [Central Archive for research of the history of Jews in Germany], Bienenstr. 5, 69117 Heidelberg
Johannes-Ronge-Archiv, Freireligiöse

Landesgemeinde der Pfalz, Wörthstr. 6 A, 67059 Ludwigshafen
Russisch-orthodoxe Diözese des orthodoxen Bischofs von Berlin und Deutschlands [Russian Orthodox Diocese of the Orthodox Bishops of Berlin and Germany], KdöR, Schirmerweg 78, 81247 München

Source: *Archive in der Bundesrepublik Deutschland, Österreich und der Schweiz,* 15. Ausgabe, Ardey-Verlag Münster, 1995.

HOW TO WORK IN A GERMAN ARCHIVE

by Friedrich R. Wollmershäuser[1]

The rules for using archival records are more or less the same at all German archives. The researcher acknowledges these rules by signing the application (*Benutzerantrag*) before using the archive.
   Before you leave home....
♦ Precisely define your research problem, determining with what kinds of records the problem may be solved and where the records may be found.
♦Determine whether the archive you plan to visit holds the records you are seeking. If so, check to find out whether such records have been microfilmed for use in the Family History Library in Salt Lake City so that you can search them first in the United States.
   After you arrive in Germany....
♦ Telephone the archive before your planned visit to make certain that it will be open on the day you plan to visit. Also, check the hours that the archive is open.
♦As you enter the archive leave your coat and belongings in a locker in the room provided (*Garderobe*). Ask the way to the reading room (*Lesesaal, Benützersaal*) to complete the application form.
♦Relate your problem to the archivist, whomay either inform you that the records for solving the problem are not available

at the archive or direct you to the appropriate catalogs or to the catalog room.

◆ Write down on an order slip the numbers of the specific files you wish to examine, then submit the slip to the archivist. Usually an archive's files may be accessed only during specified hours of the day. In some archives the number of records which may be requested per day is limited.

◆ After you receive the records you have requested, take them to your desk to examine them. When you are finished, return them to the archivist or to the place designated for this purpose.

◆ Because it is not the archivist's responsibility to read or translate entries on records you have requested, you should be sure that your language abilities are sufficient before ordering a record.

◆ Do not eat, drink, smoke, or talk loudly in the reading room.

◆ Do not take notes on paper laid on top of archive records.

◆ Reproductions of documents on paper or microfilm are usually provided upon request, but for your private use only. The copyright of archival records remains with the archive.

Without written permission, you may not forward a copy to anyone else or publish it.

If you publish a record from an archive, you must submit a free copy of the publication to the archive.

◆ Many archives will be able to refer you to a local or regional professional genealogist who is available for further research.

After you return home . . . .

Share your experiences by writing short articles for American genealogical magazines. Thus other researchers will be forewarned against mistakes you may have made and may learn about sources they had not known about before.

[1] The author: Friedrich R. Wollmershäuser, M.A., Accredited Genealogist, Herrengasse 8-10, 89610 Oberdischingen, Germany. © Friedrich R. Wollmershäuser, 1997.

CENTRAL OFFICE FOR GENEALOGY, LEIPZIG (Die deutsche Zentralstelle für Genealogie)

In the early twentieth century in Germany, a group of researchers pooled their research and created an organization, much of whose data was microfilmed following the reunification of Germany. This manuscript collection, filmed by the Church of Jesus Christ of Latter-day Saints, is available at the Family History Library in Salt Lake City and through Family History Centers. It is known as the *Ahnenlistenumlauf* (literally, "circulation of ancestor lists)," now commonly referred to as the ALU.

One of the several segments of the ALU is the 14-volume *Ahnenlistenkartei* (ancestor list cards) which is described on page 000. This body of information is the result of the decision of a group of German researchers in the 1970s to circulate their ancestor lists among contributors.

The ALA

Considerably older than the ALU is the *Ahnenlistsenaustausch* (ancestor list exchange), begun in 1921 in Dresden, and known now as the ALA.

These data, which consist of a half million German pedigrees, are indexed in a collection called *Die Ahnenstammkartei des deutschen Volkes* (pedigree index of Germans), or "ASTAKA." The index contains 2.7 million cards. This body of information, whose emphasis lies with eastern Germany and its German neighbors to the east, is housed in *Die deutsche Zentralstelle für Genealogie* (German Central Office for Genealogy) in Leipzig, generally shortened to "DZfG."

Thus researchers of German family histories have two important collections available on Family History Library microfilm: ALU and ASTAKA.

Keys to the microfilms

An index to the German pedigrees,

whose time periods range in time between 1650 and 1800, with exceptions at both ends, can be accessed by using this book:
♦ *An Introduction and Register to* Die Ahnenstammkartei des deutschen Volkes of the Deutsche Zentralstelle für Genealogie *Leipzig 1922-1991,* compiled by Thomas Kent Edlund, The Family History Library, Salt Lake City, 1993.
♦ The pedigree films are accessed through the Family History Library under computer number 677728.

Using ASTAKA

The most complete explanation of the use of the ASTAKA may be found in *"Die Ahnenstammkartei des Deutschen Volkes* Pedigree Collection from Leipzig, Germany," by Laraine K. Ferguson and Larry O. Jensen, *German Genealogical Digest,* Winter 1993, pages 110-124.

The microfilms of ASTAKA are available through local Family History Centers of the Family History Library in Salt Lake City.

INDEX TO ZENTRALSTELLE HOLDINGS

The index to the holdings of *Die deutsche Zentralstelle für Genealogie* (German Central Office for Genealogy) consists of a three-volume work, *Bestandsverzeichnis der deutschen Zentralstelle für Genealogie,* by Martina Wermes, Renate Jude, Marion Bahr and Hans-Jürgen Voigt (Verlag Degener & Co., Neustadt/Aisch, 1991-94. Vol . I, 1991; Vol. II, 1991; Vol. III, 1994)
Vol. I: *Die Kirchenbuchunterlagen der östlichen Provinzen Posen, Ost- und Westpreußen, Pommern und Schlesien.* (The Parish Registers of the Eastern Provinces of Posen, East and West Prussia, Pomerania and Silesia)
This volume lists parish registers for the German eastern provinces (1905 borders) excluding East Brandenburg.
Vol. II: *Die archivalischen und Kirchen-*

buchunterlagen deutscher Siedlungsgebiete im Ausland: Bessarabien, Bukowina, Estland, Lettland und Litauen, Siebenbürgen, Sudetenland, Slowenien und Südtirol. (The Parish Registers of the German settlements in Other Areas: Bessarabia, Bukowina, Estonia, Latvia and Lithuania, Transylvania, the Sudetenland, Slovenia and South Tyrol.)
This volume lists records for the areas mentioned above, but see Brandt, Edward R., *Germanic Genealogy: A Guide to Worldwide Sources and Migration Patterns* for specifics.
Vol. III: *Die Kirchenbuchunterlagen der Länder und Provinzen des deutschen Reiches* (The Parish Registers of theStates and Provinces of theGerman Empire)
This volume covers Berlin, Schleswig-Holstein, Thuringia, Baden, Bavaria, Brandenburg (including the part now in Poland), Hamburg, Hanover, Hesse, Mecklenburg, the Rhine province, the Kingdom of Saxony, the Prussian Province of Saxony, Westphalia, Anhalt, Brunswick, Hesse-Nassau, Lippe, Oldenburg, the Saarland, Schaumburg-Lippe, and Württemberg.
This index has been partially translated, adapted, and supplemented for English-language users by Edward Reimer Brandt, Minneapolis, 1994.

HOW TO REACH THE ZENTRALSTELLE

Deutsche Zentralstelle für Genealogie
Schongauerstraße 1
04329 Leipzig
Germany
Die deutsche Zentralstelle für Genealogie (the German Central Office for Genealogy) in Leipzig, is located in the building of the Sächsisches Staatsarchiv (Saxony State Archives) Leipzig.The home of the *Ahnenstammkartei,* or ASTAKA the *Zentralstelle* holds also a good selection of

Ortsippenbücher and *Matrikel* Registers.

To reach this archive from central Leipzig, take the number 3, 6, or 8 trolley in the direction of Sommerfeld, which is the end of the line for all three lines.

The *Sächsisches Staatsarchiv* is located in a suburb called Paunsdorf. From the end of the trolley line, go one long block on Leipzigerstraße to Schongauerstraße in the direction of Paunsdorf Center. The *Sächsisches Staatsarchiv* is on the corner, facing Schongauerstraße. The *Zenralstelle* is located on the second floor (the German "first floor").

THE BERLIN DOCUMENT CENTER

Bundesarchiv Außenstelle Berlin-Zehlendorf
Wasserkäfersteig 1
14136 Berlin
Germany
Tel: (030)81 813-0
Fax (030) 81 977 57

The Berlin Document Center is the world's largest Nazi archive, consisting of about 75 million pages of 30 million Nazi documents, filling racks 7.4 miles long. It is the most comprehensive collection of Nazi files for the years 1933-1945.

For almost 50 years the collection was in American custody, but on 1 July 1994 it was turned over to the *Bundesarchiv*, the Central Archives of Germany's federal government. It includes the almost complete membership files of the NSDAP (*Nationalsozialistische Deutsche Arbeiterpartei*, or National Socialist German Workers' Party — the Nazi party), with data on its 10.7 million party members.

Among the records are 600,000 applications for party membership, personal files on 260,000 members of the SA (*Sturmabteilung*, forerunner of the Nazi storm division in the early Nazi era), 329,000 files on the SS *(Schutzstaffel*, the

Nazi's name for the "Blackshirts"), 185,000 files on the *Kulturkammer* (the Culture Commission, NSDAP's suborganization for writers, musicians, and other artists), 500,000 files on the *NS-Lehrerbund* (the NSDAP suborganization for teachers), 238,000 files on the RaSHA (*Rasse- und Siedlungshauptamt der SS* the Race and Resettlement Department, responsible for review of marriage applications by members of the SS), 2.1 million files on the EW (*Einwandererzentralstelle Litzmannstadt*, ethnic Germans from Poland, Russia, Baltic States, etc., who were resettled in Germany), 72,000 files on the *Reichsärztekammer* (the medical directory of the NSDAP suborganization for physicians), as well as 50,000 files of the *Volksgerichtshof*, the Nazi's supreme court.

Following the United States' agreement to relinquish jurisdiction over the files to the Germans in July 1994, many scholars familiar with their content have expressed the fear that the transfer could have disastrous consequences for historians and Nazi-hunters.

Upon receipt of the master copy of the files by the National Archive in Washington, to consist of 40,000 rolls of microfilm, work was begun on making available a users copy for researchers. Already available at the National Archives in College Park, Maryland, are 4,000 rolls of the SS records, many handwritten and containing abbreviations and special terminology used by the Nazis.

Reference

For an excellent discussion of the history and post-war management of these documents, see "Secrets of the Files," by Gerald Posner, *The New Yorker*, March 14, 1994, p. 39.

THE 'GAUCK' FILES

In the 40 years before reunification of Germany, the *Staatssicherheit*, better known as the Stasi, or the East German secret police, had prepared and collected immense quantities of documents detailing the private lives of millions of East German citizens. From the 15 Stasi offices whose documents were turned over to the federal government came 35.6 million index cards and thousands of cassettes and diskettes of taped material.

Many of the records were shredded in the days just following the opening of the border. When the shredding machines broke down, Stasi members were ordered to tear up the records by hand. Thus 5,800 huge sacks of paper scraps were left waiting to be pieced together.

After the fall of the wall in November 1989, Joachim Gauck, a clergyman and a dissident from Rostock, was elected to the *Volkskammer* (the parliament of the German Democratic Republic) and became involved in the Stasi problem.

On 30 August 1989 a law was passed establishing an authority to regulate the use of the files, and Gauck was elected to head it. The new body, with headquarters in Berlin, came to be known as the *Gauck-Behörde,,* or the Gauck Authority. The official title created for the position was "The Federal Commissioner for Documentation of the State Security Service of the Former German Democratic Republic."

The mission assigned to Gauck and his 3,100 employees was to provide citizens with access to information filed about them and to protect citizens from misuse of their files. Examination of the files by private citizens began in January 1992. As of October 1995, almost 2.9 people had applied to look at their Stasi files. On 3 October 1995, Gauck was reelected for a second term to head the commission.

The address of the commission in 1995 was Glinkastraße 35, 10117 Berlin. Tel. 030-231370.

Sources:
♦"The Gauck Commission in Berlin," by Joachim Nowrocki, *Deutschland*, August 1995. pp. 138-140.
♦"East Germany's Secret Files," interview by Pilar Wolfsteller, *German Life*, February/March 1996, pp. 12-15.

Chapter 7
German genealogical aids

GERMAN GENEALOGY VOCABULARY

Abend/abends: evening/in the evening
Abendmahl: communion
Abgang: departure
Abkürzung(en): abbreviation
Abriß: synopsis, summary
Abschrift: copy, extract
Abstammungsurkunde: birth certificate
absterben: to die
Abtei: abbey
Abteilung: department, section
Ackermann: farmer (old term)
Adel: nobility
adoptieren/adoptiert: to adopt/adopted
Adreßbuch/(-bücher) address book(s), city directory(ies)
Ahne(n): ancestor(s)
Ahnenforschung: family research
Ahnenliste: ancestral line chart
Ahnentafel: pedigree chart
Akte(n): document(s), deed; records (plural)
allgemein: (adj.) general(ly), common(ly)

allhier: in this place
Almosen: welfare
alt: (adj.) old
Alter: age
älter: (adj.) elder, senior
Altertum: antiquity
Ältester: elder [noun]
Amt: office, jurisdiction
Amtsbücher: official books
Amtsgericht (AG.): district court
Amtssprache: official language
angenommenes Kind: adopted child
angezeigt durch: registered by
Anhang: appendix
Anmerkung: note, comment
Anschrift(en): address(es)
Anzeige: notice
Arbeitsgemeinschaft: society
Arbeitsmann: workman
Archiv(e): archive(s)
archivisch: (adj.) archival
arm: (adj.)poor
Armenregister: poor record
aufbieten: to publish marriage banns
Aufenthaltsort: place of residence
Aufgebote(n): proclamation(s), bann(s)

Aufstellung: list
Ausblick: outlook, prospect, view
ausgestorben: (adj.) (line) died out
Aushebungsliste: military muster rolls
Ausland: foreign country
Außenstelle: branch office
Auswanderer: emigrant
auswandern: to emigrate
Auswanderung: emigration
Auswanderungsliste: emigration record
Auszug: extract (of a record)
Baiern: Bavaria
Band/Bände: volume/volumes
Baptisten: Baptists
Bauer: peasant, farmer
Bauernhof: farm
Bauernkrieg: Peasant War (1525)
Bayern: Bavaria
beerdigt: (adj.) buried
Beerdigung: funeral, burial
Beerdigungsregister: burial register
begraben: to bury
Begräbnis, Beerdigung: burial
Begriffe: idea(s), notion(s)
Bekenntnis: religious faith (Catholic,
Lutheran, etc.)
Bemerkungen: remarks
Benutzungshinweis(e): useful comment(s)
Berg: mountain, hill
Beruf: occupation, calling
Berufsakten: occupation records
Berufsbezeichnung(en): name(s) of
occupation(s)
Beschäftigung: occupation
Bescheinigung: certificate
besonders: particular, special
Bestand/Bestände: holdings (in archive)
Beständer: leaseholder (Austria)
Bestandskataloge: catalog of holdings
Bestandsübersichten: summary of
holdings
bestatten: to bury
Bestattung: burial, funeral
Bestimmungsort: distination
Bevölkerungsliste: population list, census
Bevölkerungsgruppe(n): population
group(s)
Bevölkerungsverzeichnis: population list,
census

Bezeichnunge(n):indication(s),
representation(s)
Bezifferung: numbering
Bezirk: district
Bezirksamt: district office
Bezirkskommando (Bkdo.): district
military command
Bezugsquelle(n): source(s)
Bibliographie(n): bibliography(ies)
Bibliothek: library
Biographieforschung: biographical
research
Bischof: bishop
bischöflich: eccelesiastical
bisheriger Wohnort: former residence
Bistum: diocese
Blätter: newspaper/periodical
Blutverwandtschaft: blood relationship
Böhmen: Bohemia
Braunschweig: Brunswick
Braut: bride
Bräutigam: bridegroom
Brautkind: premarital child
Brief: letter
Brinksitzer: farmer (old term)
Bruder: brother, monk, member of a
fraternity
Brüdergemein(d)e: Moravians
Brüdergemeine: fraternity; Moravian
Brethern
Bruderschaft: brotherhood, fraternity
Buch/Bücher: book/books
Bundes: federal
Burg: fortress, castle
Bürger: person with full rights of
citizenship
Bürgerbuch/(-bücher): citizenship
record(s)
Bürgereid: citizen's oath
Bürgerrecht: citizenship
Bürgerregister: citizenship record
Burggut: castle estate
Burghof: castle court (=inside)
Christnacht: Christmas Eve
Chronik(en): chronicle(s)
Dachverband: holding, umbrella
association; parent organization
Datenschutz: (personal) data protection
Datum: date

Datum d. Abgang: date of departure
deutsche: (adj.) German
deutscher Sprachraum: German-
speaking area
Deutsches Reich: German Empire
Diakon: deacon
Diener: servant
Diener Gottes: minister
Dienstherr: employer
Dienstjunge/Dienstmagd: farmhand
(child)
Dienstmagd: maidservant
Dienststelle: government office, place of
employment, service office
Dom: cathedral
Domäne: estate
Dorf/Dörfer: village/villages
ebenda: at the same place
Ehe: marriage
Ehebrecher: adulterer
Ehebücher: marriage registers
Ehefrau: (legitimate) wife
Ehegatte: spouse, husband
Ehegattin: spouse, wife
Eheleute: married couple
ehelich: (adj.) legitimate
Ehemann: husband
Ehepaar: married couple
Ehescheidung: divorce
Eheschließung: marriage ceremony
Ehesohn: legitimate son
Ehestiftung: marriage contract
Ehetochter: legitimate daughter
Ehevertrag: marriage contract
Eid: oath
einbürgern: to naturalize
einführend: (adj.) introductory
Einführung: introduction
Eingekäufter: peasants who had
bought into the land
Einnahmsregister: receipt book
einpfarren: to assign to a parish
Einrichtung(en): regulation(s)
Eintrag, Eintragung: entry
Einwanderung: immigration
Einwilligung: permission
Einwohner: inhabitant, resident
Einwohnerliste: list of inhabitants
einzeln: (adj.) single, individual

ejusdem: (adj.) the same
Elsaß: Alsace
Eltern: parents
Erbe: heir
erben: to inherit
Erbrecht: right of succession
Erbschaft: inheritance, legacy
erfolgte am: occurred on (date)
Erforschung: research
Erschließung: development
Erstkommunionen: confirmation records
(Catholic)
Erwachsen(e): adult(s)
Erzbistum: archbishopric
evangelisch: (adj.) Protestant
Familie: family
Familienarchiv: family archive
Familienbuch: family book/register
Familienforschung: family research
Familiengeschichte: family history
Familiengeschichtsforschung: family
history research
Familienkunde: genealogy
Familienname: surname
Familienregister: family register
Familienstand: marital status
Familienverband: family organization
Filiale: branch church, branch office
Findling: foundling
firmen: to confirm (Catholic)
Firmung: confirmation (Catholic)
Firmungsbücher: confirmation books
(Catholic)
Flecken: hamlet
Flitterwochen: honeymoon
Fluß/Flüsse: river/rivers
Forscher: researcher
Forschung: research
Frankreich: France
französisch: (adj.) French
Frau: wife
Fräulein: unmarried female
Freiherr: baron
Freie Reichsstadt: free city-state
Friedhof, Friedhöfe: cemetery/cemeteries
frühe Neuzeit: early modern times
Fürst(in): prince(cess), aristocrat
Fürstbischof: prince bishop
Fürstentum: principality

Galizien: Galicia
Garnison: military garrison
Gärtner: gardener
Gäste: attendees
Gatte/Gattin: husband/wife
Gebiet(e): territory, region
geboren: to be born
geboren am: born on (birthdate)
geboren in: born at (birthplace)
geborene, geb.: maiden name
Gebühr(en): charge(s), fee(s)
Geburt: birth
Geburtsdatum: birth date
Geburtsname: maiden name
Geburtsort: place of birth
Geburtsurkunde: birth certificate
geheiratet: (adj.) married
gehören zu: to belong to
Geistlicher: clergyman
Geld: money
Gemeinde: community/parish
Gemeindelexikon: gazetteer
Gemeindeverwaltung: municipal
administration
Gemeindsmann: person with rights of
citizenship
genannt: (adj.) alias, known as, called
Genealogie: genealogy
genealogische Forschungsstelle:
genealogical research institution
Generallandesarchiv: national archives
Gericht: court
Gerichtsbuch: court record
Gerichtsprotokoll: court register
Geschichte(n): history (histories)
Geschichtsverein: historical society
geschieden: (adj.) divorced
Geschlecht: gender; family lineage
Geschlechterbuch: lineage book
Geschlechtsname: family name
Geschwister: siblings
Geselle(n): journeyman(men)
Gesellschaft: society, community, asso-
ciation
gestern: yesterday
gestorben am: died on (date)
getauft: (adj.) baptized
getraut: (adj.) married
getrennt: (adj.) separated

Gevatter: godfather, cousin, good friend
Gewerbe: trade/occupation/profession
gewesen: (adj.) former
Gilde: guild
Glaubensgemeinschaft: religious society
Glockenbuch: bell toll register
Graf/Gräfin: count/countess
Grafschaft: county
Großeltern: grandparents
Großherzogtum: grandduchy
Großmutter: grandmother
Großvater: grandfather
Grund: land
Grundbuch: land register
Gut: possessions; estate
Gutsherr: estate owner
Gutsverwalter: estate manager
Handbuch: handbook, manual
Handel: trade
Handlung: act/action, store
Handschrift: handwriting
Hannover: Hanover
Haupt-: head, main
Häuserbuch: book of houses
Häusler: cottage industries
Häusling: owns house (no farm)
Hebamme: midwife
Heft: number (of periodical)
Heimat: homeland
Heimatkunde: local history
Heimatortskartei(en): home town card-
file(s)
Heirat/heiraten: marriage/to marry
Heiratsdatum: date of marriage
Heiratsliste: list of marriages
Heiratsurkunde: marriage certificate
Heraldik: heraldry
Herkunft: origin
Herkunftsort: place of origin
Heroldsamt: heraldic office
Herrengut: noble estate
Herzog/(-tum)/-in: duke/duchy/duchess
Hesse: Hessen
hiesiger Ort: of this place
Hinterbliebene: surviving relatives
hinterlassen: to leave (behind)
Hinweis(e): comment(s), remark(s)
historisch: (adj.) historical
Hochschulmatrikel(n): roll(s)/register(s) of

school of higher education
Hochstift: independent bishopric, subject only to the Reich (similar to Freie Reichsstadt)
Hochzeit: wedding
Hof: farm, estate
Hofgut: estate
Hofland: land strictlythe property of the lord
Hofverwalter: estate manager
Hugenotten: Huguenots
Hurenkind: illegitimate child
Hutmacher: hat maker
Hypothekenbuch: mortgage book
Impfliste: vaccination record
Inhaltsverzeichnis: table of contents
Innungsregister: guild register
Institut: institution, establishment
Jahr/im Jahre: year/in the year (date)
Jahrbuch: annual register/chronicle
Jahrgang: age group (wine: vintage)
Jahrhundert: century
Judisch: Jewish
Junge: boy
jünger: (adj.) younger, junior
Jungfer: unmarried woman
Jungfrau: virgin/single woman
Junggeselle: bachelor
Jüngling: young man, bachelor
Kalender: calendar, almanac
Katholik: Catholic
katholisch: (adj.) Catholic
Kaufmann: merchant
Kind(er): child(ren)
kinderlos: (adj.) childless
Kirche: church
Kirchenbuch/-bücher: church (vital records) book(s)
Kirchenbuchduplikat: parish register duplicates
Kirchenbücherverzeichnis(se):church book list(s), register(s), index(es)
Kirchengemeinde: congregation
Kirchensprengel: diocese, parish
Kirchenvorsteher: church warden
Kirchenzehnt: tithe
Kirchenzweitschrift: parish transcript
Kirchgemeinde : parish
Kirchhof: church cemetery

kirchlich getraut: married in church
Kirchspiel: parish
Kirchsprengel: parish
Kirchweih: church dedication
Kleinstadt: small town
Kloster: cloister
Knabe: boy
Knecht: farmhand (male)
Kommunikanten: communicants (Catholic)
Konfession: religion
Konfirmation: confirmation (Protestant)
konfirmiert: (adj.) confirmed (Protestant)
König/-reich: king/kingdom
Kopfzahl: census, number of persons
Kopulation: marriage
Kötner: farmer (old term)
Krankheit: disease/illness
Krankheitbezeichnung(en): illness terminology(ies)
Kreis: district/county
Krieg: war
Kunde: science, knowledge
Kunst: arts, crafts
Kurfürst: elector
Kurfürstentum: electorate
Kusin/Kusine: cousin (male/female)
Küster: sexton
Lagerbücher: military levy books
Land/Länder: state(s)/province(s)
Landesarchiv: state archives
Landesherr: territorial ruler
Landgericht: district court
Landgraf: Landgrave (aristocrat)
Landgrafschaft: Landgraviate
Landkarte: map
Landkreis: rural administrative area (county)
Landschaft: province, district
Landwehr: militia
Landwirt: farmer (new term)
lateinisch: (adj.)Latin
lebendig: (adj.) living, alive
Lebensdokumente: vital records
ledig: (adj.) single (unmarried)
legitimieren: to legitimate
Lehrling: apprentice
Lehrlingsbuch: apprentice record
Leibzüchter: retired farmer entitled to

receive a livelihood for life
Leichen: funeral
Leichenpredigt(en): funeral sermon(s)
letzter Wille: last will
Lexikon: dictionary, encyclopedia
Literatur: literature
Lothringen: Lorraine
Mädchen: girl
Mädchenname: maiden name
Magd: farmhand (female)
Magyarország: Hungary
Mähren: Moravia
männlich: (adj.) male
Mannzahl: census, number of males
Mark: boundary/border
Markgraf: margrave
Markgrafschaft: margravate
Marktflecken: market town
Matrikel: register; enrollment
Maurermeister: master mason
Maurer: mason
Meier: leaseholder; dairy farmer
Meister: master
Meldebehörden: registration authorities
melden: to register
Mennonit/(-isch): Mennonite [noun/adj.]
Mennoniten: Mennonites
Mieter: tenant
Militär: the military
Militärverhältnis: military standing
minderjährig: underage
Mitglied(er): member(s)
Mittag: midday/noon
Mitteilung: message/news
Möbel: furniture
Monat: : month
Morgen/morgen: morning/tomorrow
morgens: in the morning
Musterungslisten: military lists
Mutter: mother
Nachfahr: descendant
Nachfahrentafel: descendancy chart
nachgelassene(r): (adj.) surviving
Nachkomme(n): descendant(s)
Nachkommenforschung: descendant
research
Nachlaß: legacy, estate
Nachlaßgericht: probate court
Nachlässe: personal effects of estate

nachmittags: in the afternoon
Nachricht: news
Nachschlagewerk: reference book
Nacht: night
Nachtrag: supplement
Name(n): name(s)
Namenlexikon: name encyclopedia
Namenregister: name index
Namensverzeichnis: name index
Nationalität: nationality
Nebenfrau: mistress, concubine
Neffe: nephew
Nichte: niece
noch lebende: still living
Nottaufe: emergency baptism
Nummer: number
Oberamt: principal government office
Oberslandesgericht: high court
Oheim: uncle
Onkel: uncle
Ort(e): location(s), place(s)
Ort der Geburt: place of birth
Ortsbuch: gazetteer
Ortschaft: village
Ortschaftsverzeichnis: gazetteer
Ortsfamilienbücher: lineage books
Ortslexikon: gazetteer
Ortsliste(n): place list(s)
Ortsnamenverzeichnis: gazetteer
Ortsregister: locality index/list
Ortssippenbuch: locality family book
Ortsteil: suburb/district
Österreich: Austria
Österreich-Ungarn: Austria-Hungary
Ostpreußen: East Prussia
Parochie: parish
Paten: witnesses, godparents
Personenregister: surname index
Personenstandsregister: civil registration
records
Pfalz: Palatinate
Pfalzgraf: Count Palatiine
Pfalzgrafschaft: Palatine county
Pfarramt: church office/parish
Pfarrbezirk: parish
Pfarrbuch: parish register
Pfarrei: parish
Pfarrer: pastor/priest
Pfarrerverzeichnis(se): index(es) of

clergymen
Pfarrkirche: parish church
Pfarrsprengel: parish district
Pflege: care, maintenance
Pflegesohn: foster son
Platz: place
Polen: Poland
Polizeiregister: police register
Polska: Poland
Polterabend: party held on eve of wedding ceremony
Pommern: Pomerania
Porzellan: porcelain/china
Postfach: post office box
Predigt: sermon
Preußen: Prussia
Priester: priest
Proklamation: banns, proclamation
protestantisch: (adj.) Protestent
Protokolle: official records
Provinz: province
Quelle(n): source(s)
Quellenverzeichnis(se): list of sources
Rangliste: list of military officers
Rathaus: town hall
Rechtsanwalt: lawyer
reformiert: (adj.) Reformed (church); Calvinistic
Regierungsbezirk (RB.) provincial district
Register: register(s)
Reich: empire
Reichsland:Area subject to the Reich itself
Reichsfreiherr: baron (prince of the Holy Roman Empire)
Reiseziel: destination
Religion: religion
Rentkammer: board of revenue
Rentner: retired person
Rheinland: Rhineland
Ritter: knight
Rittergut: knight's estate
Rufname: the given name that one goes by
Saargebiet: Saarland,Saar
Sache: thing
Sachregister: subject index
Sachsen: Saxony

Sachsen-Altenburg: Saxe-Altenburg
Sachsen-Coburg-Gotha: Saxe-Coburg-Gotha
Sachsen-Meiningen: Saxe-Meiningen
Sachsen-Weimar-Eisenach: Saxe-Weimar-Eisenach
Sammelwerk: compilation
Sammlung: collection
Scheidung: divorce
Schein: certificate
Schiffsliste: ship list
Schlesien: Silesia
Schloß: palace
Schloßgut: palace estate
Schmied: blacksmith
Schuhmacher: shoemaker
Schule: school
Schullehrer: teacher
Schweiz: Switzerland
Seelenregister: membership register
Seite: page
selbe: (adj.) same
Selbsmord: suicide
selbständig: (adj.) self-sufficient, self-employed
Selbstzeugnis(se): documentation(s) of one's own life
Siegelkunde: information about seals
siehe (abbrev.: s.): see (refer to something)
Sippe: group of related persons
Sippenforschung: ancestral research
Sippennamen: lineage names
Sippenverband: lineage
Sohn/Söhne: son/sons
Sohn von: son of
Söhnchen: son (diminutive)
Sonderdruck: special edition
sonstig: (adj) other, remaining; former
Staat: state, nation
Staatsangehörigkeit: citizenship/ nationality
Staatsarchiv: state archive; public records office
Stadt: city, town
Stadtarchiv: city archives
Stadtbuch: town or city record
Stadtchronik: town history
Stammbaum: family tree, pedigree

Stammbuch: book in which family records are kept
Stammliste: pedigree list
Stammrolle: military muster rolls
Stammtafel: pedigree
Stammvater: originating ancestor
Stand: status/position/occupation
Standesamt/(-ämter): civil registry office(s)
standesamtlich getraut: married in a civil ceremony
Standesbeamter: civil clerk at civil registry office
Standesregister: civil registry record
Stelle: place, office
Stellung im Berufe: position in profession
Sterbefall: death
sterben: to die
Sterbeurkunde: death certificate
Sterbeursache: cause of death
Steuer(n): tax(es)
Steuerbuch: tax record
Steuerrolle: tax rolls
Stiefkind: stepchild
Stift: religious institution, convent
Stiftung: foundation
Straße: street
Stunde: hour
Tag der Taufe: day of baptism
Tag : day
Tagelöhner: day laborer(s)
Tal: valley
Taufdatum: date of christening
Taufe: christening, baptism
taufen: to baptize
Taufpaten: godparents
Taufrodel: baptismal record (Swiss)
Tauftag: christening date
Taufzeuge: godfather
Taufzeugin: godmother
Teil: part (as in *part of*, or *Part I*)
Testament: will/testament
Thüringen: Thuringia
Tirol: Tyrol
Tochter/Töchter: daughter/daughters
Tochter von: daughter of
Töchterchen: daughter (diminutive)
Tochtergemeinde: church branch, filial

church
Tod: death
Todesanzeige: obituary
Todesursache: cause of death
tot: (adj.) dead
Totenbücher: death books
Totengeläutbücher: death bell tolling books
totgeborenes Kind: stillborn child
Trauung: wedding, marriage ceremony
Übersetzung: translation
Übersicht: overview
um: at about, around
unbekannt: (adj.) unknown
unehelich: illegitimate
Ungarn: Hungary
ungefähr: about, approximately
Universität: university
Universitätsmatrikel(n): university roll(s)/registry(ies)
unverheiratet: (adj.) unmarried
Urgroßvater/-mutter: great grandfather/-mother
Urkunde: old (original) document, certificate
Ursache: cause
Vater: father
Verband/Verbände: society/societies
verehelicht: (adj.) married
Verein: society, union
Vereinigte Staaten: United States
Vereinigung: association
Verfasser(in): author/writer
verheiratet: (adj.) married
Verlag: publisher
Verlobte: engaged couple
Verlobung: engagement
Verlobungsanzeige: banns
vermählt: (adj.) married
Veröffentlichung(en): publication(s)
verstorben: (adj.) deceased, defunct
verstorben am: died on
Verstorbene(r): the deceased
verwandt: (adj.) related
verwandte Publikationen: related publications
Verwandtschaft: relatives
verwitwet: (adj.) widowed
Verzeichnis(se): list(s)/index(es)

Vetter: male cousin
Viertel: town quarter
Volk: people/nation
Volkszählung: census
volljährig: (adj.) of legal age
von: of/from
Vorfahr(en): ancestor(s)
Vormund: guardian
Vormundschaft: guardianship
Vorname(n): given name(s)
Waise: orphan
Wappen: coat-of-arms
Wappenkunde: heraldry
Wäsche: laundry/underclothes
Weib: wife/woman
weiblich: female
weiland: deceased, former
Weiler: hamlet
Westfalen: Westphalia
Westpreußen: West Prussia
wichtig: (adj.) important
Wiedertäufer: Anabaptist
Wissenschaften: science
Witwe/(-r): widow/widower
wohin: where to? (destination)
wohnen: to live (reside)
Wohnhaft: place of residence
Wohnort/Wohnplatz: place of residence
Wohnsitz: residence
Wörterbuch: dictionary
wurde geboren: was born
wurde getauft: was baptized
Zehntregister: tithe register
Zeichen: symbol
Zeit: time
Zeitschrift(en): periodical(s), journal(s)
Zeitung(en): newspaper(s)
Zentral: central
Zentralstelle: center, central repository
Zeuge(n): witness(es)
Zeugnis: testimony, certificate
Ziel der Auswanderung: emigrant's
destination
Zivilstand: marital status
Zivilstandsamt: civil registry
Zivilstandsregister: civil registry (vital
records)
Zollverein: Customs Union
Zuname: surname

Zunft: guild
Zunftbuch: guild record
Zweitschriften: transcripts
Zwilling: twin

DER SCHLÜSSEL
(German periodical index)

Der Schlüssel: Gesamtinhaltsverzeichnisse für genealogische, heraldische und historische Zeitschriftenreihen mit Orts-Sach-, und Namenregistern [The Key: comprehensive index of genealogical, heraldic, and historical serials with place, subject, and name indexes], Heinz Reise-Verlag, Göttingen, Deutschland, 9 volumes, 1950ff.

This periodical index is valuable because it is an immense source of information offered through German genealogy and local history publications. Many German genealogists, in order to have their research results published, submit them to these periodicals.

Description

Der Schlüssel is a nine-volume index to more than 90 German, Austrian, and Swiss genealogical and heraldic periodicals from 1870 to 1975 (some date as early as 1860 and as late as 1981).

Indexes include titles (*Titelnachweis*), place names (*Ortsquellenverzeichnis*), subjects (*Sachverzeichnis*), and surnames (*Namenverzeichnis*).

The first three volumes are indexed within each volume; The others are indexed together. The work is written in German.

Format

The Title Index, or *Titelnachweis,* (the main body of each volume) lists authors alphabetically with the titles of their articles. The numbers assigned to each author-title are referred to in the place, subject, and surname indexes.

The Place Name Index, or *Ortsquellenverzeichnis,* lists places, areas, and countries found in the Title Index. The number following each place name is the number of the article in the Title Index.

The List of Subjects, or *Sachverzeichnis,* lists specific topics, such as emigration, census, tax, or occupation records.

The Name Index, or *Namenverzeichnis,* lists surnames found in titles of articles as they appear in the Title Index, but not surnames within particular articles. The number following each name is the article number.

Locating the periodicals

If a periodical being sought is in the collection of the Family History Library and is not under copyright protection, copies of articles may be obtained by using the Library's "Request for Photocopies" form.

Write to:

Photoduplication Service
Family History Library
35 North West Temple Street
Salt Lake City, UT 84150

Copies of periodicals may also be requested through interlibrary loan from university and public libraries.

Further information

A thorough set of instructions, from which the above information is taken, is included in "Locating a Surname, Locality or Topic in German Genealogical Periodicals: Der Schlüssel - The Key," by Laraine K. Ferguson, *German Genealogical Digest,* Vol. 9, No. 2, 1993.

Availability

Der Schlüssel is found in the Family History Library and other well stocked genealogical libraries; it is not recorded on microfilm or fiche. It may be found at the Family History Library as FHL book 943 D25sc.

GERMAN ALPHABETIZATION OF UMLAUTED VOWELS

German alphabetization can cause some confusion until it is understood that unmlauted vowels (like *a, o,* and *u*) are grouped separately and placed before umlauted vowels (*ä, ö,* and *ü*).

By this system, all words beginning with *Lü-* come before those beginning with *Lu.*

For example, in *Das Postleitzahlenbuch* (the German postal code directory), the following villages appear in this alphabetical order:

Lübz
Lüssow
Lützen
Luftschiff
Luppa

When checking alphabetized lists of German words, therefore, keep in mind this order of umlauted and unumlauted vowels: ä, a, ö, o, ü, u.

Note, however, that German lists and indexes which have been constructed by non-German researchers will likely be alphabetized with umlauted and unumlauted vowels intermingled. It is a good idea to search for a surname in an index by checking for both the umlauted and unumlauted vowels.

Words containing *ß* (the *Eszett*) are alphabetized as if the *ß* were *ss.*

GLENZDORF'S DIRECTORY

Glenzdorfs Internationales Genealogen-Lexikon **(Glenzdorf's International Directory of Genealogists) vol. 1 and 2. Wilhelm Rost Verlag, Bad Münder am Deister, 1977, 1979.**

The three volumes of the Glenzdorf directory list alphabetically the German genealogists who submitted their genealogical information to this project.

The submissions include biographical data and an index of surnames which were being researched by these German genealogists, including the submitters' names. There is also an index of the localities from which the surnames came.

All genealogists' names are listed alphabetically in Volume 3.

MEYERS ORTS- UND VERKEHRS-LEXIKON

One of the most valuable resources for German research is this gazetteer:
Meyers Orts- und Verkehrs-Lexikon des Deutschen Reichs, compiled by E. Ütrecht. Leipzig, 1912.

Printed in the old German script, which lists localities as they existed in Germany from 1871 until World War I, it may be found in FHL book (Ref. 943E5mo), film 496,640 (localities A-K) and 496,641 (localities L-Z), and microfiche 6000001-29.

Note these two major uses of this gazetteer:

1. In order to determine where the civil registration records were kept in a given locality, look for the "*StdA*" abbreviation (short for *Standesamt,* or the civil registration office). The *StdA* followed by a comma or a semicolon, indicates that the locality had its own civil registration office. If the *StdT* is not followed by a comma or semicolon, the civil registration office was located in the place named immediately following *StdA.*

2. It is possible to learn whether a church or synagogue was located in the town by looking for the abbreviations *ev.Pfk* (Lutheran church), *reform Pfk* (Reformed Church), *kath. Pfk.* (Catholic church), or *Syn.* (synagogue). If none of these terms is present, indicating that the town had no parish, it is necessary to look in other gazetteers to find the parish for the given town or village.

Reading the abbreviations

Below are listed some of the most commonly used abbreviations in the Meyers gazetteer. The first column shows abbreviations as they appear in the old German script in the gazetteer. The second column shows the same abbreviations, but in Roman type . The third column spells out the full words or phrases in German, followed by their English translations.

ABBREVIATIONS: *MEYERS ORTS- UND VERKEHRS-LEXIKON*

𝔄	A	*Amt (Amtsbezirk):* district, county
𝔄b.(e)	Ab.(e)	*Abbau(e) oder Ausbau(e):* surface mine(s)
𝔄bt.	Abt.	*Abteilung:* division, section, department
a/d	a/d	*an der, auf der:* at the, on the
𝔄g., =ag.	Ag., -ag.	*Agentur, -agentur:* agent/agency, -agency
𝔄𝔊	AG	*Amtsgericht:* lower/district court
𝔄ℌ	AH	*Amtshauptmannschaft:* main county administrative office
𝔄𝔎	AK	*Armeekorps:* army corps
𝔄ftℭes	AktGes	*Aktiengesellschaft:* joint-stock company
a.𝔏.	a.L.	*ältere Linie:* of the old lineage
𝔄ll𝔊ut.	AllGut.	*Allodialgut:* small proprietary lands; allodial estate
𝔄nh	Anh.	*Anhalt:* Anhalt (former duchy)
𝔄nsdl.	Ansdl.	*Ansiedlung:* colony, settlement
𝔄nst., =anst.	Anst., -anst.	*Anstalt, -anstalt:* institution, -institution
𝔄rb.	Arb.	*Arbeiter:* worker
𝔄rt.	Art.	*Artillerie:* artillery

Ausg.	Ausg.	*Ausgaben:* expenditures
B.	B.	*Bezirk:* district
BA	BA	*Bezirkamt:* district office
Bat.	Bat.	*Bataillon:* battalion
Batt.	Batt.	*Batterie:* battery
Bay.	Bay.	*Bayern:* Bavaria
Bgb., =bgb.	Bgb., -bgb	*Bergbau, -bergbau:* mining, -mining
BGrem.	Bgrem.	*Bezirksgremium:* district board
Bgw.	Bgw.	*Bergwerk:* mine
Bhf.	Bhf.	*Bahnhof:* train station
Bibl.	Bibl.	*Bibliothek:* library
Bk.	Bk.	*Bank:* bank
BKdo	Bkdo	*Bezirkskommando:* district military command
Bn, =bn.	Bn, -bn	*Bahn, -bahn:* railroad, -railway
Brandbg.	Brandbg.	*Brandenburg:* Brandenburg
Braunschw.	Braunschw.	*Braunschweig:* Braunschweig
=bre	-bre	*-brüche:* -swamp, moor, quarry, pit
Brgm.	Brgm.	*Bürgermeister (ei):* mayor; mayor's office
Brig.	Brig.	*Brigade:* brigade
Bsch.	Bsch.	*Baurenschaft:* farmers' association
bz.	bz.	*beziehungsweise:* respectively; or
D		*Dampfer- oderMotorbootverbindung:* steam or motorboat connection
SD		*ditto, in der Saison, -Sommer:* same as above (but boat available in summer season only)
das.	das.	*daselbst:* there, at that place
D., Dr.	D., Dr.	*Dorf, Dörfer:* village, villages
Dir., =dir.	Dir., -dir.	*Direktion, -direktion:* management, head office
Drl.	Drl.	*Darlehen:* loan
Dom.	Dom.	*Domäne, Dominium:* domain, state-owned estate
DomA.	DomA.	*Domäneamt:* estate office
dsgl.	dsgl.	*(desgleichen) bezieht sich auf unmittelbar Vorhergehendes:* (the same) refer directly to the preceding
=dt.	-dt.	*-distrikt:* -district
E		*Eisenbahnstation, Haltestelle:* train station, stop
E		*-mit Personen-und Güterverkehr:* -with passengers and goods
E		*-mit Bahntelegraph:* -with telegraph
EGt		*-nur mit Güterbeförderung:* -with transportation of goods only
EPs		*-nur mit Personenverkehr:* -with passengers only
E†		*-mit Eisenbahnauskunftsstelle:* -with railroad information desk
Ein.	Ein.	*Einöde:* wilderness, outlying (farm)house
Einn., =einn	Einn., -einn	*Einnahme, -einnahme:* income, revenue, tax office
Eis.	Eis.	*Eisenbahn:* railroad
Elktr.	Elktr.	*Der Ort hat elektr. Licht & (od.) Kraftqu.:* The place has electric light and/or a source of power

Elftrw. ......,........ Elktrw .... *Elektrizitätswerk:* power plant
Els. .... Els. .... *Elsaß:* Alsace
Esk. .... Esk. .... *Eskadro:* cavalry troop (squadron)
Etabl .... Etabl.. .... *Etablissement:* establishment
ev., Ev. .... Ev., Ev. .... *Evangelisch, Evangelische:* Protestant, (Lutheran)
F .... *Fernsprecher*   telephone
F .... *Fernsprecher und Telegraph* telephone and
                          telegraph
Fbr., =fbr. .... Fbr., -fbr. .... *Fabrik, Fabrikation*   factory, works, mill
Fil. .... Fil. .... *Filiale*   branch of an institution
Fl. .... Fl. .... *Flecken*   borough (village with some rights of a
                          township)
Först. .... Först. .... *Forst*   *Försterei* forester ranger's house
fr. .... fr. .... *früher*   former, formerly
Frht. .... Frht. .... *Freiheit*   a *Flecken* or market town (borough
                          in Rhineland and Westphalia)
Fürstt. .... Fürstt. .... *Fürstentum*   principality
G. .... G. .... *Gericht* court
Garn. .... Garn. .... *Garnison*   garrison
GB. .... GB. .... *Gerichtsbezirk*   court district
Gef. .... Gef. .... *Gefängnis*   prison, jail
geh. .... geh. .... *gehörig* belonging to
Gem. .... Gem. .... *Gemeinde*   community, congregation
Gen. .... Gen. .... *General* general, commander
Genoss. .... Genoss. .... *Genossenschaft*   company, cooperative
Ges. .... Ges. .... *Gesellschaft*   society, association
Gew., gew. .... Gew., gew. .... *Gewerbe, gewerblich*   trade, business;
                          industrial
glchn. .... Glchn. .... *gleichnamig*   of the same name
Gr., ... Gr. .... *Groß:* Great- (part of place name)
Gsth. .... Gsth. .... *Gast-, Wirtshaus, Krug:* guesthouse, inn, lodging
GTg. .... GTg. .... *Gerichtstag*   jurisdictional area of a court
Gymn. .... Gymn. .... *Gymnasium:* academically oriented high school
H. (Hr.) .... H. (Hr.) .... *Haus, (Häuser):* house (houses)
=h .... -h .... *-haus, -heim:* -house, -home
Hann. .... Hann. .... *Hannover:* Hanover (former Prussian province)
Hdl. .... Hdl. .... *Handel(s):* commerce, or business establishment
Hersch. .... Hersch. .... *Herrschaft:* manor, estate
Hessen-N. .... Hessen-N .... *Hessen-Nassau:* Hessen-Nassau (former Prussian
                          province)
Hf. .... Hf. .... *Hafen:* port, harbor
Hosp. .... Hosp. .... *Hospital:* hospital
Hpt= .... Hpt- .... *Haupt:* main
Hr. .... Hr. .... *Häuser:* houses
Hrgr.(n) .... Hrgr.(n) .... *Häusergruppe(n):* group of houses
hzl. .... hzl. .... *herzoglich:* ducal
Hzt. (=hzt.) .... Hzt. (-hzt.) .... *Herzogtum (-herzogtum):* duchy, dukedom
Ind. .... Ind. .... *Industrie:* industry
Inf. .... Inf. .... *Infantrie:* infantry

Insp. .... Insp. .... *Inspektionz:* inspection
Inst. .... Inst. .... *Institut*   institute
Int., -int. .... Int., -int. .... *Intendantur:* superintendent, quartermaster
general's department
J. .... J .... *Juden, Israeliten, israelitisch:* Jews; Israelites;
Israeli (adj.)
j.L. .... j.L. .... *jüngere Linie:* of the younger lineage
K. .... K .... *Kirche:* church
-k .... -k .... *-kasse oder -kirche:* -collecting agency; -church
Kam. .... Kam. .... *Kamme; treasury:* departments of a court (civil,
criminal, trade); houses of parliament; chamber
(like Chamber of Commerce)
Kap. .... Kap. .... *Kapelle:* chapel
Kat. .... Kat. .... *Kataster:* land-register
kath.,Kath .... kath., Kath. ...... *katholisch, Katholiken:* Roman Catholic (adj.),
Catholics
Kav. .... Kav. .... *Kavallerie:* cavalry
Kdo .... Kdo .... *Kommando:* command post
kgl. .... kgl. .... *königlich:* royal
-khlbgb. .... -khlbgb. .... *-kohlenbergbau:* coal-mine
Kl- .... Kl- .... *Klein-:* Little- (part of place names)
Klbn. .... Klbn. .... *Kleinbahn:* narrow-guage railroad
km .... km .... *Kilometer:* 1000 meters, 0.6 miles
Kol. .... Kol. .... *Kolonat, Kolonie:* hereditary leasehold to a farm
belonging to an estate
Kom. .... Kom. .... *Kommandantur:* commandant's office, garrison
headquarters
Komm. .... Komm. .... *Kommission:* commission
Kr. .... Kr. .... *Kreis:* county, district
KredVor. .... Kred.Vor .... *Kredit- & od. Vorschussverein:* loan association
Krh. .... Krh. .... *Kreishauptmannschaft:* county office
KrSt. .... KrSt. .... *Kreisstadt:* capital of a Kreis
Ksp. .... Ksp. .... *Kirchspiel:* parish
Kt. .... Kt. .... *Kanton:* county (state) in France and Switzerland
l. .... l. .... *links:* to the left
L. .... L. .... *Land(es):* land, region
Ldepl. .... Ldepl. .... *Ladeplatz:* wharf, loading point
LG. .... LG. .... *Landgericht:* county court
Lgem. .... Lgem. .... *Landgemeinde:* citizens of a county
Lherr-(en)sch. .... *Lherr-(en) sch.: Landherr(en)schaft* sovereign
possession, rulers (collectively)
Lkr. .... Lkr. .... *Landkreis:* county
Lthr., Loth. .... Lthr-, Loth. ...... *Lothringen:* Lorraine (as in Alsace-Lorraine)
LrA. .... LrA. .... *Landratsamt:* office of county commission
Lw., lw. .... Lw., lw. .... *Landwirtschaft:* farm, agriculture
m .... *Meter überm Meer:* meters above sea level
Mag. .... Mag. .... *Magazin:* warehouse, depot, armory
Masch. .... Masch. .... *Maschine(n):* machine(s)
Mdg. .... Mdg. .... *Mündung:* mouth of a river, estuary

Mekl.=Schw. .... Meckl.-Schw. ..*Mecklenburg-Schwerin:*Mecklenburg-Schwerin
Mekl.=Str. .... Meckl.-Str. .... *Mecklenburg-Strelitz:*Mecklenburg-Strelitz
Mil. .... Mil. .... *Militär:* the military
Mktfl. .... Mktfl. .... *Marktflecken:* market or small county town; a Flecken (borough) chartered to hold markets
MktGk. .... MktGk. .... *Martflecken-Gerechtigkeit:* market jurisdiction
Ml., =ml. .... Ml., -ml. .... *Mühle, -mühle:* mill, -mill
N., (n.) .... N., (n.) .... *Norden (nördlich), neben:* north, northerly; next to
=n. .... -n. .... *-nebenstelle:* -branch office
Nd.= .... Nd.- .... *Nieder-:* Lower- (part of place names)
Neum. .... Neum ....*Neumark:* eastern part of province of Brandenburg
NO. (nö.) .... NO. (Nö) .... *Nordosten, nordöstlich:* northeast, northeasterly
NW., nw. .... NW., nw. .... *Nordwesten, nordwestlich:* northwest, northwesterly
NZA. .... NZA. .... *Nebenzollamt:* branch custom office
O. .... O. Ober- .... *Upper-:* (part of place names)
O. (ö.) .... O. (ö) .... *Osten (östlich):* east (easterly)
OA. .... OA. .... *Oberamt:* county (in Württemberg)
OForst. .... Oforst. .... *Oberförsterei:*head forester's office
Oldenb. .... Oldenb. .... *Oldenburg* Oldenburg
OLG. .... OLG. .... *Oberlandesgericht:* provincial supreme court
OPDir. .... OPDir. .... *Oberpostdirektion:* top postal service administration
Ortsch. .... Ortsch. .... *Ortschaft:*(inhabited) place, village
Ostpr. .... Ostpr. .... *Ostpreußen:* East Prussia
P .... *Postanstalt:* post office
P .... *Post und Fernsprecher:* post office with telephone
P .... *Post und Telegraph:* post office with telegraph
P .... *Post, Fernsprecher und Telegraph:* post office with telephone and telegraph
Pdir. .... Pdir. .... *Postdirektion:* post authorities
Pf.= .... Pf.- .... *Pfarr.-:* parish-
Pfk. .... Pfk. .... *Pfarrkirche:* parish church
Pomm. .... Pomm. .... *Pommern:* Pomerania
Pr., (pr.) .... Pr., (pr.) .... *Preußen, (preußisch):* Prussia, Prussian
Präs. .... Präs. .... *Präsidium:*presidency, chairmanship, head office
Prov. .... Prov. .... *Provinz(ial):*province (provincial)
Pw. .... *Personenpostwagen oder Autoverkehr:* statecoach or automobile traffic
Pz. (Dt.) .... Pz. (Dt.) .... *Polizei (-distrikt):* police (police district)
r. .... r. .... *rechts:* to the right
R. .... R. .... *Regierung(s):* government, administration
Raiffbk. .... Raiffbk. .... *Raiffeisenbank:* a rural loan institution
RB. .... RB. .... *Regierungsbezirk:* provincial district
Rbkh. .... Rbkh. .... *Reichsbankhauptstelle:* main office of national bank
Rbkn. .... Rbkn. .... *Reichsbankhauptstelle:* national bank's main office

Rbkst. .... Rbkst .... *Reichsbankstelle:* German National Bank office
Ref. .... Ref. .... *Reformierte:* Calvinist, member of the Reformed Church
Reg. .... Reg. .... Regiment: *government, authority, regiment (military)*
Rg. .... Rg. .... *Rittergut:* nobleman's landed estate
Rheinl. .... Rheinl. .... *Rheinland, -provinz:* Rhineland, Rhine Province
Ritt. .... Ritt. .... *Ritterschaft(s):* knights, knighthood
RittA. .... RittA. .... *Ritteramt:* estate office
S. .... S. .... *Sankt, in Verbindung mit Ortsnamen, Kirchen, .. Stiften:* Saint, in connection with place names, churches, or monasteries
s. (a.) .... s. (a.) .... *siehe (auch):* see (also)
S. (s.) .... S. (s.) .... *Süden (südlich):* south (southerly)
Sa. .... Sa. .... *Sachsen (Staat od. Prov.):* Saxony, state or .... province
Sa.-A .... Sa.-A .... *Sachsen-Altenburg:* Saxony-Altenburg (former . duchy)
Sa-C.-G. .... Sa-C-G. .... *Sachsen-Coburg-Gotha:Saxony-Coburg-Gotha (former duchy)*
Sa.-M. .... Sa.-M. .... Sachsen-Meiningen: *Saxony-Meiningen (former duchy)*
Sa.-W.-E. .... Sa.-W.-E. .... *Sachsen-Weimar-Eisenach:* Saxony-Weimar-Eisenach (former duchy)
Sanat. .... Sanat. .... *Sanatorium:*sanatarium
Sch., =sch. .... Sch., sch. .... *Schule, -schule:*school, -school
Schaumb=L. .... Schaumb-L. ..... *Schaumburg-Lippe:*Schaumburg-Lippe
Schiff. .... Schiff. .... *Schiffahrt(s):* naval, maritime
Schl. .... Schl. .... *Schleuse:* sluice (lock)
Schles. .... Schles. .... *Schlesien:* Silesia
Schlesw=Holst. ...... Schlesw-Holst. .. *Schleswig-Holstein:*Schleswig-Holstein
Schwarzb.-Rud. .... Schwarzb.-Rud. *Schwarzburg-Rudolstadt:*Schwarzburg-Rudolstadt
Schwarzb-Sond. ...... Schwarzb.Sond.*Schwarzburg-Sondershausen:*Schwarzburg-Sondershausen
SchwG .... SchwG .... *Schwurgericht:*court with a jury
SD .... see *D (Dampfer . . . .)*
Sem. .... Sem. .... *Seminar:*seminary; training college (for teachers)
Slg. .... Slg. .... *Sammlung:*collection, compilation
SO. (sö.) .... SD. (sö) .... *Südosten (südöstlich):*southeast (southeasterly)
Soz. .... Soz. .... *Sozietät:* society, partnership, company
SpDrl. .... SpDrl. .... *Spar- & Darlehnskassenverein:* savings and loan union
Spk. .... Spk. .... *Sparkasse:*savings bank
St. .... St. .... *Stadt (städtisch):* city (municipal)
Stat. .... Stat. .... *Station:* station, stop
StdA. .... StdA. .... *Standesamt:*civil registary office
StKr. .... StKr. .... *Stadtkreis:* urban district
Strbn. (=verz.) .... Strbn. (-verz.) .. *Straßenbahn (-verzeichnis):*streetcar (-register)

Sv.	Sv.	*Servisklasse (Wohnungsgeldzuschluß):* lodging allowance for civil servants
sow.	sow.	*sovielwie:* so far as, according to
SW. (sw.)	SW. (sw.)	*S ü d w e s t e n (s ü d w e s t l i c h) :* s o u t h w e s t (southwesterly)
Syn.	Syn.	*Synogoge:* synagogue
T		*Posttelegraph* telegraph office
E		*Eisenbahntelegraph auf der Station:* railway telegraph at the station
F		*Fernsprecher und Telegraph:* telephone and telegraph
P		*Post und Telegraph:* post office and telegraph
Thür.	Thür.	*Thüringen:* Thuringia
u.	u.	*und:* and
U.	U.	*Unter-:*Lower- (part of place names)
USt.	Ust.	*Unmittelbare Stadt:* independent township
v.	v.	*von:*of, from
Ver. (e)	Ver.(e)	*Verein(e):*club(s), union(s)
Vers.	Vers.	*Versicherung:*insurance, insurance company
Verw.	Verw.	*Verwaltung:* administration, government
VerwA.	VerwA.	*Verwaltungsamt:* administration office
Vw.	Vw.	*Vorwerk:* outlying farm belonging to a main estate; first line of defense at a fortified place
=w.	-w.	*-waren (in Verbindung mit Fbr.):* -goods (as related to a factory or plant)
=w. (we.)	-W. (we.)	*-werk, (-werke):* -works
W., (w.)	W.,(w)	*Westen, westlich:* west, westerly
Westf.	Westf.	*Westfalen:* Westphalia
Westpr.	Westpr.	*Westpreußen:*West Prussia
Wlr.	Wlr.	*Weiler:* very small village
Wp.	Wp.	*Wohnplatz:* place of residence
Wst., =wst.	Wst., -wst.	*Werkstätte (-werkstätte):* workshop (-workshop)
Württ.	Württ.	*Württemberg:* Württemberg (former kingdom)
Z.	Z.	*Zoll:* custom, duty
ZA.	ZA.	*Zollamt:* customs office
Zgl.	Zgl.	*Ziegelei:* brickworks, tile works
Zh.	Zh.	*Zollhaus:* custom house
Zk.	Zk.	*Zinken:*small village (Weiler) in Baden
zw.	zw.	*zwischen:* between, among
[......]		*Verkehrsanstalt nur zu gewisser Zeit:* transportation available station (railway, bus, etc.) operating at certain times
*		*siehe dieses:* see this

Note: Population figures appearing in italics with place names indicate that they represent 1905 census numbers instead of the 1910 numbers otherwise used throughout the gazetteer.

QUERIES IN GERMAN
PUBLICATIONS: *FaNa* and *PraFo*

Two publications in Germany accept queries submitted in English, which their staffs translate into German. The cost of submitting queries varies according to the length of the query. A $20-$30 fee is common.

Query publishers

Familienkundliche Nachrichten (Genealogical News), commonly referred to as "FaNa," is a query periodical which is enclosed with virtually all regular publications of German genealogical societies. (For details, see below.)

PraFo (*Praktische Forschungshilfe* (Practical Research Help), referred to as "PraFo," is a quarterly supplement to the *Archiv für Sippenforschung* (Archive for Genealogical Research). These publications go to individual genealogists as well as to libraries in areas where many German emigrants settled worldwide. The PraFo address is Praktische Forschungshilfe, C.A. Starke Verlag, Postfach 1310, 65549 Limburg/Lahn, Germany.

To submit a query to FaNa

The following instructions are reproduced almost verbatim from the informational brochure circulated by FaNa:

Familienkundliche Nachrichten (Family Information News) is published six times a year. Its pages are devoted entirely to queries for missing ancestors. It has a circulation of more than 13,000 and is a very popular way to publicize genealogical questions.

Familienkundliche Nachrichten is added to almost every important German genealogical paper; it has also reached a wide distribution in the Netherlands and the United States within the past few years. The *Familienkundliche Nachrichten* is sent to more than 100 genealogical societies abroad where they are held at any reader's disposal.

The typical query costs about US

$20.00.

Verlag Degener prefers payment to be in the form of a German Mark check. (See "Ruesch International" in the index for information about mailing payments in marks to Germany.)

The *Familienkundliche Nachrichten* is delivered on the first days of January, March, May, July, September, and November. The publisher must receive the information at least six weeks prior to the date of publication. The address of the publisher is

Familienkundliche Nachrichten
Verlag Degener & Co.
P.O. Box 1340
D-91403 Neustadt /Aisch
Germany

Send a written narrative (in English or German) detailing all that is known about the German background of the ancestor in question, as well as the approximate date when the ancestor departed for America. Verlag Degener will take that information and formulate a precise query in German.

Verlag Degener & Co. will provide the submitter with a free copy of the issue of *Familienkundliche Nachrichten* in which the query appears.

Since this publication is widely distributed and extensively read, the submitter is almost assured of receiving responses. The submitter, upon receiving a response, is asked to send the person a note of thanks along with reimbursement for the postage. (See "International Reply Coupons" in the index for instructions on making reimubursements for German postage.)

Some organizations bind single issues of *Familienkundliche Nachrichten*, thereby providing these queries with a long-lasting effect.

Here is an example of a query for which $20.00 would be charged:

Behrmann, Emily Dorothe, Königreich Hannover, 24.3.1850; engewandert in die usa 1856. Eltern: Augustus B. und Wilhelmina Hock. Andere Kinder: Anna, William, Augusta, Ida.

1441 Lone Oak Rd., Eagan, Minnesota 55121, USA. Gary Maag

English translation: Behrmann, Emily D. Born in the kingdom of Hanover, 24 March 1850. Came to U.S. in 1856. Parents: Aug. B. & Wilhelmina Hock. Other children: Anna, William, August, Ida. Send information to: [name and address of the writer of the query]

To review queries

The Immigrant Genealogy Society (IGS) in keeps indexes to all issues of FaNa that have been published since 1964. It prints in the IGS publication *German American Genealogy* the surnames contained in FaNa submissions for six-month segments.

One may request from IGS a copy of a query containing a specific surname. Send $5.00 for each surname requested to Immigrant Genealogy Society, P.O. Box 7369, Burbank, CA 91510-7369. IGS will copy the query, translate it into English, and supply a German-English form letter to use to correspond with the submitter.

GERMAN TELEPHONE DIRECTORIES

German telephone directories may be purchased through AT&T for the towns and cities listed on the pages that follow.

With use of a German telephone directory, names and street addresses as well as names and addresses of churches, for use in correspondence, may be scanned. Surnames appearing in smaller towns and villages surrounding the locality of interest may also be searched. Still another use for the telephone directory is to check for surnames of the ancestor's neighbors in the United States, as well as for witnesses at special events.

How to order
German telephone directories

For information on current prices or to order directories, call (800) 432-6600, Monday through Friday, 7:30 am to 6 pm,

Eastern time. Fax: (800) 566-9568. To order by mail, write to AT&T, P.O. Box 19901, Indianapolis, IN 46219.

An example of costs: The white-pages directory for "Bamberg, Coburg & Area" costs $8.00. To the cost must be added a flat $5.00 shipping charge for the entire order (a total of $5.00 for shipping regardless of how many directories are ordered). The three-volume set of Berlin white pages directories costs $36.18. Yellow-pages directories are also available, but they are considerably more expensive.

How to use the list
on the following pages

The list of white-pages directories on these pages is based on the AT&T catalog available in 1996. Directories for many localities, even if the locality names are not listed in this catalog, are nevertheless available for purchase.

The two-digit numbers enclosed in brackets after each locality name on this list are not included in the AT&T catalog. The two-digit numbers added here indicate the first two digits of the five-digit zip code (*Postleitzahl*) for each locality, useful for determining whether a given locality may be represented (but unnamed) in the "& Area" phrase included in the titles of many of these directories.

AT&T representatives who take orders for these directories have no information as to whether a particular locality (other than those named) is included in a given directory.

Therefore, before ordering, the researcher should find the zip code of the place of interest in the German zip code directory (*Das Postleitzahlenbuch)*, then use the first two digits (of the five-digit code) to compare with the numbers shown in the list below.

It is necessary to use a zip code map to determine the geographic proximity of one zip code zone with another.

Localities available
•Aachen [52], Heinsberg [52] & Area
•Aalen [73], Heidenheim [91] & Area

A München scene, mid-18th century

•Altenkirchen [57], Bad Ems [56], Montabaur [56], Neuwied [56] & Area
•Amberg [92], Weiden [92], Schwandorf [92] & Area
•Ansbach [91], Erlangen [91], Hersbruck [91], Weißenburg [91] & Area
•Aschaffenburg (see Würzburg)
•Augsburg [86], Donauwörth [86] & Area
•Backnang (see Waiblingen)
•Bad Ems (see Altenkirchen)
•Bad Hersfeld (see Fulda)
•Bad Homburg [61], Hofheim [65] & Area
•Bad Kissingen [97], Schweinfurt [97] & Area
•Bad Kreuznach (see Mainz)
•Bad Mergentheim (see Schwäbisch-Hall)
•Bad Oldesloe [23], Bad Segeberg [23],Ratzeburg [23] & Area
•Bad Schwalbach (see Wiesbaden)
•Bad Segeberg (see Bad Oldesloe)
•Bad Tölz [83], Ebersberg [85], Landsberg [86], Wellheim [91] & Area
•Baden-Baden [76], Rastatt [76] & Area
•Balingen (see Reutlingen)
•Bamberg [96], Coburg [96] & Area
•Bayreuth [95], Hof [95] & Area

•Bergheim [50], Düren [52], Euskirchen [53] & Area
•Bergisch-Gladbach [51], Gummersbach [51], Leverkusen [51] & Area
•Berlin (3 vols.) [10,12,13,14]
•Biberach (see Ulm)
•Bielefeld [33], Gütersloh [33] & Area
•Böblingen [71], Ludwigsburg [71] & Area
•Bochum [44] & Area
•Bonn [53], Siegburg [53] & Area
•Borken [46], Coesfeld [48], Steinfurt [48] & Area
•Bottrop (see Gelsenkirchen)
•Braunschweig [38] & Area
•Bremen-City [28]
•Bremerhaven [27], Cuxhaven [27], Rotenburg [27], Diepholz [49] & Area
•Buchholz (see Lüneburg)
•Calw (see Pforzheim)
•Celle (see Uelzen)
•Chemnitz [09] & Area
•Coburg (see Bamberg)
•Coesfeld (see Borken)
•Cottbus [03]
•Dachau [85], Freising [85], Ingolstadt

[85] & Area
•Darmstadt [64], Dieburg [64], Gross-Garau [64] & Area
•Deggendorf [94], Passau [94], Straubing [94] & Area
•Detmold [32], Höxter [37], Paderborn [Paderborn] & Area
•Dieburg (see Darmstadt)
•Donauwörth (see Augsburg)
•Dortmund-City [44]
•Dresden [01]
•Duisburg [47] & Area
•Düren (see Bergheim)
•Düsseldorf-City [40]
•Ebersberg (See Bad Tölz)
•Erbach (see Heppenheim)
•Erfurt [99] & Area
•Erlangen (see Ansbach)
•Eschwege (see Kassel)
•Essen [45] & Area
•Esslingen [73], Göppingen [73] & Area
•Euskirchen (see Bergheim)
•Eutin (see Lübeck)
•Flensburg [24], Heide [25] and Area
•Frankfurt [60], Offenbach-City [63]
•Frankfurt/Oder [15] & Area
•Freiburg [79] & Area
•Freising (see Dachau)
•Freudenstadt (see Pforzheim)
•Fulda [36], Bad Hersfeld [36], Lauterbach [36] & Area
•Fürth-City (see Nürnberg)
•Gelsenkirchen [45], Bottrop [46], Gladbeck [45] & Area
•Gera [07] & Area
•Giessen [35], Wetzler [35] & Area
•Gifhorn (see Uelzen)
•Gladbeck (see Gelsenkirchen)
•Göppingen (see Esslingen)
•Göttingen [37] & Area
•Gross-Garau (see Darmstadt)
•Gummersbach (see Bergisch-Gladbach)
•Gütersloh (see Bielefeld)
•Hagen [58], Schwelm [58] & Area
•Halle [06] & Area
•Hamburg-City (2 vols.) [20,22]
•Hameln (see Hildesheim)
•Hamm [59], Unna [59] & Area
•Hannover Area [30], Nienburg [31], Peine

[31] & Area
•Hannover-City [30]
•Heide (See Flensburg)
•Heidelberg [69] & Area
•Heidenheim (see Aalen)
•Heilbronn (see Schwäbisch-Hall)
•Heinsberg (see Aachen)
•Heppenheim [64], Erbach [64] & Area
•Herford [32], Minden [32], Lübbecke [32] & Area
•Hersbruck (see Ansbach)
•Hildesheim [31], Hameln [31], Holzminden [37], Stadthagen [31] & Area
•Hof (see Bayreuth)
•Hofheim (see Bad Homburg)
•Holzminden (see Hildesheim)
•Homberg (see Marburg)
•Homberg (see Saarbrücken)
•Höxter (see Detmold)
•Ingolstadt (see Dachau)
•Iserlohn (see Lüdenscheid)
•Itzehoe (see Pinneberg)
•Kaiserslautern [67] & Area
•Karlsruhe [76] & Area
•Kassel [34], Eschwege [37] & Area
•Kaufbeuren [87], Kempten [87], Memmingen [87] & Area
•Kempten (see Kaufbeuren)
•Kiel [24] & Area
•Kleve [47], Wesel [47] & Area
•Koblenz [56] & Area
•Köln-City [50,51]
•Konstanz [78], Ravensburg [88] & Area
•Korbach (see Marburg)
•Krefeld [47], Mönchengladbach [41 & Area
•Landsberg (see Bad Tölz)
•Landshut[84] & Area
•Lauterbach (see Fulda)
•Leer [26], Wilhelmshaven [26] & Area
•Leipzig [04]
•Leverkusen (see Bergisch-Gladbach)
•Limburg (see Wiesbaden)
•Lingen (see Osnabrück)
•Lörrach [79], Waldshut [79] & Area
•Lübbecke (see Herford)
•Lübeck [23], Eutin [23] & Area
•Lüdenscheid [58], Iserlohn [58] & Area

•Ludwigsburg (see Böblingen)
•Ludwigshafen (see Mannheim-City)
•Lüneburg [21], Buchholz [21], Stade [21] & Area
•Madgeburg [39] & Area
•Mainz [55], Bad Kreuznach [55] & Area
•Mannheim-City [68], Ludwigshafen-City [67]
•Marburg [35], Korbach [34], Homberg [34] & Area
•Memmingen (see Kaufbeuren)
•Merzig [66], Neunkirchen[66], Saarlouis [66], St. Wendel [66] & Area
•Meschede (see Söst)
•Mettmann [40] & Area
•Minden (see Herford)
•Mönchengladbach (see Krefeld)
•Montabaur (see Altenkirchen)
•Mülheim (see Oberhausen)
•München-City (2 vols.) [80,81]
•Münster [48], Warendorf [48] & Area
•Neu Ulm (see Ulm)
•Neubrandenburg [17] & Area
•Neunkirchen (see Merzig)
•Neuss [41] & Area
•Neustadt a.d. Weinstraße [67] & Area
•Neuwied (see Altenkirchen)
•Nienburg (see Hannover Area)
•Nürnberg-City [90], Fürth-City [90]
•Oberhausen [46], Mülheim [45] & Area
Offenbach [63] & Area
•Offenbach-City (see Frankfurt)
•Offenburg [77] & Area
•Oldenburg [26] & Area
•Olpe (see Siegen)
•Osnabrück p49], Lingen [49] & Area
•Paderborn (see Detmold)
•Passau (see Deggendorf)
•Peine (see Hannover Area)
•Pforzheim [75], Calw [75], Freudenstadt [72] & Area
•Pinneberg [25], Itzehoe [25] & Area
•Potsdam [14] & Area
•Rastatt (see Baden-Baden)
•Ratzeburg (see Bad Oldesloe)
•Ravensburg (see Konstanz)
•Recklinghausen [45] & Area
•Regensburg [93] & Area
•Remscheid (see Wuppertal)

•Reutlingen [72], Tübingen [72], Balingen [72] & Area
•Rosenheim [83], Traunstein [83] & Area
•Rostock [18] & Area
•Rottweil [78], Villingen-Schwenningen [78], Tuttlingen [78] & Area
•Saarbrücken [66], Homberg [66] & Area
•Saarlouis (see Merzig)
•Schwäbisch Hall [74], Heilbronn [74], Bad Mergentheim [97] & Area
•Schwandorf (see Amberg)
•Schweinfurt (see Bad Kissingen)
•Schwelm (see Hagen)
•Schwerin [19] & Area
•Siegburg (see Bonn)
•Siegen [57], Olpe [57] & Area
•Solingen (see Wuppertal)
•Söst [59], Meschede [59] & Area
•St. Wendel (see Merzig)
•Stade (see Lüneburg)
•Stadthagen (see Hildesheim)
•Steinfurt (see Borken)
•Straubing (see Deggendorf)
•Stuttgart-City [70]
•Traunstein (see Rosenheim)
•Trier [54] & Area
•Tübingen (see Reutlingen)
•Tuttlingen (see Rottweil)
•Uelzen [29], Celle [29], Gifhorn [38] & Area
•Ulm [89], Neu Ulm [89], Biberach [89] & Area
•Unna (see Hamm)
•Villingen-Schwenningen (see Rottweil)
•Waiblingen [71], Backnang [71] & Area
•Waldshut (see Lörrach)
•Warendorf (see Münster)
•Weiden (see Amberg)
•Weißenburg (see Ansbach)
•Wellheim (see Bad Tölz)
•Wesel (see Kleve)
•Wetzler (see Giessen)
•Wiesbaden [65], Limburg [65], Bad Schwalbach [65] & Area
•Wilhelmshaven (see Leer)
•Wuppertal [42], Remscheid [42], •Solingen [42] & Area
•Würzburg [97], Aschaffenburg [63] & Area

FAMILIENGESCHICHTLICHE QUELLEN (German periodical index)

Oswald Spohr, *Familiengeschichtliche Q uellen: Zeitschrift familiengeschichtlicher Quellennachweise* [Family history sources: periodical of family history source references] 17 vols. Degener Verlag, Neustadt/Aisch, 1926-

Each volume of this index and bibliographical guide to many German genealogical publications begins with a numbered bibliography of genealogy periodicals and books. Following is the index of surnames, each citing a number listed in the bibliography. Each volume must be searched separately for the surname being sought. The researcher follows up on a named source by locating it in order to find the information cited. Written in German, but not difficult to use.

Scope

The index contains 2.5 million surname citations from more than 2,300 sources on 6,400 pages. This work indexes the first 92 volumes of *Deutsches Geschlechterbuch*.

Availability

FHL book 943 B2fq, fiche 6000817

DEUTSCHES GESCHLECHTER-BUCH (German lineage books)

Deutsches Geschlechterbuch [German lineage book]. C.A. Starke, Limburg/Lahn, 1889-. Written entirely in German.

This series of lineage books, which has reached 203 volumes (as of 1997), often provides many generations of German families.

For each family a brief history is given with a discussion of the origin of the name, a coat of arms if appropriate, places where the family lived, and a complete genealogy.

The work includes lineages from all parts of Germany, including the former German territories lost after World War II.

Many of the volumes are dedicated to specific German states (see the list below) and others deal with families from various areas.

For each family is given a brief family history, information about the origin of the surname, a coat of arms if appropriate, places where the family has lived, and a complete genealogy. All volumes are written in German; the first 119 volumes, known as "die alte Reihe" (the old series), are printed in Gothic type. The last of that series was published in 1943.

Indexes

♦Each volume contains a surname index.

♦ In 1969 a cumulative index was published for the first 150 volumes in *Stammfolgen-Verzeichnisse für das genealogische Handbuch des Adels und das deutsche Geschlechterbuch* [Index of the genealogical handbook of nobility and the German lineage books], Limburg/Lahn: C.A. Starke, 1969; FHL book 943 D2dg index 1969; or fiche 6053506. In 1994 an updated index appeared covering 199 volumes of *Deutsches Geschlechterbuch*. See the next item for information about this new index, the *Stammfolgen-Verzeichnisse 1994*.

♦The 1963 index covering volumes 1-134 has been filmed (FHL book 943 D2dg index 1963; film 1,183,565 item 5; fiche 6053506).

♦Volumes 1 through 92 have been indexed in the *Familiengeschichtliche Quellen,* by Oswald Spohr.

Availability

There are at least 190 volumes of *Deutsches Geschlechterbuch* at the Family History Library. See FHL book 943 D2dg; FHLC computer number 278503. The first 125 volumes have been microfilmed (FHL film 491876-491981), but the films of volumes published in the last 56 years ago may not be circulated to Family History Centers because of copyright restrictions. They are available at the Family History Library only.

The volumes

The numbers shown below pertain to specific volumes of *Deutsches Geschlechterbuch* as each relates to the respective area indicated:

Baden: 81,101,120,161,189
Baltic: 79
Berg (Bergische): 24,35,83,168,183
Brandenburg: 111,150,160
Darmstadt: 69,96
German-Swiss: 42,48,56,65,77
Eifel: 99,123
Hamburg: 18,19,21,23,27,44,51,63,127-128,142,171, 200 (due in 1997)
Harz: 106
Hessen: 32, 47, 52, 54, 64, 66, 69, 84, 96, 98, 107, 119, 121, 124, 138, 144, 157, 159, 175, 176
Kurpfalz (Pfalz): 58, 86, 149, 197
Lippe: 72
Magdeburg: 39
Mecklenburg: 57, 74, 88, 105
Nassau: 49
Neumark: 93
Niedersachsen: 46, 76, 89, 102, 113, 122, 129, 131, 141, 143, 151, 158, 166, 167, 180, 187
Obersachsen: 33
Ostfriesland: 26, 31, 59, 103, 134, 190
Ostpreußen: 61, 68, 117
Pommern: 40, 67, 90, 115, 136, 137, 145, 155, 174, 191
Posen: 62, 78, 116, 140
Ravensberg: 82, 194
Reutlingen: 34, 41
Sauerland: 38, 53, 97
Schlesien: 73, 112, 153, 178
Schleswig-Holstein: 91, 162, 186
Schwaben: 34, 41, 42, 55, 71, 75, 110, 146, 170
Siegerland: 95, 139, 163, 164, 198, 199
Thüringen: 87, 114,
Westfalen: 108, 152, 156, 172, 182, 184, 187, 193
Westpreußen: 126, 132, 133
General: 1-17, 20, 22, 25, 28-30, 36, 37, 45, 50, 60, 70, 80, 85, 92, 100, 104, 109,

118, 125, 130, 135, 147, 148, 154, 165, 169, 172, 177, 185, 188, 192, 195, 196, 201, 203

The first 35 volumes were titled *Genealogisches Handbuch Bürgerlicher Familien* [Genealogical Handbook of Common (non-noble) Families]. The volumes that followed were titled *Deutsches Geschlechterbuch.*

For further information

See "The German Lineage Book," by Horst Reschke, *German Genealogical Digest,* Vol. 12, No. 2, Summer, 1996.

THE NEW INDEX TO *DEUTSCHES GESCHLECHTERBUCH* (*Stammfolgen-Verzeichnesse 1994*)

Stammfolgen-Verzeichnisse 1994, C.A. Starke Verlag, Limburg, Germany.

Before this new index of 1994 was published, the index to the *Deutsches Geschlechterbuch [German lineage books]* series, published in 1969, covered the first 150 volumes. The newly published index covers 199 volumes, thus sharply increasing the number of indexed references.

As of 1997, this latest index covers all volumes except the three latest one, numbers – 200, 201, and 203

Researchers who searched the 1969 index may therefore be rewarded by continuing their exploration of *Deutsches Geschlechterbuch* through this new index.

See the previous item for information about the *Deutsches Geschlechterbuch* series.

FAMILIENGESCHICHTLICHE BIBLIOGRAPHIE: An index to German periodicals

This work, edited by Johannes Hohlfeld, Friedrich Wecken, and others

(Degener Verlag, Neustadt/Aisch, 1920-1945) is part of the Family History Center's Core Collection (fiche 600820). The first six volumes are on film 942936-942938. The first seven volumes cover German genealogical literature published between 1897 and 1945. See the explanation of this index available at the European Reference Desk at the Family History Library in Salt Lake City, entitled *Bibliography of Family History.*

DIE AHNENLISTEN-KARTEI (Ancestor List Catalog)

Die Ahnenlisten-Kartei [Ancestor List Catalog], Verlag Degener, Neustadt/Aisch, Germany, 1975-, 14 Lieferungen [volumes]

These 17 volumes serve as an index used to access the ancestor lists submitted by many German family history researchers to what is known as the *Ahnenlistenumlauf* (ancestor list exchange).

The *Ahnenlisten-Kartei* volumes index information submitted by a group of German researchers, consisting of the surnames, the locations from which these surnames originate, and the time periods in which the surnames appear. Once one finds a nearly identical match of these factors with those of his or her own ancestors, the microfilms showing these pedigrees may be ordered, to be examined for details. The microfilm numbers are listed at the right.

The *Ahnenlisten-Kartei* volumes are generally found in libraries specializing in German genealogical research.

Publication dates of volumes
The Ahnenlistenkartei volumes were published in the following years: Vol. 1, 1975; Vol. 2, 1976; Vol. 3, 1977; Vol. 4, 1978; Vol. 5, 1978; Vol. 6, 1979; Vol. 7, 1980; Vol. 8, 1981; Vol. 9, 1981; Vol. 10, 1982; Vol. 11, 1983; Vol. 12, 1985; Vol. 13, 1986; Vol. 14, 1988; Vol. 15, 1996;

Vol. 16, 1996; Vol. 17, 1996.
For further information
• Helen Boyden, "Die Ahnenlisten-Kartei." *The German Connection* (newsletter of the German Research Association), January 1988, p. 8ff.
♦ Laraine K. Ferguson, "Ahnenlistenumlauf: Circulating German Ancestor Lists a Rich Source for the Genealogist." *German Genealogical Digest*, Fall 1995.
• Betty Heinz Matyas, "Using the Ahnenlisten-Kartei." *Der Blumenbaum* (journal of the Sacramento German Genealogy Society), Vol. 11, No. 1 (Summer 1993).

THE AHNENLISTENUMLAUF ON MICROFILM

The numbers in the left column below represent the various submitters to the *Ahnenlistenumlauf* (ancestor list exchange) collection, each of whom is assigned a specific "AL" number.

In the right column are the corresponding Family History Library microfilm numbers where the pedigree and surname information donated by the respective submitters may be found. Films should be ordered by the title *Ahnenlistenumlauf.* These films are used in research that results from perusing the *Ahnenlisten Kartei.*

AL 1001-1032	FHL 1861935
AL 1032a-1075	FHL 1864551
AL 1076-1128	FHL 1864552
AL 1129-1188	FHL 1864592
AL 1181-1239	FHL 1864593
AL 1240-1284	FHL 1864594
AL 1285-1329	FHL 1864701
AL 1330-1384	FHL 1864702
AL 1385-1440	FHL 1864703
AL 1441-1504	FHL 1864870
AL 1505-1555	FHL 1864871
AL 1556-1726	FHL 1864904
AL 1727-2011	FHL 1864905
AL 2012-2079	FHL 1873641
AL 2080-2157	FHL 1873642

AL 2158-2204 .... FHL 1873643

DIE AHNENSTAMMKARTEI DES DEUTSCHEN VOLKES (ASTAKA)

ASTAKA (acronym for *Die Ahnen-stammkartei des deutschen Volkes*, or pedigree index of Germans) is an index of the ALU *(Ahnenlistenaustausch,* or ances-tor list exchange) with later ancestor lists that were added to it. These data consist of nearly 5 million names from all parts of present-day Germany and the former Ger-man lands, with emphasis on eastern ar-eas. ASTAKA is housed in *Die Deutsche Zentralstelle für Genealogie* (The German Center for Genealogy) in Leipzig.

Those who use the microfilmed ASTAKA should become familiar with the register for these films, a book entitled, *An Introduction and Register to Die Ahnenstammkartei des deutschen Volkes of the Deutsche Zentralstelle für Genealogie Leipzig 1922-1991*, compiled by Thomas Kent Edlund, The Family His-tory Library, Salt Lake City, 1993.

This register is divided into these sections:
◆"Part I, Surname Index," which is the pedigree index. The material represented by this index is recorded on 638 rolls of Family History Library microfilm. In this section of the register, microfilm numbers are listed by alphabetical order of surnames. Before a surname is searched in this index, however, its spelling must be converted according to a specific set of rules listed on pages 1 and 2 of the register.
◆ *"Ahnenlisten"* (ancestor lists): This section of the register indexes more than 12,000 pedigrees, or ancestor lists, by AL (Ancestor List) numbers. Starting on page 66, the section is headed *"Ahnentafeln* (AL) Manuscript Numbers, Part II."
◆ *Ahnenlisten Nummernkartei* (ancestor-list index): This index (page 64 of the register) gives the name of the submitter by AL numbers. Use this index to find the submitter's name, then go to the Einsend-

erkartei (see below) to find the submitter's address.
◆ *Einsenderkartei* (submitter index): This index indicates on which films the addresses of the submitters may be found (page 64 of the register).
◆ *Nummernkartei* (index of sources): This is an index (page 65 of the register) of the sources of the "literature" notations recorded on the *Ahnenstammkartei* cards in the pedigree index. (The term "literature" in this sense refers to materials other than the submitted pedigree information, such as books, manuscripts, and journal articles pertaining to specific surnames).
◆ Three other indexes, all on one roll of microfilm: *Berühmtenkartei*, for genea-logical material about well-known people; *Ortskartei*, an index of places, listed alphabetically (these locality listings were made before 1945); and *Sachkartei*, an index of miscellaneous materials.

VOCABULARY HELP WITH THE *AHNENLISTENUMLAUF*

These German words, phrases, abbre-viations and symbols may be useful for interpreting notations in the *Ahnenlisten-Kartei* and other resources contained in the *Ahnenlistenumlauf:*
Ahnenlisten: list of ancestors
Ahnenlisten-Kartei: ancestor list catalog
Ahnentafel: pedigree chart
AL-Nr.: number assigned to the submitter of the surname information
ALA: short for *Ahnenlistenaustausch,* or ancestor list exchange (established in 1921)
ALU: Ahnenlistenumlauf (ancestor list exchange), the collection of submitted pedigrees available on microfilm at the Family History Library and its centers
Anschriftenänderungen der AL Ein-sender: address changes of submitters
ASTAKA: acronym for *Ahnenstamm-kartei des deutschen Volkes*, the indexed

5-million-name collection stored at the Zentralstelle für Genealogie in Leipzig
Einsender: submitter(s)
Land: state or country
Länderschlüssel: state/country key
Name: surname
Orte: (literally, "places") The postal code for the place in which a surname is found
Ortsliste: list of places
Postleitschlüssel: zip code key
Proband: the principal or main person with which the pedigree begins, which is sometimes listed as "*Haupt,*" or "main"
Quellenverzeichnis or *Quellenangaben:* list of sources, like church books, published sources, home sources, references to other pedigrees.
Siehe Teilliste: See the continuation of the name under the wife's surname
Zeit: the century in which a surname is found (for example, "16" or "18")

MINERVA HANDBÜCHER

Minerva-Handbücher: Archive im deutschsprachingen Raum [Minerva Handbooks: Archives in German-speaking Regions]. Berlin: Walter de Gruyter. 2nd edition 1974. 2 vols.

The *Minerva Handbook* serves as a guide to the collections of archives and libraries in Germany (including East and West Germany, at the time it was written), and Austria, Switzerland, Luxembourg, Lichtenstein, Poland, and Czechoslovakia. It identifies every archive of any kind existing when the work was compiled. The work is written in German.

Most valuable for family history researchers are the listings in the *Bestände* (holdings) section for each archive entry. Records listed there are not limited to genealogical holdings; for example, listings might be given for glassworkers' archives, university archives, or other specialty areas that could tie into an ancestor's occupation. Also useful are listings for holdings in a given location that record events

in an entirely different area. The work is not useful for the archive addresses listed, as many of these have changed.

The volumes are available at the Family History Library and at larger libraries (FHL book 943 A5m 1974 Vol.1-2).

MÜLLERS GROSSES DEUTSCHES ORTSBUCH (Müller's Large German Gazetteer)

Friedrich Müller. *Müllers grosses deutsches Ortsbuch.* **Wuppertal-Barmen, Germany: Post- und Ortsbuchverlag Postmeister a.d. Friedrich Müller. 1958. 18th edition 1974**

Müllers großes deutsches Ortsbuch [Müller's large German gazetteer]lists more than 107,000 places in present-day Germany, including very small communities, as they existed before the 1990 reunification of Germany.

Useful in identifying present German states of communities that belonged to different political entities before World War II, the book is printed in modern type and is thus easier to read than gazetteers written in Gothic type.

The place-entries are listed alphabetically, with the name of the respective states given at the end of each entry.

The book also contains a section listing localities under Polish or Russian jurisdiction, which were in Germany after World War I.

Clues for use of the gazetteer
♦The abbreviation for the German state where an entity was located appears at the end of each entry.
♦Places having the same name are listed separately.
♦The Kreis (district, abbreviated as *Kr.*) appears in boldface type
♦Suburbs of large cities are listed directly after the city and are preceded with a hyphen (-)
♦Many of the indicators included in an

entry are abbreviated. See the key to abbreviations below.

Availability

This work is available on FHL Film 1,045,448; Fiche 6000340-6000354; FHL book 943 E5m 1958.

ABBREVIATIONS USED IN *MÜLLERS GROSSES DEUTSCHES ORTSBUCH*

Aa: *Arbeitsamt* [employment office]
Ab: *Abbau/Ausbau* [outskirts, suburb/ renovation]
Ag: *Amtsgericht* [local court]
Ans: *Ansiedlung* [settlement]
Arbg: *Arbeitsgericht* [labor court]
AT: *Aussichtsturm* [observation tower]
b: *bei* [at, near, by]
Bad Württ: Baden Württemberg
Bay: *Bayern* [Bavaria]
Bd: *Bad* [spa, health resort]
Bf/Bhf: *Bahnhof* [train station]
Bg: *Bauerngut, Bauernhöfe* [farm settlement]
Bgw: *Bergwerk* [mine]
Brem: *Bremen* [city of Bremen]
Bsch: *Bauernschaft* [farmers collectively]
Bz/Bez: *Bezirk* [district]
bzw: *beziehungsweise* [or else; respectively]
Chh: *Chausseehaus* [toll house]
Ctb: *Cottbus* [city of Cottbus]
D: *Dorf* [village]
DB: *Deutsche Bundesbahn* [Federal Railway]
DDR: *Deutsche Demokratische Republik* [Federal Republic of Germany— former East Germany]
Dm: *Domäne* [state-owned estate]
Dsdn: *Dresden* [city of Dresden]
E: *Eisenbahnpersonenhaltestelle bzw. Eisenbahnhof mit beschränkten Abfertigungsbefugnissen* [passenger train station with a limited schedule]
Eg: *Eisenbahngüterbahnhof* [railroad freight yard]
Eg Klb: *Eisenbahngüterbahnhof einer*

nicht bundeseigenen Eisenbahn (Kleinbahn bzw. Privatbahn) [railroad freight yard not federally owned, with small or private trains]
Ep: *Eisenbahnpersonenbahnhof* [passenger train station]
Ep Klb: *Eisenbahnpersonenbahnhof einer nicht bundeseigenen Eisenbahn* [passenger train station, not federally owned, for small or private trains]
Epg: *Eisenbahnbahnhof für Personen-, Gepäck-, Expreßgut und Güterverkehr* [train station for passengers, luggage, express freight and regular freight]
Epg (Gü b): *wie bei Epg, jedoch mit beschränkter Expreßgutabfertigung* [same as above, but with limited freight traffic]
Epg (o Gü): *Eisenbahnbahnhof für Personen-, Gepäck-, und Expreßgutverkehr (ohne Güterabfertigung)* [train station for passengers, luggage, and express freight (without regular freight)]
Epg (o Ex): *Eisenbahnbahnhof für Personen-, Gepäck-, und Güterverkehr (ohne Expressgutabfertigung)* [train station for passengers, luggage, and freight (without express freight)]
Epg (o P): *Eisenbahnbahnhof für Gepäck-, Expreßgut und Güterverkehr (ohne Personenabfertigung)* [train station for luggage, express freight and regular freight (without passengers)]
Epg Klb: *Eisenbahnbahnhof für Personen-, Gepäck-, Expreßgut und Güterverkehr einer nicht bundeseigenen Eisenbhn (Kleinbahn bzw. Privatbahn)* [small or private train station for passengers, luggage, express freight and regular freight, not federally owned]
Eft: *Erfurt* [city of Erfurt]
Fb: *Fabrik* [factory]
Fbz: *Forstbezirk* [forest area]
Ffo: *Frankfurt (Oder)* [city of Frankfurt/ Oder]
Fgbz: *Forstgutsbezirk* [forest district]
Fi: *Finanzamt* [financial office]
Fl: Flecken [small town]
Fö, Fo: *Försterei, Forsthaus* [forest area,

forester's house]
G: *Gut, Güter* [farmstead, estate]
Ga: *Gesundheitsamt* [board of health]
Gbf: *Güterbahnhof* [railroad freight station]
Gbz/Gtsbz: *Gutsbezirk* [estate district]
Geb: *Gebirge* [mountain range]
Gh: *Gasthaus, Gehöft* [inn]
GK: *Generalkarte, Deutsche* [set of maps used with Müllers]
Gm: *Gemeinde* [community]
gmfr Gebiet: *gemeindefreies Gebiet* [area independent of jurisdiction of a town or village]
Gmk: *Gemarkung* [(village, town, township) limits]
Gr: *Grube* [mine, quarry]
Grafsch/Grfsch: *Grafschaft* [county; earldom]
Gtb: *Gemeindetarifbereich* [local tariff area]
H: *Haus, Häuser, Hofstelle, Höfe, Hof* [house(s), manor, farm, estates]
Hal: *Halle* [city of Halle]
Hamb: *Hamburg* [city of Hamburg]
Hbf: *Hauptbahnhof* [main train station]
Hfe: *Höfe* [country estates]
Hess: *Hessen* [Hesse]
Hgbf: *Hauptguterbahnhof* [central freight train station]
Hgr: *Häusergruppe* [group of houses]
h.j.: *heißt jetzt* [now known as]
Hofg: *Hofgut* [domain]
Hptzo: *Hauptzollamtsbezirk* [main customs district]
Hw: *Hammerwerk, Hüttenwerk* [foundry, ironworks]
Jgh: *Jagdhaus* [hunting lodge]
K: *Kotten* [cottage]
Kirchsp: *Kirchspiel* [parish]
Kirchspeilgm, Ksplgm: *Kirchspielgemeinde* [parish congregation]
Kl: *Kloster* [monastery, convent]
Klbf: *Kleinbahnhof* [small train station]
Klg: *Klostergut* [cloister lands]
km: *Kilometer* [kilometer]
KMSt: *Karl-Marx-Stadt* [Chemnitz, formerly called Karl-Marx-Stadt]
Kol: Kolonie [colony]

Kr: *Kreis (Landkreis)* [district, rural district]
Krarbg: *Kreisarbeitsgericht* [county labor court]
kreisfr St: *kreisfreie Stadt* [city with no obligation to a kreis]
Krfi: *Kreisabgabeamt* [county revenue office]
Krg: Kreisgericht [county court]
Krkhs: *Krankenhaus* [hospital)
Krst: *Kreisstadt* [county seat]
Lchtt: *Leuchtturm* [lighthouse]
Lg: *Landgericht* [rural court]
l U: *linkes Ufer* [left bank of a river]
Lzg: *Leipzig* [city of Leipzig]
m: *mit* [with]
M: *Mühle* [mill]
Mei: *Meierei* [dairy farm]
Mfl/Marktfl: *Marktflecken* [market town]
M Fr: *Mittelfranken* [an area of Bavaria]
Mgb: *Magdeburg* [city of Magdeburg]
Mkt: *Marktgemeinde* [market community]
Neubdb: *Neubrandenburg* [city of Neubrandenburg]
NL: *Niederlausitz* [Lower Lusatia]
Niedersachs: *Niedersachsen* [Lower Saxony]
Nordrh Westf: *Nordrhein-Westfalen* [North Rhine-Westphalia]
Obus: *Kraftomnibus* [bus]
Oelm: *Ölmühle* [oil mill]
Ofö: *Oberförsterei* [chief forester's office]
O Fr: *Oberfranken* [Upper Franconia]
Okl: *Ortsklasse* [class of a locality according to size]
OL: *Oberlausitz* [Upper Lusatia]
Olg: *Oberlandesgericht* [provincial supreme court]
O Pf: *Oberpfalz* [Upper Palatinate]
Ortstl: *Ortsteil* [part of a town]
Osch: *Ortschaft* [locality, community, settlement]
P: *Zustellpostanstalt* [delivery post office]
Pbf: *Personenbahnhof* [passenger train station]
Pdm: *Potsdam* [city of Potsdam]
Prov: *Provinz* [province]

Rbz: *Regierungsbezirk* [governing district]
Rg: *Rittergut* [knightly landed estate]
Rheinl: *Rheinland* [Rhineland]
Ro: *Rotte* [squad]
Rst: *Rostock* [city of Rostock]
r U: *rechtes Ufer* [right bank of a river]
s: *siehe* [see, refer to]
Saarl: *Saarland* [Saarland]
Schl: *Schloß* [castle, fortress, manor house]
Schl Hol: *Schleswig-Holstein* [Schleswig-Holstein]
Schw: *Schwerin* [city of Schwerin]
Si: *Siedlung* [settlement]
Sgb: *Stückgutbahnhof* [parcel train station]
Sgo: *Stückgutort* [freight train station]]
spr: *sprich* [say! (pronounce)]
St: *Stadt* [city]
Sta: *Standesamt* [registrar's office]
Stadtg: *Stadtgut* [municipal property]
Stadtkr: *Stadtkreis* [(combined) city/county]
Stdttl: *Stadtteil* [section of town; ward; borough; (former) village (now) incorporated into a town]
Sw: *Sägewerk* [sawmill]
Tl: *Teil* [portion, share]
TW: *Teutoburger* [Teutoburg Forest]
u: *und* [and]
U: *Unterkunfthaus* [lodging; house of refuge]
Unterfr/U Fr: *Unterfranken* [Lower Franconia]
Va: *Verkehrsamt* [tourist office]
VB: *Verwaltungsbezirk* [administrative district]
vorl: *vorläufig* [temporary]
Vw: *Vorwerk* [residence; farm (outside castle walls)]
W: *Weiler* [hamlet; small village; farm; (hist.) Lordship]
Wh: *Wirtshaus, Wirtschaft* [inn, farm]
Wm: *Wassermühle* [watermill]
Wohnpl: *Wohnplatz* [residence, populated place]
Württ: *Württemberg* [Württemberg]
Zg: *Ziegelei* [brickyard]

Zk/Zi: *Zinken* [outlying farm]
Zo: *Zollamtsbezirk* [customs district]

BIBLIOGRAPHY OF PRINTED FAMILY HISTORIES

Bibliographie gedruckter Familiengeschichten, 1946-1960 **[Bibliography of printed family histories, 1946-1960], by Franz Heinzmann and Christoph Lenhartz, (Heinzman, Düsseldorf, 1990)**

This bibliography of printed German family histories lists 6,486 family history titles by the main family discussed in each history, and also contains indexes providing access to collateral lines, authors, and localities.

It is available as FHL book 943 D23he.

DEUTSCHES BIOGRAPHISCHES ARCHIV (DBA)

Deutsches biographisches Archiv **[The German Biographical Archive.], K.G. Saur, München, 1980-.**

Known as the "DBA," the German Biographical Archive consists of about 225,000 biographical sketches compiled from 264 biographical dictionaries, encyclopedias, almanacs, handbooks and other such collections which were published from the early 18th century through the early 20th century. Many of the subjects represented (writers, theologians, artists, philosophers and others of sufficient reputation to have earned their place in biographical publications) lived much earlier, however.

Format

Biographies are alphabetized by surname and published on 1,447 microfiche. A four-volume index (*Deutscher Biographischer Index*) of the DBA is available but is not necessary to access the DBA. The *Quellenverzeichnis* ("List of Sources") is included in each index volume.

The DBA may be used to search for an ancestor who was prominent in his time and place; to determine from what kingdom, principality, duchy or other political locality of the old German Empire persons of a specific surname came; or to find information about a specific profession or occupation by searching for it in the *Quellenverzeichnis*.

Availability

FHL fiche 6002159 (The surname being searched must accompany the request for the fiche, as the fiche copies are filed alphabetically by surname.) FHL fiche 6002158 contains the *Quellenverzeichnis*.

THE GERMAN POSTAL CODE DIRECTORY(in alphabetical order)

Das Postleitzahlenbuch: Alphabetisch geordnet [The postal code book, in alphabetical order]. Postdienst,Bonn, 1993 (updated as needed).

The *Postleitzahlenbuch* is the directory for the postal code system that was revamped (following the 1990 reunification of Germany) in 1993. On July 1 of that year all postal codes in Germany changed from four- to five-digit numbers.

Using the directory

The *Postleitzahlenbuch: Alphabetisch geordnet* is divided into three parts:

Part 1: Index of locations *(Teil 1: Orteverzeichnis)*

Part I provides an every-locality index, listing alphabetically every village, town, and city in Germany, whether it has its own post office code or is combined with the code of a nearby location. Beside each location name is the appropriate postal code — except in cases where the town or city is large enough to be assigned more than one postal code. In such case, the listing directs the user to Part 2 with this phrase:*s. Teil 2, Straßenverz.*, "(see Part 2, Street Index)."

Part 2: Street index *(Teil 2: Straßenverzeichnis)*

Part 2 provides sets of street indexes, arranged alphabetically, for all locations in Germany that have more than one postal code number. With each of these multi-code listings is a map showing the geographic borders of each of its postal code numbers. Below each map begins an A-to-Z listing of every street name in the locality, with the postal code given for each street.

Part 3: Index to suburbs *(Teil 3: Ortsteileverzeichnis)*

Part 3 lists in alphabetical order the new postal codes for multi-code localities, showing the suburbs or other subdivisions of each. For example:

51143 Köln
Langel, Porz•, Zündorf

The solid black circle (•), or *Punkt*, shown after the name *Porz* indicates that in this district or subdivision certain streets fall in postal code 51143, but other streets in Porz fall in another postal code area. In such a case, one must turn to Part 2, the Street Index, to search in the street-name index of Köln for the specific street name in order to learn the proper postal code.

No *Punkt* is shown with the district names of *Langel* and *Zündorf*, above, indicating that all the streets in these districts fall in the 51143 postal code area.

Tip

The postal zone borders do not coincide with the borders of the German states (*Länder*). It is possible, however, instantly to determine to which state (*Land*) a particular village, town, or city belongs without consulting a map. See the postal code key to the 16 German states in the section following this one.

Availability

The German postal code book may be found in most libraries with genealogy collections. (FHL book 943 E8p 1993; fiche 9,000,033-34). It may be purchased at German post offices; or through Postamt Marburg, Dienststelle 113-21, Postfach

1100, 35035 Marburg, Germany; and through some genealogical publisher outlets in the United States.

POSTAL CODES KEYED TO GERMAN STATES (*LÄNDER*)

The geographic borders of German postal codes do *not* coincide with borders of German states (*Länder*).

To determine quickly, without consulting a map, in which state (*Land*) a given locality currently lies, simply find that locality's postal code number in the list below.

For information about how to find the postal code for a specific locality, see the preceding page.

Postal codes by German state

01001-01936	Sachsen
01941-01998	Brandenburg
02601-02999	Sachsen
03001-03253	Brandenburg
04001-04579	Sachsen
04581-04639	Thüringen
04641-04889	Sachsen
04891-04907	Brandenburg
04910	Sachsen-Anhalt
04911-04938	Brandenburg
06001-06548	Sachsen-Anhalt
06551-06578	Thüringen
06601-06928	Sachsen-Anhalt
07301-07907	Thüringen
07917	Sachsen
07919-07950	Thüringen
07951	Sachsen
07952-07980	Thüringen
07982	Sachsen
07985-07989	Thüringen
08001-09669	Sachsen
10001-12527	Berlin
12529	Brandenburg
12531-12623	Berlin
12625	Brandenburg
12627-14199	Berlin
14401-16949	Brandenburg
17001-17259	Mecklenburg-Vorp.
17261-17290	Brandenburg
17301-17322	Mecklenburg-Vorp.
17323-17326	Brandenburg
17327-17331	Mecklenburg-Vorp.
17335-17337	Brandenburg
17345-19306	Mecklenburg-Vorp.
19307-19357	Brandenburg
19361-19417	Mecklenburg-Vorp.
20001-21037	Hamburg
21039	Schleswig-Holstein
21041-21149	Hamburg
21202-21218	Niedersachsen
21220	Hamburg
21221-21449	Niedersachsen
21451-21521	Schleswig-Holstein
21522	Niedersachsen
21524-21529	Schleswig-Holstein
21601-21789	Niedersachsen
22001-22143	Hamburg
22145	Schleswig-Holstein
22147-22769	Hamburg
22801-23919	Schleswig-Holstein
23921-23999	Mecklenburg-Vorp.
24001-25999	Schleswig-Holstein
26001-27478	Niedersachsen
27483-27498	Schleswig-Holstein
27499	Hamburg
27501-27580	Bremen
27607-27809	Niedersachsen
28001-28779	Bremen
28784-29399	Niedersachsen
29401-29416	Sachsen-Anhalt
29431-31868	Niedersachsen
32001-33829	Nordrhein-Westfalen
34001-34329	Hessen
34331-34355	Niedersachsen
34356-34399	Hessen
34401-34439	Nordrhein-Westfalen
34441-36399	Hessen
36401-36469	Thüringen
37001-37194	Niedersachsen
37195	Hessen
37197-37199	Niedersachsen
37201-37299	Hessen
37301-37359	Thüringen
37401-37649	Niedersachsen
37651-37688	Nordrhein-Westfalen
37689-37691	Niedersachsen
37692-37696	Nordrhein-Westfalen
37697-38479	Niedersachsen

38481-38489	Sachsen-Anhalt
38501-38729	Niedersachsen
38801-39649	Sachsen-Anhalt
40001-48432	Nordrhein-Westfalen
48442-48465	Niedersachsen
48466-48477	Nordrhein-Westfalen
48478-48480	Niedersachsen
48481-48485	Nordrhein-Westfalen
48486-48488	Niedersachsen
48489-48496	Nordrhein-Westfalen
48497-48531	Niedersachsen
48541-48739	Nordrhein-Westfalen
49001-49459	Niedersachsen
49461-49549	Nordrhein-Westfalen
49551-49849	Niedersachsen
50101-51597	Nordrhein-Westfalen
51598	Rheinland-Pfalz
51601-53359	Nordrhein-Westfalen
53401-53579	Rheinland-Pfalz
53581-53604	Nordrhein-Westfalen
53614-53619	Rheinland-Pfalz
53621-53949	Nordrhein-Westfalen
54201-55239	Rheinland-Pfalz
55240-55252	Hessen
55253-56869	Rheinland-Pfalz
57001-57489	Nordrhein-Westfalen
57501-57648	Rheinland-Pfalz
58001-59966	Nordrhein-Westfalen
59969-63699	Hessen
63701-63774	Bayern
63776	Hessen
63777-63939	Bayern
64201-64753	Hessen
64754-	Baden-Württemberg
64756-65556	Hessen
65558-65582	Rheinland-Pfalz
65583-65620	Hessen
65621-65626	Rheinland-Pfalz
65627	Hessen
65629	Rheinland-Pfalz
65701-65936	Hessen
66001-66459	Saarland
66461-66509	Rheinland-Pfalz
66511-66839	Saarland
66841-67829	Rheinland-Pfalz
68001-68309	Baden-Württemberg
68501-68519	Hessen
68520-68549	Baden-Württemberg
68601-68649	Hessen

68701-69234	Baden-Württemberg
69235-69239	Hessen
69240-69429	Baden-Württemberg
69430-69431	Hessen
69434-69469	Baden-Württemberg
69479-69488	Hessen
69489-69502	Baden-Württemberg
69503-69509	Hessen
69510-69514	Baden-Württemberg
69515-69518	Hessen
70001-74592	Baden-Württemberg
74594	Bayern
74595-76709	Baden-Württemberg
76711-76891	Rheinland-Pfalz
77601-79879	Baden-Württemberg
80001-87491	Bayern
87493-87561	Bayern
87567-87569	Bayern
87571-87789	Bayern
88001-88099	Baden-Württemberg
88101-88146	Bayern
88147	Baden-Württemberg
88149-88179	Bayern
88181-89198	Baden-Württemberg
89201-89449	Bayern
89501-89619	Baden-Württemberg
90001-96489	Bayern
96501-96529	Thüringen
97001-97859	Bayern
97861-97877	Baden-Württemberg
97888-97892	Bayern
97893-97900	Baden-Württemberg
97901-97909	Bayern
97911-97999	Baden-Württemberg
98501-99998	Thüringen

THE GERMAN POSTAL CODE DIRECTORY (in numerical order)

Das Postleitzahlenbuch: Numerisch geordnet [postal code book, in numerical order] (a partner publication of *Das Postleitzahlenbuch: Alphabetisch geordnet (postal code book in alphabetical order).*

The German postal code directory "*numerisch geordnet* (in numerical order)

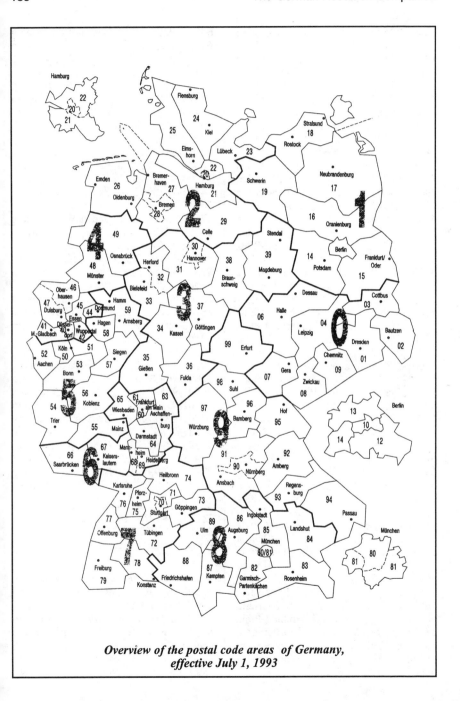

*Overview of the postal code areas of Germany,
effective July 1, 1993*

lists all postal codes in Germany in numerical order with the localities each refers to.

(The *alphabetisch geordnet* directory, on the other hand, lists localities alphabetically, with their respective matching postal codes).

Both directories are on sale at German post offices and through Postamt Marburg, Dienststelle 113-21, Postfach 1100, 35035 Marburg, Germany.

Organization

The *numerisch geordnet* directory is divided into four parts:

PART 1:
Comparison of postal codes — new to old
(Teil 1: Gegenüberstellung der Postleit-zahlen Neu/Alt)

This major section of the directory (240 pages) lists in numerical order all the "new" (post-1993) postal codes in Germany and their respective localities, starting with 01001 (part of Dresden), and ending with 99998 (Körner). These new codes are matched with the old (pre-1993) codes for the same respective localities.

♦Many of the new codes are marked in the second column with the abbreviation "Pf," for *Postfach*, meaning "post office box."

Under the new postal code system, the business which uses a post office box address has a postal code different from that of the private residence situated just next door. Therefore, in almost all cases, a postal code designated with a "Pf" should be ignored (unless one is searching for the postal code of a business). The word "Zustellung" indicates a postal code area where mail is delivered directly to the street address.

♦ Part I is organized in sections 1 to 9, in order of the first digit of each new code. The order goes like this: Leitzone 0 (postal code zone 0, in which all new codes begin with 0), Leitzone 1, Leitzone 2, Leitzone 3, etc. The zones are structured like this: : Leitzone 0: all in former East Germany

Leitzone 1: all in former East Germany except for former West Berlin codes
Leitzone 2: all in former West Germany
Leitzone 3: codes in both the former East and West Germany
Leitzone 4, 5, 6, 7, 8: all in former West Germany
Leitzone 9: codes in both the former East and West Germany:
♦This first section of the book is especially helpful for determining the names of localities geographically situated very close to a particular locality.

To look for localities in the vicinity of a town of interest, first find the postal code of the given locality in *Das Postleitzahlenbuch: Alphabetisch geordnet.*

Then find that some code number in the first section of *Das Postleitzahlenbuch: Numerisch geordnet* to find the names of surrounding localities (that is, localities with code numbers only slightly higher or slightly lower than that of the locality of interest).

PART 2:
Comparison of postal codes — old to new
(Teil 2: Gegenüberstellung der Postleitzahlen Alt/Neu)

This section of the directory (163 pages) lists in numerical order the old postal codes in Germany and their respective localities, matching them with the new codes for the same localities.

♦The beginning pages of Part 2 list in numerical order all the old postal codes of the former *East Germany* (in order of old postal codes with first digits from 0 to 9), giving their respective new codes.
♦The succeeding pages of Part 2 list in numerical order all the old postal codes of the former *West Germany* (in order of old postal codes with first digits from 0 to 9), giving their respective new codes.

PART 3:
Index to districts
(Teil 3: Orts-teileverzeichnis)

This section of the directory lists in numerical order the new postal codes for cities, showing subdivisions or outlying areas of each city.

For example, here is shown one of the postal codes for the city of Leipzig:

04349 Leipzig
Portitz,
Schönefeld-Ost •,
Thekla

The solid black circle (l), *or Punkt,* shown after the district name Schönefeld-Ost indicates that some of the streets in this district of Leipzig fall in postal code 04349, but other streets of that district fall in other postal code areas.

To determine the postal code for a particular street in the Schönefel-Ost district of Leipzig , it is necessary to go to the main postal code directory *(Das Postleitzahlenbuch: Alphabetisch geordnet)* to search in the Leipzig street-name index.

Obviously, because no *Punkt* is shown after Portitz and Thekla, all streets in these districts carry the 04349 postal code.

PART 4:
Index of place-names in bi-lingual areas of Sachsen and Brandenburg
(Teil 4: Verzeichnis der Orte im Zweisprachigen Gebiet von Brandenburg und Sachsen)

This section lists locations, in numerical order by postal code, which are known by both their Sorbish and their German names. The first column lists the postal code, the second the German name for the locality; the third the matching Sorbish name for the locality. For example:

01920 Johannisbad   Janska kupjel
01920 Lehndorf b Kamenz   Lejno p Kamjenc

Note: The designation *b Kamenz* (short for "bei Kamenz"), above, indicates that Lehndorf is an outlying locality of Kamenz.

ABBREVIATIONS USED IN THE POSTAL CODE DIRECTORIES

In the front of each of the two postal code directories (*Postleitzahlenbücher*) is a page providing a key to abbreviations (*Abkürzungen*). Some of the most commonly used follow:

a d = *an dem/an den/an der/auf der* (on the)
b = *bei/beim* (at, near)
d = *der/dem* (of the)
GE = *Postleitzahlen für Großempfänger* (special codes for recipients of great quantities of mail, such businesses handling catalog sales)
GrGE = *Postleitzahlen für Gruppen von Großempfängern* (postal code shared by several recipients of large quantities of mail)
i = *im/in* (in)
i d = *in dem/in den/in der* (in the)
Kr = *Kreis* (county)
Pf = *Postfachbezogene Postleitzahlen* (postal code for post office box)
PLZ = *Postleitzahl* (postal code)
str = *-straße* (street)

THE GERMAN RESEARCH OUTLINE

The *Research Outline: Germany,* published by the Family History Library (FHL) of the Church of Jesus Christs of Latter-day Saints in Salt Lake City, Utah, is the best brief guide (52 pages) to German genealogy available in the United States, and at the same time the cheapest, at 75 cents.

This publication provides an overview of the many resources available to the researcher of German family history, complete with book call numbers and microfilm and microfiche numbers.

The publication is particularly valuable to beginning researchers of German family history.

The outline can be purchased at most local Family History Centers, or it can be ordered by calling the Salt Lake Distribution Center at 800-537-5950.

There is a $2.00 service charge for phone orders.

Request item #34061.

The mailing address: Salt Lake Distribution Center, 1999 W. 1700 South, Salt Lake City, UT 84104.

THE ANCESTOR PASSPORT (Ahnenpaß)

During the Nazi era, Adolf Hitler's Nationalist Socialist Party required Germans to complete an *Ahnenpaß* (ancestor passport) as a means of proving their "racial purity." The *Ahnenpaß* documented what Hitler called *Der Begriff der arischen Abstammung* (the concept of Aryan descent). It was used to prove "Aryan" origins by means of a multi-generation search into the holder's ancestry.

People were obliged to conduct thorough investigations of civil and church records for past generations in order to prove their forebears' "purity."

The *Ahnenpaß* consisted of 48 pages which included a discussion of Hitler's concept of the "Aryan race," followed by an *Ahnentafel* (ancestor table) which summarized the holder's family for five generations, back to the third-great-grandparents.

Government and military personnel were required to research six generations.

On the typical *Ahnenpaß,* the holder's name is entered in the box at the bottom of the page. Moving upward on those of the holder's four grandparents (*Großeltern*), then the 8 great-grandparents (*Urgroßeltern*), the 16 great-great grandparents (*Ur-Urgroßeltern*), and finally the 32 great-great-great grandparents (*Ur-Ur-Urgroßeltern*).

On the other pages, space was provided for writing in the required information about each ancestor, including 1) surname, 2) given name, 3) birth date, 4) birth place, 5) names of parents, 6) religion, 7) death date, 8) death place, 9) occupation, 10) indication of the source of the information, 11) certification of the correctness of the information acquired from civil or church authorities. Each of the direct ancestors was assigned a number, in a manner similar to that of today's pedigree charts.

VOCABULARY ASSISTANCE FOR THE *AHNENPASS*

These words and phrases appear frequently in the *Ahnenpaß* document:
Bekenntnis .... religious faith
Beruf .... occupation
Eheschließung .... marriage
erfolgte am .... occurred on (date)
Familienname .... surname
gestorben am .... died on (date)
Mutter/Vater von .... mother/father of
Ort .... place (of residence, birth, death, etc.)
Pfarramt .... parish
Vornamen .... given (first) name

DIE QUELLENSCHAU FÜR FAMILIENFORSCHER (Index to genealogical periodicals and various records)

Quellenschau für Familienforscher [A Display of Sources for Family Research]. Köln: Paul Kuschbert, 1938. vols. 1-3.

Die Quellenschau für Familienforscher is a three-volume index to periodicals and various records, consisting of two sets, each having two parts. Both sets index localities (*Orts Register*), areas (*Gebiets Register*), subjects *(Sach Register)*, and surnames *(Personen Register)*. Written in German, in Roman print, it contains thousands of surnames and localities.

Because the indexes tie surnames to localities, the work is useful in identifying places where immigrant ancestors may have lived.

Further information

See *German Genealogical Digest,*

1989 Vol V., No. 4, for detailed instructions on the use of this resource.
Availability
FHL book 943 A3kp. Film 0924491,
items 4-6.

VILLAGE LINEAGE BOOKS
(Dorfsippenbücher,
Ortssippenbücher)

A *Sippenbuch is* a family book or local lineage book, which usually gives considerable information about most of a
town's residents. These books usually re-
count the town records from the sixteenth
century forward to the twentieth century.
Note the listings in the following two sections and the reference to Franz
Heinzmann's bibliography of German lineage books on page 197.

THE *DORFSIPPENBUCH*
PROJECT OF 1937

In 1937, the *Arbeitsgemeinschaft für*
Sippenforschung und Sippenflege was
organized, with plans to index every parish in Germany in order to provide vital
information for each individual in the parish and to link each family member and
each generation. There were an estimated
52,000 parishes in Germany. By 1938, 30
volumes of *Dorfsippenbücher* (village
"clan" books, recording all families) were
compiled, but World War II prevented the
completion of the task.

The name *Dorfsippenbücher* was
changed in 1950 to *Ortssippenbücher* (village family books), when *Sippenbücher*
were compiled for cities as well as villages
and communities.

Contents: Each book took a similar form
— a table of contents, a brief history and a
map, and a surname and locality index.
Dates and places of births, marriages, and
deaths are listed in the entries, as well as
information about citizenship and

occupations.

Scope: There are 122 volumes in Series
A *Ortssippenbucher* and 33 volumes in
Series B, which included *Sippenbücher*
from localities that had belonged to the
Austrian-Hungarian Empire and that were
later in areas that became Czechoslovakia
and Yugoslavia. (The difference between
Series A and Series B is primarily the size
of the book, not in the format or contents.)

Availability: The Family History Center
in Salt Lake City has many of the
Ortssippenbücher volumes resulting from
this project. Many are available on microfilm. To find the microfilm number for a
location, search the Locality section of the
Family History Library Catalog, under the
town name, then under "Genealogy."

Growing numbers of *Ortssippen-*
bücher are available at the *Deutsche*
Zentralstelle für Genealogie (German
Center for Genealogy) in Leipzig.

Towns and villages represented by the
work of the project described above are
combined to include all *Dorfsippenbücher*
and the A and B series of *Ortssippen-*
bücher.

Key

In the list below, *Sippenbücher* available at the Family History Library in Salt
Lake City are marked with an asterisk (*).
Those which the Library has filmed, at
least in part, are shown in italics.

ANHALT: *Grosswangen, Petersmark*
BADEN: *Altdorf (Ortenaukreis)***,
*Altenheim***, Assamstadt,* Bauschlott,
Binzen & Ruemmingen, Britzingen,
Broggingen, Büsingen, Dundenheim,
Efringen-Kirchen*, Egringen, *Eimel-*
dingen, Eppingen, Friesenheim*, *Fisch-*
ingen, Freiamt, Gochsheim, Göbrichen,
Grafenhausen, Grenzach, Haltingen,
Heidelbert-Handschuhsheim*, Heidel-
berg-Wieblingen, Herbolzheim, *Hüfingen,*
Huttingen & Istein, Ichenheim, Istein &
Huttingen, Kippenheim, Kippenheim-
weiler, *Kleinkems, Ladenburg, Lauf,*
Löffingen (Bachheim, Neuenburg),
Mahlberg-Orschweier, Meissenheim,

Mietersheim, Muellen, Münchweier, Nonnenweier, Oberacker, Obergrombach*, *Oberweier, Oetlingen, Ottoschwanden, Philippsburg, Poppenhausen, Rheinhausen,* Ringsheim*, *Rümmingen & Binzen, Rust,* Sandhausen*, *Schmieheim,* Schuttertal, *Schutterzell, Schweigern, Sexau, Tannenkirch,* Tutschfelden*, *Weingarten,* Wittenweier, *Wittlingen, Wollbach, Zaisenhausen*
BAYERN: Anhausen*, *Aschach,* Ebermergen*, Gabelbach*, Kreuth
BAYERN-PFALZ: Imsweiler, *Maudach, Mehlbach, Mittel-Hengstbach,* Mundenheim, Oppau-Edigheim*, *Pirmasens, Sambach*
BRANDENBURG: *Freyenstein, Storbeck*
BRAUNSCHWEIG: Kirchbrake*, Wedtl*enstedt*
HANNOVER: Adensen-Nordstemmen, *Dehmerbrok, Dehrenberg,* Fürstenhagen*, Gustedt*, Gladebeck*, *Hambühren,* Hannover-Grarnison*, Hohenbostel*, Krautsand*, Lenthe*, Misselwarden*, *Mulsum, Vechelade, Woquard*
HANNOVER OSTFRIESLAND: Amdorf*, *Aurich-Oldendorf, Backenmoor, Bagstede, Breinermoor, Dehrenbert, Fürstenhagen, Gustedt, Gladebeck, Hannover-Garnison, Hesel,* Holtrop*, Insel Spieckeroog*, *Insel Baltrum, Kirchborgum, Leerort, Loga, Logabirum, Middels,* Neuburg*, *Nortmoor, Ochtelbur, Reepsholt, Timmel,* Uphusen*, *Werdum,* Westerbur*, *Westerende*
HESSEN: Bickenbach*, Grüningen, *Heppenheim, Ingelheim, Vasbeck,* Volkhardingshausen
HESSEN-NASSAU: Ahausen, *Alpenrod, Altweilnau,* Ehringen, *Kassel, Schlotzau, Sontra*
MECKLENBURG: *Boitin,* Grossupahl
OLDENBURG: Neunkirchen/Nahe, Wolfersweiler
RHEINLAND: Freisen, *Fürth, Hangard,* Heide/Unterberggemeinden, Leitersweiler*, Mettlach-Keuchingen*, *Oberkirchen,* Remmesweiler*, St. Sebastian,

Stein-Wingert*, Wenau/Sankt Katharina*, Welschbillig
RIESENGEBIRGE: Rochlitz a.d. Iser*
SACHSEN: *Leutewitz*
SACHSEN (PREUSSEN): *Neuhof*
SCHAUMBURG-LIPPE: Bückeburg*
SCHLESIEN: Klitten*, Königsbruck, Winsdorf*
SCHLESWIG-HOLSTEIN: Reinbeck
THÜRINGEN: *Altenroda, Hausen, Nermsdorf,* Tottleben*, Wiegleben*
WALDECK: Affoldern*, *Berich, Berndorf,* Bringhausen-Edertal*, Bühle*, Buhlen-Edertal*, Eppe*, *Frebershausen,* Gembeck*, Goddelsheim, *Goldhausen,* Helmscheid, Helsen*, *Hillersbausen,* Immighausen*, *Landau,* Lelbach*, Lengefeld*, *Lütersheim,* Mandern*, *Mehlen,* Meineringhausen*, Mühlhausen*, *Nieder-Ense,* Niederschleidern, *Nordenbeck, Ober-Ense,* Rattlar, *Rhena,* Schmillingshausen-Arolsen, Schwalefeld, Strothe*, Twiste*, Vasbeck, Welleringhausen, Wethen*, Wetterburg*
WESTFALEN: Bergkirchen, Hartum
WÜRTTEMBERG: Altensteig*, *Altensteigdorf, Baiersbronn, Berneck, Beuren-Balzholz, Bondorf, Gaildorf, Klosterreichenbach, Mötzingen, Müster/ Unterrot,* Nagold, *Nebringen,* Oberjettingen*, *Öschelbronn, Tailfingen,* Unterjettingen*, *Walddorf*
CZECHOSLOVAKIA MORAVIA: Briesen*, Pohorsch*
HUNGARY BANAT: Apatin, *Brestowatz,* Filipowa, Gajdobra-Neugajdobra*, Hodschag*, Jahrmarkt, Miletitsch*, *Palanka,* St. Hubert-Schmidt, Stanischitsch, Ischatali, Weprowatz

Source: "Dorfsippenbücher and Ortssippenbücher," by Larry O Jensen, *German Genealogical Digest,* Vol. VII, No. 2, 1991.

SOME PUBLISHED ORTSSIPPENBÜCHER

Wolfgang Ribbe and Eckart Henning,

At the Kirchweihfest (parish fair), Upper Bavaria

***Familiengeschichtsforschung.* Verlag Degener & Co., Neustadt an der Aisch, 1995.**

In the book cited above can be found publication data concerning the *Ortssippenbücher* for the following villages and towns:

Abentheuer, Abthausen, Abtweiler, Achtelsbach, Adensen (Nordstemmen/ Niedersachsen), Affoldern (Waldeck), Ahausen, Allertshofen, Alpenrod, Alsenborn, Altdorf, Altenheim, Altenroda, Altensteig, Altensteigdorf, Altweilnau, Amdorf, Andernach, Anhausen, Anraff, Apatin/Batschka, Amsfeld (Bad Wildungen/Waldeck), Arnsfeld, Arolsen, Asbach, Aschach, Assamstadt, Asterode, Atschau-Vértesacsa, Aurich-Oldendorf, Außen (Schmelz)

Bachheim, Backemoor, Bärendorf, Bagband (Große Fehn/Ostfriesland), Bahnbrücken (Kraichtal), Baiersbronn, Baltrum, Balzholz, Bangstede, Bantorf, Barstede/Ostfreisland, Bartschdorf/ Schlesien, Bassenheim, Batschsentiwan, Bauschlott (Pforzheim/Baden), Bedekaspel (Südbrookmer/Ostfriesland), Beihingen (Nagold), Bergkirchen, Berglangenbach, Barglas, Berglicht, Berich, Berndorf/Waldeck, Berneck, Berschweiler, Bettingen (Schmelz), Beuren/Balzholz,

Beutha, Bickenbach/Bergstraße, Bierbach, Bietzen, Billings, Binzen, Birkenfeld, Bischofsdhron, Bleiderdingen, Blies, Bliesen, Bliesmengen, Blosenberg, Bobenneukirchen, Bösdorf/Elster, Bösingen, Boitin, Bondorf, Bonerath, Borr, Bosen, Brandau (Modautal), Braunsen, Braunshausen, Bredenbeck /Deister, Breinermoor, Breitenkamp, Bremm, Brensbach, Brestowatz/Batschka, Briesen (Schönhengst), Bringhausen, Britzingen, Bröckingen

Broggingen, Broich, Brücken, Brünnsee, Bubenheim, Buchhagen, Bückeburg, Bühle, Bürig, Bürstadt (Hessen), Büsingen, Buhlen (Edertal/Waldeck), Buisdorf, Burgholzhausen, Burkersdorf (Kirchberg), Burkhardtsgrün, Burscheid, Buweiler

Caßdorf, Contwig, Contwig, Cunersdorf (Zwickau)

Dambach, Damflos, Dattingen, Dechengrün, Dehmkerbrock, Dehrenbert, Derlin, Diedelsheim (Bretten/Baden), Dillingen, Dilmar, Dilshofen, Dobeneck, Dörnholzhausen/Waldeck, Dorthain, Dudweiler, Düppenweiler, Dürrbach, Dundenheim

Ebermergen, Ebersberg, Eckersweiler, Edigheim, Efringen-Kirchen, Egringen, Ehlingen, Ehringen, Eichstock:, Eicks,

Eimeldingen, Einig, Eiweiler, Eisen, Eisenach, Ellweiler, Elm, Elmern, Emmersweile, Engelhardtsgrün, Enkenbach-Alsenbom/Pfalz, Ensdorf, Eppe, Eppingen, Erbach, Erfweiler, Ernsthofen, Eschweiler, Eslarn, Ettenheim, Eulenstein, Euren, Evestorf, Eyersheim

Faha, Filipowa/Batschka, Filsch, Finsterntal, Fischingen, Flögeln, Fohren-Linden, Folperviller, Frebershausen, Freiamt, Freisen, Frei-Weinheim, Freyenstein, Friedel, Friedrichsdorf (Hugenotten),Friedrichsdorf (Dillingen), Friesenheim, Friesheim/ Pfalz, Fürstenberg (Lichtenfels/Waldeck), Fürstenhagen, Fürth/Bayern, Fürth/Odenwald

Gabelbach, Gäufelden, Gaildorf, Gajdobra/Batschka, Gappenach, Geisfeld, Geislautern, Gembeck, Gemünden/Hunsrück, Gensbach, Georgenhausen, Gering, Gersweiler, Geyer, Gierschnach, Gießen, Gilzum, Gimbweiler, Gladebeck, Gochsheim, Goddelsheim/Waldeck, Göbrichen, Göswein, Goldbach (Schmelz), Goldhausen, Grabatz/Baden, Grafenhausen, Grafenhausen, Grenzach, Gresaubach, Griesborn, Gronig, Groß-Bieberau, Großrosseln, Groß-Upahl, Großurleben, Großwangen, Großzöbern, Grüningen, Grumbach, Güdesheim, Güttigheim, Gundernhausen, Gustedt, Gusterath, Gutenbrunnen, Guthmannshausen, Gutweiler

Hägerfelde, Hahnweiler, Haiterbach, Gallerburg, Haltingen, Hambühren, Hameln, Hamm, Handschuhsteim, Hangard, Hannover-Schloßkirche, Harlingen, Harrachsdorf, Hartenau, Hartmannsdorf (Kirchberg), Hartum, Haslach (Herrenberg), Hausen, Hausen/Odenwald, Hausen (Günzburg-Krumbach), Haustadt, Heidelberg-Handschuhsheim, Heimbach (Neuwied), Heinersgrün, Heinrichshagen, Held, Helenenberg, Helmscheid, Helsen, Hengstbach, Hentern, Heppenheim, Herbitzheim, Herbolzheim, Herchenrode, Hermühlheim, Hesel, Heyda, Hilbertshausen, Hillershausen, Hinzenburg, Hinzert, Herschfeld, Hitdorf, Hochmark, Hodschag/Batschka, Höringhausen, Hohen-

bostel/Deister, Hohendorf, Holtensen (Weetzen), Holtland/Ostfriesland, Holtrop, Holzerath, Honnef, Honzrath, Hoppstädten, Horbach, Hornbach, Horsten, Hoxhol, Hüfingen, Huttingen

Ichenheim, Igelsbach, Ihrhove, Immighausen/Waldeck, Imsweiler, Imweiler, Ingelheim, Irsch,, Itzbach, Jägersfreude, Jahmen, Jahrmarkt/Banat, Kaan, Kärlich, Kaisen, Kaiserslautern, Kalt, Kappel/Rhein, Karcheez, Karden, Karlsbrunn, Kaschel, Kassel (französische Gemeinde), Kastel, Keldung, Kerben, Kesselheim, Kettig, Keuchingen, Kieselberg, Kimmlingen, Kippenheim, Kippenheimweiler, Kirchberg/Hunsrück, Kirchberg/Sachsen, Rirchborgum, Kirchbrak, Kirdorf, Kirschhausen, Klarenthal-Krughütte, Klein-Bieberau, Kleinkems, Kleinurleben, Klitten, Klosterreichenbach, Klosterreichenbach,

Klotten, Knausholz, Kobeln, Koblenz, Köllertal, Kölln, Königsbruch/Schlesien, Köppern, Kolbitzschwalde, Kolling, Kordel, Koslar (Stadt Jülich), Kostenbach, Kozma, Krautsand, Kreuth, Kreuzweiler, Kringelsdorf, Krughütte, Kürrenberg, Küttig

Ladenburg, Lambsheim, Lampaden, Landau/Waldeck, Landsweiler-Reden, Langenbach, Lasserg, Lauf, Lauschbrünn, Lauterbach/Saar, Lebach, Leerort, Leichlingen, Leitersweiler, Leitzweiler, Lelbach, Lengefeld, Lenthe, Leutewitz, Lichtenberg, Liebling/Banat, Liederbach/Taunus, Lilienthal, Limberg, Linden, Lippa/Banat, Lisdorf, Loga, Logabirum, Lohne, Longkamp, Losheim, Lovasbereny, Ludweiler-Warndt, Lübzin, Lütersheim, Lützelbach, Lützelwig, Luttringhausen, Machern/Lothringen, Magwitz, Mahlberg-Orschweiler, Mandern/Waldeck, Marbach, Marburg, Marcusgrün, Markersbach, Massenhausen, Maßweiler, Maudach, Maxdorf, Mayen, Meckenbach, Medelsheim, Mehlbach, Mehlen, Meindorf, Meineringhausen, Meißenheim, Menden, Menningen, Menzingen (Kraichtal), Merscheid, Mertloch, Merzenich, Merzkirchen,

Messbach, Metternich, Metternich, Mettlach-Keuchingen, Mettnich, Mettweiler, Middels, Mietersheim, Miletitsch/Batschka, Mimbach, Minheim, Minkelfeld, Misselwarden, Mittelbach-Hengstbach, Mittershausen, Mittweida, Modau, Möhn, Mötzingen, Monzelfeld, Morscheid, Mühlfeld, Mühlhausen/Waldeck, Mülheim/Kärlich, Mülldorf, Müllen, Münchweier, Münster (Gaildorf), Münstermaifeld, Münzesheim, Muggardt, Mulsum (Wesermünde), Mulsum (Stade), Mundenheim

Nagold (Württemberg), Nalbach, Namborn, Naunheim, Nebringen, Nermsdorf, Neuburg, Neudorf (Lippa/Banat), Neuenburg, Neugajdobra/Batschka, Neuhof, Neuhütten, Neukirchen (Boben), Neunkirchen, Neunkirchen (Nahe), Neunkirchen (Modautal), Neuried, Neutsch, Newel, Niederense, Niedergailbach,Niederhofen, Niederhofheim, Nieder-Ingelheim, Niederkainsbach, Niederliederbach, Niederlinxweiler, Nieder-Modau, Niederpleis, Nieder-Schleidern, Nitz, Nonnenweier, Nonnweiler, Nonrod, Nordenbeck, Nortmoor, Nothberg, Nüttermoor/Ostfriesland, Oberacker, Oberense, Obergrombach, Oberjettingen, Oberkirchen/Saar,Ober-Hambach, Ober-Ingelheim, Oberleuken, Oberliederbach, Oberlimberg, Ober-Modau, Oberschar, Oberschmiedeberg, Oberschwandorf/Württemberg, Obersötern, Oberthal, Oberweier (Kreis Lahr, Schwarzwald), Ochtelbur, Ochtendung, Ölsa, Öschelbronn, Öschelbronn, Ötlingen, Oftersheim, Oggersheim (Ludwigshafen), Olk, Ollmuth, Opladen, Oppau, Ormsheim, Orschweier, Osenbach, Ottengrün, Ottenhausen, Ottoschwanden

Palanka/Batschka, Pellingen, Peppenkum, Pessingshausen, Petersmark, Pferdsdorf-Spichra, Philippsburg, Pillig, Pirmasens, Plaidt, Planschwitz, Pluwig, Pohorsch, Polch, Poppenhausen, Posteholz, Potshausen-Ostrhauderfehn, Prausitz, Primstal

The beer-brewer. Regensburg, 1698

Ramstein, Rath, Rathen, Rattlar/Waldeck, Reden, Reepsholt, Rehlingen, Reinbek, Reippersberg, Remmesweiler, Reusrath, Rheindorf, Rheingönheim, Rheinhausen, Rhena, Ringsheim, Rinschheim, Riveris, Rochlitz/Iser, Rodau, Rodenbeck, Rodenkirchen (Köln), Rodenstein, Rodheim, Rohrbach, Rosenthal, Rübenach, Rüber, Rückweiler, Rümmingen, Ruitsch, Ruppertsgrün, Rust, Saarbrücken, Saar/Schildgebirge, Sambach, Sandhausen, Sarreguemines, Saupersdorf, Sausenthal, Scheuerberg, Schilliingen, Schlebuschrath, Schlotzau, Schmidt (Nideggen), Schmiedebert, Schmieheim, Schmillinghausen/Waldeck, Schönberg (Adorf/Vogtland), Schönberg, Schöndorf, Schuttertal (Lahr/Baden), Schutterzell, Schwalbach, Schwalefeld/Waldeck, Schwarzbach, Schwarzenbach/Saar, Schwarzenberg, Schweigern, Seckmauern, Sekitsch/Lavcenac, Seligenstadt, Sexau, Seyweiler, Simmern, Sindlingen, Sötern, Sonderbach, Sontra/Hessen, Spichra, Spiekeroog, Sprengen, Staffel, Stangengrün, Stanischitsch/Batschka, Stein,

Steinau, Stein-Wingert, St. Nikolaus, Storbeck, Straßberg, Strothe, St. Sebastian, Syrau, Szar

Tailfingen, Taltitz, Tannenkirch, Thalexweiler, Thalfang, Thalwinkel, Thierfeld, Thomaswalde, Timmel, Tottleben, Traunen, Treisberg, Trupe-Lilienthal, Tschatali/Batschka, Tschatalmer-Csataljer, Tutschfelden, Twiste/Waldeck

Uchtelfangen, Überberg, Überlingen,Ückesdorf, Unterhambach, Unterjettingen, Unterlicderbach, Unterrot (Gaildorf), Unterscheibe, Uphusen, Urleben, Urmitz, Utweil

Vasbeck, Vechelade, Veldenz, Vértesacsa/Otschau, Verteskozma, Vielbrunn, Völklingen, Voitersreuth, Volkhardinghausen, Vorland, Vrsenda, Wadern, Walddorf, Wald-Erlenbach, Waldfischbach, Waldstetten, Walkenried, Wallesweilerhof, Wangen, Webenheim, Webern, Wedtlenstedt, Weiersbach, Weingarten, Weisenheim, Weissenthurm, Weiten, Welferding, Welleringhausen/Waldeck, Welschbillig, Wenau, Weprowatz/Batschka, Werdum, Werschend, Westerbrak, Westerbur, Westerende, Wethen, Wetterburg, Wiblishausen, Wichtringhausen, Wieblingen/Baden, Wiedersberg, Wiegleben, Wierschen, Wiesdorf, Wildbach, Wilhelmsbruch, Wilkau, Winninghausen, Winsdorf/Oberschlesien, Winterbach, Wirschem, Wittenweier, Wittlingen, Wördeholz, Wolfersweiler, Wollbach, Woltersgrün, Woquard, Wolfskaute, Wustweiler

Zaisenhausen, Zeilhard, Zerf, Zittau, Zöbern (Groß-), Zschocken, Züsch, Zweifall

REFERENCES HELPFUL IN THE USE OF *ORTSSIPPENBÜCHER*

♦Larry O. Jensen, "Dorfsippenbücher and Ortssippenbücher," *German Genealogical Digest,* Vol. VII, No. 2, 1991.

♦Heinzmann, Franz. *Bibliographie der Ortssippenbücher in Deutschland* [Bibliography of village lineage books in Germany]. Düsseldorf: Heinzmann, 1991. (FHL book 943 D23h 1991.) Lists 668 village lineage books in alphabetical order by town name.

♦Ribbe, Wolfgang and Henning, Eckart, *Taschenbuch für Familiengeschichtsforschung.* Verlag Degener & Co., Neustadt an der Aisch. 1995. Almost 1,000 *Ortsfamilienbücher* are listed with the respective locations and time periods, and publication dates.

♦*Die deutsche Zentralstelle für Genealogie* in Leipzig holds close to 1,000 *Ortsippenbücher,* with more being added every year. As of 1996, they were not yet catalogued.

THE GERMANIC EMIGRANTS REGISTER

The Germanic Emigrants Register is an ambitious project of six genealogists in Germany by which information has been extracted concerning emigrants who were listed in German newspapers as persons ("deserters") who left their homeland without official permission and before completing their military service. The database consists of more than a half million entries.

The time period of the newspapers covered in the project, when it is complete, will range from 1820 to 1918.

That range of dates can be confusing, however: The *Reichsanzeiger,* a newspaper published by the *Reichsregierung* (Government of the Deutsches Reich) between 1871 and 1918 contained all official government announcements. (The organ fulfilling a similar purpose today is the *Bundesanzeiger*).

The database of the Germanic Emigrants Register is compiled from newspaper notices dated at the time the government discovered a specific person was missing.

This date of the published notice, therefore, could be 40 to 60 years after the emigrant's actual departure.

The Family History Library has the 1991 edition of the Register index on microfiche, containing about 118,000 names. The index shows name, event year, birth date, emigration date, destination, and last known residence. It does not give place of origin, but one may pay a fee to obtain information. The 1992 edition indexes about 177,000 emigrants names in the *Deutsch-er Reichsanzeiger* from 1820 to 1914. Contact: Germanic Emigrants Register, Postfach 1720, 49347 Diepholz, Germany.

Availability

German Emigrants Register (1991), ten microfiche: FHL microfiche 6312192; FHLC Computer Number 445448.

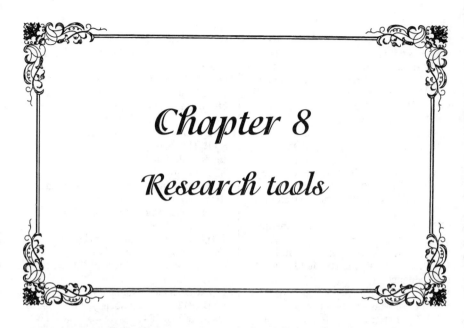

Chapter 8

Research tools

ABBREVIATIONS:
Genealogical accreditations,
organizations, resources

AAGRA: Australasian Association of Genealogists and Record Agents
AG: Accredited Genealogist
AGRA: Association of Genealogists and Record Agents (England)
AIS: Accelerateed Indexing Systems
ALA: American Library Association
AP: Association of Professional Genealogists
APG: Association of Professional Genealogists
APGQ: *Association of Professional Genealogists Quarterly*
ASG: American Society of Genealogists
BCG: Board for Certification of Genealogists.
The following titles relate to the BCG's six areas of specialty:
  ♦ **CAILS:** Certified American Indian Lineage Specialist
  ♦ **CALS:** Certified American Lineage Specialist
  ♦ **CG:** Certified Genealogist
  ♦ **CGI:** Certified Genealogical Instructor
  ♦ **CGL:** Certified Genealogical Lecturer
  ♦ **CGRS:** Certified Genealogical Record Specialist
BYU: Brigham Young University
CDA: The Colonial Dames of America
CIG: Usually a group within a society which has a special interest in using computers in genealogy
CPJG: Committee of Professional Jewish Genealogists
DAC: National Society Daughters of the American Colonists
DAR: National Society Daughters of the American Revolution
DCW: National Society Daughters of Colonial Wars
DLP: Descendants of Loyalists and Patriots
DRT: Daughters of the Republic of Texas
FASG: Fellow of the American Society of Genealogists
FGS: Federation of Genealogical Societies
FGSP: Fellow Genealogical Society of

Pennsylvania
FHC: Family History Center (one of the branches of the Family History Library)
FHL: Family History Library of the Church of Jesus Christ of Latter-day Saints (in Salt Lake City)
FHLC: Family History Library Catalog
FNGS: Fellow of the National Genealogical Society
FSAG: Fellow of the Society of Australian Genealogists
FSG: Fellow of the Society of Genealogists (England)
FUGA: Fellow of the Utah Genealogical Association
GRINZ: Genealogical Research Institute of New Zealand
GSG: Genealogical Speakers Guild
GSMD: General Society of Mayflower Descendants
HOFFM: The Hereditary Order of the first Families of Massachusetts
IGHR: Institute of Genealogy and Historical Research (Samford University)
IGI: International Genealogical Index
ISBGFH: International Society for British Genealogy and Family History
JGS: Jewish Genealogical Society
LC: Library of Congress
LDS: Church of Jesus Christ of Latter-day Saints
NARA: National Archives Records Administration
NDC: National Society of the Daughters of the American Colonists
NEHGR: *The New England Historical and Genealogical Register*
NEHGS: New England Historic Genealogical Society
NGS: National Genealogical Society
NGSQ: National Genealogical Society Quarterly
NHS: National Huguenot Society
NIGR: National Institute on Genealogical Research (National Archives)
NSCD-17: National Society of the Colonial Dames of the XVII Century
NSCDA: National Society Colonial Dames of America

NYGB: New York Genealogical and Biographical Society
NYGBR: *The New York Genealogical and Biographical Record*
OFPA: Order of the Founders and Patriots of America
OGS: Ohio Genealogical Society
PAF: Personal Ancestral File
SAC: Sons of American Colonists
SAR: National Society Sons of the American Revolution
SC: The Society of the Cincinnati
SDP: Sons and Daughters of the Pilgrims
SIW: Sons of the Indian Wars
SR: General Society Sons of the Revolution
TAG: *The American Genealogist*
TG: *The Genealogist*
UDC: United Daughters of the Confederacy
UGA: Utah Genealogical Society
USD 1812: National Society United States Daughters of 1812

QUERIES

Preparation
♦In a first draft, as a means of ensuring that the problem is focused and clear, write down the question to be posed — as simply, as directly, and as briefly as possible.
♦List the facts available concerning the question, organizing them inappropriate order
♦Cut long sentences into two or three sentences. Cross out unnecessary words.
♦Emphasize facts and other vital statistics; eliminate extraneous personal anecdotes
♦Adjust the order of items; write the second draft.
Writing the query
♦Use any form of writing the query except longhand. Use all capital letters for surnames.
♦Use standard-size paper (8½" x 11")
♦If possible, limit the length of the query to a half page, double-spaced.

Small courtesies
♦ Pose a reasonable request.
♦ Offer to pay respondents for photocopies of relevant information.

Be sure to include
♦ The name of the German village and Kreis, if known
♦ Any alternate spellings of the surname that have appeared in the research
♦ Umlauts, when known
♦ If available, the date of immigration and points of United States settlement through the ancestors' lifetimes
♦ Locations as well as dates of births, marriages, and deaths (use date estimates if necessary, but be sure to state them as estimates)
♦ The emigrant's religion, if known
♦ Your name and address; optionally, your telephone number, e-mail address, or fax number
♦ A stamped self-addressed envelope if a copy of the published query is requested

ABBREVIATIONS USED IN QUERIES

abt	about
ae	age
aft	after
anc	ancestor(s)
ans	answer
arr	arrived
b	born
bap/bapt	baptized
bdt	birthdate(s)
bef	before
bel	believed
bet	between
bp/bpl	birthplace
bro	brother
bur	buried
ca	circa, about
cem	cemetery
cen	census
cert	certificate
ch	child(ren)
CivW	Civil War
Co	County
corr/corres	correspond
csn	cousin
d	died, death
dau	daughter
desc	descendant(s)
desr	desire
div	divorced
dp/dpl	death place
dt	date(s)
em/emigr	emigrated/emigrant
Eng.	England
enl	enlisted
est	estate
f	female
fa	father
fam	family/families
1st	first
1/hus	first husband
1/w	first wife
fol	following
fr	from
g	grand-
gg	great grand-
gen	genealogy
Ger	Germany
hus	husband
id	identity
immig	immigrant/immigrated
info	information
int	interested
kn	known
/law	in-law (e.g. mo/in-law)
liv	living
loc	location
M	male
m	married
m/1	married first
m/2	married second
M.D.	doctor
mo	mother
mov	moved
Ms	manuscript
ndt	no date
npl	no place
nr	near
obit	obituary
orig	original
par	parents

per	perhaps
pl	place
pos/poss	possibly
PR	Prussia
pro	probate
prob	probably
re	regarding
rec	record
ref	reference
rel	related/relative(s)
rem	remained
req	requested
res	resided, residence
rsch	research
Rev.	Reverend
RevW	Revolutionary War
s	son(s)
SASE	self-addressed stamped envelope
2nd	second
set	settled
sib	sibling(s)
sis	sister
sol	soldier
terr	territory
tn	town
trad	tradition
twp/Tp	township
unk	unknown
unm	unmarried
V.S.	vital statistics
ver	verify
vic	vicinity
w	wife
wid	widow
widr	widower
wt	want(ed)
xch	exchange
yng	young
yr	year

PAYING IN DEUTSCHMARKS

To make a payment in deutschmarks rather than dollars (or in any of more than 120 foreign currencies), it is convenient to work through Ruesch International, Inc., a financial service specializing in foreign exchange.

This service is convenient for Americans who wish to pay for searches in German archives, for fees charged by German researchers, for subscriptions to German periodicals, or for membership fees in German genealogical societies.

The steps

♦Call any of the Ruesch numbers listed on the next page (note the nation-wide toll-free number for Washington, DC.)

♦Inform the Ruesch representative of the amount and type of foreign currency needed, as well as the name of the person or business whose name should appear on the "pay to" line. (For example, "24.50 deutschmarks, payable to Boris Heitmann"). The Ruesch representative will state Ruesch's rate of exchange and the total U.S. dollar equivalent. Once the caller approves the exchange rate quoted, Ruesch will lock in the rate and inform you of the flat $3.00 service fee to be added. The caller is assigned a transaction code number.

♦On the same day the order is executed, mail a check for the total amount, payable to "Ruesch International," to any of the Ruesch International offices listed below (usually the closest branch is chosen in the hope that the draft will arrive in the mail sooner). Be sure to write the transaction code number on the memo line of the check. It is not necessary to enclose any correspondence with the check as long as the transaction number is written on it.

♦Immediately following Ruesch International's receipt of good funds, the company will mail the draft, which may then be sent on to the payee. The process takes about a week from the time one puts the check in the mail until the draft in deutschmarks arrives.

Options are available for having the draft sent by registered mail or by overnight delivery — but still upon receipt of good funds.

In Germany, the payee may cash the draft at any time, as there is no limit on stale-dating of Ruesch's drafts issued on

German banks, but practical considerations suggest that if the check is held for a very long time before it is cashed, there may be a problem with the bank's accepting it for payment. Ruesch International can also be helpful in converting checks written in a foreign currencies, like Value Added Tax refunds, into U.S. dollars. Again, the charge is a flat $3.00 per check.

Reusch International
offices in the United States
WASHINGTON, DC
700 11th Street NW
Washington DC 20001-4507
Tel. 800-424-2923 or (202) 408-1200
NEW YORK
608 Fifth Avenue
Swiss Center
New York, NY 10020
Tel. 800-292-4685 (can be accessed only in New York and New Jersey); or (212) 977-2700
LOS ANGELES
1875 Century Park East, Suite 1450
Los Angeles, CA 90067
Tel. 800-696-7990 (can be accessed only in California); or (310)-277-7800
CHICAGO
Three First National Plaza
Chicago, IL 60602
Tel. (312) 332-5900
ATLANTA
191 Peachtree Street, Lobby Level
Atlanta, GA 30303
Tel. (404) 222-9300
BOSTON
45 Milk Street
Boston, MA 02109
Tel (617) 482-8600
Ruesch International offices are located also in London and Zürich.

INTERNATIONAL REPLY COUPONS (IRCs)

As a means of paying for postage when making a request in a letter to Germany, the International Reply Coupon (IRC) is the counterpart to the "self-addressed stamped envelope" used for such purposes in the United States.

The IRC, purchased at United States post offices (but not at postal sub-stations), may be exchanged for a set amount of postage in many foreign countries. In Germany, one IRC is exchangeable for DM 2.00 in German postage.

In 1997, the cost of a standard-weight letter (*Standardbrief*, weighing 20 grams or less), sent by airmail from Germany to the United States, was DM 3.00. A DM 3.00 stamp is sufficient, generally speaking, to carry one business-size envelope and three sheets of paper, depending on the weight of the paper. Therefore, two IRCs should be included with a letter to which a reply is expected. It is usual (and considered courteous) to enclose three IRCs.

American correspondents who frequently write to Germany have learned, however, that a generous donation of IRCs is likely to encourage German recipients who are strangers to the writer to respond. The extra IRCs are appreciated because they ease the burden of paying the high cost of German postage. Based on the exchange rate in 1997, the cost of one DM 3.00 airmail stamp for overseas use cost the equivalent of about $2.00. In contrast, a letter of the same weight sent by airmail from the United States to Germany cost 60 cents.)

In July 1995, the price of one IRC was raised from $.95 to $1.05.

Effective September 1, 1996, International Reply Coupons in Germany could no longer be exchanged for stamps, but could be used only to pay for postage at a post office as a letter or package was presented for mailing. Only one IRC per letter was permitted to be credited toward the postage due. (This change affects IRC recipients, not the purchasers.)

Post office employees in locations where customers seldom request International Reply Coupons may occasionally forget to stamp each IRC with the date of purchase. Such unstamped IRCs are not valid. Therefore, before leaving the counter, the purchaser should make certain that all IRCs purchased are date-stamped.

Validated IRCs can be used for an indefinite period of time — even after a rate increase occurs. Thus, buying them in quantity for future use can prove advantageous when IRC rates rise.

American genealogists often enclose IRCs — 10, 20 or more of them — as thank-you gifts to Germans who perform substantial research favors for them.

CHECKLIST OF SOURCES FOR LOCATING AN IMMIGRANT ANCESTOR'S PLACE OF ORIGIN

Knowing the place of origin of the immigrant ancestor is essential if one is to trace his or her family back to the homeland. The checklist below offers *some* of the sources which can reveal the immigrant's place of origin or can lead to clues to such a discovery. This is not a complete list.
•Military service records
•American church records, especially churches with heavy German immigrant members
•An all-Germany telephone search (for unusual surnames only)
•Records of fraternal organizations in the town where the immigrant settled.
•German census records on the kingdom, province, or duchy level (if the *general* area of origin is known or supposed)
•United States federal census
•Places of origins of companions on the voyage to America
•American neighbors' places of origin (see federal census, enumerated by streets)
•Places of origins of witnesses to marriages or births
•Siblings' place of origin
•Homestead Act application files and sup-

porting documents
•Tombstones
•Trade journals of immigrant's occupation
•Printed material on the occasion of a 50th wedding anniversary
•HETRINA
•Draft registration records from World War I time period (whether the immigrant served in the military or not)
•Obituaries
•Death certificate of immigrant (or of any relative of the immigrant)
•Vital records in state repositories
•State censuses in America
•United States telephone search (for unusual surname only)
•Letter to clergy in towns where the surname is strong, for posting on the church bulletin board
•Veteran organization records
•Probate records
•Alien registrations
•Official papers regarding purchase or sale of land
•Old family artifacts, which may be imprinted or otherwise marked with place of manufacture
•Family Bible (and all the papers inside)
•Old letters and their envelopes
•City directories (to find neighbors who may have come from the same town)
•Newspapers from immigrant's area of settlement in America
•Pension files, 1775-1916
•Bounty land warrant applications
•Naturalization records (after 1906)
•"First papers" (declarations of intent)
•Petition for naturalization
•Periodical Source Index (PERSI)
•Newspaper record of a marriage ceremony
♦ "Enemy Alien" lists published in 1917-1918 in various U.S. states and cities.
•Birth certificate of immigrant's child
•Social Security application
•Interviews with older relatives and distant "cousins"
•Family letters
•Passports, passport applications

•*Germans to America*, (based on passenger lists) by Glazier and Filby, and similar lists and indexes
•Records kept at hospitals, state homes, schools, universities
•Government employment records
•IGI: International Genealogical Index; (check batch number of submitter)
•Ancestral File
•Queries to genealogical societies located in the immigrant's home (U.S.) area
•Queries to German genealogical publications
◆*Die Quellenschau für Familienforscher*
•Diaries
◆Notes from previous family searches
•Public libraries in the immigrant's area of settlement in America
•Queries (paid advertisements) to newspapers in immigrant's area of settlement in America
•County histories for clues as to where some of the German settlers came from
•All town records (phone books, court records, tax lists, etc.)
•Mortuary records
•County records (birth, marriage, death, taxes, guardianships, etc.)
•Biographical sketches of fellow townspeople (for information on their places of origin)
◆German state emigration records, indexes
•Church certificates: christening, confirmation, marriage, burial
•Cemetery offices
•Published family histories
•German-American newspapers
•Surname indexes (*Familiengeschichtliche Quellen, Die Quellenschau für Familienforscher*)
•Index to German periodicals *(Der Schlüssel,* for example*)*
•Bibles, hymn books, prayer books (check place of publication)
•Queries to ethnic organizations located where the immigrant settled in America
◆ Obituaries, especially in German-language newspapers
◆Most of the above sources as means of

discovering the place of origin for a spouse, for siblings, or for other relatives

PERSI
(Periodical Source Index)

The Periodical Source Index (PERSI) is published by the Allen County [Indiana] Public Library Foundation in a joint effort with the Allen County Public Library. It indexes many genealogical and local history periodicals — by locality, subject, and surname.

Availability
The Family History Library produces the microfiche version of PERSI and makes it available to its many Family History Centers. PERSI may be accessed at Family History Centers through FHL microfiche 6016863 (for 1847-1985) and FHL 6016864 (1986 -).

The record types
Each article title is listed under one of these 22 record types:
•Biography
•Cemeteries
•Census
•ChurchCourt
•Deeds (see also Land)
•Directories
•History
•Institutions
•Land (not including deeds)
•Maps
•Military
•Naturalization
•Obituaries
•Other
•Passenger Lists
•Probate (not including Wills)
•School
•Tax
•Vital Records
•Voter
• Wills (see also Probate).

Steps for German research
To search topics related to German genealogy –

◆Select the microfiche (see microfiche numbers above, one for earlier years of periodical publication, the other for later years). From within the chosen set of microfiches for 1986 and onward, for example, select the fiche titled "1986-1990 Canada, Foreign and Research Methodologies."

◆At the beginning of the fiche, note the list of codes and their matching periodical titles. (For example: AMPM is shown as the code for *Pomeranian Society of Freistadt Newsletter*.) This periodical code list will be referred to in step 4 below.

◆ Next on the fiche comes "CAN" (Canada), and then "FOR" (Foreign Places), in which countries are listed alphabetically.

◆Move alphabetically under "FOR" to "Germany" (which includes Prussia). Here article titles are grouped by Record Types (see the list of 22 Record Types above). Therefore, in the "Germany" section one first finds all the titles related to "Biography," then all those related to "Cemeteries," then all those related to "Census," and on through the 22 Record Types as listed alphabetically above. (For example, the title, "Mennonites in Palatine Prot. church records" is listed under the Record Type "Church.")

◆Select a title of an article of interest under the column heading "Title of Article." In the next column, headed "Journal," note the code (always four capital letters). Then in the next four columns note, respectively, the volume number, the issue number, the month, and the year of the periodical in which the selected article appears.

◆To determine the name of the periodical, return to the beginning of the fiche by using the key to the four-letter periodical codes.

To obtain copies of articles

Copies of all indexed articles may be obtained from the Allen County Public Library, P.O. Box 2270, Ft. Wayne, IN 46801. Provide the full entries from PERSI and the names of the periodicals in which

the articles appear. The library bills patrons for the request, which should not include more than eight articles. No telephone or fax requests are accepted.

Another source
for locating periodicals

Check *Bibliography of Genealogy and Local Periodicals with Union List of Major U.S. Collections* (First ed., Ft. Wayne, IN: Allen County Public Library Foundation, 1990, FHL Book Ref 973 D23b), which lists titles of periodicals and their respective PERSI abbreviations, the starting dates, and publishers' addresses.

LOCATING RESEARCHERS

Lists of accredited or certified genealogists are available from these two accrediting organizations:

◆The Family History Library
35 North West Temple Street
Salt Lake City, UT 84150
(The library accredits researchers for the records of most major countries; there is no cost for the list.)

◆The Board for Certification of Genealogists
P.O. Box 5816
Falmouth, VA 22043-5816
(The Board tests and certifies researchers in the United States in various categories of services. All certified persons must agree to a code of ethics; the charge for the list is $3.50.)

Researcher lists available elsewhere

◆ The Association of Professional Genealogists supplies lists of researchers and persons supplying related services who agree to a code of professionalism:
The Association of Professional Genealogists
3421 M Street, N.W., Suite 236
Washington, DC 20007
(The list is available at public libraries or from the Association at a cost of $15.)

◆Everton's Genealogical Helper
P.O. Box 368, Logan, UT 84323-0368

(The list of researchers is printed annually in the September-October issue of this publication.)

Other sources

Lists of researchers are also generally available from libraries, archives, and courthouses as a courtesy to their patrons. No attempt is made on their part, however, to assess researchers' credentials.

Source: *Resource Guide: Hiring a Professional Genealogist,* Family History Library, Church of Jesus Christ of Latter-day Saints, Salt Lake City, Utah.

HERALDRY

Coats of arms, originally created for identification on fields of battle, are the currency of heraldry, which deals with the history and description of armorial bearings.

The following explanation of the use of arms, "Heraldry for United States Citizens,"[1] is provided as a public-service bulletin by the Board for Certification of Genealogists:[2]

"Heraldry in the United States has no legal standing unless it has been registered as a trade mark or copyrighted under United States law. Citizens of the United States may adopt and use any arms, devices, or badges of his or her own creation as long as they do not infringe on insignia covered by such a registration or copyright. However, if the citizen adopts arms, devices, or badges acknowledged by the Heraldic Offices of a foreign nation as belonging to the descendants of any of their nationals, the person using those arms, etc. may find himself guilty of violation of the laws of another country — thus subject to penalties.

"Arms do not belong to a 'family name.' They belong to individuals who are acknowledged as their owner, or who receive a grant from them (from a foreign government), or make them up for themselves. Under the laws of most countries other than ours, the rules are generally as follows:

"♦ *Unbroken male line descendants* of any person who has a legally recognized right to bear heraldic arms may use their progenitor's arms, inheriting them in the same manner that they inherit anything else. If a male line descendant changes his name — as, for instance, from Smith to Jones — he still may bear his father's arms, even though he now uses a different surname. He does not bear different arms associated in someone's mind with another person of his new surname. This is clear evidence that there is no such thing as "arms of your family name."

"♦ Daughters have the right to use their father's coat armour as long as they remain unmarried, or they may combine (by *impaling* or *escutcheon of pretense*) their father's arms with those of their husband's. If their spouses have no arms, they may continue for life to use their paternal arms, but this right is not inherited by their children and expires with their deaths. If an *armiger* (one who has the right to bear heraldic arms) has no sons but only daughters, then under British law the daughters are heraldic heiresses and their children may *quarter* the arms of their mother with those of their father. If their father has no arms, the right is lost — unless the arms are regranted to them as heirs of their maternal grandfather.

"Anyone whose uninterrupted male-line immigrant ancestor from England was entitled to use a coat of arms has the right under English law, to use this same coat of arms. If that ancestor had no such right, then neither does the descendant — unless he or she buys a grant of arms from the College of Arms. Thus, to establish the right under English (or German, French, Swiss, etc.) law to a coat-of-arms, it is necessary to prove one's uninterrupted male-line descent from someone who was legally entitled to use this coat of armour. No 'heraldry institute' or 'heraldic artist' can 'look up a surname' and provide the correct arms for a client without first proving the client's descent from the distant forebear, with legally acceptable proof at every generation. Any claim to 'research,' without proving the entire lineage, constitutes fraud.

"Several organizations in the United States seek to register and codify the use of arms. All these organizations operate on a voluntary basis. Excellent as their intentions may be, they have no legal standing and are unable to enforce the registration or uniform use of coats of arms."

Footnotes
[1] *The Report*, Ohio Genealogical Society, Spring 1996.
[2] The Board for Certification of Genealogists, P.O. Box 5816, Falmouth, VA 22403-5816

THE GERMAN *WAPPENBÜCHER*[1]

The traditions in German-speaking parts of Europe are not the same as those in England. Helmut Nickel, who has written on topics of heraldry, states, "In some countries, such as Germany and Switzerland, that once were parts of the Holy Roman Empire, it was and still is the privilege of any free man to choose and adopt his family arms, as long as they do not infringe on the rights of others."[2]

Coats of arms for non-nobles
Myron R. Falck, who writes on German heraldry, states, "Of the many Siebmacher volumes that I looked at it is clear that numerous volumes are given to the presentation of *"Bürgerliche Wappen"*; that is, coats of arms for non-noble persons and families.

A *Bürger* is described most simply as a citizen, but is also sometimes described as a free man or a burgher (a word not much in style anymore); in any case, a *Bürger* was a member of the community with rights to own property, hold office, and to participate in the governance of the community."[3]

J. Siebmacher's Wappenbuch
The best known work on German heraldry is the *Wappenbuch* (or *J. Siebmachers großes und allgemeines Wappenbuch . . .*) by Johann Siebmacher, a Nürnburg graphic artist who died in 1611. [*Wappen* means coat of arms; *Wappenbuch* means "heraldry book"; the plural is *Wappenbücher*.] This work was printed and reprinted until 1806 with revisions and additions in 18 volumes with titles that generally identify them as the "Old Siebmacher." The "New Siebmacher" was published in a series of 101 volumes from 1854 to 1961.

In the Siebmacher *Wappenbücher,* the depicted coats of arms are presented in tables. Textual material, usually independent of the table but with references to the table, is also included for most of the depicted arms. These descriptions often include significant genealogical information; for example, the names of family members, locations of land holdings, castle names, as well as other information about families. In some of the volumes, a technical description of the coat of arms, sometimes known as the blazon, is included. The language used is German in contrast to the stylized French blazon found for British arms. It usually describes the shield and its divisions, the charges on the shield, the colors to be represented, as well as the wreath, the mantling, the helmet, and the crest. There are occasional entries for persons in the extended Holy Roman Empire and the Hapsburg Empire; a few Russian and Swedish arms from the Baltic area and some Hungarian arms are also entered.

Depictions of coats of arms
A coat of arms usually has a number of parts; it includes the most important element that may stand alone: the shield (*Schild* in German). A more complete coat of arms included the helmet (*Helm*) with a wreath or binding (*Wulst*), that with six twists binds the crest (Kleinod) to the helmet; and the mantling (*Decken*) that provides an elaborate and decorative fabric

cover for the helmet, presumably for the protection of the neck and shoulders of the warrior. There are also numerous technical terms for the division of the shield, the images (charges) placed on it, and their locations, and for the stances of any animals that may be shown on the shield or crest.

Index to the Wappenbücher

The essential guide to the many volumes of the *Wappenbücher* is this index: Jäger-Sunstenau, Hanns. *General-Index zu den Siebmacher'schen Wappenbüchern 1605-1961*. Graz, Austria: Akademische Druck und Verlagsanstalt, 1964. (FHL film 1181781, No. 4).

Among other aids found in this one-volume work, an index for some 130,000 names, mostly German, is included, with a key to finding the coats of arms, as well as descriptive text as found in the Siebmacher *Wappenbücher*.

Using the index[4]

Care must be taken in going from the *Index* to the *Wappenbücher* because of the many republications.

The reverse of the title page may offer some help in decidinig which section of the books to check. The filmed version of the *Index* [FHL film number 1181781, Item #4] explains at the very beginning of the roll a conversion needed to use the books on the Family History Library shelves. As one goes through the filmed *Wappenbücher*, it may be necessary to roll through several volumes to get to the table being searched.

Beginning on page 24 of the *General-Index* is a catalog of all the *Wappenbücher* with complete bibliographic information. There is a description of the contents of each volume. At the beginning of each listing, in parentheses right after the volume or edition number, is the abbreviation for the volume that is used in the alphabetical surname index; for example, *Bg5* refers to the fifth *bürgerliche* volume. All the 14 *bürgerliche* volumes are listed beginning on page 24.

On page 39 begins a chronological list telling which volumes were published each year from 1605 to 1961. On page 43 is a list telling how the initial letters are grouped together: *b* includes *p*; *d* includes *dh*, *t*, and *th*; *f* includes *v*; *i* includes *j* and *y*; *k* includes *kh*, *c*, *ch*, *g*, and *gh*; *w* includes *v*; and *z* includes *zh*, *zs zsch*, *c*, *ch*, *cs*, and *cz*. (There are initial *v* listings under both *w* and *f*.) On page 46 are listed all the abbreviations.

This is an example of an entry in this book:

FALK- . . . .
   - . . . .
   -(Baden) Bg5 75

This entry signifies that there is a Falk family from Baden with a coat of arms described on page 75 of the fifth burgher division. One then locates the Siebmacher volume containing this division.

Footnotes

[1] The information in this section is based on and in large part excerpted, by permission of the author, from "German Coats of Arms," by Myron R. Falck, *The German Connection*, Vol. 20, No. 2 (1996)

[2] Helmut Nickel, "Heraldry," *Dictionary of the Middle Ages*, ed. Joseph Reese Strayer. New York, Charles Scribner's Sons, 1985, vol. 6, p. 172..

[3] Myron R. Falck, *Coats of Arms for the Name Falck and Variations of That Name as Found in the Siebmacher Wappenbücher*. Myron R. Falck. 1996.

[4] Helen Boyden, "Tips on Using the General-Index," *The German Connection*, Vol. 20, No. 2, 1996.

FURTHER READING ON HERALDRY

♦Fox-Davies, Arthur Charles. *The Art of Heraldry: an Encyclopedaedia of Armory*, Arno, New York, 1904, reprint 1976.

♦Neubecker, Ottfried. *Heraldry: Sources, Symbols, and Meaning*. McGraw Hill, New York, 1976.

♦Stephenson, Jean. *Heraldry for the American Genealogist.* National Genealogical Society, Washington, DC, 1959
♦Woodcock, Thomas, and John Martin Robinson. *The Oxford Guide to Heraldry.* Oxford University Press, Oxford, 1988.

SOME GERMAN-RELATED GENEALOGY AND HISTORICAL SOCIETIES IN NORTH AMERICA AND GREAT BRITAIN

♦**American-German Genealogical Association**, 4246 South 3100 East, Salt Lake City, UT 84117
♦**American Historical Society of Germans from Russia**, 631 D Street, Lincoln, NE 68502-1199. Tel. (402) 474-3363; (402) 474-7229. (*Clues; Journal; Newsletter*)
♦**American-Schleswig-Holstein Heritage Society**, P.O. Box 313, Davenport, IA 52805-0313. Tel. (319) 324-7326 (*American Schleswig-Holstsein Heritage Society Newsletter*)
♦**Anglo-German Family History Society**, 14 River Reach, Teddington, Middlesex TW11 9QL, England
♦**Bukovina Society of the Americas**, P.O. Box 81, Ellis, KS 67637-0081. E-mail owindholz@waylon.dailynews.net
♦Eastern Europe Genealogical Society, P.O. Box 2536, Winnipeg, MB R3C 4A7, Canada
♦Center for Pennsylvnia German Studies, 406 Spring Drive, Millersville, PA 17551
♦**Galizien German Descendants**, 12637 South East 214th Street, Kent, WA 98031-2215
♦**German-Bohemian Heritage Society**, P.O. Box 822, New Ulm, MN 56073-0822
♦ **German Genealogical Society of America**, P.O. Box 291818, Los Angeles, CA 90029. Tel. (909) 593-0509. [Library at 2125 Wright Avenue, Suite C-9, LaVerne, CA 91750-5814]. (*German Genealogical Society of America Bulletin*)

♦**German Interest Group,** Chicago Genealogical Society, 16828 Willow Lane Drive, Tinsley Park, IL 60477
♦**German Interest Group**, P.O. Box 2185, Janesville, WI 53547-2185 (*German Interest Group Newsletter*)
♦**German Research Association**, P.O. Box 711600, San Diego, CA 92171-1600. (*The German Conneciton*)
♦**German-Texan Heritage Society**, P.O. Box 684171, Austin, TX 78768-4171. Tel. (512) 482-0927 (*Journal; Newsletter*)
♦**Germanic Genealogy Society** (a branch of the Minnesota Genealogical Society), P.O. Box 16312, St. Paul, MN 55116-0312. Tel. (612) 777-6463 [Library materials held at Concordia College, Theodore Buenger Memorial Library, 275 N. Syndicate Street, St. Paul, MN 55104] (*Germanic Genealogy Society Newsletter*)
♦**Germans from Russia Heritage Society,** 1008 E. Central Avenue, Bismarck, ND 58501. Tel. (701) 223-6167. (*Heritage Review*)
♦**Glückstal Colonies Research Association,** 611 Esplanade, Redondo Beach, CA 90277-4130. Tel. (310) 540-1872
♦**Gottscheer Research and Genealogy Association**, 215634 American River Drive, Sonora, CA 95370-9112 (*The Gottschee Tree,* a journal)
♦**Harmonie Associates, Inc., Old Economy Village,** 14th and Church Streets, Ambridge, PA 15003. Tel. (412) 266-1803
♦**Historic Harmony/Harmony Museum,** 218 Mercer Street, P.O. Box 524, Harmony, PA 16037. Tel. (412) 452-7341 (*Newsletter*)
♦**Immigrant Genealogical Society**, P.O. Box 7369, Burbank, CA 91510-7369. Tel. (818) 848-3122 [Library at 1310-B West Magnolia Boulevard in Burbank] (*Immigrant Genealogical Society Newsletter* and *German American Genealogy*, a journal)
♦**Johannes Schwalm Historical Association,** 411 Springfield Avenue, Pennsauken, NJ 68110 (Hessian soldeirs and

their descendants)

♦**Lancaster Mennonite Historical Society,** 2215 Millstream Road, Lancaster, PA 17602-1499

♦**Lithuanian American Genealogy Society,** c/o Balzakas Museum of Lithuanian Culture, 6500 Pulaski Road, Chicago, IL 60629-5136

♦ **Mennonite Historians of Eastern Pennsylvania,** 565 Yoder Road, Box 82, Harleysville, PA 19438. Tel. (215) 256-3020. (*MHEP Newsletter*)

♦**Mid-Atlantic Germanic Society,** P.O. Box 2642, Kensington, MD 20891-2642. (*Der Kurier*)

♦**Moravian Heritage Society,** 31910 Road 160, Visalia, CA 93292-9044

♦**Orangeburgh German-Swiss Genealogical Society,** P.O.Box 974, Orangeburgh, SC 29116-0974 (*The Orangeburgh German-Swiss Newsletter*)

♦**Ostfriesian Genealogical Society,** P.O. Box 53, George, IA 51237-0053 (*Ostfriesen Genealogical Society Newsletter*)

♦**Palatines to America,** Capital University, Box 101P, Columbus, OH 43209-2394. [Library at same location] (*The Palatine Immigrant*)

♦**Pommerscher Verein Freistadt Rundschreiben,** P.O. Box 204, Germantown, WI 53022

♦**Sacramento German Genealogy Society,** P.O. Box 660061, Sacramento, CA 95866-0061. Fax (916) 421-8032. (*Der Blumenbaum*)

♦**Silesian-American Genealogy Society,** P.O. Box 21346-0346, Salt Lake City, UT

♦**Slovak Genealogical Research Center,** 6862 Palmer Court, Chino, CA 91710

♦**Slovenian Genealogy Society,** 52 Old Farm Road, Camp Hill, PA 17011

♦**Society for German American Studies,** c/o Dr. Don Heinrich Tolzmann, University of Cincinnati, Langsam Library, M.L. 33, Cincinnati, OH 45221.

♦ **Wandering Volhynians Genealogy Society,** c/o 3492 West 39th Avenue, Vancouver, BC V6N 3A2, Canada

OTHER ADDRESSES (Publications and specialized societies)

♦**Association of German Nobility in North America,** 3571 East Eighth Street, Los Angeles, CA 90023

♦**Frankenmuth Historical Museum,** 613 South Main, Frankenmuth, MI 48734 . Tel.: (517) 652-9701. (*FHA Newsletter*)

♦**Genealogical Society of Pennsylvania,** 1305 Locust Street, Philadelphia, PA 19107. Tel. (215) 545-0391. Fax: (215) 545-0936

♦**Georgia Salzburger Society,** P.O. Box 478-B, Rincon, GA 31326 (*Georgia Salzburger Society Newsletter*)

♦**German-American Family Society,** 3871 Ranfield Road, Brimfield, OH 44240

♦ **German-American Genealogical Club,** 86th CSG/RSSRR, Box 24, APO New York, NY 09012

♦**German American Heritage Association of Oklahoma,** Modern Language Department, Oklahoma City University, 2501 North Blackwelder, Oklahoma City, OK 73106

♦**German American Heritage Center,** P.O. Box 243, Davenport, IA 52805-0243

♦ **German Genealogical Digest,** 245 North Vine, Suite 106, Salt Lake City, UT 84103

♦**German Society of Pennsylvania,** 611 Spring Garden Street, Philadelphia, PA 19123. Tel. (215) 627-2332

♦**Indiana German Heritage Society,** 401 East Michigan Street, Indianapolis, IN 46204

♦**Links Genealogy Publications,** 7677 Abaline Way, Sacramento, CA 95823 (Krefeld Immigrants and Their Descendants)

♦**Pennsylvania German Society,** P.O. Box 397, Birdsboro, PA 19508. Tel.: (215) 582-1441

♦**Pommerschen Leute, Die** [publication title], 1260 South Westhaven Drive, Oshkosh, WI 54904. Tel. (414) 235-7398

(Pomeranians 1839-1899)
◆**Steuben Society of America**, 67-05 Fresh Pond Road, Ridgewood, NY 11385. Tel. (718) 381-0900. Fax: (718) 628-4874 (*The Steuben News*)
◆**Texas Wendish Heritage Museum**, Rt. 2, Box 155, Giddings TX 78942

NATIONAL GENEALOGICAL SOCIETY

National Genealogical Society
4527 17th Street North
Arlington, VA 22007
Tel. (Library): (703) 841-9065
Fax: (703) 525-0052
E-mail:
ngs.library@f302n109.zl.fidonet.org
WWW Home Page: http://genealogy.org/ NGS/
Publications
NGS Quarterly (journal); *NGS Newsletter* (bi-monthly newsletter), including the *NGS/CIG Digest*.
Library
Free to NGS members; 23,000 volumes

FEEFHS (Federation of East European Family History Societies)

Federation of East European Family History Societies (FEEFHS)
P.O. Box 510898
Salt Lake City, UT 84151-0898
E-mail: feefhs@feefhs.org.
URL: http://feefhs.org
FEEFHS is a multi-ethnic umbrella organization which disseminates information about research opportunities in Eastern and Central Europe and serves as a clearinghouse for member societies.
Of its approximately 135 organization-members, about half are genealogy societies. Others include multi-purpose societies; surname associations; publishers; archives; libraries; online services; E-mail

genealogy mailing lists or lists-servers; heraldry societies; and ethnic, religious, and national groups.
Areas of interest pertaining to ethnic origins or nationalities include Germans from Russia, Anglo-Germans, Russian-Baltic, Bukovino, Czechoslovakia and Slovakia, Croatia, Finland, Galicia, German-Bohemia, Germany, Jews, Hungary, Bessarabia, Lithuania, Moravia, Slovenia, Poland, Pomerania, Jewish Romanians, Silesia, Slavs, Switzerland, and Volhynia.
FEEFHS may be contacted for information about societies specializing in specific geographic or ethnic areas.

THE GENEALOGICAL HANDBOOK OF THE NOBILITY (*Genealogisches Handbuch des Adels*)

In 1951 C.A.Starke Verlag began publishing the *Genealogisches Handbuch des Adels*, which has since run to 51 volumes. In 1994 an index (*Stammfolgen-Verzeichnisse 1994*) was published to cover the this publication as well as the "German Lineage Book" series (*Deutsches Geschlechterbuch*)
In 1972, C.A.Starke Verlag began publication of the Adelskixikon (lexicon of nobility, covering alphabetically the families of nobility who qualify for acceptance into print except for lineages that became extinct before 1800. Six volumes have appeared between 1972 and 1989. These are (with the alphabetical range they cover) are
Vol. 1, A-Bon, 1972; vol. II, Doo-Don, 1974; vol. III, Dor-Fz, 1975; vol. !V, Ga-Har, 1978; vol. V, Has-I, 1984; vol. VI, J-Kra, 1987; and vol. VII, Kre-Lod, 1989. Additional volumes will be added.
For a thorough explanation of this and other listings of nobility, see "The Genealogical Handbook of the Nobility," by Horst A. Reschke. *German Genealogical Digest,* Vol. 12, No. 4, Winter 1996, the source of the above information.

WRITING TO GERMANY

The German-language letter below, can be adapted for mailing to -
A) a town archive (*Stadtarchiv*), or B) a local civil registration office (*Standesamt*), or C) a church office (*Pfarramt*).

The address
A) *for a village/town archive:*
Stadtarchiv [*locality name*]
[*zip code*] [*locality name*]
Germany
B) *for a local civil registry office:*
Standesamt [locality name]
[zip code] [*locality name*]
Germany
C) *for a Catholic church office:*
Katholisches Pfarramt
[*zip code*] [*locality name*]
Germany
or, *for a Lutheran church office:*
Evangelisches Pfarramt
[*zip code*] [*locality name*]
Germany

Salutation
A & B: Sehr geehrte Damen und Herren,
C: Sehr geehrter Herr Pfarrer,

Body of the letter
Vorfahren meiner Familie haben in [*locality*] gelebt. Um meine Familienchronik vervollständigen zu können, bitte ich um Kopien vorhandener Dokumente über [*last name, in all capital letters*] [*first name*] geb. [*birthdate*] in [*place of birth*] sowie gegebenen-falls auch über [seine/ihre*] Vorfahren (Eltern, Großeltern).

Ich versichere ausdrücklich, daß die erbetenen Unterlagen meine eigene Familie betreffen und nur der privaten Familienforschung dienen.

Zum Ausgleich entstehender Unkosten füge ich einen Verrechnungsscheck über DM [*amount*] bei und bitte um Nachricht, falls dies nicht ausreicht.

Für Ihre Unterstützung bedanke ich mich bereits jetzt.

Mit freundlichem Gruß
[*writer's signature and name*]

(*Use *seine* for a male immigrant, or *ihre* for a female immigrant.)

English translation
Dear Sir or Madam,
Ancestors of my family lived in [*locality name*]. To complete my family history, I request copies of any available documents concerning [*last name, in all capital letters*] [*first name*] born [*date of birth*] in [*place of birth*] as well as his/her ancestors (parents, grandparents).

I do expressly declare that these documents concern my own family and serve for private genealogical research only.

Enclosed is a check for DM [*amount*]. Please bill me for any additional expenses.

Thank you for your assistance.
Sincerely yours,
[signature of sender]
[name of sender]

Example of a finished letter
On the next page is an example of a letter modeled after the above form letter.

Note how the date is written. Months of the year in German are (in the righthand column),

January	Januar
February	Februar
March	März
April	April
May	Mai
June	Juni
July	Juli
August	August
September	September
October	Oktober
November	November
December	Dezember

Examples of the envelope address
♦Katholisches Pfarramt
36115 Ehrenberg
Germany
♦Standesamt Ehrenberg
36115 Ehrenberg
Germany
♦Stadtarchiv Ehrenberg
36115 Ehrenberg
Germany

See the example on the next page

EXAMPLE OF A LETTER TO GERMANY
(using the form letter on the previous page)

Ernest Schneider   15. März 1997
120 Beach Street
Mytown, IA 55555
U.S.A.

Evangelisches Pfarramt
36115 Ehrenberg

Sehr geehrter Herr Pfarrer,

Vorfahren meiner Familie haben in Ehrenberg gelebt. Um meine Familienchronik vervollständigen zu können, bitte ich um Kopien vorhandener Dokumente über HARTMANN Heinrich Georg geb. 22 Januar 1832 in Ehrenberg sowie gegebenenfalls auch über seine Vorfahren (Eltern, Großeltern).

Ich versichere ausdrücklich, daß die erbetenen Unterlagen meine eigene Familie betreffen und nur der privaten Familienforschung dienen.

Zum Ausgleich entstehender Unkosten füge ich einen Verrechnungsscheck über DM 10.00 bei und bitte um Nachricht, falls dies nicht ausreicht.

Für Ihre Unterstützung bedanke ich mich bereits jetzt.

Mit freundlichem Gruß

(signature)

Ernest Schneider

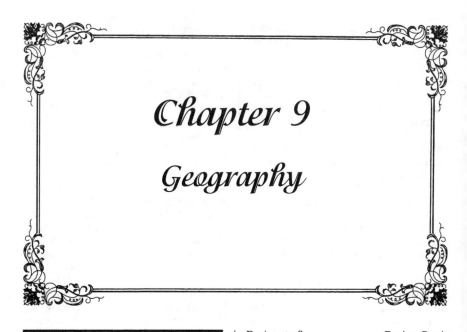

Chapter 9
Geography

GEOGRAPHIC PLACE NAMES, GERMAN-TO-ENGLISH

Adria .... Adriatic (Sea)
Ägäis .... Aegean (Sea)
Ägypten .... Egypt
Albanien .... Albania
Alpen .... Alps
Alpenvorland .... foothills of the Alps
Amerika .... America
Ardennen .... the Ardennes
Atlantik .... the Atlantic (Ocean)
Australien .... Australia
Balkanhalbinsel .... Balkan Peninsula
Balkanstaaten .... Balkan States, the Balkans
Baltikum .... the Baltic (States), the Baltics
Basel .... Basle
Bayerischen Alpen .... Bavarian Alps
Bayerische Wald .... Bavarian Forest
Bayern .... Bavaria
Belgien .... Belgium
Benelux Länder .... Benelux Countries
Beringmeer .... Bering Sea
Beringstraße .... Bering Strait
Berner Alpen .... Bernese Alps
Bessarabien .... Bessarabia
Bodensee .... Lake Constance
Böhmen .... Bohemia
Böhmen und Mähren .... Bohemia-Moravia
Böhmerwald .... Bohemian Forest
Bosnien .... Bosnia
Brandenburger Tor .... Brandenburg Gate
Brasilien .... Brazil
Breslau .... Wroclaw/Breslau
Bretagne .... Brittany
Brügge .... Bruges
Brüssel .... Brussels
Bundesrepublik .... Federal Republic
Deutschland   of Germany
Chiemsee .... Lake Chiem/Chiemsee
Dänemark .... Denmark
Danzig .... Gdansk/Danzig
Danziger Bucht .. Bay of Gdansk/Danzig
Den Haag .... The Hague
Deutsche Demokratische .... German
Republik   Democratic Republic
Deutschland .... Germany
Dnjepr .... Dnieper

Dnjestr	Dniester
Donau	Danube
Eismeer,	See *Nordpolarmeer*
Nördliches	
Eismeer, Südliches	See *Südpolarmeer*
Elsaß	Alsace
Elsaß-Lothringen	Alsace-Lorraine
Erzgebirge	Erzgebirge, Ore Mountains
Estland	Estonia
Europa	Europe
Finnischer Meerbusen	Gulf of Finland
Finnland	Finland
Franken	Franconia
Frankfurt am Main	Frankfurt (on the Main [River])
Frankfurt an der Oder	Frankfurt (on the Oder [River])
Frankreich	France
Friesische Inseln	Frisian Islands
Galicien	Galicia
Genf	Geneva
Genfer See	‚Lac Léman Lake Geneva
Gent	Ghent
Germanien	Germania
Glarner Alpen	Glarus Alps
Griechenland	Greece
Grönland	Greenland
Großbritannien	Great Britain, Britain
Helvetien	Helvetia, Switzerland
Innerasien	Central Asia
Ionisches Meer	Ionian Sea
Irische See	Irish Sea
Island	Iceland
Italien	Italy
Jugoslawien	Yugoslawien
Kanada	Canada
Karibik	Caribbean
Karpaten	Carpathians, Carpathian Mountains
Kaspisches Meer	Caspian Sea
Kaukasus	Caucasus
Kiew	Kiev
Kleinasien	Asia Minor
Köln	Cologne

Königsberg	Kaliningrad, Königsberg
Konstanz	Constance
Kroatien	Croatia
Lateinamerika	Latin America
Lettland	Latvia
Litauen	Lithania
Lothringen	Lorraine
Lüneburger Heide	Lüneburg Heath
Mähren	Moravia
Mark Brandenburg	Brandenburg Marches
Mecklenburg-Vorpommern	Mecklenburg-Western Pomerania
Mittelamerika	Central America
Mittelasien	Central Asia
Mitteldeutschland	Central Germany
Mitteleuropa	Central Europe
Mittelmeer	Mediterranean (Sea)
Mittlerer Osten	Middle East
Moldau	Moldavia
Moskau	Moscow
Mülhausen	Mulhouse
München	Munich
Naher Osten	Near East
Neufundland	Newfoundland
Neuseeland	New Zealand
Niederbayern	Lower Bavaria
Niederlande	Netherlands, Holland
Niederösterreich	Lower Austria
Niederrhein	Lower Rhine
Niedersachsen	Lower Saxony
Niederschlesien	Lower Silesia
Nordamerika	North America
Norddeutsche Tiefebene	North(ern) German Plain
Norddeutschland	North(ern) Germany
Nordeuropa	North(ern) Europe
Nordfriesischen Inseln	North Frisians
Nord-Ostsee-Kanal	Kiel Canal
Nordpol	North Pole
Nordpolarmeer	Arctic Ocean
Nordrhein-Westfalen	North Rhine-Westphalia
Nordsee	North Sea
Norwegen	Norway
Nürnberg	Nuremberg
Oberbayern	Upper Bavaria
Oberfranken	Upper Franconia

Oberitalien .... Northern Italy
Oberösterreich .... Upper Austria
Oberpfalz .... Upper Palatinate
Oberrhein .... Upper Rhine
Oberrheinische Tiefebene ... Upper Rhine
.... Valley
Oberschlesien .... Upper Silesia
Ostasien .... East Asia
Ostdeutschland .... Eastern Germany;
German Democratic
Republic, East Germany
Österreich .... Austria
Österreich-Ungarn ...... Austria-Hungary
Osteuropa .... Eastern Europe
Ostfriesische Inseln .... East Frisians
Ostpreußen .... East Prussia
Ostsee .... Baltic (Sea)
Pazifik .... Pacific (Ocean)
Peloponnes .... Peloponnese,
Peloponnesus
Persischer Golf .... Persian Gulf
Pfalz .... Palatinate
Polarkreis .... Arctic Circle
Polen .... Poland
Posen .... Poznán
Prag .... Prague
Preßburg .... Bratislava, Pressburg
Preußen .... Prussia
Pyrenäen .... Pyrenees
Rhein .... Rhine
Rheinhessen .... Rhinehessen
Rheinland .... Rhineland
Rheinland-Pfalz .... Rhineland-Palatinate
Rom .... Rome
Rotes Meer .... Red Sea
Rumänien .... Romania
Rußland .... Russia
Saargebiet .... Saar(land)
Sachsen .... Saxony
Sachsen-Anhalt .... Saxony-Anhalt
Sächsische Schweiz .... Saxon
Switzerland
Schlesien .... Silesia
Schottland .... Scotland
Schwaben .... Swabia
Schwäbische Alb .... Swabian Jura
Schwarzes Meer .... Black Sea
Schweden .... Sweden
Schweiz .... Switzerland

Schweizer Mittelland .... Swiss Midlands
Serbien .... Serbia
Siebenbürgen .... Transylvania
Skandinavien .... Scandinavia
Slowakei .... Slovakia
Slowenien .... Slovenia
Sowjetunion .... Soviet Union
Spanien .... Spain
Stettin .... Szczecin, Stettin
Straßburg .... Strasbourg
Südamerika .... South America
Süddeutschland ...... South(ern) Germany
Sudetenland .... Sudetenland,
the Sudeten
Südeuropa .... South(ern) Europe
Südpolarmeer .... Antarctic Ocean
Südsee .... South Pacific,
South Seas
Südtirol .... South Tyrol
Suezkanal .... Suez Canal
Teutoburger Wald .... Teutoburg Forest
Themse .... Thames
Thüringen .... Thuringia
Thüringer Wald .... Thuringian Forest
Tirol .... Tyrol
Totes Meer .... Dead Sea
Trient .... Trento
Tschechoslowakei .... Czechoslovakia
Türkei .... Turkey
Ungarn .... Hungary
Union der Sozia- .... Union of Soviet
listischen Sowjet-   Socialist
republiken   Republics
Unterfranken .... Lower Franconia
Ural .... Urals
Venedig .... Venice
Vereinigtes Königreich .... United
(von Großbritannien .... Kingdom (of
und Nordirland)   Great Britain and
Northern Ireland)
Vereinigte Staaten .... United States
(von Amerika)   (of America)
Vierwaldstätter See .... Lake Lucerne
Vogesen .... Vosges (Mountains)
Vorderasien .... Middle (or Near) East
Vorpommern .... WesternPomerania
Weichsel .... Vistula
Weißrußland .... B(y)elorussia,
White Russia

Westdeutschland ...... Western Germany,
       Bundesrepublik
       Deutschland
Westeuropa .... West(ern) Europe
Westfalen .... Westphalia
Westfriesische Inseln .... West Frisians
Westpreußen .... West Prussia
Wien .... Vienna
Wolga .... Volga
Zürich .... Zurich

Source: *Langenscheidts Großes Schulwörter-*
buch Deutsch-Englisch, Langenscheidt, Berlin,
1996.

PLACE NAMES, GEOGRAPHIC AREAS

✦**Allgäu:** Region in southern Germany
along the Austrian border from Lake
Constance (*Bodensee*) to Füssen in
Bavaria, Germany.
✦**Alsace:** Region of eastern France along
the southwestern border of Germany.
Called *Elsaß* in German
✦**(Das) Alte Land:** Marshy region of
northwestern Germany between the North
Sea and Hamburg.
✦**Altmark:** Region around Magdeburg,
Saxony-Anhalt, in the eastern part of
Germany.
✦**Banat:** Area around the Tisza River in
Romania.
✦**Batschka:** Part of Croatia and Hungary.
✦**Bergisches Land:** Region of Germany
east of the Rhine River in the Ruhr district
northeast of Cologne (*Köln*).
✦**Bessarabia:** Region of northeastern
Romania along the southwestern border
of the Ukraine.
✦**Black Forest:** See Schwarzwald.
✦**Bohemia:** Western portion of the Czech
Republic bounded by Germany (to the
west and north), Poland (to the east), and
Austria (to the south). Called *Böhmen* in
German.
✦**Brandenburg:** Region east of the Oder
River in the western part of Poland along

the German state of Brandenburg.
✦**Breisgau:** (1) Region of northern Baden-
Württemberg, Germany, south of
Heidelberg and lying between the Rhine
River and the Neckar River; (2) region of
the Black Forest between the Rhine River
and France around Freiburg, Germany.
✦**Bukovina:** Region of northern Romania
along the borders of the Ukraine and
Moldava.
✦**Burgenland:** Region of southeastern
Austria bordering and extending into
western Hungary.
✦**Byelorussia:** Region in Eastern Europe
between Lithuania, Poland, Russia and the
Ukraine. Also known as White Ruthenia.
✦**Carinthia:** Region of southern Austria
along the northern borders of Italy and
Slovenia.
✦**Carniola:** Region of Slovenia just south
of Croatia.
✦**Courland:** Region of western Latvia
along the Baltic coast. Known in German
as Kourland.
✦**Dobrogea:** See Dobrudscha.
✦**Dobrudscha:** Portion of eastern
Romania between the Black Sea and the
Danube River.
✦**Egerland:** Region of the Czech Republic
along the eastern border of Bavaria,
Germany.
✦**Eifel:** Mountainous southwestern part
of Northrhine-Westphalia, Germany, east
of Belgium and Luxembourg.
✦**Elsaß:** See Alsace.
✦**Emsland:** Region of northern Germany,
south of the North Sea, west of Bremen,
and along the eastern border of the
Netherlands.
✦**Ermland:** Region of Poland southeast
of Danzig.
✦**Erzgebirge:** Mountainous region along
southeastern Saxony, Germany, and
northwestern Bohemia, Czech Republic.
✦**Franconia:** Region of northern Bavaria,
Germany. Divided into Unterfranken (the
northernmost part), Mittelfranken or
Mainfranken (the middle part), and
Oberfranken (the southern part). Called

Franken in German.
◆**Franken:** See Franconia.
◆**Galicia:** Region around the upper part of the Dniester River. The western part of Galicia is in Poland and the eastern part in the Ukraine.
◆**Gorizia:** Western portion of Slovenia along the Adriatic Sea north of Trieste, Italy.
◆ **Gottschee:** Ethnic German area of northern Slovenia between Italy (on the west), Austria (on the north), Hungary (on the northeast), and Croatia (on the south).
◆**Great Poland:** The heartland of Poland.
◆**Grenzmark:** Region of eastern Pomerania, just north of Posen and now part of Poland.
◆**Gross Polen:** See Great Poland.
◆ **Haardt:** Region of the Rhineland-Palatinate, Germany, between the Rhine River at Worms, Germany, and extending west into Alsace, France.
◆ **Halich Ruthenia:** Prairie-like region along the Dniester River, Ukraine. Also known as Little Russia and better known as Galicia. Ukrainians lived in eastern Galicia and Poles in the western part known as Little Poland.
◆ **Harz:** Mountainous region of north-central Germany east of the Weser-bergland.
◆**Harzgebirge:** Mountainous region along the northern boundaries of Lower Saxony, Saxony-Anhalt, and Thuringia, Germany.
◆ **Hauerland:** Region of south central Slovakia along the northern border of Hungary.
◆ **Hegau:** Region of southwestern Germany between Lake Constance (Bodensee), the Black Forest, and the Danube and Rhine rivers.
◆**Hunsrück:** Mountainous region of the Rhineland-Palatinate state, Germany, west of the Rhine River, and north of the Saarland.
◆**Ingermanland:** Region of Russia, east of Estonia and Latvia, west of St. Petersburg, Russia.
◆**Ingria:** See Ingermanland.

◆**Karinthia:** Region of Austria south of Salzburg. Known in German as *Kärnten*.
◆**Kärnten:** See Karinthia
◆**Kashubia:** Region of Poland south and west of Danzig.
◆**Kourland:** See Courland
◆**Kraichgau:** Region east of the Rhine River between the Black Forest and the Odenwald in northern Baden-Württemberg, Germany
◆**Krain:** See Carniola.
◆**Kujawien:** Region of Poland along the Vistula River around Thorn. Also known as *Kuyavia.*
◆**Kulmerland:** Region of southwestern Poland between Kulm and Thorn.
◆**Kurpie:** Region in Russia around the Narew River, northeast of Warsaw.
◆ **Lauenburg:** Region of southern Schleswig-Holstein, Germany, north of Hamburg and west of the Elbe River
◆**Lausitz:** Region of eastern Germany between Meissen and Berlin and the Elbe and Bobr rivers.
◆**Lithuania:** An independent nation along the eastern Baltic coast between Poland, Russia and Latvia.
◆ **Little Poland:** Region along the upper Vistula River near Crakow, Poland. (See Halich Ruthenia.)
◆**Little Russia:** See Halich Ruthenia.
◆**Livland:** Region of eastern Latvia and southern Estonia.
◆ **Livonia:** Region along the Baltic coast, now known as Latvia.
◆ **Lorraine:** Region of eastern France northwest of Alsace, south of Luxembourg, and west of Germany. Known in German as *Lothringen.*
◆**Lothringen:** See Lorraine.
◆**Lusatia:** See Lausitz.
◆**Mähren:** See Moravia
◆**Markgräflerland:** Region of the Black Forest in Germany, west of the Rhine River between Basel, Switzerland, and Freiburg, Baden-Württemberg, Germany
◆**Masuria:** Region of northeastern Poland near Lithuania.
◆ **Mazovia:** Region of central Poland

between the Warthe and Vistula rivers.
◆**Memel:** Coastal region of Lithuania along the Baltic Sea.
◆**Mittelmark:** Region of Brandenburg, Germany, west of the Oder River.
◆**Moldavia:** Region lying between the Ukraine and Romania, now the independent state of Moldava.
◆**Moravia:** Region of the Czech Republic between Poland (to the north and east), the Slovak Republic (to the east and south), and Austria (to the south). Known in German as *Mähren.*
◆**Münsterland:** Region of Germany east of the Rhine River, north of the Ruhr district, and bordering the Netherlands.
◆**Neumark:** Region east of the Oder River in Brandenburg and now part of Poland.
◆**Oberland:** See Oberschwaben.
◆**Oberland:** Lake region south of Königsberg, Poland, along the Polish/Russian border.
◆**Oberpfalz:** Region of eastern Bavaria, Germany, along the Czech border.
◆**Oberschwaben:** Region of southern Germany between the Danube River, the Black Forest, Lake Constance, and the Allgäu.
◆**Palatinate:** See Pfalz.
◆**Pfalz:** (1) Region west of the Rhine River, today the southern part of the state of Rhineland-Palatinate, Germany. For most of the 19th century it was part of Bavaria, Germany; (2) Region in eastern Bavaria, Germany, known as the *Oberpfalz* (Upper Palatinate).
◆**Podhale:** Region of southern Poland just north of the Carpathian Mountains.
◆**Podlachia:** Region around Bretst-Litovsk, divided between eastern Poland and eastern Belarus. Known in German as *Podlachien.*
◆**Podlachien:** See Podlachia.
◆**Podlasie:** Region around the Bug and Narew rivers, with the western part in central Poland the eastern part in Byelorussia.
◆**Podolia:** Region between the Dniester and Boh Rivers, with the western part in central Poland and the eastern part in Byelorussia.
◆**Polesie:** Swampy region around the Pripet Marshes in southern Byelorussia.
◆**Pomerania:** See Pommern.
◆**Pomerelia:** See Pommerellen.
◆**Pommerellen:** Region in Poland south of Danzig.
◆**Pommern:** Region in northwestern Poland along the Baltic Sea. Often called Pomerania.
◆**Posen:** Region of northwestern-central Poland, just south of Pomerania.
◆**Red Ruthenia:** See Ruthenia.
◆**Rheinpfalz:** See Pfalz.
◆**Ruthenia:** Region of the Ukraine, also known as Red Ruthenia.
◆**Salzkammergut:** Region of Austria east of Salzburg.
◆**Samogita:** Region of northwestern Lithuania.
◆**Sauerland:** Region of Germany east of the Rhine River, between the Ruhr and Sieg Rivers. Not to be confused with Hauerland (which see).
◆**Schlesien:** See Silesia.
◆**Schwarzwald:** Mountainous region of southwestern Germany, west of the Rhine River along the borders of eastern France and northern Switzerland. Better known in America as the Black Forest.
◆**Samgallen:** Region in Latvia along the borders of Lithuania and Belarus.
◆**Samland:** Area of East Prussia, north of Ermland and south of Memel, around Königsburg.
◆**Semegalia:** See Semgallen
◆**Siebenburgen:** See Transylvania
◆**Silesia:** Southern border region of Poland, along the border of the Slovak Republic. Known in German as *Schlesien.*
◆**Slovonia:** Eastern region of Croatia, south of Hungary, west of Vojvodina, and north of Bosnia.
◆**Slovakia:** An independent nation, the Slovak Republic, east of the Czech Republic, south of Poland, west of the Ukraine, and north of Hungary.
◆**Srem:** See Syrmien.

◆**Steiermark:** See Styria

◆**Styria:** Region of southwestern Austria along the northern border of Slovenia. Known in German as the *Steiermark.*

◆ **Sudetenland:** Region of northern, western, and southern Czech Republic, bordered by Germany, Austria and Poland.

◆**Syrmien:** Region south of the Danube River northwest of Belgrade. Known in German as Srem.

◆**Taunus:** Hilly region of Germany in southeastern Hessen, north of the Main River.

◆**Taurida:** See Taurien.

◆**Taurien:** Region of the Crimea, Ukraine, along the Black Sea.

◆**Terek:** Region of Russia along the Terek River near the Caspian Sea.

◆**Tirol:** Region of western Austria south of Germany and north of Slovenia.

◆**Transnistria:** See Transnistrien.

◆**Transnistrien:** German name for the region of southwestern Ukraine between the Bug and Dniester Rivers.

◆ **Transylvania:** Region of central Romania. Known in German as Siebenburgen.

◆**Uckermark:** Region of northeastern Brandenburg, Germany, and eastern Mecklenburg, Vorpommern, Poland.

◆**Unterfranken:** See Franconia

◆ **Vogtland:** Region of southwestern Saxony, Germany.

◆ **Volhynia:** Region of northwestern Ukraine, south of Belarus, and east of Poland.

◆**Voralberg:** Westernmost part of Austria, south of Germany, and north of Italy and Switzerland.

◆**Walachia:** Region of southern Romania.

◆**Warmia:** See Samland

◆**Warthegau:** Region along the Warthe River, between Posen and Warsaw in west-central Poland.

◆**Wasgau:** Region of Germany, west of the Rhine River, along the eastern French border between the Vosges Mountains and the Haardt area of Germany.

◆ **Weizacker:** Region of southwestern

Pomerania along the Brandenburg, Germany, border, now partly in Poland, and mostly in Germany.

◆**Weserbergland:** Mountainous region of northern Germany along the Weser River, west of the Harz Mountains and east of the Teutoberger Forest.

◆**Westerwald:** Region of Germany east of the Rhine River and covering parts of Hessen and Rhineland-Palatinate.

◆**Westrich:** Region of Germany east of the Rhine River and covering parts of Hessen and Rhineland-Palatinate.

◆ **Wetterau:** Region of Germany in Hessen, north of the Main River above Frankfurt/Main.

◆**White Ruthenia:** See Byelorussia

Reprinted by permission of John W. Heisey. Originally published in *Antique Week,* Knightstown, IN 46148

HISTORICAL REGIONS OF GERMANY

Historical name	Present state/ country location
Allgäu	Bayern, Baden-Württemberg
Altes Land	Niedersachsen
Altmark	Sachsen-Anhalt
Ammerland	Niedersachsen
Angeln	Schleswig-Holstein
Anhalt	Sachsen-Anhalt
Baar	Baden-Württemberg
Baden	Baden-Württemberg
Baiern	Bavaria
Bergisches Land	Nordrhein-Westfalen
Böhmen	Czechia
Börde	Sachsen-Anhalt
Brandenburg	Brandenburg
Breisgau	Baden-Württemberg
Chiemgaj	Bayern
Diethmarschen	Schleswig-Holstein
Donau-Moos	Bayern
Donau-Ried	Bayern
Egerland	Czechia
Eichsfeld	Thüringen

Eiderstedt .... Thüringen	Saarland .... Saarland
Emsland .... Niedersachsen	Schlesien .... Poland
Gäuboden .... Bayern	Schleswig .... Schleswig-Holstein
Goldene Aue .... Sachsen	Schönbuch .... Baden-Württemberg
Grabfeld .... Bayern	Schwaben .... Bayern
Grenzmark .... Poland	Stormarn .... Schleswig-Holstein,
Hadeln .... Niedersachsen	.... Hamburg
Havelland .... Brandenburg	Stroh-Gäu .... Baden-Württemberg
Hessen .... Hessen	Sudetenland .... Czechia
Hohenloher Land ... Baden-Württemberg	Thüringen .... Thüringen
Holledau (Hallertau) .... Bayern	Tucheler Heide .... Poland
Holstein .... Schleswig-Holstein	Uckermark .... Brandenburg
Isarwinkel .... Bayern	Unterfranken .... Bayern
Jeverland .... Niedersachsen	Vogtland .... Thüringen
Kehdingen .... Nidersachsen	Vorpommern Mecklenburg-Vorpommern
Kraichgau .... Baden-Württemberg	Wagrien .... Schleswig-Holstein
Kulmerland .... Poland	Werdenfelser Land .... Bayern
Lüneburger Heide .... Niedersachsen	Westfalen .... Nordrhein-Westfalen
Margräfler Land ..... Baden-Württemberg	Westpreußen .... Poland
Masuren .... Poland	Wetterau .... Hessen
Mecklenburg Mechlenburg-Vorpommern	Württemberg .... Baden-Württemberg
Memelland .... Lithuania	
Mittelfranken .... Bayern	**Source:** Compiled by Rainer Thumshirn, of
Mittelmark .... Lithuania	Heimstetten, Germany
Münsterland .... Nordrhein-Westfalen	
Natangen ....Russia	
Neumark .... Poland	**MOUNTAIN RANGES**
Nieder-Lausitz .... Brandenburg	**IN AND AROUND GERMANY**
Nordfriesland .... Schleswig-Holstein	
Oberes Gäu .... Baden-Württemberg	Locations of mountain ranges listed in
Oberbayern .... Bayern	the left column are indicated in the right
Oberfranken .... Bayern	column by a nearby major town or city.
Ober-Lausitz .... Sachsen, Poland	**KEY:**
Oberpfalz .... Bayern	s = south of
Oberschlesien .... Poland	w = west of
Ostfriesland .... Niedersachsen	n = north of
Ostpreußem .... Poland, Russia	e = east of
Pfalz .... Rheinland-Pfalz	sw = southwest of
Pomesanien .... Poland	se = southeast of
Pommern ... Mecklenburg-Vorpommern,	nw = northwest of
Poland	sw = southwest of
Posen .... Poland	Adlergebirge ....sw Breslau
Prignitz .... Mecklenburg-Vorpommern	Allgäuer Alpen .... s Oberstdorf
Rangau .... Bayern	Alpen, Allgäuer- .... s Oberstdorf
Rheinhessen .... Rheinland-Pfalz	Alpen, Bayerische- .... s München
Ried .... Hessen	Alpen, Salzburger- .... s Salzburg
Ries .... Bayern	Altvater Gebirge .... s Breslau
Rodgau .... Hessen	Ardennen .... nw Luxemburg
Ruppertigau .... Bayern	Bayerische Alpen .... s München

Girl from the Gutach Valley

Bayerischer Wald .... se Regensburg
Beskiden .... s Krakau
Böhmerwald .... e Regensburg
Deister .... sw Hannover
Donnersberg .... ne Kaiserslautern
Eggegebirge .... e Paderborn
Eifel .... sw Bonn
Elbinger Höhe .... e Danzig
Elbsandsteingebirge .... s Dresden
Erzgebirge .... s Chemnitz
Eulengebirge .... sw Breslau
Fichtelgebirge .... e Bayreuth
Fläming .... sw Berlin
Fränkische Alb .... se Nürnberg
(Fränkischer Jura)
Fränkische Schweiz .... sw Bayreuth
Frankenhöhe .... e Rothenburg a. d. T.
Frankenwald .... e Coburg
Gesenke .... s Breslau
Glatzer Schneegebirge .... s Breslau
Haar .... e Dortmund
Haßberge .... nw Bamberg
Harz .... ne Göttingen
Hessisches Bergland .... s Kassel
Heuscheuer .... sw Breslau
Hohe Tatra .... s Krakau

Hohes Kenn .... w Bonn
Hunsrück .... s Koblenz
Isergebirge .... se Dresden
Kaiserstuhl .... nw Freiburg
Kaiserwald .... e Eger
Katzengebirge .... n Breslau
Kernsdorfer Höhe .... sw Allenstein
Lausitzer Gebirge .... se Dresden
Oberpfälzer Wald .... ne Regensburg
Odenwald .... ne Heidelberg
Pfälzer Wald .... s Kaiserslautern
Rheinisches Schiefergebirge .... e Köln
Rhön .... e Fulda
Reichensteiner Gebirge .... s Breslau
Riesengebirge .... sw Breslau
Rothaargebirge .... e Bonn
Sächsisches Bergland .... s Zwickau
Salzburger Alpen .... s Salzburg
Schwarzwald .... sw Stuttgart
Schwabische Alb .... s Stuttgart
(Schwäbischer Jura)
Solling .... nw Göttingen
Spessart .... se Frankfurt
Steigerwald .... w Bamberg
Süntel .... sw Hannover
Tarnowitzer Höhen .... n Gleiwitz
Taunus .... nw Frankfurt
Teutoburger Wald .... w Bielefeld
Thüringer Wald .... sw Erfurt
Turmbert .... sw Danzig
Vogelsberg .... ne Frankfurt
Vogesen (Fr. Vosges) .... w Straßburg
Wesergebirge (Weser- .... sw Hannover
bergland)
Westerwald .... ne Koblenz
Zobten .... sw Breslau

Source: Compiled by Rainer Thumshirn of
Heimstetten, Germany

LARGEST INDUSTRIAL FIRMS IN THE FEDERAL REPUBLIC OF GERMANY, 1993

1.**Daimler-Benz AG**, Stuttgart (automotive, electrical engineering, aerospace)
2. **Siemens AG**, Munich (electrical engineering)

3.**Volkswagen AG**, Wolfsburg (automotive)
4. **Veba AG**, Düsseldorf (energy, chemicals)
5. **Hoechst AG**, Frankfurt (chemicals, pharmaceuticals)
6. **RWE AG,** Essen (energy, building)
7. Bayer AG, Leverkusen (chemicals, pharmaceuticals)
8. **BASF AG,** Ludwigshafen (chemicals, pharmaceuticals)

9.**Thyssen AG**, Duisburg (steel, machinery)
10. **Bosch GmbH**, Stuttgart (electrical, engineering)
11. **Bayerische Motorenwerke**, Munich (authomotive)
12. **Mannesmann AG**, Düsseldorf (mechanical engineering, industrial installations, etc.)

Source: *Facts about Germany*, Societäts-Verlag, 1995

Chapter 10

American military sources

AMERICAN INVOLVEMENT IN WARS

Wars related to American colonization

1701-13: Queen Anne's War — between England and French/Indians. Britain gains control of French Acadia (modern Nova Scotia), Newfoundland, and the region around Hudson Bay.

1744-48: King George's War — between England and France, fought for control of North American colonial territories, but ending without significant territorial changes.

1754-63: French and Indian War — between England and France over colonial territories in North America), resulting in Great Britain's conquest of French Canada.

American national wars and engagements

1775-83: American Revolution — American forces against Great Britain allied with France and Spain (April 19, 1775 - April 11, 1783)

1791-94: Whiskey Rebellion — in Pennsylvania, near Uniontown; farmers protest whiskey tax

1812-14:War of 1812 — between United States and Great Britain (June 1812 to December 1814)

1832: Black Hawk War — Indian tribes push west across the Mississippi (began April 26, ended September21).

1835: Toledo War — Ohio-Michigan boundary dispute

1846-48: Mexican-American War — between United States and Mexico, resulting in United States' annexation of Mexican territory, comprising present United States Southwest and California

1861-65: Civil War — War Between the States (began April 12, 1861, ended April 9, 1865)

1898: Spanish-American War — United States defeats Spanish colonial forces in Philippines and Cuba (began April 25, ended July 17).

1899-1901: Philippine-American War (United States involvement) — outgrowth of the Philippine War of Independence (began February 4, 1899, ended March 23,1901)

1917-18: World War I (United States involvement) — United States enters the war April 6, 1917

1941-45: World War II (United States involvement) — United States enters the war December 8, 1941.

1950-53: Korean War — United States intervention following North Korea's attack on South Korea (began June 30, 1950, ended July 27, 1953)

1964-73: Vietnam War (United States involvement) — American participation following the 1964 attack in the Gulf of Tonkin (began February 1965, ended January 1973)

Sources

♦Bruce Wetterau, *The New York Public Library Book of Chronologies*. Prentice Hall, NY 1990.

♦ *The World Almanac and Book of Facts*. World Almanac, New York, 1993.

♦David Brownstone and Irene Franck, *Timelines of War: A Chronology of Warfare from 100,000 BC to the Present*. Little, Brown and Company, Boston 1994.

AMERICAN MILITARY RECORDS

Among the German immigrants who arrived in the mid- and later-nineteenth century waves of immigration were many who served in United States military units during those years and on into the early twentieth century. For this reason it is worth searching military records, especially for the vital records and notations of places of origin that may reside there. The following information is excerpted from a publication of the National Archives and Records Administration concerning its military service records:

United States military service

Records relating to service in the United States Regular Army by officers, 1789-1917, and enlisted men, 1789-1912, during peace and war are in the National Archives Building.

Records relating to service of Regular Army enlisted men include registers of enlistments, muster rolls of regular units, and medical and other records. Registers of enlistments show for each man his name, age, place of birth, date and place of enlistment, occupation at enlistment, regiment and company, physical description, and date and reasons for discharge.

Pension files

Records of pensions granted or applied for under laws providing for military pensions are in the National Archives Building. The pension files relate to claims based on service in the Army, Navy, or Marine Corps between 1775 and 1916.

Documents submitted in support of some pension claims include affidavits attesting to service, pages from family bibles, and copies of records of birth, marriage, and death.

For service in the Civil War and later, a pension file may also include Bureau of Pensions questionnaires sent out in 1898 and 1915, which contain genealogical information.

Information in the Records

Both pension and bounty land warrant application files usually show name, rank, and military unit of the veteran and period of his service. If a veteran applied, the file usually shows his age or date of birth and place of residence at the time he applied, and sometimes his place of death. If his widow applied, the file shows her age and place of residence, her maiden name, the date and place of their marriage, and the date and place of his birth. When application was made on behalf of minor children or by hears of the veteran, their names and sometimes their ages or dates of birth are shown.

Bounty Land Warrant
Application Files

Bounty land warrant application files relate to claims based on wartime service between 1775 and March 3, 1855. These as well as pension files are recorded at the

National Archives.

Both pension and bounty land warrant application files usually show name, rank, and military unit of the veteran and period of his service.

If a veteran applied, the file usually shows his age or date of birth and place of residence at the time he applied, and sometimes his place of death. If his widow applied, the file shows her age and place of residence, her maiden name, the date and place of their marriage, and the date and place of his birth.

When application was made on behalf of minor children or by heirs of the veteran, their names and sometimes their ages or dates of birth are shown.

Availability of unrestricted records

Photocopies of unrestricted original documents are available for a fee. The National Archives and Records Administration will conduct a search for the documents if, in addition to the full name of the serviceman, the war in which he served, and the State from which he entered service, an inquirer can supply other identifying information.

Ordering unrestricted records from the National Archives

Requests for copies of veterans records housed in the National Archives Building should be submitted on National Archives Trust Fund (NATV) Form 80, Order form, Copies of Veterans Records, which will be furnished free on request.

The form should be filled out according to the instructions and with as much information as possible and submitted to the National Archives and Records Administration, 8th and Pennsylvania Avenue, NW, Washington, DC 20408.

Source: "Military Service Records in the National Archives of the United States," General Information Leaflet, No. 7, rev. 1985 (with an address correction supplied by NARA, July 1996), National Archives and Records Administration, Washington, DC 20408

HESSIAN SOLDIERS IN THE AMERICAN REVOLUTION

Background: The number of German mercenary troops who remained in America after serving Great Britain in the American Revolution (1775-1783) is estimated at between 7,000 and 12,000 of the approximate 30,000 who were sent to North America. These Hessians comprised about 30 percent of the British forces.

"Hessian" troops in America: All German mercenaries who fought in the revolutionary war came to be referred to as "Hessians," probably because the largest contingent of troops — 15 infantry regiments, four grenadier battalions, one courier corps, one artillery corps, totaling about 15,000 men — was from Hessen-Kassel. Others came from such small kingdoms as Braunschweig, Ansbach-Bayreuth, Hesse-Hanau, Anhalt-Zerbst, and Waldeck.

The majority of the German troops arrived in August 1776. Hessians were involved in battles between 1776 and 1783. Many of the surviving troops were returned to their homelands in 1783.

Availability of records: The microfilm of *Hessische Truppen im amerikanischen Unabhängigkeitskrieg (*Hessian Troops in the American War for Independence*)* lists valuable information about individual German mercenaries. See FHL films 1,320,516 items 6-7 (A-L), and 1,320,542 items 5-6 (M-Z). (The acronym HETRINA is taken from the German name of the collection: <u>He</u>ssische <u>Tr</u>uppen <u>im [in dem]</u> <u>a</u>merikanischen Unabhängigkeitskrieg. Note: In German, im = in dem.)

Content of HETRINA microfilm: The following key is supplied with the HETRINA records, the information from which is arranged in 11 columns (the key for reading the data is shown here verbatim) —

Column 1: No. of unit in computer list
Column 2: Family name

Column 3: First name
Column 4: Yr. of birth (o/o=no statement of age)
Column 5: Place of origin (historical place names after slash; names in parentheses are aids to location)
Column 6: Code no. of towns with abbr. for the *Land* (+ = town in Hessen-Kassel)
Column 7: Rank (see list of abbreviations)
Column 8: Unit (regiment or battalion and company)
Column 9: Categories of presentation (see list)
Column 10: Date of entry in unit books (mo. and yr. in numbers)
Column 11: Archive code of the source

The researcher with a German ancestor born between 1735 and 1762 (approximately) may want to look into the possibility of descent from a Hessian soldier. The researcher working on an unusual German surname (not necessarily known to belong to a German mercenary), may want to look for that name in HETRINA. Because "place of origin" (see column 5 above) may have been the soldier's place of birth, it could be useful to search church records in the home village of a same-name Hessian soldier to see if the surname is prevalent there. Once in a while a long-shot like this can pay off.

References
◆Eckhart G. Franz, compiler. *Hessische Truppen im amerikanischen Unabhängigkeitskrieg (HETRINA).* [Hessian Troops in the American Revolution] Marburg, Germany: Archivschule. 1971-1976, 1987. 3 vols. (FHL book 943 M2mg; see film numbers above).
◆ Don Heinrich Tolzmann. *German-Americans in the American Revolution: Henry Melchior Muhlenberg Richards' History.* 1908. Reprinted by Heritage Books, Bowie, MD, 1992
◆Clifford Neal Smith, *Cumulative Surname Index and Soundex to Monographs 1 through 12 of the German-American Genealogical Research Series.* McNeal, Ariz.: Westland Publishing, 1983. (FHL

book 973 W2smn no. 13)
◆"Die Hessische Soldaten – The Hessian Soldiers," by William S. Cramer, *German American Genealogy,* Spring 1991, p. 23.

JOHANNES SCHWALM HISTORICAL ASSOCIATION

The Johannes Schwalm Historical Association researches, collects and disseminates data relating to German auxiliaries to the British Crown who fought in the Revolutionary War and their descendants.

All books and material owned by the Association are available for research and examination by the public at the Gratz Historical Society, Gratz, Pennsylvania, which is the official depository of the Association's records. JSHA issues a color certificate to authenticate a person's ties to Hessian forebearers.

Mailing address: Johannes Schwalm Historical Association, P.O. Box 99, Pennsauken, NJ 08110. ◆

AMERICAN MILITARY INDEX

The Military Index of the FamilySearch program of the Family History Library is available through *FamilySearch* at local Family History Centers and at the Family History Library in Salt Lake City. It contains death records of those who died in the Korean (1950-1957) and Vietnam (1957-1975) conflicts.Other military records are added to the program as they become available. See the publication, *FamilySearch: Military Index,* a one-page summary available through the Family History Library (Series FS, No. 2, 1991).

UNITED STATES DRAFT REGISTRATIONS (World War I)

If a male ancestor (whether native born

or alien) was born between 1873 and 1900, and lived in the United States in 1917 and 1918, his draft registration card may well be one of the 24 million collected by the Selective Service System during World War I. These draft registrations include German males who immigrated to the United States in the massive immigration period of the 1880s.

These draft records identify about 44 percent of the entire U.S. male population in 1918 and contain information important to researchers of German immigrants and their descendants.

The records do not reveal whether the registrants actually served in the military (many were not called into service), but the records do provide important information relative to the man's birthplace, his citizen status, and much more.

Registration dates

There were three World War I registrations in 1917 and 1918:

First registration: June 5, 1917, for all men between the ages of 21 and 31.

Second registration: June 5, 1918, for those who turned 21 after 5 June 1917; a supplemental registration was held on August 24, 1918 for those turning age 21 after June 5, 1918.

Third registration: September 12, 1918, for men age 18 through 45.

Record content

The contents of the three registration questionnaires are summarized below. The numbers following each item identify which of the three registration forms (from the first, second, and third registrations, listed above) asked for a response to the item.

Name: 1,2,3
Address of home: 1,2,3
Age in years: 3
Birth date: 1,2,3
Birthplace (town, state, country): 1,2,3
Father's birthplace: 2
Exemption claimed: 1
Married or Single: 1
Military Service (rank, branch, years,

nation): 1
Naturalized: 1,3
Native born: 1,2,3
Citizen by father's naturalization: 3
Alien: 1
Alien with declared intent: 1,3
Alien without declared intent: 3
Alien nationality: 1,2,3
Occupation: 1,3
Employer's name: 1,2,3
Place of business or employment: 1,2,3
Physical description: 1,2,3
Race: 1,2
Race (white, black, oriental, Indian citizen or non-white) 3
Relatives solely dependent (wife, sister, etc.): 1
Nearest relative's name: 2,3
Address of nearest relative: 2,3

National Archive records

Draft registration cards are part of Record Group 163 of the National Archives. Searches are made for a small fee as long as the full name and city and county of residence are known. For certain large cities a home address is needed (city directories may be helpful here).

A complete home address is needed for these cities: Los Angeles, San Francisco, Washington (DC), Atlanta, Chicago, Indianapolis, Louisville (KY), New Orleans, Baltimore, Boston, Minneapolis, St. Paul, Kansas City, St. Louis, Jersey City, Newark, Albany, Buffalo, New York City, Syracuse, Cincinnati, Cleveland, Luzerne County (PA), Philadelphia, Pittsburgh, Providence, Seattle, and Milwaukee.

To obtain a search form, write to
National Archives — Southeast Region
1557 St. Joseph Avenue
East Point, GA 30344.

Family History Library records

The Family History Library Catalog (1995 editions) lists 3,680 microfilms for draft cards, arranged by states, from Alabama through Tennessee, and including Wisconsin. (Look for this list of states to expand.) Microfilm readers with a 65X lens are recommended for viewing these microfilms.

The film numbers may be found in the microfiche Locality catalog under United States — Military Records — World War I, 1914-1918. In the Author-Title microfiche catalog, the records are listed as United States, Selective Service System, World War I Selective Service System draft registration cards, 1917-1918.

The records are arranged alphabetically first by state; then alphabetically by county or city; then for each draft board by an alphabetical list of the names of registrants. An individual might not have registered where he resided, but instead where it was most convenient for him on the particular day of the draft registration.

Available on microfilm is *Lists of World War I Draft Board Maps* (FHL film 1498803) providing maps of certain U.S. cities: Albany, Allegheny (PA), Atlanta, Baltimore, Birmingham, Boston, Bridgeport (CT), Bronx, Brooklyn, Buffalo, Chicago, Cincinnati, Cleveland, Dallas, Denver, hartford, Indianapolis, Jersey City, Kansas City, Los Angeles, Louisville (KY) Luzerne Co. (PA), Manhattan, Milwaukee, Minneapolis, New Haven, New Orleans, Philadelphia, Pittsburgh, Queens, Reading (PA)s, Richmond (NY), Rochester, St. Paul, San Diego, Schenectady, Seattle, Syracuse, Toledo, Washington (DC), and Westmoreland Co. (PA).

The Family History Library keeps a notebook with selective service addresses for major cities (not on microfilm or fiche). It lists the draft boards and their number and addresses for Allegheny (PA), Baltimore, Boston area, Buffalo, Chicago area, Cincinnati, Cleveland, Denver, Detroit, Indianapolis, Jersey City, Kansas City, Los Angeles, Luzerne Co. (PA), Milwaukee, Minneapolis, New Orleans, New York City, Newark, Philadelphia, Pittsburgh, Portland, Providence, St. Louis, St. Paul, San Francisco, and Seattle.

Source: "U.S. Selective Service System: Draft Registration Records, 1917-1918," by Jayare Roberts, A.G., *Genealogical Journal*. Utah Genealogical Association. Vol.24, No. 2. 1996.

GERMAN UNITS IN THE AMERICAN CIVIL WAR

German Units: Companies and regiments in the Union Army, American Civil War

NEW YORK
•5th New York Militia
•7th New York Regiment, Steuben Rifles
•8th New York Infantry, First German Rifles
•20th New York Infantry, United Turner Regiment
•29th New York Regiment, Astor Rifles
•41st New York Regiment, DeKalb Regiment
•45th New York Regiment, German Rifles No. 5 or Platt Deutsch Regiment
•46th New York Regiment, Frémont Regiment
•52nd New York Regiment, Sigel Rifles
•54th New York Regiment, Schwarze Jäger
•58th New York Regiment, First Morgan Rifles (part German)
•68th New York Volunteers, Cameron Rifles (part German)
•103rd New York Regiment, German Rifles No. 3 (one elite company composed entirely of former German officers)
•119th New York Regiment (one-third German)
•149th New York Regiment (part German)
•190th New York Regiment (part German)
Artillery:
•Brickel's artillery, 1st New York Independent Battalion Light Artillery
•Battery Sigel in the 46th New York Regiment (composed of experienced Germans)
•15th New York Heavy Artillery
•Schirmer's battery, 2nd Independent New York Battery
•Von Sturmfel's battery, Light Artillery Company A, later 13th Independent Battery
•Wiedrich's battery, 1st Regiment Light Artillery, Battery I

Cavalry:
•Dickel's mounted rifles, 4th Regiment Cavalry (largely German)
•1st Regiment New York Cavalry (four companies German)
NEW ENGLAND
Infantry:
•1st Regiment Connecticut Volunteer Infantry, Company B
•6th Regiment Connecticut Volunteer Infantry, Company H (from Bridgeport, Meriden, and New York. There was also Company B from New Haven, Norwich, and Waterbury under Captain Klein.)
•11th Connecticut Regiment, company under Captain Mögling
•17th Massachusetts Regiment, one company recruited in Boston (one-third German)
•29th Massachusetts Regiment, one company (one-third German)
PENNSYLVANIA
Infantry:
•27th Pennsylvania Regiment
•73rd Regiment, Pennsylvania Troops
•74th Pennsylvania Regiment
•75th Pennsylvania Regiment
•98th Pennsylvania Regiment, originally the 21st Männerchor Rifle Guards (Home guards)
NEW JERSEY
Cavalry:
•3rd New Jersey Cavalry, from Hoboken
Artillery:
•Battery A, 1st New Jersey Artillery
•Batteries B and C, 1st New Jersey Artillery (largely German)
OHIO
Infantry:
•9th Ohio Regiment, Ohio Turners, 1st German regiment, from Cincinnati
•28th Ohio Regiment, 2nd German regiment, from Cincinnati
•37th Ohio Regiment, 3rd German regiment, from northern Ohio
•47th Ohio Regiment (over one-half German)
•58th Ohio Regiment (over one-half German)

•74th Ohio Regiment (over one-half German)
•106th and 6th Ohio Regiment, 4th German regiment
•107th Ohio Regiment, 5th German regiment
•108th Ohio Regiment, 6th German regiment
•165th and 65th Ohio Regiment (over one-half German)
Cavalry:
•3rd Ohio Cavalry (partly German)
Artillery:
•Dilger's battery, Battery I, 1st Light Artillery, originally Von Dammert's battery from Cincinnati
•Hofman's battery, 4th Ohio Battery, from Cincinnati
•Markgraf's battery, 8th Independent Battery, from Cincinnati (half German)
•20th Ohio Independent Battery, from Cleveland (about half German)
INDIANA
Infantry:
•14th Indiana Regiment (half German; Company E, wholly German)
•24th Indiana Regiment (half German)
•32nd Indiana Regiment
•136th Indiana Regiment, from Evansville (half German)
Artillery:
•Behr's battery, 6th Independent Indiana Battery, from Indianapolis
•Klaus's battery, 1st Independent Indiana Battery, from Evansville
ILLINOIS
Infantry:
•9th Illinois Regiment, a three months regiment (half German)
•24th Illinois Regiment, Hecker's Jäger (largely but not wholly German)
•27th Illinois Regiment (half German)
•36th Illinois Regiment (half German)
•43rd Illinois Regiment (second-generation Germans from Belleville)
•44th Illinois Regiment (half German)
•45th Illinois Regiment (half German)
•45th Illinois Regiment (half German)
•57th Illinois Regiment (half German)

•58th Illinois Regiment (half German)
•82nd Illinois Regiment, second Hecker regiment
Artillery:
•Battery E, 2nd Illinois Light Artillery (almost wholly German)
Cavalry:
•12th Illinois Cavalry, Company B
•13th Illinois Cavalry (half German)
Thielemann's battalion of dragoons, Company A, 16th Illinois Cavalry
•Schambeck's independent cavalry company, or Washington Light Cavalry; later, Company B, 1st Regiment Dragoons; then Company C, 16th Illinois Cavalry (half German)
Artillery:
•Gumbert's battery of artillery, Battery E,
•2nd Light Artillery (half German)
•D'Osband's battery of artillery (half German)
•Stollemann's battery of artillery (half German)

MISSOURI
Infantry:
•1st Missouri Volunteers including three Turner companies of St. Louis and one Irish company, after the three months service, an artillery regiment (half German)
•2nd Missouri Regiment (Germans and German-Americans)
•3rd Missouri Regiment, Sigel's regiment
•4th Missouri Regiment, Black Jägers (including a few native Americans and a number of Bohemians)
•5th Missouri Regiment, from southern portion of St. Louis and adjacent counties
•7th Missouri Regiment, Company I
•12th Missouri Regiment, Osterhaus' regiment until he became brigadier general
•17th Missouri Regiment, Western Turner Rifles, composed of Turners drawn from a wide area
•18th Missouri Regiment, Company K
•39th Missouri Regiment (half German)
•40th Missouri Regiment (half German)
•41st Missouri Regiment (half German)
•Home guards, five regiments

Artillery:
•Backhoff's independent battalion light artillery, Batteries B and C, 1st Missouri Light Artillery
•Essig's Landgräber's, Mann's,
•Neustadter's, and Wölfe's batteries
•Essig's, Battery A, Franz Backhoff's independent battalion light artillery, three months service
•Neustädter's Battery C, Franz Backhoff's independent battalion light artillery
•Mann's, Battery B, Franz Backhoff's independent battalion light artillery, later Battery C, First Missouri Regiment Light Artillery
•Landgräber's, Battery F, 1st Independent
•Battery Flying Artillery, later 2nd
•Regiment Missouri Light Artillery
Pioneer Company, created by Sigel
Cavalry:
•1st Missouri Cavalry, Company A
•4th Missouri Cavalry, Frémont Hussars (almost wholly German)
WISCONSIN
•5th Wisconsin Militia (overwhelmingly German)
•6th Wisconsin Regiment, Company F (more than half German)
•9th Wisconsin Regiment, called Salomon Guards, in honor of the governor
•18th Wisconsin Regiment (more than half German)
•20th Wisconsin Regiment (more than half German)
•23rd Wisconsin Regiment (more than half German)
•26th Wisconsin Regiment
•27th Wisconsin Regiment (more than half German)
•34th Wisconsin Regiment (more than half German)
•35th Wisconsin Regiment (more than half German)
•45th Wisconsin Regiment (one-half German)
Artillery:
•2nd Wisconsin Independent Battery Light Artillery
•12th Wisconsin Battery, Platt Deutsch

Battery, from Sheboygan
IOWA
•16th Iowa Infantry, Companies B,G,K
(half German)
•5th Iowa Cavalry, Company F (two-thirds
German), from Dubuque and Burlington
(The 1st Iowa Regiment contained many
Germans, but it was not, strictly speaking,
a German unit.)
MARYLAND
•Color Company, Public Guard Regiment,
•5th Maryland Infantry
•Several companies organized just before
Gettysburg
NEBRASKA
•1st Veteran Nebraska Cavalry (half
German)
MINNESOTA
Infantry:
•1st Minnesota Regiment (more than one-
third German; Company A almost one-half
German)
•2nd, 4th, and 6th Minnesota Regiments
(one-third German)
Artillery:
•Münch's battery of Pfänder's battery, 1st
Independent Battery (a Turner unit)
Cavalry:
•Brackett's cavalry, 3rd Independent
Battalion Cavalry
KANSAS
•1st Kansas Regiment (Company A about
one-half German)
•2nd Kansas Regiment (about one-half
German)
WEST VIRGINIA
•Dilger's Mountain Howitzer Battery,
Company E, 1st Battalion Light Artillery
KENTUCKY
Infantry:
•5th Kentucky Regiment, from Louisville
(half German)
•6th Kentucky Regiment, from Louisville,
considered the best regiment of the state
(half German)
Cavalry:
•Second Kentucky Cavalry (many
Germans)
Artillery:

•(Stone's Battery, Battery A, 1st Regiment
Light Artillery, independent, contained
many Germans, though it was not, strictly
speaking, a German unit.)
TEXAS
•1st United States Regiment (almost all
of the 600 men were German)

Source: Ella Lonn, *Foreigners in the Union
Army and Navy.* Greenwood Press, New York,
1951.

RESEARCHING CIVIL WAR DOCUMENTS

The Family History Library of the
Church of Jesus Christ of Latter-day Saints
in Salt Lake City issues a guide providing
specific suggestions for researching Civil
War documents:
Service Records
Civil War military service records may
provide rank, dates of service, place of residence prior to enlistment, age, physical
description, and date and place of discharge or death.
Union records: In order use the service
records, the state of enlistment must be
known, as there is no master index to the
soldiers in the Union Army. See *Register
of United States Federal Military Records: Civil War* (vols. 2 and 4) . Available
at the Family History Library are indexes
for all states and the service records of
Union Army regiments enlisted from
southern states, but they show only the
name, rank, and unit. To obtain copies of
the service records, request NATF form 80
or write National Archives & Records
Administration, General Reference Branch
(NNRG), 7th and Pennsylvania Avenue
NW, Washington, DC 20408.
Confederate records: A general index to
the names of Confederate soldiers as well
as indexes of soldiers in each state is
available at the Family History Library.
For additional information and library
microfilm numbers, consult Register of

United States Federal Military Records: Civil War (vol. 2, pp. 145-6 and vol. 4 supplemental) .

Pension Records

Union records: Soldiers who met the proper criteria received pensions from the federal government.

Pension records may include information on a soldier's military service, family members, places of residence, and other genealogical information.

The Family History Library has three indexes to Union pensions, which have not been microfilmed. One of these indexes, *Organization Index to Pension Files of Veterans Who Served Between 1861 and 1900* (T289), may be accessed through the Family History Library Catalog under United States - Military Records - Pensions - Indexes. Use NATF Form 80 to obtain copies of a pension file.

Confederate records: Soldiers who fought in the Confederate Army did not receive pensions from the federal government.

Most of the southern states, however, paid pensions from state funds in order to compensate disabled veterans and widows. Pension files may include information on a soldier's military service, family members, places of residence, or other genealogical data. It is necessary to know the *state of residence* of a veteran after the War in order to locate his pension record.

The microfilm numbers and additional information on the records from most states are listed in *Register of United States Federal Military Records: Civil War* (vol. 2 and vol. 4 supplemental).

Union and Confederate published records

Many rosters of soldiers, lists of veteran burials, and compilations of biographical data have been published. See the Family History Library research outline for the state from which the soldier served to determine what records may be searched.

Also worth checking is the Family History Library Catalog under [State]- Military Records - Civil War, 1861-1865.

For Confederate records, see *Confederate Veteran* magazine and its index (FHL book 973 B2cv).

CONTRIBUTIONS OF GERMAN-AMERICANS BY STATES TO THE UNION ARMED FORCES IN THE CIVIL WAR 1861-1865

State	Number	Percent
New York	256,252	21%
Ohio	168,210	14%
Pennsylvania	138,244	11%
Illinois	130,804	11%
Wisconsin	123,879	10%
Missouri	88,487	7%
Indiana	66,705	5%
Maryland	43,884	4%
Michigan	38,787	3%
Iowa	38,555	3%
New Jersey	33,772	3%
Kentucky	27,227	2%
California	21,646	2%
Minnesota	18,400	1%
Massachusctts	9,961	**
Connecticut	8,525	**
Kansas	4,318	**
Territories	4,093	**
District of Columbia	3,254	**
Delaware	1,263	**
Oregon	1,078	**
Rhode Island	815	**
New Hampshire	412	**
Maine	384	**
Vermont	219	**

Total German-Americans .... 1,229,174 .... 100%

**Less than 1% from a State (District, or Territory). Aggregate total of these 11 "States" is only 5%.

Source: Ella Lonn, *Foreigners in the Union Army and Navy.* Greenwood Press, NY, 1951.

CIVIL WAR SOLDIERS AND SAILORS SYSTEM

In progress, the Civil War Soldiers and Sailors System (CWSS) is a joint project of the National Park Service, the Civil War Trust, the Federation of Genealogical Societies, the Genealogical Society of Utah, and the National Archives. Its projected completion date is the first quarter of 1998.

The system will include a computerized database containing very basic facts about soldiers who served on both sides during the Civil War; a list of regiments in both the Union and Confederate Armies; identifications and descriptions of some of the major battles of the war; references that identify the sources of the information in the database; and suggestions for where to find additional information.

The system is an indexing project to input some 3.5 million Union and Confederate soldiers of the United States Civil War from 5.5 million names (including duplicate records) of soldiers who fought in the Civil War.

It will also identify 7,000 regiments and units formed during the war and provide the location of some of the soldiers buried in Civil War cemeteries managed by the Park Service.

The first phase of the CWSS project, known as the Names Index phase, is limited to fewer than 10 pieces of information on each of 5.4 million General Index Cards. The most important pieces of information are the name of the individual, rank in and out, and the name of the organizational unit (such as regiment and sometimes the company).

Other phases of the CWSS may be able to add more information on each individual from the Compiled Military Service Records (as well as from other sources, such as pension records), but the first phase is meant to be a comprehensive index, not a complete record on every soldier.

The basis for the CWSS Names Index is the Compiled Military Service Records in the National Archives, which is the only source with a claim to being comprehensive.

The computers offering the system will be available at all National Park Service locations with computers, on the Family Search computer system of the Genealogical Society of Utah, and on the Internet.

To search the record, one needs know only the name of a soldier. The system will identify and allow access to information about the regiment to which the selected soldier served and battles in which that regiment fought.

If there is additional information available in the database, the researcher will be told how to view it. The system will also tell researchers how to request copies of the actual National Archives records for their selected soldier names.

The system is to include photographs of individual soldiers, and possibly of battlefields as they looked after battle and as they appear today.

The address for inquiries about assisting with the project is Civil War Soldiers Index, P.O. Box 3385, Salt Lake City, UT 84110-3385.

The home page of the Civil War Soldiers and Sailors system on the Internet may be found at http://www.itd.nps.gov/cwss/

MAJOR ETHNIC GROUPS IN THE UNION ARMED FORCES DURING THE CIVIL WAR, 1861-1865

Irish	1,526,541
German	1,229,174
English	414,582
British American	246,940
Scots	101,409

Source: Ella Lonn, *Foreigners in the Union Army and Navy.* Greenwood Press, NY, 1951.

SOME RESOURCES
FOR CIVIL WAR RESEARCH

◆ *Research Outline, U.S. Military Records,* Jpublished by the Family History Library, Salt Lake City, Utah, 1993, is an excellent guide to family history research relating to the Civil War (and other wars). Copies are available at the Family History Library and at many Family History Centers. This *Research Outline* provides many reference sources, directions for locating service records and draft records, as well as information about census records, cemetery records, and veteran and lineage organization records — for Union and Confederate soldiers.

◆**National Archives in Washington, DC**
The National Archives headquarters in Washington, DC holds all the original service records of Civil War soldiers. Research may be conducted there, or one may write to this address to request form NATF-80 for use in requesting information by mail: General Reference Branch (NNRG), National Archives and Record Service, Washington, DC 20408.

◆**American Civil War Home Page**
The American Civil War Home Page is found on the internet at http://funnelweb. utcc. utk.edu/~hoemann/warweb.html

◆**Published state adjutant generals' reports**

◆**Regimental histories**

◆**Confederate Descendants Society,** P.O. Box 233, Athens, AL 35611
Other sources

◆Henry Putney Beers. *A Guide to the Archives of the Government of the Confederate States of America,* Washington, D.C.: National Archives and Records Service, 1968

◆Nancy J. Carroll. "Unusual References to Confederate Military Service." *Ancestry Newsletter,* 8 (July-August 1990): 1-3.

◆Charles E. Dornsbusch. comp. *Military Bibliography of the Civil War.* New York: New York Public Library, 1961, 1967, 1972.

◆Bertram Hawthorne Groene, *Tracing Your Civil War Ancestor.* Winston-Salem, NC, John F. Blair, 1973.

◆Manrial Phillips Joslyn. "Was Your Civil War Ancestor a Prisoner of War." *Ancestry Newsletter,* 11 (July-Aug 1993): 1-5

◆Kenneth W. Munden and Henry Putney Beers. *A Guide to Federal Archives Relating to the Civil War,* Washington DC, National Archives and Records Service, 1962.

◆Michael P. Musick. "The Little Regiment. Civil War Units and Commands." *Prologue* 27 (Summer 1995): 151-171.

◆ James C. Neagles. *Confederate Research Sources: A Guide to Archive Collections.* Salt Lake City, UT: Ancestry, 1986.

◆ James C. Neagles. *U.S. Military Records: A Guide to Federal and State Sources.* Salt Lake City, UT: Ancestry, 1994

◆Ken Nelson. "Civil War Sources for Genealogical Research." *Genealogical Journal* 15 (Winter 1986): 187-199; 17 (1988)/1989)89-93.

◆*Official Records of the Union and Confederate Armies in the War of the Rebellion,* published from 1880 to 1900 by the U.S. War Department in 128 volumes.

◆ George K. Schweitzer, *Civil War Genealogy,* Knoxville, Tenn., 1988.

Chapter 11

Land in America

GLOSSARY OF LAND AND PROPERTY TERMS

Abstract of title: A history of the chain of title to a piece of property

Base line: A principal east/west line used for surveying and from which townships are numbered north and south

Bounds: Description of property boundaries by physical attributes

Bounty land: Land awarded to veterans in payment for military service

Cadaster: A public record of the extent, ownership, and value of land for taxation purposes; *adj.* cadastral

Chancery court: An equity court which decides the "reasonable justice" or the "common good," where following the letter of the law would be unjust

Chattel: Movable, personal property

Crown colony: A colony established by the king

Deed: A written document by which ownership of property is conveyed

Defendant: The party against whom a suit is brought

Fee: An estate in land, or the land so held

Fee simple: A fee without limit or restriction on transfer; highest form of ownership

Field notes: A written record of a survey

Freehold estate: The privileges of ownership extended to a tenant under a lease; e.g., voting rights

Grantee: One who receives a grant; buyer

Grantor: One who makes a grant; a seller

Hereditament: Any property that can be inherited

Homestead: n. A tract of land acquired from U.S. public lands by filing a record, living on, and improving the tract; v. to acquire or settle on land under a homestead law

Improvements: Any buildings on a piece of real property

Intestate: Having no valid will

Jurisdiction: The territorial range of authority; a political subdivision

Land warrant: A negotiable government certificate that entitles the holder to possess a designated amount of public land

Lease: A title transfer less than fee, subject to payment of rent for a certain time

Metes: Description of property boundaries by measurement; length and direction; literally, "measures"

Patent: An instrument in writing granting land ownership

Principal meridian: A principal east/west line used for surveying and from which ranges are numbered north and south

Public domain: The realm of property rights belonging to the community at large

Quitrent: An annual tax, or token payment by the tenant of a freehold estate

Range: A north-south row of townships, six miles wide, numbered east and west from the principal meridian

Survey: A delineation of a tract of land

Source: J. Loren Kemper , researcher and lecturer, P.O. Box 484, Yorba Linda, CA 92686

LAND TRANSACTIONS IN AMERICA

1606-1732: British Crown made grants (charters) to Colonies and individuals
1607-1776: Colonies transferred land to individual Colonists
1780-1876: States and foreign powers transferred land to individuals
1785-1934: Federal government transferred land to individuals
1607-present: Individuals transferred land to other individuals

Source: Janice G. Cloud, "Give Deeds Their Due: Lessons from the Land," 1996

WHAT LAND RECORDS REVEAL

Land records may tell one or more of the following:
◆Name of wife, possiblyher maiden name
◆Occupation
◆Age and marital status
◆Names of children, including son-in-law
◆Names of heirs
◆Location of previous and next home

◆Description and location of property, plus number of acres
◆Names of previous owners
◆Length of time at one location
◆Religious and educational practices (as many settlers donated land for churches and schools)
◆Economic circumstances (owned a great deal of land or land was sold to pay debts)
◆Names of neighbors and witnesses who may be relatives
◆Perhaps transactions of personal property

Source: Newsletter, St. Louis Genealogy Society, September 1994.

AMERICAN LAND MEASUREMENT TERMS

◆**Acre:** 160 square rods (43,560 square feet)
◆**Arpent:** Similar to an acre, used in French sections of the United States. The side of an arpent equals 191.994 feet; one square arpent = 0.84625 acre. In Missouri, an arpent = .8507 acres, or 192.5 square feet.
◆**Chain:** Invented by Edmund Gunter in 1620, a chain is 66 feet long with 100 links. One mile is 80 chains.
◆**Degree:** 1/360th of the distance around a circle. Used to measure direction, with 9 degrees referring to north or south. Other directions are usually given in terms of degrees from North or South.
◆**Furlong:** 660 feet
◆**Link:** 1/100th of a chain, 7.92 inches long; 25 links = 1 rod.
◆**Metes & Bounds:** A type of survey based on measurements (chains, rods, poles, perches, etc.) and country markers (trees, stakes, streams, etc.)
◆**Mile:** 5,280 feet (80 chains, 32 rods, 8 furlongs)
◆**Minute:** 1/60th of a degree
◆**Perch:** Same as a rod
◆**Rectangular Survey:** Adopted in the United States in 1785 and used in public

land states (most states west of hte Appalachian Mountains). Based on certain longitude and latitude lines (meridians and base lines), land is described in terms of range, township, sections, and quarter-sections, etc.

◆**Rod:** 16.5 feet. Measured as ¼ of a chain or 25 links. Also called pole or perch.

◆**Section:** 1 square mile (640 acres)

◆**Township:** 36 square miles

◆**Vara:** Unit of measure used in parts of the United States settled by Spain. Varying lengths, with the Texas vara being 33.3333 inches (36 varas = 100 feet), the Florida vara being larger, and the southwestern vara being smaller.

Source: Most from "Terminology Found on Plat Maps," *Antique Week*, July 15, 1996

PUBLIC LAND STATES

Alabama, Alaska, Arizona, Arkansas, California, Colorado, Florida, Idaho, Illinois, Indiana, Iowa, Kansas, Louisiana, Michigan, Minnisota, Mississippi, Missouri, Montana, Nebraska, Nevada, New Mexico, North Dakota, Ohio, Oklahoma, Oregon, South Dakota, Utah, Washington, Wisconsin, Wyoming.

FEDERAL LAND SALES

In the 19th century the U.S. government sold land at exceedingly low prices to settlers. Records are available for many of the transactions. Some of these sales are,

◆**Military Wagon Roads**: Income from sales from land lying on both sides of a proposed military road, given in order to facilitate access of troops to certain sensitive frontier areas, were used to pay for road construction. Projects were instituted in Ohio (1823, 1827), in Indiana (1827), Michigan (1863), Wisconsin (1863), and Oregon (1856-1869).

◆**Canals:** Land sales to finance canals

occurred in Indiana (1827), Ohio (1848), Illinois (1827), Wisconsin (1838, 1846, 1866), and Michigan (1852,1865,1866).

◆ **River Improvements:** Land was granted to states to sell in order to make river improvements in Alabama (1828), Wisconsin (1846), Iowa (1846), and Louisiana (1824).

◆**Railroads:** To develop the railroads, the government gave land to the states — starting in Illinois (1833). During the Civil War until 1871, Congress made huge land grants to railroad companies for construction of rail lines.

◆**"Settlement Lands":** Settlers in 1842 and 1843 were encouraged to take and develop land in Florida, Oregon/Washington, and New Mexico/Arizona.

◆ **Miscellaneous grants:** The Legislature handed out land in the unoccupied land gained by the Louisana Purchase (1803); to British Army deserters in 1776; to Hessians with the British Army in America during the Revolution (if they deserted); in Ohio, to Canadian refugees of the Revolution; and numerous others, including federal bounty and other special land grants made to American veterans of various wars and for other purposes.

Source: John W. Heisey, "Territorial expansion enhanced by federal land 'giveaway' programs," *Antique Week*, Knightstown, IN 46148.

HOMESTEAD ACT OF 1862

The Homestead Act of 1862 offered 160 acres to buyers (only 80 acres in railroad grant areas) if the settler improved the holding and lived there for five years.

The person had to be at least 21 years ol and a United States citizen, or had to have filed a declaration of intent to become a citizen. The only cost was a small fee for filing a claim.

Homesteading land was located in Alabama, Florida, Illinois, Indiana, Louisiana, Michigan, Mississippi, wisconsin, and all states west of the Mississippi River except Texas.

Other Acts of Congress making land available in the West included the Desert Reclamation Act of 1894, the Kincaid Act of 1904 (which gave out 640-acre tracts in western Nebraska), the Enlarged Homestead Act of 1909 (covering land in seven mountain states of the West), and the Stockraising Homestead Act of 1916.

Available through the Bureau of Land Management in the United States Department of the Interior are United States Government records covering more than 6.5 million patents to individuals who got public land, filed in 11,550 volumes; more than 4,000 books containing 25 million entries for tracts in public domain land; and some 8 million case records.

Information likely to be found in these records include
•A Homestead final certificate file, which should include an application form and the certificate of publication that the individual intends to complete his/her claim
•Final proof of homesteading (testimony from the claimant and witnesses)
• Certificate of naturalizaiton, if necessary
•Claimant's name
•Claimant's age
•Post office address
•Date of residence established
•Number and relationship of family members
•Citizenship
•Acres under cultivation

Homestead records are available at the Eastern States Office Bureau of Land Management, 350 South Pickett Street, Alexandria, VA 22304.

COUNTY LAND RECORDS: WHAT TO LOOK FOR

Names: All names are important, as any of them may be relatives's names. Follow up with research on people associated with the ancestor

Dates: Analysis of land records can place a family in chronological perspective by
•Estimating arrival and removal dates of a family in a county based on the earliest land purchae and final sale of land in the county.
• Estimating minimum ages of male children by the date when they first owned land (generally after they reached their majority, age 21). Or figure probable birth order of brothers based on the order in which they begin to appear in the lad records.

When a death date is not available, note the last date on which a person appears in the records and indicate on the family group sheet that he/she died after that date. Or indicate that a person died before a particular date if he/she is named in the deed as being deceased.

Places: Deeds and patents always give the place of residence (county and state) of the grantor and the grantee (or patentee).

Relationships: Relationships may be stated or implied in deeds between family members.
•Look for clues in the wording of a deed, such as "for and in consideration of $1 and the natural love and affection which I bear. . . ." This indicates a gift deed, usually between parent and child.
•Deeds resulting from probate proceedings often list names of heirs and state family relationships. This is an excellent source of information when a person dies without leaving a will.

Time frame: Deeds and patents do not have to be recorded to be legally binding. some are never recorded at all. Previously unrecorded deeds or patents are sometimes recorded when the land is subsequently sold or going through probate. Land documents may be recorded as much as 100 years after they are written.

Source:"Yes, In*deed*! American County Land Records" lecture materials, by Barbara E. Leak, Loomis, California, lecturer on land and military genealogy topics. Reprinted by permission of the author.

BUREAU OF LAND MANAGEMENT

Bureau of Land Management, Eastern States: 7450 Boston Boulevard, Springfield, VA 22153
Public Research Room: Tel. (703) 440-1600
Public Affairs Office: Tel. (703) 440-1713; Fax: (703) 440-1609

The Bureau of Land Management's Eastern States organization is the steward of the public lands and resources under the jurisdiction of BLM in the 31 states east of and bordering on the Mississippi River.

BLM's land records include some 7.5 million ownership titles covering 1.5 billion acres of present or former Public Domain land. More than 5 million of these title documents are stored and maintained at BLM's Eastern States in Virginia.

The records

As the Public Domain was surveyed, the government began transferring title of land parcels to private citizens, companies and local governments. Most titles were transferred through patents (deeds) from the federal government. Records of these patents and other conveyances of title — such as railroad grants, swamp grants, school grants, Indian allotments, and private land claims — are contained in huge tracts books.

First developed around 1800 and maintained in local land offices, tract books have long served as the essential reference source for all transactions involving public lands. They tell who obtained what land from the federal government and when.

BLM's Eastern States maintains 10,000 tract books containing the land records for the 13 public land states under its jurisdictions:

Alabama, Arkansas, Florida, Illinois, Indiana, Iowa, Louisiana, Michigan, Minnesota, Missouri, Mississippi, Ohio and Wisconsin.

Considered the largest land title office in the world, Eastern States maintains almost 5 million federal land conveyance documents which precede and follow the ratification of the constitution. These conveyance documents include homesteads, cash sales, miscellaneous warrants, private land claims, swamp lists, State selections, and railroad lists.

General Land Office Project

The GLO Automated Records System, as a result of a project begun in 1989 by the Eastern States Office, can provide information through requests from remote computer terminals.

After receiving the legal description of a parcel or parcels, BLM can locate the patent and supply a copy. The legal description should include the subdivision, section, township, range, survey meridian, and state. The name of the landowner alone has not been sufficient, since the land records of most states are not indexed by name.

Under the GLO Automated Records System, some records can now be researched by using the patentee's name, document number, patent authority, county, or land office. Title records issued through June 1908 for Arkansas, Louisiana, Florida, Michigan, Minnesota, Mississippi, Ohio, and Wisconsin are available for automated retrieval, with title records for the remaining eastern public land states well on their way toward completion.

Researchers who have personal computers with modems can access the GLO System from remote locations. Contact The Bureau of Land Management for the Remote Access Information packet. Contact Easter States Office, BLM, 7450 Boston Boulevard, Springfield, V.A 22153. Tel. (703) 440-1600.

Compact disks (CDs) available

Contact BLM concerning compact disks containing the data base only (not the images) for patents prior to 1908 by the General Land Office, available from the Government Printing Office.

Other states

Because the 13 original colonies and their territories were not part of the federal lands acquired during national expansion, BLM does not maintain the land records of 18 eastern non-public land states or the District of Columbia.

These states are,

Connecticut, Delaware, George, Kentucky, Maine, Maryland, Massachusetts, New Hampshire, New Jersey, New York, North Carolina, Pennsylvania, Rhode Island, South Carolina, Tennessee, Vermont, Virginia, and West Virginia.

Inquiries concerning land records for these states should be directed to the individual state archives, land records offices, or the National Archives in Washington, DC.

BUREAU OF LAND MANAGEMENT STATE OFFICES

◆**Alaska State Office**
Bureau of Land Management
222 W. 7th Avenue #13
Anchorage, AK 99513
(907) 271-5960

◆**Arizona State Office**
Bureau of Land Management
3707 N. 7th Street
P.O. Box 16563
Phoenix, AZ 85011
(602) 650-0528

◆**California State Office**
Bureau of Land Management
2800 Cottage Way
Sacramento, CA 95825
(916) 979-2800

◆**Colorado State Office**
Bureau of Land Management
2850 Youngfield Street
Lakewood, CO 80215
(303) 239-3600

◆**Eastern States Office**

Bureau of Land Management
7450 Boston Boulevard
Springfield, VA 22153
(703) 440-1600

◆**Idaho State Office**
Bureau of Land Management
3380 Americana Terrace
Boise, ID 83706
(208) 384-3192

◆**Montana State Office**
[North Dakota, South Dakota]
Bureau of Land Management
Granite Tower
222 N. 32nd Street
P.O. Box 36800
Billings, MT 59107
(406) 255-2885

◆**Nevada State Office**
Bureau of Land Management
850 Harvard Way
P.O. Box 12000
Reno, NV 89502
(702) 785-6500/6505

◆**New Mexico State Office**
[Oklahoma, Kansas, Texas)
Bureau of Land Management
1474 Rodeo Road
P.O. Box 27115
Santa Fe, NM 87504-1449
(505) 438-7575

◆**Oregon State Office**
[Washington]
Bureau of Land Mangement
P.O. Box 2965
Portland, OR 97208
(503) 952-6001

◆**Utah State Office**
Bureau of Land Management
324 South State Street, Suite 301
Salt Lake City, UT 84111-2303
(801) 539-4001

◆**Wyoming State Office**
[Nebraska]
Bureau of Land Management
2515 Warren Avenue
P.O. Box 1828
Cheyenne, WY 82003
(307) 775-6256

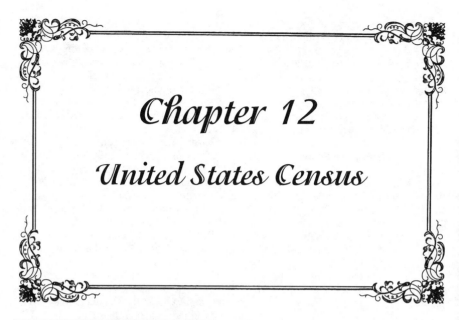

Chapter 12
United States Census

U.S. CENSUS INFORMATION RELATING TO IMMIGRATION

Census information relating to immigration or providing clues relating to immigration is categorized below according to the census years in which the various relevant questions were recorded:

◆**Place of birth of person:** 1860, 1870, 1880, 1900, 1910, 1920, 1930, 1940, 1950
◆**Place of birth of parents:** 1880, 1900, 1910, 1920, 1930
◆**Whether person or parents foreign-born:** 1870, 1880, 1900, 1910, 1920, 1930, 1940, 1950. (The 1820 and 1830 censuses ask for the number of non-naturalized foreigners in the household)
◆**Whether naturalized:** 1900, 1910, 1920, 1930, 1940,1950
◆**Year of immigration:** 1900, 1910, 1920, 1930
◆**Year of naturalization:** 1920
◆**Number of years in the United States:** 1900
◆**Number of years married**: 1900, 1910

◆**Ability to speak English:** 1900, 1910, 1920, 1930
◆**Mother tongue of person and parents:** 1910
◆**Mother tongue of foreign born:** 1920, 1930

THE SOUNDEX SYSTEM

"Soundex" is a surname index to the census schedules. The index was prepared by the Works Progress Administration between 1938 and 1940 The system was developed in order that a surname may be found even though it may have been recorded under various spellings.

Soundex Code

The Soundex index enables the researcher to search for specific surnames in the 1880, 1900, 1910, and 1920 federal census records and in some passenger list records. (The index for 1910 is called Miracode.)

The surname code (see below) is used to search in the microfilmed Soundex card index, which is organized by state, then by Soundex code, and then alphabetically by first name or initial.

The Soundex code may be determined by using a special feature of *Personal Ancestral File (PAF)*.

How to use the Soundex code

Every Soundex code consists of a the first letter of the surname plus a three-digit number.

Steps for finding the Soundex code for a surname:

1. The first letter of the surname is the first element of the Soundex code for the surname. Every surname codebegins with this first letter of the name.

2. Write down the surname. After the first letter of the name, cross out every a, e, i, o, u, w, y, and h.

3. To each of the remaining letters assign a number, according to the following guide:

```
1 .................................................. b,p,f,v
2 ....... c,s,k,g,j,q,x,z (also the German tz)
3 .......................................................... d,t
4 .............................................................. l
5 ...................................................... m,n
6 .............................................................. r
```

Exceptions

• If there are any side-by-side letters having the same number equivalents, these letters should be treated as one letter. For example, in the surname Stadtler, the *d* should be crossed out because *d* and *t* both have 3 as their code number.

• If the surname has any doubled letters, they are treated as a single letter. For example, in the surname Lloyd, the second *l* is crossed out; in Hess, the second *s* is crossed out.

• If the result is three digits, the task is finished; the three digits become the numbers of the code. For example, Rasmus = R252.

• If fewer than three digits resulted, add enough zeros so that there are three digits. For example, Kern = K650, and Hull =

H400.

• If the result is more than three digits, ignore the digits following the three needed ones. For example, Knierenschild = K565.

Special cases

• If the surname has a prefix — like Van, Von, De, Di, or Le — code it with the prefix and again without the prefix because the surname may be given either code.

• *Mc* and *Mac* are not considered prefixes.

• If the first letter of the surname could differ due to misspelling, code it in different ways. For example, Cole (C400) could be spelled Kohl (K400).

• The surnames of Catholic nuns are usually coded as "Sister."

• Be careful of a surname like Tutt, which is indexed as T300 rather than T000 because the last two Ts are doubled but are not next to the first one.

• Watch for misspellings in the records. For example, Glover may be found misspelled as Clover, and Buesch as Ruesch.

• To account for possible mistakes in the coding of surnames, try different codes for a surname.

STATEWIDE CENSUS INDEXES

Statewide Indexes exist for the 1790-1850 censuses and most of the 1860 and 1870 censuses, usually in print form, with some on microfilm or microfiche.

The Accelerated Indexing Systems International (AIS) indexes all the 1790 to 1850 censuses and a few later censuses, on microfiche.

The 1880, 1900, and 1920 censuses have been indexed through the Soundex system.

The 1880 census

All households with children aged ten and under are indexed on Soundex, on microfilm. Book indexes are available at the Family History Library for Arizona, Colorado, Idaho, Minnesota, Montana, North and South Dakota, Nevada, Ohio. Oregon, Texas, Utah, Washington, West

Virginia, and Wyoming.

1890 census

Although most of this census was destroyed, the few records remaining are indexed on FHL film 1,421,673 and on FHL film 543,341-42

1900 census

Every household is Soundexed, on microfilm.

1910 census

Soundex and "Miracode" indexes to the 1910 census are available for 21 states: Alabama, Arkansas, California, Florida, Georgia, Illinois, Kansas, Kentucky, Louisiana, Michigan, Mississippi, Missouri, North Carolina, Ohio, Oklahoma, Pennsylvania, South Carolina, Tennessee, Texas, Virginia, and West Virginia, on microfilm.

Some cities and counties are indexed separately from the state in the 1910 indexes of Alabama, Georgia, Louisiana, Pennsylvania, and Tennessee.

Published indexes are available for Hawaii, Nevada, and Wyoming.

The following resource is very helpful for searching states whose 1910 censuses are not Soundexed:

G. Eileen Buckway, compiler, *U.S. 1910 Federal Census: Unindexed States: A Guide to Finding Census Enumeration Districts for Unindexed Cities, Towns, and Villages,* compiled by C. Eileen Buckway; assisted by Marva Blalock, Elizabeth Caruso, Ray Matthews, and Kenneth Nelson (Salt Lake City: Family History Library, 1992, FHL US/CAN REF AREA 973 X2bu 1910 and microfiche 6101540, 8 microfiches)[1]

Tip

The 1910 Miracode index system can be confusing: On some of the indexed entries, a row of numbers near the upper right corner appears without any indication of what they represent. The following example illustrates how this number (always in three parts) is used:

095 0222 0162.

The first number (95), the volume number, is not always necessary for a search and can often be ignored.

The second number (222) is the Enumeration District number.

The third number (0162) is the family number, found on the census record to the left of the family name, indicating the order in which the family home was visited.

Non-Soundexed states, 1910 census

There are no statewide indexes for Alaska, Arizona, Colorado, Connecticut, Delaware, District of Columbia, Indiana, Iowa, Maine, Maryland, Massachusetts, Minnesota, Montana, Nebraska, New Hampshire, New Jersey, New Mexico, New York, North Dakota, Oregon, Puerto Rico, Rhode Island, South Dakota, Utah, Vermont, Washington, and Wisconsin.

The 1920 census

This census is completely Soundexed.

The 1930 and later censuses

The 1930 census remains closed until the year 2002, according to the agreement reached in 1952 that population schedules will "remain closed for seventy-two years after the enumeration date for each census" for privacy reasons.

[1] J. Carlyle Parker, *Going to Salt Lake City to Do Family History Research.* Rev. ed. Turlock, California: Marietta Publishing Company, 1996.

Sources:

•*Research Outline: United States,* Family History Library, Church of Jesus Christ of Latter-day Saints, Salt Lake City, Utah

•National Archives and Records Administration, Washington, DC

NON-POPULATION CENSUS SCHEDULES

The "nonpopulation" census schedules — agriculture, manufacturing, mortality, and social statistics may be found in the National Archives or in state archives.

Agriculture, mortality, and social statistics schedules are available for the census years of 1850, 1860, 1870, and 1880.

Manufacturing schedules are available

for 1820, 1850, 1860, 1870, and 1880. They are arranged by state, then by county, and then by political subdivision.

Agricultural schedules of 1850, 1860, and 1879

These schedules show for each farm listed the owner or manager's name, number of acres, the farm's cash value, farming machinery, livestock and many other details. In 1850, small farms that produced less than $100 worth of products were not included. By 1870 the minimum farm size was three acres; the minimum production, $500.

Manufacturing schedules in 1820, 1850, and 1860

These schedules provide the name of the manufacturer, the type of business, capital invested, value of materials used in the business, cost of labor, and many other details.

Mortality schedules

Recording deaths in the year preceding the taking of the census, these schedules include name, age, sex, marital status, state or country of birth, month of death, occupation, cause of death, and length of final illness.

Social statistics schedules for 1850 through 1870

This source indicates for each political subdivision the value of real estate, annual taxes, number of schools, teachers, and pupils, as well as specific information concerning libraries, newspapers, churches, paupers, criminals, wages of laborers, and more. They do not provide information about specific individuals, but rather statistical data.

The 1880 schedules provide information about deaf, dumb, blind, and criminal persons who are listed by name.

Other special censuses

For information about other special censuses (1840 List of Pensioners; Federal Territorial Censuses; and Colonial, State, and Local Censuses), see *Research Outline: United States*, Family History Library, Church of Jesus Christ of Latter-day Saints, Salt Lake City, Utah, page 13.

Source: "The Nonpopulation Census Schedules," by Claire Prechtel-Kluskens, *The Record: News from the National Archives and Records Administration*, Vol. 2, No. 1, September 1995.

'CENSUS DAY'

The "census day" is, by law, the day for which census statistics were to be taken. This list shows the dates for "census days" for each U.S. Federal Census year:

1790	August 2
1800	August 4
1810	August 6
1820	August 7
1830 through 1900	June 1
1910	April 15
1920	January 1
1930	April 1
1940	April 1

YEARS OF STATE CENSUSES (including only states in which the censuses covered the majority of the respective states)

AL	1816, 1855, 1907 Conf. Vet
AZ	1864, 1866
AR	1829
CA	1852
CO	1885
DAKOTA	1885
FL	1814, 1885
HI	1878, 1890
IL	1855, 1865
IN	1807
IA	1836, 1856, 1885, 1895, 1905, 1915, 1925
KS	1855, 1865, 1875, 1885, 1895
MD	1776
MA	1855, 1865
MI	1884, 1894
MN	1836, 1849, 1857, 1865,

	1875, 1885, 1895, 1905
MS	1810, 1816, 1841, 1845, 1853
NE	1855, 1885
NV	1875
NH	1732, 1776
NJ	1855, 1885, 1895, 1905, 1915
NY	1825, 1835, 1855, 1865, 1875,
	1892, 1905, 1915, 1925
NYC	1890, 1905, 1915, 1925
NC	1784, 1787
ND	1915, 1925
OK	1890
RI	1774, 1782, 1865, 1875,
	1885, 1915, 1925, 1936
SD	1905, 1915, 1925, 1935, 1945
TX	1840
UT	Q856
VT	1771
WI	1836, 1842, 1846, 1847,
	1855, 1875, 1895, 1905

U.S. CENSUS ABBREVIATIONS

Citizenship Status

A	Alien
NA	Naturalized
PA	First papers filed

Other abbreviations

A	aunt
Ad	adopted
AdCl	adopted child
AdD	adopted daughter
AdGcl	adopted grandchild
AdM	adopted mother
AdS	adopted son
Al	aunt-in-law
Ap	apprentice
Asst	assistant
At	attendant
B	brother
B Boy	bound boy
B Girl	bound girl
Bar	bartender
Bl	brother-in-law
Bo	boarder
Boy	boy
Bu	butler

C	cousin
Cap	captain
Cha	chambermaid
Cil	cousin-in-law
Cl	child
Coa	coachman
Com	companion
Cook	cook
D	daughter
Dl	daughter-in-law
Dla	day laborer
Dom	domestic
Dw	dishwasher
Emp	employee
En	engineer
F	father
FaH	farm hand
FaL	farm laborer
FaW	farm worker
Fi	fireman
First C	first cousin
Fl	father-in-law
FoB	foster brother
FoSi	foster sister
FoS	foster son
Gcl	grandchild
Gd	granddaughter
Gf	grandfather
GGF	greatgrandfather
GGGF	great great grandfather
GGGM	great great grandmother
GGM	great grandmother
GM	grandmother
Gml	grandmother-in-law
Gn	great or grand nephew
Gni	great or grand niece
Go	governess
God Cl	God child
Gs	grandson
Gsl	grandson-in-law
Gua	guardian
Guest	guest
H Maid	housemaid
Hb	half brother
Hbl	half brother-in-law
He	herder
Help	help
HGi	hired girl
HH	hired hand

Hk	housekeeper	Sgd	stepgranddaughter
Hlg	hireling	Sgs	stepgrandson
HSi	half sister	Si	sister
HSil	half sister-in-law	Sl	son-in-law
Husband	husband	Sm	stepmother
Hw	house worker	Ss	stepson
Inmate	inmate	Ssl	stepson-in-law
L	lodger	SSsil	stepsister-in-law
La	laborer	Su	superintendent
Lau	laundry	Ten	tenant
M	mother	U	uncle
Maid	maid	Ul	uncle-in-law
Man	manager	Vi	visitor
Mat	matron	w	wife
Ml	mother-in-law	Wa	warden
N	nephew	Wai	waitress
Ni	niece	Ward	ward
Nil	niece-in-law	wkm	workman
Nl	nephew-in-law	Wt	waiter
NU	nurse		
O	officer		
P	patient		
Pa	partner		
Ph	physician		
Por	porter		
Pr	prisoner		
Pri	principal		
Prv	private		
Pu	pupil		
R	roomer		
S	son		
Sa	sailor		
Sal	saleslady		
Sbl	stepbrother-in-law		
Scl	stepchild		
Sd	stepdaughter		
Sdl	stepdaughter-in-law		
Se	servant		
SeCl	servant's child		
Sf	stepfather		
Sfl	stepfather-in-law		

WARD MAPS

•Ward maps of 35 major cities, showing census districts and political divisions of large cities, and 232 maps representing 35 cities are available on FHL film 1,377,700; microfiche 6016554-782.

•To find which maps to use with each U.S. census, see Michael H. Shelley, *Ward Maps of United States Cities: A Selective Checklist of Pre-1900 Maps in the Library of Congress*, FHL film 928,210, item 16.

•To find U.S. county boundary maps for census decades, see William Thorndale and William Dollarhide, *Map Guide to the U.S. Federal Censuses, 1790-1920*, FHL book 973 X2th. This book shows 400 U.S. county boundary maps for the census decades from 1790 to 1920 superimposed on modern county boundaries.

Chapter 13

Newspapers, American records

UNITED STATES BOARD ON GEOGRAPHIC NAMES

The U.S.Board on Geographic Names (BGN) is the single authority in the United States to which all problems and inquiries concerning geographic names throughout the world may be addressed.

The Geographic Names Information System (GNIS) is the Nation's official data base for place names. GNIS is maintained by the U.S. Geological Survey and can often provide information on name changes. This data base contains 2 million entries, including the names of places that no longer exist as well as other or secondary names for existing places.

This automated system also contains the names of every type of feature except roads and highways. It is especially useful for genealogical research because it contains entries for very small and scattered communities as well as churches and cemeteries, including entries for those that no longer exist.

Selected place-name sources
The U.S. Geological Survey's GNIS will respond to written and phone inquiries about present past, and secondary names and locations of any of more than two million place and geographic feature names, large and small, in the United States. The service is free.

U.S. names information
To contact the U.S. Board on Geographic Names (BGN), write to:
BGN Executive Secretary and
Executive Secretary for Domestic Names
U.S. Geological Survey
523 National Center
Reston, VA 22092-0523.
Tel. (703) 648-4544

Foreign names information
For information about geographic names in foreign countries, contact:
BGN Executive Secretary for
Foreign Names
Defense Mapping Agency A-20
8613 Lee Highway,
Fairfax, VA 22031-2137.
Tel. (703) 285-9518

Geographic names software

A CD-ROM, "Geographic Names Information System, a digitized gazetteer of the United States is available and consists of three databases from the Geographic Names Information System (GNIS): 1) The National Geographic Data Base (with almost 2 million entires, 2) the Toponymic Map Names Data Base (an inventory of all USGS published topographic maps), and 3) the Reference Data Base (a collection of annotated bibliographies of all sources used in compiling information for the National Geographic Names Data Base). There are 154,243 populated places, streams, rivers, creeks, lakes, swamps, mountains, etc. and other named places such as churches and cemeteries, including 57,782 places that no longer exist, including many churches and cemeteries.

Ordering address: USGS-ESIC, 507 National Center, 12201 Sunrise Valley Drive, Reston, VA 22092. Fax: (703) 648-5548.

CEMETERIES, UNITED STATES

The following cemetery directory lists 28,000 cemeteries in the United States, with names, addresses, and locations. It is indexed by state, city, and county.

United States Cemetery Address Book, by Elizabeth Gorrell Kot and James Douglas Kot. Indices Publishing, 228 Sandy Neck Way, Vallejo, CA 94591-7850. Tel. (707) 554-4814

VETERANS BURIAL LOCATION ASSISTANCE

The National Cemetery System, Department of Veterans Affairs, provides limited burial location assistance to the next-of-kin, relatives, or close friends of decedents thought to be interred in a Department of Veterans Affairs national cemetery.

NCS personnel can research records to determine if a decedent is interred in one of the VA national cemeteries. All requests must relate to a specific individual since research cannot be conducted on groups on the basis of surname, military unit, war period or place of residence. NCS has no information on persons interred in cemeteries that are not under the jurisdiction of the Department of Veterans Affairs.

To request a burial search on a specific individual, the following information should be provided: full name, date and place of birth, date and place of death, state from which the veteran entered active duty, and branch of military (Army, Navy, Air Force, Marine Corps, Coast Guard).

No form is required and no fee is charged for this service. Send the above information in a letter addressed to Director, Executive Communications and Public Affairs Service (402B), National Cemetery System, Department of Veterans Affairs, 810 Vermont Avenue, N.W., Washington, DC 20420.

Source: National Cemetery System, Public and Consumer Affairs Division, Washington, DC 20420

FUNERAL DIRECTORS

The directory noted below lists 22,000 funeral homes with addresses and telephone numbers classified by country, state, city, and county. It also includes some international locations.

The full size edition lists also addresses for daily newspapers in the United States and Canada as well as a national hospital directory, cemeteries, and Veterans Administration information.

The Yellow Book of Funeral Directors, Nomis Publications, Inc., 1987. Address: Nomis Publications, Inc., P.O. Box 5122, Youngstown, OH 44514. Tel. 800-321-7479.

PROBATE RECORDS VOCABULARY (United States)

Administration: The process of setting in motion the legal machinery required to settle the estate of a deceased person

Administrator(trix): A person appointed by the court to settle the estate of a deceased person (usually when there is no will)

Affinity: A relationship by marriage rather than by blood

Bequeath: To give personal property by will as opposed to devise which relates to real property

Chattel: Personal property which is more than simple goods as it can include living Property. In earlier times it may act as a synonym for slaves.

Child of tender years: A child under 14

Codicil: A supplement or addition to a will

Conjoint Will: A will two or more people make together; popular with the Dutch in New York

Consanguinity: A blood relationship

Corporeal property: Property which can be seen and handled. For instance, a house is corporeal; but rent is incorporeal.

Decedent: Deceased person

Devise: A gift of real property by will

Dower: The land and tenements to which a widow has claim (in life estate) after the death of her husband, for the support of herself and her children.

Endowment: Assigning or setting off the widow's dower

Escheat: The revision of property to the state when there are no heirs

Estate: The sum total of a person's property

Et uxor: Often written "et ux," Latin for "and wife," often used in indexing

Executor(trix): The person named in the will by the testator to see that the provisions of the will are carried out after the testator's death

Friendly suit: A suit brought by a creditor against an executor or administrator (being actually a suit by the executor or administrator against himself in the name of the creditor) to compel the creditors of an estate to take an equal distribution of assets

Guardian: A person who is invested with the right, and so charged, to manage the rights and property of another person. A *testamentary guardian* is named in a deed or last will of a child's father. Otherwise the guardian is chosen by the election of the child if over 14 or by appointment if under 14.

Heir: A person who inherits or succeeds through legal means, after the death of another.

Heirs and Assigns: Under common law these words were necessary to convey any fee simple title. They are no longer necessary, but they are often used.

Holographic Will: A will written, dated, and signed in the testator's own handwriting

Infant: Any person not of full legal age; a minor

Intestate: A person who dies without make a valid will.

Issue: All lineal descendants of a common ancestor; not children only

Legacy: Same as bequest

Life Estate: An estate that lasts only during the life of a person, or for the duration of someone else's life. Often in a will a life estate is devised to a widow.

Moiety: Half of anything

Natural Affection: Affection which exists naturally between near relatives

Nuncupative Will: An oral will valid in last sickness, sudden illness or combat; it must be witnessed and be clear that it is the intent of the decedent

Probate: An inclusive term which refers to all matters over which the probate court has jurisdiction including the settling of an estate (whether testate or intestate) and guardianship matters

Real Property or **realty:** Relating to land

Relict: The surviving spouse when one has died

Testate: A person who dies leaving a valid

will

Testament: Document outlining the disposition of personal property after death
Will: Document outlining the disposition of real property after death

Source: M. Bell; definitions taken from or adapted from *Black's Law Dictionary* or from Val D. Greenwood, *The Researcher's Guide to American Genealogy,* Genealogical Publishing Co., Baltimore, 1990.

NATIONAL ARCHIVES REGIONAL CENTERS

♦**Alaska**
National Archives, Alaska Region, 654 W. Third Avenue., Room. 12, Anchorage, AK 99501. 907-271-2441
♦**Iowa, Kansas, Missouri, Nebraska**
National Archives, Central Plains Region, 2306 E. Bannister Road, Kansas City, MO 64131. 816-926-7271
♦**Illinois, Indiana, Michigan, Minnesota, Ohio, Wisconsin**
National Archives, Great Lakes Region, 7358 S. Pulaski Road, Chicago, IL 60629. 312-353-0161
♦**Delaware, Pennsylvania, Maryland, Virginia, West Virginia**
National Archives, Mid-Atlantic Region, 5000 Wissahickon Avenue, Philadelphia, PA 19144. 215-951-5588
♦**Connecticut, Maine, Massachusetts, New Hampshire, Rhode Island, Vermont**
National Archives, New England Region, 380 Trapelo Road, Waltham, MA 02154. 617-647-8100
♦**New Jersey, New York, Puerto Rico, Virgin Islands**
National Archives, Northeast Region, 201 Jarick Street, New York, NY 10014. 212-337-1300
♦**Idaho, Oregon, Washington**
National Archives, Pacific Northwest Region, 6125 Sand Point Way NE, Seattle, WA 98115. 206-442-4502

♦**California, except southern California; Hawaii; Nevada, except Clark County;** Pacific Ocean Area
National Archives, Pacific Sierra Region, 1000 Commodore Drive, San Bruno, CA 94066. 415-876-9009
♦**South Dakota, Utah, Colorado, Montana, North Dakota, Wyoming**
National Archives, Rocky Mountain Region, Denver Federal Center, Building 48, Denver, CO 80225. 303-234-5271
♦**Alabama, Georgia, Florida, Kentucky, Mississippi, North Carolina, South Carolina, Tennessee**
National Archives, Southeast Region, 1557 St. Joseph Avenue, East Point, GA 30344. 404-763-7477
♦**Arkansas, Louisiana, New Mexico, Oklahoma, Texas**
National Archives, Southwest Region, 501 W. Felix Street, P.O. Box 6216, Fort Worth, TX 76115. 817-334-5525
♦**Arizona, the southern California counties of Imperial, Inyo, Kern, Los Angeles, Orange, Rivrside, San Bernardino, San Diego, San Luis Obispo, Santa Barbara and Ventura, and Clark County, Nevada**
National Archives, Pacific Southwest Region, 24000 Avila Road, First Floor, Laguna Niguel, CA 92656-6719. 714-643-4241

NATIONAL ARCHIVES AT COLLEGE PARK (ARCHIVES II)

The following information will be helpful to the researcher who travels to Washington to do research at the National Archives at College Park (Archives II), which opened in 1996:
♦The National Archives at College Park (Archives II) is located at 8601 Adelphi Road, College Park, Maryland.
♦Unless one already has a research card, it is necessary to apply for one in the reception area.
♦ Research room hours (except legal

holidays) are 8:45 am to 5 pm, Monday and Wednesday; and 8:45 am to 9 pm, Tuesday, Thursday, and Friday. Subject matter specialists are not on duty after 5:15 pm
♦The research rooms are open also on Saturday from 8:45 am to 4:45 pm, with a small research room staff present.
♦Requests for records must be made before 3:30 pm Monday through Friday; no requests can be made on Saturday. The telephone number for the Archives II Reference Branch is (301) 713-7250.

Source: National Archives at College Park, Textual Reference Branch, 1996

SOCIAL SECURITY ACT TIMELINE

1935: Social Security Act enacted
1936 (December 1): First social security card issued
1937 (January 1): United States workers begin accumulating credits toward benefits.
1951: Domestic workers, farm and agricultural laborers, Americans working abroad for United States companies, temporary employees of the federal government, and the self-employed covered under Social Security
1955: Self-employed farmers are covered.
1957: Beginning of coverage of persons serving in the Armed Forces
1961: Internal Revenue Service begins using Social Security numbers as taxpayer identification numbers.
1963 (July 1): Persons registered with the Railroad Retirement board are no longer issued special Social Security numbers.
1965: Medicare program enacted.
1967 (July 4): Freedom of Information Act provides public access to federal government files, including the Social Security Death Master File.
1973: Starting this year, the first three digits of a person's Social Security number are determined by the zip code of the

mailing address shown on the application for a social security number.
1984 (January 1): All federal employees hired after this date earn retirement benefits under Social Security. Employees of nonprofit organizations receive mandatory coverage.
1990s: Information from the Social Security Death Master File become generally available to genealogists.

Source: "Social Security Death Master File: A Much Misunderstood Index," by Jake Gehring. *Genealogical Journal*, Utah Genealogical Association, Vol. 24, No. 2 (1996), p. 51ff.

SOCIAL SECURITY NUMBER DESIGNATIONS BY LOCALITY

001-003	NH
004-007	ME
008-009	VT
010-034	MA
035-039	RI
040-049	CT
050-134	NY
135-158	NJ
159-211	PA
212-220	MD
221-222	DE
223-231	VA
232	WV and NC
233-236	WV
237-246	NC
247-251	SC
252-260	GA
261-267	FL
268-302	OH
303-317	IN
318-361	IL
362-386	MI
387-399	WI
400-407	KY
408-415	TN
416-424	AL
425-428	MS
429-432	AR
433-439	LA

440-448	OK
449-467	TX
468-477	MN
478-485	IA
586-500	MO
501-502	ND
503-504	SD
505-508	NE
509-515	KS
516-517	MT
518-519	ID
520	WY
521-524	CO
525	NM
526-527	AZ
528-529	UT
530	NV
531-539	WA
540-544	OR
545-573	CA
574	AK
575-576	HI
577-579	DC
580	VI, PR
581-584	PR
585	NM
586	Guam,Philippine Islands, American Samoa
587	MS
700-728	Railroad Retirement Board (all states)

HELPFUL FACTS ABOUT THE SOCIAL SECURITY DEATH MASTER FILE

♦Only those who were involved with the Social Security program are included in the Social Security Death Master File.

♦A person's death is recorded only if the Social Security Administration was informed of the death, usually through family members' application for a lump sum benefit at death.

♦The file lists the state where an individual resided or the state where the Social Security card was received, which may not have been the place of the person's birth.

♦A married woman is generally listed under her married name.

♦The zip code indicated for the last residence may or may not represent the area where the death occurred.

♦Most of the deaths recorded in the index occurred after 1962, when the Social Security Administration began maintaining the file electronically.

Source: "Social Security Death Master File: A Much Misunderstood Index," by Jacob Gehring. *Genealogical Journal*, Utah Genealogical Association, Vol. 24, No. 2 (1996).

SOURCES OF THE SOCIAL SECURITY DEATH MASTER FILES

♦Banner Blue, a division of Brøderbund Software, P.O. Box 7865, Fremont, CA 94537. Tel. (415) 382-4770

♦Cambridge Statistical Research Associates, Inc., 760 Wheeling Avenue, Cambridge, OH 43725. Tel. (514) 432-6400

♦Family History Library, 35 North West Temple Street, Salt Lake City, UT 84150, tel. (800) 346-6044 (also through family history centers)

♦CompuServe (CompuTrace Deceased Individuals File), available on the Compuserve Online Service; for information, call (800) 848-8199.

♦GenRef Incorporated, 874 West 1300 North, Orem, UT 84057.Tel. (801) 225-3256

Source: "Social Security Death Master File: A Much Misunderstood Index," by Jacob Gehring. *Genealogical Journal,* Utah Genealogical Association, Vol. 24, No. 2, 1996.

SOCIAL SECURITY APPLICATIONS

It is possible to send for a copy of the SS-5 record, which is the form that social security card holders filled out when they applied for coverage.

Ordering an SS-5

SS-5 copies can be obtained for one-self, for deceased individuals, and for persons who would be over 100 years old if they were still living. Researchers should send $7.00 (if the social security number is known) or $16.50 (if the number is unknown or incorrect) to this address: Freedom of Information Officer, 4-H-8 Annex Building, 6401 Security Boulevard, Baltimore, MD 21235.

When writing to this office, request a full copy of the individual's SS-5 and his/her social security number, if known. The Social Security Death Master File provides the deceased person's social security number. If the social security number is not known, provide identifying information. Provide proof of death (such as a copy of an obituary, a death certificate, or even the printout from the Social Security Death Master File. To request a copy of a living person's SS-5, that person's signature is required. Make the check payable to "Social Security Administration."

Information provided on the SS-5

The SS-5 record provides spaces for the following information which was to be supplied by the applicant:
♦Full name of the applicant
♦Place of residence at the time of application
♦Name and address of the employer
♦Date and place of birth
♦Father's full name
♦Mother's full maiden name
♦Date of application
♦The applicant's signature

The SS-5 may be especially helpful to genealogists by providing
♦A clue to the applicant's early occupation
♦A residence address that is probably more recent than that shown on the latest available U.S. federal census
♦The maiden name of the applicant's mother
♦The full name a German-American may

have been given at christening.

Where to search for the social security number

♦Social Security Death Master File
♦Death certificate
♦Insurance policies, bank statements, income tax returns
♦Military and military discharge records
♦Pension applications
♦Employment records
♦Funeral home records
♦Voter registration rolls
♦Drivers license offices
♦Fraternal, business, trade organizations
♦Schools, colleges, alumni associations
♦Hospital records

U.S. RAILROAD RETIREMENT BOARD

The U.S. Railroad Retirement Board began keeping records of covered rail service in 1937. Its records apply only to persons covered under the Railroad Retirement Act. The Board will provide information from its records for deceased persons, but if the person of interest is still living, a written consent is required.

The Board would have no records of persons who died prior to its inception, nor would it generally have any pertinent records of persons whose rail service was performed on a casual basis and/or was of short duration.

Employers such as street, interurban, or suburban electric railways are not covered under the act.

The records are organized by the railroad employee's social security number. If the social security number is not known, it is necessary to provide the complete name, including middle name or initial, and complete dates of birth and death. This information may not be sufficient, however, if the surname is relatively common. In most cases it is not possible to make a positive identification without the employee's social security number.

The fee for searching the records is $16 for each individual for whom records are sought and is payable before the search is attempted. If the information requested cannot be located, the fee is not refundable. The check or money order should be made payable to the Railroad Retirement Board and sent to

Office of Public Affairs
Railroad Retirement Board
844 North Rush Street
Chicago, IL 60611-2092

At least 30-60 days are required for responses to genealogical inquiries.

Source: Railroad Retirement Board press release of May 30, 1996, as published in *FGS Forum*, Vol. 8, No. 2, 1996

SISTER CITIES INTERNATIONAL

Sister Cities International
120 South Payne Street
Alexandria, VA 22314
Tel. (703) 836-3535
Fax: (703) 836-4815

The following are pairings of sister cities in Germany and the United States, as organized through Sister Cities International:

Aachen: .... Arlington County, VA
Ansbach: .... Bay City, MI
Augsburg: .... Dayton, OH
Bad Königshofen: .... Arlington, TX
Bad Zwischenahn: ...... Centerville, OH
Berlin: .... Los Angeles, CA
Berlin (Spandau): .... Baca Raton, FL
Bexbach: .... Goshen, IN
Billerbeck: .... Goshen, IN
Bingen am Rhein: .... Bingen-White
                                             Salmon, WA
Braunfels: .... New Braunfels, TX
Braunschweig: .... Omaha, BE
Büdingen: .... Tinley Park, IL
Coburg: .... Garden City, NY
Cologne: .... Indianapolis, IN
Crailsheim: .... Worthington, MN

Cranzahl: .... Running Springs, CA
Dorfen: .... Constantine, MI
Dortmund: .... Buffalo, NY
Dresden: .... Columbus, OH
Eberbach: .... Ephrata, PA
Eichstatt: .... Lexington, VA
Eisenach: .... Waverly, IA
Esslingen: .... Sheboygan, WI
Eutin: .... Lawrence, KS
Freiburg im Breisgau: .... Fryburg, PA
                                             Whittier, CA
Friedrichshafen: .... Peoria, IL
Friolzheim: .... Williamsville, NY
Füssen: .... Helen, GA
Garbsen: .... Farmers Branch, TX
Garmisch-Partenkirchen: ..... Aspen, CO
Gau-Algesheim: .... Redford, MI
Gedern: .... Columbia: IL
Gießen: .... Waterloo, IA
Glückstadt: .... Fredericksburg, TX
Gotha: .... Gastonia, NC
Gottelfingen: .... Botkins, OH
Grünstadt: .... Bonita Springs, FL
Gunzenhausen: .... Frankenmuth, MI
Hamburg: .... Chicago, IL
Hamm: .... Chattanooga, TN,
                                         Santa Monica, CA
Helmstedt: .... Albuquerque, NM,
                                             Oxford, MS
Herford: .... Quincy, IL
Hof: .... Ogden, UT
Holzerlinger: .... Crystal Lake, IL
Ingelheim: .... Ridgefield, CT
Kaiserslautern: .... Davenport, IA
Kleve: .... Fitchburg, MA
Koblenz: .... Austin, TX
Königs Wusterhausen: Germantown, TN
Krefeld: .... Charlotte, NC
Kubelstein Stadt Scheßlitz: Victoria, KS
Kusel: .... Marietta, OH
Leipzig: .... Houston, TX
Leinfelden-Echterdingen: .... York, PA
Lengerich: .... Wapakoneta, OH
Leonberg: .... Seward, NE
Lichtenfels: .... Vandalia, OH
Linz am Rhein: .... Marietta, GA
Lübeck: .... Spokane, WA
Lüdinghausen: .... Deerfield, IL
Ludwigshafen am Rhein: . Pasadena, CA

Lüneburg: .... Thomasville, GA
Mainz: ....Louisville, KY
Malsch: .... Dinuba, CA
Mannheim: .... Manheim, PA
Marbach am Neckar: .. Washington, MO
Marl: .... Midland, MI
Melsungen: .... Elmira, NY
Memmingen: .... Glendale, AZ
Meßstetten: .... Toccoa, GA
Mörzheim: .... Frederick, MD
Mühlacker: .... Tolleson, AZ
München: .... Cincinnati, OH
Münster: .... Fresno, CA; Radcliff, KY
Neckargemünd: .... Missoula, MT
Neu Ulm: .... New Ulm, MN
Neusäß: .... Redwood Falls, MN
Neustadt an der Waldnaab: ..... Hays, KS
Nienburg: .... Las Cruces, NM
Ofterdingen: .... Dexter, MI
Osnabrück: .... Evansville, IN
Paderborn: .... Belleville, IL
Passau: ....Hackensack, NJ
Pfaffenweiler: .... Jasper, IN
Pinneberg: .... Rockville, MD
Porta Westfalica: .... Waterloo, IL
Potsdam: .... Sioux Falls, SD
Rastatt: ....New Britain, CT
Ratingen: .... Vermillion, SD
Regensburg: .... Tempe, AZ
Rödental: .... Eaton, OH
Saarbrücken: .... Pittsburgh, PA
Schaumburg: .... Schaumburg, IL
Schifferstadt: .... Frederick, MD
Schledehausen: .... Huntingburg, IN
Schwieberdingen: .... Belvidere, IL
Seevetal: .... Decatur, IL
Soltau: .... Coldwater, MI
Stade: .... Swarthmore, PA
Steinheim: .... Bourbonnais, IL
Stuttgart: .... St. Louis, MO
Sulzfeld: ....El Cajon, CA
Tegernsee: ....Ketchum, ID
Tirschenreuth: ...... Santa Fe Springs, CA
Trier: .... Fort Worth, TX
Tübingen: .... Ann Arbor, MI
Ulm: .... New Ulm, MN
Villingen-Schwenningen: Great Bend, KS
Walldorf: .... Astoria, OR
Wesel: ....Hagerstown, MD

Wiesloch: .... Sturgis, MI
Wiernsheim: .... New Harmony, IN
Wilhelmshaven: .... Norfolk, VA
Winterlingen: .... Shiner, TX
Wittmund: .... Simsbury, CT
Wolfach: .... Richfield, OH
Wolfenbüttel: .... Kenosha, WI
Worms: .... Mobile, AL
Würzburg: .... Rochester, NY
Zittau: .... Portsmouth, OH
Zweibrücken: .... York County, VA

BEGINNINGS OF STATEWIDE VITAL RECORDS LAWS

The beginning of registration of vital records (births, marriages, deaths) in the United States varies widely among the states. The dates shown below, indicating the year in which states began to require vital records registration, or the year in which statewide records actually began, can be misleading for these reasons:

♦Certain counties in some states often collected vital records before the state required them

♦After a statewide requirement was put in force, several years elapsed before the state came into full compliance.

♦Gaps in the years of registration activity often occurred.

♦Registration of vital records in some large cities was accomplished separately from that in the state's registration offices.

♦Some states began registering births at a different time from the year death records were collected.

♦Many states began to register marriages later than births and deaths.

For these reasons, the dates for vital records registration shown here should be considered as guidelines only. For more complete information about vital records registration history in a specific state, see the book noted as the source at the end of this list.

AL 1908
AK 1913

AZ	1909[1]
AR	1914[2]
CA	1905[3]
CO	1907
CT	1897
DE	1881[4]
DC	1874
FL	1899
GA	1919
HI	1896[5]
ID	1911
IL	1916
IN	1907[6]
IA	1880
KS	1911[7]
KY	1911
LA	1914
ME	1892[8]
MD	1898
MA	1841
MI	1867
MN	1900
MO	1863
MT	1907
NE	1905[9]
NV	1867
NH	1901
NJ	1878
NM	1880
NY	1880
NC	1913[10]
ND	1899[11]
OH	1867
OK	1908
OR	1903
PA	1906
RI	1853
SC	1915[12]
SD	1905[13]
TN	1914
TX	1903
UT	1905[14]
VT	1955[15]
VA	1912
WA	1907
WV	1917
WI	1907
WY	1909[16]

[1] Marriages: 1891
[2] Marriages: 1917
[3] Includes marriages
[4] Also 1861-63
[5] Actually began earlier, but few records in existence before this date
[6] Births, 1907; deaths 1900
[7] Marriages: 1913
[8] Includes marriage registration
[9] Marriages: 1864
[10] Deaths: 1930. Marriages: 1962
[11] Also 1893-95
[12] Marriages: 1950
[13] Includes marriages
[14] Marriages: 1887
[15] Includes marriages. Vital records were kept in the towns from 1760
[16] Marriages: 1941

Source: George B. Everton, Sr., *The Handy Book for Genealogists,* Eighth Ed., Everton Publishers, Inc., Logan, UT, 1991.

US CITIES AND STATES REQUIRING CIVIL REGISTRATION BY 1880

Cities

New Orleans	1790
Boston	1848
Philadelphia	1860
Pittsburgh	1870
Baltimore	1875

States

Delaware	1860
Florida	1865
Hawaii	1850
Iowa	1880
Massachusetts	1841
Michigan	1867
New Hampshire	1840
New Jersey	1878
New York	1880
Rhode Island	1853
Vermont	1770
Virginia	1853
Wisconsin	1876
Washington, D.C.	1871

Source: Arlene Eakle and Johni Cerny, *The Source, A Guidebook of American Genealogy.* Ancestry Publishing Co., Salt Lake City, 1984.

ACCESSING U.S. VITAL RECORDS

The following sources are helpful in tracking down vital records in the United States:
♦ *Where to Write for Vital Records: Births, Deaths, Marriages, and Divorces,* comp. U.S. Department of Health and Human Services. (DHHS Publication No. 93-1142; $2.75 in 1995).

Information provided (state by state) in this publication includes costs of certified copies, the address of the office having custody of the records, and remarks concerning the types of records available and the period of time covered by the available records.

To order, write to: U.S. Government Printing Office, Superintendent of Documents, Washington, D.C. 20402. Or telephone (202) 783-3238.
♦ **Thomas J. Kemp,** *International Vital Records Handbook,* 3rd Ed., Genealogical Publishing Co., Baltimore, 1994.

This book not only offers most of the information listed in the DHHS publication described above, but it also provides a sample copy of the necessary application forms for each office, which may be photocopied for mailing to state offices. Procedures for ordering birth, marriage, and death certificates from each state, province, territory, and country are given. The book includes addresses of key archives and libraries in 200 countries and territories.
♦ **George B. Everton, Sr.,** *The Handy Book for Genealogists,* Eighth Ed., The Everton Publishers, Inc., Logan, UT, 1991, provides county mailing addresses.
♦ **Alice Eichholz, ed.,** *Ancestry's Red Book: American State, County, and Town Sources.* Ancestry Publishing, Salt Lake City, Utah, 1989, 1992.

County addresses as well as New England town addresses may be found in this book.
♦ **Elizabeth Petty Bentley,** *County Courthouse Book.* Genealogical Publishing Co., Inc., Baltimore, 1990.

The book, arranged by state, provides a summary of each state's court system with current addresses and telephone numbers for 3,351 county courthouses. It includes location and dates of coverage for land records, naturalization records, probate records, and vital records and often gives alternative places to locate records.
♦ *Research Outlines* for the states, published by the Family History Library of the Church of Jesus Christ of Latterday Saints, Salt Lake City, Utah.

These outlines, which give specific vital records information for each state, are extremely useful. They may be purchased at most Family History Centers.

Source: "375 Years of Vital Records in the United States: Where and How to Access Them in 1995," lecture by William C. Kleese, Family History Land, Tucson, AZ, at the National Genealogy Society Conference of the States, 1995.

AERIAL PHOTOS OF GERMAN VILLAGES

The Cartographic and Architectural Branch of the National Archives is able to provide aerial photographs of German villages.

To initiate a request, send a map on which the location of the village is marked, or provide exact geographic coordinates (latitude and longitude) of the village, along with any variant spellings that the village name may have. The Cartographic and architectural Branch will reply with an order form and the negative numbers it has for the village, as well as a cost list. Address the request to the Cartographic and Architectural Branch (NNSC), National Archives and Records Administration, 8601 Adelphi Road, College Park, MD 20740-6001. Allow four to six weeks for delivery

HISTORICAL RECORDS SURVEY PROGRAM (WPA)

The Work Projects Administration, established in 1935, was responsible for the relief program associated with the "New Deal." One WPA project was the Historical Records Survey Program, which was responsible for the Soundex index to the U.S. population censuses of 1880, 1900, 1910, and 1920, as well as naturalization indexes — both areas microfilmed by the National Archives.

The goal of the Historical Records Survey Program was to locate and describe records at the county level across the United States.

Few of the projects were completed, and many records that were compiled were destroyed or lost. The agency was discontinued in 1942.

The Historical Records Survey produced bibliographies, inventories, indexes, and other historical materials. Because the projects were conducted during the lifetimes of an extraordinary number of German immigrants in America, it could be profitable to investigate specific areas of German settlements to determine whether records from the Historical Records Survey are extant.

What records remain of the Historical Records Survey are found in the National Archives' "Records of the Work Projects Administration," Record Group 69. The National Archives does not have the microfilm publications or the unpublished project material of the Historical Records Survey. These publications are listed in the Work Projects Administration *Bibliography of Research Projects Reports, Check List of Historical Records Survey Publi-*

cations, Technical Series, Research and Records Bibliography 7 (Washington: Work Projects Administration, 1943). The bibliography has been reprinted by the Genealogical Publishing Co., Baltimore, 1969. Names and addresses of the state depositories for the unpublished project material appear in an appendix to this bibliography.

Reference
The WPA Historical Records Survey: A Guide to the Unpublished Inventories, Indexes, and Transcripts, compiled by Loretta Hefner (Chicago: Society of American Archivists, 1980), contains lists of the specific holdings of HRS materials in each repository where they have been located.

CITY DIRECTORIES

The city directory serves an especially useful function as a complement to the U.S. Federal Census.

For example, during the decade of the 1880s, the number of German immigrants almost doubled that of the previous decade. The immigrants of this decade would likely have been counted in the U.S. census of 1890, but unfortunately, that census was almost completely destroyed. And even those immigrants who arrived in the 1870s and were counted in the 1880 census would not be soundexed in that census unless they were members of families with at least one child age 10 or younger.

Working against inclusion of German immigrants in the United States census during the heavy immigration decades is the fact that so many immigrants were moving about – traveling to join relatives, looking for work, heading for the gold fields, and seeking land. In this sense, the censuses were often aiming at thousands of moving targets, and when they were found, it was at only ten-year intervals.

If, however, immigrants lived in a locality where city (or other) directories were published during the second half of the nineteenth century and into the twentieth century, they could possibly be recorded in these directories – not just every ten years, but consecutively through each year of residency.

The city directory is an excellent tracking tool for German immigrants from about 1850 forward because it may provide clues as to when a person arrived in a given locality and when he or she either died or moved on.

Although city directories were published much earlier, they were at first sporadic, and it was not until around the middle of the nineteenth century that they became somewhat standardized.

City directories (as well as those for business and professional groups, members of specific industries, members of religious organizations, and social and military organizations) can offer significant clues in tracking immigrants from their ports of entry to their final destinations.

City directories generally list names of residents, their home addresses and occupations, names and addresses of businesses, and listings that include churches, cemeteries, schools, and other municipal and social institutions. Each volume of a city directory usually covers only one specific year, and occasionally two. City directories are now for the most part replaced by telephone directories.

The Library of Congress has the largest collection of city and county directories. Check first in local public and university libraries for city as well as professional organization directories.

References
• James Ethridge, ed., *Directory of Directories*, Gale Research, Detroit, 1980
• Dorothea N. Spear, *Bibliography of American Directories Through 1860*. American Antiquarian Society, Worcester, MA. 1961
• *City Directories of the United States*, Research Publications. (Available through the Family History Library and its centers; includes about 250 cities and regions from the late 1700s to 1901. Pre-1860 city directories are on more than 6,000 microfiche. Directories for 1861 to 1901 are on 1,119 microfilms. Check the Family History Library Catalog under United States - Directories.

MANUSCRIPT COLLECTIONS

Since 1959, the Library of Congress has requested from libraries and other repositories the descriptions of their manuscript collections, which have been catalogued in the *National Union Catalog of Manuscript Collections*. (NUCMC Washington, DC. Library of Congress, 1959-

This source can be valuable in identifying the ancestral home of German immigrant families.

The volumes are indexed. One might check the index using many topics, a few suggestions for which follow:
• a surname of interest
• Genealogy, then the surname of interest
• Germany
• Germans in the United States, Prussia
• specific churches, such as the Reformed Church
• localities of interest;
• Hessians or other specific interest groups
• Germans from Russia
• school records

The index provides the year the item was catalogued and the entry number for that year. Entries are arranged alphabetically in the catalog and include the title, a short description of the manuscript, location of the collection, brief description of the contents, name of the donor, and an indication as to whether a finding aid exists in the repository for the collection.

Source: "Locating the Ancestral Home: Manuscript Collections," *German Genealogical Digest*, Vol. II, No. 2, 1986.

GERMAN NEWSPAPERS IN THE UNITED STATES

The earliest German newspapers were published in Philadelphia. They included *Die Philadelphische Zeitung,* 1732; *Der Hoch-Deutsch Pensylvanische Geschicht-Schreiber,* 1739; *Die Zeitung,* 1748; and *Der Wochentliche Philadelphische Staatsbote,* 1762.

A German-language newspaper, the *Germantowner Zeitung,* holds the distinction of having first printed the news of American independence in its edition of July 3, 1776,[1] scooping all English language newspapers.

The major influence on the German press came with the immigration of the Forty-eighters (the Germans who had been active in the brief revolution in Germany in 1848), who were heavily involved in literary, musical, gymnastic, and political affairs. Forty-eighters at one time controlled a majority of all German newspapers in the United States.

In 1840 there were about 40 German newspapers publishing in the United States. That number had almost doubled in 1848. By 1852 there were 133 German-language newspapers in the United States, and by 1860 there were about 266. Between 1848 and the start of the Civil War, the United States experienced the golden age of German-language newspapers.

In 1885, of all the foreign-language newspapers in the United States, German-language papers represented 79 percent. Their popularity crested in 1894, when more than 800 papers were publishing.

The decline

World War I severely drained the energy of the German press. In 1917 Congress enacted a law whereby all war-related matters prepared for print were to be submitted to the local postmaster for censoring until the loyalty of the paper could be established. By 1920 there were found to be only 278 German-language publica-

tions, many of which were house organs for lodges, churches, and social organizations. By 1930 only 172 German-language publications remained; by 1950, only 60.[2]

[1]"Newspapers: Unique Sources for German Family and Local History," by Laraine Ferguson. *German Genealogical Digest,* Vol. 3, No. 3, 1987.
[2]La Vern J. Rippley, *The German-Americans,* University Press of America, Lan-ham, Md., 1984. pp. 163-166.

GERMAN-AMERICAN NEWSPAPER RESOURCES

♦Karl J.R. Arndt, and May E. Olson, comps. *German-American Newspapers and Periodicals, 1732-1955: History and Bibliography.* 2nd rev. ed. 1961. Reprint. Johnson Report Corp., New York. Vol. 2 (FHL film 824,091)

♦Karl J. R. Arndt and May E. Olson, *The German Language Press of the Americas 1732-1968: A History and Bibliography Die deutschsprachige Presse der Amerikas.* Munich: Verlag Dokumentation, 1973-1976

♦Clarence Saunders Brigham, *History and Bibliography of American Newspapers, 1690-1820.* 2 Vols. American Antiquarian Society, Worcester, Mass., 1947. (Additions and corrections published in 1961.)

♦*Ethnic Press in the United States: Lists of Foreign Language Nationality and Ethnic Newspapers and Periodicals in the United States,* comp. by American Council for Nationalities Service, New York, 1974.

♦ Winifred Gregory, ed. *American Newspapers, 1821-1936: A Union List of Files Available in the United States and Canada.* Reprint, Kraus Reprint Corp., New York. 1967. (FHL film 430,291)

♦Betty M. Jarboe, *Obituaries: A Guide to Sources.* Boston, G.K. Hall & Co., 1982

♦Anita Creek Milner, *Newspaper Indexes: A Location and Subject Guide for Researchers.* Scarecrow Press, Metuchen,

NJ, 1977.

◆ United States, Library of Congress. *Chronological Index of Newspapers for the Period 1801-1967 in the Collections of the Library of Congress.* Comp. by Paul E. Swigart. Washington, DC, Library of Congress, 1956.

◆ Julie Winklepeck, ed. *Gale Directory of Publications and Broadcast Media* formerly *(Ayer Directory of Publications).* Annual since 1869. Gale Research Inc., Detroit, Michigan.

◆ Grace D. Parch (ed.), *Directory of Newspaper Libraries in the U.S. and Canada.* New York: Special Libraries Association, c 1976

◆ Lubomyr R. Wynar and Anna T. Wynar, *Encyclopedic Directory of Ethnic Newspapers and Periodicals in the United States.* Littleton, Colo.: Libraries Unlimited, c 1976

◆ Lubomyr R. Wynar, *Guide to the American Ethnic Press: Slavic and East European Newspapers and Periodicals.* Kent, Ohio: Center for the Study of Ethnic Publications, 1986.

◆ *Broadcast Media. . . . an Annual Guide to Newspapers, Magazines, Journals, and Related Publications* (formerly *Ayer Directory of Publications*). Published annually since 1869. IMS Press.

◆ *Benn's Media Directory International.* Tonbridge, England: Benn's Business Information Services, annual. (Arranged by nation and city of the newspaper)

GERMAN-AMERICAN NEWSPAPERS

Listed below are United States towns and cities where German newspapers and periodicals were once published, as found in *The German Language Press of the Americas*, by K.J.R. Arndt and M.E. Olson.

Alabama: Birmingham, Cullman, Mobile, Warrior

A farmer pays his rent

Arizona: St. Michaels
Arkansas: Fort Smith, Little Rock, St. Joe
California: Anaheim, Fresno, Glendale, Lodi, Los Angeles, Mokelumne Hill, Mountain View, Oakland, Petaluma, Sacramento, San Diego, San Francisco, San Jose, Santa Barbara, Santa Rosa, Stockton
Colorado: Denver, Greeley, Leadville, Pueblo
Connecticut: Bridgeport, Hartford, Meriden, New Haven, Norwich, Rockville, Southbury, Waterbury
District of Columbia: Washington
Delaware: Wilmington
Florida: Jacksonville, Miami, Pensacola, San Antonio
Georgia: Atlanta, Savannah
Idaho: Cottonwood
Illinois: Addison, Alton, Apple River, Arlington Heights, Aurora, Beardstown, Beecher, Belleville, Bloomington, Brookfield, Cairo, Carlinville, Carlyle, Carmi, Centralia, Champaign, Chester, Chicago, Danville, Decatur, Dundee, East St. Louis, Edwardsville, Effingham, Elgin, Evanston, Forest Park, Freeport, Galena, German Valley, Hawthorne, Highland, Hoyleton, Joliet, Kankakee, Kewanee, La

An emigrant train in Berlin

Salle, Lensburg, Leonore, Lincoln, Litchfield, McHenry, Mascoutah, Mattoon, Mendota, Mundelein, Mt. Olive, Naperville, Nashville, Nauvoo, Nokomis, Okawville, Ottawa, Pekin, Peoria, Peru, Quincy, Ravenswood, Red Bud, Rock Island, Rockford, Springfield, Staunton, Sterling, Streator, Techny, Urbana, Vandalia, Warsaw, Waterloo, Wheaton, Woodstock

Indiana: Anderson, Batesville, Berne, Bowling Green, Brazil, Brookville, Collegeville, Crown Point, Elkhart, Evansville, Fort Wayne, Goshen, Hamburg, Hammone, Huntingburg, Indianapolis, Jeffersonville, Lafayette, La Port, Logansport, Michigan City, Mount Vernon, New Albany, Richmond, Rockport, St. Meinrad, Seymour, South Bend, Tell City, Terre haute, Vincennes

Iowa: Ackley, Alton, Andrew, Boone, Breda, Burlington, Carroll , Cascade, Cedar Bluffs, Cedar Rapids, Charles City, Clinton, Council Bluffs, Davenport, Decatur, Denison, Des Moines, Dubuque, Dumont, Dysart, Earling, Elkader, Esscx, Fort Dodge, Grundy Center, Guttenberg, Holstein, Ida Grove, Independence, Iowa City, Keokuk, Lansing, Le Mars, Lyons, Manning, Maquoketa, Marshalltown, Monticello, Muscatine, New Hampton, Newton, Osage, Ottumwa, Postville, Reinbeck, Remson, Rock Rapids, Rockford, Schleswig, Sigourney, Sioux City , Spirit Lake, Sumner, Tama City, Toledo, Vinton, Walcott, Waterloo, Waverly, Wellsburg, Wheatland

Kansas: Alma, Atchison, Atwood, Burrton, Canada, Ellinwood, Emporia, Fort Scott, Great Bend, Halstead, Hays, Hillsboro, Hutchinson, Inman, Kansas City, Kingman, Kinsley, Lacrosse, Lawrence, Leavenworth, Lehigh, Lindsborg, marion, Marysville, McPherson, Newton, Paola, Pittsburg, Russell, Topeka, Wichita, Winfield,

Wyandotte
Kentucky: Berea, Covington, Louisville, Newport, Stanford
Louisiana: Lafayette, New Orleans
Maryland: Baltimore, Cumberland , Fredericktown, Hagerstown, New Windsor
Massachusetts: Boston, Clinton, Fitchburg, Greenfield, Holyoke, Lawrence, Lowell, Springfield, West Roxbury
Michigan: Adrian, Ann Arbor, Au Gres, Battle Creek, Bay City, Coldwater, Detroit, Grand Rapids, Jackson, Lansing, Manistee, Marquette, Menominee, Monroe, Muskegon, Pigeon, Port Huron, Saginaw, Sebewaing, Sturgis, West Bay City
Minnesota: Carver, Chaska, Duluth, Fairmont, Freeport, Glencoe, Jordan, Lake City, Little Falls, Mankato, Melrose, Minneapolis, Mountain Lake, New Ulm, Owatonna, Perham, Red Wing, Rochester, St. Cloud, St. Paul, Shakopee, Springfield, Stillwater, Wabasha, Waconia, Winona, Wykoff
Missouri: Boonville, California, Cape Girardeau, Centreton, Chamois, Clayton, Clyde, Concordia, Festus, Franklin, Fulton, Hannibal, Hermann, Higginsville, Jackson, Jefferson City, Joplin, Kansas City, Lexington, Marthasville, Moberly, O'Fallon, St. Charles, St. Joseph, St. Louis, Ste. Genevieve, Sedalia, Springfield, Starkenburg, Stewartsville, Warrenton, Washington, Westphalia
Montana: Butte, Great Falls, Helena, Plevna
Nebraska: Arago, Auburn, Beatrice, Bellevue, Bloomfield, College View, Columbus, Crete, Deshler, Fairbury, Falls City, Fremont, Grand Island, Hartingon, Hastings, Jansen, Leigh, Lincoln, Meadow Grove, Nebraska City, Norfolk, Omaha, Schuyler, Seward, Steinauer, Sterling, Sutton, West Point, York
Nevada: Virginia City
New Hampshire: Manchester
New Jersey: Atlantic City, Bayonne, Bound Brook, Camden, Carlstadt, Egg Harbor, Elizabeth, Fairview, Hoboken, Irvington, Jersey City, Newark, New Brunswick, Orange, Passaic, Paterson, Riverside, Sea-Isle City, Town of Union, Trenton, Union, Union City
New York: Albany , Amsterdam, Auburn, Bardonia, Brooklyn, Buffalo, Camden, College Point, East New York, Elmhurst, Elmira, Erie, Forest Hills, Long Island, Haverstraw, Hicksville, Huntington, Ithaca, Jamaica, Kingston (Rondout), Lockport, Long Island City, Morrisania, Mount Vernon, Newburgh, Newown, New York, Oswego, Poughkeepsie, Rochester, Schenectady, Sea Cliff, Staten Island, Syracuse, Tonawanda, Troy, Utica, Williamsburgh, Honkers
North Carolina: Goldsboro
North Dakota: Arthur, Ashley, Berwick, Beulah, Bismarck, Dickinson, Fargo, Fessenden, Golden Valley, Harvey, Havelock, Hebron, Jamestown, Linton, McClusky, Mannhaven, Medina, Minot, New Salm, Richardton, Rugby, Stanton, Strassburg, Wahpeton, Wishek, Zap
Ohio: Akron, Baltic, Bellaire, Berea, Bluffton, Bowling Green, Bridgeport, Bucyrus, Canton, Carthagena, Celina, Chillicothe, Cincinnati, Cleveland, Columbiana, Columbus, Coshocton, Dayton, Defiance, Delphos, East Liverpool, Elyria, Findlay, Fremont, Germantown, Greenville, Hamilton, Ironton, Kenton, Kingsville, Lancaster, Lima, Lorain, Mansfield, Marietta, Marion, Massillon, Millersburg, Minster, Morrow, Napoleon, New Bremen, New Philadelphia, Newark, Norwalk, Oak Harbor, Osnaburgh, Ottawa, Pauling, Perrysburg, Piqua, Pomeroy, Port Clinton, Portsmouth, Sandusky, Sidney, Springfield, Steubenville, Teutonia, Tiffin, Toledo, Upper Sandusky, Wapakoneta, Waterloo, Weinsberg, Woodsfield, Woodville, Wooster, Worthington, Xenia, Youngstown, Zanesville, Zoar
Oklahoma: Bessie, El Reno, Enid, Guthrie, Kingfisher, Medford, Okeene, Oklahoma City, Perry

The Hofbrauhaus, München, at Bockbier time, 1865

Oregon: Astoria, Bend, Portland, St. Benedict, Salem

Pennsylvania: Aaronsburg, Abbottstown, Adamsburg, Allegheny (see Pittsburgh), Allentown, Altoona, Berlin, Bath, Berwick, Bethlehem, Boyertown, Carlisle, Cattawissa, Chambersburg, Chartiers, Chestnut-Hill, Columbia, Danville, Doylestown, Easton, Economy, Ephrata, Erie, Gap, Germantown, Gettysburg, Greensburg, Hamburg, Hanover, Harrisburg, Hazleton, Hellertown, Herman, Honesdale, Huntingdon, Jefferson, Jim Thorpe, Johnstown, Kutztown, Lancaster, Lansdale, Lebanon, Lewisburg, Mansfield, Marietta, Marklesburg, Mauchchunk, McKeesport, Meadville, Mercersbrg, Meyerstown, Middleburg, Mifflintown, Milford Square, Millheim, Nanticoke, Nazareth, New Berlin, Norristown, Orwigsburg, Pennsburg, Perkasie, Philadelphia, Philipsburg, Pittsburgh, Pottstown, Pottsville, Quakertown, Reading, Schellsburg, Scottdale, Scranton, Selinsgrove, Sharpsburg, Shrewsbury, Skippack, Somerset, Souderton, South Bethlehem, Strassburg, Stroudsburg, Sumneytown, Sunbury, Telford, Thurlow, Vincent, Weissport, West Chester, Wilkes-Barre, Williamsport, Womelsdorf, York, Zieglerville

Rhode Island: Providence

South Carolina: Charleston

South Dakota: Aberdeen, Eureka, Herreid, Java, Mitchell, Olivet, Orient, Parkston, Pierre, Redfield, Sioux Falls, Watertown, Yanktoon

Tennessee: Chaatanooga, Columbia, Hohenwald, Memphis, Nashville, Robbins

Texas: Austin, Bastrop, Bellville, Boerne, Brenham, Castroville, Comfort, Cuero, Dallas, Denison, Fort Worth, Franklin, Fredericksburg, Gainsville, Galveston, Giddings, Gonsales, Hallettsville, Houston, Independence, La Grange, Lockart, Marlin, Meyersville, New Braunfels, Rosebud, San Antonio, Schulenberg, Seguin, Shiner, Taylor, Temple, Victoria, Waco, Windhorst

Utah: Logan, Salt Lake City

Virginia: Alexandria, Bridgewater, New Market, Norfolk, Richmond, Staunton, Winchester

Washington: Bellingham, Everett, Ritzville, Seattle, South Bend, Spokane, Tacoma, Walla Walla

West Virginia: Wheeling

Wisconsin: Antigo, Appleton, Arcadia, Ashland, Athens, Beaver Dam, Beloit, Burlington, Cedarburg, Chilton,

Chippewa Falls, Clintonville, Cochrane, Columbus, Cumberland, Dorchester, Durand, Eagle, Eau Claire, Fond Du Lac, Fort Atkinson, Fountain City, Glidden, Grand Rapids, Green Bay, Hamburg, Horicon, Janesville, Jefferson, Juneau, Kaukauna, Kenosha, Kewaunee, Kiel, La Crosse, Lomira, Madison, Manitowoc, Marathon, Marinette, Marshfield, Mauston, Mayville, Medford, Menasha, Menomonie, Merrill, Merrimack, Milwaukee, Monroe, Neillsville, New Glarus, Oshkosh, Phillips, Platteville, Plymouth, Port Washington, Portage, Princeton, Racine, Reedsburg, Ripon, St. Francis, St. Nazianz, Sauk City, Schlessingerville (now Slinger), Shawano, Sheboygan, Spokane, Stevens Point, Stockbridge, Superior, Theresa, Watertown, Wasau, Wauwatosa, West Bend, Weyauwega, Wittenberg
Wyoming: Laramie

CURRENT GERMAN-AMERICAN NEWSPAPERS AND PERIODICALS

✦**Abendpost & Milwaukee Deutsche Zeitung,** 55 E. Jackson Boulevard, Suite 1820, Chicago, IL 60604. Tel. (312) 368-4884. Twice weekly.
✦**Amerika Woche,** 4732 N. Lincoln Avenue, Chicago, IL 60625. Tel. (312) 275-5054. Fax: (312) 275-5054. Weekly
✦**Aufbau,** 2121 Broadway, New York, NY 10023. Tel. (212) 873-7400. Fax (212) 496-5736. Bi-weekly
✦**California Staats-Zeitung,** 1201 N. Alvarado Street, Los Angeles, CA 90026. Tel. (213) 413-5500. Fax (213) 413-5469. Weekly
✦**Continental Reporter,** 613 9th Avenue, Seattle, WA 98104. Tel. (206) 682-1574
✦**Der Deutsch-Amerikaner, The German-American Journal,** DANK-Haus, 4740 N. Western Avenue, Chicago, IL 60625. Tel. (312) 275-1100. Fax (312) 275-4010. Monthly
✦**Deutsche Welt-USA,** P.O. Box 35831,

Houston, TX 77235. Tel (713) 721-7277
✦**Deutschland Nachrichten. Eine Wochenzeitung des German Information Center,** 950 3rd Avenue, New York, NY 10022. Tel (212) 888-9840. Fax (212) 752-6691
✦**Die Hausfrau,** 1060 Gaines School Road, Suite B-3, Athens, GA 30605. Tel (404) 548-4382
✦**Der Hermann Sohn,** 8151 Lisbon Way, Sacramento, CA 95823
✦**Eintracht,** 9456 N. Lawler Avenue, Skokie, Il 60076. Tel. (708) 677-9456. Fax (708) 677-9471 or 9456. Twice weekly
✦**International Monthly,** P.O. Box 5335, San Jose, CA 95150. Tel. (408) 227-0458
✦**Neue Presse,** 29397 Agoura Road, Suite 108, Agoura Hills, CA 91301. Tel. (818) 707-1277. Fax (818) 707-0101
✦**New-Yorker Staats-Zeitung und Herold,** 160 W. 71st Street, New York, NY 10023. Tel. (212) 875-0769. Fax (212) 875-0534. Weekly
✦**New Jersey Freie Zeitung,** 500 S. 31st Street, Kenilworth, NJ 07033. Tel. (201) 245-7995. Fax (201) 215-7997. Weekly
✦**Nordamerikanische Wochen-Post und Detroiter Abend-Post,** 1120 E. Long Lake Road, Troy, MI 48089. Tel (313) 528-2810. Fax (313) 528-2741
✦**Pazifische Rundschau,** P.O. Box 0-1, Blaine, WA 98104. Tel. (604) 270-2923. Bi-weekly
✦**San Francisco-Neue Presse,** 665 Eddy Street No. 1, San Francisco, CA 94109. Tel. (415) 441-7145
✦**Saxon News Volksblatt,** 5393 Pearl Road, Cleveland, OH 44113. Tel. (216) 842-0333
✦**Sonntagspost,** 55 E. Jackson Boulevard, Suite 1820, Chicago, IL 60604. Tel. (312) 368-4800 and 368-4884. Fax (312) 427-7829. Weekly
✦**Sonntagspost und Milwaukee deutsche Zeitung,** 120 Regency Parkway, Suite 220, Regency Court, Omaha, NE 68114. Tel. (402) 393-0142 or 1-800-228-0089
✦**Washington Journal,** 1113 National Press Building, Washington, DC 20045-

1853. Fax (703)938-2251

Source: Partially from *Adressbuch: Der deutsch-amerikanischen Zusammenarbeit,* Bonn, 1994

EMIGRATION RECORDS IN GERMAN NEWSPAPERS

by Friedrich R. Wollmershäuser

Many American genealogical researchers write to Germany to obtain copies of their ancestors' "emigration record," without really knowing what such a file might contain.. It is often assumed that such a record includes biographical information on the emigrant, the port of embarkation and debarkation, the dates of departure and arrival, and the exact destination in the country of settlement.

Actually, most of these items were of little interest to the authorities in the German countries. The main objectives for emigration records were the following:
•To have a legally valid declaration of the abandonment of citizenship
•To make sure that passports were not issued to young men under conscription
•To make proof that the emigrants had sufficient travel funds, so his home country would not have to support him when he ran out of money on the trip
•To make sure the emigrant paid his debts before he left
• To make sure that under-age emigrants had sufficient protection by accompanying adults and were protected at their place of settlement
•To collect data for statistical purposes
Emigration records therefore contain only some data to identify the emigrant (such as name, age or birthdate, and occupation) and his family members, proof that the emigrant was clear of debts or a declaration of a warrant that he would be liable for such, indication of the property he exported, agreements by the guardians of children that they have no objection,

similar agreements by military authorities, and sometimes a contract with an emigration agent. Most emigration records do not, however, include all this information.
Where to look for records
Emigration records may be searched, obviously, through the records available at or near the emigrant's place of origin. But if the specific place of origin is not known, and if all sources in the country of destination (the United States, for example) have been exhausted without finding the exact location, then one should consult the emigration indexes of the state archive for the country of origin (Bavaria, Hesse, etc.).

If this search proves unsuccessful, one may try to find the place of origin by checking the main newspapers and gazettes of the country of origin. This requires a good knowledge of the year – or even better, the months – of emigration, and it requires some trust in the lawfulness of the ancestor. Illegal emigrants are often mentioned too, but usually not close to the time when they left; therefore, such entries can be located only with the help of overall indexes.
Local newspapers
Common types of newspaper announcements that contain or may contain names of emigrants include,
•Summons to a deserter from the armed forces to appear before court
• Summons to appear before court or lose citizenship after illegal emigration
•Search for fugitive persons who are suspected of having committed a crime
•Summons to missing or absent persons to appear before court or being declared legally deceased.
•Call for missing heirs.
Official gazettes
Besides local newspapers and papers with statewide circulation (in which announce-ments appeared concerning summonses to missing persons, or notifications of emigrations of persons who may have had creditors, etc.), there were also official gazettes used for the same purpose. These had statewide circulation and gen-

erally served as enclosures in other media.

In Prussia, a "Public Advertiser" (*Öffentlicher Anzeiger*) was published as an enclosure to every issue of the "Official Newsletter of the Royal Government" (*Amtsblatt der Königlichen Regierung*) for each government seat (for example, *Amtsblatt der Königlichen Regierung Aachen*, or "Official Newsletter of the Royal Government in Aachen"). It contained warrants, names of missing heirs, names of absent divorcees, summonses to missing persons, and summonses to draft-dodgers. Similar entries were published in the *Öffentlicher Anzeiger*, an enclosure to a gazette with the following names:
1819: *Allgemeine Preußische Staatszeitung*
1843: *Allgemeine Preußische Zeitung*
1848: *Preußischer Staatsanzeiger*
1849: *Kgl. Preußischer Staatsanzeiger*
1871: *Deutscher Reichsanzeiger und Königlichen Preußischer Staatsanzeiger*
1918: *Deutscher Reichsanzeiger und Preußischer Staatsanzeiger* (to 1945)
This *Reichsanzeiger*, as a nationwide official gazette, was used as an instrument for notifications to and warrants for persons who were assumed to be somewhere in Prussia, or, from 1871 onward, somewhere in Germany or were being summoned by German authorities.

Some local papers

Listed below are a few local newspapers which carried emigration announcements:

Baden
c 1800-1871: *Karlsruher Zeitung* (indexed by Friedrich R. Wollmershäuser).
c 1800-1868: *Großherzoglich Badisches Anzeigeblatt für. . .* (from 1832 to 1856 four series, then on until 1868 by the title *Großherzoglich Badisches Allgemeines Anzeigeblatt*).
c 1800-1871: local newspapers
Württemberg
c 1800-1850: *Schwäbischer Merkur* and enclosure *Schwäbische Chronik*.

c 1800-1870: *Stuttgarter Anzeigen von allerhand Sachen (etc.)* and other titles, beginning 1850 by the name *Staatsanzeiger für Württemberg* (very incomplete to the late 1820s).
c 1820-1870: local newspapers.
Hohenzollern
1809-1834: *Wochenblatt für das Fürstentum Hohenzollern-Sigmaringen*.
1829-1836: *Wochenblatt für das Fürstentum Hohenzollern-Hechingen*.
1837-1844: *Verordnungs- und Intelligenzblatt für das Fürstentum Hohenzollern-Hechingen*
1845-1850: *Verordnungs- und Anzeigeblatt für das Fürstentum Hechingen*.
1855-1933: *Amtsblatt der Königlich Preußischen Regierung zu Sigmaringen* (and enclosure) *Oeffentlicher Anzeiger*.
Bayern (Bavaria)
Emigrations announced in local newspapers and gazettes
Braunschweig
1846-1871: *Braunschweigische Anzeigen*, and other papers. Emigration entries published by Fritz Gruhne, *Auswanderer-listen des ehemaligen Herzogtums Braunschweig ohne Stadt Braunschweig und Landkreis Holzminden. Quellen und Forschungen zur braunschweigischenGeschichte 20. Braunschweig: Geschichtsverein 1971).*
Waldeck
1829-1872: *Fürstlich Waldeckisches Regierungsblatt*. Entries on emigrants published by Karl Thomas, *Die waldeckische Auswanderung zwischen 1829 und 1872*. 2 vols. (Köln and Eslohe: privately published by the author, 1983).
Kurhessen
1831-1866: *Wochenblatt für die Provinz Niederhessen*.
Nassau
1849-1868: *Nassauisches Intelligenzblatt*. Names of emigrants published by Wolf-Heino Struck, *Die Auswanderung aus dem Herzogtum Nassau (1806-1866)*. Geschichtliche Landeskunde 4 (Wiesbaden: Steiner 1966), 133-203.

Prussia
1819-1843: *Allgemeine Preußische Staatszeitung.*
1843-1848: *Preußische Staatszeitung.*
1848: *Preußischer Staatsanzeiger.*
1849-1871: *Königlicher Preußischer Staatsanzeiger.*
German Empire
1871-1918: *Deutscher Reichsanzeiger und Königlicher Preußischer Staatsanzeiger.* (These years are being abstracted by the Germanic Emigrants Register, P.O. Box 1720, 49347 Diepholz, Germany)
Bibliography
♦ Martin Hankel, Rolf Taubert, *Die Deutsche Presse 1848-1850. Eine Bibliographie Deutsche Presseforschung,* Band 25. (München: K.G. Saur, 1986)
-The revolution of 1848-49 and the German press, with a listing of most German periodicals published then, and their current locations.
♦ Winifred Gregory (ed.), *List of the Serial Publications of Foreign Governments, 1815-1931* (New York: H.W. Wilson, 1932, reprint Millwood, NY: Kraus, 1973).
- An impressive bibliography of official gazettes published all over the world. Entries on Germany are found on pp. 226 to 271; they cover Germany in general, the German Empire from 1871 onward, and the German states alphabetically, from Alsace Lorraine, Anhalt, Baden, etc. to Württemberg.
♦ Gert Hagelweide (comp.), *Literatur zur deutschsprachigen Presse: eine BibliographieDortmunder Beiträge zur Zeitungsforschung,* Band 35. (München: K.G. Saur, 1985).
-An exhaustive bibliography of writings about the press in the German-speaking area in general, newspapers in individual states and towns, and the use and impact of newspapers. Catalogues of newspaper holdings in libraries and archives are listed on pp. 80 to 106.
♦ Oskar Michel (comp.), *Handbuch Deutscher Zeitungen 1917* (Berlin: Elsner,

1917).
-Includes all newspapers published at that date in the German Empire, with their names, publishers, years of foundation, and other details.
♦ Hartmut Walravens (ed.), *Internationale Zeitungsbestände in deutschen Bibliotheken: ein Verzeichnis von 19 000 Zeitungen, Amtsblättern und zeitungsähnlichen Periodika mit Besitznachweisen und geographischem Register* (International newspaper holdings in German libraries) (München: K.G. Saur, 1993).
-Includes the titles of 18,000 German newspapers and official gazettes with (not quite complete) references to current locations
♦ *Zeitschriften-Datenbank (ZBD)* 30th edition (Berlin: Deutsches Bibliotheksinstitut, 1994).
-419 microfiches and a manual in German and English. Includes 2,250,400 locations in Germany for 719,346 periodicals.

The author: Friedrich R. Wollmershäuser, M.A. Accredited Genealogist, Herrengasse 8-10, 89610 Oberdischingen, Germany. © Friedrich R. Wollmershäuser, 1997.

LOCATING U.S. NEWSPAPERS
(Gale Directory of Publications)

The *Gale Directory of Publications and Broadcast Media,* available on the reference shelves of many public libraries, can help the researcher determine which current newspapers (and other publications) were being published during an ancestor's residency in a particular town or city in the United States. Only publications which are still in business are listed in this reference tool, however.

Organized in three volumes, the *Gale Directory's* first two volumes list alphabetically all states of the United States, subdivided into towns and cities; the third volume contains indexes, tables, and maps.

Many of the periodicals listed are trade publications, which may be helpful if an ancestor is known to have been active in a particular business or trade.

Founding dates of newspapers and other publications which circulated in an ancestor's settlement area can be determiined in this directory. For example, the researcher may seek to learn which currently published newspapers were in business between the year an ancestor immigrated to Cincinnati in 1852, and 1898, the year he moved away. The answer is found by checking the directory first for the state, then the town or city where the immigrant settled, and by looking through the list of newspapers and magazines in that location to see if any of them were publishing between 1852 and 1898. Thus one may learn not only which current publications were in existence during an ancestor's residency in an area, but which publications should be eliminated as possibilities. The directory is updated periodically.

SPECIAL-INTEREST PERIODICALS

✦*Ancestry*, 440 South 400 West Suite D, Salt Lake City, UT 84101. Tel. (800) 531-1790. Fax. (800) 531-1798. E-mail. info@ancestry.com. Published six times annually. 32 pages. Subscription price $18 per year, $33 for two years,$45 for three years. Illustrated, wide range of topics in articles written by established genealogists. Geared toward beginning and intermediate researchers.

✦*Der Blumenbaum,* quarterly journal of the Sacramento German Genealogy Society, P.O. Box 660061-0061, Sacramento, CA 95866-0061. Fax (916)421-8032. $15.00 per year membership dues, which includes the 48-page journal. Articles on a wide range of German genealogical, historical, and cultural topics

✦ *Deutschland.* USA distributor: Edelweiss Institute, Germanic Language & Cultural Center, Nuremberg, PA 18241. Publisher: Frankfurt Societäts-Verlag, in cooperation with the Press and Information Office of the German Federal Government. Subscription DM 24.00 per year. (State choice of either English- or German-language editions.) Magazine on politics, culture, business and science, 68 pages, published six times per year. Internet: http://www.bundesregierung.de and – http://www.government de

✦*Everton's Genealogical Helper,* The Everton Publishers, Inc., P.O. Box 368, Logan, UT 84323-0368. Tel (801) 752-6022 or (800) 443-6325. Fax (801) 752-0425. Internet: http://www.everton.com. Published six times per year. 284 pages. Subscription $21.00 per year. Covers very wide range of topics, including queries, book reviews, indexes, resources.

Lists and directories regularly published by Everton in *The Genealogical Helper*

Locality Periodicals: January and February issues

Family Associations and Periodicals: March-April issue

Directory of Genealogical Libraries: May-June issue

Directory of Genealogical Societies: July-August issue

Directory of Professional Researchers: September-October issue

✦*Das Fenster,* 1060 Gaines School Road, Suite B-3, Athens, GA 30605. Monthly. $15.00 per year. Written in German. Short articles, poetry, stories, timely topics.

✦ *German-American Genealogy,* quarterly publication of the Immigrant Genealogical Society, P.O. Box 7369, Burbank, CA 91510-7369. Tel. (818) 848-3122. Internet: http://www.feefhs.org/igs/frg-igs.html. Dues include a subscription to the journal. Single copies $4.

✦ *The German Connection,* quarterly journal of the German Research Association, Inc. P.O. Box 711600, San Diego, CA 92171-1600. Annual membership includes the journal. Articles are clearly written and pertinent to many facets of interest to German genealogists.

♦ *German Genealogical Digest,* 245 North Vine, Suite 106, Salt Lake City, UT84103. E-mail: ggd@aros.net. Published quarterly. Back issues $8 ($7 each if four or more are purchased); price includes postage. In-depth articles for the intermediate and advanced German researcher. Provides information on a wealth of German resources. Often provides extensive instructions for using German resource materials which are difficult for many researchers.

♦*German Life,* P.O. Box 609, Grantsville, MD 21536. Tel. (800) 314-6843. E-mail: GWWC14A@prodigy.com. Subscription: $19.95 for 6 issues per year. Illustrated in beautiful color, wide range of topics of interest to germanophiles. First-rate presentation, style, and information.

♦ *Heritage Quest: The Genealogy Magazine,* P.O. Box 329, Bountiful, UT 84011-0329. Tel. (801) 298-5446. Fax: (801) 298-5468. E-mail: sales@agll.com. Six issues per year, 130 pages. General genealogical reference, tips, techniques.

CURRENT NEWSPAPERS IN GERMANY

The leading German national newspapers are the *Süddeutsche Zeitung* (published in Munich), *Frankfurter Allgemeine Zeitung* (published in Frankfurt am Main), *Die Welt* (published in Berlin) and the *Frankfurter Rundschau* (Frankfurt). The leading tabloid is *Bild-Zeitung*, which is published in Hamburg.

Before reunification, the official state newspaper in the German Democratic Republic was *Neues Deutschland*. It still exists as an independent paper, but with a much-reduced readership. In general, eastern German newspapers tend to be regional in scope.

The largest and most influential eastern German newspapers include *Berliner Zeitung, Leipziger Volkszeitung, Sächsische Zeitung* (published in Dresden), *Freie Presse* (Chemnitz, Saxony) and *Mitteldeutsche Zeitung* (Halle, Saxony-Anhalt).

Nearly all of the eastern newspapers have been bought up by western or foreign media concerns.

Source: German Information Center, *Federal Republic of Germany*, ed. Susan Steiner, New York, 1996.

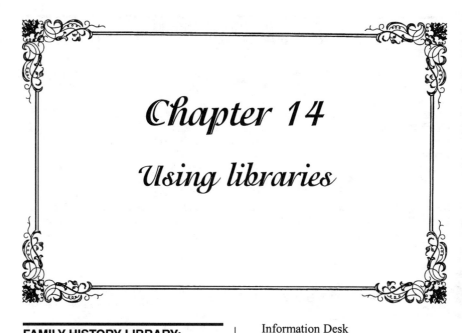

Chapter 14
Using libraries

FAMILY HISTORY LIBRARY: HOURS, TELEPHONE NUMBERS

The Family History Library in Salt Lake City is located at 35 North West Temple Street.

Hours of opening
Monday: 7:30 am - 6 pm
Tuesday-Saturday: 7:30 am - 10 pm
Sunday: closed

Holidays
Closed: New Year's Day, Fourth of July, 24 July (Pioneer Day, a Utah state holiday), Thanksgiving Day, and Christmas Day

Shortened hours
◆Day before Thanksgiving: 7:30 am - 5:00 pm
◆Christmas Eve: 7:30 am - 5 pm
◆New Year's Eve: 7:30 am - 5 pm
◆Memorial Day: 7:30 am - 6 pm
◆Labor Day: 7:30 - 6 pm

Telephone numbers
Europe Information .... (801) 240-3796 Desk
International .... (801) 240-3433

Information Desk
Library Information .... (801) 240-3702 Desk
U.S.-Canada (Books) .... (801) 240-2720
U.S.-Canada .... (801) 240-2364 (Microform)

FAMILY HISTORY LIBRARY: THE FLOORS

The researcher in Germanic ancestry will be most interested in materials on these floors of the Family History Library:

European (943-949) .... Basement 1
U.S. Family History .... Main Floor Books (929.273)
U.S. Newsletters .... Main Floor (929.27305)
U.S. Microforms .... Second Floor
Scandinavia (948) .... Basement 1
British Isles (941-942) .... Basement 2
Canada Books (971) .... Main Floor
Canada Family History .... Main Floor Books (929.271)

DEWEY DECIMAL NUMBERS
FOR MAJOR AREAS OF GERMANIC RESEARCH

	Geography	Genealogy	History
Europe, general	914	929.34	940
Germany	914.3	929.343	943
Austria	914.36	929.3436	943.6
Czech Republic	914.37	929.3437	943.7
Poland	914.38	929.3438	943.8
France	914.4	929.344	944
Russia	914.7	929.347	947
Scandanavia	914.8	929.348	948
Norway	914.81	929.3481	948.1
Sweden	914.85	929.3485	948.5
Denmark	914.89	929.3489	948.9
Other European	914.9	929.349	949
Switzerland	914.94	929.3494	949.4

DEWEY DECIMAL NUMBERS BY STATE

The beginning numbers of the Dewey Decimal Classification Scheme for the states of the United States:

Alabama	976.1
Alaska	979.8
Arizona	979.1
Arkansas	976.7
California	979.4
Colorado	978.8
Connecticut	974.6
Delaware	975.1
District of Columbia	975.3
Florida	975.9
Georgia	975.8
Hawaii	996.9
Idaho	979.6
Illinois	977.3
Indiana	977.2
Iowa	977.7
Kansas	978.1
Kentucky	976.9
Louisiana	976.3
Maine	974.1
Maryland	975.2
Massachusetts	974.4
Michigan	977.4
Minnesota	977.6
Mississippi	976.2
Missouri	977.8
Montana	978.6
Nebraska	978.2
Nevada	979.3
New Hampshire	974.2
New Jersey	974.9
New Mexico	978.9
New York	974.7
North Carolina	975.6
North Dakota	978.4
Ohio	977.1
Oklahoma	976.6
Oregon	979.5
Pennsylvania	974.8
Rhode Island	974.5
South Carolina	975.7
South Dakota	978.3
Tennessee	976.8
Texas	976.4
Utah	979.2
Vermont	974.3
Virginia	975.5
Washington	979.7
West Virginia	975.4
Wisconsin	977.5
Wyoming	978.7

DEWEY DECIMAL NUMBERS WITHIN THE 929 CATEGORY

929.0   Genealogy, names, insignia
                                    (general)
929.1 .... Genealogy
929.2 .... Family histories
929.3 .... Genealogical sources
929.4 .... Personal names
929.5 .... Cemetery records
929.6 .... Heraldry
929.7 ..... Royal houses, peerage, gentry,
                                    knighthood
929.8 .. Awards, orders, decorations, etc.
929.9 .... Forms of insignia and
                                    identifications

Source: Frank Fuqua, in Mission Oaks
Genealogy Club *Newsletter,* Winter 1997

FAMILY HISTORY LIBRARY TOOLS (FamilySearch)

FamilySearch is a computerized system of genealogical information, developed by the Family History Department of The Church of Jesus Christ of Latter-day Saints (LDS Church). It is available at the Family History Library in Salt Lake City and at many Family History Centers at other locations.

The following files of FamilySearch are described briefly below.

For detailed information about these programs, see the Research Guides published by the Family History Library. Another very helpful tool is this book: J. Carlyle Parker, *Going to Salt Lake City to Do Family History Research*, Marietta Publishing Company, Turlock, Cal., 1996.

Family History Library Catalog

The Family History Library Catalog, or FHLC, is a list of the records (books, microfilms, maps, and other materials) in the Family History Library in Salt Lake City. The FHLC provides an explanation of each of these records. It is available on compact disc on FamilySearch computers, and on microfiche.

The FHLC does not contain the records themselves, but rather it briefly describes each record, and its contents and shows where to find it in the library. New editions of the FHLC are published from time to time.

Ancestral File

The Ancestral File provides a collection of genealogies that link individuals into families and pedigrees. People throughout the world have been invited to send their genealogies to Ancestral File, the information from which is made available for research. The information includes names, with dates and places of birth, marriage, and death. The file also contains names and addresses of the individuals who have contributed the information.

Information from the Ancestral File should be carefully researched and used merely as a clue to further research. Many of the dates given in the file are estimates. Errors occur with some frequency due to individuals' reports of incorrect information

The IGI

The International Genealogical Index, or the IGI, is a worldwide index of 200 million name entries of deceased persons, based on government, church, and personal records. The bulk of the names come from vital records from the early 1500s to 1875. A very large number of names from German-speaking countries are contained in the IGI.

The IGI, prepared by the Church of Jesus Christ of Latter-day Saints is available on both microfiche and compact disk at the Family History Library in Salt Lake City and at Family History Centers. It contains about 200 million names.

The IGI is divided into two files: a main file and an addendum, which adds some 40 million more names which were acquired since publication of the main file. The index and its addendum are part of FamilySearch, available on computers at the Family History Library and Family History Centers.

A search in the country of Germany may be filtered to one of these nine German states: Alsace-Lorraine (France); Baden; Bayern; German, Misc.; Hesse-Darmstadt; Prussia; Sachsen; Thüringen; and Württemberg. Filtering to Germany, Misc. provides only the small states and free cities of Anhalt, Braunschweig, Bremen, Hamburg, Lippe, Lübeck, Mecklenburg, Oldenburg, Schaumburg-Lippe, and Waldeck.

The IGI is particularly useful for searching records of births or christenings and marriages.

To find the source of an entry in the IGI, read the directions in the Family History Library's publicaton, *Resource Guide: Finding an IGI Source,* usually available at Family History Centers as well as at the Family History Library.

Note: It is worth checking the "Country Unknown" section of the IGI, which contains about 738,000 entries on 54 microfiche, in which the computer did not recognize the place names involved. About 26 percent of the entries are from Germany.[1]

Social Security Death Benefit Index

The Social Security Death Index lists several million deceased people who had social security numbers and whose deaths were reported to the Social Security Administration. (See the index for Social Security Administration dates and other information.) Primarily, it covers deaths since 1962, but some go back to 1937. Almost a million names are added every year.

The index does not cover every person who has died or who was covered by Social Security since Social Security began.

References

◆Research Guides of the Family History Center on these individual FamilySearch programs

◆J. Carlyle Parker, *Going to Salt Lake City to Do Family History Research,* Marietta Publishing Company, Turlock, California, 3rd ed., 1996.

[1]"News of the Family History Center," *Genealogical Helper,* Nov./Dec. 1993

FHLC LOCALITY SECTIONS

When searching for information about a particular area of German lands in the Family History Library Catalog (FHLC), go first to the "Locality Section" of the Catalog, and select a geographic area from those listed below to determine the locality resources which may be available.
- Baden
- Bayern
- Bayern/Pfalz
- Braunschweig
- Elsass-Lothringen
- Hamburg
- Hessen
- Lippe
- Mecklenburg-Schwerin
- Mecklenburg-Strelitz
- Niedersachsen
- Oldenburg
- Preussen/Brandenburg
- Preussen/Hannover
- Preussen/Hessen-Nassau
- Preussen/Ostpreussen
- Preussen/Pommern
- Preussen/Posen
- Preussen/Rheinland
- Preussen/Sachsen
- Preussen/Schlesien
- Preussen/Schleswig-Holstein
- Preussen/Westfalen
- Preussen/Westpreussen
- Sachsen
- Sachsen-Altenburg
- Sachsen-Coburg-Gotha
- Sachsen-Meiningen
- Sachsen-Weimar-Eisenach
- Schaumburg-Lippe
- Schwarzburg-Rudolstadt
- Schwarzburg-Sondershausen
- Sudetenland
- Thüringen
- Waldeck
- Württemberg

ESSENTIAL FHL AIDS
FOR GERMAN RESEARCH

The following publications of the Family History Library, Church of Jesus Christ of Latter-day Saints, are extremely useful in pursuing family history research. They are usually available at Family History Centers.

♦ *Germany Research Outline*, 52 pages, three-hole drilled. This excellent guide is probably the biggest bargain among all research aids available for German research.

♦ *German Letter-Writing Guide*, 7 pages; contains sample letters and phrases for non-German speakers' use.

Publications of the Family History Library may be ordered. See address below.

ORDERING FAMILY HISTORY
LIBRARY PUBLICATIONS

Publications of the Family History Library may be oredered from:

**Salt Lake Distribution Center
1999 West 1700 South
Salt Lake City, UT 84101-4233.**
(minimum order $2.00).

FAMILY HISTORY CENTERS
IN GERMANY

Baden-Württemberg
Mannheim: Lampertheimer Str.98, 68305 Mannheim
Heidelberg: Schröderstr. 94, 69120 Heidelberg
Stuttgart: Birkenwaldstr. 46, 70191 Stuttgart
Freiberg/Neckar: Riedstr. 20, 71691 Freiberg/Neckar
Ellwangen: Seb.-Merkle-Str. 8/1, 73479 Ellwangen
Esslingen: Drosselweg 16, 73730 Esslingen
Heilbronn: Römerstr. 151, 74078 Heilbronn
Karlsruhe: Ernst-Frey-Str. 7, 76135 Karlsruhe
Offenburg: Hildastr. 55, 77654 Offenburg
Freiburg i. B.: Markgrafenstr. 87, 79115 Freiburg

Bayern
München: Rückertstr. 2, 80336 München
Rosenheim: Finsterwalder Str. 46, 83026 Rosenheim
Augsburg: Agnes-Bernauer-Str. 32, 86159 Augsburg
Nürnberg: Kesslerplatz 8, 90489 Nürnberg

Berlin
Berlin: Klingelhöfer Str. 24, 10785 Berlin

Brandenburg
Forst: Spremberger Str. 52, 03149 Forst

Bremen
Bremerhaven: Parkstr. 28, 27580 Bremerhaven
Bremen: Ottilie-Hoffmann-Str. 2, 28213 Bremen

Hamburg
Hamburg: Wartenau 20, 22089 Hamburg
Hamburg: Eberhofweg 90, 22415 HH-Langenhorn

Hessen
Frankfurt a. M.: Eckenheimer Landstr. 262-264, 60320 Frankfurt a. M.
Darmstadt: Richard Wagner Weg 78, 64287 Darmstadt
Michelstadt: Kreuzweg 10, 64720 Michelstadt
Frankfurt a. M.: Am Kapellenberg 9, 65936 Frankfurt (Hoechst)
Wetzlar: Im Amtmann 2, 35578 Wetzlar-Blankenfeld

Mecklenburg-Vorpommern
Wolgast: Tannenkampweg 81, 17438 Wolgast

Niedersachsen
Wilhelmshaven: Widukindstr. 26, 26384 Wilhelmshaven
Leer: Friesenstr. 80, 26789 Leer
Hannover: Hildesheimer Str. 344, 30519 Hannover

Stadthagen: Ecke Schacht-/Jahnstr., 31655 Stadthagen
Braunschweig: Triftweg 55, 38118 Braunschweig
Düsseldorf: Mörsenbroicher Weg 184a, 40470 Düsseldorf
Osnabrück: Rolandsmauer 13/14, 49074 Osnabrück

Nordrhein-Westfalen
Bielefeld: Hainteich Str. 80, 33613 Bielefeld
Mönchengladbach: Rheydter-Str. 220, 41065 Mönchengladbach
Wuppertal: Martin-Luther-Str. 6, 42285 Wuppertal
Dortmund: Carl-von-Ossietzky Str. 5, 44225 Dortmund
Duisburg: Essenberger Str. 251, 47059 Duisburg
Krefeld: Ungergath 25, 47805 Krefeld-Fischeln
Köln: Forststr. 130, 50767 Köln
Bonn: Rene-Schickele-Str. 8, 53123 Bonn
Hamm: Hammer Str. 215, 59075 Hamm

Rheinland-Pfalz
Bitburg: Thilmanystsr. 8, 54634 Bitburg
Idar-Oberstein: Hauptstr. 86 (Commerzbank), 55743 Idar-Oberstein
Koblenz: Moltkestr. 3, 56068 Koblenz
Kaiserslautern: Lauter Str. 1, 67657 Kaiserslautern

Saarland
Saarbrücken: Kalmanstr. 88, 66113 Saarbrücken

Sachsen
Dresden: Tiergartenstr. 40, 01219 Dresden
Leipzig: Österstr. 39, 03149 Leipzig
Zwickau: Gellertstr. 1A, 08064 Zwickau
Freiberg: Hainichener Str. 64, 09500 Freiberg

Schleswig-Holstein
Lübeck: Rabenstr. 5, 23566 Lübeck
Pinneberg: Saarlandstr. 11, 25421 Pinneberg
Kiel: Stiftstr. 17, 24103 Kiel
Neumünster: Kieler Str. 333, 24536 Neumünster

Thüringen
Erfurt: Hochheimer Str. 14, 99094 Erfurt

FAMILY HISTORY CENTERS IN AUSTRIA

Wien: Boecklinstr. 55, 1020 Wien
Linz: Spaunstr. 83, 4020 Linz
Wels: Camillo-Schulz-Str. 30, 4600 Wels
Salzburg: Andreas-Rohrbacher-Str. 20, 5020 Salzburg
Graz: Eckert Str. 136, 8020 Graz

FAMILY HISTORY CENTERS IN SWITZERLAND

Pratteln: Wartenbergstr. 31, 4133 Pratteln
Wettingen: Kapellenweg 6, 5400 Wettingen
Luzern: Matthofstrand 2, 6005 Luzern
Zürich: Herbstweg 120, 8050 Zürich
Kreuzlingen: Kirchstr. 2, 8280 Kreuzlingen
St.Gallen-Winkeln.: Kreuzbühlstr. 41, 9015 St. Gallen-Winkeln
Ebnat-Kappel: Steinfelstr. 17, 9642 Ebnat-Kappel

FAMILY HISTORY CENTER TELEPHONE NUMBERS: UNITED STATES

The following telephone numbers were compiled at various times between 1991 and 1995.

Changes in Family History Center telephone numbers occur from time to time.

ALABAMA
ANNISTON: 205-820-5841
BIRMINGHAM: 205-967-7279
CULLMAN: 205-739-0891
DECATUR: 205-350-6586
DOTHAN: 334-793-7425
EUFAULA:205-687-6146
FLORENCE: 205-766-5500

HUNTSVILLE: 205-721-0906
MOBILE: 205-344-6051
MONTGOMERY: 205-269-9041
TUSCALOOSA: 205-758-4820
ALASKA
ANCHORAGE: 907-277-8433
FAIRBANKS: 907-456-1095
JUNEAU: 907-780-4281
KETCHIKAN: 907-225-3291
SITKA: 907-747-8991
SOLDOTNA: 907-262-4253
WASILLA: 907-376-8618
ARIZONA
BENSON: 602-586-7040
BUCKEYE: 602-386-4188
CASA GRANDE: 602-836-7416
COTTONWOOD: 602-634-2349
DUNCAN: 602-359-2341
EAGAR: 602-333-4100
FLAGSTAFF: 602-774-2930
GLOBE: 520-425-9570
HOLBROOK: 520-524-6341
KINGMAN: 602-753-1316
MESA:602-964-1200
NOGALES: 602-281-2837
PAGE: 602-645-2328
PAYSON: 602-474-3788
PEORIA: 602-266-0128
PHOENIX: 602-266-0128; 602-371-0649; 602-271-7015; 602-265-7762; 602-973-0853; 602-953-1576; 602-439-1405; see also Mesa and Peoria
PRESCOTT: 602-778-2311;
SAFFORD: 602-428-3194
SCOTTSDALE: 602-947-3995
SHOW LOW: 602-537-2331
SIERRA VISTA: 602-459-1284
SNOWFLAKE: 602-536-7430
ST. JOHNS: 602-337-2543
TUCSON: 602-298-0905; 602-742-3471
WILLCOX: 602-384-2751
WINSLOW: 602-289-5496
YUMA: 602-782-6364
CALIFORNIA
Northern California
ANDERSON: 916-347-3240
CHICO: 916-343-6641
EUREKA: 707-443-7411
GRASS VALLEY: (no phone listed)

GRIDLEY: 916-846-3921
MIRANDA 707-943-3071
MT. SHASTA: 916- 926-6671
QUINCY: 916-283-3112
REDDING: 916-222-4949
SUSANVILLE: 916-257-4411
UKIAH: 707-468-5746
VACAVILLE: 707-451-8394
WEAVERVILLE: 916-623-5227
YUBA CITY: 916-673-0113
Bay Area
ANTIOCH: 510-634-9004
BERKELEY: See Oakland
CONCORD: 510-686-1766
FAIRFIELD: 707-425-2027
FREMONT: 510-623-7496; 510-790-1800
HAYWARD: See Oakland
LOS ALTOS: 415-968-1019
MILPITAS: See San Jose or Fremont
MENLO PARK: 415-325-9711
NAPA: 707-257-2887
OAKLAND: 510-531-3905
PACIFICA: 415-355-4986
PALO ALTO: See Menlo Park
SAN BRUNO: 415-873-1928
SAN FRANCISCO: See Pacifica or San Bruno
SAN JOSE: 408-274-8592; 408-259-5501
SAN MATEO: See Pacifica or Menlo Park
SANTA CLARA: 408-241-1449
SANTA CRUZ: 408-426-1078
SANTA ROSA: 707-525-0399
SUNNYVALE: See Los Altos
Central California
AUBURN: 916-888-9702
CLOVIS: 209-298-8768; 209-291-2448
DAVIS: See Woodland
EL DORADO: See Placerville
FRESNO: 209-431-3759; 209-431-4759 See also Clovis
HANFORD: 209-582-8960
MANTECA: 209-239-5516
MERCED: 209-722-1307
MODESTO: 209-571-0370; 209-545-4814
MONTEREY: See Seaside
PLACERVILLE: 916-621-1378
SACRAMENTO: 916-487-2090; 916-

688-7670
SEASIDE: 408-394-1124
SONORA: 209-536-9206
STOCKTON: 209-951-7060
SUTTER CREEK: 209-267-1139
TURLOCK: 209-643-9640
VISALIA: 209-732-3712
WOODLAND: 916-662-1538
Los Angeles County
BURBANK: 818-843-5362
CARSON: 310-835-6733
CERRITOS: 310-924-3676
CHATSWORTH: 818-885-1303
COVINA (Spanish): 818-331-7117
EL MONTE: See Pasadena
GLENDALE: 818-231-8763
HACIENDA HEIGHTS: 818-961-8765
HAWTHORNE: See Los Angeles
HUNTINGTON PARK (Spanish): 213-585-7767
INGLEWOOD: See Los Angeles
LA CRESCENTA: 818-957-0925
LAKEWOOD: See Cerritos or Buena Park
LANCASTER: 805-943-1670; 805-942-3993
LONG BEACH: See Los Alamitos
LOS ALAMITOS: 714-821-6914
LOS ANGELES: 310-474-2202
See also Monterey Park
MONTEREY PARK: 213-726-8145
NORTHRIDGE: 818-886-5953
NORWALK: 310-868-8727
PALMDALE: 805-947-1695
PALOS VERDES: See Rancho Palos Verdes
PASADENA: 818-351-8517
RANCHO PALOS VERDES: 310-541-5644
TORRANCE: 310-791-6526
VALENCIA: 805-259-9535
WHITTIER: 310-946-1880
Southern California
(excluding Los Angeles County)
ANAHEIM: 714-533-2772
BAKERSFIELD: 805-393-6403; 805-872-5683; 805-831-2036
BARSTOW: 619-252-4117
BLYTHE: 619-922-4019
BUENA PARK: 714-527-2448

CAMARILLO: 805-388-7215
CARLSBAD: 619-434-4941
CHINO: 909-393-1936
CORONA: 909-735-2619
CYPRESS: See Buena Park or Cerritos
EL CAJON: 805-588-1426
EL CENTRO: 619-353-3019
ESCONDIDO: 619-741-8441
FONTANA: 909-355-1006
GARDEN GROVE: See Westminster or Orange
HEMET: 909-658-8104
HUNTINGTON BEACH: 714-536-4736
LAKE ELSINORE: 909-245-4063
LEMON GROVE: 619-463-7236
LOMPOC: 805-735-4939
MISSION VIEJO: 714-364-2742
MORENO VALLEY: 909-247-8839
MURRIETA: See Lake Elsinore
NEEDLES: 619-326-3363
NEWBURY PARK: 805-499-1258
NORTH EDWARDS: 619-769-4345
ORANGE: 714-997-7710
OXNARD: Se Ventura or Camarillo
PALM DESERT: 619-340-6094
PALM SPRINGS: See Palm Desert
POWAY: See San Diego
REDLANDS: 909-794-3844
RIDGECREST: 619-375-6998
RIVERSIDE: 909-784-1918; 909-360-8547; 909-687-5542
SAN BERNARDINO: 909-881-5355
SAN DIEGO: 619-295-9808; 619-487-2304; see also Lemon Grove
SAN LUIS OBISPO: 805-543-6328
SANTA ANA: See Orange or Westminster
SANTA BARBARA: 805-682-2092
SANTA MARIA: 805-928-4722
SIMI VALLEY: 805-581-2456
THOUSAND OAKS: 805-495-2362
UPLAND: 909-985-8821
VENTURA: 805-643-5607
VICTORVILLE: 619-243-5632
VISTA: 619-945-6053
WESTMINSTER: 714-554-0592
ARKANSAS
FORT SMITH: 501-484-5373
HOT SPRINGS: 501-262-5640
JACKSONVILLE: 501-985-2501

LITTLE ROCK: 501-455-4998
ROGERS: 501-636-0740
RUSSELVILLE: 501-968-3114
COLORADO
ALAMOSA: 719-589-5511
ARVADA: 303-421-0920
AURORA: 303-367-0570
BOULDER: See Louisville or Longmont
COLORADO SPRINGS: 719-634-0572
CORTEZ: 303-565-7400
CRAIG: 303-824-2763
DENVER: 303-758-6460
See also Arvada, Littleton, and Northglenn
DURANGO: 303-259-1061
FORT COLLINS: 303-226-5999
FRISCO: 303-668-5633
GRAND JUNCTION: 303-243-2782
GREELEY: 303-356-1904
LA JARA: 719-274-4032
LITTLETON: 303-798-6461: 303-973-3727
LONGMONT: 303-772-4373
LOUISVILLE: 303-665-4685
MONTROSE: 303-249-4739
NORTHGLENN: 303-451-7177
PAONIA: 303-527-4084
PUEBLO: 719-564-0793
STERLING: 303-522-6407
CONNECTICUT
BLOOMFIELD: 203-242-1607
HARTFORD: See Bloomfield
MADISON: 203-245-8267
NEW CANAAN: 203-966-1305
NEW HAVEN: See Woodbridge
QUAKER HILL: 203-442-6644
WOODBRIDGE: 203-387-2012
DELAWARE
DOVER: 302-697-2700
WILMINGTON: 302-654-1911
DISTRICT OF COLUMBIA
See Kensington or Suitland, Maryland
FLORIDA
ARCADIA: 813-993-0996
BELLE GLADE: 407-996-6355
BOCA RATON (Spanish): 407-395-6644
BRADENTON: 813-755-6909
COCOA: See Rockledge
FT. LAUDERDALE: See Boca Raton or
Plantation

FT. MYERS: 813-275-0001
GAINSVILLE: 904-331-8542
HOMESTEAD: 305-246-2486
JACKSONVILLE: 904-743-0527
KEY WEST: 305-294-9400
LAKE CITY: 904-755-9432
LAKE MARY: 407-333-0137
LAKESIDE: See Orange Park
LARGO: 813-399-8018
LECANTO: 904-746-5943
MELBOURNE: See Rockledge
MIAMI: 305-265-1045
NEW PORT RICHEY: 813-863-2076
OCALA: See Gainsville
ORANGE PARK: 904-272-1150
ORLANDO: 407-895-4832
PALM BEACH GARDENS: 407-626-7989
PALM CITY: 407-287-0167
PANAMA CITY: 904-785-9290
PENSACOLA: 904-478-5211
PLANTATION (Spanish): 305-472-0524
PORT CHARLOTTE: 813-627-6446
PORT ST. LUCIE: See Palm City
ROCKLEDGE: 407-636-2431
ST. PETERSBURG: See Largo
SANFORD: See Orlando
TALLAHASSEE: 904-222-8870
TAMPA: 813-971-2869
WEST PALM BEACH: See Palm Beach
Gardens
WINTER HAVEN: 813-299-1691
GEORGIA
ALBANY: 912-436-8637
ATLANTA: See Jonesboro, Marietta,
Powder Springs, Roswell, and Tucker
AUGUSTA: See Evans
BRUNSWICK: 912-265-5912
COLUMBUS: 706-563-7216
EVANS: 706-860-1024
DOUGLAS: 912-384-0607
GAINESVILLE: 706-536-4391
JONESBORO: 404-477-5985
MACON: 912-788-5885
MARIETTA: 404-578-8758
See also Powder Springs
POWDER SPRINGS: 404-943-1983
ROME: 706-235-2281
ROSWELL: 404-594-1706

SANDY SPRINGS: See Roswell
SAVANNAH: 912-927-6543
TUCKER: 404-723-9941
WARNER ROBINS: See Macon
HAWAII
HILO, HAWAII: 808-935-0711
KAILUA-KONA, HAWAII: 808-329-4469
LIHUE, KAUAI: 808-246-9119
KAHULUI, MAUI: 808-871-8841
HONOLULU, OAHU: 808-841-4118;
808-955-8910
KANEOHE, OAHU: 808-247-3134
LAIE, OAHU: 808-293-2133
MILILANI, OAHU: 808-623-1712
WAIPAHU, OAHU: 808-678-0752
IDAHO
ARIMO: 208-254-3888
BASALT: 208-346-6011
BLACKFOOT: 208-785-5022; 208-684-3784
BOISE: 208-376-0452; 208-338-3811;
208-362-2638
BURLEY: 208-678-7286
CALDWELL: 208-454-8324
COEUR D'ALENE: 208-765-0150
DRIGGS: 208-354-2253
EMMETT: 208-365-4112
FIRTH: See Basalt
GRANGEVILLE: 208-983-2110
HAILEY: 208-788-4250
IDAHO FALLS: 208-524-5291;208-524-1038; 208-529-4087
LEWISTON: 208-746-6910
McCAMMON: 208-254-3259
MALAD: 208-766-2332
MONTPELIER: 208-847-0340
MOORE: 208-554-2121
MOUNTAIN HOME: 208-587-5249
NAMPA: 208-467-5827
POCATELLO: 208-232-9262
PRESTON: 208-852-0710
REXBURG: 208-356-2377
RIGBY: 208-745-8989; 208-745-8660
SALMON: 208-756-2371
SANDPOINT: 208-263-8721
SHELLEY: 208-357-3128
SODA SPRINGS: 208-547-3232
TERRETON: 208-663-4389

TWIN FALLS: 208-733-8073
WEISER: 208-549-1575
ILLINOIS
BUFFALO GROVE: 708-913-5387
CHAMPAIGN: 217-352-8063
CHICAGO: See Wilmette and Schaumburg
CHICAGO HEIGHTS: 708-754-2525
NAPERVILLE: 708-505-0233
NAUVOO: 217-453-6347
O'FALLON: 618-632-0210
PEORIA: 309-682-4073
ROCKFORD: 815-399-2660
SCHAUMBURG: 708-885-4130
WILMETTE: 708-251-9818
INDIANA
BLOOMINGTON: 812-333-0050
COLUMBUS: 812-376-7073
EVANSVILLE: 812-423-9832
FT. WAYNE: 219-485-9581
INDIANAPOLIS: 317-888-6002
KOKOMO: 317-453-2842
MUNCIE: 317-288-7278
NEW ALBANY: 812-949-7532
NOBLESVILLE: 317-842-6180
SOUTH BEND: 219-233-6501
TERRE HAUTE: 812-234-0269
WEST LAFAYETTE: 317-463-5079
IOWA
AMES: 515-232-3634
CEDAR FALLS: 319-266-6374
CEDAR RAPIDS: 319-363-7178
DAVENPORT: 319-386-7547
MASON CITY: 515-424-4211
SIOUX CITY: 712-255-9686
WEST DES MOINES: 515-225-0416
KANSAS
DODGE CITY: 316-225-6540
EMPORIA: 316-343-1304
HUTCHINSON: 316-665-1187
KANSAS CITY: See Olathe
OLATHE: 913-829-1775
SALINA: 913-827-2392
TOPEKA: 913-271-6818
WICHITA: 316-683-2951
KENTUCKY
CORBIN: 606-528-2898
HOPKINSVILLE: 502-886-1616
LEXINGTON: 606-269-2722

LOUISVILLE: 502-426-8174
MARTIN: 606-285-3133
MORGANTOWN: 502-728-3491
OWINGSVILLE: 606-674-6626
PADUCAH: 502-554-7203
LOUISIANA
ALEXANDRIA: 318-448-1842
BATON ROUGE: 504-769-8913
BOSSIER CITY: See Shreveport
DENHAM SPRINGS: 504-664-8979
MONROE: 318-322-7009
METAIRIE: 504-885-3936
NEW ORLEANS: See Metairie or Slidell
SHREVEPORT: 318-868-5169
SLIDELL: 504-641-3982
MAINE
AUGUSTA: See Farmingdale
BANGOR: 207-942-7310
CAPE ELIZABETH: 207-767-5000
CARIBOU: 207-492-4381
FARMINGDALE: 207-582-1827
PORTLAND: See Cape Elizabeth
MARYLAND
ANNAPOLIS: 410-757-4173
BALTIMORE: See Lutherville
ELLICOTT CITY: 301-465-1642
FREDERICK: 301-698-0406
GAITHERSBERG: 301-977-1052
KENSINGTON: 301-587-0042
LUTHERVILLE: 301-821-9880
SUITLAND: 301-423-8294
MASSACHUSETTS
BOSTON: See Weston
FOXBORO: 508-543-0298
TYNGSBORO: 508-649-9233
WESTON: 617-235-2164
WORCESTER: 508-852-7000
MICHIGAN
ANN ARBOR: 313-995-0211
BLOOMFIELD HILLS: 810-647-5671
DETROIT: See Bloomfield Hills or Westland
EAST LANSING: 517-332-2932
ESCANABA: 906-789-0370
GRAND BLANC: 313-694-2964
GRAND RAPIDS: 616-949-0070
HARVEY: 906-249-1511
HASTINGS: 616-948-2104
KALAMAZOO: 616-342-1906

LANSING: See East Lansing
LUDINGTON: 616-843-3358
MIDLAND: 517-631-1120
MUSKEGON: 616-744-3283
SAGINAW: See Midland
TRAVERSE CITY: 616-947-6500
WESTLAND: 313-459-4570
MINNESOTA
BEMIDJI: 218-751-9129
BROOKLYN PARK: 612-425-1865
DULUTH: 218-722-9508
MINNEAPOLIS: 612-544-2479
See also Brooklyn Park
ROCHESTER: 507-281-6641
ST. PAUL: 612-770-3213
MISSISSIPPI
BOONEVILLE: (no phone listed)
CLINTON: 601-924-2686
COLUMBUS: 601-328-2788
GULFPORT: 601-832-0195
HATTIESBURG: 601-268-3733
JACKSON: See Clinton
MISSOURI
CAPE GIRARDEAU: 314-334-9298
COLUMBIA: 314-443-1024
FARMINGTON: 314-756-6521
FRONTENAC: 314-993-2328
HAZELWOOD: 314-731-0034
INDEPENDENCE: 816-461-0245
JOPLIN: 417-623-6506
KANSAS CITY: 816-941-7389
LIBERTY: 816-781-8295
SPRINGFIELD: 417-887-8229
ST. JOSEPH: 816-232-2428
ST. LOUIS: See Frontenac and Hazelwood
MONTANA
BILLINGS: 406-656-8859; 406-259-3348
BOZEMAN: 406-586-3880
BUTTE: 406-494-9909
GLASGOW: 406-228-2382
GLENDIVE: 406-365-4609
GREAT FALLS: 406-453-1625
HAVRE: 406-265-7982
HELENA: 406-443-0716
KALISPELL: 406-752-5446
LEWISTON: 406-538-9058
MISSOULA: 406-543-6148
STEVENSVILLE: 406-777-2489
NEBRASKA

GORDON: 308-282-9969
GRAND ISLAND: 308-382-9418
LINCOLN: 402-423-4561
OMAHA: 402-393-7641
See also Papillion
PAPILLION: 402-339-0461
NEVADA
ELY: 702-289-2287
ELKO; 702-738-4565
FALLON: 702-423-8888
HENDERSON: 702-566-8190
LAS VEGAS: 702-382-9695
LOGANDALE: 702-398-3266
MESQUITE: 702-346-2342
RENO: 702-826-1130
TONAPAH: 702-482-5492
WINNEMUCCA: 702-623-4448
NEW HAMPSHIRE
CONCORD: 603-225-2848
NASHUA: See Tyngsboro, MA
PORTSMOUTH: 603-433-4428
NEW JERSEY
CAMDEN: See Cherry Hill
CHERRY HILL: 609-795-8841
EAST BRUNSWICK: 908-254-1480
MORRISTOWN: 201-539-5362
NEWARK: See North Caldwell or Short
Hills
NORTH CALDWELL: 201-226-8975
SHORT HILLS: 201-379-7315
NEW MEXICO
ALAMOGORDO: 505-437-8772
ALBUQUERQUE: 505-343-0456; 505-
266-4867; 505-293-5610
CARLSBAD: 505-885-1368
CLOVIS: 505-762-2021
FARMINGTON: 505-325-5813
GALLUP: 505-722-9941
GRANTS: 505-287-2305
LAS CRUCES: 505-382-0618
LOS ALAMOS: 505-662-3186
ROSWELL: 505-623-4492
SANTA FE: 505-986-8254
SILVER CITY: 505-538-5033
NEW YORK
ALBANY: See Loudonville
BINGHAMPTON: See Vestal
BROOKLYN: (No phone listed)
BUFFALO: See Williamsville

ELMHURST: (Spanish speaking) 718-
779-6859
ITHACA: 607-257-1334
JAMESTOWN: 716-487-0830
LAKE PLACID: 518-523-2889
LIVERPOOL: 315-457-5172
LOUDONVILLE: 518-463-4581
NEW YORK CITY: 212-873-1690
See also Brooklyn or Elmhurst
PITTSFORD: 716-248-9930
PLAINVIEW: 516-433-0122
QUEENS: See Elmhurst
ROCHESTER: 716-271-9454 See also
Pittsford
SCARSDALE: 914-723-4022
SCHENECTADY: See Loudonville
SYRACUSE: See Liverpool
VESTAL: 607-797-3900
WILLIAMSVILLE: 716-688-9759
YORKTOWN: 914-941-9754 See also
New Canaan, CT
NORTH CAROLINA
ASHEVILLE: See Skyland
CARY: See Raleigh
CHAPEL HILL: See Durham
CHARLOTTE: 704-541-1590; 704-535-
0238
DURHAM: 919-383-0611
FAYETTEVILLE: 910-864-2080
GOLDSBORO: 910-731-2130
GREENSBORO: 910-288-6539
HICKORY: 704-324-2823
HIGH POINT: See Greensboro or
Winston-Salem
KINSTON: 910-522-4671
RALEIGH: 919-783-7752
SKYLAND: 704-687-8339
WILMINGTON: 910-395-4456
WINSTON-SALEM: 910-768-8878
NORTH DAKOTA
BISMARCK: 701-222-2794
FARGO: 701-232-4003
GRAND FORKS: 218-746-6126
MINOT: 701-838-4486
OHIO
AKRON: See Tallmadge
CINCINNATI: 513-531-5624; 513-489-
3036
CLEVELAND: See Westlake

COLUMBUS: See Dublin and
Reynoldsburg
DAYTON: 513-854-4566
DUBLIN: 614-761-1898
FAIRBORN: 513-878-9551
KIRTLAND: 216-256-8808
PERRYSBURG: 419-872-9491
REYNOLDSBURG: 614-866-7686
TALLMADGE: 216-630-3365
TOLEDO: See Perrysburg
WESTLAKE: 216-777-1518
WINTERSVILLE: 614-266-6334

OKLAHOMA
ARDMORE: 405-226-2134
ENID: 405-234-1518
LAWTON: 405-536-1303
MUSKOGEE: 918-687-8861
NORMAN: 405-364-8337
OKLAHOMA CITY: 405-721-8455; 405-794-3800
STILLWATER: 405-377-4122
TULSA: 918-437-5690; 918-747-3966
WOODWARD: 405-256-5113

OREGON
BAKER CITY: 503-523-4901
BEAVERTON: 503-644-7782
BEND: 503-382-9947
BROOKINGS: 503-469-4079
COOS BAY: See Northbend
CORVALLIS: 503-758-1156
EUGENE: 503-343-3741
GOLD HILL: 503-664-5356
GRANTS PASS: 503-476-1926
GRESHAM: 503-665-1524
HERMISTON: 503-567-3445
HILLSBORO: 503-640-4658
JOHN DAY: (no phone listed)
KEIZER: 503-390-2095
KLAMATH FALLS: 503-884-7998
LA GRANDE: 503-963-5003
LAKE OSWEGO: 503-638-1410
McMINNVILLE: 503-434-5681
MEDFORD: 503-773-3363. See also
Gold Hill
NEWPORT: 503-265-7333
NORTHBEND: 503-269-9037
NYSSA: 503-372-5255
ONTARIO: 503-889-9359
OREGON CITY: 503-655-9908 ext. 5

PORTLAND: 503-252-1081; 503-235-9090. See also Beaverton, Gresham, and
Lake Oswego
PRINEVILLE: 503-447-1488
ROSEBURG: 503-672-1237
SCIO: 503-451-3992
ST. HELENS: 503-397-1300
SALEM: 503-363-0374; 503-371-0453.
See also Keizer
SANDY: 503- 668-4811 ext. 7
THE DALLES: 503-296-4301
TUALATIN: 503-692-0841

PENNSYLVANIA
BROOMALL: 215-356-8507
CLARKS SUMMIT: 717-587-5123
ERIE: 814-866-3611
JOHNSTOWN: 814-269-4652
KANE: 814-837-9729
LANCASTER: 717-295-1719
PHILADELPHIA: See also Broomall;
215-329-3692
PITTSBURGH: 412-921-2115
READING: 610-929-0235
SCRANTON: See Clarks Summit
STATE COLLEGE: 814-238-4560
WILKES-BARRE: See Clarks Summit
YORK: 717-854-9331

RHODE ISLAND
PROVIDENCE: See Warwick, or Quaker
Hill, CT
WARWICK: 401-463-8150

SOUTH CAROLINA
ANDERSON: See Greenville
CHARLESTON: 803-766-6017
COLUMBIA: 803-782-7141
FLORENCE: 803-665-0433
GREENVILLE: 803-627-0553
SPARTANBURG: See Greenville

SOUTH DAKOTA
GETTYSBURG: 605-765-9270
PIERRE: 605-224-2586
RAPID CITY: 605-343-8656
ROSEBUD: 605-747-2818
SIOUX FALLS: 605-361-1070

TENNESSEE
BARTLETT: 901-388-9974
CHATTANOOGA: 615-892-7632
CORDOVA: 901-754-2545
FRANKLIN: 615-794-4251

KINGSPORT: 615-245-2321
KNOXVILLE: 615-693-8252
MADISON: 615-859-6926
McMINNVILLE: 615-473-1053
MEMPHIS: See Cordova or Bartlett
NASHVILLE: See Madison
TEXAS
ABILENE: 915-673-8836
AMARILLO: 806-352-2409
AUSTIN: 512-837-3626; 512-892-7215
BAY CITY: 409-245-3152
BEAUMONT: See Port Arthur
BRYAN: 409-846-3516
CONROE: 409-756-2363
CORPUS CHRISTI: 512-993-2970
DALLAS: 214-342-2642. See also
Duncanville
DENTON: 817-387-3065
DUNCANVILLE: 214-709-0066
EL PASO: 916-565-9711; 915-581-6062
FORT WORTH: 817-292-8393; 817-284-4472
FRIENDSWOOD: 713-996-9346
GILMER: 903-843-3307
HARLINGEN: 210-421-2028
HOUSTON: 713-893-5381; 713-785-2105 (Spanish-speaking); See also
Sugarland, Spring, Friendswood and
Pasadena
KATY: 713-578-8338
KILEEN: 817-526-2918
KINGWOOD: 713-360-1352
LONGVIEW: 903-759-7911
LUBBOCK: 806-792-5040
McALLEN: 210-682-1061
MIDLAND: 915-697-6755
ODESSA: 915-337-3112
ORANGE: 409-883-7969
PASADENA: 713-487-3623
PLANO: 214-867-6479
PORT ARTHUR: 409-727-3548
SAN ANTONIO: 210-736-2940; 210-673-9404
SPRING: 713-251-5931
SUGARLAND: 713-240-1524
THE COLONY: 214-370-3537
TYLER: 903-509-8322
VICTORIA: 512-575-0055
WICHITA FALLS: (no phone listed)

UTAH
(excluding Davis, Utah,
and Salt Lake Counties)
ALTAMONT: 801-454-3422
BEAVER: 801-438-5262
BLANDING: 801-678-2728
BRIGHAM CITY: 801-723-5995
CASTLE DALE: 801-381-2899
CEDAR CITY: 801-586-2296
DELTA: 801-864-3312
DUCHESNE: 801-738-5371
ENTERPRISE: 878-2520
EUREKA: (no phone listed)
FERRON: 801-384-3288
FILLMORE: 801-743-6614, ext. 114
GOSHEN: 801-667-3232
GRANTSVILLE: See Tooele
HEBER: See Midway
HELPER: 801-472-3798
HIGHLAND: See American Fork
HUNTINIGTON: 801-687-9090
HURRICANE: 801-635-2174
HYRUM: 801-245-4551
KANAB: 801-644-5973
LAKETOWN: 801-946-3262
LOA: 801-836-2322
LOGAN: 801-755-5594; 801-755-5552
MANTI: 801-835-8888
MARION: 801-783-2921
MIDWAY: 801-654-2760
MOAB: 801-259-5563
MONTICELLO: 801-587-2139
MORGAN: 801-829-6261
MORONI: 801-436-8497
MT. PLEASANT: (no phone listed)
NEPHI: 801-623-1378
OGDEN: 801-626-1132
PANGUITCH: 801-676-2201
PARK CITY: 801-649-0725
PAROWAN: 801-477-8077
PRICE: 801-637-2071
RICHFIELD: 801-896-8057
ROOSEVELT: 801-722-3794
ST. GEORGE: 801-673-4591
TOOELE: 801-882-7514
TREMONTON: 801-257-7015
TROPIC: 801-679-8693
VERNAL: 801-789-3618

WELLINGTON: 801-637-6717
WENDOVER: 801-665-2220
Davis County
BOUNTIFUL: 801-299-4177
FARMINGTON: 801-451-1945; 801-451-
1905; 801-451-1981
KAYSVILLE: 801-543-2869; 801-543-
2853
LAYTON: 801-543-2908
SYRACUSE: 801-774-2183
Salt Lake County
DRAPER: 801-576-2821
KEARNS: 801-964-7371; 801-964-7470;
other location with no phone listed)
MAGNA: 801-252-2539; 801-252-2539
MIDVALE: 801-562-8085
MURRAY: 801-264-4161; 801-264-
4137; 801-264-4052; 801-264-4145
RIVERTON: 801-254-8126
SALT LAKE CITY: 801-240-2331 (Main
Library); 801-578-6719; 801-578-6661;
801-584-3142; 801-484-4441; 801-273-
3836; 801-273-3815; 801-273-3864; 801-
273-3784; 801-578-6769; 801-273-3719
SANDY: 801-944-2140; 801-576-2953;
801944-2094; 801-576-2949; 801-576-
2891; 801-576-2834
SOUTH JORDAN: 801-254-8169
WEST JORDAN: 801-562-8285; 801-
964-7472; 801-964-7455
WEST VALLEY CITY: 801-964-3009;
801-964-7250; 801-964-7465; 801-252-
2560; 801-964-7490;801-252-2560
Utah County
AMERICAN FORK: 801-763-2014; 801-
763-2093
LEHI: 801-768-3054
MAPLETON: 801-489-2999
OREM: 801-222-0319; 801-222-0399;
801-222-0449; 801-222-0436
PLEASANT GROVE: 801-785-0980
PROVO: 801-378-6200;801-222-0567;
801-370-6838; 801-222-3108; 801-370-
6713; 801-370-6674; 801-370-6830
SANTAQUIN: (no phone listed)
SPRINGVILLE: 801-498-2956
VERMONT
BERLIN: 802-229-0898
MONTPELIER: See Berlin

VIRGINIA
ALEXANDRIA: 703-799-3071
ANNANDALE: 703-256-5518
ARLINGTON: See Annandale,
Alexandria, or Falls Church
BASSETT: 703-629-7613
CENTREVILLE: No telephone listed
CHARLOTTESVILLE: 804-973-9856
CHESAPEAKE: 804-482-8600
DALE CITY: 703-670-5977
FALLS CHURCH: 703-532-9019
FREDERICKSBURG: 703-786-5641
HAMILTON: 703-338-9526
HAMPTON: See Newport News
MARTINSVILLE: See Bassett
NEWPORT NEWS: 804-874-2335
NORFOLK: See Chesapeake or Virginia
Beach
OAKTON: 703-626-7264
PEMBROKE: 703-626-7264
RICHMOND: 804-288-8134
ROANOKE: See Salem
SALEM: 703-562-2052
VIRGINIA BEACH: 804-467-3302
WAYNESBORO: 703-942-1036
WINCHESTER: 703-722-6055
WASHINGTON
ABERDEEN: See Elma
AUBURN: 206-735-2009
BELLEVUE: 206-454-2690
BELLINGHAM: 206-738-1849
BREMERTON: 206-479-9370; 206-698-
5552
CENTRALIA: 206-748-1316
CHENEY: 509-235-4608
COLVILLE: 509-684-6642
ELLENSBURG: 509-925-5192
ELMA: (No phone listed)
EPHRATA: 509-754-4762
EVERETT: 206-337-0457
FEDERAL WAY: 206-874-3803
KENNEWICK: See Richland
LAKE STEVENS: 206-334-0754
LONGVIEW: 360-577-8234
LYNNWOOD: See Mountlake Terrace
MARYSVILLE: See Lake Stevens or
Everett
MOSES LAKE: 509-765-8711

The German Research Companion

MOUNTVILLE TERRACE: 206-776-6678
MOUNT VERNON: 206-424-7723
NORTH BEND: 206-888-1098
OLYMPIA: 206-705-4176
OMAK: 509-826-4802
OTHELLO: 509-488-6412
PORT ANGELES: 206-452-1521
PULLMAN: 509-332-7124
PUYALLUP: 206-840-1673
QUINCY: 509-787-2521
RICHLAND: 360-946-6637
SEATTLE: 206-522-1233; 206-243-4028;
See also Bellevue
SPOKANE: 509-466-4633; 509-926-0551; 509-455-7164
SUMNER: 206-863-3383
TACOMA: 206-564-1103
VANCOUVER: 360-256-7235; 360-573-7881; 360-253-4701
WALLA WALLA: 509-525-1121
WENATCHEE: 509-884-1836
YAKIMA: 509-452-3626
WASHINGTON, DC
See Kinsington and Suitland, Maryland
WEST VIRGINIA
CHARLESTON: 304-984-9333
FAIRMONT: 304-363-0116

HUNTINGTON: 304-736-0408
MORGANTOWN: See Fairmont
WISCONSIN
APPLETON: 414-733-5358
EAU CLAIRE: 715-834-8271
HALES CORNER: 414-425-4182
KENOSHA: 414-552-8887
MADISON: 608-238-1071
MILWAUKEE: See Hales Corner
SHAWANO: 715-526-2946
WAUSAU: 715-359-7171
WYOMING
AFTON: 307-886-3905
CASPER: 307-234-3326
CHEYENNE: 307-634-3561
CODY: 307-587-3427
DIAMONDVILLE: 307-877-6821
EVANSTON: 307-789-2648
GILLETTE: 307-686-2077
GREEN RIVER: 307-875-3972
JACKSON HOLE: 307-733-6337
LARAMIE: 307-745-3234
LOVELL: 307-548-2963
LYMAN: 307-786-4559
RAWLINS: 307-324-5459
RIVERTON: 307-856-5290
ROCK SPRINGS: 307-362-8062
SHERIDAN: 307-672-8611
WORLAND: 307-347-8958

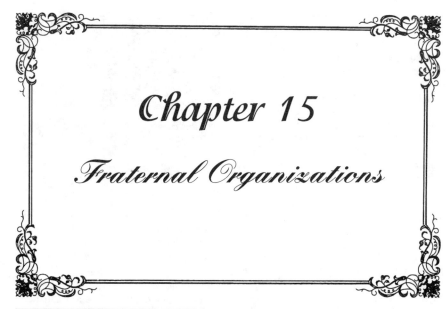

Chapter 15

Fraternal Organizations

THE TURNVEREIN IN GERMANY

In Germany today, the Turnverein serves its members as a framework for sports activities, both competitive and "just for fun." It also serves, however, as a social club. The "Vereinsheim" is virtually a guesthouse where members of all ages meet.

Organized competitive sports events are practically nil at German high schools, colleges, and universities – this is what the *Turn-* und *Sportvereine* do.

But the Turnverein has evolved through the years from a concept that began quite differently.

The 'Verein'

The word "*Verein*" is derived from "*sich vereinigen*," (to unite). Today a *Verein* is an association of people pursuing a common non-profit interest. Under German law, a *Verein* may become incorporated by registering with a court. This is shown by the abbreviated appendix of "e.V.," for "*eingetragener Verein*" (registered Verein), as in "Turnverein 1848 Schwabach e.V.," for example.

The right for Germans to found a *Verein* is guaranteed by the *Grundgesetz* (the constitution) in Article 9. The way a *Verein* may operate is regulated by 58 paragraphs (out of 2,385) in Germany's Civil Code (*Bürgerliches Gesetzbuch*).

After registration, a *Verein* becomes a legal entity which can perform legal business and transactions in its own name independently from the individual members.

Laws regulating the *Verein* system began appearing around 1867.

Historical background

The idea of the Verein developed around the turn of the eighteenth to nineteenth century as a way for people to emancipate themselves from their status as "subjects" of autocratic aristocratic (or sometimes clerical) rule.

Democratic ideas just started appearing in Germany at that time, when they were already well established in the United States.

To get listened to, individuals had to unite. That of course was not allowed because rulers realized that the emergence of political groups would mean the emergence of political power other than their own and would therefore become a threat to absolutism. Political parties were unknown then since there was nothing to vote on.

Although people didn't have any political rights other than those the ruler chose to grant them, most rulers were far from being tyrants. This is shown by their being called *"Landesvater"* or*"Landesmutter."* The rulers referred to their subjects as *"meine Landeskinder"* for whom they had to care. And mostly they did, or at least they tried to. This of course was helped by the fact that a "Germany" didn't exist, but rather consisted of a milky way of more or less sovereign states, few of which exceeded county-size. Even for a stagecoach , it was easy to cross several borders (including customs) on a single day in some areas.

So, while this kind of patriarchal rule had a mostly benevolent intent, it also created a stifling atmosphere for social and political life. There was no room to express new ideas or individualistic notions. Every aspect of life was ruled by decrees, religion or convention.

Friedrich Jahn, along with several others rediscovered some sports activities with a long history – like running, discus-throwing, and javelin-throwing – and added new ones to them, like the parallel bars and the horizontal bar. He also invented the word *"Turnen"* for these activities which he formed into a comprehensive system of physical exercises both for education in school and for the population in general.

'Frisch, Fromm, Fröhlich, Frei'

Jahn's theory was that a lively mind depended upon a physically fit body *(Frischer Körper – frischer Geist)*. The kind of person he wanted to help create was described in the motto, *Frisch, Fromm, Fröhlich, Frei* ("Lively, Pious, Merry, Free").

Jahn opened his first "Turnplatz" (ath-

The four stylized F's of the Turner motif , for "Frisch, Fromm, Fröhlich, Frei" (Lively, Pious, Merry, Free)

letic grounds) outside Berlin at Hasenheide ("rabbit's heath") in 1811 and published an important book, *Deutsche Turnkunst* (the German Art of Gymnastics) in 1816. For all this he became known as "Turnvater Jahn."

The second important idea the followers of the *Turnen* movement pursued was that of national unity, which was meant to break up the feudal mini-states and to bring more freedom to the population. The idea was natural and even overdue at that time, considering what was going on in England, France, Spain and Austria.

On the other hand, this basically sound idea was exaggerated and even perverted, especially by Friedrich Jahn and his *Turnen* movement. Jahn is accused by historians of laying the groundwork for an ugly nationalism whose outward aggressiveness did not stay purely rhetorical later on.

Soon the Turner movement worked closely together with student fraternities *(Burschenschaften)* which shared the goals of liberalization and national unity. Both groups therefore were fiercely opposed by the reactionary rulers.

Thus it was quite logical that members

of both groups also supported the 1813-1815 *Befreiungskriege* ("wars of liberation") of European states and peoples against Napoleon, which ended with his defeat at Waterloo. Many students and Turners died in this war.

Crisis for the Turner movement

After a student who happened to be a member of a *Turnverein* murdered August von Kotzebue, the publisher of a reactionary politcal magazine, all *Turnverein* activities were banned from 1820 until 1842. However, such activities were continued underground in many places. Jahn was arrested and held in custody for five years.

In 1842 this ban was lifted and the *Turnverein* movement started on a large scale both in schools and in the *Verein*.

In 1848 most of the *Turnvereinie* supported the *Nationalversammlung* in Frankfurt, which tried to find a way to German political unity and to write a constitution. When the assembly failed, many *Turnvereine* joined in the subsequent unrest and uprisings.

However, soon after that, by the middle of the nineteenth century, the *Turnverein* movement itself had become discredited in liberal circles by its nationalistic behavior.

By this time modern competitive athletics and sports as we know them today had developed in England and spread to the Continent and throughout the world. They held much greater appeal for young people than the original *Turnen*.

On the other hand, this modern sports movement, by its international character and outlook and by allowing colorful dress and even shorts, was regarded with horror by the traditionalists. This was when the more modern "*Sportverein*" movement separated from the more conservative Turnverein movement. The *Sportverein* idea thrived, while the old Turnverein idea remained more or less stagnant.

To study the history of the *Turnverein* in America is to realize that the particular Germans who founded them emigrated because they had better chances there to realize the positive ideas which the German *Turnvereine* stood for. And certainly it was the negative aspects that were among the reasons these Germans left Germany.

Germany today

In Germany today, practically all organizerd sports activities take place within a Sportverein. Even professional soccer teams are run as departments withing a Sportverein.

The sheer numbers of Sportverein members in Germany show the important role the Sportverein plays in Germany's social life. Even activities like playing chess, white-water canoeing, bowling, driving horse-drawn buggies on a slalom course, or show-dancing are conducted mostly within a Sportverein. Cardplayers have their *Vereine* too, but much to their regret, their attempts to join the *Sportsvereine* system have not been successful.

These numbers also prove the saying that whenever more than two Germans meet, they immediately form some kind of *Verein*. This tendency is described by the word *Vereinsmeierei* (clubbiness).

While the Turnvereine may be a little more tradition-minded and generally cater to more conservative interests than other *Sportvereine*, they are no longer fundamentally different. Like any other *Sportverein*, they are both service-organizations for activities of their members and centers of social life.

The best evidence of this is that while in the nineteenth century a *Turnverein* would have loudly protested at having their activities called *Sport* (a word of English! origin), today Sport is accepted as the general term, with *Turnen* as one of its branches, no longer separated by idealogical beliefs.

Source: Excerpted from "Frisch, Fromm, Fröhlich, Frei," by Rainer Thumshirn, Der Blumenbaum, Vol. 11, No. 2, 1993.

TURNERS IN AMERICA

By the time of the failure of their 1848 revolution, Germans, including many Turners, were entering the United States in droves. It was natural, then, for them to want to start up their own Turn Vereins in this country.

The earliest American Turn Vereins included those founded in Cincinnati in 1848, in San Francisco in 1852, in Milwaukee in 1853, and in Sacramento in 1854. At the peak of the movement in America, there were about 300 Turn Vereins.

Many fresh immigrants joined these clubs. The Turn Verein for them was "a home away from home," where German was spoken. The rich social life offered opportunities for camaraderie and freedom from loneliness in a new land. The athletic program was challenging.

During the American Civil War, Turner organizations raised military units and were among the first to volunteer for military service. They earned recognition for their discipline and courage. Many became war casualties.

Turn Vereins were founded in many cities and communities with heavy German immigrant populations.

The membership records and other documents produced by the these Turn Vereins in America were inventoried and published in 1996. (See below)

RECORDS OF *TURNVEREINE* IN AMERICA

The Turner organizations listed below are those for which records have been located and identified. Following the name of each organization is its founding date.

Addresses of current Turner organizations are listed in a following section.

ALABAMA
Birmingham: Deutscher Turnverein, 1887

Mobile: Mobile Turnverein, 1851

CALIFORNIA
Los Angeles: Los Angeles Turners, 1870-71 as Los Angeles Turnverein

Oakland: Oakland Turnverein, 1867

Sacramento: Sacramento Turn Verein, 1854

San Diego: San Diego Turners, 1884 as *Eintracht Turnverein*

San Francisco: San Francisco Gymnastic Club, 1852 as San Francisco Turnverein

San Jose: San Jose Turnverein, 1868

COLORADO
Boulder: Boulder Turnverein [date of organization unknown]

Denver: Denver Turnverein, Inc., 1865 as East Denver Turnverein

CONNECTICUT
Hartford: Hartford Turnerbund, 1878

Meriden: Meriden Turner Society, Inc., 1866 as Meriden Turnverein

New Britain: Socialer Turnverein, 1853 as *Sozialer Turn Verein*

New Haven: New Haven Turnverein, 1852

Rockville: Rockville Turnverein, 1857

Waterbury: *Turnverein Vorwärts*, 1893

DELAWARE
Wilmington: Wilmington Turners, 1859 as *Social Demokratischer Turnverein*

ILLINOIS
Alton: Alton Turnverein, 1864

Aurora: Aurora Turnverein, 1857; *Turnverein Frisch Auf*, 1907

Belleville: Belleville Turners, 1855 as Belleville *Turngemeinde*

Bloomington: Bloomington Turnverein, 1858

Chicago: [See *The Research Guide to the Turner Movement in the United States'* summary of the movement in Chicago]

Chicago: American Turners Northwest Chicago, 1956 (consolidation of the Social Turners, Forward (*Vorwärts*) Turners, and Swiss Turners

Chicago: Aurora Turnverein, 1864

Chicago: Chicago Turners, 1852 as Chicago Turn Verein

Chicago: Turn Verein Lincoln, Inc., 1885 as Lincoln Turn-Verein
Chicago: Turn Verein Eiche, 1890 — merger of Pullman-Kensington *Turngemeinde* (1887), *Turnverein Eintracht* (1885), and Pullman *Männerchor* (1884)
Chicago: Swiss Turners of Chicago, 1882
Chicago: Social Turners, 1886 as *Sozialer Turnverein*
Chicago: Turnverein *Vorwärts*, 1867
Columbia: Columbia Gymnastic Association, 1866 as Columbia Turnverein
Elgin: Elgin Turners, 1883 as Elgin Turnverein
Highland: Highland Gymnastic Association, 1853 as Turnverein Highland
Moline: Moline Turners, 1866 as Moline Turnverein
Mt. Olive: Mt. Olive Gymnastic Society, 1897 as Mt. Olive Turnverein
Peoria: Peoria Turnverein, 1851
Smithton: Smithton Turnverein, 1867 as Georgetown Turnverein

INDIANA
Evansville: Central Turners, 1869 as *Turnverein Vorwärts*
Fort Wayne: Fort Wayne Turners, 1897 as *Turnverein Vorwärts*
Indianapolis: Athenaeum Turners, 1851 as Indianapolis *Turngemeinde*
Indianapolis: South Side Turners, 1893 as *Südseite Turnverein*
South Bend: American Turners South Bend, 1861 as South Bend Turnverein
Tell City: Tell City *Socialer Turnverein*, 1859

IOWA
Clinton: Clinton Turners, Inc., 1883 as *Turnverein Vorwärts*
Davenport: Central Turners, 1852 as *Socialistischer Turnverein*
Davenport: Northwest Davenport Turner Society, 1871
Davenport: East Davenport Turners, 1891 as *Ost Davenport Turnverein*
Garnaville: Garnaville *Sozialer Turnverein*, 1869
Holstein: Holstein Turnverein, 1884

Keystone: Keystone Turners, Inc., 1892 as Keystone Turnverein
Muscatine: Muscatine *Turnverein Vorwärts*, 1907
Postville: Postville Turnverein, 1873

KANSAS
Atchison: Atchison Turnverein, 1859
Leavenworth: Leavenworth Turnverein, 1857
Seneca: Seneca Turnverein, 1897
Topeka: Topeka Turnverein, 1867

KENTUCKY
Covington: Covington Turner Society, 1855 as Covington *Turngemeinde*
Louisville: American Turners Louisville, 1848-1850, as Louisville *Turngemeinde*
Newport: Newport Gymnastic Association, 1852 as Newport Turnverein

LOUISIANA
New Orleans: New Orleans Turnverein, 1851

MARYLAND
Baltimore: American Turners Baltimore, Inc., 1849 as *Social Democratischer Turnverein*
Baltimore: Baltimore *Turnverein Vorwärts*, 1867

MASSACHUSETTS
Adams: Adams Turners, Inc., 1889 as Adams Turn Club [in same year changed name to Adams *Turn Verein Vorwärts*]
Boston: Boston Turnverein, 1849
Clinton: Clinton Turn Verein, 1867 as *Turnverein Frohsinn*
Fitchburg: Fitchburg Turners, Inc., 1886 as Fitchburg Turnverein
Holyoke: Holyoke Turn Verein, 1871
Holyoke: Springdale Turners, Inc., 1886 as Springdale *Vorwärts Turn Verein*
Lawrence: Lawrence Turn Verein, 1866
Malden: Malden Turn Verein, 1889
Springfield: Springfield Turnverein, Inc., 1855
Westfield: Westfield Turnverein, 1897
Worcester: Worcester *Socialer Turnverein*, 1859

MICHIGAN
Detroit: American Turners Detroit, 1852 as Detroit *Socialer Turnverein*

Saginaw: Germania Turnverein, 1856 as Saginaw Turnverein

MINNESOTA
Minneapolis: St. Anthony Turnverein, 1857

Minneapolis: West-Minneapolis Turnverein, 1866

New Ulm: *Ansiedlungsverein des Socialistischen Turnerbundes*, 1856

New Ulm: New Ulm Turnverein, 1856

St. Paul: St. Paul Turners, Inc., 1858 as St. Paul Turnverein

St. Paul: West Side Turnverein, 1888

MISSOURI
Boonville: Boonville *Turn und Gesang Verein*, about 1852 as Boonville Turnverein

Brunswick: Brunswick Turn Verein, 1866 or 1867

Kansas City: Kansas City Turners, 1858 as Kansas City *Sozialer Turnverein*

Lexington: Lexington Turner Society, 1859 as Lexington Turnverein

St. Louis: [See the summary of the Turner movement in St. Louis which introduces the section on St. Louis in *Research Guide to the Turner Movement in the United States.*]

St. Louis: St. Louis Turnverein, 1850 [other societies formed after the Civil War]

St. Louis: Carondelet *Germania Turnverein*, 1875 as Carondelet Turnverein [closed 1887, reopened 1890 as Carondelet Germania Turnverein]

St. Louis: Concordia Gymnastic Society, 1874 or 1875 as St. Louis Concordia Turnverein

St. Louis: North St. Louis Gymnastic Society, 1868 as North St. Louis *Turnschule* and *Kindergarten*

St. Louis: Schiller Turners, Inc., 1906

St. Louis: St. Louis Turnverein, 1850

St. Louis: South St. Louis Turnverein, 1864 as *Süd St. Louis Turnverein*

St. Louis: South West Gymnastic Society, 1893 as *Süd-West St. Louis Turnverein*

St. Louis: Tower Grove Gymnastic Society, 1906

St. Louis: West St. Louis Turnverein,

1879 [which was founded earlier as the Schiller Club]

Washington: Washington Turnverein, 1859 [disbanded during Civil War, reorganized 1865]

NEBRASKA
Omaha: South Side Turners, 1892 as *Süd Seite Turnverein*

NEW HAMPSHIRE
Manchester: Mancester Turnverein, 1870

NEW JERSEY
Carlstadt: Carlstadt Turnverein, 1857 as *Sozialer Turnverein von Carlstadt*

Elizabeth: Elizabeth Turnverein Vorwärts, 1872 [as successor to Turner society active prior to the Civil War]

Hoboken: Hoboken Turnverein, 1857 as Hoboken *Turngemeinde*

Jersey City: Hudson City Turnverein, 1863

New Brunswick: New Brunswick Turnverein, 1867

Newark: Newark Turnverein, 1878

North Bergen: Union Hill Turners, 1872 as Union Hill Turn Verein

Passaic: Passaic Turners, Inc., 1892

Paterson: Riverside Athletic and Singing Club, 1867 as *Socialer* Turnverein

Plainfield: Plainfield *Gesang und Turnverein*, Inc., 1886

Riverside: Riverside Turners (Turnverein Progress), 1860 as Turnverein Progress

Riverside: Riverside Turners Inc., 1897 as Riverside *Turngemeinde*

Trenton: Trenton *Turnerbund*, 1924

NEW YORK
Buffalo: Buffalo Turn Verein, Inc., 1853 as Buffalo Turn Verein

Newburgh: Newburgh Turnverein, 1863

New York City: [Turner activities began in the city in the early 1840s; in 1848 the New York *Turngemeinde* was formed. See *The Research Guide to the Turner Movement in the United States'* summary of the Turner movement in New York City, which introduces the New York City section.]

New York (Bronx): American Turners,

Bronx, Inc., 1881 as *Deutsch-Amerikanischer* Turnverein
New York (Brooklyn): American Turners of Brooklyn, Inc., 1883 as *Turnverein Vorwärts*
New York: American Turners New York, Inc., 1850 as *Sozialistischer Turnverein*
New York (Bloomingdale): Bloomingdale Turnverein, 1850s
New York (Brooklyn): Brooklyn Eastern District Turnverein, 1853 as Williamsburgh Turnverein
New York: Central Turnverein of the City of New York, 1886
New York (Long Island): Long Island Turners, Inc., 1875 as Long Island City Turnverein
New York: Mt. Vernon Turners, Inc., 1891 as Mt. Vernon Turnverein
Rochester: Rochester Turners, Inc., 1852 as *Socialer Turnverein*
Schenectady: Schenectady Turners, Inc., 1891
Syracuse: Syracuse Turners, Inc., 1854 as *Socialer Turn Verein*
Troy: Troy Turnverein, 1852
Utica: Utica Turnverein, 1854

OHIO
Akron: Akron Turner Club, 1885 as Akron Turnverein
Cincinnati: Cincinnati Central Turners Inc., 1848 as Cincinnati *Turngemeinde*
Cincinnati: North Cincinnati Gymnasium, 1881 as *Nord Cincinnati Turnverein*
Cleveland: Cleveland East Side Turners, 1849 as Cleveland Turnverein
Cleveland: Germania Turnverein [covered in history of the Cleveland East Side Turners]
Cleveland: Swiss Gymnastic Society of Cleveland, 1891 as Schweizer Turnverein
Cleveland: American Turners S.T.V. Cleveland, 1867 as *Socialer Turnverein*
Cleveland: *Turnverein Vorwärts* [covered in the history of the Cleveland East Side Turners]
Dayton: Dayton Liederkranz Turners, 1853 as Dayton *Turngemeinde*

Toledo: American Turners Toledo, 1926 [in 1930s known as the *Toledo Turn und Sport Verein* and the German-American Athletic Club]
Toledo: Toledo Turnverein, active in late 1850s, reorganized 1866
Toledo: Toledo *Turnverein Vorwärts*, 1880s

OREGON
Portland: Portland *Socialer Turnverein*, 1858 as Portland Turnverein

PENNSYLVANIA
Ambridge: *Harmonie Männerchor, Gesang und Turn Verein*, 1904
Beaver Falls: Beaver Falls Turners, 1871 as Beaver Falls Turnverein
Charleroi: Charleroi Turn Verein, 1905
Erie: East Erie Turners, 1874 as Erie Turn Verein
Homestead: Eintracht Music and Turn Hall Association, 1886 as *Turn und Gesang-Verein Eintracht von Homestead*
Johnstown: Johnstown Turners, 1866 as Johnstown Turnverein
McKeesport: McKeesport Turners, 1880 [merged with Harmony Singing Society to form the *McKeesport Turn und Gesang Verein*]
Monaca: Monaca Turn Verein, 1883
Monessen: Monessen Turn Verein, 1905
Monongahela: Monongahela Turners, 1889 as *Eintracht Gesangverein*
Philadelphia: [See *The Research Guide to the Turner Movement in the United States*' summary of the Turner movement in Philadelphia, which introduces the Philadelphia section.]
Philadelphia: Philadelphia Turners, 1849 as Philadelphia *Turngemeinde*
Philadelphia: Roxborough Turners, 1873 as *Unabhängige Turner von Roxborough* [offshoot of *Turnverein von* Manayunk, founded 1854]
Philadelphia: West Philadelphia *Turn-und Schul-Verein*, 1904
Rochester: Central Turn Verein Rochester, 1851 as *Socialer Turnverein*

RHODE ISLAND
Providence: Providence Turnverein, 1852

as Providence Turnverein
Providence: Providence Turners, 1896 as *Turnverein Vorwärts*
TENNESSEE
Chattanooga: American Turners of Chattanooga, 1866 as Chattanooga Turnverein
TEXAS
[See *The Research Guide to the Turner Movement in the United States'* summary of the Turner movement in Texas, which introduces the Texas section.]
Belleville: Piney Concordia Turnverein, about 1870
Fredericksburg: *Fredericksburg Sozialer Turnverein*, 1871
New Braunsfeld: New Braunsfeld Turnverein, 1853
WEST VIRGINIA
Morgantown: Turnverein Concordia, 1897
WISCONSIN
Farmington: Farmington Turner Society, 1862 as Farmington Turn Verein
Fond Du Lac: Fond Du Lac Turnverein, 1855 as *Sozialer Turnverein von Fond du Lac*
La Crosse: La Crosse Turnverein, 1865 as La Crosse Turnverein
Madison: Madison Turners, 1855 as Madison Turnverein
Milwaukee [See *The Research Guide to the Turner Movement in the United States'* summary of the Turner movement in Milwaukee, which introduces the Milwaukee section.]
Milwaukee: *Turnverein Bahn Frei*, 1890 as off-shoot of the North Side Turnverein
Milwaukee: Milwaukee Turner Foundation, 1853 as *Socialer Turn Verein*
Milwaukee: *Turnverein der Nordseite*, 1869 as West Hill Turning Society, changed name to *Turnverein der Nordseite* by 1870
Sheboygan: Sheboygan Turners, Inc., 1854 as *Socialer Turnverein*
Note
The entry for each organization listed in Chapter 3 of this book includes a brief historical sketch, listings of its archival collections and publications, and the location of its records. The book lists repository codes for use in locating historical records available for each society. In addition, an appendix attempts to identify all past and present Turner societies which have been active in the United States. The compilers do not, however, claim the list, which includes more than 700 Turner organizations, to be definitive.

Source: Eric L. Pumroy and Katja Rampelmann [comp.], *Research Guide to the Turner Movement in the United States,* [comp]. Greenwood Press, Westport, Conn., 1996.

TURNER ADDRESSES

National organization
National Council of the American Turners, 1127 E. Kentucky Street, P.O. Box 4216, Louisville, KY 40204. Tel. (502) 636-2395
Repository for the American Turners' archives
Ruth Lilly Special Collections and Archives, IUPUI University Library, 755 W. Michigan Street, Indianapolis, IN 46202. Tel. (317) 274-0464

LOCAL TURNER ORGANIZATIONS
* = independent society
(not belonging to the National Council of the American Turners)
California
•Los Angeles Turners, 4950 Wilshire Boulevard, Los Angeles, CA 90010
•*Sacramento Turners, 3349 J Street, Sacramento, CA 95816
Colorado
•Denver Turnverein, Inc., 1570 Clarkson Street, Denver, CO 80030
Connecticut
•*Meriden Turner Society, Inc., 800 Old Colony Road, Meriden, CT 06450
•*Concordia Turner and Singing Society, 1181 North Main Street, Waterbury, CT 06704

Delaware
•Wilmington Turners, 701 S. Claymont Street, Wilmington, DE 19805
Illinois
•Turn Verein Frisch Auf (Aurora), 1335 Mitchell Road, Aurora, IL 60504
•*Belleville Turners, YMCA Building, 15 N. 1st Street, Belleville, IL 62220
•American Turners Northwest Chicago, 6625 West Belmont Avenue, Chicago, IL 60634
•Turn Verein Lincoln, Inc. 1019 W. Diversey Parkway, Chicago, IL 60614
•*Columbia Gymnastic Association, E. Cherry Street, Columbia, IL 62236
•Elgin Turners, 112 Villa Street, Elgin, IL 60120
•Moline Turner Society, 3119 15th Street, Moline, IL 61265
•Central Turners of Rockford: Contact American Turners National Office for current address.
•*Smithton Turners, P.O. Box 73, Smithton, IL 62285
•Turn Verein Eiche, 16767 S. 80th Avenue, Tinley Park, IL 60477
Indiana
•Fort Wayne Turners, 3636 Parnell Avenue, Fort Wayne, IN 46895
•South Side Turners, 3702, Raymond Street, Indianapolis, IN 46203
•Athenaeum Turners, 401 E. Michigan Street, Indianapolis, IN 46204
•American Turners South Bend, 53666 N. Ironwood Road, South Bend, IN 46635
Iowa
•Northwest Davenport Turner Society, 1430 Warren Street, Davenport, IA 52804
•East Davenport Turners, 2113 East 11th Street, Davenport, IA 52803
•Keystone, Turners, 91 2nd Avenue, Keystone, IA 52249
Kentucky
•Covington Turner Society, 447 Pike Street, Covington, KY 41011
•River City Turners, 8009 Terry Road, Louisville, KY 40258
•American Turners Louisville, 3125 Upper River Road, Louisville, KY 40207

Maryland
•American Turners Baltimore, 9124 Lennings Lane, Baltimore, MD 21237
Massachusetts
•Adams Turners, Inc., 6 Turners Avenue, Adams, MA 01220
•Clinton Turnverein, 60 Branch Street, Clinton, MA 01510
•Springfield Turnverein, 176 Garden Street, Feeding Hills, MA 01030
•Springdale Turners, Inc., 2 Vernon Street, Holyoke, MA 01040
•Holyoke Turn Verein, 624 S. Bridge Street, Holyoke, MA 01040
Michigan
•American Turners Detroit, 26214 Virginia, Warren, MI 48091
Minnesota
•St. Paul Turners, Inc., 2500 Lexington Avenue South, Mendota Heights, MN 55120
•New Ulm Turnverein, 102 South State Street, New Ulm, MN 56073
Missouri
•Kansas City Turners, 7620 E. 79th Street, Kansas City, MO 64138
•Concordia Gymnastic Society, 6432 Gravois Road, St. Louis, MO 63116
•North St. Louis Turners, 1928 Salisbury Street, St. Louis, MO 63107
•Schiller Turners, 200 Weiss Avenue, St. Louis, MO 63125
New Jersey
•Carlstadt Turnverein, Inc., 500 Broad Street, Carlstadt, NJ 07072
•Riverside Turners Inc., 300 Rancocas Avenue, Riverside, NJ 08075
•Passaic Turners, Inc., 13 Gray Street, West Caldwell, NJ 07006
New York
•American Turners New York, 748 Clarence Avenue, Bronx, NY 10465
•Buffalo Turn Verein, 3200 Elmwood Avenue, Buffalo, NY 14217
•Long Island Turners Inc.: Contact American Turners National Office for current address.
•Schenectady Turn Verein, P.O. Box 3157, Schenectady, NY 12303

•Syracuse Turners, Inc., 619 N. Salina Street, Syracuse, NY 13208
Ohio
•Akron Turner Club, 547 S. Munroe Falls Road, Tallmadge, OH 44278
•Cincinnati Central Turners, 2200 Piney Lane, Cincinnati, OH 45231
•American Turners Toledo, 3126 Shawnee, Toledo, OH 43613
•Cleveland East Side Turners, 1616 East 55 Street, Cleveland, OH 44103
•Cleveland Turners STV, 7412 Lawn Avenue, Cleveland, OH 44103
•*Dayton Liederkranz Turners, 1400 E. Fifth Street, Dayton, OH 45402
Pennsylvania
•Beaver Falls Turners, 615 8th Street, Beaver Falls, PA 15010
•*East Erie Turnerhall, 829 Parade Street, Erie, PA 16503
•*South Erie Turners, 2663 Peach Street, Erie PA 16508
•Eintracht Music and Turn Hall Association, 218 E. 11th Avenue, Homestead, PA 15120
•Johnstown Turnverein, 632 Railroad Street, Johnstown, PA 15901
•McKeesport Turners & Gesang Verein, McKeesport, PA 15132
•Monaca Turn Verein, 1700 Broadhead Road, Monaca, PA 15061
•Monongahela Turners, 127 E. Main Street, Monongahela, PA 15063
•Roxborough Turners, 418 Leverington Avenue, Philadelphia, PA 19138
•Central Turn Verein Rochester, 338 Pennsylvania Avenue, Rochester, PA 15074
Rhode Island
•Providence Turners, 118 Glenbridge Avenue, Providence, RI 02909
Texas
•*Boerne Turn Verein, P.O. Box 711, Boerne, TX 78006
•*Houston Turn Verein, 7800 Westglen (Suite 190), Houston, TX 77063
•San Antonio Turner Club, 120 Ninth Street, San Antonio, TX 78215*
Wisconsin

•Madison Turners, Inc., 21 Butler Street, Madison, WI 53703
•Milwaukee Turners Foundation, Inc., 1034 N. 4th Street, Milwaukee, WI 53203
•St. Anthony Turnverein, P.O. Box 276, Balsam Lake, WI 54810
•Sheboygan Turners, Inc., 3714 N. 15th Street, Sheboygan, WI 53083
•*Watertown Turners, 4th Street, Watertown, WI 53094

OTHER FRATERNAL ORGANIZATIONS

The fraternal organizations which immigrants joined in the second half of the eighteenth century and the early twentieth century played a strong role in the social integration of the American newcomers.

The influence of these organizations is aptly described by Alvin J. Schmidt in his book, *Fraternal Organizations* (see "Source" at the end of this text):

As the members [of fraternal organizations] participated in their lodge sessions, they slowly learned some of the democratic processes of their newly adopted country by seeing them practiced in their fraternal society's meetings. They soon learned and appreciated the value of free speech and the expression of opinions without fear of reprisal. They also learned how to conduct meetings and the importance of voting. Having learned and internalized these American values, the immigrant became a better-integrated citizen, and much credit belonged to the fraternal societies.

The following information concerning some of the organizations to which German and East European immigrants belonged is culled from Schmidt's book, *Fraternal Organizations*. Current addresses, provided as available, come from other sources.

Aid Association For Lutherans
AAL's began its work in 1899 in Appleton, Wisconsin (as the Aid Associa-

tion for Lutherans in Wisconsin and Other States) with the purpose of establishing a fund for family protection. It received its charter from the state of Wisconsin in 1902. (AAL avoided use of the word "life insurance" or the German word *Lebensversicherung* because the purchaser of life insurance was considered to be lacking in trust in God or to be engaged in usury, which Luther had condemned.)

Each local branch is affiliated with a Lutheran congregation. See the Association's quarterly, *Correspondent*; a brief article, "Our Pioneers Are Gone, But What a Legacy They Left" appears in the summer 1969 issue of this periodical.

Address: Aid Association for Lutherans, 4321 N. Ballard Road, Appleton, WI 54919-0001. Tel. (414) 734-5721

The Alliance of Poles

The Alliance of Poles was formed in 1895 in Ohio, beginning as a fraternal benefit organization. In 1914 the name was changed to its present form, The Alliance of Poles of America. Prospective members have been required to be between 15 and 65 years old. The society's newspaper is *The Alliancer* (or, in Polish, *Zwiazkowiec*).

Address: The Alliance of Poles in America, 6966 Broadway, Cleveland, OH 44105. (216) 883-3131.

Alliance of Transylvania Saxons (ATS)

A number of Saxons founded this ethnic organization in 1902 in Cleveland, Ohio, as the *Siebenbürger Bund*. At the group's first convention the same year, the name was changed to *Central Verband der Siebenbürger Sachsen*. In 1965 the name was changed to The Alliance of Transylvania Saxons.

The society is a fraternal benefit insurance organization seeking to keep alive its 800 years of Saxon heritage. To join the society, prospective members must be "of Transylvanian Saxon birth or a descendant thereof, or married to a Saxon or descendant thereof, or of German birth or a descendant thereof." The age requirement is 16 to 60 years of age.

See the *Saxon Year Book, 1902-1977*, published in 1977 upon the society's 75th anniversary. The organization also publishes a weekly, *Saxon News (Volksblatt)*. Address: Alliance of Transylvanian Saxons, 5393 Pearl Road, Cleveland, OH 44129. Tel. (216) 842-8442.

Bavarian National Association of North America.

This organization was founded in 1884 by Bavarian immigrants as a fraternal benefit group seeking to protect families. In 1934 the society merged with Unity Life and Accident Insurance Association. See Alfred Preuss, *A Dictionary of Secret and Other Societies* (1924).

Concordia Mutual Life Association

This group was formed in 1908 to provide life insurance for Lutherans.

Address: Concordia Mutual Life Association, 3041 Woodcreek Drive, Downers Grove, IL 60515-5417. Tel. (708) 971-8000.

German Order of Harugari

This organization, also known as *Deutscher Orden der Harugari*, was formed in 1847 in New York to provide German immigrants with the opportunity to socialize and to practice speaking their mother tongue. (*"Harugari"* was selected as a name to honor the old Teutons who were called *Harugaris* because they met in the forests; *Haruc* meant grove or forest). See the society's publication, *Der Harugari*; also Albert C. Stevens, *Cyclopedia of Fraternities* (1907).

Address: German Order of Harugari, c/o Max Math, 7625 Hooker Street, Westminster, CO 80030.

Knights of Luther

This was a secret society was organized in 1912 in Des Moines, Iowa "for the purpose of fighting the Romanist Church with weapons like those with which it fights." It apparently no longer exists. See Arthur Preuss, *A Dictionary of Secret and Other Societies* (1924)

Improved Order
of Knights of Pythias

Following the refusal of the Supreme Lodge of the Knights of Pythias to allow its lodges to print the ritual of the order in any language but English, some German members seceded to form the Improved Order of Knights of Pythias in 1895 in Indianapolis. The organization dissolved around the time of World War I. See Albert C. Stevens, *Cyclopedia of Fraternities* (1907).

Lutheran Life Insurance
Society of Canada

This organization came into existence with the merger of the Aid Association of Lutherans and the Lutheran Brotherhood in 1972. Members must belong to the Lutheran church. The society offers life insurance to its members, offers mortgage funds at reduced rates to Lutheran churches, and provides scholarships to Canadian Lutheran educational institutions and individuals. The society's headquarters are in Kitchener, Ontario, Canada.

Order of Sons of Hermann

A group of German Americans in New York City in 1840 formed The Order of Sons of Hermann to protect their German culture and heritage. (Hermann, called Arminius by the Romans, is a German folk hero who led the destruction of three Ro-man legions in the Battle of Teutoberg Forest in 9 AD. The organization spread from New York to many other states.

In 1937 English rather than German began to be used in conducting meetings, and membership was opened to those of northern European lineage who did not have German ancestry.

The organization publishes a monthly periodical, *Hermann Sons News*.

Address: Order of the Sons of Hermann in Texas, P.O. Box 1941, San Antoniio, TX 78297.

United Lutheran Society

This society is the product of a merger of two organizations: 1) the Slovak Evangelical Union, founded in 1893 in Freeland, Pennsylvania (providing fraternal insurance for men who were Slovak Lutherans), and 2) the Evangelical Slovak Women's Union, organized in 1906. The two groups merged in 1962 to form the United Lutheran Society.

Address: United Lutheran Society, Ross Mt. Park Road, P.O. Box 947, Ligonier, PA 15658-0947. Tel. (412) 238-9505

Source: Alvin J. Schmidt, *Fraternal Organizations* [part of *The Greenwood Encyclopedia of American Institutions* series] Greenwood Press, Westport, Conn., 1980

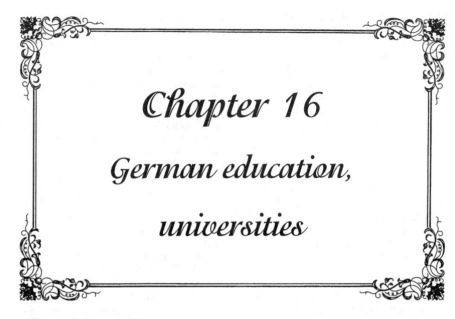

Chapter 16

German education, universities

GERMAN UNIVERSITIES

All institutions of higher education are referred to in German as *Hochschulen*. The two most common types of *Hochschulen* are universities and more specialized institutions called *Fachhochschulen* that are polytechnics and geared toward specific professions. There are *Fachhochschulen* for fields like public administration, economics, agriculture, engineering, social work, music, and the visual arts. *Fachhochschulen* offer many of the same types of academic courses as universities.

Germany also has special teacher training colleges (*pädagogische Hochschulen*) and academies of art and music *(Kunst- und Musikhochschulen)*.

There are approximately 320 institutions of higher education *(Hochschulen)* in Germany. Additional *Fachhochschulen* are scheduled to be established in the former East Germany in the late 1990s.

University faculties

The faculty of German universities commonly belong either to an academic department *(Fachbereich)* or to a school within the university *(Facultät)*. Disciplines in the humanities, natural sciences, and social sciences are often organized as *Fachbereiche*; fields like law, medicine, and theology as *Fakultäten*.

Source: *Federal Republic of Germany: Questions and Answers.* German Information Center. New York, 1996.

ACADEMIC DEGREES IN GERMANY

by Rainer Thumshirn

In Germany, an academic degree can be conferred only on graduates of a *Hochschule* which is run by the state or recognized by it.

There are basically three different kinds of *Hochschule*:

♦ *wissenschaftliche Hochschule* (a university with scientific orientation)

◆*Kunsthochschule* (art academy)
●*Fachhochschule* (similar to a college, professional orientation, requiring lesser qualifications than a university)

The student who passes the final examinations and has successfully written a *Diplomarbeit* (a lesser kind of dissertation), is awarded a *Diplom* by the *Hochschule*. A *Diplom* awarded by a university has an annex of "*Univ.*" or no annex at all. A *Diplom* awarded by a *Fachhochschule* is marked by an annex of "FH."

For example, a degree in engineering from an *Universität* is *Dipl.-Ing. Univ.* or just *Dipl.-Ing.*; from a *Fachhochschule* it is *Dipl.-Ing.(FH)*. The latter was written as *Ing. grad.* until 15 years ago.

Degrees awarded only by universities

The title most widely seen is *Doktor*, a degree that can be awarded only by universities. One earns it after obtaining the *Diplom* by staying at the university for postgraduate studies. For this the candidate must find a professor (*Doktorvater*) to assign a research project, the result of which will be the dissertation (*Doktorarbeit*). In addition, the candidate must pass an oral examination by the *Doktorvater* and two other professors. All dissertations must be published for distribution to the other universities and major scientific libraries.

Contrary to popular belief in Germany, the doctorate thus earned does not become part of one's name. However, *Doktor* may be used with one's name, have it entered on one's ID card (*Personalausweis*) or passport, or even on one's driver's license or credit card.

The highest academic degree, which can be earned only after an outstanding doctorate, is the *Habilitation* (the qualification to teach at universities). For this the candidate usually must publish the results of a major research project or other studies in a *Habilitationsschrift* and also prove one's pedagogic abilities. In many cases

this is the first and most important step toward becoming a professor at a university. Thus a physician, for example, would become a *Prof. Dr. med.* Upon choosing a non-university career, the physician would call himself or herself *Dr. med. Habil.* to show this qualification.

Universities may bestow honorary doctorates upon deserving persons, usually for special achievements in public life or for major donations to a university. This is called a *doctorate honoris causa*, abbreviated as *Dr. h.c.* However not all recipients of such an honorary degree always remember to use the *h.c.*, and thus they become indistinguishable from a *Dr.* by academic achievement, which is sometimes the intention.

Combinations of degrees

Since the *Diplom* is the prerequisite of a doctorate, usually only the *Dr.* is used, not the additional *Dipl.*; it's just *Dr. Ing.*, not *Dipl.-Ing.Dr. Ing.* However, if one has another *Diplom* in a different field, it often is added. For example, a physician may display a *"Dr. med. Dipl.-Biol."* sign on his door.

Doctorates in two or more different fields can also be earned, which could be represented as *Dr. med. Dr. Phil.*, for example.

A professor might also get a honorary doctorate and choose to use *Prof. Dr. Dr. h.c.*

A person either very active in public life or very generous might have multiple honorary doctorates and show this by adding *Dr. h.c. mult.* to his name. Chancellor Helmut Kohl, for example, holds 19 honorary doctorates.

Foreign academic degrees

Non-German academic degrees may be used in public only with express permission from German authorities. Such permission is granted only if academic qualifications similar to those in Germany are required for this academic degree.

For improper use: a misdemeanor

A person improperly using an academic degree in public can be jailed for up to one year or fined according to §132a of Germany's penal code (*Strafgesetzbuch*). An example of improper use would be to call oneself a *Doktor* without having legally acquired the degree or using an unapproved doctorate acquired at a foreign university.

The degree in everyday life

In business, the use of academic degrees, especially the *Dr.*, is thought to be of advantage where it is felt necessary to impress clients and customers with special abilities and trustworthiness of the employees they come in contact with. Business consultants or banks are good examples. A lawyer without a doctorate usually is considered of somewhat inferior quality. But otherwise the importance of a doctorate to promote a career is declining. Applicants for jobs are screened for other qualifications considered more important, like foreign languages or experience with computers.

Forms of address

Relations between employees of German companies are mostly quite formal. It is not very often that people call each other by their first names. Much less do they drop the *Doktor* when addressing a colleague or a superior unless invited to do so. Other academic degrees like the *Diplom* are not used when orally addressing another person. However, they are widely used in letterheads, company names, advertising, phone listings — and obituaries.

Even in private life the degree of *Doktor* is widely used to address a person who holds one. Two people may know one another for years and unless they are close friends who call one another by their first names, the holder of the Doktor degree would still in many cases be *Herr Doktor X* or *Frau Doktor Y*. It is also correct usage to omit the name and just say "*Herr Doktor*" or "*Frau Doktor*."

One particular use of *Frau Doktor* has gone out of fashion: Until about 30 or 40 years ago, good manners required the wife of a *Herr Doktor* (a lawyer or physician, for example) to be addressed as "*Frau Doktor*," even if she never attended a *Hochschule*. Interestingly enough, in the rare cases where the wife held a doctorate and the husband did not, he was not called "*Herr Doktor*."

A genealogical tip

When researching a person who held an academic degree, especially a doctorate, it could be helpful to contact the university in question and locate the dissertation, which usually also contains a *curriculum vitae* of the student. For example, a librarian at the law school (*Juristische Fakultät*) of Munich's Ludwig-Maximilians-Universität states that the library has all dissertations published since 1840 and "a lot" of those published before that. Unless files and archives were lost during World War II, the situation should be about the same at all German universities.

Note: The author, Rainer Thumshirn, of Heimstetten, Germany, writes for *Der Blumenbaum*, journal of the Sacramento German Genealogy Society.

GERMAN AND AMERICAN UNIVERSITYDEGREES

Three of the four types of academic degrees granted by German universities are roughly comparable to the Masters of Arts of Masters of Science degree offered by American universities.

A doctoral degree, awarded in both arts and sciences, as well as law, medicine and theology, is the equivalent of an American Ph.D. Candidates must pass a series of examinations and write a dissertation.

There are no degrees comparable to the American Bachelor of Arts or Sciences.

Source: Susan Steiner, ed., *Federal Republic of Germany: Questions and Answers,* German Information Center, 1996.

DOCTORATES AWARDED BY UNIVERSITIES   IN
GERMAN-SPEAKING COUNTRIES

The codes in parentheses after each title represent the following countries in which the
titles have been used:
D = Bundesrepublik Deutschland (the former West Germany)
DDR = Deutsche Demokratische Republik (the former East Germany)
A = Österreich (Austria)
CH = Schweiz (Switzerland)

D., ehrenhalber verliehener Doktorgrad der Ev. Theologie Doktor der .... Honorary doctor of
Protestant Theology
Dr. agr. (agronomiae), Landbauwiss., Landwirtschaftswiss. (D, DDR) .... Agriculture
Dr. disc. pol. (disciplinarum politicarum), Sozialwiss. (D) .... Social sciences
Dr. eh. (ehrenhalber), Ehrendoktor (DDR) .... Honorary doctor
Dr. e.h. (ehrenhalber), Dr. E.h. (Ehren halber), Ehrendoktor der TH, TU .... Honorary doctor of
a technical university
Dr. forest. (rerum forestalium), Forstwirtschaft (D, DDR) .... Forestry
Dr. h.c. (honoris causa), Ehrendoktor der Univ. .... Honorary doctor of a university
Dr.-Ing. (ingenieur), Ingenieurwiss. (D, DDR) .... Engineering
Dr. iur./jur. (iuris, juris), Rechtswiss. (D, DDR, A, CH) .... Law
Dr. kur. can. (iuris canonici), Kirchenrecht (D) .... Canon law
Dr. iur. utr., Dr.j.u. (iuris utriusque), weltl. und Kirchenrecht (D), CH) .... Law and canon law
Dr. med. (medicinae), Medizin (D, DDR, CH) .... Medicine
Dr. med. dent. (medicinae dentariae), Zahnmedizin (D, DDR, A, CH) .... Dentistry
Dr. med.univ. (medicinae universae), Heilkunde (A) .... Medicine
Dr. med. vet. (medicinae veterinariae), Tierheilkunde (D, DDR, A, CH) .... Veterinarian
Dr. mont. (rerum naturalium technicarum), Bodenkultur (A) .... Agriculture
Dr. oec (oeconomiae),Wirschaftswiss., Verwaltungswiss. (DDR, CH) .... Economics
Dr. oec. (oeconomiae publicae), Staatswiss., Volkswirtschaft (D,CH) .... Economics
Dr. oec. troph. (oecotrophologiae), Hauswirtschaft, Ernährungswiss. (D) .... Dietetics
Dr. paed. (paedagogiae), Erziehungswiss. (DDR) .... Educational science
Dr. pharm. (pharmaciae), Pharmazie (CH) .... Pharmaceutics
Dr. phil (philosophiae_, Philosophie, Doktorgrad der Philosoph. .... All doctorates awarded by an
Fakultät (D, DDR, A, CH)   arts faculty (i.e., languages,
history, philosophy, etc.)
Dr. phil. fac. theol. (philosophiae facultatis theologicae), Philosophie der Theolog. Fakultät .... Theology
Dr. Phil. nat. (philosophiae naturalis), Naturwiss. (soweit innerhalb der .... All doctorates in science
Philosoph Fakultät. (D, CH)   subjects, if taught
within an arts faculty
Dr. rer. agr. (rerum agrarium), Landbauwiss., Landwirtschaft und Bodenkultur (D, DDR)   Agriculture
Dr. rer. comm. (rerum commercialium), Handelswiss. (DDR, A) .... Economics
Dr. rer. forest. (rerum forestalium), Forstwiss. (D, DDR) .... Forestry
Dr. rer. hort. (rerum hortensiarum), Gartenbauwiss. (D, DDR, A, CH) .... Horticulture
Dr. rer. mont. (rerum montanarum), Bergbauwiss. (D, DDR, CH) .... Mining
Dr. rer. nat. (rerum naturalium), Naturwiss. (D, DDR, A, CH) .... All doctorates awarded
by science faculties
Dr. rer. oec. (rerum oeconomicarum), Wirtschaftswiss. (D, DDR, A)   Economics

Dr. rer. oec. publ. (rerum oeconomicarum publicarum), Staatswiss., ... Economics and
Wirtschaftswiss. (D)   political science
Dr. rer. pol. (rerum politicarum, Staatswiss., Wirtschafts- und .... Economics and
Sozialwiss., Volkswirtschaft (D, DDR, A, CH) .... political science
Dr. rer. publ (rerum publicarum), Verwaltungswiss. (CH) .... Civil service
Dr. rer. sec. (rerum securitatis), Sicherheitstechnik, -wiss. (D) .... Safety engineering
Dr. rer. silv. (rerum silvaticarum), Forstwiss. (DDR) .... Forestry
Dr. rer. soc. oec. (rerum socialium oeconomicarumque), Sozial- .... Economics and
und Wirtschaftswiss. (A) .... social science
Dr. rer. techn. (rerum technicarum), techn. Wiss. (DDR) .... Technics
Dr. sc. agr. (scientiarum agrariarum), Landbauwiss., Landwirtschaftswiss. (D, DDR) .... Agriculture
Dr. sc. jur. (scientiae juris), Rechtswiss. (DDR) .... Law
Dr. sc. math., Dr. scient. math. (scientiae mathematicae), Mathematik (CH) .... Mathematics
Dr. sc. med. (scientiae medicinae), Medizin (DDR) .... Medicine
Dr. sc. nat. Dr. scient. nat. (scientiae naturalium), Naturwiss. .... All doctorates awarded
(DDR, CH)   by science faculties
Dr. sc. oec., Dr. scient. oec. (scientiae oeconomiae), Wirtschaftswiss. (DDR) .... Economics
Dr. sc. paed. (scientiae paedagogiae), Erziehungswiss. (DDR) .... Educational science
Dr. sc. phil. (scientiae philosophiae), Philosophie (DDR) ... All doctorates awarded by an arts faculty
Dr. sc. pol. (scientiarum politicarum), Staatswiss., Sozialwiss., ... Political science
Volkswirtschaft (D)   and economics
Dr. sc. silv. (scientiae silvaticae), Forstwiss. (DDR) .... Forestry
Dr. sc. techn., Dr. scient. techn. (scientiarum technicarum), techn. Wiss. (CH) ...... Technical science
Dr. techn. (technicae), techn. Wiss. (A) .... Technical science
Dr. theol. (theologiae), Theologie (D, DDR, A, CII) .... Theology
Dr. troph. (trophologiae), Ernährungswiss. (D) .... Dietetics
Dr. vet. (veterinariae), Tierheilkunde (DDR) .... Veterinarian

DIPLOM DEGREES AWARDED BY GERMAN UNIVERSITIES

Diplom-Agrarbiologe (Dipl.-Agr.Biol.) .... Agricultural biologist
Diplom-Agraringenieur (Dipl.-Ing.agr.) .... Agricultural engineer
Diplom-Agrarökonom .... Agricultural economist
Diplom-Anglist .... English philologist
Diplom-Architekt (Dipl.-Arch.) .... Architect
Diplom-Betriebswirt (Dipl.-Betriebsw.) .... Business management
Diplom-Bibliothekar (Dipl.-Bibl.) .... Librarian
Diplom-Biochemiker (Dipl.-Biochem.) .... Biochemist
Diplom-Biologe (Dipl.-Biol.) .... Biologist
Diplom-Chemieingenieur (Dipl.-Chem.Ing.) .... Chemical engineer
Diplom-Chemiker (Dipl.-Chem.) .... Chemist
Diplom-Designer (Dipl.-Des.) .... Designer
Diplom-Dokumentar .... Documentarian
Diplom-Dolmetscher (Dipl.-Dolm.) .... Interpreter
Diplom-Ernährungswissenschaftler .... Dietician
Diplom-Fachsprachenexperte .... Technical translator
Diplom-Forstwirt .... Forestry
Diplom-Geograph (Dipl.-Geogr.) .... Geographer

Diplom-Geologe (Dipl.-Geol.) .... Geologist
Diplom-Geophysiker (Dipl.-Geophys.) .... Geophysicist
Diplom-Handelslehrer (Dipl.-HdL.) .... Teacher at a commercial school
Diplom-Haushaltsökonom .... Housekeeping economist
Diplom-Informatiker (Dipl.-Inform.) .... Computer specialist
Diplom-Ingenieur (Dipl.-Ing.) .... Engineer
Diplom-Journalist (Dipl.-Journ.) .... Journalist
Diplom-Kaufmann (Dipl.-Kfm.), -Kauffrau .... Economics and business administration
Diplom-Laborchemiker (Dipl.-Lab.Chem.) .... Laboratory chemist
Diplom-Landschaftsplaner .... Landscape architect
Diplom-Landwirt (Dipl.-Landw.) .... Agriculture
Diplom-Lebensmittelchemiker .... Food chemist
Diplom-Lebensmittel-Ingenieur .... Food engineer
Diplom-Lebensmitteltechnologe .... Food technology
Diplom-Literaturübersetzer .... Translator of literature
Diplom-Mathematiker (Dipl.-Math.) .... Mathematician
Diplom-Meteorologe (Dipl.-Met.) .... Meteorologist
Diplom-Mineraloge (Dipl.-Min.) .... Mineralogist
Diplom-Oecotrophologe (Dipl.oec.troph.) .... Dietetics
Diplom-Ökonom (Dipl.oec.) .... Economist
Diplom-Ozeanograph .... Oceanographer
Diplom-Pädagoge (Dipl.-Päd) .... Teacher
Diplom-Pharmakologe .... Pharmacologist
Diplom-Physiker (Dipl.-Phys.) .... Physicist
Diplom-Physikingenieur (Dipl.-Phys.Ing.) .... Physics engineer
Diplom-Politologe (Dipl.-Pol.) .... Political scientist
Diplom-Psychologe (Dipl.Psych.) .... Psychologist
Diplom-Romanist .... Romance philologist
Diplom-Sozialökonom .... Sociologist
Diplom-Sozialwissenschaftler (Dipl.-Soz.Wiss.) .... Sociologist
Diplom-Soziologe (Dipl.-Soz.) .... Sociologist
Diplom-Sportlehrer (Dipl.SportL.) .... Teacher of sports
Diplom-Sprachenlehrer (Deutsch als Fremdsprache) .... Teacher of German
                                                                                        as a foreign language
Diplom-Statistiker (Dipl.-Stat.) .... Statistician
Diplom-Übersetzer (Dipl.-Übers.) .... Translator
Diplom-Theaterwissenschaftler .... Theater studies, dramaturgy
Diplom-Theologe (Dipl.-Theol.) .... Theologian
Diplom-Umweltwissenschaftler .... Environmentalist
Diplom-Verfahrenschemiker (Dipl.-Verf.Chem.) .... Chemist
Diplom-Volkswirt (Dipl.-Volksw.) .... Economist
Diplom-Wirtschaftsingenieur (Dipl.-Wirtsch.Ing.) .... Economist and engineer

DIPLOM DEGREES AWARDED BY GERMAN FACHHOCHSCHULEN

Diplom-Bauingenieur .... Civic engineer
Diplom-Betriebswirt (Dipl.-Betriebsw.) .... Managerial economics
Diplom-Bibliothekar (Dipl.-Bibl.) .... Librarian

Diplom-Chemieingenieur .... Chemical engineer
Diplom-Designer (Dipl.-Des.) .... Designer
Diplom-Dokumentar (Dipl.-Dok.) .... Documentarian
Diplom-Dolmetscher (Dipl.-Dolm.) .... Interpreter
Diplom-Elektroingenieur .... Electrical engineer
Diplom-Fachlehrer .... Teacher specializing in ...
Diplom-Finanzwirt (Dipl.-Finanzw.) .... Public finance
Diplom-Forstingenieur .... Forestry engineer
Diplom-Heilpädagoge (Dipl.-Heilpäd.) .... Therapeutic pedagogist
Diplom-Informatiker (Dipl.-Inform.) .... Computer specialist
Diplom-Ingenieur (dipl.-Ing.) .... Engineer
Diplom-Maschinenbauingenieur .... Mechanical engineer
Diplom-Mathematiker .... Mathematician
Diplom-Nautiker .... Navigation
Diplom-Oecotrophologe (Dipl.-oec.troph.) .... Dietetics
Diplom-Physikingenieur .... Physics engineer
Diplom-Rechtspfleger (Dipl.-Rpfl.) .... Judicial officer
Diplom-Sozialarbeiter (Dipl.-Soz.Arb.) .... Welfare worker
Diplom-Sozialpädagoge (Dipl.-Soz.Päd.) .... Teacher of social studies
Diplom-Übersetzer (Dipl.Übers.) .... Translator
Diplom-Verwaltungsbetriebswirt .... Economist with the Civil Service
  (Dipl.-Verwaltungsbetriebsw.)
Diplom-Verwaltungswirt (Dipl.-Verwaltungsw.) .... Civil servant
Diplom-Wirtschaftsinformatiker .... Computer specialist and economist

Source: ***Brockhaus Encyclopaedia;*** **English translations by Rainer Thumshirn**

SELECTED EUROPEAN UNIVERSITIES *(Hochschulen)* FOUNDED BEFORE 1920

Institutions in Germany are listed by their last-known German name, alphabetically by name of geographical location. Names of those in other countries are listed by their names in English.
KEY:
f = founded
* = no longer extant
German universities
Rheinisch-Westfälische Technische Hochschule (Rhenish-Westphalian Technical University of Aachen); f 1870 as Polytechnikum; 1880 became Technische Hochschule; 1948 present title
Universität Altdorf*; f 1578
Universität Bamberg*; f 1648

Hochschule für Schauspielkunst Berlin (College of Theatrical Arts Berlin); f 1905; 1981 present title
Technische Universität Berlin; f 1799 as Bauakademie; 1879 Technische Hochschule; 1916 Bergakademie, founded 1770, incorporated; 1946 reopened as Technische Universität
Humboldt-Universität zu Berlin (Humboldt University, Berlin); f 1809 as Friedrich-Wilhelms Universität;1948 renamed with present name
Rheinische Friedrich-Wilhelms-Universität Bonn (Rhenish Friedrich-Wilhelms-Universität Bonn); f 1777; raised to university rank 1786; dissolved 1794 during French occupation; refounded 1818
Universität Breslau; refounded 1811
Technische Universität Clausthal; f 1775; became Bergakademie Clausthal

1864; acquired university status 1920; present title conferred 1968
Technical Universität Carolo-Wilhelmina zu Braunschweig (Carolo-Wilhelmina Technical University of Brunswick); f 1745 as Collegium Carolinum; became Technische Hochschule 1877; Technische Universität 1968
Technische Universität Chemnitz; f 1836; became college of engineering 1953; Technische Hochschule 1963; renamed Technische Universität 1986
Hochschule für Bauwesen Cottbus (College of Building Technology Engineering of Cottbus); f 1836 as Höhere Gewerbeschule; became Technische Hochschule 1877; acquired university status 1895
Technische Hochschule Darmstadt (University of Darmstadt); acquired university status 1895
Universität Dillinger*; f 1554
Technische Universität Dresden; f 1826; renamed Polytechnische Schule, Technische Hochschule 1890; conferred university status 1961
Heinrich-Heine-University Düsseldorf; f 1907 as academy for practical medicine; university status 1923
Universität Erfurt*; f 1382
Friedrich-Alexander-Universität Erlangen-Nürnberg; f 1743; 1961 the former Hochschule für Wirtschafts-und Sozialwissenschaften Nürnberg was incorporated, and"Nürnberg" was added to the name.
Johann-Wolfgang-Goethe-Universität Frankfurt a. M; f 1914; Goethe name adopted 1932
Universität Frankfurt a. O.; f 1506; 1811 united with Universität Breslau
Bergakademie Freiberg (Freiberg Mining Academy); f 1765; university status 1905
Albert-Ludwigs-Universität Freiberg im Breisgau; f 1457
Justus-Liebig-Universität Gießen (Justus Liebig University of Giessen); f 1607

Georg-August-Universität Göttingen; f 1737
Ernst-Moritz-Arnt-Universität Greifswald; f 1456; 1648 came under control of Sweden; became a Prussian university in 1815
Martin-Luther-Universität Halle-Wittenberg; University of Wittenburg f 1502; University of Halle f 1694; 1817 merged; 1933 name changed to Martin-Luther-Universität
Universität Hamburg; f 1919
Tierarztliche Hochschule Hannover (Hannover School of Veterinary Medicine); f 1778; 1887 university status
Universität Hannover; f 1831 as secondary vocational school; 1847 became Polytechnische Hochschule; 1879 Königliche Technische Hochschule; 1880 acquired university status
Ruprecht-Karls-Universität Heidelberg; f 1386
Universität Helmstedt*; f 1576
Universität Herborn*; f 1654
Universität Hohenheim; f 1818; 1904 became Hochschule; 1919 acquired university status
Universität Ingolstadt*; f 1472
Friedrich-Schiller-Universität Jena; f 1558 (as academy; 1558 became university
Pädagogische Hochschule Karlsruhe (College of Education Karlsruhe); f 1768 as Scul-Seminarium; 1962 became college
Universität Fridericiana Karlsruhe (Technische Hochschule); f 1825 as Polytechnische Schule; 1865 acquired university status
Christian-Albrechts-Universität zu Kiel; f 1665; 1773 became *Landesuniversität* for Schleswig-Holstein; 1867 became a Prussian university; 1945 reestablished as *Landesuniversität*
Universität Köln; f 1388; closed from 1798 under French occupation; 1919 refounded
Universität Königsberg i. Pr.; f 1544
Universität Landshut*; f 1800; 1826 moved to München
Universität Leipzig; f 1409; 1953 became

Karl-Marx-Universität; 1991 acquired present title
Universität Löwen; f 1426
Johannes Gutenberg-Universität Mainz; f 1477; 1816 closed, but Catholic theology faculty continued as a seminary; 1946 reestablished
Universität Mannheim; f 1907 as Stadtische Handelshochschule; 1933 attached to University of Heidelberg; 1946 became Wirtschaftshochschule; 1967 university title conferred.
Philipps Universität Marburg a. d. Lahn; f 1527
Technische Universität München; f 1827 as Polytechnische Zentralschule; 1868 became Polytechnisch Schule; 1877 became Technische Hochschule; 1970 acquired university status
Ludwig-Maximilians-Universität München; f 1472 at Ingolstadt; 1800 transferred to Landshut; 1826 to München
Westfalische Wilhelms Universität Münster; f 1780 as university; 1818 became an academy of Philosophy and theology; 1902 restored to university status; 1907 acquired present title
Universität Osnabrück*; f 1630
Universität Paderborn*; f 1614
Universität Rostock; f 1419; 15th century moved temporarily to Greifswald and Lübeck; 1946 reorganized and reopened
Pädagogische Hochschule Schwäbisch Gmünd (University of Education of Schwäbisch Gmünd); f 1825 as University College
Universität Stuttgart; f 1829 as grammar and vocational school; 1840 became Polytechnische Schule; 1890 became Technische Hochschule; 1967 present title conferred
Universität Trier*; f 1473
Eberhard-Karls-Universität Tübingen; f 1477
Hochschule für Architektur und Bauwesen Weimar: f 1860 as academy of fine arts; 1926 became college; 1954 acquired university status
Universität Wittenberg*; f 1502; 1817 united with Halle
Bayerische-Julius-Maximilians Universität Würzburg; f 1582

Switzerland
Universität Basel; f 1460
Universität Berne; f 1528 as school; 18th century became academy; 1834 became university
Université de Fribourg; f 1889
Université de Genève; f 1559 as Schola Genevensis by Calvin; 1873 established as university
École polytechnique federale de Lausanne; f 1853 as private school; 1890 part of Faculty of Science in University of Lausanne; 1946 autonomous institute
Université de Lausanne; f 1537 as Académie de Lausanne, a theological seminary; 1890 became university
Université de Neuchâtel; f 1838 as academy; 1909 became university
Hochschule St. Gallen für Wirtschafts-Rechts- und Socialwissenschaften (University of St. Gallen for Business Administration, Economics, Law, and Social Sciences); f 1898
Eidgenössische Technische Hochschule Zürich (Swiss Federal Institute of Technology); f 1855
Universität Zürich; f 1523 as a school; 1838 became university

Austria
Hochschule für Musik und darstellende Kunst in Graz (College of Music and Dramatic Art Graz); f 1803 as provincial School of Music; 1815 conservatory; 1963 Akademie; 1970 university institution with title of Hochschule
Karl-Franzens-Universität Graz; f 1585/86; 1782 university status withdrawn; 1827 reestablished as Karl Franzens Universität
Technische Universität Graz; f 1811; 1865/66 university rank
Leopold-Franzens-Universität Innsbruck; f 1669
Montauniversität Leoben (University of

Mining and Metallurgy Leoben); f 1840 as mining institute; 1904 university status; 1975 present title

Hochschule für Musik und darstellende Kunst 'Mozarteum' in Salzburg; f 1841; 1914 conservatory; 1921 state institution; 1953 Akademie; 1970 university institution with title of Hochschule

Universität Salzburg; f 1617 as school; 1622 university; 1810 dissolved; 1962 reestablished

Akademie der bildenden Künste in Wien (Academy of Fine Arts Vienna); f 1692

Hochschule für Musik und darstellende Kunst in Wien (College of Music and Dramatic Art Vienna); f 1812 as a Conservatory; 1920 became Academy; 1970 university with title of Hochschule

Universität für Bodenkultur Wien (University of Agriculture Vienna); f 1872 as Hochschule; 1975 present title

Hochschule für angewandte Kunst in Wien (University of Applied Arts Vienna); f 1868 as school; 1948 academy; 1970 university institution with title of Hochschule

Technische Universität Wien; f 1815 as institute of technology; 1872 university rank

Universität Wien; f 1365

Wirtschaftuniversität Wien (Vienna University of Economic and Business Administration); f 1898 as academy for foreign trade; 1919 became Hochschule für Welthandel, with university rank

Veterinärmedizinische Universität Wien (Vienna University of Veterinary Medicine); f 1767 as school; 1908 university status; 1975 present title

Czechoslovakia (Czech Republic)

Masaryk University Brno; f 1919; 1939 closed; 1945 reopened as Jana Evangelista Purkyn University; 1989 reverted to former name

Technical University of Brno; f 1849; closed during German occupation; 1945 reopened

University of Agriculture Brno; f 1919

University of Veterinary Sciences Brno; f 1918; 1969 became university

Palacky University Olomouc; f 1573; closed during German occupation; 1946 reopened

Technical University of Mines and Metallurgy Ostrava; f 1716 as School of Mining and Metallurgy at Jáchymov in Bohemia; 1763 became part of University of Prague; 1770 moved to Slovakia; 1849 to Stiavnica and Pribram, Bohemia; 1894 acquired university status; 1945 moved to present location, Ostrava

Charles University Prague; f 1348; 1882 divided into separate Czech and German universities, each bearing title Charles-Ferdinand; 1918 present title adopted; November 1939 closed during German occupation; 1945 reopened when the German university was abolished

Czech Technical University of Prague; f 1707 as Czech State Engineering School; 1803 became Polytechnic; 1864 acquired university status; 1939 closed during German occupation; 1945 reopened

University of Agriculture Prague; f 1906; 1939 closed during the German occupation; 1945 reopened; 1952 detached and reestablished as separate institution

Lithuania

Vilnius University; f 1579 as Academica and Universitas Vilnensis; 1781 and 1803 reorganized as Imperial University of Vilnius; 1832 closed; 1919 reopened; 1943 closed during German occupation

Luxembourg

University Centre of Luxembourg; f 1848

Netherlands

Free University Amsterdam; f 1880

University of Amsterdam; f 1632; 1876 became university

Delft University of Technology; f 1842 as "Royal Academy"; 1986 acquired present title

University of Groningen; f 1614
Leiden University; f 1575
Utrecht University; f 1636
Wageningen Agriculture University; f 1876 as national agricultural college; 1918 acquired university status

Poland
Crakow University of Technology; 1945 succeeded Polytechnic Institute (1835); 1878 suppressed; 1970 reorganized
Jagiellonian University Cracow; f 1364; 1939 closed during the German occupation; after 1942 operated as an underground university
The Stanis aw Staszic University of Mining and Metallurgy Cracow; f 1919 as Akademia Gornicza, Academy of Mining; 1949 name changed to Akademia Gorniczo-Hutnicza
Technical University of Gdansk; f 1904 as Technische Hochschule Gdansk, Prussia
Catholic University of Lublin; f 1918; 1939 closed during the German occupation; 1944 reopened
Adam Mickiewicz University of Poznan; f 1919
Technical University of Poznan; f 1919 as college; 1939 closed; 1945 reopened; 1955 acquired full university status
University of "Agriculture Poznan; f 1870 as Agricultural School; 1919 became Faculty of Agriculture and forestry, Adam Mickiewicz University Poznan; 1951 detached as college; 1972 took present title
University of Wroclaw; f 1702 as Generale Litterarum Gymnasium; 1811 became university after union with the University of Frankfurt/Oder; 1945 German university closed and Polish university opened
University of Warsaw f 1808 as school of law; 1816 became university; almost completely destroyed during World War II; 1945 reopened
Warsaw University of Technology; f 1826 as polytechnic institute; 1830 closed; 1898-1915 operated with Russian as

medium of instruction; 1915 reorganized as Technical University of Warsaw; 1939-1944 closed during the German occupation

Slovak Republic
Comenius University Bratislava; f 1919 to replace former Hungarian University established 1914
Technical University of Košice; f 1864 as Mining and Metallurgical School at Banskabystrica
University of Forestry and Wood Technology Zvolen; f 1807 at Banska Stiaynica as School of Forestry

Yugoslavia
University of Belgrade; f 1808 as a school; 1838 lyceum; 1863 became college; 1905 university status

¯ Sources:
♦*International Handbook of Universities*. 13th ed. International Association of Universities. The Macmillan Press Ltd., London. 1993.
♦*Meyers Lexikon*, Bibliographisches Institut, Leipzig, 1930.

ARCHIVES IN SELECTED GERMAN AND AUSTRIAN UNIVERSITIES

Aachen: Rheinisch-Westfälische Technische Hochschule Aachen Historisches Institut, Abt. Hochschularchiv, Templergraben 57, 52062 Aachen; Post: Kopernikusstr. 16, 52074 Aachen
Augsburg: Universität Augsburg, Universitätsarchiv, Alter Postweg 120, 86159 Augsburg
Bamberg: Otto-Friedrich-Universität Bamberg, Universitätsarchiv, Kapuzinerstr. 16, 96047 Bamberg; Postanschrift: 96045 Bamberg
Bautzen: Sorbisches Kulturarchiv, Bahnhofstr. 6, 02625 Bautzen
Bayreuth: Universität Bayreuth, Universitätsarchiv, Dezernat HB/ID, Universitätsstr. 30, 95447 Bayreuth

Berlin: Freie Universität Berlin, Universitätsarchiv, Kaiserswerther Str. 16-18, 14195 Berlin
- Hochschule der Künste Berlin, Hochschularchiv, Postfach 126720, 10595 Berlin, Bundesalle 1-12, 10719 Berlin
- Humboldt-Universität zu Berlin, Universitätsarchiv, Unter den Linden 6, 10099 Berlin
- Technische Fachhochschule Berlin, Historisches Archiv, Luxemburger Str. 10, Haus Grashof, Raum 802, 13353 Berlin
- Technische Universität Berlin, Universitätsbibliothek/Hoschschularchiv, Straße des 17. June 135, 10623 Berlin
- HEROLD, Verein für Heraldik, Genealogie und verwandte Wissenschaften, Archiv, Archivstr. 12-14, 14195 Berlin
Bochum: Ruhr-Universität Bochum, Universitätsarchiv, Ruhr-Universität, 44780 Bochum (im Aufbau)
Bonn: Rheinische Friedrich-Wilhelms-Universität Bonn, Universitätsarchiv, Am Hof, 53113 Bonn
Braunschweig: Technische Universität Carolo-Wilhelmina Braunschweig, Universitätsarchiv, Pockelsstr. 4, 38106 Braunschweig
Bremerhaven: Förderverein Deutsches Auswanderermuseum e.V., Archiv, Inselstr. 6, 27568 Bremerhaven
Chemnitz: Technische Universität Chemnitz-Zwickau, Universitätsarchiv, Reichenhainer Str. 41, 09126 Chemnitz; Postfach 964, 09009 Chemnitz
Clausthal: Technische Universität Clausthal, Universitätsarchiv, Leibnizstr. 2, 38678 Clausthal-Zellerfeld
Darmstadt: Technische Hochschule Darmstadt, Dokumentation und Hochschularchiv, Karolinenplatz 3, 64289 Darmstadt
Dortmund: Universität Dortmund, Universitätsarchiv, August-Schmidt-Str. 4, 44227 Dortmund-Eichlinghofen; Postanschrift: 44221 Dortmund
Dresden: Technische Universität Dresden, Universitätsarchiv, Mommenstr. 13, 01069 Dresden

Duisberg: Gerhard-Mercator-Universität-Gesamthochschule Duisburg, Archiv, Lotharstr. 65, 47048 Duisburg
Eichstätt: Katholische Universität Eichstätt, Archiv, Ostenstr. 26, 85071 Eichstätt
Erfurt: Pädagogische Hochschule Erfurt/ Mühlhausen, Hochschularchiv, Nordhäuser Str. 63, 99089 Erfurt; Postfach 307, 99006 Erfurt
Erlangen-Nürnberg: Friedrich-Alexander-Universität Erlangen-Nürnberg, Universitätsarchiv, Schuhstr. 1a, 91052 Erlangen
Flensburg: Fachhochschule Flensburg, Hochschularchiv, Kanzleistr. 91-93 Block B, 24943 Flensburg
Frankfurt am Main: Johann Wolfgang Goethe-Universität Frankfurt (Main), Universitätsarchiv, Senckenberganlage 31, 60325 Frankfurt
Freiberg: Technische Universität Bergakademie Freiberg, Universitätsarchiv, Akademiestr. 6, 09596 Freiberg
Freiberg im Breisgau: Albert-Ludwigs-Universität Freiburg, Universitätsarchiv, Werthmannplatz 2, 79098 Freiburg im Breisgau; Postfach 1629, 79016 Freiburg im Breisgau
Gießen: Justus-Liebig-Universität Gießen, Universitätsarchiv, c/o Universitätsbibliothek, Otto-Behaghel-Str. 8, 35394 Gießen
Göttingen: Georg-August-Universität Göttingen, Universitätsarchiv, Goßlerstr. 12a, 37073 Göttingen; Postfach 3744, 37027 Göttingen
Graz (Austria): Karl-Franzens-Universität Graz, Universitätsarchiv, Universitätsplatz 3, A-8010 Graz
Halle: Martin-Luther-Universität Halle-Wittenberg, Universitätsarchiv, Weidenplan 12, 06108 Halle (Saale)
Hamburg: Universitätsarchiv Hamburg, Staatsarchiv der Freien und Hansestadt Hamburg, ABC-Str. 19 A, 20354 Hamburg
Hannover: Universität Hannover, Universitätsarchiv, Welfengarten 1 B,

30167 Hannover
Heidelberg: Ruprecht-Karls-Universität Heidelberg, Universitätsarchiv, Friedrich-Ebert-Platz 2, 69117 Heidelberg; Postfach 105760, 69047 Heidelberg
-Zentralarchiv zur Erforschung der Geschichte der Juden in Deutschland, Bienenstr. 5, 69117 Heidelberg
Hohenheim: Universität Hohenheim, Universitätsarchiv, Museum zur Geschichte Hohenheims, Speisemeistereiflügel, Schloß Hohenheim, Postfach, 70599 Stuttgart (Hohenheim)
Ilmenau: Technische Universität Ilmenau, Universitätsarchiv, Dezernat Akademische und Rechtsangelegenheiten, Max-Planck-Ring 14, 98693 Ilmenau; Postfach 327, 98684 Ilmenau
Innsbruck (Austria): Universität Innsbruck, Universitätsarchiv, Innrain 52, A-6020 Innsbruck
Jena: Friedrich-Schiller-Universität Jena, Thüringer Universitäts- und Landesbibliothek, Universitätsarchiv, Postfach, 07740 Jena
- Fachhochschule Jena, Hochschularchiv, Tatzendpromenade 1b, 07745 Jena; Postfach 100314, 07703 Jena
Karlsruhe: Universität Fridericiana Karlsruhe (Technische Hochschule), Universitätsarchiv, Kaiserstr. 12, 76131 Karlsruhe; Postfach 6980, 76128 Karlsruhe
Kiel: Universitätsarchiv Kiel, Landesarchiv Schleswig-Holstein, Prinzenpalais, 24837 Schleswig
Köln: Universität Köln, Universitätsarchiv, Universitätsstr. 33 [entrance on Kerpener Str.], 50931 Köln
Konstanz: Universität Konstanz, Universitätsarchiv, Universitätsstr. 10, 78464 Konstanz; Postfach 5560, D75, 78434 Konstanz
Leipzig: Universitätsarchiv Leipzig, Beethovenstr. 6, 04107 Leipzig
- Hochschule für Technik, Wirtschaft und Kultur Leipzig (FH), Hochschularchiv, eichendorffstr. 2, 04277 Leipzig; Postfach 66, 04251 Leipzig

Lüneberg: Universität Lüneburg, Hochschularchiv, Wilschenbruchweg 84, 21335 Lünebert
Magdeburg: Otto-von-Guericke-Universität, Universitätsarchiv, Universitätsplatz 2, 39106 Magdeburg; Postfach 4120, 39016 Magdeburg
Mainz: Johannes Gutenburg-Universität Mainz, Universitätsarchiv, Forum 2, 55128 Mains; Postfach 3980, 55099 Mainz
Mannheim: Universität Mannheim, Universitätsarchiv, Schloß, Dezernat I, Postfach 103462, 68034 Mannheim
Marburg/Lahn: Philippss-Universität Marburg (Lahn), Universitätsarchiv, Hessisches Staatsarchiv Marburg, Friedrichsplatz 15, Postfach 540, 35037 Marburg
München: Ludwig-Maximilians-Universität München, Universitätsarchiv, Geschwister-Scholl-Platz 1, 80539 München
Münster: Westfälische Wilhelms-Universität Münster, Universitätsarchiv, Steinfurter Str. 107, 48149 Münster
Oldenburg: Carl von Ossietzky-Universität Oldenburg, Universitätsarchiv, Hermann-Helmers-Archiv, BIS, Postfach 2541, 26015 Oldenburg
Paderborn: Universität-Gesamthochschule Paderborn, Universitätsarchiv, Warburger Str. 100, 33098 Paderborn
Passau: Universität Passau, Universitätsarchiv, Dr.-Hans-Kapfinger-Str. 22, 94032 Passau
Potsdam: Universität Potsdam, Universitätsarchiv, UNI-Potsdam, Postfach 601553, 14415 Potsdam
Reutlingen: Fachhochschule für Technik und Wirtschaft Reutlingen, Hochschularchiv, Alteburgstr. 150, 72762 Reutlingen
Rostock: Universität Rostock, Universitätsarchiv, Universitätsplatz 1, 188051 Rostock
Saarbrücken: Universität des Saarlandes, Universitätsarchiv, Postfach 151150, 66041 Saarbrücken
Salzburg (Austria): Universität Salzburg, Universitätsarchiv, Residenzplatz 1,

Postfach 505, A-5010 Salzburg
Stuttgart: Universität Stuttgart, Universitätsarchiv, Universitätsbibliothek, Postfach 104941, 70043 Stuttgart
Tübingen: Eberhard-Karls-Universität Tübingen, Universitätsarchiv, Wilhelmstr. 32, 72074 Tübingen
Ulm: Universität Ulm, Universitätsarchiv, 89069 Ulm
Wien (Austria): Universität Wien, Universitätsarchiv, Postgasse 9 (Alte Universität), A1010 Wien
- Technische Universität Wien, Universitätsarchiv, Karlsplatz 13, A-1040 Wien
Würzburg: Bayerische Julius-Maximilians-Universität Würzburg, Universitätsarchiv, Sanderring 2, 97070 Würzburg
Zwickau: Hochschule für Technik und Wirtschaft Zwickau (FH), Hochschularchiv, Dr.-Friedrich-Ring 2a, 08056 Zwickau; Postfach 35, 08001 Zwickau

UNIVERSITIES, TECHNICAL SCHOOLS, AND LIBRARIES OF THE SECOND EMPIRE

Second Empire universities

The 21 universities of the Second German Empire are listed below, with their respective dates of founding (in parentheses). All had faculties of theology, law, medicine, and philosophy except Münster, which had no faculty of medicine.

Berlin (1809); Bonn* (1818); Breslau* (1811); Erlangen (1743); Freiburg**(1457); Giessen (1607); Göttingen (1737); Griefswald (1456); Halle (1694); Heidelberg (1385); Jena (1558); Kiel (1665); Königsberg (1544); Leipzig (1409); Marburg (1527); Munich** (1826); Münster** (1902); Rostock (1418); Strassburg (1872); Tübingen* (1477); Würzburg** (1582)

* = both Protestant and Catholic faculties for school of theology
** = exclusively Catholic faculty for school of theology
All others: exclusively Protestant fac-

ulty for school of theology

Technical High Schools (Polytechnica)

Ten technical high schools, with departments of architecture, building, civil engineering, chemistry, metallurgy and, in some cases, anatomy, had the power to grant certain degrees. They were Berlin (Charlottenburg), Munich, Darmstadt, Karlsruhe, Hanover, Dresden, Stuttgart, Aix-la-Chapelle, Brunswick, and Danzig.

Among other higher technical schools were three mining academies of Berlin, Clausthal, in the Harz, and Freiberg in Saxony.

For instruction in agriculture were agricultural schools attached to several universities — notably Berlin, Halle, Göttingen, Königsberg, Jena, Poppelsdorf near Bonn, Munich and Leipzig.

Noted academies of forestry were those of Tharandt (in Saxony), Eberswalde, Münden on the Weser, Hohenheim near Stuttgart, Brunswick, Eisenach, Giessen, and Karlsruhe.

Five veterinary academies were located at Berlin, Hanover, Munich, Dresden, and Stuttgart.

For military science there were the academies of war *(Kriegsakademien)* in Berlin and Munich, a naval academy in Kiel, and various cadet and non-commissioned officers' schools.

Libraries

The best known libraries were in these locations:
Berlin (1,000,000 volumes, 30,000 manuscripts)
Munich (1,000,000 volumes, 40,000 manuscripts)
Heidelberg (563,000 volumes, 8,000 manuscripts)
Göttingen (503,000 volumes, 6,000 manuscripts)
Strassburg (760,000 volumes)
Dresden (500,000 volumes, 6,000 manuscripts)
Hamburg (municipal library 600,000 volumes, 5,000 manuscripts)
Stuttgart (400,000 volumes, 3,500 manu-

scripts)
Leipzig (university library 500,000 volumes, 5,000 manuscripts)
Würzburg (350,000 volumes)
Tübingen (340,000 volumes)
Rostock (318,000 volumes)
Breslau (university library 300,000 volumes, 7,000 manuscripts)
Freiburg-im-Breisgau (250,000 volumes)
Bonn (265,000 volumes)
Königsberg (230,000 voumes, 1,100 manuscripts)

There were also famous libraries at Gotha, Wolfenbüttel, and Celle.

Source: *Encyclopedia Britannica: Dictionary of Arts, Sciences, Literature and General Information,* University Press, NY, 1910, 11th edition

---

EARLY EDUCATION IN GERMANY

At the age of six, children enter elementary school (*Grundschule*), which lasts four years, except in Berlin, where it lasts six years. All children attend elementary school together. With the start of secondary school, they begin to follow more specialized courses of study. During the fifth and sixth years of school, known in most states as the "orientation stage" (*Orientierungsstufe*), they make the transition to either pre-university or vocational high school programs.

There are three traditional types of high school in Germany and a newer fourth type that combines features of the other three.
1) The *Gymnasium* (academic high school), which, including the orientation stage, lasts nine years in the western states, through grade 13, and eight years in four of the five of the eastern states, through grade 12. Students who successfully complete their studies at academic high schools receive a diploma known as the *Abitur*. The *Abitur* is the basic requirement for admission to a university.

In 1990, the officials of the Federal Republic and the German Democratic Republic negotiating the terms of German unification agreed to defer making a decision on a common length for Gymnasium study until 1996. The state ministers of education decided in 1994, however, to postpone "educational unification" until 2000, after they undertake a comprehensive review of the country's school system.
2) The *Realschule* (commercial high school), which offers instruction in both academic and business-related subjects and lasts through the tenth grade. Graduates of *Realschulen* receive diplomas that normally entitle them to admission to business and technical colleges, or, depending on their grades, to the last three years of *Gymnasium*.
3) The *Hauptschule* (general high school), which is vocationally oriented. After completing the ninth or tenth grade, depending on the state, *Hauptschule* students receive the diploma necessary to enter formal three-year training programs for technical and clerical professions. During those three years, students in training programs attend a mandatory eight to twelve hours of classroom instruction a week at a *Berufsschule* (vocational school).

In recent years, comprehensive schools, *Gemsamtschulen*, that offer academic, commercial, and vocational programs have become increasingly common. There are also special schools for disabled students.

Source: German Information Center, *Federal Republic of Germany: Questions and Answers,* ed. Susan Steiner, New York, 1996.

UNIVERSITY ADMISSION REQUIREMENTS

The basic entrance requirement is the *Abitur*, the diploma awarded to students who have passed a series of final exami-

THE GERMAN EDUCATION SYSTEM

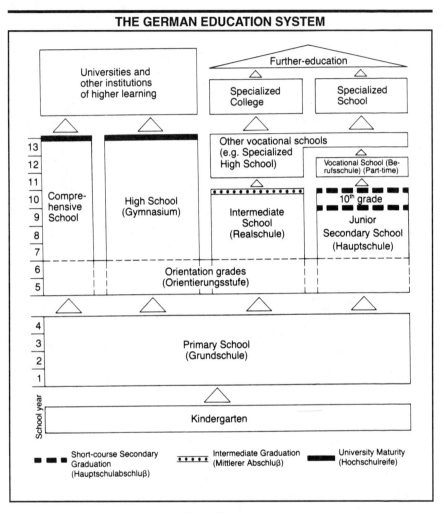

Source: German Information Center, New York

nations in grade 13 of an academic high school or its equivalent.

Some university-level programs, particularly in technical fields and specialized subjects like agriculture, are open to graduates of two-year vocational colleges (*Fachoberschulen*). It is possible for individuals who did not attend either an academic high school or a *Fachoberschule*

to earn the *Abitur* at night school or in a general education institution called a Kolleg. Some vocational programs have also begun increasing the number of general education courses they offer, thereby opening the possibility for students in those programs to go on to study for the *Abitur*. These efforts to give individuals who did not attend Gymnasium the opportunity for university-level study are known as "Second Chance Education" (*Zweiter Bildungsweg*).

German universities once offered virtually open enrollment to all holders of an *Abitur*. But the number of young people choosing to pursue an *Abitur* has been growing steadily, which has put tremendous pressure on the university system.

Overcrowding is common in many German universities, and admission to some fields of study is now restricted. Young people hoping to study medicine, dentistry, and veterinary medicine must take special admissions exams. Students wanting to study other high-demand fields, including architecture, law, economics, psychology, and pharmacy, must apply to the Central Office for the Allocation of Study Places (*ZVS: Zentralstelle für die Vergabe von Studienplätzen*) in Dortmund (North Rhine-Westphalia), which ranks students on the basis of their grades on the *Abitur* exams and how long they have been on the waiting list to enter the desired program. The limitation on the number of students admitted to study certain fields is known as the *Numerus Clausus*.

Source: *Federal Republic of Germany: Questions and Answers,* ed. Susan Steiner . German Information Center, New York, 1996

GLOSSARY OF THE GERMAN EDUCATION SYSTEM

Abendgymnasium: General secondary night school for employed adults providing university entrance qualification

Allgemeine Hochschulreife: General university entrance qualification, as a rule obtained by taking a final examination (*Abiturprüfung*) after 13 years of schooling, including upper secondary education, in general at a *Gymnasium*. The holder has the right to study at all institutions of higher education without restrictions with regard to subject areas.

Berufliches Gymnasium: Vocational school at the upper level of secondary education (grades 11, 12, 13) which leads to a general university entrance qualification. Career oriented-subject areas and focuses such as economics and engineering are added to the subjects otherwise available at the general education *Gymnasium*.

Berufsaufbauschule: Vocational extension school giving access to the upper level technical types of education by providing a qualification equivalent to that of the *Realschule* leaving certificate.

Berufsfachschule: Vocational school at the upper level of secondary education that prepares students for jobs or provides them with vocational training promoting at the same time general education. Depending on the objective of training, the requirements for admission (*Hauptschule* or *Realschule* certificate) vary as well as the period of training (from 1 year to 3 years).

Berufsgrundbildungsjahr: Basic vocational training year as the first stage of vocational training either in a full-time school or in the cooperative form of part-time school and on-the-job training.

Berufsschule: Part-time vocational school at the upper level of secondary education providing general and career-oriented education for students in initial vocational training; special attention is paid to the requirements of training in the dual system (part-time school and on-the-job training).

Fachgymnasium: See *Berufliches Gymnasium.*

Fachhochschule: Institution of higher education offering academic training with a practical bias, particularly in engineering, economics, social work, agriculture and design.

Fachhochschulreife: Qualification obtained, as a rule, by taking a final examination after 12 years of schooling, the last two years at a *Fachoberschule*. It provides access to studies at *Fachhochschulen* and the corresponding courses of study at *Gesamthochschulen*.

Fachoberschule: Technical secondary school (grades 11 and 12) specialized in various areas and providing access to *Fachhochschulen.*

Fachschule: Technical school providing advanced vocational training.

Gesamthochschule: Institution of higher education existing in two *Länder* combining functions of the universities, *Fachhochschulen* and, in some cases, colleges of art and music. It offers courses of study of various durations and leading to different degrees.

Gesamtschule: Comprehensive school existing in two forms: the cooperative comprehensive school combinies the schools of the traditional tripartite system under one roof and harmonizes the curicula in order to facilitate student transfer between the different coexisting types; the integrated comprehensive school admits all pupils of a certain age without differentiating between the traditional school types. In 1989, 5.9 per cent of the student population at the lower secondary level attended comprehensive schools. A number of the integrated comprehensive schools also have the upper secondary level, usually the *Gymnasiale Oberstufe*

Gymnasiale Oberstufe: Upper level of the *Gymnasium* (grades 11, 12, 13); the final examination *(Abiturprüfung)* provides a general university entrance qualification.

Gymnasium: General education secondary school (grades 5 to 13) providing general university entrance qualification. See also *Allgemeine Hochschulreife.*

Hauptschule: General education secondary school – lower level – providing full-time compulsory education and leading normally to vocational education and training.

Kolleg: Institute of general education preparing adults for higher education.

Kunsthochschule: College of arts

Mittlerer Bildungsabschluss: Equivalent to the *Realschule* certificate; this qualification can also be obtained in vocational schools *(Berufsschule, Berufsaufbauschule, Berufsfachschule)* in combination with a vocational qualification.

Musikhochschule: College of music

Orientierungsstufe: Grades 5 and 6 may be organized as an orientational stage during which the decision on a particular school type is left open. In some *Länder* the orientation stage may be a separate organizational unit independent of the traditional school types which then start with grade 7.

Pädagogische Hochschule: Teacher training college which exists in only three *Länder* where teachers are traiined for careers in primary and lower secondary as well as special education. In the other *Länder*, courses for the above-mentioned teaching careers are offered by universities, *Gesamthochschulen* and colleges of art and music.

Realschule: General education secondary school – lower level, normally grades 5 to 10 – going beyond the level of the *Hauptschule* and granting access to upper secondary education where a higher education entrance qualification or a vocational qualification may be obtained.

Sonderschule: Special schools for children with learning disabilities, schools for the blind and visually handicapped, schools for the deaf and hard of hearing, schools for children with speech handicaps, schools for the physically handicapped, schools for mentally handicapped children, and schools for children with behavioral disturbances.

Technische Universität/Technische Hochschule: Technical university.

Verwaltungsfachhochschule: Special type of *Fachhochschule* offering administrative studies which include periods of on-the-job training for future civil servants at the middle echelon level in federal, *Land* or local authorities.

Source: Secretariat of the Standing Conference of the Ministers of Education and Cultural Affairs of the *Länder,* in the Federal Republic of Germany, 1990.

VOCATIONAL EDUCATION IN GERMANY

Germany's vocational education program is known as the "dual system." Students combine on-the-job training, often as apprentices, and classroom instruction. Apprentices and job trainees usually spend three or four days a week in the work place and one or two days attending classes in trade schools (*Berufsschulen*). Usually about 40 percent of their school work is in basic academic subjects such as languages, mathematics, and and sciences, and about 60 percent in subjects directly related to their chosen professions.

The dual system is a collaboration between the state, private employers, and trade unions. It offers a means of assuring that nationwide training standards for every occupation are maintained. Large companies often run their own trade schools, which must be state accredited.

In 1994, young people could participate in training programs in 380 different occupations ranging from automobile repair to diamond cutting. About a third of the young men and half the young women participating in vocational programs pursue the ten most popular careers: retail sales, engine repair, industrial sales and purchasing, banking, clerical work, wholesale trade, electrical installation, hair dressing, assisting doctors, and industrial mechanics.

Source: *The Federal Republic of Germany: Questions and Answers,* ed. Susan Steiner. German Information Center, 1996

UNIVERSITIES, ACADEMIES, AND COLLEGES IN GERMANY TODAY

Aachen: Rheinisch-Westfälische Technische Hochschule Aachen
Templergraben 55
52056 Aachen

Augsburg: Universität Augsburg
Universitätsstr. 2
86135 Augsburg
Bamberg: Otto-Friedrich-Universität Bamberg
Kapuzinerstr. 16
96045 Bamberg
Bayreuth: Universität Bayreuth
Universitätsstr. 30
95440 Bayreuth
Berlin: Freie Universität Berlin
Kaiserswerther Straße 16-18
14195 Berlin
Berlin: Humboldt-Universität zu Berlin
Unter den Linden 6
10099 Berlin
Berlin: Technische Universität Berlin
Straße des 17. Juni 135
10623 Berlin
Berlin: EAP Europäische Wirtschaftshochschule Berlin
Europa-Center
10789 Berlin
Bielefeld: Universität Bielefeld
Universitätsstr. 25
Postfach 100131
33510 Bielefeld
Bochum: Ruhr-Universität Bochum
Universitätsstr. 150
44780 Bochum
Bonn: Rheinische Friedrich-Wilhelms-Universität Bonn
Regina-Pacis-Weg 3
Postfach 2220
53012 Bonn
Braunschweig: Technische Universität Carolo-Wilhelmina zu Braunschweig
Pockelsstr. 14
Postfach 3329
38023 Braunschweig
Bremen: Hochschule Bremen
Neustadtswall 30
28199 Bremen
Bremen: Universität Bremen
Bibliothekstr. 1
Postfach 330440
28334 Bremen
Bremerhaven: Hochschule Bremerhaven
An der Karlstadt 8

27568 Bremerhaven
Chemnitz: Technische Universität
Chemnitz-Zwickau
Straße der Nationen 62
09107 Chemnitz
Clausthal: Technische Universität
Clausthal
Adolph-Roemer-Straße 2a
38678 Clausthal-Zellerfeld
Cottbus: Technische Universität Cottbus
Karl-Marx-Straße 17
Postfach 101344
03013 Cottbus
Darmstadt: Technische Hochschule
Darmstadt
Karolinenplatz 5
64289 Darmstadt
Dortmund: Universität Dortmund
August-Schmidt-Straße 4
44221 Dortmund
Dortmund: International School of
Management ISM
Otto-Hahn-Straße 37
44227 Dortmund
Dresden: Technische Universität Dresden
Mommsensstr. 13
01062 Dresden
Duisburg: Gerhard-Mercator-Universität-
Gesamthochschule - Duisburg
Lotharstr. 65
47057 Duisburg
Düsseldorf: Heinrich-Heine-Universität
Düsseldorf
Universitätsstr. 1
40225 Düsseldorf
Düsseldorf: Robert-Schumann-
Hochschule Düsseldorf
Fischerstr. 110
40476 Düsseldorf
Erfurt: Universität Erfurt
Krämerbrücke 9-11
99084 Erfurt
Erfurt: Pädagogische Hochschule
Erfurt-Mühlhausen
Nordhäuser Straße 63
Postfach 307
99006 Erfurt
Erlangen: Friedrich-Alexander-
Universität Erlangen-Nürnberg

Schloßplatz 4
Postfach 3520
91023 Erlangen
Essen: Folkwang-Hochschule Essen
Klemensborn 39
Postfach 4428
45224 Essen
Essen: Universität-Gesamthochschule-
Essen
Universitätsstr. 2
45117 Essen
Flensburg: Bildungswissenschaftliche
Hochschule Flensburg - Universität
Mürwiker Straße 77
24943 Flensburg
Frankfurt/Main: Johann-Wolfgang-
GoethepUniversität
Senckenberganlage 31
60054 Frankfurt/Main
Frankfurt/Oder: Europa-Universität
Viadrina Frankfurt/Oder
Große Scharmstr. 59
Postfach 776
15207 Frankfurt/Oder
Freiberg: Technische Universität
Bergakademie Freiberg
Akademiestr. 6
09596 Freiberg
Freiburg/Breisgau: Albert-Ludwigs-
Universität Freiburg/Breisgau
Heinrich-von-Stephan-Straße 25
79100 Freiburg/Breisgau
Freiburg/Breisgau: Pädagogische
Hochschule Freiburg/Breisgau
Kunzenweg 21
79117 Freiburg/Breisgau
Gießen: Justus-Liebig-Universität
Gießen
Ludwigstr. 12
Postfach 111440
35359 Gießen
Göttingen: Georg-August-Universität
Göttingen
Goßlerstr. 5-7
Postfach 3744
37027 Göttingen
Greifswald: Ernest-Moritz-Arndt-
Universität Greifswald
Domstr. 11

17487 Greifswald
Hagen: Fernuniversität -
Gesamthochschule - Hagen
Feithstr. 152
58084 Hagen
Halle: Martin-Luther-Universität Halle-
Wittenberg
Universitätsplatz 10
06099 Halle/Saale
Hamburg: Hochschule für Wirtschaft und
Politik
Von-Melle-Park 9
20146 Hamburg
Hamburg: Technische Universität
Hamburg-Harburg
Denikestr. 22
21071 Hamburg
Hamburg: Universität Hamburg
Edmund-Siemers-Allee 1
20146 Hamburg
Hamburg: Universität der Bundeswehr
Hamburg
Holstenhofweg 85
22043 Hamburg
Hannover: Medizinische Hochschule
Hannover
Konstanty-Gulschow-Straße 8
30623 Hannover
Hannover: Tierärztliche Hochschule
Hannover
Bünteweg 2
30559 Hannover
Hannover: Universität Hannover
Welfengarten 1
30167 Hannover
Heidelberg: Hochschule für Jüdische
Studien Heidelberg
Friedrichstr. 9
69117 Heidelberg
Heidelberg: Ruprecht-Karls-Universität
Heidelberg
Grabengasse 1
Postfach 105760
69047 Heidelberg
Heidelberg: Pädagogische Hochschule
Heidelberg
Keplerstraße 87
69120 Heidelberg
Hildesheim: Universität Hildesheim

Marienburger Platz 22
Postfach 101363
31113 Hildesheim
Ilmenau: Technische Universität
Ilmenau
Max-Planck-Ring 14
Postfach 327
98684 Ilmenau
Jena: Friedrich-Schiller-Universität
Fürstengraben 1
07740 Jena
Kaiserslautern: Universität Kaisers-
lautern
Erwiin-Schrödlinger-Straße
Postfach 3049
67653 Kaiserslautern
Karlsruhe: Universität Fridericiana zu
Karlsruhe - Technische Hochschule
Kaiserstr. 12
76131 Karlsruhe
Karlsruhe: Pädagogische Hochschule
Karlsruhe
Bismarckstr. 10
Postfach 4960
76032 Karlsruhe
Kassel: Gesamthochschule Kassel -
Universität
Mönchebergstr. 19
34109 Kassel
Kiel: Christian-Albrechts-Universität zu
Kiel
Olshausenstr. 40
24098 Kiel
Kiel: Muthesius-Hochschule
Lorenzendamm 6-8
24103 Kiel
Köln: Deutsche Sporthochschule Köln
Carl-Diem-Weg 6
50927 Köln
Köln: Universität Köln
Albertus-Magnus-Platz
50923 Köln
Konstanz: Universität Konstanz
Universitätsstr. 10
78464 Konstanz
Leipzig: Universität Leipzig
Augustusplatz 9-11
04081 Leipzig
Leipzig: Ostdeutsche Hochschule für

Berufstätige
Konradstr. 52
04315 Leipzig
Ludwigsburg: Pädagogische
Hochschule Ludwigsburg
Reuteallee 46
Postfach 220
71602 Ludwigsburg
Lübeck: Medizinische Universität zu
Lübeck
Ratzeburger Allee 160
23538 Lübeck
Lüneburg: Universität Lüneburg
Wilschenbrucher Weg 84
21332 Lüneburg
Mainz: Johannes-Gutenberg-Universität
Mainz
Saarstr. 21
55099 Mainz
Mainz: Universität Koblenz-Landau
Hegelstr. 59
Postfach 1864
55008 Mainz
Magdeburg: Otto-von-Guericke-
Universität Magdeburg
Universitätsplatz 2
Postfach 4120
39016 Magdeburg
Mannheim: Universität Mannheim
Schloß
68131 Mannheim
Marburg/Lahn: Philipps-Universität
Marburg
Biegenstr. 10
35032 Marburg/Lahn
München: Hochschule für Philosophie
Kaulbachstr.33
80539 München
München: Ludwig-Maximilians-
Universität München
Geschwister-Scholl-Platz 1
80539 München
München: Technische Universität
München
Arcisstr. 21
80290 München
Münster: Westfälische Wilhelms-
Universität Münster
Schloßplatz 2

48149 Münster
Neuendettelsau: Augustana-
Hochschule in Neuendettelsau
Waldstr. 11
Postfach 20
91561 Neuendettelsau
Neubiberg: Universität der Bundeswehr
München
Werner-Heisenberg-Weg 39
85579 Neubiberg
Oestrich-Winkel: European Business
School
Schloß Reichartshausen
65375 Oestrich-Winkel
Oldenburg: Carl-von-Ossietzky-
Universität Oldenburg
Ammerländer Heerstr. 114-118
26111 Oldenburg
Osnabrück: Universität Osnabrück
Neuer Graben - Schloß
49069 Osnabrück
Paderborn: Universität -
Gesamthochschule - Paderborn
Warburger Straße 100
33098 Paderborn
Passau: Universität Passau
Dr.-Hans-Kapfinger-Straße 22
94030 Passau
Potsdam: Universität Potsdam
Am Neuen Palais 10
Postfach 601553
14415 Potsdam
Regensburg: Universitsät Regensburg
Universitätsstr. 31
93040 Regensburg
Rostock: Universität Rostock
Universitätsplatz 1
18051 Rostock
Saarbrücken: Hochschule für Technik
und Wirtschaft des Saarlandes (HTW)
Goebenstr. 40
66117 Saarbrücken
Saarbrücken: Universität des
Saarlandes im Stadtwald
Postfach 151150
66041 Saarbrücken
Schwäbisch-Gmünd: Pädagogische
Hochschule Schwäbisch-Gmünd
Oberbettringer Straße 200

73525 Schwäbisch-Gmünd
Siegen: Universität - Gesamthochschule
- Siegen
Herrengarten 3
57068 Siegen
Speyer: Hochschule für Verwaltungs-
wissenschaften Speyer
Freiherr-vom-Stein-Straße 2
67324 Speyer
Stuttgart: Universität Stuttgart
Keplerstr. 7
70174 Stuttgart
Stuttgart: Universität Hohenheim
Schloß 1
70593 Stuttgart
Trier: Universität Trier
Universitätsring 15
54286 Trier
Tübingen: Eberhard-Karis-Universität
Tübingen
Wilhelmnstr. 7
72074 Tübingen
Ulm/Donau: Universität Ulm
Albert-Einstein-Allee
89069 Ulm/Donau
Vallendar: Wissenschaftliche
Hochschule für Unternehmensführung -
Otto-Beisheim-Hochschule -
Burgplatz 2
56179 Vallendar
Vechta: Hochschule Vechta
Driverstr. 22
49377 Vechta
Weilheim-Bierbronnen: Gustav-
Siewerth-Akademie
Oberbierbronnen 1
79809 Weilheim-Bierbronnen
Weimar: Hochschule für Architektur
und Bauwesen
Geschwister-Scholl-Straße 8
99421 Weimar
Weingarten: Pädagogische Hochschule
Weingarten
Kirchplatz 2
88250 Weingarten
Witten: Private Universität Witten-
Herdecke
Alfred-Herrhausen-Straße 50
58448 Witten

Würzburg: Bayerische Julius-
Maximilians-Universität Würzburg
Sanderring 2
97070 Würzburg
Wuppertal: Bergische Universität -
Gesamthochschule - Wuppertal
Gaußstr.20
42097 Wuppertal

Art and music academies
(*Kunst- und Musikhochschulen*)

Berlin: Hochschule der Künste Berlin
Ernst-Reuter-Platz 10
Postfach 126720
10595 Berlin
Berlin: Hochschule für Musik „Hans
Eister" Berlin
Charlottenstr. 55
Postfach 147
10104 Berlin
Berlin: Hochschule für Schauspielkunst
„Ernst Busch" Berlin
Schnellerstr. 104
12439 Berlin
Berlin: Kunsthochschule Berlin-
Weißensee Hochschule für Gestaltung
Bühringstr. 20
13086 Berlin
Braunschweig: Hochschule für Bildende
Künste Braunschweig
Johannes-Selenka-Platz 1
Postfach 2538
38015 Braunschweig
Bremen: Hochschule für Künste
Am Wandrahm 23
28195 Bremen
Detmold: Hochschule für Musik Detmold
Neustadt 22
32756 Detmold
Dresden: Hochschule für Bildende Künste
Dresden
Günzstr. 34
01288 Dresden
Dresden: Hochschule für Musik „Carl
Maria von Weber" Dresden
Wettiner Platz 13
Postfach 120039
01001 Dresden
Düsseldorf: Kunstakademie Düsseldorf
Eiskellerstr. 1

40213 Düsseldorf
Frankfurt/Main: Staatliche Hochschule
für Bildende Künste (Städelschule)
Dürerstsr. 10
60596 Frankfurt/Main
Frankfurt/Main: Hochschule für Musik
und Darstellende Kunst Frankfurt/Main
Eschersheimer Landstraße 29-39
60322 Frankfurt/Main
Freiburg/Breisgau: Staatliche
Hochschule für Musik Freiburg/
Breisgau
Schwarzwaldstr. 141
79095 Freiburg/Breisgau
Halle: Hochschule für Kunst und Design
Burg Giebichenstein
Neuwerk 7
Postfach 200252
06003 Halle
Hamburg: Hochschule für Bildende
Künste Hamburg
Lerchenleid 2
22081 Hamburg
Hamburg: Hochschule für Musik und
Theater Hamburg
Harvestehuder Weg 12
20148 Hamburg
Hannover: Hochschule für Musik und
Theater Hannover
Emmichplatz 1
30175 Hannover

Mannheim: Staatliche Hochschule für
Musik Heidelberg-Mannheim
N 7, 18
68161 Mannheim
Karlsruhe: Staatliche Akademie der
Bildenden Künst Karlsruhe
Reinhold-Frank-Straße 67
Postfach 6267
76042 Karlsruhe
Karlsruhe: Staatliche Hochschule für
Gestaltung Karlsruhe
Durmersheimer Straße 55
75185 Karlsruhe
Karlsruhe: Statliche Hochschule für
Musik Karlsruhe
Wolfahrtsweierer Straße 7a
Postfach 6040
76040 Karlsruhe
Köln: Kunsthochschule für Medien Köln
Peter-Welter-Platz 2
50676 Köln
Köln: Hochschule für Musik Köln
Dagobertstr. 38
50668 Köln
Leipzig: Hochschule für Musik und
Theater „Felix Mendelsson-Bartholdy"
Leipzig
Grassistr.8
Postfach 809
04008 Leipzig

Chapter 17
Language

GERMANIC LANGUAGES

Germanic languages are spoken by more that 480 million people in northern and western Europe, North America, South Africa, and Australia.

About 7 million people in Austria, about 300,000 in Luxembourg, 3,400,000 in northern Switzerland, and about 1,500,000 in Alsace-Lorraine speak German – in addition to about 330,000 people in Canada, 550,000 in Brazil, and 250,000 in Argentina.

The largest number of people outside Europe using German as their mother tongue live in the United States. The Pennsylvania Germans, who immigrated from the Palatinate during the late 17th and the 18th centuries and who settled in southeastern Pennsylvania, speak the Rhine-Franconian dialect mixed with some English.

In seven countries of the world German is an official language. In Germany, Austria, and Liechtenstein it is the only official language. In Switzerland it is a co-official language, together with French and Italian. In Luxembourg it is also a co-official language, together with French and Letzeburgisch. It is a reagional official language in Italy, in Bolzano-South Tyrol (together with Italian) and in Belgium, in the German-speaking community in the eastern part of the country.

Sources:
•"The German Language: Lingua Franca Overshadowed by English?" by Ulrich Ammon. *Deutschland,* No. 1, 2/1994
•"German Language," *Microsoft Encarta,* Funk & Wagnalls Corp., 1994

HISTORICAL OVERVIEW OF THE GERMAN LANGUAGE

•**Until middle of 14th century:** Latin was the official written language of the Holy Roman Empire (comprising most of the German-speaking regions of present-day Europe)

•**In reign of Louis IV, Holy Roman Empire, 1314-47):** German was adopted as the language of official court documents

•**Between 1480 and 1500:** German was introduced for official use in many municipalities and courts of Saxony and Meissen and was adopted by the universities of Leipzig and Wittenberg

•**By 1500:** German generally was accepted as the official language of all parts of Saxony and Thuringia and was the written language of the educated classes. Publication of books i n German increased in Wittenberg, Erfurt, and Leipzig as well as in Mainz, Straßbourg, Basel, Nürnberg, and Augsburg, resulting in a reduction of regional differences and the standardization of the literary language.

•**First quarter of 16th century:** Standard written German emerged in areas such as Erfurt, Meissen, Dresden, and Leipzig, where the dialect spoken was based on Middle and Upper German dialects of High German. The High German standard, due largely to Luther's translations and writings, spread throughout the rest of Germany.

•**By 1600:** The literary language was well established, even though it did not become recognizable in its present form until about the middle of the 18th century.

•**Until the 20th century:** Different standards of spelling were adhered to in various parts of Germany and in other parts of Europe where German was spoken.

♦In 1898 a commission of university professors and respresentatives of the German theater formed the basis of codified rules of pronunciation in *Deutsche Buhneaussprache* (German Stage Pronunciation), published first in 1898 and later in 1957 as *Deutsche Hochsprache* (Standard German).

Following the spread of High German, that term came to have two meanings: It referred to all German dialects except those included in the Low German branch of the language, as well as to the literary language of Germany.

Source: "German Language," *Microsoft Encarta.* Funk & Wagnalls corp., 1994

AN OVERVIEW OF GERMAN LANGUAGE REFORM

Before Germany became a nation in 1871, no binding rules governing spelling existed for the entire German-speaking area of Europe.

♦In 1901 representatives of northern and southern Germany, Austria, and Switzerland participated in a conference through which they devised a uniform system of orthography which was later accepted.

This system is outlined in *Rechtschreibung der deutschen Sprache* (Orthography of the German language) by the famous German philologist Konrad Duden. This work became the official German spelling guide, and has gone through 20 editions.

♦The Vienna Conference of 1994 again discussed the standardization of the language.

The resulting reforms are expected to be adopted incrementally by the year 2005. The 20th edition of *Duden – Die deutsche Rechtschreibung* already contains the major innovations and recommendations in a special index.

In 1996 a group of 100 writers, literary scholars, teachers and publishers from around the German-speaking nations put their names to a strongly critical declaration that was presented to the public during the Frankfurt Book Fair.

The "Frankfurt Declaration" called on public officials in Austria, Germany and Switzerland to reconsider their plans to introduce modifications in German spelling rules in the autumn of 1998. The declaration contended that the changes would "waste millions of working hours, create decades of confusion, harm the standing of the German language at home and abroad, and cost more than a billion marks." Among the best known of the Germans to put their names to the declaration were the novelists Günter Grass, Siegried Lenz, and Martini Walser.

As of late 1996, the 212 spelling and punctuation rules governing German were to be trimmed to 112 by the reform. In all, 185 words in German's "basic vocabulary" of 12,000 words were to be affected.

Examples of proposed changes

Standard	New
Kuß, bißchen	Kuss, bisschen
Eislaufen	Eis laufen
Panther	Panter
Mayonnaise	Majonäse
Open-Air Festival	Openairfestival

A recommendation of the conference affects the written forms of *Du* and *Sie*, both meaning "you.." Formerly, both had to be spelled with capital letters in correspondence. Under the reform, the *du* forms (the familiar forms) and their derivatives would remain in lower case letters, and the *Sie* would continue to be capitalized, increasing its value as a form of respect.

Sources:
•"German Language," *Microsoft Encarta.* Funk & Wagnalls Corp., 1994
•"'Frankfurt Declaration Attacks Much Debated Language Reform," *The Week in Germany,* German Information Center, October 11, 1996, p. 6
•*Munich Found,* August/September 1996, p. 6
•"German Spelling in the 21st Century," by Gerhard Weiss. *German Life,* October/November 1995, p. 64.

SOME BASIC GERMAN ALPHABET AND LANGUAGE CHARACTERISTICS

•**Umlauted vowels:** The German alphabet has three additional vowels called umlauts *(Umlaute).* They are ä. ö, and ü (Ä. Ö, and Ü). In certain lists and dictionaries created by Germans, the lists put an umlauted vowel before the same vowel that is unumlauted. Sometimes the umlaut is omitted, and the letter *e* is added. (For example, *Schröder* becomes *Schroeder.*)

•**The** *Eszett:* This letter (ß) is the equivalent of *ss* and is alphabetized as if it were *ss.* In a headline or other printed form using all capital letters, the ß is printed as *SS.* The ß is used only with lower-case forms of printed words.Thus the word *Haß* retains the *Eszett* when the word is written in lower case; but when it is composed in all capital letters, it is shown as *HASS.*

Handwritten letters

Although the old German Gothic handwritten script is another topic altogether, it may be useful to list here two other special features of German spelling.

•**The** *U-Haube* or *U-Häubchen* (u-cap, or little u-cap): This is a little cap (like a smiling mouth) that was placed over the letter *u* to help the reader distinguish it from the many up-and-down strokes that appear in German-script letters like *m, n, c,* and *e.* (See the handwritten alphabet in the section, "German Script.")

•**The** *Verdoppelungsstrich* (doubling dash) or *Faulheitsstrich* (lazy dash): This little "dash," or straight line placed over the handwritten *m* or *n* was used as an indication that the respective letter was to be doubled. For example, the surname *Hammer* might be written as *Hamer,* with a little dash placed over the *m* to indicate that the *m* should be doubled. Thus writers using the "lazy dash" saved themselves the bother of writing two letters, instead writing just one with a simple little straight-line dash on top of it.

HIGH, MIDDLE, LOW GERMAN

The names "high German," "middle German," and "low German" take their names from the geographical altitude of the areas where they are spoken.

High German is a blend of *Oberdeutsch* (upper, or mountain) German and *Mitteldeutsch* (midway German or middle upland) German.

Remnants of Low German (north of an imaginary boundary called the Benrath line), which is no longer spoken officially, are found as *Plattdeutsch* in rural areas north of the Benrath line. *Platt* is much like English. The Low Franconian dialect farther south merges with the Rhenish Franconian dialects.

It was a coincidence that led to High German rather than Low German becoming the accepted dialect. As a result of the attempt by the duke of Saxony in the early 1500s to standardize the dialects in his duchy, a language for state affairs called *Kanzleisprache* was adopted. This occurred just at the time Martin Luther translated the Bible from Latin, using the very same German dialect.

Luther explained his task in these words: *"Ich habe keine gewisse, sonderlich, eigene Sprache im Deutschen, sondern brauche die gemeine deutsche Sprache, daß mich beide, Ober- und Niederländer verstehen können."* (I have no special, definitive language in German, but I am using the common German tongue so that both High German and Low German will be able to understand me.)

Martin Luther was compromising between the extremes of upper and lower German. The real coincidence was that he came from the Saxon area and wrote many manuscripts, including he Bible, in the *Kanzleisprache.*

This blending of dialects grew into what is called New High German, with a grammar taught in the schools to all Germans. It is sometimes called *Bühnensprache* (stage language) or *Schriftdeutsch* (written German).

Ironically, although everyone writes High German, almost no one speaks it all the time. At home and among friends, Germans speak in their own local dialects. This tradition reflects the reverence and devotion of the German to his local region, hometown, and territorial district.

The common parent of English and

German is Saxon. Both also share a single grandfather, Gothic.

Long before the Romans moved into German territory, many Germanic tribes roamed Europe, one of which was the Goths. After the Christian era began, the Goths migrated to southern Russia. There, in about 350 AD, Bishop Wulfilas translated the Bible into Gothic. It is from this document that linguists have been able to compare the Gothic language with later Saxon documents — and to determine that Saxon evolved from the root language of Gothic.

Thus the parent language of modern English was Anglo-Saxon, and that of modern German was Saxon.

Source: *Of German Ways,* by LaVern Rippley. Dillon Press, Minneapolis, 1970

FRAKTUR

The decorated manuscripts made primarily by the Pennsylvania Germans are called fraktur. Most of them are birth and baptism certificates (*Geburts und Taufschein*) produced from about 1760 to the early years of the twentieth century, almost always in German. By around 1900, fraktur are frequently found written in English.

From about 1760 to 1818, freehand fraktur were created by schoolmasters. Later fraktur, from about 1810 to 1900, were preprinted and filled out by persons highly skilled in producing decorative handwriting.

The areas in which Fraktur were common are the present states of Pennsylvania, Virginia, West Virginia, Ohio, Maryland, New Jersey, New York, Indiana, the Carolinas, and Ontario, Canada. Their heaviest concentration was in southeast Pennsylvania. They were most popular among Lutheran and Reformed families because the majority of them were baptism certificates, representing an important sacrament among followers of these faiths.

The word Fraktur (pronounced FROCK-tur), short for *Frakturschriften* (broken writing) derives from a Latin word meaning "fractured," or "broken," for as the letters are formed, instead of writing cursively, without lifting the pen, the writer lifts the pen, which is thus "broken" from the page.

Usually the fraktur birth and baptism certificates include the father's name, the mother's name including her maiden name, the date of birth of the child, the place of birth, the name of the child, the date of baptism, and the name of the pastor who baptized the child. Names of witnesses or sponsors at the baptism, who were usually related to the child, are also listed.

Fraktur are highly prized for their beauty and historical value. The data they preserve have been found to be highly reliable

Collections of fraktur may be found at the Free Library of Philadelphia; the Abby Aldrich Rockefeller Folk Art Center in Williamsburg, Virginia; and The Henry Francis du Pont Winterhur Museum in Winterthur, Delaware. They are also held at the National Archives, the Library of Congress, and in some public libraries.

A great many fraktur have been published and indexed by Russell and Corinne Earnest in East Berlin, Pennsylvania. Among the books they have published on fraktur are *Papers for Birth Dayes: Guide to the Fraktur Artists and Scriveners, The Genealogist's Guide to Fraktur: For Genealogists Researching German-American Families*; and most recently the three-volume series, *German-American Family Records in the Fraktur Tradition* (1991), which translates and transcribes the genealogy texts in fraktur.

To submit photocopies of fraktur to the Earnests for sharing with others, or for information about publications, write to Russell D. Earnest Associates, P.O. Box 1007, East Berlin, PA 17316, being sure to enclose a long, self addressed stamped envelope. Tel. (717) 259-0299.

Sources: Corinne P. Earnest, *Antique Week*; and Kenneth L. Marple, Palatines to America National Conference, June 1994.

'THE GERMAN CARD'

The German Card, laminated and when folded the size of a credit card, is a helpful tool for researchers to carry with them as they conduct research in libraries and archives.

Containing eight panels that fold up, accordion-style, The German Card, created by the Sacramento German Genealogy Society, contains the following information:

•The complete German alphabet in the old Gothic script (the most popular feature of the card), both printed and handwritten (the old Gothic script), upper and lower case letters. For easy comparison, each letter can be placed directly under the German word being investigated.

•A brief list of immigration information found in the various United States Federal Census records from 1850 through 1920

•The key for interpreting the German genealogy symbols (birth, death, burial, christening, etc.) Commonly used in German vital statistic records

•The rules and the code for the Soundex system for finding surname entries in the United States census

•A list of some basic German genealogy resources

•Dates of civil records in Germany

Cost

The German Card costs $3.00 plus a stamped (first class postage) long self-addressed envelope. If no envelope is included with the order, add 50 cents for postage and handling. For two or three cards, affix 55 cents in postage to the envelope, or if no self-addressed envelope is included with the order, add 75 cents for postage and handling.

To order send a check payable to "S.G.G.S." with the self-addressed stamped envelope to Sacramento German Genealogy Society, P.O. Box 660061, Sacramento, CA 95866-0061.

NUMBERS VOCABULARY

0	null
1	eins
2	zwei
3	drei
4	vier
5	fünf
6	sechs
7	sieben
8	acht
9	neun
10	zehn
11	elf
12	zwölf
13	dreizehn
14	vierzehn
15	fünfzehn
20	zwanzig
21	einundzwanzig
30	dreißig
31	einunddreißig
40	vierzig
41	einundvierzig
50	fünzig
51	einundfünzig
60	sechzig
61	einundsechzig
70	siebzig
71	einundsiebzig
80	achtzig
81	einundactzig
90	neunzig
91	einundneunzig
100	hundert
101	hundert(und)eins
200	zweihundert
300	dreihundert
1000	tausend
2000	zweitausend

Cramped conditions of the voyage

1,000,000	eine Million
1,000,000,000	eine Milliarde

**Ordinal numbers
(first, second, third, etc.)**

1	erste
2	zweite
3	dritte
4	vierte
5	fünfte
6	sechste
7	sieb(en)te
8	achte
9	neunte
10	zehnte
11	elfte
20	zwanzigste
21	einundzwanzigste
30	dreißigste
40	vierzigste
50	fünfzigste
60	sechzigste
70	siebzigste
80	achtzigste
90	neunzigste
100	hundertste
101	hundert(und)erste
1000	tausendste
1,000,000	millionste
2,000,000	zweimillionste

The Old German Alphabet

𝔄	a	𝔑	r				
𝔅	b	𝔖	ſs				
ℭ	c	𝔗	t				
𝔇	d	𝔘	u				
𝔈	e	𝔙	v				
𝔉	f	𝔚	w				
𝔊	g	𝔛	x				
ℌ	h	𝔜	y				
ℑ	i	ℨ	z				
𝔍	j	ch					
𝔎	k	ck					
𝔏	l	ng					
𝔐	m	pf					
𝔑	n	ph					
𝔒	o	ſch					
𝔓	p	ſſ					
𝔔	q	tz					

IDENTIFYING GERMAN SCRIPT

O	A	U	Y*		c*	c*	i	d	sch
G	Q	P	H*		e	n	nn	u	m
I	T	F*	J		o	a	acht	nach	
J	Y*	H*	Z		r	v	w	vier	
B	L	C	Ch		b	k	l	d	s (final) t* t*
E	F*	D			g	q	j	p	x y z
K	R	X*	X*		f	h	s	ss	sz st
S	St	N	M		ein	er	en		
V	W				ie	und	zwei		

* alternate forms

Gothic—Roman Alphabet Comparison

Gothic	Roman
𝔄	A
𝔘	U
𝔅	B
𝔙	V
𝔓	P
ℭ	C
𝔈	E
𝔊	G
𝔖	S
𝔇	D
𝔒	O
𝔔	Q
𝔍	I
𝔍	J
𝔉	F
𝔎	K
𝔑	N
𝔕	R
𝔐	M
𝔚	W
𝔥	H
𝔏	L
𝔗	T
𝔛	X
𝔜	Y
𝔷	Z

Gothic	Roman
a	a
o	o
b	b
d	d
v	v
c	c
e	e
r	r
x	x
g	g
p	p
q	q
f	f
s	s
i	i
j	j
k	k
l	l
t	t
n	n
u	u
h	h
y	y
m	m
w	w
s	s
z	z
ss	ss

THE SÜTTERLIN ALPHABET

The Sütterlin alphabet (Sütterlinschrift) was named after
an art teacher from Berlin, Ludwig Sütterlin, who first
published his proposal for this simplification of the
standard script in 1917. It was adopted by Prussian
schools in 1922 and soon spread to the other parts of
Germany. The teaching of the Sütterlin alphabet was
discontinued about 1942.

THE GERMAN HANDSHAKE PACKET

Travelers to German-speaking countries who do not speak German may be interested in ordering a set of personalized introductory materials to ease the way. The German Handshake Packet is prepared by the Sacramento German Genealogy Society specifically for non-German speaking members in search of information about their German ancestors.

The Packet consists of several items designed to be helpful in communicating with German-speaking officials encountered in libraries, archives, and municipal offices, as well as to help in communicating with community members who may have information to offer. The Packet includes the following items:

Letter 1

This letter is written in German on the society's official letterhead (embossed with its official seal) and signed by the Society's president.

It introduces the traveler by name as a valued member of the Sacramento German Genealogy Society and states that, although the bearer of the letter does not speak German, he or she is researching his or her German ancestry during the trip abroad. It also states that the Society will appreciate any consideration the reader of the letter shows on behalf of the traveler.

The traveler carries one copy of this letter to each of the archives or libraries visited..

Letter 2

This letter, also written in German, is headed with the traveler's own address and carries the traveler's signature.

It explains that the bearer of the letter does not speak German but that the traveler's purpose in making the journey is to conduct research concerning one or more German ancestors.

It states that attachments to this letter provide whatever vital records the traveler has learned concerning the immigrant. The letter asks for the reader's suggestions for further research of the named ancestor and thanks the reader for any help given. Both letters (this one and the letter described above) are written in formal, polite German by a native German speaker.

The traveler carries about ten copies of this letter, to be used as needed.

Attached items

A set of attachments to Letter 2 consists of the major data thus far known about the ancestor(s) being researched. Written entirely in German, this information gives name, birth date, birth place, residence, year of emigration, and place of residence in the United States (insofar as such information is known) for the immigrant and for the immigrant's father and mother (as applicable). Attachments for more than one immigrant (each including the immi-grant's parents) may be prepared at additional cost.

Translations

English translations of all three documents named above are included in the Packet.

Ordering

The German Handshake Packet must be ordered at least one month before the traveler's departure date. All applications must be submitted on the application form supplied by the Society. It is necessary to complete a separate application form for each additional immigrant. To obtain an application form, write to Sacramento German Genealogy Society, P.O. Box 660061, Sacramento, CA 95866-0061

Cost

The Packet is individually prepared for Society members for $6 for one immigrant ancestor (and parents). Preparation of data concerning additional immigrant ancestors (with parents) cost $4 each.

Applicants who are not members of the Sacramento German Genealogy Society pay an additional $15, the cost of annual dues in the Society. (The letters introduce travelers as *members of the Society*.)

Bride from the Baar region

LATIN GENEALOGICAL VOCABULARY

a, ab .... from, out
aedituus church guardian, church warden
aetas suae .... aged
aetatis .... age
aetakis suae .... his age
affinis .... related through marriage
agricola .... peasant
ambo ex .... both from
amita .... father's sister
amita magna .... grandfather's sister
ancilla .... maid, maiden
anno .... in the year of
annorum .... years
annus .... year
arx .... castel, fortress
Ascensio Domini .... Ascension Day
avia .... grandmother
avuncula .... mother's sister
avunculus .... mother's brother
avus .... grandfather
balneator .... bather, surgeon,
barber

baptisma .... the baptism
baptizatus .... baptized
baptizatus est .... was baptized
beatae memoriae ...... of blessed memory
calendae ianuariis .... first of January
cantor .... singer
capellanus .... chaplain
carnifex .... executioner
chirurg, chirurgus .... surgeon
Circumcisio Domini .... January 1
coelebs .... single, unmarried
cognatus .... related; uncle
commorantes in .... residing in
concionator .... preacher
coniugalis .... legitimate
coniugata .... married
coniugatus .... married
coniuges .... spouses
coniugo .... married
coniiugium .... marriage
coniugum .... husband
coniugum ex .... husband from
coniunctus .... married
coniunx .... husband
coniux .... spouse
conjunx, conjux .... wife
consobrinus .... child of siblings
consobrini .... children of siblings
copulati .... the ones who were married
copulatio, copulation .... marriage
coriarius .... the tanner
cum .... with
decem .... ten
defuncta .... deceased (female)
defunctus .... deceased (male)
diaconus .... deacon, assistant minister
dierum .... days
die, dies ....day
dies Jovis .... Thursday
dies Lunaw .... Monday
dies Martis .... Tuesday
dies Mercurii .... Wednesday
dies Sabbathi .... Saturday
dies Solis .... Sunday
dies Veneris .... Friday
domi .... at home
Dum medium .... Sunday after Christmas
ecclesia .... church
ecclesia parrochiali .... parish church

ejusdem .... same day, as above
emeritus .... retired, emeritus
eodem...................................... same day
eodem dienatus .... was born
et baptizatus .... and baptized
on the same day
Epiphanie .... 6th of January
eques .... rider, knight, servant
et .... and
ex .... from, out(of), of
Exaudi .... 6th Sunday after Easter
exinde .... of the same place
extra .... beyond
extra matrimonium .... illigitimate
faber .... smith
faber lignarius .... woodworker
famula .... servant (female)
famulus .... servant (male)
feria quarta .... Wednesday
feria quinta .... Thursday
feria secunda .... Monday
feria sexta .... Friday
feria tertia .... Tuesday
filia .... daughter
filia legitima .... legitimate daughter
filia putativa .... daughter who had
a child before marriage
or had cohabited
filiola .... little daughter
filiolus .... little son
filius .... son
filius legittimus .... legitimate son
figulus .... potter
frater .... brother
frater germanus .... half-brother
fratria .... brother's wife
gemelli .... twins
gener .... son-in-law
gens..clan
glos .... husband's sister
heri .... yesterday
hic jacet .... here lies
inferior .... the lower
in periculo mortis .... in danger of death
in praesente .... in the presence of
inquilinus   house resident, renter,
inhabitant
institor .... merchant
judex .... judge

junior .... the younger
juvenis .... youth
levantes .... witness, godparent
liber .... book
liber baptizatorum .... baptismal book
liber matrimoniorum .... marriage book
liber mortuorum .... death book
ludimoderafor .... schoolmaster
ludirector .... school director
maritus .... husband, spouse
mater .... mother
maternitas .... motherhood
materta .... sister of the mother
materta magna .... great aunt
matrimonialis   legitimate, pertaining
to marriage
matrimonium .... marriage
matrina .... godmother
mensis .... month
mensium .... months
miles .... soldier
molitor .... miller
mortuus .... died
nata .... born (female)
natale .... birthday
natales .... origin, birth
natalis dies .... birthday
nativitas Domini .... Christmas (25 Dec.)
natus .... born (male)
natus est .... was born
nepos .... nephew; grandson
neptis .... niece; granddaughter
N.N. ..... nomen nescio (unknown name)
nobilis .... noble, nobility
novem .... nine
noverca .... stepmother
nurus .... daughter-in-law
nutrix ....nurse
obit. .... died
obstetrix .... midwife
octo .... eight
opilio .... shepherd
pannifex .... clothmaker
parentes ....parents
parochus .... minister
partus ....birth
Pascha .... Easter
pastor .... pastor, minister
pater .... father

patrini .... godparents, witnesses
patrinus .... godfather
patruus .... father's brother
patruus magnus .... great uncle
pharmacopola .... pharmacist
physicus .... doctor
piscator .... fisherman
pistor .... baker
postero die .... on the following day
post pascha .... Monday after Easter
postridie baptizatus   baptized on the
                                           following day
practious .... lawyer
praeceptor .... house teacher
praefectus .... adminstrator, director
preces .... blessing
pridie idus septembris   on the 12th of
                                            September
pridie natur .... bortn the day before
primogenita .... first born (female)
primogenitus .... first born (male)
prius .... previous
privigna .... step-daughter
privignus .... step-son
proamita .... great grandfather's sister
proavia .... great grandmother
proavus .... great grandfather
proclamatio .... banns, the ones
                                          who planned
                                   on getting married
promaterta .... great great aunt
pronepos .... great grandson
proneptis .... great granddaughter
propatruus .... great granduncle
puella .... girls
puer .... boy
quasi modo geniti .... first Sunday
                                         after Easter
quaestor .... tax collector
quam primum natus fuit . right after birth
rector .... rector, minister
rector ecclesia .... minister
relicta .... left behind,
                                     surviving (female)
relictus ...... left behind, surviving (male)
renata .... baptized (female)
renatus .... baptized (male)
sabbato .... Saturday
sartor .... tailor

schola .... school
scriba .... scribe, write
senator .... councilman, counsilor
senatus .... city council
septum .... seven
sepultatio .... the burial
sepultus .... buried
sequenti die .... on the following day
servus .... servant, knight
socer .... stepfather
socrus .... stepmother
soror .... sister
soror germana .... half sister
sororius .... sister's husband
sponsa .... the engaged (female)
sponsalia .... engagement
sponsus .... the engaged (male)
spuria .... illigitimate (female)
spurius .... illegitimate (male)
superattendens .... superinitendent
superior .... the above
susceperunt ... they lifted (out of baptism
suscipientes .... godparents, witnesses
sutor .... shoemaker
testes .... witnesses, godparents
testis .... witness, godparent
textor .... linenweaver
trigemini .... triplets
tutor .... guardian
unica .... the only one (female)
unicus .... the only one (male)
uxor .... wife
vicarius .... vicar
vidua .... widow
viduus .... widower
vietor .... basketweaver
vilicus .... gardener; administrator
virgo .... virgin, unmarried
vitricus .... step-father
vivus .... living
xenodochium .... hospital,
                                       pilgrim's house

Abbreviated Latin
date indicators

7bris .... in September
VIIber .... in September
8bris .... in October
VIIIber .... in October
9bris ....in November

IXber .... in November
10bris .... in December
Xber .... in December
Note: See *septem, octo, novem, decem*
above.

ROMAN NUMERALS

I.. 1
II 2
III 3
IV 4
V 5
VI.. 6
VII 7
VIII 8
IX 9
X 10
XI 11
XII 12
XIII 13
XIV 14
XV 15
XX 20
XXIV 24
XXIX 29
XXXI 31
XL 40
L... 50
LX 60
LXX 70
LXXX 80
XC 90
C 100
CI 101
CV 105
CXI 111
CXLI 141
CL 150
CC.. 200
CCC 300
CCCC 400
CD 400
D 500
DC 600
DCLV 655
DCC.. 700
DCCC 800

DCCCC 900
CM 900
M 1000
MDCCVI 1606
MDCCCLXV 1865
MDCCCXC 1890
MCMIX 1909
MCMXLVIII 1948
MCMXCVIII 1998

GENEALOGICAL AIDS IN INTERPRETING LATIN

♦C. Russell Jensen, Ph.D., *Parish Register Latin: an Introduction.* Vita Nova Books, Salt Lake City, 1988. Out of print (FHL book 475 J453p)
♦ Kenneth L. Smith, *German Church Books; Beyond the Basics.* Picton Press, Camden, Maine, 1989.
♦ Ernest Thode, *German-English Genealogical Dictionary.* Genealogical Publishing Company, Baltimore, 1992. *[Note: Besides German, this dictionary contains many Latin words and phrases.]*
♦Wolfgang Ribbe and Eckart Henning, *Taschenbuch für Familiengeschichtsforschung.* Verlag Degener & Co., Inh., Neustadt an der Aisch, 1995.

TOMBSTONE LATIN

A.D. – Anno Domini: In the Year of Our Lord . . .
Ad perpetuam rei memoriam: For a perpetual record of the matter
Adsum: Here I am
Ars longa, vita brevis: Art is long, life is short
Beatae memoriae: Of blessed memory
Carpe diem: Enjoy the present day
Dei gratia: By the grace of God
Deo volente (D.V.): God willing
Dominus vobiscum: The Lord be with you
Durante vita: During life
Elapso tempore: The time having passed

Errare humanum est: To err is human
Et sequentes (sequentia): And those who follow
Ex voto: According to one's wishes
Faber suae fortunae: A self-made man
Fecit.: Made it. Executed it
Fidei defensor: Defender of the faith
Filius terrae: A son of the soil.
Gloria patri: Glory be to the Father
Hic jacet: Here lies
Hoc nomine: In his name.
In articulo mortis: At the point of death
In facie ecclesiae: Before the church
In futuro: Henceforth
In memoriam: In memory of . . . .
In nomine Domini: In the name of the Lord . . . .
In perpetuum: For ever
In secula seculorum: For ever and ever
Jubilate Deo: Rejoice in God
Laus Deo: Praise to God
Monumentum aere perennius: A monument more lasting than brass
Mors omnibus communis: Death is common to all
Natus est: Was born
Obit: Died
Pace tua: By your leave
R.I.P. – Requiescat in pace: May he (she) rest in peace
Scripta litera manet: The written word remains.
Sic transit gloria mundi: Thus passes away the glory of the world.
Taedium vitae: Weariness of life
Tempus fugit: Time flies.
Ubi supra: Where above mentioned
Ut infra: As below
Ut supra: As above

Source: Raymond Lamont Brown, *A Book of Epitaphs*. Taplinger Publishing Co., New York, 1969

DAYS, MONTHS IN LATIN

Sunday: dominica, dies dominica (dominicus), dies Solis, feria prima

Monday: feria secunda, dies Lunae
Tuesday: feria tertia, dies Martis
Wednesday: feria quarta, dies mercurii
Thursday: feria quinta, dies Jovis
Friday: feria sexta, dies Veneris
Saturday: feria septima, sabbatum, die sabbatinus, dies Saturni

Months
(nominative form)

January: Januarius
February: Februarius
March: Martius
April: Aprilis
May: Maius
June: Junius
July: Julius
August: Augustus
September*: September
October*: October
November*: November
December*: December

*For other representations of these months, see "Latin Genealogical Vocabulary"

FRENCH GENEALOGICAL VOCABULARY

accoucher .... to give birth
actes de naissance .... birth records
actes de notaire .... notary records
alliance .... marriage
l'an, l'année .... year
aujourd'hui .... today
avec .... with
le baptême .... baptism
bans .... banns
le célibataire .... bachelor
le citoyen .... citizen
la commune .... community
conjoindre .... marriage
les conjoints .... couple
le cordonnier .... shoemaker
le curé .... priest, minister
de, de la, de l', du .... of (the)
le décès .... death
décédé .... deceased
le défunt .... the deceased

demain	tomorrow		naguit	born
le demeurant	residing in		né, née	born
le domicile	residence		nom	surname
l'église	church		nom de baptême	given name
Église Catholique Romaine	Roman Catholic Church		nom de famille	surname
l'emploi	occupation		parents	parents
enfant	child		la paroisse, paroissiaux, paroissiales	parish
enseveli	burial		le parrain, la marraine	godfather, godmother
enterré	burial		le pére	father
l'enterrement	burial		pére et mére	parents
épouser	to marry; marriage		pour	for
époux	husband		le prénom	given name
et	and		le prêtre	priest
expiré	death		publications	banns
la famille	family		registres paroissiaux	parish registers
la fille	girl, daughter		registres de l'État Civil	civil registers
la fille légitime	legitimate daughter		répertoire	index
le fils	son		la sépulture	burial
le fils naturel	illigitimate son		la soeur	sister
le frére	brother		le soir	evening
funébre	burial		tables	index
le garçon	boy		la tante	aunt
le grand-pére	grandfather		le témoin	witness
la grand-mere	grandmother		le temps	time
hébreu	Jewish		le testament	will
l'heure	hour, time of day		le tome	volume
hier	yesterday		unir	marriage
l'homme	man		veuve, veuf	widow, widower
hôtel de ville	town hall		(de cette) ville	(from this) city
inanimé	death			
inhumé	burial			
israélite	Jewish			
le jour	day			
juif	Jewish			
juive	Jewish			
le lieu	place			
mairie	town hall			
maison de ville	town hall			
le mari	husband			
marié	husband			
le mariage	marriage			
le même mois	the same month			
mensuel	month			
la mére	mother			
le mois	month			
la mort	death			
mort-né	stillborn			
la naissance	birth			

NUMBER WORDS IN FRENCH

1	un
2	deux
3	trois
4	quatre
5	cinq
6	six
7	sept
8	huit
9	neuf
10	dix
11	onze
12	douze
13	treize

14	....	quatorze
15	....	quinze
16	....	seize
17	....	dix-sept
18	....	dix-huit
19	....	dix-neuf
20	....	vingt
21	....	vingt-et-un
30	....	treinte
40	....	quarante
50	....	cinquante
60	....	soixante
70	....	soixante-dex, septante
80	....	quatre-vingts, huitante
90	....	quatre-vingt-dix
100	....	cent
1000	....	mil, mille

DAYS, MONTHS IN FRENCH

Days

lundi	....	Monday
mardi	....	Tuesday
mercredi	....	Wednesday
jeudi	....	Thursday
vendredi	....	Friday
samedi	....	Saturday
dimanche	....	Sunday

Months

janvier	....	January
février	....	February
mars	....	March
avril	....	April
mai	....	May
juin	....	June
juillet	....	July
août	....	August
septembre (7bre)	....	September
octobre (8bre)	....	October
novembre (9bre)	....	November
décembre (10bre)	....	December

ABBREVIATIONS
OF FRENCH GIVEN NAMES

A.	....	Albert
Ch.	....	Charles
Fr^s		François
Fr^{se}		Françoise
G.	....	Ghislain
G^e		Ghislaine
H.	....	Henri
H^e		Henriette
J.	....	Joseph
J^e		Josèphe
J^{ne}		Joséphine
L.	....	Louis
L^e		Louise
M.	....	Marie
P.	....	Pierre
Th.	....	Thérèse

Chapter 18
German life

ABBREVIATIONS
German and Latin

a. .... *am, an/aus*: at/from

Abb. .... *Abbildung:* illustration, figure (fig.)

a. St. .... *alten Stils*: old style (ofcalendar)

a.a.O. .... *am angeführten Orte [= loc. cit]:* the place cited

abb. .... *Abbildung*; illustration

abds. .... *abends*; in the evening

Abf. .... *Abfahrt:* departure

Abk. .... *Abkürzung*: abbreviation

Abs. .... *Absender*: sender

Abt. .... *Abteilung*, department

a.c. .... *anno currente*, Lat.: of the current year

A.C. .... *anno Christi*, Lat.: in the year of the Lord

a.D. .... *außer Dienst:* retired

A.D. .... *anno Domini*, Lat.: in the year of our Lord

ADAC .... *Allgemeiner Deutscher Automobil-Club:* General German Automobile Association

Adr. .... *Adresse*: address

a.e. .... *anno edicto*, Lat.: in the year mentioned

AG .... *Aktiengesellschaft:* a corporation whose shares can be traded on the German stock exchanges

AG. .... *Amtsgericht*: district court

A.H. .... *alter Herr*: old gentleman

allg. .... *allgemein;* general

Ank. .... *Ankunft*; arrival

Anm. .... *Anmerkung*: note; *Anmeldung:* registration

ao. .... *anno*, *Lat.:* in the year

a.pr. .... anno prioris (Lat.): in the previous year

ARD .... *Arbeitsgemeinschaft der Rundfunkanstalten Deutschlands:* Germany's first public TV network

Ausg. .... *Ausgabe*: edition

b. .... *bei(m)* (with persons) [=c/o]: in care of

B.-Rhin .... *Bas-Rhin*: Lower Rhine

b.w.   *bitte wenden:* please turn
                over (page)
BA. .... *Bezirksamt:* district office
BAFöG .... Federal   Education
                Promotion Act, which
                provides scholarship money
                for German university
                students
Bd. .... *Band:* volume (book)
Bde. .... *Bände:* volumes (books)
begr. .... *Begräbnis:* burial;begraben
                buried
beil. .... *beiliegend:* enclosed
Bem. .... *Bemerkung:* remark
bes. .... *besonders:* especially
betr. .... *betreffend:* concerning,
                about
bez.,bz. .... *bezahlt:* paid
Bez. .... *Bezirk:* district
Bhf. .... *Bahnhof:* train station
bisw. .... *bisweilen:*   sometimes,
                occasionally
Br. .... *Bruder; Breite:* brother;
                latitude
BRD .... *B u n d e s r e p u b l i k*
                Deutschland; FRG, Federal
                Republic of Germany, West
                Germany
Bz. .... *Bezirk:* district
bzgl. .... *bezüglich:* with reference to
bzw. .... *b e z i e h u n g s w e i s e :*
                respectively; or
C .... *T s c h e c h o s l o w a k e i :*
                Czechoslovakia
c. .... *copuliert* (Lat.): married
c. .... *currentis/circa* (Lat.); of the
                current year\about
c.a., ca. .... *currentis anni* (Lat.): of the
                current year
CDU .... *Christlich Demokratische*
                Union: the Christian
                Democratic Union (a
                political party)
c.f.l. .... *conjugium filius legitimus/*
                filia legitima (Lat.):
                legitimate child
CH .... *Confoederatio Helvetica:*
                Latin for "Swiss
                Confederation"

c.l. .... *citato loco,* Lat.: in the place
                cited
C.N. .... *Code Napoléon:* Code
                Napoleon
ca. .... *circa, Lat.:* approximately
Chr. .... *Christus,* Lat.: Christ
conj .... *conjux,* Lat.: wife
Cop. .... *copulatio,* Lat.: marriage
cr. .... *currentis,* Lat.: of the current
                year
CSU .... *Christlich-Soziale Union:*
                Christian Social Union,
                Bavarian sister party of
                CDU
CVJM .... *Christlicher Verein Junger*
                .... *Männer:* YMCA
d. .... *den; des:* on the (date); of the
D. .... *Deutschland:* Germany
d.a. .... *dicti anni,* Lat.: of the year
                .... mentioned
d.Ä. .... *der Ältere:* the elder; senior
DAX .... *Deutscher Aktien-Index:*
                index of stocks in Germany
                (similar to the Dow-Jones
                index)
DB .... *Deutsche Bahn AG:* German
                Rail
d.Bl. .... *dieses Blattes:* of this page
d.d. .... *de dato,* Lat.: on this date
DDR. .... *Deutsche Demokratische*
                Republik: (former)
                East Germany
D.dw .... *Euer dienstwilliger:* your
                obedient servant
dgl. .... *dergleichen:* the like
d.Gr. .... *der Große;* the Great
d.h. .... *das heißt:* that is [i.e.]
d.i. .... *das ist:* that is
Di. .... *Dienstag:* Tuesday
DIN .... *Deutsche Industrie-Norm:*
                German Industry Standards
Dipl. .... Diplom (holding a)
d.J. .... *der Jüngere/des Jahres*
                (Lat.): the younger; junior/
                of the year
d.l. .... *dicto loco,* Lat.: in the place
                mentioned
d.l.J. .... *des laufenden Jahres:* of the
                current year

d.M. .... *dieses Monats:* this month [=inst.]

DM .... *Deutsche Mark:* German mark(s)

d.M. .... *dieses Monats:* this month; instant

D.N. .... *Dominus Noster* (Lat.): Our Lord

d.O. .... *der Obige:* the above

Do. .... *Donnerstag:* Thursday

dom. .... *dominica (Lat.):* Sunday

dch. .... *durch:* through

dgl. .... *dergleichen/desgleichen:* (of) the same

Di. .... *Dienstag:* Tuesday

do./dto. .... *ditto:* ditto

Do. .... *Donnerstag:* Thursday

dom. .... *dominica,* Lat.: Sunday

dpa ....Deutsche Presse-Agentur: German Press Agency

Dr. .... [See "university degrees"]

ds.J. .... *dieses Jahres:* of this year

ds.M(ts) ...... *dieses Monats:* of this month

d.s.p. .... *decessit sine prole,* Lat.: he/she died without issue

d.s.p.l. .... *decessit sine prole legitima,* Lat.: he/she died without legitimate issue

d.s.p.m. .... *decessit sine prole mascula,* Lat.: he/she/died without male issue

d.s.p.s. .... *decessit sine prole supersite,* Lat.: he/she/died without surviving issue

dt. .... *deutsch:* German

d.Verf. .... *der Verfasser:* the author

dz. .... *derzeit:* then, at that time

e.a. .... *ejusdem anni,* Lat.: of the same year

e.a. .... *ejusdem anni:* of the same year

ebd. .... *ebenda:* ib(id), in the same place

eccl. .... *ecclesia (Lat.):* church

Ecu .... European Currency Unit

e.g. .... *exempli gratia:* for example

EG .... Europäische Gemeinschaft: European Community (EC), now known as the European Union (EU)

E.K. .... *Eisernes Kreuz:* Iron Cross (military medal)

E.K.D. .... *Evangelische Kirche in Deutschland:* Lutheran Church in Germany

e.m. .... *ejusdem mensis,* Lat.: in the same month

e.o. .... *ex officio,* Lat.: by virtue of one's office

e.p. .... *en personne,* Fr.: in person

e.V. .... *eingeschriebener Verein:* a registered association, usually a nonprofit organization

E.v. .... *Eltern von:* parents of

ead. .... *eadem,* Lat.: likewise

ebd. .... *ebenda(selbst):* in the same place; ibidem

eccl. .... *ecclesia,* Lat.: church

Ehefr. .... *Ehefrau:* wife, married woman

ehel. .... *ehelich:* legitimate (child)

Ehl. .... *Eheleute:* a married couple

eigtl. .... *eigentlich:* actually; proper(ly)

ejusd. .... *Ejusdem:* of the same

EKD .... *Evangelische Kirche in Deutschland:* Protestant Church in Germany

eod. .... *eodem:* the same

eod.q.s. .... *eodem quo supra,* Lat.: on the same day as above

Ep. .... *Epiphania:* Epiphany

EU .... *Europäische Union:* European Union

ev.luth. .... *evangelish-lutherisch:* Evangelical Lutheran

ev.ref. .... *evangelisch-reformiert:* Evangelical Reformed

evtl. .... *eventuell:* possibly

Expl. .... Exemplar: sample, copy

f. .... *für/folgende/folium:* for/following (page)/page

f. .... *filius/filia,* Lat.: son/daughter

F. .... *Frankreich:* France

Fa. .... *Firma:* firm, company

F.-Geb. .... *Fehlgeburt:* stillbirth; abortion

Ropemaker workshop *(woodcut, late 16th century)*

f.c. .... *filius/filia civis*, Lat.: son/ daughter of a citizen

f.d.A. .... *für die Ausfertigung*: attesting to this document

FDJ .... *Freie Deutsche Jugend:* Free German Youth, youth wing of SED (in former East Germany)

FDP .... *Freie Demokratische Partei:* Free Democratic Party

ff. .... *folgende (Seiten):* following (pages)

ff. ....*filii*, Lat.: sons

fr. ....*frater*, Lat.: brother

f.l. .... *filia legitima, filius legitimus*, Lat.: legitimate child

Fr. .... *Frau:* wife, Mrs

Fr. ....*Freitag:* Friday.

Frdh. .... *Friedhof:* cemetery

Frl. .... *Fräulein:* Miss; unmarried young woman

frz ....*französisch:* French

geb. .... *geboren:* born

gem. .... *gemelli/gemellae (Lat.):* male/female twins

Gev. .... *Gevatter(n):* sponsor(s)

g.f. .... *generis femini*, Lat.: of female sex

g.g.F. .... *gegebenen Falls:* in that case

G.G. .... *Grundgesetz:* Basic Law (federal Constitution)

G.K. .... *Gregoranischer Kalender*, Lat.: Gregorian calendar

g.m. .... *generis masculini*, Lat: of male sex

g.z. .... *gehört zu:* belongs to

geb. .... *geboren/geborene:* born: birthname

gefl. .... *gefälligst:* if you please

gegr. .... *gegründet:* founded

gem. .... *gemelli/gemellae*, Lat.: male/female twins; *gemäß:* according to

gen. .... *genannt:* named, mentioned

gesch. .... *geschieden*: divorced; *geschätzt: estimated*

geschr. .... *geschrieben:* written

gest. .... *gestorben:* died

Gestapo ...... *Geheimesstaatspolizei:* Secret State Police (Nazi)

get. .... *getauft:* baptized, christened

getr. .... *getraut:* married

gez. .... *gezeichnet:* signed

GmbH .... *Gesellschaft mit beschränkter haftung:* a closed corporation or limited liability company (Ltd.)

h .... *hora*, Lat.: hour; o'clock

H .... *Helvetica:* Switzerland; *Herr*: Mr.

h. .... *hora*, Lat.: hour

H. .... *Hafen:* port

h.a. .... *hoc anno*, Lat.: in this year

h.a. .... *hoc anno/hujus anni*, Lat.: in this year/of this year

ha .... *Hektar:* hectare (about 2.47 acres)

Hapag .... *Hamburg-Amerikanische Paketfahrt-Aktien-Gesellschaft:* German merchantshipping company
Hausfr. .... *Hausfrau:* wife, housewife
Hbf. .... *Hauptbahnhof:* main train station
h.e. .... *hoc est,* Lat.: that is
hins. .... *hinsichtlich:* with regard to
h.l. .... *hoc loco,* Lat.: at this place
H.R.I.P. .... *Hic Requiescat In Pace,* Lat.: here rests in peace
H.R.R. .... *Heiliges Römisches Reich:* Holy Roman Empire
h.t. .... *hoc tempore,* Lat.: at this time
Hg.,Hrsg. ... *Herausgeber:* editor
hl. .... *heilig:* holy
Hpt. .... *Haupt-:* chief, main
Hr. .... *Herr:* Mr.
I .... *Italien:* Italy
i.D.. .... *im Durchschnitt:* on the average
i. .... *in; im:* (in place names)in
I. .... *Iesus,* Lat.: Jesus
i.allg. .... *im allgemeinen:* in general
IC .... *InterCity* (German long-distance train)
ICE .... *InterCity Express* (German high speed train)
i.d. .... *in der, in dem:* in the
i.e. .... *id est,* Lat.: that is
i.f. .... *ipso facto,* Lat.: by its very nature
i.f. .... *in fine,* Lat.: in conclusion
i.f., i.folg. ..... *im folgenden:* in the following
i.J. .... *im Jahre:* in the year
inkl. .... *Inklusive:* including
i.R .... *im Ruhestand:* retired
ib(d). .... *ibidem,* Lat.: in the same place
J .... *Johann/Jahr(e):* Johann/ years
j. .... *jährlich:* annually
Jg. .... *Jahrgang:* year (of issue of a publication)
Jgfr. .... *Jungfrau:* unmarried young woman

Jh./Jhdt. ...... *Jahrhundert:* century
jhrl. .... *jährlich:* yearly, annually
Jngfr. .... *Jungfrau:* unmarried young woman
Joes .... *Johannes*
Joh. .... *Johann:* Johann
jr. .... *junior:* younger of two people of same name
jun. .... *junior:* younger of two people of same name
juv. .... *juvenis,* Lat.: young, youth
-k. .... *-keit/-kunde/-kunst:* -ness/ knowledge/-skill
Kap. .... *Kapitel:* chapter
kath. .... *katholisch:* Catholic
K.B. .... *Kirchenbuch:* church record book
k.J. .... *kommenden/künftigen Jahres:* of the coming year
k.M. .... *kommenden/künftigen Monats:* of the coming month
k.W. .... *kommende Woche:* next week
KG .... *Kommanditgesellschaft:* a limited partnership
KGaA .... *Kommanditgesellschaft auf Aktien:* a partnership, with the partners holding stock
Kl. .... *Klasse:* class
Kr(s). .... *Kreis:* district
Kripo .... *Kriminalpolizei:* criminal investigation department (C.I.D.)
Kt. .... *Kanton:* canton
k.u.k. .... *kaiserlich und königlich:* imperial and royal
L .... *Luxemburg:* Luxembourg
l. .... *legitimata,* Lat.: legitimate
l. .... *lies!/links:* read!/left
L.-Nr. .... *Listennummer:* list number
l.b. .... *liegen bei:* (documents) are enclosed
l.c. .... *loco citato,* Lat.:the place cited
led. .... *ledig:* unmarried
L.G. .... *Landgericht:* district court
l.J. .... *laufenden Jahres/letzten Jahrs:* of the current year/ of

last year
Lkw .... *Lastkraftwagen*: truck, semi
l.l. .... *loco laudato*, Lat.: in the
.... place cited
l.o. .... *links oben*: top left
l.p.m.s. .... *legitimatus per matri-*
            monium subsequens, Lat.:
            legitimized by subsequent
            marriage
l.p.r.p. .... *legitimatus per rescriptum*
            principis: legitimate by
            order of the ruler
l.p.s.m. .... *legitimatus persubsequens*
            matrimonium, Lat.: legiti-
            mitzed by subsequent
            marriage
l.u. .... *links unten*: bottom left
LB .... *Landesbezirk*: administra-
            tive district
lfd. .... *laufend*: current
lt. .... *laut*: according to
luth. .... *lutherisch*: Lutheran
m. .... *mit*: with
M. .... *Magister, Meister*: master
MA .... *Mittelalter*: Middle Ages
m.a. .... *mit anderen*: with other
            things
m.a.W. .... *mit anderen Worten*: in other
            words
m.m.p. .... *manu mea propria*, Lat.:
            with my own hand
m.n. .... *more novo*, Lat.: according
            to the new custom
m.p. .... *manu propria*, Lat.: with
            one's own hand
Mstr. .... *Meister*: master
m.v. .... *more vetere*, Lat.: old style
            of calendar
m.Vn. .... *männerlicher Vorname*:
            male given name
m.W. .... *meines Wissens*: as far as I
            know
Mwst. .... *Mehrwertsteuer*: value-
            added tax, VAT
männl. .... *männlich*: masculine
MA. .... *Mittelalter/Meldeamt*:
            Middle Ages/registration
            office
m.E. .... *meines Erachtens*: in my

opinion
MEZ .... *Mitteleuropäische Zeit*:
            Central European Time
            (CET)
Mgl. .... *Mitglied*: member
Mi. .... *Mittwoch*: Wednesday
mlat. .... *mittellatein*: Middle Latin
Mo. .... *Montag/Monat*: Monday/
            month
Mskr. .... *Manuskript*: manuscript
MW Mittelwelle*: medium wave,
            AM radio
N .... *Nord(en)/Niederlande*:
            .... north/Netherlands
n. .... *nördlich*: north
n. .... *nata/natus*, Lat.: born
nat. .... *nata/natus*, Lat.: born
N.B. .... *nota bene! (Lat.)*: note well
n. Chr. nach Christus*: after Christ,
            A.D.
n. Chr.G. .... *nach Christus Geburt*: after
            the birth of Christ, A.D.
n.J. .... *nächsten Jahres*: next year
n.M. .... *nächsten Monat(s)*: next
            month
N.N./n.n. ..... *nomen nescio*, Lat.: name
            unknown
N.S. .... *Nachschrift*: postscript (P.S.)
nachm. .... *nachmittags*: in the
            afternoon; P.M.
NSDAP .... *National sozialistische*
            Deutsche Arbeiterpartei:
            National Socialist German
            Workers' Party, or Nazis
nep. .... *nepos, neptis*, Lat.: nephew/
            grandson
NL .... *Niederlande*: Netherlands
Nr(n). .... *Nummer(n)*: Number(s)
NVA .... *National Volksarmee*:
            National People's Army,
            GDR army
o. .... *obiit*, Lat.: died
o.ä. .... *oder ähnliche(s)*: or similar
ÖBB .... *Österreichische Bundes-*
            bahnen*: Austrian Federal
            Railways
o.g. .... *oben genannt*: mentioned
            above
oHG .... *offene Handelsgesellschaft*:

general partnership

o.J. .... *ohne Jahr:* without a year; no\ date

o.O. .... *ohne Ort:* without place

o.O.u.J. .... *ohne Ort und Jahr:* without place and year

O. .... *Ost(en):* east

od. .... *oder:* or

P. .... *Pater,* Lat.: father, pastor

p.a. .... *per annum,* Lat.: per year

p.A(dr) .... *per Adresse:* in care of (c/o)

par .... *parentes, Lat.:* parents

pat. .... *pater, Lat.:* father

patr. .... *patrini; Lat.:* godparents

p.Chr. .... *post Christi,* Lat.: after Christ; A.D.

p.d. .... *post datum,* Lat.: after the date

PDS .... *Partei Deutscher Sozialisten:* Party of German Socialists, Communist successor to SED after 1990

Pkw .... *Personenkraftwagen:* automobile

P.L. .... *Pastor Loci, Lat.:* pastor of this parish

p.m. .... *post mortem, Lat.:* after death

p.m.s.l. .... *per subsequens matrimonium legitimatus:* legitimized by subsequent marriage

p.m.s.l. .... *per subsequens matrimonium legitimatus,* Lat.: legitimized by subsequent marriage

p.n.Chr. ...... *post nativitatem Christi:* after the birth of Christ; A.D.

par. .... *parentes,* Lat.: parents

pat. .... *pater,* Lat.: father

pd. .... *pridie,* Lat.:the day before

Pf. .... *Pfennig:* penny

Pfd. .... *Pfund:* German pound(s)

Pfl. .... *Pflege:* ward; care

Pr. .... *Preußen:* Prussia

prot. .... *protestantisch:* Protestant

Prov. .... *Province:* province

p.t. .... *pro tempore:* for the time

pzt. .... *prozentig:* percent

q.e. .... *quod est:* which is

Q.I.P. .... *quiescat in pace:* may he/she rest in peace

qkm .... *Quadratkilometer:* square . kilometer

qm .... *Quadratmeter:* square meter

Q.M.O. .... *qui mortem obiit,* Lat.: the one who died

qu. .... *quasi (Lat.):* questioned, questionable

q.v. .... *quod vide:* which see

q.v._annos:. who lived _years

R.-Bez .... *Regierungsbezirk:* government district

rd. .... *rund:* approximately

rel. .... *relictus, relicta,* Lat.: widower, widow

ren./renat. .. *renata, renatus,* Lat.: baptized

resp. .... *respektive:* respectively

Rh. .... *Rhein:* Rhine (River)

R.I.P. .... *Requiescat in pace:* rest in peace

Rr. .... *Richter:* judge

röm .... römisch: Roman

ß .... *Schilling:* coin

s. .... *siehe:* see, refer to

S. .... *Süd(en):* south

S. .... *Seite:* page

S., sel. .... *selig:* late, deceased

s.a. .... *sine anno,* Lat.: without the year

s.a. .... *(S)siehe auch (Seite):* see also (page)

SA .... *Sturmabteilung:*storm troops of the NSDAP, founded 1921

Sa. .... *Samstag:* Saturday

SAE .... *saeculum,* Lat.: century

s.a.e.l. .... *sine anno et loco,* Lat.: without year and place

Sa. .... *Samstag:* Saturday

SAE .... *saeculum (Lat.):* century

SBB .... *Schweizerische Bundesbahnen:* Swiss Federal Railways

SCL .... *saeculo, Lat.:* in the century

s.d. .... *siehe dies!:* see this!

S.d. .... *Sohn der/desson:* son of (the)

SD .... *Sicherheitsdienst:* Nazi

Security Service

SED .... *Sozialistische Einheitspartei Deutschlands:* Socialist Unity Party of Germany, East German Communist party

sen. .... *senior:* older; elder (of the two)

sep. .... *sepulta, sepultus, Lat.:*buried

seq. .... *sequens,*Lat.: (the) following

s.o. .... *siehe oben!:* see above!

So. .... *Sonntag:* Sunday

SPD .... *Sozialdemokratische Partei Deutschlands:*Social Democratic Party of Germany

s.p.l. .... *sine prole legitima:* without legitimate issue

s.p.m. .... *sine prole mascula*: without male issue

spons. .... *sponsus, sponsa,* Lat.: bridegroom, bride

spur. .... *spurius, spuria,* Lat. illegitimate child

sq. .... *sequens,* Lat.: following

s.R. .... *siehe Rückseite:* see reverse (side)

sr. .... *senior:* the older of two people of the same name

SS .... *Schutzstaffel:* special formation of the NSDAP; founded as the bodyguard for National Socialist leaders

Stasi .... *Staatssicherheitsdienst:* former East Germany's state security agency

StB .... *Staatsbibliothek:* state library

Std./Stdn ..... *Stunde(n)*: hour(s)

StdA. .... *Standesamt:* civil registration office

Str. .... *Straße:* Street, Road

stud. .... *studiosus, Lat.:* student

susc. .... *susceptor, susceptores, susceptrix,Lat.):* godparents, Lat.

s.u. .... *siehe unten: see* below

S.v. .... *Sohn von:* son of

SW .... *Schweiz:* Switzerland

s.Z. .... *seinerzeit:* in those times, formerly

T. .... *Tag(e):* day(s)

T.d. .... *Tochter des/der:* daughter of

testes .... testes(Lat.): godparents

Tr. .... *Trinitatis:* Trinity

TT .... *testamentum (Lat.):* will

TÜV .... *Technische Überwachungsverein:* German auto safety testing agency

T.v. .... *Tochter von:* daughter of

T.V. .... *Turnverein*: gymnastic society

To. .... *Tochter:* daughter

Tsd. .... *Tausend:* thousand

Tz. .... *Taufzeuge:* male baptismal sponsor

Tzi. .... *Taufzeugin:* female baptismal sponsor

u. .... *und:* and

u.Ä. .... *und Ähnliches:* and similar

u.a. .... *und ander(s) or unter anderem/anderen:* and others, among other things

u.a.m. .... *und andere mehr:* among others

U-Bahn .... *Untergrundbahn:* subway

u.d. .... *und der/und des*: and of (the) *u. desgl. und desgleichen (mehr)*: and the like

Ufa .... *Universum Film-Aktiengesellschaft*: German film studio founded in the 1920s

u.ff. .... *und folgende (Seiten):* and the following (pages)

u.i. .... *ut infra:* as below

UKW .... *Ultrakurzwellen:* FM radio

ult. .... *ultimo, Lat.:* last day of month or year

u.s. .... *ut supra:* as above

usw. .... *und so weiter:* etc.

u.U. .... *unter Umständen*: in (certain)circumstances, possibly

u.v.a. .... *und viel anderes:* and much more

u.W. .... *unseres Wissens:* as far as we know

u.zw. .... *und zwar:* that is; namely; in fact

Umgeb. .... *Umgebung:* vicinity

unehel. .... *unehelich:* illegitimate (child)
usf. .... *und so forth:* and so forth
usw. .... *und so weiter:* and so forth
ux. .... *uxor:* wife, spouse
v. .... *von, vom:* from (the)
v.Chr.G. ..... *vor Christi Geburt:* before Christ's birth; B.C.
v. Chr. .... *vor Christus:* before Christ, B.C.
v.d. .... *vor dem/der:* before the
Verf. .... *Verfasser:* author
verw. .... *verwitwet:* widowed
v.H. .... *vom Hundert:* percent
vid. .... *vide, Lat.:* see
vid. .... *viduus, vidua* (*Lat.*): widower, widow
v.J. .... *vorigen Jahres:* of last year
v.M. .... *vorigen Monats:* of last month
v.v. .... *vice versa:* the other way around
vdt. .... *vidit,* Lat.: has seen
verh. .... *verheiratet:* married
verl. .... *verlobt:* engaged (to marry)
verm. .... *vermählt:* married
verw. .... *verwitwetet/verwundet:* widowed/wounded
Verw.-Bez. ... *Verwaltungsbezirk:* administrative district
Verz. .... *Verzeichnis:* list
vgl. .... *vergleiche!:* compare!; see!
VID .... *vidua, viduus (Lat.):* widow, widower
v.s.p .... *vide subsequente pagina (Lat.):* see the following page
vw. .... *verwitwet:* widowed
W. .... *West(en):* west
WC .... *water closet:* rest room, toilet
w.o. .... *wie oben:* as above
w.u. .... *wie unten:* as below
w.v. .... *wie vorher:* as previously
weibl. .... *weiblich:* feminine
weil. .... *weiland:* late, deceased
weyl. .... *weyland:* deceased
Wlr. .... *Weiler:* hamlet
Wo. .... *Woche:* week
Wwe. .... *Witwe:* widow
X; Xs. .... *Christus:* Christ

Candlemaker, 1568

Xstnacht ..... *Christnacht:* Christmas
Z. .... *Zeile/Zahl/Zeuge:* line (on a page)/number/witness
z.B. .... *zum Beispiel:* for example
ZDF .... *ZweitesDeutsches Fernsehen:* Germany's second public TV network/channel
Zi. .... *Zimmer:* room (number)
z.J. .... *zum Jahr:* in the year
z.T .... *zum Teil:* partly, to some extent
Ztg. .... *Zeitung:* newspaper
z.Zt. .... *zur Zeit:* at this time; *zum Teil:* partly

Other short forms:
September:
7br. 7ber. 7bris. VIIber.:
October:
8br. 8ber. 8bris. VIIIber.
November:
9br. 9ber. 9bris. IXber.
December:
Xbr. Xber. Xbris. 10ber. 10bris
Christ:
Xus or *Xg:* Christus
Christianus, Christian: *Xian. Xiang:*

House construction (woodcut, 1526)

DESIGNATIONS FOR GERMAN OCCUPATIONS, TRADES, AND TITLES (*Berufsbezeichnungen*)

Abdecker .... skinner
Abortfeger .... toilet cleaner
Ackerer, Acker(s)mann .... farmer
Adeliger .... nobleman
Aderlasser .... blood-letter, surgeon
Akademiker .... academician
Amtmann .... magistrate, warden, district judge
Amtsdiener .... court usher
Amtsverweser .... deputy
Anbauer .... peasant
Angestellter .... employee
Anstreicher .... painter
Anwalt .... lawyer, guardian, notary
Apotheker .... pharmacist
Arbeiter .... worker, laborer
Architekt .... architect
Arzt .... physician
Aufseher .... guard, supervisor
Auktionator .... auctioneer
Ausgeber .... distributor
Ausländer .... foreigner
Ausrufer .... town crier
Auswanderer .... emigrant
Auszahler .... paymaster
Bader .... barber, surgeon
Bauer .... farmer
Bäcker .... baker
Badeknecht/-magd . baths servant (male/female)

Bader .... bathhouse operator, barber
Ballierer .... polisher
Bamutter .... midwife
Bandfabrikant .... ribbon maker
Bankangestellte .... bank employee
Barbier .... barber
Bauarbeiter .... construction worker
Bauer .... farmer
Bartscherer .... barber
Bauhandwerker .... assigner of building contracts
Baumeister .... master builder
Baumgärtner .... gardener
Beamter .... official
Beauftragter .... deputy, representative
Becherer .... turner
Bechermacher .... mugs or cups maker
Becker .... baker
Beinhauer .... butcher
Beisitzer .... assessor
Berater .... counselor, advisor
Bergleute .... miners
Bergmann .... miner
Berittener .... mounted horseman
Bernsteinschleifer .... amber gem cutter
Beschlägemacher .... tinsmith
Beschleißer .... custodian, caretaker
Beschneider .... animal castrator
Besenbinder .... broom maker
Besitzer .... owner, proprietor
Bettler .... beggar
Beutler .... (leather) bagmaker
Bewaffneter .... arms bearer
Bienenpfleger .... bee-keeper
Bienenzüchter .... bee cultivator

Bierbrauer .... beer brewer
Bierfahrer .... beer delivery man
Bierschenk(er) .... tavern keeper
Biersieder .... beer brewer
Bildhauer .... sculptor
Bildschnitzer .... woodcarver
Bildweber .... wood-cutter
Binder .... binder
Bischof .... bishop
Blaufärber .... dyer of blue cloth
Blecharbeiter .... sheet metal worker
Blechschmied .... sheet metal/tin smith
Bleicher .... bleacher
Bleigießer .... lead smelter
Bogenmacher .... bowmaker
Bogenschütze .... archer
Bogner .... bowmaker
Bohrerschmied .... drill smith
Bortenwirker .... lace worker
Bote .... messenger
Böttcher .... cooper, barrelmaker
Brandweinbrenner .... distiller
Brauer .... brewer
Brauknecht .... brewery worker
Brettschneider .... sawyer
Briefbote, -träger .... mailman
Brinksitzer .... farmer
Bruchschneider .... physician, surgeon
Brunnengraber .... well digger
Brunnenmeister   supervisor of well
                                          construction
Buchbinder .... bookbinder
Buchdrucker .... printer
Buchführer .... bookkeeper
Buchhalter .... bookkeeper
Buchhändler .... book dealer
Buchschließenmacher .... maker
                                   of miniature locks
                                            for books
Büchsenmacher .... gunsmith, armorer
Büchsenschmied .... gunsmith
Büdner .... stallkeeper
Bürge .... guarantor, sponsor
Bürger .... citizen
Bürgermeister .... mayor
Burggraf .... baron
Burgmann .... castle steward
Bürstenmacher .... brush maker
Büttel .... overseer, bailiff

Büttner .... cooper
Chemiker .... chemist
Chirurg .... surgeon
Civilbeamt .... civil officer
Colon .... farmer, settler
Conditor .... see Konditor
Dachdecker .... thatcher, roof tiler
Dechanat .... dean
Dekan .... dean
Dengler .... blademaker (scythes)
Dichter .... author, poet
Dieb .... thief
Diener/-in . servant (male/female), waiter
Dienstbote .... domestic servant
Dienstmädchen .... servant woman
Dirne ... female servant, maid, farm hand
Doktor .... learned person
Domherr .... canon
Dosenfasser .... tinsmith
Dosenmacher .... can maker
Dragoner .... dragoon
Drahtzieher .... wire drawer/maker
Drechsler .... thresher, (wood) turner
Dreher .... turner
Drogist .... druggist, chemist
Drucker .... printer
Edelmann .... nobleman
Edelsteinhändler .... dealer in
                                      precious stones
Eichbeamter   weights and measures
                                       representative
Eierhändler .... egg dealer
Eigengärtner .... independent gardener
Eigenkätner .... independent cottager
Eigentümer .... property owner
Einlieger .... lodger, tenant farmer
Einnehmer .... collector (of money)
Einwohner .... inhabitant
Eisengießer .... iron founder
Einsiedler .... hermit, recluse
Eisengießer .... iron founder
Eisenhändler .... iron monger
Eisenhauer .... miner, iron-hewer
Eisenmeister .... iron master
Eisenschmied .... blacksmith
Erntearbeiter .... harvester
Erzbischof .... archbishop
Erzgießer .... caster
Erzherzog/(-in) .... archduke/archduchess

Erzieher .... educator
Eseltreiber .... donkey driver
Estrichmacher .... stone floor maker
Fabricant ... manufacturer, factory owner
Fächermacher .... fan maker
Fackelträger .... torch carrier
Fadenmacher .... threadmaker
Fahnträger .... flagbearer
Fährmann .... ferryman
Faktor .... manager, supervisor
Falkner .... falconer
Färber .... dyer
Färbergeselle .... dyer journeyman
Faßbinder .... cooper, barrel-maker
Federschmücker   feather maker,
                                              plumassier
Federviehhändler .... poultry merchant
Feldmesser .... surveyor
Feldsher .... army surgeon
Feldschütz .... sergeant
Feldwebel .... sergeant
Ferkelbeschneider .... pig castrator
Fertigmacher . finisher, foreman, adjuster
Feuerwehrleute .... fire brigade workers
Feuerwerker .... explosives expert
Fiedler .... fiddler
Finanzbeamte .... finance official
Fischer .... fisherman
Flachshändler .... flax merchant
Flachshausierer .... flax peddler
Flaschenmacher .... bottlemaker
Flaschner .... plumber
Flecksieder .... cleaner/boiler of animal
                              entrails for further use
Fleischer.................................. butcher
Fleischhauer .... butcher
Flicker .... mender
Flickschneider .... tailor who mends
Flickschuster .... cobbler, shoe repairman
Flieger .... aviator
Flötenbläser .... flute player
Fluchting .... refugee, deserter
Fohlenbeschneider .... foal castrator
Förster .... forest ranger
Franziskaner .... monk
Freibauer .... independent peasant,
Freiherr/(-in) .... baron/baroness
                                              freeholder
Friseur .... barber, hairdresser (male)

Führerdirector, manager, driver, conductor
Fuhrknecht .... grooms attendant
Fuhrleute .... freight haulers
Fuhrmann .... coachman, wagoner, driver
Fürsprech .... advocate
Fürst/(-in) .... prince/princess
Füselier .... light infantryman
Fußsoldat .... foot soldier
Fußvolk .... footmen
Futterhändler ...... animal feed tradesman
Galanteriearbeiter ...... worker with fancy
                                    goods and jewelry
Garkoch .... cook
Garmmeister .... fisherman
Gärtner .... gardener
Gastwirt(h) .... innkeeper
Gaukler ...... juggler, vagabond, minstrel
Geächteter .... outlaw
Gebißmacher .... bridle bit maker
Gefäßformer .... ceramic mold maker
Geflügelhändler .... poulterer
Geheimschreiber .. confidential secretary
Gehilfe .... assistant, helper
Geiger .... violinist
Geißhirte .... goat herder
Geistlicher .... priest, pastor, clergyman
Geldleiher .... money lender
Geldwechsler .... money changer
Gelehrter .... scholar
Geistlicher .... clergyman
Gemeindemann .... officer
Gemüsegärtner .... market gardener
Gerber .... tanner
Gerichtsdiener .... servant in the court
Gerichtsmann des Gerichts .... magistrate
                                              of the court
Gerichtsschreiber .... clerk of the court
Geschäft .... trade, business
Geschäftsführer .... manager
Geschäftsmann .... businessman
Geselle .... journeyman
Getreidehändler .... grain dealer
Gewandschneider .... garment cutter
Gewehrschmied .... gun smith
Gewerbe .... trade, occupation
Gewürtz -krämer/-händler .... grocer,
                                              spice dealer
Gießer .... founder, caster, molder
Gilde .... guild

Gipser .... plasterer
Glasgeselle .... glazier
Glaser .... glassmaker, glazier
Glasmacher .... glassmaker
Glasmaler .... glass painter
Gläubiger .... creditor, mortgagee
Glockengießer .... bell founder
Glöckner .... sexton, bellringer
Goldarbeiter .... gold worker
Goldschlager .... maker of gold leaf
Goldschmied .... goldsmith
Graveur .... engraver
Grobschmied .... blacksmith
Großhändler .... wholesaler
Großherzog/(-in) .... grand duke/grand
 duchess
Großuhrmacher .... maker of big clocks
 (for churches, etc.)
Grützer .... grain miller
Gurtelmacher .... beltmaker
Gürtler.................................. beltmaker
Gutsbesitzer .... estate owner
Häcker............................... vine grower
Hafner .... potter
Halbbauer .... half-share farmer
Hammerschmied .... blacksmith
Handarbeiter .... manual laborer
Handelsmann .... merchant
 trader
Händler .... dealer, trader, retailer
Handschumacher .... glove maker
Handwerker.............. artisan, craftsman
Handwerksmann .... craftsman
Harfner .... harpist
Harnischmacher .... armor maker
Häscher .... bailiff
Hauer .... miner
Hauptmann .... captain, chief
Hausdiener .... house servant
Hausgenosse .... household member
Hausierer .... door-to-door salesman,
 peddler
Häusler .... cottager, landless laborer
Hausmeister .... caretaker
Hebamme .... midwife
Heizer............................. stoker, fireman
Hellebardenmacher .... halberd maker
Helmmacher .... helmet maker
Helmschmied .... helmet smith

Coppersmith and maiden (woodcut from the seventeenth century)

Hemd(en)macher .... shirtmaker
Henker................. hangman, executioner
Herr .... master, lord, Lord
Herstellen .... manufacturer
Herzog/(-in) .... duke/duchess
Heuerling .... day laborer
Hirte .... shepherd, cowherd
Hochseefischer .... deep sea fisherman
Hofleute .... bondsmen, courtiers
Hofmann .... courtier, bailiff, steward
Hofmarschall .... master of ceremonies
Holzarbeiter .... woodworker
Holzbitschenmacher .... cooper
Holzdrechsler .... turner (wood)
Holzflösser .... raftsman

Weapon maker, around 1470

Holzhändler .... lumber dealer
Holzhauer .... woodcutter
Holzschläger .... woodcutter
Holzschuhhändler .... trader in
                                 wooden shoes
Holzschuhmacher .. wooden shoe maker
Holztroghauer maker of wooden troughs
Homusikus .... crowns musician
Hopfenbauer .... hops grower
Hornrichter .... comb maker
Hospitaler .... nursing home resident
Hucker .... peddler
Hüfener .... farmer with full size farm
Hufschmied .... farrier, blacksmith
Hüter .... guardian, warden, herdsman
Hutmacher .... hatmaker, milliner
Hüttenarbeiter .... foundryman
Imker .... beekeeper
Ingenieur .... engineer
Jäger .... huntsman
Journalist .... journalist
Jurist .... lawyer
Juwelier .... jeweler
Kacheler .... tiler
Kachelmacher .... tiled stove maker

Kalkbrenner .... chalk burner
Kalkmacher .... chalkmaker
Kaminkehrer .... chimneysweep
Kammerdiener .... butler
Kämmerer . (city) treasurer, chamberlain
Kammmacher .... comb maker
Kampferer .... warrior
Kannengießer .... pewter worker
Karrenmann .... coachman
Karrenzieher .... cart puller
Kantor .... choirmaster, organist
Kaplan .... chaplain
Kärrner, Karrer .... coachman
Käsehändler .... cheese dealer
Käser .... cheesemaker
Käsmacher .... cheesemaker
Kastellan .... steward
Kastenmacher .... boxmaker
Kastrierer .... castrator
Kattunweber .... cotton weaver
Kaufbudeninhaber .... shop/stall owner
Kaufleute .... Merchants, businessmen
Kaufmann .... shopkeeper, merchant,
                                 businessman
Kehrrichtlader .... rubbish collector
Kelchmaker .... cup maker
Kellereiverwalter .... keeper of
                             the wine cellar
Kellermeister ...... cellarmaster/cellarman
Kellner .... waiter
Kerkermeister .... jailer
Kerkenzieher .... candlemaker
Kesselflicker .... tinker
Kesselschmied .... boilermaker
Kessler .... boilermaker
Kettenschmied .... chainsmith
Kieffer .... cooper
Kielfedernschneider .. quill feather cutter
Kindermagd .... nanny
Kirschner .... cherry brandy maker
Kistenmacher .. cratemaker, woodworker
Klausner .... hermit, recluse
Kleidermacher .... clothesmaker
Kleinbauer .... peasant, farmer
Kleinbüttscher .... cooper
Kleinverschlüssen .... maker of
                        fasteners and locks
Klempner .... plumber, tinsmith
Klingenschmied .... sword smith

Klopffechter .. fencing artist (circus, etc.) or fencing teacher
Klosterschaffner .... financial adviser .... of an abbey
Knappe .... page, squire
Knecht .... (male) servant, farmhand
Knochenhauer .... butcher
Knopfmacher .... buttonmaker
Koch/Köchin .... cook (male/female)
Kohlenbrenner .... coal-maker/sorter
Köhler .... charcoalmaker
Kolonist .... settler
pioneer
Konditor .... pastry-cook
Kopist .... copyist
Korbflechter .... basket weaver
Korbmacher .... basket weaver
Korbwagenmacher .... basket-carriage maker
Kornfruchthändler .... cereals dealer
Kornhändler .... grain merchant
Kornhausverwalter .... granary administrator
Kornmüller .... grain miller
Korsettmacher .... corsetmaker
Kostgänger .... board
Kötner .... farmer
Krämer .... shopkeeper, tradesman
Krankenpfleger ..... caregiver for the sick
Krankenschwester .... nurse
Kräutermann .... herbalist
Krautkrämer .... druggist
Krüger .... innkeeper, publican
Krugführer .... innkeeper
Kuchenbäcker .... confectioner
Kuchenmeister .... head cook
Küfer .... cellarman; (dial.) cooper
Kuhirt .... cowherd
K.U.K. Oberleutnant .... regimental sergeant major
Künstler .... artist
Kunstschlosser .... art metal worker
Kunsttischler .... cabinetmaker
Kupferdrucker .... copperplate printer
Kupferschmied .... coppersmith
Kupferstecher .... copperplate engraver, etcher
Kuppler .... matchmaker
Kürschner .... furrier

Kutscher .... coachman
Küster .... sexton
Kutscher .... coachman
Kuttler .... offal seller
Landarbeiter .... farm laborer, farmhand
Landmann .... farmer
Landmesser .... surveyor
Landwirt(h) .... farmer
Landwirt(h) .... farmer
Lastträger .... porter
Laternenmacher .... lanternmaker
Läufer .... messenger
Lebkuchner .... gingerbread maker
Lederbereiter .... leather dresser
Lederbeutelmacher ..... leather bag maker
Lederer .... leather maker
Lederhändler .... leather dealer
Lehmarbiter .... potter or brickmaker
Lehrmeister .... master of a trade
Lehmfahrer .... clay pit transportation worker
Lehmverstreicher .... grouter
Lehnsmann .... vassal (slave)
Lehrer/(-in) .... teacher (male/female)
Lehrling .... apprentice
Leibarzt .... personal physician
Leibzüchter .... retired farmer
Leichenbestatter .... undertaker
Leichenbitter .... inviter to funerals
Leichenlader ..... undertaker or inviter to funerals
Lein(en)weber .... linen weaver
Leitender Arzt .... head physician
Leiter .... director
Leutnant .... lieutenant
Lichtzieher .... candlemaker
Litterati .... writer
Lodenfärber .... wool or cloth dyer
Lohgerber .... tanner
Lohnarbeiter .... hired worker
Lohnkutscher .... hired coachman
Lumpensammler .... ragpicker
Magd ..... female domestic servant, maid
Magister .... schoolmaster
Mahler .... painter, artist
Maier .... overseer
Major .... major
Makler .... broker, jobber
Maler .... painter, artist

Mälzer .... beer distiller, malt miller
Malzmüller .... malt miller
Mantelmacher .... coatmaker
Marktaufseher .... market supervisor
Marktschreier .... charlatan
Matratzenmacher .... mattressmaker
Matrose .... sailor
Maurer .... mason
Mechaniker .... fitter, mechanic
Mehlhändler .... flour merchant
Meier .... dairy farmer
Meister .... master
Melker .... milker (male)
Messerschmied .... cutler, knifemaker
Messergriffmacher .. knife-handle maker
Messerschneidenmacher ...... knife-blade
                                                maker
Messingschmied .... brassworker
Messner .... sexton
Metzger .... butcher
Mietling .... male renter, tenant,
                                         mercenary
Mietsgärtner .... tenant gardener
Mietsmann .... male tenant
Milchträger .... milkman
Milchviehzüchter .... dairy farm leaser
Milizer .... militiaman
Möbelhändler .... furniture merchant
Modist .... milliner
Mönch .... monk, friar
Müller .... miller
Münzer .... (coin) minter
Münzscheider .... assayer
Musiker, Musikant .... musician
Nachahmer .... copyist
Nachtwächter .... night watchman
Nadelfertiger .... needle finisher
Nadelhändler .... needle merchant
Nadelmacher .... needlemaker
Nadler .... needlemaker, haberdasher
Nagelschmied .... nailsmith
Näherin .... dressmaker
Nestler .... shoelace maker
Neuling .... novice
Niederrichter .... lower judge
Notar .... notary, civil lawyer
Oberkoch .... master chef
Oberpfarrer .... rector
Oberst .... colonel

Obsthändler .... fruit seller
Ofensetzer .... stove fitter
Ölmacher .... oilman, chandler
Ölmüller .... oil-miller
Ölschlager .... oil press operator
                                         (oil from seeds)
Örgelbauer .... organ builder
Orgelmacher .... organ builder
Pächter .... lessee, tenant
Packer .... packer
Paneelenmacher .... panelmaker
Pantoffelmacher .... slipper maker
Panzermacher .... maker of body armor
Papierarbeiter .... paper worker
Papierhändler . stationer, paper merchant
Papiermacher .... papermaker
Parfümmacher .... perfume maker
Pastetenverkäufer .... pie seller
Pauker .... kettle drummer, duellist
Pelzhändler .... fur dealer
Pergamentmacher .... parchment maker
Perück(en)macher .... wigmaker
Pfalzgraf .... Earl, count palatine
Pfandnehmer .... pawnbroker
Pfannenschmied .... pan smithy
Pfarrer .... clergyman, pastor, priest
Pfarrkind .... parishioner
Pfeifenfabrikant .... pipe maker
Pfeifenmacher .... pipe maker
Pfeifer .... fife player
Pfeilmacher .... arrowmaker
Pferdehändler .... horse merchant
Pferdeknecht .... stable worker
Pferdeschlächter .... horse butcher
Pferdeverleiher .... livery stable worker
Pflasterer .... street paver
Pfleger .... nurse (male)
Pflüger .... plowman
Pförtner .... doorman, porter
Philosoph .... philosopher
Pilger .... pilgrim
Piscator .... fisherman
Plattner .... (flattening) smith,
                                         body armor maker
Polierer.................... burnisher, polisher
Polizei .... police
Polsterer .... upholsterer
Porträtmaler .... portrait painter

Posamentierer .. braidmaker, lacemaker, haberdasher
Postbeamte .... postal worker
Posthalter .... post-horse keeper
Postillion .... coachman
Prediger ....preacher
Priester .... priest
Prinz/(essin) .... prince/princess
Probst .... dean
Prüfer ....examiner
Puppenmacher........................ dollmaker
Putzfrau .... cleaning woman
Quacksalber ...... quack doctor, charlatan
Rademacher .... wheelwright
Ratsdiener ....council employee
Ratsherr .... town councilman
Ratsmitglied ....member of council
Rauchfleischmetzger .... smoked meat dealer
Rechenmeister .... accountant
Rechtsanwalt .... attorney
Rechenmeister .... accountant
Regenschirmmacher ...... umbrella maker
Reisender .... traveler
Rektor ....dean
Rentner .... retired person (male)
Richter .... judge,justice
Riemenschneider .... harness maker
Riemer .... saddler, strapmaker
Rinderhirt .... cowherd
Ritter .... knight, cavalryman
Rosenkranzmacher .... maker of rose garlands
Roßtäuscher .... horse merchant
Rotgerber .... red tanner

Rotgießer .... coppersmelter
Rutenbinder .... broommaker
Sachwalter .... attorney
Säckler .... sackmaker
Sägenmacher .... sawmaker
Säger .... sawyer
Salbenhändler .... dealer in ointments
Salpetergräber ....saltpeter digger
Salzhändler .... salt merchant
Salzsieder .... salt works laborer
Salzverlader .... salt trader
Sämann .... sower
Samtweber .... velvet weaver
Sattelmacher .... saddle maker
Sattler .... saddlemaker, harnessmaker
Sauhirt .... swineherd
Schachtelmacher .... boxmaker
Schäfer .... sheepherder
Schaffner .... conductor
Schaftstiefelmacher ...... sheepskin maker
Schalknarr .... clown
Schankwirt .... publican
Scharfrichter .... executioner
Schätzer .... (expert) valuer, adjuster
Schatzmeister .... treasurer
Schauspieler/-in .... actor/actress
Schenkwirt ....innkeeper
Scheibler .... salt carrier
Schellenmacher .... bell maker
Scherenschleifer .... scissors sharpener
Schiedsrichter .... arbiter, judge
Schieferdecker .... roofer
Schiffbauer .... ship builder
Schiffer .... sailor

Cooper's workshop (woodcut, 1516)

Schiffsführer .... ship captain
Schiffstaumacher .... ship cable maker
Schindelhändler .... shingle merchant
Schindelhauer .... shinglemaker
Schinder .... renderer, skinner
Schirmer .... umbrella maker
Schirmmaker .... umbrella maker
Schlächter .... butcher
Schleierverkäufer .... veil dealer
Schleifer .... grinder, polisher, gem-cutter
Schlosser .... locksmith
Schlüsselträger .... key carrier
Schmelzer .... caster, founder, molder
Schmid, Schmied .... blacksmith
Schnallengiesser/macher ... buckle maker
Schneider .... tailor
Schnitter .... harvester, reaper
Schnittwarenhändler .... dry goods
                                                merchant
Schnurmacher .... lace maker
Schöffer .... juror
Schornsteinfeger .... chimneysweep
Schrader .... tailor, cutter
Schrammermeister .... scratcher for
                                          washer boards
Schreiber .... writer, scribe, clerk
Schreiner .... joiner, cabinetmaker
Schriftgießer .... type founder
Schriftsetzer .... compositor, typesetter
Schriftsteller .... author
Schröter .... tailor, carter, cooper
Schuhflicker .... shoemaker
Schuhknecht .... book-jack
Schuhmacher .... shoemaker
Schuldiener .... school caretaker
Schüler . student (below university level)
Schulhalter .... teacher
Schullehrer .... teacher
Schulmeister .... schoolmaster
Schultheiß .... village mayor
Schulze .... village mayor
Schuster .... cobbler
Schwarzbrotbäcker .... baker of
                                             black bread
Schwarzkünstler .... sorcerer
Schwarzschmied .... blacksmith
Schweinebeschneider ..... swine castrator
Schweinehändler .... swine dealer
Schweinehirt .... swineherd

Wool-comber (1818)

Schwerdtfeger .... armorer, bladesmith
Schwerdtschleifer .... sword sharpener
Schwörer .... public servant/
               official sworn by oath
        to perform his duties correctly
           (surveyor, inspector of
           seawalls, weights, etc.)
Seeleute .... seamen
Segelmacher .... sail maker
Seifensieder .... soapmaker
Seidenkrämer .... silk merchant
Seidenmacher .... silk maker
Seidenstricker ... (male) silk embroiderer
Seidenwirker .... silk worker
Seifensieder .... soapmaker
Seigner .... fisherman
Seiler .... rope maker, rope merchant
Seilmacher .... ropemaker
Seiltänzer .... tightrope walker
Sensenschmied .... scythe smith
Siebmacher .... sieve maker
Siedler .... settler

Siegelbewahrer .... keeper of the seal
Silberschmied .... silversmith
Silhouetteur .... silhouette cutter
Soldat .... soldier
Sonnenschirmmacher .... parasolmaker
Spangenmacher .... brass worker
Spediteur .... (freight) forwarder
Spengler .... tinsmith
Spenhauer .... carpenter
Spezereihändler .... grocer
Spiegelmacher .... mirror maker
Spiegler .... mirror maker
Spielmann .... minstrel
Spinnermann .... spinner
Spinrockenmacher .... maker of spinning
distaffs
Spion .... spy
Spitalpfleger .... male nurse
Sporenmacher, Sporer .... spur maker
Sprechmeister .... musician
Stadtknecht .... town worker
Stallknecht .... stable servant
Stallmeister .... riding master
Steinhauer .... stone cutter
Steinmetz .... stone mason
Stecknadelmacher .... pinmaker
Steinbrecher .... quarryman
Steinhauer .... stone cutter
Stellmacher .... wheelwright
Steinbrecher .... stone mason
Steinhauer .... stone mason
Steinmetz .... stone mason
Steinschneider .... gem cutter, lapidary
Steinsetzer .... paver
Stellmacher .... wheelwright
Stellvertreter .... deputy, substitute
Stempeischneider .... stamp cutter
Steuereinnehmer .... tax collector
Steuereintreiber .... tax collector
Steurrat .... tax board
Stockmeister .... jailer
Straßenfeger .... road sweeper
Strumpffabrikant .... stocking producer
Strumpfstricker .... stocking weaver
Stückweber .... piece weaver
Student .... student
Sulzer .... saltmaker
Tafelmacher .... carpenter (for tables)
Tag(e)löhner .... day laborer

Tagwerker .... day laborer
Tambour .... drummer
Tapezierer .... paperhanger, decorator,
upholsterer
Taschnmaker .... bagmaker
Taschner .... leather bag maker
Taucher .... diver
Teppichweber .... carpet weaver
Teppichwirker .... carpet worker
Theologe .... theologian
Tierarzt .... veterinarian
Tischler .... carpenter, cabitnetmaker
Töpfer .... potter
Topfhändler/-krämer .... pots merchant
Torwächter .... gatekeeper
Torwart .... gatekeeper
Totengräber .... gravedigger
Träger .... porter
Trödler .. secondhand, old clothes dealer
Trommler .... drummer
Trompeter .... trumpeter
Troßbube .... baggage servant
Tuch .... cloth, fabric, material
Tücher .... whitewasher
Tüchermacher .... cloth maker
Tuchhändler .... cloth dealer, draper
Tuchmacher .... fabric maker
Tuchscherer .... cloth cutter
Tuchschneider .... tailor
Tüncher .... whitewasher
Turner .... gymnast
Tütenmacher .... paper bag maker
Uhrmacher .... watch- or clock-maker
Unterhändler .... agent
Unteroffizier .... corporal
Unvermögende .... pauper
Vergolder .... gilder
Verkäufer .... salesman
Vermögensverwalter estate administrator
Vertreter .... agent, representative
Verwalter .... administrator, manager
Verwaltungsbeamter .... administrative
official
Verweser .... administrator
Viehbeschneider .... cattle castrator
Viehhändler .... cattle dealer
Vogeler .... bird-catcher, fowler
Vogt .... overseer, warden
Vormund .... legal guardian

Vorsänger .... choir leader
                        officiating minister
Vorsteher .... director, manager, chief
Waagemeister ..... master of weights and
                                measures
Wachszieher .... candle maker or seller
Wächter .... watchman, guard
Waffenschmied .... weapon maker,
                                gunsmith
Wagenbauer .... coachbuilder, cartwright
Wagenmacher coach builder, cartwright
Wagenmeister .... wagonmaster
Wagner ...... coach builder, wheel maker
Wahrsager .... fortune-teller
Wäscher/-in .... laundry man/
                                washerwoman
Wasenmeister .... skinner, renderer
Wassermüller .... watermill operator
Weber .... weaver
Webergeselle .... weaver
Wechsler .... money changer
Weg(e)macher .... road mender
Wehmutter .... midwife
Weinbauer .... wine farmer
Weingärtner .... vine-dresser
Weinprüfer .... wine tester
Weinschenker .... waiter
Weinwirt .... keeper of a wine tavern
Weißbinder .... cooper, whitewasher
Weißbrotbäcker .... white bread baker
Weißgerber .... tanner (of fine leather)
Werbeberater .... publicity agent
Werghändler .... hemp tradesman
Wiedertäufer .... Anabaptist
Wildhändler .... game dealer
Wildzaunwärter .... game keeper
Winzer .... vintner, wine farmer
Wirt(h) .... innkeeper, landlord, hotel/
                        restaurant proprietor
Wissenschaftler .... scientist
Wollkämmer .... wool comber
Wollspinner .... wool spinner
Woll(en)weber .... wool weaver
Wucherer .... money lender
Wundarzt .... surgeon
Würdenträger .... high official
Würfelmacher .... wood turner for dice
Würfelspieler .... dice player
Wurstmacher .... sausage maker

Zahlmeister .... paymaster
Zahnbrecher .... dentist
Zangenschmied .... blacksmith
Zauberer .... magician
Zaumschmied .... bridle maker
Zaumstricher .... bridle maker
Zeichner .... graphic artist, draftsman
Zeidler .... beekeeper
Zeiner .... basketmaker
Zerrenner .... blacksmith, especially
                        one who smelts iron
Zeuge .... witness
Zeugkrämer .... cloth merchant
Zeugmacher .... clothmaker
Zeugschmied .... toolsmith
Ziegelbrenner, Ziegler .... brickmaker
Ziegelbrenner .... brick/tile maker
Ziegler .... brick/tile maker
Zigeuner .... gypsy
Zimmermädchen .... (chamber)maid
Zimmermann .... carpenter, joiner
Zinkenbläser .... bugler
Zinngießer .... tin founder, pewterer
Zinsbauer .... farmer who pays tithes
Zinsnehmer ...... collector of taxes or rent
Zofe .... chambermaid
Zögling .... trainee, pupil
Zöller .... customs official
Zöllner .... toll collector
Zuchtmeister .... taskmaster
Zuckerbäcker .... confectioner
Zuhälter .... pimp
Zunftmeister .... master of a guild
Zwirnmacher ...... thread or twine maker
Zwischenhändler .... (commission) agent,
                                intermediary

LATIN DESIGNATIONS FOR OCCUPATIONS, TRADES AND TITLES

abatissa .... abbess
abbas .... abbot
abiectarius .... cabinetmaker
actionarius .... shopkeeper (Krämer)
acupictor .... embroiderer
adumbrator .... draftsman
advocatus .... lawyer

The pilot's examination (Düsseldorf, 1810)

aedilis .... chief, head	arator .... farmer
aedituus .... sexton	arcarius faber .... box/cabinet maker
aerarius veteramentarius .... tinker	archiater, archigenes .... physician
aerarius faber .... coppersmith	architriclinus .... conductor, master of
agaso .... stable boy	ceremonies
agittarius .... crossbow maker	arcularius .... cabinetmaker
agricola .... farmer	argentarius .... banker, money changer
albator .... bleacher	armbruster .... bow maker
altarista inhaber .... chaplain	aromatopola .. herb/spice dealer/peddler
alumnus .... boarding student	arrendator .... lessee
amiger .... page, squire	artifex calcarium .... spur maker
ampularius .... bottle maker	artifex loricarius .... harnessmaker
anachoreta .... hermit	artopoeus .... baker
ancilla .... female servant	assator .... cook
annonarius .... dealer in grain	aucellator .... falconer
annutarius faber .... armor maker,	aulaeorum opifex .... carpet weaver
chainsmith	aurifaber .... gold and silver smith
antistes .... clergyman	auriga .... wagoner
apiarius .... bee-keeper	baccalaureus .... scholar, lowest degree
apothecarius .... pharmacist	academedician
apparitor .... overseer, bailiff	baiulus .... messenger, porter

balistarius	bowmaker, archer
bapirifex	paper maker
barbarius	barber
becharius	(wood) turner
bedellus	bailiff
bergarius	sheepherder
biadarius	grain dealer
bibliopegus........................	bookbinder
birmenter	parchment maker
bombardarius	tinsmith
bombicinator	silk maker
bractearius...........................	gold beater
brasiator	maltser
breiser	haberdasher
bubulcus................................	cowherd
burgravius	baron
bursarius	bag maker
cacubarius	tiled stove maker
caduceator	agent, bridge and road mender
caelator..................................	engraver
caementarius	stonemason
caicariator	spur maker
calciator	shoemaker
califex	pewterer
calopedarius	wooden shoe maker
calvarius	nail smith
cambiator	money changer
campanarius	sexton
campsor	money changer
candidarius	bleacher
caniparius	waiter

cantafusor	pewterer
capellanus	curate
capillamentarius	wig maker
capsarius	box maker
carator	nurse (male)
carbonarius....................	charcoal maker
carnarius	butcher
carnifex	hangman, knacker, butcher
carpentarius........................	cartwright
carrucarius	driver
casier	cheese maker
castellanus...............................	steward
castrator	cattle castrator
catopticus	mirror maker
cauno	publican
caupo	innkeeper
cellarius.............................	cellarmaster
cementarius	mason
cerdo	tanner
cereficiarius	wax chandler
cerevisiarius	brewer
cervillarius	helmet smith
chaicographus	copper plate engrver
chelista	violinist
chelius	violinist
chirothecarius	glove maker
chirurgus	surgeon
chymiater	alchemist
cingularius	belt maker
circulator	tramp, vagrant
cistarius	box/chest maker
claustrarius	doorkeeper, janitor
clausurmacher	lockmaker
claviorum artifex	art metal worker
clericus	clergyman
clibanarius...........................	oven caster
clusor	smith
coctor	brewer
cocus	cook
collector	tax collector
colonus	settler, peasant farmer
colorator	painter
comes	Count Palatine
commissarius	deputy, agent
commutator	money changer
concionator	clergyman
conducticius	day worker
conflator	foundryman
consiliarius, consul ..	councilman, mayor

Sign of a hatmaker, around 1800

conterfetter .... portrait painter
coqua .... cook (female)
coquus .... cook (male)
corbo .... basket maker
cordarius .... rope maker
coreator, coriarius tanner, leather worker
corrigiarius .... strap maker
credenzer .... waiter
crumenarius .... bottle and bag maker
crustularius .... confectioner
culcitarius .... coat maker
cuparius .... cooper
cupendinarius .... confectioner
cuprifaber .... coppersmith
custodius .... watchman
custos .... custodian, guard
dantler .... peddler
dapifer .... lord high steward
deaurator .... gilder
decanus .... dean, prior, provost
deglubitor .... knacker, flayer
dignitarius .... high official
disceptator .... arbiter, judge
discipulus .... student
dispensator .... conductor
doliarius .... cooper
domicellus .... nobleman
dulciarius .... confectioner
ebursator .... paymaster
edentarius .... dentist
ennoyeus .... goat herder
ephipparius .... saddler
ephorus .... director, manager
episcopus .... bishop
eques .... cavalryman, knight
equester .... mounted horseman
equicida .... horse butcher
equicius .... horse dealer
eremita .... hermit, recluse
ergastularius .... taskmaster, jailer
eruginator .... sword sharpener
exactor .... tax collector
exclamator .... town crier
faber, Fabricius .... smithy
faber lignarius .... woodworker
falcarius .... scythe sharpener
falconarius .... falconer
famula/famulus ... servant (female/male)
farcher .... swine dealer

fartor .... sausage maker
feniseca .... harvester, reaper
fibulator .... plumber
fidicen .... fiddler, minstrel
figulus .... potter, tiler
filicarius .... paver, stone mason
fistulator .... fife/flute player
flator .... caster, foundryman
flebotomarius .... blood-letter
foeniseca .... reaper, harvester
forestarius .... forester
fornacarius .... stove fitter
fossarius .... grave digger
fossor .... gravedigger, ditch digger
fragner .... tradesman
frenarius .... strapmaker
frumentarius .... grain salesman
fuderer .... feed tradesman
fullo .... fuller, draper
funarius .... rope maker
funicularius ...... belt/strap/thongs maker
funifex .... rope maker
furnarius .... oven fitter
gailer .... tramp, begger
gantier .... glove maker
garcifer .... cook
gemmarius .... jeweler
geraria .... nanny
gerulus .... messenger, porter
girator .... tramp, vagrant
gladiarius .... swordsmith
grammaticus .... schoolmaster
guardianus .... guard
haragius .... magician, fortune teller
harpator .... harpist
hauderer .... cabman
herbarius .... dealer in herbs
hortulanus .... gardener
hospes .... innkeeper
hospinianus .... innkeeper
impressor .... printer
inbursator .... money collector
incisor .... tailor
indusiarius .... shirt maker
infector .... painter
institor .... peddler, shopkeeper
ioculator .... juggler
iudex .... judge
judex .... judge

kaviller .... knacker
laaber .... cheesemaker
laborator .... worker, day worker
laborius .... worker, laborer
lacticinator .... milker
laganator .... plumber
laminarius .... sheet metal smith
laniator .... butcher
lanifex .... clothmaker
lanio .... butcher
lanitextor .... clothmaker
lapidarius .... quarryman
lapper .... jobbing cobbler
lapsator .... gem polisher
lasiterer .... saltpeter digger
laterator .... brickmaker
lavandarius .... laundryman
leno .... matchmaker
lepper .... cobbler
liber rusticus .... free peasant
librarius .... book dealer
libripens .... inspector of weights and
                                    measures
lictor .... bailiff, jailer
ligator .... cooper
lignarius .... joiner, cabinetmaker
lignicidus .... woodcutter
ligularius .... thong/shoelace maker
limbolarius .... braid maker, haberdasher
linarius .... hemp and flax dealer
linifex .... linen weaver
lintearius .... hemp and flax dealer
liticen .... minstrel
lodex .... weaver, coatmaker
lorarius .... strap maker
ludimagister .... schoolmaster, teacher
ludimoderator .. teacher of lower classes
ludirector .... school director
lutorissa .... washer woman
lychnopoeus .... candlemaker
macellator .... butcher
mactator .... butcher
magirus .... cook
magister civium .... mayor
magister .... master, teacher
magus .... magician
malleator .... blacksmith
mamburnus .... administrator
mansuarius .... farmer

marcellarius .... butcher
marinarius .... sailor
marpahis .... riding master
marsuparius .... purse/satchel maker
massarius .... dairy farmer
materialista .... merchant
matiarius .... sausage maker
medicus .... physician
medicus equarius .... veterinarian
medicus dentium .... dentist
mellicida .... bee farmer
membranarius .... parchment maker
mendicus .... beggar
mensator .... cabinetmaker
mercator .... merchant, businessman
mercenarius .... daylaborer
meretrix .... prostitute
messor .... examiner (check)
miles .... soldier, knight
mindrita .... shepherd, monk
minutor .... bloodletter, surgeon
molendarius .... miller
molineus .... miller
molitor .... miller
murarius .... mason
mylius .... miller
nauta .... sailor
navector .... ferryman
negotiant .... businessman, merchant
netor .... tailor
netrix .... seamstress
nigromanticus .... sorcerer, magician
notarius .... clerk, notary
nummularius .... minter
nuntius .... messenger
nutrix .... wet-nurse
obsequa .... domestic servant (female)
obstetrix .... midwife
oenopola .... tavern keeper
official, officialis .... agent
olearius .... oil presser (from seeds)
operarius .... laborer
operator .... laborer
opifex .... craftsman
opilio .... sheepherder
ornitander .... fowler
ostiarius .... caretaker, guard
palaeopater .... patriarch
panifex .... baker

Housewife and kitchen hands

pannarius .... clothmaker
pannicida .... cloth-, drapery cutter
pannifex .... clothmaker
pantopola .... wholesaler
papyrifex .... paper worker
paramentier .... lace maker
parochus .... clergyman
pastellator .... pan smithy
pastor .... shepherd, pastor
paternosterer ..... maker of rose garlands
paur .... farmer
pectinator .... wool comber
pellifex .... furrier
pellificator .... furrier
pellio .... furrier
pelviarius .... boilermaker
pelvifex .... boilermaker
pelzer .... furrier
penesticus .... second-hand dealer
pensator .. weights and measures official
perator .... leather bag maker
pharmacopola .... pharmacist, scented
                                        oil merchant
phlebotomarius ..... bloodletter, surgeon
picarius .... cooper
picator .... cooper

pictaciarius .... mender
pictor .... painter
pilearius .... drayman
pileo .... drayman
piscator .... fisherman
pistor .... baker
plastes .... sculptor
plebanus .... clergyman
plumbarius .... tin founder, pewterer
poeta .... poet
polentarius ...... maltzer, brewery worker
polio .... flattening smith
pollinctor .... undertaker
pomarius .... fruit dealer
pontifex .... bishop
popinarius .... cook
practious .... lawyer
praeceptor .... schoolmaster
praeco .... town crier
praefectus .... adminstrator, overseer
praefectus .... magistrate
praepositus .... dean
praestes .... director, manager
praetor .... manager, mayor
praetorius .... mayor, judge
praxator .... brewer
presser .... printer
procarius .... swineherd
procurator .... deputy, advocate
proirnus .... head cook
promocondus .... cellarmaster, steward
proreta .... ship captain
proxeneta .... (commission-) agent
puer exercitus .... baggage boy
quaestor .... tax collector, treasurer
rector ecclesia .... minister
reddituarius .... lessee, tenant
redemptor .... dealer, merchant
regius, Rex .... king
repositor .... treasurer
restiarius .... ship cable/rope maker
restio .... ship cable/rope maker
rhedarius .... wagoner
ribaldus .... tramp, vagrant
rurensis .... brewer
rusticus .... peasant, farmer
saccellarius .... treasurer
sacellanus .... chaplain
sacerdos .... priest

sagittarius .... bow and arrow maker, marksman
sakristan .... sexton
salarius .... salt works laborer
salifex .... salt dealer
salinator .... salt dealer
sallarius .... salt works laborer
salpista .... trumpeter
salsuciarius .... prepares entrails for further use (sausage, strings, etc.)
samiator .... grinder, gem polisher
sapicida .... stone mason
sartor .... tailor
satellites .... servant, farmhand
sator .... sower
scabinus .... juror
scandularius .... shinglemaker
schacherer .... peddler
sclopetarius .... handler of guns
scoparius .... road sweeper
scorifex .... tanner
scriba....................... scribe, writer, clerk
scriniarius .... confidental secretary, archivist, cabinetmaker
scrutarius................. second-hand dealer
scultetus .... village mayor
segristanus .... sexton
sellarius .... saddler
sensal .... broker, jobber
serator .... locksmith
sericarius .... silk worker
serrarius .... saw maker
servus .... servant, knight
similarius .... bread baker
simulator .... copyist
smigator .... soapmaker
socius .... apprentice, comrade
speciarius .... herb peddler
speculator .... guard, spy
sportularius .... basketmaker
stabularis .... stable servant
stannarius .... pewterer
staterarius .... wagonmaker
stationarius .... shopkeeper
stipus .ּ... beggar
stratarius .... saddler
stupenator .... baths owner
subulcus .... swineherd
sufferator .... blacksmith

superattendens .... superintendent
sutor .... cobbler, shoemaker
tabellarius .... messenger
talemetarius .... baker
tector .... roofer
tegularius .... brickmaker
teleonarius .... tax collector
textor .... weaver
tinctor .... dyer
tiro .... novice, student
tomeator .... thresher
tomio .... thresher
tonsor .... gem cutter
tritor .... thresher
tunnarius .... cooper
tutor .... guardian
tyropola .... cheese dealer
unguentarius .... perfume and scented oil maker
urinator .... diver
usurarius .... money lender
vadius .... guarantor
valvarius .... custodian, caretaker
vassus .... servant, vassal
vector .... coachman
venator .... hunter
venditor .... merchant, businessman
verganter .... auctioneer
vespillo .... gravedigger
vestiarius .... tailor
veteramentarius ...... second-hand dealer
viego .... cooper
vietor.. cooper
vigilarius .... guard
villicus .... lower court judge, overseer
vinctor .... cooper
vinitor .... vintner

virgulator .... broom maker
vitriarius .... glassmaker
xylocopus .... carpenter
zonarius .... belt maker
zythopepta .... brewer
zytopoeus .... brewer

MEDICAL TERMS, ILLNESSES, CAUSES OF DEATH (German and Latin)

Abreibung .... abortion
Abseß .... abscess
Abweichen .... diarrhea
Abzehrung .... consumption, emaciation
Agonia .... throes of death
Albschoß .... rheumatic pain
Alter .... age, old age
Altersschwäche ...... weakness of old age
Alterentkräftung .... debility of old age
(St.-)Andreas-Krankheit .... gout
Anfall .... stroke
Angina ..... angina, tonsillitis, sore throat
Angst .... cramping, pain
Antrax .... bleeding ulcer, sore
Apoplexie .... apoplexy, stroke
Apostema .... abscess,
Ardura .... inflammation
Aussatz .... leprosy
Außerer Schaden .... external damage
Auszehrung .... consumption, tuberculosis
Balbina .... goiter
Bandwurm .... tapeworm
Bereden .... bewitched
Berle .... bleeding tumor
Beulenpest .... bubonic plague
Beuschel (Bäuschel .... consumption
Blärr (Plarre) .... ulcer, abscess
Blattern .... smallpox
Blätterrose .... shingles
Blinddarmentzündung .... appendicitis
Blödigkeit .... debility, sickness
Blödigkeit der Augen .... failing eyesight
Blutfluß .... hemorrhage, dysentery
Blutgang .... hemorrhage

Blutsturz .... violent hemorrhage
Blutvergiftung .... blood poisoning, toxemia
Brand .... burning pain, typhus
Brand am Fuß .... gangrene on the foot
Bräune .... angina, diphtheria
Brechruhr .... cholera
bresthaft .... maimed, sick
Bruchschaden .... hernia
Brustenzündung .... pleurisy-bronchitis
Brustfieber .... bronchitis or inflammation of the chest
Brustkiste .... difficult breathing, asthma
Brustkrämpfe .... cramps, spasms, convulsions of the chest
Brustkrankheit .... lung disease, tuberculosis
Brustwassersucht ...... dropsy of the chest
Bürzel .... influenza
Busse .... bone decay, cancer
cachexicus .... consumptive
Cancer, Carcinoma .... cancer
Cepphalea .... head pain
Certamen .... death throes
Cholera .... cholera
Ciballium passio .... digestive system malady
clinicus .... confined to bed
Dampf .... difficult breathing
Debilitas .... weakness, debility
Debilitatio .... paralysis, palsy
decrepitus .... infirm, decrepid
Delocatio, Dislocatio .... dislocation
Diarrhöe .... diarrhea
Diptherie .... diphtheria
Dissenteria, Dysenteria .... dysentery
Dissolutio .... infirmity
Durchfall .... diarrhea
Durchlauf, Durchschlechten ... diarrhea, dysentery
Eiß .... abscess, carbuncle
Elend .... severe illness
Eiterbeule .... abscess
Emanatio .... discharge, secretion
Emissio .... contagion, pestilence
empicus .... suffering from lung disease

Engerling   skin disease (usually with itching)
Entkräftung .... weakening, exhaustion, debilitation
Ertränkung .... drowning
Eructatio .... vomiting
Excrementum .... phlegm
Excretio .... excretion, excrement
Exitus .... death
Fallsucht .... epilepsy
Faulfieber .... putrid fever
Fäule .... body odor
Falbel (Fallübel, -sucht) .... epilepsy
Faulfieber .... typhus
febricare .... fevered
Febris .... fever
Fehlgeburt .... miscarriage
Fieber .... fever
Flecken, rote .... rubella
Fleckenkrankeit .... dry scab
Fleckfieber .... typhus
Flecktyphus .... typhoid fever
Fleisch, faules .... wound, cancer
Fluß (Fluvius) .... catarrh, eczema, rheumatism, arthritis
Flußfieber .... rheumatic fever
foitidus .... foul smelling
Fomentationes .... flatulence
Fraisen .... convulsions, epilepsy, seizures
Fruhgeburt .... premature birth
Gallenfieber .... typhus
Gallfluß .... bone cancer, decay
Gallsucht .... jaundice
Gehirnschlag .... cerebral apoplexy, heart attack
Gelbsucht .... jaundice
Gelenkrheumatismus .... arthritis
Geschwulst .... swelling, tumor, goiter
Geschwür .... ulcer, abscess, running sore
Geschwür im Hals .... ulcer in throat
Gesichtsrose .... erysipelas
Gicht .... arthritis, gout
Gichter .... convulsions
Gift .... poison
Glandines .... lymph tumors
Glaucoma .... glaucoma

(grüner Star)
Gravitas .... pregnancy, frailty
Gravitas mentis .... depression
Gürtelrose .... shingles
haemorrhoia .... hemorrhaging
Hals abgeschnitten .... throat cut
Halsbräune (-gichter,   diphtheria, -krankheit)   croup
Halsentzündung ...... throat inflammation
Halsschwindsucht .... throat consumption
Härte .... rickets
Häulige .... croup
Hauptkrankheit .... contagious disease, epidemic
Hauptschuß .... rheumatism
häutige Bräune .... croup
Hebetudo .... feeble-mindedness
Heisch .... inflammation, swelling
Hemicrania .... migraine
Herznot .... heart ailment
Herzschlag .... heart attack
Hictericus (Icterus) .... jaundice (in children)
Hinfallendes .... epilepsy
Hirnentzündung .... brain infection
Hirnfluß .... head cold
Hitze, böse .... fever
hitziges Fieber .... high fever (typhoid)
Höchsten, am   epilepsy, (innerlichen)   convulsions
Hüftweh .... sciatica
Hünsch .... Bubonic plague
Husten .... coughing
Husten, blauer .... whooping cough
Icterus (Hictericus) .... jaundice (in children)
Imago mortis .... appearance of death
Impfung .... vaccination (smallpox)
Inflammatio .... inflammation
Inflatio .... flatulence
innerlichs Krankheit ...... internal disease
inokulation .... (smallpox) vaccination
insanus .... mental illness
insatanatus .... possessed of the devil
instivus .... congenital, hereditary
Ischias .... sciatica
Jammer .... crying of infants due to stomach-intestinal infection
(St.-) Jobst-Krankheit .... scurvy

Juck .... itching of the skin
Kaat .... tumor discharging pus
Kalte (Kaltweh) .... chills, intermittent
fever, malaria
Kancer .... malignant ulcer, cancer
Kartanie .... four-day intermittent fever
Kaule .... swelling, growth
(in the throat)
Kehlfluß .... cold in larynx, influenza
Kelch .... goiter
Keuchhusten .... whooping cough
Kindbettfieber .... childbed fever
Kinderbett gestorben, im....... died while
giving birth
Kinderblattern (-flecken)   pocks,
measles
Kinderlähmung .... infantile paralysis
Kinderpocken .... chicken pox
Knochenfraß .... caries, cancer
Knochenkrebs .... bone cancer
Knollsucht .... leprosy, scab, mange
Knüttel .... boil, tumor, lump
Kohl(e) .... carbuncle, bubo
Kolic .... colic
Kontagion .... contagious disease
Kontraktur .... cramp, paralysis
Kopfwasser .... hydrocephalus
Kofpwüstigkeit .... influenza
Korn .... glandular swelling
Kot .... carbuncle, cancer
Kotz .... coughing up, vomiting
Krampf .... cramps, convulsions
Krämpfe .... brain, nerve disease
Kränke .... general sickness,
also epilepsy
Krankheit, englische .... rickets
Krankheit, fallende .... epilepsy
Krankheit, flechtende .... dysentery
Krankheit, hitzige .... typhus
Krankheit, schlechte .... cancer
Krankheit, französische .... syphilis
(or spanische)
Krankheit, ungarische .... intermittent
fever, typhus,
dysentery
Krätze .... scabies
in Krämpfen bewusstlos   convulsions
while unconscious
krank .... sick, ill

Krankheit .... illness
Krebs .... cancer
Krebsgeschwür .... cancer
Krips .... grippe, influenza
Kropf .... goiter
Krupp .... croup
Landlauf .... (dysentery-) epidemic
Leid .... sickness, epilepsy
Lethargus .... somnolence, lethargy
Letze .... injury and its aftermath
Lues .... infectious disease
(not only venereal)
Lungenentzündung .... pneumonia
Lungenkatarrh .... pulmonary disease
Lungenschwindsucht   consumption,
tuberculosis
Lustfeuche .... syphilis
Magenkatarrh .... gastritis
Magenschwäche .... stomach disease
Mager .... frailty, skin abscess
Maledey (Maltzey, ... leprosy,
Malatzie)   cancer
malesanus .... mentally ill
mancus .... lame, maimed
Mandelbräune .... tonsillitis
Mandelentzündung .... tonsillitis
Mania .... madness
Marasmus (senilis) .... senility
Mase .... scar from wound or disease
Masel-, Miselsucht .... skin disease,
leprosy
Maser .... skin lumps, pimples;
measles
Masern .... measles
Melancholie .... depression
Meuchel .... concealed illness
Milzverhärtung .... anthrax
Miserere .... stomach-intestinal
infection; incurable
malady
Morbus regius .... leprosy
Mortalitas sacra .... epidemic, plague
Mückele, Mügele .... abscess, tumor
Möckele ....close to death
Mumps .... mumps
Mutterfrais .... convulsions
Mutter, grimme .... colic
Nachtschaden .... nightmares
Nascendiae .... labor pains

In a family stube

Nerven fieber .... typhus	(nürnbergischer, spanischer)
Nesselwurm .... tapeworm	Plage chronic disease, epidemic,
Noli me tangere .... tumor,	intermittent fever
("touch me not") cancer	Plemen .... wound
Nösch (Nosch) arthritis, rheumatismus,	Podagra, podager (foot) gout/
delirium	arthritis, lame
Not, kleine .... urinary disorder	Porpeln .... smallpox, measles, rubella
Not, schwere .... diarrhea, epilepsy	Puerperium .... delivery (of a child),
Ölschenkel .... running sore, ulcer	with child
orbus .... blind	Punctio laterum .... stitch in the side
Orexis .... vomiting	Pus .... pus, decay
Orke .... hoarseness	Pusseln (Pustella, ... pustules,
Palo .... contagious disease	Pustula) pimples, smallpox
Papula .... skin growths, eczema	Quartanfieber .... intermittent fever,
paralyticus .... lame	malaria
Paucken .... large tumor	(St.) Quirins-Marter ... cancer, pestilence
Pest .... plague	Rachenbräune .... diphtheria
Pestbeulen .... bubo	Räcke (Rähe) .... joint stiffness
Pfies .... tumor	Raude (böse .... itching skin
Pfneche .... asthma	Räudigkeit) disease
Pfnusel .... head cold	Rheuma .... head cold
Pocken .... smallpox	Riesel .... scarlet fever,
phlebotomare .... bleeding	measles, rubella
Phrenesia .... mental illness	Ritt .... chills, shivering
Pipf, Pips .... influenza	

Rittung .... shooting pains, rheumatism
Röt .... dysentery
rote Ruhr .... dysentery, measles
Rose .... inflammation
Röteln .... German measles
Rugitus .... stomach-intestinal complaints
Ruhr .... dysentery
ruhrartig .... dysenteric
ruhrkrank .... suffering from dysentery
Samenfluß .... gonorrhea
Sanies .... pus, discharge
Saucium .... wound
Scabea (Scabies) .... scabies
Schabe (Schapp) .... skin disease, scabies
Schäuerchen .... epilepsy
Scharbock .... scurvy
Scharre .... scabies, mange
Scharlach .... scarlet fever
Scharlachfieber .... scarlet fever
Scharte .... scars, mutilation
Schaumlöffelgeschwür .... carbuncle
Schlacht ....rash
Schlafkrankheit .... influenza (comafebrile)
Schlag(anfall) ....stroke
Schlagfluß .... apoplexy, stroke
Schleimfieber .... gastric fever, typhus
Schlier .... running sore, abscess
Schütt .... fever, chills
Schwäche .... debility, infirmity
Schwamm .... (cancer) tumor
Schwämme .... fungus
Schwartzgalligkeit .... depression
Schweine (Schwinde)........... emaciation
Schweißsucht .... heavy fever,
(englischer Schweiß, ... tuberculosis
Sudor anglicus) ....
Schwinden aller Glieder ....muscular atrophy
Schwindsucht .... consumption
Schwulst (Scirrhus) swelling, generally cancer
Scotonia .... fainting
Secund(in)ae ....afterbirth
Sehr .... inflammation, painful disease
Selbstmord .... suicide

Senium .... old-age debility
sensibus excessus .... unconscious
Seuche, ziehende epidemic, shooting pains
Sirey .... parasitic skin disease, leprosy
Soda .... abscess, typhus, headache following an infectious sickness
Sonnenschuß .... sunstroke
Spasmus .... cramp, convulsion
Speer .... muscle cramps
Squinantia .... tonsillitis, angina, sore throat
Staupe .... chills, plague as God's punishment
Staupe böse epilepsy, purulent skin disease with fever
Sterbensläufe .... (plague) epidemic
Stickfluß .... bronchitis, asthma
Stickfraisen .... convulsive coughing
Stigma .... scar, burn-scar
Stilopus .... swelling on the face, stye
Stranguria .... strangury, dysuria
Strumm, Struma .... goiter
Stuch .... influenza, rheumatism
Sucht .... epidemic with fever
Sucht, fallende .... epilepsy
Sudor letalis .... death fever
Suffosio .... cataract
Surdamen .... deafness
Sumpfieber .... swamp fever
Syncopa .... fainting, unconsciousness
Sync(h)lus .... continuous fever
Tabes (Tabitudo) .... consumption, tuberculosis
Tabes dorsalis .... spinal tuberculosis
Tabum .... pus, plague
Tannwätschel .... influenza
Terror leti .... foreboding of death
Tobsucht .... raving madness
Tod schwarzer ....plague
Torment .... stomach-intestinal infection, especially in children, dysentery, stomach cramps
Tortio .... stomach ache

Totenübel .... leprosy, cancer,
                                                   syphilis
toxicus .... poisoned, poisonous
Tribulatio .... ailments, distress
Trumsel .... dizziness,
                                              somnolence
Truncato .... mutilation, maiming
Tuberkulose .... tuberculosis
Typhus .... typhus
Ulceratio ....ı.............. stomach ulcer
Unflat .... excrement,
                                         feverish delirium
unbekannt .... unknown
unbestimmte .... undefined disease
Krankheit
Unfall .... accident
Unglück .... epilepsy, serious
                                          (chronic) illness
Unterleibstyphus .... typhoid
Urschlächten .... smallpox, smallpox
                              scars, measles, rubella
Varicosus .... varicose veins
Variola .... pockmarks
Venae sectio .... blood-letting
Vergicht .... rheumatism, arthritis
Verzehrung .... wasting away,
                                            consumptive
Vergiftung .... poisoning
Vesania .... mental illness
Vesicae petrae .... bladder stones
Veternus .... lethargy, somnolence
Vipex .... welts
Viscera .... viscera, intestines
Wasser am Auge ...... growths on the eye
Wasserkopf .... hydrocephalus
Wassersucht .... dropsy
Wehtag .... pain on certain days
                                              (e.g. at birth),
                                          epileptic seizure
Wesen, böses .... cramps, epilepsy,
                                        St. Vitus' dance
Wolf .... cancer, skin
                                           inflammation,
                                             bone caries
Weichselzopf matted hair infested by lice
weisse Ruhr .... diarrhea
Windpocken .... chicken pox
Wochenbettfieber .... childbed fever
Würgengel .... pestilence

Würmer .... worms
Wurmfieber .... intestinal cold,
                                                   typhus
Zahnfleischentzündung .... gingivitis
Zahnfieber .... gingivitis
Zahnung .... teething
Zehrmilbe   skin disease
                              (traceable to worms)
Zips .... influenza
Zwang .... diarrhea
Ziegenpeter .... mumps
Zuckung .... cramps, convulsions

FAMILY RELATIONSHIPS
VOCABULARY
German and Latin

Ahn(e) .... ancestor
Ahnfrau .... female ancestor
Ahnherr .... male ancestor
angenommenes Kind .... adopted child
Artschwager/(in) .... brother/
                              ˙ (sister)-in-law
Awwe .... grandmother
Base .... female cousin
Bessmoder, Bessmoer .... grandmother
Blutsfreund .... blood relative
Bruder .... brother
conius/conjus, ... spouse
coniux/conjus, Lat.
Cousin .... male cousin
Cousine .... female cousin
dogter (Dutch) .... daughter
Ehefrau .... wife
Ehegatte .... husband
Ehegattin .... wife
Ehem .... mother's brother: uncle
Ehemann .... husband
Ehni .... grandfather
Eltern .... parents
Elternpaar .... parents
En(c)kel-in .... grandson: -daughter
En(c)kelkind .... grandchild
En(c)kelsohn .... grandson
En(c)keltochter .... granddaughter
et exor, *Lat.* .... and wife
Findling .... foundling

FAMILY RELATIONSHIPS

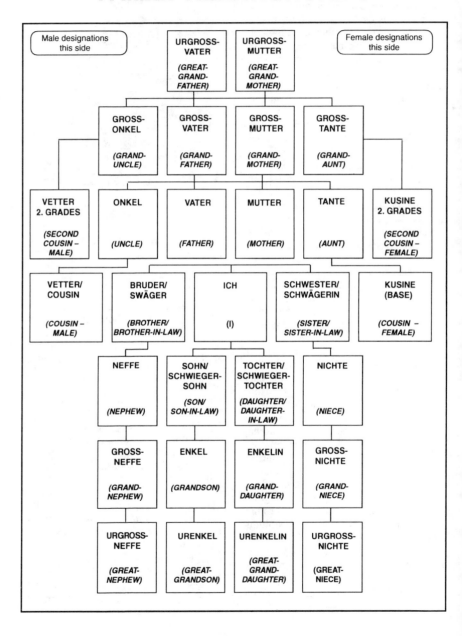

frater *Lat.* .... brother: cousin;
                brother-in-law; kinsman
frater consanguineus *Lat.* .... half-brother
frater germanus Lat. ...... son of a brother
frater uterinus *Lat.* .... half-brother
                (with same mother)
Frau .... woman; wife; Mrs./Ms.
Fräulein .... unmarried woman, miss
Gatte .... husband
Gattin .... wife
Gebärerin .... mother
Gemahl .... (male) spouse;
                (esteemed) husband
Gemahlin .... (female) spouse;
                (esteemed) wife
genetor *Lat.* .... father; begetter
genitores *Lat.* .... parents
genetrix *Lat.* .... mother
germanus *Lat.* .... (full) brother
germen *Lat.* .... descendant; son; junior
Geschäger .... brother-in-law
Geschwei/Geschwey   mother-in-law;
                sister-in-law
Geschwister .... siblings
Geswige .... sister-in-law
Geswiger .... brother-in-law
Gevatter .... godfather
Gevatterin .... godmother:
Grememm .... grandmother
grootmoeder (Dutch) .... grandmother
grootvader (Dutch) .... grandfather
Großeltern .... grandparents
Großen(c)kel/-in .... grandson,
                granddaughter
Großkind .... grandchild
Großmama/Großmutter   grandma,
                grandmother
Großpapa/Großvater   grandpa,
                grandfather
Großsohn .... grandson
Großtochter .... granddaughter
Halbbruder .... half-brother
Halbgeschwister .... half-siblings
Halbschwester .... half-sister
Halfbole .... half-brother
Hausehre .... wife; housewife
Hausvater ..... (father and) head of family
Hussfrow, Hußfraw .... wife
Kusine .... female cousin

liberi, *Lat.* .... children; grandchildren
Majoratserbe .... first son;
                heir by primogeniture
mater meretrix, *Lat.* .... mother of child
                born out of wedlock
matrinia, *Lat.* .... stepmother
Mauser .... son born out of wedlock
Nachfahr(e)/Nachkomme ..... descendant
Neffe .... nephew
Nichte .... niece
noverca, *Lat.* .... stepmother
novercus, *Lat.* .... stepfather
Omi/Oma .... grandma
Onkel .... uncle
Opi/Opa .... grandpa
Pate/Pathe .... godparents
Patenkind/Pathenkind .... godchild
Patensohn/Pathensohn .... godson
Patin, Pathin .... godmother,
                sometimes goddaughter
pater,*Lat.* .... father
pater familias, *Lat.* ..... father of a family
pater ignoratus, *Lat.* ...... father unknown
pater patris, *Lat.* .... father's father
pater sponsae, *Lat.* ..... father of the bride
patrui Lat. .... father's brother
Pflegekind .... ward; foster child
Pflegemutter .... foster mother

Pflegesohn/tochter ... foster son/daughter
Pflegevater .... foster father
prefigna/prefignus,Lat .... step-
daughter/stepson
progenita, *Lat.* .... daughter
progenitor *Lat.* (male) .... progenitor;
ancestor
progenitrix *Lat.* .... female ancestor
progenitus *Lat.* .... son
protavus Lat. .... great-grandfather
rechte Geschwister .... full siblings
Schnorr .... mother-in-law
Schnur(r) .... daughter-in-law
Schwager .... brother-in-law
Schwägerin .... sister-in-law
Schwägerschaft .... relationship
(through the spouse)
Schwäher .... father-in-law;
brother-in-law
Schweher, Schwehr .... father-in-law
Schwester .... sister
Schwesterkind .... sister's child
Schwestermann .... sister's husband;
brother-in-law
Schwestersohn .... sister's son; nephew
Schwestertochter .... sister's daughter;
niece
Schwieger .... mother-in-law
Schwieger- .... -in-law
Schwiegermutter .... mother-in-law
Schwiegereltern .... parents-in-law
Schwiegerkind .... child relative
through marriage
Schwiegersohn .... son-in-law
Schwiegervater .... father-in-law
Schwieger/Schwiegermutter ...... mother-
in-law
Schwippschwager/wägerin .... brother/
sister of one's brother-
in-law or sister-in-law
Schwöster .... sister
Seitenverwandte .... collateral relatives
Sibbe .... relatives
sobrina, *Lat.* .... (female)
(maternal first) cousin
socer, *Lat.* .... father-in-law
soceri, *Lat.* .... parents-in-law
socrinus, *Lat.* .... brother-in-law
socrus, *Lat.* .... mother-in-law

Sohn .... son
Söhnin/Sohnsfrau .... daughter-in-law
soror germana, *Lat.* .... half-sister
soror patruelis, *Lat.* .... nephew or niece
sororis filia, *Lat.* .... niece;
sister's daughter
sororis filius, *Lat.* ... nephew; sister's son
sororius, *Lat.* .... brother-in-law;
husband of sister
Stammverwandte(r) .... kin
Stiefbruder .... stepbrother; half-brothr
Stiefkind .... stepchild
Stiefmutter .... stepmother
Stiefschwester .... stepsister; half-sister
Stiefsohn .... stepson
Stieftochter .... stepdaughter
Stiefvater stepfather
struprator (Lat.): .... father of child born
out of wedlock
Suhnerin .... daugher-in-law
Süster .... sister
Tante .... aunt
Taufpaten .... godfather
Taufpatin .... godmother
Taufzeuge .... godfather
Taufzeugin .... godmother
Tochter .... daughter
Tochtermann .... son-in-law
Ullersmann .... father of the bride
Uren(c)kel .... great-grandson
Uren(c)kelin .... great-granddaughter
Uren(c)kelkind .... great-grandchild
Urgroßeltern .... great-grandparents
Urgroßkind .... great-grandchild
Urgroßmutter/vater .... great-
grandmother/grandfather
Urur- .... great-great-
uterini, Lat. .... half-siblings by
the same mother
uxor Lat. .... wife, spouse
vader (Dutch) .... father
Vater .... father
Vatersschwester .... father's sister
Vedeke .... cousin, aunt
vedova/vedovus, *Lat.* ... widow/widower
Verhältnis .... family relationship
Verwandtschaft .... relationship
Vetter .... cousin (male), relative
Vetternschaft .... cousins; relatives

vitrica, *Lat.* .... stepmother
vitricus, *Lat.* .... stepfather
Vorkinder .... stepchldren from
a former marriage
Vorsohn/Vortochter ..... stepson/daughter
from a previous marriage
Vorvater .... forefather
vrouw (Dutch) .... wife
Wäschen .... cousin; aunt
Weib(e); Wyb, Wyp .... wife
Witwe .... widow
Witwer .... widower
zuster (Dutch) .... sister
Zwillingsbruder/schwester .... twin
brother/sister
Zwillingskind .... twin child

Source: Most of the definitions above are based
on *German-English Genealogical Dictionary*,
by Ernests Thode. Genealogical Publishing Co.,
Inc., Baltimore, 1992

BIRTHS, CHRISTENINGS, GUARDIANSHIPS VOCABULARY

angenommenes Kind .... adopted child
Brautkind .... premarital child
ehelich .... born legitimate(ly),
in marriage
ehelos .... unmarried
geboren .... born
Geborene .... born
gebornene .... née (with maiden/birth
name)
Geburt .... birth
gebürtig: native .... by birth
Geburtsakt .... birth record
Geburtsanzeige .... printed birth
announcement
Geburtsbrief: .... birth letter
Geburtsdatum .... birth date
Geburtsfest .... celebration of a birth
Geburtshelfer(in) ... obstetrician, midwife
Geburtsjahr .... year of birth
Geburtsort .... place of birth
Geburtsregister .... birth register
Geburtsschein, ... birth certificate
Geburtszeugnis

Geburtsstätte: ...... house or place of birth
Geburtsurkunde .... birth documents
Geburtsverzeichnis .... birth index
getauft .... baptized
Getaufte .... the person baptized
Hebamme .... midwife
Herkunftszeugnis: .... proof of origin
Hurenkind .... illegitimate child
infans adulterinus .... child born out of
(or spurius) [Lat.]   wedlock
infantulus [Lat.] .... little child, infant
Jungfernkind .... child born out of
wedlock; first-born
Jüngste .... youngest one   (female)
Jüngster .... youngest one (male)
Kinderheim .... children's home,
foster home
kinderlos .... childless
Kindermädchen .... nanny
Kindervater .... father of a child
Kinderverding, ... contract for placement
Kinderzug   of a child
Kinderzahl .... number of children
Kindesabtreibung .... abortion
Kindesmutter .... (unmarried) mother;
Kindestaufe .... baptism of a child
Kindesvater .... father (of an out-of-
wedlock child)
Mutter .... mother
mutterlos .... motherless
Nottaufe .... emergency baptism
Pate .... godfather
Paten .... godparents
Pateneltern .... godparents
Patenkind .... godchild
Patin .... godmother
Söhnchen .... little son(s)
Stiefkind .... stepchild
Taufbücher .... christening records
Taufeltern .... godparents
Taufkind .... child being christened
Taufpate .... godfather
Taufpaten .... godparents
Taufpatin .... godmother
Taufprotokolle .... christening records
Taufregister .... christeninig register
Taufurkunde .... christening record
Taufzeuge .... godfather
Taufzeugin .... godmother

Emigrants on the Rhine

Totgeburt	stillbirth
unehelich	illegitimate
Vater	father
Vorkind(er)	stepchild(ren)
Vormund	guardian
Waise	orphan

MARRIAGE VOCABULARY

Ablobung:	(arranged) marriage
ac quaestus coniugalis	community property
acte de mariage (Fr.)	marriage certificate
Äe, Aee	marriage
affinitas (Lat.)	relationship through marriage
alliance (Fr.)	marriage
amensa et toro (Lat.)	divorced
angeheiratet	married into (a family)
ante nuptius (Lat.)	before the marriage; prenuptial
Anulehe s	ecret marriage
Anulfrau	secretly married woman
anverwandt	related by marriage
aufbieten	proclaim (marriage banns)
Aufgebotsverzeichnis	list of proclations (of marriage banns)
bans (Fr.)	(marriage) banns
bestatten (sich)	marry; (lit."bury oneself")
bigami (Lat.)	remarried widower
binuba/ binubus (Lat.)	woman/man married for second time
Braut	bride
Brautausstattung,- aussteuer	trousseau; dowry
Brautbitter	marriage arranger
Brauteltern	parents of the bride
Bräutigam	bridegroom
Brautkind	child born to an engaged couple
Brautleute/ Brautpaar	engaged couple; bride and bridegroom
Brautmacher	bridegroom
Brautmesse:	(Catholic) nuptial mass
Brautschatz:	dowry

Brautstand .... time of engagement;
                              betrothal
Brautsuche .... search for a wife
Brautmutter/-vater: .... bride's
                         mother/father
Brautwein: tax payable by newly married
couples
Brautwerber .... marriage arranger
Bruthavent .... dowry
Brutlacht .... wedding
Brutmaker/ .... bridegroom
Brutmann .... bridegroom;
                         witness at wedding
Brutschat(t) .... dowry
Civilehe .... civil marriage
collateralis (Lat.) .... wife
conjus, conjux: (Lat.) .... spouse
conjugatis (Lat.) .... married
Connubium .... marriage
connubius (Lat.) .... marriage
copulatio (Lat.) .... marriage
discidium (Lat.) .... separation; divorce
dos inter nuptias (Lat.) .... dowry
dos adventitia (Lat.) .. woman's property
                          brought to marriage
dos profectitia .... man's property
(Lat.)   brought to marriage
Eheberedung: .... marriage contract
Ehebücher .... marriage registers
Ehebündis .... wedlock
Ehefrau: wife .... married woman
Ehegatte .... husband
Eheherr(in) .... husband/wife
eheherrlich .... of husband's rights in a
                              marriage
Ehejahr .... year of marriage
Ehekonsens .... (parental) consent
                              to a marriage
Eheleute .... married couple
ehelichen: .... marry; wed
ehelos .... unmarried
Ehemakler .... matchmaker
Ehemangel .... reason for nullity
                              of a marriage
Ehemann .... husband; married man
Ehemittler(in) .... matchmaker
ehemündig .... of legal age to marry
Ehepaar .... married couple
Ehepaktenbuch .. marriage contract book

Ehepartner(in) .... spouse
Eheregister .... marriage register
Ehesakrament ..... sacrament of marriage
Ehescheidung .... divorce
Ehescheidungsklage .... petition for
                              divorce
Ehescheidungsurteil .... divorce decree
Eheschließung .... marriage
Ehestand .... matrimony
Ehestifter/(in) .... matchmaker \(male/
                              female)
eheunmündig ... not of legal age to marry
Eheverbot .... prohibition to marry
Eheverkündigung .... marriage
                              announcement
Ehevertrag .... marriage contract
eingeheiratet .... married into
enviandé/(e) .... married (male/female
épouse (Fr.) .... bride; wife
épouser (Fr.) .... marry
Fastenehe .... secret marriage
geheurat(h)et .... married
geschieden .... divorced
Heirat .... marriage
heiraten .... to marry
Heirat(h)sbüro .... marriage bureau
Heirat(h)sgesuch .... petition for marriage
                              permit
Heiratsakt .... marriage record
Heiratserlaubnis .... arriage permit
Heiratsgesuch .... petition for marriage
                              permit
Heiratsgut .... dowry
Heiratsregister register of marriages
Heiratsrottel .... marriage contract
Heiratsstifter .... matchmaker
Heiratsurkunde .... marriage record
Heiratsvermittler .... matchmaker
Heiratsversprechen .... engagement
                              (to marry)
Heiratsvertrag .... marriage contract
Heurat(h) .... marriage
heymelike Ehe .... secret marriage
Hillcheit .... marriage
Hochzeitsbrauch .... marriage rites
Hochzeitszeremoniell .... wedding
                              ceremony
Hürat(h)en .... to marry
innuba, innupta (Lat.) .... unmarried

Amana Colony: Grace before meat
Courtesy of the German Information Center

innubus, innupta (Lat.) .... unmarried (female) (male)
iugere (Lat.) .... join; marry
Josephsehe .... quasi-marriage
Keuschheitsehe .... unconsummated marriage
kirchenrufen .... proclaim (marriage) banns
Konkubinat .... common-law marriage
Konleute .... married couple
Kopulation .... marriage
Kriegstrauung .... wartime wedding
ledig .... unmarried; single
Ledige/r .... unmarried woman/man
liber matrimoniorum ... marriage register
Liebesheirat .... marriage for love; love match
marier (Fr.) .... get married
mariés (Fr.) .... married couple
matrimonia (Lat.) .... marriage
matrimonium .... secret marriage clandestinum (Lat.)

matrimonium .... secret marriage conscientiae (Lat.)
matrimonium .... unconsummated claudicans (Lat.) marriage
matrimonium .... unequal (in status) morganaticum (Lat.) marriage
matrimonium .... invalid marriage putativum (Lat.)
matrimonium .... unconsummated virgineum (Lat.) marriage
neosponsa/ .... bride/bridegroom neosponsus (Lat.)
Notzivilehe .... emergency civil marriage
nouveaux-mariés (Fr.) .... newlyweds
nuptiae (Lat.) .... marriage
Nupturienten .... bride and groom
ongehuwd (Dutch) .... unmarried
pacta dotalia (Lat.) ..... marriage contract
pactum connubiatis .... marriage contract (Lat.)
Proclamation(en) .... proclamation of the marriage banns
Quasimatrimonium .... quasi-marriage;

unconsummated marriage
reconciliatio .... (second) marriage,
this time before
clergy with jurisdiction
Reinigungseid .... oath of marital fidelity
relicta/relictus (Lat.) ..... widow/widower
Ringehe .... secret marriage
(esp. of priests in Middle Ages)
sacro ledo .... married after a mass
copulati (Lat.)
schecken .... get engaged
without parental permission
Scheidung .... divorce
secunda vota (Lat.) .... second marriage
sedes vidualis (Lat.) .... widowhood
separatio a .... separation from bed
T(h)oro et   and board
Trauzeuge,   best man at a wedding
erster
Trauzeuge, ... groomsman
zweiter   (at a wedding)
Trauzeugnis .... marriage certificate
Truwe l .... oyalty; marriage
Truwe, heymelike .... secret marriage
Ullersmann .... father of the bride
unverheiratet .... unmarried
vacara/ .... unmarried
vacarus (Lat.)   (female/male)
verehelichungsbücher .... marriage
registers
uxor (abbrev. ux.) (Lat.) .... wife; spouse
uxor militaris (Lat.) .... soldier's wife
uxorata/-is (Lat.) .... female/male
uxoratis (Lat.) .... married
vacara/-us (Lat.) .... unmrried
(female/male)
verehelichen .... marry
verehelicht .... married
Verehelichung .... marriage; wedding
Verkündigen .... proclaim
(marriage banns)
Verkündigung .... proclamation
(of marriage banns)
verlobt .... engaged
Vermühlen (sich) .... (formally) marry
vermählt .... (formally married)
Vermählung .... (formal) marriage
Vermählungsanzeige .... marriage
announcement

Verwandtenehe .... marriage between
(blood) relatives
vierge (Fr.) ...... virgin; unmarried woman
wiederverheiratet, ... remarried
wiedergeheiratet
Wiederheirat, ... remarriage
Wiederverehelichung
wiederverehelicht .... remarried
Witfrau, Witib, ... widow
Wittib, Wittwe
Witmann, Wittiber, ... widower
Wittler, Wittling, Wittmann
Wittwenschaft .... widowhood
Würt .... husband
Why, Wyp .... wife; woman

DEATH VOCABULARY

acte de décès (Fr.) .... death certificate
annales funesti (Lat.) .... death register
beerdigen .... to bury, inter
Beerdigung .... burial
Begräbnis .... burial
Bestattung .... burial, funeral
Erbschaft .... inheritance
Erbsteuer .... death or estate duties
Friedhofsparzelle .... cemetery lot
Friedhof .... cemetery
Friedhofsprotokoll .... cemetery record
gesetzlicher Erbe .... legal heir
gestorben .... dead, died
Grab .... grave, tomb, sepulchre
Grabgeleit .... funeral procession
Grabgewölbe .... tomb, vault
Grablegung ..... burial, interment, funeral
Grabrede .... funeral oration, eulogy
Grabschrift .... epitaph, inscription
Grabstätte .... burial place, grave, tomb
Grabstein .... grave stone
Graburne .... funeral urn
Hinterlassenschaft .... (testator's) estate
Leiche .... corpse, remains
Leichenacker .. cemetery, burying ground
Leichenausgrabung .... exhumation
Leichenbegängnis .... funeral, burial
Leichenbegleiter .... mourner
Leichenbegleitung ..... funeral procession
Leichenbeschau .... inspection of body;

The customs house, Jena

inquest
Leichenbeschauer .... coroner; medical examiner
Leichenbesichtigung .... inspection of body; inquest
Leichenbesorger .... undertaker
Leichenbestatter .... undertaker
Leichenbestattung .... funeral, burial
Leichenbitter .... person who invites persons to a funeral
Leichenbuch .... book of the deceased
Leicheneröffnung .... autopsy
Leichenfeier .... funeral service
Leichengeburt ...... birth of child after its mother's death
Leichengefolge .... funeral procession
Leichengewölbe .... burial vault
Leichengruft .... burial vault
Leichenhalle, Leichenhaus .... mortuary
Leichenkapelle .... mortuary chapel
Leichenpredigt .... funeral sermon
Leichenrede .... funeral sermon
Leichenschauhaus .... morgue
Leichenschmaus .... funeral meal
Leichenstein .... tombstone
Leichenträger .... pallbearer
Leichenverbrennung .... cremation

Leichenwache .... death vigil, wake
Leichenwagen .... hearse
Leichenzug .... funeral procession
Leichnam .... corpse
Leichsstein .... burial stone in a church
Leicht .... burial
Leich(t)mann .... undertaker, funeral director
Leich(t)versorger ..... undertaker, funeral director
letzter Wille .... last will
letztwillig .... in the will
Mord .... murder
obiit (Lat.) .... (he; she; it) died
obire (Lat.) .... die; go away
obita (Lat.) .... dead (female)
obitus (Lat.) .... dead (male)
Parta .... obituary notice
Sterbedatum .... date of death
Sterbeeintrag .... death record
Sterbegeld .... death benefit (of mutual aid society)
Sterbekasse ..... (funeral) benefit fund (of mutual aid society)
Sterbelager .... deathbed
sterben .... die
sterbenskrank .... deathly sick

Sterberegister .... register of deaths
Sterbesakrament .... last rites
Sterblichkeit .... mortality (statistic)
Testament .... last will and testament
Tod .... death
Todesanzeige .... death notice
Todesdatum .... date of death
Todeseintrag .... death entry
Todeserklärung ... (official) declaration of
death of a missing person
Todesfall .... a death (or casualty,
as in war)
Todeskampf .... death struggle;
death throes
Todesmesse .... funeral mass
Todesnachweis .... proof of death
Todestag .... anniversary of a death
Todesursache .... cause of death
Todfallsgeld .... money paid by a
burial fund
todkrank .... deathly ill
tot .... dead
To(d)tenbuch .... book of deaths
To(d)tenhof .... cemetery
To(d)tenregister .... death register
to(d)tgeboren .... stillborn
Totenacker .... cemetery
Totenamt .... burial service
Totenausleger .... undertaker
Totenbahre .... bier
Totenbeschauer .... physician
attesting death;
medical examiner;
coroner
Totenbett .... deathbed
Totenbuch .... book of the dead
Totenfeier .... funeral rites
Totenfest .... festival in
commemoration
of the dead
Totenfrau .... female undertaker
Totengebet .... prayer for the dead
Totengedächtnis .... memorial service
for the dead
Totengeläutbuch .... death knell record
Totengeleit .... funeral cortege
Totengesang .... funeral dirge
Totenglocke .... death knell
Totengottesdienst .... funeral service;

memorial service
Totengräber ...... grave digger, undertaker
Totengruft .... vault, sepulchre
Totenhalle, Totenhaus .... mortuary;
funeral home
Totenhof .... cemetery
Totenkirche .... memorial chapel
Totenklage .... dirge, wake
Totenlade .... coffin
Totenlied .... funeral dirge
Totenliste .... list of deaths
Totenmann .... undertaker
Totenmesse .... mass for the dead
Totenname .... name of the deceased
Totenregister .... register of deaths
Totenschein .... death certificate
Totenschau .... coroner's inquest;
post-mortem examination
Totenverbrennung .... cremation
Totenwache .... death vigil; wake
Totenwagen .... hearse
Totenzeugnis .... death certificate
toter Leib .... dead body
totgeboren .... stillborn
Totgeburt .... stillbirth
totgesagt .... reported dead
totsagen .... declare dead
Trauergottesdienst .... funeral service
Tumulus (Lat.) .... grave
Verstorbene .... deceased (person)
Waise .... orphan
wijlen (Dutch) .... deceased
Wurmfrass .... being eaten by worms

LEGAL AND COURT TERMINOLOGY

Abhilfe .... remedy or cure
Aburteilung .... trial
Advocat .... lawyer
Amtmann .... district judge
Amtsrichter .... county judge
Amtsvogt .... district judge
Anwalt .... lawyer
Appellationsgericht .... court of appeal
Behörde .... authority, board,
department

Berufungsgericht .... appeals court
Beweismittel .... evidence
Bundesgericht .... federal court
                                                    or tribunal
Bundesverfassungs- .... federal
gericht   constitutional court
Entscheidung .... legal decision
Erbgericht i .... nheritance court
Erlaß .... decree, edict
Gau(Go-) .... regional district,
Gericht   provincial court
gelehrte Richter .... learned judge
Gemeindegericht .... municipal court
Gerichts Buch .... court record
Gerichts Protokolle .... court record
Gerichts Schöffen ..... court of lay judges
                                          or or jury courts
Gerichtsakten .... court records
Gerichtsbezirk .... circuit court,
                                          judicial district court
Gerichtshof ... court of justice, law court
Gerichtsurteil ...... judgment of the court
Handelsgericht .... court dealing
                                            with commerce
Hofgericht .... appellate court
Kammergericht .... supreme court
Kirchengericht .... ecclesiastical court
Kreisgericht .... court of an
                                    administrative district
Kreisrichte ...... r county or district judge
Landesgericht .... law ofthe land/
                                          municipal law
Landmarschallschen- .... appellate
gericht   court
öffentlich .... public
Patrimonialgericht .... court on a
                                            noble estate
Polizeibehörden .... police authorities
Prozeß .... lawsuit, trial, litigation
Recht .... right, law, justice,
               '   due process of law
Rechtsanwalt .... lawyer
Rechtsordnung .... legal system
Reichsgesetz .... federal law
Reichsverfassung .... constitution of
                                          the German Empire
Richter .... judge
Scharfrichter ...... executioner, hangman
Schöffe .... lay judge

Schöffengericht .... court with trial
                                          by jury
Schultheißegericht .... local or
                                          communal court
Staatsrecht ... consitutional or public law
Stadtgericht .... city court
Stadtrecht .... city law, municipal law
Strafgericht .... criminal court
Strafmittel .... disciplinary matters
Untergericht .... lower court
Urteil .... judgment, decision,
                                          sentence, verdict
Verbrechen .... crime, felony
Vorschriften .... rule, regulation
Zivilprozeß .... civil action

COURTS OF THE GERMAN EMPIRE

German courts of the German Empire, from 1877, from lowest to highest:

♦*Amtsgericht* (county court): jurisdiction in petty criminal and civil cases; the *Amtsrichter* was the judge. The *Amtsgericht* was presided over by a single judge, whose jurisdiction covered petty criminal and civil cases, up to 300 marks. Petty criminal cases were heard by the Amtsrichter sitting with two *Schöffen* (assessors) selected by lot from the jury lists. Prisoners were tried for offenses punishable with a fine not exceeding 600 marks or confinement, or with imprisonment of not more than three months.

♦*Landgericht:* (regional court): revised the decisions of the *Amtsgerichte*, had original jurisdiction in criminal and civl cases and in divorce proceedings The *Landgericht* could revise the decisions of the *Amtsgerichte*.

♦ *Oberlandesgericht* (higher regional court): had original jurisdiction in grave offences; it was composed of seven judges. There were 28 such courts in the empire in 1910. Only Bavaria had an *Oberstes Landesgericht* which could revise the action of the *Oberlandesgericht*.

♦*Reichsgericht* (supreme court): composed of 92 judges, called *Reichsgerichts-räte*, appointed by the emperor. The supreme court seat was at Leipzig.

The *Rechtsanwalt*, or advocate, was required to study law at a university for four years and to pass two state examinations in order to be admitted to practice by the *Amtsgericht* or *Landgericht*.

Source: *Encyclopedia Britannica: Dictionary of Arts, Sciences, Literature and General Information.* University Press, New York, 11th ed. 1910

NOBILITY AND ROYALTY TERMINOLOGY

Adel .... nobility, aristocracy
Adeliger .... nobleman
Adelsstand .... nobility
Baron .... baron
Burggraf .... burgrave
Edelknecht .... squire
Edelmann .... nobleman
Freiherr/Freiherrin .... baron/baroness or *Freifrau*
Fürst/(-in) .... prince/princess
Fürstentum .... principality
Graf/Gräfin .... count/countess
Grafschaft .... county
Großherzog/-in .... grand duke/grand duchess
Großherzogtum .... duchy
Herr .... master, lord, Lord
Herrengut .... noble estate
Herrschaft .... domain
Herzog/(-in) .... duke/duchess
Herzogtum .... duchy
Kaiser/(-in) .... emperor/empress
Kanzler .... chancellor
König/-in .... king/queen
Königreich .... kingdom
Krönprinz .... crown prince
Kurfürst .... elector
Kurfürstentum .... electorate
Landgraf .... landgrave, count
Landgräfin .... landgravine/landraviate, countess
Landgrafschaft ...... landgraviate, county
Landgut .... country estate
Mark .... march, borderland
Markgraf/ .... margrave/margravine
Markgräfin marquis/marquise
Markgrafschaft .... margraviate, marquisage
Pfalzgraf .... Earl, count palatine
Pfalzgraf .... Count Palatinate/Palatine
Prinz/-essin .... prince, princess
Reichsfreiherr .... baron (prince of the Holy Roman Empire)
Ritter .... knight
Rittergut .... knight's estate
Ritterorden .... order of knighthood
Ritterschaft .... knighthood
Truchseß .... lord high steward

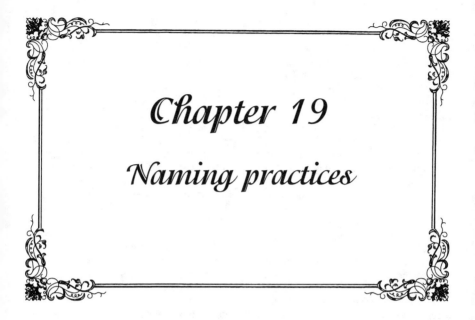

Chapter 19
Naming practices

A BRIEF HISTORY OF GERMAN NAMES

Germanic names

Originally, sons and daughters born into Germanic tribes had but one name, which consisted mostly of two words or syllables like,

Bernhart: *bêr* (bear) + *hart* (strong)
Kuonrad: *kuon* (bold) + *rad* (advise)

Other words or syllables like these were often used –

- ✦*ger* (spear)
- ✦*hari* (army)
- ✦*brant* (sword)
- ✦*wulf* (wolf)
- ✦*run* (magic)

– showing that Germanic names usually revolved around bravery, glory, honor, battles, victory, prosperity – things and ideas held in high esteem.

Very early abbreviations and endearing short forms of these names – today called *Kosename* (endearing or shortened famil-iar forms of names) came into use, especially for children:

Bernhart >> Bernd
Kuonrad >> Kuno, Kurt
Audomar >> Otto
Hugibert >> Hugo

Many of these old Germanic names, especially their abbreviated forms, still exist and are widely used as given names (*Vorname*) today.

Christian names (Taufnamen)

During the early days of Christianity in Germany, it was mostly adults who converted and were baptized. The church did not require them to change their Germanic names, but this happened nevertheless, following the example of the Roman Saulus, who became *Paulus*. In this way, biblical names and names of saints and martyrs of Hebrew, Greek and Latin origin came into use.

When the idea of baptizing infants (around the third century) gained ground, this ceremony usually coincided with the naming of the child. The name given to the child was therefore called the *Taufname* (Christian name).

Only after the Council of Trent, in the catechism of 1566, did the Roman Catholic Church require that a child must be given the name of a saint. Often (but not always) the name of the saint was chosen whose day of commemoration the calendar showed on the child's birthday. In case the dates differed, this created a tradition of celebrating the child's *Namenstag* (name day) in addition to (or instead of) his or her birthday. For example, a boy born on July 10 and named Nikolaus celebrates his *Namenstag* on December 6. This tradition is still alive today in predominantly Catholic regions like Bavaria and the Rhineland.

Maria and *Joseph* (*Josef*) thus became the most popular names – to such a degree that boys were named *Maria* (in addition to another first name – like the composer Carl-Maria von Weber) or girls *Josephine* or *Josefa*. Other popular Christian names were *Joachim* and *Anna* (names ascribed to the parents of Maria) and *Elisabeth*, the name ascribed to the mother of John, the Baptist (*Johannes der Täufer*). Next were the four evangelists *Matthäus, Markus, Lukas and Johannes* – followed by the apostles *Andreas, Bartholomäus, Jakobus, Thomas, Johannes, Matthäus, Matthias, Petrus, Philippus, Simon and Thaddäus* (*Judas* was omitted).

Archangels chosen as namesakes were *Gabriel, Michael,* and *Raphael.* The names of the 14 *Nothelfer* (saints as helpers in need) also were used: *Achatius, Ägidius, Barbar, Blasius, Christopherus, Cyriak, Dionysius, Erasmus, Eustachius, Georg, Katharina, Margarete, Pantalon,* and *Vitus.* Even popes' names became popular choices: *Alexander, Anastasius, Benedict, Eugen, Felix, Gregor, Klemens, Leo, Linus, Paul, Pius, Stephan.*

Some of these Latin names were germanized: *Antonius* >>*Anton*; *Augustus* >> *August*; *Aemilius* >>*Emil.*

Greek names were introduced and adopted in a similar way, including *Agatha, Andreas, Barbara, Christoph, Helene, Katharina, Peter, Petra, Sophie,* and *Theodor.*

The use of the names of saints and popes was of course restricted to Roman Catholic areas, as Protestants did not believe in these ideas. They used names from the Old and New Testaments as Christian names or (later, in the Pietist movement of the seventeenth and eighteenth centuries) invented new names like *Gottlieb* (loves God or loved by God), *Leberecht* (live a decent life), or *Fürchtegott* (fear God).

Family names
(last names)

With an increasing population and interaction between its members, soon one Christian name was no longer sufficient for distinguishing persons from one another. Thus, "important," aristocratic families started to add the name of their origin (region or location of a castle) to their Christian names (Rudolf von Habsburg), thus creating in Germany by the eleventh century the concept of the *Familien* name (family name). Since it was added to the Christian name – that is, it came after it – it is also called *Nachname* or *Zuname* (last name).

This same idea was employed by commoners (*Konrad von Würzburg, Walter von der Vogelweid*). Not until about 1800 was the prefix "von" definitely restricted to show an aristocratic lineage.

By the thirteenth/fourteenth century, the use of family names had spread to most of the population. Either the name of the father (*Patronym*) was added (*Martin, Ernst, Paul*), or the region of origin (*Schwab* = Swabia, *Heß* = Hessia), the hometown (*Nürnberger, Darmstädter*), the profession (*Bäcker* = baker, *Bauer* = farmer, *Schmidt* = smith, *Schneider* = tailor) or bodily or intellectual characteristics (*Klein* = small, *Klug* = smart).

Most of the Jewish population adopted

family names only after being forced to do so by local laws in the eighteenth and early nineteenth centuries. These names ranged from choices like *Lilienthal* (valley of the lilies) and neutral names like *Schwabacher* to obvious insults forced upon the unfortunate applicant by antisemitic bureaucrats (*Kanalgeruch* = smell from the sewer, *Bauchfleck* = birthmark on the belly).

The Humanist period (around the sixteenth/seventeenth centuries) with its revival of ancient Greek and Roman ideals led some families to use Latin versions (*Molitor* for *Müller, Pastorius* for *Schäfer*) or Greek versions (*Melanchthon* for *Schwarzerd*) of their German names.

In Germany, the general practice was always for a woman to adopt her husband's family name upon marriage. However, sometimes a husband would add his wife's family name to his own (*Mendelssohn - Bartholdy*).

Some confusion can arise from the fact that some names, like *Karl, Otto* or *Heinrich* can be used both as first and last names, so documents should be checked carefully as to which name is the *Vorname* and which one is the *Nachname* or *Familienname*.

Hofnamen
(names of farms)

In rural areas, the owners of a farm sometimes are known to their neighbors by a totally different family name than the one shown in the birth or marriage register. This can happen when the original, often centuries-old, name of a farm is passed on despite changes in the owners' names. So a farm once owned by a family named *Pfleger* was known as *Pflegerhof* (Pfleger's farm). Today's owner may still be called Pfleger (now deriving his name from the farm), even though his official name is Maier.

This is called his *Hofname* (name of the farm).

When a farmer has taken on the name of his farm, a double surname may result.

Look for the words *oder* (or) and *genannt* (called) connecting double surnames.

Vornamen
(given names) today

A *Vorname* is basically the same as the *Taufname* except that this word takes into account that, with the start of the Age of Enlightenment in Germany (around the seventeenth century), religious influences generally receded. Therefore the naming of children was less likely to be connected with their baptism. The word *Vorname* states neutrally that this name is the one that stands before the family name.

Choice of first names was increasingly secularized and in the nineteenth and early twentieth centuries turned to names of kings, emperors, and other political leaders (*Friedrich, Wilhelm, Ludwig*). For obvious reasons, the popularity of *Adolf* dropped abysmally after 1945.

Although most Germans today have more than one "first" name, this additional name is rarely used or represented by a middle initial. While the conventional view on this may change, its use is often considered "showy" like a loud tie. When two "first" names are used, it is most often in hyphenated form, like *Franz-Xaver* or *Hans-Jochen*.

Official registration
of names

Since the fourteenth century (there are regional variations), parishes kept track of their members by entries and updates in the *Kirchenbücher* or *Pfarrbücher* (church registers). It belonged to the priest's or pastor's most important duties to keep current the *Tauf-, Firmungs-, Trauungs* and *Totenbücher* (baptism-, confirmation-, marriage- and death records). The names recorded therein became the official, legally binding names of a person.

While these church records are still kept today for church purposes, since 1876 and the introduction of the law called the *Reichspersonenstandsgesetz,* the legally binding names are those officially registered by the *Standesamt* (registry office).

The Rufname

Often more than one first name is given to a child (aristocrats may have a dozen or so) and entered in the birth register. Usually the first one of those names was the one by which the parents wanted the child to be primarily known and called – therefore this is the *Rufname*, sometimes called the *Nenner*. As further clarification, the registrar underlines the *Rufname* when it is recorded in the church registry. This is not forever binding for the person involved, who later on in life may choose one of his other names as a *Rufname*. However, a person may not – in a legal and officially binding way – choose an altogether new name.

Source: Rainer Thumshirn, of Heimstetten, Germany

SOME ODDITIES IN NAMING PRACTICES

♦ The surname of a woman was often represented by an *-in* ending —for example, *Schneiderin* as the female form of *Schneider*. The *-chen* ending on a given name signifies smallness, as in *Gretchen* (little Grete).

♦ A name may have been recorded or transcribed in different languages in different time periods. For example, the German name *Johann (Hans)* might have been recorded as *Jean* in French, as *Johannes* in Latin, or as *Jan* in Polish.

♦ Variant spellings of names occurred according to similarities in pronunciation of certain letters of the alphabet, like these, for example,

♦ v and f	♦ j and y
♦ b and p	♦ k and g
♦ b and v	♦ ch and gh
♦ f and ph	♦ s and z
♦ t and d	♦ k and c
♦ m and n	♦ g and ch
♦ z and tz	

♦ In past times, how a name was spelled was unimportant. How it was pronounced was what counted. Many people could pronounce their own names, but they could not write or spell them.

♦ Persons in a community with identical names were distinguished from one another by adding terms that separated them by age, like *alt-* (old), *älter* (older), *ältest* (oldest); *jung-* (young), *junger* (younger), *jungst* (youngest); *mitteln* (middle); and I, II, and III. These indicators usually pointed to differences in the ages of same-name persons, not blood relationships. For example, three men named Karl Hartmann, might be recorded as *Karl Hartmann d. [der] jungste,* (Karl Hartmann the youngest), *Karl Hartmann d. mittlere* (the Karl Hartmann who is not the eldest or the youngest), and *Karl Hartmann d. älteste* (Karl Hartmann the eldest). Likewise, the identifiers I, II, and III separate men by age and do not necessarily infer family relationships.[1]

[1] Arta F. Johnson, *How to Read German Church Records without Knowing Much German.* The Copy Shop, Columbus, OH, 1981.

ABBREVIATED VERSIONS OF GERMAN GIVEN NAMES

The names in the left column below are abbreviated versions of the first names shown at the right, which persons may prefer to use in everyday life instead of their officially registered first names:

Male names

Achim	Joachim
Adi	Adolf
Alex	Alexander
Alf	Alfred
Alois	Aloysius
Andi, Andrä, Anderl	Andreas
Armin	Hermann
Arno	Arnold, Arnulf
Ben	Benedikt, Benjamin
Bernd	Bernhard

Bert, Berti .... Albert, Herbert, Hubert,
                    Norbert, Bertram,
                    Engelbert
Chris, ... Christian,
Christoph   Christopherus
Claus .... Claudius, Nikolaus
Curd, Curt, Conny .... Konrad
Didi, Dieter .... Diethelm, Dietmar,
                                       Dietrich
Dolf   Adolf
Edi .... Edgar, Eduard
Ferdi, Fertl .... Ferdinand
Fips .... Philipp
Fonse .... Alfons
Fred .... Alfred
Friedel, Frieder .... Gottfried, Friedrich
Fritz, Fred .... Friedrich
Gerd, Gert .... Gerhard(t), Gernot
Götz .... Gottfried
Gus, Gustl, Gussi .... Gustav, August
Hans, Hannes .... Johannes
Harry .... Harald, Heinrich
Hein, Heini, Heiner, ... Heinrich
Heinz, Heiko,
Heino, Hinz
Herbert .... Hubertus
Hias .... Matthias
Ingo .... Ingolf
Iwan .... Johannes
Jan, Janosch .... Johannes
Jackel .... Jakob
Jochen, Jockel .... Joachim
Jörg .... Georg
Jos .... Joseph
Juan .... Johannes
Jupp .... Joseph
Kirsten .... Christian
Klaus .... Nikolaus
Konny .... Konrad
Lenz .... Lorenz
Leo .... Leonard(t), Leopold
Lois .... Alois
Louis .... Ludwig
Luggi .... Ludwig, Lukas
Lutz .... Ludwig
Manne, Manni, Männer .... Manfred
Max .... Maximilian
Matz, Matthes .... Matthias
Mewes .... Bartholomäus

Naz, Nazi .... Ignaz
Niels .... Nikolaus
Olli .... Oliver
Pit .... Peter
Poldi .... Leopold, Luitpold
Rolf, Ralf .... Rudolph
Roger .... Rüdiger
Rudi .... Rudolph
Schorsch .... Georg
Sepp .... Joseph
Sigi .... Siegfried
Simmerl .... Simon
Steffen .... Stephan
Stoffel .... Christoph
Theo, Teo .... Theodor
Thies .... Matthias
Thilo .... Dieter
Tim .... Timotheus
Tobi .... Tobias
Tom .... Thomas
Toni .... Anton
Ulf .... Wolfgang
Uli, Ulli .... Ulrich
Wasti, Wastl .... Sebastian
Wiggerl .... Ludwig
Willi, Willy, Wim .... Wilhelm
Winni .... Winfried
Wolf, Wulf .... Wolfgang

Female names

Alex .... Alexandra
Alice...................................... Elisabeth
Andi .... Andrea
Angela, Angi .... Angelika
Anja, Änne, Anna, Antje .... Annette
Annegret .... Anna Margarete
Annemarie, Annamirl .... Anna Maria
Babsi .... Babette
Bärbel .... Barbara
Bea .... Beate
Bessie .... Elisabeth
Betty .... Elisabeth, Bettina,
                                       Babette
Birgit .... Brigitte
Burgi, Burgl .... Walburga
Carola .... Caroline
Christa, Christel .... Christina
Claire .... Clara, Klara
Conny .... Cornelia, Constanze
Dorte, Dörte .... Dorothea

Edda	Adelheid
Elfi	Elfriede
Elke, Ellen, Elise, Else	Elisabeth
Erna	Ernestine
Emma	Emmerentia
Eva	Evelyn
Fanny, Franzi	Franziska
Finny, Fine	Josefine
Friedl	Friederike
Gabi	Gabriele
Geli	Angelika
Gerda, Gerdi	Gertrude
Gigi	Gisela, Brigitte
Gila	Gisela
Gina	Regina
Gitte, Gitti	Brigitte
Grete	Margarete
Gunda, Gundi	Gundula, Gunhild, Kunigunde
Gusti	Augustine, Gustava
Hanna	Johanna
Hedda	Hedwig
Heidi	Heidemarie
Hella	Helene, Helena
Helma	Wilhelmine
Henny	Henriette
Hetty	Henriette
Hilde	Hildegard, Brunhilde, Gernhilde, Mathilde
Inge	Ingeborg
Ika	Veronika
Ilona	Helene
Ilse	Elisabeth
Ina, Ines	Agnes
Irma, Irmi	Irmengard
Isa, Isabella	Elisabeth
Jean, Jenny	Johanna
Jella	Gabriele
Karin, Katrin, Käthe, Kati, Katja	Katharina
Karola	Karoline
Kerstin	Christine
Lena, Lene, Leni	Magdalena, Marlene, Helene
Lia, Lisa, Lise, Liesel, Lissi	Elisabeth, Lieselotte
Lilo	Lieselotte
Lina, Line	Pauline
Lore	Eleanore, Hannelore

Lotte	Lieselotte
Magda	Magdalena
Margit, Margot, Margret	Margaretha
Marion	Maria
Marlene	Maria Helena
Marlis	Maria Elisabeth
Mascha, Mia	Maria
Minna	Wilhelmiine
Mirjam	Maria
Nelli	Cornelia
Nora	Eleonore
Resi	Therese
Rita	Roswitha
Rose	Rosemarie, Roswitha
Sandra	Alexandra
Sigi	Sigrid, Sieglinde
Silke	Gisela
Sissi, Sissy	Elisabeth
Stasi	Anastasia
Steffi	Stephanie
Susi	Susanne
Thea	Dorothea, Theolinde
Tina, Tine	Christina
Toni	Antonia
Traudl	Gertraud, Waltraud, Edeltraud
Trude, Trudi	Gertrude, Wiltrud
Ulla, Ursel, Uschi	Ursula
Uli, Ulli	Ulrike
Vera, Vroni	Veronika, Verena
Wally	Walburga, Waltraud
Wilma	Wilhelmine
Zenzi	Creszenzia

PATRONYMIC NAMES

The patronymic naming system incorporated the name of the father into the name of the child. Generally, in Scandanavia a male infant would be named after the father's given name, followed by "son" or "sen." For females it would be followed by "datter" or "dotter."

For example Carl, the son of Peter Hansen, would be named Carl Peterson, not Carl Hansen.

The use of this system was prevalent in the areas of Schleswig-Holstein,

Hannover, northern Rheinland, and Westfalen.

Laws were passed in various areas in the eighteenth and nineteenth centuries to establish permanent surnames: In 1771 such a law was passed in the Schleswig area; in 1811 in Ostfriesland; in Prussia in 1816.[1]

[1] "The World of Germanic Names: Or, a German by Any Other Name May Be Your Ancestor," *German Genealogical Digest,* Vol. IV, No. 1, 1988.

FURTHER READING ON NAMING PRACTICES

♦Hans Bahlow, *Dictionary of German Names,* translated by Edda Gentry. Friends of the Max Kade Institute for German-American Studies, Inc. Madison, Wisconsin, 1993.

♦George F. Jones, *German American Names,* 2nd Edition. Genealogical Publishing Co., Baltimore, MD, 1995.

♦"The World of Germanic Names, or A German by Any Other Name May be Your Ancestor," by Larry O Jensen, *German Genealogical Digest.* Part I, Vol. 4, No. 1, 1988; Part II, Vol 4, No. 2, 1988.

♦Larry O. Jensen, *A Genealogical Handbook of German Research,* rev. ed. Logan, UT, 1995.

♦ *Germany Research Outline,* Family History Library, The Church of Jesus Christ of Latter-day Saints, Salt Lake City, UT, 1994.

ADDRESSING GERMANS: *USING DU AND SIE*

The German language offers two ways to address a person: "You" translates as either *Du* or *Sie.*

Du is usually reserved for addressing relatives, close friends, and children (up to about 16 years of age) together with the first name.

Sie should be used in all other cases, together with appropriate titles, like *Herr* (Mr.), *Frau* (Mrs.) Or *Fräulein* (Miss) and also together with the last name.

When in doubt, always use *Sie* and wait for the other person to use *Du.*

Avoid addressing an adult by his or her first name unless invited to do so.

Also avoid offering to be called by your own first name ("Hi, I'm Bob") – at least right away and unless you really want to start a closer relationship.

Addressing persons in writing

In writing, the letter should start with, *Sehr geehrte Damen und Herren* (if no specific name is known) or, if the name is known, *Sehr geehrte/r Frau/Herr Maier.* (The literal German translation of "Dear Mr. Maier" would be *Lieber Herr Maier,* which would be appropriate only if you know Herr Maier very well.)

End with *Hochachtungsvoll* (very formal), or with *Mit freundlichen Gruß* (less formal but appropriate).

Titles

If the person addressed (either orally or in writing) holds a doctorate in any field, the title should be used:

Frau Doktor (Dr.) Maier

Herr Doktor (Dr.) Maier

Wait for him or her to invite you to drop this "Doctor" – then call him (or her) *Herr (Frau) Maier.*

Almost all other titles (academic or otherwise) may be omitted without serious "breach of etiquette" – even if you should know what those titles are.

GERMAN, NON-GERMAN GIVEN NAMES

On the next pages are listed given names of Germanic and foreign origin. During the Third Reich, parents were urged to choose names having Germanic roots. Lists of such names were published to help them choose "approved" names.

FEMALE GIVEN NAMES OF GERMANIC ORIGIN

Ada	Ellen	Hedda	Kunhild	Siegberta
Adda	Ellengard	Hedwig	Kunigard	Sieghild(e)
Adele	Elvira	Heide	Kunigund	Sieglinde
Adelgard	Emma	Heilburg	Leopolda	Siegrun
Adelgund	Engelberta	Heimtr(a)ud	Leopoldine	Sigberta
Adelheid	Engelgard	Helga	Liebgunde	Sigburg
Adeltraut	Erda	Helgard	Lina	Sighild
Adolfine	Erdmut(e)	Helma	Ludwiga	Siglind
Alberta	Erika	Helmtrud	Luitgard	Sigmut
Albertine	Ermgard	Henrike	Malwine	Sigrun
Almgard	Erna	Hergard	Mathild(e)	Sigtrub
Almtrud	Ernestine	Herma	Mechthild(e)	Solweig
Almut	Ferdinande	Hermine	Meinhild	Swanhild
Aloisia	Folkhild	Herta	Merlind	Theadelinde
Alrun	Frida	Hertr(a)ud	Miltrud	Thekla
Altrud	Friderun	Hildburg	Minna	Thusnelda
Alwine	Fridgarb	Hilde	Nortrud	Tilla
Amalie	Fridhild	Hildegard	Northild(e)	Traudlind(e)
Anselma	Fried(e)gard	Hildegund	Notburg(a)	Trude
Arngard	Frieda	Hildrun	Olga	U(da)lberta
Arnhild	Friedegund	Hiltr(a)ud	Orthild	Ulla
Arntrud	Friederike	Hulda	Ortlind	Ulrike
Berchthild	Frigga	Ida	Ortraud	Undine
Bernhild(e)	Froburg	Ilsa	Ortrud	Uta
Berta	Gesine	Ilse	Ortrun	Ute
Berthild(e)	Gelmut	Ingala	Osilde	Walburg
Bertraud	Genoveva	Inge	Oslinde	Walfriede
Bertrun	Gerburg	Ingeborg	Oswine	Walpurga
Borghild	Gerda	Ingeburg	Ottilie	Waltraud
Bothild	Gerharde	Ingeltrud	Radegund	Waltrud
Brita	Gerhild(e)	Ingrid	Reglind	Wanda
Brunhild(e)	Gerlind(e)	Irma	Reimunde	Werngard
Burghild	Gertraud	Irmburg	Reingard	Wernhild
Daglind	Gertrud	Irmela	Reinhild(e)	Wilburg
Dagmar	Gislinde	Irmfriede	Richarda	Wilfriede
Dietburg	Gisa	Irmgard	Roberta	Wilgard
Dietgard	Gisela	Irmhild	Rosa	Wilhelma
Dietlind	Giselheid	Irmlind	Rosamund(e)	Wilhelmine
Edelburg	Giseltr(a)ud	Irmlind(e)	Roswitha	Wilma
Edelgard	Gislind	Irmtr(a)ud	Rotraut	Wiltrud(t)
Edeltr(a)ud	Gotlind	Ishild(e)	Rotrud	Winfriede
Edith	Gudrun	Isolde	Rudolfine	Wolfhild
Ehrengard	Gudula	Karla	Runfrid	Wunhild
Eiltraut	Gunhild	Karoline	Runhild(e)	
Elfride	Gunthild(e)	Klothild(e)	Ruperta	
Elfriede	Hadburg	Kriemhild(e)	Selma	
Ella	Hadmut	Kunigunde	Senta	

MALE GIVEN NAMES OF GERMANIC ORIGIN

Adalbert	Dietger	Fritz	Helmbrecht	Lienhard
Adelbert	Diethard	Fromund	Helmund	Lothar
Adelhard	Diethelm	Frowein	Helmut	Ludolf
Adolf	Diether	Frowin	Helmuth	Ludwig
Alarich	Dietmar	Fürchtegott	Helwig	Luitpold
Albert	Dietrich	Gebhard	Helwin	Lutz
Albrecht	Dietwalt	Gerald	Henning	Manfred
Alfons	Eberhard	Gerd	Herbert	Markward
Alfred	Eckehard	Gerfried	Heribert	Markwart
Alois	Eckmar	Gerhard	Hermann	Markwin
Alwig	Edgar	Gerhold	Herwart	Marwig
Alwin	Edmund	Germut	Herwig	Meinhard
Anshelm	Eduard	Gernot	Hilbert	Meinhold
Armin	Edward	Gero	Hildebert	Meinrad
Arnhelm	Edwin	Gerolf	Hildebrand	Neidhard
Arno	Egbert	Gerwig	Hildemar	Neithard
Arnold	Eginhard	Gerwin	Hilmar	Norbert
Arnulf	Egon	Gilbert	Hinz	Norfried
Balduin	Eilert	Gisbert	Horstmar	Notker
Baldur	Eilhard	Giselher	(Horst)	Odilo
Baldwin	Einhard	Godecke	Hubert	Odo
Benno	Eisenhard	Gottfried	Hubert	Olaf
Bernd	Emmerich	Gotthard	Hugbert	Ortfrid
Bernhard	Erhard	Gotthelf	Hugo	Ortwig
Bernold	Erich	Gotthold	Humbert	Ortwin
Bernwart	Erkmar	Gottlieb	Ingbert	Oskar
Berther	Ernst	Gottwald	Ingo	Oswald
Berthold	Erwin	Götz	Ingolf	Oswin
Bertram	Ewalt	Guido	Ingomar	Otfrid
Bodmar	Falk	Gumprecht	Iwein	Otger
Bodo	Falko	Gundolf	Karl	Otmar
Bodwin	Ferdinand	Gunter	Karlmann	Otto
Bruno	Folker	Günter	Klodwig	Ottobert
Brunold	(Volker)	Guntram	Knut	Ottokar
Burckhard	Folkhard	Guntwig	Konrad	Ottomar
Burghard	Folkmar	Gustav	Kraft	Radbod
Dagabert	Folkrat	Hagen	Kunibert	Radulf
Dagbert	Frank	Harold	Kuno	Rainer
Dagmar	Franz	Harro	Kunold	Ralf
Dagobert	Fridbalt	Hartlieb	Kurt	Rambert
Dagomar	Fridbert	Hartmann	Lambrecht	Randolf
Dankmar	Fridhelm	Hartmut	Landhelm	Ratwin
Dankwart	Fridrich	Hartwig	Landolf	Reimar
Degenhard	Fridwalt	Hartwin	Lebrecht	Reimund
Detlef	Friedel	Heinrich	Leonhard	Reinalt
Diepold	Friedolin	Heinz	Leopold	Reiner
Dietbert	Friedrich	Helmar	Leuthold	Reinhard

Reinhold	Siegfried	Tejo	Volkwin	Willibalt
Reinulf	Siegmar	Theodebald	Waldemar	Willrich
Richard	Siegmund	Theoderich	Walter	Wilmar
Robert	Siegward	Tilmann	Walther	Winand
Roderich	Sigbert	Tilo	Warmund	Winfrid
Rodewalt	Sigfrid	Timm	Wernand	Winfried
Rodewin	Sighard	Traugott	Werner	Winild
Roger	Sigisbert	Tujoho	Widukind	Winrich
Roland	Sigismund	Udo	Wieland	Wiprecht
Rudolf	Sigmar	Ulbert	Wigand	Wittich
Rupert	Sigmund	Ulrich	Wigbert	Wolf
Ruprecht	Sigolf	Utz	Wighard	Wolfgang
Ruthard	Sigurd	Volker	Wilfrid	Wolfhard
Schwerthelm	Sigwart	Volkbert	Wilfried	Wolfram
Sebald	Sturmhard	Volkhard	Wilhelm	Wulf
Sebalt	Tassilo	Volkmar	Willi	
Siegbert	Tasso	Volkrad	Willibald	

FEMALE GIVEN NAMES OF FOREIGN ORIGIN

Agathe	Christel	Gabriele	Laura	Paula
Agnes	Christene	Grete(l)	Lene	Pauline
Alice	Crescentia	Hanna	Leonore	Renate
Alma	Dora	Helene	Liesbeth	Ruth
Angela	Dorothea	Henriette	Liese	Sophie
Angelika	Dörthe	Irene	Lieselotte	Stefanie
Anna	Elisabeth	Isabella	Lilli	Susanne
Anneliese	Elise	Johanna	Lore	Suse
Annemarie	Elsa	Josefa	Lotte	Therese
Auguste	Elsbeth	Josephine	Luise	Tine
Babette	Else	Jutta	Magdalene	Toni
Barbara	Emilie	Katharina	Margarete	Trine
Beate	Eugenie	Käthe	Marianne	Ursel
Bettina	Eva	Kathrein	Marie	Ursula
Brigitte	Fanni	Kathrine	Marie-Luise	Vareria
Cäcille	Florentine	Klara	Martha	Veronika
Charlotte	Franziska	Kreszenz	Meta	Viktoria

MALE GIVEN NAMES OF FOREIGN ORIGIN

Achim	Benedikt	Hans	Johann(es)	Klemeno
Alexander	Christian	Ignatz	Jörg	Leo
Andrä	Christoph	Immanuel	Josef	Lorenz
Andreas	Emil	Jakob	Julius	Martin
Anton	Felix	Joachim	Jürgen	Matthias
Artur	Florian	Jobst	Karsten	Max
August	Georg	Jochem	Kaspar	Merten
Bartel	Gregor	Jochen	Klaus	Michael

Michel	Peter	Sepp	Theo	Veit
Moritz	Philipp	Simon	Theodor	Viktor
Paul	Sebastian	Stefan	Thomas	Vinzenz

NAME DAYS *(Namenstage)*
IN GERMAN-SPEAKING AREAS

Below is a *selection* of the best known and most popular "name days" (*Namenstage*) in Germany and neighboring German-speaking areas. Regional variations in popularity may apply.

The "name day" is a tradition mostly in the Roman Catholic Church. It is less popular in predominantly Protestant areas.

According to Roman Catholic tradition, the date shown is usually the death date (historically correct or as traditionally assumed).

It used to be customary for children to be named according to the day on which they were born.

Key
S = Patron saint for . . .
H = Helpers in case of . . . ;
appealed to for or against . . .

January 6: Kaspar, Melchior, Balthasar [the Three Wise Men]
S: city of Köln, travelers, pilgrims, game card producers
H: thunderstorm, epilepsy
January 14: Engelmar [hermit, martyr]
S: town of St. Englmar (Bavaria), farmers
H: good harvest, cattle diseases
January 20: Sebastian [martyr]
S: the dying, soldiers, wells, hardware dealers, potters, pewter makers, gardeners, tanners, stone masons, gunsmiths, brush makers, rifle marksmen
H: wounds, epidemics, cattle diseases
January 21: Agnes [martyr]
S: young women, the engaged, gardeners, chastity
January 22: Vinzenz [martyr]

S: vintners, sailors, roofers, lumberjacks
H: lost objects
January 28: Thomas von Aquin [monk]
S: Order of Dominican Monks, Catholic universities, students, book dealers, pencil makers, clergy
H: thunderstorms
February 1: Brigitta von Kildare [abbess]
S: city of Essen, pregnant women, children, cattle
H: disaster, persecution
February 3: Blasius [bishop, martyr]
S: physicians, wool traders, cobblers, tailors, weavers, bakers, construction workers, hat makers, musicians, domestic animals, horses
H: coughing, sore throats, diseases of the bladder, bleeding, toothaches, pestilence
February 4: Veronika [disciple]
S: priest's housekeepers, washerwomen, weavers
H: gentle death, severe injuries, bleeding
February 5: Agatha [martyr]
S: Midwives, weavers, female shepherds, bell founders, miners, goldsmiths
H: fire, thunderstorm, earthquake, disaster, famine, infected wounds, diseases of the breast
February 6: Dorothea [martyr]
S: gardeners, miners, newlyweds, brides, pregnant women
H: birth labor, poverty, dying, false accusations
February 14: Valentin von Tern [bishop]
S: youth, travelers, beekeepers
H: good marriage, pestilence
February 24: Matthias [apostle]
S: dioceses of Trier, Goslar, Hanover, Hildesheim; construction workers; butchers; pastry makers; blacksmiths; tailors
H: coughing, infertility, start of school year for boys

"Land of milk and honey" (woodcut)

February 25: Walburga [abbess]
S: diocese of Eichstätt, pregnant women, farmers, domestic animals
H: Coughing, dog bite, rabies, eye diseases, good harvest
March 17: Gertrud [nun]
S: hospitals, pilgrims, travelers, poor, widows, gardeners, crops
H: mice and rats
March 17: Patrick [bishop, missionary]
S: Ireland, barbers, blacksmiths, miners, coopers, cattle
H: vermin, cattle diseases, evil
March 19: Joseph von Nazareth [husband of Mary]
S: Catholic Church, Austria, Bavaria, Bohemia, Tyrol, Styria, Carinthia, dioceses of Osnabrück and Cologne, families, children, orphans, artisans, carpenters, engineers, travelers, teachers, undertakers, expatriates
H: eye diseases, temptation, desperation, homelessness
March 26: Kastulus [martyr]
S: herdsmen

H: lightning, flooding, horse theft
April 23: Adalbert [bishop, martyr]
S: Prussia, Bohemia
April 23: Georg [martyr]
S: diocese of Limburg, boy scouts, farmers, miners, saddlers, blacksmiths, coopers, artists, horses, cattle, hikers, hospitals, soldiers, prisoners, horsemen
H: war, temptation, bad weather, fever, pestilence
April 25: Markus [evangelist, martyr]
S: notaries, construction workers, basket makers, glaziers
H: favorable weather, good harvest, hail, lightning, sudden death
May 4: Florian [martyr]
S: Upper Austria, fire brigades, chimney sweeps, beer brewers, coopers, potters, blacksmiths, soap makers
H: fire, flooding, drought, infertility of fields, storm, burn injuries
May 12 Pankraz [martyr]
S: communicants, young plants, blossoms
H: headache, cramps, perjury, wrongful accusation

May 13: Servatius [bishop, martyr]
S: cities of Goslar, Limburg/Lahn, Quedlinburg; diocese of Worms; locksmiths; cabinetmakers
H: rheumatism, fever, sore feet, frost, mice and rats
May 16: Johannes von Nepomuk [vicar, martyr]
S: Bohemia, priests, bridges, sailors, rafters, millers, Hapsburg Dynasty
H: libel, confessional secrets, flooding, protection of property
June 2: Erasmus, also known as Elmo [bishop, martyr]
S: sailors (St. Elm's fire), rope makers, weavers, domestic animals
H: cramps, colic, ulcers, childbirth, cattle diseases
June 3: Klothilde (Clothilde) [Queen of Franconia]
S: women, notaries, the lame
H: fever, sick children, sudden death, conversion of husband to Christianity
June 5: Bonifatius, also known as Winfrid ("Apostle to Germany")
S: diocese of Fulda, Thüringen, tailors, file makers, beer brewers
June 13: Antonius von Padua [monk]
S: cities of Paderborn and Hildesheim, Franciscan monks, lovers, women, matrimony, children, the poor, travelers, bakers, miners
H: lost objects, childbirth, infertility, fever, cattle diseases, shipwreck, war, pestilence, emergencies of any kind
June 15: Veit, also known as Vitus [child martyr]
S: Lower Saxony; Bohemia; cities of Prague, Mönchengladbach, Ellwangen, Krems; youth; innkeepers; pharmacists; vintners; actors; beer brewers; miners; blacksmiths; domestic animals; dogs; poultry; springs; the mute; the deaf
H: rabies, epilepsy, hysterics, cramps, diseases of eyes and ears, bedwetting, lightning, thunderstorms, fire, infertility, good harvest
June 16: Benno von Meissen [bishop]
S: Bavaria, city of München, diocese of

Dresden-Meissen, fishermen, weavers
H: pestilence, drought, thunderstorms
June 21: Alban von Mainz [priest, missionary, martyr]
S: city of Mainz, farmers
H: headache, sore throat, epilepsy, diseases of the urinal tract, thunderestorms
June 21: Aloisius von Gonzaga [monk]
S: youth, students
H: choosing a profession, pestilence, eye diseases
June 24: Johannes der Taufer (John the Baptist)
S: weavers, tailors, furriers, tanners, dyers, saddlers, vintners, innkeepers, coopers, chimney sweeps, blacksmiths, masons, carpenters, movie theater owners, farmers, herdsmen, architects, musicians, dancers, singers, vineyards, domestic animals, sheep, lambs
H: abstinence, epilepsy, headache, sore throat, dizziness, sick children, fear, hail
June 29: Paul (Paulus) [apostle, martyr]
S: the Pope, diocese of Osnabrück, butchers, carpenters, glaziers, watchmakers, locksmiths, potters, blacksmiths, construction workers, tile makers, bridge builders, weavers, net makers, fishermen, fish merchants, sailors, virgins, the repentant, stonemasons
H: snake bites, fever, rabies, sore feet, obsessions, theft, shipwreck
June 30: Otto von Bamberg [bishop]
S: dioceses of Bamberg and Berlin
H: fever, rabies
July 3: Thomas (apostle)
S: architects, construction workers, carpenters, masons, the clergy
H: backache, good marriage
July 4: Ulrich von Augsburg [bishop]
S: diocese and city of Augsburg, village of St. Ulrich in South Tyrol, vintners, fishermen, weavers, travelers, the dying
H: complications at childbirth, all kins of illness, fever, rabies, mice and rats, flooding
July 11: Benedikt von Nursia [monk]
S: Europe, teachers, miners, coppersmiths, spelunkers, schoolchildren, the dying

H: fever, infections, poisoning, kidney stones, gallstones, witchcraft

July 13: Heinrich (German emperor)
S: diocese and city of Bamberg, diocese and city of Basel

July 13: Kunigunde (wife of Heinrich)
S: diocese of Bamberg, pregnant women, sick children

July 16: Irmgard (Irmengard) [abbess]
S: Lake Chiemsee district (Bavaria)
H: all kinds of needs

July 20: Margareta von Antiochien [martyr]
S: farmers, virgins, girls, midwives, wives, pregnant women
H: difficult childbirth, wounds, fertility

July 22: Maria Magdalena [present at Jesus' death]
S: women, penitents, students, prisoners, barbers, gardeners, vintners, coopers, wiine merchants, glove makers, perfume makers
H: for children to learn to walk, eye infections, thunderstorms, pests

July 24: Christopher [martyr]
S: traffic, vehicle operators, rafters, coachmen, sailors, ferries, pilgrims, travelers, athletes, miners, carpenters, hatters, dyers, bookbinders, treasure hunters, gardeners, fruit dealers, fortifications, children
H: pestilence, sudden death, epidemics, fire, flooding, drought, thunderstorms, hail, eye diseases, toothaches, wounds

August 10: Lorenz (Laurentius) [martyr]
S: cities of Nürnberg, Wuppertal, and Kulm; librarians, archivists, cooks, beer brewers, innkeepers, washerwomen, pastrymakers, fire brigades, students
H: eye diseases, lumbago fever, skin diseases, fire, torments in purgatory, good grape harvest, pestilence

August 19: Sebald (Sebaldus) [missionary]
S: City of Nürnberg
H: cold weather

August 24: Bartholomäus [apostle]
S: cities of Frankfurt/Main, Pilsen, and Altenburg; miners; butchers; tailors; farmers; bookbinders; vintners; bakers

H: nervous diseases, skin diseases

August 25: Ludwig (king of France)
S: cities of München, Saarbrücken, Berlin, Saarlouis; science;'pilgrims; bakers; barbers; painters; masons; merchants; jewelry makers; button makers; bailiffs
H: blindness, deafness, pestilence

September 1: Aegidius, also known as Egid, Till, Gilles [French hermit]
S: Carinthia, Styria, cities of Nürnberg, Osnabrück, Braunschweig, Graz; hungers; herdsmen; horse traders; the shipwrecked; beggars, lepers, breast-feeding mothers
H: infertility (human and livestock), mental diseases, drought, fire, storm, desolation, good confessions

September 8: Maria, mother of Jesus
S: All of Christianity, Bavaria, dioceses of Aachen and Speyer, innkeepers, cooks, furriers, cloth makers, potters, sailors, gingerbread bakers, silk weavers, vinegar brewers
H: thunderstorms, lightning, in all kinds of distress and need

September 21: Matthäus [apostle]
S: bookkeepers, customs officials, tax collectors, bankers
H: alcoholism

September 22: Mauritius, also known as Moritz, Maurice [martyr]
S: soldiers, merchants, dyers, hat makers, glaziers, armorers, blade smiths, cloth makers, horses, vineyards
H: in wartime, gout, obsessions, diseases of the ears, horse diseases

September 24: Rupert von Salzburg [bishop]
S: city and diocese of Salzburg, salt miners, dogs

September 29: Michael [archangel]
S: the Catholic Church, all Germans, soldiers, Pharmacists, tailors, glaziers, painters, cabinetmakers, merchants, scales makers, calibrators of scales, gilders, bankers, radio mechanics, cemeteries
H: painless death, lightning, thunderstorms

October 4: Franz von Assisi [monk]
S: Diocese of Basel, Franciscan monks,

the poor, social workers, animals, environment, merchants, tailors, weavers
H: headache, pestilence
October 16: Hedwig von Andechs und Schlesien [duchess]
S: Silesia; cities of Berlin, Breslau, Trebnitz and Krakau; expatriates, engaged couples
October 21: Ursula [martyr]
S: city of Köln, youth, female teachers, cloth merchants
H: good marriage, painless death, sick children
October 31: Wolfgang von Regensburg [bishop]
S: Bavaria, city and diocese of Regensburg, charcoal burners, herdsmen, carpenters, sculptors, bargemen, lumber-jacks, innocent prisoners, cattle
H: gout, paralysis, eye diseases, bleeding, sore feet, stroke, dysentery, skin diseases, infertility, deformed child
November 3: Hubert (Hubertus) [bishop]
S: hunters, rifle marksmen, butchers, furriers, wood turners, opticians, metalworkers, mathematicians, hounds
H: dog bites (in French, *mal de St. Hubert*), snake bites, fear of water
November 11: Martin von Tours [bishop]
S: dioceses of Mainz and Rottenburg, province of Burgenland (Austria) and Schwyz (Switzerland), soldiers, cavalry, horsemen, farriers, armorers, weavers, tailors, tanners, glove makers, hat makers, hotel owners, millers, coopers, vintners, herdsmen, travelers, innkeepers, the poor, beggars, teetotalers, domestic animals, horses, geese
H: skin diseases, snakebite, good harvests
November 19: Elisabeth von Thüringen [countess]
S: Hessen, Thüringen, welfare organizations (Caritas), widows and orphans, beggars, innocently persecuted, the sick, the needy, bakers
November 22: Cäcilia [martyr]
S: sacred music, musicians, singers, builders of musical instruments, poets
November 25: Katharina von Alexandria [martyr]
S: girls, wives, teachers, students, libraries, orators, hospitals, attorneys
H: headaches, diseases of the tongue, discovery of drowned persons, good harvests
November 30: Andreas [apostle]
S: fishermen, fish merchants, butchers, miners, rope makers
H: gout, sore throat, cramps, swine fever, good marriage
December 3: Franz Xaver [missionary]
S: missionaries, sailors, Catholic newspapers
H: painless death, storms, pestilence
December 4: Barbara [martyr]
S: towers, miners, farmers, architects, construction workers, roofers, bell founders, masons, carpenters, undertakers, cooks, prisoners, girls, artillery, fortifications, fire brigades, the dying
H: painless death, fire, fever, thunderstorms, pestilence
December 6: Nikolaus von Myra [bishop]
S: province of Lothringen, altar boys, children, pilgrims, travelers, attorneys, merchants, judges, pharmacists, innkeepers, bargemen, fishermen, sailors, rafters, millers, bakers, butchers, beer brewers, farmers, distillers, weavers, masons, quarry workers, coopers, candle makers, prisoners, fire brigades
H: good marriage, shipwreck, retrieval of stolen property, protection from thieves
December 24: Adam und Eva [first humans]
S: tailors, gardeners
December 26: Stephan [martyr]
S: horses, horsemen, coachmen, construction workers, tailors, masons, carpenters, weavers, coopers
H: headaches, kidney stones, gallstones, stitches, obsessions, painless death
December 27: Johannes [apostle]
S: the clergy, civil servants, notaries, sculptors, painters, writers, book dealers,

printers, bookbinders, paper makers,
vintners, butchers
H: poisoning, burns, sore feet, epilepsy,
hail, good harvests
December 29: David [king of Israel]
S: Musicians, singers, poets, miners
December 31: Silvester [pope]
S: domestic animals
H: good harvests of animal food, for a
"happy new year"

Source: Vera Schauber, *Pattloch-Namenstagskalender*. Pattloch Verlag, Augsburg 1994. English translations by Rainer Thumshirn.

OTHER NAME DAYS (*Namenstage*)

Achim	Aug. 16
Ada, Viktor	Jul. 28
Adalbert	Jun. 20
Adalbert	Apr. 23
Adam	Dec. 24
Adelheid	Dec. 16
Adolf	Jun. 17
Adolf	Jan. 3
Agatha	Feb. 5
Agnes	Jan. 21
Agnes	Mar. 2
Aja	Apr. 18
Alberich	Nov. 14
Alberich	Oct. 17
Albert	Apr. 8
Albert	Aug. 7
Albert	Sep. 5
Albert	Nov. 15
Albin	Mar. 1
Alexander	May 3
Alexander	Feb. 26
Alexander	Feb. 27
Alexandra	Feb. 21
Alexandra	Mar. 21
Alf	Aug. 2
Alfons	Aug. 1
Alfons R.	Oct. 30
Alfons	Aug. 1
Alfons	Oct. 30
Alfred	Oct. 28
Alfred	Feb. 2

Alice	Apr. 4
Alice	Feb. 5
Alice	Jun. 12
Almud	Mar. 12
Alois	Jun. 21
Altmann	Aug. 9
Alwin	May 19
Alwin	Jan. 15
Amadeus	Mar. 30
Amanda	Mar. 19
Ambrosius	Dec. 7
Anastasia	Dec. 25
Andrea	Jul. 12
Andreas	Feb. 4
Andreas	Sep. 20
Andreas	Jun. 19
Andreas	Nov. 30
Andreas	Nov. 10
Angela	Jan. 4
Angela	Jun. 1
Angela	Jan. 27
Angela	Nov. 2
Angelina	Dec. 10
Anke	Jul. 26
Anna	Feb. 9
Anna	Jul. 26
Anno	May 23
Anonius	Oct. 24
Anselm	Mar. 18
Ansgar	Feb. 3
Anton	Jan. 17
Anton	Jul. 5
Anton v. P.	Jun. 13
Anton	Feb. 12
Antonia	May 6
Antonius	Jun. 13
Antonius	Jan. 17
Apolonia	Feb. 9
Ariane	Aug. 2
Armin	Jun. 2
Arno	Jan. 24
Arnold	May 1
Arnold	Jan. 15
Arnulf	Sep. 19
Arnulf	Jan. 29
Arthur	Sep. 1
Arthur	Nov. 1
Asta	Apr. 15
Astrid	Aug. 10

Athanasius .... May 2
Attila .... Oct. 5
Augustin .... Aug. 28
Augustin v. C. .... May 27
Augustin .... May 27
Augustinus .... Aug. 28
Aurelia .... Oct. 13
Axel .... Mar. 21
Barbara .... Dec. 4
Barbara .... Mar. 9
Bärbel .... Dec. 4
Barnabas .... Jun. 11
Bartholomaüs .... Aug. 24
Basilius .... Jan. 2
Beata .... Sep. 6
Beate .... May 9
Beate .... Aug. 8
Beate .... Mar. 12
Beate .... Apr. 8
Beatrix .... Mar. 12
Beatrix .... Aug. 29
Beatrix .... Jan. 17
Benedikt .... Feb. 12
Benedikt .... Jul. 11
Benedikt .... Oct. 8
Benedikt .... Apr. 16
Benekikt .... Mar. 21
Benjamin .... Mar. 31
Benno .... Aug. 3
Benno .... Jun. 16
Benno .... Jul. 28
Bernard .... Apr. 30
Bernadette .... Feb. 18
Bernadette .... Apr. 16
Bernhard .... Aug. 20
Bernhard .... Nov. 20
Bernhard .... May 20
Bernhard .... Oct. 30
Bernulf .... Jul. 19
Berta .... Jul. 4
Berta .... May 1
Berta .... Mar. 24
Berthilde .... Nov. 5
Bertold .... Jul. 27
Bertold .... Jul. 13
Bertold .... Sep. 19
Bertram .... Jun. 30
Bertram .... Jun. 6
Bertram .... May 10

'Bärbele' und 'Gustele'

Bettina .... Jul. 8
Bibiana .... Dec. 2
Birgit .... Jul. 23
Birgitta .... Jul. 23
Blandina .... Nov. 5
Blanka .... Dec. 1
Blasius .... Feb. 3
Bodo .... Feb. 2
Bonifatius .... May 14
Bonifaz .... Jun. 5
Boris .... May 2
Brigitta .... Feb. 1
Brunhilde .... Dec. 17
Bruno .... Oct. 6
Bruno .... Oct. 11
Bruno .... May 17
Bruno .... Dec. 10
Bruno .... Mar. 9
Burchard .... Apr. 7
Burkhard .... Oct. 14
Burkhard .... Jun. 14
Cäcilia .... Nov. 22
Camilla .... Sep. 16
Camillus .... Jul. 14

Carlo	Dec. 15	Dietrich	Jul. 1
Carmen	Jul. 16	Dietrich	Sep. 27
Carola	Aug. 17	Dolores	Sep. 15
Carolina	Apr. 6	Dominikus	Aug. 4
Cäsar	Apr. 1	Donald	Jul. 15
Charlotte	Jul. 17	Donatus	Aug. 7
Christa	Jun. 4	Dorothea	Feb. 6
Christian	May 14	Dorothea	Jun. 25
Christian	Dec. 4	Eberhard	Jan. 9
Christian	Feb. 4	Eberhard	Apr. 17
Christiana	Dec. 15	Eckart	Nov. 27
Christiane	Jul. 26	Eckart	Jul. 1
Christine	Jul. 24	Edeltraud	Jun. 23
Christine	Jun. 22	Edgar	Sep. 10
Christine	Nov. 6	Edgar	Jul. 8
Christine	Dec. 15	Edith	Jan. 26
Christophorus	Jul. 24	Edith	Aug. 9
Claudia	Mar. 20	Edith	Dec. 8
Claudia	May 18	Edith	Sep. 16
Claudia	Aug. 18	Edmund	Oct. 20
Claudia	Sep. 10	Edmund	Nov. 20
Clementia	Mar. 21	Eduard	Jan. 5
Constance	Jun. 25	Eduard	Mar. 18
Corinna	May 14	Eduard	Oct. 13
Cornelia	Sep. 14	Eduard	Mar. 18
Corona	May 16	Edwin	Oct. 4
Dagmar	May 24	Edwin	Oct. 11
Dagobert	Dec. 23	Egbert	Nov. 25
Damian	Sep. 26	Egbert	Aug. 26
Daniel	Dec. 11	Egbert	Apr. 24
Daniel	Jul. 21	Egmont	Sep. 26
Daniel	Jun. 27	Egolf	Sep. 3
Daniel(a)	Jul. 21	Egon	Jul. 15
Daria	Oct. 25	Ekkehard	Jun. 28
David	Jul. 15	Eleanore	May 27
Debor	Sep. 21	Eleonore	Feb. 21
Detlef	Nov. 23	Elfriede	May 20
Detlef	Apr. 28	Elfriede	Dec. 8
Diana	Jun. 9	Elfriede	Feb. 8
Diana	Jun. 10	Elias	Mar. 24
Dieger	Jan. 2	Elisabeth v. Th.	Nov. 19
Diethard	Sep. 10	Elisabeth	Apr. 3
Diethard	Dec. 10	Elke	Feb. 5
Diethilde	Jun. 28	Elmar	Mar. 22
Dietmar	Sep. 28	Elmar	Aug. 28
Dietmar	Mar. 5	Emanuel	Oct. 1
Dietmar	May 17	Emil	Dec. 6
Dietrich	Oct. 29	Emil	Mar. 10
Dietrich	Dec. 16	Emil	May 22

Emil	Nov. 12	Florian	May 4
Emilia	Jan. 5	Folkard	Nov. 30
Emilie	Jan. 4	Frank	Oct. 6
Emma	Apr. 19	Franz	Oct. 4
Emma	Dec. 3	Franz Xaver	Dec. 3
Emmerich	Nov. 5	Franz	Apr. 2
Engelbert	Jul. 10	Franz v. P.	Apr. 2
Engelbert	Nov. 7	Franz v. S.	Jan. 24
Engelbert	Apr. 10	Franz v. A.	Oct. 4
Engelbert	Jun. 8	Franz	Jan. 24
Ephräm	Jun. 9	Franz. B.	Oct. 10
Erhard	Jan. 8	Franziska	Mar. 9
Erich	May 18	Franziska	Dec. 14
Erika	Jul. 10	Fridolin	Mar. 6
Erna	Jan. 12	Frieda	Oct. 19
Ernst	Nov. 7	Friedrich	Nov. 29
Ernst	Jun. 30	Friedrich	Jul. 18
Ernst	Jan. 12	Gabriel	Mar. 24
Esther	May 23	Galesius	Nov. 21
Eucharius	Dec. 9	Gangolf	May 11
Eugen	Jun. 2	Gebhard	Jun. 16
Eugen	Dec. 20	Gebhart	Aug. 27
Eugen	Nov. 13	Genofeva	Jan. 3
Eugen	Jan. 23	Georg	Apr. 23
Eugenie	Sep. 26	Gerald	Mar. 13
Eva	May 26	Gerald	Dec. 5
Eva	Mar. 14	Gerda	Mar. 5
Eva	Dec. 24	Gerda	May 29
Ewald	Oct. 3	Gerfried	Sep. 12
Ewald	Mar. 23	Gerhard	Apr. 23
Fabian	Jan. 20	Gerhard	Jan. 27
Fabiola	Dec. 27	Gerlinde	Feb. 13
Falko	Feb. 20	Gerlinde	Dec. 3
Farah	Dec. 7	German	May 28
Felicia	Jun. 18	Gernot	Sep. 24
Felix	Mar. 26	Gerold	Apr. 19
Felix	Jul. 12	Gerold	Apr. 10
Felix	Sep. 11	Gertrud	Aug. 13
Felix	Feb. 14	Gertrud	Nov. 17
Felix	Nov. 20	Gertrud	Mar. 17
Felix	Jan. 14	Gervin	Apr. 17
Ferdinand	May 30	Gerwich	Oct. 26
Fides	Aug. 1	Gerwin	Apr. 17
Flora	Jul. 29	Gilbert	Aug. 6
Flora	Oct. 9	Gilbert	Oct. 24
Flora	Nov. 24	Gisela	May 7
Flora	Jun. 11	Gislar	Sep. 28
Florence	Oct. 10	Gordian	May 12
Florentina	Jun. 20	Goswin	Jul. 31

Gottfried	Jan. 13	Herald	Jun. 27
Gottfried	Nov. 8	Heribert	May 25
Gottfried	Feb. 16	Heribert	Mar. 16
Gottfried	Jul. 9	Heribert	Apr. 27
Gotthelf	Sep. 25	Heribert	Aug. 29
Gottlieb	Mar. 30	Heribert	Aug. 30
Gottschalk	Jun. 7	Hermann	May 21
Gregor	Jan. 2	Hermann	Oct. 2
Gregor	Aug. 26	Hermann	Apr. 25
Gregor	Nov. 17	Hermann	May 21
Gregor	May 9	Hermelindis	Oct. 29
Gregor d. Gr.	Sep. 3	Hermine	Apr. 13
Gudrun	Jan. 8	Hermine	Dec. 30
Guido	Mar. 31	Herta	Nov. 24
Guido	May 4	Hieronymus	Feb. 8
Guido	Sep. 12	Hilaria	Aug. 12
Gundula	May 6	Hilde	Jan. 12
Gundula	Mar. 3	Hildebald	Oct. 2
Gunnar	Mar. 16	Hildebrand	May 25
Gunther	Nov. 28	Hildegard	Sep. 17
Günther	Oct. 9	Hildegard	Apr. 30
Günther	Oct. 8	Hildegund	Oct. 14
Gustav	Aug. 8	Hildegund	Apr. 20
Gustav	Mar. 10	Hiltrud	May 31
Gutmar	Oct. 11	Hiltrud	Nov. 17
Hadrian	Sep. 8	Himana	Oct. 21
Hadwig	Feb. 19	Holger	Oct. 7
Hanno	Mar. 27	Horst	Oct. 12
Hanno	Sep. 20	Hubert	Nov. 3
Harald	Nov. 1	Hugo	Apr. 28
Hartmann	Dec. 12	Hugo	Apr. 1
Hartwig	Apr. 13	Hyppolyt	Aug. 13
Hartwig	Jun. 14	Ida	May 8
Hedwig	Oct. 16	Ida	Nov. 26
Hedwig	Feb. 19	Ida	Feb. 24
Hedwig	Apr. 14	Ida	Apr. 13
Hedwig	Oct. 16	Ida	Sep. 4
Heiko	Feb. 5	Ignatius	Jul. 31
Heinrich	Jan. 23	Ignaz	Oct. 17
Heinrich	Jul. 13	Ignaz v. L.	Jul. 31
Helene	Aug. 18	Ines	Mar. 1
Helene	Apr. 26	Ingbert	Oct. 22
Helga	Sep. 11	Ingeborg	Jul. 30
Helga	Jun. 8	Ingrid	Sep. 2
Helga	May 7	Inis	Mar. 2
Helmtrud	May 30	Irene	Sep. 18
Helmut	Mar. 29	Irene	Apr. 3
Helmut	Apr. 24	Irene	Apr. 1
Hemma	Jun. 27	Irene	Feb. 21

Irene	Jan. 22	Josef	Mar. 19
Iris	Sep. 4	Joseph	Mar. 19
Irmgard	Mar. 20	Judas	Oct. 28
Irmgard	Feb. 19	Judith	Sep. 7
Irmgard	Feb. 24	Judith	Mar. 25
Irmgard	Sep. 14	Judith	Mar. 13
Irmgard	Dec. 30	Julia	May 22
Irmgard	Sep. 4	Julian	Jan. 9
Irmgard	Jul. 17	Julian	Jan. 17
Irmtrud	May 29	Julian	Mar. 8
Isabella	Feb. 22	Juliana	Feb. 16
Isabella	Jun. 8	Juliana	Jun. 19
Isabella	Aug. 21	Julius	Apr. 12
Isador	Apr. 4	Justus	Feb. 25
Isador	May 10	Jutta	Aug. 17
Isolde	Aug. 23	Jutta	Jan. 13
Isolde	Apr. 6	Jutta	Feb. 13
Ivo	Dec. 23	Jutta	Dec. 22.
Jakob	Oct. 6	Jutta	Nov. 29
Jakobus	May 3	Jutta	Mar. 25
Jakobus	Jul. 25	Jutta	May 5
Jaqueline	Jul. 23	Kajetan	Aug. 7
Jaqueline	Feb. 26	Karin	Nov. 7
Jeanne	May 30	Karin	Apr. 30
Jeanne d'Arc	May 29	Karl L.	Jun. 3
Jenniver	Jan. 3	Karl	Mar. 2
Joachim	Oct. 16	Karl	Jan. 28
Joachim	May 11	Karl Borromäus	Nov. 4
Johann Bosco	Jan. 31	Karl	Aug. 12
Johann B.	Apr. 7	Karl	Mar. 2
Johanna	Dec. 12	Karola	Aug. 17
Johanna	Aug. 21	Kasimir	Mar. 4
Johannes	Jan. 31	Kaspar	Jan. 6
Johannes	Jan. 11	Kastor	Feb. 13
Johannes	Sep. 13	Katharina	Nov. 25
Johannes	Oct. 23	Katharina	Mar. 23
Johannes	Jun. 12	Katharina	Feb. 9
Johannes	Apr. 7	Katharina v. S	Apr. 29
Johannes Ev.	Dec. 27	Katharina	Nov. 24
Johannes v. G.	Mar. 8	Katharina	Apr. 29
Johannes der Täufer	Jun. 24	Kilian	Jul. 8
Johannes	Dec. 14	Klara	May 8
Johannes	Jun. 26	Klara	Aug. 11
Jolanda	Dec. 17	Klara	Jun. 15
Jolande	Nov. 29	Klaus	Sep. 25
Jonas	Sep. 21	Klemens	Mar. 15
Jordan	Feb. 20	Klemens	Nov. 23
Josef	May 21	Klemens	Mar. 15
		Kleopatra	Apr. 9

Klothilde ....Jun. 3
Klothilde ....Jun. 4
Knut .... Jul. 10
Konrad Jun.1
Konrad .... Nov. 26
Konrad .... Apr. 9
Konrad .... Nov. 26
Konrad .... Mar. 14
Konrad .... Apr. 21
Konrad .... Dec. 19
Konstantia .... Feb. 18
Konstantin .... Apr. 12
Konstantin .... Feb. 17
Kordula ....Jun. 1
Kordula .... Oct. 22
Kunibert ....Nov. 12
Kunigunde .... Jul. 13
Kunigunde .... Mar. 3
Kuno .... May 19
Kuno .... Mar. 8
Kurt .... Feb. 14
Kurt .... Apr. 19
Kurt .... Nov. 26
Lambert .... Sep. 18
Larissa .... Mar. 26
Laura .... Oct. 19
Laurentius .... Jul. 21
Laurentius .... Aug. 10
Laurentz .... Sep. 5
Lea .... Mar. 22
Leander .... Feb. 27
Leo .... Jul. 3
Leo .... Jun. 12
Leo der Große .... Nov. 10
Leo .... Feb. 20
Leo .... Apr. 11
Leo .... Apr. 19
Leo d. W. .... Feb. 20
Leonhard .... Nov. 6
Leopold .... Nov. 15
Liane .... Apr. 12
Lisbeth .... Jun. 18
Lothar ....Jun. 15
Lothar .... Dec. 29
Lucas .... Feb. 17
Lucia .... Dec. 13
Lucius .... Mar. 4
Lucius .... Dec. 2
Ludger .... Mar. 25

Heir of the grandduchess of Baden in Wiesbach costume

Ludia .... Sep. 16
Ludwig .... Aug. 25
Ludwig .... Oct. 25
Ludwig .... Apr. 28
Ludwig .... Aug. 19
Ludwig .... Oct. 10
Luise .... Apr. 15
Luise .... Jan. 31
Lukas Ev. .... Oct. 18
Lutz .... Aug. 19
Lydia .... Aug. 3
Lydia .... Mar. 27
Magnus .... Sep. 6
Manfred .... Jan. 28
Marc ....Jun. 18
Margareta .... Aug. 26
Margareta Jul.20
Margarete .... Feb. 22
Margarete ....Nov. 16
Margot .... Dec. 30
Margot ....Jun. 10
Maria .... Feb. 11
   von Lourdes
Maria .... Aug. 5

Maria Königin	Aug. 22	Nadine	Sep. 14
Maria	Jul. 6	Natalie	Dec. 1
Maria Magdalena	Jul. 22	Natalie	Jul. 27
Mariam	Feb. 22	Natalie	Dec. 1
Marian	Dec. 22	Niels	Dec. 5
Marina	Jul. 17	Nikolaus	Dec. 6
Mario	Jan. 19	Norbert	Jun. 6
Marion	Apr. 24	Oda	Nov. 27
Marita	Jul. 20	Oda	Oct. 23
Marius	Jan. 4	Odo	Nov. 18
Mark	Jun. 18	Olaf	Feb. 15
Markus	Oct. 7	Olaf	Jul. 29
Markus	Apr. 25	Olaf	Jul. 10
Marlene	Jul. 22	Olga	Jul. 11
Martha	Jul. 29	Oliver	Mar. 5
Martha	Jan. 19	Oliver	Jul. 11
Martha	Oct. 20	Olivia	Jun. 10
Martha	Jul. 29	Oranna	Sep. 15
Martin v. T.	Nov. 11	Orthold	Sep. 9
Martin	Apr. 13	Oskar	Feb. 3
Martina	Jul. 2	Oswald	Aug. 5
Martina	Jan. 30	Oswald	Feb. 28
Martina	Nov. 11	Oswin	Mar. 13
Maternus	Sep. 11	Otmar	Nov. 16
Mathilde	Mar. 14	Otmar	Sep. 9
Matthäus	Sep. 21	Ottilie	Dec. 13
Matthias	Feb. 24	Otto	Dec. 28
Mauritius	Sep. 22	Otto	Jun. 30
Maximilian	Mar. 12	Otto	Feb. 23
Maximilian	Aug. 21	Otto	Jun. 30
Maximilian	Oct. 12	Otto	Jul. 2
Maximilian	Aug. 14	Otto	Jan. 16
Mechthild	Jul. 6	Otwin	Jun. 13
Mechthild	May 31	Pankratius	May 12
Mechthild	Mar. 5	Patricia	Aug. 25
Mechthild	Feb. 26	Patricia	Aug. 15
Meinhard	Aug. 14	Patrick	Mar. 17
Meinhart	Aug. 14	Paul	Oct. 19
Meinolf	Oct. 5	Paul Eins.	Jan. 15
Meinrad	Jan. 21	Paul	Jun. 29
Melanie	Dec. 31	Paul	Feb. 8
Mercedes	Sep. 24	Paula	Jun. 3
Michael(a)	Sep. 29	Paula	Jun. 11
Michaela	Aug. 24	Pauli B.	Jan. 25
Mona Oct. 18		Pauline	Jan. 11
Monika	Aug. 27	Paulinus	Aug. 31
Monika	May 4	Paulus	Jan. 10
Moritz	Sep. 22	Paulus	Jun. 29
Nabor	Jul. 12	Paulus	Jun. 26

Peter	Jun. 29	Roger	Mar. 1
Peter	Jun. 23	Roland	May 13
Petri Stuhlf.	Feb. 22	Roland	Jul. 14
Petrus	Feb. 21	Roland	Sep. 15
Petrus	Jul. 30	Roland	Jan. 16
Petrus	Jun. 29	Roland	Nov. 9
Philipp	May 26	Roman	Aug. 9
Philipp	Feb. 8	Roman	Nov. 18
Philipp	Dec. 18	Roman	Oct. 1
Philipp	May 3	Roman	Feb. 28
Pia	Jan. 19	Romana	Feb. 23
Pius	Jul. 11	Ronald	Aug. 20
Priska	Jan. 18	Rosa	Aug. 23
Priska	Feb 18	Rosa	Aug. 24
Radegund	Aug. 12	Rosalie	Aug. 23
Raimund	Jan. 7	Rosalinde	Oct. 7
Raimund	Aug. 31	Rose	Aug. 29
Rainer	Jun. 17	Rosina	Mar. 13
Rainer	Aug. 4	Roswitha	Apr. 29
Rainer	Apr. 11	Rotraut	Jun. 22
Ralf	Feb. 1	Rudger	Dec. 27
Ralph	Sep. 7	Rüdiger	Mar. 1
Raphael	Sep. 29	Rudolf	Jul. 27
Rasso	Jun. 19	Rudolf	Oct. 17
Rebekka	Mar. 23	Rudolf	Nov. 6
Regina	Dec. 20	Rudolf	Apr. 17
Regina	Sep. 7	Rudolf	Jun. 21
Regina	Aug. 22	Rufus	Nov. 21
Regine	May 10	Rupert	Sep. 24
Regine	Jan. 18	Rupert	Aug. 15
Reimund	Jan 7	Rupert	Mar. 4
Reinbert	May 16	Ruth	Sep. 1
Reiner	Feb. 7	Rupert	May 15
Reiner	Jan. 14	Sabine	Feb. 1
Reinhard	Mar. 7	Sabine	Aug. 29
Reinhild	May 30	Sabine	Oct. 27
Reinhild	Feb. 13	Sandrina	Apr. 2
Renate	May 22	Sebald	Aug. 19
Renate	May 23	Sebastian	Jan. 20
René	Sep. 2	Sella	Sep. 22
Rheinhard	Nov. 4	Senta	Apr. 5
Richard	Feb. 7	Serena	Jan. 30
Richard	Nov. 15	Servatius	May 13
Richard	Apr. 3	Seuse	Jan. 23
Richard	Jun. 9	Severin	Oct. 25
Rita	May 22	Severin	Jan. 8
Robert	May 13	Sibylle	Oct. 9
Robert	Jun. 7	Sidonie	Oct. 14
Robert	Sep. 17	Sidonie	Nov. 14

Siegfried	Feb. 15	Thomas	Jul. 3
Sigismund	May 2	Thomas	Jun. 22
Sigrid	Aug. 4	Thomas	Jul. 3
Sigrid	May 5	Thomas Becket	Dec. 29
Sigrid	Jan. 7	Timotheus	Jan. 26
Sigurd	Feb. 10	Titus	Jan. 26
Silvana	Feb. 10	Titus	Jan. 25
Silvester	Dec. 31	Tobias	Mar. 3
Silvinus	Feb. 17	Tobias	Sep. 13
Simon	Oct. 28	Torsten	May 5
Sissy	Nov. 22	Trudbert	Apr. 26
Sixtus	Aug. 6	Uda	Dec. 28
Sola	Dec. 5	Uda	Oct. 3
Sophie	May 15	Ulrich	Mar. 11
Sophie	May 24	Ulrich	Feb. 26
Stanislaus	Apr. 11	Ulrich	Jan. 16
Stanislaus	Nov. 13	Ulrich	Jul. 4
Stefan	Aug. 2	Urban	May 25
Stefan	Dec. 26	Urban	Dec. 19
Stephan	Dec. 26	Ursula	Jan. 20
Susanna	Aug. 11	Ursula	Oct. 21
Susanne	Aug. 11	Ursus	Sep. 30
Susanne	Jan. 18	Uschi	Oct. 21
Sven	Mar. 1	Valentin	Feb. 14
Sylvia	Nov. 3	Valerian	Apr. 14
Tamara	Dec. 29	Valerie	Dec. 9
Tassilo	Dec. 11	Valerius	Jan. 29
Tasso	Jan. 11	Valerius	Apr. 14
Thea	Jul. 25	Veit	Jun. 15
Thea	Jan. 11	Vera	Aug. 29
Thea	Apr. 5	Vera	Jan. 24
Thekla	Sep. 23	Verena	Jul. 22
Thekla	Oct. 15	Verena	Sep. 1
Theo	Aug. 16	Veronika	Feb. 28
Theo	Apr. 20	Veronika	Feb. 4
Theobald	Jul. 1	Veronika	Jul. 9
Theobald	Jan. 16	Victoria	Dec. 23
Theodor	Dec. 28	Viktor	Jan. 31
Theodor	Feb. 11	Viktor	Sep. 30
Theodor	Aug. 16	Viktor	Jul. 28
Theodor	Feb. 7	Viktoria	Nov. 2
Theodor	Nov. 9	Vinzenz	Jan. 22
Theresia v. A.	Oct. 15	Vinzenz Ferr.	Apr. 5
Theresia	Mar. 11	Vinzenz	Sep. 27
Theresia	Oct. 1	Viola	May 3
Thikla	Mar. 26	Virgil	Nov. 27
Thomas	Dec. 21	Volker	Mar. 7
Thomas B.	Dec. 29	Volkmar	Jul. 18
Thomas	Jan. 28	Volkmar	May 9

Walburga	Feb. 25	Wilhelm	Mar. 28
Waldo	Dec. 18	Wilhelm	May 28
Walfried	July. 7	Willibald	Jul. 7
Walpurga	Feb. 25	Willibald	Nov. 8
Walter	May 17	Willibald	Jul. 7
Walter	Jan. 22	Wilma	Sep. 19
Walter	Oct. 15	Wilpert	May 23
Walter	Apr. 8	Wiltrud	May 21
Waltmann	Apr. 15	Winfried	Jun. 5
Waltraud	Apr. 9	Wolf	Apr. 21
Waltrud	Apr. 9	Wolf	Mar. 8
Wendelin	Oct. 20	Wolf	Oct. 31
Wenzel	Sep. 28	Wolf	Jul. 19
Werner	Apr. 18	Wolfgang	Oct. 31
Werner	Jun. 4	Wolfgang	Mar. 23
Wigbert	Aug. 13	Wolfhard	Oct. 27
Wigbert	Apr. 18	Wolfhelm	Apr. 22
Wigmann	Nov. 2	Wolfram	Jan. 25
Wilhelm	Jan. 10	Wulf	Oct. 31
Wilhelm	Jul. 5	Wunibald	Dec. 18
Wilhelm	Feb. 10	Zita	Apr. 27

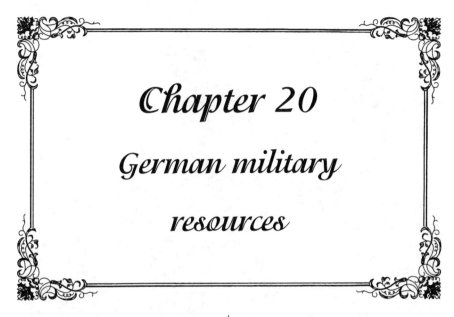

Chapter 20

German military resources

SELECTED EUROPEAN WARS AND WORLD WARS SINCE 1500 INVOLVING GERMANIC PEOPLE AND THEIR NEIGHBORS

1524-25: Peasants Revolt — Lutheran peasants revolt in southern Germanic area and are suppressed (Austria, southern Germany)

1562-98: ... Wars of Religion — Civil wars between Catholics and Protestants (Huguenots) in France

1618-48: Thirty Years War — Denmark, Sweden, France against the Hapsburg dynasty and the Holy Roman Empire, which is devastated by the war

1652-78: Dutch Wars — Trade wars — one between England and United Provinces (Netherlands) in 1652-54, and another a general European war resulting from French expansionism, 1672-1678

1689-97: War of the Grand Alliance — Expansionist aims of French king Louis XIV result in invasion of the Rhineland

1700-21: ..... Great Northern War — Russia gains Baltic territories.

1701-14: .... War of the Spanish Succession — Great Britain, Netherlands, Holy Roman Empire, Poland, and others wage war against Spain and France.

1733-38: War of the Polish Succession — Struggle for Polish throne; France on one side, Austria and Russia on the other

1740-48: War of Austrian Succession — France, Spain, Prussia and others against Great Britain and Austria; known in America as King George's War

1756-63: Seven Years War — France, Austria, Russia, Saxony, Sweden, and Spain against Great Britain and Prussia. Prussia, under Prussian king Frederick the Great wins more territory and establishes Prussia as an important European power.

1789-1802: French Revolution and Re-volutionary Wars — Austria and Prussia become allies against France.

1803-15: Napoleonic Wars — Between

A bitter farewell

France and Great Britain, Russia, Austria, and Sweden. German troops serve throughout Europe. France temporarily occupies the Rheinland.

1864: Austro-Prusso-Danish War — Schleswig and Holstein are ceded to Prussia and Austria

1866: Prusso-Austrian War (Seven Weeks War) — Prussian chancellor Otto von Bismarck provokes war between Prussia and Austria, resulting in Prussia's exclusion of Austria from confederation of northern German states and leading to the establishment of the Austro-Hungarian Empire in 1867

1867: Prussia absorbs the armies of all other states except Bavaria, Saxony, and Württemberg.

1870-71: Franco-German War — France defeated. Germany annexes province of Alsace-Lorraine

1912-13: Balkan Wars — Two wars,

becoming precursors to World War I

1914-18: World War I — Between Allies, including France, Great Britain, Russia, Italy, United States; and Central Powers, including Germany, Austria-Hungary, and Ottoman Empire. Alsace-Lorraine returned to France. (War ends 11 November 1918.)

1917-22: Russian Revolution and Civil War — Result in formal adoption of the name "Union of Soviet Socialist Repub-lics"

1918-20: Baltic War of Liberation — Estonia, Latvia, and Lithuania successfully fight off invasions of Bolsheviks and Germans at end of World War I.

1919-20: Russo-Polish War — Poland gains some territory in Ukraine and Byelorussia.

1936-39: Spanish Civil War — Spanish nationalists defeat Loyalists, resulting in dictatorship of General Francisco Franco and contributing to outbreak of World War II

1939-45 World War II — Allies, including United States, Great Britain, France, Russia and Russia, defeat Axis, including Germany, Italy, and later Japan, resulting in westward shift in Polish border and large gains in territory for USSR. Many German records destroyed. (War began 1 September 1939, ended 8 May 1945)

1939-40 Russo-Finnish War Soviet Union fights for Finnish territory.

Sources:

•Bruce Wetterau, *The New York Public Library Book of Chronologies.* Prentice Hall, New York 1990

•The World Almanac and Book of Facts. Pharos Books, New York, 1993.

•David Brownstone and Irene Franck, Timelines of War: *A Chronology of Warfare from 100,000 BC to the Present.* Little, Brown and Company, Boston 1994

GERMAN MILITARY RECORDS VOCABULARY

Bataillon .... battalion
Corporal .... corporal
Dragoner .... dragoon
Fähnrich .... flagbearer (military)
Feldschreiber .... military clerk
Feldwebel .... sergeant major,
        sergeant first class
Fourier   quartermaster
Füselier .... light infantryman
Fußsoldat .... foot soldier
Fußsoldaten mit Gewehr   armed foot
           soldier
Garnisonskirchenbuch .... garrison
         church book
Generalfeldmarschall .... general
         of the army
Generalleutnant .. (army) major general
Generalmajor .... (army) brigadier
          general
Generaloberst .... (army) general
Grenadier .... grenadier, infantryman
Hauptmann .... captain
Heer .... army
Heeresdienst .... military service
Heeresmacht .... (military) forces
Kapitän (navy) .... captain
Königlich [sächsische] Armee   Royal
         [Saxon] Army
Krieg .... war
Kriegsdienst .... military service
Leutnant (army) ...... second lieutenant
Major .... major
Mannschaftsstammrollen .... troop rolls
Militärarzt ...... military medical officer
Militärgericht .... military court
Militärkirchenbücher   military parish
          records
Musterungslisten .... muster rolls
Oberleutnant (army) .... first lieutenant
Oberst (army) .... colonel
Oberstleutnant (army) lieutenant colonel
Offiziersstammrollen .... officer rolls
Quartiermeister .... quartermaster
Rangliste ... table of ranks, officer rolls
Regimentsgeschichten .... regimental

histories
Regimentsquartiermeister .... regiment
quartermaster
Reiter .... rider, cavalry soldier
Rittmeister .... captain (of cavalry)
Soldat .... soldier
Stammrollen .... records of
common soldiers and
noncommissioned officers
Unteroffizier .... corporal
Wachsoldat .... military guard
Wachtmeister .... sergeant major

GERMAN MILITARY RECORDS: AN OVERVIEW

Before 1871, when the Franco-Prussian War ended, there was no "German" army, but rather armies of the many states and principalities. In 1867, however, many of the non-Prussian troops in Germany

Infantry staff-officer

were combined with the Prussian Army, which meant that after that year there was no longer an army consisting of solely Prussian soldiers. (The exceptions were Bavaria, Saxony, Württemberg, and Austria.)

Military records, dating from the 17th century, consist of military church records, records of common soldiers and noncommissioned officers, officers' rolls, and regimental histories.

The excellent 12-page pamphlet, *German Military Records as Genealogical Sources,* by Horst A. Reschke is essential as an orientation to military record searches. It outlines in general term which German military records are available, in which German states they can be found, and what time period they cover.

This work is available on microfiche (FHL fiche 6001596). It may be purchased for $4.00, postpaid, from the author, Horst A. Reschke, P.O. Box 27161, Salt Lake City, UT 84127-0161.

Source: *German Military Records as Genealogical Sources*, by Horst A. Reschke, 1990

GERMAN 'IMPERIAL' ARMIES

Research in German military records must always begin by first determining the army in question, i.e., Prussian, Saxon, Bavarian, etc. If family tradition reports military service in the 'imperial' (German = *Kaiserliche*) army, it never refers to the Prussian army, but, prior to 1804, would always indicate the Austrian army, and after 1804 would have reference to Napoleon's French army and all of its attached allied regiments. During the second half of the nineteenth century, the letters 'k. u. k.' (German = *kaiserlich und königlich,* i.e. imperial and royal) always denoted Austro-Hungarian troops.

Source: From Horst A. Reschke, *Military Record Sources in Germany* (FHL microfiche 6,001,596)

GERMAN MILITARY CHURCH BOOKS

Information about available German military church records may be found through the *Verzeichnis der Militär-kirchenbücher in der Bunderspublik Deutschland* (List of the Military Church Books in the Federal Republic of Germany).[1]

This list is limited to the locations of military churchbooks in the old Federal Republic (the former West Germany), including Berlin, as well as the 678 volumes (as of September 25, 1990) stored at the Zentralstelle für Genealogie in Leipzig.[2]

Some of the items included in this book (written entirely in German) include (in translation),

•"Table of Contents" (Check the *Lagerorte,* storage locations, for locations of military churchbooks in specific cities or provinces.)

• .... "On the History of Military Churchbooks and the Field Chaplain System"

• .... "On the Storage Locations of the Military Church Books"

•"Military Church Books as Family History Resources"

•"Using the Military Church Book List"

•"Storage Locations of Military Church-books" (In this section on pages 314-315 are included commanders of Prussian infantry regiments numbered 1-52 and 54-60 by sequential regiment numbers with their dates of command. On pages 431-445, is "Register of Military Units," listing alphabetically the names of units.)

•"Index of the Regimental Church books at the German Center for Genealogy in Leipzig" (useful if the name of the military regiment or the name of its commander is known.)

• ...."Register of Towns and Areas of Origin, and Persons Who Commissioned or Commanded Military Units" (Alphabeti-cally listed, the places include towns, cities, states, and provinces in which the military church books originated. The persons include names of nobles, military commanders, and others after whom military units were named.)

•"Register of Military Units" (Names of military units are listed alphabetically.)

•"List of Publications of Working Group for the Archive and Library System in the Evangelical Church"

On the topic of the use of military church records, Horst A. Reschke ad-vises:

"Military parish records . . . are only good, i.e., contain information, if a sol-dier either got married in a garrison church (*Garnisonkirche*) or, as a mar-ried soldier, had children who were bap-tized or confirmed and thus made it into the record books. If a soldier died or was killed while on active status, his death might be recorded. Regimental church records were kept by the regiment's chaplain and were regarded as his per-sonal property."

Footnotes

[1]Wolfgang Eger: *Verzeichnis der Militärkirchenbücher in der Bundes-republik Deutschland (nach dem Stand vom 30. September 1990). Veröffent-lichungen der Arbeitsgemeinschaft der Archive und Bibliotheken in der evangelischen Kirche 18.* (List of the Military Church Books in the Federal Republic of Germany (as of 30 September 1990). Publications of the Working Group of the Archives and Libraries in the Evangelical Church, No. 18.) Verlag Degener & Co., Neustadt an der Aisch 1993, XXII, 446 pages, DM 60,--.

[2]*Die deutsche Zentralstelle für Genealogie* is located at the Deutsches Staatsarchiv Leipzig, Schongauerstr. 1, 04329 Leipzig, Germany.

The retreat (1854)

Source: "A Guide to Military Churchbooks," by Merriam M. Moore. *The German Connection* (German Research Association), Vol. 20, No. 3 (1996), page 59.

References
♦ *Index der Regimentskirchenbücher* (Index of Regimental Churchbooks), at the *Deutsche Zentralstelle für Genealogie* in Leipzig
♦ *Findbuch der Regiments Kirchenbücher* 1714-1942 (Inventory of Military Parish Registers of the Prussian Army), FHL Microfilm #0492737.
♦"A Guide to Military Churchbooks," by Merriam M. Moore (see "Source" above)

Note
German military church records are usually listed in the Family History Library Catalog with other church records.

FINDING A GERMAN ANCESTOR'S 'LOCAL DRAFT BOARD'

To find the location of the military authority/office to which a male ancestor was obliged to report, see the gazetteer *Meyers Orts- und Verkehrs-Lexikon des Deutsch-en Reichs*[1] under the ancestor's native place name, to see whether the abbreviation: *BKdo* appears, followed by a place name. *BKdo* stands for *Bezirkskommando*, or district military authority.

Note this explanation by Horst A. Reschke: "Most native places were too small to have their own *Bezirkskommando*. Look in *Meyers* for the *Kreis*, or *Bezirksamt*, or *Domäneamt*, or *Amt*, or *Oberamt* – all terms for an administrative body akin to our American "county" – and find the *BKdo* which applies to it. (The reason for the variety of terminology being that the different German states did not have a uniform word for *their* "county" seat, usually a city.) By doing so you have identified the 'local draft board' at which your ancestor was obliged to show up, register, and report for military duty."

The unit designations and garrisons of the German army are listed in the *Einteil-ung und Standorte der deutschen Wehr-macht.* beginning on page 53 of theAppen- dix of *Meyers* (at the end of fiche number 28). The sixth column of this tabular listing, with the heading *Standort* (garrison), contains the name of the town in which each listed regiment was garrisoned.

To find the location of non-Prussian military records (Prussian records were almost completely destroyed by fire in 1945), refer to *Military Record Sources in Germany,* by Horst A. Reschke or to "Beginning Your Military Research," by Horst A. Reschke (see "Source," below).

Source: "Beginning Your Military Research," by Horst A. Reschke, *The German Connection* , Vol. 20, No. 3, 1996
Footnote
[1]FHL microfiche 6,000,001 through 6,000,029; FHL microfilms 496,640 and 496,641

GERMAN PRISONERS OF WAR IN THE UNITED STATES DURING WORLD WAR II

More than three million prisoners of war were held by the Allies during World War II, of which about 425,000 were encamped in the continental United States. Of these, between 360,000 and 372,000 prisoners (estimates vary) were Germans. In World War I, Americans held a total of only 1,346 prisoners of war.[1]

Three general groups of German prisoners were sent to the United States: 1) Germans captured during the fighting in North Africa in late 1942 and in 1943 (by the end of 1943 there were 123,440 German POWs in the United States), 2) about 50,000 Germans, most of whom were captured in the fighting in Italy, and 3) the 182,000 Germans captured after the landing at Normandy on June 6, 1944.[2]

It was decided in 1942 that all prisoners taken by the United States would be shipped to the States, rather than keeping them in Europe, to be transported in ships that were returning to our shores practically empty after carrying troops and supplies overseas.

At first, prisoner-of-war encampments were established in old Civilian Conservation Corps (CCC) camps or in unused camps built in the Southwest for enemy aliens. In the first few months quarters were prepared to hold 76,218 more men, and structures for 144,000 more were begun in case they were needed. At first tents were generally used to hold the prisoners until more substantial structures could be built.

At that time, the pertinent treaty in effect was the 1929 Geneva Convention Relative to the Treatment of Prisoners of War, under which prisoners were to be treated humanely.

Under this convention, prisoners were to get the same housing, food, clothing, pay and work hours as provided to soldiers of the capturing nation. Only enlisted men (if they were healthy) could be put to work. Non-commissioned officers could be required only to supervise enlisted men, and officers could not be required to work.[3]

Americans honored the Geneva Convention almost to the letter, and often beyond its minimum requirements. Reasons for this strict attention to international law were, 1) prisoners were entitled to humanitarian treatment, 2) the United States felt a duty to live up to an agreement which it had signed, 3) liv-

A Swede reconnoitering before Danzig

ing up to the agreement would not give the German government justification not to treat American prisoners humanely, 4) the belief that well-treated prisoners would make better workers, and 5) German soldiers might well be encouraged to surrender, knowing they would be well treated by the Americans.[4]

Under the Geneva Convention, prisoners were not to be "reeducated" or denationalized. At the urging of Eleanor Roosevelt, however, the United States government did secretly undertake an extensive effort to inculcate democratic principles among German prisoners of war.

In 1944, the Prisoner of War Special Projects Division was created, whose personnel put together in a matter of weeks a program to reeducate 372,000 Germans. The project and its results form an intriguing undertaking that had distinguished if controversial effects.[5]

A sampling of some of the courses offered to the prisoners includes
◆The Democratic Way of Life
◆The Constitution of the United States

◆ Political Parties, Elections, and Parliamentary Procedures
◆Education in the United States
◆American Family Life
◆The American Economic Scene
◆American Military Government
◆Democratic Traditions in Germany
◆ Why the Weimar Republic Failed; Democratic Traditions in Germany
◆The World of Today and Germany
◆New Democratic Trends in the World Today[6]

The interpreter shortage

The problem of interpreters was severe. It was not unusual for only a single translator to be available for up to 10,000 prisoners. The choices related to such a dilemma were not attractive: either use English-speaking German prisoners, (Nazis or anti-Nazis), or just forget about he prisoners and let them run themselves. Between these two choices it was decided that the better plan was to use the English-speaking Germans for communication, although the Nazi influence in the camps was a definite risk, which often backfired.[7]

Prisoner segregation

Only superficial separation of German personnel took place, with army personnel separated from air force, and officers from enlisted men. Nazis and anti-Nazis were housed together, causing serious problems later on. By 1945, only a total of 4,500 visibly loyal Nazis were interned at Alva, Oklahoma, and 3,300 of the most visibly dedicated anti-Nazis were shipped to Fort Devens, Massachusetts, and Camp Campbell, Kentucky. There were numerous incidents in which rabid Nazis tried (and too often succeeded) in murdering or harming anti-Nazi prisoners of war.[8]

Escape attempts

Fewer than 1 percent of the total number of German prisoners in the United States made attempts to escape. Working in favor of the War Department in this respect were three major factors: 1) the Germans formed a tightly obedient military unit, with each rank responsible to its immediate superior, 2) the prisoners were immediately attracted to a comprehensive recreational and educational program offered to them, and 3) there was simply no place to go (long train rides had impressed on prisoners the vastness of the American landscape).

Yet some prisoners tried to escape, and indeed, not only was it legal under the Geneva Convention of 1929, but it was the duty of captured soldiers to escape, charged by their oath of service to escape at every opportunity.

A "Memorandum Addressed to German Soldiers," provided to all German POWs as guaranteed by the Geneva Convention, reminded the soldiers that they were to keep physically strong, to become fully familiar with their rights, and to take every opportunity to escape.

The number of escapes was small: monthly about 3 escapees per 10,000 captives, a record better than that of the American penitentiary system. The great majority of escapees were returned to

military control within 24 hours of their escape, when they were routinely interrogated, given a token punishment as required under the Geneva Convention, and returned to the prisoner community.

The War Department reported that 46 percent of the escapes occurred at base camps, 16 percent from branch camps, and 30 percent from work details.[9]

Of the total of 2,222 German prisoners of war who escaped, only 17 remained at large in late 1947; by 1951 only six were at large. Four were discovered or surrendered by 1959. The last escapee, Georg Gaertner, who escaped in September 1945, was never located [10]

A time of horrors

In 1945 the big news from Europe was that of the millions who had perished in the Nazi extermination camps. The War Department made mandatory the showing of films of the Nazi atrocities to German prisoners of war. The orders were the same for all camps: all prisoners were forced to attend, silence was to be maintained during the film, and no discussion afterwards was permitted.

Responses varied. Some were horrified, destroyed their German uniforms, and even took up collections for concentration camp survivors.

Others credited the films as Hollywood fabrications, or as Russian propaganda. The most common response: "Why did they show that to us? We didn't do it."[11]

The reaction of the War Department, in May 1945, was to reduce the food allowances of the prisoners. At Camp Stark, New Hampshire, for example, the daily food ration was reduced from 5,500 to 1,800 calories; the canteen no longer sold beer, milk, cigarettes, or candy; and the lumber-cutting work quota was raised.[12]

In the midst of this new anxiety, the German prisoners at Camp Stark got word of another piece of news that put

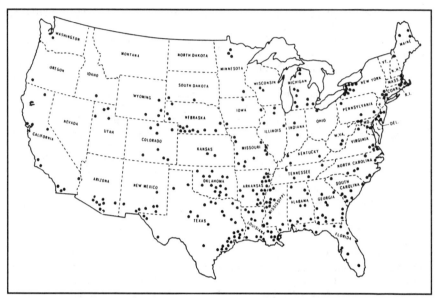

Major Prisoner of War camps in the U.S. as of June 1944. (U.S. Army photo)

fear in their hearts: Some new guards were coming into the camp, American soldiers who had just returned to the United States after suffering as prisoners of war in Germany. These men, captured during the Battle of the Bulge, had been marched without food for four days from Belgium to Germany, and had endured a four-day rail journey locked in a box car with 60 men without food or water. Then they were marched to Bad Orb where for the next 100 days they existed on grass soup with a few potatoes. These men, the War Department declared, "who have experienced captivity and detention by the enemy, are considered to be eminently qualified for these duties."

The big surprise came when the American prisoners of war arrived and bore no animosity to the German prisoners. Rather, close friendships were formed between these two groups who shared the experience as prisoners of war. The Germans heard first-hand news of the situation in Germany from their new guards – and as bad as the news was, at least it was reliable. Also, the Americans empathized with the plight of the German prisoners of war. When rations were cut for the German prisoners, the American guards slipped food and cigarettes to the Germans in order to communicate their lack of support for the American policy.[13]

Dashed hopes

The end of the war raised great hopes for the Germans that they could return home. But the end the emptying out of the American prisoner of war camps triggered great disappointment and resentment in many Germans who had come to admire the United States. About half the German prisoners of war found that they were not going to go home after all, but that they were instead to be traded off primarily to France and England to help reconstruct those war-damaged countries. The anger stirred in the prisoners by this deal made by the Allies was remembered for years after.[14]

The majority of the prisoners shunted off to France, England, Netherlands, Scandinavia, Czechoslovakia, Yugoslavia, and Greece served in labor battalions for about four to six months, although many thousands were held much longer.[15]

Footnotes

[1] Allen V. Koop, *Stark Decency: German Prisoners of War in a New England Village* (New York: Hanover: University Press of New England, 1988), 24.

[2] Helmut Hörner, *A German Odyssey: The Journal of a German Prisoner of War* (Golden, Colorado: Fulcrum Publishing, 1991) ix.

[3] Hörner, *A German Odyssey: The Journal of a German Prisoner of War*, viii.

[4] Hörner, *A German Odyssey: The Journal of a German Prisoner of War*, viii.

[5] Judith M. Gansberg, *Stalag: U.S.A. The Remarkable Story of German POWs in America,* (New York: Thomas Y. Crowell Company, 1977).

[6] Hörner, *A German Odyssey: The Journal of a German Prisoner of War*, 360.

[7] Arnold Krammer, *Nazi Prisoners of War in America* (New York: Stein and Day, 1979), 5

[8] Krammer, *Nazi Prisoners of War in America*, 169-174

[9] Krammer, *Nazi Prisoners of War in America*, 116-121

[10] Krammer, *Nazi Prisoners of War in America*, 136-139

[11] Koop, *Stark Decency:German Prisoners of War in a New England Village,* 99-100.

[12] Koop, *Stark Decency: German Prisoners of War in a New England Village*, 99-101.

[13] Koop, *Stark Decency: German Prisoners of War in a New England Village*, 103.

[14] Koop, *Stark Decency: German Prisoners of War in a New England Village*, 111.

[15] Krammer, *Nazi Prisoners of War in America*, 248

MAJOR GERMAN PRISONER OF WAR INTERNMENT CAMPS IN THE UNITED STATES

- Camp Algoma, Idaho
- Camp Aliceville, Alabama
- Camp Alva, Oklahoma
- Camp Angel Island, California
- Camp Ashby, Virginia
- Camp Ashford, West Virginia
- Camp Atlanta, Nebraska
- Camp Atterbury, Indiana
- Camp Barkeley, Texas
- Camp Beale, California
- Camp Blanding, Florida
- Camp Bowie, Texas
- Camp Brady, Texas
- Camp Breckinridge, Kentucky
- Camp Butner, North Carolina
- Camp Campbell, Kentucky
- Camp Carson, Colorado
- Camp Chaffee, Arkansas
- Camp Claiborne, Louisiana
- Camp Clarinda, Iowa
- Camp Clark, Missouri
- Camp Clinton, Mississippi
- Camp Como, Mississippi
- Camp Concordia, Kansas
- Camp Cooke, California
- Camp Croft, South Carolina
- Camp Crossville, Tennessee
- Camp Crowder, Missouri
- Camp David, Maryland
- Camp Dermott, Arkansas
- Camp Douglas, Wyoming
- Camp Edwards, Massacnusetts
- Camp Ellis, Illinois
- Camp Evelyn Michigan
- Camp Fannin, Texas
- Camp Farragut, Idaho
- Camp Florence, Arizona
- Camp Forrest, Tennessee
- Camp Gordon Johnston, Florida
- Camp Grant, Illinois
- Camp Gruber, Oklahoma
- Camp Hale, Colorado
- Camp Hearne, Teas
- Camp Hood, Texas

•Camp Houlton, Maine
•Camp Howze,. Texas
•Camp Hulen, Texas
•Camp Huntsville, Texas
•Camp Indianola, Nebreaska
•Camp Jerome, Arkansas
•Camp Lee, Virginia
•Camp Livingston, Louisiana
•Camp Lordsburg, New Mexico
•Camp McAlester, Oklahoma
•Camp McCain, Mississippi
•Camp McCoy, Wisconsin
•Camp McLean, Texas
•Camp Mackall, North Carolina
•Camp Maxey, Texas
•Camp Mexia, Texas
•Camp Monticello, Arkansas
•Camp New Cumberland, Pennsylvania
•Camp Ogden, Utah
•Camp Opelika, Alabama
•Camp Papago Park, Arizona
•Camp Peary, Virginia
•Camp Perry, Ohio
•Camp Phillips, Kansas
•Camp Pickett, Virginia
•Camp Pima, Arizona
•Camp Polk, Louisiana
•Camp Popolopen, New York
•Camp Pryor, Oklahoma
•Camp Reynolds, Pennsylvania
•Camp Jos. T. Robinson, Arkansas
•Camp Roswell, New Mexico
•Camp Rucker, Alabama
•Camp Rupert, Idaho
•Camp Ruston, Louisiana
•Camp Scottsbluff, Nebraska
•Camp Shelby, Mississippi
•Camp Sibert, Alabama
•Camp Somerset, Maryland
•Camp Stewart, Georgia
•Camp Stockton, California
•Camp Sutton, North Carolina
•Camp Swift, Texas
•Camp Tonkawa, Oklahoma
•Camp Trinidad, Colorado
•Camp Van Dorn, Mississippi
•Camp Wallace, Texas
•Camp Wheeler, Georgia
•Camp White, Oregon

•Camp Wolters, Texas
•Fort Benjamin Harrison, Indiana
•Fort Benning, Georgia
•Fort Bliss, Texas
•Fort Bragg, North Carolina
•Fort Crockett, Texas
•Fort Curtis, Virginia
•Fort Custer, Michigan
•Fort Devens, Massachusetts
•Fort Dix, New Jersey
•Fort DuPont, Delaware,
•For Eustis, Virginia
•Fort Gordon, Georgia
•Fort Greely, Colorado
•Fort Jackson, South Carolina
•Fort Kearny, Rhode Island
•Fort Knox, Kentucky
•Fort Leavenworth, Kansas
•Fort Leonard Wood, Missouri
•Fort Lewis, Washington
•Fort McClellan, Alabama
•Fort Meade, Maryland
•Fort Niagara, New Hork
•Fort Oglethorpe, Georgia
•Fort Ord, California
•Fort Patrick Henry, Virginia
•Fort Reno, Oklahoma
•Fort Riley, Kansas
•Fort Robinson, Nebraska
•Fort D.W. Russell, Texas
•Fort Sam Houston, Texas
•Fort Sheridan, Illinois
•Fort Sill, Oklahoma
•Fort F.E. Warren, Wyoming
•Edgewood Arsenal, Maryland
•Eglin Army Air Field, Florida
•Glennan General Hospital, Oklahoma
•Halloran General Hospital, Neew York
•Hampton Roads Port of Embarkation, Virginia
•Indiantown Gap Military Reservation, Pennsylvania
•Holabird Signal Depot, Maryland
•McCloskey General Hospital, Texas
•Memphis General Depot, Tennessee
•New Orleans Port of Embarkation, Louisiana
•Olmsted Field, Pennsylvania
•Pine Bluff Arsenal, Arkansas

•Richmond ASF Depot, Virginia
•Tobyhanna Military Reservation, Pennsylvania
•Westover Field, Massachusetts

[1] ..... Arnold Krammer, *Nazi Prisoners of War in America,* Stein and Day, New York, 1979

RESEARCHING GERMAN PRISONERS OF WAR IN THE UNITED STATES

After World War II, the United States sent relevant prisoner-of-war personnel files to Germany. The holder of such records is the *Wehrmachtsauskunftsstelle* ("information center on members of the former German army") abbreviated as "WAST," according to this pattern: Wehrmachtsauskunftsstelle
     For information , contact
     WAST
     Eichborndamm 179, Tor 6
     13403 Berlin, Germany
     Tel. 030-419040
     Open Monday-Thursday, 9 am - 2 pm; Friday 9 am - 1 pm
Most of the records in the custody of the National Archives and Records Administration (NARA) as they relate to POW camps in the United States can be found in Record Group 389, Records of the Office of the Provost Marshal General.

Many POW camp records were destroyed after the war. While NARA usually has some material about the major camps in the United States, it has very little documentation about the small branch or satellite camps which existed. RG 389 files in NARA's custody which are camp specific include the following:

Inspection Reports
These include reports by the United States War Department, and by neutral observers such as the International Red Cross and the Swiss Legation. These files document camp facilities and activities, and may include blueprints and maps.

Special Projects Division Files
Include documents related to prisoner re-education and cultural activities.

Detention Rosters
Although not necessarily complete for each camp, the rosters contain name, service number, POW number, birth date, date of capture and possible SS affiliation.

Labor Report Forms
Forms covering a two-week period and list total POW man-hours available and how those hours were broken down into various activities. Sometime the "remarks" section of these forms was used to record important administrative events.

Technical Service Division Files
Containing contain examples of admin-istrative forms and some reports relating to the operation of the camps.

Construction Files
Documents relating to the construction of camps, although many of the enclosures and attachments described in cover sheets are not in these files.

Administrative Files
Containing information about the transfer of specific POWs in and out of the camps. Correspondence contains some lists of POWs.

In addition to the camp-specific files described above, RG 389 contains several correspondence files relating to Axis POWs interned in the United States.

Other record groups in NARA's custody also contain related information. For example, Record Group 211, Records of the War Manpower Commission, contains several series of records relating to the use of POW labor in the United States during World War II.

Sources:
* National Archives II, Textual Reference Branch, 1996
* WAST information: Rainer Thumshirn, of Heimstetten, Germany

SUGGESTED READING ON GERMAN PRISONERS OF WAR

*Judith M. Gansberg, *Stalag U.S.A.: The Remarkable Story of German POWs in America*. Thomas Y. Crowell Co., New York, 1977.
*Arnold Krammer, *Nazi Prisoners of War in America*. Stein and Day, New York, 1979.

* Allen V. Koop, *Stark Decency: German Prisoners of War in a New England Village*. University Press of New England, Hanover, 1988.
*Helmut Hörner, *A German Odyssey: The Journal of A German Prisoner of War*. Fulcrum Publishing, Golden, Colorado, 1991.
*Glenn Thompson, *Prisoners on the Plains: German POWs in America*. Gamut Publications, 1993.
*R. Robin, *The Barbed-Wire College: Reeducating German POWs in the United States During World War II*. Princeton University Press, 1995

Chapter 21

Religions

THE CHURCH IN MODERN GERMANY

In 1993, about 35 percent of the German population was Catholic (about 28.4 million church members). Some 36.5 percent of the population at that time (27.5 million) was affiliated with the established Protestant (Evangelical) Church. In addition, there were some 1.9 million Moslems in the country. The number of Jews has risen steadily due to an influx from eastern Europe and now lies at about 50,000, while the two large churches have seen a small but steady decline in membership and attendance in recent years.

The Protestant Church in Germany (*Evangelische Kirche in Deutschland*) is a federation of the Lutheran, Reformed (Calvinist) and United (Calvinist and Lutheran) churches. Its legislative body is the Synod.

The Roman Catholic Church in Germany is organized into 27 dioceses, five of which are in eastern Germany. The Catholic Church hierarchy is headed by the German Bishops Conference, the main governing body of the Church.

Although many Germans are members of a church, few attend regularly. The number of churchgoers has been on the decline in recent years. In 1993, 5.4 million Catholics – 19 percent of registered Catholics in the country – attended Sunday mass. That is down from the 25.3 percent recorded in 1984. Only 1.2 million, or four percent, of the Protestants in Germany regularly attended Sunday services in 1992.

Germany has no state religion. The Basic Law guarantees freedom of faith and freedom of religion or ideological creed. Historical development, however, has resulted in religious concentrations in certain areas. Northern Germany is primarily Protestant, while the population in the West and South is primarily Catholic.

These regional groupings, however, are gradually being leveled out through the increasing migration and mobility of fami-
(continued on page 429)

RELIGIOUS PREFERENCE
OF THE STATES OF THE GERMAN EMPIRE, 1880

	% Prot.	% Cath.	% Jews
Anhalt	97	2	1
Baden	35	63	2
Bayern	28	71	1
Berlin	88	7	5
Brandenburg	97	2	1
Braunschweig	97	3	-
Bremen	96	4	1
Elsaß-Lothringen	20	78	3
Hamburg*	93	3	4
Hannover	87	12	1
Hessen*	68	29	3
Hessen-Nassau	70	27	3
Hohenzollern	3	95	1
Lippe	96	3	1
Lübeck	98	1	1
Mecklenburg-Schwerin	99	-	-
Mecklenburg-Strelitz	99	-	1
Oldenburg	77	22	1
Ostpreußen*	86	13	1
Pommern	97	2	1
Posen	31	65	3
Preußen	65	34	1
Reuß ältere Linie	99	1	-
Reuß jüngere Linie	99	1-	
Rheinland	26	72	1
Sachsen (Kingdom)	97	3	-
Sachsen (Preußen)	93	6	-
Sachsen-Altenburg	99	1	-
Sachsen-Coburg-Gotha	99	1	-
Sachsen-Meiningen	98	1	1
Sachsen-Weimar-Eisenach	96	3	-
Schaumburg-Lippe	98	2	-
Schlesien	47	52	1
Schleswig-Holstein	99	1	-
Schwarzburg-Rudolstadt	99	1	-
Schwarzburg-Sondershausen	99	1	-
Waldeck	96	3	2
Westfalen	46	52	1
Westpreußen	49	49	2
Württemberg	69	30	1
GERMANY	63	36	1

*In addition, showed a 1% count of religious preference for "other."

Source: *Germany Genealogical Research Guide,* by Steven W. Blodgett. The Genealogical
Department of the Church of Jesus Christ of Latter-day Saints. rev. 1989. Reprinted by permission of
the author.

lies since World War II.

Church financing

Germans who are members of a church support it through their taxes, not directly as in the United States.

When taxpayers list their religious affiliation on their employment record, an amount between eight and nine percent of their income tax is collected by the tax authorities and given to the church to which the taxpayer belongs. Churches pay the administration cost.

Thus, churches in the Federal Republic have a guaranteed annual income from their members. They do not engage in the kinds of fund-raising activities familiar in the United States.

Religious instruction

Religion is a subject in public schools. Children attend classes according to their faith. Parents may decide wich class their children attend, or whether they should attend any class at all. From the age of 14 on, a student can decide whether or not to continue religious instruction. There are also parochial schools in Germany, but they have become less important in the last few decades.

Religion in everyday life

Churches play an important role in the field of public welfare and social services, and foreign aid. They take part in the debate about peace and disarmament, foreign worker and labor market policy, abortion, and protection of the environment.

In the former German Democratic Republic, the churches played an important political role by sheltering dissidents and providing a free space for discussion. They were instrumental in supporting the grassroots movements that eventually paved the way for unification.

Church holidays are often national holidays, and the religious pageantry associated with these holidays has become a part of the public spectrum of customs and festivals.

In the former East Germany, some religious ceremonies were replaced by secular ones. For example, the *Jugend-weihe*, a non-religious coming-of-age ceremony took the place of confirmation.

The *Jugendweihe* was discarded after unification, like many other eastern German customs, but is now making a comeback.

Despite the celebration of religious holidays, however, Germans are generally less involved in religious activities on a daily basis than are Americans, though this varies from region to region. German leisure-time activities generally do not center around the church.

Source: Courtesy of the German Information Center; excerpted from *Federal Republic of Germany: Questions and Answers*, ed. Susan Steiner, German Information Center, New York, 1996

OFFICIALLY RECOGNIZED RELIGIONS

Following the Reformation, the Roman Catholic Church was strongest in Bavaria; the Lutheran church in the northern states; and the Reformed church in the Palatinate. Catholic (*katholisch*) records have been kept since 1563, usually written in Latin. Lutheran and Reformed records date from 1550, written in German.

Also written in German were the Evangelical records.

Through the treaty that ended the Thirty Years War (1648), it was stipulated that only three religious confessions would be tolerated in the German nations: Catholic, Lutheran, and Reformed.

Any sects outside these religions were outlawed. Thus it was understandable why so many of the emigrants were of Pietist persuasions who sought freedom to practice their religion in America.

Up to the time of Napoleon, the Protestant churches — Lutheran and Reformed — were separate but legal entities. Then in 1806 in the Palatinate, in 1807 in other southern German states, and in 1817 in Prussia, they were decreed legally to be one "Protestant Evangelical Christian Church."

Thus the records since that time show a person's religion to be either *katolisch* or *evangelisch*.

Other smaller religious groups included Huguenots (French Protestants), Anabaptists (Mennonites and others), Waldensians, Moravians, Amish, Quakers, Dunkers, Separatists, and Schwenkfelders.

Further reading

For an informative overview of religious groups in Germany, including a bibliography and addresses of organizations, see *Germanic Genealogy: A Guide to Worldwide Sources and Migration Patterns*, by Edward R. Brandt, Ph.D. et al, Germanic Genealogy Society, 1995, pp. 110-121.

Sources:

♦Ruth Bailey Allen, "Church Records Relating to the Pennsylvania Germans," Palatines to America: Publications Plus, 1992, No. 2
♦Wolfgang Glaser, *Americans and Germans*. Verlag Moos&Partner. Munich, 1985.

THE PIETISTS

The Pietists participated in a seventeenth and eighteenth century Lutheran reform movement in which the focus was placed on individual conversion and "living faith."

The term Pietism stems from the *collegia pietatis* (informal devotional meetings) which became the basis for the movement through the efforts of Philipp Jakob Spener, a Frankfurt pastor. In small groups involving study and prayer, the participants emphasized faith in Christ, not just acceptance of correct theological concepts, as well as the importance of education.

The University of Halle became the intellectual center of Pietism, which influenced younger Halle-educated pastors in Protestant Germany who subsequently became pastors in colonial America.

The pietist reform movement, beginning in the late seventeenth century with its focus on individual conversion and a devout way of life, strengthened Lutheranism in Germany and spread to other countries.[1]

These pietistic sects were represented in good numbers in the early German settlements in the United States, largely as a result ofthe stipulation of the Peace of Westphalia in 1648 (ending the Thirty Years' War), that only the Catholic, Lutheran, and Reformed religions were to be permitted in Germany. Other sects or religions were forbidden In order to continue practicing their religion, they were forced to emigrate.[2]

[1]"Pietism," Microsoft (R) Encarta. 1994 Microsoft Corporation, Funk & Wagnalls Corporation, 1994
[2]La Vern Rippley, The German-Americans, University Press of America, Inc. 1984.

ANABAPTISTS

In the early 1520s religious leaders who were to become known as Anabaptists spoke out against the church and social practices of the time, in Switzerland, Germany, and Austria. They stressed the need for personal faith and for independent judgment, at the same time rejecting the formal ritualistic practices of the established churches.

Originally named *Täufer* (baptizers), they took their name from their belief in adult baptism, or "believer's baptism. They were also called *Wiedertäufer* (rebaptizers) and *"Taufgesinnte"* (baptism-minded) because of their belief in adult baptism.[1]

The history of the Anabaptists in Europe is one of persecution resulting in migrations.

Anabaptist groups were found spread through Europe under a number of different names, one being that of the Mennonites.

[1]Hermann Guth, *Amish Mennonites in Germany: Their Congregations, the Estates Where They Lived, Their Families.* Masthof Press, Morgantown, Pa., 1995.

MENNONITES (ANABAPTISTS)

The Mennonites whose faith grew out of Huldreich Zwingli's Reformation, take their name from the religious leader Menno Simons. ·

The views that were later called Mennonite originated in Zürich, where in 1523 a small community left the state church and shortly thereafter adopted the tenet of believers' baptism. Because of their belief in adult baptism, the term "Anabaptists," meaning "rebaptizers," came into being. The Mennonites' original name was *Täufer* (baptizers) or *Taufgesinnte* (baptism-minded).

Anabaptists were most active during the Reformation and shortly afterward in Germany and the Netherlands. They were forced to flee following the fierce opposition and persecutions by both Catholic and Protestant authorities. Their congregations survived only in isolated parts of Switzerland and Frisia, with a few in the Palatinate.

In the Netherlands, the Frisian priest Menno Simons preached believers' baptism and nonresistance, which led to years of persecution of his Anabaptist followers. Mennonites took their name from that of Menno Simons.

Groups of the same persuasion appeared in southern Germany and in Austria (led by Jakob Hutter and his Hutterites).

In the 1520s in Switzerland, Mennonites broke with Zwingli over infant baptism.

In 1620 the Swiss Mennonites broke into two parties, the Uplanders, known as Amish (after Jakob Amen or Ammann, their leader), and the Lowlanders.

Mennonites were persecuted in Switzerland, Germany, Holland, and France.

In the 18th century, the Swiss Brethren fled to the Rhineland, the Netherlands, Pennsylvania, and eastern Europe. Many Dutch Mennonites emigrated to Pennsylvania, Prussia, and Poland.

Large numbers of German Mennonite colonies were formed in southern Russia following the invitation by Catherine II, where they were attracted by religious liberty and freedom from military service.

Of the many colonies which emigrated to America the oldest, a group of 13 families from Krefeld (Crefeld), was settled in 1683 at Germantown, Pennsylvania, under the leadership of Francis Daniel Pastorius, whose colonists were warmly welcomed by William Penn.

Germantown was the first permanent German settlement in North America. The Krefelders were later joined by some of the Quaker Mennonites from Kriegsheim.

The date of the Krefelders' arrival in Philadelphia, 6 October 1683 is a date celebrated to this day as the beginning of German-American history. (In recent years, 6 October has been declared German-American Day.)

Following the Krefelders were Dutch and Swiss Mennonites. Among them were the Amish Mennonites.

In the first half of the 19th century, Mennonites from Switzerland and southern Germany settled in Ohio, to the west, and into Missouri.

Following the Civil War, Mennonites emigrated to Kansas, Nebraska, and South Dakota. After World War I, Mennonite groups migrated to Canada, primarily Saskatchewan.

Sources:
♦ *Encyclopedia Britannica: Dictionary of Arts, Sciences, Literature and General Information,*

University Press, New York, Eleventh Edition, 1905

♦ *The American Immigration Collection: The German Element in the United States*, Albert Bernhardt Faust, Arno Press and New York Times, New York 1969. Vol. I.

♦ *Amish Mennonites in Germany*, Herman Guth, Masthof Press, Morgantown, PA. 1995. Original work: *Amische Mennoniten in Deutschland*

RESOURCES FOR MENNONITE RESEARCH

Libraries and societies

♦ **Lancaster Mennonite Historical Society** (Landis Library), 2215 Millstream Road, Lancaster, PA 17602 (See 000)

♦ **Fresno Pacific Library,** 1717 S. Chestnut, Fresno, CA 93702

♦ **Associated Mennonite Seminary,** 3003 Benham, Elkhart, IN 46517

♦ **Mennonite Historical Library,** Goshen College, Goshen, IN 46526 (See 000)

♦ **Mennonite Library and Archives,** Bethel College, North Newton, KS 67117

♦ **Center for Mennonite Brethren Studies,** 4824 East Butler, Fresno, CA 93727-5097.

♦ **Center for Mennonite Brethren Studies,** Tabor College, 400 South Jefferson, Hillsboro, KS 67063

♦ **Germantown Mennonite Historic Trust,** 6133 Germantown Avenue, Philadelphia, PA 19144 (Collections: Hymnals, prayerbooks printed in Germantown in the eighteenth and nineteenth centuries; mostly Mennonite and Brethren, some Lutheran; Germantown Mennonite history)

♦ **Illinois Mennonite Historical and Genealogical Society,** State Route 16, P.O. Box 819, Metamora, IL 61548

♦ **Menno Simons Historical Library and Archives,** Eastern Mennonite University, Harrisonburg, VA 22801-2462. (See 000)

♦ **Mennonite Family History,** 10 West Main Street, P.O. Box 171, Elverson, PA 19520-0171

♦ **Mennonite Historians of Eastern Pennsylvania,** 565 Yoder Road, Box 82, Harleysville, PA 19438 (Collections: Local Mennonites; local genealogy, history, biography and churches in Bucks, Montghomery, Berks, Lehigh and Philadelphia Counties; General Mennonite and Anabaptist history and theology; Pennsylvania German studies, peace and non-resistance, Mennonite missions; congregational histories; congregational and conference archival collections for theEastern District and Franconia Conferences; manuscript collections from families, ministers, former organizations and businesses relating to Mennonite in the region; local cemetery records)

♦ **Mennonite Historical Association of the Cumberland Valley**, 4850 Molly Pitcher Highway South, Chambersburg, PA 17201 (Collections: General history of Mennonite and related church groups; genealogy books; Mennonite journals; archival collection focusing on Mennonite and related church groups in the Cumberland Valley of Maryland and Pennsylvania)

♦ **Mifflin County Mennonite Historical Society,** Walnut Street, P.O. Box 5603, Belleville, PA 17004 (Collections: Books on genealogy, local and church history; old family Bibles; church and local periodi-cals; Amish-related materials; Mennonite and Anabaptist local history; deeds, letters, local newspapers, pictures and records of the local Mennonite congregations)

♦ **Muddy Creek Farm Library**, 376 N. Muddy Creek Road, Denver, PA 17517 (Collection: Old Order Mennonites and some kindred groups; many Old Order Mennonite and Old Order Amish magazines and many Mennonite periodicals; Mennonite biographies, county histories, fraktur, general church histories, congregational and conference histories; empha-sis on collecting of all known Mennonite devotional books from the sixteenth century to the present)

◆**Pequea Bruderschaft Library**, P.O. Box 25, Gordonville, PA 17529 (Collections: Old Order Amish and some Mennonite publications, genealogies, church and secular histories; books used in Amish schools; diaries, account books and ledgers, cemetery records of Lancaster County from 1794 to 1985; Amish death records in Lancaster County from 1794 to the present; newspaper clippings on the Amish)

◆**Mennonite Historical Society of Iowa, Mennonite Historical Museum,** 411 Ninth Street, P.O. Box 576, Kalona, IA 52247

◆**Mennonite Library and Archives,** Bethel College, 300 East 27th, North Newton, KS 67117

◆**Brethren in Christ Archives/Historical Society,** Messiah College, Grantham, PA 17027 (Collection: Focus on Brethren in Christ; also Anabaptism, Pietism and Wesleyanism)

◆**Home Messenger Library,** 1438-H West Main Street, Ephrata, PA 17522 (Collections: Old Order Mennonites; biographies, historical, devotional and secular books; letters, diaries, records and out-of-print material)

◆**Juniata District Mennonite Historical Society,** P.O. Box 81, Richfield, PA 17086 (Collections: Herald Press publications, local church histories, local county and state histories and family Bibles; genea-logies, published and unpublished; Juniata County newspapers; Juniata District church records, community papers and records; deeds; land title records for Juniata and Snyder Counties)

◆**Mennonite Heritage Centre,** 600 Shaftesbury Blvd., Winnipeg, Manitoba, Canada, R3P OM4

◆**OMII Genealogical Project** (Ohio, Michigan, Indiana, Illinois), of the California Mennonite Historical Society, titled the "GRANDMA" project, placing information about Swiss and South German Mennonite and Amish families into a database, with primary focus on families coming into the four states from Europe after 1815.

Information on earlier immigrant families from Pennsylvania, Virginia, and other states is also included.

The coordinator of the program is David Habegger, 6929 Hillsboro Court, Fort Wayne, IN 46835.

Publications

◆*Mennonite Cyclopedic Dictionary*, ed. Daniel Kaufman. Scottdale, PA: Mennonite Publishing House 1937; reprinted 1978 by The Bookmark, Knightstown, IN

◆*Amish Mennonites in Germany,* Herman Guth, Masthof Press, Morgantown, PA. 1995. Originally published as *Amische Mennoniten in Deutschland.*

◆*The Palatine Immigrant*, Vol. V, No. 2 (autumn 1979). Issue deals completely with Mennonites

◆*Historic Background and Annals of the Swiss and German Pioneer Settlers of Southeastern Pennsylvania, and of Their Remote Ancestors,* by H. Frank Eschleman, 1917. Reprinted by The Genealogical Publishing Co., Inc., Baltimore, 1969.

◆Kraybill, Paul N., *Mennonite World Handbook: A Survey of Mennonite and Brethren in Christ Churches.* Mennonite World Conference, Lombard, Ill., 1978

◆"Swiss Mennonite Family Names, An Annotated Checklist," Leo Schelbert and Sandra Luebking. *Newsletter* of the Swiss American Historical Society, Vol. XIV No. 2, June 1978.

◆*Krefeld Immigrants and Their Descendants,* LINKS Genealogy Publications, 7677 Abaline Way, Sacramento, CA 95823-4224. Creator of bi-annual publications for the descendants of the Krefeld immigrants, their families, and neighbors of those who established Germantown, Pennsylvania, their migration, religion, and history.

Back issues of the publications are available.

Source: Library holdings information partially based on Ray K. Hacker, comp., *The Eastern Mennonite Associated Libraries and Archives Directory.* Masthof Press, Morgantown, Pa., 1996

LANCASTER MENNONITE HISTORICAL SOCIETY

Lancaster Mennonite Historical Society
2215 Millstream Road
Lancaster, PA 17602-1499
Tel. (717) 393-9745

The library and archives of the Lancaster Mennonite Historical Society emphasize Pennsylvania Mennonite and Amish history, genealogy, and theology. The Society serves as the official repository of the Mennonite Church.

The collection includes historical and genealogical materials related to southeastern and south-central Pennsylvania and other areas to which Mennonites moved from Pennsylvania, especially concerning denominations with a Swiss and German background such as the Church of the Brethren, United Brethren, Brethren in Christ, River Brethren, Moravians, Lutherans, and German Reformed.

Materials available include approximately 230,000 individual name cards in the genealogical card file, including all obituaries indexed from a major Mennonite periodical (*Herald of Truth/Gospel Herald*) since 1864; major Mennonite, Brethren and Amish periodicals; about 1,900 published genealogies; census records and court-related documents for Lancaster County and surrounding counties; important works pertinent to Pennsylvania genealogical research; and collections of notes and other documents of significance to researchers.

Availability

Open Tuesday through Saturday, 8:30 am - 4:30 pm, except holidays. Users fee for non-members is $3.00 per day.

MENNO SIMONS HISTORICAL LIBRARY AND ARCHIVES

Eastern Mennonite University
Harrisonville, VA 22801-2462
Fax: (540) 432-4977
E-mail: huberhe@emu.edu

The Menno Simons Historical Library and Archives is located in the Hartzler Library on the campus of Eastern Mennonite University. The library's primary purpose is to "collect, preserve and make available for study and research the recorded history, doctrines, life, and arts of Anabaptist and Mennonite groups." Provided also are materials on Shenan-doah Valley history, culture and genealogy.

Holdings

The collection. spanning the years from 1501 to the present, has special strengths in the Protestant Reformation, Dutch and German Anabaptist Mennonite history and thought, the life and ideas of Mennonites and related groups in North America, and materials on history of Swiss and German immigrants as well as genealogical information.

The collections include Pennsylvania German materials such as Ephrata and Saur imprints, extensive materials pertaining to the Amish and an outstanding collection of central Shenandoah Valley imprints. The library focuses on the collecting of materials from the East and Southeast, including small Mennonite groups in the Southeast.. Genealogical collections are listed in a seven-page handout.

Availability

Hours are Monday through Friday, 10 am to 5 pm; Saturday 10 am - 1 pm (no Saturday hours during summers/holidays). Archives hours largely by appointment. Persons traveling from a distance should contact the library in advance.

MENNONITE HISTORICAL LIBRARY

Mennonite Historical Library
Goshen College
Goshen, IN 46526
Tel. (219) 535-7418
Fax: (219) 535-7438
The Mennonite Historical Library, located on the third floor of the Harold and Wilma Good Library of Goshen College, owns a genealogical collection of more than 2,800 volumes, including genealogical aids. It is particularly strong in the genealogy of Amish and Mennonite families coming from Switzerland and South Germany. Many Dutch, West Prussian and Russian families are also represented.

Holdings

The broadest areas of the general collection are publications of Pennsylvania German records and German immigration in the 18th and 19th centuries.

The collection includes 41,000 volumes (books, pamphlets, bound periodicals) documenting Reformation and Anabaptist history and the various Mennonite and related groups throughout the world.

The library maintains an obituary index to the *Herald of Truth* (1864-1908) and its successor, the *Gospel Herald.* There is also a computerized index to about 120 Amish genealogies.

AMISH

In 1663 occurred the "Amish Division," a split among the "Swiss Brethren" Mennonites.

The division was instigated by a Mennonite preacher in the canton of Bern, Jacob Amman, who pushed for the doctrine of *Meidung* (avoidance, or shunning). Most Swiss Brethren of the Palatinate and of the Emmenthal were not willing to ac-

cede to Amman's demand.

When an Amish person is put "under the ban," of shunning, the result is total ostracism – business social, religious, and domestic.

He is totally isolated from his fellow church members. Even his wife and children are forbiddent to sit at the same table with him.

The Amish set for themselves restrictions in styles of dress and implemented the practice of footwashing. They were known as *Häftler* ("hook-and eyers") because of their use of hooks and eyes instead of buttons on their clothing, and *Bartmänner* ("beardsmen") because of their prefernce for full beards, without mustaches. Liberal Mennonites who had refused to accede to Amman's principles were called *Knöpfler* (button-wearers).

In 1712, King Louis XI banished all "Anabaptists" from France. Many Amish groups migrated into Germany. None of these congregations survives.

All but one of the following congregations were located in what is present-day Germany (each represents a chapter in the Hermann Guth book, *Amish Mennonites in Germany* – see "Source" listing below):
1. The Congregation of the Upper Palatinate
2. The Congregation of the Lower Palatinate
3. The Hofstätten Congregation
4. The Darmstadt Congregation
The Durlach Congregation
6. The Hochburg Congregation
7. The Weilburg Congregation
8. The Zweibrücken Congregation
9.The Frönsburg (Froensbourg) Congregation, today in France
10. The Waldeck Congregation (with Wittgenstein and neighboring areas)

In North America, the Amish are formally referred to as Old Order Amish Mennonites.

Known as the Plain People, they began migrating to North America in 1728, traveling to Pennsylvania, then to Ohio,

Illinois, and Iowa, and more recently to Wisconsin, Minnesota, and Canada.

Note: *The Guidebook to Amish Communities in North America and Business Directory,* by Ottie A. Garrett, Hitching Post Enterprises, 1996 contains a list of all known Amish communities, as well as some families and church districts. It is available through Masthof Bookstore, Morgantown, Pennsylvania.

Sources:
♦Hermann Guth, *Amish Mennonites in Germany.* Masthof Press, Morgantown, PA, 1995
♦Fredric Klees, *The Pennsylvania Dutch.* The Macmillan Company, New York, 1950.
♦La Vern J. Rippley, *The German Americans.* University Press of America, Inc., Lanham, Md., 1984.

THE SCHWENKFELDERS

Kaspar Schwenkfeld von Ossig (1490-1561), a German nobleman from Silesia who led the Reformation there, and a theologian, was maligned by Catholic and Protestant groups and was unable to settle a theological dispute with the reformer Martin Luther.

At his death in 1561, he left behind a band of loyal followers known as Schwenkfeldians, who continued his mission by forming a sect in Silesia.

When, in 1720, a Commission of Jesuits set out to convert the sect by force, most members fled to Saxony, then to Holland, England, and North America. All Schwenkfelder immigrants came from either Silesia or Saxony, and many from Silesia moved to Saxony shortly before going to Pennsylvania.[1]

During the period 1731-1737, about 206 Schwenkfelders fled persecution and settled in eastern Pennsylvania — in Philadelphia as well as in Montgomery, Bucks, Lehigh, and Berks counties.

In 1782 the Society of Schwenkfelders was organized. In 1909, descendants of these immigrants incorporated themselves under the name of The Schwenkfelder Church.

Schwenkfelders practice adult baptism, dedication of children and open communion. They serve in the armed forces when called.

The churches teach the right, privilege and obligations of individual conscience.

Five congregations exist today in southeastern Pennsylvania: Palm (in Montgomery County, founded soon after arrival of the Schwenkfelder immigrants in Philadelphia in 1734), Norristown (organized as a mission in 1904), Lansdale (begun in 1916), Worcester (in Montgomery County, where members originally worshiped in private homes, later in meeting houses in Salfor, Towamencin, and Worcester, after which a church building was constructed in 1951), and Philadelphia (at 30th and Cumberland Streets, originating as a mission in 1895), with a total membership of about 3000.

Organizations
♦Schwenkfelder Church, One Seminary Street, Pennsburg, PA 18073
♦ Schwenkfelder Historical Society Library, Carnegie Library Building, Pennsburg, PA 18073
♦The Society of the Descendants of the Schwenkfeldian Exiles, c/o Schwenkfelder Historical Society Library (see address above). This society seeks to maintain interest in the genealogical and cultural heritage of the Schwenkfelder exiles and refugees of the eighteenth century.
♦ Samual K. Brecht, *A Genealogical Record of the Schwenkfelder Families.* .Board of Publications of the Schwenkfelder Church, Pennsburg, Pa., Chicago, 1923.
♦*Selections from the Genealogical Record of the Schwenkfelder Families,* the Schwenkfelder Church, Pennsburg, PA: Rand McNally, Chicago, 1923. 1923.
♦ Howard Wiegner Kriebel, *The*

Schwenkfelders in Pennsylvania: A Historical Sketch. Pennsylvania German Society Proceedings, vol. 13, 1904. Reprint. AMS Press, New York, 1971.

[1]Aaron Spencer Fogleman, Hopeful Journeys: German Immigration, Settlement, and Political Culture in colonialAmerica, 1717-1775. University of Pennsylvania Press, Philadelphia, 1996.

HUGUENOTS

The Huguenot Confession originated in France. Followers of the faith were influ-enced by John Calvin who, in Geneva, Switzerland, trained hundreds of exiles from France to serve as missionaries in their own country.

Following the revocation of the Edict of Nantes in 1685 (whereby Huguenots were generally granted freedom of reliTelegraph Road, Alexandria, VA 22303

♦*Hugenotten in der Pfalz,* FHL microfiche 6001626

♦*Archiv für Sippenforschung,* Vol. 28, 1967 (a special edition of this periodical on Huguenots) and the August 1975 issue

♦*Der deutsche Hugenott,* March and June 1966, references provided by Helmut Cellarius to literature, libraries, archives, and museums in France, Netherlands, England, and Germany

HUGUENOT CHRONOLOGY

1536: John Calvin's leadership role in Geneva enables him to train hundreds of exiles from France, who return as missionary pastors.

1560: Aristocratic families in France begin to accept the Calvinist religion. Rival factions emerge (Roman Catholic extremists and supporters of royalty), leading to ten wars.

1562-1563: First Huguenot war

1567-1568: Second Huguenot war
1568-1570: Third Huguenot war
1572-1573: Fourth Huguenot war
1574-1576: Fifth Huguenot war
1577 (April-September): Sixth Huguenot war
1579-1580: Seventh Huguenot war
1586-1598: Eighth Huguenot war
1598: King Henry IV promulgates the Edict of Nantes, reaffirming the position of the Catholic church as the official religion and granting freedom of religion to Huguenots in much of France.
1617: Louis XIII becomes king
1621-1622: Ninth Huguenot war
1624: Cardinal Richelieu becomes part of the king's council; he destroys the political power of the Huguenots.
1625-1629: Tenth Huguenot war
1685: King Louis XIV revokes the Edict of Nantes; thousands of Huguenots flee France for Holland, America, British Isles, and Germany. About 30,000 flee to Germany, traveling through Elsaß-Lothringen, Saar, Pfalz, North Baden, North Württemberg, Hessen, South Hannover, Anhalt, Brandenburg and the Vorpommern area.
1787: Edict of Toleration restores most of the civil rights of Protestants.
1802: Napoleonic Code grants full religious equality.

Source: "The Huguenots in Germanic Areas," *German Genealogical Digest,* Vol. 2, No. 4, 1986.

THE HARMONISTS

Georg Rapp of Iptingen, in Württemberg, led members of a nineteenth century sect who had left the Protestant church in order to worship in a more informal and pietistic manner.

These Separatists, as they came to be known, were called upon to submit a declaration of their position. The "Articles of Faith" of 1798 defined their beliefs concerning the church, baptism, communion, the church school, government and oaths, and military service — and constituted the formal beginning of the Separatist movement.

In 1803 Rapp and a few other Separatists sailed to Philadelphia and built a prosperous community called Harmony in Pennsylvania, near Pittsburgh.

They became a corporate body in 1805, from which time they were called either Harmonists or Rappites.

In 1814 the group resettled south of Vincennes, Indiana, building the town of New Harmony. Here they thrived from 1814 to 1824 and experienced phenomenal economic success, at one point even lending money to the new State of Indiana. Frederick Rapp, the adopted son of Georg Rapp, became a representative to Indiana's constitutional convention in 1816.

Then in 1824 the Harmonists moved again, back to Pennsylvania, purchasing land on the Ohio River near Pittsburgh and building the town of Economy (now called Ambridge, after the American Bridge Company). All the Harmonists had moved there by 1825.

Not long after, the religious faith of the Harmonists began to decline, especially among the young. In 1906 the society was dissolved.

Of genealogical interest is a document that discloses the membership of the Harmonists — a power of attorney given by the membership in Indiana to Frederick Rapp to sell their property.

This document, dated 21 May 1824 and recorded 20 April 20 1825, is found in Deed Record Book D, pages 116-127, at the Posey Conty courthouse in Mount Vernon, Indiana.

Nearly 500 names, male and female, are listed. The document, with a complete list of names, was published in the *Indiana Magazine of History*, Vol. XLVII, pp. 313-319 (1951).

The definitive work on the Harmony Society is Karl J.R. Arndt's *George Rapp's Harmony Society, 1785-1847*, revised edition, Fairleigh Dickinson Press, Rutherford, New Jersey, 1972.

Source: Based primarily on "Württembergers to America: The Harmonists," by Keith Boger. *The German Connection*, Vol. 14, No. 4, October 1990.

THE AMANA COLONIES

The Amana community had its beginnings in eighteenth century Europe when a group of German, Swiss, and French pietists founded a religion based on a belief in divine revelation through *Werkzeuge*, or "inspired prophets."

The denominational name became Community of True Inspiration.

In 1843 some 600 Inspirationists, beset by political and religious persecution, emigrated to the United States from German lands under the leadership of a pietist, Christian Metz, and founded the Ebenezer Society community near Buffalo, New York. Around 1855 they moved west to the Iowa River Valley. There they lived a communal life for 77 years in seven villages that they founded, the oldest of which was Amana.

The Amana Society was incorporated in 1859.

References

◆ Shambaugh, Bertha Maud (Horack), *Amana That Was and Amana That Is*. State Historical Society of Iowa, Iowa City, 1932. Reprint. Benjamin Blom, New York, 1971

◆ Perkins, William Rufus, and Barthinius L. Wick, *History of the Amana Society or Community of True Inspiration*. Reprint. Radical Tradition in America, Westport, Conn., Hyperion Press, 1976.

Source: "Iowa's Enduring Amana Colonies," by Laura Longley Babb; *National Geographic*, Dec. 1975.

THE MORAVIAN CHURCH

The Moravian Church has its roots in the provinces of Bohemia and Moravia in the present-day Czech Republic. The name of the church when it was founded was "Unitas Fratrum" (United Brethren), The church goes back to the time of John Hus, burned at the stake in 1415 as an early Protestant heretic, whom the Moravian church honored as a martyr.

After 1458 when the first association of the church organized in Bohemia, the church was referred to as *Jednota Bratrska* (The Union of Brethren) or *Unitas Fratrum* (Unity of the Brethren).

The Unitas Fratrum, or Moravians, should not be confused with the United Brethren in Christ, which did not form until around 1800.

The Moravians, however adopted the name United Brethren in Christ in the midwest.

In 1740, by invitation of Count von Zinzendorf, a small group of the faithful took refuge on the his estate in Saxony, where they built the town of Herrnhut. Under Zinzendorf's leadership, in 1741, members of the church arrived in Philadelphia and settled in Northampton and Lehigh counties, Pennsylvania, founding the town of Bethlehem — and later Nazareth, Lititz, and Emaus, also in Pennsylvania.

The group failed at their attempts to form colonies in Georgia, in Hope, New Jersey, and in Salem, North Carolina.

Almost all Moravian emigrants left Europe from Herrnhut (Saxony), Wetteravia, the Netherlands, or London.[1]

The count named the group Moravians because they came from northern Moravia. (Although Moravia was attached to Bohemia from the eleventh century, it became an Austrian crownland after the Revolution of 1848. When Czechoslovakia was formed in 1918, Moravia became a part of that country.)

Moravian Church members, a German-speaking pietist sect, were the most successful missionaries among American Indians in American history.

They settled around Winston-Salem, North Carolina, in 1753.

Their numbers have been greatest in Pennsylvania, North Carolina, and Wisconsin, in that order.

The United Brethren has consolidated with the Methodist Episcopal Church to become the United Metho-dists. In the midwest, the Moravians adopted the name "United Brethren in Christ."

Resources
for further study

♦**Moravian Archives,** 41 West Locust Street, Bethlehem, PA 18018 ["Northern Province"].

♦**Moravian Archives**, 4 East Bank Street, Winston-Salem, NC 27101-5307. Tel. (910) 722-1742 ["Southern Province"]. This is the repository of the Southern Province, Moravian Church. Records go back to 1753. The Archives provides research for a fee.

♦**Salem College, Granly Library**, Salem Square, Winston-Salem, NC 27108

♦**Gnadenhutten Public Library**, 160 N. Walnut, Gnadenhutten, OH 44629

♦**Moravian College Library**, Main and Elizabeth, Bethlehem, PA 18018

♦**Moravian Heritage Society**, 31910 Road 160, Visalia, CA 93292. Tel. (209) 798-1490. Fax: (209) 798-1922. A Moravian surnames database may be accessed for $2 per surname. Other research services are available.

References

♦Hamilton, John Taylor, *A History of the Church Known as the Moravian Church, or the Unitas Fratrum, or the Unity of the Brethren, During the Eighteenth and Nineteenth Centuries.* 1900. Reprint, AMS Press, New York, 1971

♦ "Old Moravian Cemeteries," by Arta F. Johnson. *Palatine Immigrant*, Vol. V, No. 1, Summer 1979.

◆Reichel, Levin T., *The Moravians in North Carolina, an Authentic History.* 1857. Reprint, Genealogical Publishing, Baltimore, 1968.

[1]Aaron Spencer Fogleman, Hopeful Journeys: German Immigration, Settlement, and Political Culture in Colonial America, 1717-1775, University of Pennsylvania Press, Philadelphia, 1996.

HUTTERIAN BRETHREN

Known as Hutterites, the Hutterian Brethren began in an Anabaptist community in Moravia during the Reformation.

Their name is derived from their original leader, Jakob Hutter of Austerlitz, burned as a heretic in 1536.

In the seventeenth and eighteenth centuries the Hutterites lived for more than a century in a German-language enclave in Slavic Moravia.

To escape persecution, they settled in Russia and stayed there for about 100 years, until 1874.

When Russia mandated the use of Russian in the schools and required military service, they emigrated to settle in Dakota territory during the period between 1874 to 1879, and later in Canada in Manitoba and Alberta. An early colony settled near Yankton, South Dakota in 1884. There still remain more than 50 Hutterite colonies in South Dakota.

The Hutterites retain the German language in school instruction and in the home.

Resources
◆Horsch, John, *Hutterite Brethren: 1528-1931.* The Mennonite Historical Society, Goshen, IN., 1931
◆Gross, Paul S., *The Hutterite Way; the Inside Story of the Life, Customs, Religion, and Traditions of the Hutterites.* Freeman Publishing, Saskatoon, Saskatchewan, 1965

CHURCH OF THE BRETHREN, OR GERMAN BAPTIST BRETHREN (DUNKERS)

Dunkers (or Tunkers, after the German verb *tunken,* "to dip," based on their method of baptismal immersion) were members of a late seventeenth century pietist sect, which became the Church of the Brethren.

They have also been known as German Baptist Brethren or German Brethren.

The sect's members followed the teachings of Andrew Mack of Swartzenau, Germany.

Shortly after the new sect was organized in Germany in 1708, its members took refuge in Holland to escape persecution, but then emigrated to Pennsylvania between 1719 and 1729. The sect left none of its members behind in Germany.

The first German Baptists in America, who settled in Germantown, Pennsylvania, came from Krefeld in the Rhineland.

The first congregation in America was organized in 1723 by Peter Becker at Germantown. There, in 1743, Christopher Saur, a printer by trade and one of the sect's first pastors, printed the first Bible published in a European language in America.

The Dunkers moved westward and south from Pennsylvania, settling also in Maryland, Virginia, Ohio, Indiana, Illinois, Iowa, Missouri, Nebraska, Kansas, and North Dakota.

A few of them separated from the original teachings and went to Ephrata Cloister in Pennsylvania, with Conrad Beissel. This group believed in celibacy and gradually died out. Ephrata Cloister disbanded in 1830.

By the time of the American Revolution, the Dunkers were called Brethren.

In the 1880s the church divided into the Old-Order and Progressive Brethren and eventually formed separate organizations. The Progressive Brethren divided again in 1939.

The parent church today is called the Church of the Brethren (Conservative Dunkers).

Branches of the Brethren which consider themselves as outgrowths of the original group are the Old German Baptist Brethren, organized in 1881; Brethren Church, 1883; Fellowship of Grace Brethren Churches, 1939; and the Dunkard Brethren, 1926.

References
♦Brumbaugh, Martin Grovek, *A History of the German Baptist Brethren in Europe and America.* Bookmark, Knightstown,Ind., 1977
♦ Doll, Eugene Edgar, *The Ephrata Cloister: An Introduction.,* Ephrata Cloister Associates, Ephrata, Pa., 1958.
♦Falkenstein, George N., "The German Baptist Brethren or Dunkers," *Pennsylvania German Society Proceedings* and Addresses 10 (1900): 1-48. Pennsylvania German Society, Lancaster, Pa., 1900.
♦Fitzkee, Donald R. , *Moving Toward the Mainstream: 20th Century Change Among the Brethren of Eastern Pennsylvania,* Good Books, 1995.
♦ "Migration of Early German Baptist Brethren Within the United States," by Lester H. Binnie. *The Palatine Immigrant,* Vol. V, No. 1, Summer 1979.

Archives
♦ Church of the Brethren Historical Library, 1421 Dundee Avenue, Elgin, IL 60120
♦Church of the Brethren Library, 2710 Kingston Road, York, PA 17402
♦ Bethany Theological Seminary, Butterfield and Meyers Roads, Oak Brook, IL 60521
♦Ashland Theological Seminary, Ashland, OH 44805
♦Ephrata Cloister, Ephrata, PA 17522
♦ Juniata College, 18th and Moore, Huntington, PA 16652
♦ McPherson College, Miller Library, McPherson, KS 67460
♦ Messiah College, Murray Center,

Grantham, PA 17027
♦ Juniata College, 18th and Moore, Huntington, PA 16652
♦Ephrata Cloister, Ephrata, PA 17522

Sources:
♦*Encyclopedia Britannica: Dictionary of the Arts, Sciences, Literature and General Information,* University Press, New York, 11th ed., 1910.
♦La Vern J. Rippley,*The German-Americans.* University Press of America, Inc., Lanham, MD, 1984
♦Microsoft (R) Encarta, 1994 Microsoft Corp., Funk & Wagnalls Corporation, 1994

UNITED BRETHREN IN CHRIST

The Church of the United Brethren in Christ was founded in 1800 in Pennsylvania primarily through the efforts of a German-born clergyman, Philip William Otterbein, and a German Mennonite preacher, Martin Boehm. Services were initially conducted in German.

In 1946 the United Brethren in Christ united with the former Evangelical church to form the Evangelical United Brethren church, which joined with the Methodist church in 1968 to form the United Methodist Church.

Resource
The Center for Evangelical United Brethren Heritage, United Theological Seminary Library, 1810 Harvard Boulevard, Dayton, OH 45406. Tel. (513) 278-5817.

The Center's library contains denominational resources of the United Brethren in Christ Church, the Evangelical Church, and the Evangelical United Brethren Church; research is performed for a fee.

Generally, the Center advises, it is more profitable to inquire into local church records to find family information. The Center can help to direct searches by locating a church or by attempting to trace the history of a local church.

Source: "United Brethren in Christ," Microsoft

(R) Encarta. Microsoft Corporation 1994. Funk & Wagnalls Corporation 1994.

Kurier, Mid-Atlantic Germanic Society, Vol. 14, No. 2, June 1996.

REFORMED CHURCH IN THE UNITED STATES

Founders of the Reformed Church emigrated to America from the Rhine area and from the German cantons of Switzerland in the early 18th century. Other emigrants included French and Dutch families of the Reformed faith. The Dutch Reformed arrived before the German emigrants.

In 1793 the congregations adopted the name German Reformed Church. In 1869 the church was renamed the Reformed Church in the United States.

In the mid 1980s, it merged, except for a group of 34 churches, with the Evangelical Synod of North America as the Evangelical and Reformed Church. The latter became part of the United Church of Christ in 1957.

Beliefs of the German Reformed Church were based on the thinking of such men as John Calvin, Heinrich Bullinger, and Ulrich Zwingli.

The document that best expresses the doctrine of the German Reformed churches is the Heidelberg Catechism, written in 1563.

The German Reformed Church limited baptism to children of communicants.

References

◆Good, James Isaac, "The Founding of the German Reformed Church in America by the Dutch," *American Historical Association,* Annual Report, 1897.

◆Dubbs, Joseph Henry, "History of the Reformed Church, German, by Joseph Henry Dubbs." *The American Church History Series 8*, 1895.

Sources:

◆"Reformed Church in the United States," Microsoft (R) Encarta. Microsoft Corporation 1994, Funk & Wagnalls Corporation 1994.

◆Humphrey, John T.,"Baptismal Records: Understanding Their Meaning & Use." *Der*

UNITED CHURCH OF CHRIST

This church resulted from a merger of the Evangelical and Reformed Church (mostly German in background) and the General Council of the Congregational Churches.

EVANGELICAL AND REFORMED HISTORICAL SOCIETY

The Evangelical and Reformed Historical Society
555 West James Street
Lancaster, PA 17603
Tel.: (717) 290-8734

This Society, located at the Lancaster Theological Seminary, is the repository for the records of the former German Reformed Church, the Reformed Church in the United States, and the Evangelical and Reformed Church

Merger

Since the merger in 1957 with the Congregational Christian Churches, the denomination has been known as the United Church of Christ.

Holdings

In addition to denominational records, the Society holds records from some former German Reformed congregations, especially in the southeastern and central Pennsylvania areas.

Most of the local church records, which include baptisms, marriages, and burials, have been microfilmed by and are available through the LDS Family History Library.

The Society's holdings do not include records from other German denominations or sects.

Availability

The facility is open Monday through

Thursday. A $5.00 fee for a day of genea-
logical research is charged; memberships
are also offered, at $25 per year.

The Society does not consider itself to
be primarily a genealogical research organization. Researchers are encouraged to
call in advance if they wish to use the
Society's resources.

EXPULSION OF
THE SALZBURG PROTESTANTS

In 1686 the Archbishop of Salzburg expelled 621 Protestants from his bishopric.
All children under the age of 15 had to be
left behind to be reared by Catholics.

Then 45 years later, Salzburg's Archbishop Leopold Anton Freiherr von
Firmian, seeking to stop the rise of Protestantism, signed into law on November
11, 1731 the *Emigrationspatent* (emigration order) forcing all domestic servants
and employed workers to renounce Protestantism or to leave Salzburg by November 30.

This meant an immediate exodus in the
middle of winter with nowhere specific to
go. Farmers, artisans, and merchants were
given an additional five months in which
they could try to sell their property, being
under order to leave by April 24, 1732.

The majority of the more than 30,000
emigrants headed for East Prussia, and
smaller groups settled in southern Germany and Holland. One group headed for
the British colonies in North America and
settled near Savannah, Georgia. Altogether, more than 20,000 Protestants were
evicted from their homeland. Estimates are
that approximately a quarter of them perished on their flight to a new homeland.
A band of Lutheran Salz-burgers settled
in the United States on the Savannah River
in Purysburg, Georgia, in 1731. Many of
these settlers later moved to the nearby
village of New Ebenezer, founded in 1736.

The Georgia Salzburger Society is publishing an updated, multi-volume geneal-

ogy of the Salzburgers, *Georgia Salzburgers and Allied Families*. Contact: Georgia Salzburger Society, 9345 Whitfield
Avenue, Savannah, GA 31406. Tel. (912)
754-7001/754-6333

Source: "Exodus of the Salzburg Protestants to
Georgia," by Rainer Thumshirn. *Der
Blumenbaum*, Vol. 13, No. 3, 1996.

HIGHLIGHTS
OF LUTHERAN CHURCH
HISTORY IN THE UNITED STATES

1623: First permanent settlement of
European Lutherans arrives at Manhattan
Island from Holland.

1748: Congregations in Pennsylvania,
New Jersey, New York and Maryland
organize the country's first Lutheran
synod, "the ministerium of Pennsylvania," under Pastor Henry Melchior
Mühlenberg.

1838: German immigrants, forerunners of
the Lutheran Church-Missouri Synod,
arrive in Missouri (also in Michigan).

1918: Groups of Germans, Norwegians,
Danes, Icelanders, Finns and Slovaks start
a cooperative group, the National Lutheran
Council

1930: Norwegian and other groups united
in "old" American Lutheran Church.

1960: American Lutheran Church, largely
of Norwegian, Danish and German roots,
is formed by "old" American Lutheran
Church, Evangelical Lutheran Church,
and United Evangelical Lutheran Church.
Three years later, Lutheran Free Church
joins.

1962: Lutheran Church in America is
formed by four bodies, largely of Swedish,
German, Finnish and Danish background:
Augustana, United Lutherans, Suomi
Synod, and American Evangelical
Lutherans.

1966: Lutheran Church in America,
American Lutheran Church, and Missouri
Synod form the Lutheran Council in the
USA, successor to the National Lutheran

Council (formed in 1918)
1972: American Lutheran Church, Lutheran Church of America, and Missouri Synod form the Consultation on Lutheran Unity
1975: Consultation on Lutheran Unity dissolved by mutual consent of the three denominations.
1976: "Moderates" who split from the Missouri Synod form the Association of Evangelical Lutheran Churches.
1982: Lutheran Church in America, American Lutheran Church, and Association of Evangelical Lutheran Churches begin work toward merger
1988: The new Evangelical Lutheran Church in America begins functioning

Source: Based on "A Brief History of Lutheran Union in America," *The German Connection*, Vol. 11, No. 1, January 1987, as reprinted from *Perspective* (date not given)

RECENT LUTHERAN CHURCH MERGERS IN THE UNITED STATES

As of the early 1980s these five Lutheran bodies were active:
LCA: Lutheran Church in America
LCMS: Lutheran Church - Missouri Synod
ALC: American Lutheran Church
WELS: Wisconsin Evangelical Lutheran Synod
AELC: Association of Evangelical Lutheran Churches
ELCA: Beginning in 1988, LCA, ALC, and AELC were consolidated to form the Evangelical Lutheran Church in America (ELCA).
Lutheranism is the third largest Protestant denomination in the United States.
The LCA
The Lutheran Church in America (LCA), based in New York and Philadelphia, formed in 1962 from the union of four separate Lutheran bodies. The LCA

dated from the mid-1660s, when Dutch Lutherans formed congregations in the New York area.
The ALC
The American Lutheran Church (ALC), with headquarters in Minneapolis, formed in 1960 as the result of a merger of four separate Lutheran groups.
The AELC
The Association of Evangelical Lutheran Churches (AELC), based in St. Louis, was established in 1976 as a result of separation from the Lutheran Church-Missouri Synod.
The ELCA
The Evangelical Lutheran Church in America (ELCA), based in Chicago, is the largest of the United States-based Lutheran bodies.
Lutheran Church – Missouri Synod
This is the second largest Lutheran church in the United States. *Missouri* is part of the name because the denomination was founded in that state by German emigrants in 1847.
The church's headquarters are in St. Louis.
Wisconsin Evangelical Lutheran Synod
This synod was organizaed in 1850 in Milwaukee as the German Evangelical Lutheran Synod of Wisconsin. It merged with two other synods – Minnesota and Michigan – in 1917, to become the Evangelical Lutheran Joint Synod of Wisconsin and Other States. The present name was adopted in 1959.
Source: Frank Spencer Mead, *Handbook of Denominations in the United States*. Abingdon Press, Nashville, TN., new 9th ed., rev. by Samual S. Hill, 1990.

CONCORDIA HISTORICAL INSTITUTE

Concordia Historical Institute
Department of Archives and History
801 DeMun Avenue
St. Louis, MO 63105

Tel.: (314) 721-5934

Concordia Historical Institute is the Department of Archives for The Lutheran Church – Missouri Synod.

Most of the resources in its collection are related to the pastors and congregations of the Missouri Synod, which was organized in 1847. The Institute does not have a computer listing of all Lutherans, as functioning parishes should still have their own records.

In order for the Institute to determine whether its holdings contain information that would interest a researcher, it needs as specific information as possible, including the name of a specific Lutheran congregation or minister who served the family, or some other such specific connection with the Lutheran Church.

Such information will enable the Institute to determine whether its holdings will be useful in researching a given request.

EVANGELICAL AND REFORMED HISTORICAL SOCIETY

The Evangelical and Reformed
Historical Society
555 West James Street
Lancaster, PA 17603
Tel. (717) 393-0654

This Society is a sponsored agency of the Historical Council of the United Church of Christ and serves as a denominational archives for the records of the former German Reformed Church in the United States.

Merger

The United Church of Christ is the product of a merger of the Evangelical and German Reformed churches and some Congregational churches.

The Society performs only the most limited genealogical research.

The researcher would need to know the name of a specific Reformed church in which an ancestor was once a member before a search can be made to determine whether records for that church are available.

Holdings

The Society holds original records or copies from central and southeastern Pennsylvania churches of this denomination, but there are no surname indexes to records.

Availability

Mosts of the Society's records have been microfilmed by the Church of Jesus Christ of Latter-day Saints.

THE WENTZ LIBRARY

The Wentz Library
Lutheran Theological Seminary
Gettysburg, PA 17325

The Wentz library building at the Seminary serves as a repository for the archives of synods in central Pennsylvania and Maryland. Original parish registers stored there are not available for genealogical research.

All information contained in the records is available on microfilm through the Family History Library of the Church of Jesus Christ of Latter-day Saints.

Many records are also available through
The Genealogical Society of Pennsylvania
Hall of the Historical Society
1300 Locust Street
Philadelphia, PA 19107

Typed transcripts of a limited number of parish registers from central Pennsylvania and Maryland are available at
Adams County Historical Society
Drawer A
Gettysburg, PA 17325
Tel. (717) 334-4723

A researcher is available, for a fee, for responses to written requests for service through the microfilms created by the Church of Jesus Christ of Latter-day Saints.

WELS HISTORICAL INSTITUTE

The WELS Historical Institute, Dept. of Archives
Rev. Martin O. Westerhaus, Archivist
11831 N. Seminary Drive 65W
Mequon, WI 53092
WELS Historical Institute maintains archives of the Wisconsin Evangelical Lutheran Synod (WELS), which dates back to 1850 when the German Evangelical Lutheran Synod of Wisconsin and other states was organized in Milwaukee. Pastors and members of this church were recent immigrants from Germany. For some decades, services were conducted in the German language.

Although WELS has member congregations in all 50 states, the largest concentration of churches is in the upper Midwest, especially the states of Wisconsin, Minnesota, and Michigan.

The WELS Archives primarily gather and preserve records of the Wisconsin Synod itself as well as historical information about member congregations and biographical information about pastors and teachers of the Synod. The Institute does not have records of sacred acts of member congregations, which are kept by the congregations themselves.

Records of closed or merged congregations usually went to the congregation which most members of the closing congregation joined.

The Institute can usually provide names and addresses of congregations where ancestors might have been members, and information on pastors.

ELCA ARCHIVES

The Evangelical Lutheran Church in America has a network of archival centers, most associated with its college or seminary archives/libraries.

ELCA rents and sells microfilms of congregational records.

The Archives staff will inform researchers as to whether a particular set of records has been filmed.

These films are not available through inter-library loan. Typically, the films contain records of baptisms, confirmations, marriages, and funerals. Some contain membership lists and official meeting minutes.

Write to the Archives office in Chicago (address below) for specific information about loans and purchases of films and its research fee schedule.

The archives in New York and Pennsylvania will be of particular interest to researchers of German colonial ancestors; those in the Midwest to those researching the 19th century immigration waves.

The following list represents regional/synodical collections only.

Churchwide archives
Evangelical Lutheran Church in America Archives
8765 West Higgins Road
Chicago, IL 60631-4198
Tel. (312) 380-2818
Fax: (312) 380-2977
E-Mail: archives@ELCA.ORG
♦**Alaska, Idaho, Montana, Oregon, Washington**
ELCA Region 1 Archives
Archives and Special Collections
Mortvedt Library
Pacific Lutheran University
Tacoma, WA 98447
Tel. (206) 535-7586
♦**Arizona, California, Colorado, Hawaii, New Mexico, Nevada, Utah, Wyoming**
ELCA Region 2 Archives
Pacific Lutheran Theological Seminary
2770 Marin Avenue
Berkeley, CA 94708-1597
Tel. (510) 524-5264
♦**Minnesota, North Dakota, South Dakota**
ELCA Region 3 Archives

2481 Como Avenue West
Saint Paul, MN 55108-1445
Tel. (612) 641-3205
♦**Arkansas, Oklahoma**
Arkansas-Oklahoma Synod
4803 South Lewis Avenue
Tulsa, OK 74105-5199
Tel. (918) 747-8617
♦**Kansas, Missouri**
Bethany College
Wallerstedt Learning Center
421 North First Street
Lindsborg, KS 67456-1897
Tel. (913) 227-3311, Ext. 8299
E-Mail:
PearsonJ@Bethany.BethanyLB.edu
♦**Texas, Louisiana**
The Rev. Arnold Moede
205 Coventry
Seguin, TX 78155
Tel. (210) 379-6450
♦**Nebraska**
Vivian Peterson
1325 North Platte Avenue
Fremont, NE 68025
Tel. (402) 721-9119
♦**llinois, Iowa, Wisconsin, Upper Michigan**
ELCA Region 5 Archives
333 Wartburg Place
Dubuque, IA 52003-7797
Tel. (319) 589-0320
♦**Indiana, Kentucky, Michigan, Ohio**
ELCA Region 6 Archives
Trinity Lutheran Seminary
2199 East Main Street
Columbus, OH 43209
Tel. (614) 235-4136, Ext. 4002
♦**New York, New Jersey, Eastern Pennsylvania, New England and the non-geographic Slovak-Zion Synod**
–For all synods named above except
Metropolitan New York:
Lutheran Archives Center
Northeast Region Archives ELCA
7301 Germantown Avenue
Philadelphia, PA 19119-1799
Tel. (215) 248-4616, ext. 34
Fax: (215) 248-4577

E-Mail:
LUTTHELIB@SHRSYS.HSLC.ORG
–For Metropolitan New York Synod:
Lutheran Church Archives
Hormann Library
Wagner College
Staten Island, NY 10301
Tel. (516) 271-2466
–For Western Pennsylvania, West
Virginia, Western Maryland
Tri-Synod Archives
Thiel College
College Avenue
Greenville, PA 16125
Tel. (412) 589-2131
–For Central Pennsylvania, Delaware-
Maryland , and Metropolitan Washing-
ton, DC
A.R. Wentz Library
Lutheran Theological Seminary
Gettysburg, PA 17325
Tel. (717) 334-6286, Ext. 407
♦ **North Carolina:**
ELCA North Carolina Synod
1988 Lutheran Synod Drive
Salisbury, NC 28144
Tel. (704) 633-4861
♦ **South Carolina**
ELCA South Carolina Synod
P.O. Box 43
Columbia, SC 29202-0043
Fax: 803-252-5558
♦**Alabama, Florida-Bahamas, Georgia, Mississippi, Tennessee, and the Caribbean Synod:**
Archives, Lutheran Theological Southern
Seminary
4201 North Main Street
Columbia, SC 29203
Tel (803) 786-5150, ext. 234
♦**Virginia**
ELCA Virginia Synod
P.O. Drawer 70
Salem, VA 24153
Tel. (540) 389-5962
E-Mail: VASYNOD.parti@ecunet.com

LUTHERAN CHURCHES WITH GERMAN-SPEAKING CONGREGATIONS

German Evangelical Lutheran Conference in North America
Deutsche Evangelisch-Lutherische Konferenz in Nordamerika
9715 Lake Avenue
Cleveland, OH 44102
Tel. (216) 631-5007
Fax: (216) 961-1735
[Purpose: Promotion and development of the work of German-speaking Lutheran churches in North America]

GERMAN METHODISTS

The German Methodist movement developed from the work of William Nast, who descended from a long line of Swabian pastors of the Lutheran church in Württemberg.

Germans joined with the church through the Methodists Episcopal Church.

The growth in numbers of German Methodists grew especially fast after the Civil War[1]

Resources
◆**Methodist Historical Society**, Old St. George Church, 326 New Street, Philadelphia, PA 19106
◆**United Methodist Archives Center,** General Commission on Archives and History of the United Methodist Church, Drew University Library, Madison, NJ 07940
◆**Nippert Collection of German Methodism** (full title: "Bethesda Hospital and Deaconess Association/Rev. Louis and Ida E. Nippert Memorial Library and Museum of German Methodism in America and Germany Records").

The materials relate to the conferences, churches, schools, hospitals, deaconess institutions, orphanages, missions, and individuals in the German Methodist Church in the United States, Germany, Switzerland, and China.

Contact: Dr. Jonathan Dembo, Archivist, The Museum Center, Cincinnati Union Terminal, Cincinnati, OH 45203. Tel. (513) 287-7030
◆**Archives of Indiana United Methodism,** Roy O. West Library, DePauw University, Greencastle, IN 46153
◆**Garrett-Evangelical Theological Seminary,** 2121 Sheridan Road, Evanston, IL 60201
◆ **The Historical Center of the Free Methodist Church,** Winona Lake, IN 46590
◆**Methodist Historical Library,** Perkins School of Theology, Southern Metho-dist University, Dallas, TX 75222
◆**New England Methodist Historical Society Library**, Boston University, School of Theology, 745 Commonwealth Avenue, Boston, MA 02215
◆**Pacific School of Religion,** Charles Holbrook Library, 1798 Scenic Avenue, Berkeley,CCA 94709
Publications
◆General Commission on Archives and History of the United Methodist Church, *The Directory*. United Methodist Church, Madison, N.J., 1981
◆Harmon, Nolan B., ed. *The Encyclopedia of World Methodism.* World Methodist Council and Com-mission on Archives and History, United Methodist Publishing House, Nashville, 1974. 2 vols.

ROMAN CATHOLICS

After the Thirty Years War, only Catholic, Lutheran, and Reformed churches were recognized state churches.

Almost half the German-Americans in the 1880s were Roman Catholics. John Martin Henni, appointed bishop of Milwaukee in 1844, was a leader among the German-Americans by building a foundation for a German-American clergy in his Midwest archdiocese.[1]

Left to right: Priest from ancient Byzantium; bishop in vestment for a festive mass; bishop in vestment for regular mass, dean of a cathedral (second in rank to the bishop); cardinal; deacon; secular cleric (priest not belonging to an order)

Some Catholic records may be found in local and state historical societies and other secular libraries.

Organizations

◆**American Catholic Historical Society of Philadelphia**, P.O. Box 84, Philadelphia, PA 19105.

◆**The National Conference of Catholic Bishops (NCCB)**
3211 Fourth Street, NE
Washington, DC 20017-1194
Tel. (202) 541-3000
Fax: (202) 541-3322

◆**United States Catholic Conference (USCC)**
3211 FourthStreet, NE
Washington, DC 20017-1194
Tel. (202) 541-3000
Fax: (202) 541-3322

◆**American St. Boniface Society**
P.O. Box D
Bronx, NY 10466-0604
Tel. (718) 994-0989
Fax: (718) 994-6119

[Supports the Catholic church in the eastern German states]

◆**Archives of the University of Notre Dame,** South Bend, IN 46624. (Archdiocese of New Orleans Records (1576-1865)

◆**Barry University,** 11300 NE Second Avenue, Miami Shores, FL 33161

◆**Boston College Library,** Chestnut Hill, MA 02167

◆**Catholic University of America,** 620 Michigan Avenue N.E., Washington, DC 20013

◆**College of the Holy Cross,** College Street, Worcester, MA 01610

◆**Conception Abbey Library,** Conception, MO 64433

◆**Diocese of Fresno Library,** 1510 N. Fresno, Fresno, CA 93703

◆**Kenrich Seminary,** 7800 Kenrick Road, St. Louis, MO 63119

◆**LeMoyne College Library,** LeMoyne Heights, Syracuse, NY 13214

◆**Loyola University Library,** 6525 N.

Left to right: Cartesian monk; Capuchin monk; Dominican monk; Franciscan monk, Jesuit; Carmelite monk

Sheridan, Chicago, IL 60626
◆**Loyola University Library**, 6363 St. Charles, New Orleans, LA 70118
◆**Providence College, Phillips Library,** Providence, RI 02918
◆**St. Anselm College, Geisel Library,** Manchester, NH 03102
◆**St. Mary's College**, St. Albert Hall, Moraga, CA 94575
◆**St. Bonaventure University**, Library Center, St. Bonaventure, NY 14778
◆**St. Francis Seminary Library**, 3257 S. Lake Drive, Milwaukee, WI 53207
◆**St. Michaels College**, 56 College Parkway, Winooski, VT 05404
◆**St. Paul Seminary, Ireland Library**, St. Paul, MN 55105
◆**St. Vincent College Library**, Latrobe, PA 15650
◆**Seton Hall University**, McLaughlin Library, South Orange, NJ 02079
◆**SS Cyril and Methodius Seminary,** 3605 Perrysville Highway, Pittsburgh, PA 15214

◆**Stamford Catholic Library**, 195 Glenbrook, Stamford, CT 06902
◆**Texas Catholic Historical Society,** 16th & Congress, Austin, TX 78711
◆**Villanova University, Falvey Library**, Villanova, PA 19085

Publication

The Official Catholic Directory. P.J. Kennedy & Sons. Wilmette, Ill, published annually.

[1]La Vern J. Rippley, *The German Americans.* University Press of America, Inc., Lanham, Md. 1984

JEWS

Jews were living in Germany since medieval times, but from about 1400 they were not permitted to hold citizenship in German towns and had to live on assigned streets in a Ghetto.

Left to right: Russian Orthodox Patriarch Nikon; Italian abbots; Protestant minister

Left to right: Bridgetian nun; Dominican nun; Cistercian nun from the FrenchMonastery of Port-Royal; Carmelite nun

They were forced to take official family names starting in 1808, before which time children were named after their fathers or paternal grandfathers, or they held the name of the house where they lived.

After 1808, many Jewish people took their names from towns of their ancestors. Following the "emancipation" of the early nineteenth century, when Jews were given the full rights of citizenship, there were created special civil registers for Jews, which were in effect until enactment of a general civil registsration law in Germany, effective January 1, 1876.

The best records exist in Württemberg, where 209 of the 213 communities there still exist, and records back to 1750 or sometimes earlier are available, but in other areas of Germany, the situation is much more difficult.

Source: Wolfgang Glaser, *Americans and Germans: Deutsche und Amerikaner.* Verlag Moos & Partner, Müchen, 1986

BEGINNINGS OF JEWISH FAMILY NAMES

Laws by which Jews were mandated to take family names took effect on the following dates for given areas:

Austria . 17 July and 11 November 1787
Galicia .... 7 May 1789
South and East Prussia ...... 17 July 1797
Russia .... 9 December 1804
West Galicia .... 21 February 1805
Westphalia .... (Decree by Jérome Napoleon 31 March 1808, repeated 4 July 1811)
France .... (Including theGerman area left of the Rhine) 20 July 1808
Hesse .... 15 December 1808

Planting of the freedom oak at the freedom fest in Jena

Baden .... 13 January 1812
Lippe .... 16 December 1809 and
                                    10 November 1840
Mecklenburg .... 22 February 1812
Prussia .... 11 March 1812
Bavaria .... 10 June 1813
Denmark .... 29 March 1814
Kurhessen .... 14 May 1816
Saxony-Anhalt .... 20 June 1811 and
                                    4 November 1821
Saxony-Weimar-Eisenach . 20 June 1823
Württemberg .... 25 April 1828
Saxony .... 16 November 1834
Oldenburg 1852
Breslau .... 30 April 1791
Frankfurt/Main .... 30 November 1807
                                    and 1811
Posen .... 1 June 1833
                            and 22 December 1833

Source: Wolfgang Ribbe, Eckart Henning,
Taschenbuch für Familiengeschichtsforschung.
Verlag Degener & Co., Neustadt an der Aisch,
1995, p. 169

EXAMPLES OF TYPES OF JEWISH RECORDS RECORDED IN GERMAN

The examples of types of Jewish records listed below were kept by municipal offices and Christian churches, as well as by Jewish synagogues.

All these types are available through the Family History Library in Salt Lake City, Utah.

♦ **Bürgerbücher:** Citizenship records, records of residents without citizenship
♦ **Dissidentenregister:** Dissenter Registers, in which Jews were often included
♦ **Gerichtsakten:** Court records registering and verifying birth, marriage and death. Verification Jews were baptized
♦ **Judenregister:** Register of Jews
♦ **Juden Taufen:** Baptismal records of Jews
♦ **Jüdische Familienliste:** List of Jewish families
♦ **Kirchbücher (Lutheran):** Includes non-conformist and Jewish birth, marriage and

death records

◆Kirchenbücher (Catholic): Includes Protestants and Jewish birth, marriage, and death records

◆Matrikeln (Registers), a general term which included —

-Aufnahme neuer Mitglieder: Admission of new members

-Austritte: Record of people leaving the Jewish faith

-Beschneidungsbuch: Circumcision records

-Ehescheidungen: Divorce records

-Eingebürgerung: Naturalization record

-Familienbuch: Family books

-Friedhofsregister: Cemetery record

-Gottesdienst: Services held in the synagogue

-Gräberliste: List of graves

-Judenliste: List of Jews

-Mitgliederlisten: Membership list

-Namensannahme: Register of Jewish name changes

-Personenstandsfälle: Legal status records

-Seelenliste: List of members

-Synagogenbuch: Synagogue records (in Hebrew)

-Übertritte: Record of people joining the Jewish faith

-Wittwen u. Waisenunterstützungsfond: Widow and orphan fund

◆ Passover charity collections and disbursements: Written in either Hebrew or Yiddish

◆Schutzverwanten Protokolle: Tax on persons with limited citizenship rights

◆Volkszählung: Census record (1938-39, of non-Germanic minorities with emphasis on the Jews)

◆Vormundschaftsprotokolle: Guardianship records

◆Zivilstandsregister: Civil registration — vital records (births, marriages and deaths)

◆Heiratsbelege: Verification of marriage

Source: Larry O. Jensen, "Jewish Records," *German Genealogical Digest,* Vol. 9, No. 1, 1993.

Weapon-makers at work.
Augsburg, 1479

THE TWO GROUPS OF JEWS IN GERMANY

Historically, the two distinct groups of Jews in Germany are these:

The Ashkenazim are descendants of Jews who settled in central Europe, especially along the Rhine River as early as Roman times. They lived in Cologne by 321 AD. The Ashkenazim Jews came to speak a special dialect of medieval German called *Jüdisch* (Yiddish). They centered mainly in southwestern Germany in the seventeenth through thenineteenth centuries. Also they moved eastward into Slavic countries, particularly Poland, where occupational restrictions were not severe.

The Sephardim, also called Maranos, were the Jews who fled Spain and Portugal in the late 15th century during the time of the Inquisition. About 120 families of Marano Jews settled in and near Hamburg in the early sixteenth century. Their language, Ladino, is based on medieval Spanish. Their cemetery was at Altona, then Danish territory, and they had synagogues at Altona, Hamburg, and Wandsbek.

Source: Clifford Neal Smith and Anna Piszczan-Czaja Smith. *Encyclopedia of German-American Genealogical Research.* R.R. Bowker Co., New York, 1976

Potter at work
Augsburg 1537

JEWISH ORGANIZATIONS

Organizations in the United States
♦**Jewish Genealogy Society**
P.O. Box 6398
New York, NY 10128
Tel. (212) 330-8257
♦**World Jewish Genealogy Organization**
P.O. Box 190420
Brooklyn, NY 11219-0009
♦**Jewish Genealogical Society of Cleveland**
996 Eastlawn Drive
Highland Heights, OH 44143
♦**Jewish Genealogical Society of Illinois**
P.O. Box 515
Northbrook, IL 60065-0515
♦**Jewish Genealogical Society of Los Angeles**
P.O. Box 55443
Sherman Oaks, CA 91413-5544
♦ **Jewish Genealogical Society of Pittsburgh**
2131 Fifth Avenue
Pittsburgh, PA 15219
♦**Jewish Genealogical Society of Rochester**
265 Viennawood Drive

Rochester, NY 14618
♦**Jewish Historical Society**
914 Royal Avenue, S.W.
Calgary, Alberta
Canada T2T 0L5
♦**Leo Baeck Institute**
129 East 73rd Street
New York, NY 10021
Tel. (212) 744-6400
Fax: (212) 988-1305
[Researches and preserves the cultural heritage of the Jews in Germany and in German-speaking countries; houses a public reference center consisting of a library, an archive, and an art collection.]
♦**United States Holocaust Memorial Museum**
100 Raoul Wallenberg Place, SW
Washington, DC 20024-2150
Tel. (202) 488- 0400
Web site: http://www.ushmm.org
[Includes the exhibition section, a library, an archive, and an educational section]
♦**Holocaust Memorial Center**
6602 West Maple Road
West Bloomfield, MI 48322
Tel. (313) 661-0840
Fax: (313) 661-4204
[Includes an exhibit section and a library]
♦**Beit Hashoah-Museum of Tolerance**
9786 West Pico Boulevard
Los Angeles, CA 90035-4792
Tel. (310) 553-9036
Fax: (310) 277-5558
[Holocaust memorial of the Simon Wiesenthal Center; includes an archive, a theater, and an educational section]
Organizations in Germany and Austria
♦**Genkstätte, Haus der Wannsee-Konferenz**
Großen Wannsee 56-58
14109 Berlin
Tel. (030) 80 50 01-0, -26
♦**Stiftung Brandenburgische Gedenkstätten mit den Gedenkstätten Sachsenhausen und Ravensbrück,**
JVA Brandenburg
Heinrich-Grüber-Platz

16515 Oranienburg
Tel. (03301) 81 09 18
and
Gedenkstätte Ravensbrück
16798 Fürstenberg
Tel. (03 30 93) 20 25
[Foundation dedicated to documenting Nazi persecution in former concentration camps and to performing international youth and educational services]
♦**Gedenkstätte Bergen-Belsen**
29303 Lohheide
Tel. (05051 60 11
♦**Gedenkstätte Buchenwald**
99427 Buchenwald
Tel. (03643) 43 10 41
♦**KZ-Gedenkstätte Dachau**
Alte Römerstraße 75
85221 Dachau
Tel. (08131) 17 41-42
♦**Gedenkstätte Plötzensee für die Opfer des Nationalsozialismus aus dem In- und Ausland**
Hüttigpfad
13627 Berlin
(030) 3 44 32 26
♦**Stiftung Topographie des Terrors**
Budapester Str. 40
10787 Berlin
Tel. (030) 25 45 09-15
Fax: (030) 26 13 00-2
[Documents National-Socialist persecution to which an exhibit on the grounds of the former Gestapo headquarters in Berlin is dedicated]
♦[Jewish archive in Vienna]: **Israelitische Kulturgemeinde**
Schottenring 25
A-1010 Wien, Austria
♦**Zentralrat der Juden in Deutschland**
Rüngsdorfer Strasse 6
53173 Bonn, Germany
Tel. (0228) 35 70 23/24
Fax: (0228) 36 11 48
[consisting of 16 state associations including 65 Jewish congregations joined together under the Central Council of Jews in Germany]
♦**Hochschule für jüdische Studien**

Wie die Alten sungen,
so zwitschern auch die Jungen
(As the old folks sing,
so twitter the young ones –
"like father, like son")

Friedrichstr. 9
69117 Heidelberg
Tel. (06221) 16 31 31
Fax: (06221) 16 76 96
[University for Jewish Studies, with close partnership with the Hebraic University in Jerusalem]
♦ **B'nai B'rith International**
1640 Rhode Island Avenue, NW
Washington, DC 20036
Tel. (202) 857-6600
Fax. (202) 857-1099
[Founded in 1843 as a fraternal order of Jews who had emigrated mainly from Germany and Austria]
♦**American Jewish Congress**
Stephen Wise Congress House
15 East 84th Street
New York, NY 10028
Tel. (212) 879-4500
Fax: (212) 249-3672
♦**Anti-Defamation League (ADL)**
823 United Nations Plaza
New York, NY 10017

Geographical Distribution of Religious Faiths, German Empire, Early 20th Century

States	Evangelicals	Catholics	Other Christians	Jews
Prussia	21,817,577	12,113,670	139,127	392,322
Bavaria	1,749,206	4,363,178	7,607	54,928
Saxony	3,972,063	198,265	19,103	12,416
Württemberg	1,497,299	650392	9,426	11,916
Baden	704,058	1,131,639	5,563	26,132
Hesse	746,201	341,570	7,368	24,486
Mecklenburg-Schwerin	597,268	8,182	487	1,763
Saxe-Weimar	347,144	14,158	361	1,188
Mecklenburg-Strelitz	100,568	1,612	62	331
Oldenburg	309,510	86,920	1,334	1,359
Brunswick	436,976	24,175	1,271	1,824
Saxe-Meiningen	244,810	4,170	395	1,351
Saxe-Altenburg	189,885	4,723	206	99
Saxe-Coburg-Gotha	225,074	3,330	515	608
Anhalt	301,953	11,699	794	1,605
Schwarzburg-Sondershausen	79,593	1,110	27	166
Schwarzburg-Rudolstadt	92,298	676	37	48
Waldeck	55,285	1,831	164	637
Reuss-Greiz	66,860	1,043	444	48
Reuss-Schleiz	135,958	2,579	466	178
Schaumburg-Lippe	41,908	785	177	257
Lippe	132,708	5,157	205	879
Lübeck	93,671	2,190	213	670
Bremen	208,815	13,506	876	1,409
Hamburg	712,338	30,903	3,149	17,949
Alsace-Lorraine	372,078	1,310,450	4,301	32,379
Total	35,231,104	20,327,913	203,678	586,948

Source: *Encyclopedia Britannica: Dictionary of the Arts, Sciences, Literature and General Information,* University Press, New York, 1910. 11th edition.

Tel. (212) 490-2525
Fax: (212) 867-0779
◆**Union of Orthodox Jewish Congregations of America**
333 Seventh Avenue
New York, NY 10001
◆**Simon Wiesenthal Center**
New York:
342 Madison Avenue, Suite 633
New York, NY 10173

Tel. (212) 370-0320
Fax: (212) 883-0895
Los Angeles:
9760 West Pico Boulevard
Los Angeles, CA 90035
Tel. (310) 553-9036
Fax: (310) 553-8007
Publications
◆*Stammbaum* [German-Jewish journal],
1601 Cougar Court, Winter Springs, FL

32708-3855
✦*Avotaynu: The International Review of Jewish Genealogy*, 155 N. Washington Avenue, Bergenfield, NJ 07621. Tel. (800) 286-9298
✦Mokoloff, Gary, *How to Document Victims and Locate Survivors of the Holocaust.* Genealogy Unlimited, Orem UT.
✦ Segall, Aryeh, ed., *Guide to Jewish Archives*, World Council on Jewish Archives, Jerusalem, New York, 1981.
✦Goldstein, Irene Saunders, ed., *Jewish Genealogy Beginner's Guide.* Jewish Genealogy Society of Greater Washington, 2nd ed., Vienna, VA, 1991
✦ Arnstein, George, "Genealogical Resources for German Jewish Ancestry," Chap. XII of *Germanic Genealogy: A Guide to Worldwide Sources and Migration Patterns*, by Edward R.Brandt et al., Germanic Genealogy Society, St. Paul, Minn., 1994.
✦Gilbert, Martin, *The Atlas of Jewish History.* William Morrow and Co., New York, rev. ed. 1993.
✦Kurzweil, Arthur, *From Generation to Generation: How to Trace Your Jewish Genealogy and Personal History.* Harper Collins, New York, 2nd ed. 1994
✦Rottenberg, Dan, *Finding Our Fathers:*
✦Weiner, Miriam, *Bridging the Generations: Researching Your Jewish Roots.* Secaucus, NJ, 1987
✦Zubatsky, David S., and Irwin M. Berent, *Jewish Genealogy: A Sourcebook of Family Histories and Genealogies.* Garland Publishing Co., New York, Rev. ed., 2 vols., 1991.
✦ Beider, Alexander, *A Dictionary of Jewish Surnames from the Former Russian Empire.* Avotaynu, Teaneck, NJ, 1993.
✦ Beider, Alexander, *A Dictionary of Jewish Surnames from the Kingdom of Poland.* Avotaynu, Teaneck, NJ, 1995.

Miners at their frugal meal

STAMMBAUM: JOURNAL OF GERMAN-JEWISH GENEALOGICAL RESEARCH

Stammbaum is an English-language journal which supports research and publication of reliable family histories and facilitates the exchange of information, techniques, sources, and archival material.

The scope of *Stammbaum*, while focusing on Germany, includes Austria, Switzerland, Alsace, Bohemia, and other areas with linguistic and historic relevance.

This journal is published twice yearly by the Leo Baeck Institute. Back issues are available. Send all correspondence to :Stammbaum, Leo Baeck Institute, 129 E. 73rd Street, New York, NY 10021. E-mail: frank@1bi.com

SOME JEWISH ARCHIVES

[See the Leo Baeck Institute, page 454]
American Jewish Archives
Hebrew Union College
Jewish Institute of Religion
3101 Clifton Avenue

Cincinnati, OH 45220
Gesamtarchiv der deutschen Juden
Joachimstaler Str. 13
10719 Berlin, Germany
International Tracing Service
35534 Arolsen, Germany
Bundesarchiv
Am Wöllershof 12
56068 Koblenz, Germany
Archiv des Institutum Judaicum
Delitzschianum
Wilmergasse 1-4
48143 Münster, Germany
Israelitische Kultusgemeide [Austria]
Schottenring 25
A-1010 Wien, Oesterreich

YIVO Institute for Jewish Research
1048 Fifth Avenue (at 86th Street)
New York, NY 10028
Central Archive for the History of the Jewish People
Sprimzak Building, Givat Ram Campus
Hebrew University
P.O. Box 1149
IL- Jerusalem
Israel
The Jewish National and University Library
Givat Ram Campus
Hebrew University
IL- Jerusalem
Israel

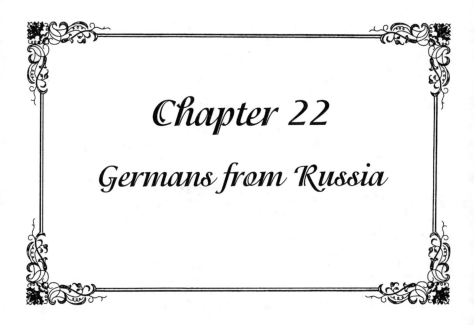

Chapter 22
Germans from Russia

eye examinations are given to potential emigrants before boarding ships in Europe. (Trachoma plagues the Germans from Russia during this period.)

1912: The *Welt-Post*, newspaper devoted to Volga German interests, begins publication; continuing (in Omaha and Lincoln) until 1954.

1917: Russian and Bolshevik revolutions. Conditions temporarily improve for Germans in Russia.

1920: *The Dakota Freie Presse* moves to New Ulm, Minnesota.

1921-22: Crop failure and famine

1928-29: Stalin begins ruthless collectivization. Churches close.

1932-33: Crop failure and famine

1936-38: Peak of the period of banishment and liquidation of pastors, teachers, doctors, and officials

1941: Russia begins resettlement of Germans in the Crimea, South Caucasus and banishment of the Volga Germans to Siberia and Central Asia

1955: Civil rights restored to ethnic Germans, but confiscated property is not returned. Germans denied right to return to their original homes.

1964: Soviets lift deportation order of 1941.

1992: Autonomous Volga Republic established.

PROVISIONS OF MANIFESTOS OF CATHERINE II AND ALEXANDER I

Catherine II's Manifesto, 1763
- Free practice of religion
- Tax exemption for ten years
- Freedom from military service
- Cash grant, to be repaid in 20 years
- Treatment equal to that of native Russians
- Each family may bring into the country 500 rubles in cash or property duty-free.
- Professionals and laboreres permitted to join guilds and unions
- After 10 years, an annual tax to be paid

on land received
- Freedom to depart, but only after paying debts to crown and five years real estate taxes

Alexander I's Manifesto, 1804
The decree of 1804 was similar to that of Catherine II, but its intent was to restrict immigration into Russia to colonists who were well-to-do experienced farmers who could serve as models for agricultural occupations and handicrafts.

GERMANS IN RUSSIA, BY SETTLEMENT AREAS

- Black Sea Germans
- Baltic Germans
- Lithuanian Germans
- Polish and Volhynian Germans
- Petersburg Germans
- Volga Germans
- Germans in Transcaucasia
- Germans in other parts of European and Asiatic Russia

GERMANS FROM RUSSIA, SETTLEMENTS IN THE UNITED STATES

Black Sea emigrants
Settled primarily in the Dakotas and were mostly Protestant. These were the first to arrive in America, in 1873.

Volga River emigrants
Settled shortly after the Black Sea emigrants in the central Great Plains states and were as a rule Catholic. The center of their settlements was Ellis and Rush Counties, Kansas, south and east of the town of Hays. Protestant Volga Germans tended to settle in Lincoln or Sutston, Nebraska, and later worked in the sugar beet fields of Colorado.

Emigrants from other areas
Small numbers from Bessarabia, Volhynia, Caucasus and elsewhere. They were Catholic, Protestant (Reformed or Luth-

eran), and Mennonite.

Source: La Vern J. Rippley, The German-Americans, University Press of America, Inc., Lanham MD, 1984.

PHASES OF GERMAN MIGRATIONS

By Arthur E. Flegel, C.G.

The "Germans from Russia," seeing freedom from oppressive rulers and an opportunity of self-determination, accepted the inducements that included numerous privileges to become colonists in czarist Russia.

The German homelands included principally Hesse, the Rhinelands, Baden, Württemberg, and Bavaria — in fact, most of southwest Germany, the German-speaking French Alsace, and the northern portion of Switzerland along with the Danzig region adjacent to the Vistula River in Polish Prussia.

Notwithstanding the fact that Germans had been living in the Baltic Regions since the return of the Teutonic Knights from the Crusades in the 1300s, the settlements in Russia were developed in several distinct phases:

1763-1768: The Volga German colonies extending from Saratov to Kamyschin on both sides of the lower Volga under Czarina Catherine II to develop the virgin lands and to act as a buffer against the marauding Khirgiz and Kalmuck tribes. Also in this period, some 2,000 people who did not make it to the Volga settled in the St. Petersburg area where they engaged in small truck farming.

1764-1768: The Chernigov and Voronezh separated colonies by immigrants who were probably destined for but did not reach the Volga Region

1789-1820: The Mennonite colonies along the Kneper River by a pietistic religious sect that obtained special autonomy under Catherine II and Paul I

1790-1850: The Volhynian Germans in the Zhitomir region of Russia from Polish areas that became their homelands after the Partitions of Poland (1772-1795)

1804-1840: The Black Sea German colonies established in the Odessa region of South Russia under Alexander I for the purpose of developing those lands agriculturally which they also succeeded in making into the bread-basket of Europe

1814-1830: The Bessarabian German colonies between the Dniester and Prut Rivers following Russian acquisition of that area of the Treaty of Bucharest in 1812

Mennonites on their way to Kansas or Nebraska
Harper's Weekly, May 30, 1874

1818-1820: The Trans-Caucasus German settlements in the Tiflis (Tbilisi) region of the Caucasus under Alexander I by a separatist religious group

1850-1900: The Don River, North Caucusus along the Kuban River and East of the Urals settlements developed by new immigrants along with settlers from earlier established and later overpopulated communities.

With the development of the Plains Regions, the western United States and Canada in the latter half of the nineteenth century, these eastern European Germans joined the mass immigration to the western hemisphere where they again became pioneers.

They brought along the Red Turkey wheat that had made Ukraine so prosperous and with that as a basis, succeeded in creating the "bread basket of the world" in the states of North Dakota and Kansas, and in the Province of Saskatchewan.

The millions who remained in the eastern European regions fell prey to the Russian Revolution and communism and suffered their personal holocaust. Millions perished during the contrived famines. Those who survived that holocaust but were unwilling to accept forced collectivization were systematically disappropriated, driven out of their homes and dispersed into forced (slave) labor camps throughout Asiatic Russia and Siberia — a process that again caused the untimely deaths of thousands.

Reprinted by permission of the author, from "Phases of the German Migrations," *Der Blumenbaum,* Vol. 12, No. 3, 1995.

SOME GERMAN SETTLEMENTS OUTSIDE RUSSIA

By Arthur E. Flegel, C.G.

Germans settled in what had previously been parts of the Austro-Hungarian Empire. These peoples include:

♦ The Polish Galician, Bohemian and Moravian Germans from the northern areas of the Hapsburg Empire
♦ The Germans who settled in Slovenia, the Batschka (Bazca) and Banat along the Danube River basin (1740-1800)
♦ The Siebenbürgen (Transylvanian) Germans in Central Romania whose ancestors had been in that region as early as the 1200s
♦ The Bukowina Germans, who settled from 1770-1790 in northern Moldavia where Romania borders the Ukraine.
♦ The Romanian Germans of the Dobrudscha (Dobruja, Dobrogea) region, who settled along the Black coast of Eastern Romania from 1850-1900 when it was part of the Ottoman Turkish Empire.

MAJOR RESOURCES FOR GERMANS-FROM-RUSSIA RESEARCH

♦**American Historical Society of Germans from Russia**, 631 D Street, Lincoln, NE 68502.
Collection emphasis:
Bessarabian, Black Sea, Crimean, Volga, and Volhynian Germans
♦**Germans from Russia Heritage Society,** 1008 East Central Avenue, Bismarck, ND 58501.
Collection emphasis:
Bessarbian, Black Sea, and Crimean Germans
♦**Germans from Russia Heritage Collection,** North Dakota State University Libraries, P.O. Box 5599, Fargo, ND 58105-5599.
Collection emphasis: Bessarabian and Black Sea Germans. Annotated bibliography to the collection: *Researching the Germans from Russia: Annotated Bibliography of the Germans from Russia Heritage Collection*
♦**Heimatmuseum der Deutschen aus Bessarabien e.V.**, Florianstraße 17, 70188 Stuttgart, Germany.

Collection emphasis: Bessarabian Germans
Landsmannschaft der Deutschen aus Russland, Raitelsbergerstraße 49, 70188 Stuttgart, Germany.
Collection emphasis: Black Sea, Crimean, Mennonite, Volga, and Volhynian Germans
Source: Contribution of collections emphases by Professor Michael M. Miller, Germans from Russia bibliographer, Germans from Russia Heritage Collection, North Dakota Institute for Regional Studies, North Dakota State University

MICROFILMED CARDFILE: GERMANS FROM RUSSIA

The FHL microfilms titled *Bestandskartei der Ruslanddeutschen, 1750-1943* (Card file of Russian Germans, 1750-1943) are described in the Family History Library Catalog as follows:
"Index cards of ethnic Germans in Russia, arranged alphabetically by surname.
While not all the cards contain the same amount of information, many of them supply the given name, present address, birth place and date, place and date of death, earlier and present citizenship; place of origin, year of emigra-tion, and names of ancestors who first emigrated from Germany; places of residence in Russia; year of emigration from Russia; earlier occupation and later activities; religion, whether pedigrees exist; name, places and dates of birth, marriage, and death, occupation for spouse; names, birthplaces and dates for children; and documentary sources."

Aab-Anton 1335722
Antoni-Bastian, Alexander 1335723
Bastian, Alexander-Bekker
(Becker) 1335724
Belajeff-Bleeck, Alfred 1335725
Bleeck, Alfred-Braun, Ida 1335726
Braun, Ida-Busse, Arthur 1335727
Busse, Arthur-Dietrich 1457135
Dietsch-Eckhard 1457136
Eckhard-Esch 1528980
Esch-Fischer, Josef 1528981
Fischer, Josef-Fritz, Elisabeth .. 1528982
Fritz, Elisabeth-Geissler 15288983
Geist-Goltz 15288984
Goltz-von Bynz-Rekowski 15288985
Haab-Hartman 15288986
Hartman-Helke 15288987
Hell-Hilzendeger 1529015
Hilzendeger-Hornbacher 1529016
Hornbacher-Janzen 1529017
Janzen-Kalkowski 1529018
Kalkowski-Kircher 1529019
Kircher-Knecht 1457323
Knechtel-Kox 1457324
Kraas-Krscheminski 1457325
Krüber-Lang, Daniel 1457326
Lang, Daniel-Lindt 1457327
Lindt-Mahn 1538533
Mahn-Mayer 1538534
Mayer-Mössner 1538535
Mössner-Neufeld 1538536
Neufeld-Ozenberger 1538537
Pabst-Prieb 1538538
Prieb-Reinbold 1538539
Reinbold-Roduner 1538540
Röchert-Sattler 1538541
Sattler-Scheydemanns 1538542
Schibat-Schmied 1538613
Schmied-Schuhmacher, Karl 1538614
Schuhmacher, Karl-Sell 1538615
Sell-Starke 1538616
Starke-Subarewa 1538617
Subarewa-Trost 1538714
Trost-Vüst 1538715
Waade-Webert 1538716
Wechinger-Wieb 1538717
Wieb-Wößner 1538718
Wogaraki-Zimmerman, C. 1538830
Zimmerman, C.-Zyres 1538831

OTHER RESOURCES FOR GERMANS-FROM-RUSSIA RESEARCH

*Ruben Goertz Collection: Germans-from-Russia materials at Augustana College, Collections of the Center for

Western States, 2113 South Summit, Sioux Falls, SD 57105
♦ Mennonite Library and Archives, Information and Research Center, North Newton, KS 67117
♦Mennonite Historical Library, Goshen College, Goshen, IN 46526.

Suggested reading
♦ Adam Giesinger, *From Catherine to Khruschev*, Marian Press, Battleford, Saskatchewan, Canada, 1974
♦Joseph S. Height, *Homesteaders on the Steppe*, Gulde-Druck, Tübingen, Germany; Bismarck, ND, 1975
♦ Joseph S. Height, *Paradise on the Steppe*, Gulde-Druck, Tübingen, Germany; Bismarck, ND, 1972
♦P.Conrad Keller, *The German Colonies in South Russia: 1804-1904*, vols I and II, translated by A. Becker, Mercury Printers,

Ltd., Saskatoon, Saskatchewan, Canada, 1973
♦Timothy J. and Rosalinda Kloberdanz, *Thunder on the Steppe*, American Historical Society of Germans from Russia, 1993
♦ Richard Sallet, *Russian-German Settlements in the United States*, translated by LaVerne Rippley and Armond Bauer, Institute for Regional Studies, Fargo, North Dakota, 1974
♦ Karl Stumpp, *The Emigration from Germany to Russia in the Years 1763-1862*. Translation by Prof. Joseph S. Height and others. American Historical Society of Germans from Russia, Lincoln, NE, 1978
♦Karl Stumpp, *The German-Russians: Two Centuries of Pioneering*, Atlantic Forum, 1971

Chapter 23

Pennsylvania

THE PENNSYLVANIA GERMANS ('Pennsylvania Dutch')

"Pennsylvania Dutch" describes the Germans who came to Pennsylvania in the late 1600s and in the 1700s, mostly from the Rhineland, Württemberg, Baden, and Alsace. Also among these emigrants, but in smaller numbers were French Huguenots and the Swiss.

The word "Dutch" came from English-speaking settlers' mispronunciation of the word these Germans used to describe themselves — the *Deutsche* (Germans). Thus non-German settlers, especially the English, were led to think of the Pennsylvania Germans as Dutch, as if they had emigrated from the Netherlands.

Between 1702 and 1704 two books praising the new lands of William Penn circulated widely in Germany. One of them, *Curieuse Nachright von Pensylvania in Norden-America* (A Novel Report from Pennsylvania in North America) by a German, Daniel Falckner,

was written upon his return home from a 1699 visit to Pennsylvania. In it he wrote glowing accounts of the New World and gave specific advice on how to emigrate to Penn's colony. A book published by Gabriel Thomas in 1698 supplied similar information about Penn's settlements.

Many Pennsylvania Germans, besides representing the Lutherans and German Reformed churches, belonged to several sects — like the Amish, Brethern, Mennonites, French Huguenots, Moravians, and Schwenkfelders — growing out of the religious movement in Europe called pietism, which rejected formal religious practices. These separatist sects generally opposed formal religious practices. Even today many Pennsylvania Germans, most of whom settled in southeastern Pennsylvania, are referred to as "plain people."

These German emigrants tended to stay together, traveling in groups across the ocean and then colonizing the new lands. They governed themselves and maintained their language and customs to such an extent that Benjamin Franklin urged the English Parliament to restrict the high immigration of "Palatine Boors" for fear that the English colonists "be not able to preserve our language, and even our government will become precarious."

In 1790, the Pennsylvania Germans made up a third of the state's population. Their dialect has only recently been dying out.

Although it is impossible to draw a strict boundary line around the Pennsylvania German communities, one writer, Fredric Klees, in his book, *The Pennsylvania Dutch* (1952) includes a map of Pennsylvania Dutch settlements that covers the area from the New Jersey line on the east, through Huntington County, Pennsylvania, on the west, and Luzerne County, Pennsyulvania in the north, to Baltimore, Maryland, in the south.

There still remain pockets, especially in rural areas, where "Dutch" is spoken in the home.

Suggested reading
♦ Fredric Klees. *The Pennsylvania Dutch*. The Macmillan Co. New York, 1952. (out of print)
♦ Annette K. Burgert. "Are Your Pennsylvania Dutch Ancestors Really Swiss?" *The German Connection,* First quarter 1995
♦ Edward W. Hocker, Genealogical Data Relating to the German Settlers of Pennsylvania and Adjacent Territory from Advertisements in German Newspapers Published in Philadelphia and Germantown, 1743-1800. Genealogical Publishing Co., Baltimore, 1980
♦ *Pennsylvania German Church Records: Births, Baptisms, Marriages, Burials, Etc.* with an introduction by Don Yoder,. 3 vols. Baltimore: Genealogical Publishing Co. 1983
♦ Ralph B. Strassburger and William J. Hinke. *Pennsylvania German Pioneers, 1727-1808.* Pennsylvania German Society, Norristown, PA.
♦ *Rhineland Emigrants: Lists of German Settlers in Colonial America.* Don Yoder, ed. Baltimore: Genealogical Publishing Co. 1981. Reprinted 1985.

THE LORD'S PRAYER IN PENNSYLVANIA GERMAN

Em Herr Sei Gebaed
Unser Vadder, os ist im Himmel.
    Geheilicht is Dei Naame.
Dei Kaenichreich soll kumme.
    Dei wille soll geduh warre uff die Erd
    graat wie im Himmel.
Geb unns heit unser daeglich Brod.
    Vergeb unns unser schulde, wie mier
    anner ehre schulde vergewwe.
Fiehr unns net in versuchung awwer
    erlase unns vunn iwwel.
Ver Dei is es Keenichreich, unn die grofft,
    unn die Harlichkeit, in Aewichkeit.
        Amen

THE LORD'S PRAYER IN STANDARD GERMAN (Hochdeutsch)

Das Gebet des Herrn
Vater unser, der du bist im Himmel.
    Geheiliget werde dein Name.
Dein Reich komme.
Dein Wille geschehe, wie im Himmel, also auf Erden.
Unser Täglich Brot gib uns heute.
Und vergib uns unsere Schuld, als wir
    vergeben unserm Schuldigern.
Und führe uns nicht in Versuchung,
    sondern erlöse uns von Übel.
Denn dein ist das Reich, und die Kraft
und die Herrlichkeit in Ewigkeit.
        Amen

PENNSYLVANIANS' GERMAN ANCESTRY

The number of Pennsylvanians claiming German as a single ancestry rose by 9.7 percent during the 1980s, according to the Pennsylvania State Data Center at Penn State Harrisburg. Almost 1.9 million of all Pennsylvanians who reported a single ancestry in the 1990 Census claimed German ancestry. That works out to 28.4 percent of the total in that category.

Source: *Focus Magazine*, 1 September 1992.

RESOURCES FOR PENNSYLVANIA RESEARCH

♦*Research Outline: Pennsylvania*, Family History Library, Church of Jesus Christ of Latter-day Saints. Available in most Family History Centers.
♦Florence Clint, *Pennsylvania Area Key: A Guide to the Genealogical Records of the State of Pennsylvania; Including Maps, Histories, Charts, and Other Helpful Materials.* 2nd ed. Area Keys, Denver, 1976. (An area key is also available for each county.)
♦John W. Heisey, *Handbook for Genealogical Research in Pennsylvania.* Heritage House, Indianapolis, Ind., 1985.
♦Floyd G. Hoenstine, *Guide to Genealogical and Historical Research in Pennsylvania.* 3rd ed., F. Hoenstine, Hollidaysburg, PA., 1978.
♦*Pennsylvania Line: A Research Guide to Pennsylvania Genealogy and Local History.* 3rd ed. Southwest Pennsylvania Genealogical Services, Laughlintown, Pa., 1983.
♦George K. Schweitzer, *Pennsylvania Genealogical Research.* G. Schweitzer, Knoxville, Tenn., 1986.
♦Center for Pennsylania German Studies,

406 Spring Drive, Millersville, PA 17551-2021

SOME SOURCES OF COLLECTIONS OF PENNSYLVANIA CHURCH RECORDS

♦Genealogical Society of Pennsylvania, 1300 Locust Street, Philadelphia, PA 19107
♦ Evangelical & Reformed Historical Society, James and College Street, Lancaster, PA 17603
♦State Library of Pennsylvania, P.O. Box 1601, Harrisburg, PA 17126
wLutheran Theological Seminary, 61 West Confederate Avenue, Gettysburg, PA 17325
♦Lutheran Theological Seminary, 7310 Germantown Avenue, Mt. Airy, Philadelphia, PA 19119
♦Moravian Archives, 41 West Locust Street, Bethlehem, PA 18018
♦ Family History Library, Salt Lake City, Utah

Source: Annette K. Burgert, "Locating Your Ancestor in the Keystone State: Genealogical Research in Pennsylvania, NGS Conference in the States, 1995.

THE PENNSYLVANIA STATE ARCHIVES

Records of the Pennsylvania State Archives in Harrisburg date from 1664 to the present and cover a wide range of topics relating to almost every aspect of Pennsylvania history.

Records of specific genealogical interest include passenger lists, primarily of German and Swiss arrival at the port of Philadelphia, 1727-1808; official naturalization lists, 1740-1773; oaths of allegiance, 1777-1790; septennial census returns, 1779-1863; naturalization records of the Pennsylvania Supreme Court, Eastern District, 1794-1868; Western District 1812-1867; and Southern District, 1815-1829; and records relating to military service.

Available on microfilm are certain records of 58 counties, including wills, deeds, slave registers, and tax lists.

Federal population schedules

Microfilm holdings include copies of the federal population schedules for Pennsylvania, 1800-1920 (1790 being published and indexed), the 1880-1920 Soundexes and the 1870 and 1880 censuses on industry and manufacturers.

Military service records

Official records relating to service with Pennsylvania military units covering the period 1775-1945 are found among the records of the Departments of Military Affairs, Treasury, Auditor General, and State; and also of the Office of the Comptroller General, and Pennsylvania's Revolutionary Governments. They consist primarily of muster rolls, military returns, clemency petitions, bonus files, pension records, commissions, and military accounts.

Land records

The State Archives holds the records of Pennsylvania's Land Office, which document the original purchases of land from the Penn Family or the Commonwealth, consisting of applications, warrants, surveys, patents, and other related records. Papers relating to Donation and Depreciation Lands are available for finding grants of land to soldiers of the Pennsylvania Line in the Revolution. Also on file are warrant tract maps for about 48 percent of the counties, showing the locations of original surveys within current township boundaries. A list of the maps of counties and townships completed may be obtained upon request.

Published State Archives

Of the nine series of the Pennsylvania Archives, consisting altogether of about 120 volumes, the series that are of most use to genealogists are the Second, Third, Fifth, Sixth, and Seventh. See the *Guide to the Published Archives of Pennsylvania*.

Ethnic studies

Individual collections of personal papers, organizational records, runs of foreign-language newspapers, and church anniversary histories are part of a general ethnic studies collection.

Maps

The map collection consists of more than 900 maps and panoramic views. Dating from 1681 to the present, these maps are mainly state road and turnpike, political subdivision and boundary, and military maps.

Address

The Pennsylvania State Archives is located at the corner of Third and Forster streets in Harrisburg. Mailing address: Pennsylvania State Archives, P.O. Box 1026, Harrisburg, PA 17108-1026. Tel. (717) 783-3281

Hours

The library is open Tuesday through Friday, and Saturday (for microfilm only) except state and legal holidays. Check for hourly schedule.

THE STATE LIBRARY OF PENNSYLVANIA

The State Library of Pennsylvania in Harrisburg is not the holder of offical or unofficial records but rather it holds compilations made from other sources, as well as an extensive collection of Pennsylvania newspapers.

A microfiche group titled Genealogy/ Local History, is a collection of local histories, genealogies and primary source materials indexed by author, title, geographical area, and name. The collection also contains unpublished compilations of church and cemetery records and a file of miscellaneous family materials.

Surname/Place Name indexes

The Surname/Place Name Indexes contain almost 2 million cards, with information gathered from the indexes of titles which were in the collection proior to 1968 and from seveeral special collections. Since 1968 no new cards have been added to either of these indexes.

Pennsylvania newspapers

The State Library's collection of retrospective Pennsylvania newspapers, the largest known to exist, is a primary source for identifying birth and death dates. More than 61,000 microfilm reels are maintained by the library. Staff at libraries with access to OCLC can search for specific newspaper holdings by means of the "Pennsylvania Union List of Newspapers," a database maintained on the OCLC computer. Reels of newspaper microfilm are available for interlibrary loan for use in any library in North America

Online catalog

Dial access to LUIS, the library's online catalog, is available to libraries and individuals with the capability to access it. For complete instructions, write to the State Library (address below) to request its publication, "Dial Access to LUIS."

Librarians at local public libraries may borrow a copy of the Reel Index to the Microfilm Collection of Pennsylvania County and Regional Histories. The librarian should specify the titles being requested, as well as the reel numbers, on the interlibrary loan form.

Address

The library is located in the Forum building on Commonwealth Avenue at Walnut Street, Harrisburg. Write to Pennsylvania Department of Education, State Library of Pennsylvania, Library Services Division, Box 1601, Harrisburg, PA 17105-1601. Tel.: (717) 787-4440 (Reference). Fax: (717) 783-2070 (Interlibrary Loan)

Hours

Monday-Saturday, 9:30 am - 4:30 pm, on Tuesday until 8 pm, as of 1997. For confirmation of hours call (717) 783-5991.

PENNSYLVANIA LIBRARIES

The book noted below is a county-by-county compilation of Pennsylvania libraries where it is known that genealogical and/or local history information is found in collections. The book includes library addresses, telephonee numbers, and comments, including special genealogical/local history holdings, restrictions on use, and user fees, if known.

John W. Heisey, *Pennsylvania Genealogical Library Guide*. Masthof Press, Route 1, Box 20, Mill Road, Morgantown, PA 19543-9701 (formerly Old Springfield Press)

SOUTHEASTERN AND OTHER PENNSYLVANIA GERMAN COUNTIES, WITH THEIR PARENT COUNTIES

Listed below are some southeastern and nearby counties in Pennsylvania, the dates they formed, and their respective parent counties (in the right column). Germans who immigrated into Pennsylvania in the early years settled in these (and some other) counties.

Adams (1800) .... York
Berks (1752) .... Chester, Lancaster,
.... Philadelphia
Bucks (1662) .... Original County
Chester (1682) .... Original County
Cumberland (1750) .... Lancaster
Dauphin (1785) .... Lancaster
Delaware (1789) .... Chester
Juniata (1831) .... Mifflin
Lancaster (1729) .... Chester
Lebanon (1813) ..... Dauphin, Lancaster
Lehigh (1812) .... Northampton
Northampton (1752) .... Bucks

Northumberland (1772) .... Bedford,
                    Berks, Lancaster
Perry (1820) .... Cumberland
Philadelphia (1682)...... Original County
Schuylkill (1811) ... Berks, Northampton
York (1749) .... Lancaster

Source: John W. Heisey, *Pennsylvania
Genealogical Library Guide*, Masthoff Press,
Route 1, Box 20, Mill Road, Morgantown, PA
19543-6860.

Some Miscellaneous Data

GERMAN-AMERICAN UNIONS OF NEW YORK CITY, 1860-1890

The number of members is shown in parentheses
1860s: German Joiners Association (1,000)
1860s: Cabinetmakers (550)
1860s: United Piano Forte Union (250)
1870: Cigarmakers (9,292) (U.S.)
1870: Shoemakers (19,631) (U.S.)
1871: German Social Democratic Workingmen's Union (293)
1881: ... Brewery Workmen's Union of New York City and Vicinity, Local 1, AFL (121)
1890: Brewery Worker's Local 69, #3 Knights of Labor (1,000)
1890: New York Typographia [German] Local #6 (1,400)

Source: James Sigurd Lapham, "The German-American, New York City 1860-1890," Ph. D. dissertation, St. John's University, New York, 1977.

SUICIDES IN NEW YORK CITY, 1870

The Nationality of Suicides in New York City, October to December 1870

Nationality and number of suicides:
German 50
American 25
Irish 20
English 4
"Uncanny" Scot 1

The German suicide rate remained at a high level into the 1870s. In 1875, the percentage of German suicides among the foreign element (one third of the foreign population was German) of the city was 37 percent.

Source: James Sigurd Lapham, "The German-Americans of New York City 1860-1890." Ph. D. dissertation, St. John's University, New York, 1977.

Chapter 24
Beyond Germany

CHRONOLOGY OF AUSTRIA AND THE AUSTRIAN-HUNGARIAN EMPIRE AFTER THE THIRTY YEARS WAR

1740-48: War of the Austrian Succession. Prussia gains Silesia from Austria.

1781: The Patent of Tolerance provides new freedoms to non-Catholics, opening the way for Protestants to settle in Austria. (Therefore, all immigrants before this date would have been Catholics.)

1784: Under Emperor Joseph II, ministers must keep separate registers of christenings, marriages, and death records.

1804-13: Napoleonic Wars

1848: Insurrections throughout the Austrian Empire

1866: Seven Weeks War. Prussia defeats Austria, forcing Austria to share power with Hungary as Austrian-Hungarian Empire is established in 1867.

1914-18: World War I. End of the Austrian-Hungarian Empire (1919), with its division into Austria, Czechoslovakia, Hungary, Italy, Poland, Romania, Russia and Yugoslavia. (In 1914, the Austrian-ruled half consisted of Austria proper, Bohemia, Bosnia and Herzegovina, Bukovina, Carinthia, Carniola, Dalmatia, Galicia, Istria, Moravia, Salzburg, the Austrian part of Silesia, Styria, Trent, Tyrol, and Vorarlberg. Hungary ruled Croatia, Slavonia, and Transylvania, in addition to Hungary proper, then much larger than today. After World War I, Austria and Hungary each became a separate, small country. A part of the ethnically mixed Burgenland region, which hitherto had belonged to Hungary, became part of Austria pursuant to a plebiscite.[1])

1938: Hitler annexes Austria and the Sudetenland region of Czechoslovakia.

1939-1945: World War II. Following the war, Austria's previous boundaries are restored.

1955: Austria becomes an independent state.

[1]Brandt, Edward R., et al, *Germanic Genealogy: A Guide to Worldwide Sources and Migration Patterns.* Germanic Genealogy Society, St. Paul. 1995.

FOUNDING DATES AND CAPITALS OF AUSTRIAN STATES

State	Anglicized name	Date	Capital
Burgenland	(Burgenland)	1945	Eisenstadt
Kärnten	(Carinthia)	1920	Klagenfurt
Niederösterreich	(Lower Austria)	1920	St. Pölten
Oberösterreich	(Upper Austria)	1918	Linz
Salzburg	(Salzburg)	1920	Salzburg
Steiermark	(Styria)	1945	Graz
Tirol	(Tyrol)	1919	Innsbruck
Voralberg	(Vorarlberg)	1919	Bregenz
Wien	(Vienna)	1922	

RELIGIOUS PREFERENCE OF THE STATES
OF THE AUSTRO-HUNGARIAN EMPIRE

Includes Catholics (Roman and Greek), Protestants (Evangelical and Reformed), Eastern Orthodox, Jews, Other.

	%Cath	%Prot.	%Orth.	%Jews	%Other
Böhmen	96	2	-	1	1
Bukowina	15	3	69	13	-
Dalmatien	84	-	16	-	-
Galizien	88	-	-	11	1
Kärnten	94	5	-	-	-
Krain	100	-	-	-	-
Küstenland	99	-	-	-	1
Mähren	95	3	-	2	-
Niederösterreich	92	2	-	-	-
Oberösterreich	98	2	-	-	-
Salzburg	85	13	-	2	-
Schlesien	85	13	-	2	-
Steiermark	99	1	-	-	-
Tirol	99	-	-	-	1
Vorarlberg	99	1	-	-	-
Austria	91	2	2	5	-
Hungary	58	23	14	5	1
Austria-Hungary	78	10	7	5	-

Source: Steven W. Blodgett, *Germany Genealogical Research Guide*. The Genealogical Department of the Church of Jesus Christ of Latter-day Saints. rev. 1989. Reprinted by permission of the author.

LANDS OF THE AUSTRIAN EMPIRE 1806-1867
AND THE AUSTRO-HUNGARIAN EMPIRE 1867-1918

English	German	Other
Banat	Banat	Vojvodina
Bohemia	Böhmen	Cechy
Bosnia	Bosnien	Bosna
Bucovina	Bukowina	Bukovina
Carinthia	Kärnten	Koroska
Carniola	Krain	Kranjska
Coastland	Düstenland	
Croatia	Kroatien	Hrvatska
Dalmatia	Dalmatien	Dalmacija
Galicia	Galizien	Halicz
Goritz	Görz	Gorizia, Gorica
Hercegoviina	Herzegowina	Hercegovina
Hungary	Ungarn	Magyarorszag
Istria	Istrien	Istra
Lombarday	Lombardie	Lombardia
Lower Austria	Niederösterreich	Österreich unter der Enns
Montenegro	Montenegro	Crna Gora
Moravia	Mähren	Morava
Salzburg	Salzburg	
Silesia	Schlesien	Slezsko
Slavonia	Slavonien	Slavonija
Styria	Steiermark	Stajersko
Transylvania	Siebenbürgen	Erdely, Transilvania
Triest	Triest	Trieste, Trst
Tyrol	Tirol	Tirolo
Upper Austria	Oberösterreich	Österreich ob der Enns
Venice	Venedig	Venezia
Vorarlberg	Vorarlberg	
Austria	Österreich	
Austria-Hungary	Österreich-Ungarn	

Source: Steven W. Blodgett, Germany Genealogical Research Guide. The Genealogical Department of the Church of Jesus Christ of Latter-day Saints, rev. 1989. Reprinted by permission of the author.

AUSTRIAN HUNGARIAN EMPIRE (ENDING IN 1919)

Austrian Crownlands
- Niederösterreich/Lower Austria
- Oberösterreich/Upper Austria
- Salzburg/Salzburg
- Kärnten/Carinthia
- Steiermark/Styria
- Krain/Carniola
- Goerz and Gradiska/Goritz
- Triest and surrounding area/Triest
- Istrien/Istria
- Dalmatien/Dalmatia
- Tirol/Tyrol
- Vorarlberg/Vorarlberg
- Böhmen/Bohemia
- Mähren/Moravia
- Schlesien/Silesia
- Galizien/Galicia
- Bukowina/Bukovina

Hungarian Crownlands
- Ungarn with Siebenbürgen/Hungary with Siebenbürgen
- Kroatien-Slovonien/Croatien-Slovenia
- Fiume and surrounding area/Fiume and surrounding area

Occupied Areas
- Bosnien/Bosnia
- Herzegowina/Hercegovina

RESEARCH SUGGESTIONS FROM THE AUSTRIAN NATIONAL TOURIST OFFICE

The Austrian National Tourist Office provides the following advice and caution:

For any birthdates prior to November 1918, make certain the town listed as the birthplace is within present-day Austria. Generally, Austria is given as a country of birth prior to 1918 for any birth in the provinces of the Austrian Empire and, later on, the Austro-Hungarian Monarchy. At the end of World War I, this entity disintegrated into a number of different countries, and a birthplace listed as being in Austria may actually be in any of these modern-day countries. In the past, the following organizations in some of these successor countries to the Austro-Hungarian Monarchy and the Austrian Empire have been genealogically helpful:

- Czech Republic: Archivni Sprava, Trida Obrancy Miru 133 Prague 6
- Hungary: Magyar Leveltar Orszagos, Becsi Kapu ter 4, Budapest
- Poland: Naczelna Dyrekcja Archiwow Panstwowych, ul. Wicza 9a, Warsaw 10

Nobility

Contact this organization (which keeps complete lists of families and coats of arms) about any degree of nobility discovered:

Heraldisch-Genealogische Gesellschaft Adler, Landstrasser Hauptstrasse 140, A-1030 Wien, Austria

Military records

Files on military personnel (*Militärmatrikeln*) may be accessed at the address below. Note, however, that the person being searched would have to be positively identified as having served in the Imperial Army or the Imperial Navy, and basic data on the time and location of military postings or assignments or a date of discharge would have to be known as well.

Bundesministerium für Inneres Abteilung 9/M, Karl-Schweighofer-Gasse 3, A-1070 Wien, Austria

Church records

In general, under the administrative system introduced by Empress Maria Theresia, personal documents such as certificates of birth, marriage or death were issued and the corresponding records kept by the religious communities in the respective localities. Therefore, it is necessary to establish, through documents, letters, the correct affiliation (Roman Catholic, Lutheran, Calvinist, Jewish) and then contact the respective religious community in that town, such as a parish (*Pfarramt*) or a synagogue.

In some cases, files have been transferred to regional archives (such as those of a diocese) of the various religious denominations,

and it may be helpful to contact those. After 1870, the administrative districts and self-administering cities started registers (*Meldeamt*) for persons without religious affiliation
See the Austrian church archive addresses below.

CHURCH ARCHIVES IN AUSTRIA (*Kirchenarchive*)

Catholic diocesan archives (Diözesanarchive)
♦Diözese Eisenstadt: Diözenanarchiv, St. Rochus-Str. 21, A-7001 Eisenstadt
♦Diözese Feldkirch: Archiv der Diözese, Bahnhofstr. 13, A-6800 Feldkirch
♦Diözese Graz-Seckau: Diözesanarchiv, Bischofsplatz 4, A-8010 Graz
♦Diözese Gurk in Klagenfurt, Archiv der Diöze, Mariannengasse 6, A-9020 Klagenfurt
♦ Diözese Innsbruck: Diözesanarchiv, Riedgasse 9, A-6021 Innsbruck
♦ Diözese Linz: Diözesanarchiv, Harrachstr. 7, A-4020 Linz
♦Diözese St. Pölten: Diözesanarchiv, Domplatz 1, A-3100 St. Pölten
♦ **Archdiocese:** Erzdiözese Salzburg, Konsistorialarchiv, Kapitelplatz 2, A-5010 Salzburg
♦**Archdiocese:** Erzdiözese Wien,: Diözesanarchiv, Wollzeile 2, A-1010 Wien
Protestant church archives
Protestant church archives
♦Archiv des Evangelischen Oberkirchenrates A.u.H.B., Severin Schreiber-Gasse 3, A-1180 Wien
♦Archiv des Evangelischen Oberkirchenrates H.B., Archiv der Evangelischen Pfarrgemeinde H.B. Wien-Innere Stadt, Dorotheergasse 16, A-1010 Wien
Jewish archive
♦Israelitische Kulturgemeinde, Schottenring 25, A-1010 Wien
Sources: *Archive in der Bundesrepublik Deutschland, Österreich und der Schweiz,*

Ardey-Verlag, Münster, 1995; and Austrian National Tourist Office.

AUSTRIAN CITY/TOWN ARCHIVES (*Stadtarchive*)

Amstetten: Stadtarchiv, Rathausstr. 1, A-3300 Amstetten
Baden bei Wien: Standtarchiv, Weikersdorfer-platz 1, A-2500 Baden bei Wien
Bludenz: Stadtarchiv, Rathaus, Postfach 120, A-6700 Bludenz
Braunau am Inn: Stadtarchiv, Palmplatz 8, A-5280 Braunau am Inn
Bregenz: Stadtarciv, Rathausstr. 4, A-6900 Bregenz
Bruck an der Leitha: Stadtarchiv, Rathaus, Hauptplatz 16, A-2460 Bruck an der Leitha
Dornbirn: Stadtarchiv, Rathaus, A-6850 Dornbirn
Drosendorf: Stadarchiv, Rathaus, Hauptplatz 1, A-2098 Drosendorf
Durnstein: Stadtarchiv, Rathaus, A-3601 Dürnstein
Eferding (Oberösterreich): Stadtarchiv, Stadtplatz 31, A-4070 Eferding (Oberösterreich)
Eisenstadt: Stadtarchiv Eisenstadt (stored in *Burgenländischen Landesarchiv Eisenstadt*)
Enns: Stadtarchiv, Hauptplatz 16, A-4470 Enns
Feldkirch: Stadtarchiv, Palais Liechtenstein, A-6800 Feldkirch (Vorarlberg)
Gleisdorf (Steiermark): Stadtarchiv, Rathaus, A-8200 Gleisdorf (Steiermark)
Gmunden (Oberösterreich): Stadtarchiv (stored in Oberösterreichischen Landesarchiv Linz)
Graz: Stadtarchiv, Hans-Sachs-Gasse 1, A-8010 Graz
Grein Oberösterreich: Stadarchiv (stored in Oberösterreichischen Landsarchiv Linz)
Groß-Siegharts: Stadtarchiv, Rathaus, Schloßplatz 1, A-3812 Groß-Siegharts
Haag (Niederösterreich) : Stadtarchiv,

Rathaus, A-3350 Haag (Niederösterreich)
Hainburg an der Donau: Stadtarchiv
Bauhof der Stadtgemeinde, Dorrekstr.
2, A-2410 Hainburg an der Donau
Hall in Tirol: Stadtarchiv, Oberer
Stadtplatz 1, A-6060 Hall in Tirol
Hallein (Salzburg): Stadtarchiv, Kelten-
museum, A-5400 Hallein (Salzburg)
Horn: Stadtarchiv, Rathausplatz 4, A-
3580 Horn
Innsbruck: Stadtarchiv, Badgasse 2, A-
6020 Innsbruck
Kitzbühel (Tirol): Stadtarchiv, Kirch-
gasse 2, A-6370 Kitzbühel (Tirol) (Stadt-
gemeinde, Kulturreferat, Rathaus, A-6370
Kitzbühel)
Klosterneuburg: Stadtarchiv, Rathaus-
platz 1, A-3400 Klosterneuburg
Korneuburg: Stadtarchiv, Hauptplatz 39,
A-2100 Korneuburg
Krems an der Donau: Stadtarchiv, Kör-
nermarkt 13, A-3500 Krems an der Donau
Laa an der Thaya: Stadtarchiv, Rathaus,
A-2126 Laa an der Thaya
Langenlois (Niederösterreich): Stadt-
archiv, Rathausstr. 2, A-3550 Langenlois
(Niederösterreich)
Leoben: Stadtarchiv, Kirchgasse 6, A-
8700 Leoben
Lienz: Stadtarchiv, Museum Schloß
Bruck, A-9900 Lienz
Linz: Stadtarchiv, Hauptstr. 1-5, Postfach
1000, A-4041 Linz
Mödling: Stadtarchiv, Rathausgasse 8, A-
2340 Mödling
Neunkirchen: Stadtarchiv, Heimatmus-
eum, Dr. Stockhammergasse 13, A-2620
Neunkirchen
Pinkafeld (Burgenland): Stadtarchiv,
Hauptplatz 1, A-7423 Pinkafeld (Burgen-
land) (handled through the *Burgen-
ländische Landesarchiv Eisenstadt)*
Pöchlarn (Niederösterreich): Stadt-
archiv, Regensburger Str. 11, A-3380
Pöchlarn (Niederösterreich)
Retz: Stadtarchiv, Stadtamt, Hauptplatz
30, A2070 Retz
Ried im Innkreis: Stadtarchiv, Kirchen-
platz 13, A-4910 Ried im Innkreis

Rust (Burgenland): Stadtarchiv, Con-
radplatz 1, A-7071 Rust (Burgenland)
Salzburg: 1) Stadtarachiv mit Archiv des
Salzburger Museums Carolino-August-
eum, Museumsplatz 6, A-5020 Salzburg
2) Archiv der Stadt Salzburg, Magistrats-
Abt.ZV/o4, Fürbergstr. 47, Postfach 63,
A-5024 Salzburg
St. Pölten: Stadtarchiv, Prandtauerstr. 2,
A-3100 St. Pölten
Schwechat: Stadtarchiv, Stadtamt, A-
2320 Schwechat
Steyr (Oberösterreich): Stadtarchiv,
Stadtplatz 27, A-4400 Steyr (Oberöster-
reich)
Stockerau: Stadtarchiv, Belvederschlößl,
Belvederegasse 5, A-2000 Stockerau
Traiskirchen (Niederösterreich): Stadt-
archiv, Hauptplatz 13, A-2514 Trais-
kirchen (Niederösterreich)
Tulln (Niederösterreich): Stadtarchiv,
Nußalle 4, A-3430 Tulln (Niederöster-
reich)
Villach: Stadtarchiv, Widmanngasse 38,
A-9500 Villach
Vöcklabruck (Oberösterreich): Stadt-
archiv Vöcklabruck (Oberösterreich)
(stored in Oberösterreichischen Landes-
archiv Linz)
Bad Vöslau: Stadtarchiv, Altes Rathaus,
A-2540 Bad Vöslau
Waidhofen an der Thaya: Stadtarchiv,
Rathaus, Hauptplatz 1, A-3830 Waidhofen
an der Thaya
Waidhofen an der Ybbs: Stadtarchiv,
Ybsitzerstr. 18, A-3340 Waidhofen an der
Ybbs
Weitra (Niederösterreich): Stadtarchiv,
Rathausplatz 1, A-3970 Weitra (Nieder-
österreich)
Wels: Stadtarchiv, Rathaus, A-4601 Wels
Wiener Neustadt: Stadtarchiv, Wienerstr.
63, A-2700 Wiener Neustadt
Ybbs an der Donau: Stadtarchiv, Haupt-
platz 1, A-3370 Ybbs an der Donau
Zwettl (Niederösterreich): Stadtarchiv,
Stadtamt, Gartenstr. 3, A-3910 Zwettl
(Niederösterreich)

Source: *Archive in der Bundesrepublik Deutschland, Österreich und der Schweiz,* Ardey-Verlag, Münster, 1995.

AUSTRIAN WAR ARCHIVES (*Kriegsarchiv*)

The address of the War Archives (*Kriegsarchiv*) in Vienna is,
Kriegsarchiv
Nottendorfergasse 2-4
1030 Wien
Austria

This archive contains holdings of the central ;military offices, the territorial authorities, and the field chancelleries of the Imperial Army and the Royal Army.

Records older than 30 years are opened to the public if they do not fall under the provisions of the Information Protection Act and the Personal Information Act.

A *partial* list of holdings follows:

Personnel records
♦Roll call records (personnel lists) 1740-1820
♦Basic service sheets 1820-1918
♦Enlistment registers and enrollment lists 1862-1918
♦Retirement and pension books 1749-1920
♦Pay registers for persons on staff '753-1819
♦Records of soldiers' children 1770-1870
♦Death notices and press clippings 1918-1996

Parish registers and war casualties
♦Military parish registers
♦ Military units and institutions 17th century-1920
World War I 1914-1918
♦Military hospitals (death registers) 1779-1922
♦Card index to military parish registers 1914-1918*
♦Lists of war casualties 1914-1918
♦Prisoners of war (lists and card indexes) 1914-1918*
♦ Military hospitals (patients' sheets)

1914-1918
♦Burial records 1914-1918
♦Soldiers' returns 1918-1920*
* = restricted access

AUSTRIAN NATIONAL TOURIST OFFICES

New York
Austrian National Tourist Office
P.O. Box 1142
New York, NY 10108-1142
Tel.: (212) 944-6880
FAX: (212) 730-4568

Los Angeles
Austrian National Tourist Office
P.O. Box 491938
Los Angeles, CA 90049
Tel.: (310) 477-3332
FAX: (310) 477-5141

Toronto
Austrian National Tourist Office
Toronto
2 Bloor Street East, Suite 3330
Toronto, Ontario M4W 1A8
Tel. (416) 967-4867, 967-3381
FAX (416) 967-4101

Montreal
Austrian National Tourist Office
National Autrichien du Tourisme
1010 Sherbrooke Street West/ouest,
rue Sherbrooke, Suite 1410
Montreal, Quebec H3A 2R7
Tel. (514) 849-3709/9
FAX (514) 849-9577

RIVERS OF AUSTRIA

The Danube River, which runs paas Linz and Vienna, is the main river of Austria.

Its tributaries include the Inn, which forms part of Austria's border with Germany; the Traun; the Enns; and Ybbs rivers.

The Mur and Mürz rivers are in the south.

SWISS CANTONS WITH FOUNDING DATES, CANTON CAPITALS, LANGUAGES SPOKEN AND RELIGIONS IN CANTONS

Canton/founding date	Capital	Language(s) spoken/ religion
Aargau (1803)	Aarau	Sw-Ger 90.5% / [Prot. 52.4%]
Appenzell- Inner-Rhoden (1513)	Appenzell	Sw-Ger.95.8% / [Prot. 96.2%]
Appenzell- Ausser-Rhoden (1513)	Herisau	Sw-Ger 93% / [Prot. 76.6%]
Bern (1353)	Bern	Sw- Ger, Fr
Basel-Land(1501)	Liestal	Sw-Ger 88.1% ,Fr. / [Prot.65.3]
Basel-Stadt (1501)	Basel	Sw-Ger 89.4% / [Prot. 59.8%]
Fribourg (1481)	Fribourg	Sw-Ger 34%, Fr. 63.4% / [Cath. 86.3%]
Genèva (1815)	Genèva	Sw-Ger 13.3%, Fr. 70%, It. 9.6% [Cath. c. 50% / Prot. c. 50%]
Glarus (1352)	Glarus	Sw-Ger 86.9% / [Prot. 58.8%]
Graubünden (1803)	Chur	Sw-Ger 56.6%, It. 16.1%, Ro. 26.1% [Cath. c. 50% / [Prot. c. 50%]
Luzern (1332)	Luzern	Sw-Ger 94.3% / [Cath. 85.1%]
Neuchâtel (1815)	Neuchâtel	Fr 78.3% / [Prot. 68.5%]
Unterwalden- Nidwalden (1291)	Stans	Sw-Ger
Obwalden (1291)	Sarnen	Sw-Ger
Gallen (1803)	St. Gallen	Sw-Ger
Schaffhausen (1501)	Schaffhausen	Sw-Ger
Solothurn (1481)	Solothurn	Sw-Ger 90.3% / [Cath. 57.7%]
Schwyz (1291)	Schwyz	Sw-Ger 94.3% / [Cath.93.6%]
Thurgau (1803)	Frauenfeld	Sw-Ger 91.7% / [Prot. 60.9]
Ticino (1803)	Bellinzona	It. / [Cath. 91.2%]
Uri (1291)	Altdorf	Sw-Ger 94.5% / [Cath. 92.5%]
Vaud (1803)	Lausanne	Fr.
Valais (1815)	Sion	Fr., It., Sw-Ger
Zug (1352)	Zug	Sw-Ger.
Zürich (1351)	Zürich	Sw-Ger

KEY: Sw-Ger = Swiss-German; Fr. = French;
It. = Italian; Ro.=Romansh; Cath. = Catholic;
Prot. = Protestant

©John W. Heisey, 1997. Reprinted by permission. Based on *Handy Guide to Swiss Genealogical Records,* by Jared H. Suess, Everton Publishers, UT 1978.

CIVIL REGISTRATION IN SWITZERLAND (Zivilstands-Register)

Civil registration was required in all Cantons beginning January 1, 1876. Some of the areas in which it was started earlier include:

Basel-Land	1827
Fribourg	1849
Genève	1798
Glarus	1849
Neuchâtel	1825
Schaffhausen	1849
Solothurn	1836
St. Gallen	1867
Ticino	1855
Valais	1853
Vaud	1821

SWISS PARISH REGISTERS (Pfarrbücher)

Protestant areas

Parish registers began in the 1520s (especially the Zürich and Bern areas); they were kept in village churches in the second half of the 16th and the early 17th centuries.

Catholic areas

Most began in the first part of the 17th century (usually in Latin).

Parish registers include: Baptism records *(Taufbücher)*, marriage records *(Ehebücher)*, and burial records *(Beerdigungen)*.

Parish register inventories

These inventories, listing years for which parish registers are accessible, are available for Cantons Solothurn, Basel, Aargau, Zürich, Schaffhausen, St. Gallen (FHL film 908,641, item 4), Glarus (FHL film 908,641, item 5), and Luzern. (The inventories are available at the Family History Library in print form for all these Cantons, as well as on microfilm for the two Cantons noted above.)

SWISS CITIZENSHIP

In Switzerland, each family name is connected to its original place of origin or citizenship, or *Burgerort*. A Swiss person is first and foremost a citizen of a community, and as such a citizen of the canton, and automatically a Swiss citizen. (A child born outside Switzerland is born a Swiss citizen if his or her father is Swiss.)

Vital records are registered at the place where the person lives but also at the "home community," which is in charge of the family registry. A Swiss citizen may never see his or her home community.

The place of origin is necessary for the proper identification of the family, as there are often several unrelated families with the same surname. Places of birth, baptism, marriage and death are also important, but the place of civil registration is always the place of birth.

SWISS CIVIL REGISTERS

Civil registration began officially on January 1, 1876. It began earlier in some areas.

Civil registers are of two types:

A-Registers: Recorded all births, marriages, and deaths *within* a political community

B-Registers: Recorded vital events of citizens of a political community occurring *outside* the jurisdiction of that community. In 1928 these records were discontinued and the information was continued in th Family Registers *(Familienregister)*, which consist of a page of vital records for each married couple and their children. Before Family Registers were in use, Citizens' Books *(Bürgerbücher)* were kept.

Church censuses began in 1634 and were continued until the early 1700s.

Bürgerbücher (citizens' books), similar to family registers, began around 1820.

SWISS POSTAL ABBREVIATIONS

The postal abbreviations below represent Switzerland's 23 cantons , three of which are divided into half-cantons.

Asterisks signify half-cantons, which were formed for administrative convenience.

Postal Abbreviation	Canton
AG	Aargau
AI	*Appenzell (Inner Rhoden)
AR	*Appenzell (Ausser Rhoden)
BE	Bern
BL	*Basel-Land
BS	*Basel-Stadt
FR	Freibourg
GE	Geneva (Genève)
GL	Glarus
GR	Graubünden (Grisons)
JU	Jura
LU	Lucerne (Luzern)
NE	Neuchâtel
NW	*Nidwalden
OW	*Obwalden
SG	Sankt Gallen
SO	Solothurn (Soleure)
SH	Schaffhausen
SZ	Schwyz
TG	Thurgau
TI	Ticino
UR	Uri
VD	Vaud
VS	Valais
ZG	Zug
ZH	Zürich

SWITZERLAND CHRONOLOGY

58 BC: The Helvetii, earliest inhabitants of Switzerland, conquered by the Romans. (The Romanstsch language, still spoken in the canton of Graubunden, derives from this period.)

1518: Huldreich Zwingli sparks the Protestant Reformation in Switzerland; city of Zürich, supported by its merchants, revolts against church dogma and with other towns such as Basel and Bern, supports independence from the Roman Catholic Church and the Holy Roman Empire.

1536: Geneva, newly adopted home of the French theologian John Calvin who organizes his new church here, revolts against the duchy of Savoy and refuses recognition of the Roman Catholic bishop.

1541-1564: Geneva is the stronghold of Calvinism.

1648: Through the Peace of Westphalia following the Thirty Years War, Switzerland is recognized as a completely independent state.

1798: Swiss revolutionaries of the French Revolution occupy all Swiss territory. Napoleon unifies the country under the name Helvetic Republic, instituting a constitution strongly resented by the Swiss.

1803: Napoleon withdraws his occupation forces; by Act of Mediation, a new constitution is established, with Swiss approval

1815: The Congress of Vienna guarantees the perpetual neutrality of Switzerland.

1847: The Roman Catholic cantons form the *Sonderbund*, a league denounced by the federal government as a violation of the constitution, and civil war resulted. The federal government defeats the *Sonderbund*.

1848: The resulting constitution greatly increases federal power.

1874: Another constitution is enacted, basically still in force today, turning a group of cantons into a federal state which in turn relegating power to the cantons and their individual communes. A law is enacted to require all cantons to begin civil registration as of January 1, 1876

1876: Civil registration begins

Source: *Microsoft Encarta,* Microsoft Corporation, Funk & Wagnall's Corporation, 1994.

STATE ARCHIVES, SWITZERLAND (Staatliche Archive)

♦ Schweizerisches Bundesarchiv, Archivstr. 24, CH-3003 Bern
♦ Staatsarchiv des Kantons Aargau, Obere Vorstadt 6, CH-5001 Aarau
♦ Staatsarchiv des Kantons Appenzell Ausserrhoden, Regierungsgebäude, CH-9100 Herisau
♦ Landesarchiv Appenzell Innerrhoden, Landeskanzlei, CH-9050 Appenzell
♦ Staatsarchiv des Kantons Basel-Landschaft, Wiedenhubstr. 35, CH-4410 Liestal
♦ Staatsarchiv des Kantons Basel-Stadt, Martinsgasse 2, CH-4001 Basel
♦ Staatsarchiv des Kantons Bern, Falkenplatz 4, CH-3012 Bern
♦ Archives de l'Etat de Fribourg, 4 chemin des Archives, CH-1700 Fribourg
♦ Archives d'Etat de Genève, 1 rue de l'Hotel de Ville, Case postale 164, CH-1211 Genève 3
♦ Landesarchiv des Kantons Glarus, Postgasse 29, CH-8750 Glarus
♦ Staatsarchiv des Kantons Graubünden, Karlihofplatz, CH-7001 Chur
♦ Archives historiques de la Rèpublique et Canton du Jura, Office du patrimoine historique, Hotel des Halles, CH-2900 Porrentruy 2
♦ Staatsarchiv des Kantons Luzern, Schützenstr. 9, Postfach, CH-6000 Luzern 7
♦ Archives de l'Etat de Neuchâtel, Chateau de Neuchâtel, CH-2001 Neuchatel
♦ Staatsarchiv des Kantons Nidwalden, Mürgstr. 12, CH-6370 Stans
♦ Staatsarchiv des Kantons Obwalden, Rathaus, CH-6060 Sarnen
♦ Staatsarchiv des Kantons St. Gallen, Regierungsgebäude, CH-9001 St. Gallen
♦ Staatsarchiv Schaffhausen, Rathausbogen 4, CH-8200 Schaffhausen
♦ Staatsarchiv des Kantons Schwyz, Bahnhofstr. 20. Postfach 357, CH-6430 Schwyz
♦ Staatsarchiv des Kantons Solothurn, Bielstr. 41, CH-4500 Solothurn
♦ Staatsarchiv des Kantons Thurgau, Regierungsgebäude, CH-8500
♦ Frauenfeld, Archivio cantonale del Ticino, Via Carlo Salvioni 14, CH-6501 Bellinzona
♦ Staatsarchiv des Kantons Uri, Ankenwaage, CH-6460 Altdorf
♦ Archives cantonales vaudoises, Rue de la mouline 32, CH-1022 Chavanne-près-Renens
♦ Staatsarchiv des Kantons Wallis, 9 rue des Vergers, CH-1951 Sion
♦ Staatsarchiv des Kantons Zürich, Winterthurerstr. 170, CH-8057 Zürich
♦ Staatsarchiv des Kantons Zug, Verwaltungszentrum an der Aa, Aabachstr. 5, Postfach 897, CH-6301 Zug

TOWN ARCHIVES, SWITZERLAND (Stadtarchive)

♦ Stadtarchiv, Rathaus, Rathausgasse 1, CH-5000 Aarau
♦ Stadtarchiv, Rathaus, CH-4663 Aarburg Talarchiv Ursern, Rathaus, CH-6490 Andermatt
♦ Archives communales d'Avenches, Municipalité, CH-1580 Avenches
♦ Stadtarchiv c/o Historisches Museum Baden, Landvogteischloß, CH-5400 Baden
♦ Stadtarchiv und Dokumentationsdienst, Erlacherhof, Junkerngasse 47, CH-3011 Bern
♦ Stadtarchiv, E.-Schülerstr. 23, CH-2502 Biel
♦ Stadtarchiv, Rathaus, CH-5620 Bremgarten
♦ Stadtarchiv, Stadthaus, CH-5200 Brugg Burgerarchiv (= altes Stadtarchiv), Bernstr. 5, CH-3400 Burgdorf
♦ Stadtarchiv (= neues Stadtarchiv ab 1832), Rathaus, Kirchbühl 19, CH-3400 Burgdorf
♦ Stadtarchiv, Rathaus, CH-7002 Chur

Bürgerarchiv (= altes Stadtarchiv), Bürgergemeinde, CH-8500 Frauenfeld
◆Stadtarchiv (= neues Archiv), Rathaus, CH-8500 Frauenfeld
Archives de la Ville, Maison de Ville, CH-1700 Fribourg
◆Archives de la Ville, Palais Eynard, rue de la Croix-Rouge 4, CH-1211 Genève 3
◆ Stadtarchiv, Schulhaus I, CH-2540 Grenchen
◆Stadtarchiv, Rathaus, CH-8434 Kaiserstuhl
◆Stadtarchiv, Propsteigebäude, CH-5313 Klingnau
◆ Archives communales, c/o Musée d'Histoire et Médaillier, rue des Musées 31, CH-2300 La Chaux-de-Fonds
◆Stadtarchiv, Rathaus, CH-4335 Laufenburg
◆Archives de la Ville, rue du Maupas 47, Case postale CH-1000 Lausanne 9
◆Stadtarchiv, Rathaus, CH-5600 Lenzburg
◆ Archivio della città di Locarno, Via Rusca 1, CH-6600 Locarno
◆Archivio della città di Lugano, strada di Gandria 4, CH-6976 Castagnola
◆Stadtarchiv, Industriestr. 6, CH-6005 Luzern
◆ Stadtarchiv, Rathaus, CH-5507 Mellingen
◆Archives de la Commune de Montreux, p.a. Greffe municipal, Grand-Rue 73, CH-1820 Montreux
◆Archives communales, Place de l'Hôtel de Ville 1, CH-1110 Morges
◆Stadtarchiv, Rathaus, CH-3280 Murten
◆ Archives de la Ville, Départment Historique du Musée d'Art et d'Histoire, Quai Léopold-Robert, case postale 876, CH-2001 Neuchâtel
◆Stadtarchiv, Stadthaus, Dornacherstr. 1, CH-4600 Olten
◆Stadtarchiv der Ortsgemeinde, Rathaus, CH-8640 Rapperswil
◆ Stadtarchiv, Rathaus, CH-4310 Rheinfelden
◆Stadtarchiv (Vadiana), Notherstr. 22, CH-9000 St. Gallen
◆Stadtarchiv, Fronwagplatz 24, CH-8200

Black Forest maiden

Schaffhausen
◆Archives communales, Hôtel de Ville, Grand-Pont 12, CH-1950 Sion
◆ Bürgerarchiv, Bürgergemeindehaus, Unterer Winkel 1, CH-4500 Solothurn
◆Stadtarchiv, Rathaus, CH-8260 Stein am Rhein
◆Stadtarchiv, Rathaus, CH-6210 Sursee
Stadtarchiv, Hofstettenstr. 14, CH-3600 Thun
◆Burgerarchiv, Rathausplatz 1, CH-3600 Thun
◆Archives communales de Vevey, Hôtel de Ville, rue du Lac 2, CH-1800 Vevey
◆ Bürgerarchiv (= altes Stadtarchiv), Ortsbürgergemeinde, Präsidium, Toggenburgerstr. 86, CH-9500 Wil
◆Stadtarchiv, Stadthaus, CH-8400 Winterhur
◆Stadtarchiv, Hintere Hauptstr. 20, CH-4800 Zofingen
◆ Bürgerarchiv (= altes Stadtarchiv), Rathaus, CH-6300 Zug
◆ Stadtarchiv, St.-Oswalds-Gasse 21, Postfach 362, CH-6301 Zug
◆ Stadtarchiv, Neumarkt 4, CH-8001 Zürich

Source: *Archive in der Bundesrepublik Deutschland, Österreich und der Schweiz,* Ardey-Verlag Münster, 15th ed., 1995

SWISS CHURCH ARCHIVES
(Kirchliche Archive)

Diocesan archives
(Diözesanarchive)
Diocese and Prince-Bishopric, Basel [before 1815]: Fondation des Archives de l'ancien Evêché de Bâle, Hôtel de Gléresse, 10 rue des Annonciades, CH-2900 Porrentruy
Bishopric of Basel (since 1828): Bischôfliches Archiv, Baselstr. 58, CH-4501 Solothurn
Bishopric of Lausanne, Genève and Fribourg: Archives épiscopales, 86 rue de Lausanne, case postale 271, CH-1701 Fribourg
Bishopric of Lugano: Bischöfliches Archiv, Curia Vescovile, via Borghetto 6, DH-6900 Lugano
Bishopric of St. Gallen: Bischöfliches Archiv, Klosterhof 6 B, CH-9000 St. Gallen
Bishopric of Sitten/Sion: Archives épiscopales, Avenue de la Tour 12, CH-1950 Sion
Protestant archive
(Evangelische Kirchenarchiv)
Archiv der Basler Mission, Missionsstr. 11, CH-4003 Basel

Source: *Archive in der Bundesrepublik Deutschland, Österreich und der Schweiz.* Ardey-Verlag Münster. 15th ed., 1995

MICROFILMED RECORDS

Records from Switzerland have been microfilmed and are available through the Family History Library in these cantons:
- Basel-Land
- Basel-Stadt
- Zürich
- Sankt Gallen
- Thurgau
- Ticino
- Vaud
- Geneva
- Lucerne
- Appenzell-Ausser-Rhoden
- Appenzell-Inner-Rhoden
- Neuchâtel
- Graubünden
- Solothurn
- Jura
- Uri

The city of Küssnacht, canton of Schwyz, has been filmed.

Records of Bern are in the process of becoming available.

SWISS EMBASSY
AND CONSULATES GENERAL
IN THE UNITED STATES
AND CANADA

UNITED STATES
Washington, DC
Swiss Embassy
2900 Cathedral Ave. NW
Washington, DC 20008
Tel. (202) 745-7900
Fax: (202) 387-2564
Atlanta
Swiss Consulate General
1275 Peachtree Street NW, Suite 425
Atlanta, GA 30309
Tel. (404) 870-2000
Fax: (404) 874-6655
Chicago
Swiss Consulate General
Olympia Center, Suite 2301
737 N. Michigan Avenue
Chicago, IL 60611
Tel. (312) 915-0061
Fax: (312) 915-0388
Houston
Swiss Consulate General
First Interstate Bank Plaza, Suite 5670
1000 Louisiana

Houston, TX 77002
Tel. (713) 650-0000
Fax: (714) 650-1321
Los Angeles
Swiss Consulate General
11766 Wilshire Blvd., Suite 1400
Los Angeles, CA 90025
Tel. (310) 575-1145
Fax: (310) 575-1982
New York
Swiss Consulate General
665 Fifth Avenue
Rolex Bldg., 8th floor
New York, NY 10022
Tel. (212) 758-2560
Fax: (212) 207-8024
San Francisco
Swiss Consulate General
456 Montgomery Street, Suite 1500
San Francisco, CA 94104
Tel. (415) 788-2272
Fax: (415) 788-1402
CANADA
Ottawa
Swiss Embassy
5 Ave. Marlborough
Ottawa Ont. K1N 8E6
Canada
Tel. (613) 235-1837
Fax: (613) 563-1394
Montreal
Swiss Consulate General
1572 Ave. Dr. Penfield
Montreal P.Q. H3G 1C4
Canada
Tel. (514) 932-7181
Fax: (514) 932-9028
Toronto
Swiss Consulate General
154 University Ave.
Toronto, Ontario M5H 3Y9
Canada
Tel. (416) 593-5371
Fax: (416) 593-5083
Vancouver
Swiss Consulate General
790-999 Canada Place
Vancouver, B.C. V6C 3E1
Canada

Tel. (604) 684-2231
Fax: (604) 684-2806

SWISS TOURISM CONTACTS, UNITED STATES AND CANADA

UNITED STATES
New York
Swiss Center
608 Fifth Avenue
New York, NY 10020
Tel. (212) 757-5944
Fax: (212) 262-6116
Chicago
Switzerland Tourism
150 North Michigan Avenue
Chicago, IL 60601-7525
Tel. (312) 630-5840
Fax: (312) 630-5848
El Segundo, California
Switzerland Tourism
222 North Sepulveda Boulevard
Suite 1570
El Segundo, CA 90245-4300
Tel. (310) 335-5980
Fax: (310) 335-5982
CANADA
Switzerland Tourism
926 The East Mall
Etobicoke, ON M9B 6K1
Canada
Tel. (416) 695-2090
Fax: (416) 695-2774

Switzerland Tourism on the World Wide Web
http://www.SwitzerlandTourism.ch/

CONTACTS FOR SWISS GENEALOGICAL RESEARCH

Swiss genealogy newsletter
The Swiss Connection
c/o Maralyn Wellauer
2845 North 72nd Street
Milwaukee, WI 53210

Tel. (414) 778-1224
Fax: (414) 778-2109
Quarterly newsletter on Swiss genealogy, with Swiss-American genealogical
queries. For information: Maralyn
Wellauer, 2845 North 72nd Street, Milwaukee, WI 53210.

Organizations
♦**Swiss-American Historical Society**
6440 N. Bosworth Avenue
Chicago, IL 60626
♦**Lancaster Historical Society**
2215 Mill Stream Road
Lancaster, PA 17602
♦**Zentralstelle für genealogische Aus-
künfte**
[Central Office for Genealogical Informa-
tion]
Manuel Aicher, Manager
Vogelaustrasse 34
CH-8953 Dietikon
Switzerland
One may communicate in English with
this organization, which, for a fee, handles
inquiries about names or places of inter-
est.
This office can supply information
about the kinds of records available.
♦ **Schweizerische Vereinigung für
jüdische Genealogie**
c/o Rene Loeb
P.O. Box 876
CH-8021 Zürich
Switzerland
(Jewish Genealogical Society of Switz-
erland)

Library
Craven County Library
New Bern, NC 28650

**Information and research
on Swiss coats of arms**
Heraldik & Genealogie
Atelier Galloway
Museggstrasse 25
6004 Lucerne
(Private firm offering heraldic and
genealogical information)

MAJOR RESOURCES
FOR SWISS RESEARCH

General reference works
♦Bartholdi, Albert, ed. *Prominent Ameri-
cans of Swiss Origin*. James T. White &
Co., New York, 1932.
♦ *Familiennamenbuch der Schweiz*,
[Register of Swiss Surnames], 3rd edition.
Schulthess Polygraphischer Verlag, Zür-
ick, 1989. 3 vols.

Official inventory of names of families
which in 1962 possessed citizenship in a
Swiss community. Surnames are followed
by cantons, arranged in alphabetical order, according to the official names of the
place of citizenship; the year in which citizenship was granted (acquired before
1800, acquired in the nineteenth century,
1801-1900; or citizenship acquired 1901-
1962.

The first edition was published in two
volumes in 1940. In 1968/71 an expanded,
six-volume edition appeared. Regulations
governing the release of information since
1962 and the large amount of data gener-
ated since that time, have made an update
of the inventory of names beyond 1962
impossible. The third edition will ac-
knowledge the new Canton Jura which
came into existence after the second edition was released and it will also include
numerous other revisions and additions.)
♦Faust, Albert B. and Galus M. Brumbaugh. *Lists of Swiss Emigrants in the
Eighteenth Century to the American
Colonies*. National Genealogical Society,
Washington, DC, 1925. Reprinted with
Dr. Leo Schelbert's "Notes on Swiss
Emigrants," Genealogical Publishing Co.,
Inc., Baltimore, MD, 1976.

Contains descriptive lists of early emigrants from Zürick, 1734-1744; Bern,
1706-1795; and Basel, 1734-1794, compiled from records found at the state archives in Switzerland. Indexed.
♦Strassburger, Ralph B. andWilliam J.
Hinke, eds., *Pennsylvania German Pio-*

neers. 3 vols. Pennsylvania German Society, Norristown, PA, 1934.

Transcriptions of the original lists of arrival at the port of Philadelphia.

♦Turier, Prof. Dr. Heinrich, Dr. Marcel Godet and Victor Attinger, *Historisch-Biographisches Lexikon der Schweiz*. 7 vols. plus supplement. Administration des Historisch-Biographisches Lexikons, Neuenburg, 1921-1934.

This is a very useful set of biographical and genealogical pieces on Swiss families and places, submitted by experts in the field, accompanied by good bibliographies for further consultation. Important activities such as emigration are discussed in well-rounded articles.

♦von Grueningen, John Paul, ed., *The Swiss in the United States*. Swiss American Historical Society, Madison, WI, 1940.

Contains information derived from census data explaining the distribution of the Swiss throughout the United States and presents stories on some prominent Swiss-Americans.

♦ Macco, Herman Friedrich, *Swiss Emigrants to the Palatinate in Germany and to America, 1650-1800*, and Huguenots in the Palatinate and Germany. 6 vols. and index. FHL microfilms 823,861 and 823,862 (index in latter film).

Research Guides

♦Nielson, Paul A., *Swiss Genealogical Research: An Introductory Guide*. Donning Co. Publishers, Virginia Beach, VA, 1979.

♦Suess, Jared H., *Handy Guide to Swiss Genealogical Records*. Everton Publishers, Inc., Logan, UT, 1979.

♦Wellauer, Maralyn A., *Tracing Your Swiss Roots*. Wellauer, Milwaukee, WI, 1979. (1988, 1991).

Place names

♦Jacot, Arthur, *Schweizerisches Ortslexikon*. C.J. Bucher, Luzern.

♦ United States Board on Geographic Names. *Preliminary Gazetteer: Switzerland*, Washington, DC, 1950.

Source: Maralyn A. Wellauer, editor of *The Swiss Connection*. Reprinted by permission.

MORE RESOURCES FOR SWISS RESEARCH

♦Mario von Moos, *Bibliography of Swiss Genealogies*. Picton Press, Camden, ME, 1993. Lists published genealogies of non-noble Swiss families, with a place index and a surname index]

♦ *Schweizerisches Geschlechterbuch* (Swiss lineage books). Kommissionverlag von C.F. Lendorff, Basel, Verlag Genealogisches Institut Zwicky, Zürich, 1904-65. 12 vols.

♦*Deutsches Geschlechterbuch: Genealogisches Handbuch Bürgerlicher Familien*. Verlag von C.A. Starke, Limburg an der Lahn, Görlitz, 1889. See volumes 42, 48, 56, 65, and 77.

NETHERLANDS RESEARCH BASICS

♦Civil registration was introduced in some southern parts of Netherlands in 1796; it was in general use in 1811. Records are available through 1912, with indexes, on microfilm through the Family History Library of the Church of Jesus Christ of Latter-day Saints

♦Population registers (by families), show birth and death dates and places, and frequently arrival and departure dates. Passport applications are found in these records.

♦Church records were kept by the Dutch Reformed Church during the time of the Republic of the United Netherlands (1586-1795); within these records are often found records of Catholics, Mennonites, Jews, and others.

Most registers were handed over to civil authorities during the French occupation (1796-1813), and they are now in custody of the archives.

◆Notarial records (wills, divisions of estates, marriage contracts, deeds and other items) date from 1531.
◆Copies of almost all original church registers are available through the Family History Library.
Source: "Dutch Research," by Gene Weston Cheney. Presentation at 1995 NGS Conference in the States

NETHERLANDS-RELATED ADDRESSES

◆Consulate General of the Netherlands
303 E. Wacker Drive, Suite 410
Chicago, IL 60601
◆Algemeen Rijksarchief
Bleijenburg 7
NL-2500's Gravenhage
The Netherlands
(The central state archive)
◆Central Bureau for Genealogy
Postbus 11755
2502 at The Hague
Netherlands
Tel. 011-31-70/3814651
Genealogy/heritage societies
Nederlandse Genealogische Vereniging,
Postbus 976,
NL-1000 AZ Amsterdam
The Netherlands
◆**Germans of Dutch Werkgroep Genealogisch Onderzoek Duitsland**
P.C. Hooftlaan 9
NL-3818 HG Amersfoort
The Netherlands
(This society is geared to the needs of amateur German genealogists with Dutch roots.)
◆**Dutch Family Heritage Society**
2463 Ledgewood Drive
West Jordan, UT 84084-5738
◆ **Netherlands Board of Tourism in Chicago**
(800) 348-9015
Libraries
◆**Herrick Public Library**

300 South River Avenue
Holland, MI 49423-3290
Tel. (616) 394-1400
Fax: (616) 355-1426
E-mail: holrh@lakeland.lib.mi.us
(The Genealogy Department holds records of Dutch emigrants to America, primarily 1820-1880.)
◆**Hope College, Van Zoeren Library**
Holland, MI 49423
◆**Western Theological Seminary Library**
Holland, MI 49423
Further reading
◆Franklin, Charles M., *Dutch Genealogical Research*, C.M. Franklin, c 1982.
◆ Swierenga, Robert P., comp. *Dutch Immigrants in U.S. Ship Passenger Manifests, 1820-1880: An Alphabetical Listing by Household Heads and Independent Persons.* 2 vols. Wilmington, Del.: Scholarly Research, 1983.
◆ Wijnaendts van Resandt, Willem, *Searching for Your Ancestors in the Netherlands.* Central Bureau voor Genealogie, The Hague, 1972.

GENEALOGICAL SOCIETIES IN THE NETHERLANDS

◆Zentraal Bureau voor Genealogie
Prins WIllem-Alexanderhof 22
Postbus 11755
NL-2595 BE's Gravenhage
Netherlands
◆Nederlandse Genealogische Vereniging
Postbus 976
NL-1000 AZ Amsterdam
Netherlands

DUTCH-ENGLISH GENEALOGICAL TERMS

Gezinsblad .... family group sheet
Acternaam .... family name
Voornamen .... given names
Geb. plaats .... birth place

Geb. datum .... birth date
Ged. plaats .... place of baptism
Ged. datum .... date of baptism
Ovl datum .... place of death
Beg. plaats .... place of burial
Geloof .... religion
Beroep .... profession
Ouders (man) .... parents (father)
Getrouwd .... marriage
Tr. plaats .... wedding place
Tr. plaats (K) ..... wedding place (church)
Kinderen .... children

Source: *German-American Genealogy,*
Immigrant Genealogical Society, Spring
1996.

ARCHIVES IN LIECHTENSTEIN

◆Liechtensteinisches Landesarchiv, FL-
9490 Vaduz
◆Hausarchiv der regierenden Fürsten von
Liechtenstein, Schloß, FL-9490, Vaduz
◆ Civil registry office:Kanzlei der
Regierung des Fürstentums Liechten-
stein, FL-9490 Vaduz, Liechtenstein

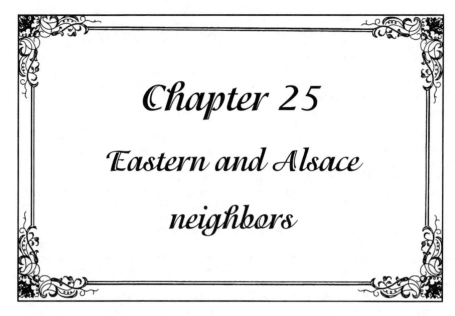

Chapter 25
Eastern and Alsace
neighbors

POLAND SINCE THE 16TH CENTURY: PARTITIONS, BOUNDARY CHANGES

1569: The two realms of Poland and Lithuania are united (including Prussia, Volhynia, Podolia, and Ukraine). Poland has taken a leading position in Europe since the early 15th century. Protestantism is no longer a significant religion after 1600.

1572: Polish nobility takes complete control of the country.

1772, 1793,1795: Three partitions result in treaties whereby the Russian Empire, Prussia, and Austria divide the territory under their respective controls, causing the Polish state to disappear from the map of Europe for almost 125 years. (In the third partition, in 1795, nearly all of western and central Poland , beyond the Vistula River, comes under Prussian rule.)

1808: Napoleon establishes civil registration in the Russian part of Poland (with records written in Polish — one copy remaining in the parish, the other going to the appropriate civil court).

1815: Congress of Vienna creates the kingdom of Poland ruled by the Russian emperor, establishes Kraków as a city republic, and gives the rest of the country to Russia, Austria, and Prussia.

1831: Russians squelch a powerful movement for Polish independence and severe Russianization activities ensue.

1848, 1861, 1863: Polish insurrections result in intensification of Russian repressions. Russian language is introduced in Polish schools in an attempt to replace Polish. Those parts of Poland ruled by Russians become mere provinces of the Russian Empire. Those under Prussian rule are made to endure a Germanization policy; but Austrian Poles are treated more liberally.

1917: A Polish government, following the downfall of the Russian Empire, is established, controlled by Germans.

1918-1919: The Republic of Poland is recreated as an independent state, with its boundary with Germany running east of the Oder River. Treaty of Versailles grants

490	The German Research Companion

Poland territory along Vistula River (the "Polish corridor") and large sections of Posen and West Prussia. The former Austrian province of Galicia becomes part of the republic.

1920-1921: Following war with Soviet Russia, Poland annexes parts of Belarussia and Ukraine.

1921-1922: Poland acquires parts of Upper Silesia.

1939: German invasion of Poland results in its partition by Germany and USSR.

1944-1945: Many Germans in central Poland flee before advancing Soviet armies or are expelled.

1945: Following World War II, Poland, as an independent state, is given administrative rights over Upper and Lower Silesia, Danzig, and parts of Brandenburg, Pomerania, and East Prussia. Poland's eastern boundary of 1939 is restored, and the western border moves to the Oder-Neisse line. Most Germans living east of the Oder-Neisse line who had not already fled are expelled. The German Democratic Republic (East Germany) recognizes the line as the German-Polish border, but the German Federal Republic (West Germany) does not. USSR acquires considerable formerly Polish territory.

1947-1989: Poland is dominated by a Communist-ruled government.

1990: Reunited Germany approves treaty recognizing the Oder-Neisse line as the German-Polish border, and the following year a treaty of friendship and cooperation is ratified.

Sources:
◆"Poland," Microsoft (R) Encarta; Microsoft Corporation and Funk & Wagnalls Corporation. 1994
◆"Family Origins in Eastern Europe: Using the Records of the Genealogical Society of Utah, Modern Poland," by Zdenka Kucera. Church of Jesus Christ of Latter-day Saints, 1980.
◆"Chronology of German-Polish Relations," *German Life*, December 1996/January 1997

RESOURCES FOR POLISH RESEARCH

Many of the Polish records held by the Family History Library in Salt Lake City come from the Polish state archive system, including:
◆ Civil registration records (beginning 1808 or later) from the area of Napoleon's Duchy of Warsaw and later under Imperial Russian rule. These include many Jewish communities.
◆Civil/church registration records from the former province of Galicia, some going back to 1784.
◆Catholic and Protestant parish registers from as early as 1529, most starting in the mid to late 1700s (most from parishes in former German and Russian-ruled areas).

For records later than 1865 or 1870, one must write to the headquarters of the Polish State Archives in Warsaw

Publications
◆ Chorzempa, Rosemary A. *Korzenie Polskie: Polish Roots*, Genealogical Publishing Co., Baltimore, 1993
◆ Müllerowa, Lidia, *Roman Catholic Parishes in the Polish People's Republic in 1984*. Genealogy Unlimited, Orem, Ut.
◆ Budrewicz, Olgierd, *Introduction to Poland*. American Institute of Polish Culture, Miami, 1985
◆ Lewanski, Richard Casimir, comp., *Guide to Polish Libraries and Archives*. East European Monographs, No. VI. Boulder, Colorado, 1974.
◆Schlyter, Daniel M., *Poland/Prussia, How to Locate Vital Records of Former Prussian Areas of Poland in the Genealogical Library*. GENUN Publishers, Buffalo Grove, IL, 1985.
◆"Poland: Maps, Gazetteers, Aids," by Dolores Semon. *The German Connection*, Vol. 17, No. 1, January 1993.
◆"Acquiring Polish Records" by Dolores Semon. *The German Connection*, Vol. 17, No. 1, January 1993.
◆Wellauer, Maralyn A., *Tracing Your*

Polish Roots. Private printing, Milwaukee, WI, 1991

◆Palmer, Michael P., *Genealogical Resources in Eastern Germany (Poland).* Privately published, Claremont, CA 1993.

Resources

◆ **Polish Genealogical Society of America**, 984 N. Milwaukee Avenue,Chicago, IL 60622-4199

◆ **Polish Genealogical Society of the Northeast,** 8 Lyle Road, New Britain,CT 06053-2104

◆ **Polish Genealogical Society of Michigan,** c/o Burton Historical Collection, Detroit Public Library, 5201 Woodward Avenue, Detroit, MI 48202-4007

◆**Polish Genealogical Society of Texas,** 15917 Juneau Drive, Houston, TX 77040-2155

◆ **Polish Genealogical Society of California,** P.O. Box 713, Midway City, CA 92655-0713

◆**Polish Genealogical Society of Greater Cleveland**, 906 College Avenue, Cleveland, OH 44113

◆ **Polish Genealogical Society of Massachusetts,** P. O. Box 381, Northhampton, MA 01061-0381

◆ **Polish Genealogical Society of Minnesota,** P.O. Box 16069, St. Paul, MN 55116-0069

◆**Polish Genealogical Society of New Zealand**, 16 Nugent Street, Plymouth, New Zealand

◆ **Polish Genealogical Society of Western New York,** 299 Barnard Street, Buffalo, NY 14206-3212

◆ **Polish Genealogical Society of Wisconsin,** 3731 Turnwood Drive, Richfield, WI 53076

Sources:

◆"Poland: Maps, Gazetteers, Aids," by Dolores Semon. *The German Connection,* Vol. 17, No. 1, January 1993.

◆ "Acquiring Polish Records," by Dolores Semon. *The German Connection*, Vol. 17, No. 1,

Bessarabien girl

January 1993.

◆Edward R. Brandt, et al., *Germanic Genealogy: A Guide to Worldwide Sources and Migration Patterns.* Germanic Genealogy Society, St. Paul, Minn.,1994

GALICIA (Galizien)

Galicia, now part of southeastern Poland and western Ukraine, was formerly an Austrian crown land. The background:

11th, 12th centuries: An important Slavic principality, later belonged to Poland

1772: Galicia becomes part of the Austrian Empire (as a result of the first partition of Poland) and remains an Austsrian Crown land until 1918, when it was claimed by the new Polish Republic.

1919: West Galicia is assigned to Poland by the Treaty of Versailles following World War I. East Galicia is later given the right of self-determination

1919: East Galicia is given autonomy under a Polish protectorate that lasted 20 years. Galicia comprises the Polish provinces of Kraków, Lwów, Stanislawów and Tarnopol.

1939: The provinces of Kraków, Tarnopol, and part of Lwów, after the invasion of Poland by Germany and the Union of Soviet Socialist Republics, are included in the Soviet zone of Occupation.

1945: Galicia is assigned to the USSR and incorporated into the Ukrainian SSR under a Polish-Soviet agreement.

1991: Ukraine becomes independent.

Resources
♦**Ukrainian Genealogical & Historical Society of Canada,** R.R. #2, Cochrane, AB TOW 0W0, Canada

Source: Microsoft (R) Encarta. Copyright 1994 Microsoft Corporation; Funk & Wagnall's Corporation 1994.

SILESIA (Schlesien)

Silesia (in German, *Schlesien*) fall mostly in what is now southwestern Poland. It also included parts of North Moravia,, the Czech Republic, and the states of Brandenburg and Saxony in eastern Germany.

In the eleventh century it was part of the kingdom of Poland. In the fourteenth century its was acquired by Bohemia.

In 1742 it was annexed by Prussia, after having been ruled for more than 200 years by the Austrian Habsburgs.

The German population was expelled after World War II when almost all of Prussian Silesia reverted to Poland.

Societies
♦**Silesian-American Genealogy Society** [for U.S. and Canada], P.O.Box 21346-0346, Salt Lake City, UT 84121-0346
♦**Silesian Genealogical Society** [Poland], PL 50-950, Wroclaw 2, P.O. Box 312, Poland

Source: Microsoft (R) Encarta. Copyright 1994

Microsoft Corp., Funk & Wagnalls Corporation, 1994.

CZECHOSLOVAKIA (Czech Republic, Slovakia)

1918: Czechoslovakia is born from the disbanded Austro-Hungarian Empire after World War I. (The regions of Bohemia, Moravia, and Silesia – now known as the Czech Republic – had fallen under the rule of the Austrian crown. Before 1918, Czechs were known as Austrians. The Slovaks were occupied by the Hungarian monarchy, and later the dual Austro-Hungarian Empire.) The 1918 creation of Czecho-Slovakia soon beccomes referred to simply as Czechoslovakia.

1938: Bohemia and Moravia become a Protectorate of the Third Reich following the Nazi invasion. Slovakia becomes an "independent" puppet state of the Nazi government.

1945: At the end of World War II, the nation once more becomes Czechoslovakia

1946: With the Communist takeover, the country becomes the Czechoslovak Socialist Republic.

1989: Through the "Velvet Revolution," the Czechoslovak Federal Republic is born, soon followed by the Czech and Slovak Federal Republic

1993: The country divided into the Czech Republic and the Slovak Republic, more commonly known as Slovakia.

Archives
The Czech Republic archives are divided into regional branches, with five Bohemian archives and two Moravian archives. All parish registers, beginning in the 1890s, remain in the city or village repositories.

Books completed during the last decade of the nineteenth century and those prior to them were sent to regional archives for preservation and cataloging. They may be accessed, but with some rather stringent restrictions.

Slovak records for the three major regional archives in Slovakia are available through the Family History Library.

Source: Dr. Paul S. Valasek, "Multiple border, national boundary changes test skills of the Czech, Slovak researchers." *AntiqueWeek,* February 10, 1997. (Dr. Valasek is a founding member of the Czech & Slovak American Genealogy Society of Illinois and serves as the editor to its journal, *Koreny* ("roots"). He is also a member of the Slovak Heritage & Folklore Society International and serves as the Illinois Represntative for the Moravian Heritage Society (see addresses below). He welcomes letters and comments and may be reached at 2643 W. 51st Street, Chicago, IL 60632-1559.

Societies
♦ **Czech and Slovak American Genealogy Society of Illinois,** P.O. Box 303, Sugar Grove, IL 60554
♦**Slovak Heritage & Folklore Society International,** 151 Colebrook Drive, Rochester, NY 14617-2215.
♦ **Moravian Heritage Society,** 31910 Road 160, Visalia, CA 93292-9044

GERMAN BOHEMIANS

The *Böhmisch* (Bohemians) descend from Germanic peoples who lived outside of what was until recently Czechoslovakia (for example: Bavaria, Silesia, and Austria), though they forged a distinct identity after living as long as 900 years in Bohemia.

German-Bohemians were settlers from as long ago as the seventh century in the mountainous area that extend around Bohemia and Moravia, which much later, in 1918, became Czechoslovakia.

Around 1900 these areas came to be known as the Sudetenland and the people as Sudeten-Germans. By this time ethnic Germans constituted 35 percent of Bohemia's population, and almost 28 percent of the population of Moravia; these populations were overwhelmingly Roman Catholic.

In 1938, these territories were taken over by Germany until the end of World War II, when Czechoslovakia's pre-war borders were restored. Most ethnic Germans were expelled from the country. In 1948, most of the border villages were bulldozed to the ground.

Many of the *Böhmisch* emigrants settled near New Ulm, Minnesota in Brown and Nicollet counties, starting in 1856 and continuing until 1914. Early emigrants settled near Dubuque, Iowa, but then moved on toward New Ulm to find better land.

Church registers
Church registers in Bohemia and Moravia were taken into state possession in 1952. No civil registration existed until the twentieth century.

Resources and further reading
♦La Vern Rippley and Robert Paulson, *The German-Bohemians: The Quiet Immigrants.* St. Olaf College Press, Northfield Minnesota. 1995.
♦Ken Meter and Robert Paulson, *Border People: The Bohemisch* [German-Bohemians] *in America.* Crossroads Resource Center and the German-Bohemian Heritage Society. 1993.

Genealogy societies
See the list of representative *Heimatbücher* on page 494.
♦**German-Bohemian Heritage Society,** P.O. Box 822, New Ulm, MN 56073-0822
E-mail: LALGBHS@aol.com
– [GBHS founder] Robert Paulson, 800 W. Idaho Avenue, St. Paul, MN 55117.
E-mail: RpaulGBHS@aol.com
Publication: German-Bohemian Heritage Society Newsletter (quarterly; free queries) (This is the primary society in the United States for German-Bohemian research, with a German-Bohemian Family Data Base available on the internet.)
♦ **Vereinigung Sudetendeutscher**

(continued on page 495)

REPRESENTATIVE GERMAN-BOHEMIAN *HEIMATBÜCHER* HELD BY THE CZECHOSLOVAK GENEALOGICAL SOCIETY INTERNATIONAL

The following is a representative list of German locations for which *Heimatbücher* (lineage books for specific localities) exist. There are many more. Those listed are available at the Czechoslovak Genealogical Society International.

German District	Czech Version	Locality of country
Bischofteinitz	Horšovsk	West Bohemia
Gablonz	Jablonec nad Nisou	North Bohemia
Budweis	Ceské Bud jovice	South Bohemia
Luditz	Zlutice	Northwest Bohemia
Landskron	Lanškroun	East Bohemia
Bilin	Bilina	North Bohemia
Reichenberg	Liberec	North Bohemia
Mies	St íbro	West Bohemia
Aussig	Ustí nad Labem	North Bohemia
Falkenau	Falknov	Northwest Bohemia
Warnsdorf	Varnsdorf	North Bohemia
Mährisch-Schönberg	Šumperk	North Bohemia
Mährisch-Trübau	T eba ov	West Moravia
Zwittau	Svitavy	West Moravia
Tachau	Tachov	West Bohemia
Braunau	Broumov	Northeast Bohemia
Bergreichenstein	Kašpersk Hory	West Bohemia
Elbogen	Locket	Northwest Bohemia
Freiwaldau	Fr valdov	West Silesia
Wishau	Vyškov	Central Moravia
Hohenstadt	Záb eh	North Moravia
Prachatitz	Prachatice	South Bohemia
Znaim	Znojmo	Southwest Moravia
Freudenthal	Bruntál	West Silesia
Markt-Eisenstein	Zelezná Ruda	
Bergreichenstein	Kašpersk Hory	West Bohemia
Troppau	Opava	North Silesia (Moravia)
Brünn	Brno	South Moravia
Herrnskretschen	H ensko (Tetschen Dist)	North Bohemia
Alt-Moletein	Star Maletín	West Moravia

Familien-forscher (VSFF), Erikaweg 58, 93053 Regensburg

♦**Czechoslovak Genealogical Society International**, P.O. Box 16225, St. Paul, MN 55116-0255

♦ **Minnesota Genealogical Society Library**, 1650 Carroll Avenue, St. Paul, MN 55104

♦**Minnesota Historical Society**, 345 Kellog Blvd. West, St. Paul, MN 55102-1906

♦**Brown County Historical Society**, 2 North Broadway, New Ulm, MN 56073

Publications

The best English-language guide to ethnic German genealogical research in the former Czechoslovakia is,

♦ Arbeitsgemeinschaft ostdeutscher Familienforscher e.V., Herne, *Genealogical Guide to German Ancestors from East Germany and Eastern Europe* (AGoFF-Wegweiser - English Edition), translated by Joachim O.R. Nuthack and Adalbert Goertz. Verlag Degener, Neustadt/Aisch, 1984.

♦Leo Baca, ed., *Czech Immigration Passenger Lists*. 2 vols. Old Homestead Publishing Co., Hallettsville, Tex., 1983-1985

Archive

Sudetendeutsches Archiv, Hochstraße 8/11, 81669 München. Tel. (089) 48 00 03-30

The Sudeten German Archive collects historic primary sources, documents, newspapers, magazines, pictures and recordings of the political, economic and cultural development of the Sudeten Germans before and after their expulsion. Its focus is local historical and geographical history and the Sudeten German and Czechoslovakian press.

District archives

Archives in the Czech Republic are divided into these eight districts:

1. West Bohemian district: State district archives Pilsen (Pilzen)
2. North Bohemian district: State district archives Leitmeritz (Litomerice)

3. Middle Bohemian district: State district archives Prague (Praha)
4. South Bohemian district: State district archives Wittingau (Trebon)
5. East Bohemian district: State district archives Zamrsk
6. North Moravian district: State district archives Troppau (Opava)
7. South Moravian district: State district archives Brünn (Brno)
8. Prague: Archive of the capital of Prague (Praha)

BUKOVINA GERMANS

Formerly a province of Romania, Bukovina lies in the foothills of the eastern Carpathian Mountains. Until 1769 it was ruled by the Ottoman Turks and occupied by Russia. In 1775, having been taken over by Ausstria, Bukovina became part of Galicia until 1849, when it was made a separate crownland or province. In the late 1700s and early 1800s, the ruling Hapsburg family recruited German-speaking people to settle its virgin forests.

The German colonists consisted of three groups: 1) Swabians and Palatines from what is now Baden-Württemberg and Rheinland-Pfalz, in southwest Germany; 2) German Bohemians, from the Bohemian forest (*Böhmerwald)*, now in the Czech Republic; and 3) Zipsers, from the Zips mountains, now Spis county, Slovakia. The Bukovina Germans never exceeded 10 percent of the population of the province. Although a minority, they lived in ethnic German villages and communities, preserving their language and customs.

After one to two generations in Bukovina, land became scarce and the New World looked promising. Agents for the railroads passed out flyers throughout Europe to recruit the hard-working Germans to settle along their lines. Newspapers brimmed with ads announcing free homestead land, and, in the case of South America, free passage. Some 70 familiies chose Ellis, Kansas as their destination during a span of 15 years beginning in 1886. Later arrivals located in Rooks, Trego, Ness and other western Kansas counties. Two other colonies were started, one in Yuma County, Colorado, and one in Lewis County, Washington. After 1900, some Bukovina Germans located in New York and Chicago. Stepping off the train in western Kansas in the middle of a vast prairie was a stark contrast to their forested ancestral lands, but the hardy pioioneers carved out successful lives as the largest concentration of Bukovina Germans in the United States.

At the end of World War I, when the Austro-Hungarian Empire was dissolved, Bukovina became independent and joined Romania as a province. During World War II (in 1940), Bukovina and Bessarabia were ceded to the Soviet Union but were occupied by German and Romanian forces from 1941-1944. Through an armistice in 1944, northern Bukovina and Bessarabia became part of the Soviet Union, and southern Bukovina remained in Romania. The ancestral villages of the Ellis Bukovina Germans today are in Romania.

Societies
♦**Bukovina Society of the Americas**, P.O. Box 81, Ellis, KS 67637-0081.
♦**Landsmannschaft der Buchenland-deutschen e.V.**, Bukowina Institut, Alter Postweg 97a, 86159 Augsburg, Germany. (This organization was formed in 1949 by refugees who had resettled from Bukovina to Germany and Austria during and after World War II.)
♦ **Raimund Friedrich Kaindl-Gesellschaft e.V.**, Waldburgstr. 251, 70655 Stuttgart, Germany (a genealogical society)

Publications
♦ Irma Bornemann, *The Bukovina Germans;* published in Germany as *Die Buchenlanddeutschen*, vol. 13 of *Kulturelle Arbeitschelfte*, ed. Barbara

Konitz (Bonn: Bund der Vertriebenen, 1986). English translation by Sophie A. Welisch, © 1990 by the Bukovina Society of the Americans, Ellis, Kansas.
♦Sopie A Welisch, *Bukovina Villages/Towns/Cities and Their Germans.* Published 1990 by the Bukovina Society of the Americas, Ellis, Kansas.
♦ Oneita Jean Bollig, Extracted parish records from Ellis, Kansas. Each book includes the Register of Baptisms, Register of Confirmations, Register of Marriages, and Register of Funerals for the cited years.
♦Irmgard Hein Ellingson, *The Bukovina Germans in Kansas: A 200 Year History of the Lutheran Swabians.* No. 6 of Ethnic Heritage Studies, published by Fort Hays State University, 1987. (Irmgard Ellingson, P.O. Box 97, Ossian, IA 52161-0097)
♦Oren Windholz, *Bohemian Germans in Kansas: A Catholic Community from Bukovina.* Published by the author, 1993 (Oren Windholz, P.O.Box 1083, Hays, KS 67601)
♦Almar Associates, *Bukovina Families: 200 Years.* Almar Associates, Ellis, Kansas, 1993. Primary emphasis on families from Pojana Mikuli. (Almar Associates, 300 N. Washington Street, Ellis, KS 67637)

Records
After World War II, many of the Roman Catholic and Lutheran parish records were brought out of Romania when the Bukovina Germans left there in the *Umsiedlung* (resettlement) of 1940. Most of them were collected in *Die deutsche Zentralstelle für Genealogie* in Leipzig. All these records have been microfilmed for the Family History Library in Salt Lake City and are available through Family History Centers.

'DANUBE SWABIANS'

A large-scale migration of Germans into eastern and southeastern Europe during the eighteenth century resulted in many settling in the Austrian Empire, who became known as Hungarian Germans because the area was part of Greater Hungary of that day. Since 1919 these settlers have been referred to as the "Danube Swabians" because a majority of these settlements were now in Romania or Yugoslavia.

Genealogist and author Edward R. Brandt, conjecturing on why they were called "Swabians," places credence on the explanation that the settlers became known as "Swabians" because they embarked at Ulm inSwabia and sailed down the Danube to their destination near Belgrade.

Society

Society of Danube Swabians, 4219 N. Lincoln Avenue, Chicago, IL 60618

LITHUANIAN RESEARCH

Lithuanian American Genealogy Society
Balzekas Museum of Lithuanian Culture, IHG/LAGS
6500 S. Pulaski Road
Chicago, IL 60629-5136
The Lithuanian American Genealogy Society (LAGS), part of the Balzekas Museum of Lithuanian Culture, maintains the largest collection of Lithuanian library and research materials outside Lithuania and is the only American genealogy organization that holds an institutional relationship with the Lithuanian Archives, whose records date back to the year 1359.

Research services are offered by LAGS and the Immigration History & Genealogy Department (IHG) of the Balzekas Museum.

WENDS

Wends was the name that Germans in medieval times gave to the Slavic tribes from an area west of the Oder River. Some 500 of these Wends (who called themselves Sorbs) sailed from their homes in Lusatia (Lausitz), the area now divided between Upper Lusatia in Saxony and Lower Lusatia in Brandenburg.

Led by their spiritual leader, The Rev. Jan Killian, they arrived at the harbor at Galveston, Texas in 1854, seeking religious liberty and the right to speak their Wendish tongue. Their settlement was established on 4254 purchased acres in what is now Lee County. They named their new town Serbin, near Giddings. In Serbin, they established what became the first Missouri Synod Lutheran church in Texas, with the only Wendish school in America.

The colonists moved on into other parts of Texas in the late 1800s, and they founded sub-colonies in places like Austin, Houston, Warda, Fedor, Swiss Alp, Giddings, Port Arthur, Manheim, Copperas Cove, Vernon, Walburg, The Grove, Bishop, and the Rio Grande Valley – in each place building a new church affiliated with the Missouri Synod, thus helping to spread its congregations throughout Texas.

Many more Wends immigrated in the second half of the nineteenth century.

Wends manuscript collections
♦Texas Wendish Heritage Museum, Rt. 2, Box 155, Giddings, TX 78942 (archives, library, museum). Tel. (409) 366-2441
♦Sophienburg Museum, 401 W. Coll, New Braunfels, TX 78130. Tel. (210) 629-1572.
♦Sophienburg Archives, 200 N. Seguin Avenue, New Braunfels, TX 78130. Tel. (512) 629-1900.
♦Gillespie County Historical Society, 312 West San Antonio, P.O. Box 765, Fredericksburg, TX 78624 (archives, historical society). Tel. (512) 997-2835.
♦Winedale Historical Center, University of Texas, Farm Road 2714-Winedale, P.O. Box 11, Round Top, TX 78954 (historical center). Tel. (409) 278-3530. Fax: (409) 3531
♦University of Texas Institute of Texan Cultures, Library (library, museum,

research institution). Tel. (210) 226-7651. Fax: (210) 222-8564
• Barker Texas Historical Center, University of Texas at Austin, SRH 2.101, Austin, TX 78712. Tel. (512) 495-4515. FAX 512-495-4542

Sorb museum

•Sorbisches Museum, Ortenburg 3, 02065 Bautzen, Germany. Tel. (03591) 42403. Fax: (03591) 42425

GERMAN-CANADIANS

German-speaking and German-descended populations are found in the greatest numbers in the rural areas of Manitoba, Saskatchewan, and Alberta. They are found in Ontario in and near the cities of Kitchener (formerly Berlin) and Waterloo, the town of New Hamburg and the Niagra area, and in the Royal York area of metropolitan Toronto.

The following potential resource locations have been published by *German Life* (February/March 1996):

Alberta

Alberta Travel Information
10155-102 Street
Commerce Place
Edmonton, Alberta, Canada

Manitoba

•Manitoba Industry Trade and Tourism
1670 Portage Avenue
Winnipeg, Manitoba, Canada
•Mennonite Heritage Center
600 Shaftesbury Boulevard
Winnipeg, Manitoba R3_ 0M4, Canada
Tel. (204) 888-6781
Fax: (204) 831-5675
•Winnipeg Tourist and Visitor Information
3rd Floor, Johnson Terminal
Winnipeg, Manitoba, Canada

Ontario

Archives of the Province of Ontario
77 Grenville
Toronto, Ontario, Canada
Tel. (416) 327-1600 (inquiries)
Tel.: (416) 327-1602 (archivist)

•Austrian Club Edelweiss
207 Beverley
Toronto, Ontario, Canada
Tel.: (416) 977-0466
•Danube Swabian Association
c/o Blue Danube
1686 Ellesmere Road
Scarborough, Ontario M1H 2V5, Canada
Tel. (416) 290-6186
•German Canadian Royal Congress
605 Royal York Road
Toronto, Ontario, Canada
Tel. (416) 503-3904
•Mennonite Central Committee
11 Madison
Toronto, Ontario, Canada
Tel. (416) 921-3927
•Multicultural History Society of Ontario
43 Queen's Park Crescent East
Toronto, Ontario, Canada
Tel. (416) 979-2973
•Ontario Ministry of Citizenship
77 Bloor Street West (5th Floor)
Toronto, Ontario M7A 2R9, Canada
Tel. (416) 314-7726/7724
•For information on Mennonite Heritage in Ontario, the largely German Canadian Kitchener-Waterloo, New Hamburg, and fruit-growing (Niagra) areas, call (519) 748-0800
•Swiss Canadian Chamber of Commerce
21 Iron
Toronto, Ontario, Canada
Tel. (416) 243-1201

Quebec

Festival Folklorique du Monde
405 rue Saiint-Jean
Drummondville, Quebec J2B 5L7, Canada
Tel. (819) 472-1184
Fax: (819) 474-6585

Saskatchewan

Saskatchewan Tourism
1900 Albert Street, Suite 500
Regina, Saskatchewan S4P 4L9, Canada

ARCHIVES

The National Archives of Canada
395 Wellington Street
Ottawa, Ontario, Canada K1A 0N3
Publications

Regional archives
Montreal Federal Records Centre
665A Montee de Liesse
Ville St. Laurent, Quebec, Canada H4T
1P5
♦Quebec City Federal Records Centre
75 de Hambourg
St. Augustan, Quebec, Canada G3A 1S6
♦Ottawa Federal Records Centre
Bldg. #15 Tunneys Pastsure, Goldenrod
Street
Ottawa, Ontario, Canada K1A 0N3
♦Toronto Federal Land Record Centre
190 Carrier Drive
Rexdale, Ontario, Canada M9W 5R1
♦Winnipeg Federal Records Center
201 Weston Street
Winnipeg, Manitoba, Canada R3E 3H4
♦Edmonton Federal Records Centre
8707 51st Avenue
Edmonton, Alberta, Canada T6E 5H1
♦Vancouver Federal Records Centre
2751 Production Way
Lake City Industrial Park
Buraby, British Columbia, Canada V5A
3G7
♦Halifax Federal Records Centre
131 Thornhill Drive
Halifax, Nova Scotia, Canada B3B 1S2

St. Albans passenger arrival records
The St. Albans Passenger Arrival Records record those people who crossed the border from Canada to the United States, including passengers arriving by train through substtions,ports, or along the borders from Washington State to Maine.

The Immigration and Naturalization Service at St. Albans, Vermont, maintained these records, which are part of Group 85 records of the Immigration and Naturalization Service. It has been estimated that as many as 40 percent of the passengers arriving in Canada were actually bound for the United States. They were traveling through Canada because of the low railway and steamship fares.

Records Group 85 indexes
The four indexes for this INS Records Group 85 are,

♦**M1461** (400 rolls of microfilm), "Soundex Index to Canadian Border Entries through the St. Albans, Vermont, District, 1895-1924"
M1462 (6 rolls of microfilm), "Alphabetical Index to Canadian Border Entries through Small Ports in Vermont, 1895-1924.
♦**M1463** (98 rolls of microfilm), "Soundex Index to Entries into theSt. Albans, Vermont, District through Canadian Pacific and Atlantic Ports, 1924-1958."
♦**M1478** (117 rolls of microfilm), "Card Manifests (Alphabetical) of Individuals Entering through the Port of Detroit, Michigan, 1906-1954"

Immigrants who came to the United States through any Canadian port were reported to the St. Albans Immigration office, the records for which are found in the #M1463 index.

For more information, see "St. Albans Passenger Arrival Records," by Constance Potter, Prologue, National Archives, Washington, Spring 1990, pp 90-93.

Canadian passenger ship manifests
Manifests are available to researchers for the ports of Montreal/Quebec City, 1865-1919; Halifax, 1880-1919; North Sydney, 1906-1919; Saint John, 1900-1918; Vancouver, 1905-1919; Victoria and small coastal ports, 1905-1919.

Microfilms of these manifests are available at Family History Centers of the Family History Library of the Church of Jesus Christ of Latter-day Saints in Salt Lake City, as well as at locations in Canada. Almost none of the manifests is indexed. The information is arranged chronologically by year and date. For further information, see "Canadian Passenger Ship Manifests," by Glen Eker. *Ancestry*, March/April 1996.

Publications
♦ Baxter, Angus, In Search of Your Canadian Roots. Genealogical Publishing Co., Inc., Baltimore. 2nd ed. 1994
♦Lehman, Heinz, *The German Canadians*, 1750-1937, trans. Prof. Gerhard P.

Bassler. Jesperson Press, St. John's, Newfoundland, 1986.
(This is a very detailed history of German settlements in Canada, including place of origin for many settlers)

Consulate General
Canadian Consulate General
300 S. Grand Avenue, Suite 1000
Los Angeles, CA 90071
Tel. (213) 346-2700

Sources:
♦"Road less travelled used by some 'back door' immigrant ancestors," by John W. Heisey, *AntiqueWeek*, August 28, 1995.
♦ "A History of German Canadians," by William A. Hynes. *German Life*, February/March 1996.
♦"Canadian Passenger Ship Manifests," by Glen Eker. *Ancestry*, March/April 1996

CANTONS OF LUXEMBOURG

♦Capellen
♦Clervaux
♦Diekirch
♦Echtermach
♦Esch-sur-Alzette
♦Grevenmacher
♦Luxembourg-Campagne
♦Luxembourg-Ville
♦Mersch
♦Redange
♦Remich
♦Vianden
♦Wiltz

'BLACK DUTCH'

Although the term "Black Dutch" has been used to denote a number of different ethnic or cultural groups, there seems to be little agreement as to just what the phrase means.

Several genealogical organizations have made attempts to investigate the origin of the term "Black Dutch," yet no specific clarification, no pedigree charts, and no documentation of any kind have been forthcoming.

Numerous accounts have circulated to the effect that the "Black Dutch" can be identified as groups of Irish, Cherokees, Amish, Swiss, Sephardic Jews, Dutch-Indonesians, and Hollanders — to name just a few.

The conclusion drawn by those who have attempted to define the term is that "Black Dutch" ancestry seems to be based on folklore and hearsay.

CHRONOLOGY OF ALSACE JURISDICTIONS

Before 1648: Alsace is part of the Holy Roman Empire
1648: Most of Alsace becomes part of France.
1766: Lorraine becomes part of France.
1871: Alsace and part of Lorraine ("German Lorraine") are annexed by Germany under the name Elsaß-Lothringen. Bismarck takes from Napoleon III the French départements of Bas-Rhin, Haut-Rhin, and Moselle. The western part of Haut-Rhin becomes the territory of Belfort.
1919: Alsace becomes part of France, following World War I. (The old Alsatian départements of Bas-Rhin and Haut-Rhin are restored. The Lothringen section becomes the département of Moselle.)
1939-1945: Alsace becomes part of Germany during World War II.
1946 to present: Alsace is part of France. (Alsace takes in the departments of Bas-Rhin, Haut-Rhin and, since 1871 the Territory of Belfort; Lorraine corresponds to the departments of Moselle, Meurthe-et-Moselle, and parts of the départements of Meuse and of Vosges.)

RESOURCES FOR ALSACE-LORRAINE RESEARCH

♦"Alsace Family History Research," by Adeline Vigelis. *The German Connection*

(The German Research Association), Vol. 18, No. 3, 1994.
◆Annette Kunselman Burgert, *Eighteenth Century Emigrants from the Northern Alsace to America*. Picton Press, Camden, Maine, 1992
◆Hugh T. Law, "Locating the Ancestral Home in Elsaß-Lothringen (Alsace Lorraine)," *German Genealogical Digest*, Vol. VI, No. 3, 1990.
◆Cornelia Schrader-Muggenthaler, *Alsace Emigration Book*, 3 vols. Apollo, PA: Closson Press. 1989-1991
◆Friedrich Müller. *Ortsbuch für Eupen-Malmedy, Elsass-Lothringen und Luxemburg* [Gazetteer for Eupen-Malmedy (Belgium), Alsace-Lorraine, and Luxembourg]. 1942.

ARCHIVES FOR ALSACE-LORRAINE RESEARCH

Alsace
(Elsaß)
◆Archives Departementales du Bas-Rhin, 5-9 rue Fischart, 67000 Strasbourg, France
◆Archives Departementales du Haut-Rhin, Cité administrative, 68026 Colmar Cedex, France
◆Archives Departementales du Territoire de Belfort, 2 rue de l'Ancien Théâtre, 90020 Belfort Cedex, France

Lorraine
(Lothringen)
◆Archives Departementales de Meurthe et Moselle, 1, rue de la Monnaie, 54052 Nancy Cedex, France
◆Arcives Departementales de la Meuse, 20, rue Mgr. Aimond, 55012 Bar-le-Duc, France
◆Archives Departementales de la Moselle, 1, allée du Château, 57070 St.-Julien-lès-Metz, France
◆Archives Departementales des Vosges, Allée des Hêtres, Z.I. La Voivre, 88000 Épinal, France

ALSACE EMIGRATION INDEX

FHL microfilm numbers for the Alsace Emigration Index for surnames beginning with the specified letters of the alphabet are listed below:

A-C	1,125,002
D-G	1,125,003
H-K	1,125,004
L-P	1,125,005
Q-S	1,125,006
T-Z	1,125,007

Birthplaces, ages and dates of emigration found on these films can become the basis for searches in French civil or parish records.

After 1792, civil records for Alsace and the department of Moselle are mostly in German.

Parish records of Lutherans are usually in German. Parish records of Catholics are in Latin, or sometimes in French.

'OPTIONS OF ALSATIANS AND LORRAINERS'

After Germany annexed much of Alsace and Lorraine after the Franco-Prussian War in 1871, about 160,000 residents of the area, as well as many others, recorded their options to leave.

A list of 523,000 persons who registered their options are recorded on FHL microfilm. Included are names, birth dates, and places of birth.

Some places of destinations are also given.

These lists were originally published in supplements to the *Bulletin des Lois* (Bulletin of the Laws).

Microfilm numbers for these "Options of Alsatians and Lorrainers" are 787,154 (beginning in the middle) to 787,166. Film numbers 787,165 and 787,166 contain information about persons whose destinations were given as New York, New Orleans, Louisville, St. Louis, San Fran-

cisco, Baltimore, Boston, Chicago, Cincinnati, Washington, Quebec, etc.
Source: Hugh T. Law, M.A., A.G., "Locatiing the Ancestral Home in Elsass-Lothringen," *German Genealogical Digest,* Vol. VI, No. 3 (1990), p. 83.

THE ANDRIVEAU COLLECTION

The Andriveau family in Paris has made available indexes of civil and church records of many French cities. These have been filmed and are available through the Family History Library. The index to the 1,068 rolls of microfilm may be found on microfiche in the Family History Library Catalog, Author section (fiche #0032).

The collection's manuscript card index of parish registers includes,
Paris 1700-1860; **Bruxelles**, 1800-1880; **Anvers**, 1760-1880; **Le Mans**, 1700-1888; **Le Merlerault**, 1700-1830; **Argentan**, 1700-1830; **Bordeaux**, 1700-1820; **Ancenis**, 1700-1820; **Niort**, 1700-1882; **Poitiers**, 1700-1882; **Tours**, 1700-1882; **Montpellier**, 1700-1875; **Mortain**, 1759-1863; **Le Havre**, 1700-1883; **Amiens**, 1700-1885; **Louviers**, 1700-1883; **Arras**, 1700-1885; **Valenciennes**, 1759-1909; **Dijon**, 1700-1869; **Epernay**, 1700-1862; **Chalon-sur-Marne,** 1700-1862; **Laon**, 1700-1890; **Lure**, 1700-1890; **Vitry-le-Francois**, 1700-1890; **Strasbourg**, 1700-1870; **Metz**, 1700-1870; **Nancy**, 1700-1870; **Reims**, 1750-1891.

The contents of the films are listed in the index as follows:
Paris: baptisms, marriages, 1800-1860; deaths, 1795-1850; marriages 1700-1850. **Bruxelles:** marriages, 1800-1880. **Anvers:** marriages, 1760-1880. **Le Mans:** marriages, 1700-1888. **Le Merlerault:**

marriages 1700-1830. **Argentan:** marriages 1700-1830. **Bordeaux:** marriages 1700-1820. **Ancenis:** marriages 1700-1820. **Niort:** marriages, 1700-1882. **Poitiers:** marriages, 1700-1882. **Tours:** marriages, 1700-1882. **Montpellier:** marriages, 1700-1875. **Mortain:** marriages, 1759-1863. **Le Havre:** marriages, 1700-1883. **Louviers:** marriages, 1700-1883. **Amiens:** marriages, 1700-1885. **Arras:** marriages, 1700-1885. **Valenciennes:** marriages, 1759-1909. **Dijon:** marriages, 1700-1869. **Epernay:** marriages, 1700-1862. **Chalons-sur-Marne:** marriages, 1700-1862. **Laon:** marriages, 1700-1890. **Lure:** marriages, 1700-1890. **Vitry-le-Francois:** marriages, 1700-1890. **Strasbourg:** marriages, 1700-1870. **Metz:** marriages, 1770-1870. **Nancy:** marriages, 1750-1869. **Reims:** marriages, 1750-1891.

FHL microfilm numbers range (with breaks) from 1147628 through 1296860.

See the microfiche noted above (Family History Library Catalog, Author section, microfiche #0032) for the listing of microfilm numbers arranged alphabetically by surname.

ALSACE EMIGRATION INDEX
The Family History Library's Alsace Emigration Index on microfilm is a list of some 25,000 perions, mostly French, with thousands of Germans and some Swiss and Italian. Places of birth or residence, dates, and destinations are shown.

Overall dates are 1817-1866.
Surname initials with corresponding microfilm numbers:

A-C	1,125,002
D-G	1,125-003
H-K	1,125,004
L-P	1,125,005
Q-S	1,125,006
T-Z	1,125,007

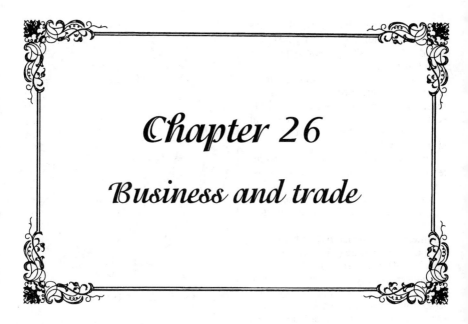

Chapter 26
Business and trade

THE GUILDS (Zünfte)

Background

Guilds (*Gilden, Zünfte, Innungen*) were associations of craftsmen or merchants, organized for self-protection and economic and social gain, which flourished between the 11th and 16th centuries in Europe. They became possible only after the rise of towns in the 10th and 11th centuries, enjoying their heyday from the 12th to the 15th centuries.

The guilds governed practices by which apprentices in the crafts gained experience in their respective trades. A decree abolishing craft associations was enacted in Germany in 1859-60.

Stages of guild training

Apprentices *(Lehrlinge, Lehrjunge)* were young boys who lived with the family of a master *(Meister)*, an established craftsman, who trained him for at least three years (usually five to nine years). Instead of wages, the apprentice received board and keep in addition to his training. To enroll a son as an apprentice, the family was required to pay a large sum of money to the master.

At the end of the apprenticeship, the *Lehrling* could take an examination *(Gesellenprüfung),* which, if he passed, earned him a journeyman's certificate *(Gesellenbrief),* and allowed him to go on to become a journeyman *(Geselle)*. Traditionally the journeyman then set off on travels around the country *(Wanderschaft)* to work for master craftsmen and guilds in towns along his way.

The journeyman's goal was to become accepted as a *Meister* so that he could in

Workmen's seals: shoemaker and butcher

turn open a shop and train apprentices. Another examination was in many cases required (*Meisterprüfung*) before he could reach this stage.

Another step toward becoming a master was the construction of a *Meisterstück* (masterpiece) as a demonstration of his technical competence in the given field and as a determiner of the journeyman's admission into the guild.

Often apprenticeships came to be limited to the sons or other relatives of masters.

Men who passed the master's test were recorded in a book of masters *(Meisterbuch)*.

Some records associated with guilds
◆The birth certificate (*Geburtsbrief*) or a statement of birth and origin (*Geburts- und Herkunftszeugnisse)* to prove "honorable birth and origin." (Illegitimately born persons were not accepted into guilds.)
◆Apprentice records were called *Ein- und Ausschreiben der Burschen* and *Lehrbriefe* (apprenticeship certificates).
◆The traveling pass *(Wanderzettel)*, a record in which the journeyman's guild attested to his skills and verified his identity, and in which the various masters for whom he worked wrote to certify the quality of his performance.
◆The journeyman was given a *Wanderbuch* (journey book) as he set out on his travels. In it each employer would write down the nature of his work and the manner in which he performed it. Thus it became a record of his travels.
◆ The certificate of employment and conduct (*Kundschafts-Zettel*).

Availability of records
Guild records (*Zunftbücher*) may be found in state and city archives, in modern guilds, and sometimes in the Family History Library Catalog. Few have been published or filmed.

When available on film, they are found on the FLHC under "Occupations" (under Germany, or a German state, or a German town).

Sign of the Lucas Guild, Würzburg

FHL-filmed guild records
A few guild records are available on microfilm through the Family History Library. Records for one or more guilds are available for:
◆**Bavaria:** Augsburg, Nürnberg, München
◆**Brandenburg:** Potsdam
◆**Braunschweig**
◆**Saxony:** Magdeburg
◆**West Prussia:** Garnsee
◆**Württemberg:** Göppingen
◆**East Prussia:** Angerburg, Bartenstein, Bialla, Bischofstein, Braunsberg, Christburg, Darkehmen, Drengfurt, Frauenburg, Friedland, Gerdauen, Goldap, Gumbinnen, Heiligenbeil, Insterburg, Johannisburg, Königsberg, Kreuzburg, Labiau, Lötzen, Lyck, Mehlsack, Memel, Mohrungen, Mühlhausen, Neidenburg, Ortelsburg, Osterode, Pillau, Preußisch Holland, Rastenburg, Rössel, Saalfeld, Schippenbeil, Seeburg, Soldau, Tapia, Tilsit, Wehlau, Zinten (Source of record list: *German Genealogial Digest,* Winter 1994)

NUMBERS OF CRAFTSMEN
EMPLOYED IN THE CITY OF JENA IN 1800

Schuster (cobblers)	55
Fleischhauer (butchers)	46
Bäcker (bakers)	33
Sattler, Gürtler, Riemer, Beutler (workers in leather belts, bags, saddles, and harnesses)	24
Tuchmacher, -färber und -scherer (cloth makers, dyers, and cutters	16
Schmiede — Huf-, Nagel-, und Kuperferschmiede (blacksmiths, nailsmiths, coppersmiths)	16
	16
Stumpfwirker (stocking makers)	15
Leineweber (linen weavers)	11
Tischler (cabinetmakers)	11
Glaser (glassmakers)	8
Seiler (rope makers)	8
Töpfer (potters)	8
Böttcher (coopers)	7
Buchbinder (bookbinders)	7
Müller (millers)	7
Schlosser (locksmiths)	7
Sporer (spur makers)	7
Seifensieder (soapmakers)	7
Hutmacher (hatmaker)	6
Wagner (coach-, wheelmaker)	6
Drechsler (wood turners)	4
Kürschner (furriers)	4
Nadler (needlemakers)	4
Zinngießer (tin founders)	4
Klempner (tinsmiths)	3
Goldarbeiter (gold workers)	3
Knopfmacher (button makers)	3
Mechaniker (fitters, mechanics)	3
Gerber (tanners)	3
Kammmacher (combmakers)	2
Korbmacher (basketmakers)	2
Posamentierer (lace/braid makers)	2
Bürstenmacher (brushmaker)	1
Papiermacher (papermaker)	1
Samtwirker (velvet worker)	1
Polierer (burnisher, polisher)	1
Schriftgießer (type founder)	1

Source: Stadtmuseum, Jena, 1996 exhibit.

COSTS OF LIVING IN JENA (PRUSSIA) IN 1804

	Taler	Groschen	Pfennige
1 *Scheffel Weizen* (wheat)	12	x	x
1 *Scheffel Hafer* (oats)	3	x	x
1 *Pfund Rindfleisch* (beef)	x	2	8-10
1 *Pfund Schweinefleisch* (pork)	x	2	0
1 *Rindszunge* (beef tongue)	x	10-12	x
1 *Bratwurst* (sausage)	x	1	x
1 *Kalbsleber* (calves liver)	x	3-4	x
1 *Pfund Blutwurst* (blood sausage)	x	4	x
1 *Pfund Speck* (bacon)	x	8	x
1 *Pfund Seife* (soap)	x	5	x
1 *Pfund gegossener Lichter* (candle)	x	7	6
½ Pfund Butter	x	2	3-6
1 *Kanne Erbsen* (peas)	x	1	2
1 *Pfund Aal* (eel)	x	12-14	x
1 *Pfund Karpfen* (carp)	x	4	6
1 *Maß Graupen* (barley)	x	2	8
1 *Hase* (hare)	x	10-18	x
1 *Pfund Wildbret* (venison)	x	2	x
1 *Gans* (goose)	x	16	x
1 *Ente* (duck)	x	8	x
1 *Paar Tauben* (2 pigeons)	x	2	6
1 *Huhn* (chicken)	x	4	6
1 *alte Henne* (old hen)	x	6-7	x
1 *Maß Dorf- und Stadtbier* (local beer)		x	x 7
1 *Maß englisches Bier* (English beer)	x	2	10
1 *Mandel Eier* (eggs)	x	3	x
1 *Pfund Leinöl* (flax)	x	9	x

IN JENA, IN 1804 –
A craftsman earned between 8 and 15 Talers per month.
1 Taler = 24 Groschen
1 Groschen = 12 Pfennige
1 Jenaer Scheffel = 160.12 Liter
1 Kanne = 0.89 Liter
1 Elle = 0.56 Meter

Source: Stadtmuseum, Jena. "Lebensmittelpreise 1804," 1996 exhibit.

The Burgkeller at Jena

Further information

See "Guild Records in Germany," adapted from a lecture of Gerhard Jeske, *German Genealogical Digest*, Vol. 10, No. 4, Winter 1994.

CHRONOLOGY OF GUILDS

1106: For the first time, guild regulations are put into writing (Fishermen in Worms)

1156: The guilds are mentioned as organizations in the Augsburg city code.

1356: Augsburg guilds are guaranteed in the laws of Augsburg. Since that time, guilds exist and are fully recognized in all towns. Between 20 and 50 masters belong to a guild. Augsburg develops into the world center of crafts. In 1466 there are 749 masters in the weavers guild alone.

1731: Cities forbid the guilds to hold meetings, to establish dues, and to create their own seals without the consent of the authorities.

18th century: Under pressure of the authorities and as a result of the French Revolution and several wars, the guilds disintegrate even furtheer.

1848: Competition by industry, but also among the craftsmen themselves, puts the craftsmen in danger. As a result of the need for the maintenance of quality and performance, in this year occurs the first German trade congress in Frankfurt. There, 100 craftsmen from all over Germany draft trade regulations for mandatory guilds, as successors to guilds, which are adopted and given semi-official status.

1869: The North German Confederation proclaims free trade. Guild associations and laws are abolished.

1881: The government recognizes the guilds as corporations under public law and puts them in charge of the apprentice system.

1897: The reform movement of the craftsmen, out of which the last of the guilds developed, is acknowledged through the law protecting craftsmen.

Source: "Zunft: von den Anfängen bis zu den Innungen von heute" [Guilds: From Their

Vorderseite   *Rückseite*

A Franconian Gulden, two sides, 1496

Beginnings to the Craftsmen's Associations Today], *Das Große Illustrierte Wörterbuch der deutschen Sprache*. Verlag Das Beste, Stuttgart, Zürich, Wien, 1996.

MONETARY HISTORY

The value of coins in circulation always was based on the weight and purity of gold or silver they contained and therefore differed widely. Karl V was the first emperor to decree (in 1524) that a standard coin, the *Taler*, should be minted for universal use in his *Reich*.

The basis was the weight measure of the *Mark* (=½ lb.) as defined in Cologne at 233,855 grams. Out of 1 Mark of 93.75 percent pure silver, 8 *Taler* could be minted.

However this was only parallel to a considerable variety (both locally and over time) of other coins also called *Taler* – but of different value.

To add to the confusion, the number of *Kreuzer, Groschen*, or *Pfennige* into which a *Taler* was divided, also could vary. The monetary systems reflected territorial variety.

It was not until the foundation of the *Deutsches Reich* in 1871 that a single currency was installed. It consisted of 1 *Mark* = 1/2790 kg of gold and was divided into 100 *Pfennige*.

Equivalencies shown below, commonly used as standards for around 1800, don't really mean much unless they can be attributed to a particular territory.

No such specific territorial area has been established for them.

1 *Taler* = 1½ *Gulden* = 24 *Groschen* = 288 *Pfennige*
1 *Gulden* = 16 *Groschen* = 192 *Pfennige*
1 *Groschen* = 12 *Pfennige*

Source: Rainer Thumshirn, of Munich, Germany

MONEY EQUIVALENCIES AROUND 1800

Thaler
The Thaler was in use from 1486 in Tirol until 1872 in Königreich Sachsen.
1 Thaler = 1½ Gulden = 24 Groschen = 288 Pfennige (but note the caution stated in the item above)

Other Thaler equivalencies
1 Thaler = 24 Gute Groschen = 48 Sechser = 96 Dreier = 288 Pfennige
1 Thaler = 3 Mark = 9 Schillinge = 18 Flinderken = 72 Grote = 360 Schwaren

Note: In 1857 a monetary agreement attempted to unify the value of the Thaler by setting a weight of 18.518 grams and a composition of 90 percent silvered, but its value nevertheless fluctuated. In Austria it was worth 1½ Austria gulden, 1¾ gulden in the southern German states, and 30 silber groschen if it was a Prussian coin. In 1871 when the Empire was formed by Prussia, the new unit of coinage became the mark.

Gulden and Groschen
1 Gulden = 16 Groschen = 192 Pfennige
1 Groschen = 12 Pfennige

Louis d'or
The louis d'or served as a trade coin which became the most important French gold coin of the seventeenth and eighteenth centuries. It was first struck in 1640 under Louis XIII and was valued at 10 livres. During the reign of Louis XV (ruled 1715-1774) the louis d'or was valued at 20, and later 24 livres.

The last of the coins were struck in

1793, followed by issuing of 24-livre pieces, which were the old louis d'or, whose official name had been changed. A few years later, France adopted a decimal system, which did not include the louis d'or.

Sources:

♦Helmut Kohnt and Berndt Knorr, *Alte Maße, Münzen und Gewichte*. Bibliographisches Institut Mannheim, Meyers Lexikonverlag. 1987.

♦Richard G. Doty, *The Macmillan Encyclopedic Dictionary of Numismatics*. Macmillan Publishing Co., Inc., New York, 1982

EXAMPLES OF MEASUREMENTS IN GERMAN-SPEAKING AREAS OF EUROPE AROUND 1800

Important: Before converting old measurements, make sure of the state and year in which they were used.

Key

m = meters; ltr = liters; g = grams; q, QU = square

Acker

Schwarzburg-Sondershausen: 1 Acker = 1877.3m²

Sachsen-Altenburg: 1 Acker = 6443.1 m²

Meisenheim: 1 Acker = 2500 m²

Ar (a)
(plural Are)

Land measure

1 Ar = 100 square meters (119.5993 square yards, or .024711 acres) [Guth]

Becher

Baden: 1 Becher = 0.15 ltr.

Lippe: 1 Becher = 2.768 ltr.

Österreich: 1 Becher = 0.48 ltr.

Dutzend

1 Dutzend = 1/12 Gros = 1/144 Maß = 12 Stück

Elle

Schleswig-Holstein: 1 Elle = 2 Fuß = 0.573 m

Weimar: 1 Elle = 0.564 m

Hamburg:

Kurze [short] Elle = 0.573 m

Lange [long] Elle = 0.691 m

Braunschweig: 1 Elle = 2 Fuß = 0.571 m

Gera: 1 Elle = 0.579 m

Nürnberg: 1 Elle = 0.656 m

Fuder

A cart-load of hay, produce or wood; measure for wine equal to contents of cart-sized barrel (210-475 U.S. gallons or 800 - 1,800 liters, depending on locality.

Fuß

Bayern: 1 Fuß = 0.292 m

Bremen: 1 Fuß (old) = 0.605 m; (new) = 0.289 m

Pommern: 1 Fuß = 0.292 m

Württemberg: 1 Fuß = 0.287 m

Gros

1 Gros = 12 Dutzend = 144 Stück

Hectar (ha)

1 ha = 4 Morgen = 2.47 acre = 0.067 Hufe

100 ha = 1 square kilometer = 0.39 square miles

1 ha = 100 Are (10,000 square meters), or about 2.5 acres

Hektoliter (hl)

100 liters, or 26.418 gallons for liquids, or 2.838 bushels as a dry measure [Guth]

Hufe

1 Hufe = 60 Morgen = 36.9 acres = 15 ha

Joch

Archaic measure, originally the area of land a team could plow in a day.

1 Joch = about 60 Are, or about 1.5 acres

Kanne

Dresden: 1 Kanne = 0.937 ltr.

Oldenburg: 1 Kanne = 1.368 ltr.

Lot

Frankfurt/Main, Nassau, Hollenzollern: 1 Lot = 4 Quentchen = 15.625g

Kurhessen, Lippe: 1 Lot = 10 Quentchen = 16.667g

Malter

(singular and plural)

Antique German dry measure for grain; about 150 liters or 4.257 bushels; but sizes varied

Mandel

1 große (large) Mandel (or "Bauern") = 16 Stück (pieces)

1 kleine (small) Mandel = ¼ Schock = 15 Stück (pieces)

Maß

Generally: 1 Maß = 1 ltr.
Baden: 1 Maß = 10 Becher = 1.5 ltr.
Gotha: 1 Maß = 0.910 ltr.
Rheiinland: 1 Maß = 4 Achtel = 1.783 Ltr.
Württemberg: 1 Maß = 1.831 ltr

Meile

Generally: 1 Meile = 7420.4385 m
Baden: 1 Meile = 2 Wegstunden =
8888.89 m
Sachsen: 1 Meile = 16,000 Ellen =
9062.08 m
Hannover: 1 Meile = 1587.5 Ruten =
25400 Fuß = 7419.205 m

Morgen

(The Morgen was theoretically the amount
of land that one man and an ox could plow
in a morning. *Morgen* in German means
also "morning.")
Aachen: 1 Morgen = 150 Qu-Ruten =
3053.26 m
Danzig: 1 Morgen = 300 Qu-Ruten =
5555.46 qm
Koblenz: 1 Morgen = 160 Qu-Ruten =
3459.44 qm
Leipzig: 1 Morgen = 3273.2 qm
Preußen: 1 Morgen = 180 Qu-Ruten =
2553.224 qm
Sachsen: 1 Morgen = ½ Acker = 150
Quadratruten = 2767.100m^2)
Bayern: 1 Morgen = 4 Viertel = 400
Quadratruten = 3437 m^2; or 34.073 Are
(about .85 acre)
Württemberg: 1 Morgen = 31.5 Are, or
about .79 acre

Pfund (#)

Frankfurt/Main: 1 Pfund = 32 Lot = 500g
(about 1.10 U.S. pounds)
Hamburg: 1 Old Pfund = 551.23 g; middle
19th century = 484.848g

Österreich:

Wiener Pf. = 560g
Tiroler Pf = 564.26g
Apotheker Pf. = 420g
Schokoladen Pf = 490g

Zollpfund = 500g
Preußen: 1 Pfund = 32 Lot = 467.404g

Quentchen

Generally: 1 Quentchen (new) =
4 Gewichtspfennig = 4.385g
Hannover: 1 Quentchen = 3.654g
Preußen: 1 Quentchen = 4 Pfenniggewicht
= 3.651g

Rute

Aachen: 1 Rute = 16 Fuß = 4.602 m
Bayern: 1 Alte (old) Rute = 15 Fuß = 4.378
m
Hamburg: 1 Rute = 16 Fuß = 4.585 m
Köln: 1 Rute = 16 Fuß = 4.602 m
Ulm: 1 Rute = 18 Fuß = 5.202 m

Schock

1 Schock = 4 Mandel = 5 Dutzend = 60
Stück (pieces)

Sheffel (Scheffel)

Bremen: 1 Sheffel = 79.201 ltr.
Dresden: 1 Sheffel = 106.298 ltr.
Hessen: 1 Sheffel = 8 Metzen = 80.368
ltr.
Potsdam before 1814: 1 Sheffel - 53.2 ltr.

Simmer/Simri

(plural *Simmeren)*
Dry measure
Palatinate: 1 Simmer = .25 Malter
Württemburg: 1 Simmer = .629 bushel

Zentner

1 Zentner = 100 German pounds, or about
110.23 U.S. pounds

Sources:

•Fritz Verdenhalven, *Alte Maße, Münzen und
Gewichte aus dem deutschen Sprach-
gebiet,*Verlag Degener & Co. Neustadt an der
Aisch. 1968.
•Helmut Kohnt and Berndt Knorr, *Alte Maße,
Münzen und Gewichte,*Bibliographisches Institut
Mannheim, Meyers Lexikon-Verlag. 1987.
•Helmut Guth, *Amish Mennonites in Germany:
Their Congregations, The Estates Where They
Lived, Their Families.* Masthof Press, Morgan-
town, PA, 1995.

Chapter 27

Keeping track of time

CALENDARS: JULIAN, GREGORIAN, FRENCH REPUBLICAN

Old Style Julian calendar

Up to 1582, the Julian calendar (commonly referred to as the "Old Style," or "OS") was established by Julius Caesar in 46 BC, with 12 months, 365 days in the year for three years and a leap year of 366 days. It was based on one year equaling 365.25 days instead of the actual length of the year which is only 365.2422 days. By 1582, the calendar had lost 10 days — the vernal equinox had moved from 21 March to 10 March. The Julian calendar compensated for the loss by observing the leap year. New Years Day was observed on 25 March in medieval times in Christian nations under the Old Style Julian calendar.

New Style Gregorian calendar

In 1582, Pope Gregory XIII made a correction. He revised the calendar (commonly referred to as the "New Style," or "NS"), announcing that the day after 5 October 1582 would be 15 October 1582 and that century years not divisible evenly by 400 would no longer be counted as leap years. Instead of 25 March, New Years Day would change to 1 January. The New Style (NS) Gregorian calendar was adopted by Catholic areas in Germany in 1583-1585, but it was not accepted in Protestant areas until much later.

In Great Britain and America, the Gregorian calendar began on 1 January 1753. The beginning dates of the Gregorian Calendar are listed on the next page.

French Republican Calendar

The French Republican Calendar was established during the French Revolution, and remained in effect only from 24 October 1793 to 31 December 1805. This calendar affected civil registration records in France and areas ruled by the French including modern Belgium, Luxembourg, and parts of Netherlands, Germany, Switzerland, and Italy.

The calendar was divided into 12 months, with 30 days each. The 5 or 6 extra days were added at the end of the year. The months were named *Vendémiaire, Brumaire, Frimaire, Nivôse, Pluviôse, Ventôse, Germinal, Floréal, Prairial, Messidor, Thermidor* (sometimes *Fervidor* was used instead), and *Fructidor*. (These months do not correspond to the standard months of January through December.)

To calculate the standard date for a French Republican calendar date, see the *Research Outline: French Republican Calendar*, Family History Library, Salt Lake City, Utah. 1990.

See also John Dahl, *Conversion Tables, French Republican Calendar: An Aid for Family Research in France and Germany*, 2nd Edition. Deseret Books, Salt Lake City, 1972. FHL 944 A9d.

GREGORIAN CALENDAR: BEGINNING DATES

The Gregorian calendar was put in effect on the following dates in various areas of Europe and Asia:

Aachen .... 11 Jan. 1583
Appenzell .... Nov. 1724
Augsburg (diocese) .... 24 Feb. 1783
Augsburg (city) .... 16 Oct. 1583
Baden (margraviate) .... 27 Nov. 1583
Basel (diocese) .... 31 Oct. 1783
Basel (city) .... 12 Jan. 1701
Bayern/Bavaria (duchy) .... 16 Oct. 1582
Böhmen/Bohemia .... 17 Jan. 1584
Brabant .... 1 Jan. 1583
Breisgau .... 24 Oct. 1583
Brixen (South Tyrol) .... 16 Oct. 1583
Bulgarien/Bulgaria .... 1 Jan 1916
Cleve (duchy) .... 28 Nov. 1583
Dänemark/Denmark .... 1 Mar. 1700
Danzig 1582
Deutschland/Germany 1583-85
  (Catholic)
Deutschland/Germany ... 1 Mar. 1700-76
  (Protestant)

Dorpat .... 1617, after 1625 until
                                           World War I
Eichstätt .... 16 Oct. 1583
Elsaß/Alsace   1648 in the areas ceded
      through the Treaty of Westphalia;
      österreichisches Oberelsaß/Austrian
      Upper Alsace: 24 Dec. 1583
England .... 14 Sep. 1752
Estland/Estonia .... after World War I
Finnland/Finland 1753
Flandern/Flanders .... 1 Jan. 1583
Frankreich/France .... 20 Dec. 1582
                            (later in some parts)
Freiburg .... 22 Jan. 1584
Freising (diocese) .... 16 Oct. 1583
Friesland .... 12 Jan. 1701
Galizien/Galicia .... in World War I
(Greek-Orthodox dioceses)
Graubünden 1812
Griechenland/Greece .... 1 Mar. 1923
Hennegau .... 1 Jan. 1583
Hildesheim (diocese) .... 26 Mar. 1631
Holland .... 1 Jan. 1583
Italien/Italy .... 15 Oct. 1582
                            (predominantly)
Jülich-Berg (duchy) .... 13 Nov. 1583
Jugoslawien/ .... after World War I
Yugoslavia   except for the Serbian-
                              Orthodox Church
Köln/Cologne .... 14 Nov. 1583
(Archdiocese and city)
Kurland .... Partially from 1607
                until 28 Jan. 1796, then
                until World War I back
                to the Julian calendar
Lausitz .... 23 Jan. 1584
Lettland .... 18 Nov. 1918
Litauen/Lithuania .... Partially until
                13 Jan. 1800, then
                returning to the Julian
                Calendar until World War I
Lothringen/Lorraine .... 20 Dec. 1582
Lüttich .... 21 Feb. 1583
Luzern/Luzerne .... 22 Jan. 1584
Mainz (archdiocese) .... 22 Nov. 1583
Minden 1630
Mühlhausen .... 31 Oct. 1583
Münster (diocese) .... 28 Nov. 1583
Neuburg/Pfalz .... 24 Dec. 1615

Niederlande/Netherlands:
- ◆Staatskanzlei/chancery ... 25 Dec. 1583
- ◆Antwerpen, Artois, ... 25 Dec. 1582

Brabant, Flandern,   or 1 Jan. 1583
Hennegau, Mecheln,
Limburg, Luxemburg,
Namur
- ◆Bistum/Diocese Lüttich .. 21 Feb. 1583
- ◆Holland and .... 25 Dec. 1582 or
Zeeland   1 Jan. 1583
- ◆Groningen .... 11 Mar. 1583
           (until summer 1594,
           ultimately 12 Dec.
        1700/12 January 1701)
- ◆Friesland .... 12 Jan. 1801
- ◆Gelderland ..... 12 July or 12 Dec. 1700
- ◆Overijssel .... 12 Dec. 1700
- ◆Utrecht .... 1 Mar. 1700

Norwegen/Norway .... 1 Mar. 1700
Oberelsaß/UpperAlsace .... 24 Oct. 1583
(Austrian)
Osnabrück 1624
Österreich/Austria .... 29 Dec. 1583
(above the Enns)
Österreich .... 16 Oct. 1583
 (below the Enns)
Paderborn (diocese) .... 27 Jun 1585
Passau .... Feb. 1583
Polen/Poland 1583
           (in Poland both
        calendars were used)
Portugal .... 15 Oct. 1582
Preußen/Prussia (duchy) ..... 2 Sep. 1612
Regensburg .... 16 Oct. 1583
Rumänien/Romania .... after 1917
Rußland/Russia .... after 1917
Salzburg .... 16 Oct. 1583
Schaffhausen .... 12 Jan. 1701
Schlesien/Silesia ... 17 Jan.-23 Jan. 1584
Schweden/Sweden .... 1 Mar. 1753
     (with an interruption around
        1600; in 1700 the extra day
        in the calendar was omitted)
Schwyz/Switzerland .... 22 Jan. 1584
Siebenbürgen .... 25 Dec. 1590
Solothurn .... 22 Jan. 1584
Spanien/Spain .... 15 Oct. 1582
(and all Philipp II's lands)
St. Gallen 1724

Steiermark/Styria .... 25 Nov. 1503
Straßburg (diocese) .... 27 Nov. 1583
Straßburg (city) ..... 16 Feb.-1 Mar. 1682
Tirol/Tyrol .... 16 Oct. 1583
Trient .... 21 Feb. 1583
Trier .... 15 Oct. 1583
Türkei/Turkey 1926
Ungarn/Hungary .... 2 Feb. 1584;
        first by law 1 Nov. 1587
Unterwalden .... Jun. 1584
Uri .... 22 Jan. 1584
Westfalen/Westphalia .... 12 Jul. 1584
(duchy)
Würzburg (diocese) .... 15 Nov. 1583
Zug .... 22 Jan. 1584
Zürich .... 12 Jan. 1701

Source: Wolfgang Ribbe, Eckart Henning, *Taschenbuch für Familiengeschichtsforschung.* Verlag Degener & Co., Neustadt an der Aisch, 1995.

PERPETUAL CALENDAR

Use the perpetual calendar to determine the day of the week of a particular event since the Gregorian calendar was introduced in 1582, when Pope Gregory XIII corrected the errors in the Julian Calendar, starting on the day following October 4, which became 15 October. The calendar as revised is known as the New Style (NS) Gregorian calendar.

Note

The "Gregorian Date Calculator," of Personal Ancestral File (PAF) will also calculate day of the week as well as birth date from death date and age as found on headstone inscriptions .

See the calendar on the next two pages for dates between 1776 and 2000. The key for the years 1583 to 1775 appears on page 516.

1776-2000 CALENDARS

Year/Cal	Year/Cal	Year/Cal	Year/Cal	Year/Cal	Year/Cal
1776 … 9	1814 … 7	1852 … 12	1890 … 4	1928 … 8	1966 … 7
1777 … 4	1815 … 1	1853 … 7	1891 … 5	1929 … 3	1967 … 1
1778 … 5	1816 … 9	1854 … 1	1892 … 13	1930 … 4	1968 … 9
1779 … 6	1817 … 4	1855 … 2	1893 … 1	1931 … 5	1969 … 4
1780 … 14	1818 … 5	1856 … 10	1894 … 2	1932 … 13	1970 … 5
1781 … 2	1819 … 6	1857 … 5	1895 … 3	1933 … 1	1971 … 6
1782 … 3	1820 … 14	1858 … 6	1896 … 11	1934 … 2	1972 … 14
1783 … 4	1821 … 2	1859 … 7	1897 … 6	1935 … 3	1973 … 2
1784 … 12	1822 … 3	1860 … 8	1898 … 7	1936 … 11	1974 … 3
1785 … 7	1823 … 4	1861 … 3	1899 … 1	1937 … 6	1975 … 4
1786 … 1	1824 … 12	1862 … 4	1900 … 2	1938 … 7	1976 … 12
1787 … 2	1825 … 7	1863 … 5	1901 … 3	1939 … 1	1977 … 7
1788 … 10	1826 … 1	1864 … 13	1902 … 4	1940 … 9	1978 … 1
1789 … 5	1827 … 2	1865 … 1	1903 … 5	1941 … 4	1979 … 2
1790 … 6	1828 … 10	1866 … 2	1904 … 13	1942 … 5	1980 … 10
1791 … 7	1829 … 5	1867 … 3	1905 … 1	1943 … 6	1981 … 5
1792 … 8	1830 … 6	1868 … 11	1906 … 2	1944 … 14	1982 … 6
1793 … 3	1831 … 7	1869 … 6	1907 … 3	1945 … 2	1983 … 7
1794 … 4	1832 … 8	1870 … 7	1908 … 11	1946 … 3	1984 … 8
1795 … 5	1833 … 3	1871 … 1	1909 … 6	1947 … 4	1985 … 3
1796 … 13	1834 … 4	1872 … 9	1910 … 7	1948 … 12	1986 … 4
1797 … 1	1835 … 5	1873 … 4	1911 … 1	1949 … 7	1987 … 5
1798 … 2	1836 … 13	1874 … 5	1912 … 9	1950 … 1	1988 … 13
1799 … 3	1837 … 1	1875 … 6	1913 … 4	1951 … 2	1989 … 1
1800 … 4	1838 … 2	1876 … 14	1914 … 5	1952 … 10	1990 … 2
1801 … 5	1839 … 3	1877 … 2	1915 … 6	1953 … 5	1991 … 3
1802 … 6	1840 … 11	1878 … 3	1916 … 14	1954 … 6	1992 … 11
1803 … 7	1841 … 6	1879 … 4	1917 … 2	1955 … 7	1993 … 6
1804 … 8	1842 … 7	1880 … 12	1918 … 3	1956 … 8	1994 … 7
1805 … 3	1843 … 1	1881 … 7	1919 … 4	1957 … 3	1995 … 1
1806 … 4	1844 … 9	1882 … 1	1920 … 12	1958 … 4	1996 … 9
1807 … 5	1845 … 4	1883 … 2	1921 … 7	1959 … 5	1997 … 4
1808 … 13	1846 … 5	1884 … 10	1922 … 1	1960 … 13	1998 … 5
1809 … 1	1847 … 6	1885 … 5	1923 … 2	1961 … 1	1999 … 6
1810 … 2	1848 … 14	1886 … 6	1924 … 10	1962 … 2	2000 … 14
1811 … 3	1849 … 2	1887 … 7	1925 … 5	1963 … 3	
1812 … 11	1850 … 3	1888 … 8	1926 … 6	1964 … 11	
1813 … 6	1851 … 4	1889 … 3	1927 … 7	1965 … 6	

Directions: The number opposite each year indicates the number of the calendar for that year, as provided on these pages.

Calendar 1

```
JANUARY               FEBRUARY              MARCH                 APRIL
 S  M  T  W  T  F  S    S  M  T  W  T  F  S    S  M  T  W  T  F  S    S  M  T  W  T  F  S
 1  2  3  4  5  6  7                1  2  3  4             1  2  3  4                      1
 8  9 10 11 12 13 14    5  6  7  8  9 10 11    5  6  7  8  9 10 11    2  3  4  5  6  7  8
15 16 17 18 19 20 21   12 13 14 15 16 17 18   12 13 14 15 16 17 18    9 10 11 12 13 14 15
22 23 24 25 26 27 28   19 20 21 22 23 24 25   19 20 21 22 23 24 25   16 17 18 19 20 21 22
29 30 31               26 27 28               26 27 28 29 30 31      23 24 25 26 27 28 29
                                                                     30

MAY                   JUNE                  JULY                  AUGUST
 S  M  T  W  T  F  S    S  M  T  W  T  F  S    S  M  T  W  T  F  S    S  M  T  W  T  F  S
    1  2  3  4  5  6             1  2  3                         1          1  2  3  4  5
 7  8  9 10 11 12 13    4  5  6  7  8  9 10    2  3  4  5  6  7  8    6  7  8  9 10 11 12
14 15 16 17 18 19 20   11 12 13 14 15 16 17    9 10 11 12 13 14 15   13 14 15 16 17 18 19
21 22 23 24 25 26 27   18 19 20 21 22 23 24   16 17 18 19 20 21 22   20 21 22 23 24 25 26
28 29 30 31            25 26 27 28 29 30      23 24 25 26 27 28 29   27 28 29 30 31
                                              30 31

SEPTEMBER             OCTOBER               NOVEMBER              DECEMBER
 S  M  T  W  T  F  S    S  M  T  W  T  F  S    S  M  T  W  T  F  S    S  M  T  W  T  F  S
                1  2    1  2  3  4  5  6  7                1  2  3                   1  2
 3  4  5  6  7  8  9    8  9 10 11 12 13 14    5  6  7  8  9 10 11    3  4  5  6  7  8  9
10 11 12 13 14 15 16   15 16 17 18 19 20 21   12 13 14 15 16 17 18   10 11 12 13 14 15 16
17 18 19 20 21 22 23   22 23 24 25 26 27 28   19 20 21 22 23 24 25   17 18 19 20 21 22 23
24 25 26 27 28 29 30   29 30 31               26 27 28 29 30         24 25 26 27 28 29 30
                                                                     31
```

Calendar 2

```
JANUARY               FEBRUARY              MARCH                 APRIL
 S  M  T  W  T  F  S    S  M  T  W  T  F  S    S  M  T  W  T  F  S    S  M  T  W  T  F  S
    1  2  3  4  5  6                1  2  3                1  2  3    1  2  3  4  5  6  7
 7  8  9 10 11 12 13    4  5  6  7  8  9 10    4  5  6  7  8  9 10    8  9 10 11 12 13 14
14 15 16 17 18 19 20   11 12 13 14 15 16 17   11 12 13 14 15 16 17   15 16 17 18 19 20 21
21 22 23 24 25 26 27   18 19 20 21 22 23 24   18 19 20 21 22 23 24   22 23 24 25 26 27 28
28 29 30 31            25 26 27 28            25 26 27 28 29 30 31   29 30

MAY                   JUNE                  JULY                  AUGUST
 S  M  T  W  T  F  S    S  M  T  W  T  F  S    S  M  T  W  T  F  S    S  M  T  W  T  F  S
       1  2  3  4  5                   1  2    1  2  3  4  5  6  7                1  2  3
 6  7  8  9 10 11 12    3  4  5  6  7  8  9    8  9 10 11 12 13 14    4  5  6  7  8  9 10
13 14 15 16 17 18 19   10 11 12 13 14 15 16   15 16 17 18 19 20 21   11 12 13 14 15 16 17
20 21 22 23 24 25 26   17 18 19 20 21 22 23   22 23 24 25 26 27 28   18 19 20 21 22 23 24
27 28 29 30 31         24 25 26 27 28 29 30   29 30 31               25 26 27 28 29 30 31

SEPTEMBER             OCTOBER               NOVEMBER              DECEMBER
 S  M  T  W  T  F  S    S  M  T  W  T  F  S    S  M  T  W  T  F  S    S  M  T  W  T  F  S
                   1       1  2  3  4  5  6                1  2  3                      1
 2  3  4  5  6  7  8    7  8  9 10 11 12 13    4  5  6  7  8  9 10    2  3  4  5  6  7  8
 9 10 11 12 13 14 15   14 15 16 17 18 19 20   11 12 13 14 15 16 17    9 10 11 12 13 14 15
16 17 18 19 20 21 22   21 22 23 24 25 26 27   18 19 20 21 22 23 24   16 17 18 19 20 21 22
23 24 25 26 27 28 29   28 29 30 31            25 26 27 28 29 30      23 24 25 26 27 28 29
30                                                                   30 31
```

Calendar 3

```
JANUARY               FEBRUARY              MARCH                 APRIL
 S  M  T  W  T  F  S    S  M  T  W  T  F  S    S  M  T  W  T  F  S    S  M  T  W  T  F  S
       1  2  3  4  5                   1  2                   1  2             1  2  3  4
 6  7  8  9 10 11 12    3  4  5  6  7  8  9    3  4  5  6  7  8  9    5  6  7  8  9 10 11
13 14 15 16 17 18 19   10 11 12 13 14 15 16   10 11 12 13 14 15 16   12 13 14 15 16 17 18
20 21 22 23 24 25 26   17 18 19 20 21 22 23   17 18 19 20 21 22 23   19 20 21 22 23 24 25
27 28 29 30 31         24 25 26 27 28         24 25 26 27 28 29 30   26 27 28 29 30
                                              31

MAY                   JUNE                  JULY                  AUGUST
 S  M  T  W  T  F  S    S  M  T  W  T  F  S    S  M  T  W  T  F  S    S  M  T  W  T  F  S
          1  2  3  4                      1       1  2  3  4  5  6                1  2
 5  6  7  8  9 10 11    2  3  4  5  6  7  8    7  8  9 10 11 12 13    3  4  5  6  7  8  9
12 13 14 15 16 17 18    9 10 11 12 13 14 15   14 15 16 17 18 19 20   10 11 12 13 14 15 16
19 20 21 22 23 24 25   16 17 18 19 20 21 22   21 22 23 24 25 26 27   17 18 19 20 21 22 23
26 27 28 29 30 31      23 24 25 26 27 28 29   28 29 30 31            24 25 26 27 28 29 30
                       30                                            31

SEPTEMBER             OCTOBER               NOVEMBER              DECEMBER
 S  M  T  W  T  F  S    S  M  T  W  T  F  S    S  M  T  W  T  F  S    S  M  T  W  T  F  S
 1  2  3  4  5  6  7       1  2  3  4  5  6                   1  2    1  2  3  4  5  6  7
 8  9 10 11 12 13 14    7  8  9 10 11 12 13    3  4  5  6  7  8  9    8  9 10 11 12 13 14
15 16 17 18 19 20 21   14 15 16 17 18 19 20   10 11 12 13 14 15 16   15 16 17 18 19 20 21
22 23 24 25 26 27 28   21 22 23 24 25 26 27   17 18 19 20 21 22 23   22 23 24 25 26 27 28
29 30                  28 29 30 31            24 25 26 27 28 29 30   29 30 31
```

Calendar 4

```
JANUARY               FEBRUARY              MARCH                 APRIL
 S  M  T  W  T  F  S    S  M  T  W  T  F  S    S  M  T  W  T  F  S    S  M  T  W  T  F  S
          1  2  3  4                      1                      1          1  2  3  4  5
 5  6  7  8  9 10 11    2  3  4  5  6  7  8    2  3  4  5  6  7  8    6  7  8  9 10 11 12
12 13 14 15 16 17 18    9 10 11 12 13 14 15    9 10 11 12 13 14 15   13 14 15 16 17 18 19
19 20 21 22 23 24 25   16 17 18 19 20 21 22   16 17 18 19 20 21 22   20 21 22 23 24 25 26
26 27 28 29 30 31      23 24 25 26 27 28      23 24 25 26 27 28 29   27 28 29 30
                                              30 31

MAY                   JUNE                  JULY                  AUGUST
 S  M  T  W  T  F  S    S  M  T  W  T  F  S    S  M  T  W  T  F  S    S  M  T  W  T  F  S
             1  2  3    1  2  3  4  5  6  7          1  2  3  4  5                   1  2
 4  5  6  7  8  9 10    8  9 10 11 12 13 14    6  7  8  9 10 11 12    3  4  5  6  7  8  9
11 12 13 14 15 16 17   15 16 17 18 19 20 21   13 14 15 16 17 18 19   10 11 12 13 14 15 16
18 19 20 21 22 23 24   22 23 24 25 26 27 28   20 21 22 23 24 25 26   17 18 19 20 21 22 23
25 26 27 28 29 30 31   29 30                  27 28 29 30 31         24 25 26 27 28 29 30
                                                                     31

SEPTEMBER             OCTOBER               NOVEMBER              DECEMBER
 S  M  T  W  T  F  S    S  M  T  W  T  F  S    S  M  T  W  T  F  S    S  M  T  W  T  F  S
    1  2  3  4  5  6             1  2  3  4                      1       1  2  3  4  5  6
 7  8  9 10 11 12 13    5  6  7  8  9 10 11    2  3  4  5  6  7  8    7  8  9 10 11 12 13
14 15 16 17 18 19 20   12 13 14 15 16 17 18    9 10 11 12 13 14 15   14 15 16 17 18 19 20
21 22 23 24 25 26 27   19 20 21 22 23 24 25   16 17 18 19 20 21 22   21 22 23 24 25 26 27
28 29 30               26 27 28 29 30 31      23 24 25 26 27 28 29   28 29 30 31
                                              30
```

Calendar 5

```
JANUARY               FEBRUARY              MARCH                 APRIL
 S  M  T  W  T  F  S    S  M  T  W  T  F  S    S  M  T  W  T  F  S    S  M  T  W  T  F  S
             1  2  3    1  2  3  4  5  6  7    1  2  3  4  5  6  7                1  2  3  4
 4  5  6  7  8  9 10    8  9 10 11 12 13 14    8  9 10 11 12 13 14    5  6  7  8  9 10 11
11 12 13 14 15 16 17   15 16 17 18 19 20 21   15 16 17 18 19 20 21   12 13 14 15 16 17 18
18 19 20 21 22 23 24   22 23 24 25 26 27 28   22 23 24 25 26 27 28   19 20 21 22 23 24 25
25 26 27 28 29 30 31                          29 30 31               26 27 28 29 30

MAY                   JUNE                  JULY                  AUGUST
 S  M  T  W  T  F  S    S  M  T  W  T  F  S    S  M  T  W  T  F  S    S  M  T  W  T  F  S
                1  2       1  2  3  4  5  6             1  2  3  4                      1
 3  4  5  6  7  8  9    7  8  9 10 11 12 13    5  6  7  8  9 10 11    2  3  4  5  6  7  8
10 11 12 13 14 15 16   14 15 16 17 18 19 20   12 13 14 15 16 17 18    9 10 11 12 13 14 15
17 18 19 20 21 22 23   21 22 23 24 25 26 27   19 20 21 22 23 24 25   16 17 18 19 20 21 22
24 25 26 27 28 29 30   28 29 30               26 27 28 29 30 31      23 24 25 26 27 28 29
31                                                                   30 31

SEPTEMBER             OCTOBER               NOVEMBER              DECEMBER
 S  M  T  W  T  F  S    S  M  T  W  T  F  S    S  M  T  W  T  F  S    S  M  T  W  T  F  S
       1  2  3  4  5                1  2  3    1  2  3  4  5  6  7             1  2  3  4  5
 6  7  8  9 10 11 12    4  5  6  7  8  9 10    8  9 10 11 12 13 14    6  7  8  9 10 11 12
13 14 15 16 17 18 19   11 12 13 14 15 16 17   15 16 17 18 19 20 21   13 14 15 16 17 18 19
20 21 22 23 24 25 26   18 19 20 21 22 23 24   22 23 24 25 26 27 28   20 21 22 23 24 25 26
27 28 29 30            25 26 27 28 29 30 31   29 30                  27 28 29 30 31
```

Calendar 6

```
JANUARY               FEBRUARY              MARCH                 APRIL
 S  M  T  W  T  F  S    S  M  T  W  T  F  S    S  M  T  W  T  F  S    S  M  T  W  T  F  S
                1  2       1  2  3  4  5  6             1  2  3  4                1  2  3
 3  4  5  6  7  8  9    7  8  9 10 11 12 13    7  8  9 10 11 12 13    4  5  6  7  8  9 10
10 11 12 13 14 15 16   14 15 16 17 18 19 20   14 15 16 17 18 19 20   11 12 13 14 15 16 17
17 18 19 20 21 22 23   21 22 23 24 25 26 27   21 22 23 24 25 26 27   18 19 20 21 22 23 24
24 25 26 27 28 29 30   28                     28 29 30 31            25 26 27 28 29 30
31

MAY                   JUNE                  JULY                  AUGUST
 S  M  T  W  T  F  S    S  M  T  W  T  F  S    S  M  T  W  T  F  S    S  M  T  W  T  F  S
                   1       1  2  3  4  5                1  2  3    1  2  3  4  5  6  7
 2  3  4  5  6  7  8    6  7  8  9 10 11 12    4  5  6  7  8  9 10    8  9 10 11 12 13 14
 9 10 11 12 13 14 15   13 14 15 16 17 18 19   11 12 13 14 15 16 17   15 16 17 18 19 20 21
16 17 18 19 20 21 22   20 21 22 23 24 25 26   18 19 20 21 22 23 24   22 23 24 25 26 27 28
23 24 25 26 27 28 29   27 28 29 30            25 26 27 28 29 30 31   29 30 31
30 31

SEPTEMBER             OCTOBER               NOVEMBER              DECEMBER
 S  M  T  W  T  F  S    S  M  T  W  T  F  S    S  M  T  W  T  F  S    S  M  T  W  T  F  S
          1  2  3  4                1  2       1  2  3  4  5  6                1  2  3  4
 5  6  7  8  9 10 11    3  4  5  6  7  8  9    7  8  9 10 11 12 13    5  6  7  8  9 10 11
12 13 14 15 16 17 18   10 11 12 13 14 15 16   14 15 16 17 18 19 20   12 13 14 15 16 17 18
19 20 21 22 23 24 25   17 18 19 20 21 22 23   21 22 23 24 25 26 27   19 20 21 22 23 24 25
26 27 28 29 30         24 25 26 27 28 29 30   28 29 30               26 27 28 29 30 31
                       31
```

7

JANUARY

S	M	T	W	T	F	S
						1
2	3	4	5	6	7	8
9	10	11	12	13	14	15
16	17	18	19	20	21	22
23	24	25	26	27	28	29
30	31					

FEBRUARY

S	M	T	W	T	F	S
		1	2	3	4	5
6	7	8	9	10	11	12
13	14	15	16	17	18	19
20	21	22	23	24	25	26
27	28					

MARCH

S	M	T	W	T	F	S
		1	2	3	4	5
6	7	8	9	10	11	12
13	14	15	16	17	18	19
20	21	22	23	24	25	26
27	28	29	30	31		

APRIL

S	M	T	W	T	F	S
					1	2
3	4	5	6	7	8	9
10	11	12	13	14	15	16
17	18	19	20	21	22	23
24	25	26	27	28	29	30

MAY

S	M	T	W	T	F	S
1	2	3	4	5	6	7
8	9	10	11	12	13	14
15	16	17	18	19	20	21
22	23	24	25	26	27	28
29	30	31				

JUNE

S	M	T	W	T	F	S
			1	2	3	4
5	6	7	8	9	10	11
12	13	14	15	16	17	18
19	20	21	22	23	24	25
26	27	28	29	30		

JULY

S	M	T	W	T	F	S
					1	2
3	4	5	6	7	8	9
10	11	12	13	14	15	16
17	18	19	20	21	22	23
24	25	26	27	28	29	30
31						

AUGUST

S	M	T	W	T	F	S
	1	2	3	4	5	6
7	8	9	10	11	12	13
14	15	16	17	18	19	20
21	22	23	24	25	26	27
28	29	30	31			

SEPTEMBER

S	M	T	W	T	F	S
				1	2	3
4	5	6	7	8	9	10
11	12	13	14	15	16	17
18	19	20	21	22	23	24
25	26	27	28	29	30	

OCTOBER

S	M	T	W	T	F	S
						1
2	3	4	5	6	7	8
9	10	11	12	13	14	15
16	17	18	19	20	21	22
23	24	25	26	27	28	29
30	31					

NOVEMBER

S	M	T	W	T	F	S
		1	2	3	4	5
6	7	8	9	10	11	12
13	14	15	16	17	18	19
20	21	22	23	24	25	26
27	28	29	30			

DECEMBER

S	M	T	W	T	F	S
				1	2	3
4	5	6	7	8	9	10
11	12	13	14	15	16	17
18	19	20	21	22	23	24
25	26	27	28	29	30	31

8

JANUARY

S	M	T	W	T	F	S
1	2	3	4	5	6	7
8	9	10	11	12	13	14
15	16	17	18	19	20	21
22	23	24	25	26	27	28
29	30	31				

FEBRUARY

S	M	T	W	T	F	S
			1	2	3	4
5	6	7	8	9	10	11
12	13	14	15	16	17	18
19	20	21	22	23	24	25
26	27	28	29			

MARCH

S	M	T	W	T	F	S
				1	2	3
4	5	6	7	8	9	10
11	12	13	14	15	16	17
18	19	20	21	22	23	24
25	26	27	28	29	30	31

APRIL

S	M	T	W	T	F	S
1	2	3	4	5	6	7
8	9	10	11	12	13	14
15	16	17	18	19	20	21
22	23	24	25	26	27	28
29	30					

MAY

S	M	T	W	T	F	S
		1	2	3	4	5
6	7	8	9	10	11	12
13	14	15	16	17	18	19
20	21	22	23	24	25	26
27	28	29	30	31		

JUNE

S	M	T	W	T	F	S
					1	2
3	4	5	6	7	8	9
10	11	12	13	14	15	16
17	18	19	20	21	22	23
24	25	26	27	28	29	30

JULY

S	M	T	W	T	F	S
1	2	3	4	5	6	7
8	9	10	11	12	13	14
15	16	17	18	19	20	21
22	23	24	25	26	27	28
29	30	31				

AUGUST

S	M	T	W	T	F	S
			1	2	3	4
5	6	7	8	9	10	11
12	13	14	15	16	17	18
19	20	21	22	23	24	25
26	27	28	29	30	31	

SEPTEMBER

S	M	T	W	T	F	S
						1
2	3	4	5	6	7	8
9	10	11	12	13	14	15
16	17	18	19	20	21	22
23	24	25	26	27	28	29
30						

OCTOBER

S	M	T	W	T	F	S
	1	2	3	4	5	6
7	8	9	10	11	12	13
14	15	16	17	18	19	20
21	22	23	24	25	26	27
28	29	30	31			

NOVEMBER

S	M	T	W	T	F	S
				1	2	3
4	5	6	7	8	9	10
11	12	13	14	15	16	17
18	19	20	21	22	23	24
25	26	27	28	29	30	

DECEMBER

S	M	T	W	T	F	S
						1
2	3	4	5	6	7	8
9	10	11	12	13	14	15
16	17	18	19	20	21	22
23	24	25	26	27	28	29
30	31					

9

JANUARY

S	M	T	W	T	F	S
	1	2	3	4	5	6
7	8	9	10	11	12	13
14	15	16	17	18	19	20
21	22	23	24	25	26	27
28	29	30	31			

FEBRUARY

S	M	T	W	T	F	S
				1	2	3
4	5	6	7	8	9	10
11	12	13	14	15	16	17
18	19	20	21	22	23	24
25	26	27	28	29		

MARCH

S	M	T	W	T	F	S
					1	2
3	4	5	6	7	8	9
10	11	12	13	14	15	16
17	18	19	20	21	22	23
24	25	26	27	28	29	30
31						

APRIL

S	M	T	W	T	F	S
	1	2	3	4	5	6
7	8	9	10	11	12	13
14	15	16	17	18	19	20
21	22	23	24	25	26	27
28	29	30				

MAY

S	M	T	W	T	F	S
			1	2	3	4
5	6	7	8	9	10	11
12	13	14	15	16	17	18
19	20	21	22	23	24	25
26	27	28	29	30	31	

JUNE

S	M	T	W	T	F	S
						1
2	3	4	5	6	7	8
9	10	11	12	13	14	15
16	17	18	19	20	21	22
23	24	25	26	27	28	29
30						

JULY

S	M	T	W	T	F	S
	1	2	3	4	5	6
7	8	9	10	11	12	13
14	15	16	17	18	19	20
21	22	23	24	25	26	27
28	29	30	31			

AUGUST

S	M	T	W	T	F	S
				1	2	3
4	5	6	7	8	9	10
11	12	13	14	15	16	17
18	19	20	21	22	23	24
25	26	27	28	29	30	31

SEPTEMBER

S	M	T	W	T	F	S
1	2	3	4	5	6	7
8	9	10	11	12	13	14
15	16	17	18	19	20	21
22	23	24	25	26	27	28
29	30					

OCTOBER

S	M	T	W	T	F	S
		1	2	3	4	5
6	7	8	9	10	11	12
13	14	15	16	17	18	19
20	21	22	23	24	25	26
27	28	29	30	31		

NOVEMBER

S	M	T	W	T	F	S
					1	2
3	4	5	6	7	8	9
10	11	12	13	14	15	16
17	18	19	20	21	22	23
24	25	26	27	28	29	30

DECEMBER

S	M	T	W	T	F	S
1	2	3	4	5	6	7
8	9	10	11	12	13	14
15	16	17	18	19	20	21
22	23	24	25	26	27	28
29	30	31				

10

JANUARY

S	M	T	W	T	F	S
		1	2	3	4	5
6	7	8	9	10	11	12
13	14	15	16	17	18	19
20	21	22	23	24	25	26
27	28	29	30	31		

FEBRUARY

S	M	T	W	T	F	S
					1	2
3	4	5	6	7	8	9
10	11	12	13	14	15	16
17	18	19	20	21	22	23
24	25	26	27	28	29	

MARCH

S	M	T	W	T	F	S
						1
2	3	4	5	6	7	8
9	10	11	12	13	14	15
16	17	18	19	20	21	22
23	24	25	26	27	28	29
30	31					

APRIL

S	M	T	W	T	F	S
		1	2	3	4	5
6	7	8	9	10	11	12
13	14	15	16	17	18	19
20	21	22	23	24	25	26
27	28	29	30			

MAY

S	M	T	W	T	F	S
				1	2	3
4	5	6	7	8	9	10
11	12	13	14	15	16	17
18	19	20	21	22	23	24
25	26	27	28	29	30	31

JUNE

S	M	T	W	T	F	S
1	2	3	4	5	6	7
8	9	10	11	12	13	14
15	16	17	18	19	20	21
22	23	24	25	26	27	28
29	30					

JULY

S	M	T	W	T	F	S
		1	2	3	4	5
6	7	8	9	10	11	12
13	14	15	16	17	18	19
20	21	22	23	24	25	26
27	28	29	30	31		

AUGUST

S	M	T	W	T	F	S
					1	2
3	4	5	6	7	8	9
10	11	12	13	14	15	16
17	18	19	20	21	22	23
24	25	26	27	28	29	30
31						

SEPTEMBER

S	M	T	W	T	F	S
	1	2	3	4	5	6
7	8	9	10	11	12	13
14	15	16	17	18	19	20
21	22	23	24	25	26	27
28	29	30				

OCTOBER

S	M	T	W	T	F	S
			1	2	3	4
5	6	7	8	9	10	11
12	13	14	15	16	17	18
19	20	21	22	23	24	25
26	27	28	29	30	31	

NOVEMBER

S	M	T	W	T	F	S
						1
2	3	4	5	6	7	8
9	10	11	12	13	14	15
16	17	18	19	20	21	22
23	24	25	26	27	28	29
30						

DECEMBER

S	M	T	W	T	F	S
	1	2	3	4	5	6
7	8	9	10	11	12	13
14	15	16	17	18	19	20
21	22	23	24	25	26	27
28	29	30	31			

11

JANUARY

S	M	T	W	T	F	S
			1	2	3	4
5	6	7	8	9	10	11
12	13	14	15	16	17	18
19	20	21	22	23	24	25
26	27	28	29	30	31	

FEBRUARY

S	M	T	W	T	F	S
						1
2	3	4	5	6	7	8
9	10	11	12	13	14	15
16	17	18	19	20	21	22
23	24	25	26	27	28	29

MARCH

S	M	T	W	T	F	S
1	2	3	4	5	6	7
8	9	10	11	12	13	14
15	16	17	18	19	20	21
22	23	24	25	26	27	28
29	30	31				

APRIL

S	M	T	W	T	F	S
			1	2	3	4
5	6	7	8	9	10	11
12	13	14	15	16	17	18
19	20	21	22	23	24	25
26	27	28	29	30		

MAY

S	M	T	W	T	F	S
					1	2
3	4	5	6	7	8	9
10	11	12	13	14	15	16
17	18	19	20	21	22	23
24	25	26	27	28	29	30
31						

JUNE

S	M	T	W	T	F	S
	1	2	3	4	5	6
7	8	9	10	11	12	13
14	15	16	17	18	19	20
21	22	23	24	25	26	27
28	29	30				

JULY

S	M	T	W	T	F	S
			1	2	3	4
5	6	7	8	9	10	11
12	13	14	15	16	17	18
19	20	21	22	23	24	25
26	27	28	29	30	31	

AUGUST

S	M	T	W	T	F	S
						1
2	3	4	5	6	7	8
9	10	11	12	13	14	15
16	17	18	19	20	21	22
23	24	25	26	27	28	29
30	31					

SEPTEMBER

S	M	T	W	T	F	S
		1	2	3	4	5
6	7	8	9	10	11	12
13	14	15	16	17	18	19
20	21	22	23	24	25	26
27	28	29	30			

OCTOBER

S	M	T	W	T	F	S
				1	2	3
4	5	6	7	8	9	10
11	12	13	14	15	16	17
18	19	20	21	22	23	24
25	26	27	28	29	30	31

NOVEMBER

S	M	T	W	T	F	S
1	2	3	4	5	6	7
8	9	10	11	12	13	14
15	16	17	18	19	20	21
22	23	24	25	26	27	28
29	30					

DECEMBER

S	M	T	W	T	F	S
		1	2	3	4	5
6	7	8	9	10	11	12
13	14	15	16	17	18	19
20	21	22	23	24	25	26
27	28	29	30	31		

12

JANUARY

S	M	T	W	T	F	S
				1	2	3
4	5	6	7	8	9	10
11	12	13	14	15	16	17
18	19	20	21	22	23	24
25	26	27	28	29	30	31

FEBRUARY

S	M	T	W	T	F	S
1	2	3	4	5	6	7
8	9	10	11	12	13	14
15	16	17	18	19	20	21
22	23	24	25	26	27	28
29						

MARCH

S	M	T	W	T	F	S
	1	2	3	4	5	6
7	8	9	10	11	12	13
14	15	16	17	18	19	20
21	22	23	24	25	26	27
28	29	30	31			

APRIL

S	M	T	W	T	F	S
				1	2	3
4	5	6	7	8	9	10
11	12	13	14	15	16	17
18	19	20	21	22	23	24
25	26	27	28	29	30	

MAY

S	M	T	W	T	F	S
						1
2	3	4	5	6	7	8
9	10	11	12	13	14	15
16	17	18	19	20	21	22
23	24	25	26	27	28	29
30	31					

JUNE

S	M	T	W	T	F	S
		1	2	3	4	5
6	7	8	9	10	11	12
13	14	15	16	17	18	19
20	21	22	23	24	25	26
27	28	29	30			

JULY

S	M	T	W	T	F	S
				1	2	3
4	5	6	7	8	9	10
11	12	13	14	15	16	17
18	19	20	21	22	23	24
25	26	27	28	29	30	31

AUGUST

S	M	T	W	T	F	S
1	2	3	4	5	6	7
8	9	10	11	12	13	14
15	16	17	18	19	20	21
22	23	24	25	26	27	28
29	30	31				

SEPTEMBER

S	M	T	W	T	F	S
			1	2	3	4
5	6	7	8	9	10	11
12	13	14	15	16	17	18
19	20	21	22	23	24	25
26	27	28	29	30		

OCTOBER

S	M	T	W	T	F	S
					1	2
3	4	5	6	7	8	9
10	11	12	13	14	15	16
17	18	19	20	21	22	23
24	25	26	27	28	29	30
31						

NOVEMBER

S	M	T	W	T	F	S
	1	2	3	4	5	6
7	8	9	10	11	12	13
14	15	16	17	18	19	20
21	22	23	24	25	26	27
28	29	30				

DECEMBER

S	M	T	W	T	F	S
			1	2	3	4
5	6	7	8	9	10	11
12	13	14	15	16	17	18
19	20	21	22	23	24	25
26	27	28	29	30	31	

13

JANUARY

S	M	T	W	T	F	S
					1	2
3	4	5	6	7	8	9
10	11	12	13	14	15	16
17	18	19	20	21	22	23
24	25	26	27	28	29	30
31						

FEBRUARY

S	M	T	W	T	F	S
	1	2	3	4	5	6
7	8	9	10	11	12	13
14	15	16	17	18	19	20
21	22	23	24	25	26	27
28	29					

MARCH

S	M	T	W	T	F	S
		1	2	3	4	5
6	7	8	9	10	11	12
13	14	15	16	17	18	19
20	21	22	23	24	25	26
27	28	29	30	31		

APRIL

S	M	T	W	T	F	S
					1	2
3	4	5	6	7	8	9
10	11	12	13	14	15	16
17	18	19	20	21	22	23
24	25	26	27	28	29	30

MAY

S	M	T	W	T	F	S
1	2	3	4	5	6	7
8	9	10	11	12	13	14
15	16	17	18	19	20	21
22	23	24	25	26	27	28
29	30	31				

JUNE

S	M	T	W	T	F	S
			1	2	3	4
5	6	7	8	9	10	11
12	13	14	15	16	17	18
19	20	21	22	23	24	25
26	27	28	29	30		

JULY

S	M	T	W	T	F	S
					1	2
3	4	5	6	7	8	9
10	11	12	13	14	15	16
17	18	19	20	21	22	23
24	25	26	27	28	29	30
31						

AUGUST

S	M	T	W	T	F	S
	1	2	3	4	5	6
7	8	9	10	11	12	13
14	15	16	17	18	19	20
21	22	23	24	25	26	27
28	29	30	31			

SEPTEMBER

S	M	T	W	T	F	S
				1	2	3
4	5	6	7	8	9	10
11	12	13	14	15	16	17
18	19	20	21	22	23	24
25	26	27	28	29	30	

OCTOBER

S	M	T	W	T	F	S
						1
2	3	4	5	6	7	8
9	10	11	12	13	14	15
16	17	18	19	20	21	22
23	24	25	26	27	28	29
30	31					

NOVEMBER

S	M	T	W	T	F	S
		1	2	3	4	5
6	7	8	9	10	11	12
13	14	15	16	17	18	19
20	21	22	23	24	25	26
27	28	29	30			

DECEMBER

S	M	T	W	T	F	S
				1	2	3
4	5	6	7	8	9	10
11	12	13	14	15	16	17
18	19	20	21	22	23	24
25	26	27	28	29	30	31

14

JANUARY

S	M	T	W	T	F	S
						1
2	3	4	5	6	7	8
9	10	11	12	13	14	15
16	17	18	19	20	21	22
23	24	25	26	27	28	29
30	31					

FEBRUARY

S	M	T	W	T	F	S
		1	2	3	4	5
6	7	8	9	10	11	12
13	14	15	16	17	18	19
20	21	22	23	24	25	26
27	28	29				

MARCH

S	M	T	W	T	F	S
			1	2	3	4
5	6	7	8	9	10	11
12	13	14	15	16	17	18
19	20	21	22	23	24	25
26	27	28	29	30	31	

APRIL

S	M	T	W	T	F	S
						1
2	3	4	5	6	7	8
9	10	11	12	13	14	15
16	17	18	19	20	21	22
23	24	25	26	27	28	29
30						

MAY

S	M	T	W	T	F	S
	1	2	3	4	5	6
7	8	9	10	11	12	13
14	15	16	17	18	19	20
21	22	23	24	25	26	27
28	29	30	31			

JUNE

S	M	T	W	T	F	S
				1	2	3
4	5	6	7	8	9	10
11	12	13	14	15	16	17
18	19	20	21	22	23	24
25	26	27	28	29	30	

JULY

S	M	T	W	T	F	S
						1
2	3	4	5	6	7	8
9	10	11	12	13	14	15
16	17	18	19	20	21	22
23	24	25	26	27	28	29
30	31					

AUGUST

S	M	T	W	T	F	S
		1	2	3	4	5
6	7	8	9	10	11	12
13	14	15	16	17	18	19
20	21	22	23	24	25	26
27	28	29	30	31		

SEPTEMBER

S	M	T	W	T	F	S
					1	2
3	4	5	6	7	8	9
10	11	12	13	14	15	16
17	18	19	20	21	22	23
24	25	26	27	28	29	30

OCTOBER

S	M	T	W	T	F	S
1	2	3	4	5	6	7
8	9	10	11	12	13	14
15	16	17	18	19	20	21
22	23	24	25	26	27	28
29	30	31				

NOVEMBER

S	M	T	W	T	F	S
			1	2	3	4
5	6	7	8	9	10	11
12	13	14	15	16	17	18
19	20	21	22	23	24	25
26	27	28	29	30		

DECEMBER

S	M	T	W	T	F	S
					1	2
3	4	5	6	7	8	9
10	11	12	13	14	15	16
17	18	19	20	21	22	23
24	25	26	27	28	29	30
31						

GREGORIAN CALENDAR KEY FOR 1583-1775

Find the year to be searched below for the years 1583-1775. The numbers beside each year are keyed to the 14 calendars on the previous two pages.

Note: The Gregorian Calendar began on October 15, 1582. From that date to 31 December 1582, use calendar 6.)

1583 7	1620 .. 11	1657 2
1584 8	1621 6	1658 3
1585 3	1622 7	1659 4
1586 4	1623 1	1660 .. 12
1587 5	1624 9	1661 7
1588 .. 13	1625 4	1662 1
1589 1	1626 5	1663 2
1590 2	1627 6	1664 .. 10
1591 3	1628 .. 14	1665 5
1592 .. 11	1629 2	1666 6
1593 6	1630 3	1667 7
1594 7	1631 4	1668 8
1695 1	1632 .. 12	1669 3
1596 9	1633 7	1670 4
1597 4	1634 1	1671 5
1598 5	1635 2	1672 .. 13
1599 6	1636 .. 10	1673 1
1600 .. 14	1637 5	1674 2
1601 2	1638 6	1675 3
1602 3	1639 7	1676 .. 11
1603 4	1640 8	1677 6
1604 .. 12	1641 3	1678 7
1605 7	1642 4	1679 1
1606 1	1643 5	1680 9
1607 2	1644 .. 13	1681 4
1608 .. 10	1645 1	1682 5
1609 5	1646 2	1683 6
1610 6	1647 3	1684 .. 14
1611 7	1648 .. 11	1685 2
1612 8	1649 6	1686 3
1613 3	1650 7	1687 4
1614 4	1651 1	1688 .. 12
1615 5	1652 9	1689 7
1616 .. 13	1653 4	1690 1
1617 1	1654 5	1691 2
1618 2	1655 6	1692 .. 10
1619 3	1656 .. 14	1693 ... 5

1694 6	1722 5	1750 5
1695 7	1723 6	1751 6
1696 8	1724 .. 14	1752 .. 14
1697 3	1725 2	1753 2
1698 4	1726 3	1754 3
1699 5	1727 4	1755 4
1700 6	1728 .. 12	1756 .. 12
1701 7	1729 7	1757 7
1702 1	1730 1	1758 1
1703 2	1731 2	1759 2
1704 .. 10	1732 .. 10	1760 .. 10
1705 5	1733 5	1761 5
1706 6	1734 6	1762 6
1707 7	1735 7	1763 7
1708 8	1736 8	1764 8
1709 3	1737 3	1765 3
1710 4	1738 4	1766 4
1711 5	1739 5	1767 5
1712 .. 13	1740 .. 13	1768 .. 13
1713 1	1741 1	1769 1
1714 2	1742 2	1770 2
1715 3	1743 3	1771 3
1716 .. 11	1744 .. 11	1772 .. 11
1717 6	1745 6	1773 6
1718 7	1746 7	1774 7
1719 1	1747 1	1775 1
1720 9	1748 9	
1721 4	1749 4	

REFERENCES FOR HELP WITH DATING

•*French Republican Calendar Research Outline,* Family History Library, Church of Jesus Christ of Latter-day Saints, 1991.
• Larry O. Jensen, *A Genealogical Handbook of German Research,* Pleasant Grove, Utah, 1983; Vol. 2
•George K. Schweitzer, *German Genealogical Research,* Knoxville, 1995
•"Variations and Uses of Calendars," *German Genealogical Digest,* Vol. 3, No. 2, 1987
•Kenneth L. Smith, *A Practical Guide to Dating Systems for Genealogists*
•"Church Year Calendar," *The German Connection,* German Research Association, Vol. 9, No. 3, August 1985.

MONTHS OF THE YEAR IN FIVE LANGUAGES				
ENGLISH	**GERMAN**	**SWISS**	**FRENCH**	**LATIN**
January	Januar/Hartung/ Eismonat	Januar/Jänner/ Jenner/Erster Monat	janvier	Januarius
February	Februar/Hornung/ Regenmonat	Februar/ Hornung	février	Februarius
March	März/Lenzing/ Lenzmond/ Windmonat	März/Lenz Frühlingsmonat	mars	Martius
April	April/Ostermond/ Ostermonat/ Wandelmonat	April/ Ostermonat	avril	Aprilis
May	Mai/Weidemonat/ Wonnemond/ Blütenmonat	Mai/ Wonnemonat	mai	Maius
June	Juni/Brachet/ Brachmonat/ Wiesenmonat	Juni/ Brachmonat	juin	Junius
July	Juli/Heuert/ Heumonat	Juli/ Heumonat	juillet	Julius
August	August/Ernting/ Erntemonat/ Hitzmonat	August/Augst/ Augstmonat/ Erntemonat	août	Augustus
September	September/ Fruchtmonat/ Scheiding/7ber	September/ Herbstmonat/ 7ber	septembre/ 7bre	September/ Septembris
October	Oktober/Gilbhard Weinmonat/8ber	Oktober/ Weinmonat/ 8ber	octobre/ 8bre	October/ Octobris
November	November/ Reifmonat/ Nebelmonat/9ber	November/ Wintermonat/ 9ber	novembre/ 9bre	November/ Novembris
December	Dezember/ Julmonat/ Schneemonat/ Christmonat/10bre	Dezember Christmonat/ Wolfmonat/ 10ber/Xber	décembre/ 10bre Xbre	December/ Decembris

DAYS OF THE WEEK IN FIVE LANGUAGES

ENGLISH	GERMAN	SWISS	FRENCH	LATIN
Sunday	Sonntag	Suntig	dimanche	dies dominica/dies Solis/feria prima
Monday	Montag	Mäntig	lundi	dies Lunae/feria secunda
Tuesday	Dienstag	Ziestig/ Zinstag	mardi	dies Martis/feria tertia
Wednesday	Mittwoch	Mittwuch	mercredi	dies Mercurii/feria quarta
Thursday	Donnerstag	Dunstig	jeudi	dies Jovis/feria quinta
Friday	Freitag/ Freytag/Frytig	Fritag/Frytig	venredi	dies Veneris/feria sexta
Saturday	Samstag/ Sonnabend	Samstag	samedi	dies Saturnia/feria septima/ sabbatum

HOLIDAYS AND OBSERVANCES IN GERMAN-SPEAKING AREAS

•**January 1:** *Neujahr, 1. Januar* (New Year); New Years Day is celebrated with fireworks and parties on New Year's Eve (*Silvester*); observed in Christendom since the sixth century

•**January 6:** *Heilige drei Könige* (Holy Three Kings), *Epiphanias*; Epiphany; observed in Austria, Baden-Württemberg, and Bavaria in Germany, and in Catholic areas of Switzerland; since the ninth century A.D.

•**February 3:** *Maria Reinigung*; Purification

•**February/March:** *Aschermittwoch;* Ash Wednesday; first day of Lent (*Fasten*), 46 days before Easter

•**February/March:** *Fastnacht*; Shrove Tuesday; the day before Ash Wednesday

•**February/March:** *feister Sonntag*; fat Sunday; last Sunday before Lent

•**February/March:** *Rosenmontag;* 42 days before Easter; the climax of the *Karneval* celebrations, especially in the Rhineland

•**March 19:** *Josefstage*; Feast of St. Joseph

•**March 25:** *Verkündigung*; Annunciation

•**March/April:** *Palmsonntag*; Palm Sunday; Sunday before Easter

•**March/April:** *grüner Donnerstage*; Maundy Thursday; Thursday before Easter

•**March/April:** *Karfreitag, Stiller Freitag*; Good Friday; Friday before Easter; observance of the crucifixion of Jesus; since the second century A.D.; the week before Easter is called "*Karwoche*"

•**March/April:** *Ostersonntag* (Easter Sunday); commemorates the resurrection of Jesus; Sunday after the first full moon after March 21 (always between March 22 and April 25); the basis for all movable Church feast days; established by the Council of Nicäa in 325 A.D; a legal holiday.

•**March/April:** *Ostermontag* (Easter Monday); Monday after Easter

•**March/April:** *Quasimodogeniti*; Low Sunday; Sunday after Easter

•**May 1:** *Tag der Arbeit, Maifeiertag* (Labor Day); celebrated in most of Europe; a legal holiday; observed since 1890

•**May/June:** *Christi Himmelfahrt* (Ascension Day); fortieth day after Easter, always on a Thursday; observed in Catholic regions; began in the fourth century A.D.; a legal holiday

•**May/June:** *Pfingstsonntag* (Whitsunday); also called Pentecost Sunday (Pfingsten) or Whitsun in English; seventh Sunday after Easter; the season from Pentecost Sunday to Advent; a legal holiday; observed since about 130 A.D.

•**May/June:** *Pfingstmontag* (Whitmonday); Monday after Pfingsten; Pfingstsonntag and Pfingstmontag fall between May 9 and June 13; a legal holiday

•**May/June:** *Fronleichnam* (Corpus Christi Day); first Sunday after Pfingsten; not observed in the northern and eastern states; since 1254, prescribed by Urban IV.

•**June 24:** *Johannistage (Johannis des Täufers)*; Feast of St. John the Baptist

•**July 2:** *Heimsuchung Maria;* Visitation

•**August 1:** *Bundesfeier,* **Swiss National Day;** celebrates the founding of the Swiss Confederation, with fireworks, Alpine bonfires, lantern-lit nighttime parades, and political speeches

•**August 15:** *Mariä Himmelfahrt* (Assumption of the Blessed Virgin); observance of Mary's ascension into heaven, in Catholic regions of Germany; celebrated since Pope Pius XII announced the dogma of Mary's Assumption in 1950

•**September:** *Buß und Bettag* (Day of Repentance and Prayer); third Sunday in September; day of meditation in the Lutheran Church in Switzerland.

•**October 3:** *Tag der deutschen Einheit* (Day of German Unity); became a legal holiday in 1992; celebrates the official date of German reunification in 1990.

•**October:** *Erntedankfest* (Harvest Thanksgiving); celebrated in many rural areas on the first Sunday in October (or first Sunday after Michaelmas, which is September 29); not a legal holiday.

•**October 26:** *Flag Day* in Austria, observing the restoration of full sovereignty after World War II and declaration of neutrality on October 26, 1955.

•**October 31:** *Reformationstag*; Feast of the Reformation; only in Protestant areas

•**October:** *Königsfest Christi:* Feast of Christ the King; first Sunday of October

•**November 1:** *Allerheiligen,* All Saints Day; observed in Austria and the Catholic regions of Germany and Switzerland; commemoration of all saints; since 835 A.D.

•**November 2:** *Allerseelen*; All Souls Day; Catholic memorial day for all saints not accorded special days in the church calendar

•**November/December:** *Buß und Bettag* (Day of Repentance and Prayer); Wednesday before *Totensonntag* (Memorial Sunday), observed as a day of meditation in the Lutheran Church in Germany; introduced in Prussia in 1816, then spread through Protestant areas; no longer a federal legal holiday since 1995

•**November 11:** St. Martin's Day *(Martinstag)*; celebrated with lantern marches and a goose for dinner

•**November:** *Volkstrauertag,* national (Protestant) day of mourning; Sunday before *Totensonntag;* dedicated to victims of the National Socialist terror and the dead of the two World Wars

•**November:** *Totensonntag,* or *Ewigkeitssonntag*; last Sunday before the first Advent; memorial day, for visiting graves of the dead and remembering the dead in church services.

•**November/December:** Advent; starts on fourth Sunday before Christmas

•**December 6:** *Nikolaustag* (St. Nicholas Day); not a legal holiday; the day when Sankt Nikolaus (not Santa Claus) brings small gifts to children

•**December 8:** *Mariä Empfängnis, unbefleckte Empfängnis*; Day of the Immaculate Conception; since the eighteenth century

•**December 24:** *Heiligabend, Weihnachtsabend,* Christmas Eve; the most important day of the Christmas season; presents are exchanged

•**December 25:** *Weihnachtstag,* Christmas Day (commemoration of the birth of Jesus); celebrated on this day since 354 A.D.; a legal holiday in Germany

•**December 26:** *Weihnachtstag* (Second Christmas); a legal holiday in Germany

Sources:

•Hyde Flippo, *The German Way.* Passport Books, Lincolnwood, Illinois, 1997

•Dieter Kramer, *German Holidays and Folk Customs,* Atlantik-Brücke, Bonn, 1986

•German Research Association, *The German Connection.* Vol. 16, No. 1, January 1992

•Susan Steiner ed., *Federal Republic of Germany: Questions and Answers.* German Information Center, New York, 1996

FEAST DAYS

Events marking the church calendar, rather than dates from the secular calendars, were in many cases used in recording births, marriages, and deaths in both Protestant and Catholic church records.

The church year was based on the two major church events, Christmas (December 25) and Easter (in March or April, date varies).

Major feast days of the church calendar are listed below.

An asterisk (*) indicates that the observance date changes from year to year, based on solar-lunar cycles.

Advent (*Advents*)

♦ *Adventssonntag* (first Sunday in Advent, fourth Sunday before Christmas)

♦*Andreas* (St. Andrew), 30 November

♦*Second Sunday in Advent, third Sunday before Christmas

♦*Third Sunday in Advent, second Sunday before Christmas

♦*Thomas* (St. Thomas), 21 December

♦Fourth Sunday in Advent, first Sunday before Christmas

♦*Weihnachts* (Christmas), 25 December

Christmas (*Weihnachts*)

♦*Stephanus* (St. Stephen), 26 December

♦*First Sunday after Christmas

♦*Johannes* (St. John), 27 December

♦*Unschuldige Kindlein* (Holy Innocents), 28 December

♦*Second Sunday after Christmas

♦*Beschneidung Christi* (Circumcision of Our Lord), 1 January

Epiphany (*Epiphanie/Erscheinung*)

♦*Epiphanie* (Epiphany), 6 January

♦*Septuagesima* (Septuagesima Sunday), ninth Sunday before Easter

♦ *Sexagesima* (Sexagesima Sunday), eighth Sunday before Easter

♦ *Quinquasgesima* (Quinquagesima Sunday), seventh Sunday before Easter

♦*Pauli Bekehrung/Conversio* (Conversion of St. Paul), 25 January

♦*Praesentatio Domini Nostrum* (Presentation of Our Lord), 2 February

♦*Matthias* (St. Matthias), 24 February

Lent (*Fastenzeit*)

♦ *Aschermitwoch* (Ash Wednesday), 46 days before Easter

♦ *I Invocavit* (first Sunday in Lent), sixth Sunday before Easter

♦*II Reminiscere* (second Sunday in Lent), fifth Sunday before Easter

♦*III Oculi* (third Sunday in Lent), fourth Sunday before Easter

♦*IV Laetare* (fourth Sunday in Lent), third Sunday before Easter

♦*Passionssonntag* (fifth Sunday in Lent), second Sunday before Easter

♦*Palmsonntag* (sixth Sunday in Lent), first Sunday before Easter

♦*Karwoche* (Holy Week)

Montag (Monday)
Dienstag (Tuesday)
Mittwoch (Wednesday)
Gründonnerstag (Maundy Thursday)
Karfreitag (Good Friday)
Samstag (Easter Eve)
Easter (*Osternzeit*)
♦*Ostern (Easter Sunday)
♦*Berkündigung Maria* (Annunciation), 25 March
♦**I Quasi Modo Geniti* (second Sunday of Easter), first Sunday after Easter
♦*II Misericordia (third Sunday of Easter), second Sunday after Easter
♦*III Jubilate (fourth Sunday of Easter), third Sunday after Easter
♦*IV Cantate (fifth Sunday of Easter), fourth Sunday after Easter
♦**V Rogate/Vocem Juncunditatis* (sixth Sunday of Easter), fifth Sunday after Easter
♦ **Himmelfahrt Christi* (Ascension Thursday), 40 days after Easter
♦*VI Exaudi (7th Sunday of Easter), 6th Sunday after Easter
♦*Marcus* (St. Mark), 25 April
♦*Philippus und Jacobus* (St. Philip and St. James), 1 May
♦ *Pfingsten (Pentecost/Whitsunday), seventh Sunday or 50 days after Easter
Trinity (*Trinititatis*)
♦(*Trinity Sunday), eighth Sunday after Easter
♦ *Johannes der Täufer* (St. John the Baptist), 24 June
♦*Petrus und Paulus* (Sts. Peter and Paul), 29 June
♦*Heimsuchung Mariä* (Visitation), 2 July
w*Jacobus der Ältere* (St. James the Elder), 25 July
♦ *Umgestaltung/Verklärung* (Transfiguration of Our Lord), 6 August
♦ *Himmelfahrt Maria* (Assumption of Mary), 15 August
♦*Bartholomäus* (St. Bartholomew), 24 August
♦*Matthaeus* (St. Matthew), 21 September
w*Michael* (St. Michael and All Angels), 29 September
♦*Lucas* (St. Luke), 18 October

♦*Simeon und Judas* (Sts. Simon and Jude), 28 October
♦*Reformations-Fest* (Reformation Day-Protestant), 31 October
♦*Allerseelen/Allerheiligen* (All Souls'/All Saints' Day), 1 November

Source: George K. Schweitzer, *German Genealogical Research*, 1995.

OKTOBERFEST

Munich's Oktoberfest, a traditional celebration dominated by beer tents, music, and parades, is scheduled each year for 16 days, beginning on the third Saturday in September and running through the first Sunday in October.

The *Oktoberfest* tradition began in 1810 with a horserace on October 17 with a parade of military riders, music, and waving flags, on the occasion of the wedding feast of Bavarian King Maximilian Joseph's son, Prince Ludwig, and Princess Therese of Saxony-Hildburghausen.

The *Theresienwiese* (Therese's Meadow) where the *Oktoberfest* is held, is named after the bride.

The king, known as Max Josef, went so far as to invite Bavarian farmers, considered then as crude peasants, to join in the observance of the horse race in an attempt to revive patriotism, tradition, and the old ways

Until the mid 1800s, the *Oktoberfest's* most popular attractions remained the horse race and the marksmen competitions. By the mid nineteenth century, the *Oktoberfest* became more of a country fair, where the beer tents were added.

Today's *Oktoberfest* horse race is held ten miles from the beer tents, at the Reims track.

The opening parade, *Wies'n Einzug der Festwirte und Brauereien* (Meadow Appearance of Festival Hosts and Breweries), dates back to 1887. The main attraction is the horse-drawn beer wagons.

On the second day, Sunday, the *Oktoberfest Trachten und Schützen* (Oktoberfest Costume and Marksmen's) parade, which goes back to 1835, takes place, the largest *Oktoberfest* parade.

The grounds are open at 10 am on weekdays, 9 am on weekends. Beer tents stay open until 10:30 pm. Rides stop at about 10:30 pm

For more information about Munich's Oktoberfest, call the German National Tourist offices in New York (212) 661-7200, Los Angeles (310) 575-9799, or Toronto (416) 968-1570

Source: Dennis Burnside, "Oktoberfest Horses," *German Life*, October/November, 1996.

COMPUTING BIRTHDATES FROM GRAVESTONE AGES

Gravestones often list the death date and athe age at death expressed in years, months, and days. The "8870 method" is a simple way to calculate the birthdate.

Example: Date of death is May 6, 1889, and the age is given as 78 years, 3 months, and 27 days.

Death date is expressed as 18890506
Age is expressed as 780327
Difference 8110179
Subtract correction factor 8870
Result 8101309

This translates as the 9th day of the 13th month of 1810. Since there is not a 13th month, add one to the year and subtract 12 from the months. The birthdate becomes January 9, 1811.

Source: *Cemetery Q&A's* of Janesville, Wisconsin, December 1996

DOOR-MARKING RITUAL DURING EPIPHANY

On or around January 6 (Epiphany in the church calendar), groups of children disguised as the "Three Wise Men" plus a leader carrying a representation of the star of Bethlehem wander from house to house, sing Christmas carols, and ask for donations either for charities or for themselves.

In return they mark the door with the abbreviation of "*Christus mansionem benedicat,*" (C + M + B), or, "May Christ bless this house)"and the year. The chalking of a door on Epiphany in 1997 would look like this: *19 C + M + B 97*

Until about 300 years ago, the New Year started on Epiphany Day until Pope Innozenz XII moved it up five days.

People, especially in rural areas, who did not know Latin, interpreted the letters C + M + B as the abbreviations of the Three Wise Men's biblical names of Caspar, Melchior and Balthasar.

Chapter 28

This and that

DOLLARS/MARKS CONVERSIONS

To convert dollars to deutschmarks
Multiply dollars by the exchange rate. For example, to change $200 to deutschmarks when the exchange rate is 1.49 ($1 = 1.49 DM): $200 x 1.49 = 298 DM

To convert deutschmarks to dollars
Divide deutschmarks by the exchange rate. For example, to change 88 DM to dollars when the exchange rate is 1.49 ($1 = 1.49 DM): 88 DM ÷ 1.49 = $59.06

KILOMETERS/MILES CONVERSIONS

1 kilometer = 0.621 miles
1 mile = 1.609 kilometers
To convert miles to kilometers
Divide the number of miles by 0.62; for example, 24 miles divided by 0.62 equals 38.7 kilometers.

To convert kilometers to miles
Divide the number of kilometers by 1.6; for example, 204 kilometers divided by 1.6 equals 127.5 miles.

FAHRENHEIT/CELSIUS

Degrees Celsius/ Centigrade	Degrees Fahrenheit
-20	-4
-17.8	0
-15	5
-10	14
-5	23
0	32
1	33.8
2	35.6
3	37.4
4	39.2
5	41
6	42.8
7	44.6
8	46.4
9	48.2

10	50
15	59
20	68
25	77
30	88
35	95
40	104

VACATION DAYS IN GERMANY

Federal law in Germany requires a legal minimum for vacation time of 18 work days for adults, and 25-30 days for young adults up to the age of 18 years. However, due to collective bargaining agreements, 70 percent of all employees enjoy at least six weeks of paid vacation, and most of hte others get between five and six weeks.

As for school children, in all the federal states they have six weeks of summer vacation, two or three weeks at Easter and at Christmastime, and a one-week vacation in the fall. Additional days off from school vary from state to state. The major summer vacations are scheduled by the various states each year according to a staggered timetable. This is done to alleviate traffic congestion on the highways, because German families tend to travel when summer vacations begin.

Source: German Information Center, Federal Republic of German: Questions and Answers, ed. Susan Steiner (New York, 1996)

SPEED LIMITS IN GERMANY

Speed limits in Germany exist on state and local highways (100 km/h or 62 mph), and in towns and cities (50 km/h or 31 mph). The Autobahns have a recommended maximum speed of 130 km/h or 81 mph, but normally no mandatory speed limit.

The legal age for driving is 18 for driving cars and trucks, 16 for mopeds and motorscooters.

VIDEO SYSTEMS: GERMANY VS. UNITED STATES

Video equipment systems in Germany and the United States are for the most part different. Germany uses the PAL system, which is not compatible with the NTSC system prevalent in the United States. There are, however, some films in Germany which are specially made with NTSC equipment for the United States market and can be run on American VCRs.

It is common to have video cassettes recorded on the PAL system converted electronically to NTSC for use on American systems.

THE WANDERING MUSICIANS OF THE PFALZ

By Rainer Thumshirn[1]

As an economic necessity for many families in the Pfalz, migrant German bands began traveling first in Europe, then to the United States and many other countries of the world beginning in the mid-19th century.

The economic problems in the Pfalz go back to Napoleon, who annexed the Pfalz in 1801. Trade and manufacturing were then deregulated, resulting in an influx of cheaper and unskilled labor. This cheap labor undermined the system of artisans' guilds and lowered the incomes of workers.

Combined with this decrease in incomes were the improvements occurring in medical care and hygiene, resulting in lower infant mortality and longer life expectancy. Thus the size of the population needing to be fed was rising. Add to these predicaments the disastrous harvests in three successive years, 1838, 1839, and 1840, and it becomes clear why economic chaos developed.

There were attempts to achieve some political liberalization (Hambacher Fest of 1832, and the "revolution" of 1848), but they were mostly futile.

All these influences led to an immense increase of emigration from the Pfalz – especially to the United States.

The appearance of migrant workers

One particular result of the economic pressures in the Pfalz in the early 19th century was the appearance of migrant workers (*Wanderarbeiter*). These were men who were forced to leave their home towns to find jobs or at least to find part-time second jobs. It is the Pfälzers' search for work outside standard occupations like farmer, shoemaker, and butcher that led to the occupation of *Wandermusikant* (wandering minstrel).

In the area northwest of Kaiserslautern, many of these migrant workers chose music as their profession. Archival records often give people's professions as "carpenter and musician," or "farmer and musician."

Musikantenland

The area where these musicians came from became known as "*Musikantenland*," roughly identical with today's Kreis Kusel, containing towns and villages like Mackenbach, Aschbach, Jettenbach, Meisenheim, Otterberg, Landstuhl, Waldmohr, Kusel, and Lauterecken, with Wolfstein as an economic center.

After playing at first in towns of the Pfalz, the *Wandermusikanten* made France and then other European counties their destinations in the 1830s. By the middle of the 19th century, overseas countries like Australia, South Africa and primarily the United States were added. In the heydays after 1900, approximately 2,500 *Wandermusikanten* from this small part of the Pfalz roamed the far corners of the world.

Bands were all male, although in some cases the wife of the bandleader would accompany the band as cook and housekeeper. But the wives of the *Wandermusikanten* mostly stayed at home, working the small farms and raising the children.

The *Musikanten* 'season'

Preparations for the trip started in the fall during the *Kirchweih* season, when festivities and fairs provided excellent opportunities for bandleaders and musicians to meet and put together the bands for the next season. The bands numbered anywhere from about 5 to about 15 members. Bandleaders often took on as apprentices young boys, merely 13 years old and just out of school.

Preparations continued with the filing of applications for passports and exit visas. During winter the bands would practice and have their uniforms tailored. In spring they would set out on their journey. Those bands staying in Europe would usually return in the fall of the same year. Bands heading overseas mostly stayed away for two to three years.

Most often, the *Musikanten* started out by walking to a German, Dutch, or French port for embarkation. If they were lucky, they would be hired to play on board a vessel headed for America.

Some bands traveled to one of the big cities like Boston, New York, Philadelphia and stayed for two or three years, renting a house for the duration. Others would move from town to town seeking whatever engagements they could find. Because of the milder climate, they would often start their tour in the South, slowly working their way north in summer and fall.

The bands played in the streets and parks for donations, but the work they preferred was long-term engagements at hotels and river boats. However, they would play for anyone willing to pay – for example, at fairs, horse races, parties, weddings, funerals or rallies by political parties (especially the Democrats).

The repertoires of the bands included internationally popular opera melodies and dancing music, as well as ethnic specialties like Polish krakowiaks, Hungarian csardas, Irish reels, English jigs, and Bohemian polkas.

Especially in the United States, the *Wandermusikanten* served as a bridge between the immigrants from the Pfalz (and other parts of Germany) and their old country. They settled mainly in industrial towns in the eastern United States, as well as Ohio and Texas.

Texan farmers of German origin had an especially good reputation for their generosity among the *Wandermusikanten,* so bands stayed in that area as long as possible. (*The San Antonio Express* described them in 1913 as "a happy family of wandering minstrels who possess all the romantic spirit of their tribe.")

In some folk songs the cuckoo is mentioned (as in *"Kuckuck, Kuckuck, ruft's aus dem Wald"*) and to imitate its call the drummer blew a special kind of whistle or flute. There always had to be a cuckoo in every performance! The call of the cuckoo sometimes made the musicians as homesick as their audiences and they cried in happy unison.

Many of the *Wandermusikanten* found positions with professional American orchestras and stayed iin the United States. One source mentions that around 1900 about two-thirds of the Boston Symphony Orchestra's members were former *Pfälzer Wandermusikanten.* Another source calls the Pfalz "America's conservatory for the period from 1865 to 1914."

The impact back home

The activities of the *Wandermusikanten* had a strong impact on the small region of the Pfalz they called home and whose economy largely depended upon them.

An industry producing musical instruments sprang up, a textile industry was needed for the uniforms, and two banks financed the tours and deposited the earnings.

On their travels to the United States and elsewhere, the *Wandermusikanten* took back to the Pfalz new liberal ideas they had encountered.

They had become worldly-wise in the literal sense of the word, making them for a long time objects of suspicion to the ruling conservative political and church authorities.

Many of the *Wandermusikanten* made much more money abroad than the artisans and laborers in the Pfalz. Such opportunities enabled them to buy land and build homes, sometimes with the savings accumulated during a single two- or three-year trip.

After Germany's war against France in 1870, the *Musikanten* were no longer welcome in most of France.

The outbreak of World War I in 1914 closed the rest of the world for them. But even if this had not happened, the increased use of the radio by about 1920 and the spreading of the phonograph probably would have greatly diminished the popularity (and income) of street-musicians anyway.

Still standing in *Musikantenland* are many of the houses built by the *Musikanten,* with the typical ornamental gables (*Musikantengiebel*) and the decorations and inscriptions above the doors of the homes and on tombstones, most often that of the lyra, the ancient symbol for music.

The exporting of music to faraway countries allowed many of the people of the Pfalz to survive and even made some of them fairly well off.

[1]Rainer Thumshirn, of Heimstetten (Bavaria), Germany, is the foreign correspondent for *Der Blumenbaum,* journal of the Sacramento German Genealogy Society. This article is adapted from "There Always Had to Be a Cuckoo," published in Vol. 11, No. 2 (1993) of that publication.

Sources:
•*Westricher Heimatblätter,* Vol. 20, No. 3, Sept. 1989
•Ibid., Vol. 10, No. 2, May 1979
•*Pfälzer Bergland – Kuseler Musikanten-land: Der schöne Landkreis Kusel* (special edition taken from *Pfalz am Rhein* from the years 1981, 1986, 1987, and 1988)
•*San Antonio Express,* April 13, 1913.

TRAVELS OF WANDERING MUSICIANS FROM PFALZ VILLAGES, 1861-1922

The numbers of passports (*Paßregister*) issued to wandering musicians (*Wandermusikanten*) from the Pfalz, as listed here for the various villages, indicate the degree of traveling activity by the *Wandermusikanten* of these villages between 1861 and 1922.

The source of this list is the *Musikantenmuseum* in Burg Lichtenberg, just outside Thallichtenberg, near Kusel. Located there is a 379-page *Paßregister* listing, by year, those who applied for passports during this period. The list includes the name of the traveler, his birth year, his town of residence, and the foreign location for which he was given permission to travel. (Starting in 1905, the age of the passport holder is given rather than the birth year.) All passport-holders are from the villages listed below.

The register contains 12,901 names, of which 12,343 represented *Wandermusikanten*.

No passports were issued in 1911, 1912, or 1915; only one passport was issued in 1919. Destinations as recorded on the passport records include Africa, America, Argentinia, Asia, Australia, Baden, Belgium, Brazil, China, Denmark, Germany, England, Finland, France, Greece, Holland, India, Italy, Japan, North America, Norway, Austria, Sweden, Switzerland, Siberia, South America, South Africa, Turkey, and Hungary. In 1996 the museum was open daily (except for some holidays) from 10 am until noon and from 2 until 5 pm.

Address: Musikantenmuseum, Burg Lichtenberg, 66871 Thallichtenberg, Germany. Tel. 06381/8429 or 06381/424109.

Passports issued 1861-1922

Adenbach	60
Albersbach	62
Altenglan	40
Aschbach	307
Becherbach	49
Bedesbach	25
Berzweiler	12
Blaubach	40
Bledesbach	10
Bosenbach	746
Cronenberg	73
Dennweiler-Frohnbach	15
Diedelkopf	1
Ehweiler	5
Einöllen	136
Eisenbach	5
Elzweiler	94
Eßweiler	904
Eschenau	16
Erdesbach	20
Etschberg	44
Föckelberg	83
Frankelbach	264
Friedelhausen	209
Frutzweiler	6
Gangloff	9
Gensweiler	71
Godelhausen	13
Gumbsweiler	39
Hachenbach	31
Haschbach	8
Hefersweiler	116
Heinzhausen	89
Herchweiler	25
Herschweiler-Pettersheim	28
Hinzweiler	365
Hohenöllen	275
Hoof	101
Horschbach	159
Hüffler	41
Hundheim	149
Jettenbach	2,695
Kaulbach	356
Kollweiler	256
Konken	28
Körborn	10
Kreimbach	334
Krottelbach	15
Kusel	33
Lauterecken	35
Liebsthal	20
Lohnweiler	99
Marth	6

*Journeyman tailor and seamstress,
mid-16th century*

GERMANY'S SCENIC ROUTES
(Ferienstraße)

♦ *Grüne Küstenstraße,* "Green Coastal
Route" (coastal marsh and meadowlands):
Pinneberg, North Sea coast, Tønder in
Denmark

♦ *Störtebekerstraße,* "Störtebecker Route"
(famous pirate, a kind of Robin Hood of
the seas): Leer, East Frisian coast, Cuxhaven, Stade

♦ *Alte Salzstraße,* "Old Salt Route" (salt
transport): Lüneburg, Nature Park of
Lauenburg Lakes, Lübeck

♦ *Deutsche Märchenstraße,* "German
Fairy Tale Route" (locations mentioned in
fairy tales by the Grimm brothers): Hanau,
Kassel, Weser valley, Bremen

♦ *Hamalandroute,* "Hamaland Route"
(region of Hamaland): Western Münsterland, Raesfeld, Wulfen

♦ *Osning-Route,* "Osnig Route" (Osnig
Mountain, part of the Teutoburg Forest):
Bad Laer, Osnabrück, Teutoburg Forest,
Detmold

♦ *Ahr-Rotweinstraße/Grüne Straße
Eifel-Ardennen/Deutsche Wildstraße,*
"Red Wine Route along River Ahr/Green
Route from Eifel Mountains to Ardennes/
German Game Route": Sinzig, Ahr Valley,
Daun, the Eifel, meeting point of Ger-
many, Belgium, and Luxemburg

♦ *Mosel-Wein-Straße,* "Mosel Wine Route":
French border, Trier, Mosel valley, Koblenz

♦ *Kannebäcker-/Bäderstraße,* "Pottery

Route/Spa Route": Montabauer, the Taunus mountans, Wiesbaden
* *Rheingau-Riesling-Route/Rheingoldstraße,* " Rhineland Route/Rhinegold Route" (Nibelungen saga): Wiesbaden, the Rheingau, castles of the Middle Rhine, Koblenz
* *Deutsche Edelsteinstraße,* "German Gem Route" (gem cutting and polishing industries): Idar-Oberstein, Idar Forest
w*Deutsche Weinstraße,* "German Wine Route": Bockenheim, Rheinhessen and Pfalz wine areas, Schweigen
* *Nibelungenstraße/Siegfriedstraße,* "Nibelungen Route/Siegfried Route": Worms, the Odenwald, Miltenberg
* *Burgenstraße,* "Route of Castles," Mannheim, the Odenwald, Rothenburg o.d.T., Nürnberg
•Bergstraße, "Mountain Route" (western slopes of the Odenwald mountains, Rhine): Darmstadt, Heidelberg, Karlsruhe
•Straße der Staufer, " Staufer Route" (Staufen dynasty of German kings and emperors, c. 1050-1268, Friedrich I, Barbarossa): Lorch, Schwäbisch Gmünd, Göppingen
* *Schwäbische Albstraße,* "Swabian Mountain Route": Aalen, Tuttlingen,
•Schwarzwaldbäderstraße, "Black Forest Spas Route": Northern Black Forest, Pforzheim, Hirsau, Nagold, and Freudenstadt, Wildbad, Bad Herrenalb
•Schwarzwaldhochstraße, "Black Forest Mountains Ridge Route": Black Forest, Baden-Baden, the Mummelsee, Kniebis, Gutachtal, Titisee, Waldshut-Tiengen
* *Oberschwäbische Barockstraße,* "Upper Swabian Baroque Route": Ochsenhausen, Birnau,Steinhausen, Zwiefalten
•Badische Weinstraße, "Wine Route of Baden,": Baden-Baden, wine area of the upper Rhine valley, Freiburg, Kaiserstuhl
* *Romantische Straße,* "Romantic Route": Würzburg, Dinkelsbühl, Nördlingen, Augsburg, Füssen, Neuschwanstein
* *Straße der Residenzen,* "Route of

Palaces": Aschaffenburg, Coburg, Bamberg, Nürnberg, Regensburg, Landshut, Salzburg
* *Fichtelgebirgsstraße/Bayerische Ostmarkstraße,* "Fichtelgebirge Route/ Bavaria's Eastern Region Route": Bad Berneck, Luisenburg, Oberpfälzer Forest, National Park of the Bavarian Forest, Passau
•Deutsche Alpenstraße, "German Alpine Route,": Allgäu Alps, Wetterstein- and Karwendelgebirges, Watzmann Mountain at Königsee
•Artlandroute, "Artland Route" (region of Artland): Dinklage, Ankum, Berge, Dinklage
* *Bier- und Burgenstraße,* "Beer and Castles Route": Kulmbach,Kronach, Lauenstein
•Bramgauroute, "Region of Bramgau": Neuenkirch, Hagenbeck, Neuenkirchen
•Deutsche Ferienstraße Alpen, "German Vacation Route from the Alps to the Baltic Sea": Puttgarden, Celle, Michelstadt, Kehlheim, Traunstein, Berchtesgaden
•Deutsche-französische Touristikroute, "German-French Tourist Route": Schweigen, Neustadt/Weinstraße, Bitche, Schweigen
•Deutsche Hopfenstraße, "German Hops Route" (hops growing area): Zolling, Au, Abensberg
* *Deutsche Schuhstraße,* "German Shoes Route" (shoe manufacturing industries): Waldfischbach, Leimen, Pirmasens, Dahn
* *Eichenlaubstraße,* "Oak Leaf Route" (oak forests): Oberlenken, Nonnweiler, Oberkirchen
* *Elbufer-Straße,* "Banks of the River Elbe Route": Schnackenburg, Gorleben, Niedermarschacht
•Elmhochstraße, "Elm Mountains Ridge Route": Helmstedt, Worlenbüttel
* *Feldbergstraße,* "Feldberg Route (mountain in the BlackForest): Freiburg, Titisee, Neustadt, Feldberg
•Ferienstraße Südeifel, "Soutern Eifel Mountains Route": Baustert, Nattenheim, Baustert

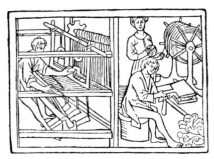

Wool-weaver at the loom and preparation of yarn, 1479

◆ *Frankenwaldhochstraße,* "Frankenwald Mountains Ridge Route": Steinwiesen, Nordhalben, Reichenbach, Rothenkirchen
◆ *Frankenwaldstraße,* "Frankenwald Mountains Route": Mitwitz, Kronach, Hof
◆ *Freundschaftsstraße,* "Friendship Route" (in commemoration of Franco-German friendship): Stuttgart, Straßburg, Metz
◆ *Glasstraße,* "Glass Route," (glassmaking industries): Fichtelberg, Warmensteinach, Bayreuth
◆ *Grüne Straße/Route Verte,* "Green Route" (dense forests): Epinal, Colmar, Freiburg, Donaueschingen, Lindau or Konstanz
w*Harz-Heide-Straße,* "Harz Mountains - Heathlands Route": Lüneburg, Braunschweig, Göttingen
◆ *Harz-Hochstraße,* "Harz Mountains Ridge Route": Seesen, Braunlage
◆ *Hochrhönring,* "Upper Rhön Mountains Circular Route": Kleinsassen, Oberhausen, Kleinsassen
◆*Hochrhönstraße,* "Upper Rhön Mountains Route,": Bischofsheim, Leu-bach, Fladungen
◆ *Hochtaunusstraße,* "Upper Taunus Mountains Route": Bad Homburg, Oberursel, Camberg
◆ *Hunsrück-Höhenstraße* "Hunsrück Mountains Ridge Route": Koblenz, Moorbach, Saarburg

◆ *Hunsrück Schieferstraße,* "Hunsrück Mountains Slate Route" (slate quarries): Kirn, Bundenbach, Simmern
◆ *Idyllische Straße,* "Idyllic Route": Welzheim, Spiegelberg, Eschach, Welzheim
◆*Kehlsteinstraße,* "Kehlstein Mountain Route" (to Adolf Hitler's mountain retreat): Obersalzberg, Kehlstein
◆ *Kesselbergstraße,* "Kesselberg Mountain Route": Kochel am See, Kesselberg, Walchensee
◆*Liebfrauenstraße,* "Route of Our Lady": Worms, Mainz
◆ *Loreley-Burgenstraße,* "Loreley and Castles Route": Kamp, St. Goarshausen, Kaub
◆*Nahe-Weinstraße,* "River Nahe Wine Route": Bad Kreuznach, Sobernheim, Schweppenhausen, Bad Kreuznach
◆*Nordstraße,* "Northern Route": Flensburg, Gundelsby, Kappeln
◆ *Obstmarschenweg,* "Marshlands-Orchards Route": Itzwörden, Stade, Neuenfelde
◆*Ostsee-Bäderstraße,* "Baltic Sea Spas Route": Travenmünde, Burg auf Fehmarn, Eckernförde, Glücksburg
◆*Panoramastraße,* "Panoramic Route": Bischofsgrün, Ochsenkopf, Fichtelberg
◆*Panoramastraße,* "Panoramic Route": Heppenschwant, Attlisberg, Höchenschwand
◆ *Panorama- und Saaletalstraße,* "Panoramic and Saale Valley Route":
◆*Porzellanstraße,* "China Route" (china manufacturing industries): Selb, Marktredwitz
◆*Roßfeld-Ringstraße,* "Rossfeld Mountain Circular Route": Berchtesgaden, Roßfeld, Berchtesgaden
◆ *Schauinslandstraße,* "Schauinsland Mountain Route": Freiburg, Todtnau
◆*Schwäbische Bäderstraße,* "Swabian Spas Route": Bad Buchau, Bad Wurzach, Bad Wörishofen
◆*Schwäbische Dichterstraße,* "Swabian Poets' Route": Bad Mergentheim, Marbach, Tübingen, Meersburg

Wool weaver with shuttle, shears and knife

♦ ***Schwäbische Weinstraße***, "Swabian Wine Route": Gundelsheim, Heilbronn, Esslingen

♦ ***Schwarzwald-Tälerstraße***, "Valleys of the Black Forest Route": Karlsruhe, Freudenstadt, Schenkenzell

♦ ***Spessart-Höhenstraße***, "Spessart Mountains Ridge Route": Steinau, Wiesen, Hösbach

♦ ***Spitzingstraße***, "Spitzing Mountain Area Route": Schliersee, Spitzingsee

♦ ***Steigerwald-Höhenstraße***, "Steigerwald Mountains Ridge Route": Ebersbach, Neustadt/Aisch, Uffenheim

♦ ***Totenkopfstraße***, "Skull Mountain Route (Route passes Skull Mountain, where ancient skeletons were found): Neustadt, Johanniskreuz

♦ ***Wesertalstraße***, "River Weser Valley Route": Münden, Höxter, Hameln, Minden

Partial Source: "Die schönsten Ferienstraßen in Deutschland," Grieben Reiseführer, Grieben Verlag, 1987.

POSTAL CODES: UNITED STATES AND CANADA

United States

AL	Alabama
AK	Alaska
AZ	Arizona
AR	Arkansas
CA	California
CO	Colorado
CT	Connecticut
DC	District of Columbia
DE	Delaware
FL	Florida
GA	Georgia
HI	Hawaii
ID	Idaho
IL	Illinois
IN	Indiana
IA	Iowa
KS	Kansas
KY	Kentucky
LA	Louisiana
ME	Maine
MD	Maryland
MA	Massachusetts
MI	Michigan
MN	Minnesota
MS	Mississippi
MO	Missouri
MT	Montana
NE	Nebraska
NV	Nevada
NH	New Hampshire
NJ	New Jersey
NM	New Mexico
NY	New Hork
NC	North Carolina
ND	North Dakota
OH	Ohio
OK	Oklahoma
OR	Oregon
PA	Pennsylvania
PR	Puerto Rico
RI	Rhode Island
SC	South Carolina
SD	South Dakota
TN	Tennessee

TX .... Texas
UT .... Utah
VT .... Vermont
VA .... Virginia
WA .... Washington
WV .... West Virginia
WI .... Wisconsin
WY .... Wyoming

Canada

AB .... Alberta
BC .... British Columbia
MB .... Manitoba
NB .... New Brunswick
NF .... Newfoundland
NS .... Nova Scotia
NT .... Northwest Territory
ON .... Ontario
PE .... Prince Edward Island
PQ .... Quebec
SK .... Saskatchewan
YK .... Yukon

TELEPHONING
TO AND FROM GERMANY

Calling Germany
from the United States

◆Dial 011, the code for reaching Europe; but a different code may be required for some long distance carriers and calling cards.

◆ Next, dial 49, the country code for Germany.

◆Next, dial the remaining digits of the telephone number, which consist of the area code* and the recipient's individual telephone number.

*The area code (*Vorwahl*), as usually printed on a business card, a letterhead, or an advertisement, begins with a zero. Note that German area codes may have 3, 4, or 5 digits, including the 0. The telephone number itself (the digits following the area code) consists of from 3 to 8 digits.

When calling from the United States, do not dial the zero which precedes the area code. It is needed only if the call is

placed within Germany from a location outside the calling area of the recipient. In other words, the zero serves the same purpose in Germany that the "1" serves in the United States; it is used in Germany only when the call is directed outside the caller's telephone area.

Example: Calling 0 64 32 4501, dial 011 49 64 32 4501

Calling the United States
from Germany

◆ Dial 001* (the country code for the United States and Canada).

◆Next, dial the area code and the individual's telephone number.

Example: Calling (415) 232-5555, dial 001 415 232 5555.

*Some calling cards may be used to call the United States.

Look for the toll-free access number in *USA Today* (European edition) or the *International Herald Tribune*.

SOME TELEPHONE
COUNTRY CODES

The following country codes are needed to call the respective countries *from the United States*.

To call these countries from Germany, add 00 before each code (Austria, 0043, etc.)

Note that the German words for the countries listed below are shown in parentheses:

◆Austria (*Österreich*): 43

◆Czech Republic (*Tschechische Republik*): 42

◆Denmark (*Dänemark*): 45

◆Finland (*Finnland*): 358

◆France (*Frankreich*): 33

◆Germany (*Deutschland*): 49

◆Great Britain and North Ireland (*Großbritannien und Nordirland*): 44

◆Hungary (*Ungarn*): 36

◆Ireland (*Irland*): 353

◆Italy (*Italien*): 39

◆Japan: 0081

Community life

•Latvia (*Lettland*): 371
•Liechtenstein: 41
•Lithuania (*Litauen*): 370
•Luxemburg: 352
•Netherlands (*Niederlande*): 31
•Northern Ireland (*Nordirland*): 0044
•Poland (*Polen*): 48
•Russia (*Russische Föderation*): 7
•Spain (*Spanien*): 34
•Sweden (*Schweden*): 46
•Switzerland (*Schweiz*): 41
•Norway (*Norwegen*): 47

TELEPHONE CONVERSATION ALPHABET KEY

The following set of spelling aids is commonly used in the German language, especially in telephone conversations when it may be difficult to distinguish the difference, for example, between the sounds d and t, s and f, p and b, and so on.

A	Anton
Ä	Ärger
B	Berta
C	Cäsar
CH	Charlotte
D	Dora
E	Emil
F	Friedrich
G	Gustav
H	Heinrich
I	Ida
J	Julius
K	Kaufmann
L	Ludwig
M	Martha
N	Nordpol
O	Otto
Ö	Ökonom
P	Paula
Q	Quelle
R	Richard

S .... Samuel
Sch .... Schule
T .... Theodor
U .... Ulrich
Ü .... Übermut
V .... Viktor
W .... Wilhelm
X .... Xanthippe
Y .... Ypsilon
Z... Zacharias

HOME AND COMMUNITY SOURCES FOR SEARCHING GERMAN FAMILY HISTORY

Clues useful to family history projects may surface through examination of any of the following sources — from one's own family members, as well as from the community.

From family members

◆Family Bible: For family birth-marriage-death records, also for scraps of papers, programs, letters, and other miscellanea tucked haphazardly among the pages

◆Old letters: Some letters may be from Germany. If they are still inside their envelopes, they may reveal a location and a date. Old letters mailed from within the United States may be equally valuable.

◆Newspaper clippings

◆ Old photographs and albums: The pictures may themselves provide clues; also, names and dates may be written on their reverse sides.

◆Family scrapbooks, journals, diaries, histories, autograph books, personal address books, receipt books

◆Needlework containing a family name or date

◆Newspaper clippings or notes on births, marriages, deaths, retirements, awards, and other events

◆Certificates of any kind

◆Birth announcements

◆Baptismal certificates

◆Wedding announcements, invitations

◆Memorial cards or funeral cards/folders

◆Passports (often contain names of parents and grandparents)

◆ Citizenship papers: Particularly the "Declaration of Intent" papers, or naturalization papers, or citizenship certificates

◆Land records: Deeds, mortgage papers, other official papers regarding purchase or sale of land

◆ Military records: Pension files, applications, correspondence, discharge papers — all papers regarding military service

◆School report cards, diplomas

◆School notebooks or essays containing biographical information

◆School yearbooks

◆Passports

◆Family traditions and treasures: Stories collected through interviews of family members

◆ Old family artifacts, which may be imprinted or otherwise marked with the name of a place of origin or of manufacture

From community sources

◆Cemetery office records

The baker

♦Tombstone inscriptions
♦Mortuary records
♦Vital records (birth, marriage, and death records)
♦Paraphernalia and records from professional organizations, lodges, fraternal societies
♦City directories
♦German-American newspapers, other newspapers
♦Trade journals
♦County atlases, county plat books, insurance maps
♦County histories
♦Family genealogies, family histories
♦Local histories
♦Genealogical magazines, newsletters
♦ Wills, probate records, other papers related to a death
♦Other court records
♦Passenger arrival lists, ship arrival lists
♦Federal census records
♦State census records
♦Alien registrations

GERMAN WEIGHTS AND MEASURES

Linear measure
1mm **Millimeter** (millemeter)
=1/1000 meter
=0.03937079 inches
1 cm **Zentimeter** (centimeter)
=1/100 meter
=0.9370 inches
1 dm **Dezimeter** (decimeter)
=1/10 meter
=3.9370 inches
1 m **Meter** (meter)
=1.0936 yards
=3.2809 feet
=39.37079 inches
1 km **Kilometer** (kilometer)
=1,000 metres
=1,093.637 yards
=3,280.8692 feet
=39,370.79 inches

Square measure
1m Quadratmeter (square meter)
=1.19599 square yards
=10.7641 square feet
=1,550 square inches
1 **a Ar** (are)
=100 square meters
=119.5993 square yards
=1,076.4103 square feet
1 **ha Hektar** (hectare)
=100 acres
= 10,000 square meters
= 247.11 acres
=0.3861 square miles
1km^2 **Quadratkilometer** (square kilometer)
=1,000 cubic millimeters
=0.061 cubic inches
Cubic measure
1cm^3 **Kubikzentimeter** (cubic centimeter)
1 m^3 **Kubikmeter** (cubic meter),
1 rm **Raummeter** (cubic meter),
1 fm Festmeter (cubic meter)
=1,000 cubic decimeters
=1.3079 cubic yards
=35.3156 cubic feet
1 RT **Registertonne** (register ton)
=2.832m^3
=100 cubic feet
1l Liter (liter)
=10 deciliters
=1.7607 pints (Br.)
= 7.0431 gills (Br.
=0.2201 gallons (Br.)
=2.1134 pints (Am.)
=8.4534 gills (Am.)
=1.0567 quarts (Am.)
=0.2642 gallons (Am.)
1 hl Hektoliter (hectoliter
=100 liters
=22.009 (Br.)
=2.751 bushels (Br.)
=26.418 gallons (Am.)
=2.84 bushels (Am.)
Weights
1 mg Milligram (milligram)
=1/1000 gram
=0.0154 grains

1 **g Gramm** (gram)
    =1/1000 kilogram
    =15.4324 grains
1 **Pfd Pfund** pound (German)
    =½ kilogram
    =500 grams
    = 1.1023 pounds (avdp.)
    = 1.3396 pounds (troy)
1 **kg Kilogramm**, Kilo (kilogram)
    =1,000 grams
    =2.2046 pounds (advp.)
    =2.6792 pounds (troy)

1 **Ztr Zentner** (centner)
    =100 pounds (German)
    =50 kilograms
    =110.23 pounds (advp)
1 **dz Doppelzentner**
    =100 kilograms
    =1.9684 British hundred-
    weights
    2.2046 U.S. hundred-weights
1 **t Tonne** (ton)
    =1,000 kilograms
    =0.984 British tons
    =1.1023 U.S. tons

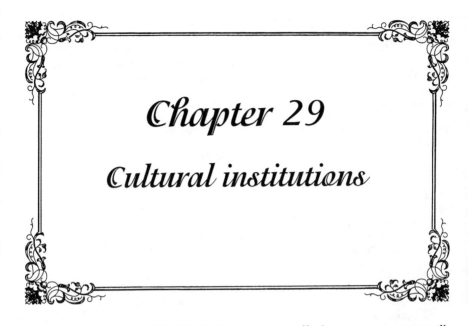

Chapter 29

Cultural institutions

GOETHE INSTITUT

The Goethe-Institut is a worldwide organization whose mission is to foster appreciation for the German language and culture in its host countries, to contribute to international understanding, and to enhance the intercultural dialog with other countries.

The organization has some 170 centers in 80 countries around the world, 15 of which are in North America.

Activities

◆The Language Division develops and implements continuing education projects for teachers of German in association with universities, education departments, and teachers' associations.

◆The German American Partnership Program enables students to experience life in German schools and families through exchange.

◆The 17 Goethe-Institutes in Germany offer intensive language courses for all levels. Most Goethe-Institutes in North America offer language courses as well.

◆Together with North American cultural institutions, Goethe-Institut organizes programs in the arts and humanities, exploring topics pertinent to German-American and German-Canadian relations, cohosting and cosponsoring film series, conferences, readings, lectures, exhibitions, concerts, dance and theater performances and media and computer-related events.

◆Most of the 15 branch institutes which have opened since the end of the Cold War are located in the countries of eastern Europe and the former Soviet Union. The first in eastern Germany opened in Weimar in May 1996.

Libraries

Almost all the Goethe-Institutes in North America offer resource centers, most in the form of libraries containing works in both English and German, with emphasis on reference materials and on modern communication technologies.

Goethe-Institut's homepage may be reached at http://www.goethe.de.

GOETHE-INSTITUT
IN THE UNITED STATES

•**Ann Arbor**
Goethe-Institut
City Center Building
220 East Huron, Suite 210
Ann Arbor, MI 48104
Tel: (313) 996-8600
Fax (313) 996-0777
E-mail:
goethe@goetheannarbor.org

•**Atlanta**
Goethe-Institut
German Cultural Center
Colony Square, Plaza Level
1197 Peachtree Street, NE
Atlanta, GA 30361-2401
Tel: (404) 892-2388
Fax (404) 892-3832
E-mail:
goethe@post.peach.net

•**Boston**
Goethe-Institut
German Cultural Center for New England
170 Beacon Street
Boston, MA 02116
Tel: (617) 262-6050
Fax (617) 262-2615
E-mail:
100627.1010@compuserve.com

•**Chicago**
Goethe-Institut
German Cultural Center
401 North Michigan Avenue
Chicago, IL 60611
Tel: (312) 329-0915, 329-0917
Fax (312) 329-2487
E-mail:
gipro@interaccess.com

•**Cincinnati**
Goethe-Institut
559 Liberty Hill, Pendelton House
Cincinnati, OH 45210
Tel: (513) 721-2777
Fax (513) 721-4136
E-mail:
goethe@uc.edu

•**Houston**
Goethe-Institut
German Cultural Center
3120 Southwest Freeway, Suite 100
Houston, TX 77098
Tel: (713) 528-2787
Fax (713) 528-4023
E-mail:
goethehou@aol.com

•**Los Angeles**
Goethe-Institut
5700 Wilshire Boulevard 110
(corner of Masselin)
Los Angeles, CA 90036
Tel: (213) 525-3388
Fax (213) 934-3597
E-mail:
gila@artnet.net

•**New York**
Goethe House New York/
German Cultural Center
1014 Fifth Avenue
New York, NY 10028
Tel: (212) 439-8700
Fax (212) 439-8705
E-mail:
library@goethenewyork.org

•**San Francisco**
Goethe-Institut
530 Bush Street
San Francisco, CA 94108
Tel: (415) 391-0370
Fax (415) 391-8715
E-mail:
gisfprog@aol.com

•**Seattle**
Goethe-Institut
Mutual Life Building
605 First Avenue, Suite 401
Seattle, WA 98104
Tel: (206) 622-9694
Fax (206) 623-7930
E-mail:
goethe@eskimo.com

•**St. Louis**
Goethe-Institut
326 North Euclid Avenue, 2nd Floor
South
St. Louis, MO 63108

Tel: (314) 367-2452
Fax (314) 367-9439
E-mail:
goethesl@attmail.com
◆**Washington, DC**
Goethe-Institut
1607 New Hampshire Avenue, N.W.
Washington, D.C. 20009
Tel: (202) 319-0702
Fax (202) 319-0705
E-mail:
goethedc@artswire.org

GOETHE-INSTITUTE IN CANADA

◆**Toronto**
Goethe-Institut Canada
Goethe-Institut
1067, Younge Street
Toronto, Ont., M4W 2L2
Tel: (416) 924-3327
Fax (416) 924-0589
E-mail:
goethetoront@cis.compuserve.com
◆**Vancouver**
Goethe-Institut
German Cultural Center
944, West 8th Avenue
Vancouver, B.C., V5Z 1E5
Tel: (604) 732-3966
Fax (604) 732-5062
E-mail:
libr@goethe-van.org
◆**Montreal**
Goethe-Institut
418, Sherbrooke est
Montreal, P.Q., H2L 1J6
Tel: (514) 499-0159
Fax (514) 499-0905
E-mail:
goethe-institut.montreal @uqam.ca

GOETHE-INSTITUT IN GERMANY

◆**Berlin**
Goethe Institut

Friedrichstrasse 209
10969 Berlin
Germany
E-mail:
berlin@goethe.de
Fax: (030) 25906-3
◆**Bonn**
Goethe Institut
Friedrich-Ebert Strasse. 11
53177 Bonn
E-mail:
bonn@goethe.de
Fax: (0228) 95756-23
◆**Boppard**
Goethe-Institut
Helene-Pagés-Strasse 9
56154 Boppard
E-mail:
boppard@goethe.de
Fax: (06742) 81619
◆**Bremen**
Goethe Institut
Fedelhören 78
28203 Bremen
E-mail:
 bremen@goethe.de
Fax: (0421) 325242
◆**Düsseldorf**
Goethe-Institut
Willi-Becker-Allee 10
Postfach 102603
40227 Düsseldorf
E-mail:
duesseldorf@goethe.de
Fax: (0211) 771084
◆**Frankfurt am Main**
Goethe-Institut
Hedderichstr. 108-110
60596 Frankfurt am Main
E-mail:
frankfurt@goethe.de
Fax: (069) 20395
◆**Freiburg**
Goethe-Institut
Wilhelmstr. 17
79098 Freiburg
E-mail:
freiburg@goethe.de
Fax: (0761) 38671-15

◆**Göttingen**
Goethe-Institut
Merkelstr. 4
Fridtjof-Nansen-Haus
37085 Göttingen
E-mail:
goettingen@goethe.de
Fax: (0551) 43103
◆**Iserlohn**
Goethe-Institut
Stennerstr. 4
58636 Iserlohn
E-mail:
iserlohn@ goethe.de
Fax: (02371) 828333
◆**Mannheim** Goethe-Institut
Steubenstsr. 44
68163 Mannheim
E-mail:
mannheim@goethe.de
◆**München]:**
Goethe-Institut
Sonnenstr. 25
80331 München
E-mail:
muenchen@goethe.de
Fax: (089) 55190335
◆**München**
Goethe Institut
Goethestr. 20
80336 München
Germany
Fax: (089) 55190345
◆**Murnau**
Goethe Institut
Seidlstr. 17
82418 Murnau
E-mail:
murnau@goethe de
Fax: (08841) 3391
◆**Prien**
Goethe-Institut
Goethestr. 1
83209 Prien
E-mail:
prien@goethe.de
Fax: (08051) 61625
◆**Rothenburg**
Goethe-Institut

Herrengasse 17
91541 Rothenburg o.d.T.
E-mail:
rothenburg@goethe.de
Fax: (09861) 86418
◆**Schwäbisch Hall**
Goethe- Institut
Am Spitalbach 8
74523 Schwäbisch Hall
E-mail:
schwaebisch-hall@goethe.de
Fax: (0791) 8713
◆**Staufen**
Goethe Institut
Grunerner Str. 3
79219 Staufen
E-mail: staufen@goethe.de
Fax: (07633) 950622

THE GERMAN INFORMATION CENTER

German Information Center
950 Third Avenue
New York, NY 10022*
Tel. (212) 888-9840
Fax: (212) 752-6691
E-mail: Compuserve 74667,3145;
Internet gic1@ix.netcom.com
Internet: http://www.germany-info.org
***Note:** The address of the German Information Center is scheduled to change around 1998 to: 871 United Nations Plaza, NY 10016. It is uncertain at this writing as to whether the telephone number will remain the same.

Hours
Monday-Thursday, 8:30 am to 12 noon and 1 pm to 5 pm; Friday 8:30 am to 12 noon and 1 pm to 3:30 pm.

Programs
The German Information Center in New York welcomes media professionals, students, and researchers to use its resources for information about many aspects of German life.

The German Information Center should not, however, be considered a genealogical resource.

Fact-checkers from major publications regularly use German Information Center services to ensure accuracy in writing stories pertaining to individual Germans and topics concerning Germany.

Library

The library's 3,500-volume library is open to the public. Most of its books are written in German, although quite a few English-language books are included as well. Political, historical and economic texts make up the bulk of the collection.

Access to the German Information Center's archive is available upon request. Since 1961, it has collected newspaper clippings, press releases, and government publications on a broad range of topics.

Areas of particular concentration are German domestic politics, German-American relations, German social policy, and environmental protection.

The German Information Center is a major source of information on Germany, but it does *not* cover such topics as family history, tourism, culture, and business.

Publications

The Week in Germany, an eight page free newsletter in English, provides to 40,000 readers the latest information on politics, the economy, sports and the arts in Germany.

The editors of *The Week in Germany*, who work hard to guard against its becoming a propaganda tool, present a comprehensive and balanced picture of German life.

Deutschland Nachrichten is an eight-page weekly newsletter in German that covers politics, economics, cultural, and spports news from Germany, as well as a review of German newspaper editorials.

Subscriptions to both these publications are free upon request.

DEUTSCHE WELLE

Deutsche Welle, Germany's international broadcasting service since 1953, provides radio and TV programs geared toward portraying accurate and comprehensive pictures of political, cultural and economic life in Germany, as well as to present objective reports on world events.

Deutsche Welle tv (DW-tv)

Produced in Berlin and Cologne, current affairs television programming via satellite operates 24 hours a day: 12 hours in German, 10 in English and two in Spanish. Several hundred television stations and cable operators rebroadcast DW-tv's satellite programs.

Deutsche Welle radio (DW-radio)

Deutsche Welle's radio programs are broadcast from Cologne in German and in 38 other languages via satellite to all regions of the world, on short, medium, and ultra-short wave.

The centerpiece of DW-radio is the German program, transmitted in an eight-hour format: the news is broadcast on the hour, short news bulletin every half hour, and a current affairs magazine program every two hours. Topics focus on politics, economics, culture and sports. Deutsche Welle-radio can be received worldwide in German and English.

Reception of DW-tv and DW-radio

DW-tv can be received everywhere in the world via a global satellite network. It is received via INTELSAT-K on the American East Coast and Latin America, and via SATCOM C-4 in North America and the Caribbean.

To learn on what channel Deutsch Welle tv may be found, check with the local cable company.

DW-radio programs are broadcast to all regions of the world via 37 short wave

Menno Simons, Mennonite founder

and 2 medium wave transmitters. Several thousand rebroadcasting partners distribute the programming worldwide.

Online-service

Deutsche Welle may be accessed worldwide via its online service Internet http://www-dw.gmd.de/DW and Compu-Serve (Forum "Germany Online," section "Deutsche Welle," data file DWINFO).

For further information

Deutsche Welle
Raderberggürtel 50
50968 Köln, Germany
Tel.: 0221/389-2041/42
Fax: 0221/389-2047

DEUTSCHE WELLE TELEVISION PROGRAMS

Abbreviations

G: broadcast in German
E: broadcast in English
AE: American English
(Languages in which these programs are broadcast other than German and English are not indicated in the list below.)

Programs

◆Journal: The News Magazine [*Journal:*

Das Nachrichtenmagazin], 30 min./G,E
◆Journal, 15 min./G,E
◆News & Compact: The Week in Review [*Compact: Der Wochenrückblick*], G,E
◆ Perspectives: Magazine on Politics [*Standpunkte: Das Politik-Magazin*], once weekly/G,E
◆Inside Bonn: German Politics [*Plenum: Das bundespolitische Magazin*], once weekly/G,E
◆D 16: Germany's Federal States [*D 16: Das Bundesländer-Magazin*], once weekly/G,E
◆Regarding. . . The Story of the Week [*Betrifft. . . Das Thema der Woche*], once weekly/G,E
◆*Das Interview*, 30 min., twice monthly/G
◆ Made in Germany: The Business Maga-zine [*Made in Germany: Das Wirtschafts-magazin*], once weekly/G,E
◆ Boulevard Germany [*Boulevard Deutschland*], 45 min., weekdays/G,E
◆Germany Live [Schauplatz Deutschland], view of everyday German life, once month-ly/G,E
◆Alice [magazine on German regional cultures], once monthly/G,E
◆ European Journal [*Drehscheibe Europa*], everyday European life, once weekly/G,E
◆Focus on Europe [*Focus Europa*] twice monthly, G,E
◆ H.E.A.T.: Hits, Entertainment and Topics [*100 Grad: Das junge Magazin*], week-ends/G,E
◆Arts Unlimited [*Kunst & Co.*], weekly/G,E
◆ Bookmark: Reports for Readers [*Buchhandlung: Ein Magazin für Leser*], once monthly/G,E
◆*Lesezeit: Große deutsche Schauspieler lesen große deutsche Literatur*, 30 min./G
◆Eco/Echo: The Environment Magazine [*Noah: Das Umweltmagazin*]/G,E
◆Tomorrow - Today: Millennium Magazine [*Leonardo: Das Zukunftsmagazin*] once monthly/G,E

◆Sport-Report, 15 min., weekends/G
◆ *Doppelpass*, on the German soccer league/G
◆Sports Report/G,E
◆World Sport Special: A Week of International Sport [*Sport Special: Eine Woche Sport international*], 30 min., weekly/G,E
◆*Streifzüge durch die Klassik*, interpretations of classical music, monthly/G
◆B.I.G. : Big in Germany: Top 10, Big in Germany: Top 40 [*B.I.G.: Die deutschen Top 10, die deutschen Top 40*], 30 min., Wednesdays and Thursdays/G,E
◆ *Das deutsche Schlagermagazin*, German music chart hits, once monthly/G
◆ *Lustige Musikanten*, folk music program, one hour/G
◆*Presseclub*, current events roundtable/G
◆Inside Report [*Die ZDF-Reportage*]/G,E
◆*Politbarometer*, once monthly/G
◆ Theme: Germany, News from the Federal States [*Länderspiegel*]/G,E
◆ *Boulevard Bio: Talkshow mit Alfred Biolek*/G
◆Health-Cast [*Tele-Praxis*]/G,E
◆ *Forscher-Fakten-Visionen: Das Wissen-schaftsmagazin*, science magazine/G
◆ *Zukunftsgespräche* [guest conversations] /G
◆Treasures of the World: Heritage of Mankind [*Schätze der Welt: Erbe der Menschheit*], once weekly/G,E
◆Church & Society [*Zur Zeit*], 15 min., once weekly/G,E
◆Oldtimers: Youthful Love for Old Brass [*Oldtimer: Altes Blech, junge Liebe*], old cars/G,E
◆Video Timeline [*Video-Chronik*], postwar documentaries/G,E
◆ *Bilder aus der Schweiz: Ländermagazin*, events, stories from German-speaking part of Switzerland, once weekly/G
◆*Bilder aus Österreich: Ländermagazin*,

focus on Austria, once weekly/G
◆*Das Fernsehspiel*, drama, Saturdays/G
◆Apropos, behind-the-scenes of drama production, once weekly/G
◆The Current Feature Report [*Nahaufnahme*], varied topics, 30 min., Mondays/G,E
◆ Was?: The Language Course [*Was? Der Sprachkurs*], for young viewers learning German/G, AE

GENEALOGICAL INSTITUTES CONFERENCES, LEARNING PROGRAMS

◆**National Institute of Genealogical Research (NIGR)**
P.O. Box 14274
Washington, DC 20044-4274
◆**Samford University's Institute of Genealogy and Historical Research (IGHR)**
Samford University Library
Birmingham, AL 35229
Tel. (205) 870-2780
◆**Institute of Genealogical Studies (IGS)**
Dallas Genealogical Society
P.O. Box 25556
Dallas, TX 75225-1556
◆**Ohio Genealogical Society Workshop**
P.O. Box 2625
Mansfield, OH 44906-0625
◆**Genealogical Institute of Mid-America**
University of Illinois at Springfield
Springfield, IL 62794-9243
Tel. (217) 786-7464
◆**Salt Lake Institute of Genealogy**
P.O. Box 1144
Salt Lake City, UT 84110-1144
◆**Virginia Institute of Genealogical Research (VIGR)**
Virginia Genealogical Society
5001 West Broad Street, Suite 115
Richmond, VA 23230-3023
National conferences
◆**NGS Conference in the States**
4527 17th Street, North

Arlington, VA 22207-2399
◆FGS Conference for the Nation's Genealogists
P.O. Box 830220
Richardson, TX 75083
◆Brigham Young University, Genealogy and Family History Conference
Conferences and Workshops
136 Harman Building
Provo, UT 84602
◆GENTECH, Inc.[computers and genealogy conference]
P.O. Box 28021
Dallas, TX 75228-0021
Home study courses
◆The National Genealogical Society's Home Study Course
NGS Education Division
4527 17th Street, North
Arlington, VA 22207-2399
◆The Brigham Young University Independent Study Course
Brigham Young University
Department of Independent Studies
P.O. Box 21514
Provo, UT 84602-1514
(801) 378-6053

Source: Patricia Law Hatcher, "Educational Opportunities in Genealogy: Part I, Formal Instruction. *Ancestry*, Salt Lake City, May/June 1996.

BALCH INSTITUTE FOR ETHNIC STUDIES

Balch Institute for Ethnic Studies
18 South Seventh Street
Philadelphia, PA 19106
Tel. (215) 925-8090
Fax: (215) 925-8195

The Balch Institute for Ethnic Studies is devoted to the ongoing collection and interpretation of materials focusing on American ethnic, racial and immigration experiences from an historical and contemporary perspective.

The Library of the Balch Institute is the only library in the country that collects printed and manuscript sources on all racial and ethnic groups in America. Its collections consist of more than 60,000 volumes, 5,000 linear feet of manuscript materials, 6,000 reels of microfilm, and 12,000 photographs documenting the experiences of more than 80 ethnic and racial groups in the United States.

Records relating to Germans are reflected through newspapers, diaries, church histories, German organizations, and original documents, to name a few. The registers and inventories described in the "Guide to Manuscript and Microfilm Collections of the Research Library of the Balch Institute for Ethnic Studies" are available through interlibrary loan.

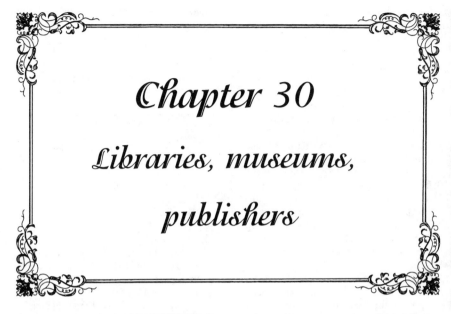

Chapter 30

Libraries, museums, publishers

PUBLIC LIBRARIES IN GERMANY

The most important public research libraries are in Munich (Bavarian State Library), Berlin (State Library of the Prussian Cultural Heritage Foundation), Frankfurt am Main (The German Library, including the Federal Republic's bibliographical center) and Leipzig (German Library). The German Library in Frankfurt am Main has at least one copy of all books published in the German language since 1945.

Source: *Federal Republic of Germany: Questions and Answers,* ed. Susan Steiner. German Information Center, New York, 1996.

TOWARD A 'NATIONAL' LIBRARY IN GERMANY

Great libraries of all sizes and specialties Germany has in abundance. What it lacks is a central national library like the

Library of Congress or the British Library that serves as a copyright repository collection. The German Library (*Die deutsche Bücherei*) in Leipzig took on that role, but only beginning in 1913, some four and a half centuries after Gutenberg opened the age of print with the invention of movable type.

With the division of Germany after World War II, the German Library (*Die deutsche Bibliothek*) in Frankfurt has also functioned as a copyright collection, but only for books printed during the 20th century. Books printed before 1913, however, are scattered in various collections around the country; the lack of a central registry or catalog often renders them inaccessible to any but the most determined researcher.

In 1990, in recognition of the lack of a national library, five major libraries joined forces to build as complete a collection as possible of books printed in Germany since 1450. The "Collection of German Imprints 1450-1912" is to be a "virtual" one – each of the five libraries has been assigned a period of time and asked to collect the books printed in Germany (or in the lands that became part of modern Germany) during that period as completely as possible. The researcher will be able to find the location of books through a general catalog that can be accessed online.

Responsibility for making acquisitions has been divided among the five libraries according to their existing strengths:
◆**Bavarian State Library, Munich:** First centuryand a half of printing
◆**Herzog August Library, Wolfenbüttel (Lower Saxony):** Seventeenth century
◆**University Library of Göttingen (Lower Saxony):** Eighteenth century
◆**Frankfurt's Public and University Library:** 1801-1870
◆**Prussian State Library, Berlin:** 1871-1912

Although the results of the libraries' first five years of collecting were impressive, many titles are still lacking.

Of the estimated one million titles printed during the nineteenth century, for example, about one-third were destroyed and are lost forever.

Of the two-thirds remaining, experts estimate, the Frankfurt Public and University Library's comprehensive collection of early- and mid nineteenth-century works encompasses all but 100,000-150,000 titles.

Coming up with those missing works could take another half century.[1]

Note: Although the German words *Bücherei* and *Bibliothek* both translate as "library," it is important to distinguish between *Die deutsche Bücherei Leipzig,* which was the first site of collected German works, and *Die deutsche Bibliothek,* the national collection held in five locations.

Addresses of the two traditional sites for the German library system are,
◆**Deutsche Bücherei Leipzig**
Deutscher Platz 1
04103 Leipzig
Tel.: (0341) 22 7a-309

◆**Deutsche Bibliothek Frankfurt a.M.**
Zeppelinallee 4 - 8
60325 Frankfurt am Main
Tel.: (069) 75 66-372

[1]*The Week in Germany,* October 20, 1995. German Information Center, New York.

SELECTED LARGE AMERICAN LIBRARIES WITH GERMAN GENEALOGICAL HOLDINGS

◆**Allen County Public Library**
900 Webster Street
P.O. Box 2270
Fort Wayne, IN 46801-2270
Tel. (219) 424-7241, ext. 3315
Fax: (219) 422-9688
Library hours: Every day, but closed on Sundays from Memorial Day weekend through Labor Day.

The Fred J. Reynolds Historical Genealogy Department holds 220,000 printed volumes and 253,000 items of microfilm and microfiche; also, among many other items, all federal populations schedules and many state censuses; more than 30,000 R.L. Polk city directories; almost 40,000 family histories; *Deutsches Geschlecterbuch*; Siebmacher's *Grossem Allgemeinem Wappenbuch*; headquarters of the Periodical Source Index (PERSI).

See Karen B. Cavanaugh, *A Genealogist's Guide to the Fort Wayne Indiana Library,* 3rd ed., Cavanaugh, Fort Wayne, 1983.

◆**Denver Public Library**
Western History/Genealogy
10 West Fourteenth Avenue Parkway
Denver, CO 80204-2731
Tel. (303) 640-8800; Social Sciences/Genealogy: (303) 640-8870
Fax, Social Sciences/Genealogy: (303) 640-4726
◆**Detroit Public Library**
5201 Woodward Avenue
Detroit, MI 48202
Tel. (313) 833-1000

Fax: (313) 832-0877
[The library's Burton Historical Collection holds all the sources used in Filby's Passenger and Immigration Lists Index. A library form is sent upon request for sources, requiring a $10 research fee in advance. Copies are 20 cents per page; $2.00 is charged for postage and handling.]
♦Los Angeles Library System
630 W. Fifth Street
Los Angeles, CA 90071-2097
Tel. (213) 228-7000
Fax: (213) 228-7429
[Among the library's holdings are all 203 volumes of the Deutsches Geschlechterbuch; about 10,000 family history titles, of which about 20 percent of which are not in the Library of Congress; 102 volumes of J. Siebmacher's Grosses und Allgemeines Wappenbuch; passenger arrival lists of ships docking in San Francisco, Boston, and Philadelphia, and records for New York ships between 1820 and 1846; many local histories; an exellent map and newspaper collection.]
♦New York Public Library
Fifth Avenue at 42nd Street
New York, NY 10018
Tel. (212) 930-0800
U.S. History, Local History, and Genealogy Division: (212) 930-0829
Fax: (212) 921-2546
♦Newberry Library
60 W. Walton Street
Chicago, IL 60610-3394
Tel. (312) 943-9090
Reference: (312) 255-3506
Genealogy: (312) 255-3512
[See Guide to Local and Family History at the Newberry Library, by Peggy Sinko, 1989 (available through Heritage Quest].
♦Sutro Library
[branch of the California State Library, Sacramento]
480 Winston Drive
San Francisco, CA 94132
Tel. (415) 731-4477
Fax: (415) 557-9325

[The Sutro Library houses the largest collection of genealogical materials west of Salt Lake City, including more than 10,000 family histories]
Special collections: Royal and noble genealogy; heraldry and vexillology; Crusades, knighthood, chivalry; historical maps; insignia, medials and decorations; medieval Europe; the Celts; archaeology and anthropology)
♦State Historical Society of Wisconsin Library
816 State Street
Madison, WI 53706
Tel. (608) 264-6534
Fax: (608) 264-6520
[This library has probably the largest collection of German newspapers and the largest general newspaper collection except for the National Archives. It also holds all Wisconsin newspapers and many ethnic newspapers.]
♦Major resources
See elsewhere in this book for information about the Family History Library in Salt Lake City and about the National Archives and Records Administration.

LIBRARY OF CONGRESS

♦The Library of Congress
Washington, DC 20540
Tel.: (202) 707-5000
Fax: (202) 707-5844
Reference tel.: (202) 707-6200
Reference fax: (202) 507-1389
Recorded information
numbers
Reading room hours: (202) 707-6400
Researchers: (202) 707) 6500
Directions: (202) 707-4700
Thomas Jefferson Building
1st Street, SE between East Capitol Street and Independence Avenue
James Madison
Memorial Building
Independence Avenue between 1st and 2nd Streets, SE

John Adams Building
2nd Street, SE between East Capitol Street and Independence Avenue
Maps
Library of Congress
Geography and Map Division
Washington, DC 20540
Photoduplication
Library of Congress
Photoduplication Service
Washington, DC 20540-5230
Publications
Library of Congress
Catalog Distribution Service
Customer Services Division
Washington, DC 20540-5017
Local History and Genealogy Reading Room
Location: Thomas Jefferson Building ("LJ"), ground floor
Card catalogs for this reading room:
♦Family Name Index

♦Analyzed Surname Index
♦U.S. Biographical Index
♦Coats-of-arms Index
♦Subject Catalog
♦Local History Shelf List
♦Computer catalog (for books added to the collection since 1980)

For a comprehensive guide to the Library of Congress, for use by genealogists, see *The Center: A Guide to Genealogical Research in the National Capital Area*, by Christina K. Schaefer. Genealogical Publishing Company, Inc. , Baltimore, 1996; this guide is the source of the information above.

SAMPLING OF SMALLER U.S. LIBRARIES WITH GERMAN-AMERICAN HOLDINGS

Below are listed a few of the many United States libraries with collections offering information related to German family history research.

In brackets after most listings is a brief description of the collection or holding that gives the library its special interest to German family historians. Each holdings category named below is only one of several other special-interest topics for which the library is known.

♦**Weld Library District**
Lincoln Park Branch, Special Collections
919 7th Street
Greeley, CO 80631
Tel.: (970) 350-9210
[Germans from Russia: history, genealogy, personal reminiscences]
♦**University of Illinois**
Illinois Historical Survey
346 Main Library
1408 W. Gregory Drive
Urbana, IL 61801
Tel.: (217) 333-0790
Fax: (217) 244-4358
[German immigration]
♦**St. Louis Public Library**

Rare Book & Special Collections
Department
Central Library
1301 Olive Street
St. Louis, MO 63103-2389
Tel.: (314) 241-2288
Fax: (314) 241-3840
[German-American Heritage Archives]
◆**Wagner College**
Horrmann Library
631 Howard Avenue
Staten Island, NY 10301
Tel.: (718) 390-3401
Fax: (718) 390-3107
[German-American Newspapers – 118
reels of microfilm]
◆**University of Cincinnati**
German-Americana Collection
Blegen Library
P.O. Box 210033
Cincinnati, OH 45221-0133
Tel. (513) 556-1515
Fax: (513) 556-6325
[German-American literature, history,
and culture]
◆**Ursinus College**
Myrin Library
Special Collections
Collegeville, PA 19426-1000
Tel.: (610) 489-4111
Fax: (610) 489-0634
[Pennsylvania German culture, German
Reformed Church]
◆**Washington State University**
Manuscripts, Archives, & Special
Collections
Pullman, WA 99164-5610
Tel.: (509) 335-4558
Fax: (509) 335-6721
[Germans from Russia]
◆**Historical Society of Berks County**
Library
940 Centre Avenue
Reading, PA 19601
Tel.: (610) 375-4375
Fax: (610) 375-4376
[German-Americans in Pennsylvania]
◆**German Society of Pennsylvania**
Joseph Horner Memorial Library

611 Spring Garden Street
Philadelphia, PA 19123
Tel.: (215) 627-4365
Fax: (215) 627-5297
[German history, biography, literature –
85% in German language; Americana-
Germanica special collection]
◆**Franklin and Marshall College**
Shadek-Fackenthal Library
P.O. Box 3003
Lancaster, PA 17604-3003
Tel.: (717) 291-4216
Fax: (717) 291-4160
E-mail: K_Spencer@FandM.edu
[German American Imprint Collection –
2500 volumes, 350 fraktur]
◆**Muhlenberg College**
Harry C. Trexler Library
2400 Chew Street
Allentown, PA 18104-5586
Tel.: (610) 821-3500
Fax: (610) 821-3511
E-mail: mccallis@max.muhlberg.edu
[Muhlenberg Papers; Pennsylvania
Germans – 2000 items]
◆**American Historical Society of**
Germans from Russia Library
631 D Street
Lincoln, NE 68502-1199
Tel.: (402) 474-3363
Fax: (402) 474-7229
E-mail: ahsgr@aol.com
[Germans from Russia – culture, history,
genealogy]
◆**Deutschheim State Historic Site**
Library
109 W. Second Street
Hermann, MO 65041
Tel.: (573) 486-2200
[19th century Germans and 19th century
Missouri Germans – art, architecture,
daily life; 19th century German rare book
and manuscript collection; 10 rare maps
of the Germanys – earliest dated 1807]
◆**Colorado State University**
Germans from Russia Project Library
University Libraries
Fort Collins, CO 80523-1019
Tel.: (970) 491-1833

Fax: (970) 491-1195
[Germans from Russia]
♦**Catholic Central Union of America Central Bureau Library**
3835 Westminster Place
St. Louis, MO 63108
Tel.: (314) 371-1653
[German-Americana]
♦**Ellis County Historical Society Archives**
100 W. Seventh Street
Hays, KS 67601
Tel.: (913) 628-2624
[Volga-Germans migration; Volga-German Centennial photograph collection – 2000]
♦**German Genealogical Society of America Library**
2125 Wright Avenue, Suite C-9
La Verne,CA 91750-5541
Tel.: (909) 593-0509
[German genealogy and ethnic history]
♦ **Immigrant Genealogical Society Library**
1310-B West Magnolia Blvd.
Burbank, CA
Mailing address:
P.O. Box 7369
Burbank, CA 91510-7369
Tel.: (818) 848-3122
[German genealogy and ethnic history]
♦**Milwaukee County Historical Society Library and Archives**
910 N. Old World Third Street
Milwaukee, WI 53203
Tel.: (414) 273-8288
[Germans and other immigrant groups; German-American Studies]
♦**Missouri Historical Society Archives Library and Collections Center**
P.O. Box 11940
St. Louis, MO 63112-0040
Tel.: (314) 746-4500
[German immigrants]
♦**Lebanon County Historical Society Library**
924 Cumberland Street
Lebanon, PA 17042-5186
Tel.: (717) 272-1473

[Germans in Pennsylvania]
♦**Eastern Mennonite College and Seminary, Menno Simons Historical Library and Archives**
Harrisonburg, VA 22801-2462
Tel.: (540) 432-4170
Fax: (540) 432-4977
E-mail: lehmanjo@aemu.edu
[Anabaptist and Mennonite history; German culture in Eastern United States; genealogy]
♦**German Historical Institute Library**
1607 New Hampshire Avenue NW
Washington, DC 20009
Tel.: (202) 387-3355
Fax: (202) 483-3430
E-mail:DHIVSA@TRIBECA.IOS.COM
Germany
♦**The Augustan Society Library**
P.O. Box P
Torrance, CA 90508-0210
    Tel.: (310) 320-7766
    Fax: (310) 320-2315
[Specializes in royal and noble genealogy, heraldry and vexillology, insignia, medals and decorations, medieval Europe.]

SOME PRINTED RESOURCES FREQUENTLY USED IN GERMAN GENEALOGY

♦ Arndt, Karl J.R. and May E. Olson, comp. *German-American Newspapers and Periodicals, 1732-1955*. 2nd rev. ed., Johnson Reprint Corporation, New York, 1965.
♦ _____, *The German Language Press of the Americas, 1732-1968*. Verlag Dokumentation, Pullach, 1973.
♦ Bahlow, Hans, *Deutsches Namenlexikon* [Encyclopedia of German (family and first) names]. Keysersche Verlagsbuchhandlung, Munich, 1967
♦ _____, *Dictionary of German Names*. Translated by Edda Gentry. Ed. Henry Geitz and Charlotte L. Brancaforte. Max Kade Inststitute for German-American

Studies Translation Series, ed. Henry Geitz, University of Wisconsin-Madison, 1993.

♦ Baxter, Angus, *In Search of Your German Roots: A Complete Guide to Tracing Your Ancestors in the Germanic Areas of Europe.* Genealogical Publishing Co., Inc., Baltimore, 3rd ed., 1994.

♦Bentley, Elizabeth Petty, *County Courthouse Book.* Genealogical Publishing Co., Inc., Baltimore, 1995.

♦_____, *Directory of Family Associations.* Genealogical Publishing Co., Inc., Baltimore, 1993.

♦_____, *The Genealogists's Address Book.* Genealogical Publishing Co., Inc. Baltimore, 3rd ed., 1995.

♦ Bentz, Edna M., *If I Can You Can Decipher Germanic Records.* Edna M. Bentz, 1982

♦Blodgett, Steven W., *Germany: Genealogical Research Guide.* Genealogical Society of Utah, Salt Lake City, 1989

♦ Brandt, Edward R., Ph.D., Mary Bellingham, Kent Cutkomp, Kermit Frye, and Patricia Lowel, *Germanic Genealogy: A Guide to Worldwide Sources and Migration Patterns.* Germanic Genealogy Society, St. Paul, MN, 1995

♦ *Cassell's German-English, English-German Dictionary,* rev. by Harold T. Betteridge. MacMillan Publishing Co., New York, 1978

♦Crowe, Elizabeth Powell, *Genealogy Online: Researching Your Roots.* Windcrest/McGraw-Hill, Blue Ridge Summit, PA, 1995

♦Dearden, Fay and Douglas Dearden, *The German Researcher: How to Get the Most Out of Our Family History Center.* Family Tree Press, Minneapolis, MN, 1983. 4th ed., revised and expanded 1990.

♦Eakle, Arlene and Johni Cerny, *The Source: A Guidebook of American Genealogy.* Ancestry, Inc., 1984.

♦ Edlund, Thomas Kent, comp., *An Introduction and Register to Die Ahnenstammkartei des deutschen Volkes of the Deutsche Zentralstelle für Genealogie Leipzig 1922-1991.* Family History Library, Salt Lake City, UT, 1993.

♦Eichholz, Alice, ed., *Ancestry's Red Book: American State, County, and Town Sources.* Ancestry Publishing, Salt Lake City, UT, 1989, 1992.

♦Everton, George B., Sr., ed. *The Handy Book for Genealogists,* 8th ed., Everton Publishers, Inc., Logan, UT, 1991.

♦Ferguson, Laraine, "Locating Church and Civil Registration Records," *German Genealogical Digest,* vol. 1, No. 3, pp. 202-203, 1985

♦Filby, P. William, and Mary K. Meyer, *Passenger and Immigration Lists Index: A Guide to Published Arrival Records of about 500,000 passengers who came to the United States and Canada in the Seventeenth, Eighteenth, and Nineteenth Centuries.* 1st ed., 3 vol. plus annual supplements, Gale Research Co., c 1981.

♦Filby, P. William, ed., *Passenger and Immigration Lists Bibliography, 1538-*

1900: Being a Guide to Published Lists of Arrivals in the United States and Canada. 1st ed., Gale Research Co., Detroit, MI, c1981

◆Glazier, Ira A. and P. William Filby, ed., *Germans to America: Lists of Passengers Arriving at U.S. Ports, 1850-1855.* Scholarly Resources, Wilmington, DE, c 1988.

◆Greenwood, Val D., *The Researcher's Guide to American Genealogy.* Genealogical Publishing Co., Inc. Baltimore, 1990.

◆ Gregory, Winifred, ed. *American Newspapers, 1821-1936, and Canada.* W.H. Wilson, New York, 1937.

◆Hall, Charles M., *The Atlantic Bridge to Germany,* 9 vols. The Everton Publishers, Inc., Logan, UT.

◆Haller, Charles R., *Across the Atlantic and Beyond: The Migration of German and Swiss Immigrants to America.* Heritage Books, Inc. , 1993

◆Jensen, Larry O., "Basic Principles in Resolving Naming Practice Problems," *German Genealogical Digest,* vol. 4, no. 1, 1988, pp. 17-19.

◆ Jensen, Larry O., *A Genealogical Handbook of German Research.* Pleasant Grove, UT, Everton Publishers, Logan, UT, 2 vol., 1980-1983.

◆Johnson, Dr. Arta F., ed. *Bibliography and Source Materials for German-American Research.* Vol. 1, Arta F. Johnson, 1982. Updated 1984.

◆Jones, George F., *German-American Names.* Genealogy Unlimited, Inc. Orem, UT, 2nd. ed., 1995.

◆Kemp, Thomas Jay, *International Vital Records Handbook.* Genealogical Publishing Co., Inc., 1990.

◆Kirkham, E. Kay. *A Survey of American Church Records: Major Denominations before 1880,* vol. 1. Everton Publishers, Logan, UT, 1971

◆_____, *A Survey of American Church Records: Minor Denominations,* vol. 2. Everton Publishers, Logan, UT, 1969.

◆Law, Hugh T., *How to Trace Your Ancestors to Europe.* Cottonwood Books,

Salt Lake City, 1989

◆*Langenscheidts Großes Schulwörterbuch, Deutsch-Englisch.* Langenscheidt, Berlin & München, 1996.

◆Meyer, Mary K., *Meyer's Directory of Genealogical Societies in the U.S. and Canada,* 9th ed., Mount Airy, MD, 1992.

◆ Müller, Friedrich, *Müllers großes deutsches Ortsbuch* (Müller's large German gazetteer). Post- und Ortsbuchverlag Postmeister a.d. Friedrich Müller, Wuppertal-Barmen, Germany, 1958

◆Neagles, James C. and Lila Lee Neagles, *Locating Your Immigrant Ancestor: A Guide to Naturalization Records.* Everton Publishing Co., Logan, UT, 1975.

◆Newman, John J., *American Naturalization Processes and Procedures, 1790-1985.* Family History Section, Indiana Historical Society, Indianapolis, 1985.

◆Parker, J. Carlyle, *Going to Salt Lake City to Do Family History Research.* Marietta Publishing Company, Turlock, CA, 3rd ed. 1996.

◆ Pence, Richard A., ed., *Computer Genealogy: A Guide to Research Through High Technology.* Ancestry, Salt Lake City, UT, 1991, rev. ed.

◆Przecha, Donna and Joan Lowrey, *Guide to Genealogy Software.* Genealogical Publishing Co., Baltimore, 1993.

◆Ribbe, Wolfgang, and Eckhard Henning, *Taschenbuch für Familiengeschichteforschung.* Verlag Degener, Neustadt/Aisch, 1995

◆ Schenk, Trudy and Ruth Froelke, *Württemberg Emigration Index.* Ancestry, Inc., Salt Lake City, UT, 1986 ff.

◆ Schweitzer, George K., *German Genealogical Research.* George K. Schweitzer, 407 Ascot Court, Knoxville, TN 37923, 1995.

◆Smith, Clifford Neal and Anna Piszczan-Czaja Smith, *Encyclopedia of German-American Genealogical Research,* R.R. Bowker Co., New York, 1976.

◆Smith, Kenneth L., *German Church Books: Beyond the Basics.* Picton Press, Camden, Maine, 1989.

♦Stumpp, Dr. Karl, *The Emigration from Germany to Russia in the Years 1763-1862*. Translation by Prof. Joseph S. Height and others. American Historical Society of Germans from Russia, Lincoln, NE, 1978
♦ Suess, Jared H., *Central European Genealogical Terminology*. Everton Publishers, Logan, UT, 1978.
♦Thode, Ernest J., Jr., Thode, *Address Book for Germanic Genealogy*. Genealogical Publishing Co., Baltimore, 5th ed. 1994.
♦_____, *Atlas for Germanic Genealogy*, Heritage House, Marietta, OH, 1982, 1988.
♦_____, *German-English Genealogical Dictionary*. Genealogical Publishing Co., Inc., Baltimore, 1992
♦"Tracking Immigrant Origins," in *The Source: A Guidebook of American Genealogy*, Arlene Eakle and Johni Cerny, ed. Ancestry Publishing Co., Salt Lake City, UT, 1984.
♦Ütrecht, Dr. E., ed. *Meyers Orts- und Verkehrs-Lexikon des deutschen Reichs*. (Meyer's Directory of Places and Commerce in the German Empire). Bibliographisches Institut, Leipzig, Germany. 1912, 2 vols.
♦ *Where to Write for Vital Records: Births,Deaths, Marriages and Divorces*. U.S. Department of Health and Human Services.
♦Wittke, Carl, *The German-Language Press in America*. University of Kentucky Press, Lexington, 1957.
♦ Zimmerman, Gary J. and Marion Wolfert, *German Immigrants: Lists of Passengers Bound from Bremen to New York 1847-1854 with Places of Origin*. Genealogical Publishing Co., Inc., Baltimore, 1993.

SOME PUBLISHERS OF GENEALOGICAL MATERIALS

♦**Adam Apple Press,**

1249 Edge Hill Road, Box E
Bedminster, PA 18910
Tel. (215) 795-2149.
Fax: (215) 795-2694.
♦**AGLL**
593 West 100 North
P.O. Box 329
Bountiful, UT 84011-0329
Tel. (801) 298-5446.
Fax: (801) 298-5468
♦**AKB Publications**
691 Weavertown Road
Myerstown, PA 17067-2642
Tel. (717) 866-2300
♦**Ancestry, Inc.**
P.O. Box 476
Salt Lake City, UT 84110-0476.
Tel. (800) 262-3787
Fax: (801) 51-1798
E-mail: info@ancestry.com.
Internet: http://www.ancestry.com
♦**Atlantik-Brücke e.V.**
P.O. Box 1147
53001 Bonn, Germany
Tel. (49-228) 21 41 60
Fax: (49-228) 21 46 59
♦**Edna M. Bentz**
13139 Old West Avenue
San Diego, CA 92129-2406.
♦**Carl-Bertelsmann AG**
Carl-Bertelsmann-Str. 270
Postfach 111
33311 Gütersloh
Fax: (05241) 75166
♦**Böhlau Verlag GmbH & Co.**
Theodor-Heuss-Strasse 76
51149 Köln, Germany
Fax" (02203) 307349
♦**R.R. Bowker & Co.**
121 Chanlon Road
New Providence, NJ 07974
Tel. Sales: (800) 521-8110
Fax: (908) 464-3553
E-mail: info@reedref.com
(908) 464-6800.
♦**Edward R. Brandt**
13 - 27th Avenue S.E.
Minneapolis, MN 55414-3101
♦Clearfield Company, Inc.

200 E.Eager Street
Baltimore, MD 21202-3761
Tel. (410) 625-9004
♦**Degener & Co.**
Manfred Dreiss Verlag
Nürnberger Str. 27
71413 Neustadt a d Aisch
 Germany
Mailing address:
 Postfach 1360
91403 Neustadt a d Aisch
Germany.
♦**Deseret Book Direct**
0 E. South Temple
Salt Lake City 84130
Tel. (800) 453-3876
Fax: (801) 578-3338
♦**The Everton Publishers, Inc.**
3223 S. Main Street
P.O. Box 368
Logan, UT 84323-0368
Tel. (800) 443-6325 or
 (801) 752-6022
Fax: (801) 752-0425
♦**Facts On File, Inc.**
11 Penn Plaza
New York, NY 10001
Tel. (800) 322-8755; (212) 967-8800
♦**Family Line Publications**
Rear 63 E. Main Street
Westminster, MD 21157
Tel.: (800) 876-6103
♦**Family Tree Press**
2912 Orchard Avenue N.
Minneapolis, MN 55422
Tel. (612) 588-5824
♦**Frontier Press**
15 Quintana Drive, Suite 2
Galveston, TX 77554-9350.
Tel. (800) 772-7559 (to order).
Fax: (409) 740-0138
E-mail: kgfrontier@aol.com
URL: http://www.doit.com/frontier
♦**Gale Research Inc.**
The Thomson Corp.
835 Penobscot Building
Detroit, MI 48226-4094
Tel. (800) 521-0707,
or   (800) 877-GALE (customer service)

(313) 961-2242
Fax: (313) 961-6083
E-mail: gale.com
♦**Genealogical Publishing Co. Inc.**
1001 N. Calvert Street
Baltimore, MD 21202-3897.
Tel. (800) 296-6687; (410) 837-8271
Fax: (410) 752-8492
E-mail: orders@genealogical.com
♦**Genealogical Sources Unlimited**
407 Ascot Court
Knoxville, TN 37923-5807
Tel. (423) 690-7831
♦**Genealogists Bookshelf**
Box 468
343 E. 86th Street
New York, NY 10028-4550
♦**Genealogy Unlimited, Inc.**
P.O. Box 537
Orem, UT 84059-0537
Tel. (800) 666-4363 or (801) 763-7132
Fax: (801) 763-7185
E-mail: genun@itsnet.com
♦ **German Genealogical Digest,** 245
North Vine, Suite 106, Salt Lake City, UT
84103.
♦**German Information Center**
950 Third Avenue,
New York, NY 10022-2781.
Tel. (212) 888-9840
♦**Germanic Genealogy Society**
P.O. Box 16312
St. Paul, MN 5116
♦**Greenwood Publishing Group**
88 Post Road West
P. O. Box 5007
Westport, CT 06881
Tel. (800) 225-5800; (203) 226-3571
Fax: (203) 222-1502
E-mail: bookinfo@greenwood.com
♦**Hearthside Press**
8405 Richmond Highway, Suite H
Alexandria, VA 22309-2425
Tel. (703) 360-6900
♦**Heritage Books, Inc.**
1540-E Pointer Ridge Place
Bowie, MD 20716-1800
Tel. (800) 398-7709 or (301) 390-7708
Fax: (800) 276-1760

E-mail: heritagebooks@usa.pipeline.com
◆**Heritage House**
Div. of Ye Olde Genealogie Shoppe
P.O. Box 39128
Indianapolis, IN 46239
 Tel.: (317) 862-3330; (800) 419-0200
Fax: (317) 862-2599
◆**Heritage Quest,**
P.O. Box 40
Orting, WA 98360-0040
Tel. (800) 442-2029
◆**Institut für pfälzische Geschichte und Volkskunde**
Benzinoring 6
67657 Kaiserslautern
Tel. (0631) 3647302
Fax: (0631) 63597
◆**Dr. Arta F. Johnson**
153 Aldrich Road
 Columbus, OH 43214-2625
◆**Kinship**
60 Cedar Heights Road
Rhinebeck, NY 12572
Tel. (914) 876-4592
E-mail: 71045,1516@compuserve.com
◆**Links Genealogy Publications**
Iris Carter Jones,
7677 Abaline Wy
Sacramento, CA 95823-4224
Tel. (916) 428-2245
E-mail: ralphj@ix.netcom.com
◆**Lorelei Press**
P.O. Box 221356
 Sacramento, CA 95822-8356
Fax: (916) 421-8032
E-mail: lorelei@softcom.net
◆**Marietta Publishing Company,**
2115 North Denair Avenue,
Turlock, CA 95382
Tel. (209) 634-9473
◆**Masthof Press**
[formerly Olde Springfield Shoppe]
Route 1, Box 20
Morgantown, PA 19543-9701.
Tel. (610) 286-0258
Fax: (610) 286-6860
E-mail: masthof@ptdprolog.net
◆**The Memorabilia Corner**
1312 McKinley Avenue

Norman, OK 73072
Tel. (405) 321-8366
◆**National Archives and Records Administration**
601 Pennsylvania Ave. NW, Rm. G9
Washington, DC 20408
Tel. (202) (501) 5212
(800) 234-8861 (orders).
Fax: (202) 501-7170
Home page: http://www.nara.gov
◆**Olde Springfield Shoppe**
(see Masthof Press)
◆**Origins**
4327 Milton Avenue
Janesville, WI 53546
Tel. (608) 757-2777
◆**Picton Press**
P.O. Box 1111
Camden, ME 04843-1111
Tel. (203) 236-6565
◆**Verlag Degener & Company**
 Nürnberger Strasse 27
Postfach 1360,
91403 Neustadt/Aisch,
Germany.
◆**Gerhard Rautenberg Druckerei und Verlag GmbH & Co. KG**
Blinke 8
26787 Leer
Germany
Mailing address:
Postfach 1909
26767 Leer
Germany
◆**Horst Reschke**
3083 W. 4900 S
Salt Lake City, UT 84118-2527
◆**Roots International**
3239 N. 58th Street
Milwaukee, WI 53216-3123
Tel. (414) 871-7421
◆**K.G. Saur**
Subsidiary of R.R. Bowker Co.,
121 Chanlon Road
 New Providence, NJ 07974-1541
Tel. (908) 665-3576
(800) 521-8110 (orders only)
Fax (908) 771-7792
◆**Helmut Scherer Verlag**

Boothstr. 21a
12207 Berlin
Germany
✦Scholarly Resources, Inc.,
104 Greenhill Avenue
Wilmington, DE 19805-1897
Tel. (800) 772-8937 or (302) 654-7713
Fax: (302) 654-3871
E-mail: sales@scholarly.com
✦ Dr. George K. Schweitzer: See
Genealogical Sources Unlimited
✦Kenneth L. Smith
523 S. Weyant Avenue
Columbus, OH 43213-2275
✦C.A. Starke Verlag,
Frankfurter Strasse 51-53
Postfach 1310
65549 Limburg/Lahn, Germany
Fax: (06431) 43927
✦Suhrkamp Publishers New York, Inc.
175 Fifth Avenue
New York, NY 10010-7703
Tel. (212) 460-1653
✦Ernest Thode (Thode Translations)
RR 7, Box 306 Kern Road
Marietta, OH 45750-9437
Tel. (614) 373-3728
✦University of Utah Press
University of Utah
101 University Service Building
Salt Lake City, UT 84112
Tel. (800) 773-6672; (801) 581-6771
Fax: (801) 581-3365
E-mail: mkeele@media.utah.edu

✦University Press of America, Inc.
4720 Boston Way
Lanham, MD 20706
Tel. (301) 459-3366; (800) 462-6420
Fax: (301) 459-2118
✦ Westkreuz-Verlag   Bonn/Berlin
Vühlenstrasse 10-14
53902 Bad Münstereifel
Germany
✦Westland Publications
P.O. Box 117
McNeal, AZ 85617-0117
Tel. (602) 642-3500
✦Zielke-Verlag
Stadtlohnweg 13 C407
48161 Münster
Germany

SELECTED MUSEUMS PORTRAYING GERMAN ETHNOLOGY

Below are listed just a few of the many museums in Germany which present the culture and living conditions of Germans in centuries past. Many are *Freilichtmuseen* (open-air museums) where demonstrations of crafts and other everyday work of the times are scheduled.

In addition to these are the hundreds of local museums which fall under the category of the *Heimatmuseum*, too numerous in Germany to list here. The *Heimatmuseum*, or "hometown" museum, portrays the clothing, tools, furniture, crafts, and other articles of everyday life in the locale where the museum is situated.

✦**Berlin :** Museum für deutsche Volkskunde SMPK (Museum of German Ethnology), devoted to the popular culture, urban and rural, of German-speaking central Europe, from the 16th century to the present
✦ **Böblingen (Baden-Württemberg):** Deutsches Fleischermuseum (German Butchers' Museum), displaying the history of the butcher trade in Germany and the slaughtering and processing techniques

used at different periods

◆ **Bochum (Northrhine-Westphalia):** Deutsches Bergbau-Museum (German Mining Museum), showing the past and present of mining in Germany, with demonstration mine galleries beneath the museum building

◆**Cloppenburg (Lower Saxony):** Museumsdorf (Museum Village), the largest open-air museum in Germany

◆ **Detmold (Northrhine-Westphalia):** Westfälisches Freilichtmuseum Detmold, Landesmuseum für Volkskunde, Krummes Haus (Westphalia Open-Air Museum), with rural houses, farm buildings, and workshops from different parts of Westphalia

◆**Dortmund (Northrhine-Westphalia):** *Deutsches Kochbuchmuseum,* literally, the German cookbook museum, which presents a cultural history of eating and drinking

◆**Grossweil (Upper Bavaria):** *Freilichtmuseum des Bezirks Oberbayern* (Open-Air Museum of Upper Bavaria) contains a large collection of rural buildings, including farmhouses, granaries, barns, mills, flax-kilns, and a fisherman's hut

◆**Hagen** (Northrhine-Westphalia): *Westfälisches Freilichtmuseum, Landesmuseum für Handwerk und Technik* (Westphalian Open-Air Museum of Technology), offering regular demonstrations of, for example, a scythe mill, a rope-walk, different forges, a printing shop, a paper mill, and a sawmill

◆ **Hamburg:** *Museumsdorf* (Museum Village), with a reconstruction of a Holstein village, including a village inn, smithy, drive-through barn, mill, and farmhouse

◆ **Hersbruck (Bavaria):** *Deutsches Hirtenmuseum* (German Shepherds' Museum), illustrating the life and duties of shepherds and cowboys from all over the world, but especially from Germany, with the traditional life of rural Franconia

◆ **Iphofen (Bavaria):** *Fränkisches Bauern- und Handwerkermuseum* (Fran-

Cooper making a barrel
(16th century woodcut)

conian Museum of Farming and Handicrafts), with 17 craftsmen's workshops, 12 galleries showing farm implements and 6 for vineyard cultivation and wine production

◆**Kiel (Schleswig-Holstein):** *Schleswig-Holsteinisches Freilichtmuseum* (Schleswig-Holstein Open-Air Museum), includes rural houses, mills, barns and workshops, with regular demonstrations of basket-making, weaving and blacksmith's work

◆ **Marktrodach (Bavaria):** *Flössermuseum Unterrodach* (Unterrodach Raftsmen's Museum), illustrating the history and techniques of log-floating in the Frankenwald region

◆**Molfsee (Schleswig-Holstein):** *Schleswig-Holsteinisches Freilichtmuseum* (Schleswig-Holstein Open-Air Museum), with 16th-19th century buildings and their furniture, domestic equipment, agricultural implements, windmills, farmhouses, and an apothecary's shop

◆**Neu-Anspach (Hesse):** *Freilichtmuseum Hessenpark* (Hessenpark Open-Air Museum), a market place, surrounded by old buildings, contains restaurants, shops in which regional handicrafts are on sale, and exhibition rooms

◆**Sobernheim (Rhineland-Palatinate):** *Rheinland Pfälzisches Freilichtmuseum* (Open-Air Museum of the Rhineland Palatinate), comprising rural buildings which include houses, farm buildings, and workshops

◆**Tann (Hesse):** *Freilichtmuseum 'Rhöpner Museumsdorf* (Rhön Museum Village), illustrating the way of life of a well-to-do rural family around 1800

◆ **Triberg (Baden-Württemberg):** *Schwarzwald-Museum* (Black Forest Museum), dealing mainly with traditional handicrafts of the Black Forest

◆**Ulm (Baden-Württemberg):** *Deutsches Brotmuseum* (German Bread Museum), concerned with the history of breadmaking, including a display of the history of hunger in the 19th and 20th centuries

Source: Kenneth Hudson and Ann Nichols, *The Cambridge Guide to the Museums of Europe*. Cambridge University Press, New York and Cambridge, 1991.

MUSEUMS AND SITES IN ROMAN GERMANY

After 400 years of existence, the Roman Empire left hundreds of thousands of ruins that lie in present-day Germany, mostly still unexplored. A few of these ruins and Roman artifacts can be seen in these locations:

◆*Via Romana*: The 50-mile-long "Roman Road" that runs from Nijmegan, Holland to Xanten, Germany, connecting eight towns, each of which has Roman ruins, excavations, and outdoor museums or archaeological theme parks

◆**Roman Route:** 175 miles of ancient Roman roads from Xanten to Detmold. (For information: Münsterland Touristik "Grünen Band," Hohe Schule 13, 48565 Steinfurt, Germany)

◆**Xanten:** The *Archaeologischer Park*. (For information: Xanten Tourist Office, Karthaus 2, 46509 Xanten, Germany)

◆ **Osnabrück-Kalkriese:** Kulturgeschichtliches Museum (Museum of Cultural History), Heger-Tor-Wall28.

◆**Cologne:** *Römisch-Germanisches Museum* (Roman-Germanic Museum), at Roncalliplatz 4. (Information: Tourist Office, Unter Fettenhennen 19, 50667 Köln.)

◆**Trier:** *Rheinisches Landesmuseum*, Ostallee 44 (has the most comprehensive collection of Roman finds); also the Porta Nigra, Amphitheater, Imperial Baths and Basilika. (For information: Verkehrsamt-Touristik Informaion, An der Porta Nigra, 54292 Trier

◆ **Mainz:** *Antikes Schiffahrtsmuseum* (Antique Ships Museum), 2-B Neutorstrasse; also the *Römisch-Germanisches Zentralmuseum* in Kurfürstliches Schloss; and the *Mittelrheinisches Landesmuseum*, on Grosse Bleiche. (For information: Verkehrsverein Mainz, Bahnhofstrasse 15, 55116 Mainz)

◆**Saalburg:** The castellum, just outside Bad Homburg. (For information: Saalburgmuseum, Saalburg-Römerkastell, 61352 Bad Homburg)

◆ **Schwarzenacker:** *Römermuseum*. (Schwarzenacker is a suburb of Homburg/Saarland.)

◆**Köngen:** Römerpark

◆ **Hechingen:** *Villa Rustica* and the *Römisches Freilichtmuseum* (Roman Open Air Museum) in the suburb of Steir

◆**Aalen:** The *Limes Museum*, St. Johann-Strasse 5

◆**Rottweil:** *Stadtmuseum*, Hauptstrasse 20

◆**Augsburg:** *Römisches Museum*, in the former Dominican St. Magdalene church at Dominikaner Strasse 15

◆ **Kempten:** *Archaeologischer Park*, Campodonum Weg 3

◆ **Regensburg:** *Museum der Stadt Regensburg*, Dachauplatz 2-4 (For information: Krauterermarkt 3, 93047 Regensburg

Source: "Living Roman Legacy," by John Dornberg. *German Life*, April/May 1995

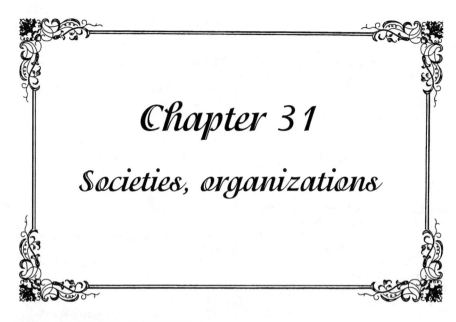

Chapter 31
Societies, organizations

GENEALOGY-RELATED ORGANIZATIONS IN GERMANY

The boldfaced words preceding each address below represent the English translation of the name of the organization. It has been added merely for the reader's convenience and should not be used as part of the mailing address. In correspondence be sure to add "Germany" as the last line of each address (except for one address in The Netherlands).

The abbreviation *e.V.* stands for *eingetragener Verein,* a court-registered society that is incorparated.

Brühl: German Association of Genealogy Societies
Deutsche Arbeitsgemeinschaft genealogischer Verbände e.V.
Schloßstr. 12
50321 Brühl

Herne: Society of East German Genealogical Researchers
Arbeitsgemeinschaft ostdeutscher Familienforscher e.V. (AgoFF)
Detlef Kühn
Zum Block 1 a
01561 Medessen

München: Bavarian Genealogy Society
Bayerischer Landesverein für Familienkunde e.V.
Ludwigstr. 14/I
80539 München

Garbsen: Lower Saxony, Bremen, and Eastfalia Genealogy Society
Familienkundliche Kommission für Niedersachsen und Bremen sowie angrenzende ostfälische Gebiete e.V.
Steinfeldstr. 34
30826 Garbsen

Hamburg: Genealogy Society at Hamburg
Genealogische Gesellschaft, Sitz Hamburg, e.V.
Postfach 302042
20307 Hamburg

Göttingen: Genealogy and Heraldry Society at Göttingen
Genealogisch-Heraldische Gesellschaft Göttingen, e.V.

Postfach 2062
37010 Göttingen
Nürnberg: Society for Family History Research in Franconia
Gesellschaft für Familienforschung in Franken e.V.
Archivstr. 17 (Staatsarchiv)
90408 Nürnberg
Kassel: Society for Family History Research in Kurhessen and Waldeck
Gesellschaft für Familienkunde in Kurhessen und Waldeck e.V.
Postfach 101346
34013 Kassel
Berlin: HEROLD, Society for Heraldry, Genealogy, and Related Studies
HEROLD, Verein für Heraldik, Genealogie und verwandte Wissenschaften
Archivstr. 12-14
14195 Berlin (Dahlem)
Berlin: Genealogy Society of Berlin
Interessengemeinschaft Genealogie Berlin
Heinrich-Heine-Str. 11
10179 Berlin
Hessian Family History Society
Hessische familiengeschichtliche Vereinigung e.V. (HFV)
Karolinenplatz 3 (Staatsarchiv)
64289 Darmstadt
Bretten: Baden Homeland Society for Historical and Cultural Studies
Landesverein Badische Heimat e.V.
Heilbronner Str. 3
75015 Bretten
Bonn: Organization of Genealogy Societies
Bund der Familienverbände e.V.
Lorenz-von-Stein-Ring 20
24340 Eckernförde
Hannover: Lower Saxony Society for Genealogy
Niedersächsischer Landesverein für Familienkunde e.V.
Am Bokemahle 14-16 (Stadtarchiv)
39171 Hannover
Oldenburg: Oldenburg Genealogical Society
Oldenburgische Gesellschaft für Familien-

kunde
Lerigauweg 14
26131 Oldenburg
Hamburg: Hamburg Society for Genealogy in East- and West Prussia
Verein für Familienforschung in Ost- und Westpreussen e.V.
In der Krümm 10
21147 Hamburg
Stuttgart: Society for Family History and Heraldry in Württemberg and Baden
Verein für Familien- und Wappenkunde in Württemberg und Baden e.V.
Postfach 10 54 41
70047 Stuttgart
Köln: West German Genealogical Society
Westdeutsche Gesellschaft für Familienkunde e.V., Sitz Köln
Unter Gottes Gnaden 34
50859 Köln
Münster: Westphalia Society for Genealogy and Family History
Westfälische Gesellschaft für Genealogie und Familienforschung
Postfach 6125
48133 Münster
Friedrichsdorf: Central Office for Genealogy and Family History
Zentralstelle für Personen- und Familiengeschichte (Institut für Genealogie)
Birkenweg 13
61381 Friedrichsdorf
Marburg: German Nobility Archive
Deutsches Adelsarchiv
Schwanallee 21
35037 Marburg
Kiel: Schleswig-Holstein Society for Genealogy and Heraldry
Schleswig-Holsteinische Gesellschaft für Familienforschung und Wappenkunde e.V.
Postfach 3809
24037 Kiel
Berlin: Sponsors and Supporters of the Central Office for Genealogy and Family History
Verein zur Förderung der Zentralstelle für

Personen- und Familiengeschichte e.V. (Zentralstellenverein)
Archivstr. 12-14
14195 Berlin (Dahlem)
Ludwigshafen: Society for Palatine and Rhineland Genealogy
Arbeitsgemeinschaft für Pfälzisch-Rheinische Familienkunde e.V.
Rottstr. 17
67061 Ludwigshafen
Berlin: Siemens Employees of Berlin Society for Family History
Arbeitsgemeinschaft für Familiengeschichte im Kulturkreis Siemens e.V.
Göbelstr. 143-145
13629 Berlin
Bremen: "The Mouse" Society for Genealogy
Die Maus, Gesellschaft für Familienforschung e.V.
Am Staatsarchiv 1/Fedelhöen (Staatsarchiv)
28203 Bremen
Wiesbaden: Genealogical Society for Nassau and Frankfurt
Familienkundliche Gesellschaft für Nassau und Frankfurt e.V. (Hessisches Hauptstaatsarchiv)
 Mosbacher Str. 55
65187 Wiesbaden
Markkleeberg: Society for Middle Germany Genealogy
Arbeitsgemeinschaft für mitteldeutsche Familienforschung e.V.
Frau Marlene Müller
Waldweg 5
04416 Markkleeberg
Erlangen: Siemens Employees of Erlangen Genealogical Society
Genealogischer Kreis in der Kameradschaft Siemens Erlangen e.V.
Postfach 3240
z.H. Th. Lonicer, Abt. VT 611
91050 Erlangen
Dortmund: Roland at Dortmund
Roland zu Dortmund e.V.
Postfach 103326
44033 Dortmund 1
Hagen: Society for Genealogy in Hagen

Arbeitskreis für Familienforschung im Hagener Heimatbund e.V.
Hochstr. 74
58095 Hagen
Düren: Lineage Society of Wallmichrath
Sippenverband Wallmichrath e.V.
Rütger-von-Scheven-Str. 63a
52349 Düren
Lübeck: Society for Genealogy Lübeck
Arbeitskreis für Familienforschung Lübeck e.V.
Mühlentorplatz 2 (Mühlentorturm)
23552 Lübeck
Ilmenau: Organization of Genealogical Societies
Bund der Familienverbände e.V.
Kirchgasse 18
98693 Ilmenau
Bielefeld: Salzburger Society
Salzburger Verein e.V.
Memeler Str. 35 (Wohnstift Salzburg)
33605 Bielefeld
Bensheim: Friedrich Wilhelm Euler Society for Genealogical Research
Friedrich-Wilhelm-Euler-Gesellschaft für personengeschichtliche Forschung e.V. (Ehem. Institut zur Erforschung historischer Führungsschichten e.V.)
Ernst-Ludwig-Str. 21
64625 Bensheim
Regensburg: Association of Sudeten German Genealogists
Vereinigung Sudetendeutscher Familienforscher
Sudetendeutsches Genealogisches Archiv
Erikaweg 58
93053 Regensburg
Peine: Railway Employees' Society for Genealogy and Heraldry
Gruppe Familien- und Wappenkunde im Bundesbahn-Sozialwerk
Weissdornstr. 10
31228 Peine
Sindelfingen: Society of Danube Swabian Genealogy
Arbeitskreis donauschwäbischer Familienforscher
Goldmühlestr. 30

71065 Sindelfingen
**Bad Karlshafen: German Huguenots
Society**
Deutscher Hugenotten-Verein e.v.
Deutsches Hugenotten-Zentrum
Hafenplatz 9 a
34385 Bad Karlshafen
**Brühl: North Rhine-Westphalia
Genealogical Archive, Rhineland
Section**
Nordrhein-Westfälisches Personen-
standsarchiv Rheinland
Schlossstr. 12
50321 Brühl
**Wuppertal: Society for Genealogy of the
Bergisches Land Region**
Bergischer Verein für Familienkunde e.V.
Dr. Wolfram Lang
Zanellastr. 52
42287 Wuppertal
**Lünen: Society for the Promotion of
Computer-Assisted Genealogical
Research**
Verein zur Förderung EDV-gestützter
familienkundlicher Forschungen e.V.
Schlorlemmerskamp 20
44536 Lünen
**Heidelberg: Genealogical Association
of English-Speaking Researchers in
Europe**
Genealogical Association of English-
Speaking Researchers in Europe
c/o Alexander Fülling
Kaiserstraße 12
51643 Gummersbach
**Ratingen-Lintorf: Dusseldorf Society
for Genealogy**
Düsseldorfer Verein für Familienkunde
e.V.
Krummenweger Str. 26
40885 Ratingen-Lintorf
**Braunschweig: Academy for Genea-
logy, Heraldry, and Related Studies**
Akademie für Genealogie, Heraldik und
verwandte Wissenschaften e.V.
Gutenbergstr. 12 B
38118 Braunschweig
**Erfurt: Genealogical Society of
Thuringia**

Arbeitsgemeinschaft   Genealogie
Thüringen e.V.
Martin-Andersen-Nexö-Str. 62
99096 Erfurt
**Püttlingen: Society for Saarland
Genealogy**
Arbeitsgemeinschaft für Saarländische
Familienkunde e.V.
Hebbelstr. 3
66346 Püttlingen
**Leipzig: German Central Office of
Genealogy**
Deutsche Zentralstelle für Genealogie
Sächsisches Staatsarchiv Leipzig
Abt. Deutsche Zentralstelle für Genealogie
Schongauer Str. 1
04329 Leipzig
**Hemau: Society for Genealogy in the
Upper Palatinate** (Bavaria)
Gesellschaft für Familienforschung in der
Oberpfalz e.V.
Karl-Heinz Kriegelstein
Pustetstr. 13
93155 Hemau
**Kleve: Mosaik Genealogical Society for
the Kleve District**
Mosaik Familienkundliche Vereinigung
für das Klever Land e.V.
Mosaik-Archiv
Lindenallee 54
47533 Kleve
**Netherlands: Research Group for
German Genealogy** (in the Netherlands)
Werkgröp Genealogisch Onderzök
Duitsland
P.C. Hooftlaan 9
NL-3838 HG Amersfoort
Niederlande
Leipzig: Leipzig Genealogical Society
Leipziger Genealogische Gesellschaft e.V.
Marion Bähr
c/o Deutsche Zentralstelle für Genealogie
Postfach 274
04002 Leipzig
**Wilhelmshaven: Genealogical Society
for East Frisia**
Upstalsboom-Gesellschaft für historische
Personenforschung und Bevölkerungs-
geschichte in Ostfriesland e.V.

Prof. Dr. Harro Buss
Flotowweg 4
26386 Wilhelmshaven
Düsseldorf: Stoye Foundation
Stiftung Stoye
Jürgen Wagner
Rheinallee 159
40545 Düsseldorf
Köln: Leps-Milke Foundation
Leps-Milke Stiftung
Gerhard Leps
Neusser Wall 12
50670 Köln
Herdecke: Society for Eastern Central European Studies
Gesellschaft für ostmitteleuropäische Landeskunde und Kultur e.V.
Klaus-Dieter Kreplin
Zum Nordhang 5
58313 Herdecke
Magdeburg: Magdeburg Genealogical Society
Arbeitsgemeinschaft Genealogie Magdeburg
Thiemstr. 7
39104 Magdeburg
Beckedorf: Registry of Pedigrees for the *Deutsche Arbeitsgemeinschaft Genealogischer Verbänd*
Ahnenlistenumlauf der DAGV
Rainer Bien
Hauuptstr. 70
31699 Beckedorf
Bolanden: Mennonite History Society
Mennonitischer Geschichtsverein e.V.
Am Hollerbrunnen 7
67295 Bolanden
Darmstadt: German-Baltic Genealogical Society
Deutsch-Baltische Genealogische Gesellschaft e.V.
Herdweg 79
64285 Darmstadt
Hannover: Heraldry Society of "Clover Leaf"
Heraldischer Verein zum Kleeblatt e.V.
Erhardt Haacke
Berliner Str. 14E
30457 Hannover

Söhlde: Hildesheim Genealogical Society
Familienkundlicher Verein Hildesheim
Nr 66
31185 Söhlde
Mörfelden-Walldorf: Historical Society of Walldorf
Arbeitsgemeinschaft für Walldorfer Geschichte
Waldstr. 100
64546 Mörfelden-Walldorf
Worms: Historical Society for the Siebenbürg Region (Romania) **Genealogical Section**
Arbeitskreis für Siebenbürgische Landeskunde e.V.
Abteilung Genealogie
Michäl Fleischer
Holderbaumstr. 9
67549 Worms
Kassel: Society of Genealogical Organizations in Hessen
Arbeitsgemeinschaft der familienkundlichen Gesellschaften in Hessen
Gräfestr. 35
34121 Kassel
München: Document Center for German Expatriates and Refugees from Eastern Europe (Silesia, East Prussia, Pomerania, etc.)
Zentralstelle der Heimatsortskarteien
Lessingstr. 1
80336 München
Dresden: Genealogy Society of Dresden
Interessengemeinschaft Genealogie Dresden
c/o Eberhard Stimmel
Krenkelstr. 9
01309 Dresden
Halle: Halle Researchers "Ekkehard"
Hallischer Familienforscher "Ekkehard" e.V.
c/o Bernd Hofestädt
Otto-Hahn-Str.2
06122 Halle-Neustadt
Langen: Genealogical Work Group of the "Männer vom Morgenstern, Heimatbund an Elb- und Wesermündung e.V."

Merchant with abacus, 15th century

Familienkundliche Arbeitsgemeinschaft der „Männer vom Morgenstern, Heimatbund an Elb- und Wesermündung e.v. **Marburg: Work Group for Central German Research** Arbeitsgemeinschaft für mitteldeutsche Familienforschung e.v. Waldweg 5 04416 Markkleeberg **Neuenhaus: Historical and Cultural Society of Emsland Region, Genealogical Section** Arbeitskreis Familienforschung der „Emländischen Landschaft e.v." c/o Jan Ringena Grafenstraße 11 49828 **Plauen: Society for History and Culture of Vogtland Region Genealogical Section** Arbeitskreis Vogtländische Familienforscher" im Verein für vogtländische Geschichte, Volks- und Landeskunde e.v. c/o Frau Andrea Hanisch Alfred-Schlagk-Str. 12 08523 Plauen **Chemnitz: Genealogical Society of Chemnitz** Fachgruppe Genealogie Chemnitz

c/o Armin Lippmann
Straße Usti nad Labem 23
09119 Chemnitz

HISTORICAL SOCIETIES IN GERMANY

Aachen: Aachener Geschichtsverein e.v. Fischmarkt 3 (Stadtarchiv) 52062 Aachen **Bad Aibling:** Historischer Verein für Bad Aibling und Umgebung Wilhelm-Leibl-Platz 2 (Heimatmuseum Bad Aibling) Geschäftsstelle: Frühlingstr. 34 83043 Bad Aibling. **Alsfeld:** Geschichts- und Museumsverein Rittergasse 3-5 (Regionalmuseum) 36304 Alsfeld. **Ansbach:** Historischer Verein für Mittelfranken e.v. Staatliche Bibliothek (Schloßbibliothek) Reitbahn 5 91522 Ansbach **Arolsen:** Waldeckischer Geschichtsverein e.v. Schloßstr. 24 (Schreibersches Haus) 34454 Arolsen. **Aschaffenburg:** Geschichts- und Kunstverein Aschaffenburg e.V. Wermbachstr. 15 (Schönborner Hof) 63739 Aschaffenburg. **Augsburg:** Heimatverein für den Landkreis Augsburg, e.V. Prinzregentenplatz 4 (Landratsamt) 86150 Augsburg. -Historischer Verein für Schwaben, Schaezlerstr. 25 86152 Augsburg. -Schwäbische Forschungsgemeinschaft bei der Kommission für bayerische Landesgeschichte bei der Bayerischen Akademie der Wissenschaften Universitätsstr. 10 (Universität Augsburg) 86159 Augsburg. **Bamberg:** Historischer Verein für die Pflege der Geschichte des ehemaligen Fürstbistums Bamberg

Postfach 1624
96007 Bamberg.
Bayreuth: Historischer Verein für Ober-
franke
Ludwigstr. 21 (Neues Schloß)
95444 Bayreuth.
Berchtesgaden: Verein für Heimatkunde
des Berchtesgadener Landes e.V.
2. Vorsitzender: Hellmut Schöner
Salzburger Str. 18
83471 Berchtesgaden.
Berlin: Historische Kommission zu
Berlin, Kirchweg 33
14129 Berlin.
-Historische Gesellschaft zu Berlin
Habelschwerdter Allee 39-45
14195 Berlin.
-Landesgeschichtliche Vereinigung für die
Mark Brandenburg
Britzer Damm 23
12169 Berlin.
-Verein für die Geschichte Berlins
Geschäftsstelle: Frau Ingeborg-Schröter
Brauerstr. 31
12209 Berlin
Biberach: Gesellschaft für Heimatpflege,
Kunst- und Altertumsverein Biberach e.V.
Gustav E. Gerster
Memminger Str. 36
88400 Biberach.
Bielefeld: Historischer Verein für die
Grafschaft Ravensburg e.V.
Rohrteichstr. 19
33602 Bielefeld
Bingen: Vereinigung der Heimatfreunde
am Mittelrhein e.V.
Sitz Bingen
Geschäftsstelle: Rheinkai 21 (Städtisches
Verkehrsamt)
55411 Bingen/Rh.
Bischofsheim: Heimat- und Geschichts-
verein Bischofsheim
Geschäftsführer: Hans Leoff
Schillerstr. 25
65474 Bischofsheim.
Böblingen: Heimatgeschichtsverein für
Schönbuch und Gäu e.V.
Parkstr. 16
71005 Böblingen

Bonn: Bonner Heimat- und Geschichts-
verein e.V,
Berliner Platz 2 (Stadtarchiv)
53111 Bonn
-Verein für geschichtliche Landeskunde
der Rheinlande
Am Hofgarten 22
53113 Bonn
-Historischer Verein für den Niederrhein,
insbesondere für das alte Erzbistum Köln
Geschäftsstelle: Prof. Dr. Giesbert Knopp
GrafZeppelin-Str. 36
53757 Sankt Augustin
Braunschweig: Braunschweigischer
Geschichtsverein e.V.
Löwenwall 18 b (Stadtarchiv)
38100 Braunschweig.
-Harzverein für Geschichte und Alter-
tumskunde
Burgplatz 1
38100 Braunschweig.
Bremen: Historische Gesellschaft Bremen
e.V.
Am Staatsarchiv 1
28203 Bremen
Bremerhaven: „Männer vom Morgen-
stern," Heimatbund an Elb- und Weser-
mündung
Geschäftsstelle: Bernd Behrens
Müggenburgweg 2
27607 Langen.
Bückeburg: Schaumburg-Lippischer
Heimatverein
Vorsitzende: Frau Dr. Roswitha Sommer
Lübingstr. 4
31675 Bückeburg.
Büdingen: Büdinger Geschichtsverein
1. Vorsitzender: Leitender Schulamts-
direktor Willi Luh
In der Langgewann 58
63654 Büdingen.
Burghhausen: Heimatverein Burghausen/
Salzach
Burg 40 (Josef Schneider)
84469 Burghausen.
Butzbach: Geschichtsverein für Butzbach
und Umgebung
Brudergasse 8 (Winfried Schunk)
35510 Butzbach.

Coburg: Historische Gesellschaft Coburg e.V.
Eupenstr. 108 (Oberstudiendirektor Harald Bachmann)
96450 Coburg.
Darmstadt: Hessische Historische Kommission
Karolinenplatz 3 (Staatsarchiv)
64289 Darmstadt
-Historischer Verein für Hessen
Carolinenplatz 3 (Staatsarchiv)
64289 Darmstadt
-Hessische Kirchengeschichtliche Vereinigung
Ahastr. 5 a (Zentralarchiv der Evangelischen Kirche in Hessen und Nassau)
64285 Darmstadt.
Detmold: Naturwissenschaftlicher und Historischer Verein für das Land Lippe
Willi-Hofmann-Str. 2 (Staatsarchiv)
32756 Detmold
Dillingen: Fürstl. und Gräfl. Fuggersches Familien- und Stiftungsarchiv
Ziegelstr. 29
89407 Dillingen/Donau
-Historischer Verein Dillingen/Donau
Westendstr. 34 (OstudDir. Dieter M. Schienhammer)
89407 Dillingen.
Donauschingen: Verein für Geschichte und Naturgeschichte der Baar
Haldenstr. 3 (Fürst. Fürstenbergisches Archiv)
78166 Donaueschingen.
Dortmund: Gesellschaft für Westfälische Wirtschaftsgeschichte e.V.
Märkische Str. 120
44009 Dortmund
-Historischer Verein für Dortmund und die Grafschaft Mark e.V.
Geschäftsstelle: Stadtarchiv Dortmund
Friedensplatz 5
44135 Dortmund
Düren: Dürener Geschichtsverein
Vorsitzender: Dr. Hans J. Domsta
Stadt- und Kreisarchiv Düren
Postfach 356
52303 Düren
Düsseldorf: Düsseldorfer Geschichts-verein e.V.
Mauerstr. 55 (Hauptstaatsarchiv)
40476 Düsseldorf.
Duisburg: Mercator-Gesellschaft
Karmelplatz 5 (Stadtarchiv)
47049 Duisburg
Eichstätt: Historischer Verein Eichstätt
Kobenzl-Schlößchen
85072 Eichstätt
Erlangen: Heimat- und Geschichtsverein Erlangen e.V.
Marktplatz 1
91054 Erlangen
-Zentralinstitut für Fränkische Landeskunde und allgemeine Regionalforschung der Universität Erlangen-Nürnberg
Kochstr. 4
91054 Erlangen.
Essen: Historisher Verein für Stadt und Stift Essen
Vorsitzender: Dr. G. Annen
Laubendakler Landstr. 1
45239 Essen.
Esslingen: Geschichts- und Altertumsverein am Neckar e.V., Stadtmuseum
Hafenmarkt 7
73728 Esslingen.
Euskirchen: Verein der Geschichts- und Heimatfreunde Euskirchen e.V.
Kreisverwaltungsarchiv
Jülicher Ring, Postfach 1145
53861 Euskirchen.
Flensburg: Gesellschaft für Flensburger Stadtgeschichte e.V.
Am Pferdewasser 1
24937 Flensburg.
Frankfurt (Main): Frankfurter Historische Kommission
Karmelitergasse 5 (Stadtarchiv)
60311 Frankfurt/M.
-Frankfurter Verein für Geschichte und Landeskunde e.V.
Karmelitergasse 5 (Stadtarchiv)
60311 Frankfurt/M.
-Verein für Geschichte und Altertumskunde e.V.
Frankfurt/M.-Höchst
Museum im Höchster Schloß
Schloßplatz 16

65929 Frankfurt/M.-Höchst.
Freiburg: Breisgau-Geschichtsverein
Schau ins Land
Grünwälder Str. 15
79098 Freiburg i. Br.
Freising: Historischer Verein Freising e.V.
Rathaus/Stadtarchiv
85354 Freising.
Friedberg: Friedberger Geschichtsverein
e.V.,
Augustinergasse 8
Bibliothekzentrum Klosterbau
61169 Friedberg i. Hessen.
Fürth: „Alt-Fürth," Verein für Geschichte
und Heimatforschung e.V.
Schloßhof 12
90768 Fürth.
Fulda: Fuldaer Geschichtsverein
Stadtschloß/Kulturamt
Postfach 1020
36010 Fulda.
Geldern: Historischer Verein für Geldern
und Umgebung e.V.
Kapuzinerstr. 34 (Kreisarchiv)
47608 Geldern.
Gelsenkirchen-Buer: Verein für Orts-
und Heimatkunde Gelsenkirchen-Buer
Postfach 200417
45839 Gelsenkirchen
Gießen: Oberhessischer Geschichtsverein
Gießen e.V.
Ostanlage 45
35390 Gießen
Göppingen: Geschichts- und Altertums-
verein Göppingen
Postfach 809 (Kreisarchiv)
Orcher Str. 6
73033 Göppingen
Göttingen: Geschichtsverein für Götting-
en und Umgebung e.V.
Geismarlandstr. 4 (Neues Rathaus)
37083 Göttingen
-Historische Kommission für ost- und
westpreußische Landesforschung
Eichener Str. 32
53902 Bad Münstereifel-Houverath
(Prof. Dr. Udo Arnold).
Goslar: Geschichts- und Heimatschutz-
verein Goslar

Cehntstr. 24 (Stadtarchiv)
Postfach 2569
38615 Goslar.
Grafing: Arbeitsgemeinschaft für
Heimatkunde e.V.
Dobelweg 16 (Dr. Rolf Klinger)
85567 Grafing b. München
Großostheim: Geschichtsverein Bachgau
Stettiner Str. 6
63762 Großostheim II
Günzburg: Historischer Verein Günzburg
e.V.
Sophienstr. 3
89312 Günzburg.
Gunzenhausen: Verein für Heimatkunde
Gunzenhausen e.V.
Sonnenstr. 8
91710 Gunzenhausen.
Hamburg: Verein für Hamburgische
Geschichte
ABC-Str. 19 (Staatsarchiv)
20354 Hamburg.
Hanau: Hanauer Geschichtsverein
Schloßplatz 3
63450 Hanau.
Hannover: Gesellschaft für Niedersächs-
ische Kirchengeschichte
Rote Reihe 6
30169 Hannover.
-Historischer Verein für Niedersachsen
Am Archiv 1 (Hauptstaatsarchiv)
30169 Hannover
Heilbronn: Historischer Verein Heilbronn
e.V.
Eichgasse 1 (Stadtarchiv)
Postfach 2030
74010 Heilbronn.
Heiligenhaus: Geschichtsverein Heiligen-
hause e.V.
Rathaus
42579 Heiligenhaus.
Herborn: Geschichtsverein Herborn e. V.
Schloßstr. 3 (Rechtsanwalt J. Wienecke)
55758 Herborn
Hof: Nordoberfränkischer Verein für
Natur-, Geschichts- und Landeskunde e.V.
Unteres Tor 9 (Stadtarchiv)
95028 Hof/Saale.
Bad Homburg v.d. Höhe: Verein für

Geschichte und Landeskunde e.V.
Bad Homburg v.d. Höhe
Ernst-Moritz-Arndt Str. 2 b
61348 Bad Homburg v. d. Höhe.
Hünfeld: Hünfelder Kultur- und Mus-
eumsgesellschaft e.v.
Geschäftsstelle Kirchplatz 4
36088 Hünfeld
Ingelheim: Historischer Verein Ingelheim
Museum bei der Kaiserpfalz
Am alten Rathaus
55218 Ingelheim a. Rh.
Ingolstadt: Historischer Verein
Ingolstadt Geschäftsstelle: Auf der
Schanz 4 (Stadtarchiv)
85049 Ingolstadt.
Kassel: Verein für hessische Geschichte
und Landeskunde e.V.
Mönchebergstr. 19 (Gesamthochschule
Kassel)
34125 Kassel
(Vorsitzender: Leitender Bibliotheks-
director Dr. H.-J. Kahlfuß).
Kempten: Heimatverein Kempten e.V. im
Heimatbund Allgäu e.V. (Anton J. Keil)
Amselweg 5
87439 Kempton/Allgäu.
Kiel: Gesellschaft für Kieler Stadtge-
schichte
Rathaus/Stadtarchiv
24103 Kiel.
Koblenz: Verein für Kunst und Geschichte
des Mittelrheins
Karmeliterstr. 1/3 (Landeshauptarchiv)
56068 Koblenz.
Köln: Gesellschaft für Rheinische
Geschichtskunde
Severinstr. 222-228
50676 Köln
-Kölnischer Geschichtsverein, Universi-
täts und Stadtbibliothek
Universitätsstr. 33
50923 Köln
Königstein: Verein für Heimatkunde
Königstein im Taunus
Hauptstr. 3
61462 Königstein i. Ts.
Konstanz: Verein für Geschichte des
Bodensees und seiner Umgebung

Deutsche Geschäftsstelle: Stadtarchiv
Konstanz
Benediktinerplatz 5 (Prof. Dr. Mauerer)
78467 Konstanz
Koslar: Geschichtsverein Koslar e.V.
Lebsgasse 15
52428 Koslar
Bad Kreuznach: Verein für Heimatkunde
für Stadt und Kreis Bad Kreuznach e.V.
Geschäftsstellen: Dr. Horst Silbermann
Dienheimer Berg 11
55545 Sobernheim,
und in der Bücherei im Hauses der
Kreisverwaltung
Salinenstr. 47
55543 Bad Kreuznach
Kronberg: Verein für Geschichte und
Heimatkunde der Stadt Kronberg im
Taunus e.V.
Geschäftsstelle: Dr. Bruno Langhammer
Kronberger Str. 7
61462 Königstein.
Kulmbach: Freunde der Plassenburg e.V.
E.-C.-Baumann-Str. 5
95326 Kulmbach
Landsberg a. Lech: Historischer Verein
für Stadt und Kreis Landsberg a. Lech
Klaus Münzer
Galgenweg 17
86899 Landsberg a. Lech.
Landshut: Historischer Verein für
Niederbayern
Altstadt 79
Residenz
84028 Landshut.
Lauterbach: Lauterbacher Museum
Berliner Platz 1 (Hochhaus)
66333 Lauterbach.
Lichtenfels: Colloquium Historicum
Wirsbergense
Heimat und Geschichtsfreunde am
Obermain e.V.
Vorsitzender: Dr. Emil Singer
Neubaustr. 2
96257 Redwitz.
Limburg/Lahn: Bischöfliches Ordinariat
Limburg
Roßmarkt 4
65549 Limburg a. d. L.

Lindau: Museumsverein Lindau
Dr. Karl Bachmann
Schweizerhofweg 18
88131 Lindau.
Ludwigsburg: Historischer Verein Ludwigsburg für Stadt und Kreise e.V.
Stadtarchiv
Kaiserstr. 14
71636 Ludwigsburg.
Lübeck: Hansischer Geschichtsverein
Mühlendamm 1-3 (Archiv der Hansestadt Lübeck)
23552 Lübeck.
-Verein für Lübeckische Geschichte und Altertumskunde
Mühlendamm 1-3 (Archiv der Hansestadt Lübeck)
23552 Lübeck.
Lüneburg: Museumsverein für das Fürstentum Lüneburg
Wandrahmstr. 10 (Museum)
21335 Lüneburg
Mainz: West- und Süddeutscher Verband für Altertumsforschung
Institut für Vorund Frühgeschichte
Schillerstr. 11
55166 Mainz.
Marburg: Hessisches Landesamt für geschlichtliche Landeskunde
Wilhelm-Roepke-Str. 6 c
35039 Marburg/Lahn.
-Historische Kommission für Hessen
Friedrichsplatz 15
35037 Marburg/Lahn.
-Gesellschaft für Hessen, Friedrichsplatz 15, 35037 Marburg/Lahn
-Gesellschaft für pommersche Geschichte, Altertumskunde und Kunst e.V.
Johann-Gottfried-Herder-Institut
Gisonenweg 5-7
35307 Marburg/Lahn
Minden: Mindener Geschichtsverein Tonhallenstr.7 (Kommunalarchiv Minden)
32423 Minden.
Monschau: Geschichtsverein des Monschauer Landes
Dr. E. Neuß M.A.
Görlitzer Str. 33
48157 Münster.

München: Collegium Carolinum e.V.
Forschungsstelle für böhmische Länder
Hochstr. 8/II
81669 München
-Historische Kommission der Sudetenländer e.v.
Hochstr. 8
81669 München
-Historischer Verein von Oberbayern
Winzererstr. 68
80797 München
-Institut für bayerische Geschichte an der Universität München
Ludwigstr. 14
80539 München
-Kommission für bayerische Landesgeschichte bei der Bayerischen Akademie der Wissenschaften
Marstallplatz 8
80539 München
-Studiengruppe für Sächsische Geschichte und Kultur e. V.
Geschäftsstelle: Grünwalder Str. 225 d
81445 München
-Verband für Orts- und Flurnamenforschung in Bayern e.V.
Leonrodstr. 57
80636 München.
Münster: Kopernikus-Vereinigung zur Pflege der Heimatkunde und Geschichte Westpreußens e.V.
Sitz Münster/Westfalen
Geschäftsstelle: Norbert Str. 29
48151 Münster.
-Historische Kommission für Westfalen
Warendorfer Str. 24
48145 Münster
-Historischer Verein für Ermland
Ermlandweg 22 (Ermlandhaus)
48159 Münster
-Westfälisches Institut für Regionalgeschichte
Warendorfer Str. 14
48745 Münster.
-Verein für Geschichte und Altertumskunde Westfalens Abt. Münster
Geschäftsstelle: Warendorfer Str. 14
48133 Münster
-Verein für Westfälische Kirchenge-

schichte
An der Apostelkirche 1-3
48143 Münster
Neu-Ulm: Verein für Heimatgeschechte
Nagold e.V.
Haiterbacher Str. 58
72202 Nagold
-Historischer Verein Neu-Ulm
Illerholzweg 18
89231 Neu-Ulm.
-Verband zur Vorbereitung der Kreisbeschreibung für die Stadt- und Landkreise Günzburg
Illertissen
Krumbach und Neu-Ulm e.V.
Geschäftsführender Vorstand:Rechtsanwalt Horst Gaiser
Donaucenter
Marienstr. 1
89231 Neu-Ulm.
Nördlingen: Historischer Verein für
Nördlingen und das Ries
Stadtarchiv Nördlingen
Rathaus, Marktplatz 1
86720 Nördlingen.
Northeim: Heimat- und Museumsverein
für Northeim und Umgebung
Postsfach 1323
37154 Northeim.
Nürnberg: Abteilung für Vorgeschichte
der Naturhistorischen Gesellschaft e.V.
Gewerbemuseumsplatz 4 (Luitpoldhaus)
90403 Nürnberg
-Verein für die Geschichte der Stadt
Nürnberg
Egidienplatz 23 (Stadtarchiv)
90403 Nürnberg
Oberursel: Verein für Geschichte und
Heimatkunde Oberursel (Taunus) e.V.
Postfach 1146
61401 Oberursel/Ts.
Offenburg: Historischer Verein für
Mittelbaden
Postfach 1569
77605 Offenburg.
Osnabrück: Verein für Geschichte und
Landeskunde von Osnabrück
Schloßstr. 29 (Staatsarchiv)
49072 Osnabrück.

Osterrode: Heimat- und Geschichtsverein
Osterrode am Harz und Umgebung e.V.
Martin-Luther-Platz 2
Altes Rathaus
37520 Osterrode a. H.
Paderborn: Verein für Geschichte und
Altertumskunde Westfalens
Abt. Paderborn
Leostr. 21
33098 Paderborn
Pottenstein: Heimatverein Pottenstein
Hauptstr. 19
91278 Pottenstein
Ratzeburg: Heimatbund und Geschichtsverein Herzogtum Lauenburg e.V. Domhof
12 (Kreismuseum)
23909 Ratzburg.
Recklinghausen: Verein für Orts und
Heimatkunde Recklinghausen
Stadtarchiv, Hohenzollernstr. 12
45659 Recklinghausen
Regensburg: Fürst Thurn und Taxis Zentralarchiv-Hofbibliothek
Emeramsplatz
93047 Regensburg
-Historischer Verein für Oberpfalz und
Regensburg
Dachauplatz 4
93047 Regensburg
Rosenheim: Historischer Verein Rosenheim
Stadt und Landkreis
Geschäftsstelle: Kulturamt
Max-Bram-Platz 2 a
83022 Rosenheim.
Rott: Heimatverein für Wasserburg am
Inn und Umgebung (Historischer Verein)
e.V.
Arnikaweg 10
83543 Rott am Inn.
Rottenburg: Sülchgauer Altertumsverein
Geschäftsführer: Karlheinz Geppert M.A.
Stadtarchiv
Postfach 29
72101 Rottenburg a. N.
Saarbrücken: Historischer Verein für die
Saargegend e.V.
Stadtarchiv
Postfach 439

66104 Saarbrücken.
-Institut für Landeskunde im Saarland, Universität
Bau 35 (Herr Güth)
66123 Saarbrücken.
-Kommission f. Saarländische Landesgeschichte u. Volksforschung
Scheidter Str. 114
66130 Saarbrücken.
Schleswig: Gesellschaft für Schleswig-Holsteinische Geschichte
Frau Sylvia Günther
Harder Koppel 15
24217 Schönberg/Holstein.
Schrobenhausen: Historischer Verein Schrobenhausen
Paarstr. 5
86529 Schrobenhausen
Schwäbisch-Hall: Historischer Verein für Württembergisch Franken
Münzstr. 1
74523 Schwäbisch-Hall.
Schweinfurt: Historischer Verein Schweinfurt e. V.
Petersgasse 3
97421 Schweinfurt.
Siegburg: Geschichts- und Altertumsverein und dem Rhein-Sieg-Kreis e.V.
Rathaus
53721 Siegburg
Sigmaringen: Hohenzollerischer Geschichtsverein
Karlstr. 3
72488 Sigmaringen
-Landeskundliche Forschungsstelle Hohenzollern in der Kommission für geschichtliche Landeskunde in Baden-Württemberg
Karlstr. 3
72488 Sigmaringen
Singen: Verein für Geschichte des Hegau e.V.
August-Ruf-Str. 7 (Stadtarchiv)
78224 Singen (Hohentwiel)
Soest: Verein für Geschichte und Heimatpflege Soest e.V.
Jakobistr. 13 (Stadtarchiv und wissenschaftliche Stadtbibliothek)
49494 Soest.

Spalt: Heimatverein Spalter Land e.V.
Heinrich Heubusch
Lerchenbuck 28
91174 Spalt.
Speyer: Historischer Verein der Pfalz e.V. Domplatz (Historisches Museum der Pfalz)
67324 Speyer.
-Pfälzische Gesellschaft zur Förderung der Wissenschaften
Große Pfaffengasse 7 (Historisches Museum der Pfalz)
67346 Speyer.
Stade: Niedersächsisches Staatsarchiv Stade
Am Sande 4 c
21682 Stade.
-Stader Geschichts- und Heimatverein
Rathaus
Postfach 2025
21660 Stade.
Straubing: Historischer Verein für Straubing und Umgebung e.V.
Fraunhoferstr. 9
94315 Straubing.
Stuttgart: Württembergischer Geschichts- und Altertumsverein e.V.
Konrad-Adenauer-Str. 4 (Hauptstaatsarchiv),
70173 Stuttgart
Tittmoning: Historischer Verein Tittmoning e.V.
Poschacher Str. 2 a
84529 Tittmoning.
Traunstein: Historischer Verein für den Chiemgau zu Traunstein e.V.
Heimathaussstr.
Postfach 1829
83268 Traunstein
Trier: Gesellschaft für nützliche Forschungen Trier
a) Ostalled 44
54290 Trier
Ihre Sektion: Arbeitsgemeinschaft für Landesgeschichte und Volkskunde des Trierer Raumes
Weberbachstr. 25 (Stadtarchiv)
54290 Trier
Ulm: Verein für Kunst und Altertum in

Ulm und Oberschwaben
Weinhof 12 (Stadtarchiv)
89073 Ulm.
Waldshut-Tiengen: Geschichtsverein
Hochrhein e.V.
Waldshut-Tiengen
Vorsitzender: Fritz Schächtelin
Rathausstr. 19
79761 Waldshut-Tiengen.
Weiden: Heimatkundlicher Arbeitskreis
im Oberpfälzer Waldverein
Geschäftsstelle: Pfarrplatz 4
(Stadtarchiv) 92637 Weiden (Oberpfalz).
Weißenhorn: Heimat- und Museums-
verein Weißenhorn und Umgebung Wolf-
gang Ott M. A.
Kirchplatz 4
89264 Weißenhorn (Schwaben)
Wertheim: Historischer Verein Wertheim
e.V.
Rathausgasse 10
97877 Wertheim/Main
Wetzlar: Wetzlarer Geschichtsverein
e.V.
Vorsitzende: Ingeburg Schäfer
Engelsgasse 8
35578 Wetzlar.
Wiesbaden: Historische Kommission für
Nassau
Mosbacher Str. 55 (Hessisches Haupt-
staatsarchiv)
65187 Wiesbaden.
-Verein für Nassauische Altertumskunde
und Geschichtsforschung e.V.
Mosbacher Str. 55 (Hessisches
Hauptstaatsarchiv)
65187 Wiesbaden.
Würzburg: Bischöfliches Ordinariat
Würzburger Diözesangeschichtsverein
Vorsitzender: Prof. Dr. Klaus Wittstadt
Universität Würzburg
Sanderring 2
97070 Würzburg.

Source: Wolfgang Ribbe and Eckart Henning,
Taschenbuch für Familiengeschichtsforschung.
Verlag-Degener &Co., Neustadt an der Aisch,
1995.

CASTLES AND PALACES

Deutsche Burgenvereinigung e.V.
Marksburg
56338 Braubach/Rhein
Germany

The full name of the *Deutsche Burgenvereinigung e.V. zur Erhaltung der
historischen Wehr- und Wohnbauten* (address above), translates as "German castle
association for the preservation of the historic defense and residential structures."

With a library of some 20,000 volumes
of castle-related titles, *Deutsche Burgenvereinigung* researches the history of
castles and palaces. It also advises owners of these structures on how to preserve,
utilize and restore their historic sites.

The library staff responds to inquiries,
with fees ranging from 50 Pfennig for one
page to 25 Marks for extensive projects.

The librarian reports, "As a rule the
society does not research genealogical
questions."

The society's headquarters is the
Marksburg Castle, eight miles south of
Koblenz.

The society's membership is open. It
publishes a semi-annual journal, *Burgen
und Schlösser* (castles and palaces) and
other publications.

Source: Horst A. Reschke, "Preserving Castles &
Fortresses." *German Genealogical Digest*, Vol.
12, No. 2, Summer, 1996.

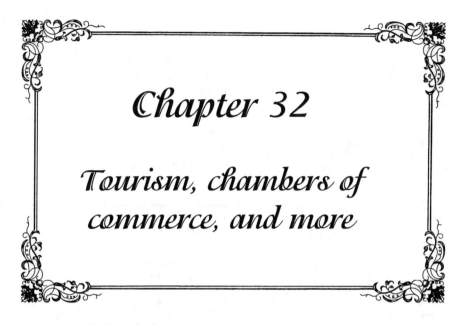

Chapter 32

Tourism, chambers of commerce, and more

GERMAN EMBASSIES

United States

♦Embassy of the Federal Republic of Germany
4645 Reservoir Road N.W.
Washington, DC 20007
Tel. (202) 298-4000
Fax: (202) 298-4249

♦ **Atlanta:** Consulate General of the Federal Republic of Germany
Marquis Two Tower, Suite 901
285 Peachtree Center Avenue, NE
Atlanta, GA 30303-1221
Tel.: (404) 659-4760-4762
Fax: (404) 659-1280

Jurisdiction: Alabama, Georgia, Mississippi, North Carolina, South Carolina, Tennessee

♦ **Boston:** Consulate General of the Federal Republic of Germany
3 Copley Place, Suite 500
Boston, MA 02116
Tel: (617) 536-8172 (overseas calls)
(617) 536-4414 (calls with the U.S.)

Jurisdiction: Connecticut (except Fairfield County), Maine, Massachusetts, new Hampshire, Rhode Island, Vermont

♦ **Chicago:** Consulate General of the Federal Republic of Germany
676 North Michigan Avenue, Suite 3200
Chicago, IL 60611
Tel.: (312) 580-1199
Fax: (312) 580-0099

Jurisdiction: Illinois, Iowa, Kansas, Minnesota, Minnesota, Missouri, Nebraska, North Dakota, South Dakota, Wisconsin

♦ **Detroit:** Consulate General of the Federal Republic of Germany
Edison Plaza, Suite 2100,
660 Plaza Drive
Detroit, MI 48226-1271
Tel: (313) 963-6526
Fax: (313) 962-7345

Jurisdiction: Indiana, Kentucky, Michigan, Ohio

♦ **Houston:** Consulate General of the Federal Republic of Germany
1330 Post Oak Blvd., Suite 1850
Houston, TX 77056-3018
Tel.: (713) 627-7770-7773

Fax: (713) 627-0506
Jurisdiction Arkansas, Louisiana, New Mexico, Oklahoma, Texas
◆ **Los Angeles:** ConsulateGeneral of theFederal Republic of Germany
6222 Wilshire Boulevard, Suite 500
Los Angeles, CA 90048
Tel.: (213) 930-2703
Fax: (213) 930-2805
Jurisdiction: Counties Imperial, Kern, Los Angeles, Orange, Riverside, San Bernardino, SanDiego, SanLuis obispo, Santa Barbara, and Ventura of the state of California; Arizona
◆**Miami:** Consulate General of the Federal Republic of Germany
100 N. Biscayne Bouevard, Suite 2200
Miami, FL 33132
Tel.: (305) 358-0290
Fax: (305) 358-0307
Jurisdiction: Florida, Puerto, Rico, American Virgin Islands
◆**New York:** Consulate General ofthe Federal Republic of Germany
460 Park Avenue
New York, NY 10022
Tel.: (212) 308-8700
Fax: (212) 308-3422
Jurisdiction: New York; New Jersey; Pennsylvania; Fairfield County; Connecticut; Bermuda
◆**San Francisco:** Consulate General of the Federal Republic of Germany
1960 Jackson Street
San Francisco, CA 94109
Tel.: (415) 775-1061
Fax: (415) 775-0187
Jurisdiction: California (except Imperial, Kern, Los Angeles, Orange, Rivrside, San Bernardino, San Diego, San Luis Obispo, Santa Barbara, and Ventury Counties); Colorado, Hawaii, Nevada, Utah, Wyoming, and the U.S. territories (Baker Island, Howland Island, Jarvis Island, Johnston Island, Midway, and Palmyra Island)
◆**Seattle:** Consulate General of the Federal Republic of Germany
One Union Square, Suite 2500

600 University Street
Seattle, WA 98101
Tel.: (206) 682-4312
Fax: (206) 682-3724
Jurisdiction: Alaska, Idaho, Montana, Oregon, Washington

Canada
Embassy of the Federal Republic of Germany
275 Slater Street, 14th Floor
Ottawa, Ontario K1P 5H9
Tel. (613) 232-1101
Fax: (613) 594-9330

U.S. EMBASSY OFFICES IN GERMANY

◆**Bonn** – Embassy of the United States of America: Botschaft der Vereinigten Staaten von Amerika
Deichmanns Aue 29
53170 Bonn
Tel.: (0228) 3 39 - 1/ -20 53
Fax: (0228) 33 27 12
Jurisdiction: North Rhine-Westphalia
◆**Berlin office** – Außenstelle Berlin
Neustädtische Kirch-straße 4-5
Tel.: (030) 2 38 - 51 74
Fax: (030) 2 38 - 6 90
◆**Consular Section of the Berlin Office:**
Konsularabteilung der Außenstelle Berlin
Clayallee 170
14195 Berlin
Tel.: (030) 8 19 74 54
Fax: (030) 8 31 49 26
Consular jurisdiction: Berlin, Brandenburg, Bremen, Hamburg, Mecklenberg-Western Pomerania, Lower Saxony, Saxony, Saxony-Anhalt, Schleswig-Holstein, Thuringia
◆**Frankfurt** – Consulate General of the United States of America: Generalkonsulat der Vereinigtenb Staaten von Amerika
Siesmayerstraße 21
60323 Frankfurt (Main)
Tel.: (069) 7 53 50
Fax: (069) 74 89 38
Consular jurisdiction: States of Hesse,

Rhineland-Palatinate, Saarland; Lower Franconia County of the state of Bavaria; Baden-Württemberg
♦**München** – Consulate General of the United States of America: Generalkonsulat der Vereinigten Staaten von Amerika
Königinstraße 5
80538 München
Tel.: (089) 28 88 - 0
Fax: (089) 2 80 51 63
Consular jurisdiction: State of Bavaria (except Lower Franconia County).
The consulate general in Munich does not issue any entry visas.
♦**Hamburg** – Consulate General of the United States of America: Generalkonsulat der Vereinigten Staaten von Amerika
Alsterufer 27
20354 Hamburg
Tel.: (040) 41 17 10
Fax: (040) 44 30 04
The consulate general in Hamburg does not issue any entry visas.

Scene at the "Donisl" in München

GERMAN CHAMBERS OF COMMERCE IN THE UNITED STATES

♦**Atlanta:** German American Chamber of Commerce
3475 Lenox Road N.E., Suite 620
Atlanta, GA 30326
Tel. (404) 239-9494
Fax (404) 264-1761
Jurisdiction: Alabama, Florida, Georgia, North Carolina, South Carolina, Tennessee
♦**Chicago:** German American Chamber of Commerce
401 North Michigan Avenue, Suite 2525
Chicago, IL 60611-4212
Tel. (312) 644-2662
Fax (312) 644-0738
Jurisdiction: Illinois, Indiana, Iowa, Kansas, Kentucky, Michigan, Minnesota, Missouri, Nebraska, North Dakota, Ohio, South Dakota, Wisconsin
♦**Houston:** German American Chamber of Commerce
5599 San Felipe, Suite 510
Houston, TX 77056
Tel. (713) 877-1114
Fax (713) 877-1602.
Jurisdiction: Arkansas, Louisiana, Mississippi, Oklahoma, Texas
♦ **Los Angeles:** German American Chamber of Commerce
5220 Pacific Concourse Drive
Los Angeles, CA 90045
Tel. (310) 297-7979
Fax (310) 297-7966
Jurisdiction: Arizona, California (south of Fresno), Colorado, Nevada (southern part – Las Vegas), New Mexico, Utah
♦**New York:** German American Chamber of Commerce.
40 West 57th Street, 31st Floor
New York, NY 10019-4092
Tel (212) 974-8830
Fax (212) 974-8867
Jurisdiction: Connecticut, Delaware, Maine, Massachusetts, New Hampshire, New Jersey, New York, Rhode Island, Vermont, Puerto Rico
♦**Philadelphia:** German American Cham-

ber of Commerce
Philadelphia Chapter
1515 Market Street, Suite 505
Philadelphia, PA 19102
(215) 665- 1585
Fax: (215) 665-0375
Jurisdiction: Delaware, southern New
Jersey (including Princeton), eastern
Pennsylania (including Harrisburg)
♦ **San Francisco:** German American
Chamber of Commerce
465 California Street, Suite 910
San Francisco, CA 94104
Tel (415) 392-2262
Fax (415) 392-1314
Jurisdiction: Alaska, Bahamas, Cali-
fornia (north of Fresno), Hawaii, Idaho,
Montana, northern Nevada (Reno),
Oregon, Washington, Wyoming

GERMAN TOURIST ASSOCIATIONS

German National Tourist Board
Deutsche Zentrale für Tourismus e.V. -
DZT
Beethovenstr. 69
60325 Frankfurt a. Main
Tel. (069) 757 20
Fax: (069) 75 1903
♦**Bonn**:
Deutscher Fremdenververkehrs-verband
Niebuhrstr. 16 b
53113 Bonn
Tel. (0228)2140 71
Fax: (0228) 2191 08
♦**Stuttgart**:
Landesfremdenverkehrsverband
Baden-Württemberg
Esslinger Str. 8
70182 Stuttgart
Tel. (0711) 238580
Fax: (0711) 23899
♦**Freiburg**:
Fremdenverkehrsverband
Schwarzwald e.V.
Bertoldstr. 45
Postfach 1660
79098 Freiburg

Tel. (0761) 313 17 18
Fax: (0761) 360 21
♦**Heilbronn:**
Touristikverband
Neckarland-Schwaben e.V.
Lohtorstr. 21
74072 Heilbronn
Tel. (07131) 7 85 20
Fax: (07131 6 86 38
♦**Konstanz:**
Fremdenverkehrsverband
Bodensee-Oberschwaben
Schützenstr. 8
78462 Konstanz
Tel. (07531) 222 32
Fax: (07531) 164 43
♦**München**:
Landesfremdenverkehrsverband
Bayern e.V.
Prinzregentenstr. 18
Postfach 22 13 52
80538 München
Tel. (089) 2123 97 0
Fax: (089) 293582
♦**Nürnberg**:
Fremdenverkehrsverband
Franken e.V.
Am Plärrer 14
90429 Nürnberg
Tel. (0911) 26 42 02
Fax: (0911) 2705 47
♦**Regensburg**:
Fremdenverkehrsverband
Ostbayern e.V.
Landshuter Str. 13
93047 Regensburg
Tel. (0941) 58 53 90
Fax: (0941) 58 53 939
♦**München**:
 Fremdenverkehrsverband
München/Oberbayern e.V.
Bodenseestr. 13
81243 München
Tel. (089) 82-9218-0
Fax: (089)82 9218-28
♦**Augsburg**:
Tourismusverband
Allgäu/Bayerisch-Schwaben e.V.
Fuggerstr. 9

Emigrants at Columbus Quay in Bremerhaven

86150 Augsburg
Tel. (0821) 333-35
Fax: (0821) 383 31
◆**Berlin:**
 Berlin-Tourismus Marketing
GmbH (BTM)
Am Karlsbad 11
10785 Berlin
Tel. (030) 26 47 48 0
Fax: (030) 26 47 48 99
◆**Brandenburg:**
Landesfremdenverkehrsverband
Brandenburg
Friedrich-Ebert-Str. 115
14467 Potsdam
Tel. (0331) 25632
Fax: (0331) 26683
◆**Hamburg:**
Tourismus-Zentrale
Hamburg GmbH
Burchardstr. 14
Postfach 10 22 49

20095 HamburgTel. (040) 300 51-0
Fax: (040 3005 12 53
◆**Harz:**
Harzer Verkehrsverband e.V.
Marktstr. 45
38640 Goslar
Tel. (05321) 34040
Fax: (05321) 340466
◆**Hesse:**
Hessischer Fremdenverkehrsverband
e.V.
Abraham-Lincoln Str. 38-42
65189 Wiesbaden
Tel. (0611) 7788 00
Fax: (0611) 7788 - 40
◆**Lower Saxony, Bremen:**
 Fremdenverkehrsverband Nordsee
Lower Saxony-Bremen
Bahnhofstr. 19-20
26122 Oldenburg
Tel. (0441) 921 71 0
Fax: (0441) 921 71 90

◆**Lüneburg Heath:**
Fremdenverkehrs-verband   Lüneburger
Heide e.V.
Am Sande 5
Postfach 2160
21335 Lüneburg
Tel. (04131) 52063
Fax: (04131) 52442
◆**Mecklenburg-Vorpommern:**
Landes-fremdenverkehrsverband
Mecklenburg-Vorpommern e.V.
Platz der Freundschaft 1
18059 Rostock
Tel. (0381) 448426
Fax: (0381) 448423
◆**Rhineland:**
Landesverkehrsverband
Rheinland e.V.
Rheinallee 69
Postfach 20 08 61
53173 Bonn
Tel. (0228) 3629 21 22
Fax: (0228) 3639 29
◆ **Rhineland-Palatinate:**
Fremdenver-kehrs- und
Heilbäderverband
Rheinland-Pfalz e.V.
Lohrstr. 103-105
Postfach 1420
56068 Koblenz
Tel. (0261) 310 79
Fax: (0261) 183 43
◆**Saarland:**
Fremdenverkehrsverband Saarland e.V.
Dudweiler Str. 53
Postfach 242
66133 Saarbrücken
Tel. (0681) 353 76 / 37088
Fax: (0681) 358 41
◆**Saxony:**
Landesfremdenverkehrsverband Sachsen
Friedrichstr. 24
01067 Dresden
Tel. (0351) 496-97 03
Fax: (0351) 496 93 06
◆**Saxony-Anhalt:**
Sachsen-Anhalt Tourismusverband
Grosse Diesdorfer Str. 12
39108 Magdeburg

Tel. (03917) 38 43 00
Fax: (03917) 38 43 02
◆**Schleswig-Holstein:**
Fremdenverkehrsverband Schleswig-
Holstein e.V.
Niemannsweg 31
24105 Kiel
Tel. (0431) 5600 0
Fax: (0431) 569810
◆**Thuringia:**
Landesfremdenverkehrsverband
Thüringen e.V.
Stauffenbergallee 18
99085 Erfurt
Tel: (0361) 6022-34/12
Fax: (0361) 6461 475
◆**Weser Hills:**
Fremdenverkehrsverband
Weserbergland-Mittelweser e.V.
Inselstr. 3
Postfach 10 03 39
31787 Hameln
Tel. (05151) 245 66
Fax: (05151) 268 32
◆**Westphalia:**
Landesverkehrsverband Westfalen e.V.
Friedensplatz 3
44135 Dortmund
Tel. (0231) 5275 06 / 07
Fax: (0231) 5245 08
Other countries
Offices are available also in
Amsterdam, Brussels, Copenhagen, Lon-
don, Madrid, Milan, Paris, Stockholm
Tokyo, Vienna, and Zürich.

GERMAN TOURIST OFFICES IN THE UNITED STATES AND CANADA

United States
◆**Los Angeles:** German National Tourist
Office
11766 Wilshire Blvd., Suite 750
Los Angeles, CA 90025
Tel. (310) 575-9799
Fax: (310) 575-1565

◆New York:
German National Tourist Office
122 East 42nd Street; Chanin Building,
52nd Floor
New York, NY 10168-0072
Tel: (212) 661-7200
Fax (212) 661-7174
◆Chicago:
German National Tourist Office
c/o German-American Chamber of
Commerce [for trade only in IL, IN, MI,
MN & WI]
401 North Michigan Avenue, Suite 2525
Chicago, IL 60611-4212
Tel. (312) 644-0723
Fax: (312) 644-0724

Canada

◆Toronto:
German National Tourist Office
175 Bloor Street East, North Tower, Suite
604
Toronto, Ontario M4W 3R8
Tel. (416) 968-1570
Fax: (416) 968-1986

DER TOURS

◆U.S. Corporate Office
11933 Wilshire Blvd.
Los Angeles, CA 90025
Tel.: (310) 479-4140
◆Chicago Sales Office/German Rail
9501 W. Devon Avenue
Rosemont, IL 60018-4832
Tel.: (847) 692-6300
Fax: (847) 692-4506

TOURISM OFFICES IN GERMANY

◆Frankfurt:
Deutsche Zentrale für Tourismus e.V.
(DZT)
Beethovenstraße 69
60325 Frankfurt (Main)
Tel.: (069) 75 72 - 0
Fax: (069) 75 19 03

◆Frankfurt:
Fremdenverkehrsamt der USA (U.S.
Travel and Tourism Adminis-tration)
Bethmannstraße 56
60311 Frankfurt (Main)
Tel.: (069) 9 20 03 60
Fax: (069) 74 64 36
◆Frankfurt:
Deutsches Reisebüro GmbH (DER)
Emil-von-Behring-Str. 6
60439 Frankfurt (Main)
Tel.: (069) 95 88 17 58
Fax: (069) 95 88 17 67
(DER is the German general agent for
Amtrak service and Greyhound bus
transportation.)

AMERICAN UNIVERSITIES IN GERMANY

◆Stanford Univeristy (Berlin)
Pacelli-Allee 18-20
14195 Berlin
Tel.: (030) 8 31 30 88
Fax: (030) 8 31 30 - 79
**◆University of Southern California
(USC), Germany**
Hohenstaufenstr. 1
80801 München
Tel.: (089) 34 59 54
Fax: (089) 33 60 04
◆University of Maryland (Mannheim)
Grenadierstr. 4, Gebäude 485
68167 Mannheim
Tel.: (0621) 337 40
Fax: (0621) 337 4103
◆University of Maryland (Heidelberg)
Im Bosseldorn 30
69126 Heidelberg
Tel.: (06221) 3 78 - 0
Fax: (06221 3 78 - 300
**◆University of Maryland University
College**
Postfach 20 23
73510 Schwäbisch Gmünd
Tel.: (07171) 18070
Fax: (07171) 37525, or 37776
◆ Schiller International University

(Heidelberg)
Admissions Office and Central
Administration
Bergstraße 106
69121 Heidelberg
Tel.: (06221) 4 91 59
Fax: (06221) 40 27 03

GERMAN-AMERICAN ORGANIZATIONS

◆**Atlantik-Brücke e.V.**
Adenauerallee 131
53113 Bonn
Postfach 11 47
53001 Bonn
Tel.: (0228) 2 14 1 60 or -2 60
Fax: (0228) 2 14 - 6 59
◆**American Council on Germany**
14 East 60th Street, Suite 606
New York, NY 10022
Tel.: (212) 826-3636
Fax: (212) 758-3445
E-Mail: aicgsdoc@jhunix.hcf.jhu.edu
◆**American Institute for Contemporary German Studies**
The Johns Hopkins University
1400 16th Street, N.W., Suite 420
Washington, D.C. 20036-2217
Tel.: (202) 332-9312
Fax: (202) 265-9531
E-mail: aicgsdoc@jhunix.hcf.jhu.edu
◆**"Städte-Brücke" e.V.**
Deutsch-Amerikanischer Rundfunk - und
Fernseh-Arbeitskreis
Postfach 76 04 44
22054 Hamburg
Tel.: (040) 20 46 47
Fax: (040) 2.00 26 55
(This organization organizes private and professional exchanges between Germans and Americans. It focuses on arranging meetings between Germans and Americans with the same surname.)
◆**Verband der Deutsch-Amerikanischen Clubs e.V.**
Kniebisstraße 16
68163 Mannheim

Tel./Fax: (0621) 81 78 89
◆**German American Joint Action Committee (GAJAC)**
P.O. Box 5488
Washington, DC 20016-5488
(This is the umbrella organization of the three largest German-American organizations, listed immediately below. The three organizations work together in preparing German American Day as well as in other areas.)
◆**German-American National Congress (DANK)**
Deutsch-Amerikanischer Nationalkongreß Executive Offices
4740 N. Western Avenue - 2nd Floor
Chicago, IL 60625-2097
Tel.: (312) 275-1100
Fax: (312) 275-4010
◆**Steuben Society of America**
National Council
6705 Fresh Pond Road
Ridgewood, NY 11385
Tel.: (718) 381-0900
Fax: (718) 628-4874
◆**United German-American Committee of the USA**
Vereinigtes Deutsch-Amerikanische
Komitee (VDAK)
515 Huntingdon Pike
Rockledge, PA 19046-4451
TEl.: (215) 379-1722
Fax: (215) 663-8533

OTHER ORGANIZATIONS

◆**German Wine Information Bureau**
79 Madison Avenue, 9th Floor
New York, NY 10016
Tel.: (212) 213-7028
Fax: (212) 213-7042
◆**German Village Meeting Haus**
588 Third Street
Columbus, OH 43215
Tel.: (614) 221-8888
◆**American Association of Teachers of German, Inc. (AATG)**
112 Haddontowne Court No. 104

Cherry Hill, NJ 08034-3668
Tell.: (609) 795-5553
Fax: (609) 795-9398
◆German Studies Association
Arizona State University
Box 87 32 04
Tempe, AZ 85287-3204
Tel.: (602) 965-4839
Fax: (602) 965-8989
◆German Language Society
P.O. Box 4811
Washington, DC 20008
Tel.: (202) 333-6281
◆Society for German American
Studies
Blegen Library
University of Cincinnati
P.O. Box 210 113
Cincinnati, OH 45221-0113
Tel.: (513) 556-1959
Fax: (513) 556-2113
◆Center for German & European
Studies
Edmund A. Walsh School of Foreign

Service
Georgetown University
Washington, DC 20057
Tel.: (202) 687-5602
Fax: (202) 687-8359
◆Center for German & European
Studies
University of California
254 Moses Hall
Berkeley, CA 94720-2316
Tel. (510) 643-5777
Fax: (510) 643-5996
◆Deutsches Historisches Institut
1607 New Hampshire Avenue, NW
Washington, DC 20009
Tel. (202) 387-3355
Fax: (202) 483-3430
◆Center for Immigration Research
Temple University - Balch Institute
18 South 7th Street
Philadelphia, PA 19106
Tel.: (215) 922-3454
Fax: (215) 922-3201
◆The German Marshall Fund of the

United States
Berlin Office
Friedrichstr. 113a
10117 Berlin
Tel.: (030) 2 83 48 33; 2 83 48 43
Fax: (030) 2 83 48 53
♦**The German Marshall Fund of the
United States**
11 Dupont Circle, NW
Washington, DC 20036
Tel. (202) 745-3950
Fax: (202) 265-1662
♦**Institute for German-American
Relations**
9380 McKnight Road, Suite 102
Pittsburgh, PA 15237
Tel: (412) 364-6554
Fax: (412) 364-7752
♦**Ellis Island Immigration Museum**
Statue of Liberty National Monument
Ellis Island/Liberty Island
New York, NY 10044
Tel.: (212) 363-7620 or 7772
Fax: (212) 363-8347

GERMAN SCHOOLS
IN THE UNITED STATES

♦**Deutsche Schule Washington, DC**
8617 Chateau Drive
Potomac, MD 20854
Tel.: (301) 365-4400
Fax: (301) 365-3905
♦**Deutsche Schule New York**
50 Partridge Road
White Plains, NY 10605
Tel.: (914) 948-6514
Fax: (914) 948-6529
♦**Deutsch-Amerikanische Schule San
Francisco**
275 Elliott Drive
Menlo Park, CA 94025
Tel.: (415) 324-8617
Fax: (415) 324-9548
♦**German Language School Conference
(GLSC)**
154 Middle River Road
Danbury, CT 06810

Tel.: (203) 792-2795
(An association of private German
language schools in the United States (for
the most part Saturday schools.)

AMERICAN AND INTERNATIONAL
SCHOOLS IN GERMANY

♦**John-F.-Kennedy-Schule**
Teltower Damm 87-93
14167 Berlin
Tel.: (030) 8 07 - 27 10
Fax: (030) 8 07 - 33 77
♦**International School of Düsseldorf e.V.**
Leuchtenberger Kirchweg 2
40489 Düsseldorf
Tel.: (0211) 94 066
Fax: (0211) 4 08 07 74
♦**The Frankfurt International School**
An der Waldlust 15
61440 Oberursel
Tel.: (06171) 2 02 - 0
Fax: (06171) 2 02 - 3 84
♦**Hamburg International School**
Internationale Schule Hamburg
Holmbrook 20
20605 Hamburg
Tel.: (040) 8 83 00 10
Fax: (040) 8 81 14 05
♦**Europäische Schule Karlsruhe**
Albert-Schweitzer-Straße 1
76139 Karlsruhe-Waldstadt
Tel.: (0721) 68 00 90
Fax: (0721) 68 72 33
♦**Europäische Schule München**
Elise-Aulinger-Straße 21
81739 München
Tel.: (089) 6 37 84 18
♦**Munich International School**
Percha-Schloß Buchhof
82319 Starnberg
Tel: (08151) 366 - 0
Fax: (08151) 366 119

MAX KADE INSTITUTES

◆Max Kade Institute for German-
American Studies at the University of
Wisconsin-Madison
901 University Bay Drive
Madison, WI 53705
Tel.: (608) 262-7546
Fax: (608) 265-4640
E-mail: maxkade@macc.wisc.edu
◆Max Kade German-American
Research Institute
304 Burrowes Building
Pennsylvania State University
University Park, PA 16802-6203
Tel.: *814) 863-9537
Fax: (814) 865-5482
E-mail: gari@psu.edu
◆Max Kade German-American
CenterIndiana University-Purdue
University at Indianapolis
401 East Michigan Street
Indianapolis, IN 46204
Tel. (317) 464-9004
Fax: (317) 630-0035
◆Max Kade German-American
Document and Research Center
Department of Germanic Languages and
Literatures
University of Kansas
Lawrence, KS 66045

AMERICAN HOUSES
(Amerika-Häuser)

◆Amerika-Haus Berlin
Hardenbergstr. 22-24
10623 Berlin
Tel.: (030) 31 00 01 13/14
Fax: (030) 31 00 01 27
e-mail: covbera@usia.gov
◆Amerika-Haus Frankfurt
Staufenstsr. 1
60232 Frankfurt (Main)
Tel.: (069) 97 14 48 28
Fax: (069) 17 49 62
e-mail: bibifran@usia.gov

◆Amerika-Haus Hamburg
Tesdorpfstsr. 1
20148 Hamburg
Tel.: (040) 45 01 04 23
Fax: (040) 44 80 96 98
e-mail: csghamb@usia.gov
◆Amerika-Haus Köln
Apostelnkloster 13-15
50672 Köln
Tel.: (0221 209 01 47
Fax: (0221) 209 01 57
e-mail-ahlcolo@usia.gov
◆Amerika-Haus Leipzig
Wilhelm-Seyfferth-Straße 4
04107 Leipzig
Tel.: (0341) 2 13 84 25
Fax: (0341) 2 13 84 43
e-mail: ustleip@usia.gov
◆Amerika-Haus München
Karolinenplatz 3
80333 München
Tel.: (089) 55 25 37 21
Fax: (089) 55 35 78
e-mail: mapmuni@usia.gov

GERMAN HOUSES
(Deutsche Häuser)

◆Deutsches Haus
Columbia Univeresity
420 West 116th Street
New York, NY 10011
Tel.: (212) 280-3964
◆Deutsches Haus
New York University
42 Washington Meews
New York, NY 10003
Tel.: (212) 998-8660
Fax: (212) 998-4142

THE TWO MAJOR
GERMAN LIBRARIES

◆Deutsche Bibliothek Frankfurt a.M.
Zeppelinallee 4 - 8
60325 Frankfurt am Main
Tel.: (069) 75 66-372

◆**Deutsche Bücherei Leipzig**
Deutscher Platz 1
04103 Leipzig
Tel.: (0341) 22 7a-309

GERMAN-AMERICAN INSTITUTES IN GERMANY

◆**Carl-Schurz Haus**
Kaiser-Joseph-Straße 266
79098 Freiburg
Tel.: (0761) 3 16 45
Fax: (0761) 3 98 27
◆**Deutsch-Amerikanisches Institut**
Sofienstr. 12
69115 Heidelberg
Tel.: (06221) 2 47 71
Fax: (06221) 1 49 25
◆**Kennedy-Haus**
Holtenauerstr. 9
24103 Kiel
Tel.: (0431 55 48 66
◆**Deutsch-Amerikanisches Institut**
Gleissbühlstr. 13
90402 Nürnberg
Tel.: (0911) 20 33 27
Fax: (0911) 20 87 67
◆**Deutsch-Amerikanisches Institut**
Haidplatz 8
93047 Regensburg
Tel.: (0941) 5 24 76
Fax: (0941) 5 21 98

◆**Deutsch-Amerikanisches Institut**
Berliner Promenade 15
66111 Saarbrücken
Tel.: (0681) 3 11 60
Fax: (0681) 37 26 24
◆**Deutsch-Amerikanisches Institut**
Karlstr. 3
72072 Tübingen
Tel.: (07071) 3 40 71/2
Fax: (07071) 3 18 73

SISTER-CITY PARTNERSHIPS

◆**Deutscher Städtetag (DST)**
Lindenallee 13 - 17
50968 Köln
Tel.: (0221) 37 71 - 0
Fax: (0221) 37 71 - 1 27 or -8
(Issues information on sister-city partnerships)
◆**Sister Cities International**
120 Payne Street, Suite 400
Alexandria, VA 22314
Tel.: (703) 836-3535
Fax: (703) 836-4815
◆**Institut für europäische Partnerschaft-en und internationale Zusammen-arbeit e.V. (IPZ)**
Mirecourtstr. 7
53225 Bonn
Tel.: (0228) 46 72 83
Fax: (0228) 47 72 86
(Promotes sister-city partnerships)

Index

A

$\mathcal{B}$

𝒟

𝓔

𝓕

G

$\mathcal{H}$

𝓘

𝒥

$\mathcal{K}$

$\mathcal{L}$

$\mathcal{N}$

O

P

Q

R

$\mathcal{S}$

T

U

V

W

Y

Z

Cited Sources and References

Adressbuch: Der deutsch-amerikanischen Zusammenarbeit, Bonn, 1994 and 1996.

Die Ahnenlisten-Kartei. Verlag Degener, Neustadt/Aisch, Germany, 1975- 14 vols.

Ruth Bailey Allen, "Church Records Relating to the Pennsylvania Germans." Palatines to America: Publications Plus, 1992

Almar Associates, *Bukovina Families: 200 Years.* Almar Associates, Ellis, Kansas, 1993.

American Council for Nationalities Service, comp., *Ethnic Press in the United States: Lists of Foreign Language Nationality and Ethnic Newspapers and Periodicals in the United States.New York, 1974.*

Ulrich Ammon, "The German Language: Lingua Franca Overshadowed by English?" *Deutschland*, No. 1,2/1994.

Archive in der Bundesrepublik Deutschland, Österreich und der Schweiz. 15. Ausgabe, Ardey-Verlag Münster, 1995.

Karl J.R. Arndt, and May E. Olson, comps., *German-American Newspapers and Periodicals, 1732-1955: History and Bibliography.* 2nd rev. ed. 1961. Reprint. Johnson Report Corp., New York. Vol. 2.

_____, *The German Language Press of the Americas 1732-1968: A History and Bibliography. Die deutschsprachige Press der Amerikas.* Verlag Dokumentation, München, 1973-1976.

Laura Longley Babb, "Iowa's Enduring Amana Colonies." *National Geographic*, December 1975.

George Arnstein, "Genealogical Resources for German Jewish Ancestry," Chap. XII of *Germanic Genealogy: A Guide to Worldwide Sources and Migration Patterns*, by Edward R. Brandt et al., Germanic Genealogy Society, St. Paul, Minn., 1994.

Leo Baca, ed., *Czech Immigration Passenger Lists.* 2 vols. Old Homestead Publishing Co., Hallettsville,Tex., 1983-1985.

Hans Bahlow, *Dictionary of German Names*, trans. Edda Gentry. Friends of the Max Kade Institute for German-American Studies, Inc., Madison, Wisc., 1993.

E.M.C. Barraclough, ed., *Flags of the World.* Warne & Co., New York, 1971.

Albert Bartholdi, *Prominent Americans of Swiss Origin.* James T. White & Co., New York, 1932.

Angus Baxter, *In Search of Your German Roots: A Complete Guide to Tracing Your Ancestors in the Germanic Areas of Europe.* Genealogical Publishing Co., Inc., Baltimore, 3rd ed., 1994.

Henry Putney Beers, *A Guide to the Archives of the Government of the Confederate States of America.* National Archives and Records Service, Washington, D.C., 1968.

Alexander Beider, *A Dictionary of Jewish Surnames from the Former Russian Empire.* Avotaynu, Teaneck, NJ, 1993.

_____, *A Dictionary of Jewish Surnames from the Kingdom of Poland.*
    Avotaynu, Teaneck, NJ, 1995.
Benn's Media Directory International. Benn's Business Information Services,
    Tonbridge, England. Annual
Elizabeth Petty Bentley, *County Courthouse Book.* Genealogical Publishing Co.,
    Inc., Baltimore, 1995.
_____, *Directory of Family Associations.* Genealogical Publishing Co., Inc.,
    Baltimore, 1993
_____, *The Genealogists' Address Book.* Genealogical Publishing Co., Inc.,
    Baltimore, 3rd ed., 1995.
Edna M. Bentz, *If I Can You Can Decipher Germanic Records.* Edna M. Bentz,
    1982.
*Bibliography of Genealogy and Local Periodicals with Union List of Major U.S.
    Collections.* First ed., Allen County Public Library Foundation, Fort
    Wayne, 1990.
Lester H. Binnie, "Migration of Early German Baptist Brethren Within the United
    States." The *Palatine Immigrant,* Vol. V, No. 1, Summer 1979.
Steven W. Blodgett, *German Genealogical Research Guide.* The Genealogical
    Department of the Church of Jesus Christ of Latter-day Saints, 1989.
Keith Boger, "Württembergers to America: The Harmonists." *The German
    Connection,* Vol. 14, No. 4, October 1990.
August C. Bolino, *The Ellis Island Source Book.* Kensingon Historical Press,
    Washington,DC, 1985.
Irma Bornemann, *The Bukovina Germans (Die Buchenlanddeutschen,* Vol. 13 of
    Kulturelle Arbeitschelfte, ed. Barbara Konitz. Bonn: Bund der
    Vertriebenen, 1986) English trans. Sophie A. Welisch, Bukovina Society
    of the Americas, Ellis, Kansas, 1990.
Helen Boyden, "Die Ahnenlisten-Kartei." *The German Connection,* January
    1988.
Clarence Saunders Brigham, *History and Bibliography of American
    Newspapers, 1690-1820.* 2 vols. American Antiquarian Society,
    Worcester, Mass., 1947. (Additions and corrections published in 1961)
Edward R. Brandt, Mary Bellingham, Kent Cutkomp, Kermit Frye, and Patricia
    Lowe, *Germanic Genealogy: A Guide to Worldwide Sources and
    Migration Patterns.* Germanic Genealogy Society, St. Paul, Minn., 1994.
*Broadcast Media. . . an Annual Guide to Newspapers, Magazines, Journals, and
    Related Publications (*formerly *Ayer Directory of Publications).* IMS
    Press. Published annually since 1869.
Brockhaus Enzyklopädie, Sechster Band. F.A. Brockhaus, Mannheim, 1988.
Raymond Lamont Brown, *A Book of Epitaphs.* Taplinger Publishing Co., New
    York, 1969.
David Brownstone and Irene Franck, *Timelines of War: A Chronology of Warfare
    from 100,000 BC to the Present.* Little, Brown and Company, Boston,
    1994.
Ekkehard Brose, Betsy Wittleder, Ina-Marie Blomeyer, Andrea Metz, eds.,
    "German Americans." German Embassy, March 1996.
Martin Grovek Brumbaugh, *A History of the German Baptist Brethren in Europe*

and America. Bookmark, Knightstown, Ind., 1977.

Olgierd Budrewicz, *Introduction to Poland.* American Institute of Polish Culture, Miami, 1985.

Annette K. Burgert, Eighteenth Century Emigrants from German-Speaking Lands to North America. Pennsylvania German Society, Breinigsville, Pa., 1983 and 1985.

_____, *Eighteenth Century Emigrants from Northern Alsace to America.* Picton Press, Camden, Maine, 1992.

_____, "Are Your Pennsylvania Dutch Ancestors Really Swiss?" *The German Connection,* First Quarter, 1995.

Dennis Burnside, "Oktoberfest Horses," *German Life,* October/November 1996.

Michelle Buswinka, "A Ballot for Americans: A Famous Vote That Was Never Taken." *Munich Found,* April 1992.

Nancy J. Carroll, "Unusual References to Confederate Military Service." *Ancestry Newsletter,* 8 (July-August 1990).

Cassell's German-English, English-German Dictionary, rev. by Harold T. Betteridge. Macmillan Publishing Co., New York, 1978.

Florence Clint, *Pennsylvania Area Key: A Guide to the Genealogical Records of the State of Pennsylvania; Including Maps, Histories, Charts, and Other Helpful Materials.* 2nd ed. Area Keys, Denver, 1976.

John P. Colletta, *They Came in Ships.* Ancestry Publishing, Salt Lake City, 1989.

William S. Cramer, "Die Hessische Soldaten – The Hessian Soldiers." *German American Genealogy,* Spring 1991.

Elizabeth Powell Crowe, *Genealogy Online: Researchng Your Roots.* Windcrest/ McGraw-Hill, Blue Ridge Summit, Pa., 1995.

John Dahl, Conversion Tables, *French Republican Calendar: An Aid for Family Research in France and Germany.* 2nd ed., Deseret Books, Salt Lake City, Ut. 1972.

Fay and Douglas Dearden, *The German Researcher: How to Get the Most Out of Our Family History Center.* Family Tree Press, Minneapolis, Minn., 1983. 4th ed., revised and expanded 1990.

Deutsches biographisches Archiv, D.G. Saur, München, 1980-.

Deutsches Geschlechterbuch. C.A. Starke, Limburg/Lahn, Germany, 1889-. 203 vols.

Martin A. Diestler, "Some suggestions on tracing emigrants through Hamburg police records," *The Palatine Immigrant,* Vol. 14, no. 1, March 1989.

Eugene Edgar Doll, *The Ephrata Cloister: An Introduction.* Ephrata Cloister Associates, Ephrata, Pa., 1958.

John Dornberg, "Living Roman Legacy." *German Life,* April/May 1995.

Richard G. Doty, *The Macmillan Encyclopedic Dictionary of Numismatics.* Macmillan Publishing Co., Inc., New York, 1982.

Arlene Eakle and Johni Cerny, *The Source: A Guidebook of American Genealogy.* Ancestry Publishing Co., Salt Lake City, Ut., 1984.

Corinne P. Earnest, *AntiqueWeek;* and Kenneth L. Marple; Palatines to America National Conference, June 1994.

Thomas Kent Edlund, comp, *An Introduction and Register to Die Ahnenstammkartei des deutschen Volkes of the Deutsche Zentralstelle für Genealogie Leipzig 1922-1991.* Family History Library, Salt Lake City, Ut., 1993.

Wolfgang Eger, *Verzeichnis der Militärkirchenbücher in der Bundesrepublik Deutschland (nach dem Stand vom 30. September 1990). Veröffentlichungen der Arbeitsgemeinschaft der Archive und Bibliotheken in der evangelischen Kirche 18.* Verlag Degener & Co., Neustadt/Aisch, 1993.

Alice Eichholz, ed., *Ancestry's Red Book: American State, County, and Town Sources.* Ancestry Publishing, Salt Lake City, Ut., 1989, 1992.

Glen Eker, "Canadian Passenger Ship Manifests." *Ancestry,* March/April 1996.

Irmgard Hein Ellingson, *The Bukovina Germans in Kansas: A 200 Year History of the Lutheran Swabians.* No. 6 of Ethnic Heritage Sstudies. Fort Hays State University, 1987.

Encyclopedia Britannica: Dictionary of Arts, Sciences, Literature and General Information. University Press, New York, 11ᵗʰ ed., 1910.

Rolf Engelsing, *Bremen als Auswandererhafen 1683/1880. Ein Beitrag zur bremischen Wirtschaftsgeschichte des 19. Jahrhunderts.* Schünemann, Bremen, 1961.

H. Frank Eschleman, *Historic Background and Annals of the Swiss and German Pioneer Settlers of Southeastern Pennsylvania, and of Their Remote Ancestors.* 1917. Reprint, Genealogical Publishing Co., Inc. Baltimore, 1969.

James Ethridge, ed., *Directory of Directories,* Gale Research, Detroit, 1980.

George B. Everton, Sr., *The Handy Book for Genealogists.* 8ᵗʰ ed., Everton Publishers, Inc., Logan Ut., 1991.

Facts about Germany. Societäts-Verlag, 1995.

Myron R. Falck, "German Coats of Arms." *The German Connection,* Vol. 20, No. 2, 1996.

George N. Falkenstein, "The German Baptist Brethren or Dunkers." *Pennsylvania German Society Proceedings and Addresses* 10, 1900. Pennsylvania German Society, Lancaster, Pa., 1900.

Familiennamenbuch der Schweiz, 3ʳᵈ ed. Schultheiss Polygraphischer Verlag, Zürich, 1989. 3 vols.

Albert Bernhardt Faust, *The American Immigration Collection: The German Element in the United States.* Arno Press and New York Times, New York, 1969. Vol. I.

Albert B. Faust and Galus M. Brumbaugh., *Lists of Swiss Emigrants in the Eighteenth Century to the American Colonies.* National Genealogical Society, Washington, D.C., 1925. Reprinted with Dr. Leo Schelbert's "Notes on Swiss Emigrants," Genealogical Publishing Co., Inc., Baltimore, Md., 1976.

Laraine K. Ferguson and Larry O. Jensen, "Die Ahnenstammkartei des deutschen Volkes Pedigree Collection from Leipzig, Germany." *German Genealogial Digest,* Vol. 9 No. 4, 1993.

Laraine K. Ferguson, "Ahnenlistenumlauf: Circulating German Ancestor Lists, a Rich Source for the Genealogist." *German Genealogical Digest,* Fall 1995.

_____, "Hamburg, Germany, Gateway to the Ancestral Home." *German Genealogical Digest,* Vol. 2, No. 1, 1985.

_____ "Locating Church and Civil Registration Records," *German Genealogical Digest, Vol. 1, No. 3, 1985.*

_____, "Newspapers: Unique Sources for German Family and Local History." *German Genealogical Digest,* Vol. 3, No. 3, 1987.

Wilfried Fest, *Dictionary of German History, 1806-1945.* St. Martin's Press, New York, 1978.

P. William Filby, *Passenger and Immigration Lists Bibliography, 1538-1900: Being a Guide to Published Lists of Arrivals in the United States and Canada.* Gale Research Co., Detroit, 1988.

_____ , with Mary K. Meyer, eds. *Passenger and Immigration Lists Index: A Guide to Published Arrival Records of about 500,000 Passengers Who Came to the United States and Canada in the 17th, 18th, and 19th Centuries.* 3 vols. Gale Research Co., 1981. Supplemental volumes.

Donald R. Fitzkee, *Moving Toward the Mainstream: 20th Century Change Among the Brethren of Eastern Pennsylvania.* Good Books, 1995.

Hyde Flippo, *The German Way.* Passport Books, Lincolnwood, Ill., 1997.

Aaron Spencer Fogleman, *Hopeful Journeys: German Immigration, Settlement, and Political Culture in Colonial America,* 1717-1775. University of Pennsylvania Press, Philadelphia, 1996.

Arthur Charles Fox-Davies, *The Art of Heraldry: an Encyclopedia of Armory,* Arno, New York, 1904, reprint 1976.

"Frankfurt Declaration Attacks Much Debated Language Reform," *The Week in Germany,* German Information Center, October 11, 1996.

Charles M. Franklin, *Dutch Genealogical Research,* C.M. Franklin, c 1982.

Eckhart G. Franz, comp., *Hessische Truppen im amerikanischen Unabhängigkeitskrieg (HETRINA).* Archivschule, Marburg, Germany. 1971-1976, 1987. 3 vols.

Frank Fuqua, "Dewey Decimal Numbers,." *Mission Oaks Genealogy Club Newsletter,* Winter 1997.

Judith M. Gansberg, *Stalag USA: The Remarkable Story of German POWs in America.* Thomas Y. Crowell Co., New York, 1977.

Farley Grubb, *German Immigration Servant Contracts: Registered at the Port of Philadelphia, 1817-1831.* Genealogical Publishing Co., Baltimore, 1994.

Jake Gehring, "Social Security Death Master File: A Much Misunderstood Index." *Genealogical Journal,* Utah Genealogical Association, Vol. 24, No. 2, 1996.

Birgit Gelbert, *Auswanderung nach Übersee. Soziale Probleme der Auswandererbeförderung in Hamburg und Bremen von der Mitte des 19. Jahrhunderts bis zum ersten Weltkrieg.* (Beiträge zur Geschichte Hamburg 10). Hamburg: Christiansen, 1973.

Genealogisches Handbuch des Adels. C.A. Starke Verlag, 1951-. 51 vols.

Wolfgang Glaser, *Americans and Germans.* Verlag Moos&Partner, München, 1985.

Ira A. Glazier and P. William Filby, ed., *Germans to America: Lists of Passengers*

Arriving at U.S. Ports, 1850-1855. Scholarly Resources, 104 Greenhill
    Avenue, Wilmington, Del. 19805-2897.
Adam Giesinger, *From Catherine to Khruschev.* Marian Press, Battleford,
    Saskatchewan, Canada, 1974.
Martin Gilbert, *The Atlas of Jewish History.* William Morrow and Co., New York,
    rev. ed. 1993.
Irene Saunders Goldstein, ed. *Jewish Genealogy Beginner's Guide.* Jewish
    Genealogy Society of Greater Washington, 2nd ed., Vienna, Va., 1991.
Val D. Greenwood, *The Researcher's Guide to American Genealogy.*
    Genealogical Publishing Co., Baltimore, 1990.
Glenzdorfs Internationales Genealogen-Lexikon. Wilhelm Rost Verlag, Bad
    Münder am Deister, 1977. 2 vols.
Winifred Gregory, ed., *American Newspapers, 1821-1936: A Union List of Files
    Available in the United States and Canada.* Reprint, Kraus Reprint
    Corp., New York, 1967.
_____, ed., *List of the Serial Publications of Foreign Governments, 1815-1931.*
    H.W. Wilson, New York, 1932. Reprint Kraus, Millwood, NY, 1973.
Paul S. Gross, *The Hutterite Way; the Inside Story of the Life, Customs, Religion,
    and Traditions of the Hutterites.* Freeman Publishing, Saskatoon,
    Saskatchewan, 1965.
Helmut Guth, *Amish Mennonites in Germany: Their Congregations, The Estates
    Where They Lived, Their Families.* Masthof Press, Morgantown, Pa.,
    1995.
Gert Hagelweide, comp., *Literatur zur deutschsprachigen Presse: eine
    Bibliogrphie Dortmunder Beiträge zur Zeitungsforschung*, K.G. Saur,
    München, 1985.
Charles M. Hall, *The Atlantic Bridge to Germany*, 9 vols. The Everton Publishers,
    Inc., Logan Ut.
Charles R. Haller, *Across the Atlantic and Beyond: The Migration of German and
    Swiss Immigrants to America.* Heritage Books, Inc., 1993.
John Taylor Hamilton, *A History of the Church Known as the Moravian Church,
    or the Unitas Fratrum, or the Unity of the Brethren, During the
    Eighteenth and Nineteenth Centuries.* 1900. Reprint. AMS Press, New
    York, 1971.
Martin Handel, Rolf Taubert, *Die deutsche Presse 1848-1850. Eine Bibliographie
    deutsche Presseforschung.* K.G. Saur, München, 1986.
"The Hamburg Passenger Lists," *The Genealogical Helper* 44, 1990.
The Hamburg Passenger Lists. Genealogical Society of Utah, Salt Lake City,
    1984.
Patricia Law Hatcher, "Educational Opportunities in Genealogy: Part I, Formal
    Instruction." *Ancestry*, Salt Lake City, May/June 1996.
Bertram Hawthorne Groene, *Tracing Your Civil War Ancestor.* John F. Blair,
    Winston-Salem, N.C., 1973.
Joseph S. Height, *Homesteaders on the Steppe.* Gulde-Druck, Tübingen,
    Germany; Bismarck, ND, 1975.
Franz Heinzmann and Christoph Lenhartz, *Bibliographie gedruckter
    Familiengeschichten, 1946-1960.* Heinzman, Düsseldorf, 1990.

Franz Heinzmann, *Bibliographie der Ortssippenbücher in Deutschalnd.* Henzmann, 1991.

John W. Heisey, *Handbook for Genealogical Research in Pennsylvania.* Heritage House, Indianapolis, Ind., 1985.

_____, "Fire insurance documents may offer valuable information about ancestors." *AntiqueWeek,* September 9, 1996.

_____, *Pennsylvania Genealogical Library Guide.* Masthoff Press, Morgantown, Pa.

_____, "Road less travelled used by some 'back door' immigrant ancestors." *AntiqueWeek,* August 28, 1995.

_____, "Territorial expansion enhanced by federal land 'giveaway' programs." *AntiqueWeek,* Knightstown, IN.

Herne, *Genealogical Guide to German Ancestors from East Germany and Eastern Europe* (AgoFF-Wegweiser - English Edition), Arbeitsgemeinschaft ostdeutscher Familienforscher e.V. Trans., Joachim O. R. Nuthack and Adalbert Goertz. Verlag Degener, Neustadt/Aisch, 1984.

Bodo Heyne, "Über bremische Quellen zur Auswanderungsforschung." *Bremisches Jahrbuch 41,* 1944.

Edward W. Hocker, *Genealogical Data Relating to the German Settlers of Pennsyllvania and Adjacent Territory from Advertisements in German Newspapers Published in Philadelphia and Germantown, 1743-1800.* Genealogical Publishing Co., Baltimore, 1980.

Floyd G. Hoenstsine, *Guide to Genealogical and Historical Research in Pennsylvania.* 3rd ed., F. Hoenstsine, Hollidaysburg, Pa., 1978.

Johannes Hohlfeld, Friedrich Wecken, et al, eds. *Familiengeschichtliche Bibliographie.* Verlag Degener, Neustadt/Aisch, 1920-1945.

Helmut Hörner, *A German Odyssey: The Journal of a German Prisoner of War,* Fulcrum Publishing, Golden, Colorado, 1991.

John Horsch, *Hutterite Brethren: 1528-1931.* The Mennonite Historical Society, Goshen, Ind., 1931.

Kenneth Hudson and Ann Nichols, *The Cambridge Guide to the Museums of Europe.* Cambridge University Press, New York and Cambridge, 1991.

"The Huguenots in Germanic Areas," *German Genealogical Digest,* Vol. 2, No. 4, 1986.

John T. Humphrey, "Baptismal Records: Understanding Their Meaning and Use." *Der Kurier,* Mid-Atlantic Germanic Society, Vol. 14, No. 2, June 1996.

William A. Hynes, "A History of German Canadians." *German Life,* February/March 1996.

"Insights to Research: German Census and Other Population Records." *German Genealogical Digest,* Vol. VI, No. 1.

International Handbook of Universities. 13th ed., International Association of Universities. The Macmillan Press Ltd., London, 1993.

Arthur Jacot, *Schweizerisches Ortslexikon.* C.J. Bucher, Luzern.

Betty M. Jarboe, *Obituaries: A Guide to Sources.* G.K. Hall & Co., Boston, 1982.

C. Russell Jensen, *Parish Register Latin: an Introduction.* Vita Nova Books, Salt

Lake City, 1988. Out of print

Larry O. Jensen, "Dorfsippenbücher and Ortssippenbücher." *German Genealogical Digest,* Vol. VII, No. 2, 1991.

_____, "Basic Principles in Resolving Naming Practice Problems." *German Genealogical Digest,* Vol. 4, No. 1, 1988.

_____, *A Genealogical Handbook of German Research,* rev. ed., Everton Publishers, Logan, Ut. 2 vols. 1980-1983.

_____, "Jewish Records." *German Genealogical Digest,* Vol. 9, No. 1, 1993.

_____, "The World of Germanic Names, or A German by Any Other Name May be Your Ancestor." *German Genealogical Digest.* Part I, Vol. 4, No. 1, 1988; Part II, Vol. 4, No. 2, 1988.

Gerhard Jeske, "Guild Records in Germany." *German Genealogical Digest,* Vol. 10, No. 4, Winter 1994.

Arta F. Johnson, ed. *Bibliography and Source Materials for German-American Research,* Arta F. Johnson, 1982. Updated 1984.

_____, *How to Read German Church Records without Knowing Much German.* The Copy Shop, Columbus, Ohio, 1981.

_____, "Old Moravian Cemeteries." *Palatine Immigrant,* Vol. V, No. 1, Summer 1979.

George F. Jones, *German American Names,* 2nd ed.. Genealogical Publishing Co., Baltimore, 1995.

Manrial Phillips Joslyn, "Was Your Civil War Ancestor a Prisoner of War?" *Ancestry Newsletter,* 11 (July-August 1993).

Daniel Kaufman, ed., *Mennonite Cyclopedic Dictionary.* Mennonite Publishing House, Scottdale, Pa., 1937. Reprinted 1978 by The Bookmark, Knightstown, Ind.

P. Conrad Keller, *The German Colonies in South Russia: 1804-1904.* A. Becker, trans. Mercury Printers, Ltd., Saskatoon, Saskatchewan, Canada, 1973. 2 vols.

Thomas Jay Kemp, *International Vital Records Handbook.* Genealogical Publishing Co., Inc., Baltimore, 1990.

E. Kay Kirkham, *A Survey of American Church Records: Major Denominations before 1880,* Vol. 1. Everton Publishers, Logan, Ut., 1971.

_____, *A Survey of American Church Records: Minor Denominations,* Vol. 2. Everton Publishers, Logan, Ut., 1969.

Fredric Klees, *The Pennsylvania Dutch.* The Macmillan Co., New York, 1952. (out of print)

William C. Kleese, "375 Years of Vital Records in the United States: Where and How to Access Them in 1995." National Genealogy Society Conference of the States, 1995 program book.

Timothy J. and Rosalinda Kloberdanz, *Thunder on the Steppe.* American Historical Society of Germans from Russia, Lincoln, Neb., 1993.

Karl-Werner Klüber, "Die Hamburger Auswanderlisten (Schiffslisten)". *Mitteilungen der westdeutschen Gesellschaft für Familienkunde* 56, 1968.

_____, "Die Hamburger Schiffslisten." *Archiv für Sippenforschung,* 1964.

Luke B. Knapke, comp., ed.,: *Liwwät Böke 1807-1882: Pioneer.* The Minster Historical Society, Minster, Ohio, 1987.
Helmut Kohnt and Berndt Knorr, *Alte Maße, Münzen und Gewichte.* Bibliographisches Institut Mannheim, Meyers Lexikonverlag, 1987.
Allen V. Koop, *Stark Decency: German Prisoners of War in a New England Village.* University Press of New England, New York, Hanover, 1988.
Rosemary A. Korzenie *Polskie: Polish Roots.* Genealogical Publishing Co., Baltimore, 1993.
"Chronology of German-Polish Relations." *German Life,* December 1996/January 1997.
Elizabeth Gorrell Kot and James Douglas Kot, *United States Cemetery Address Book.* Indices Publishing, Vallejo, Cal.
Dieter Kramer, *German Holidays and Folk Customs.* Atlantik-Brücke, Bonn, 1986.
Arnold Krammer, *Nazi Prisoners of War in America.* Stein And Day, New York, 1979.
Paul N. Kraybill, *Mennonite World Handbook: A Survey of Mennonite and Brethren in Christ Churches.* Mennonite World Conference, Lombard, Ill., 1978.
Zdenka Kucera, "Family Origins in Eastern Europe: Using the Records of the Genealogical Society of Utah, Modern Poland." Church of Jesus Christ of Latter-day Saints, 1980.
Arthur Kurzweil, *From Generation to Generation: How to Trace Your Jewish Genealogy and Personal History.* HarperCollins, New York, 2nd ed. 1994.
James Sigurd Lapham, "The German-American, New York City 1860-1890." Ph.D. dissertation, St. John's University, New York, 1977.
Hugh T. Law, "Locating the Ancestral Home in Elsaß-Lothringen (Alsace Lorraine)." *German Genealogical Digest,* Vol. VI, No. 3, 1990.
Barbara E. Leak, "Yes, In*deed!* American County Land Records." Lecture materials, June 1, 1996.
Neil Stuckey Levine, Ursula Roy, and David J. Rempel Smucker, "Trans-Atlantic Advice: An 1822 Letter by Louis C. Jüngerich (1803-1882)." *Pennsylvania Mennonite Heritage,* Vol. XIX, No. 3, July 1996
Richard Casimir Lewanski, comp., *Guide to Polish Libraries and Archives.* East European Monographs, No. VI. Boulder, Colo., 1974.
Jo White Linn, "Sanborn City Maps." *Heritage Quest* #32.
"Locating the Ancestral Home: Manuscript Collections." *German Genealogical Digest,* Vol. II, No. 2, 1986.
Ella Lonn, *Foreigners in the Union Army and Navy.* Greenwood Press, New York, 1951.
Herman Friedrich Macco, *Swiss Emigrants to the Palatinate in Germany and to America, 1650-1800, and Huguenots in the Palatinate and Germany.* 6 vols.
Peter Marschalck, comp., *Inventar der Quellen zur Geschichte der Wanderungen, besonders der Auswanderung, in Bremer Archiven.* Staatsarchiv Bremen, Bremen, 1986.

Betty Heinz Matyas, "Using the Ahnenlisten-Kartei. " *Der Blumenbaum,* Vol. 11, No. 1, 1993.

Hans-Georg Mercker, *Alphabetisches Register der von und über Harburg ausgewanderten Personen von 1841 bis 1884,* 1964.

Mary K. Meyer, *Meyer's Directory of Genealogial Societies in the U.S. and Canada,* 9th ed. Mount Airy, Md., 1992.

Meyers Lexikon, Bibliographisches Institut, Leipzig, 1930.

Meyers Memo: Das Wissen der Welt nach Sachgebieten. Meyers Lexikonverlag, Mannheim, 1991.

Oskar Michel, comp., *Handbuch deutscher Zeitungen 1917.* Elsner, Berlin, 1917.

Microsoft Encarta, Funk & Wagnalls Corp., 1994.

Anita Creek Milner, *Newspaper Indexes: A Location and Subject Guide for Researchers.* Scarecrow Press, Metuchen, N.J., 1977.

Minerva Atlas, Leipzig, 1927.

Minerva-Handbücher: Archive im deutschsprachingen Raum. Walter de Gruyter. 2nd ed. 1974. 2 vols.

Gary Mokoloff, *How to Document Victims and Locate Survivors of the Holocaust.* Genealogy Unlimited, Orem, Ut.

Merriam M. Moore, "A Guide to Military Churchbooks." *The German Connection,* Vol. 20, No. 3, 1996.

Morton Allan Directory of European Passenger Steamship Arrivals: For the Years 1890 to 1930 at the Port of New York and for the Years 1904 to 1926 at the Ports of New York, Philadelphia, Boston and Baltimore, Genealogical Publishing Company, Inc., Baltimore, 1993.

Friedrich Müller, *Müllers grosses deutsches Ortsbuch.* Wuppertal-Barmen, Germany: Post- und Ortsburchverlag Postsmeister a.d. Friedrich Müller, 1958. 18th ed. 1974.

_____, *Ortsbuch für Eupen-Malmedy, Elsaß-Lothringen und Luxemburg,* 1942.

Lidia Müllerowa, *Roman Catholic Parishes in the Polish People's Republic in 1984.* Genealogy Unlimited, Orem, Ut.

Kenneth W. Munden and Henry Putney Beers, *A Guide to Federal Archives Relating to the Civil War,* National Archives and Records Service, Washington, D.C., 1962.

Michael P. Musick, "The Little Regiment. Civil War Units and Commands." *Prologue* 27 (Summer 1995).

National Archives and Records Administration, "Military Service Records in the National Archives of the United States," General Information Leaflet, No. 7, rev. 1985.

National Archives Trust Fund Board, *Immigrant and Passenger Arrivals: A Select Catalog of National Archives Microfilm Publications.* National Archives Trust Fund Board, Washington, D.C., 1983.

James C. Neagles. *Confederate Research Sources: A Guide to Archive Collections.* Ancestry, Salt Lake City, Ut., 1986.

James C. Neagles and Lila Lee Neagles, *Locating Your Immigrant Ancestor: A Guide to Naturalization Records.* Everton Publishing Co., Logan, Ut., 1975.

Gunnar Nebelung, "Auswanderung über Bremerhaven," *Genealogie* 41, 1992.

Ken Nelson, "Civil War Sources for Genealogical Research." *Genealogical Journal*, 15 (Winter 1986) ; 17 (1988).

Ottfried Neubecker, *Heraldry: Sources, Symbols, and Meaning*. McGraw Hill, New York, 1976.

John J. Newman, *American Naturalization Processes and Procedures, 1790-1985*. Family History Section, Indiana Historical Society, Indianapolis, 1985.

"News of the Family History Library, Salt Lake City, Utah." *Genealogical Helper*, Nov./Dec. 1993.

Paul A. Nielson, *Swiss Genealogical Research: An Introductory Guide*. Donning Co. Publishers, Virginia Beach, Va., 1979.

Joachim Nowrocki, "The Gauck Commission in Berlin." *Deutschland*, August 1995.

Richard O'Connor, *The German-Americans: An Informal History*. Little, Brown and Co., Boston, 1968

Diane L. Oswald, "Fire insurance maps are 'hot' with collectors." *AntiqueWeek*, August 5, 1996.

Michael Palmer, *Genealogical Resources in Eastern Germany (Poland)*. Privately published, Claremont, Cal., 1993.

_____, "Published Passenger Lists: A Review of German Immigrants and Germans to America." *German Genealogical Society of America Bulletin*, vol. 4, 1990.

Grace D. Parch, ed., *Directory of Newspaper Libraries in the U.S. and Canada*. Special Libraries Association, New York, c 1976.

J. Carlyle Parker, *Going to Salt Lake City to Do Family History Research*. Marietta Publishing Company, Turlock, Calif., 3rd ed., 1996.

Richard A. Pence, ed., *Computer Genealogy: A Guide to Research Through High Technology*. Ancestry, Salt Lake City, Ut., 1991. Rev. ed.

Pennsylvania German Church Records:Births, Baptisms, Marriages, Burials, Etc., with an introduction by Don Yoder. 3 vols. Genealogical Publishing Co., Baltimore, 1983.

The Pennsylvania-German Society Proceedings and Addresses at Ephrata, Oct. 20, 1899. Vol. X, 1900; Chap. III.

Pennsylvania Line: A Research Guide to Pennsylvania Genealogy and Local History. 3rd ed. Southwest Pennsylvania Genealogical Services, Laughlintown, Pa., 1983.

William Rufus Perkins, and Barthinius L. Wick, *History of the Amana Society or Community of True Inspiration*. Reprint. Radical Tradition in America, Westport, Conn., Hyperion Press, 1976.

Gerald Posner, "Secrets of the Files." *The New Yorker*, March 14, 1994.

Das Postleitzahlenbuch: Alphabetisch geordnet. Postdienst, Bonn, 1993.

Das Postleitzahlenbuch: Numerisch geordnet. Postdienst, Bonn, 1993.

Claire Prechtel-Kluskens, *The Record: News from the National Archives and Records Administration*, Vol. 2, No. 1, September 1995.

Donna Przecha and Joan Lowrey, *Guide to Genealogy Software*. Genealogical Publishing Co., Baltimore, 1993.

Eric L. Pumroy and Katja Rampelmann, comp., *Research Guide to the Turner*

Movement in the United States. Greenwood Press, Westport, Conn., 1996.

Die Quellenschau für Familienforscher. Paul Kuschbert, Köln, 1938. 3 vols.

Register and Guide to the Hamburg Passenger Lists, 1850-1934. Research Paper Series C, No. 30. The Genealogical Department of The Church of Jesus Christ of Latter-day Saints, Salt Lake City.

Levin T. Reichel, *The Moravians in North Carolina, an Authentic History.* 1857. Reprint. Genealogical Publishing Co., Inc., Baltimore, 1968.

Horst A. Reschke, "Beginning Your Military Research." *The German Connection,* Vol. 20, No. 3, 1996.

_____, "The German Lineage Book." *German Genealogical Digest,* Vol. 12, No. 2, Summer 1996.

_____, *German Military Records as Genealogical Sources,* Horst A. Reschke, 1990.

_____, *Military Record Sources in Germany,* Salt Lake City, Utah.

_____, "Preserving Castles and Fortresses." *German Genealogical Digest,* Vol. 12, No. 2, Summer, 1996.

Research Outline: French Republican Calendar. Family History Library, Salt Lake City, Ut., 1990.

Research Outline: Germany, Family History Library, Church of Jesus Christ of Latter-day Saints, Salt Lake City, Ut.

Research Outline: Pennsylvania, Family History Library, Church of Jesus Christ of Latter-day Saints, Salt Lake City, Ut.

Wolfgang Ribbe and Eckart Henning, *Taschenbuch für Familiengeschichtsforschung.* Verlag Degener & Co., Neustadt/Aisch, 1995.

LaVern J. Rippley, *The German Americans.* University Press of America, Lanham, Md., 1984.

_____, *Of German Ways.* Dillon Press, Minneapolis, 1970.

LaVern J. Rippley and Robert J. Paulson, *German Bohemians: The Quiet Immigrants.* St. Olaf College Press, Northfield, Minn., 1995

Jayare Roberts, "U.S. Selective Service System: Draft Registration Records, 1917-1918." *Genealogical Journal,* Utah Genealogical Association, Vol. 24, No. 2, 1996.

R. Robin, *The Barbed-Wire College: Reeducating German POWs in the United States During World War II.* Princeton University Press, 1995.

Richard Sallet, *Russian-German Settlements in the United States,* trans. By LaVern Rippley and Armond Bauer. Institute for Regional Studies, Fargo, North Dakota, 1974.

Christina K. Schaefer, *The Center: A Guide to Genealogical Research in the National Capital Area.* Genealogical Publishing Company, Inc., Baltimore, 1996.

Vera Schauber, *Pattloch-Namensstagskalender.* Pattloch Verlag, Augsburg, 1994.

Leo Schelbert and Sandra Luebking, "Swiss Mennonite Family Names, An Annotated Checklist." *Newsletter* of the Swiss American Historical Society, Vol. XIV, No. 2, June 1978.

Trudy Schenk and Ruth Froelke, comps., *The Württemberg Emigration Index.* Ancestry, Salt Lake City, Ut., 1986-88.

Der Schlüssel: Gesamtinhaltsverzeichnisse für genealogische, heraldische und historische Zeitschriftenreihen mit Orts- Sach- und Namenregistern. Heinz Reise-Verlag, Göttingen, Germany. 9 vols.

Daniel M. Schlyter, *Poland/Prussia, How to Locate Vital Records of Former Prussian Areas of Poland in the Genealogical Library.* GENUN Publishers, Buffalo Grove, Il., 1985.

Alvin J. Schmidt, *Fraternal Organizations*, Greenwood Press, Westport, Conn., 1980.

Ingrid Schöberl, "Emigration Policy in Germany and Immigration Policy in the United States." *Germans to America: 300 Years of Immigration 1683-1983*, ed. Günter Moltman, Institute for Foreign Relations, Stuttgart, in cooperation with Inter Nationes, Bonn, Bad Godesberg, 1982.

"Die schönsten Ferienstraßen in Deutschland," *Grieben Reiseführer*, Grieben Verlag, 1987.

Cornelia Schrader-Muggenthaler, *Alsace Emigration Book*, 3 vols. Closson Press, Apollo, Pa., 1989-1991.

Karl-Egbert Schultze, "Zur Bearbeitung der Hamburger Auswandererlisten, insbesondere: kann man sie Drucken?" *Zeitschrift für niedersächsische Familienkunde* 41, 1966.

George K. Schweitzer, *Civil War Genealogy*, Knoxville, Tenn., 1988.

_____, *German Genealogial Research,* Knoxville, Tenn., 1995

_____, *Pennsylvania Genealogical Research.* G. Schweitzer, Knoxville, Tenn., 1986.

Schweizerisches Geschlechterbuch. Kommissionverlag von C.F. Lendorff. Basel, Verlag Genealogisches Institut Zwicky, Zürich, 1904-1965. 12 vols.

Aryeh Segall, ed., *Guide to Jewish Archives.* World Council on Jewish Archives, Jerusalem, New York, 1981.

Dolores Semon, "Acquiring Polish Records." The German Connection, Vol. 17, No. 1, January 1993.

_____, "Poland: Maps Gazetteers, Aids." *The German Connection*, Vol. 17, No. 1, January 1993.

Bertha Maud (Horack) Shambaugh, *Amana That Was and Amana That Is.* State Historical Society of Iowa, Iowa City, 1932. Reprint. Benjamin Blom, New York, 1971.

Michael H. Shelley, *Ward Maps of United States Cities: A Selective Checklist of Pre-1900 Maps in the Library of Congress.*

Clifford Neal Smith, *Cumulative Surname Index and Soundex to Monographs 1 through 12 of the German-American Genealogical Research Series.* Westland Publishing, McNeal, Ariz., 1983.

Clifford Neal Smith and Anna Piszczan-Czaja Smith, *Encyclopedia of German-American Genealogical Research*, New York, R.R. Bowker, 1976.

Kenneth L. Smith, *German Church Books: Behond the Basics.* Picton Press, Camden, Maine, 1989.

_____, *A Practical Guide to Dating Systems for Genealogists.* Picton Press, Camden, Maine.

Dorothea N. Spear, *Bibliography of American Directories Through 1860.* American Antiquarian Society, Worcester, Mass., 1961.

Oswald Spohr, *Familiengeschichtliche Quellen: Zeitschrift familiengeschichtlicher Quellennachweise.* Verlag Degener, Neustadt/ Aisch, 1926-. 17 vols.

Susan Steiner, ed., *Federal Republic of Germany: Questions and Answers.* German Information Center, New York, 1996.

Jean Stephenson, *Heraldry for the American Genealogist.* National Genealogical Society, Washington, D.C., 1959.

Ralph Beaver Strassburger, comp., and William John Hinke, ed., *Pennsylvania German Pioneers: A Publication of the Original Lists of Arrivals in the Port of Philadelphia from 1727 to 1808.* Pennsylvania German Society, Norristown, Pa., 1934.

Joseph R. Strayer, ed., *Dictionary of the Middle Ages.* Charles Scribner's Sons, New York, 1985.

Karl Stumpp, *The Emigration from Germany to Russia in the Years 1763-1862.* Trans. by Joseph S. Height et al. American Historical Society of Germans from Russia, Lincoln, Neb., 1978.

_____, *The German-Russians: Two Centuries of Pioneering*, Atlantic Forum, 1971.

Erika Suchan-Galow, "Hamburger Quellen zur Auswandererforschung." *Deutsches Archiv für Landes- und Volksforschung* 7, 1943.

Jared H. Suess, *Handy Guide to Swiss Genealogical Records.* Everton Publishers, Ut. 1978.

Robert P. Swierenga, comp., *Dutch Immigrants in U.S. Ship Passenger Manifests, 1820-18808: An Alphabetical Listing by Household Heads and Independent Persons.* 2 vols. Scholarly Research, Wilmingon, Del., 1983.

Paul E. Swigart, comp., *Chronological Index of Newspapers for the Period 1801-1967 in the Collections of the Library of Congress.* Library of Congress, Washington, D.C., 1956.

Michael H. Tepper, *American Passenger Arrival Records: A Guide to the Records of Immigrants Arriving at American Ports by Sail and Steam.* Genealogical Publishing Co., 1988.

Ernest Thode, *Address Book for Germanic Genealogy.* Genealogical Publishing Co., Baltimore, 5th ed., 1994.

_____, *Atlas for Germanic Genealogy.* Heritage House, Marietta, Ohio, 1932. 3rd ed. 1988.

_____, *German-English Genealogical Dictionary.* Genealogical Publishing Co., Inc., Baltimore, 1992.

Glenn Thompson, *Prisoners on the Plains: German POWs in America.* Gamut Publications, 1993.

Rainer Thumshirn, "Frisch, Fromm, Fröhlich, Frei." *Der Blumenbaum*, Vol. 11, No. 2, 1993.

_____ "Exodus of the Salzburg Protestants to Georgia." *Der Blumenbaum,* Vol. 13, No. 3, 1996.

_____, "There Always Had to be a Cuckoo." *Der Blumenbaum*, Vol. 11, No. 2, 1993.

William J. Toeppe, "Dewey and His System (Part 3A)," *German Genealogical*

Society Newsletter, Vol. IV, No. 6, July, 1995.

Don Heinrich Tolzmann, *German-Americans in the American Revolution: Henry Melchior Muhlenberg Richards' History, 1908.* Reprinted by Heritage Books, Bowie, Md. 1992.

Heinrich Turier, Marcel Godet, and Victor Attinger, *Historisch-Biographisches Lexikon der Schweiz.* 7 vols. Plus supplement. Administration des Historisch-Biographisches Lexikons, Neuenburg, 1921-1934.

U.S. Board on Geographic Names. *Preliminary Gazetteer: Switzerland.* Washington, DC, 1950.

U.S. War Department, *Official Records of the Union and Confederate Armies in the War of the Rebellion,* published from 1880 to 1900. 128 vols.

Ütrecht, Dr. E., ed. *Meyers Orts- und Verkehrs-Lexikon des deutschen Reichs.* Bibliographisches Institut, Leipzig, 1912. 2 vols.

"Variations and Uses of Calendars," *German Genealogical Digest,* Vol. 3, No. 2, 1987.

Fritz Verdenhalven, *Alte Maße, Münzen und Gewichte aus dem deutschen Sprachgebiet .* Verlag Degener & Co., Neustadt/Aisch, 1968.

Adeline Vigelis, "Alsace Family History Research." *The German Connection,* Vol. 18, No. 3, 1994.

John Paul von Grueningen, ed., *The Swiss in the United States.* Swiss American Historical Society, Madison, Wisc., 1940.

Mario von Moos, *Bibliography of Swiss Genealogies.* Picton Press, Camden, Me., 1993.

Hartmut Walravens, ed., *Internationale Zeitungsbestände in deutschen Bibliotheken: ein Verzeichnis von 19 000 Zeitungen, Amtsblättern und zeitungsähnlichen Periodika mit Besitznachweisen und geographischem Register,* K.G. Saur, München, 1993.

Bruce Walthers and Rolf Wasser, "How Our Ancestors Got to the Sea." *The German Connection,* Vol. 18, No. 2, 1994.

Gustav Wehner, "Das Schicksal der Bremer Auswanderer-Listen." *Norddeutsche Familienkunde* 1, 1952.

Miriam Weiner, *Bridging the Generations: Researching Your Jewish Roots.* Secaucus, NJ, 1987.

Gerhard Weiss, "Banner of Unity, Flag of Hope." *German Life,* August/ September 1995.

_____, "German Spelling in the 21st Century." *German Life,* November 1995.

Sopie A. Welisch, Bukovina *Villages/Towns/Cities and Their Germans.* Bukovina Society of the Americas,Ellis, Kansas, 1990.

Maralyn A. Wellauer, *Tracing Your Polish Roots.* Private printing, Milwaukee, Wisc., 1991.

_____, *Tracing Your Swiss Roots.* Wellauer, Milwaukee, Wisc., 1979, 1988, 1991.

Martina Wermes, Renate Jude, Marion Bahr and Hans-Jürgen Voigt, *Bestandsverzeidchnis der deutschen Zentralstelle für Genealogie.* Verlag Degener & Co., Neustadts/Aisch, 1991-1994. 3 vols.

Bruce Wetterau, *The New York Public Library Book of Chronologies.* Prentice Hall, NY 1990.

Where to Write for Vital Records: Births, Deaths, Marriages and Divorces. U.S. Department of Health and Human Services.

Willem Wijnaendts van Resandt, *Searching for Your Ancestors in the Netherlands.* Central Bureau voor Genealogie, The Hague, 1972.

Oren Windholz, *Bohemian Germans in Kansas: A Catholic Community from Bukovina.* Privately published, 1993.

Julie Winklepeck, ed., *Gale Directory of Publications and Broadcast Media* (formerly *Ayer Directory of Publications*). Gale Research Inc., Detroit Mich. Annual since 1869.

Carl Wittke, *The German-Language Press in America.* University of Kentucky Press, Lexington, 1957.

Pilar Wolfsteller, interviewer, "East Germany's Secret Files." *German Life,* February/March 1996.

Thomas Woodcock and John Martin Robinson. *The Oxford Guide to Heraldry.* Oxford University Press, Oxford, 1988

The World Almanac and Book of Facts. Pharos Books, New York, 1993.

Lubomyr R. Wynar and Anna T. Wynar, *Encyclopedic Directory of Ethnic Newspapers and Periodicals in the United States.* Libraries Unlimited, Littleton, Colo., c 1976.

Lubomyr R.Wynar, *Guide to the American Ethnic Press: Slavic and East European Newspapers and Periodicals.* Center for the Study of Ethnic Publications, Kent, Ohio, 1986

The Yellow Book of Funeral Directors. Nomis Publications, Inc. Youngstown, Ohio, 1987

Don Yoder, ed., *Pennsylvania German Immigrants, 1709-1786: Lists Consolidated from Yearbooks of The Pennsylvania German Folklore Society.* Genealogical Publishing Co., Baltimore, 1980.

_____, ed., *Rhineland Emigrants: Lists of German Settlers in Colonial America.* Genealogical Publishing Co., Baltimore, 1981. Reprinted 1985.

Zeitschriften-Datenbank (ZBD), 30th ed.., Deutsches Bibliotheksinstitut, Berlin, 1994.

Gary J. Zimmerman and Marion Wolfert, comps., *German Immigrants: Lists of Passengers Bound from Bremen to New York, 1847-1854.* Genealogical Publishing Co., Baltimore, 1985.

David S. Zubatsky and Irwin M. Berent, *Jewish Genealogy: A Sourcebook of Family Histories and Genealogies.* Garland Publishing Co., New York, rev. ed., 2 vols, 1991.

"Zunft: von den Anfängen bis zu den Innungen von heute." *Das Große Illustrierte Wörterbuch der deutschen Sprache.* Verlag Das Beste, Stuttgart, Zürich, Wien, 1996.

NOTES

NOTES

NOTES

Another publication
of Lorelei Press

Four times a year, *Der Blumenbaum*, journal of the Sacramento German Genealogy Society, delivers to its members facts and ideas related to German genealogy, history, and culture.

Der Blumenbaum is a 48-page journal chock-full of useful facts, resource ideas, how-to instructions, German-American background stories, down-to-earth tips, surname indexes, research techniques, translator and mentor contacts, information about archives, and an occasional feature, "Libraries for Genealogists."

To join the Sacramento German Genealogy Society and receive four issues of *Der Blumenbaum* per year, send your check ($15.00 for individuals, $20 for couples), payable to "SGGS," to

Sacramento German Genealogy Society
P.O. Box 660061
Sacramento, CA 95866-0061

**These are only a few of the topics found in
THE GERMAN RESEARCH COMPANION
(see the next page)**

- The German Länder (states)
- German occupations/ translations
- State archive addresses
- Immigration periods
- Ellis Island, Castle Garden, timelines
- wIllnesses/ translations
- German government offices
- German military records
- Parish inventories
- Requesting INS records
- German-Americans in U.S.
- How to use German archives
- Early trades, occupations
- Germans in the American civil War
- Topics covered in U.S. censuses
- German funeral sermons
- German address books
- Statue of Liberty
- Ortssippenbücher
- Meyers Orts-Verkehrslexikon abbreviations, etc.
- Common German male/female given names
- Perpetual calendar for two centuries
- Formula for finding days of week in any year
- German civil registration dates
- European wars
- Hessian troops in Amer. Revolution
- Place-name endings, clues
- Vocabulary for German politial subdivisions
- German house books
- Gregorian, Julian calendars
- German feast days, reckoning
- Emigration ships

- Ports of entry
- Sister Cities, U.S. and Germany
- Chronology: Holy Roman Empire
- Civil War Soldiers System
- Selective Service records
- German units in American Civil War
- German embassies, tourist offices
- Old German measurements
- German education, university degrees
- Old German and other universities
- German privacy laws
- Military church books
- German flag, history
- Towns/cities over 100,000 population
- German gov't structure
- Guilds in Germany
- German fraternal organizations
- Pennsylvania "Dutch"
- The Turn Verein movement
- German courts
- Family relationships
- Ahnenpaß
- Occupations, Latin
- Early railroads
- Major rivers of Europe
- Passenger departure lists
- Salzburgers to Georgia
- German holidays
- Religions, pietist sects in U.S., Germany
- U.S. census abbreviations
- Redemptioners
- Shipping lines
- Hamburg passenger lists
- Passport applications
- Degrees granted by German universities
- Naming practices
- Abbreviations

- Naturalization laws: chronology
- Immigration/ emigration
- Germans to Russia
- Non-political place names
- German newspapers
- Social security, railroad retirement
- U.S. Death Master File
- Emigration record
- Germans from Austria
- German empires
- Alsace-Lorraine research
- Germans from Bohemia
- Social security dates, files
- Pennsylvania research
- Der Schlüssel
- German telephone books
- Queries in German publications
- Goethe Haus in U.S.
- Gazetteers by area
- Family Search
- Ruesch payments in marks
- German zip codes by state
- German prisoners of war in U.S.
- German Information Center
- Ahnenlisten-Kartei
- Family History Library Catalog
- Deutsches Biographisches Archiv
- Lineage books: Deutsches Geschlechterbuch
- Works Progress Adminstration, projects
- U.S. libraries
- Soundex code
- Non-populations schedules
- German-American newspapers
- Periodical Source Index
- Minerva Handbuch
- U.S. German-

- related institutes
- Berlin Document Center
- Jewish archives
- Saints days
- Oktoberfest
- Zentralstelle für Genealogie, Leipzig
- Dewey Decimal System
- Directories
- Query abbreviations
- Marks, dollars
- Regional church archives
- Deutsche Welle
- Postal codes, U.S., Canada
- Fahrenheit/Celsius
- Familiengeschichtlich Quelle
- Müllers Orts abbreviations
- Homestead Act
- Land area terms
- Mennonites
- County land records
- Kilometers/miles
- Geneology societies
- Publishers
- German medical terminology
- Births, christenings, guardianship vocabulary
- Useful German genealogy terms
- German genealogical symbols terminology
- Poland dateline
- Death vocabulary
- Church archives
- Pietists
- Telephoning to Germany
- Postleitzahlenbuch (zip code book)
- English language "vote"
- French vocabulary for genealogy
- Library of Congress
- Stadtarchive, addresses
- Ahnenstammkartei
- Lutherans in USA
- "Black Dutch"
- German script

The German Resource Companion

by Shirley J. Riemer

◆Contains many topics relating to German family history research
(see the other side for a sampling of these topics)
◆A book you will keep at your elbow through all your German
family history research projects
◆Ideal for discovering the resources you never knew as possible
avenues of research
◆You don't read German? No "mystery" language here. All
German words and phrases are translated into English.
◆Make room in your research bag for this book – the necessary
companion for every trip to a library or archive
◆Softcover; 622 pages of text; illustrated; indexed
◆Price: $34.95 (includes shipping, handling, and tax)

ORDER FORM

Enclosed is my check for $_____. Please ship _____copy/copies
of *The German Research Companion*, at $34.95 each (which
includes shipping, handling, and tax) to the address below. Make
checks payable to "Lorelei Press."
                    Amount enclosed: _____

NAME_____

ADDRESS_____

_____

Mail this order form with your check to:

Lorelei Press
P.O. Box 221356
Sacramento, CA 95822-8356

These are only a few of the topics found in
THE GERMAN RESEARCH COMPANION
(see the next page)

- The German Länder (states)
- German occupations/ translations
- State archive addresses
- Immigration periods
- Ellis Island, Castle Garden, timelines wIllnesses/ translations
- German government offices
- German military records
- Parish inventories
- Requesting INS records
- German-Americans in U.S.
- How to use German archives
- Early trades, occupations
- Germans in the American civil War
- Topics covered in U.S. censuses
- German funeral sermons
- German address books
- Statue of Liberty
- Ortssippenbücher
- Meyers Orts-Verkehrslexikon abbreviations, etc.
- Common German male/female given names
- Perpetual calendar for two centuries
- Formula for finding days of week in any year
- German civil registration dates
- European wars
- Hessian troops in Amer. Revolution
- Place-name endings, clues
- Vocabulary for German politial subdivisions
- German house books
- Gregorian, Julian calendars
- German feast days, reckoning
- Emigration ships

- Ports of entry
- Sister Cities, U.S. and Germany
- Chronology: Holy Roman Empire
- Civil War Soldiers System
- Selective Service records
- German units in American Civil War
- German embassies, tourist offices
- Old German measurements
- German education, university degrees
- Old German and other universities
- German privacy laws
- Military church books
- German flag, history
- Towns/cities over 100,000 population
- German gov't structure
- Guilds in Germany
- German fraternal organizations
- Pennsylvania "Dutch"
- The Turn Verein movement
- German courts
- Family relationships
- Ahnenpaß
- Occupations, Latin
- Early railroads
- Major rivers of Europe
- Passenger departure lists
- Salzburgers to Georgia
- German holidays
- Religions, pietist sects in U.S., Germany
- U.S. census abbreviations
- Redemptioners
- Shipping lines
- Hamburg passenger lists
- Passport applications
- Degrees granted by German universities
- Naming practices
- Abbreviations

- Naturalization laws: chronology
- Immigration/ emigration
- Germans to Russia
- Non-political place names
- German newspapers
- Social security, railroad retirement
- U.S. Death Master File
- Emigration record
- Germans from Austria
- German empires
- Alsace-Lorraine research
- Germans from Bohemia
- Social security dates, files
- Pennsylvania research
- Der Schlüssel
- German telephone books
- Queries in German publications
- Goethe Haus in U.S.
- Gazetteers by area
- Family Search
- Ruesch payments in marks
- German zip codes by state
- German prisoners of war in U.S.
- German Information Center
- Ahnenlisten-Kartei
- Family History Library Catalog
- Deutsches Biographisches Archiv
- Lineage books: Deutsches Geschlechterbuch
- Works Progress Adminstration, projects
- U.S. libraries
- Soundex code
- Non-populations schedules
- German-American newspapers
- Periodical Source Index
- Minerva Handbuch
- U.S. German-

- related institutes
- Berlin Document Center
- Jewish archives
- Saints days
- Oktoberfest
- Zentralstelle für Genealogie, Leipzig
- Dewey Decimal System
- Directories
- Query abbreviations
- Marks, dollars
- Regional church archives
- Deutsche Welle
- Postal codes, U.S., Canada
- Fahrenheit/Celsius
- Familiengeschichtlich Quelle
- Müllers Orts abbreviations
- Homestead Act
- Land area terms
- Mennonites
- County land records
- Kilometers/miles
- Geneology societies
- Publishers
- German medical terminology
- Births, christ-enings, guardianship vocabulary
- Useful German genealogy terms
- German genealogical symbols terminology
- Poland dateline
- Death vocabulary
- Church archives
- Pietists
- Telephoning to Germany
- Postleitzahlenbuch (zip code book)
- English language "vote"
- French vocabulary for genealogy
- Library of Congress
- Stadtarchive, addresses
- Ahnenstammkartei
- Lutherans in USA
- "Black Dutch"
- German script

The German Resource Companion

by Shirley J. Riemer

◆Contains many topics relating to German family history research (see the other side for a sampling of these topics)
◆A book you will keep at your elbow through all your German family history research projects
◆Ideal for discovering the resources you never knew as possible avenues of research
◆You don't read German? No "mystery" language here. All German words and phrases are translated into English.
◆Make room in your research bag for this book – the necessary companion for every trip to a library or archive
◆Softcover; 622 pages of text; illustrated; indexed
◆Price: $34.95 (includes shipping, handling, and tax)

ORDER FORM

Enclosed is my check for $_____. Please ship _____copy/copies of *The German Research Companion*, at $34.95 each (which includes shipping, handling, and tax) to the address below. Make checks payable to "Lorelei Press."
                    Amount enclosed: _____

NAME_____

ADDRESS_____

_____

Mail this order form with your check to:

Lorelei Press
P.O. Box 221356
Sacramento, CA 95822-8356